CASES AND MATERIALS ON
EMPLOYMENT DISCRIMINATION AND EMPLOYMENT LAW
THE FIELD AS PRACTICED

Fifth Edition

■ ■ ■

Samuel Estreicher
Dwight D. Opperman Professor of Law
New York University

Michael C. Harper
Barreca Labor Relations Scholar and Professor of Law
Boston University

Elizabeth C. Tippett
Assistant Professor of Law
University of Oregon

AMERICAN CASEBOOK SERIES®

WEST
ACADEMIC
PUBLISHING

American Casebook Series is a trademark registered in the U.S. Patent and Trademark Office.

© West, a Thomson business, 2000, 2004, 2008
© 2012 Thomson Reuters
© 2016 LEG, Inc. d/b/a West Academic
    444 Cedar Street, Suite 700
    St. Paul, MN 55101
    1-877-888-1330

West, West Academic Publishing, and West Academic are trademarks of West Publishing Corporation, used under license.

Printed in the United States of America

ISBN: 978-1-63460-460-4

To my little wing and our life together . . .
SE

To Marvis, silver to gold
MH

To Kevin
ET

PREFACE

This text is the fifth edition of a work that grew out of our initial text, Cases and Materials on the Law Governing the Employment Relationship. We are also publishing this year a new edition of our shorter texts on employment discrimination law, and employment law, respectively.

The book captures the breadth of expertise demanded of practitioners in our field. While employment lawyers can and do specialize, a working knowledge of the field is as critical for defense lawyers counseling an employer as it is for plaintiffs' lawyers evaluating a case. An employer inquiring about an employee discipline issue may implicate discrimination and retaliation-related liability. A plaintiff complaining about discriminatory treatment may have a weak Title VII claim but an excellent wage and hour claim. Students exposed to the breadth of the field are best positioned to issue spot from a complex fact pattern, and educate their future clients about available options.

The book also provides considerable flexibility for instructors planning to sample from many different topics, emphasize topics reflecting their area of specialty, or focus on issues most heavily litigated in their jurisdiction. The book also supports intensive courses and courses that extend across multiple semesters. The teaching website accompanying the fifth edition offers several options for tailoring the course to suit your needs.

The notes and questions that follow the principal readings are organized into two categories: "Test Your Understanding of the Material" and "Related Issues." The former encourage students to gain a basic understanding of the material on their own, liberating instructors to spend more class time on rule application and advanced topics. The "Related Issues" notes explain important points of law not covered in the principle cases and explore policy questions and debates. The note material is intended primarily as a teaching tool rather than as a vehicle for expressing our particular viewpoints. In this text, as well as in earlier editions, we have not tried to reach complete consensus concerning the wording and the balance of each of our notes.

We also hope to entice students to join this exciting area of practice through the "Practitioner Perspectives" interspersed through the book. Each one provides a glimpse into the day-to-day practice of leading practitioners in our field, and their area of sub-specialization.

In order to avoid excessive use of asterisks in our editing of cases and secondary material, we indicate ellipses only when our excerpt deletes substantive material from the original text. We do not typically indicate the fact that the excerpt we use may come from the middle of an opinion, or that its ending does not correspond with the end of the opinion. Although we have preserved case citations where appropriate, so that students can check the court's authorities on their own, we have not included references to prior lower court opinions in the same case or to trial or appellate records and briefs or internal references to majority or dissenting opinions. We also often do not include subheadings. These omissions, made in the interest of readability, are not always indicated in our excerpts. For Supreme Court decisions in which a majority of the Justices have not joined a single opinion, we include both the plurality and important concurring opinions. As a general matter, however, we do not indicate the position taken by every single member of the Court.

Samuel and Michael wish to again express their debt to their spouses, Aleta G. Estreicher, Marvis Ann Knospe, and children, Michael Simon Estreicher, Jessica Aronson, Hannah Rose Estreicher, Oliver Louis and Nicholas Skelly Harper. Elizabeth thanks the wonderful caregivers at the Vivian Olum Child Development Center for providing the time and peace of mind to work on this project. In addition to those students whom we have thanked in prior editions, we would like to thank the following students for their research assistance for this edition: Matt Carhart (N.Y.U.), Claire Metcalf (B.U.), River Finken (N.Y.U.), Sean Ahern (B.U.), Sarah Kushner (N.Y.U.), Trevor Mauck (N.Y.U.), Cassandra Bow (Oregon), Zach Conway (Oregon), Ariana Denley (Oregon), Joel Janke (Oregon), Alisha Kormondy (Oregon), Elizabeth Miller (Oregon), Anastasya Raichart (Oregon), Alina Salo (Oregon), and Kalia Walker (Oregon). We also note again that the text benefitted from the comments of students and instructors who used our predecessor texts.

SAMUEL ESTREICHER
MICHAEL HARPER
ELIZABETH TIPPETT

SUMMARY OF CONTENTS

PART 4. TORTS IN THE EMPLOYMENT RELATIONSHIP

PART 5. REGULATION OF COMPENSATION AND BENEFITS

PART 6. REMEDIAL ISSUES IN EMPLOYMENT LAW

TABLE OF CONTENTS

PART 4. TORTS IN THE EMPLOYMENT RELATIONSHIP

PART 5. REGULATION OF COMPENSATION AND BENEFITS

TABLE OF CASES

The principal cases are in bold type.

———————

CASES AND MATERIALS ON

EMPLOYMENT DISCRIMINATION AND EMPLOYMENT LAW

THE FIELD AS PRACTICED

Fifth Edition

INTRODUCTION

■ ■ ■

Frank Tannenbaum opened his 1951 work, A Philosophy of Labor, with the observation: "We have become a nation of employees" increasingly dependent on the job as the critical resource of our lives. The continuing contraction of American farming and other self-employment makes this even truer today. For most members of modern society, no public relationship is more important than their relation to the entity for which they work or would like to work. This book is an introductory exploration of the role of law in regulating the employment relationship.

Organization of the Book

The exploration focuses on the legal rules governing the commencement, development and termination of employment relationships. It does so by considering how American law affects decisions to hire, promote, compensate, otherwise reward, discipline, and fire employees. The opening chapter considers the threshold coverage question of whether the individual seeking the protection of the employment laws is an employee warranting that protection, and the related issue of whether claims may be asserted against not only the immediate employer but other firms that have an effective influence over employment terms and conditions. Part 1 then examines evolving developments in the legislatures and courts to move away from the "at will" premise of U.S. employment contracts: that absent an express contract for a definite term, the employment relationship can be terminated by either party at any time, with or without a nondiscriminatory cause.

Part 2 discusses laws designed to protect individuals from employment decisions that affect them unfairly because of an immutable status (such as race, sex, sexual orientation and identity, age and disability) apparently irrelevant to their productivity as employees.

Part 3 considers the extent to which the law prevents employers from retaliating against employee activity that our society for one reason or another highly values or seeks to protect, perhaps because unrestrained employer authority may entail adverse effects on third-party interests.

Part 4 explores torts that arise in the employment context. First, we examine torts that typically arise in the course of hiring and terminating employees—misrepresentation, tortious interference with contract, and defamation. Next, we examine the legal framework through which employees are compensated for workplace injuries, primarily consisting of workers' compensation. Then we examine common law and statutory

1

protections for employee privacy, with a particular focus on informational privacy and electronic intrusions.

In Part 5, we examine statutory protections for employee compensation and benefits. The final chapters of the book (Part 6) take up the remedial systems that apply in the employment law context.

Identifying the Purposes of Regulation

Some might suppose that the project of this book should primarily consist of determining how the force of law can be best employed to most quickly and effectively eliminate undesirable employer decisionmaking. Questions of regulatory efficacy are certainly an important part of this book. However, they do not exhaust the range of issues that careful students of the law in this area must confront.

We need, initially, to go beyond a statement of generally laudatory goals to define as precisely as possible the purposes of employment laws. Precise definition can illuminate critical regulatory choices. Social advancement of unfairly treated status groups, for instance, may require more than the elimination of employment decisions motivated by hostility or even lack of equal regard for members of the groups. Are all employment decisions that are not directly related to firm productivity and that have an unequal effect on particular groups to be prohibited? Similarly, the regulation of employer decisions affecting socially valued activity requires a consideration of the kinds of activity that should be protected, and why. For instance, should the law's protection be confined to employee speech on matters of public interest or are there circumstances in which speech on matters of private interest also should be insulated from employer power? A similar elaboration is required for regulations that seek to curb arbitrary and intrusive decisionmaking by employers. Is the purpose of such rules to protect longevity of service, to check supervisory judgments, or to displace private judgments entirely with a regulated system akin to the civil service laws governing public employment? "Minimum terms" laws also must be evaluated in terms of their underlying purpose to avoid undesirable over- and under-regulation.

Assessing the Justifications for Regulation

Thorough analysis of our society's regulation of the employment relationship does not end with a determination of how precisely defined goals can be most effectively achieved through regulation. We also must confront the more fundamental question of whether such goals should or need to be achieved through particular forms of legal intervention rather than through passive reliance on market forces to curb undesirable behavior.

1.   *Traditional Economic Model of Labor Markets.* To provide a basis for assessing this question, economists employ a model of individual

decisionmaking that assumes that human beings, and the economic entities that they control, are rational actors who know their true preferences and generally act to further those preferences, never trading something that is more valuable to them for something less valuable. This model, as conventionally formulated, also weighs equally everyone's preferences, regardless of their content, and defines social welfare as the aggregation of individual welfare decisions. It is then argued that, given any particular distribution of wealth, human satisfaction can be maximized by permitting unregulated free trading. Free trading is said to ensure that any good, including rights to engage in or be protected from particular activity, will be allocated to those parties who value it most highly, and hence will make most productive use of that good. Regulation is thus said to be presumptively undesirable: it will tend to prevent trades from being made that would further the preferences of the contracting parties, or otherwise distort the outcomes that would be reached by private bargaining.

Applied to the employment context, this theory argues for allowing an employer to purchase, say, the right to be free of restrictions in personnel decisionmaking by giving its employees some good in exchange which is more valuable to them than a right to be treated fairly, but is less valuable to the employer than the right to act with complete discretion. Such exchanges, because they reflect actual preferences, will presumably make both the employer and the employees better off than arrangements that prevent the parties from acting on their preferences. Regulation that seeks to curb arbitrary treatment of employees can only prevent such mutually beneficial exchanges from occurring in labor markets and thus can only detract from social welfare.

The same analysis follows for any form of status or protected activity discrimination. For example, Gary Becker of the University of Chicago and other economists have posited that some employers may have a "taste for discrimination," either because the employers personally hold such preferences or because they defer to the preferences of their existing employees or customers. If all preferences are to be considered equally worthy, the argument goes, the satisfaction of even such "tastes" should be part of a welfare calculus.

Economists also may argue that competitive market forces adequately check preferences that are irrational in the sense that they obstruct maximization of profit. For instance, a discriminatory firm artificially limits the available supply of workers bidding for jobs and hence pays a premium for the workers it does employ. Nondiscriminatory competitor firms will then emerge to take advantage of the potentially lower labor costs and to offer the same product or service more cheaply. Similarly, a firm intent on treating its employees arbitrarily will be vulnerable to competition from other firms that fairly reward productive employee behavior and fairly penalize unproductive behavior. The economic argument concludes that firms that do not discriminate or treat their employees arbitrarily will earn higher profits and be able to raise more capital for expansion. Firms that persist in engaging in unfair practices in the long run will be driven from the market.

2. *Questioning the Premises of the Model.* One form of counterargument is to question whether the assumptions underlying this economic model are applicable to the employment relationship. Several conditions are assumed: (1) employment decisions are made in the context of competitive markets, where there are many firms bidding for workers and many workers bidding for jobs; (2) such decisions are based on perfect knowledge, in that the parties know their preferences, can accurately value the various goods being exchanged, and are fully aware of alternative opportunities; (3) the parties to the relationship are mobile, in that if either party is dissatisfied with the proposed bargain, it can readily terminate the relationship and seek more advantageous terms elsewhere; and (4) there are no significant transaction costs to the making of beneficial trades.

a. *The Market for Human Capital.* It may be argued that the market for human labor does not always satisfy these conditions. First, in some settings employers may enjoy a measure of monopoly (or monopsony) power, where they are relatively insulated from product market competition or they function in somewhat isolated labor markets free of any real competition for the services of their employees. "Internal labor market" considerations often may be more important to employers and employees than external market forces; where both parties have made investments in firm-specific training, the employment relationship may be better viewed as a "bilateral monopoly." Second, trades may be distorted when one or both parties have less than perfect information about what they are trading. Employees may not, for instance, understand what it means to have no contractual protection against arbitrary discharge, because they make erroneous assumptions about what employers lawfully may do or fail accurately to assess the probability that they may be terminated unjustifiably. Third, mobility in labor markets may be questionable. Individuals often find it difficult to uproot their families in order to take advantage of better opportunities elsewhere. Moreover, a variety of forces, including investments in firm-specific training, bonuses for outstanding past services, and pension and other fringe-benefit policies, may bind the employee to the job. Firms often pay workers more than would be required by supply and demand forces because they want to attract and retain workers willing to compete to work more productively to avoid the risk of losing especially attractive employment. Finally, while the transactions costs of contract-making are, on one level, relatively low in the employment setting, the parties at the outset of a relationship may find it difficult to talk about and bargain for certain terms, such as job-security provisions governing the termination of the relationship. These aspects of the real economic world all suggest that there may be situations where private bargains between employers and employees do not in fact reflect a mutually advantageous exchange.

b.   *"Agency Costs" of Firms.* Aspects of the real economic world also suggest that market forces might not be as effective in checking employer practices that have an adverse effect on firm productivity as a simple economic model might posit. Thus, while some discriminatory or arbitrary treatment of employees by agents of a firm may detract from firm profits, the costs to the firm in lost productivity may be lower than the costs entailed in identifying and eliminating such treatment. It may be a long time before firms see a pattern of terminations which may create a basis for questioning the judgments of particular supervisors. Hence, economically rational owners of the firm who otherwise would be inclined to minimize unfair practices do not in fact do so because of the costs of controlling prejudiced or arbitrary agents.

c.   *Attenuated Product Market Competition.* Moreover, given the many market imperfections in the real world, the short run in which inefficient employment practices persist can become quite a long period for many employers and their employees. Any employer with a monopolistic position in its product market, for instance, would only detract from its monopoly profits by continuing inefficient discrimination; it would not be threatened with extinction. Market imperfections created by other government regulations, often in place perhaps for good independent justifications, might also serve to perpetuate inefficient discrimination. Minimum wage legislation, for example, may make it more difficult for nondiscriminatory employers to reduce their relative labor costs by hiring the disfavored and thereby undercutting the prices of discriminatory employers. Similarly, "prevailing wage" requirements for federal construction projects may affirmatively erect barriers to entry by new firms. Also, because of the tendency of firms to adopt the personnel practices of other firms, product market competition may have to be quite vigorous before its influence filters down to the personnel department. Regulation might therefore be justified as a means of accelerating the elimination of persistent, albeit inefficient, employment practices.

d.   *Do All Preferences Count Equally?* Other arguments against the economic model question whether social welfare should be computed by an aggregation of individual welfare decisions. Society collectively may be quite willing to overcome scruples about judging some human preferences less worthy than others. We may, for instance, wish to exclude the satisfaction of human "tastes" for at least some forms of discrimination from the welfare calculus. Indeed, one role of law might be to reshape the preferences of even a majority of citizens in accord with deeper (or at least higher) social values. The purpose of regulation might also be avowedly redistributive, in contrast with an economic argument that accepts the existing distribution of wealth and bargaining power as a given. Regulation might be premised either on a society's judgments that the marginal satisfaction of the desires of some of its less fortunate members is worth more than the marginal satisfaction of some of its more fortunate, or on a recognition that employers often can afford to bid more for what is actually worth more to workers. Also, the simplified economic model presented above ignores the effects of trades on third parties such as the general community. To the extent the parties to an agreement do not bear fully the costs of their activity, there may be a need for the law's intervention. Thus, some regulation of employment decisionmaking may be justified by the benefits it ultimately provides to society, rather than to the parties directly affected.

Such arguments suggest that society might wish to eliminate some discriminatory or arbitrary preferences even when they contribute to firm productivity. First, some discriminatory employment practices may be consistent with profitability only because of the prejudice of employees or customers. Members of socially favored groups may find it distasteful to work alongside, or especially under the supervision, of members of socially disfavored groups. If so, the socially favored groups might demand a wage premium which could increase a nondiscriminating employer's labor costs and reduce its profits. Potential customers also might find certain goods or services less valuable if they are dispensed by members of disfavored social groups. If so, the customers will be willing to pay less and profits could be reduced. Our society, however, may no more wish to include the discriminatory tastes of employees and customers in its welfare calculus than when similar tastes are indulged in by employers. As suggested, even if a prejudice pervades the culture, we may wish to attempt to transform that culture by forcing ourselves to live up to our higher values.

Second, we may wish to prohibit reliance on some generalizations or stereotypes that are sufficiently accurate to be efficient, because their use is nonetheless unfair to many individuals or will have a cumulative deleterious social impact. An employer, for instance, might rationally conclude that membership in a particular social group or engagement in a particular activity is a good predictor of a job applicant's potential productivity and indeed may be less costly than other means of assessing qualifications. Our society might insist, however, that such a screening device not be used because it penalizes even individuals who would be productive, and either aggravates the social disabilities of all members of the excluded group or discourages the activity even more than is warranted by productivity concerns.

More generally, as suggested above, we might wish to regulate the employment relationship either to reduce third-party effects or to redistribute wealth to employees. Profit maximization may serve neither of these goals. An employer who threatens to discharge an employee for disclosing the firm's price-fixing activity to public authorities in violation of the antitrust laws may be acting as a rational profit-maximizer; society may, however, wish to encourage such disclosure to avert harmful impact on the community. Similarly, from the standpoint of the individual firm, it may be quite rational to discharge older workers who, because of seniority-based compensation policies, are paid at a level higher than the value they currently contribute to the firm; society may, however, wish to bolster the economic position of older workers because of the difficulties they confront in securing alternative employment. Even the intentional arbitrary discharge of easily replaced unskilled workers may be efficient for firms that wish to maintain unquestioned control of their workplace; but society may want to prevent such practices to provide a minimum level of dignity to all its workers.

Assessing the Costs of the Regulation

Analysis cannot stop, however, with a determination that some form of regulation to address a particular undesirable employment practice is warranted. The student must also consider the appropriateness of the particular systems of regulation that have been adopted, which in turn requires consideration of the costs of these systems as well as their benefits.

Administrative, Litigation and Error Costs. The costs of regulation include the administrative, litigation and error costs of enforcement. This book should enable the reader to assess the efficacy of alternative systems of implementation. The sixth and final part of the text is devoted to a consideration of the processes by which the substantive regulations are to be achieved. Moreover, a consideration of the costs of enforcement and the merits of alternative schemes is a necessary part of the analysis of each area of substantive law treated below.

Over-Enforcement? Other costs of regulation also need to be treated, however. One important set are the costs of over-enforcement. Legal presumptions provide a good example. The most effective way to eliminate a particular practice may be to reduce the difficulty of proving that practice has occurred by establishing such presumptions. For instance, as a means of facilitating challenges to employment decisions motivated by prejudice against a particular status group, the law might erect a conclusive presumption that employment practices having a significant adverse effect on members of that group are tainted by prejudice. Such a presumption may effectively extirpate prejudicial decisionmaking; but it may also encourage other kinds of inefficient decisionmaking, such as absolute preferences for less qualified members of the particular status group, that we may not wish to encourage. Even rules precisely tailored to cover only that which we want to proscribe may have some over-enforcement costs, as employers attempt to insure against costly litigation by compromising otherwise efficient practices.

"Backlash" Costs? Two other kinds of costs of regulation ought also to be noted in this introduction. Both might be described as backlash costs. Political backlash can occur when those who are not included in groups directly benefited by the regulation, and who may even be adversely affected by it, react against not only the regulation, but also its beneficiaries. Economic backlash can occur when employers forced to provide benefits to certain groups of workers respond by denying other benefits or even employment. For example, employers faced with costly litigation or regulatory oversight when they have members of a statutorily protected group on their payroll may seek to avoid those difficulties by not hiring members of the group, confident that lawsuits are not likely to be brought. Employers may even move work sites to towns or regions of the country where they are less likely to have job applications from members of a group more likely to generate litigation. Such a reaction may be economically rational, and depending on the nature of the labor market and the content and enforcement of other laws, a predictable response to regulation.

PART 1

THE EMPLOYMENT RELATIONSHIP

■ ■ ■

The laws dealt with in this book involve regulations of the employment relationship. With a few notable exceptions like 42 U.S.C. § 1981, which bars racial and certain forms of national origin discrimination in the making of any contract, these laws protect individuals only if they are employees of an employer. Customers or vendors of the employer are not regulated. Nor are independent contractors who may provide services for the employer that resemble services provided by undisputed employees. Defining the employment relationship, moreover, has become increasingly important with the growth of temporary agencies, remote work, and the on-demand economy. Our first chapter thus deals with the threshold questions of whether the individual seeking the law's protection is in an employment relationship, and if so, with which employers.

In Chapter 2, we begin with a discussion of the American common law doctrine of "employment at will," and look at the growing statutory and decisional exceptions to the rule that have emerged in recent decades.

CHAPTER 1

DEFINING EMPLOYEE AND EMPLOYER STATUS

■ ■ ■

Introduction

Most employment statutes cover only employees and impose obligations only on employers. These critical terms of coverage are generally not defined in the legislation, requiring resort to background principles, including the common law of agency and employment relations.

A. EMPLOYEES OR INDEPENDENT CONTRACTORS?

NATIONWIDE MUTUAL INSURANCE COMPANY v. DARDEN
Supreme Court of the United States, 1992.
503 U.S. 318, 112 S.Ct. 1344, 117 L.Ed.2d 581.

JUSTICE SOUTER delivered the opinion of the Court.

In this case we construe the term "employee" as it appears in § 3(6) of the Employee Retirement Income Security Act of 1974 (ERISA), 88 Stat. 834, 29 U.S.C. § 1002(6), and read it to incorporate traditional agency law criteria for identifying master-servant relationships.

I

From 1962 through 1980, respondent Robert Darden operated an insurance agency according to the terms of several contracts he signed with petitioners Nationwide Mutual Insurance Co. et al. Darden promised to sell only Nationwide insurance policies, and, in exchange, Nationwide agreed to pay him commissions on his sales and enroll him in a company retirement scheme called the "Agent's Security Compensation Plan" (Plan). The Plan consisted of two different programs: the "Deferred Compensation Incentive Credit Plan," under which Nationwide annually credited an agent's retirement account with a sum based on his business performance, and the "Extended Earnings Plan," under which Nationwide paid an agent, upon retirement or termination, a sum equal to the total of his policy renewal fees for the previous 12 months.

Such were the contractual terms, however, that Darden would forfeit his entitlement to the Plan's benefits if, within a year of his termination

11

and 25 miles of his prior business location, he sold insurance for Nationwide's competitors. The contracts also disqualified him from receiving those benefits if, after he stopped representing Nationwide, he ever induced a Nationwide policyholder to cancel one of its policies.

In November 1980, Nationwide exercised its contractual right to end its relationship with Darden. A month later, Darden became an independent insurance agent and, doing business from his old office, sold insurance policies for several of Nationwide's competitors. The company reacted with the charge that his new business activities disqualified him from receiving the Plan benefits to which he would have been entitled otherwise. Darden then sued for the benefits, which he claimed were nonforfeitable because already vested under the terms of ERISA. 29 U.S.C. § 1053(a). Darden brought his action under 29 U.S.C. § 1132(a), which enables a benefit plan "participant" to enforce the substantive provisions of ERISA. The Act elsewhere defines "participant" as "any employee or former employee of an employer . . . who is or may become eligible to receive a benefit of any type from an employee benefit plan. . . ." § 1002(7). Thus, Darden's ERISA claim can succeed only if he was Nationwide's "employee," a term the Act defines as "any individual employed by an employer." § 1002(6).

* * *

II

We have often been asked to construe the meaning of "employee" where the statute containing the term does not helpfully define it. Most recently we confronted this problem in *Community for Creative Non-Violence v. Reid*, 490 U.S. 730, 104 L. Ed. 2d 811, 109 S. Ct. 2166 (1989), a case in which a sculptor and a nonprofit group each claimed copyright ownership in a statue the group had commissioned from the artist. The dispute ultimately turned on whether, by the terms of § 101 of the Copyright Act of 1976, 17 U.S.C. § 101, the statue had been "prepared by an employee within the scope of his or her employment." Because the Copyright Act nowhere defined the term "employee," we unanimously applied the "well established" principle that

> "where Congress uses terms that have accumulated settled meaning under . . . the common law, a court must infer, unless the statute otherwise dictates, that Congress means to incorporate the established meaning of these terms. . . . In the past, when Congress has used the term 'employee' without defining it, we have concluded that Congress intended to describe the conventional master-servant relationship as understood by common-law agency doctrine. * * * "

While we supported this reading of the Copyright Act with other observations, the general rule stood as independent authority for the decision. So too should it stand here. ERISA's nominal definition of "employee" as "any individual employed by an employer," 29 U.S.C. § 1002(6), is completely circular and explains nothing. As for the rest of the Act, Darden does not cite, and we do not find, any provision either giving specific guidance on the term's meaning or suggesting that construing it to incorporate traditional agency law principles would thwart the congressional design or lead to absurd results. Thus, we adopt a common-law test for determining who qualifies as an "employee" under ERISA, a test we most recently summarized in *Reid*:

> "In determining whether a hired party is an employee under the general common law of agency, we consider the hiring party's right to control the manner and means by which the product is accomplished. Among the other factors relevant to this inquiry are the skill required; the source of the instrumentalities and tools; the location of the work; the duration of the relationship between the parties; whether the hiring party has the right to assign additional projects to the hired party; the extent of the hired party's discretion over when and how long to work; the method of payment; the hired party's role in hiring and paying assistants; whether the work is part of the regular business of the hiring party; whether the hiring party is in business; the provision of employee benefits; and the tax treatment of the hired party." 490 U.S. at 751–752 (footnotes omitted).

Cf. Restatement (Second) of Agency § 220(2) (1958) (listing nonexhaustive criteria for identifying master-servant relationship); Rev. Rul. 87–41, 1987–1 Cum. Bull. 296, 298–299 (setting forth 20 factors as guides in determining whether an individual qualifies as a common-law "employee" in various tax law contexts). Since the common-law test contains "no shorthand formula or magic phrase that can be applied to find the answer, . . . all of the incidents of the relationship must be assessed and weighed with no one factor being decisive." *NLRB v. United Ins. Co. of America*, 390 U.S. [254,] 258 [(1968)].

In taking its different tack, the Court of Appeals cited *NLRB v. Hearst Publications, Inc.*, 322 U.S. [111,] 120–129 [(1944)], and *United States v. Silk*, 331 U.S. [704,] 713 [(1947)], for the proposition that "the content of the term 'employee' in the context of a particular federal statute is 'to be construed "in the light of the mischief to be corrected and the end to be attained." ' " *Darden*, 796 F.2d at 706, quoting *Silk, supra*, at 713, in turn quoting *Hearst, supra*, at 124. But *Hearst* and *Silk*, which interpreted "employee" for purposes of the National Labor Relations Act and Social Security Act, respectively, are feeble precedents for unmooring the term from the common law. In each case, the Court read "employee," which neither statute helpfully defined,[4] to imply something broader than the common-law definition; after each opinion, Congress amended the statute so construed to demonstrate that the usual common-law principles were the keys to meaning. * * *

* * * At oral argument, Darden tried to subordinate *Reid* to *Rutherford Food Corp. v. McComb*, 331 U.S. 722, 91 L. Ed. 1772, 67 S. Ct. 1473 (1947), which adopted a broad reading of "employee" under the Fair Labor Standards Act (FLSA). And amicus United States, while rejecting Darden's position, also relied on *Rutherford Food* for the proposition that, when enacting ERISA, Congress must have intended a modified common-law definition of "employee" that would advance, in a way not defined, the Act's "remedial purposes." * * * But *Rutherford Food* supports neither position. The definition of "employee" in the FLSA evidently derives from the child labor statutes, see *Rutherford Food, supra*, at 728, and, on its face, goes beyond its ERISA counterpart. While the FLSA, like ERISA, defines an "employee" to include "any individual employed by an employer," it defines the verb "employ" expansively to mean "suffer or permit to work." 52 Stat. 1060, § 3, codified at 29 U.S.C. §§ 203(e), (g). This latter definition, whose striking breadth we have previously noted, *Rutherford Food, supra*, at 728, stretches the meaning of "employee" to cover some parties who might not qualify as such under a strict application of traditional agency law principles. ERISA lacks any such provision, however, and the textual asymmetry between the two statutes precludes reliance on FLSA cases when construing ERISA's concept of "employee." * * *

III

While the Court of Appeals noted that "Darden most probably would not qualify as an employee" under traditional agency law principles, *Darden, supra*, at 705, it did not actually decide that issue. We therefore reverse the judgment and remand the case to that court for proceedings consistent with this opinion.

SECRETARY OF LABOR V. LAURITZEN
U.S. Court of Appeals, Seventh Circuit, 1987.
835 F.2d 1529.

HARLINGTON WOOD, JR., J.

This, as unlikely as it may at first seem, is a federal pickle case. The issue is whether the migrant workers who harvest the pickle crop of defendant Lauritzen Farms, in effect defendant Michael Lauritzen, are employees for purposes of the Fair Labor Standards Act of 1938 ("FLSA"), or are instead independent contractors not subject to the requirements of

---

[4]   The National Labor Relations Act simply defined "employee" to mean (in relevant part) "any employee." 49 Stat. 450 (1935). The Social Security Act defined the term to "include," among other, unspecified occupations, "an officer of a corporation." 49 Stat. 647.

the Act. The Secretary, alleging that the migrant harvesters are employees, not independent contractors, brought this action seeking to enjoin the defendants from violating the minimum wage requirements and to enforce the record-keeping and child labor provisions of the Act.

* * * The district court granted the Secretary partial summary judgment, determining the migrants to be employees, not independent contractors. * * *

On a yearly basis the defendants plant between 100 to 330 acres of pickles on land they either own or lease. The harvested crop is sold to various processors in the area. The pickles are handpicked, usually from July through September, by migrant families from out of state. Sometimes the children, some under twelve years of age, work in some capacity in the fields alongside their parents. Many of the migrant families return each harvest season by arrangement with the defendants, but, each year, other migrant families often come for the first time from Florida, Texas and elsewhere looking for work. The defendants would inform the families, either orally or sometimes in writing, of the amount of compensation they were to receive. Compensation is set by the defendants at one-half of the proceeds the defendants realize on the sale of the pickles that the migrants harvest on a family basis. Toward the end of the harvest season, when the crop is less abundant and, therefore, less profitable, the defendants offer the migrants a bonus to encourage them to stay to complete the harvest, but some leave anyway.

Wisconsin law requires a form "Migrant Work Agreement" to be signed, and it was used in this case. It provides for the same pay scale as is paid by the defendants except the minimum wage is guaranteed. The Wisconsin Migrant Law invalidates agreements that endeavor to convert migrant workers from employees to independent contractors. Wis. Stat. Ann. § 103.90–.97 (West 1987); 71 Op. Att'y Gen. Wis. 92 (1982). Accompanying the work agreement is a pickle price list purporting to set forth what the processors will pay the defendants for pickles of various grades. This price list is the basis of the migrant workers' compensation. The workers are not parties to the determination of prices agreed upon between the defendants and the processors.

All matters relating to planting, fertilizing, insecticide spraying, and irrigation of the crop are within the defendants' direction, and performed by workers other than the migrant workers here involved. Occasionally a migrant who has worked for the defendant previously and knows the harvesting will suggest the need for irrigation. In order to conduct their pickle-raising business, the defendants have made a considerable investment in land, buildings, equipment, and supplies. The defendants provide the migrants free housing which the defendants assign, but with regard for any preference the migrant families may have. The defendants also supply migrants with the equipment they need for their work. The migrants need supply only work gloves for themselves.

The harvest area is subdivided into migrant family plots. The defendants make the allocation after the migrant families inform them how much acreage the family can harvest. Much depends on which areas are ready to harvest, and when a particular migrant family may arrive ready to work. The family, not the defendants, determines which family members will pick the pickles. If a family arrives before the harvest begins, the defendants may, nevertheless, provide them with housing. A few may be given some interim duties or be permitted to work temporarily for other farmers. When the pickles are ready to pick, however, the migrant family's attention must be devoted only to their particular pickle plot.

The pickles that are ready to harvest must be picked regularly and completely before they grow too large and lose value when classified. The defendants give the workers pails in which to put the picked pickles. When the pails are filled by the pickers the pails are dumped into the defendants' sacks. At the end of the harvest day a family member will use one of the defendants' trucks to haul the day's pick to one of defendants' grading stations or sorting sheds. After the pickles are graded the defendants give the migrant family member a receipt showing pickle grade and weight. The income of the individual families is not always equal. That is due, to some extent, to the ability of the migrant family to judge the pickles' size, color, and freshness so as to achieve pickles of better grade and higher value.

* * *

It is well recognized that under the FLSA the statutory definitions regarding employment[5] are broad and comprehensive in order to accomplish the remedial purposes of the Act. See, e.g., *United States v. Rosenwasser*, 323 U.S. 360, 362–63, 89 L. Ed. 301, 65 S. Ct. 295 (1945); *Real v. Driscoll Strawberry Associates, Inc.*, 603 F.2d 748, 754 (9th Cir.1979). Courts, therefore, have not considered the common law concepts of "employee" and "independent contractor" to define the limits of the Act's coverage. We are seeking, instead, to determine "economic reality." *Brock v. Mr. W Fireworks, Inc.*, 814 F.2d 1042, 1043 (5th Cir.1987); *Karr v. Strong Detective Agency, Inc.*, 787 F.2d 1205, 1207 (7th Cir.1986). For purposes of social welfare legislation, such as the FLSA, " 'employees are those who as a matter of economic reality are dependent upon the business to which they render service.' " *Mednick v. Albert Enterprises, Inc.*, 508 F.2d 297, 299 (5th Cir.1975) (quoting *Bartels v. Birmingham*, 332 U.S. 126, 130, 91 L. Ed. 1947, 67 S. Ct. 1547 (1947)).

---

5   The Act defines an employee simply as "any individual employed by an employer." 29 U.S.C. § 203(e)(1). An "employer" is defined to include "any person acting directly or indirectly in the interest of an employer in relation to an employee." 29 U.S.C. § 203(d). To "employ includes to suffer or permit to work." 29 U.S.C. § 203(g).

In seeking to determine the economic reality of the nature of the working relationship, courts do not look to a particular isolated factor but to all the circumstances of the work activity. *Rutherford Food Corp. v. McComb*, 331 U.S. 722, 730, 91 L. Ed. 1772, 67 S. Ct. 1473 (1947). Certain criteria have been developed to assist in determining the true nature of the relationship, but no criterion is by itself, or by its absence, dispositive or controlling.

Among the criteria courts have considered are the following six:

1) the nature and degree of the alleged employer's control as to the manner in which the work is to be performed;

2) the alleged employee's opportunity for profit or loss depending upon his managerial skill;

3) the alleged employee's investment in equipment or materials required for his task, or his employment of workers;

4) whether the service rendered requires a special skill;

5) the degree of permanency and duration of the working relationship;

6) the extent to which the service rendered is an integral part of the alleged employer's business.

* * *

We cannot say that the migrants are not employees, but, instead, are in business for themselves and sufficiently independent to lie beyond the broad reach of the FLSA. They depend on the defendants' land, crops, agricultural expertise, equipment, and marketing skills. They are the defendants' employees. * * *

EASTERBROOK, J., concurring.

People are entitled to know the legal rules before they act, and only the most compelling reason should lead a court to announce an approach under which no one can know where he stands until litigation has been completed. * * *

Consider the problems with the balancing test. These are not the factors the Restatement (Second) of Agency § 2(3) (1958) suggests for identifying "independent contractors." The Restatement takes the view that the right to control the physical performance of the job is the central element of status as an independent contractor. My colleagues, joining many other courts, say that this approach is inapplicable because we should "accomplish the remedial purposes of the Act":

Courts, therefore, have not considered the common law concepts of "employee" and "independent contractor" to define the limits of the Act's coverage. We are seeking, instead, to determine "economic reality."

This implies that the definition of "independent contractor" used in tort cases is inconsistent with "economic reality" but that the seven factors applied in FLSA cases capture that "reality." In which way did "economic reality" elude the American Law Institute and the courts of 50 states? What kind of differences between FLSA and tort cases are justified? * * *

* * *

We should abandon [the court's] unfocused "factors" and start again. The language of the statute is the place to start. Section 3(g), 29 U.S.C. § 203(g), defines "employ" as including "to suffer or permit to work". This is "the broadest definition ' . . . ever included in any one act.' " *United States v. Rosenwasser*, 323 U.S.360, 363 n. 3, 89 L. Ed. 301, 65 S. Ct. 295, 297 n. 3 (1945), quoting from Sen. Hugo Black, the Act's sponsor, 81 Cong.Rec. 7657 (1937). No wonder the common law definition of "independent contractor" does not govern. * * *

Unfortunately there is no useful discussion in the legislative debates about the application of the FLSA to agricultural workers. This drives us back to more general purposes—those of the FLSA in general, and those of the common law definition of the independent contractor. Section 2 of the FLSA, 29 U.S.C. § 202, supplies part of the need. Courts are "to correct and as rapidly as practical eliminate", § 2(b), the "labor conditions detrimental to the maintenance of the minimum standard of living necessary to health, efficiency, and general well-being of workers", § 2(a) * * * .

The purposes Congress identified * * * strongly suggest that the FLSA applies to migrant farm workers. [T]he statute was designed to protect workers without substantial human capital, who therefore earn the lowest wages. No one doubts that migrant farm workers are short on human capital; an occupation that can be learned quickly does not pay great rewards.

The functions of the FLSA call for coverage. How about the functions of the independent contractor doctrine? This is a branch of tort law, designed to identify who is answerable for a wrong (and therefore, indirectly, to determine who must take care to prevent injuries). To say "X is an independent contractor" is to say that the chain of vicarious liability runs from X's employees to X but stops there. This concentrates on X the full incentive to take care. It is the right allocation when X is in the best position to determine what care is appropriate, to take that care, or to spread the risk of loss. See *Anderson v. Marathon Petroleum Co.*, 801 F.2d 936, 938–39 (7th Cir.1986); Alan O. Sykes, The Economics of Vicarious Liability, 93 Yale L.J. 1231 (1984). This usually follows the right to control the work. Someone who surrenders control of the details of the work—often to take advantage of the expertise (human capital) of someone else—cannot determine what precautions are appropriate; his ignorance may have been the principal reason for hiring the independent contractor. Such a person or firm specifies the outputs (design the building; paint the fence) rather than the inputs. Imposing liability on the person who does not control the execution of the work might induce pointless monitoring. All the details of the common law independent contractor doctrine having to do with the right to control the work are addressed to identifying the best monitor and precaution-taker.

The reasons for blocking vicarious liability at a particular point have nothing to do with the functions of the FLSA. * * *

The migrant workers are selling nothing but their labor. They have no physical capital and little human capital to vend. This does not belittle their skills. Willingness to work hard, dedication to a job, honesty, and good health, are valuable traits and all too scarce. Those who possess these traits will find employment; those who do not cannot work (for long) even at the minimum wage in the private sector. But those to whom the FLSA applies must include workers who possess only dedication, honesty, and good health. So the baby-sitter is an "employee" even though working but a few hours a week, and the writer of novels is not an "employee" of the publisher even though renting only human capital. The migrant workers labor on the farmer's premises, doing repetitive tasks. Payment on a piecework rate (e.g., 1 cents per pound of cucumbers) would not take these workers out of the Act, any more than payment of the sales staff at a department store on commission avoids the statute. The link of the migrants' compensation to the market price of pickles is not fundamentally different from piecework compensation. Just as the piecework rate may be adjusted in response to the market (e.g., to 1 cents per 1.1 pounds, if the market falls 10%), imposing the market risk on piecework laborers, so the migrants' percentage share may be adjusted in response to the market (e.g., rising to 55% of the gross if the market should fall 10%) in order to relieve them of market risk. Through such adjustments Lauritzen may end up bearing the whole market risk, and in the long run must do so to attract workers.

There are hard cases under the approach I have limned, but this is not one of them. Migrant farm hands are "employees" under the FLSA—without regard to the crop and the contract in each case.

RESTATEMENT OF EMPLOYMENT LAW § 1.01
American Law Institute (2015).

§ 1.01   General   Conditions   for   Existence   of   Employment Relationship

(a)   Except as provided in §§ 1.02 and 1.03, an individual renders services as an employee of an employer if

(1)   the individual acts, at least in part, to serve the interests of the employer;

(2)   the employer consents to receive the individual's services; and

(3)   the employer controls the manner and means by which the individual renders services, or the employer otherwise effectively prevents the individual from rendering those services as an independent businessperson.

(b)   An individual renders services as an independent businessperson and not as an employee when the individual in his or her own interest exercises entrepreneurial control over important business decisions, including whether to hire and where to assign assistants, whether to purchase and where to deploy equipment, and whether and when to provide service to other customers.

NOTES AND QUESTIONS

Test Your Understanding of the Material

1.   Review the common-law "right to control" factors referenced in *Darden* and the "economic reality" test applied in *Lauritzen*. How are the tests different? Which way does each factor cut? For example, if the job involves a high level of skill, does that favor employee status or independent contractor status? How much weight should be given to each of the factors? Does skill level provide a useful dividing line between employee and independent contractor?

2.   Would application of the "economic reality" test change the outcome in a case like *Darden*? Conversely, would application of the common-law control test have changed the outcome in a case like *Lauritzen*? Are there cases where the difference between the test might affect outcomes?

3.   *Recurring Cases.* How should the following economic relationships be treated under the "right to control" and "economic reality" tests as well as the approach of the Employment Restatement?

a.   taxicab drivers who rent their cabs from fleet owners and charge fares as regulated by government, but are free to adopt any route they wish or work on any shift they wish;

b.   owner-drivers of trucks who service a single customer, say, the area's single large department store;

c.   registered nurses who perform home health-care services for elderly patients, but are not actively supervised by a referring organization;

d.   lawyers who "telecommute" at home drafting briefs and papers for a number of law firms, although 80% of their work is done for one major law firm;

e.   freelance musicians who as "regular players" for local orchestras must accept the majority of work offered, see Lerohl v. Friends of Minn. Sinfonia, 322 F.3d 486 (8th Cir. 2003); also Lancaster Symphony Orchestra, 357 N.L.R.B. No. 152 (2011).

f.   licensed real estate brokers who work exclusively for a real estate brokerage firm on a commission-only basis as independent contractors; who are required to obtain brokerage licenses; who are expected to attend training classes, take turns being in the office to handle calls and welcome off-the-street customers; who are not paid at all unless they help make a sale, in which the standard 6% commission is shared with the brokerage firm and the broker on the other side of the transaction; and who are expected to develop their own clients but sometimes take on clients on referral from the brokerage firm. See Monell v. Boston Pads LLC, 471 Mass. 566, 31 N.E.3d 60 (2015).

Related Issues

4.   *"Entrepreneurial   Control"   Test.*   The Restatement uses an "entrepreneurial control" test for assessing employment status. Is this test a break from the Restatement 2d of Agency § 220, discussed in *Darden*, or does it simply elaborate the non-physical-control factors in the § 220 formulation? Is "entrepreneurial capacity" or opportunity sufficient or must the putative independent contractors actually make nontrivial entrepreneurial decisions? For decisions addressing entrepreneurial control, see, e.g., NLRB v. Friendly Cab Co., 512 F.3d 1090 (9th Cir. 2008) (placing "particular significance on [employer's] requirement that its drivers may not engage in any entrepreneurial opportunities"); Corporate Express Delivery Sys. v. NLRB, 292 F.3d 777 (D.C. Cir. 2002) (finding employee status because of the absence of "entrepreneurial opportunity"). See also Estrada v. FedEx Ground Package System, Inc., 154 Cal.App.4th 1, 64 Cal.Rptr.3d 327 (2007) (drivers who lacked a "true entrepreneurial opportunity" were employees); FedEx Home Delivery v. NLRB, 563 F.3d 492 (D.C. Cir. 2009) (finding FedEx drivers to be independent contractors, applying an entrepreneurial-control test). See generally Michael C. Harper, Defining the Economic Relationship Appropriate for Collective Bargaining, 38 B.C.L. Rev. 329 (1998); and his Fashioning a General Common Law for Employment in an Age of Statutes, 100 Corn. L. Rev. 1281 (2015).

5.   *Department of Labor Interpretive Guidance on "Suffer or Permit" Standard.* In 2015, the DOL issued an Administrator's Interpretation of the "suffer or permit" language in the FLSA. Department of Labor Wage and Hour Division, Administrator's Interpretation No. 2015–1 (July 15, 2015). The Interpretation emphasized that the "opportunity for profit or loss" element should not depend on working more hours but should be a function of managerial decisions associated with running an independent business. The DOL also argued that "an employer's lack of control over workers is not particularly telling if the workers work from home or offsite. . . . Technological

advances and enhanced monitoring mechanisms may encourage companies to [use contractors] yet maintain stringent control over aspects of the workers' job." Is this Interpretation in accord with the Restatement test?

Consider the role of the "suffer or permit" language in the DOL's analysis:

The history of the "suffer or permit" standard highlights its broad applicability. Prior to the FLSA's enactment, the phrase "suffer or permit" (or variations of the phrase) was commonly used in state laws regulating child labor and was "designed to reach businesses that used middlemen to illegally hire and supervise children." *Antenor v. D & S Farms*, 88 F.3d 925, 929 n.5 (11th Cir. 1996). A key rationale underlying the "suffer or permit" standard in child labor laws was that the employer's opportunity to detect work being performed illegally and the ability to prevent it from occurring was sufficient to impose liability on the employer. *See, e.g., People ex rel. Price v. Sheffield Farms-Slawson-Decker Co.*, 225 N.Y. 25, 29–31 (N.Y. 1918). * * *

Unlike the common law control test, which analyzes whether a worker is an employee based on the employer's control over the worker and not the broader economic realities of the working relationship, the "suffer or permit" standard broadens the scope of employment relationships covered by the FLSA. Indeed, the FLSA's statutory definitions (including "suffer or permit") rejected the common law control test that was prevalent at the time.

Does the history of the "suffer or permit" standard speak only to the extent of knowledge the putative employer must have of the child's services, or does it more broadly support the agency's Interpretation?

6.   *Origins of the Right-to-Control Test.* As Judge Easterbrook points out in his concurrence in *Lauritzen*, courts originally developed the "right to control" test for the purpose of determining when it is appropriate to impose respondeat superior (i.e., strict) liability on a principal, as a "master," for the torts of an agent, as a "servant." See also Marc Linder, The Employment Relationship in Anglo-American Law: A Historical Perspective 133–70 (1989); Richard R. Carlson, Why the Law Still Can't Tell an Employee When It Sees One and How It Ought to Stop Trying, 22 Berk. J. of Emp. & Lab. L. 295, 302–06 (2001). The test clearly makes sense in this context; only a principal that controls the details of an agent's work should be given the incentive of potential liability to monitor that work. Consider in the course of reading this text whether the test serves equally well the purposes of antidiscrimination and employment laws.

Comparative Note

Some countries have developed in their statutes an intermediate category of workers, falling between the employee and independent contractor poles. German law, for instance, extends some labor and antidiscrimination protections to "employee-like persons" ("Arbeitnehmerahnliche Personem") who may be technically self-employed, but are nonetheless economically dependent on the users of their services; unjust dismissal law protection, however, is not offered to this group. See Wolfgang Daubler, Working People in Germany, 21 Comp. Lab. L. & Pol. J. 77, 94–95 (1999).

Should U.S. statutes be read to include a "dependent contractor" category? Can they be read in this manner? Professor Sprague argues that the economic-reality test is a poor fit for on-demand workers who provide services through Uber or Amazon's MTurk platform. See Robert Sprague, Worker (Mis)Classification in the Sharing Economy: Square Pegs Trying to Fit in Round Holes, 31 ABA J. of Lab & Emp. L. (2015). For these workers, "there is still some control exercised by the employer but less worker dependence on that employer." Sprague's proposed test would focus instead on the "dependence of the employers on the workers." Are there ways to promote independent contractor access for certain employment law benefits and protections without creating an intermediate category? Should Uber or other platforms establish, or be required to establish, a fund for workers' compensation coverage for their on-demand workers? E.g., N.Y. Exec. L. § 160-cc et seq. To what extent should antidiscrimination laws be amended to provide coverage for independent contractors?

NOTE: VOLUNTEERS AND INTERNS

Volunteers. Agents under the full control of their principals are treated as employees by the common law for purposes of vicarious liability, regardless of whether they perform their work without compensation. See § 7.07(3)(b) of the Restatement Third) of Agency. Some courts have held, however, that those who work voluntarily without compensation are not employees for purposes of certain employment laws. See, e.g., York v. Association of the Bar of the City of N.Y., 286 F.3d 122 (2d Cir. 2002) (prospect of future employment through networking in volunteer position not sufficient for employee status under Title VII); Mendoza v. Town of Ross, 128 Cal.App.4th 625, 27 Cal.Rptr.3d 452 (2005) (case holding the same under California Fair Employment and Housing Act, Cal. Gov. §§ 12900 et seq.). See generally Mitchell H. Rubinstein, Our Nation's Forgotten Workers: The Unprotected Volunteers, 9 U. Pa. J. Lab. & Emp. L. 147 (2006). The exclusion of volunteers extends to the FLSA, notwithstanding its broad definition of "employ" as "to suffer or permit to work." See Walling v.

Portland Terminal Co., 330 U.S. 148, 152, 67 S.Ct. 639, 91 L.Ed. 809 (1947) (brakemen not employees while in training and not compensated). See Employment Restatement § 1.02 ("An individual is a volunteer and not an employee if the individual renders uncoerced services to a principal without being offered a material inducement.")

Interns. According to the Department of Labor ("DOL"), an intern is not exempt from protection as an employee by the FLSA unless all six factors of the following test are satisfied:

1. The internship, even though it includes actual operation of the facilities of the employer, is similar to training which would be given in an educational environment;

2. The internship experience is for the benefit of the intern;

3. The intern does not displace regular employees, but works under close supervision of existing staff;

4. The employer that provides the training derives no immediate advantage from the activities of the intern, and on occasion its operations may actually be impeded;

5. The intern is not necessarily entitled to a job at the conclusion of the internship; and

6. The employer and the intern understand that the intern is not entitled to wages for the time spent in the internship.

See DOL Wage and Hour Division's Fact Sheet #71—Internship Programs Under the Fair Labor Standards Act (Apr. 2010), available at www.dol.gov/whd/regs/compliance/whdfs71.pdf.

The DOL's six-factor test is derived from Walling v. Portland Terminal Co., 330 U.S. 148 (1947), involving railroad brakemen who were not paid for their participation in a training program. In *Portland Terminal*, the Court discussed each of the six factors before holding that the trainees were not employees under the FLSA, although the Court did not state that each factor was necessary to its holding.

Several courts of appeals recently have rejected the DOL six-factor test in favor of a test that considers whether the intern or the employer is the "primary beneficiary" of the relationship. See, e.g., Schumann v. Collier Anesthesia, P.A., 803 F.3d 1199 (11th Cir. 2015); Glatt v. Fox Searchlight Pictures, Inc., 791 F.3d 376 (2d Cir. 2015).

Consider the following fact patterns, and assess whether the workers would be considered volunteers, interns, independent contractors, or employees:

a. Under the auspices of the Seventh Day Adventist church, Laurelbrook operates a boarding school for students in grades nine through twelve, an elementary school for children of staff members, and a 50-bed intermediate-care nursing home that assists in the students' practical training (the Sanitarium). The school has been approved and accredited by the Tennessee Department of Education since the 1970s. Students in Laurelbrook's boarding school learn in both academic and practical settings, spending four hours of each school day in the classroom and four hours learning practical skills. Students learn practical skills, in part, so they can later serve as missionaries in foreign lands. Boarding students keep busy with "wholesome activities" that teach them practical skills about "work, responsibility, [and] the dignity of manual labor" and that contribute to maintaining Laurelbrook's operations. See Solis v. Laurelbrook Sanitarium and School, Inc., 642 F.3d 518 (6th Cir. 2011) (applying a "primary benefit" standard rather than six-factor DOL test).

b.   The city's unpaid firefighters are required to be certified to render Basic Life Support (BLS) services to individuals they encounter in the performance of their duties. It is not uncommon for firefighters to be dispatched on emergency medical calls if they are able to arrive before a rescue squad. Rescue squads are separately organized non-profit entities that provide "Advanced Life Support" (ALS). The city itself does not possess an ALS license and does not require its firefighters to become certified to provide ALS care. Benshoff, a city firefighter, freely volunteered to join a rescue squad and now seeks compensation from the city for time he spends on rescue squad service rendered on occasions when he is dispatched on emergency calls. See Benshoff v. City of Virginia Beach, 180 F.3d 136 (4th Cir.1999).

c.   Defendant employs piece-rate workers to pick and peel the seafood it processes and packs. The workers provide their own hairnets, aprons, gloves and knives. Defendant enforces hygiene rules but otherwise does not regulate their work. The workers come and go as they please and are free to work for competitors (though few in fact do so). See McLaughlin v. Seafood, Inc., 867 F.2d 875, modifying 861 F.2d 450 (5th Cir.1988).

B. JOINT EMPLOYERS

Where more than one entity exercises control over an individual, courts must assess whether each entity qualifies as a joint employer. The first Supreme Court decision to address the issue of joint employment was a 1947 FLSA decision, Rutherford Food Corp. v. McComb, 331 U.S. 722, 67 S. Ct. 1473, 91 L. Ed 1772 (1947). In that case, the meat company contracted with a "boning supervisor", who was the nominal employer of all of the workers responsible for removing the meat from the bones. As boning supervisors left, the meat company replaced them with other supervisors under similar terms, while the workers performing the deboning remained at the slaughterhouse.

The Supreme Court concluded that the workers were jointly employed by the meat company and the boning supervisors, but did not articulate a test for assessing joint-employer status. *Rutherford* generated a number of approaches. The case which follows applies *Rutherford* to the garment industry.

ZHENG V. LIBERTY APPAREL COMPANY INC.

U.S. Court of Appeals, Second Circuit, 2003.
355 F.3d 61.

CABRANES, J.:

This case asks us to decide whether garment manufacturers who hired contractors to stitch and finish pieces of clothing were "joint employers" within the meaning of the Fair Labor Standards Act of 1938 ("FLSA"), 29 U.S.C. § 201 et seq., and New York law. Plaintiffs, garment workers in New York City who were directly employed by the contractors, claim that the manufacturers were their joint employers because they worked predominantly on the manufacturers' garments, they performed a line-job that was integral to the production of the manufacturer's product, and their work was frequently and directly supervised by the manufacturers' agents. The manufacturers respond that the contractors, who, among other things, hired and paid plaintiffs to assemble clothing for numerous manufacturers, were plaintiffs' sole employers. Both plaintiffs and the manufacturers moved for summary judgment on the issue of joint employment.

The United States District Court for the Southern District of New York * * * applying the four-factor test set forth in *Carter v. Dutchess Community College*, 735 F.2d 8 (2d Cir. 1984), granted the manufacturers' motion, and held that the manufacturers could not be held liable for violations of the *FLSA* or its New York statutory analogues. The District Court also declined to exercise supplemental jurisdiction over a surviving New York claim.

* * *

Plaintiffs-Appellants are 26 non-English-speaking adult garment workers who worked in a factory at 103 Broadway in New York's Chinatown. They brought this action against both (1) their immediate employers, six contractors doing business at 103 Broadway ("Contractor Corporations") and their principals (collectively, "Contractor Defendants"), and (2) Liberty Apparel Company, Inc. ("Liberty") and its principals, Albert Nigri and Hagai Laniado (collectively, "Liberty Defendants"). Because the Contractor Defendants either could not be located or have ceased doing business, plaintiffs have voluntarily dismissed their claims against those defendants with prejudice. Accordingly, plaintiffs now seek damages only from the Liberty Defendants.

Liberty, a "jobber" in the parlance of the garment industry, is a manufacturing company that contracts out the last phase of its production process. That process, in broad terms, worked as follows: First, Liberty employees developed a pattern for a garment, cut a sample from the pattern, and sent the sample to a customer for approval. Once the customer approved the pattern, Liberty purchased the necessary fabric from a vendor, and the vendor delivered the fabric to Liberty's warehouse. There, the fabric was graded and marked, spread out on tables, and, finally, cut by Liberty employees.

After the fabric was cut, Liberty did not complete the production process on its own premises. Instead, Liberty delivered the cut fabric, along with other essential materials, to various contractors for assembly. The assemblers, in turn, employed workers to stitch and finish the pieces, a process that included sewing the fabrics, buttons, and labels into the garments, cuffing and hemming the garments, and, finally, hanging the garments. The workers, including plaintiffs, were paid at a piece rate for their labor.

From March 1997 through April 1999, Liberty entered into agreements with the Contractor Corporations under which the Contractor Corporations would assemble garments to meet Liberty's specifications. During that time period, Liberty utilized as many as thirty to forty assemblers, including the Contractor Corporations. Liberty did not seek out assemblers; instead, assemblers came to Liberty's warehouse looking for assembly work. In order to obtain such work, a prospective assembler was required by Liberty to sign a form agreement.

Plaintiffs claim that approximately 70–75% of their work during the time period at issue was for Liberty. They explain that they knew they were working for Liberty based on both the labels that were sown into the garments and the specific lot numbers that came with the garments. Liberty's co-owner, Albert Nigri, asserts that the percentage of the Contractor Corporations' work performed for Liberty was closer to 10–15%. He derives that figure from individual plaintiffs' handwritten notes and records.

The parties do not dispute that Liberty employed people to monitor Liberty's garments while they were being assembled. However, the parties dispute the extent to which Liberty oversaw the assembly process. Various plaintiffs presented affidavits to the District Court stating that two Liberty representatives—a man named Ah Sen and "a Taiwanese woman"—visited the factory approximately two to four times a week for up to three hours a day, and exhorted the plaintiffs to work harder and faster. In their affidavits, these plaintiffs claim further that, when they finished working on garments, Liberty representatives—as opposed to employees of the Contractor Corporations—inspected their work and gave instructions directly to the workers if corrections needed to be made. One of the plaintiffs also asserts that she informed the "Taiwanese woman" that the workers were not being paid for their work at the factory.

* * *

Lopez v. Silverman, 14 F. Supp. 2d 405 (S. D.N.Y. 1998), [drawing on] the Supreme Court's decision in *Rutherford Food Corp. v. McComb*, 331 U.S. 722, 91 L. Ed. 1772, 67 S. Ct. 1473 (1947), Judge Cote concluded that the following *seven* factors should be considered in determining whether garment workers are jointly employed by a "jobber":

(1) the extent to which the workers perform a discrete line-job forming an integral part of the putative joint employer's integrated process of production or overall business objective;

(2) whether the putative joint employer's premises and equipment were used for the work;

(3) the extent of the putative employees' work for the putative joint employer;

(4) the permanence or duration of the working relationship between the workers and the putative joint employer;

(5) the degree of control exercised by the putative joint employer over the workers;

(6) whether responsibility under the contract with the putative joint employer passed "without material changes" from one group of potential joint employees to another; and

(7) whether the workers had a "business organization" that could or did shift as a unit from one putative joint employer to another.

* * *

We conclude, for the reasons set forth below, that the District Court erred when * * * it determined that the Liberty Defendants were not, as a matter of law, joint employers under the *FLSA*. In our view, the broad language of the *FLSA*, as interpreted by the Supreme Court in *Rutherford*, demands that a district court look beyond an entity's formal right to control the physical performance of another's work before declaring that the entity is not an employer under the *FLSA*. * * *

* * *

Rutherford confirmed that the definition of "employ" in the *FLSA* cannot be reduced to formal control over the physical performance of another's work. In *Rutherford*, the Supreme Court held that a slaughterhouse jointly employed workers who de-boned meat on its premises, despite the fact that a boning supervisor—with whom the slaughterhouse had entered into a contract—directly controlled the terms and conditions of the meat boners' employment. Specifically, the supervisor, *rather than the slaughterhouse*, (i) hired and fired the boners, (ii) set their hours, and, (iii) after being paid a set amount by the slaughterhouse for each one hundred pounds of de-boned meat, paid the boners for their work. *Rutherford*, 331 U.S. at 726, 730.

In determining that the meat boners were employees of the slaughterhouse notwithstanding the role played by the boning supervisor, the Court examined the "circumstances of the whole activity," *id. at 730*, but also isolated specific relevant factors that help distinguish a legitimate contractor from an entity that "suffers or permits" its subcontractor's employees to work. First, the Court noted that the boners "did a specialty job on the production line"; that is, their work was "a part of the integrated unit of production" at the slaughterhouse. *Id. at 729–30*. The Court noted also that responsibility under the boning contracts passed from one boning supervisor to another "without material changes" in the work performed at the slaughterhouse; that the slaughterhouse's premises and equipment were used for the boners' work; that the group of boners "had no business organization that could or did shift as a unit from one slaughterhouse to another"; and that the managing official of the slaughterhouse, in addition to the boners' purported employer, closely monitored the boners' performance and productivity. *Id.* Based on its analysis of these factors, the Court imposed *FLSA* liability on the slaughterhouse.

Like the case at bar, *Rutherford* was a joint employment case, as it is apparent from the Supreme Court's opinion that the boners were, first and foremost, employed by the boning supervisor who had entered into a contract with the slaughterhouse. *See id. at 724–25* (explaining that the boning supervisor exercised the prerogatives of an employer, including hiring workers, managing their work, and paying them). *Rutherford* thus held that, in certain circumstances, an entity can be a joint employer under the *FLSA* even when it does not hire and fire its joint employees, directly dictate their hours, or pay them.

* * *

The factors we find pertinent in these circumstances, listed in no particular order, are (1) whether Liberty's premises and equipment were used for the plaintiffs' work; (2) whether the Contractor Corporations had a business that could or did shift as a unit from one putative joint employer to another; (3) the extent to which plaintiffs performed a discrete line-job that was integral to Liberty's process of production; (4) whether responsibility under the contracts could pass from one subcontractor to another without material changes; (5) the degree to which the Liberty Defendants or their agents supervised plaintiffs' work; and (6) whether plaintiffs worked exclusively or predominantly for the Liberty Defendants. *See Rutherford*, 331 U.S. at 724–25, 730; *see also Lopez*, 14 F. Supp. 2d at 416–18 (summarizing the factors considered in *Rutherford*).

* * *

The first two factors derived from *Rutherford* require minimal discussion. The first factor—namely, whether a putative joint employer's premises and equipment are used by its putative joint employees—is relevant because the shared use of premises and equipment may support the inference that a putative joint employer has functional control over the plaintiffs' work. Similarly, the second factor—namely, whether the putative joint employees are part of a business organization that shifts as a unit from one putative joint employer to another—is relevant because a subcontractor that seeks business from a variety of contractors is less likely to be part of a subterfuge arrangement than a subcontractor that serves a single client. Although neither shared premises nor the absence of a broad client base is anything close to a perfect proxy for joint employment (because they are both perfectly consistent with a legitimate subcontracting relationship), the factfinder can use these readily verifiable facts as a starting point in uncovering the economic realities of a business relationship.

* * *

Rutherford * * * offers no firm guidance as to how to distinguish work that "in its essence, follows the usual path of an employee," [331 U.S. at 730], from work that can be outsourced without attracting increased scrutiny under the *FLSA*. In our view, there is no bright-line distinction between these two categories of work. On one end of the spectrum lies the type of work performed by the boners in *Rutherford*—*i.e.*, piecework on a producer's premises that requires minimal training or equipment, and which constitutes an essential step in the producer's integrated manufacturing process. On the other end of the spectrum lies work that is not part of an integrated production unit, that is not performed on a predictable schedule, and that requires specialized skills or expensive technology. In classifying business relationships that fall in between these two poles, we are mindful of the substantial and valuable place that outsourcing, along with the subcontracting relationships that follow from outsourcing, have come to occupy in the American economy. * * * Accordingly, we resist the temptation to say that any work on a so-called production line—no matter what product is being manufactured—should attract heightened scrutiny. Instead, in determining the weight and degree of factor (3), we believe that both industry custom and historical practice should be consulted. Industry custom may be relevant because, insofar as the practice of using subcontractors to complete a particular task is widespread, it is unlikely to be a mere subterfuge to avoid complying with labor laws. At the same time, historical practice may also be relevant, because, if plaintiffs can prove that, as a historical matter, a contracting device has developed in response to and as a means to avoid applicable labor laws, the prevalence of that device may, in particular circumstances, be attributable to widespread evasion of labor laws. Ultimately, this factor, like the other factors derived from *Rutherford* is not independently determinative of a defendant's status, because the mere fact that a manufacturing job is not typically outsourced does not necessarily mean that there is no substantial economic reason to outsource it in a particular case. However, as *Rutherford* indicates, the type of work performed by plaintiffs can bear on the overall determination as to whether a defendant may be held liable for an FLSA violation.

The fourth factor the Court considered in *Rutherford* is whether responsibility under the contracts could pass from one subcontractor to another without material changes. * * * Under *Rutherford*, * * * this factor weighs in favor of a determination of joint employment when employees are tied to an entity such as the slaughterhouse rather than to an ostensible direct employer such as the boning supervisor. In such circumstances, it is difficult *not* to draw the inference that a subterfuge arrangement exists. Where, on the other hand, employees work for an entity (the purported joint employer) only to the extent that their direct employer is hired by that entity, this factor does not in any way support the determination that a joint employment relationship exists.

The fifth factor listed above—namely, the degree to which the defendants supervise the plaintiffs' work—also requires some comment, as it too can be misinterpreted to encompass run-of-the-mill subcontracting relationships. Although *Rutherford* indicates that a defendant's extensive supervision of a plaintiff's work is indicative of an employment relationship, *see Rutherford*, 331 U.S. at 730 (noting that "the managing official of the plant kept close touch on the operation"), *Rutherford* indicates also that such extensive supervision weighs in favor of joint employment only if it demonstrates effective control of the terms and conditions of the plaintiff's employment, *see Rutherford*, 331 U.S. at 726 (suggesting the slaughterhouse owner's close scrutiny of the boners' work played a role in setting the boners' schedule); * * * By contrast, supervision with respect to contractual warranties of quality and time of delivery has no bearing on the joint employment inquiry, as such supervision is perfectly consistent with a typical, legitimate subcontracting arrangement. * * *

Finally, the *Rutherford* Court considered whether the purported joint employees worked exclusively or predominantly for the putative joint employer. In describing that factor, we use the words "exclusively or predominantly" on purpose. * * * In those situations, the joint employer may *de facto* become responsible, among other things, for the amount workers are paid and for their schedules, which are traditional indicia of employment. On the other hand, where a subcontractor performs merely a majority of its work for a single customer, there is no sound basis on which to infer that the customer has assumed the prerogatives of an employer.

* * *

Although summary judgment might also be granted to plaintiffs even when isolated factors point against imposing joint liability, * * * the District Court's conclusion that, in the present circumstances, the record cannot support summary judgment in plaintiffs' favor, remains undisturbed. This case is quite different from *Rutherford*, in which the Supreme Court concluded that the slaughterhouse was a joint employer as a matter of law. In *Rutherford*, unlike in this case, *every* relevant factor described above weighed in favor of a joint employment relationship, and the record as a whole compelled the conclusion that the slaughterhouse exercised functional control over the boners. *See Rutherford*, 331 U.S. at 730.

[*Eds*. The court's discussion of the state law claims is omitted.]

RESTATEMENT OF EMPLOYMENT LAW § 1.04
American Law Institute (2015).

§ 1.04   Employees of Two or More Employers

(a) An individual is an employee of two or more separate employers if (i) the individual renders services to each of the employers on a separate basis during a given day, week, or other time period and (ii) during such time period is subject solely to that employer's control or supervision as provided in § 1.01(a)(3).

(b) An individual is an employee of two or more joint employers if (i) the individual renders services to at least one of the employers and (ii) that employer and the other joint employers each control or supervise such rendering of services as provided in § 1.01(a)(3).

NOTES AND QUESTIONS

Legislative Response

As *Zheng* illustrates, garment workers may be employed by small, thinly-capitalized firms that are difficult to monitor and, even when caught violating the employment laws, may be judgment-proof as a practical matter. As one response to this problem, the New York legislature amended the state labor law to make manufacturers and contractors jointly liable for unpaid wages owed contractors' employees. See New York Labor Law §§ 340–45 & 348.

Test Your Understanding of the Material

1.   The Court distinguishes *Rutherford* on the ground that not every factor weighs in favor of joint employer status. Which factors in *Zheng* did not weigh in favor of joint employer status?

2.   Consider again Judge Easterbrook's criticism of the "economic reality" test in *Lauritzen*. Does the *Zheng* court's multi-factor test provide a predictable and coherent guidepost for potential employers?

Related Issues

3.   *Control over Essential Terms and Conditions of Employment.* The Third Circuit has adopted a test for joint employment under the FLSA that emphasizes control over essential terms and conditions of employment:

> 1) the alleged employer's authority to hire and fire the relevant employees; 2) the alleged employer's authority to promulgate work rules and assignments and to set the employees' conditions of employment: compensation, benefits, and work schedules, including the rate and method of payment; 3) the alleged employer's involvement in day-to-day employee supervision, including employee discipline; and 4) the alleged employer's actual control of employee records, such as payroll, insurance, or taxes.

In re Enterprise Rent-A-Car Wage & Hour Employment Practices Litigation, 683 F.3d 462 (3d Cir. 2012). See also NLRB v. Browning-Ferris Indus. of Penn., 691 F.2d 1117 (3d Cir. 1982) (applying similar test under National Labor Relations Act).

4.   *Common Ownership and Control.* Is Common ownership and control of integrated enterprises sufficient for joint-employer status? Chao v. A-One Medical Servs., Inc., 346 F.3d 908 (9th Cir. 2003) (common ownership and control sufficient to establish joint-employer status). Cf. In re Enterprise, supra note 3 (no joint employer relationship where parent company only made "recommendations" as to employment matters of subsidiary). Do parent companies always "control" their subsidiaries in the relevant sense?

5.   *Joint Employers of Farmworkers.* Agriculture is another economic sector that has posed frequent questions of joint employment status. Farm operator-growers often use labor contractors to recruit and supervise farm-laborers. Are the farm operators joint employers with the contractors? Decisions finding joint employment status have emphasized the operators' supervision of the laborers and the contractors' limited capital investment. See, e.g., Reyes v. Remington Hybrid Seed Co., 495 F.3d 403 (7th Cir. 2007) (Easterbrook, J.); Charles v. Burton, 169 F.3d 1322 (11th Cir. 1999); Torres-Lopez v. May, 111 F.3d 633 (9th Cir. 1997); Antenor v. D & S Farms, 88 F.3d 925 (11th Cir. 1996). But see Aimable v. Long & Scott Farms, 20 F.3d 434 (11th Cir. 1994) (farm operator not an employer of workers provided by a contractor who also provided housing and transportation and had sole supervisory control); Gonzalez-Sanchez v. International Paper Co., 346 F.3d 1017 (11th Cir. 2003) (laborers who hand-planted seedlings in forests owned by International

Paper were not IP's employees where only contractors supervised and supplied housing, equipment and transportation).

6.   *"Temp" Agencies.* Temporary employment agencies and their clients may be considered joint employers of employees supplied by the agencies when the agencies set and pay wages while the clients control the details of the work. See, e.g., NLRB v. Western Temporary Serv., 821 F.2d 1258 (7th Cir. 1987) (temporary agency and client joint employers under NLRA); Ansoumana v. Gristede's Operating Corp., 255 F.Supp.2d 184 (S.D. N.Y. 2003) (drug store was joint employer under FLSA of delivery workers provided by contractors); Amarnare v. Merrill Lynch, 611 F.Supp. 344 (S.D.N.Y. 1984) (temporary employment agency and client both employers under Title VII).

7.   *Reason for Invoking Joint-Employer Issue?* Should the test for joint-employer status vary with the reasons for invoking the issue? There may be one test for holding two firms as joint employers at the outset of the litigation and perhaps a broader test providing more latitude to bring claims against franchisors or clients where the primary employer is effectively insolvent or at least judgment-proof. Is this approach available under the existing legal framework?

C. EMPLOYEES OR EMPLOYERS?

CLACKAMAS GASTROENTEROLOGY ASSOCIATES, P.C. v. WELLS
Supreme Court of the United States, 2003.
538 U.S. 440, 123 S.Ct. 1673, 155 L.Ed.2d 615.

JUSTICE STEVENS delivered the opinion of the Court.

The Americans with Disabilities Act of 1990 (ADA or Act), 104 Stat. 327, as amended, 42 U.S.C. § 12101 *et seq.*, like other federal antidiscrimination legislation, is inapplicable to very small businesses. Under the ADA an "employer" is not covered unless its workforce includes "15 or more employees for each working day in each of 20 or more calendar weeks in the current or preceding calendar year." § 12111(5). The question in this case is whether four physicians actively engaged in medical practice as shareholders and directors of a professional corporation should be counted as "employees."

I

Petitioner, Clackamas Gastroenterology Associates, P. C., is a medical clinic in Oregon. It employed respondent, Deborah Wells, as a bookkeeper from 1986 until 1997. After her termination, she brought this action against the clinic alleging unlawful discrimination on the basis of disability under Title I of the ADA. Petitioner denied that it was covered by the Act and moved for summary judgment, asserting that it did not have 15 or more employees for the 20 weeks required by the statute. It is undisputed that the accuracy of that assertion depends on whether the four physician-shareholders who own the professional corporation and constitute its board of directors are counted as employees.

The District Court, adopting the Magistrate Judge's findings and recommendation, granted the motion. Relying on an "economic realities" test adopted by the Seventh Circuit in *EEOC v. Dowd & Dowd, Ltd.*, 736 F.2d 1177, 1178 (1984), the District Court concluded that the four doctors were "more analogous to partners in a partnership than to shareholders in a general corporation" and therefore were "not employees for purposes of the federal antidiscrimination laws."

A divided panel of the Court of Appeals for the Ninth Circuit reversed. [*Eds.* The panel majority refused to engage in inquire into whether the physician-shareholders functioned as partners because they operated under a corporate form: "While the shareholders of a corporation may or may not be "employees," they can never be partners in that corporation because the roles are "mutually exclusive." Finding they were employees because they "actively participated in the management and operation of the medical practice and literally were employees of the corporation under employment agreements," the panel concluded that Clackamas had sufficient employees to be a covered "employer" under ADA § 12111(5). 271 F.3d 903, 905–906 (9th Cir. 2000).]

II

"We have often been asked to construe the meaning of 'employee' where the statute containing the term does not helpfully define it." *Nationwide Mut. Ins. Co. v. Darden*, 503 U.S. 318, 322, 117 L.Ed. 2d 581, 112 S.Ct. 1344 (1992). The definition of the term in the ADA simply states that an "employee" is "an individual employed by an employer." 42 U.S.C. § 12111(4). * * *

In *Darden* * * * we adopted a common-law test for determining who qualifies as an "employee" under ERISA. * * * We explained that " 'when Congress has used the term 'employee' without defining it, we have concluded that Congress intended to describe the conventional master-servant relationship as understood by common-law agency doctrine.' " *Darden*, 503 U.S., at 322–323.

Rather than looking to the common law, petitioner argues that courts should determine whether a shareholder-director of a professional corporation is an "employee" by asking whether the shareholder-director is, in reality, a "partner." The question whether a shareholder-director is an employee, however, cannot be answered by asking whether the shareholder-director appears to be the functional equivalent of a partner. Today there are partnerships that include hundreds of members, some of whom may well qualify as "employees" because control is concentrated in a small number of managing partners. Cf. *Hishon v. King & Spalding*, 467

U.S. 69, 80, n. 2, 81 L.Ed. 2d 59, 104 S.Ct. 2229 (1984) (Powell, J., concurring) ("An employer may not evade the strictures of Title VII simply by labeling its employees as 'partners' "); *EEOC v. Sidley Austin Brown & Wood*, 315 F.3d 696, 709 (CA7 2002) (Easterbrook, concurring in part and concurring in judgment); *Strother v. Southern California Permanente Medical Group*, 79 F.3d 859 (CA9 1996). Thus, asking whether shareholder-directors are partners—rather than asking whether they are employees—simply begs the question.

Nor does the approach adopted by the Court of Appeals in this case fare any better. The majority's approach, which paid particular attention to "the broad purpose of the ADA," 271 F.3d at 905, is consistent with the statutory purpose of ridding the Nation of the evil of discrimination. See 42 U.S.C. § 12101(b).[6] Nevertheless, two countervailing considerations must be weighed in the balance. First, as the dissenting judge noted below, the congressional decision to limit the coverage of the legislation to firms with 15 or more employees has its own justification that must be respected—namely, easing entry into the market and preserving the competitive position of smaller firms. See 271 F.3d at 908 (opinion of Graber, J.) * * * . Second, as *Darden* reminds us, congressional silence often reflects an expectation that courts will look to the common law to fill gaps in statutory text, particularly when an undefined term has a settled meaning at common law. Congress has overridden judicial decisions that went beyond the common law in an effort to correct "the mischief" at which a statute was aimed. See *Darden*, 503 U.S., at 324–325.

Perhaps the Court of Appeals' and the parties' failure to look to the common law for guidance in this case stems from the fact that we are dealing with a new type of business entity that has no exact precedent in the common law. State statutes now permit incorporation for the purpose of practicing a profession, but in the past "the so-called learned professions were not permitted to organize as corporate entities." 1A W. Fletcher, Cyclopedia of the Law of Private Corporations § 112.10 (rev. ed. 1997–2002). Thus, professional corporations are relatively young participants in the market, and their features vary from State to State. See generally 1 B. Bittker & J. Eustice, Federal Income Taxation of Corporations and Shareholders ¶ 2.06 (7th ed. 2002) (explaining that States began to authorize the creation of professional corporations in the late 1950's and that the momentum to form professional corporations grew in the 1970's).

---

[6] The meaning of the term "employee" comes into play when determining whether an individual is an "employee" who may invoke the ADA's protections against discrimination in "hiring, advancement, or discharge," 42 U.S.C. § 12112(a), as well as when determining whether an individual is an "employee" for purposes of the 15-employee threshold. [citations omitted] Consequently, a broad reading of the term "employee" would—consistent with the statutory purpose of ridding the Nation of discrimination—tend to expand the coverage of the ADA by enlarging the number of employees entitled to protection and by reducing the number of firms entitled to exemption.

Nonetheless, the common law's definition of the master-servant relationship does provide helpful guidance. At common law the relevant factors defining the master-servant relationship focus on the master's control over the servant. The general definition of the term "servant" in the Restatement (Second) of Agency § 2(2) (1958), for example, refers to a person whose work is "controlled or is subject to the right to control by the master." * * * In addition, the Restatement's more specific definition of the term "servant" lists factors to be considered when distinguishing between servants and independent contractors, the first of which is "the extent of control" that one may exercise over the details of the work of the other. *Id.*, § 220(2)(a). We think that the common-law element of control is the principal guidepost that should be followed in this case.

This is the position that is advocated by the Equal Employment Opportunity Commission (EEOC), the agency that has special enforcement responsibilities under the ADA and other federal statutes containing similar threshold issues for determining coverage. It argues that a court should examine "whether shareholder-directors operate independently and manage the business or instead are subject to the firm's control." According to the EEOC's view, "if the shareholder-directors operate independently and manage the business, they are proprietors and not employees; if they are subject to the firm's control, they are employees."

Specific EEOC guidelines discuss both the broad question of who is an "employee" and the narrower question of when partners, officers, members of boards of directors, and major shareholders qualify as employees. See 2 Equal Employment Opportunity Commission, Compliance Manual §§ 605:0008–605:00010 (2000) (hereinafter EEOC Compliance Manual). With respect to the broad question, the guidelines list 16 factors—taken from *Darden*, 503 U.S., at 323–324—that may be relevant to "whether the employer controls the means and manner of the worker's work performance." EEOC Compliance Manual § 605:0008, and n. 71. The guidelines list six factors to be considered in answering the narrower question, which they frame as "whether the individual acts independently and participates in managing the organization, or whether the individual is subject to the organization's control." *Id.*, § 605:0009.

We are persuaded by the EEOC's focus on the common-law touchstone of control, see *Skidmore v. Swift & Co.*, 323 U.S. 134, 140, 89 L.Ed. 124, 65 S.Ct. 161 (1944), and specifically by its submission that each of the following six factors is relevant to the inquiry whether a shareholder-director is an employee:

Whether the organization can hire or fire the individual or set the rules and regulations of the individual's work

Whether and, if so, to what extent the organization supervises the individual's work

Whether the individual reports to someone higher in the organization

Whether and, if so, to what extent the individual is able to influence the organization

Whether the parties intended that the individual be an employee, as expressed in written agreements or contracts

Whether the individual shares in the profits, losses, and liabilities of the organization." EEOC Compliance Manual § 605:0009.[10]

As the EEOC's standard reflects, an employer is the person, or group of persons, who owns and manages the enterprise. The employer can hire and fire employees, can assign tasks to employees and supervise their performance, and can decide how the profits and losses of the business are to be distributed. The mere fact that a person has a particular title—such as partner, director, or vice president—should not necessarily be used to determine whether he or she is an employee or a proprietor. See *ibid.* ("An individual's title . . . does not determine whether the individual is a partner, officer, member of a board of directors, or major shareholder, as opposed to an employee"). Nor should the mere existence of a document styled "employment agreement" lead inexorably to the conclusion that either party is an employee. See *ibid.* (looking to whether "the parties intended that the individual be an employee, as expressed in written agreements or contracts"). Rather, as was true in applying common law rules to the independent-contractor-versus-employee issue confronted in *Darden*, the answer to whether a shareholder-director is an employee depends on " 'all of the incidents of the relationship . . . with no one factor being decisive.' " 503 U.S., at 324 (quoting *NLRB v. United Ins. Co. of America*, 390 U.S. 254, 258, 19 L.Ed. 2d 1083, 88 S.Ct. 988 (1968)).

III

Some of the District Court's findings—when considered in light of the EEOC's standard—appear to weigh in favor of a conclusion that the four director-shareholder physicians in this case are not employees of the clinic. For example, they apparently control the operation of their clinic, they share the profits, and they are personally liable for malpractice claims. There may, however, be evidence in the record that would contradict those findings or support a contrary conclusion under the EEOC's standard that we endorse today.[11] Accordingly, as we did in *Darden*, we reverse the

---

[10] The EEOC asserts that these six factors need not necessarily be treated as "exhaustive." We agree. The answer to whether a shareholder-director is an employee or an employer cannot be decided in every case by a " 'shorthand formula or magic phrase.' " *Nationwide Mut. Ins. Co. v. Darden*, 503 U.S. 318, 324, 117 L.Ed. 2d 581, 112 S.Ct. 1344 (1992) (quoting *NLRB v. United Ins. Co. of America*, 390 U.S. 254, 258, 19 L.Ed. 2d 1083, 88 S.Ct. 988 (1968)).

[11] For example, the record indicates that the four director-shareholders receive salaries, that they must comply with the standards established by the clinic, and that they report to a personnel manager.

judgment of the Court of Appeals and remand the case to that court for further proceedings consistent with this opinion.

JUSTICE GINSBURG, with whom JUSTICE BREYER joins, dissenting.

Are the physician-shareholders "servants" of Clackamas for the purpose relevant here? The Restatement defines "servant" to mean "an agent employed by a master to perform service in his affairs whose physical conduct in the performance of the service is controlled or is subject to the right to control by the master." Restatement (Second) of Agency § 2(2) (1958) (hereinafter Restatement). When acting as clinic doctors, the physician-shareholders appear to fit the Restatement definition. The doctors provide services on behalf of the corporation, in whose name the practice is conducted. See Ore. Rev. Stat. Ann. § 58.185(1)(a) (1998 Supp.) (shareholders of a professional corporation "render the specified professional services *of the corporation*" (emphasis added)). The doctors have employment contracts with Clackamas, under which they receive salaries and yearly bonuses, and they work at facilities owned or leased by the corporation. In performing their duties, the doctors must "comply with . . . standards [the organization has] established." See Restatement, ch. 7, tit. B, Introductory Note, p. 479 ("Fully employed but highly placed employees of a corporation . . . are no less servants because they are not controlled in their day-to-day work by other human beings. Their physical activities are controlled by their sense of obligation to devote their time and energies to the interests of the enterprise.").

The physician-shareholders, it bears emphasis, invite the designation "employee" for various purposes under federal and state law. The Employee Retirement Income Security Act of 1974 (ERISA), much like the ADA, defines "employee" as "any individual employed by an employer." 29 U.S.C. § 1002(6). Clackamas readily acknowledges that the physician-shareholders are "employees" for ERISA purposes. Indeed, gaining qualification as "employees" under ERISA was the prime reason the physician-shareholders chose the corporate form instead of a partnership. Further, Clackamas agrees, the physician-shareholders are covered by Oregon's workers' compensation law, a statute applicable to "persons . . . who . . . furnish services for a remuneration, subject to the direction and control of an employer," Ore. Rev. Stat. Ann. § 656.005(30) (1996 Supp.). Finally, by electing to organize their practice as a corporation, the physician-shareholders created an entity separate and distinct from themselves, one that would afford them limited liability for the debts of the enterprise. §§ 58.185(4), (5), (10), (11) (1998 Supp.). I see no reason to allow the doctors to escape from their choice of corporate form when the question becomes whether they are employees for purposes of federal antidiscrimination statutes.

RESTATEMENT OF EMPLOYMENT LAW § 1.03

American Law Institute (2015).

§ 1.03   Controlling Owners Are Not Employees for Purposes of Laws Governing Employment Relationship

An individual is not an employee of an enterprise if the individual through an ownership interest controls all or a part of the enterprise.

NOTES AND QUESTIONS

Test Your Understanding of the Material

1.   What test does the Court instruct the lower court to apply on remand?

2.   Is the position of the EEOC and that of the Court in *Clackamas* consistent with the Restatement of Employment Law?

3.   Under the common law as stated in the Restatement (Second) of Agency in 1958, "highly placed employees of a corporation, such as presidents and general managers, are not less servants because they are not controlled in their day-to-day work by other human beings. Their physical activities are controlled by their sense of obligation to devote their time and energies to the interests of the enterprise." Restatement (Second) of Agency, introductory note, p. 479. Furthermore, working partners in some circumstances also can be employees: "When one of the partners is in active management of the business or is otherwise regularly employed in the business, he is a servant of the partnership." Id. § 14 A Is the EEOC's position in *Clackamas* consistent with that of the 1958 Agency Restatement?

Related Issues

4.   *Partners as Employees?* Before *Clackamas*, the courts of appeals were split as to whether partners in a formal partnership should ever be treated as employees under the antidiscrimination laws. Compare Simpson v. Ernst & Young, 100 F.3d 436 (6th Cir. 1996) (treating individual denominated as a partner and charged with full liability for firm losses, as employee under federal antidiscrimination and employment laws), with Wheeler v. Hurdman, 825 F.2d 257 (10th Cir. 1987) (rejecting EEOC test and holding bona fide general partners are nonemployees under antidiscrimination laws). See also EEOC v. Sidley Austin Brown & Wood, 315 F.3d 696 (7th Cir. 2002) (discovery dispute turning on employee status; majority opinion by Judge Posner and partial concurrence by Judge Easterbrook).

The partnership-consideration process is covered by the antidiscrimination laws, even if once admitted into the partnership the plaintiff would then be excluded from the laws' reach. See Hishon v. King & Spalding, 467 U.S. 69, 104 S.Ct. 2229, 81 L.Ed.2d 59 (1984); Price Waterhouse v. Hopkins, 490 U.S. 228, 109 S.Ct. 1775, 104 L.Ed.2d 268 (1989). In the *Price Waterhouse* litigation, a Title VII violation was found and the court ordered that the plaintiff be admitted to the partnership. See Hopkins v. Price Waterhouse, 920 F.2d 967 (D.C.Cir.), affirming 737 F.Supp. 1202 (D.D.C.1990).

CHAPTER 2

EMPLOYMENT-AT-WILL AND ITS CONTRACTUAL EXCEPTIONS

■ ■ ■

Introduction

We start with the U.S, common law doctrine of employment at-will upon which statutory and other developments in employment law have been built.

A. THE DEFAULT RULE OF AT-WILL EMPLOYMENT

U.S. courts generally construe employment for an indefinite or unstated term as a relationship which may be terminated "at will" by either party. In the absence of a contractual qualification or statutory limitation (of the sort set forth in Chapters 3 through 10 of this book), or a recognized common law exception (such as the "public policy" cause of action explored in Chapter 12), the employment relationship is terminable at the will of either party.

RESTATEMENT OF EMPLOYMENT LAW § 2.01
American Law Institute (2015).

§ 2.01   Default Rule of an At-Will Employment Relationship

Either party may terminate an employment relationship with or without cause unless the right to do so is limited by a statute, other law or public policy, or an agreement between the parties, a binding employer promise, or a binding employer policy statement.

NOTES AND QUESTIONS

Test Your Understanding of the Material

1.   Is the at-will default rule consistent with general contract principles? What is the basic exchange between the employer and the employee? Is there mutuality of obligation? Does there have to be? Consider the following analysis from a 1921 Illinois ruling:

> While consideration is essential to the validity of a contract, mutuality of obligation is not. Where there is no other consideration for a contract, the mutual promises of the parties constitute the

41

consideration, and these promises must be binding on both parties or the contract fails for want of consideration, but, where, there is any other consideration for the contract, mutuality of obligation is not essential. If mutuality, in a broad sense, were held to be an essential element in every valid contract to the extent that both contracting parties could sue on it, there could be no such thing as a valid unilateral or option contract.

Armstrong Paint & Varnish Works v. Continental Can Co., 301 Ill. 102, 108, 133 N.E. 711, 714 (1921). See also Mark Pettit, Jr., Modern Unilateral Contracts, 63 B.U.L.Rev. 551 (1983). See Samuel Estreicher & Beverly Wolff, At-Will Employment and the Problem of Unjust Dismissal, 36 Record of Assn. of the Bar of the City of N.Y. 170, 187–88 (April 1981).

Related Issues

2.   Critics of the American default rule of employment at-will make two core points. First, they claim that the doctrine erects a virtually irrebuttable presumption of at-will status that may be at variance with the actual intentions of the parties to establish a different rule. Second, the doctrine has been challenged, principally as a matter of policy, for providing an inadequate level of job security. The two criticisms lead to distinct modes of legal intervention. The response to the former criticism is to abandon any rigid presumption of at-will status and instead allow open consideration of the available evidence as to the joint intentions of the parties. Such a program is in keeping with the traditional function of contract law—to facilitate private determination. The response to the latter criticism is to mandate some form of job security irrespective of the agreement of the parties. This is not a traditional role for contract law but rather a call for legislative intervention that must be justified as such.

3.   The default rule stated in § 2.01 of the Employment Restatement is recognized in all U.S. jurisdictions save for Montana, see Mont. Code Ann. § 39–2–901 et seq., and Puerto Rico, see P.R. Law 80, 29 L.P.R.A. § 185a, which have enacted statutes to deal with employment termination. See Employment Restatement § 2.01, App. A to Reporters' Notes, at 54–60. A "cause" limitation on termination is characteristic of union-represented employment and government employment. Most developed nations outside of the United States have enacted wrongful-termination laws, which are evaluated against the U.S. system in Samuel Estreicher & Jeffrey M. Hirsch, Comparative Wrongful Dismissal Law: Reassessing American Exceptionalism, 92 N.Car. L. Rev. 343 (2014). The Canadian approach, which combines legislation and common law remedies, is described id. at 370–378.

4.   *Historical Accounts.* For historical accounts regarding the development of the employment-at-will doctrine, see Jay Feinman, The Development of the Employment At Will Rule, 20 Amer.J. of Legal Hist. 118 (1976); Mary Ann Glendon & Edward R. Lev, Changes in the Bonding of the Employment Relationship: An Essay on the New Property, 20 B.C.L.Rev. 457 (1979); Sanford Jacoby, The Duration of Indefinite Employment Contracts in

the United States and England: A Historical Analysis, 5 Comp.Lab.L. 85 (1982); Charles McCurdy, The Roots of "Liberty of Contract" Reconsidered: Major Premises in the Law of Employment, 1867–1937, 1984 Y.B.Sup.Ct.Hist. Soc'y 20; Gary Minda, The Common Law of Employment At Will in New York, 36 Syracuse L.Rev. 939, 966–90 (1985).

5. *A Property Right in One's Job?* Some writers have suggested that contract law is the wrong starting point for analyzing the termination of the employment relationship. Rather, the employee should be viewed as having a property right in his job defeasible only upon "cause" for termination. See William B. Gould, IV, The Idea of the Job as Property in Contemporary America: The Legal and Collective Bargaining Framework, 1986 B.Y.U.L.Rev. 885; Jack Beermann & Joseph Singer, Baseline Questions in Legal Reasoning: The Example of Property in Jobs, 23 Ga.L.Rev. 911 (1989). On what basis should the courts recognize such property rights?

6. *Procedural Due Process.* Government workers may claim some protection under the Fourteenth Amendment's due process clause's command that "property" not be taken by the state without "due process of law." The Supreme Court has held that the clause does not create property rights, but rather reaches only interests already recognized by state or other positive law, including in some cases interests in continued public employment absent "cause" for termination. See Board of Regents of State Colleges v. Roth, 408 U.S. 564, 92 S.Ct. 2701, 33 L.Ed.2d 548 (1972); Perry v. Sindermann, 408 U.S. 593, 92 S.Ct. 2694, 33 L.Ed.2d 570 (1972). Interests so recognized are due some process before they may be impaired; sometimes such process may be an appropriate combination of a limited hearing prior to termination of employment and a prompt post-termination hearing. See Cleveland Board of Educ. v. Loudermill, 470 U.S. 532, 105 S.Ct. 1487, 84 L.Ed.2d 494 (1985); Gilbert v. Homar, 520 U.S. 924, 117 S.Ct. 1807, 138 L.Ed.2d 120 (1997).

B. WRONGFUL TERMINATION: CONTRACT THEORIES OF RECOVERY

The courts have proceeded on two fronts to mitigate the rigid presumption erected by early formulations of the employment at-will doctrine. One approach has been to show greater receptivity to finding express contractual promises of job security. Second, a minority of jurisdictions has recognized in particular circumstances implied promises restricting the employer's at-will authority. The modern U.S at-will default rule and its established contract-law exceptions are reflected in the Employment Restatement as set forth below and in the materials discussed in this Part of the Chapter.

RESTATEMENT OF EMPLOYMENT LAW §§ 2.02–2.03

American Law Institute (2015).

§ 2.02 Agreements and Binding Employer Promises or Statements Providing for Terms Other Than At-Will Employment

The employment relationship is not terminable at will by an employer if:

(a) an agreement between the employer and the employee provides for (i) a definite term of employment, or (ii) an indefinite term of employment and requires cause (defined in § 2.04) to terminate the employment (§ 2.03); or

(b) a promise by the employer to limit termination of employment reasonably induces detrimental reliance by the employee (§ 2.02, Comment c); or

(c) a binding policy statement made by the employer limits termination of employment (§ 2.05); or

(d) the implied duty of good faith and fair dealing applicable to all employment relationships (§ 2.07) limits termination of employment; or

(e) other established principles recognized in the general law of contracts limits termination of employment (§ 2.02, Comment d).

§ 2.03 Agreements for a Definite or Indefinite Term

(a) An employer must have cause (§ 2.04) for terminating

(1) an unexpired agreement for a definite term of employment, or

(2) an agreement for an indefinite term of employment requiring cause for termination.

(b) In the absence of an employee's express agreement providing otherwise, the employee is under no reciprocal obligation to have cause to terminate the employment relationship.

1. AGREEMENTS FOR A DEFINITE OR INDEFINITE TERM

a. Express Contracts

OHANIAN V. AVIS RENT A CAR SYSTEM, INC.

United States Court of Appeals, Second Circuit, 1985.
779 F.2d 101.

CARDAMONE, J.

Defendant Avis Rent A Car System (Avis) appeals from a judgment entered on a jury verdict in the Eastern District of New York (Weinstein, Ch.J.) awarding $304,693 in damages to plaintiff Robert S. Ohanian for lost wages and pension benefits arising from defendant's breach of a lifetime employment contract made orally to plaintiff.

* * *

Plaintiff Ohanian began working for Avis in Boston in 1967. Later he was appointed District Sales Manager in New York, and subsequently moved to San Francisco. By 1980 he had become Vice President of Sales for Avis's Western Region. Robert Mahmarian, a former Avis general manager, testified that Ohanian's performance in that region was excellent. During what Mahmarian characterized as "a very bad, depressed economic period," Ohanian's Western Region stood out as the one region that was growing and profitable. According to the witness, Ohanian was directly responsible for this success.

In the fall of 1980, Avis's Northeast Region—the region with the most profit potential—was "dying." Mahmarian and then Avis President Calvano decided that the Northeast Region needed new leadership and Ohanian was the logical candidate. They thought plaintiff should return to New York as Vice President of Sales for the Northeast Region. According to Mahmarian, "nobody anticipated how tough it would be to get the guy." Ohanian was happy in the Western Region, and for several reasons did not want to move. First, he had developed a good "team" in the Western Region; second, he and his family liked the San Francisco area; and third, he was secure in his position where he was doing well and did not want to get involved in the politics of the Avis "World Headquarters," which was located in the Northeast Region. Mahmarian and Calvano were determined to bring Ohanian east and so they set out to overcome his reluctance. After several phone calls to him, first from then Vice President of Sales McNamara, then from Calvano, and finally Mahmarian, Ohanian was convinced to accept the job in the Northeast Region. In Mahmarian's words, he changed Ohanian's mind[:]

> On the basis of promise, that a good man is a good man, and he
> has proven his ability, and if it didn't work out and he had to go

back out in the field, or back to California, or whatever else, fine. As far as I was concerned, his future was secure in the company, unless—and I always had to qualify—unless he screwed up badly. Then he is on his own, and even then I indicated that at worst he would get his [severance] because there was some degree of responsibility on the part of management, Calvano and myself, in making this man make this change.

Ohanian's concerns about security were met by Mahmarian's assurance that "[u]nless [he] screwed up badly, there is no way [he was] going to get fired * * * [he would] never get hurt here in this company." Ohanian accepted the offer and began work in the Northeast Region in early February 1981.

In April 1981 Ohanian told Fred Sharp, Vice President of Personnel, that he needed relocation money that had been promised, but not yet received. Sharp subsequently sent two form letters to Ohanian: one from Sharp to Ohanian and the other, prepared by Avis, from Ohanian to Sharp. The second letter was a form with boxes for Ohanian to check to signify his choice of relocation expense plans. Ohanian checked one of the boxes, signed the form, and returned it to Sharp.

The following language appeared on the form that Ohanian signed and returned:

I also hereby confirm my understanding that nothing contained herein or in connection with the change in my position with Avis shall be deemed to constitute an obligation on the part of Avis to employ me for any period of time, and both the company and I can terminate my employment at will.

There are no other agreements or understandings in respect of my change in position with Avis or the moving of my residence except as is set forth or referred to herein, and in your confirmation letter to me dated April 21, 1981, and the agreements and undertakings set forth therein cannot be modified or altered except by an instrument in writing signed by me and by an executive officer of Avis.

At trial, Ohanian said that he did not believe he read the letter other than to check the relocation plan he desired. He testified that he did not intend this letter to be a contract or to change the terms of his prior agreement with Avis.

Seven months after Ohanian moved to the Northeast Region, he was promoted to National Vice President of Sales and began work at Avis World Headquarters in Garden City, New York. He soon became dissatisfied with this position and in June 1982, pursuant to his request, returned to his former position as Vice President of Sales for the Northeast Region. A month later, on July 27, 1982, at 47 years of age, plaintiff was fired without severance pay. He then instituted this action. Within three months of termination, plaintiff obtained a job as Vice President of Sales for American International Rent A Car. His first year's salary at American International was $50,000 plus a $20,000 bonus. When Ohanian was fired by Avis, his yearly salary was $68,400, and the jury found that he was owed a $17,100 bonus that he had earned before being fired.

* * *

Avis does not challenge the jury's finding that it had not proved that plaintiff was terminated for just cause. Neither has it appealed the awards for the bonus and relocation expenses. Both parties agree that New York law applies.

Defendant's principal argument is that the oral contract that the jury found existed is barred under the statute of frauds, § 5–701 (subd. a, para. 1) of the General Obligations Law. Section 5–701 provides in relevant part:

> Every agreement, promise or undertaking is void, unless it or some note or memorandum thereof be in writing, and subscribed by the party to be charged therewith, or by his lawful agent, if such agreement, promise or undertaking * * * [b]y its terms is not to be performed within one year from the making thereof or the performance of which is not to be completed before the end of a lifetime.

It has long been held that the purpose of the statute is to raise a barrier to fraud when parties attempt to prove certain legal transactions that are deemed to be particularly susceptible to deception, mistake, and perjury. *See D & N Boening, Inc. v. Kirsch Beverages*, 63 N.Y.2d 449, 453–54, 483 N.Y.S.2d 164, 472 N.E.2d 992 (1984). The provision making void any oral contract "not to be performed within one year" is to prevent injustice that might result either from a faulty memory or the absence of witnesses that have died or moved. *See id.; 2 Corbin on Contracts* § 444 at 534 (1950).

* * *

In fact, New York courts perhaps * * * believing that strict application of the statute causes more fraud than it prevents, have tended to construe it warily. The one-year provision has been held not to preclude an oral contract unless there is "not * * * the slightest possibility that it can be fully performed within one year." 2 *Corbin on Contracts* § 444 at 535; *Warner v. Texas and Pacific Railway*, 164 U.S. 418, 434, 17 S.Ct. 147, 153, 41 L.Ed. 495 (1896) ("The question is not what the probable, or expected, or actual performance of the contract was; but whether the contract, according to the reasonable interpretation of its terms, required that it should not be performed within the year."); *Boening*, 63 N.Y.2d at 455, 483 N.Y.S.2d 164, 472 N.E.2d 992. ("this court has continued to analyze oral agreements to determine if, according to the parties' terms, there might be any possible means of performance within one year"). * * *

When does an oral contract not to be performed within a year fall within the strictures of the statute? A contract is not "to be performed within a year" if it is terminable within that time only upon the breach of one of the parties. *Boening*, 63 N.Y.2d at 456, 483 N.Y.S.2d 164, 472 N.E.2d 992. That rule derives from logic because "[p]erformance, if it means anything at all, is 'carrying out the contract by doing what it requires or permits' * * * and a breach is the unexcused failure to do so." *Id. (citing Blake v. Voigt,* 134 N.Y. at 72, 31 N.E. 256) [(1892)]. The distinction is between an oral contract that provides for its own termination at any time on the one hand, and an oral contract that is terminable within a year only upon its breach on the other. The former may be proved by a plaintiff and the latter is barred by the statute.

Avis contends that its oral agreement with Ohanian is barred by the statute of frauds because it was not performable within a year. Avis claims that it could only fire plaintiff if he breached the contract, and breach of a contract is not performance. * * *

What defendant fails to recognize is that under New York law "just cause" for termination may exist for reasons other than an employee's breach. * * *

In the instant case, just cause for dismissing Ohanian would plainly include any breach of the contract, such as drinking on the job or refusing to work, since the agreement contemplates plaintiff giving his best efforts. But, as noted, just cause can be broader than breach and here there may be just cause to dismiss without a breach. To illustrate, under the terms of the contract it would be possible that despite plaintiff's best efforts the results achieved might prove poor because of adverse market conditions. From defendant's standpoint that too would force Avis to make a change in its business strategy, perhaps reducing or closing an operation. That is, there would be just cause for plaintiff's dismissal. But if this is what occurred, it would not constitute a breach of the agreement. Best efforts were contemplated by the parties, results were not. Defendant was anxious to have plaintiff relocate because of his past success, but plaintiff made no guarantee to produce certain results. Thus, this oral contract could have been terminated for just cause within one year, without any breach by plaintiff, and is therefore not barred by the statute of frauds.

* * *

Defendant next urges that any claims based on the oral agreement between Ohanian and Avis are barred by the parol evidence rule. Avis says that the clear and unambiguous letter of April 21, 1981 was signed by plaintiff, and it contradicts plaintiff's assertion that he was promised lifetime employment and severance on termination. It is, of course, a fundamental principle of contract law "that, where parties have reduced their bargain, or any element of it, to writing, the parol evidence rule applies to prevent its variance by parol evidence." *Laskey v. Rubel Corp.,* 303 N.Y. 69, 71, 100 N.E.2d 140 (1951).

Avis's argument fails for a very basic reason: the jury found that the April 21st letter did not constitute a contract between it and Ohanian. The trial judge had correctly instructed the jury that if it found the letter to be a contract it could not find for plaintiff, and the jury found for plaintiff. Parol evidence is excluded only when used as an attempt to vary or modify the terms of an existing written contract. *See Kirtley v. Abrams,* 299 F.2d 341, 345 (2d Cir.1962) (the rule does not preclude a party "from attempting to show that there never was any agreement such as the writing purported to be"); *Whipple v. Brown Brothers Co.,* 225 N.Y. 237, 244, 121 N.E. 748 (1919) ("One cannot be made to stand on a contract he never intended to make."); 3 *Corbin on Contracts* § 577 at 385 (1960).

* * *

Avis says that inasmuch as the evidence of an oral promise of lifetime employment was insufficient as a matter of law, that issue should not have gone to the jury. It relies on *Brown v. Safeway Stores, Inc.,* 190 F.Supp. 295 (E.D.N.Y.1960), as support for this argument. Defendant can draw little solace from *Brown.* In that case the claimed assurances were made in several ways including meetings of a group of employees—the purpose of which was not to discuss length of employment—or during casual conversation. *Id.* at 299–300. The conversations were not conducted in an atmosphere, as here, of critical one-on-one negotiation regarding the terms of future employment. Further, in *Brown* the district court found as a matter of fact that the alleged promise of lifetime employment was never made. In contrast, in the instant case the evidence was ample to permit the jury to decide whether statements made to Ohanian by defendant were more than casual comments or mere pep talks delivered by management to a group of employees. All of the surrounding circumstances—fully related earlier—were sufficient for the jury in fact to find that there was a promise of lifetime employment to a "star" employee who, it was hoped, would revive a "dying" division of defendant corporation.

NOTES AND QUESTIONS

Test Your Understanding of the Material

1. Ohanian's claim is based on an oral agreement with Avis. New York's statute of frauds provides that any unwritten agreement is void if "such agreement, promise or undertaking * * * [b]y its terms is not to be performed within one year from the making thereof." How does the court overcome the statute of frauds? For a contrary view, see note 5 below.

2.   As you may recall from your contracts class, the parol evidence rule prohibits a party from introducing extrinsic evidence to alter the meaning of an integrated written contract. See Restatement Second of Contracts § 213 (1981). Why didn't the April 1981 letter preclude Ohanian from introducing evidence of the prior oral agreement?

Related Issues

3.   *Promises of "Lifetime" or "Permanent" Employment.* Modern courts generally have rejected the position of the early common law that express promises of "permanent" or "lifetime" employment are per se unenforceable either for want of consideration or mutuality of obligation. See, e.g., Weiner v. McGraw-Hill, Inc., 57 N.Y.2d 458, 457 N.Y.S.2d 193, 443 N.E.2d 441 (1982). The courts remain, however, wary of purported *oral* agreements of lifetime employment. See e.g., *Woolley v. Hoffman La Roche, Inc.*, infra p. 67 (discussion of Savarese v. Pyrene Mfg. Co., 9 N.J. 595, 9 N.J. 595, 89 A.2d 237 (1952)); see also Murray v. Commercial Union Insurance Co., 782 F.2d 432 (3d Cir.1986) (applying Pennsylvania law); Veno v. Meredith, 357 Pa.Super. 85, 515 A.2d 571 (1986). See generally Employment Restatement § 2.03, Comment c.

4.   *Definite vs. Indefinite Promises.* At the beginning of Mike Tyson's boxing career, he was placed under the supervision of Cus D'Amato, a renowned boxing figure and manager, who became Tyson's legal guardian. In 1982 D'Amato and Kevin Rooney, a trainer, agreed they would train Tyson without compensation until he became a professional fighter. The two further agreed that when Tyson advanced to professional ranks, Rooney would be Tyson's trainer "for as long as [Tyson] fought professionally." Rooney trained Tyson for 28 months without compensation. After Tyson entered professional ranks in 1985, D'Amato died and James Jacobs became Tyson's manager in 1986. To quell rumors, Tyson authorized Jacobs to state publicly that Rooney would be Tyson's trainer "as long as Mike Tyson is a professional fighter." In 1988, Tyson terminated his relationship with Rooney. The latter then sued Tyson in federal court claiming breach of the 1982 oral agreement. On certified questions from the Second Circuit, the New York Court of Appeals agreed that Rooney's suit could proceed under New York law:

> A sensible path to declare New York law starts with these two steps:
> (1) if the duration is definite, the at-will doctrine is inapplicable, on
> the other hand, (2) if the employment term is indefinite or undefined,
> the rebuttable at-will presumption is operative and other facts come
> into the equation. * * *
>
> * * *
>
> When an agreement is silent as to duration * * * it is presumptively
> at-will, absent an express or implied limitation on an employer's
> otherwise unfettered ability to discharge an employee. * * * Only
> when we discern no term of definiteness or no express limitation does
> the analysis switch over to the rebuttable presumption line of cases.
> They embody the principle that an employment relationship is
> terminable upon even the whim of either the employer or the

employee. The agreement in this case is not silent and manifestly provides a sufficiently limiting framework.

* * *

* * * [A]lthough the exact end-date of Tyson's professional boxing career was not precisely calculable, the boundaries of beginning and end of the employment period are sufficiently ascertainable. That is enough to defeat a matter-of-law decision by a judge, in substitution for resolution * * * by jury verdict. * * *

The range of the employment relationship * * * is established by the definable commencement and conclusion of Tyson's boxing career. Though the times are not precisely predictable and calculable to dates certain, they are legally and experientially limited and ascertainable by objective benchmarks. * * *

Rooney v. Tyson, 91 N.Y.2d 685, 689–90, 692–93, 674 N.Y.S.2d 616, 697 N.E.2d 571 (1998). The court did not consider the applicability of the statute of frauds, which presumably would not have barred the action because Tyson's professional career might have ended within a year.

5.   *Continuing Relevance of Statute of Frauds.* In McInerney v. Charter Golf, Inc., 176 Ill.2d 482, 223 Ill.Dec. 911, 680 N.E.2d 1347 (1997), the court rejected the approach taken in *Ohanian*, holding an oral promise of lifetime employment unenforceable under the statute of frauds:

A "lifetime" employment contract is, in essence, a permanent employment contract. Inherently, it anticipates a relationship of long duration—certainly longer than one year. In the context of an employment-for-life contract, we believe that the better view is to treat the contract as one "not to be performed within the space of one year from the making thereof." To hold otherwise would eviscerate the policy underlying the statute of frauds and would invite confusion, uncertainty and outright fraud. Accordingly, we hold that a writing is required for the fair enforcement of lifetime employment contracts.

Id. at 490–91, 680 N.E.2d at 1351–52.

6.   *Promissory Estoppel Theory.* Can a promissory estoppel claim be pursued when the alleged promise is for employment-at-will rather than employment for a definite term? Section 2.02(b) of the Employment Restatement recognizes that the employment relationship is not terminable at will if "a promise by the employer to limit termination of employment reasonably induces detrimental reliance by the employee. . . ." See also id. § 2.02, Comment c. For issues regarding remedies under this theory, see id. § 9.01(d).

In Bower v. AT&T Technologies, Inc., 852 F.2d 361 (8th Cir.1988), the federal court held that a claim under Missouri law was stated by employees alleging detrimental reliance on their employer's promise that they would be rehired as clerical workers once their repair jobs were phased out as a result of the divestiture of AT & T subsidiaries. Subsequently, the Missouri Court of Appeals ruled that promissory estoppel theory was not available to enforce a promise for at-will employment. See Rosatone v. GTE Sprint Communications, 761 S.W.2d 670 (Mo.App.1988). But cf. Peck v. Imedia, Inc., 293 N.J.Super. 151, 679 A.2d 745 (App.Div.1996); Comeaux v. Brown & Williamson Tobacco Co., 915 F.2d 1264, 1272–73 (9th Cir.1990) (damages under California law for detrimental reliance on withdrawn job offer). See also Cal. Labor Code § 970 (prohibiting employers from inducing employees to relocate "by means of knowingly false representations").

b.   "Implied in Fact" Contracts

FOLEY V. INTERACTIVE DATA CORPORATION
Supreme Court of California, en banc, 1988.
47 Cal.3d 654, 254 Cal.Rptr. 211, 765 P.2d 373.

LUCAS, C.J.

According to the complaint, plaintiff is a former employee of defendant, a wholly owned subsidiary of Chase Manhattan Bank that markets computer-based decision-support services. Defendant hired plaintiff in June 1976 as an assistant product manager at a starting salary of $18,500. As a condition of employment defendant required plaintiff to sign a "Confidential and Proprietary Information Agreement" whereby he promised not to engage in certain competition with defendant for one year after the termination of his employment for any reason. The agreement also contained a "Disclosure and Assignment of Information" provision that obliged plaintiff to disclose to defendant all computer-related information known to him, including any innovations, inventions or developments pertaining to the computer field for a period of one year following his termination. Finally, the agreement imposed on plaintiff a continuing obligation to assign to defendant all rights to his computer-related inventions or innovations for one year following termination. It did not state any limitation on the grounds for which plaintiff's employment could be terminated.

Over the next six years and nine months, plaintiff received a steady series of salary increases, promotions, bonuses, awards and superior performance evaluations. In 1979 defendant named him consultant manager of the year and in 1981 promoted him to branch manager of its Los Angeles office. His annual salary rose to $56,164 and he received an additional $6,762 merit bonus two days before his discharge in March 1983. He alleges defendant's officers made repeated oral assurances of job security so long as his performance remained adequate.

Plaintiff also alleged that during his employment, defendant maintained written "Termination Guidelines" that set forth express grounds for discharge and a mandatory seven-step pretermination procedure. Plaintiff understood that these guidelines applied not only to employees under plaintiff's supervision, but to him as well. On the basis of these representations, plaintiff alleged that he reasonably believed defendant would not discharge him except for good cause, and therefore he refrained from accepting or pursuing other job opportunities.

The event that led to plaintiff's discharge was a private conversation in January 1983 with his former supervisor, vice president Richard Earnest. During the previous year defendant had hired Robert Kuhne and subsequently named Kuhne to replace Earnest as plaintiff's immediate supervisor. Plaintiff learned that Kuhne was currently under investigation by the Federal Bureau of Investigation for embezzlement from his former employer, Bank of America. Plaintiff reported what he knew about Kuhne to Earnest, because he was "worried about working for Kuhne and having him in a supervisory position * * * , in view of Kuhne's suspected criminal conduct." Plaintiff asserted he "made this disclosure in the interest and for the benefit of his employer," allegedly because he believed that because defendant and its parent do business with the financial community on a confidential basis, the company would have a legitimate interest in knowing about a high executive's alleged prior criminal conduct.

In response, Earnest allegedly told plaintiff not to discuss "rumors" and to "forget what he heard" about Kuhne's past. In early March, Kuhne informed plaintiff that defendant had decided to replace him for "performance reasons" and that he could transfer to a position in another division in Waltham, Massachusetts. Plaintiff was told that if he did not accept a transfer, he might be demoted but not fired. One week later, in Waltham, Earnest informed plaintiff he was not doing a good job, and six days later, he notified plaintiff he could continue as branch manager if he "agreed to go on a 'performance plan.' Plaintiff asserts he agreed to consider such an arrangement." The next day, when Kuhne met with plaintiff, purportedly to present him with a written "performance plan" proposal, Kuhne instead informed plaintiff he had the choice of resigning or being fired. Kuhne offered neither a performance plan nor an option to transfer to another position.

* * *

Although plaintiff describes his cause of action as one for breach of an oral contract, he does not allege explicit words by which the parties agreed that he would not be terminated without good cause. Instead he alleges that a course of conduct, including various oral representations, created a reasonable expectation to that effect. Thus, his cause of action is more properly described as one for breach of an implied-in-fact contract. * * *

The absence of an express written or oral contract term concerning termination of employment does not necessarily indicate that the employment is actually intended by the parties to be "at will," because the presumption of at-will employment may be overcome by evidence of contrary intent. Generally, courts seek to enforce the actual understanding of the parties to a contract, and in so doing may inquire into the parties' conduct to determine if it demonstrates an implied contract. "[I]t must be determined, as a question of fact, whether the parties acted in such a manner as to provide the necessary foundation for [an implied contract], and evidence may be introduced to rebut the inferences and show that there is another explanation for the conduct." (*Silva v. Providence Hosp. of Oakland* (1939) 14 Cal.2d 762, 774, 97 P.2d 798; * * *). Such implied-in-fact contract terms ordinarily stand on equal footing with express terms. ([Restatement Second of Contracts] §§ 4, 19.) At issue here is whether the foregoing principles apply to contract terms establishing employment security, so that the presumption of Labor Code section 2922 [of at-will employment] may be overcome by evidence of contrary implied terms, or whether such agreements are subject to special substantive or evidentiary limitations.

* * *

The limitations on employment security terms on which defendant relies were developed during a period when courts were generally reluctant to look beyond explicit promises of the parties to a contract. "The court-imposed presumption that the employment contract is terminable at will relies upon the formalistic approach to contract interpretation predominant in late nineteenth century legal thought: manifestations of assent must be evidenced by definite, express terms if promises are to be enforceable." (Note, *Protecting At Will Employees*, 93 Harv.L.Rev. [1816, 1825 (1980)].) In the intervening decades, however, courts increasingly demonstrated their willingness to examine the entire relationship of the parties to commercial contracts to ascertain their actual intent, and this trend has been reflected in the body of law guiding contract interpretation. (See, Goetz & Scott, *The Limits of Expanded Choice: An Analysis of the Interactions Between Express and Implied Contract Terms* (1985) 73 Cal.L.Rev. 261, 273–276 ["The (Uniform Commercial) Code, now joined by the Second Restatement of Contracts, effectively reverses the common law presumption that the parties' writing and the official law of contract are the definitive elements of the agreement. Evidence derived from experience and practice can now trigger the incorporation of additional, implied terms"].)

* * *

In the employment context, factors apart from consideration and express terms may be used to ascertain the existence and content of an employment agreement, including "the personnel policies or practices of the employer, the employee's longevity of service, actions or communications by the employer reflecting assurances of continued employment, and the practices of the industry in which the employee is engaged." * * * Pursuant to Labor Code section 2922, if the parties reach no express or implied agreement to the contrary, the relationship is terminable at any time without cause. But when the parties have enforceable expectations concerning either the term of employment or the grounds or manner of termination, Labor Code section 2922 does not diminish the force of such contractual or legal obligations. The presumption that an employment relationship of indefinite duration is intended to be terminable at will is therefore "subject, like any presumption, to contrary evidence. This may take the form of an agreement, express or implied, that * * * the employment relationship will continue indefinitely, pending the occurrence of some event such as the employer's dissatisfaction with the employee's services or the existence of some 'cause' for termination." * * *

Finally, we do not agree with the Court of Appeal that employment security agreements are so inherently harmful or unfair to employers, who do not receive equivalent guarantees of continued service, as to merit treatment different from that accorded other contracts. On the contrary, employers may benefit from the increased loyalty and productivity that such agreements may inspire. * * * Permitting proof of and reliance on implied-in-fact contract terms does not nullify the at-will rule, it merely treats such contracts in a manner in keeping with general contract law. * * *

Defendant's remaining argument is that even if a promise to discharge "for good cause only" could be implied in fact, the evidentiary factors * * * relied on by plaintiff are inadequate as a matter of law. This contention fails on several grounds.

First, defendant overemphasizes the fact that plaintiff was employed for "only" six years and nine months. Length of employment is a relevant consideration but six years and nine months is sufficient time for conduct to occur on which a trier of fact could find the existence of an implied contract. * * *

Second, an allegation of breach of written "Termination Guidelines" implying self-imposed limitations on the employer's power to discharge at will may be sufficient to state a cause of action for breach of an employment contract. * * *

Finally, * * * plaintiff alleges that he supplied the company valuable and separate consideration by signing an agreement whereby he promised not to compete or conceal any computer-related information from defendant for one year after termination. The noncompetition agreement and its attendant "Disclosure and Assignment of Proprietary Information, Inventions, etc." may be probative evidence that "it is more probable that the parties intended a continuing relationship, with limitations upon the employer's dismissal authority [because the] employee has provided some benefit to the employer, or suffers some detriment, beyond the usual rendition of service."

In sum, plaintiff has pleaded facts which, if proved, may be sufficient for a jury to find an implied-in-fact contract limiting defendant's right to discharge him arbitrarily—facts sufficient to overcome the presumption of Labor Code section 2922. On demurrer, we must assume these facts to be true. In other words, plaintiff has pleaded an implied-in-fact contract and its breach, and is entitled to his opportunity to prove those allegations.

NOTES AND QUESTIONS

Test Your Understanding of the Material

1.   How does the court in *Foley* reconcile its recognition of an "implied in fact" contract with the otherwise applicable (indeed, in California, statutorily grounded) presumption of at-will employment?

2.   Implied terms are common in employment contract law. See Employment Restatement § 2.03, Comment g ("In some cases, the parties to an otherwise enforceable employment agreement expressly or impliedly refer to stated policies or established practices of the employer or in the trade to supply omitted terms in the agreement."). Is the *Foley* court going beyond recognition of certain terms implicit in the parties' relationship to dispense with the need for express promises or other manifestations of the intention of both parties to enter into a binding agreement?

3.   What exactly does the court mean by the "implied-in-fact contract"? What are the elements of such a contract? Is it different from a traditional contract?

Related Issues

4.   *"Implied in Fact" Doctrine in Other Jurisdictions.* In other jurisdictions, courts may invoke the language of "implied in fact" contracts to permit enforcement of indefinite oral obligations contained in unilateral employer promulgations or recognize implied terms in employment agreements negotiated between employers and employees. For example, in Torosyan v. Boehringer Ingelheim Pharms., 234 Conn. 1, 662 A.2d 89 (1995); see also Boothby v. Texon, Inc., 414 Mass. 468, 608 N.E.2d 1028 (1993), the court used the terminology of "implied contract" apparently in the belief that "express" contracts, at least in that jurisdiction, require a particular form of words. The case would appear to have involved sufficient evidence of an agreement for indefinite employment containing a limit on termination of employment by the employer. As the state high court noted and held to be not clearly erroneous: "The trial court found that, in the circumstances of this case, the oral and written statements constituted promises to the plaintiff" and "that, by working for the defendant, the plaintiff accepted those promises." 234 Conn. at 22. The state supreme court further reasoned:

> Pursuant to traditional contract principles . . . the default rule of employment at will can be modified by the agreement of the parties. Accordingly, to prevail on the . . . count of his complaint (that) alleged the existence of an implied agreement, the plaintiff had the burden

of proving by the fair preponderance of the evidence that (the employer) had agreed either by words or conduct, to undertake (some) form of actual contract commitment to him under which he could not be terminated without cause.

Id. at 15. Employment Restatement § 2.03, Comments g–h & Illus. 6–7.

GUZ v. BECHTEL NATIONAL, INC.

Supreme Court of California, En Banc, 2000.
24 Cal.4th 317, 100 Cal.Rptr.2d 352, 8 P.3d 1089.

BAXTER, J.

This case presents questions about the law governing claims of wrongful discharge from employment as it applies to an employer's motion for summary judgment. Plaintiff John Guz, a longtime employee of Bechtel National, Inc. (BNI), was released at age 49 when his work unit was eliminated and its tasks were transferred to another Bechtel office. Guz sued BNI and its parent, Bechtel Corporation (hereinafter collectively Bechtel), alleging * * * breach of an implied contract to be terminated only for good cause * * *. The trial court granted Bechtel's motion for summary judgment and dismissed the action. In a split decision, the Court of Appeal reversed. The majority found that Bechtel had demonstrated no grounds to foreclose a trial on any of the claims asserted in the complaint.

Having closely reviewed the Court of Appeal's decision, we reach the following conclusions:

First, the Court of Appeal used erroneous grounds to reverse summary judgment on Guz's implied contract cause of action. The Court of Appeal found triable evidence (1) that Guz had an actual agreement, implied in fact, to be discharged only for good cause, and (2) that the elimination of Guz's work unit lacked good cause because Bechtel's stated reason-a "downturn in . . . workload"—was not justified by the facts, and was, in truth, a pretext to discharge the unit's workers for poor performance without following the company's "progressive discipline" policy. We acknowledge a triable issue that Guz, like other Bechtel workers, had implied contractual rights under specific provisions of Bechtel's written personnel policies. But neither the policies, nor other evidence, suggests any contractual restriction on Bechtel's right to eliminate a work unit as it saw fit, even where dissatisfaction with unit performance was a factor in the decision. The Court of Appeal's ruling on Guz's implied contract claim must therefore be reversed. The Court of Appeal did not reach the additional ground on which Guz claims a contractual breach—i.e., that Bechtel failed to follow its fair layoff policies when, during and after the reorganization, it made individual personnel decisions leading to Guz's release. Accordingly, we leave that issue to the Court of Appeal on remand.

* * *

Guz alleges he had an agreement with Bechtel that he would be employed so long as he was performing satisfactorily and would be discharged only for good cause. Guz claims no express understanding to this effect. However, he asserts that such an agreement can be inferred by combining evidence of several *Foley* factors, including (1) his long service; (2) assurances of continued employment in the form of raises, promotions, and good performance reviews; (3) Bechtel's written personnel policies, which suggested that termination for poor performance would be preceded by progressive discipline, that layoffs during a work force reduction would be based on objective criteria, including formal ranking, and that persons laid off would receive placement and reassignment assistance; and (4) testimony by a Bechtel executive that company practice was to terminate employees for a good reason and to reassign, if possible, a laid-off employee who was performing satisfactorily.

During this time, Bechtel maintained Personnel Policy 1101, dated June 1991, on the subject of termination of employment (Policy 1101). Policy 1101 stated that "Bechtel employees have no employment agreements guaranteeing continuous service and may resign at their option or be terminated at the option of Bechtel."

Policy 1101 also described several "Categories of Termination," including "Layoff" and "Unsatisfactory Performance." With respect to Unsatisfactory Performance, the policy stated that "[e]mployees who fail to perform their jobs in a satisfactory manner may be terminated, provided the employees have been advised of the specific shortcomings and given an opportunity to improve their performance." A layoff was defined as "a Bechtel-initiated termination [ ] of employees caused by a reduction in workload, reorganizations, changes in job requirements, or other circumstances. . . ." Under the Layoff policy, employees subject to termination for this reason "may be placed on 'holding status' if there is a possible Bechtel assignment within the following 3-month period." Guz understood that Policy 1101 applied to him. * * *

Guz also submitted additional Bechtel documents discussing specific company personnel policies and practices, including those policies pertaining to laid-off employees. These documents included Bechtel's 1989 Reduction-in-Force Guidelines (RIF Guidelines) and Bechtel's Personnel Policy 302 (Policy 302).

Policy 302 described a system of employee ranking (sometimes hereafter called force ranking), which was to be "used alone or in conjunction with other management tools in making personnel decisions in such areas as . . . [s]taffing." Rankings were to be based on the fair, objective, and consistent evaluation of employees' comparative job-relevant skills and performance. However, Policy 302 also provided that "[u]nique situations may occur in which employee ranking may be inapplicable based on the nature of the personnel decision or the limited size of the ranking group." (Italics omitted.)

The RIF Guidelines specified that when choosing among employees to be retained and released during a reduction in force, the formal ranking system set forth in Policy 302 was to be employed. For this purpose, the RIF Guidelines said, employees should "[i]deally" be ranked, by similarity of function or level of work activity, in groups of from 20 to 100. * * *

The RIF Guidelines also explained the term "holding status" and its benefits. According to the RIF Guidelines, this status could be granted upon layoff, for a renewable three-month period, while the employee awaited possible reassignment. The employee would not receive salary, but Bechtel would maintain his medical, dental, voluntary personal accident, and term life insurance. Bechtel should also provide the employee with "[t]ransfer and [p]lacement [a]ssistance."

* * *

As we shall explain, we find triable evidence that Bechtel's written personnel documents set forth implied contractual limits on the circumstances under which Guz, and other Bechtel workers, would be terminated. On the other hand, we see no triable evidence of an implied agreement between Guz and Bechtel on additional, different, or broader terms of employment security. As Bechtel suggests, the personnel documents themselves did not restrict Bechtel's freedom to reorganize, reduce, and consolidate its work force for whatever reasons it wished. Thus, contrary to the Court of Appeal's holding, Bechtel had the absolute right to eliminate Guz's work unit and to transfer the unit's responsibilities to another company entity, even if the decision was influenced by dissatisfaction with the eliminated unit's performance, and even if the personnel documents entitled an individual employee to progressive discipline procedures before being fired for poor performance.

* * *

At the outset, Bechtel insists that the existence of implied contractual limitations on its termination rights is negated because Bechtel expressly disclaimed all such agreements. Bechtel suggests the at-will presumption of Labor Code § 2922 was conclusively reinforced by language Bechtel inserted in Policy 1101, which specified that the company's employees "have no . . . agreements guaranteeing continuous service and may be terminated at [Bechtel's] option." As Bechtel points out, Guz concedes he understood Policy 1101 applied to him.[9]

---

[9]   As noted, Bechtel's disclaimer appears in Policy 1101, part of the general body of Bechtel personnel documents submitted by the parties in connection with the motion for summary judgment. The date on which Policy 1101 was promulgated is uncertain. However, we do not understand Guz to claim that he had an employment security agreement that *predated* and *arose independently of* Policy 1101 and therefore could not be *rescinded or cancelled* by virtue of Policy

This express disclaimer, reinforced by the statutory presumption of at-will employment, satisfied Bechtel's initial burden, if any, to show that Guz's claim of a contract limiting Bechtel's termination rights had no merit. But neither the disclaimer nor the statutory presumption necessarily foreclosed Guz from proving the existence and breach of such an agreement.

* * *

Cases in California and elsewhere have held that at-will provisions in personnel handbooks, manuals, or memoranda do not bar, or necessarily overcome, other evidence of the employer's contrary intent[.] * * * 10

We agree that disclaimer language in an employee handbook or policy manual does not necessarily mean an employee is employed at will. But even if a handbook disclaimer is not controlling * * * in every case, neither can such a provision be ignored in determining whether the parties' conduct was intended, and reasonably understood, to create binding limits on an employer's statutory right to terminate the relationship at will. Like any direct expression of employer intent, communicated to employees and intended to apply to them, such language must be taken into account, along with all other pertinent evidence, in ascertaining the terms on which a worker was employed. We examine accordingly the evidence cited by Guz in support of his implied contract claim.

[I]t is undisputed that Guz received no individual promises or representations that Bechtel would retain him except for good cause, or upon other specified circumstances. * * * Nor does Guz seriously claim that the practice in Bechtel's industry was to provide secure employment. Indeed, the undisputed evidence suggested that because Bechtel, like other members of its industry, operated by competitive bidding from project to project, its work force fluctuated widely and, in terms of raw numbers, was in general decline.

However, Guz insists his own undisputed long and successful service at Bechtel constitutes strong evidence of an implied contract for permanent employment except upon good cause. Guz argues that by retaining him for over 20 years, and by providing him with steady raises, promotions, commendations, and good performance reviews during his tenure, Bechtel engaged in "actions . . . reflecting assurances of continued employment." (*Foley, supra*, 47 Cal. 3d 654, 680.) Bechtel responds that an individual employee's mere long and praiseworthy service has little or no tendency to

---

1101's belated disclaimer. On the contrary, Guz admits Policy 1101 (necessarily including its disclaimer) applied to him, and he premises his contractual claim on an amalgam of factors, *significantly including certain language in Policy 1101 itself.* (See discussion herein.) Hence, we may, and do, assume that the disclaimer included in Policy 1101 is a material factor in ascertaining the terms and conditions on which Guz individually was employed by Bechtel.

10   On the other hand, most cases applying California law, both pre-and post-Foley, have held that an at-will provision in an express written agreement, signed by the employee, cannot be overcome by proof of an implied contrary understanding. * * *

show an implied agreement between the parties that the employee is no longer terminable at will.

* * *

We agree that an employee's mere passage of time in the employer's service, even where marked with tangible indicia that the employer approves the employee's work, cannot alone form an implied-in-fact contract that the employee is no longer at will. Absent other evidence of the employer's intent, longevity, raises and promotions are their own rewards for the employee's continuing valued service; they do not, in and of themselves, additionally constitute a contractual guarantee of future employment security. A rule granting such contract rights on the basis of successful longevity alone would discourage the retention and promotion of employees.

On the other hand, long and successful service is not necessarily irrelevant to the existence of such a contract. Over the period of an employee's tenure, the employer can certainly communicate, by its written and unwritten policies and practices, or by informal assurances, that seniority and longevity do create rights against termination at will. The issue is whether the employer's words or conduct, on which an employee reasonably relied, gave rise to that specific understanding.

Read in context, *Foley, supra*, 47 Cal. 3d 654, did not hold otherwise. In the first place, *Foley*'s reference to lengthy, successful service as evidence of an implied contract not to terminate at will was simply quoted, with little independent analysis, from *Pugh* [*v. See's Candies, Inc.*,] 116 Cal. App. 3d 311, at page 328 [(1981)]. *Pugh*, in turn, had adopted wholesale the reasoning of *Cleary v. American Airlines, Inc.* (1980) 111 Cal. App. 3d 443, 168 Cal. Rptr. 722 that " 'termination of employment without legal cause [after long service] offends the implied-in-law covenant of good faith and fair dealing contained in all contracts, including employment contracts.' " (*Pugh, supra*, 116 Cal. App. 3d at p. 328, quoting *Cleary*, supra, 111 Cal. App. 3d at p. 455 * * * .) In other words, these cases suggested, because the arbitrary termination of a veteran employee is neither fair nor in good faith, such conduct violates the implied covenant contained in every employment contract, regardless of its terms.

But *Foley* itself discredited this line of reasoning. There we "reiterated that the employment relationship is fundamentally contractual" (*Foley, supra*, 47 Cal. 3d 654, 696), and we made clear that the implied covenant of good faith and fair dealing cannot supply limitations on termination rights to which the parties have not actually agreed. * * *

We therefore decline to interpret *Foley* as holding that long, successful service, standing alone, can demonstrate an implied-in-fact contract right not to be terminated at will. In the case before us, there is no indication that employee longevity is a significant factor in determining the existence or content of an implied contract limiting the employer's termination rights. Guz claims no particular "actions or communications by [Bechtel]" (*Foley, supra,* 47 Cal. 3d 654, 680), and no industry customs, practices, or policies, which suggest that by virtue of his successful longevity in Bechtel's employ, he had earned a contractual right against future termination at will.

If anything, Bechtel had communicated otherwise. The company's Policy 1101 stated that Bechtel employees had no contracts guaranteeing their continuous employment and could be terminated at Bechtel's option. Nothing in this language suggested any exception for senior workers, or for those who had received regular raises and promotions. While occasional references to seniority appear in other sections of Bechtel's personnel documents, the narrow context of these references undermines an inference that Bechtel additionally intended, or employees had reason to expect, special immunities from termination based on their extended or successful service.

* * *

Finally, Guz asserts there is evidence that, industry custom and written company personnel policies aside, Bechtel had an unwritten "policy or practice[ ]" (*Foley, supra,* 47 Cal. 3d 654, 680) to release its employees only for cause. As the sole evidence of this policy, Guz points to the deposition testimony of Johnstone, BNI's president, who stated his understanding that Bechtel terminated workers only with "good reason" or for "lack of [available] work." But there is no evidence that Bechtel employees were aware of such an unwritten policy, and it flies in the face of Bechtel's general disclaimer. This brief and vague statement, by a single Bechtel official, that Bechtel sought to avoid arbitrary firings is insufficient as a matter of law to permit a finding that the company, by an unwritten practice or policy on which employees reasonably relied, had contracted away its right to discharge Guz at will.

In sum, if there is any significant evidence that Guz had an implied contract against termination at will, that evidence flows exclusively from Bechtel's written personnel documents. It follows that there is no triable issue of an implied contract on terms broader than the specific provisions of those documents. In reviewing the Court of Appeal's determination that Bechtel may have breached contractual obligations to Guz by eliminating his work unit, we must therefore focus on the pertinent written provisions.

As noted above, Bechtel's written personnel provisions covering termination from employment fell into two categories. The parties do not dispute that certain of these provisions, expressly denominated "Policies" (including Policies 1101 and 302), were disseminated to employees and were intended by Bechtel to inform workers of rules applicable to their employment. There seems little doubt, and we conclude, a triable issue exists that the specific provisions of these Policies did become an implicit part of the employment contracts of the Bechtel employees they covered, including Guz.

Guz also points to another Bechtel document, the RIF Guidelines, that addressed procedures for implementing reductions in the workforce. Evidence suggesting the contractual status of this document is somewhat closer. On the one hand, the "Guidelines" label and evidence indicating this document was distributed primarily to supervisors for their use, weighs against an inference that Bechtel intended a widely disseminated policy on which employees might directly rely. * * * Moreover, there was some evidence that even some Bechtel managers were unaware of the force ranking system set forth in Policy 302 and the RIF Guidelines.

On the other hand, the formality, tone, length, and detail of the RIF Guidelines suggests they were not intended as merely precatory. The RIF Guidelines comprised a minimum of six single-spaced pages, and were distributed under a cover letter suggesting that they represented "corporate policy." In some instances, the RIF Guidelines defined or supplemented terms and provisions directly set forth in Policies 302 and 1101, such as the holding status described in Policy 1101 and the formal personnel ranking system described in Policy 302. There was also some evidence that Bechtel employees, including Guz, were aware of RIF Guideline procedures such as force ranking, had observed that the company followed these procedures in the past, and believed them to be Bechtel's policy. Goldstein, Guz's supervisor at BNI-MI, declared that as a supervisor, he received and was "instructed to follow" the RIF Guidelines. On balance, we are persuaded a triable issue exists that the RIF Guidelines, like the formally denominated Policies, formed part of an implied contract between Bechtel and its employees.

As Bechtel stresses, Policy 1101 itself purported to disclaim any employment security rights. However, Bechtel had inserted other language, not only in Policy 1101 itself, but in other written personnel documents, which described detailed rules and procedures for the termination of employees under particular circumstances. Moreover, the specific language of Bechtel's disclaimer, stating that employees had no contracts "guaranteeing . . . continuous service" * * * and were terminable at Bechtel's "option," did not foreclose an understanding between Bechtel and all its workers that Bechtel would make its termination decisions within the limits of its written personnel rules. Given these ambiguities, a fact finder could rationally determine that despite its general disclaimer, Bechtel had bound itself to the specific provisions of these documents.

In holding that Bechtel may have breached the terms of an implied contract with Guz by eliminating his work unit, the Court of Appeal relied on two premises. Focusing on one reason Guz was given for this decision— a "downturn in . . . workload"—the Court of Appeal concluded that even if this reason were taken at face value, the evidence permitted a determination that it was arbitrary and unreasonable, and thus without good cause, because it lacked support in the facts. Second, the Court of Appeal found triable evidence that this stated reason was pretextual, in that it masked Bechtel's true purpose to dismiss BNI-MI's workers on the basis of the unit's poor performance, but without affording each member the benefit of the progressive discipline rules set forth in the company's personnel documents.

On the facts before us, we conclude that both these premises were in error. Bechtel's written personnel documents—which, as we have seen, are the sole source of any contractual limits on Bechtel's rights to terminate Guz—imposed no restrictions upon the company's prerogatives to eliminate jobs or work units, for any or no reason, even if this would lead to the release of existing employees such as Guz.

Policy 1101 itself did address a category of termination labeled "Layoff." However, this section simply defined that term as a "Bechtel-initiated termination[ ] of employees caused by a reduction in workload, reorganizations, changes in job requirements, or other circumstances such as failure to meet [a] client's site access requirements." [Italics omitted.] Policy 1101 further provided that persons scheduled for layoff were entitled to advance notice to facilitate reassignment efforts and job search assistance, and that "[a] surplus employee[ ] [might] be placed on 'holding status' if there [was] a possible Bechtel reassignment within the following 3-month period." By proceeding in this fashion, Policy 1101 confirmed that Bechtel was free to "reorganize" itself, or to "change[ ] . . . job requirements," and to "initiate[ ]" employee "terminations . . . caused by" this process, so long as Bechtel provided the requisite advance notice.

The RIF Guidelines set forth more detailed procedures for selecting individual layoff candidates, and for helping such persons obtain jobs elsewhere within the company. But the RIF Guidelines, like the Policies, neither stated nor implied any limits on Bechtel's freedom to implement the reorganization itself.

Guz, like the Court of Appeal, focuses on a separate section of Policy 1101, titled "Unsatisfactory Performance." This section, the so-called progressive discipline provision, stated that "employees who fail to perform their jobs in a satisfactory manner may be terminated, provided the employees have been advised of the specific shortcomings and given an opportunity to improve their performance." * * * Like the Court of Appeal, Guz cites BNI president Johnstone's disclosure that he was unhappy with BNI-MI's work product as evidence that the elimination of BNI-MI was a pretext for firing its individual members without resort to the progressive discipline policy.

However, as Bechtel suggests, Policy 1101 cannot reasonably be construed to conflate the separate Unsatisfactory Performance and Layoff provisions in this manner. Whatever rights Policy 1101 gave an employee threatened with replacement on account of his or her individual poor performance, we see nothing in Bechtel's personnel documents which, despite Bechtel's general disclaimer, limited Bechtel's prerogative to eliminate an entire work unit, and thus its individual jobs, even if the decision was influenced by a belief that the unit's work would be better performed elsewhere within the company.

Accordingly, we conclude the Court of Appeal erred in finding, on the grounds it stated, that Guz's implied contract claim was triable. Insofar as the Court of Appeal used these incorrect grounds to overturn the trial court's contrary determination, and thus to reinstate Guz's contractual cause of action, the Court of Appeal's decision must be reversed.

The Court of Appeal did not address Guz's second theory, i.e., that Bechtel also breached its implied contract by failing, during and after the reorganization, to provide him personally with the fair layoff protections, including force ranking and reassignment help, which are set forth in its Policies and RIF Guidelines. This theory raises difficult questions, including what the proper remedy, if any, should be if Guz ultimately shows that Bechtel breached a contractual obligation to follow certain procedural policies in the termination process. * * * On remand, the Court of Appeal should confront this issue and should determine whether Guz has raised a triable issue on this theory.

NOTES AND QUESTIONS

Test Your Understanding of the Material

1.   What argument does each party make based on Policy 1101?

2.   In what respects has the *Guz* court narrowed the scope of the "implied in fact" contract doctrine in California; and in what respects does the doctrine continue to be viable in that jurisdiction?

3.   Do you understand why the court agreed there was a triable issue of fact with respect to Bechtel's RIF guidelines but not the other aspects of Guz's implied-contract claims?

2.   PERSONNEL MANUALS/EMPLOYEE HANDBOOKS AND BINDING EMPLOYER POLICY STATEMENTS

RESTATEMENT OF EMPLOYMENT LAW §§ 2.05–2.06
American Law Institute (2015).

§ 2.05   Binding Employer Policy Statements

Policy statements by an employer in documents such as employee manuals, personnel handbooks, and employment policy directives that are provided or made accessible to employees, whether by physical or electronic means, and that, reasonably read in context, establish limits on the employer's power to terminate the employment relationship, are binding on the employer until modified or revoked (as provided in § 2.06).

§ 2.06 Modification or Revocation of Binding Employer Policy Statements

(a) An employer may prospectively modify or revoke its binding policy statements if it provides reasonable advance notice of, or reasonably makes accessible, the modified statement or revocation to the affected employees.

(b) Modifications and revocations apply to all employees hired, and all employees who continue working, after the notice is given and the modification or revocation becomes effective.

(c) Modifications and revocations cannot adversely affect vested or accrued employee rights that may have been created by the statement, an agreement based on the statement (covered by § 2.03), or reasonable detrimental reliance on a promise in the statement (covered by § 2.02, Comment c).

WOOLLEY V. HOFFMANN-LA ROCHE, INC.
Supreme Court of New Jersey, 1985.
99 N.J. 284, 491 A.2d 1257.

WILENTZ, C.J.

Plaintiff, Richard Woolley, was hired by defendant, Hoffmann-La Roche, Inc., in October 1969, as an Engineering Section Head in defendant's Central Engineering Department at Nutley. There was no written employment contract between plaintiff and defendant. Plaintiff began work in mid-November 1969. Some time in December, plaintiff received and read the personnel manual on which his claims are based.

In 1976, plaintiff was promoted, and in January 1977 he was promoted again, this latter time to Group Leader for the Civil Engineering, the Piping Design, the Plant Layout, and the Standards and Systems Sections. In March 1978, plaintiff was directed to write a report to his supervisors about piping problems in one of defendant's buildings in Nutley. This report was written and submitted to plaintiff's immediate supervisor on April 5, 1978. On May 3, 1978, stating that the General Manager of defendant's Corporate Engineering Department had lost confidence in him, plaintiff's supervisors requested his resignation. Following this, by letter dated May 22, 1978, plaintiff was formally asked for his resignation, to be effective July 15, 1978.

Plaintiff refused to resign. Two weeks later defendant again requested plaintiff's resignation, and told him he would be fired if he did not resign. Plaintiff again declined, and he was fired in July.

* * *

The trial court, relying on *Savarese v. Pyrene Mfg. Co.,* 9 N.J. 595, 89 A.2d 237 (1952), *Hindle v. Morrison Steel Co.,* 92 N.J.Super. 75, 223 A.2d 193 (App.Div.1966), and *Piechowski v. Matarese,* 54 N.J.Super. 333, 148 A.2d 872 (App.Div.1959), held that in the absence of a "most convincing[ ]" demonstration that "it was the intent of the parties to enter into such long-range commitments * * * clearly, specifically and definitely expressed" (using, almost verbatim, the language of *Savarese, supra,* 9 N.J. at 601, 89 A.2d 237), supported by consideration over and above the employee's rendition of services, the employment is at will. Finding that the personnel policy manual did not contain any such clear and definite expression and, further, that there was no such additional consideration, the court granted summary judgment in favor of defendant, sustaining its right to fire plaintiff with or without cause.

The Appellate Division, viewing plaintiff's claim as one for a "permanent or lifetime employment," found that the company's policy manual did not specifically set forth the term, work, hours or duties of the employment and "appear[ed] to be a unilateral expression of company policies and procedures * * * not bargained for by the parties," this last reference being similar to the notion, relied on by the trial court, that additional consideration was required. Based on that view, it held that the "promulgation and circulation of the personnel policy manual by defendant did not give plaintiff any enforceable contractual rights." * * *

We are thus faced with the question of whether this is the kind of employment contract—a "long-range commitment"—that must be construed as one of indefinite duration and therefore at will unless the stringent requirements of *Savarese* are met, or whether ordinary contractual doctrine applies. In either case, the question is whether Hoffmann-La Roche retained the right to fire with or without cause or whether, as Woolley claims, his employment could be terminated only for cause. * * *

This Court has clearly announced its unwillingness to continue to adhere to rules regularly leading to the conclusion that an employer can fire an employee-at-will, with or without cause, for any reason whatsoever. Our holding in *Pierce v. Ortho Pharmaceutical Corp.,* 84 N.J. 58, 72, 417 A.2d 505 (1980), while necessarily limited to the specific issue of that case (whether employer can fire employee-at-will when discharge is contrary to a clear mandate of public policy), implied a significant questioning of that rule in general.

* * *

The rule of *Savarese, supra,* 9 N.J. 595, 89 A.2d 237, which the trial court and the Appellate Division transported to this case, was derived in a very different context from that here. The case involved an unusual transaction not likely to recur (promise by company officer, made to induce employee to play baseball with company team, for lifetime employment even if employee became disabled as a result of playing baseball). * * *

What is before us in this case is not a special contract with a particular employee, but a general agreement covering all employees. There is no reason to treat such a document with hostility.

* * *

Given the facts before us and the common law of contracts interpreted in the light of sound policy applicable to this modern setting, we conclude that the termination clauses of this company's Personnel Policy Manual, including the procedure required before termination occurs, could be found to be contractually enforceable. Furthermore, we conclude that when an employer of a substantial number of employees circulates a manual that, when fairly read, provides that certain benefits are an incident of the employment (including, especially, job security provisions), the judiciary, instead of "grudgingly" conceding the enforceability of those provisions, *Savarese, supra*, 9 N.J. at 601, 89 A.2d 237, should construe them in accordance with the reasonable expectations of the employees.

* * *

In determining the manual's meaning and effect, we must consider the probable context in which it was disseminated and the environment surrounding its continued existence. The manual, though apparently not distributed to all employees ("in general, distribution will be provided to supervisory personnel * * * "), covers all of them. Its terms are of such importance to all employees that in the absence of contradicting evidence, it would seem clear that it was intended by Hoffmann-La Roche that all employees be advised of the benefits it confers.

We take judicial notice of the fact that Hoffmann-La Roche is a substantial company with many employees in New Jersey. The record permits the conclusion that the policy manual represents the most reliable statement of the terms of their employment. At oral argument counsel conceded that it is rare for any employee, except one on the medical staff, to have a special contract. Without minimizing the importance of its specific provisions, the context of the manual's preparation and distribution is, to us, the most persuasive proof that it would be almost inevitable for an employee to regard it as a binding commitment, legally enforceable, concerning the terms and conditions of his employment. Having been employed, like hundreds of his co-employees, without any individual employment contract, by an employer whose good reputation made it so attractive, the employee is given this one document that purports to set forth the terms and conditions of his employment, a document obviously carefully prepared by the company with all of the appearances of corporate legitimacy that one could imagine.

* * *

The mere fact of the manual's distribution suggests its importance. Its changeability—the uncontroverted ability of management to change its terms—is argued as supporting its non-binding quality, but one might as easily conclude that, given its importance, the employer wanted to keep it up to date, especially to make certain, given this employer's good reputation in labor relations, that the benefits conferred were sufficiently competitive with those available from other employers, including benefits found in collective bargaining agreements. The record suggests that the changes actually made almost always favored the employees.

Given that background, then, unless the language contained in the manual were such that no one could reasonably have thought it was intended to create legally binding obligations, the termination provisions of the policy manual would have to be regarded as an obligation undertaken by the employer. It will not do now for the company to say it did not mean the things it said in its manual to be binding. Our courts will not allow an employer to offer attractive inducements and benefits to the workforce and then withdraw them when it chooses, no matter how sincere its belief that they are not enforceable.

* * *

Many of these workers undoubtedly know little about contracts, and many probably would be unable to analyze the language and terms of the manual. Whatever Hoffmann-La Roche may have intended, that which was read by its employees was a promise not to fire them except for cause.

Having concluded that a jury could find the Personnel Policy Manual to constitute an offer, we deal with what most cases deem the major obstacle to construction of the terms as constituting a binding agreement, namely, the requirement under contract law that consideration must be given in exchange for the employer's offer in order to convert that offer into a binding agreement.

We conclude that these job security provisions contained in a personnel policy manual widely distributed among a large workforce are supported by consideration and may therefore be enforced as a binding commitment of the employer.

* * * In most of the cases involving an employer's personnel policy manual, the document is prepared without any negotiations and is voluntarily distributed to the workforce by the employer. It seeks no return promise from the employees. It is reasonable to interpret it as seeking continued work from the employees, who, in most cases, are free to quit since they are almost always employees at will, not simply in the sense that the employer can fire them without cause, but in the sense that they can quit without breaching any obligation. Thus analyzed, the manual is an

offer that seeks the formation of a unilateral contract—the employees' bargained-for action needed to make the offer binding being their continued work when they have no obligation to continue.

The unilateral contract analysis is perfectly adequate for that employee who was aware of the manual and who continued to work intending that continuation to be the action in exchange for the employer's promise; it is even more helpful in support of that conclusion if, but for the employer's policy manual, the employee would have quit. *See generally* M. Pettit, "Modern Unilateral Contracts," 63 B.U.L.Rev. 551 (1983) (judicial use of unilateral contract analysis in employment cases is widespread).

* * * In *Toussaint* [*v. Blue Cross and Blue Shield of Michigan,*] 408 Mich. 579, 292 N.W.2d 880 [1980,] one main issue was the contractual force of an oral assurance given to the employee when he was hired that he would not be discharged so long as he was "doing his job." In addition to that assurance, Toussaint was at the same time handed a manual, which provided that an employee would not be discharged without cause and without following certain procedures. The court noted in *dictum* that the oral assurance was not necessary to its holding. The court's discussion of the effect of distributing a manual is worth noting:

> * * * It is enough that the employer chooses, presumably in its own interest, to create an environment in which the employee believes that, whatever, the personnel policies and practices, they are established and official at any given time, purport to be fair, and are applied consistently and uniformly to each employee. The employer has then created a situation "instinct with an obligation." [292 N.W.2d at 892 (footnotes omitted).]

A footnote concluded that "[i]t was therefore unnecessary for Toussaint to prove reliance on the policies set forth in the manual."

Similarly, in *Anthony v. Jersey Cent. Power & Light Co.,* 51 N.J.Super. 139, 143 A.2d 762 [(1958)], practically every contractual objection that could be made here was disposed of by the Appellate Division in the context of a claim for pension rights by supervisory personnel based on a company manual (entitled "General Rules"). There, the defendant-employer argued that its severance-pay rule was a mere gratuitous promise, not supported by consideration. The court responded, analyzing the promise as an offer of a unilateral contract and the employees' continued services as sufficient acceptance and consideration therefor. *Id.* at 143, 143 A.2d 762. To the defendant's argument that there was no evidence of reliance upon its promise, the *Anthony* court responded that reliance was to be presumed under the circumstances. *Id.* at 145–46, 143 A.2d 762. We agree.[10]

---

[10] If reliance is not presumed, a strict contractual analysis might protect the rights of some employees and not others. For example, where an employee is not even aware of the existence of the manual, his or her continued work would not ordinarily be thought of as the bargained-for detriment. See S. Williston, *Contracts* §§ 101, 102A (1957). But see A. Corbin, *Contracts* 59 (1963)

The lack of definiteness concerning the other terms of employment—its duration,[11] wages, precise service to be rendered, hours of work, etc., does not prevent enforcement of a job security provision. Realistically, the objection has force only when the agreement is regarded as a special one between the employer and an individual employee. There it might be difficult to determine whether there was good cause for termination if one could not determine what it was that the employee was expected to do. That difficulty is one factor that suggests the employer did not intend a lifetime contract with one employee. Here the question of good cause is made considerably easier to deal with in view of the fact that the agreement applies to the entire workforce, and the workforce itself is rather large. Even-handedness and equality of treatment will make the issue in most cases far from complex; the fact that in some cases the "for cause" provision may be difficult to interpret and enforce should not deprive employees in other cases from taking advantage of it. If there is a problem arising from indefiniteness, in any event, it is one caused by the employer.

* * *

We therefore reverse the Appellate Division's affirmance of the trial court's grant of summary judgment and remand this matter to the trial court for further proceedings consistent with this opinion. Those proceedings should have the benefit of the entire manual that was in force at the time Woolley was discharged. The provisions of the manual concerning job security shall be considered binding unless the manual elsewhere prominently and unmistakably indicates that those provisions shall not be binding or unless there is some other similar proof of the employer's intent not to be bound. The ordinary division of issues between the court and the jury shall apply. If the court concludes that the job security provisions are binding (or submits that issue to the jury), it shall either determine their meaning or, if reasonable men could differ as to that meaning, submit that issue as well to the jury. If either the court or the jury under those circumstances concludes that the Personnel Policy

---

(suggesting that knowledge of an offer is not a prerequisite to acceptance). Similarly, if it is quite clear that those employees who knew of the offer knew that it sought their continued work, but nevertheless continued without the slightest intention of putting forth that action as consideration for the employer's promise, it might not be sufficient to form a contract. See S. Williston, Contracts § 67 (1957). But see *Pine River* [*State Bank* v. *Mettille*,] 333 N.W.2d at 622, 627, 630 [(Minn.1983).] In this case there is no proof that plaintiff, Woolley, relied on the policy manual in continuing his work. Furthermore, as the Appellate Division correctly noted, Woolley did "not bargain for" the employer's promise. The implication of the presumption of reliance is that the manual's job security provisions became binding the moment the manual was distributed. Anyone employed before or after became one of the beneficiaries of those provisions of the manual. And if *Toussaint* is followed, employees neither had to read it, know of its existence, or rely on it to benefit from its provisions any more than employees in a plant that is unionized have to read or rely on a collective-bargaining agreement in order to obtain its benefits.

[11] The parties agree that Woolley's employment was for an indefinite period. We therefore need not determine the impact of a job security clause where the employment is alleged to be for a fixed term, *e.g.,* because of the stated salary period. See *Willis v. Wyllys Corp.,* 98 N.J.L. 180, 119 A. 24 (E. & A. 1922) (when employment contract states annual salary, the term of employment is not indefinite, but by the year).

Manual constituted a promise that an employee in Woolley's position could not be fired except for good cause, the only issue remaining shall be Woolley's damages. Woolley need not prove consideration—that shall be presumed. Furthermore, it shall not be open to defendant to prove that good cause in fact existed on the basis of which Woolley could have been terminated. If the court or jury concludes that the manual's job security provisions are binding, then, according to those provisions, even if good cause existed, an employee could not be fired unless the employer went through the various procedures set forth in the manual, steps designed to rehabilitate that employee in order to *avoid* termination. On the record before us the employer's failure to do so is undeniable. If that is the case, we believe it would be unfair to allow this employer to try now to recreate the facts as they might have existed had the employer given to Woolley that which the manual promised, namely, a set of detailed procedures, all for Woolley's benefit, designed to see if there was some way he could be retained by Hoffmann-La Roche. This is especially so in view of Woolley's death. Hoffmann-La Roche chose to act without complying with those procedures. It would not be fair now to allow the employer to claim that these procedures, of which it wrongfully deprived him, would have done him no good, when the only party who could effectively counter that claim—Woolley—is dead.

* * *

We are aware that problems that do not ordinarily exist when collective bargaining agreements are involved may arise from the enforcement of employment manuals. Policy manuals may not generally be as comprehensive or definite as typical collective bargaining agreements. Further problems may result from the employer's explicitly reserved right unilaterally to change the manual. We have no doubt that, generally, changes in such a manual, including changes in terms and conditions of employment, are permitted. We express no opinion, however, on whether or to what extent they are permitted when they adversely affect a binding job security provision.

* * *

All that this opinion requires of an employer is that it be fair. It would be unfair to allow an employer to distribute a policy manual that makes the workforce believe that certain promises have been made and then to allow the employer to renege on those promises. What is sought here is basic honesty: if the employer, for whatever reason, does not want the manual to be capable of being construed by the court as a binding contract, there are simple ways to attain that goal. All that need be done is the inclusion in a very prominent position of an appropriate statement that there is no promise of any kind by the employer contained in the manual; that regardless of what the manual says or provides, the employer promises nothing and remains free to change wages and all other working conditions without having to consult anyone and without anyone's agreement; and that the employer continues to have the absolute power to fire anyone with or without good cause.

[*Eds.* The Appendix to the *Woolley* decision containing the termination provisions of the defendant's personnel policy can be found in the Statutory Supplement.]

NOTES AND QUESTIONS

> *Historical Note*
>
> Before courts recognized claims based on employee handbooks or other unilateral employer statements they "routinely ignored or discounted evidence of employer statements" inducing employee reliance. "In Bird v. J.L. Prescott Co. [99 A.380 (N.J. 1916)], for example, the plaintiff was injured at work and agreed not to sue his employer in exchange for a written promise of lifetime employment. The New Jersey appellate court held that the writing was 'no more than a friendly assurance of employment and . . . not sufficiently definite to make an enforceable contract.'" J.H. Verkerke, The Story of Woolley v. Hoffmann-La Roche: Finding a Way to Enforce Employee Handbook Promises, Employment Law Stories 27 (Samuel Estreicher & Gillian Lester eds. 2007).

Test Your Understanding of the Material

1. To what extent does *Woolley* depart from traditional contract principles? Consider the following key principles of contract law drawn from the Restatement Second of Contracts:

Assent (§§ 18–19) "Manifestation of mutual assent to an exchange requires that each party either make a promise or begin or render a performance. . . . The conduct of a party is not effective as a manifestation of his assent unless he intends to engage in the conduct and knows or has reason to know that the other party may infer from his conduct that he assents."

Consideration (§ 71) "To constitute consideration, a performance or a return promise must be bargained for. . . The performance may consist of an act other than a promise, or a forbearance, or the creation, modification or destruction of a legal relation"

Certainty (§ 33) "Even though a manifestation of intention is intended to be understood as an offer, it cannot be accepted so as to form a contract unless the terms of the contract are reasonably certain."

2. Consider the following Handbook excerpt from Valve Corporation, a video game company:

"Nobody has ever been fired at Valve for making a mistake. It wouldn't make sense for us to operate that way. Providing the freedom to fail is an important trait of the company—we couldn't expect so much of individuals if we also penalized people for errors. Even expensive mistakes, or ones which result in a very public failure, are genuinely looked at as opportunities to learn." See Valve Software Handbook for New Employees, http://www.valvesoftware. com/company/Valve_Handbook_LowRes.pdf (last visited March 16, 2016).

Is this language sufficient to support a breach of contract claim by an employee fired for accidentally introducing a bug to the software that caused the game to crash? What if the handbook included an italicized disclaimer on the front page that all employees are at-will? What if all employees signed an acknowledgement of receipt of the handbook and disclaimer?

3.   *Effect on the Uniformity of Employer Terms?* Under the *Woolley* court's reasoning, could an employer argue that just as its unilateral contract offer to impose a job security term could be accepted by the employees' continued performance, so could its new unilateral contract offer to remove the job security term be accepted by the employees' continued performance? Consider three groups of employees: (1) one group hired during the earlier at-will era; (2) one group hired after the job security term was imposed; and (3) a third group hired after the job security term was rescinded. Do the rights of these employees differ? If employees in group (2) are terminated after the job security term was rescinded, are their rights based on the job security term or the revived at-will rule?

Related Issues

4.   *Other "Handbook" Rulings.* Virtually all jurisdictions that have considered the question have concluded that unilaterally promulgated personnel manuals and employee handbooks in appropriate circumstances can give rise to enforceable promises of job security. In addition to *Woolley*, see, e.g., Dillon v. Champion Jogbra, Inc., 175 Vt. 1, 819 A.2d 703 (2002); Demasse v. ITT Corp., 194 Ariz. 500, 984 P.2d 1138 (1999) (en banc); Leikvold v. Valley View Community Hospital, 141 Ariz. 544, 688 P.2d 170 (1984); O'Brien v. New England Telephone & Telegraph Co., 422 Mass. 686, 664 N.E.2d 843 (1996); Feges v. Perkins Restaurants, Inc., 483 N.W.2d 701 (Minn. 1992); cf. Pine River State Bank v. Mettille, 333 N.W.2d 622 (Minn.1983); Duldulao v. St. Mary of Nazareth Hospital Center, 115 Ill.2d 482, 106 Ill.Dec. 8, 505 N.E.2d 314 (1987); Thompson v. St. Regis Paper Co., 102 Wash.2d 219, 685 P.2d 1081 (1984); Gates v. Life of Montana Ins. Co., 205 Mont. 304, 668 P.2d 213 (1983); Weiner v. McGraw-Hill, Inc., 57 N.Y.2d 458, 457 N.Y.S.2d 193, 443 N.E.2d 441 (1982); Simpson v. Western Graphics Corp., 293 Or. 96, 643 P.2d 1276 (1982); Toussaint v. Blue Cross and Blue Shield of Michigan, 408 Mich. 579, 292 N.W.2d 880 (1980). See generally Stephen F. Befort, Employee Handbooks and the Legal Effect of Disclaimers, 13 Indus. Rels. L.J. 326 (1991/1992).

5. *Disclaimers.* In keeping with the suggestion in the last paragraph of the *Woolley* opinion and similar invitations in other cases such as *Toussaint*, 408 Mich. at 610, 292 N.W.2d at 890–91 (as further confirmed in *Lytle*, supra), and *Thompson,* 102 Wash.2d at 230, 685 P.2d at 1088, employers have revised their manuals and handbooks by inserting prominent disclaimers of any promise of job security. The courts have held that such disclaimers are generally sufficient to defeat a *Woolley*-type contract claim. See, e.g., Rowe v. Montgomery Ward & Co., 437 Mich. 627, 473 N.W.2d 268 (1991); Suter v. Harsco Corp., 184 W.Va. 734, 403 S.E.2d 751 (1991); Pratt v. Brown Machine Co., 855 F.2d 1225 (6th Cir.1988); Uebelacker v. Cincom Systems Inc., 48 Ohio App.3d 268, 549 N.E.2d 1210 (Ohio App.1988) (disclaimer in employee benefit book held effective); Eldridge v. Evangelical Lutheran Good Samaritan Soc'y, 417 N.W.2d 797 (N.D.1987); Reid v. Sears, Roebuck & Co., 790 F.2d 453 (6th Cir.1986); Larose v. Agway, Inc., 147 Vt. 1, 508 A.2d 1364 (1986); Bailey v. Perkins Restaurants, Inc., 398 N.W.2d 120, 122–23 (N.D.1986).

Nevertheless, the employer's disclaimer may be ineffective if the wording is ambiguous or if it has not been adequately communicated to the employee. See Schipani v. Ford Motor Co., 102 Mich.App. 606, 302 N.W.2d 307 (1981); Ferraro v. Koelsch, 124 Wis.2d 154, 368 N.W.2d 666 (1985). In Nicosia v. Wakefern Food Corp., 136 N.J. 401, 643 A.2d 554 (1994), the employer's manual contained the following disclaimer:

> This manual contains statements of Wakefern Food Corp. and its subsidiaries' Human Resource policies and procedures. * * * The terms and procedures contained therein are not contractual and are subject to change and interpretation at the sole discretion of the Company, and without prior notice or consideration to any employee.

The New Jersey Supreme Court held the disclaimer to be ineffective both because it was not "set off in a way to attract attention" and its message did not make clear the employer's reservation of at-will authority:

> Nicosia should not be expected to understand that Wakefern's characterization of its manual as "not contractual" or "subject to change and interpretation at the sole discretion of the Company" meant that the employer, despite the discipline and termination provisions of its manual, reserved the "absolute power to fire anyone with or without cause" without actually changing those provisions.

643 A.2d at 560–61.

Some courts have allowed juries to evaluate disclaimers in light of the employer's actual practice. See McGinnis v. Honeywell, Inc., 110 N.M. 1, 791 P.2d 452, 457 (1990); Zaccardi v. Zale Corp., 856 F.2d 1473, 1476–77 (10th Cir.1988), or on proof of detrimental reliance on the employer's representations. See McDonald v. Mobil Coal Producing, Inc., 789 P.2d 866 (Wyo.1990).

6. *Promissory Estoppel.* Would the doctrine of promissory estoppel have provided a firmer basis for a handbook exception to the at-will rule? Some courts like the New York Court of Appeals effectively have limited the

exception to circumstances that would support a promissory estoppel claim. Weiner v. McGraw-Hill, Inc., 57 N.Y.2d 458, 457 N.Y.S.2d 193, 443 N.E.2d 441 (1982); Horn v. New York Times, 100 N.Y.2d 85 (2003). See note 6 on p. 51, supra (following Ohanian v. Avis Rent a Car System, Inc.).

7.   *Distribution of Handbooks.* In a post-*Woolley* ruling, the New Jersey Supreme Court seemed to reaffirm that dissemination of the personnel manual in its entirety is not required. See Nicosia v. Wakefern Food Corp., 136 N.J. 401, 408–12, 643 A.2d 554, 558–59 (1994) (entire manual was distributed to only 300 of 1500 nonunion employees; plaintiff received only eleven-page section of the manual dealing with discipline procedures but had to rest his claim on the manual as a whole). By contrast, the Pennsylvania Supreme Court appears to require actual dissemination to employees before a handbook will create binding commitments. See Morosetti v. Louisiana Land and Exploration Co., 522 Pa. 492, 495, 564 A.2d 151, 152 (1989): "A handbook distributed to employees as inducement for employment may be an offer and its acceptance a contract. The employees here, however, could * * * show [only] an internal consideration of policy for what might be given, if and when they announced a policy for all employees. It is not sufficient to show only that they had a policy. It must be shown that they intended to offer it as a binding contract."

8.   *"Wrongful Demotion"?* Does the cause of action recognized in *Woolley* extend to adverse personnel decisions short of dismissal? In Scott v. Pacific Gas and Electric Co., 11 Cal.4th 454, 46 Cal.Rptr.2d 427, 904 P.2d 834 (1995), Scott and Johnson were engineers employed by the defendant utility in a managerial capacity who were demoted for failure to properly supervise overtime and establishing a side business that gave rise to a number of conflicts of interest with their employer. The demotion resulted in a 25 percent reduction in salary and benefits, as well as loss of all supervisory authority. Plaintiffs claimed their demotion violated the employer's implied "cause" promise gleaned in part from its discipline guidelines that stressed "positive," i.e., progressive discipline. The California high court held:

> Conceptually, there is no rational reason why an employer's policy that its employees will not be demoted except for good cause, like a policy restricting termination or providing for severance pay, cannot become an implied term of an employment contract. In each of these instances, an employer promises to confer a significant benefit on the employee, and it is a question of fact whether that promise was reasonably understood by the employee to create a contractual obligation.

Id. at 464, 904 P.2d at 839. See also discussion on pp. 642–643, (Chapter 12, Note 4, following *Tameny v. Atlantic Richfield Co.*); Employment Restatement 5.01, Reporters' Notes, Comment c. See generally Gregory Mark Munson, A Straightjacket for Employment At-Will: Recognizing Breach of Implied Contract Actions for Wrongful Demotion, 50 Vand. L. Rev. 1577 (1997).

9.   *Arbitration Provisions in Handbooks.* When employers include binding arbitration provisions in handbooks, employees might challenge the

provisions as unconscionable, or argue that they did not knowingly waive their right to a judicial proceeding. To decide these issues, courts must apply state contract law within the constraints of the Federal Arbitration Act, 9 U.S.C § 1 et seq., which creates a strong federal policy favoring arbitration. See Chapter 21, pp. 982 to 999 (Private Grievance Arbitration and Federal Statutory Claims).

NOTE: UNILATERAL MODIFICATION/RESCISSION OF HANDBOOK PROMISES

Consider the *Woolley* court's reservation of the question whether the employer could unilaterally change the handbook in a manner that would "adversely affect a job security provision." From the standpoint of traditional contract law, an employer cannot effect a midterm modification of a prior contractual commitment to employ an individual for a stated term (or under stated conditions) simply by announcing that it is changing the contract for the future. The employee's continued performance of services in the face of such an announcement would not constitute an agreement to the change; and the employer's continued provision of employment (albeit under different terms) would not provide consideration for the midterm modification because of the employer's pre-existing duty. See generally E. Allan Farnsworth, Contracts, supra, §§ 4.21–.22 (1990) (questioning pre-existing duty rule).

By contrast, where employment is truly at will, each day provides the setting for a new contract. Below, is a summary of different positions states have taken on the issue of unilateral modification.

1. *Michigan-California Position.* In Bankey v. Storer Broadcasting Co., 432 Mich. 438, 443 N.W.2d 112 (1989) (en banc), the Michigan Supreme Court, responding to a certified question from the Sixth Circuit, rejected the implications of the "unilateral contract" theory utilized in *Woolley*. The court held that contractual rights based on the "handbook exception" to the "at will" rule recognized in *Toussaint* could be unilaterally modified by an employer even without explicit reservation at the outset of the right to do so:

> Without rejecting the applicability of unilateral contract theory in other situations, we find it inadequate [here]. We look, instead, to the analysis employed in *Toussaint* which focused upon the benefit that accrues to an employer when it establishes desirable personnel policies. Under *Toussaint,* written personnel policies are not enforceable because they have been "offered and accepted" as a unilateral contract; rather, their enforceability arises from the benefit the employer derives by establishing such policies. * * *

> Under the *Toussaint* analysis, an employer who chooses to establish desirable personnel policies, such as a discharge-for-cause employment policy, is not seeking to induce each individual employee to show up for work day after day, but rather is seeking to promote an environment conducive to collective productivity. The benefit to the employer of promoting such an environment, rather than the

traditional contract-forming mechanisms of mutual assent or individual detrimental reliance, gives rise to a situation "instinct with an obligation." When * * * the employer changes its discharge-for-cause policy to one of employment-at-will, the employer's benefit is correspondingly extinguished, as is the rationale for the court's enforcement of the discharge-for-cause policy. * * *

It is one thing to expect that a discharge-for-cause policy will be uniformly applied while it is in effect; it is quite a different proposition to expect that such a personnel policy, having no fixed duration, will be immutable unless the right to revoke the policy was expressly reserved. * * *

Were we to [hold] that once an employer adopted a policy of discharge-for-cause, such a policy could never be changed short of successful renegotiation with each employee who worked while the policy was in effect, the uniformity stressed in *Toussaint* * * * would be sacrificed. If an employer had amended its policy from time to time * * * , the employer could find itself obligated in a variety of different ways to any number of different employees, depending on the modifications that had been adopted and the extent of the work force turnover.

443 N.W.2d at 119–20. The *Bankey* court stressed, however, that changes cannot be made in "bad faith," giving the example of a temporary suspension of a for-cause policy for the purpose of facilitating the termination of a particular employee; and that "reasonable notice of the change must be uniformly given to affected employees." Id. at 120. For the California Supreme Court's somewhat similar view, see Asmus v. Pacific Bell, 23 Cal.4th 1, 96 Cal.Rptr.2d 179, 999 P.2d 71, 73–78–79 (2000) (en banc) (on certified question from Ninth Circuit).

2. *Illinois-Connecticut-Wyoming Position.* The Illinois high court took a very different view in Doyle v. Holy Cross Hospital, 186 Ill.2d 104, 237 Ill.Dec. 100, 708 N.E.2d 1140 (1999):

* * * Given the contractual rationale of *Duldulao* [*v. St. Mary of Nazareth Hospital Center*, 115 Ill.2d 482, 106 Ill.Dec. 8, 505 N.E.2d 314 (1987)], we find it difficult to reconcile defendant's position with the requirements for contract formation and modification. Applying "traditional principles" of contract law, as *Duldulao* did, we conclude * * * that the defendant's unilateral modification to the employee handbook lacked consideration and therefore is not binding on the plaintiffs. A modification of an existing contract, like a newly formed contract, requires consideration to be valid and enforceable. * * * Consideration consists of some detriment to the offeror, some benefit to the offeree, or some bargained-for exchange between them. * * * In the present case, we are unable to conclude that consideration exists that would justify our enforcement of the modification against existing employees. Because the defendant was seeking to reduce the

rights enjoyed by the plaintiffs, it was the defendant, and not the plaintiffs, who would properly be required to provide consideration for the modification. But in adding the disclaimer, the defendant provided nothing of value to the plaintiffs and did not itself incur any disadvantage. * * *

* * * [T]o accept the defendant's reasoning, that the plaintiffs must supply consideration for a change in the contract to their detriment, and to locate consideration in the plaintiffs' continued work, * * * would paradoxically require the plaintiffs to quit their jobs in order to preserve the rights they previously claimed under the employee handbook.

Id. at 111–15, 708 N.E.2d at 1144–46. The Connecticut and Wyoming supreme courts follow a similar approach. See Torosyan v. Boehringer Ingelheim Pharm., 234 Conn. 1, 662 A.2d 89 (1995) (Peters, C.J.; arguably prior "cause" term was based on bilateral agreement); Brodie v. General Chem. Corp., 934 P.2d 1263 (Wyo.1997). See also Demasse v. ITT Corp., 194 Ariz. 500, 984 P.2d 1138 (1999) (on certified questions from the Ninth Circuit); McIlravy v. Kerr-McGee Corp., 119 F.3d 876 (10th Cir.1997) (applying Arizona law).

Is the problem identified in *Doyle* one of lack of consideration for the sought-for modification or one of lack of adequate notice? The Arizona Supreme Court in *Demasse*, for example, left open the question whether continued employment could provide consideration for a rescission of an "implied in fact" job security term where the employee was given "adequate notice of the modification": "An employee must be informed of any new term, aware of its impact on the pre-existing contract, and affirmatively consent to it to accept the offered modification." 194 Ariz. at 508, 984 P.2d at 1146.

What would be adequate consideration for changing a handbook-based job security term? The Wyoming high court in *Brodie* stated: "Consideration to modify an employment contract to restore at-will status would consist of either some benefit to the employee, detriment to the employer, or a bargained for exchange. The question of what type of consideration is sufficient cannot be answered with specificity because we have long held that absent fraud or unconscionability, we will not look into the adequacy of consideration." 934 P.2d at 1268 (citations omitted). Does the employer provide sufficient consideration by conditioning some improvement in benefits or a promotion on the employee's continuing to work in accordance with the terms of the modified employee handbook? Are employees likely to change their position by quitting? If, say, a promotion is withheld on this basis, does the disappointed employee have a retaliation claim (see note 6, p. 643 supra)? What about the firm's interest in uniform treatment of employees otherwise similarly situated: Does it make sense to have some of the workers covered by a "good cause" and others subject to "at will" status, when the terms and conditions of the workers are supposedly governed by the same underlying, ostensibly uniform personnel manual/employee handbook?

3. *Restatement of Employment Law*. As noted, § 2.05 of the Employment Restatement recognizes that "[p]olicy statements by an employer in documents such as employee manuals, personnel handbooks, and employment policy directives that are provided or made accessible to employees, whether by physical or electronic means, and that, reasonably read in context, establish limits on the employer's power to terminate the employment relationship, are binding on the employer until modified or revoked." Such obligations can be revoked prospectively under § 2.06:

§ 2.06   Modification or Revocation of Binding Employer Policy Statements

(a) An employer may prospectively modify or revoke its binding policy statements if it provides reasonable advance notice of the modified statement or revocation to the affected employees.

(b) Modifications and revocations apply to all employees hired, and all employees who continue working, after the notice is given and the modification or revocation becomes effective.

(c) Modification and revocations cannot adversely affect vested or accrued employee rights that may have been created by the statement, an agreement based on the statement (covered by § 2. 03), or reasonable detrimental reliance on a promise in the statement (covered by § 2.02, Comment *c*).

4. *A Doctrine Akin to "Administrative Estoppel"?* *Woolley* and similar cases can be understood as an instance of estoppel akin to the administrative law doctrine that agencies are bound to self-imposed restrictions on their discretionary authority until formally rescinded. See Accardi v. Shaughnessy, 347 U.S. 260, 74 S.Ct. 499, 98 L.Ed. 681 (1954). For a similar rationale, see Bankey v. Storer Broadcasting, discussed supra, note 1, pp. 77–78. See Restatement of Employment Law § 2.05, Comment b:

> Some courts have tried to fit this class of unilateral employer statements into a conventional contract-law framework, reasoning that employees "accept" or "rely on" these unilateral employer "offers" by continuing to provide services after the statements are disseminated. This has proved to be a conceptually awkward fit. . . .
>
> Against that background, other courts, and this Restatement, rest the binding effect of unilateral employer statements on general estoppel principles. Employers make certain unilateral statements about personnel policy to govern the operational decisions of their supervisors and managers. Employers do so to serve their own interests in advancing productivity, improving employee morale, or achieving some other organizational objective. Absent contrary language in the statement, the employer's purpose in promulgating a unilateral policy statement is to have it govern operational decisions while the statement is in effect but not to bind the employer to continued adherence after changing the policy and giving reasonable

notice to employees of the change. . . . Such statements are analogous to rules of practice promulgated by administrative agencies to govern their operational decisions. As a matter of administrative law, such rules bind the agency until properly modified or revoked on a theory of "administrative agency estoppel," even though no statute or regulation may have required their promulgation in the first place. Similarly, unilateral employer statements that, reasonably read in context, are intended to govern operational personnel decisions should be binding on the employer until properly modified or revoked.

3. WHAT CONSTITUTES "CAUSE" OR "GOOD CAUSE"?

This section examines how courts interpret employment agreements that limit termination of employment except for "cause." The next case, *Cotran v. Rollins*, considers whether a requirement of "cause" or "good cause" for terminating an employment relationship requires "cause in fact," even if the employer acted on an erroneous, but reasonable, good faith belief that it had cause for the decision.

RESTATEMENT OF EMPLOYMENT LAW § 2.04
American Law Institute (2015).

§ 2.04 Cause for Termination of Employment Agreements

Unless other provided for in the agreement:

(a) An employer has cause for early termination of an agreement for a definite term of employment if the employee has materially breached the agreement, including by persistent neglect of duties; by engaging in misconduct or other malfeasance, including gross negligence; or by being unable to perform the duties of the position due to a long-term disability.

(b) In addition to the grounds stated in subsection (a), an employer has a ground for terminating an agreement for an indefinite term of employment requiring cause for termination when a significant change in the employer's economic circumstances means that the employer no longer has a business need for the employee's services.

COTRAN V. ROLLINS HUDIG HALL INT'L
Supreme Court of California, 1998.
17 Cal.4th 93, 69 Cal.Rptr.2d 900, 948 P.2d 412.

BROWN, J.

When an employee hired under an implied agreement not to be dismissed except for "good cause" is fired for misconduct and challenges the termination in court, what is the role of the jury in deciding whether misconduct occurred? Does it decide whether the acts that led to the decision to terminate happened? Or is its role to decide whether the employer had reasonable grounds for believing they happened and otherwise acted fairly? * * *

* * * The better reasoned view, we conclude, prescribes the jury's role as deciding whether the employer acted with " 'a fair and honest cause or reason, regulated by good faith.' " That language is from *Pugh v. See's Candies, Inc.* (1981) 116 Cal. App. 3d 311, 330 [171 Cal. Rptr. 917] (*Pugh I*), the font of implied-contract-based wrongful termination law in California. Recently, in *Scott v. Pacific Gas & Electric Co.* (1995) 11 Cal. 4th 454, 467 [46 Cal. Rptr. 2d 427, 904 P.2d 834] (*Scott*), we elaborated on the content of good or just cause by enumerating what it is not: reasons that are " 'trivial, capricious, unrelated to business needs or goals, or pretextual.' " * * * 8

[Facts and Procedural Background]

In 1987, Rollins Hudig Hall International, Inc. (Rollins), an insurance brokerage firm, approached plaintiff, then a vice-president of a competitor, with a proposal to head its new West Coast international office. Following a series of telephone conferences, meetings and exchanges of letters, plaintiff joined Rollins in January 1988 as senior vice-president and western regional international manager. He held that position until 1993 when he was fired.

The events leading to plaintiff's termination began in March 1993, when an employee in Rollins's international department reported to Deborah Redmond, the firm's director of human resources, that plaintiff was sexually harassing two other employees, Carrie Dolce and Shari Pickett. On March 24, Redmond called both women to her office. In separate interviews, she asked each if they had been harassed. Both said yes; each accused plaintiff as the harasser. Two days later, both women furnished statements to Redmond stating that plaintiff had exposed himself and masturbated in their presence more than once; both also accused plaintiff of making repeated obscene telephone calls to them at home. Redmond sent copies of these statements to Rollins's equal employment opportunity (EEO) office in Chicago. Rollins's president, Fred Feldman, also was given copies. He arranged for a meeting with plaintiff

---

8 In this case, the contractual limitation on the employer's at-will power of termination is implied, arising, as the trial judge apparently determined, from preliminary negotiations and the text of a letter defendants sent plaintiff in response to a request for additional assurances of "permanent employment" before accepting their employment offer. The letter stated that if plaintiff's efforts to develop an international brokerage department failed to succeed, "other opportunities" within the organization would be "made available" to him. The Court of Appeal held it was error for the trial court to take from the jury the issue whether there was an implied contract not to terminate plaintiff except for good cause, a holding we do not review. Wrongful termination claims founded on an explicit promise that termination will not occur except for just or good cause may call for a different standard, depending on the precise terms of the contract provision.

at Rollins's Chicago office, attended by Robert Hurvitz, the firm's head of EEO, and Susan Held, Rollins's manager for EEO compliance. At the meeting, Feldman reviewed the accusations made by Dolce and Pickett against plaintiff. He explained that an investigation would ensue and that its outcome would turn on credibility. After reading the Dolce and Pickett statements to plaintiff, Held explained how the investigation would proceed. Plaintiff said nothing during the meeting about having had consensual relations with either of his two accusers, and offered no explanation for the complaints.

Pending completion of the EEO investigation, Rollins suspended plaintiff. Over the next two weeks, Held interviewed 21 people who had worked with plaintiff, including 5 he had asked her to interview. Held concluded that both Dolce and Pickett, who reiterated the incidents described in their statements, appeared credible. Her investigation failed to turn up anyone else who accused plaintiff of harassing them while at Rollins. One Rollins account executive, Gail Morris, told Held that plaintiff had made obscene telephone calls to her when they both worked for another company, soon after a sexual relationship between the two had ended. Susan Randall, one of those plaintiff had asked to be interviewed and who had described plaintiff as a "perfect gentleman," later called Held to relate "a strange early morning phone call" from plaintiff which "was not for any business purpose." Randall "couldn't figure out what [plaintiff] wanted, * * * yelled at him, told him to leave her alone, and never to call her in the middle of the night again." Held's investigation also confirmed that plaintiff had telephoned Dolce and Pickett at home. In April, both women signed sworn affidavits reciting in detail the charges made against plaintiff in their original statements.

On the basis of her investigation, her assessment of Dolce's and Pickett's credibility, and the fact that no one she interviewed had said it was "impossible" to believe plaintiff had committed the alleged sexual harassment, Held concluded it was more likely than not the harassment had occurred. She met with Feldman and Hurvitz to present her conclusions and gave Feldman copies of the affidavits of Dolce, Pickett, and Gail Morris. After reviewing Held's investigative report and the affidavits, Feldman fired plaintiff on April 23, 1993. This suit followed.

[The Trial]

Rollins defended its decision to fire plaintiff on the ground that it had been reached honestly and in good faith, not that Rollins was required to prove the acts of sexual harassment occurred. Plaintiff objected to Rollins's defense theory, and the trial court rejected it as not available in a breach of contract action, the only one of plaintiff's claims to go to the jury. Boiled down, the trial judge remarked, the case was nothing more than "a contract dispute" and it was Rollins's burden to prove plaintiff committed the acts that led to his dismissal; "whether [Rollins] in good faith believed [plaintiff] did it is not at issue." The trial court told the jury: "What is at issue is whether the claimed acts took place. * * * The issue for the jury to determine is whether the acts are in fact true. * * * Those are issues that the jury has to determine." The trial court also read * * * the standard instruction defining "good cause" in employment discharge litigation.[9] It refused an instruction requested by Rollins directing the jury not to substitute its opinion for the employer's.

The jury returned a special verdict. Asked whether plaintiff "engaged in any of the behavior on which [Rollins] based its decision to terminate plaintiff's employment," it answered "no." It set the present cash value of plaintiff's lost compensation at $1.78 million. Rollins appealed from the judgment entered on the verdict. The Court of Appeal reversed. We granted review to clarify the standard juries apply in wrongful termination litigation to evaluate an employer's "good cause" defense based on employee misconduct. We decide, in other words, the question the jury answers when the discharged employee denies committing the acts that provoked the decision to terminate employment. The question of the jury's role in resolving the related but separate issue of whether the reasons assigned by an employer for termination are legally sufficient to constitute good cause is one we leave for another case.

[Discussion]

* * * As several courts have pointed out, a standard permitting juries to reexamine the factual basis for the decision to terminate for misconduct—typically gathered under the exigencies of the workaday world and without benefit of the slow-moving machinery of a contested trial—dampens an employer's willingness to act, intruding on the "wide latitude" the court in [*Pugh v. See's Candies, Inc.*, 203 Cal.App.3d 743, 250 Cal.Rptr. 195 (1988) (*Pugh II*),] recognized as a reasonable condition for the efficient conduct of business. We believe the [actual-cause] standard is too intrusive, that it tips unreasonably the balance between the conflicting interests of employer and employee that California courts have sought to sustain as a hallmark of the state's modern wrongful termination employment law. * * *

Equally significant is the jury's relative remoteness from the everyday reality of the workplace. The decision to terminate an employee for misconduct is one that not uncommonly implicates organizational judgment and may turn on intractable factual uncertainties, even where the grounds for dismissal are fact specific. * * *

* * *

---

[9] [This standard instruction] states: "Where there is an employment agreement not to terminate an employee except for good cause, an employer may not terminate the employment of an employee unless such termination is based on a fair and honest cause or reason. In determining whether there was good cause, you must balance the employer's interest in operating the business efficiently and profitably with the interest of the employee in maintaining employment."

The proper inquiry for the jury, in other words, is not, "Did the employee in fact commit the act leading to dismissal?" It is, "Was the factual basis on which the employer concluded a dischargeable act had been committed reached honestly, after an appropriate investigation and for reasons that are not arbitrary or pretextual?" The jury conducts a factual inquiry in both cases, but the questions are not the same. In the first, the jury decides the ultimate truth of the employee's alleged misconduct. In the second, it focuses on the employer's response to allegations of misconduct. * * *

We give operative meaning to the term "good cause" in the context of implied employment contracts by defining it, under the combined *Scott-Pugh* standard * * * as fair and honest reasons, regulated by good faith on the part of the employer, that are not trivial, arbitrary or capricious, unrelated to business needs or goals, or pretextual. A reasoned conclusion, in short, supported by substantial evidence gathered through an adequate investigation that includes notice of the claimed misconduct and a chance for the employee to respond.

The law of wrongful discharge is largely a creature of the common law. Hence, it would be imprudent to specify in detail the essentials of an adequate investigation. * * *

All of the elements of the governing standard are triable to the jury.

[The Disposition]

Because it was error to instruct that Rollins could prevail only if the jury was satisfied sexual harassment actually occurred, the case must be retried. On retrial, the jury should be instructed, in accordance with the views we have expressed, that the question critical to defendants' liability is not whether plaintiff in fact sexually harassed other employees, but whether at the time the decision to terminate his employment was made, defendants, acting in good faith and following an investigation that was appropriate under the circumstances, had reasonable grounds for believing plaintiff had done so. * * *

KENNARD, J. [dissenting in part].

* * * To determine the parties' intent, a court or jury must examine all evidence relating to the formation of the implied agreement. Only if the court or jury concludes that the parties' intent cannot be determined from this evidence should it undertake to bridge this gap by supplying the meaning that comports with community standards of fairness and public policy.

Moreover, if the court must flesh out the meaning of an implied "good cause" limitation, it should choose the meaning that achieves the fairest and most workable result consistent with the normal practices and expectations of employers and employees in modern society. In my view, the meaning that best satisfies these requirements is one that permits the employer to discharge the employee only for specific acts of misconduct that the employee actually committed. Recognizing that a limitation of this kind puts the employer in a difficult position, and that it may impose liability even on employers who have used their best efforts to determine the truth of misconduct allegations fairly and accurately, I would hold that if an employer agrees to reinstate a falsely accused and wrongfully discharged employee, it should be liable in damages only for backpay.

NOTES AND QUESTIONS

Test Your Understanding of the Material

1.   Is the court's standard only a "default" rule that the parties could modify by express contract terms? If so, what sort of language would suffice to give Cotran the protection of an objective standard? Compare the default rules stated in the Employment Restatement.

2.   Is the *Cotran* court suggesting that the "implied in fact" contract is not entitled to the full level of protection that would be accorded an express contract for a definite term requiring "cause" for mid-term dismissal? Consider in particular the Court's statement in footnote 8.

3.   How would the *Cotran* court treat a situation where an employer acquires post-discharge evidence of the employee's resume fraud? Can the good-faith standard be met by an employer who did not know of the fraud at the time of its initial decision? Is there any reason to treat "implied in fact" contract cases differently from Title VII claims, where after-acquired evidence of misconduct may affect entitlement to reinstatement and other prospective relief but does not negate the underlying violation? See pp. 135–140 supra. But see Crawford Rehabilitation Services, Inc. v. Weissman, 938 P.2d 540 (Colo.1997) (holding that "after-acquired" evidence of "resume fraud" provided a complete defense to claims of breach of implied contract and promissory estoppel).

Related Issues

4.   *Elaboration of "Cause" in the Employment Restatement*

RESTATEMENT OF EMPLOYMENT LAW § 2.04, Comments b–e (2015):

(b)   *Definite-term agreements.* Where the parties have entered into an express agreement for a fixed term, that agreement ordinarily provides for a special payout in the event of early termination without cause. Often the parties will also specify what constitutes "cause" for early termination without breach. Under this Section, if not defined in the parties' agreement, "cause" refers to material breach of the agreement, such as persistent neglect of duties; misconduct or other malfeasance by the employee, including gross negligence; or inability to perform the duties of the position due to a long-term disability. Absent explicit language in the agreement, "cause" does not include changes in the employer's economic condition, such as a downturn in demand for the employer's product, a fall in the employer's share price, or the sale of the business.

(c) *Indefinite-term agreements.* When parties have negotiated an indefinite-term agreement containing a cause limitation on the employer's power to terminate, the definition of cause to which the parties have agreed controls. However, if the agreement is silent on the question, then given the potential length of indefinite-term agreements, the reasonable assumption is that the parties intended, in addition to the grounds stated in § 2.04(a), to include significant changes in the employer's economic circumstances.

(d) *Factual cause.* When the parties agree to a definite term of employment or for an indefinite term with a cause limitation on the employer's power to terminate, the reasonable assumption is that the parties intend any cause requirement to be undisputed or proven employee material breach, misconduct or malfeasance, or inability to perform the work due to long-term disability; and do not intend also to permit termination based on the employer's reasonable, good-faith but erroneous belief that there was cause for termination. This is in keeping with conventional views of cause as an objective concept. It is also consistent with the understanding that a good-faith but erroneous belief that early termination of a definite-term contract is justified, even if based on facts after an appropriate investigation, is not legally sufficient cause to terminate such an agreement.

(e) *Procedural dimension.* The cause required to terminate an agreement under this Section also may have a procedural dimension. When the agreement specifies termination procedures, those terms control. If those terms, for example, require the terminated employee to exhaust certain internal remedies, such as an appeal to the board of directors, those remedies ordinarily—absent proof of futility— must be reasonably exhausted before the employee may bring a lawsuit claiming that the termination was not based on a proper cause. Even where the agreement is silent on termination procedures, the fact that the parties have provided a cause limitation on the employer's power to terminate normally requires the employer to give reasons for the dismissal. The cause limitation also requires the employer to apply the grounds for termination in a regular and even-handed manner.

C. EVALUATING THE CASE FOR WRONGFUL DISCHARGE LEGISLATION

The preceding sections of this chapter have surveyed the various approaches the courts have taken to modify the employment-at-will doctrine in response to the job-security claims of employees who are not covered by collective bargaining agreements or civil service laws. However, judicial action, whether based on contract, tort or property principles, is not a likely (or arguably even legitimate) source for enduring "just cause" protection for all employees. Because of the limits of the common law both in working a radical change in background employment norms and in fashioning the necessary procedures and exceptions from coverage, general "just cause" protection requires legislation. The case for and against such legislation, and the form such measures might take, is treated in this section. Consider first Professor Epstein's defense of existing arrangements.

1.   IS LEGISLATION WARRANTED?

Richard Epstein's article, *In Defense of the Contract at Will*, 51 U.Chi. L. Rev. 947 (1984), makes four principle arguments in favor of an at-will system:

1. *"Monitoring Behavior."* Epstein argues that it is difficult for employers to police employee misconduct and overcome employee incentives to work unproductively. "In order to maintain internal discipline, the firm may have to resort to sanctions against individual employees. It is far easier to use those powers that can be unilaterally exercised: to fire, to demote, to withhold wages, or to reprimand."

2. *"Reputational Losses.* * * * The employer who decides to act for bad reason or no reason at all may not face any legal liability under the classical common law rule. But he faces very powerful adverse economic consequences. If coworkers perceive the dismissal as arbitrary, they will take fresh stock of their own prospects, for they can no longer be certain that their faithful performance will ensure their security and advancement."

3. *"Risk Diversification and Imperfect Information.* * * * The at-will contract * * * allows both sides to take a wait-and-see attitude to their relationship so that new and more accurate choices can be made on the strength of improved information."

4. *"Administrative Costs.* There is one last way in which the contract at will has an enormous advantage over its rivals. It is very cheap to administer. Any effort to use a for-cause rule will in principle allow all, or at least a substantial fraction of, dismissals to generate litigation."

NOTES AND QUESTIONS

Test Your Understanding of the Material

1.   Professor Epstein argues that the at-will doctrine offers advantages for both parties to the employment relationship. Is it likely that movement to a "cause" regime will make employers significantly less likely to hire at the

margin, and to forestall hiring until completion of extensive pre-employment screening and satisfactory performance of a probationary period?

2.   In the absence of racial, gender or ethnic discrimination or retaliation for whistleblowing, it is never in the interest of the employer to discharge long-term productive employees? Even if the firm as a whole may be considered a rational economic actor, can the same be said for line supervisors who may be acting out of pique or preservation of a power relationship and whose decisions are routinely deferred to by the firm?

3.   Are reputational sanctions sufficient to deter employers from arbitrary termination—particularly in light of social media and employer rating sites like glassdoor.com? For more on this issue, see Samuel Estreicher, Employer Reputation at Work, 27 Hofstra Lab. & Emp. L. J. 1 (2009).

Related Issues

4.   *Employer Opportunism in Internal Labor Markets?* A decision to fire a productive employee may be economically rational if the employee's compensation exceeds his or her marginal productivity to the firm. Professors Wachter and Cohen suggest that a "backloaded" compensation structure may be characteristic of firms seeking to promote long-term commitment and investment by employees in "firm-specific skills" (which add value to the employer but do not enhance the employee's portable skills). Such a compensation structure is often referred in the economics literature as an "internal labor market" or "relational" contract.

Although descriptions vary, the central feature of the arrangement is that after an initial training period, both the firm and the employee derive gains that they would not achieve in its absence. The employee's productivity exceeds not only his wage but what he could earn in the external labor market; and the firm reaps the benefit of a specially trained, committed workforce. During this phase, because both sides benefit, the arrangement is fully self-enforcing. However, because compensation is backloaded over the course of the employee's career—in part to motivate long-term commitment and in part because employees derive satisfaction from a compensation structure that improves over time—there comes a point where the interests of the firm and the employee begin to diverge. The employee continues to enjoy a wage exceeding what he could obtain elsewhere, but his wage also exceeds his productivity contribution to the firm. See Michael L. Wachter & George Cohen, The Law and Economics of Collective Bargaining: An Introduction and Application to the Problems of Subcontracting, Partial Closure, and Relocation, 136 U.Pa.L.Rev. 1349, 1362–64 (1988).

In bad times, employers may have an incentive to "cheat" on this relational contract; hence, candidates for staff reductions are likely to come from the ranks of long-term, usually older, workers who are being paid above their marginal value. Age discrimination laws may be animated by similar concerns. Professor Schwab applies such reasoning to explain California decisions like *Pugh*, *See's Candies*, and *Foley* finding an "implied in fact" job security term in the case of long-service employee facing late-career discharges. See Stewart J. Schwab, Life-Cycle Justice: Accommodating Just Cause and Employment at Will, 92 Mich. L. Rev. 8 (1993). A similar analysis may apply as an explanation for age discrimination laws, see p. 439 supra.

Professor Ehrenberg has argued, on the other hand, that long-term employees do not need the law's assistance because reputational costs would discourage firms from unjustly dismissing workers who were in the stage of their life-cycles in which marginal productivity falls below wages. In his view, the problem of unjust dismissal is largely confined to low-skilled workers in casual labor markets. For such workers, the appropriate legal response is not to increase marginal labor costs (through mandatory job security), but to prod state unemployment insurance systems to more rigorously examine dismissals for "misconduct" and to encourage the award of unemployment benefits without extra waiting periods. See Ronald Ehrenberg, Workers' Rights: Rethinking Protective Labor Legislation, in Rethinking Employment Policy 137, 142–50 (D.L. Bawden & F. Skidmore eds. 1989).

5.   *Incidence of Wrongful Dismissal*. Does the fact that arbitrators under collective bargaining agreements overturn approximately one-third of all discharges that go to arbitration suggest that unjust dismissal does in fact occur with some regularity? See Jack Stieber & Michael Murray, Protection Against Unjust Discharge: The Need for a Federal Statute, 16 U. Mich. J.L. Ref. 319 (1983); Jack Stieber, The Case for Protection of Unorganized Employees Against Unjust Discharge, IRRA 32nd Annual Proc. 155, 160–61 (1979).

Estimates of the incidence of wrongful dismissal vary. Extrapolating from the labor arbitration experience, and on the assumption that the reversal rate in the arbitration setting would also hold true for nonunion firms under a statutory "cause" regime, Professor Peck estimated that approximately 300,000 discharge or discipline cases would be overturned annually. See Cornelius J. Peck, Unjust Discharges from Employment: A Necessary Change in the Law, 40 Ohio St.L.J. 1, 8–10 (1979). Professor Frug puts the figure at 150,000 cases a year. See Gerald E. Frug, Why Courts Are Always Making Law, Fortune, Sept. 25, 1989, at 247, 248. Professors Freed and Polsby estimate that a nonunion worker faces a probability of wrongful dismissal of no more than 0.5769% (under Peck's estimate) or 0.2083% (under Frug's): "All of these probabilities are low enough that a person who disregarded them would not be acting unreasonably." Mayer Freed & Daniel Polsby, Just Cause for Termination Rules and Economic Efficiency, 38 Emory L.J. 1097, 1106–07 (1989). The methodology of the Stieber-Peck estimates is criticized in Andrew P. Morriss, Bad Data, Bad Economics, and Bad Policy: Time to Fire Wrongful Discharge Law, 74 Tex. L. Rev. 1901 (1996).

NOTE: CRITIQUE OF THE EMPLOYMENT-AT-WILL DOCTRINE

An economist might defend Epstein's position and the employment-at-will doctrine by arguing that employers and employees who would benefit from checks on arbitrary terminations could freely contract for such checks without governmental regulation. To the extent that any such check is more valuable to a group of employees than its absence is valuable to their employer, they will "purchase" the check by trading other parts of the compensation package that their labor market position enables them to command. Such purchases do in fact occur, the economist might note, when employees support unions that negotiate "just cause" provisions in collective agreements and when some high-level management employees negotiate contracts for a definite term containing sanctions for termination without cause. Mandatory job security protection, however, may force employees to accept a benefit that is more expensive to their employers than it is valuable to them. Employers may respond by eliminating (or reducing) other compensation that the employees would have preferred or by hiring fewer employees because of increased marginal labor costs. Either way, under this view, private autonomy will be frustrated and net social welfare will be reduced. See Jeffrey L. Harrison, The "New" Terminable-at-Will Employment Contract: An Interest and Cost Incidence Analysis, 69 Iowa L.Rev. 327 (1984).

There are two kinds of counterarguments that can be made to this kind of criticism of governmental regulation. First, a society may wish to reject the valuation that many individual workers are willing to give a particular good, such as job security. It may wish to do so because the rejected individual priorities offend certain fundamental values by which the society wishes to be defined, such as the importance of assuring some minimum level of dignity to all who work, or the principle reflected in § 6 of the Clayton Act of 1914 that the labor of a human being is not a commodity to be dispensed with at will. A society may also reject certain individual values because it is convinced that requiring people to live under new values will transform their priorities, creating a different welfare calculus in accord with the new values. Such paternalistic justifications, however, may be more difficult to accept for a general mandatory job security law than for minimum employment terms such as those established by the Occupational Safety and Health Act and minimum wage legislation.

The second kind of counterargument questions some of the assumptions of the free market economist's attack on regulation. Some would argue, for instance, that the grant of minimum benefits to workers, whether it be minimum job safety or job security, can help effect some redistribution of social wealth from the holders of capital to the contributors of labor. Employers operating in imperfect labor markets cannot necessarily recoup what they must grant workers by lowering other parts of the compensation package. Most economists would view unrestricted redistributions of social wealth in the form of tax and spending power subsidies as more efficient and therefore preferable vehicles. Those interested in pursuing wealth redistribution policies, however, may find that redistribution is socially acceptable only when it occurs as an incident to rules that accord with dominant social values.

Furthermore, some would question the assumption that the rarity of individual employee bargaining for job security protections proves that workers are not willing to incur the costs of such protections. The inclusion in almost all collective bargaining agreements of prohibitions of termination without "just cause" certainly suggests that many employees are willing to bargain and pay for job security. It may be that free bargaining over job security does not occur in most nonunionized labor markets—because of barriers to information about the availability of such protections, inaccurate assessments of the likelihood of unjust dismissal, difficulties in raising questions concerning termination at the outset of a relationship, obstacles to mobility, or employer monopsony. For an elaboration of this view, see Paul C. Weiler, Governing the Workplace: The Future of Labor and Employment Law 72–78 (1990).

2. WHAT FORM SHOULD THE LEGISLATION TAKE?

As an example of how wrongful discharge legislation might be framed, consider the Montana Wrongful Discharge from Employment Act, the first of its kind in this country.

MONTANA WRONGFUL DISCHARGE FROM EMPLOYMENT ACT

Mont.Code Ann. §§ 39–2–901 to –914.

Plaintiff Bar Oppostion to the Montana Law

The most vociferous opponents of the Montana Wrongful Discharge statute were plaintiffs' attorneys, who disliked the legislation's cap on damages. Prior to the 1987 statute, the Montana courts "steadily increased the scope of the implied covenant theory" and made punitive damages available for wrongful termination claims. The legislation sought to provide more predictability in resolving employment disputes, and drew "wide support in the House, including from representatives whose support for it 'shocked the hell' out of the bill's opponents." Andrew Morriss, The Story of the Montana Wrongful Discharge from Employment Act: A Drama in 5 Acts, from Employment Law Stories (Samuel Estreicher & Gillian Lester eds. 2007).

NOTES AND QUESTIONS

1. *"Good Cause" Standard.* The substantive standard for wrongful termination—"good cause"—is defined only in general terms. Consider the previous discussion of the Employment Restatement § 2.04, pp. 81–87.

Montana decisions suggest a fairly deferential standard. In Buck v. Billings Montana Chevrolet, Inc., 248 Mont. 276, 811 P.2d 537 (1991), the court held that a new purchaser of an automobile dealership had "a legitimate business reason," within the meaning of the "good cause" concept as defined in the statute, to terminate the former manager and replace him with a manager from the purchaser's other operations, even though the decision was admittedly not based on the prior work performance of the former manager. The *Buck* court defined a "legitimate business reason" as one that is

> neither false, whimsical or capricious, and it must have some logical relationship to the needs of the business. In applying this definition, one must take into account the right of an employer to exercise discretion over who it will employ and keep in employment. Of equal importance to this right, however, is the legitimate interest of the employee to secure employment.

Id. at 281–82, 811 P.2d at 540. The court explained, however, that its holding was limited "to those who occupy sensitive managerial confidential positions," and that the balance might tip the other way in the case of non-managerial employees. Id. at 283, 811 P.2d at 541. The Montana high court also apparently draws a distinction between decisions eliminating managerial positions and decisions replacing one employee with another. See Kestell v. Heritage Health Care Corp., 259 Mont. 518, 858 P.2d 3 (1993) (setting aside summary judgment against former director of hospital's chemical dependency unit). See generally Donald C. Robinson, The First Decade of Judicial Interpretation of the Montana Wrongful Discharge from Employment Act, 57 Mont. L. Rev. 375 (1996).

2. *Montana's Post-Dispute Arbitration Option.* The Montana statute contemplates resort to a civil action and presumably a jury trial. However, final and binding arbitration is offered as an alternative and is creatively encouraged by fee-shifting provisions. See Mont. Code. Ann. §§ 39–2–914, 39–2–915. Are there advantages to this approach over either committing disputes exclusively to the courts or to arbitration? Does the Montana statute require that there must be an agreement to arbitrate before the attorney's fees provisions are triggered? In 1993, the Montana legislature amended the statute to make clear that a unilateral offer to arbitrate that is refused triggers the attorney's fees provisions. See Mont. Code Ann. § 39–2–915.

3. *Implications of Damages Cap.* Note that Montana legislature placed a four-year "cap" on lost wages and fringe benefits, excluded recovery for emotional distress and compensatory damages, and limited punitive damages to cases of fraud or malice. In view of the statutory cap on recovery and the preemption of preexisting common law contract remedies, are plaintiffs as a class made less well off than they were under an at-will regime? Does the Montana measure, in effect, confer upon employees as a group some measure of job security in exchange for a ceiling on employer liability? Would it have been preferable from a policy standpoint, and fairer to employee interests, to have provided either for (i) a strict liability-based administrative process resembling workers' compensation systems, or (ii) if a fault-based civil action were desired, authority to award attorney's fees to prevailing claimants, as is true under Title VII and ADEA?

The Montana Supreme Court rejected a challenge to the Montana statute brought under the state constitution's guaranty of equal protection and "full legal redress for injury incurred in employment" in Meech v. Hillhaven West, Inc., 238 Mont. 21, 776 P.2d 488 (1989).

4. *Exclusions from Coverage.* Note that the act contains several exclusions from coverage. The "good cause" standard only applies to employees who have completed a probationary period, presumably to give employers time to determine the suitability of a new hire. In addition, the act exempts any discharge (i) that is remediable by any other state or federal statute; (ii) that affects employees covered by a collective bargaining agreement; or (iii) that affects employees "covered by a written contract for a specific term." The first exemption avoids duplicative adjudication. The second exemption may do so as well, but it raises the question of whether the state should require unionized employees to expend bargaining leverage to extract protection that is granted as a statutory right to nonunion workers.

What is the explanation for the third exclusion? Is the legislature effectively providing an opportunity for the parties to "contract out" of the statute? Will employees be better off if they are compelled to enter into written contracts for two-or one-year, or even shorter terms, rather than open-ended indefinite employment arrangements? Montana decisions make clear that nonrenewal of specific-term contracts are not covered by the "good cause" requirement. See Farris v. Hutchinson, 254 Mont. 334, 838 P.2d 374 (1992).

5. *Adverse Actions Short of Discharge.* Note also that the statute covers constructive discharges, but this term does not include refusals to promote or improve wages or other working conditions. Some courts have applied the new common law "wrongful discharge" doctrine to constructive discharges. See, e.g., Scott v. Pacific Gas and Electric Co., 11 Cal.4th 454, 46 Cal.Rptr.2d 427, 904 P.2d 834 (1995), discussed at note 8, p. 76 supra; Mitchell v. Connecticut General Life Ins. Co., 697 F.Supp. 948 (E.D.Mich.1988) (applying Michigan's *Toussaint* doctrine).

6. *Preemption of Common Law Claims.* Note also that implied-contract claims are barred by the preemption provision of the statute, Mont. Code Ann. § 39–2–913; however, contract claims bearing on matters other than discharge, such as compensation, are not barred. See Beasley v. Semitool, Inc., 258 Mont. 258, 853 P.2d 84 (1993).

NOTE: THE MODEL EMPLOYMENT TERMINATION ACT

In August 1991, the National Conference of Commissioners of Uniform State Laws approved a "Model Employment Termination Act" and recommended its enactment in every state; for text, see the Statutory Supplement. The proposed model act embodies essentially the tradeoff reflected in the Montana law: certainty of a right of action to challenge wrongful termination in exchange for limitations on remedies, particularly the exclusion of punitive damages, compensatory damages, or other recovery for emotional distress and pain and suffering. Covered employees are granted a substantive right to "good cause" protections against discharge, which cannot be waived except by an individually executed agreement guaranteeing a minimum schedule of severance payments keyed to length of service. The proposed law contemplates that state-appointed arbitrators will adjudicate claims with authority to award reinstatement, with or without backpay, and severance pay if reinstatement is infeasible. Unlike the Montana law, attorney's fees may be awarded to a prevailing claimant.

SAMUEL ESTREICHER, UNJUST DISMISSAL LAWS: SOME CAUTIONARY NOTES

33 Am.J.Comp.L. 310 (1985)*

III. Some General Characteristics of Unjust Dismissal Laws Abroad

A.   Reinstatement

The most striking point about the foregoing schemes is that, irrespective of formal legal position, reinstatement is simply not an important feature in practice (at least outside of Canada, Italy and perhaps Germany). The measures surveyed here do not in fact vindicate a right to a job. At best, they provide a much needed transfer payment to cushion displacement and perhaps an opportunity to clear one's name.

The evidence from England and from studies of NLRB reinstatees, as compared with labor arbitration reinstatees, suggests that the reinstatement remedy is difficult to police effectively outside of the context of union representation. Germany's works councils seem to play a supportive role, similar to that of a union, and Italy's statute is aided by its labor movement's willingness to assist nonmember dischargees (in the hopes of recruiting them). One may venture here the generalization that perhaps such protective support mechanisms are necessary to the success of the reinstatement remedy.

B.   Size of Awards

Outside of Canada and possibly Italy, the monetary awards, while not insignificant, are at modest, predictable levels—certainly in comparison to American jury recoveries. The English awards are striking in this regard, which goes a long way toward explaining the English employers' reluctance to reinstate and the high settlement rate prior to hearing.** Punitive damages are also not a significant feature, although punitive concepts explain the additional award in Great Britain's statute and other similar provisions.

---

* As updated in Global Issues in Employment Law 74–85 (Samuel Estreicher & Miriam A. Cherry eds. 2008).

** [Eds. Under pressure from the European Community's International Court of Justice, the United Kingdom has amended its laws to provide for uncapped monetary recoveries in discrimination cases, and has raised its monetary cap for unfair dismissal cases to £50,000 (approximately $75,000).]

C.   Exclusions from Coverage and Fixed-Term Contracts

None of the countries in question provides universal protection; throughout we find qualifying periods of continuous service (in Great Britain, now 52 continuous weeks and two years for small firms); and exclusions or special provision for small sized companies (again, in Great Britain, by nearly doubling the qualifying period).

Managerial employees apparently are not per se excluded from coverage. (Italy does provide a separate set of procedures.) Great Britain's exclusion of employees under fixed-term contract of at least one year's duration may operate to disqualify most managers. Even if formally excluded, however, managerial employees may have common law rights to dismissal only upon notice.

As to fixed-term contracts, Great Britain permits exclusion in the case of employees under a fixed-term contract of at least one year's duration who sign a written waiver of statutory rights. On the other hand, Germany, France and Italy, sensing here a potentially significant evasive tactic, seek to discourage repeated renewal of fixed-term contracts.

D.   Delegation of "Just Cause" Criteria to the Tribunal

None of the statutes here attempt to spell out the standards, the criteria of "just cause." Rather, they are broad delegations to the tribunals to develop procedural and substantive criteria, usually without guidance from a well-developed body of labor arbitration law.

The British model, as it has evolved, seems to be one of deferential review of managerial prerogative, rather than *de novo* review—similar in theory to our judicial review of administrative agency action. This model of thoroughgoing deference seems not to have taken hold elsewhere on the Continent.

E.   Use of Specialized Tribunals

With the exception of Japan and Italy, the statutes in question all utilize specialized labor tribunals that, at least in theory, are thought to dispense a cheaper, quicker, more accessible and expert justice. These tribunals, while often tripartite, do not offer the same opportunity for party selection of decisionmaker as would U.S. labor arbitration.

F.   Absence of Labor Union Opposition

Although at first unions were skeptical, even opposed, to these new statutes, the evidence strongly suggests that the European unions have not only made their peace but also have assisted nonmember utilization of the statutory procedures (as an organizing tactic).

G.   Relation to Redundancy Dismissal Legislation

Virtually all of the countries under review have also enacted some protections against economic dismissals, individual or group. In Great

Britain, redundancy laws preceded the unjust dismissal statute. Although I am not sure of the precise relationship between these schemes, I suspect that unjust dismissal laws appeared to many as at least logically inevitable once the inviolability of the at-will concept was breached by redundancy laws. Moreover, in many situations, both disciplinary and economic reasons may be potentially available to an employer bent on terminating an employee. Effective policing of either scheme may well require enactment of the other.

NOTES AND QUESTIONS

Test Your Understanding of the Material

1. By U.S. standards, U.K. employment tribunal awards would seem low, even in discrimination cases where caps are no longer imposed on awards. Might this be the source of a desirable trade-off for the U.S.—relatively prompt recovery provided in employee-friendly employment tribunals but lower awards?

2. Under what conditions is an effective reinstatement remedy possible in a nonunionized environment or one without a support mechanism similar to the German works councils? Who would police post-reinstatement compliance? Should the law require the reinstatement of wrongly dismissed high-level executives or other employees whose jobs depend on maintenance of a high degree of employer trust and confidence?

3. Europeans tend to provide for special administrative tribunals or labor courts to handle employment cases, including discrimination claims. Would the U.S. need a similar set of institutions to administer a general unfair dismissal regime? Is the Canadian federal government's use of "adjudicators" from the ranks of private labor arbitrators an attractive possibility for the U.S.? See Estreicher, Arbitration of Employment Disputes Without Unions, supra.

Related Issues

4. *Relationship Between Discrimination and Unfair Dismissal Claims.* Because of the availability of unfair dismissal remedies in most of the European countries, there is less of an incentive to frame one's case as a discrimination case where the gravamen of the claim is a challenge to the fairness of a termination decision. Thus, for example, only 18% of cases in the U.K. tribunal system in 2011–12 involved discrimination claims. See Government of the United Kingdom, Annual Employment Tribunal and Employment Appeal Tribunal Statistics: Statistical Tables, https://www.gov. uk/government/statistics/employment-tribunal-and-employment-appeal-tribunal-statistics (last visited March 16, 2016). In the U.S., by contrast, given the absence of unfair dismissal legislation (outside of Montana), plaintiffs look to the anti-discrimination laws as their principal recourse. Over time, litigants in Europe may be more attracted to pursuing discrimination claims which, under EU law, cannot be subject to a maximum level of recovery.

5.   *Resistance to Change?* Although many European observers believe that a greater measure of flexibility is needed in dismissal laws to encourage employment growth, change to these laws faces considerable obstacles. See, e.g., John C. Reitz, Political Economy and Contract Law, in New Features in Contract Law (Reiner Schulze, ed., 2007) (available at http://ssrn.com/abstract=964476):

> In April–May, 2006, French students and labor unions, joined by teachers, the jobless, and even retirees, took to the streets in an escalating series of actions to protest government proposals to amend the labor laws to give employers a limited right to terminate young, first-time permanent employees on an at will basis. The proposed law would have created a new two-year labor contract (the so-called *contrat première embauche* or *C.P.E.*) for businesses with over twenty workers and for workers younger than twenty-six [when] employed for their first job. The new contract would have permitted employers to terminate without notice, severance pay, or the obligation to show that the employee has violated the contract. Over a two-month period of disruptions, the protestors managed to * * * shut down universities, threatened to hurt tourism and economy, and brought violent clashes between young people and police. Eventually, the French political leaders bowed to public opposition and rescinded the law that promulgated the *C.P.E.* contract.

6.   For a recent assessment of dismissal laws across countries, see Samuel Estreicher & Jeffrey Hirsch, Comparative Unjust Dismissal Law: Reassessing American Exceptionalism, 92 N.C. L.Rev. 343 (2014).

PART 2

EMPLOYMENT DISCRIMINATION LAW

■ ■ ■

This major Part examines American employment law designed to outlaw disadvantageous treatment in employment on account of irrelevant criteria like race, gender, national origin, or religion. Its first two chapters consider the basic principles through which the principal federal law (Title VII of the 1964 Civil Rights Act) regulates employment discrimination on account of race and other prohibited characteristics. The third chapter looks at the legality of race- and gender-based remedial action, whether required by government or undertaken voluntarily by the employer. The final five chapters in Part 2 consider special issues that arise in connection with the regulation of discrimination against individuals on account of their sex (or gender), sexual orientation, gender identity, age, disability, and religion.

CHAPTER 3

DISPARATE TREATMENT

■ ■ ■

Introduction

This chapter introduces Title VII of the Civil Rights Act of 1964, 42 U.S.C. § 2000e et seq., a significant part of one of the major statutes passed in response to the mid-twentieth century's civil rights movement. There are two basic theories of liability under Title VII and related federal and state laws. The first, a theory of intentional discrimination, generally called "disparate treatment" discrimination, is treated in this chapter. The second theory, which focuses on the unjustified "disparate impact" of some employment practices, is treated in the next chapter.

A. TITLE VII OF THE 1964 CIVIL RIGHTS ACT AND OTHER FEDERAL INITIATIVES AGAINST RACE DISCRIMINATION IN EMPLOYMENT

The federal government did not begin to take seriously the problem of racial discrimination until the 1960s. Eighty years before, a modest legislative effort to challenge certain barriers was rebuffed by the Supreme Court in the In re Civil Rights Cases, 109 U.S. 3, 3 S.Ct. 18, 27 L.Ed. 835 (1883), which adopted a very narrow view of Congress's authority to enforce the antidiscrimination commands of the Thirteenth and Fourteenth Amendments. See Samuel Estreicher, Note, Federal Power to Regulate Private Discrimination: The Revival of the Enforcement Clauses of the Reconstruction Amendments, 74 Colum. L. Rev. 449 (1974).

During the Second World War, President Roosevelt created the Fair Employment Practices Committee, which investigated discriminatory practices and attempted to pressure federal contractors and others to hire black workers. The Court, too, began during this period to enforce more aggressively equal protection principles against segregationist political parties, labor unions and land-use regulations. However, it was not until the Court's 1954 decision in Brown v. Board of Education, 347 U.S. 483, 74 S.Ct. 686, 98 L.Ed. 873 (1954), and the ensuing decade of resistance to integration and the emergence of a national civil rights movement, that federal involvement began in earnest. In 1962, President Kennedy issued an executive order that authorized enforcement mechanisms to give effect to the ban on discrimination by federal contractors put in place by his predecessors. Three years later, President Johnson issued Executive Order

11246, which remains in force to this day. As elaborated below at pp. 315–317, the Executive Order extends beyond antidiscrimination commands to require all federal contractors to ensure the utilization of qualified minority group workers. Furthermore, in the 1970s the Supreme Court held that a reconstruction-era civil rights law, 42 U.S.C. § 1981, proscribes racial discrimination by private sector employers.

The most important federal initiative, however, was Title VII of the Civil Rights Act of 1964, 78 Stat. 253, 42 U.S.C. 2000e et seq. Passed over considerable opposition by representatives from the Southern states, Title VII extended antidiscrimination commands to private employment, and sought to promote the economic integration of blacks into the mainstream of American society. President Johnson and the Congress witnessed the civil rights movement's hard-fought, successful attack on the most blatant legacy of slavery, the de jure system of segregation and discrimination in public facilities in the South. They recognized, however, that blacks in the North as well as the South confronted other discriminatory barriers in private as well as public employment. See discussion in United Steelworkers of America v. Weber, 443 U.S. 193, 202, 99 S.Ct. 2721, 2727, 61 L.Ed.2d 480 (1979). See generally Hugh Davis Graham, The Civil Rights Era: Origins and Development of National Policy (1990).

After amendments in 1972, Title VII covers not only all private employers affecting interstate commerce with fifteen or more employees, but also all governmental employers—federal, state and local—as well.

The central prohibition of Title VII provides:

Sec. 703.(a)   It shall be an unlawful employment practice for an employer—

(1)   to fail or refuse to hire or to discharge any individual, or otherwise to discriminate against any individual with respect to his compensation, terms, conditions, or privileges of employment, because of such individual's race, color, religion, sex, or national origin; or

(2)   to limit, segregate, or classify his employees or applicants for employment in any way which would deprive or tend to deprive any individual of employment opportunities, or otherwise adversely affect his status as an employee, because of such individual's race, color, religion, sex, or national origin.

Title VII also proscribes discriminatory practices by labor organizations and employment agencies.

Title VII establishes an executive agency, the Equal Employment Opportunity Commission (EEOC). The EEOC investigates complaints by or on behalf of persons claiming to be aggrieved by a violation of the Act as well as any charges of discrimination lodged by one of its members. If the

EEOC determines that there is good cause to believe that the complaint is well-founded, it attempts to remedy the problem through informal conciliation with the party charged. If it cannot do so satisfactorily, the agency has the authority to bring a court action against that party. The EEOC has no authority to issue enforcement orders itself; it must obtain relief from courts, which are granted power to enjoin illegal practices and to provide "any other equitable relief as the court deems appropriate * * * ."

Aggrieved individuals have a private right of action under the statute. Since passage of the Civil Rights Act of 1991, they may seek limited legal damages, as well as equitable relief, to compensate for intentional discrimination. However, complainants cannot exercise their Title VII right of action until they first give the EEOC an opportunity to conciliate and to bring its own public suit. Moreover, aggrieved individuals must also give state and local agencies possessing antidiscrimination authority an opportunity to remedy the problem before proceeding to court. This system was framed as a compromise to encourage conciliation and to allay the concerns of certain members of Congress that "zealous" federal regulators would unduly disrupt private decisionmaking.

The economically adverse position of sections of the black community remains a stubborn reality even after almost five decades since the passage of Title VII. The median income of black families is less than two thirds that of white families. See Council of Economic Advisors, Economic Report of the President, Table B-9 (2016). Since 1972 the unemployment rate for African-Americans has ranged from a high of 19.5% in 1983 to a low of 7.6% in 2000. It was at 9.6% in 2015. See Economic Report of the President, supra, at Table B-12. Between 1972 and 2010 the unemployment rate for blacks was more than twice that for whites. Id. Over 25% of black families were below the poverty line in 2014. Id. at Table B-9.

Black men's wages rose relative to those of white males until the middle to late 1970s, but their relative pay declined over the next decade, and the record to the mid-1990s showed no further clear improvement in relative pay until the economic expansion of the late 1990s seemed to push their income to about three fourths that of white males. Council of Economic Advisors, Changing America: Indicators of Social Well-Being by Race and Hispanic Origin, 23, 28 (1998). This ratio has settled around 80% in recent years. See Economic Report of the President, supra, at Table B-9 (data through 2014). Black women have fared better relative to white women, with full-time black female workers almost achieving parity with their white counterparts in weekly wages in the mid-1970s; yet black women failed to keep full pace with the increases in the income of white women over the next thirty five years. Id.; Changing America, supra, at 23, 31.

Scholars have continued to debate the reasons for these persistent disparities. See, e.g., Glenn Loury, The Anatomy of Racial Inequality (2002); Stephen Thernstrom & Abigail Thernstrom, America in Black and

White (1998); Orlando Patterson, The Ordeal of Integration (1997); William J. Wilson, When Work Disappears: The World of the New Urban Poor (1996). Most agree, however, that discrimination against black Americans continues to be a problem in this country.

B.   PROVING INDIVIDUAL DISPARATE TREATMENT

McDONNELL DOUGLAS CORP. v. GREEN
Supreme Court of the United States, 1973.
411 U.S. 792, 93 S.Ct. 1817, 36 L.Ed.2d 668.

JUSTICE POWELL delivered the opinion of the Court.

Petitioner, McDonnell Douglas Corp., is an aerospace and aircraft manufacturer headquartered in St. Louis, Missouri, where it employs over 30,000 people. Respondent, a black citizen of St. Louis, worked for petitioner as a mechanic and laboratory technician from 1956 until August 28, 1964 when he was laid off in the course of a general reduction in petitioner's work force.

Respondent, a long-time activist in the civil rights movement, protested vigorously that his discharge and the general hiring practices of petitioner were racially motivated. As part of this protest, respondent and other members of the Congress on Racial Equality illegally stalled their cars on the main roads leading to petitioner's plant for the purpose of blocking access to it at the time of the morning shift change. The District Judge described the plan for, and respondent's participation in, the "stall-in" as follows:

* * *

"Acting under the 'stall in' plan, plaintiff [respondent in the present action] drove his car onto Brown Road, a McDonnell access road, at approximately 7:00 a.m., at the start of the morning rush hour. Plaintiff was aware of the traffic problems that would result. He stopped his car with the intent to block traffic. The police arrived shortly and requested plaintiff to move his car. He refused to move his car voluntarily. Plaintiff's car was towed away by the police, and he was arrested for obstructing traffic. Plaintiff pleaded guilty to the charge of obstructing traffic and was fined."

On July 2, 1965, a "lock-in" took place wherein a chain and padlock were placed on the front door of a building to prevent the occupants, certain of petitioner's employees, from leaving. Though respondent apparently knew beforehand of the "lock-in," the full extent of his involvement remains uncertain.

Some three weeks following the "lock-in," on July 25, 1965, petitioner publicly advertised for qualified mechanics, respondent's trade, and respondent promptly applied for re-employment. Petitioner turned down respondent, basing its rejection on respondent's participation in the "stall-in" and "lock-in." Shortly thereafter, respondent filed a formal complaint with the Equal Employment Opportunity Commission, claiming that petitioner had refused to rehire him because of his race and persistent involvement in the civil rights movement, in violation of §§ 703(a)(1) and 704(a) of the Civil Rights Act of 1964, 42 U.S.C. §§ 2000e–2(a)(1) and 2000e–3(a). The former section generally prohibits racial discrimination in any employment decision while the latter forbids discrimination against applicants or employees for attempting to protest or correct allegedly discriminatory conditions of employment.

The Commission made no finding on respondent's allegation of racial bias under § 703(a)(1), but it did find reasonable cause to believe petitioner had violated § 704(a) by refusing to rehire respondent because of his civil rights activity. After the Commission unsuccessfully attempted to conciliate the dispute, it advised respondent in March 1968, of his right to institute a civil action in federal court within 30 days.

[*Eds.* The Court reported that the District Court, with the affirmance of the Court of Appeals, found that the plaintiff's participation in illegal demonstrations was not protected by § 704(a), and that plaintiff did not seek further review of this issue. Justice Powell also noted that the District Court had dismissed plaintiff's § 703(a) claim because the EEOC had failed to make a determination of reasonable cause to believe that a violation of that section had been committed. The Supreme Court, however, agreed with the Court of Appeals that an EEOC "cause" finding was not required. The Court stressed that Title VII "does not restrict a complainant's right to sue to those charges as to which the Commission has made findings of reasonable cause * * * ." It was thus necessary to remand the case for trial of plaintiff's § 703(a) discrimination claim, and the Court offered the following instructions to guide the trial on remand:]

The complainant in a Title VII trial must carry the initial burden under the statute of establishing a prima facie case of racial discrimination. This may be done by showing (i) that he belongs to a racial minority; (ii) that he applied and was qualified for a job for which the employer was seeking applicants; (iii) that, despite his qualifications, he was rejected; and (iv) that, after his rejection, the position remained open and the employer continued to seek applicants from persons of complainant's qualifications.[13] In the instant case, we agree with the Court of Appeals that respondent proved a prima facie case. Petitioner sought mechanics,

---

[13]   The facts necessarily will vary in Title VII cases, and the specification above of the prima facie proof required from respondent is not necessarily applicable in every respect to differing factual situations.

respondent's trade, and continued to do so after respondent's rejection. Petitioner, moreover, does not dispute respondent's qualifications and acknowledges that his past work performance in petitioner's employ was "satisfactory."

The burden then must shift to the employer to articulate some legitimate, nondiscriminatory reason for the employee's rejection. We need not attempt in the instant case to detail every matter which fairly could be recognized as a reasonable basis for a refusal to hire. Here petitioner has assigned respondent's participation in unlawful conduct against it as the cause for his rejection. We think that this suffices to discharge petitioner's burden of proof at this stage and to meet respondent's prima facie case of discrimination.

The Court of Appeals intimated, however, that petitioner's stated reason for refusing to rehire respondent was a "subjective" rather than objective criterion which "carr[ies] little weight in rebutting charges of discrimination". This was among the statements which caused the dissenting judge to read the opinion as taking "the position that such unlawful acts as Green committed against McDonnell would not legally entitle McDonnell to refuse to hire him, even though no racial motivation was involved * * * ." Regardless of whether this was the intended import of the opinion, we think the court below seriously underestimated the rebuttal weight to which petitioner's reasons were entitled. Respondent admittedly had taken part in a carefully planned "stall-in," designed to tie up access to and egress from petitioner's plant at a peak traffic hour. Nothing in Title VII compels an employer to absolve and rehire one who has engaged in such deliberate, unlawful activity against it.[17]

* * *

Petitioner's reason for rejection thus suffices to meet the prima facie case, but the inquiry must not end here. While Title VII does not, without more, compel rehiring of respondent, neither does it permit petitioner to use respondent's conduct as a pretext for the sort of discrimination prohibited by § 703(a)(1). On remand, respondent must, as the Court of Appeals recognized, be afforded a fair opportunity to show that petitioner's stated reason for respondent's rejection was in fact pretext. Especially relevant to such a showing would be evidence that white employees involved in acts against petitioner of comparable seriousness to the "stall-in" were nevertheless retained or rehired. Petitioner may justifiably refuse to rehire one who was engaged in unlawful, disruptive acts against it, but only if this criterion is applied alike to members of all races.

---

[17] The unlawful activity in this case was directed specifically against petitioner. We need not consider or decide here whether, or under what circumstances, unlawful activity not directed against the particular employer may be a legitimate justification for refusing to hire.

Other evidence that may be relevant to any showing of pretext includes facts as to the petitioner's treatment of respondent during his prior term of employment; petitioner's reaction, if any, to respondent's legitimate civil rights activities; and petitioner's general policy and practice with respect to minority employment. On the latter point, statistics as to petitioner's employment policy and practice may be helpful to a determination of whether petitioner's refusal to rehire respondent in this case conformed to a general pattern of discrimination against blacks. *Jones v. Lee Way Motor Freight, Inc.*, 431 F.2d 245 (C.A.10 1970); Blumrosen, Strangers in Paradise: Griggs v. Duke Power Co., and the Concept of Employment Discrimination, 71 Mich.L.Rev. 59, 91–94 (1972).[19] In short, on the retrial respondent must be given a full and fair opportunity to demonstrate by competent evidence that the presumptively valid reasons for his rejection were in fact a coverup for a racially discriminatory decision.

NOTES AND QUESTIONS

Background Note

Percy Green, the plaintiff in the *McDonnell Douglas* case, is a well-known civil rights activist in St. Louis. When McDonnell Douglas fired him, he was the "only black worker among 600 involved in research and development related to the Gemini space program."

He is perhaps best known for climbing 125 feet up the partially constructed St. Louis arch in July 1964 to protest the failure to hire African-American contractors and employees on the project. In a 2014 interview, Green reflected, "[w]e thought we better not wait until it was almost built before we started raising the question" of hiring discrimination. See Kevin McDermott, 50 years after Arch-climbing protest, 'We still have work to do' on minority hiring, St. Louis Post-Dispatch, July 14, 2014.[1]

---

[19] The District Court may, for example, determine, after reasonable discovery that "the [racial] composition of defendant's labor force is itself reflective of restrictive or exclusionary practices." See Blumrosen, *supra,* at 92. We caution that such general determinations, while helpful, may not be in and of themselves controlling as to an individualized hiring decision, particularly in the presence of an otherwise justifiable reason for refusing to rehire. See generally *United States v. Bethlehem Steel Corp.*, 312 F.Supp. 977, 992 (W.D.N.Y.1970), order modified, 446 F.2d 652 (C.A.2 1971); Blumrosen, *supra,* n. 19, at 93.

[1] See also David B. Oppenheimer, The Story of Green v. McDonnell Douglas, Employment Discrimination Stories, (Joel Friedman, ed. 2006).

Test Your Understanding of the Material

1.   What does the Court mean when it uses the term "pretext"? How does proof of pretext help prove discriminatory motive? How does one go about proving pretext?

2.   Review the language of § 703, which prohibits employers from refusing to hire an employee "because of race." Does the *McDonnell Douglas* framework make it easier or harder for plaintiffs to prove that an employer's decision was "because of race"? (Note that the Court subsequently made clear in a series of decisions that plaintiffs need not use the framework if they can otherwise prove a discriminatory motive.)

3.   The introduction posits two possible purposes for antidiscrimination legislation: (1) to purify employer decisionmaking by penalizing decisions that are significantly influenced by consideration of the presumptively irrelevant characteristic of group membership, and (2) to prohibit employment decisions that, even in the absence of discriminatory intent, significantly disadvantage members of particular social groups without adequate justification. Does the *McDonnell Douglas* framework advance either or both of these purposes?

Related Issues

4.   *Modifying the* McDonnell Douglas *Formulation for Discharges*. The four *McDonnell Douglas* factors seem framed for a hiring or promotion case. How would the factors have to be reformulated for a discharge or on-the-job treatment case? See, e.g., Perry v. Woodward, 199 F.3d 1126 (10th Cir. 1999) (plaintiff must establish: "(1) she belongs to a protected class; (2) she was qualified for her job; (3) despite her qualifications, she was discharged; and (4) the job was not eliminated after her discharge."): Pivirotto v. Innovative Systems, Inc., 191 F.3d 344 (3d Cir. 1999) (collecting cases).

5.   *Adverse Employment Actions Other than Failure to Hire and Discharges*. Section 703 of Title VII expressly prohibits an employer from "fail[ing] or ref[using] to hire or discharg[ing]" an employee on the basis of his/her membership in a protected category. It also prohibits an employer from "discriminat[ing] against any individual with respect to his compensation, terms, conditions or privileges of employment" or "limit[ing], segregat[ing], or classify[ing]" an employee based on a protected category.

In Burlington Northern & Santa Fe Ry. v. White, 548 U.S. 53, 126 S.Ct. 2405, 165 L.Ed.2d 345 (2006), excerpted in Chapter 11 infra, the Court held that § 704, the anti-retaliatory provision of Title VII, protects employees from employer actions that are "materially adverse", stressing the importance of separating "significant from trivial harms" under Title VII. The *Burlington* Court's indication that some employment actions do not entail sufficiently "materially adverse" consequences to be actionable accords with the approach the lower courts have taken under § 703. See, e.g., Jones v. Spherion Atl. Enter., LLC, 493 F. App'x 6, 9 (11th Cir. 2012) ("criticisms of an employee's performance, whether written or oral, which do not lead to tangible job consequences, are generally not sufficient to constitute a violation of Title VII."); Mitchell v. Vanderbilt Univ., 389 F.3d 177 (6th Cir. 2004) (reduction of laboratory space and not being selected for desired lateral transfer not materially adverse where medical professor retained salary and tenured employment status); Herrnreiter v. Chicago Housing Authority, 315 F.3d 742, 744 (7th Cir.2002) (§ 703(a) does not reach *"any* action that displeases the employee", but only those that reduce either the employee's financial terms or his "career prospects by preventing him from using the skills in which he is trained and experienced" or that subject "him to a humiliating, degrading, unsafe, unhealthful, or otherwise significantly negative alteration in his working environment"). For treatment of workplace harassment as discrimination, see pp. 364–388 infra.

6.   *Does the Plainfiff Have to Show He/She Was More Qualified than the Individual Hired?* The *McDonnell Douglas* formulation of the prima facie showing assumes that the position that plaintiff sought remained open after the plaintiff was rejected. If another individual has been hired, the courts sometimes require the plaintiff, as part of a prima facie proof, to show that he or she was more qualified than the other individual. Compare Brown v. Ala. Dep't of Transp., 597 F.3d 1160, 1174 (11th Cir. 2010), with Walker v. Mortham, 158 F.3d 1177 (11th Cir.1998). The plaintiff in any event will have to prove this if the employer articulates relative qualifications as a reason for its refusal to hire or promote the plaintiff. See Young v. Lehman, 748 F.2d 194 (4th Cir.1984). See also Ash v. Tyson Foods, Inc., 546 U.S. 454, 126 S.Ct. 1195, 163 L.Ed.2d 1053 (2006) ("qualification evidence may suffice, at least in some circumstances, to show pretext").

7.   Can *White Plaintiffs Complaining of Race Discrimination Use the* McDonnell Douglas *Framwork?* In McDonald v. Santa Fe Trail Transp. Co., 427 U.S. 273, 96 S.Ct. 2574, 49 L.Ed.2d 493 (1976), the Court held that white employees can challenge adverse treatment on account of their race under Title VII as well as 42 U.S.C. § 1981. Does this mean that the first *McDonnell Douglas* factor, belonging to a racial minority, can be ignored? Does *McDonnell Douglas* assume that belonging to a racial minority is relevant to creating a suspicion of discrimination? In what situations might suspicion of discrimination against a white be equally appropriate? See Harding v. Gray, 9 F.3d 150, 153 (D.C.Cir.1993) (plaintiff established a prima facie case because he proved "background circumstances [that] support the suspicion that the defendant is that unusual employer who discriminates against the majority"). For discussion of affirmative action, see Chapter 5 infra.

8.   *Can the Plaintiff Establish a Prima Facie Case If the Replacement Hired is Someone from the Same Title VII Protected Class?* Most courts of appeals have held in discharge cases that plaintiffs are not "precluded from meeting the prima facie burden by an inability to demonstrate that the replacement employee does not share her protected attribute." Perry v. Woodward, 199 F.3d 1126, 1138 (10th Cir.1999). See also, e.g., Bates v. City of Chi., 726 F.3d 951, 954 n.4 (7th Cir. 2013); Stella v. Mineta, 284 F.3d 135 (D.C.Cir.2002); Pivirotto v. Innovative Systems, Inc., 191 F.3d 344 (3d Cir.1999). But see Miles v. Dell, Inc., 429 F.3d 480 (4th Cir. 2005) (requiring that replacement be outside protected class except in special circumstances).

Should courts require the proof of special circumstances to raise an inference of discrimination to establish a *McDonnell Douglas* prima facie case where a job *applicant* lost out to another member of the same protected class? Should a disappointed black job applicant at least be able to sue an employer for maintaining a higher qualification threshold for employing black applicants, or for penalizing certain personality traits only among black applicants, even when the person ultimately selected is black?

TEXAS DEPT. OF COMMUNITY AFFAIRS V. BURDINE

Supreme Court of the United States, 1981.
450 U.S. 248, 101 S.Ct. 1089, 67 L.Ed.2d 207.

JUSTICE POWELL delivered the opinion of the Court.

I

Petitioner, the Texas Department of Community Affairs (TDCA), hired respondent, a female, in January 1972, for the position of accounting clerk in the Public Service Careers Division (PSC). PSC provided training and employment opportunities in the public sector for unskilled workers. When hired, respondent possessed several years' experience in employment training. She was promoted to Field Services Coordinator in July 1972. Her supervisor resigned in November of that year, and respondent was assigned additional duties. Although she applied for the supervisor's position of Project Director, the position remained vacant for six months.

PSC was funded completely by the United States Department of Labor. The Department was seriously concerned about inefficiencies at PSC. In February 1973, the Department notified the Executive Director of TDCA, B.R. Fuller, that it would terminate PSC the following month. TDCA officials, assisted by respondent, persuaded the Department to continue funding the program, conditioned upon PSC's reforming its operations. Among the agreed conditions were the appointment of a permanent Project Director and a complete reorganization of the PSC staff.

After consulting with personnel within TDCA, Fuller hired a male from another division of the agency as Project Director. In reducing the PSC staff, he fired respondent along with two other employees, and retained another male, Walz, as the only professional employee in the division. It is undisputed that respondent had maintained her application for the position of Project Director and had requested to remain with TDCA. Respondent soon was rehired by TDCA and assigned to another division of the agency. She received the exact salary paid to the Project Director at PSC, and the subsequent promotions she has received have kept her salary and responsibility commensurate with what she would have received had she been appointed Project Director.

Respondent filed this suit in the United States District Court for the Western District of Texas. She alleged that the failure to promote and the subsequent decision to terminate her had been predicated on gender discrimination in violation of Title VII. After a bench trial, the District Court held that neither decision was based on gender discrimination. The court relied on the testimony of Fuller that the employment decisions necessitated by the commands of the Department of Labor were based on consultation among trusted advisors and a nondiscriminatory evaluation of the relative qualifications of the individuals involved. He testified that the three individuals terminated did not work well together, and that TDCA thought that eliminating this problem would improve PSC's efficiency. The court accepted this explanation as rational and, in effect, found no evidence that the decisions not to promote and to terminate respondent were prompted by gender discrimination. * * *

[handwritten margin note: District = no discrimination]

The Court of Appeals, however, reversed the District Court's finding that Fuller's testimony sufficiently had rebutted respondent's prima facie case of gender discrimination in the decision to terminate her employment at PSC. The court reaffirmed its previously announced views that the defendant in a Title VII case bears the burden of proving by a preponderance of the evidence the existence of legitimate nondiscriminatory reasons for the employment action and that the defendant also must prove by objective evidence that those hired or promoted were better qualified than the plaintiff. The court found that Fuller's testimony did not carry either of these evidentiary burdens. It, therefore, reversed the judgment of the District Court and remanded the case for computation of backpay.

[handwritten margin note: wrong standard]

II

In *McDonnell Douglas Corp. v. Green,* 411 U.S. 792, 93 S.Ct. 1817, 36 L.Ed.2d 668 (1973), we set forth the basic allocation of burdens and order of presentation of proof in a Title VII case alleging discriminatory treatment. * * *

The nature of the burden that shifts to the defendant should be understood in light of the plaintiff's ultimate and intermediate burdens. The ultimate burden of persuading the trier of fact that the defendant intentionally discriminated against the plaintiff remains at all times with the plaintiff. See *Board of Trustees of Keene State College v. Sweeney,* 439 U.S. 24, 25, n. 2, 99 S.Ct. 295, 296, n. 2, 58 L.Ed.2d 216 (1978); *id.,* at 29, 99 S.Ct., at 297 (Stevens, J., dissenting). See generally 9 J. Wigmore, Evidence § 2489 (3d ed. 1940) (the burden of persuasion "never shifts"). The *McDonnell Douglas* division of intermediate evidentiary burdens serves to bring the litigants and the court expeditiously and fairly to this ultimate question.

The burden of establishing a prima facie case of disparate treatment is not onerous. The plaintiff must prove by a preponderance of the evidence that she applied for an available position for which she was qualified, but was rejected under circumstances which give rise to an inference of unlawful discrimination.[6] The prima facie case serves an important function in the litigation: it eliminates the most common nondiscriminatory reasons for the plaintiff's rejection. See *Teamsters v. United States,* 431 U.S. 324, 358, and n. 44, 97 S.Ct. 1843, 1866, n. 44, 52 L.Ed.2d 396 (1977). As the Court explained in *Furnco Construction Corp. v. Waters,* 438 U.S. 567, 577, 98 S.Ct. 2943, 2949, 57 L.Ed.2d 957 (1978), the prima facie case "raises an inference of discrimination only because we presume these acts, if otherwise unexplained, are more likely than not based on the consideration of impermissible factors." Establishment of the prima facie case in effect creates a presumption that the employer unlawfully discriminated against the employee. If the trier of fact believes the plaintiff's evidence, and if the employer is silent in the face of the presumption, the court must enter judgment for the plaintiff because no issue of fact remains in the case.[7]

The burden that shifts to the defendant, therefore, is to rebut the presumption of discrimination by producing evidence that the plaintiff was rejected, or someone else was preferred, for a legitimate, nondiscriminatory reason. The defendant need not persuade the court that it was actually motivated by the proffered reasons. See *Sweeney, supra,* at 25, 99 S.Ct., at 296. It is sufficient if the defendant's evidence raises a genuine issue of fact as to whether it discriminated against the plaintiff.[8] To accomplish this, the defendant must clearly set forth, through the introduction of admissible evidence, the reasons for the plaintiff's rejection. The explanation provided must be legally sufficient to justify a judgment for the defendant. If the defendant carries this burden of production, the presumption raised by the prima facie case is rebutted,[10] and the factual

---

[6] In the instant case, it is not seriously contested that respondent has proved a prima facie case. She showed that she was a qualified woman who sought an available position, but the position was left open for several months before she finally was rejected in favor of a male, Walz, who had been under her supervision.

[7] The phrase "prima facie case" not only may denote the establishment of a legally mandatory, rebuttable presumption, but also may be used by courts to describe the plaintiff's burden of producing enough evidence to permit the trier of fact to infer the fact at issue. 9 J. Wigmore, Evidence § 2494 (3d ed. 1940). *McDonnell Douglas* should have made it apparent that in the Title VII context we use "prima facie case" in the former sense.

[8] This evidentiary relationship between the presumption created by a prima facie case and the consequential burden of production placed on the defendant is a traditional feature of the common law. "The word 'presumption' properly used refers only to a device for allocating the production burden." F. James & G. Hazard, Civil Procedure § 7.9, p. 255 (2d ed. 1977) (footnote omitted). See Fed.Rule Evid. 301. See generally 9 J. Wigmore, Evidence § 2491 (3d ed. 1940). Cf. J. Maguire, Evidence, Common Sense and Common Law 185–186 (1947). Usually, assessing the burden of production helps the judge determine whether the litigants have created an issue of fact to be decided by the jury. In a Title VII case, the allocation of burdens and the creation of a presumption by the establishment of a prima facie case is intended progressively to sharpen the inquiry into the elusive factual question of intentional discrimination.

[10] See generally J. Thayer, Preliminary Treatise on Evidence 346 (1898). In saying that the presumption drops from the case, we do not imply that the trier of fact no longer may consider evidence previously introduced by the plaintiff to establish a prima facie case. A satisfactory explanation by the defendant destroys the legally mandatory inference of discrimination arising from the plaintiff's initial evidence. Nonetheless, this evidence and inferences properly drawn therefrom may be considered by the trier of fact on the issue of whether the defendant's

inquiry proceeds to a new level of specificity. Placing this burden of production on the defendant thus serves simultaneously to meet the plaintiff's prima facie case by presenting a legitimate reason for the action and to frame the factual issue with sufficient clarity so that the plaintiff will have a full and fair opportunity to demonstrate pretext. The sufficiency of the defendant's evidence should be evaluated by the extent to which it fulfills these functions.

The plaintiff retains the burden of persuasion. She now must have the opportunity to demonstrate that the proffered reason was not the true reason for the employment decision. This burden now merges with the ultimate burden of persuading the court that she has been the victim of intentional discrimination. She may succeed in this either directly by persuading the court that a discriminatory reason more likely motivated the employer or indirectly by showing that the employer's proffered explanation is unworthy of credence.

* * *

III

The Court of Appeals has misconstrued the nature of the burden that *McDonnell Douglas* and its progeny place on the defendant. We stated in *Sweeney* that "the employer's burden is satisfied if he simply 'explains what he has done' or 'produc[es] evidence of legitimate nondiscriminatory reasons.'" 439 U.S., at 25, n. 2, 99 S.Ct., at 296 n. 2, quoting *id.,* at 28, 29, 99 S.Ct., at 297–298 (Stevens, J., dissenting). It is plain that the Court of Appeals required much more: it placed on the defendant the burden of persuading the court that it had convincing, objective reasons for preferring the chosen applicant above the plaintiff.[11]

* * * We have stated consistently that the employee's prima facie case of discrimination will be rebutted if the employer articulates lawful reasons for the action; that is, to satisfy this intermediate burden, the employer need only produce admissible evidence which would allow the trier of fact rationally to conclude that the employment decision had not been

---

explanation is pretextual. Indeed, there may be some cases where the plaintiff's initial evidence, combined with effective cross-examination of the defendant, will suffice to discredit the defendant's explanation.

[11] The court reviewed the defendant's evidence and explained its deficiency:

"Defendant failed to introduce comparative factual data concerning Burdine and Walz. Fuller merely testified that he discharged and retained personnel in the spring shakeup at TDCA primarily on the recommendations of subordinates and that he considered Walz qualified for the position he was retained to do. Fuller failed to specify any objective criteria on which he based the decision to discharge Burdine and retain Walz. He stated only that the action was in the best interest of the program and that there had been some friction within the department that might be alleviated by Burdine's discharge. Nothing in the record indicates whether he examined Walz' ability to work well with others. This court [previously has] found such unsubstantiated assertions of 'qualification' and 'prior work record' insufficient absent data that will allow a true *comparison* of the individuals hired and rejected."

motivated by discriminatory animus. The Court of Appeals would require the defendant to introduce evidence which, in the absence of any evidence of pretext, would *persuade* the trier of fact that the employment action was lawful. This exceeds what properly can be demanded to satisfy a burden of production.

The court placed the burden of persuasion on the defendant apparently because it feared that "[i]f an employer need only *articulate*—not prove—a legitimate, nondiscriminatory reason for his action, he may compose fictitious, but legitimate, reasons for his actions." *Turner v. Texas Instruments, Inc.,* [555 F.2d 1251, 1255 (C.A.5 1977)] (emphasis in original). We do not believe, however, that limiting the defendant's evidentiary obligation to a burden of production will unduly hinder the plaintiff. First, as noted above, the defendant's explanation of its legitimate reasons must be clear and reasonably specific. See *Loeb v. Textron, Inc.,* 600 F.2d 1003, 1011–1012, n. 5 (C.A.1 1979). This obligation arises both from the necessity of rebutting the inference of discrimination arising from the prima facie case and from the requirement that the plaintiff be afforded "a full and fair opportunity" to demonstrate pretext. Second, although the defendant does not bear a formal burden of persuasion, the defendant nevertheless retains an incentive to persuade the trier of fact that the employment decision was lawful. Thus, the defendant normally will attempt to prove the factual basis for its explanation. Third, the liberal discovery rules applicable to any civil suit in federal court are supplemented in a Title VII suit by the plaintiff's access to the Equal Employment Opportunity Commission's investigatory files concerning her complaint. See *EEOC v. Associated Dry Goods Corp.,* 449 U.S. 590, 101 S.Ct. 817, 66 L.Ed.2d 762 (1981). Given these factors, we are unpersuaded that the plaintiff will find it particularly difficult to prove that a proffered explanation lacking a factual basis is a pretext. We remain confident that the *McDonnell Douglas* framework permits the plaintiff meriting relief to demonstrate intentional discrimination.

The Court of Appeals also erred in requiring the defendant to prove by objective evidence that the person hired or promoted was more qualified than the plaintiff. *McDonnell Douglas* teaches that it is the plaintiff's task to demonstrate that similarly situated employees were not treated equally. 411 U.S., at 804, 93 S.Ct., at 1825. The Court of Appeals' rule would require the employer to show that the plaintiff's objective qualifications were inferior to those of the person selected. If it cannot, a court would, in effect, conclude that it has discriminated.

The court's procedural rule harbors a substantive error. Title VII prohibits all discrimination in employment based upon race, sex, and national origin. "The broad, overriding interest, shared by employer, employee, and consumer, is efficient and trustworthy workmanship assured through fair and * * * neutral employment and personnel decisions." *McDonnell Douglas, supra,* at 801, 93 S.Ct., at 1823. Title VII, however, does not demand that an employer give preferential treatment to minorities or women. 42 U.S.C. § 2000e–2(j). See *Steelworkers v. Weber,* 443 U.S. 193, 205–206, 99 S.Ct. 2721, 2728–2729, 61 L.Ed.2d 480 (1979). The statute was not intended to "diminish traditional management prerogatives." *Id.,* at 207, 99 S.Ct., at 2729. It does not require the employer to restructure his employment practices to maximize the number of minorities and women hired. *Furnco Construction Corp. v. Waters,* 438 U.S. 567, 577–578, 98 S.Ct. 2943, 2949–2950, 57 L.Ed.2d 957 (1978).

The views of the Court of Appeals can be read, we think, as requiring the employer to hire the minority or female applicant whenever that person's objective qualifications were equal to those of a white male applicant. But Title VII does not obligate an employer to accord this preference. Rather, the employer has discretion to choose among equally qualified candidates, provided the decision is not based upon unlawful criteria. The fact that a court may think that the employer misjudged the qualifications of the applicants does not in itself expose him to Title VII liability, although this may be probative of whether the employer's reasons are pretexts for discrimination. *Loeb v. Textron, Inc., supra,* at, n. 6; see *Lieberman v. Gant,* 630 F.2d 60, 65 (C.A.2 1980).

In summary, the Court of Appeals erred by requiring the defendant to prove by a preponderance of the evidence the existence of nondiscriminatory reasons for terminating the respondent and that the person retained in her stead had superior objective qualifications for the position.[12] When the plaintiff has proved a prima facie case of discrimination, the defendant bears only the burden of explaining clearly the nondiscriminatory reasons for its actions. The judgment of the Court of Appeals is vacated, and the case is remanded for further proceedings consistent with this opinion.

NOTES AND QUESTIONS

Test Your Understanding of the Material

1.   What evidence did the Texas Department of Community Affairs proffer in support of its decision? Was this evidence sufficient to support the defendant's burden of production? Why? By comparison, a general statement about the employer's practices, without any specific application to plaintiff's individual case, has been deemed insufficient by lower courts. See, e.g., IMPACT v. Firestone, 893 F.2d 1189, 1193–94 (11th Cir.1990) (averment of general practice of hiring the more qualified not sufficient).

---

[12] Because the Court of Appeals applied the wrong legal standard to the evidence, we have no occasion to decide whether it erred in not reviewing the District Court's finding of no intentional discrimination under the "clearly erroneous" standard of Federal Rule of Civil Procedure 52 (a). Addressing this issue in this case would be inappropriate because the District Court made no findings on the intermediate questions posed by *McDonnell Douglas*.

2.   *Burdine* states that a plaintiff may sustain its ultimate persuasion burden "either directly by persuading the court that a discriminatory reason more likely motivated the employer or indirectly by showing that the employer's offered explanation is unworthy of credence." What is the difference between these two types of proof? Which type is proof of pretext? Provide examples of each type of proof.

3.   If the employer fails to carry its burden of production, must the court find for the plaintiff upon the four-factor *McDonnell Douglas* showing, or does it retain discretion to find for the defendant? See footnote 7 in *Burdine*. On the other hand, if the employer succeeds in carrying its burden, must the court find for the defendant unless the plaintiff enters additional evidence? See footnote 10 in *Burdine*.

Related Issues

4.   *"Same Decisionmaker" Defense?* Plaintiffs face a tougher case when the same decisionmaker both hired (or promoted) the plaintiff in the first place and is responsible for the plaintiff's discharge or demotion. While all courts find "same decisionmaker" evidence relevant, the courts of appeals differ on the amount of weight that it should be given. Compare, e.g., Wexler v. White's Fine Furniture, Inc., 317 F.3d 564, 573 (6th Cir.2003) (rejecting "the idea that a mandatory inference must be applied * * * whenever the claimant has been hired and fired by the same individual"), with Proud v. Stone, 945 F.2d 796, 797 (4th Cir.1991) ("where the hirer and firer are the same individual and the termination of employment occurs within a relatively short time span following the hiring, a strong inference exists that discrimination was not a determining factor"). But see Linda Hamilton Krieger & Susan T. Fiske, Behavioral Realism in Employment Discrimination Law: Implicit Bias and Disparate Treatment, 94 Cal. L. Rev. 997, 1046 (2006) (suggesting that "an employer might be unaware of his own stereotypical view . . . at the time of hiring") (quoting Johnson v. Zema Sys. Corp., 170 F.3d 734, 745 (7th Cir. 1999)).

5.   *Statistical Proof.* Statistics are generally insufficient on their own to establish or defeat an individual discrimination case. See, e.g., Deloach v. Delchamps, Inc., 897 F.2d 815, 820 (5th Cir.1990) (plaintiff cannot prove pretext with statistical evidence alone); Cross v. United States Postal Service, 639 F.2d 409 (8th Cir.1981) (defendant's statistics demonstrating hiring of member's class not an absolute defense).

6.   *"Me Too" Evidence.* In *Sprint/United Mgmt. Co. v. Mendelsohn*, 552 U.S. 279,388, 128 S.Ct. 1140, 170 L.Ed. 2d 1 (2008), the Supreme Court considered whether to categorically exclude evidence of discrimination by supervisors other than the particular supervisor responsible for the adverse employment action. The Supreme Court declined to impose a categorical rule: "[t]he question whether evidence of discrimination by other supervisors is relevant . . . is fact based and depends on many factors, including how closely related the evidence is to the plaintiff's circumstances and theory of the case."

The next case, *Reeves v. Sanderson Plumbing*, is the successor to a 1993 Supreme Court ruling, St. Mary's Honor Center v. Hicks, 509 U.S. 502, 113 S. Ct. 2742, 125 L. Ed. 2d 407 (1993). In *St. Mary's*, the trial judge as the trier of fact concluded that the defendant employer had provided a false reason for its demotion and later discharge of Hicks. However, the trial court ruled that Hicks nonetheless could not prevail because he had failed to prove that the real reason for his adverse treatment was racial rather than personal animus. The Court of Appeals set this determination aside, holding that a plaintiff who proves all of a defendant's "proffered reasons for the adverse employment actions to be pretextual" is "entitled to judgment as a matter of law."

The Supreme Court in *St. Mary's* disagreed. It held that since "the *McDonnell Douglas* framework—with its presumptions and burdens—is no longer relevant" after the defendant carries its burden of production by proffering some legitimate reason for its actions, the plaintiff's proof of the defendant's pretext does not compel the trier of fact to find illegal discriminatory intent. 509 U.S. at 510. The trier of fact must determine whether the plaintiff has proven such intent based on all the evidence, both inculpatory and exculpatory.

In a dissenting opinion in *St. Mary's*, Justice Souter identified some uncertainty in the majority's ruling:

> "In one passage, the Court states that although proof of the falsity of the employer's proffered reasons does not 'compe[l] judgment for the plaintiff,' such evidence, without more, 'will permit the trier of fact to infer the ultimate fact of intentional discrimination.' . . . But other language in the Court's opinion supports a more extreme conclusion . . . the Court twice states that the plaintiff must show '*both* that the reason was false, *and* that discrimination was the real reason.' In addition, in summing up its reading of our earlier cases, the Court states that '[i]t is not enough . . . to disbelieve the employer.'" 509 U.S. at 535.

As you read *Reeves*, consider how it resolves the uncertainty that Justice Souter identified in *St. Mary's*.

REEVES V. SANDERSON PLUMBING PRODUCTS, INC.

Supreme Court of the United States, 2000.
530 U.S. 133, 120 S.Ct. 2097, 147 L.Ed.2d 105.

JUSTICE O'CONNOR delivered the opinion of the Court.

* * *

In October 1995, petitioner Roger Reeves was 57 years old and had spent 40 years in the employ of respondent, Sanderson Plumbing Products, Inc., a manufacturer of toilet seats and covers. Petitioner worked in a department known as the "Hinge Room," where he supervised the "regular line." Joe Oswalt, in his mid-thirties, supervised the Hinge Room's "special line," and Russell Caldwell, the manager of the Hinge Room and age 45, supervised both petitioner and Oswalt. Petitioner's responsibilities included recording the attendance and hours of those under his supervision, and reviewing a weekly report that listed the hours worked by each employee.

In the summer of 1995, Caldwell informed Powe Chesnut, the director of manufacturing and the husband of company president Sandra Sanderson, that "production was down" in the Hinge Room because employees were often absent and were "coming in late and leaving early." Because the monthly attendance reports did not indicate a problem, Chesnut ordered an audit of the Hinge Room's timesheets for July, August, and September of that year. According to Chesnut's testimony, that investigation revealed "numerous timekeeping errors and misrepresentations on the part of Caldwell, Reeves, and Oswalt." Following the audit, Chesnut, along with Dana Jester, vice president of human resources, and Tom Whitaker, vice president of operations, recommended to company president Sanderson that petitioner and Caldwell be fired. In October 1995, Sanderson followed the recommendation and discharged both petitioner and Caldwell.

In June 1996, petitioner filed suit in the United States District Court for the Northern District of Mississippi, contending that he had been fired because of his age in violation of the Age Discrimination in Employment Act of 1967 (ADEA), 81 Stat. 602, as amended, 29 U. S. C. § 621 *et seq.* At trial, respondent contended that it had fired petitioner due to his failure to maintain accurate attendance records, while petitioner attempted to demonstrate that respondent's explanation was pretext for age discrimination. Petitioner introduced evidence that he had accurately recorded the attendance and hours of the employees under his supervision, and that Chesnut, whom Oswalt described as wielding "absolute power" within the company, had demonstrated age-based animus in his dealings with petitioner. During the trial, the District Court twice denied oral motions by respondent for judgment as a matter of law under Rule 50 of the Federal Rules of Civil Procedure, and the case went to the jury. The court instructed the jury that "[i]f the plaintiff fails to prove age was a determinative or motivating factor in the decision to terminate him, then your verdict shall be for the defendant." So charged, the jury returned a verdict in favor of petitioner * * * .

The Court of Appeals for the Fifth Circuit reversed, holding that petitioner had not introduced sufficient evidence to sustain the jury's finding of unlawful discrimination. * * *

We granted certiorari to resolve a conflict among the Courts of Appeals as to whether a plaintiff's prima facie case of discrimination (as defined in

McDonnell Douglas Corp. v. Green, 411 U. S. 792, 802 (1973)), combined with sufficient evidence for a reasonable factfinder to reject the employer's nondiscriminatory explanation for its decision, is adequate to sustain a finding of liability for intentional discrimination. *issue*

* * *

II

* * *

In this case, the evidence supporting respondent's explanation for petitioner's discharge consisted primarily of testimony by Chesnut and Sanderson and documentation of petitioner's alleged "shoddy record keeping." Chesnut testified that a 1993 audit of Hinge Room operations revealed "a very lax assembly line" where employees were not adhering to general work rules. As a result of that audit, petitioner was placed on 90 days' probation for unsatisfactory performance. In 1995, Chesnut ordered another investigation of the Hinge Room, which, according to his testimony, revealed that petitioner was not correctly recording the absences and hours of employees. Respondent introduced summaries of that investigation documenting several attendance violations by 12 employees under petitioner's supervision, and noting that each should have been disciplined in some manner. Chesnut testified that this failure to discipline absent and late employees is "extremely important when you are dealing with a union" because uneven enforcement across departments would keep the company "in grievance and arbitration cases, which are costly, all the time." He and Sanderson also stated that petitioner's errors, by failing to adjust for hours not worked, cost the company overpaid wages. Sanderson testified that she accepted the recommendation to discharge petitioner because he had "intentionally falsif[ied] company pay records."

Petitioner, however, made a substantial showing that respondent's explanation was false. First, petitioner offered evidence that he had properly maintained the attendance records. Most of the timekeeping errors cited by respondent involved employees who were not marked late but who were recorded as having arrived at the plant at 7 a.m. for the 7 a.m. shift. Respondent contended that employees arriving at 7 a.m. could not have been at their workstations by 7 a.m., and therefore must have been late. But both petitioner and Oswalt testified that the company's automated timeclock often failed to scan employees' timecards, so that the timesheets would not record any time of arrival. On these occasions, petitioner and Oswalt would visually check the workstations and record whether the employees were present at the start of the shift. They stated that if an employee arrived promptly but the timesheet contained no time of arrival, they would reconcile the two by marking "7 a.m." as the employee's arrival time, even if the employee actually arrived at the plant earlier. On cross-examination, Chesnut acknowledged that the timeclock sometimes malfunctioned, and that if "people were there at their work station[s]" at the start of the shift, the supervisor "would write in seven o'clock." Petitioner also testified that when employees arrived before or stayed after their shifts, he would assign them additional work so they would not be overpaid.

Petitioner similarly cast doubt on whether he was responsible for any failure to discipline late and absent employees. Petitioner testified that his job only included reviewing the daily and weekly attendance reports, and that disciplinary writeups were based on the monthly reports, which were reviewed by Caldwell. Sanderson admitted that Caldwell, and not petitioner, was responsible for citing employees for violations of the company's attendance policy. Further, Chesnut conceded that there had never been a union grievance or employee complaint arising from petitioner's recordkeeping, and that the company had never calculated the amount of overpayments allegedly attributable to petitioner's errors. Petitioner also testified that, on the day he was fired, Chesnut said that his discharge was due to his failure to report as absent one employee, Gina Mae Coley, on two days in September 1995. But petitioner explained that he had spent those days in the hospital, and that Caldwell was therefore responsible for any overpayment of Coley. Finally, petitioner stated that on previous occasions that employees were paid for hours they had not worked, the company had simply adjusted those employees' next paychecks to correct the errors.

Based on this evidence, the Court of Appeals concluded that petitioner "very well may be correct" that "a reasonable jury could have found that [respondent's] explanation for its employment decision was pretextual." Nonetheless, the court held that this showing, standing alone, was insufficient to sustain the jury's finding of liability: "We must, as an essential final step, determine whether Reeves presented sufficient evidence that his age motivated [respondent's] employment decision." And in making this determination, the Court of Appeals ignored the evidence supporting petitioner's prima facie case and challenging respondent's explanation for its decision. The court confined its review of evidence favoring petitioner to that evidence showing that Chesnut had directed derogatory, age-based comments at petitioner, and that Chesnut had singled out petitioner for harsher treatment than younger employees. It is therefore apparent that the court believed that only this additional evidence of discrimination was relevant to whether the jury's verdict should stand. That is, the Court of Appeals proceeded from the assumption that a prima facie case of discrimination, combined with sufficient evidence for the trier of fact to disbelieve the defendant's legitimate, nondiscriminatory reason for its decision, is insufficient as a matter of law to sustain a jury's finding of intentional discrimination.

In so reasoning, the Court of Appeals misconceived the evidentiary burden borne by plaintiffs who attempt to prove intentional discrimination through indirect evidence. This much is evident from our decision in *St. Mary's Honor Center* [*v. Hicks*, 509 U.S. 502 (1993)]. There we held that the factfinder's rejection of the employer's legitimate, nondiscriminatory reason for its action does not *compel* judgment for the plaintiff. 509 U. S., at 511. The ultimate question is whether the employer intentionally discriminated, and proof that "the employer's proffered reason is unpersuasive, or even obviously contrived, does not necessarily establish that the plaintiff's proffered reason . . . is correct." *Id.*, at 524. In other words, "[i]t is not enough * * * to *dis*believe the employer; the factfinder must *believe* the plaintiff's explanation of intentional discrimination." *Id.*, at 519.

[handwritten: Have to believe discrimination, but can infer it from employer falsity]

In reaching this conclusion, however, we reasoned that it is *permissible* for the trier of fact to infer the ultimate fact of discrimination from the falsity of the employer's explanation. Specifically, we stated:

> "The factfinder's disbelief of the reasons put forward by the defendant (particularly if disbelief is accompanied by a suspicion of mendacity) may, together with the elements of the prima facie case, suffice to show intentional discrimination. Thus, rejection of the defendant's proffered reasons will *permit* the trier of fact to infer the ultimate fact of intentional discrimination." *Id.*, at 511.

Proof that the defendant's explanation is unworthy of credence is simply one form of circumstantial evidence that is probative of intentional discrimination, and it may be quite persuasive. See *id.*, at 517 ("[P]roving the employer's reason false becomes part of (and often considerably assists) the greater enterprise of proving that the real reason was intentional discrimination"). In appropriate circumstances, the trier of fact can reasonably infer from the falsity of the explanation that the employer is dissembling to cover up a discriminatory purpose. * * * Once the employer's justification has been eliminated, discrimination may well be the most likely alternative explanation, especially since the employer is in the best position to put forth the actual reason for its decision. * * * Thus, a plaintiff's prima facie case, combined with sufficient evidence to find that the employer's asserted justification is false, may permit the trier of fact to conclude that the employer unlawfully discriminated.

[handwritten: Holding]

This is not to say that such a showing by the plaintiff will *always* be adequate to sustain a jury's finding of liability. Certainly there will be instances where, although the plaintiff has established a prima facie case and set forth sufficient evidence to reject the defendant's explanation, no rational factfinder could conclude that the action was discriminatory. For instance, an employer would be entitled to judgment as a matter of law if the record conclusively revealed some other, nondiscriminatory reason for the employer's decision, or if the plaintiff created only a weak issue of fact as to whether the employer's reason was untrue and there was abundant and uncontroverted independent evidence that no discrimination had occurred. See *Aka v. Washington Hospital Center*, 156 F. 3d 1284, 1291–1292 (D.C.Cir.1998) see also *Fisher v. Vassar College*, 114 F.3d, 1332, 1338 (2d Cir.1997) ("[I]f the circumstances show that the defendant gave the false explanation to conceal something other than discrimination, the inference of discrimination will be weak or nonexistent"). To hold otherwise would be effectively to insulate an entire category of employment discrimination cases from review under Rule 50, and we have reiterated that trial courts should not " 'treat discrimination differently from other ultimate questions of fact.' " *St. Mary's Honor Center*, *supra*, at 524 (quoting *Aikens*, 460 U. S., at 716).

Whether judgment as a matter of law is appropriate in any particular case will depend on a number of factors. Those include the strength of the plaintiff's prima facie case, the probative value of the proof that the employer's explanation is false, and any other evidence that supports the employer's case and that properly may be considered on a motion for judgment as a matter of law. For purposes of this case, we need not—and could not—resolve all of the circumstances in which such factors would entitle an employer to judgment as a matter of law. It suffices to say that, because a prima facie case and sufficient evidence to reject the employer's explanation may permit a finding of liability, the Court of Appeals erred in proceeding from the premise that a plaintiff must always introduce additional, independent evidence of discrimination.

III

The remaining question is whether, despite the Court of Appeals' misconception of petitioner's evidentiary burden, respondent was nonetheless entitled to judgment as a matter of law. Under Rule 50, a court should render judgment as a matter of law when "a party has been fully heard on an issue and there is no legally sufficient evidentiary basis for a reasonable jury to find for that party on that issue." Fed. Rule Civ. Proc. 50(a); * * * .

* * * [T]he standard for granting summary judgment "mirrors" the standard for judgment as a matter of law, such that "the inquiry under each is the same." *Anderson v. Liberty Lobby, Inc.*, 477 U. S. 242, 250–251 (1986); see also *Celotex Corp. v. Catrett*, 477 U. S. 317, 323 (1986). It therefore follows that, in entertaining a motion for judgment as a matter of law, the court should review all of the evidence in the record. In doing so, however, the court must draw all reasonable inferences in favor of the nonmoving party, and it may not make credibility determinations or weigh the evidence. * * * Thus, although the court should review the record as a whole, it must disregard all evidence favorable to the moving party that the jury is not required to believe. That is, the court should give credence to the evidence favoring the nonmovant as well as that "evidence

supporting the moving party that is uncontradicted and unimpeached, at least to the extent that that evidence comes from disinterested witnesses."

Applying this standard here, it is apparent that respondent was not entitled to judgment as a matter of law. In this case, in addition to establishing a prima facie case of discrimination and creating a jury issue as to the falsity of the employer's explanation, petitioner introduced additional evidence that Chesnut was motivated by age-based animus and was principally responsible for petitioner's firing. Petitioner testified that Chesnut had told him that he "was so old [he] must have come over on the Mayflower" and, on one occasion when petitioner was having difficulty starting a machine, that he "was too damn old to do [his] job." * * *

Direct evidence

Further, petitioner introduced evidence that Chesnut was the actual decisionmaker behind his firing. Chesnut was married to Sanderson, who made the formal decision to discharge petitioner. * * *

In holding that the record contained insufficient evidence to sustain the jury's verdict, the Court of Appeals misapplied the standard of review dictated by Rule 50. Again, the court disregarded critical evidence favorable to petitioner-namely, the evidence supporting petitioner's prima facie case and undermining respondent's nondiscriminatory explanation. The court also failed to draw all reasonable inferences in favor of petitioner. For instance, while acknowledging "the potentially damning nature" of Chesnut's age-related comments, the court discounted them on the ground that they "were not made in the direct context of Reeves's termination." And the court discredited petitioner's evidence that Chesnut was the actual decisionmaker by giving weight to the fact that there was "no evidence to suggest that any of the other decision makers were motivated by age." Moreover, the other evidence on which the court relied—that Caldwell and Oswalt were also cited for poor recordkeeping, and that respondent employed many managers over age 50—although relevant, is certainly not dispositive. * * *

NOTES AND QUESTIONS

Test Your Understanding of the Material

1.   How does the Court in *Reeves* resolve the uncertainty identified by Justice Souter in *St. Mary's*?

2.   What was Reeves's evidence of pretext? What other evidence did Reeves have of discriminatory intent?

3.   The *Reeves* Court expressly states that "judgment as a matter of law" may be appropriate in some cases against plaintiffs who offer adequate proof of pretext along with their prima facie case. What exculpatory evidence might support an employer's summary judgment or Rule 50 motion despite a plaintiff's proof of pretext?

Related Issues

4.   *Practical Impact of* Reeves. *St. Mary's* presumably continues to govern a case where the trier of fact finds pretext but not discrimination, while *Reeves* governs a case where the trier of fact finds discrimination on the basis of pretext. Which type of case is more likely? Are triers of fact, especially juries, likely to often find in favor of an employer that they believe has offered a false explanation for a challenged employment decision? Does this depend on the reason for the prevarication? What if the employer simply wanted to soften the blow of a termination by calling it a "resignation"?

5.   *Jury Instructions.* Is a jury instruction tracking the *McDonnell Douglas* framework legally required or will a simpler instruction suffice (e.g. "You must determine whether plaintiff has demonstrated by a preponderance of the evidence that race was a motivating factor in the defendant employer's decision not to employ the plaintiff.") Compare Townsend v. Lumbermens Mutual Casualty Co., 294 F.3d 1232, 1241 (10th Cir.2002) (pretext instruction mandatory), with Conroy v. Abraham Chevrolet-Tampa, Inc., 375 F.3d 1228, 1235 (11th Cir.2004) ("district courts, though permitted, are not required to give the jury a specific instruction on pretext in employment discrimination cases"); Browning v. United States, 567 F.3d 1038 (9th Cir. 2009) (same as *Conroy*).

6.   *Pleading Standards.* A plaintiff in an employment case can prove his or her case indirectly (using the *McDonnell Douglas* framework) or directly (by producing evidence the decision was motivated by race). Because Title VII affords these alternate methods of proof, the Supreme Court has held that a complaint need not allege a prima facie *McDonnell Douglas* case in order to survive a motion to dismiss on the pleadings. Swierkiewicz v. Sorema, 534 U.S. 506, 122 S.Ct. 992, 152 L.Ed.2d 1 (2002). The Court did not question the *Swierkiewicz* holding in subsequent decisions that seemed to tighten pleading requirements in federal courts. See Ashcroft v. Iqbal, 556 U.S. 662, 129 S.Ct. 1937, 173 L.Ed.2d 868 (2009); Bell Atlantic Corp. v. Twombly, 550 U.S. 544, 127 S.Ct. 1955, 167 L.Ed.2d 929 (2007). See also, e.g., Keys v. Humana, 684 F.3d 605 (6th Cir. 2012) (*McDonnell Douglas* prima facie case not a minimum pleading standard). See generally Charles A. Sullivan, Plausibly Pleading Employment Discrimination, 52 Wm. And Mary L. Rev. 1613 (2011).

PRACTITIONER'S PERSPECTIVE: EVALUATING A CASE

Laurie Berke-Weiss
Principal, Berke-Weiss Law PLLC.

I represent plaintiffs in employment cases in New York. People who come to my office for a consultation generally are in the process of losing their jobs or they have been fired. Sometimes, though, they are still working but have suffered negative treatment at work and want to see if they have "a case" in an effort to keep their job or to simply make work more tolerable. Often they are nervous and unhappy, but some are relieved to be finished with an untenable job. In each situation I want to know all about what has been going on at work to evaluate the case. Thus, the initial consultation is a detailed exploration of the facts and circumstances that brought the client to the office.

Sometimes I speak to the client on the phone first to get a brief idea of what is going on, and whether it makes sense to have the person meet with me. Usually this approach does not provide enough information for an evaluation, nor is it generally advisable to make a snap judgment on the phone. If the client agrees to come in for a consultation (generally it is paid), I ask that the client prepare a detailed chronology, and gather all the paperwork (including electronic communications) that relates to their situation. At the meeting, we review this information together.

I meet clients in a conference room and, with some prompting, they tell me the story of the problems that brought them to the office. I take notes on a yellow pad. Occasionally, I know something about the employer in question. Sometimes, I recognize familiar patterns of a work relationship gone sour because of a new boss, a bad actor in the workplace, outside economic pressures, or a change in the client's own circumstances. Sometimes, the facts depict a classic case of illegal discrimination. Other times, there are hints of wrongdoing that amount to mean bullying or just plain intemperate behavior, none of which may signal illegal discrimination. The information I gather plays out against a backdrop of "employment at will" and the vagaries of individual performance, which also are part of the analysis of whether the matter is actionable.

If the employer has made a severance offer, I review it in detail with the client, to evaluate the monetary offer, as well as the terms on which it is conditioned. I assess the offer against the possibility there is a more valuable claim to be made. To reach that conclusion, numerous factors come into play, such as the client's tolerance for risk, his or her financial situation, and prospects for new employment. I also assess the facts against what I know, research applicable law, and consider whether the client prefers to put the matter to rest sooner rather than later. If there is a viable case, an attempt to negotiate with the employer with or without mediation often precedes litigation. In many cases, the client does not want to sue his or her employer, and that must be taken into account as well.

There are usually deadlines to consider. Under many severance agreements, the client will have 21 or 45 days to consider the settlement offer, and time flies, particularly if the client did not seek legal advice immediately on its receipt. Occasionally, there is a statute of limitations about to run, which creates even more urgency. These deadlines must be taken seriously, and sometimes play a significant role in determining how the matter will be resolved.

The process of exploring the facts, reviewing relevant documents, discussing applicable law, and considering available options can lead to a resolution which is often short of litigation.

DESERT PALACE, INC. v. COSTA

Supreme Court of the United States, 2003.
539 U.S. 90, 123 S.Ct. 2148, 156 L.Ed.2d 84.

JUSTICE THOMAS delivered the opinion of the Court.

The question before us in this case is whether a plaintiff must present direct evidence of discrimination in order to obtain a mixed-motive instruction under Title VII of the Civil Rights Act of 1964, as amended by the Civil Rights Act of 1991 (1991 Act). We hold that direct evidence is not required.

I

A

Since 1964, Title VII has made it an "unlawful employment practice for an employer . . . to discriminate against any individual . . . , *because of* such individual's race, color, religion, sex, or national origin." 78 Stat. 255, 42 U.S.C. § 2000e–2(a)(1) (emphasis added). In *Price Waterhouse v. Hopkins*, 490 U.S. 228, 104 L. Ed. 2d 268, 109 S. Ct. 1775 (1989), the Court considered whether an employment decision is made "because of" sex in a "mixed-motive" case, *i.e.*, where both legitimate and illegitimate reasons motivated the decision. The Court concluded that, under § 2000e–2(a)(1), an employer could "avoid a finding of liability . . . by proving that it would have made the same decision even if it had not allowed gender to play such a role." Id., at 244; see id., at 261, n. (White, J., concurring in judgment); id., at 261 (O'Connor, J., concurring in judgment). The Court was divided, however, over the predicate question of when the burden of proof may be shifted to an employer to prove the affirmative defense.

Justice Brennan, writing for a plurality of four Justices, would have held that "when a plaintiff . . . proves that her gender played a *motivating* part in an employment decision, the defendant may avoid a finding of liability only by proving by a preponderance of the evidence that it would have made the same decision even if it had not taken the plaintiff's gender into account." Id., at 258 (emphasis added). The plurality did not, however, "suggest a limitation on the possible ways of proving that [gender] stereotyping played a motivating role in an employment decision." Id., at 251–252.

Justice White and Justice O'Connor both concurred in the judgment. Justice White would have held that the case was governed by *Mt. Healthy City Bd. of Ed. v. Doyle*, 429 U.S. 274, 50 L. Ed. 2d 471, 97 S. Ct. 568 (1977), and would have shifted the burden to the employer only when a plaintiff "showed that the unlawful motive was a *substantial factor* in the adverse employment action." *Price Waterhouse, supra*, at 259. Justice O'Connor, like Justice White, would have required the plaintiff to show that an illegitimate consideration was a "substantial factor" in the employment decision. 490 U.S., at 276. But, under Justice O'Connor's view, "the burden on the issue of causation" would shift to the employer only where "a disparate treatment plaintiff [could] show by *direct evidence* that an illegitimate criterion was a substantial factor in the decision." *Ibid.* (emphasis added).

Two years after *Price Waterhouse*, Congress passed the 1991 Act "in large part [as] a response to a series of decisions of this Court interpreting the Civil Rights Acts of 1866 and 1964." *Landgraf v. USI Film Products*, 511 U.S. 244, 250, 128 L. Ed. 2d 229, 114 S. Ct. 1483 (1994). In particular, § 107 of the 1991 Act, which is at issue in this case, "responded" to *Price Waterhouse* by "setting forth standards applicable in 'mixed motive' cases" in two new statutory provisions.[1] 511 U.S., at 251. The first establishes an alternative for proving that an "unlawful employment practice" has occurred:

> " 'Except as otherwise provided in this subchapter, an unlawful employment practice is established when the complaining party demonstrates that race, color, religion, sex, or national origin was a motivating factor for any employment practice, even though other factors also motivated the practice.' " 42 U.S.C. § 2000e–2(m).

The second provides that, with respect to " 'a claim in which an individual proves a violation under section 2000e–2(m),' " the employer has a limited affirmative defense that does not absolve it of liability, but restricts the remedies available to a plaintiff. The available remedies include only declaratory relief, certain types of injunctive relief, and attorney's fees and costs. 42 U.S.C. § 2000e–5(g)(2)(B). In order to avail itself of the affirmative defense, the employer must "demonstrate that [it] would have taken the same action in the absence of the impermissible motivating factor." *Ibid.*

Since the passage of the 1991 Act, the Courts of Appeals have divided over whether a plaintiff must prove by direct evidence that an impermissible consideration was a "motivating factor" in an adverse employment action. See 42 U.S.C. § 2000e–2(m). Relying primarily on Justice O'Connor's concurrence in *Price Waterhouse*, a number of courts have held that direct evidence is required to establish liability under § 2000e–2(m) [citations omitted]. In the decision below, however, the Ninth Circuit concluded otherwise.

---

[1]   This case does not require us to decide when, if ever, § 107 applies outside of the mixed-motive context.

B

Petitioner Desert Palace, Inc., dba Caesar's Palace Hotel & Casino of Las Vegas, Nevada, employed respondent Catharina Costa as a warehouse worker and heavy equipment operator. Respondent was the only woman in this job and in her local Teamsters bargaining unit.

Respondent experienced a number of problems with management and her co-workers that led to an escalating series of disciplinary sanctions, including informal rebukes, a denial of privileges, and suspension. Petitioner finally terminated respondent after she was involved in a physical altercation in a warehouse elevator with fellow Teamsters member Herbert Gerber. Petitioner disciplined both employees because the facts surrounding the incident were in dispute, but Gerber, who had a clean disciplinary record, received only a 5-day suspension.

Respondent subsequently filed this lawsuit against petitioner in the United States District Court for the District of Nevada, asserting claims of sex discrimination and sexual harassment under Title VII. The District Court dismissed the sexual harassment claim, but allowed the claim for sex discrimination to go to the jury. At trial, respondent presented evidence that (1) she was singled out for "intense 'stalking'" by one of her supervisors, (2) she received harsher discipline than men for the same conduct, (3) she was treated less favorably than men in the assignment of overtime, and (4) supervisors repeatedly "stacked" her disciplinary record and "frequently used or tolerated" sex-based slurs against her.

Based on this evidence, the District Court denied petitioner's motion for judgment as a matter of law, and submitted the case to the jury with instructions, two of which are relevant here. First, without objection from petitioner, the District Court instructed the jury that " 'the plaintiff has the burden of proving . . . by a preponderance of the evidence that she "suffered adverse work conditions" and that her sex "was a motivating factor in any such work conditions imposed upon her." ' "

Second, the District Court gave the jury the following mixed-motive instruction:

> You have heard evidence that the defendant's treatment of the plaintiff was motivated by the plaintiff's sex and also by other lawful reasons. If you find that the plaintiff's sex was a motivating factor in the defendant's treatment of the plaintiff, the plaintiff is entitled to your verdict, even if you find that the defendant's conduct was also motivated by a lawful reason.

> However, if you find that the defendant's treatment of the plaintiff was motivated by both gender and lawful reasons, you must decide whether the plaintiff is entitled to damages. The plaintiff is entitled to damages unless the defendant proves by a preponderance of the evidence that the defendant would have

treated plaintiff similarly even if the plaintiff's gender had played no role in the employment decision.

Petitioner unsuccessfully objected to this instruction, claiming that respondent had failed to adduce "direct evidence" that sex was a motivating factor in her dismissal or in any of the other adverse employment actions taken against her. The jury rendered a verdict for respondent, awarding backpay, compensatory damages, and punitive damages. The District Court denied petitioner's renewed motion for judgment as a matter of law.

* * *

The Court of Appeals reinstated the District Court's judgment after rehearing the case en banc. The en banc court saw no need to decide whether Justice O'Connor's concurrence in Price Waterhouse controlled because it concluded that Justice O'Connor's references to "direct evidence" had been "wholly abrogated" by the 1991 Act. And, turning "to the language" of § 2000e–2(m), the court observed that the statute "imposes no special [evidentiary] requirement and does not reference 'direct evidence.'" Accordingly, the court concluded that a "plaintiff . . . may establish a violation through a preponderance of evidence (whether direct or circumstantial) that a protected characteristic played 'a motivating factor.'" Based on that standard, the Court of Appeals held that respondent's evidence was sufficient to warrant a mixed-motive instruction and that a reasonable jury could have found that respondent's sex was a "motivating factor in her treatment." Four judges of the en banc panel dissented, * * * .

II

* * *

Our precedents make clear that the starting point for our analysis is the statutory text. And where, as here, the words of the statute are unambiguous, the "'judicial inquiry is complete.'" Section 2000e–2(m) unambiguously states that a plaintiff need only "demonstrate" that an employer used a forbidden consideration with respect to "any employment practice." On its face, the statute does not mention, much less require, that a plaintiff make a heightened showing through direct evidence. Indeed, petitioner concedes as much.

Moreover, Congress explicitly defined the term "demonstrates" in the 1991 Act, leaving little doubt that no special evidentiary showing is required. Title VII defines the term "'demonstrates'" as to "meet the burdens of production and persuasion." § 2000e(m). If Congress intended the term "'demonstrates'" to require that the "burdens of production and persuasion" be met by direct evidence or some other heightened showing, it could have made that intent clear by including language to that effect in § 2000e(m). Its failure to do so is significant, for Congress has been unequivocal when imposing heightened proof requirements in other circumstances, including in other provisions of Title 42. * * *

In addition, Title VII's silence with respect to the type of evidence required in mixed-motive cases also suggests that we should not depart from the "conventional rule of civil litigation [that] generally applies in Title VII cases." *Ibid.* That rule requires a plaintiff to prove his case "by a preponderance of the evidence," *ibid.* using "direct or circumstantial evidence," *Postal Service Bd. of Governors v. Aikens*, 460 U.S. 711, 714, n. 3, 75 L. Ed. 2d 403, 103 S. Ct. 1478 (1983). We have often acknowledged the utility of circumstantial evidence in discrimination cases. For instance, in *Reeves v. Sanderson Plumbing Products, Inc.*, 530 U.S. 133, 147 L. Ed. 2d 105, 120 S. Ct. 2097 (2000), we recognized that evidence that a defendant's explanation for an employment practice is "unworthy of credence" is "one form of *circumstantial evidence* that is probative of intentional discrimination." Id., at 147 (emphasis added). The reason for treating circumstantial and direct evidence alike is both clear and deep-rooted: "Circumstantial evidence is not only sufficient, but may also be more certain, satisfying and persuasive than direct evidence." *Rogers v. Missouri Pacific R. Co.*, 352 U.S. 500, 508, n. 17, 1 L. Ed. 2d 493, 77 S. Ct. 443 (1957).

The adequacy of circumstantial evidence also extends beyond civil cases; we have never questioned the sufficiency of circumstantial evidence in support of a criminal conviction, even though proof beyond a reasonable doubt is required. And juries are routinely instructed that "the law makes no distinction between the weight or value to be given to either direct or circumstantial evidence." 1A K. O'Malley, J. Grenig, & W. Lee, Federal Jury Practice and Instructions, Criminal § 12.04 (5th ed. 2000); see also 4 L. Sand, J. Siffert, W. Loughlin, S. Reiss, & N. Batterman, Modern Federal Jury Instructions P74.01 (2002) (model instruction 74–2). * * *

Finally, the use of the term "demonstrates" in other provisions of Title VII tends to show further that § 2000e–2(m) does not incorporate a direct evidence requirement. See, e.g., 42 U.S.C. §§ 2000e–2(k)(1)(A)(i), 2000e–5(g)(2)(B). For instance, § 2000e–5(g)(2)(B) requires an employer to "demonstrate that [it] would have taken the same action in the absence of the impermissible motivating factor" in order to take advantage of the partial affirmative defense. Due to the similarity in structure between that provision and § 2000e–2(m), it would be logical to assume that the term "demonstrates" would carry the same meaning with respect to both provisions. But when pressed at oral argument about whether direct evidence is required before the partial affirmative defense can be invoked, petitioner did not "agree that . . . the defendant or the employer has any heightened standard" to satisfy. Absent some congressional indication to the contrary, we decline to give the same term in the same Act a different meaning depending on whether the rights of the plaintiff or the defendant are at issue.

For the reasons stated above, we agree with the Court of Appeals that no heightened showing is required under § 2000e–2(m).

In order to obtain an instruction under § 2000e–2(m), a plaintiff need only present sufficient evidence for a reasonable jury to conclude, by a preponderance of the evidence, that "race, color, religion, sex, or national origin was a motivating factor for any employment practice." Because direct evidence of discrimination is not required in mixed-motive cases, the Court of Appeals correctly concluded that the District Court did not abuse its discretion in giving a mixed-motive instruction to the jury. Accordingly, the judgment of the Court of Appeals is affirmed.

NOTES AND QUESTIONS

Test Your Understanding of the Material

1.   Under *Desert Palace*, can the plaintiff always obtain a "mixed-motive" instruction like that used in *Desert Palace* even if the defendant does not assert a "same decision" affirmative defense? In what sort of cases would the plaintiff want such an instruction?

2.   How might a defendant prove that it would have taken the same action in the absence of the impermissible motivating factor? In jury-tried cases will defendants often be reluctant to assert "same decision" defenses?

3.   What social policies underlying the regulation of status discrimination are served by making it illegal to consider an impermissible status when making a personnel decision if such consideration would not have changed the decision? Are there reasons that our society might want to condemn employer consideration of certain status categories even when such consideration in fact does not influence a decision?

In formulating your answer, consider the limited relief available in mixed motive cases where the defendant proves that it would have taken the same action in the absence of the impermissible motivating factor. This relief does not include "damages or * * * an order requiring any admission, reinstatement, hiring, promotion" or back pay. A court may grant only "declaratory relief, injunctive relief * * * , and attorney's fees and costs."

Related Issues

4.   *Does § 107 Apply Outside of the Mixed-Motive Context?* In footnote 1, the Court suggests that § 107 (which references §§ 703(m) and 706(g)(2)(B)) may not apply "outside of the mixed-motive context." Does this mean that § 107 is relevant only in mixed-motive and not in pretext caseswhere the plaintiff's proof all concerns eliminating non-discriminatory motives? For lower court interpretations of *Desert Palace*, see, e.g., Fogg v. Gonzales, 492 F.3d 447 (D.C. Cir. 2007) (§ 703(a)(1) and § 703(m) offer alternative standards for liability to be analyzed separately; no affirmative defense to pretext, single motive proof);

Wright v. Murray Guard, Inc., 455 F.3d 702 (6th Cir. 2006) (applying *Desert Palace* to summary judgment motions, but separating analysis of pretext and mixed-motive claims). See generally Michael C. Harper, The Causation Standard in Federal Employment Law: *Gross v. FBL Financial Services, Inc.*, and the Unfulfilled Promise of the Civil Rights Act of 1991, 58 Buff. L. Rev. 69, 112–132 (2010).

5.   *Does § 107 Provide a Cause of Action Separate from § 703?* Does § 107 simply provide a causation standard for all § 703 causes of action, or does it provide a separate cause of action that a plaintiff must plead and litigate independently? Some lower court decisions, see, e.g., *Fogg*, supra, have assumed plaintiffs must plead and litigate a § 107 "mixed motive" cause of action independently. However, in University of Texas Southwestern Medical Center v. Nassar, 570 U.S. ___, 133 S.Ct. 2517 (2013), the Court explained that § 107 "is not itself a substantive ban on discrimination. Rather, it is a rule that establishes the causation standard for proving a violation defined elsewhere in Title VII."

NOTE: RELIEF AVAILABLE TO INDIVIDUALS FOR TITLE VII VIOLATIONS

Section 706(g) governs judicial remedial authority in Title VII cases. Some major remedial issues raised by this section, such as the availability of class-based affirmative relief and the impact of seniority systems on remedial orders, will be discussed in later chapters. However, some basic Title VII remedial doctrine, especially that governing the monetary relief obtainable by successful plaintiffs in individual disparate treatment cases, should be presented at this point. See also Chapter 20 pp. 914–925 (discussing statutory remedies).

In an early Title VII case, Albemarle Paper Co. v. Moody, 422 U.S. 405, 421, 95 S.Ct. 2362, 2373, 45 L.Ed.2d 280 (1975), the Supreme Court held that trial courts should grant back pay in most cases for any wages that were lost because of the defendant's illegal actions: "[B]ack pay should be denied only for reasons which, if applied generally, would not frustrate the central statutory purposes of eradicating discrimination throughout the economy and making persons whole for injuries suffered through past discrimination." The *Albemarle* Court also held that an employer's good faith was not a sufficient reason to deny back pay inasmuch as Title VII remedies were primarily compensatory, rather than penal.

Section 713(b) of the Act, however, does provide that no person shall be subject to any liability for good faith reliance "on any written interpretation or opinion" of the EEOC. This can include opinion letters, matter published in the Federal Register and designated as a written interpretation of the Commission, and a Commission interpretation of "no reasonable cause" when such determination states that it is a written interpretation of the Commission. In subsequent decisions concerned with widely used discriminatory pension practices, the Court denied retroactive back pay relief out of a concern that such relief could bankrupt some pension funds and thereby harm many innocent employees. Florida v. Long, 487 U.S. 223, 108 S.Ct. 2354, 101 L.Ed.2d

206 (1988); Arizona Governing Committee v. Norris, 463 U.S. 1073, 103 S.Ct. 3492, 77 L.Ed.2d 1236 (1983); City of Los Angeles, Dept. of Water & Power v. Manhart, 435 U.S. 702, 98 S.Ct. 1370, 55 L.Ed.2d 657 (1978).

Section 706(g) requires plaintiffs to mitigate their damages: "Interim earnings or amounts earnable with reasonable diligence by the person or persons discriminated against shall operate to reduce the back pay otherwise allowable." In Ford Motor Co. v. EEOC, 458 U.S. 219, 102 S.Ct. 3057, 73 L.Ed.2d 721 (1982), the Court stated that although this mitigation requirement does not demand that an unemployed claimant "go into another line of work, accept a demotion, or take a demeaning position, he forfeits his right to backpay if he refuses a job substantially equivalent to the one he was denied." Id. at 231. See Restatement of Employment Law § 9.01, comments f–h (2015) (discussing mitigation in the employment context). Backpay claimants who have suffered discrimination short of discharge usually have to remain in their jobs unless they can claim "constructive discharge"—that is, the discrimination would force a "reasonable person" to feel compelled to resign.

The courts are divided over whether backpay awards should be reduced by funds plaintiffs have received from collateral governmental sources, such as social security, welfare, or unemployment compensation. Supreme Court precedent under the National Labor Relations Act (NLRA) suggests that such collateral income may be disregarded. See NLRB v. Gullett Gin Co., 340 U.S. 361, 71 S.Ct. 337, 95 L.Ed. 337 (1951) (not an abuse of discretion for Board to decline to deduct unemployment compensation from backpay award because "payments of unemployment compensation were not made to the employees by [the employer] but by the state out of state funds derived from taxation"). See also Employment Restatement § 9.01, Reporter's Notes, comment f (2015) (describing the "collateral source" doctrine). The backpay period normally terminates when the plaintiff is unconditionally offered, either through judicial decree or unilateral employer action, the disputed position or whatever else has been denied. Id ("in the absence of special circumstances, an employer's unconditional offer of reinstatement to discharged employees cuts off the employee's post-offer economic damages, whether or not the offer is accepted."). Back pay has been denied for periods in which the plaintiff was not able to work because of sickness or disability, or is otherwise ineligible for or unable to fill the disputed position.

In addition to back pay, courts normally have offered successful plaintiffs instatement or reinstatement in jobs from which they have wrongfully been denied, or in lieu thereof "front pay" in cases where the work environment would be too hostile for plaintiffs to return. See, e.g., Griffith v. State of Colo., Div. of Youth Services, 17 F.3d 1323, 1330 (10th Cir.1994). Courts also have offered plaintiffs promotions that they were wrongfully denied. For instance, on remand in the *Price Waterhouse* case, Hopkins was awarded the partnership that the court found she had been denied because of her sex. Hopkins v. Price Waterhouse, 920 F.2d 967 (D.C.Cir.1990), affirming 737 F.Supp. 1202 (D.D.C.1990). The Court of Appeals stressed the broad "make whole" remedial reach of § 706(g), and the Supreme Court's holding in Hishon v. King &

Spalding, 467 U.S. 69, 104 S.Ct. 2229, 81 L.Ed.2d 59 (1984), that the discriminatory denial of partnership can constitute a violation of Title VII. The court concluded that the "mere fact that elevation to partnership may place the beneficiary beyond Title VII's reach in no way proves that Title VII is powerless to elevate a victim of discrimination to that position in the first place." 920 F.2d at 978. Restatement of Employment Law § 9.04, comment c (2015).

Before the Civil Rights Act of 1991 compensatory and punitive damages were not available to successful plaintiffs, and Title VII litigants had no right to a jury trial. Section 102 of the 1991 Act provides that Title VII complainants may recover compensatory damages for "unlawful intentional discrimination". Section 102 authorizes compensatory damages for "future pecuniary losses, emotional pain, suffering, inconvenience, mental anguish, loss of enjoyment of life, and other nonpecuniary losses". 42 U.S.C. § 1981a(b)(3).

Section 102 also allows punitive damages for intentional discrimination engaged in by a private employer "with malice or with reckless indifference to the federally protected rights of an aggrieved individual". 42 U.S.C. § 1981a(b)(1). The sum of compensatory and punitive damages is capped at levels ranging from $50,000 to $300,000, depending on the number of employees employed by a defendant employer. See Hernandez-Miranda v. Empresas Diaz Masso, Inc. 651 F.3d 167 (1st Cir. 2011) (cap based on number of employees at time of discrimination, not time of award). Section 102 also provides that if a complaining party seeks damages, "any party may demand a trial by jury". 42 U.S.C. § 1981a(c)(1).

The capping of compensatory and punitive damages presents numerous issues. In Pollard v. E.I. du Pont de Nemours & Co., 532 U.S. 843, 121 S.Ct. 1946, 150 L.Ed.2d 62 (2001), the Court unanimously held that front pay, like back pay, is not an element of compensatory damages and therefore is not subject to the damages cap. When there are multiple plaintiffs in an individual suit, each plaintiff presumably should be able to recover the full cap amount. The EEOC also has asserted a separate cap should be applied to each individual for whom it brings suit. See EEOC v. W. & O., Inc., 213 F.3d 600 (11th Cir. 2000) (agreeing with EEOC). See also Guidance: Compensatory and Punitive Damages Available Under § 102 of the Civil Rights Act of 1991, supra; Donald R. Livingston, The Civil Rights Act of 1991 and EEOC Enforcement, 23 Stet.L.Rev. 53 (1993). For further discussion of remedial issues, see Chapter 20 infra. For the history of the compromise that led to the allowance of capped damages, and a discussion of the case for elimination of the caps, see Michael C. Harper, Eliminating the Need for Caps on Title VII Damage Awards: The Shield of *Kolstad v. American Dental Association*, 14 N.Y.U. J. of Leg. & Pub. Pol. 477, 496–596 (2011).

McKENNON v. NASHVILLE BANNER PUBLISHING COMPANY

Supreme Court of the United States, 1995.
513 U.S. 352, 115 S.Ct. 879, 130 L.Ed.2d 852.

JUSTICE KENNEDY delivered the opinion of the Court.

The question before us is whether an employee discharged in violation of the Age Discrimination in Employment Act of 1967 is barred from all relief when, after her discharge, the employer discovers evidence of wrongdoing that, in any event, would have led to the employee's termination on lawful and legitimate grounds.

I

For some 30 years, petitioner Christine McKennon worked for respondent Nashville Banner Publishing Company. She was discharged, the Banner claimed, as part of a work force reduction plan necessitated by cost considerations. McKennon, who was 62 years old when she lost her job, thought another reason explained her dismissal: her age. She filed suit in the United States District Court for the Middle District of Tennessee, alleging that her discharge violated the Age Discrimination in Employment Act of 1967 (ADEA). * * * McKennon sought a variety of legal and equitable remedies available under the ADEA, including backpay.

In preparation of the case, the Banner took McKennon's deposition. She testified that, during her final year of employment, she had copied several confidential documents bearing upon the company's financial condition. She had access to these records as secretary to the Banner's comptroller. McKennon took the copies home and showed them to her husband. Her motivation, she averred, was an apprehension she was about to be fired because of her age. When she became concerned about her job, she removed and copied the documents for "insurance" and "protection." A few days after these deposition disclosures, the Banner sent McKennon a letter declaring that removal and copying of the records was in violation of her job responsibilities and advising her (again) that she was terminated. The Banner's letter also recited that had it known of McKennon's misconduct it would have discharged her at once for that reason.

For purposes of summary judgment, the Banner conceded its discrimination against McKennon. The District Court granted summary judgment for the Banner, holding that McKennon's misconduct was grounds for her termination and that neither backpay nor any other remedy was available to her under the ADEA. The United States Court of Appeals for the Sixth Circuit affirmed on the same rationale. * * *

II

We shall assume, as summary judgment procedures require us to assume, that the sole reason for McKennon's initial discharge was her age, a discharge violative of the ADEA. Our further premise is that the misconduct revealed by the deposition was so grave that McKennon's immediate discharge would have followed its disclosure in any event. The District Court and the Court of Appeals found no basis for contesting that proposition, and for purposes of our review we need not question it here. We do question the legal conclusion reached by those courts that after-acquired evidence of wrongdoing which would have resulted in discharge bars employees from any relief under the ADEA. That ruling is incorrect.

The Court of Appeals considered McKennon's misconduct, in effect, to be supervening grounds for termination. That may be so, but it does not follow, as the Court of Appeals said in citing one of its own earlier cases, that the misconduct renders it " 'irrelevant whether or not [McKennon] was discriminated against.' " We conclude that a violation of the ADEA cannot be so altogether disregarded. * * *

The ADEA and Title VII share common substantive features and also a common purpose: "the elimination of discrimination in the workplace." *Oscar Mayer & Co. v. Evans*, 441 U.S. 750, 756, 60 L. Ed. 2d 609, 99 S. Ct. 2066 (1979). Congress designed the remedial measures in these statutes to serve as a "spur or catalyst" to cause employers "to self-examine and to self-evaluate their employment practices and to endeavor to eliminate, so far as possible, the last vestiges" of discrimination. *Albemarle Paper Co. v. Moody*, 422 U.S. 405, 417–418, 45 L. Ed. 2d 280, 95 S. Ct. 2362 (1975) (internal quotation marks and citation omitted); see also *Franks v. Bowman Transportation Co.*, 424 U.S. 747, 763, 47 L. Ed. 2d 444, 96 S. Ct. 1251 (1976). Deterrence is one object of these statutes. Compensation for injuries caused by the prohibited discrimination is another. *Albemarle Paper Co. v. Moody, supra*, at 418; *Franks v. Bowman Transportation Co., supra*, at 763–764. The ADEA, in keeping with these purposes, contains a vital element found in both Title VII and the Fair Labor Standards Act [the statute that provides the model for ADEA's procedural provisions]: it grants an injured employee a right of action to obtain the authorized relief. 29 U.S.C. § 626(c). The private litigant who seeks redress for his or her injuries vindicates both the deterrence and the compensation objectives of the ADEA. * * * It would not accord with this scheme if after-acquired evidence of wrongdoing that would have resulted in termination operates, in every instance, to bar all relief for an earlier violation of the Act.

The objectives of the ADEA are furthered when even a single employee establishes that an employer has discriminated against him or her. The disclosure through litigation of incidents or practices which violate national policies respecting nondiscrimination in the work force is itself important, for the occurrence of violations may disclose patterns of noncompliance resulting from a misappreciation of the Act's operation or entrenched resistance to its commands, either of which can be of industry-wide significance. * * *

* * *

* * * [T]he case comes to us on the express assumption that an unlawful motive was the sole basis for the firing. McKennon's misconduct was not discovered until after she had been fired. The employer could not have been motivated by knowledge it did not have and it cannot now claim that the employee was fired for the nondiscriminatory reason. Mixed motive cases are inapposite here, except to the important extent they underscore the necessity of determining the employer's motives in ordering the discharge, an essential element in determining whether the employer violated the federal antidiscrimination law. * * *

Our inquiry is not at an end, however, for even though the employer has violated the Act, we must consider how the after-acquired evidence of the employee's wrongdoing bears on the specific remedy to be ordered. Equity's maxim that a suitor who engaged in his own reprehensible conduct in the course of the transaction at issue must be denied equitable relief because of unclean hands, a rule which in conventional formulation operated in limine to bar the suitor from invoking the aid of the equity court, 2 S. Symons, Pomeroy's Equity Jurisprudence § 397, pp. 90–92 (5th ed. 1941), has not been applied where Congress authorizes broad equitable relief to serve important national policies. We have rejected the unclean hands defense "where a private suit serves important public purposes." *Perma Life Mufflers, Inc. v. International Parts Corp.*, 392 U.S. 134, 138, 20 L. Ed. 2d 982, 88 S. Ct. 1981 (1968) (Sherman and Clayton Antitrust Acts). That does not mean, however, the employee's own misconduct is irrelevant to all the remedies otherwise available under the statute. The statute controlling this case provides that "the court shall have jurisdiction to grant such legal or equitable relief as may be appropriate to effectuate the purposes of this chapter, including without limitation judgments compelling employment, reinstatement or promotion, or enforcing the liability for [amounts owing to a person as a result of a violation of this chapter]." 29 U.S.C. § 626(b); see also § 216(b). In giving effect to the ADEA, we must recognize the duality between the legitimate interests of the employer and the important claims of the employee who invokes the national employment policy mandated by the Act. The employee's wrongdoing must be taken into account, we conclude, lest the employer's legitimate concerns be ignored. The ADEA, like Title VII, is not a general regulation of the workplace but a law which prohibits discrimination. The statute does not constrain employers from exercising significant other prerogatives and discretions in the course of the hiring, promoting, and discharging of their employees. * * * In determining appropriate remedial action, the employee's wrongdoing becomes relevant not to punish the employee, or out of concern "for the relative moral worth of the parties," but to take due account of the lawful prerogatives of the employer in the usual course of its business and the corresponding equities that it has arising from the employee's wrongdoing.

The proper boundaries of remedial relief in the general class of cases where, after termination, it is discovered that the employee has engaged in wrongdoing must be addressed by the judicial system in the ordinary course of further decisions, for the factual permutations and the equitable considerations they raise will vary from case to case. We do conclude that here, and as a general rule in cases of this type, neither reinstatement nor front pay is an appropriate remedy. It would be both inequitable and pointless to order the reinstatement of someone the employer would have terminated, and will terminate, in any event and upon lawful grounds.

The proper measure of backpay presents a more difficult problem. Resolution of this question must give proper recognition to the fact that an ADEA violation has occurred which must be deterred and compensated without undue infringement upon the employer's rights and prerogatives. The object of compensation is to restore the employee to the position he or she would have been in absent the discrimination, *Franks v. Bowman Transportation Co.*, 424 U.S. at 764, but that principle is difficult to apply with precision where there is after-acquired evidence of wrongdoing that would have led to termination on legitimate grounds had the employer known about it. Once an employer learns about employee wrongdoing that would lead to a legitimate discharge, we cannot require the employer to ignore the information, even if it is acquired during the course of discovery in a suit against the employer and even if the information might have gone undiscovered absent the suit. The beginning point in the trial court's formulation of a remedy should be calculation of backpay from the date of the unlawful discharge to the date the new information was discovered. In determining the appropriate order for relief, the court can consider taking into further account extraordinary equitable circumstances that affect the legitimate interests of either party. An absolute rule barring any recovery of backpay, however, would undermine the ADEA's objective of forcing employers to consider and examine their motivations, and of penalizing them for employment decisions that spring from age discrimination.

Where an employer seeks to rely upon after-acquired evidence of wrongdoing, it must first establish that the wrongdoing was of such severity that the employee in fact would have been terminated on those grounds alone if the employer had known of it at the time of the discharge. The concern that employers might as a routine matter undertake extensive discovery into an employee's background or performance on the job to resist claims under the Act is not an insubstantial one, but we think the authority of the courts to award attorney's fees, mandated under the statute, 29 U.S.C. §§ 216(b), 626(b), and in appropriate cases to invoke the provisions of Rule 11 of the Federal Rules of Civil Procedure will deter most abuses.

NOTES AND QUESTIONS

Test Your Understanding of the Material

1.   What is the *McKennon* Court's holding on after-acquired evidence of employee misconduct? Does such evidence ever provide the employer a complete defense to liability? When does such evidence limit the remedies available to plaintiffs?

2.   Is *McKennon* a federal common law rule or does it only apply in ADEA cases? Are state courts free to disagree with *McKennon* in interpreting state law?

3.   The EEOC has issued an Enforcement Guidance on the *McKennon* decision, EEOC Notice No. 915.002 (Dec. 14, 1995). Evaluate whether the following portions of the EEOC guidance are consistent with *McKennon*:

- If an employer fails to prove that it would have taken the challenged disciplinary action on the basis of after-acquired evidence of misconduct, relief may not be limited by such evidence.

- Where evidence of misconduct is discovered as part of a "retaliatory investigation," defined as an investigation "initiated in response to a complaint of discrimination in an attempt to uncover derogatory information about the complaining party or discourage other charges or opposition", back pay until the date a charge or complaint is resolved may be awarded.

- Agency personnel should seek relief for emotional harm, though not out-of-pocket expenses, caused by discriminatory conduct even to the extent that harm continues after a legitimate reason for the adverse action has been discovered.

- Punitive damages are not barred by after-acquired evidence when the charged party has been shown to have acted initially with malice or reckless indifference to the charging party's rights.

Related Issues

4.   *Application to Title VII.* The courts have applied *McKennon* to Title VII cases. See, e.g., Wallace v. Dunn Const. Co., 62 F.3d 374 (11th Cir.1995); Wehr v. Ryan's Family Steak Houses, Inc. 49 F.3d 1150 (6th Cir.1995).

5.   *Does* McKennon *Encourage Retaliatory Investigations?* Justice Kennedy for the Court acknowledges the not "insubstantial" concern that employers as a routine matter might undertake extensive discovery of the files and background of any employee who claims discriminatory treatment. See Melissa Hart, Rethinking Litigation Tactics: The Chilling Effect of "After-Acquired Evidence", 40 Ariz. St. L.J. 401 (2008). Do the prohibitions of retaliation against discrimination complainants (treated in Chapter 11 infra) adequately address those concerns?

6. *Compensatory Damages in After-Acquired Evidence Cases.* Are compensatory damages available despite a successful after-acquired evidence defense? See Crapp v. City of Miami Beach, 242 F.3d 1017 (11th Cir.2001) (proper to deny backpay and reinstatement, but allow compensatory damages).

7. *After-Acquired Evidence Under State Law.* Some states have applied an after-acquired evidence rule as a defense to certain state common law claims. See e.g. Gassmann v. Evangelical Lutheran Good Samaritan Society, Inc., 261 Kan. 725, 933 P.2d 743 (1997) (breach of implied contract); O'Day v. McDonnell Douglas Helicopter Co., 191 Ariz. 535, 959 P.2d 792 (1998) (after acquired evidence full defense to breach of contract claim, limits damages in wrongful termination in violation of public policy claim); Horn v. Dept. of Corrections, 216 Mich. App. 58, 548 N.W.2d 660 (Mich Ct. App. 1996) (discrimination). See also Restatement of Employment Law § 2.04, Reporters' Notes, Comment *e*.

STAUB V. PROCTOR HOSPITAL
Supreme Court of the United States, 2011.
562 U.S. 411, 131 S.Ct. 1186, 179 L.Ed.2d 144.

JUSTICE SCALIA delivered the opinion of the Court.

We consider the circumstances under which an employer may be held liable for employment discrimination based on the discriminatory animus of an employee who influenced, but did not make, the ultimate employment decision.

I

Petitioner Vincent Staub worked as an angiography technician for respondent Proctor Hospital until 2004, when he was fired. Staub and Proctor hotly dispute the facts surrounding the firing, but because a jury found for Staub in his claim of employment discrimination against Proctor, we describe the facts viewed in the light most favorable to him.

While employed by Proctor, Staub was a member of the United States Army Reserve, which required him to attend drill one weekend per month and to train full time for two to three weeks a year. Both Janice Mulally, Staub's immediate supervisor, and Michael Korenchuk, Mulally's supervisor, were hostile to Staub's military obligations. Mulally scheduled Staub for additional shifts without notice so that he would " 'pa[y] back the department for everyone else having to bend over backwards to cover [his] schedule for the Reserves.' " She also informed Staub's co-worker, Leslie Sweborg, that Staub's " 'military duty had been a strain on th[e] department,' " and asked Sweborg to help her " 'get rid of him.' " Korenchuk referred to Staub's military obligations as " 'a b[u]nch of smoking and joking and [a] waste of taxpayers['] money' " He was also aware that Mulally was " 'out to get' " Staub.

In January 2004, Mulally issued Staub a "Corrective Action" disciplinary warning for purportedly violating a company rule requiring him to stay in his work area whenever he was not working with a patient. The Corrective Action included a directive requiring Staub to report to Mulally or Korenchuk " 'when [he] ha[d] no patients and [the angio] cases [we]re complete[d].' " According to Staub, Mulally's justification for the Corrective Action was false for two reasons: First, the company rule invoked by Mulally did not exist; and second, even if it did, Staub did not violate it.

On April 2, 2004, Angie Day, Staub's co-worker, complained to Linda Buck, Proctor's vice president of human resources, and Garrett McGowan, Proctor's chief operating officer, about Staub's frequent unavailability and abruptness. McGowan directed Korenchuk and Buck to create a plan that would solve Staub's " 'availability' problems." But three weeks later, before they had time to do so, Korenchuk informed Buck that Staub had left his desk without informing a supervisor, in violation of the January Corrective Action. Staub now contends this accusation was false: he had left Korenchuk a voice-mail notification that he was leaving his desk. Buck relied on Korenchuk's accusation, however, and after reviewing Staub's personnel file, she decided to fire him. The termination notice stated that Staub had ignored the directive issued in the January 2004 Corrective Action.

Staub challenged his firing through Proctor's grievance process, claiming that Mulally had fabricated the allegation underlying the Corrective Action out of hostility toward his military obligations. Buck did not follow up with Mulally about this claim. After discussing the matter with another personnel officer, Buck adhered to her decision.

Staub sued Proctor under the Uniformed Services Employment and Reemployment Rights Act of 1994, 38 U.S.C. § 4301 *et seq.,* claiming that his discharge was motivated by hostility to his obligations as a military reservist. His contention was not that Buck had any such hostility but that Mulally and Korenchuk did, and that their actions influenced Buck's ultimate employment decision. A jury found that Staub's "military status was a motivating factor in [Proctor's] decision to discharge him," and awarded $57,640 in damages. *[handwritten: Trial court]*

The <u>Seventh Circuit reversed</u>, holding that Proctor was entitled to judgment as a matter of law. The court observed that Staub had brought a " 'cat's paw' case," meaning that he sought to hold his employer liable for the animus of a supervisor who was not charged with making the ultimate employment decision. It explained that under Seventh Circuit precedent, a "cat's paw" case could not succeed unless the nondecisionmaker exercised such " 'singular influence' " over the decisionmaker that the decision to terminate was the product of "blind reliance." It then noted that "Buck looked beyond what Mulally and Korenchuk said," relying in part on her *[handwritten: 7th Cir. reversed]* conversation with Day and her review of Staub's personnel file. The court "admit[ted] that Buck's investigation could have been more robust," since it "failed to pursue Staub's theory that Mulally fabricated the write-up." But the court said that the " 'singular influence' " rule "does not require the decisionmaker to be a paragon of independence": "It is enough that the decisionmaker is not wholly dependent on a single source of information and conducts her own investigation into the facts relevant to the decision." (internal quotation marks omitted). Because the undisputed evidence established that Buck was not wholly dependent on the advice of Korenchuk and Mulally, the court held that Proctor was entitled to judgment.

II

Statute

The Uniformed Services Employment and Reemployment Rights Act (USERRA) provides in relevant part as follows:

> "A person who is a member of . . . or has an obligation to perform service in a uniformed service shall not be denied initial employment, reemployment, retention in employment, promotion, or any benefit of employment by an employer on the basis of that membership, . . . or obligation." 38 U.S.C. § 4311(a).

It elaborates further:

> "An employer shall be considered to have engaged in actions prohibited . . . under subsection (a), if the person's membership . . . is a motivating factor in the employer's action, unless the employer can prove that the action would have been taken in the absence of such membership." § 4311(c).

The statute is very similar to Title VII, which prohibits employment discrimination "because of . . . race, color, religion, sex, or national origin" and states that such discrimination is established when one of those factors "was a motivating factor for any employment practice, even though other factors also motivated the practice." 42 U.S.C. §§ 2000e–2(a), (m).

The central difficulty in this case is construing the phrase "motivating factor in the employer's action." When the company official who makes the decision to take an adverse employment action is personally acting out of hostility to the employee's membership in or obligation to a uniformed service, a motivating factor obviously exists. The problem we confront arises when that official has no discriminatory animus but is influenced by previous company action that is the product of a like animus in someone else.

In approaching this question, we start from the premise that when Congress creates a federal tort it adopts the background of general tort law. Intentional torts such as this, "as distinguished from negligent or reckless torts, . . . generally require that the actor intend 'the *consequences*' of an act,' not simply 'the act itself.'" *Kawaauhau v. Geiger*, 523 U.S. 57, 61–62, 118 S. Ct. 974, 140 L. Ed. 2d 90 (1998).

Staub contends that the fact that an unfavorable entry on the plaintiff's personnel record was caused to be put there, with discriminatory animus, by Mulally and Korenchuk, suffices to establish the tort, even if Mulally and Korenchuk did not intend to cause his dismissal. But discrimination was no part of Buck's reason for the dismissal; and while Korenchuk and Mulally acted with discriminatory animus, the act they committed—the mere making of the reports—was not a denial of "initial employment, reemployment, retention in employment, promotion, or any benefit of employment," as liability under USERRA requires. If dismissal was not the object of Mulally's and Korenchuk's reports, it may have been their result, or even their foreseeable consequence, but that is not enough to render Mulally or Korenchuk responsible.

Here, however, Staub is seeking to hold liable not Mulally and Korenchuk, but their employer. Perhaps, therefore, the discriminatory motive of one of the employer's agents (Mulally or Korenchuk) can be aggregated with the act of another agent (Buck) to impose liability on Proctor. Again we consult general principles of law, agency law, which form the background against which federal tort laws are enacted. See *Meyer v. Holley*, 537 U.S. 280, 285, 123 S. Ct. 824, 154 L. Ed. 2d 753 (2003); *Burlington, supra*, at 754–755, 118 S. Ct. 2257, 141 L. Ed. 2d 633. Here, however, the answer is not so clear. The Restatement of Agency suggests that the malicious mental state of one agent cannot generally be combined with the harmful action of another agent to hold the principal liable for a tort that requires both. See Restatement (Second) Agency § 275, Illustration 4 (1958). Some of the cases involving federal torts apply that rule. See *United States v. Science Applications Int'l Corp.*, 626 F.3d 1257, 1273–1276 (CADC 2010); *Chaney v. Dreyfus Service Corp.*, 595 F.3d 219, 241 (CA5 2010); *United States v. Philip Morris USA Inc.*, 566 F.3d 1095, 1122, 386 U.S. App. D.C. 49 (CADC 2009). But another case involving a federal tort, and one involving a federal crime, hold to the contrary. See *United States ex rel. Harrison v. Westinghouse Savannah River Co.*, 352 F.3d 908, 918–919 (CA4 2003); *United States v. Bank of New England, N.A.*, 821 F.2d 844, 856 (CA1 1987). Ultimately, we think it unnecessary in this case to decide what the background rule of agency law may be, since the former line of authority is suggested by the governing text, which requires that discrimination be "a motivating factor" *in the adverse action*. When a decision to fire is made with no unlawful animus on the part of the firing agent, but partly on the basis of a report prompted (unbeknownst to that agent) by discrimination, discrimination might perhaps be called a "factor" or a "causal factor" in the decision; but it seems to us a considerable stretch to call it "a motivating factor."

Proctor, on the other hand, contends that the employer is not liable unless the *de facto* decisionmaker (the technical decisionmaker or the agent for whom he is the "cat's paw") is motivated by discriminatory animus. This avoids the aggregation of animus and adverse action, but it seems to us not the only application of general tort law that can do so. Animus and responsibility for the adverse action can both be attributed to the earlier agent (here, Staub's supervisors) if the adverse action is the intended consequence of that agent's discriminatory conduct. So long as the agent intends, for discriminatory reasons, that the adverse action occur, he has the scienter required to be liable under USERRA. And it is axiomatic under tort law that the exercise of judgment by the decisionmaker does not prevent the earlier agent's action (and hence the earlier agent's discriminatory animus) from being the proximate cause of the harm. Proximate cause requires only "some direct relation between the injury asserted and the injurious conduct alleged," and excludes only those "link[s] that are too remote, purely contingent, or indirect." *Hemi Group, LLC v. City of New York*, 559 U.S. 1, ___, 130 S. Ct. 983, 175 L. Ed. 2d 943, 951 (2010) (internal quotation marks omitted).[2] We do not think that the ultimate decisionmaker's exercise of judgment automatically renders the link to the supervisor's bias "remote" or "purely contingent." The decisionmaker's exercise of judgment is *also* a proximate cause of the employment decision, but it is common for injuries to have multiple proximate causes. See *Sosa v. Alvarez-Machain*, 542 U.S. 692, 704, 124 S. Ct. 2739, 159 L. Ed. 2d 718 (2004). Nor can the ultimate decisionmaker's judgment be deemed a superseding cause of the harm. A cause can be thought "superseding" only if it is a "cause of independent origin that was not foreseeable." *Exxon Co., U.S.A. v. Sofec, Inc.*, 517 U.S. 830, 837, 116 S. Ct. 1813, 135 L. Ed. 2d 113 (1996) (internal quotation marks omitted).

Moreover, the approach urged upon us by Proctor gives an unlikely meaning to a provision designed to prevent employer discrimination. An employer's authority to reward, punish, or dismiss is often allocated among multiple agents. The one who makes the ultimate decision does so on the basis of performance assessments by other supervisors. Proctor's view would have the improbable consequence that if an employer isolates a personnel official from an employee's supervisors, vests the decision to take adverse employment actions in that official, and asks that official to review the employee's personnel file before taking the adverse action, then the employer will be effectively shielded from discriminatory acts and recommendations of supervisors that were *designed and intended* to

---

[2]   Under the traditional doctrine of proximate cause, a tortfeasor is sometimes, but not always, liable when he intends to cause an adverse action and a different adverse action results. See Restatement (Second) Torts §§ 435, 435B and Comment *a* (1963 and 1964). That issue is not presented in this case since the record contains no evidence that Mulally or Korenchuk intended any particular adverse action other than Staub's termination.

produce the adverse action. That seems to us an implausible meaning of the text, and one that is not compelled by its words.

Proctor suggests that even if the decisionmaker's mere exercise of independent judgment does not suffice to negate the effect of the prior discrimination, at least the decisionmaker's independent investigation (and rejection) of the employee's allegations of discriminatory animus ought to do so. We decline to adopt such a hard-and-fast rule. As we have already acknowledged, the requirement that the biased supervisor's action be a causal factor of the ultimate employment action incorporates the traditional tort-law concept of proximate cause. See, *e.g., Anza v. Ideal Steel Supply Corp.*, 547 U.S. 451, 457–458, 126 S. Ct. 1991, 164 L. Ed. 2d 720 (2006); *Sosa, supra*, at 703, 124 S. Ct. 2739, 159 L. Ed. 2d 718. Thus, if the employer's investigation results in an adverse action for reasons unrelated to the supervisor's original biased action (by the terms of USERRA it is the employer's burden to establish that), then the employer will not be liable. But the supervisor's biased report may remain a causal factor if the independent investigation takes it into account without determining that the adverse action was, apart from the supervisor's recommendation, entirely justified. We are aware of no principle in tort or agency law under which an employer's mere conduct of an independent investigation has a claim-preclusive effect. Nor do we think the independent investigation somehow relieves the employer of "fault." The employer is at fault because one of its agents committed an action based on discriminatory animus that was intended to cause, and did in fact cause, an adverse employment decision.

* * *

We therefore hold that if a supervisor performs an act motivated by antimilitary animus that is *intended* by the supervisor to cause an adverse employment action,[3] and if that act is a proximate cause of the ultimate employment action, then the employer is liable under USERRA.[4]

holding

III

Applying our analysis to the facts of this case, it is clear that the Seventh Circuit's judgment must be reversed. Both Mulally and Korenchuk were acting within the scope of their employment when they took the

---

[3] Under traditional tort law, " 'intent' . . . denote[s] that the actor desires to cause consequences of his act, or that he believes that the consequences are substantially certain to result from it." *Id.,* § 8A.

[4] Needless to say, the employer would be liable only when the supervisor acts within the scope of his employment, or when the supervisor acts outside the scope of his employment and liability would be imputed to the employer under traditional agency principles. See *Burlington Industries, Inc. v. Ellerth*, 524 U.S. 742, 758, 118 S. Ct. 2257, 141 L. Ed. 2d 633 (1998). We express no view as to whether the employer would be liable if a co-worker, rather than a supervisor, committed a discriminatory act that influenced the ultimate employment decision. We also observe that Staub took advantage of Proctor's grievance process, and we express no view as to whether Proctor would have an affirmative defense if he did not. Cf. *Pennsylvania State Police v. Suders*, 542 U.S. 129, 148–149, 124 S. Ct. 2342, 159 L. Ed. 2d 204 (2004).

actions that allegedly caused Buck to fire Staub. A "reprimand . . . for workplace failings" constitutes conduct within the scope of an agent's employment. *Faragher v. Boca Raton*, 524 U.S. 775, 798–799, 118 S. Ct. 2275, 141 L. Ed. 2d 662 (1998). As the Seventh Circuit recognized, there was evidence that Mulally's and Korenchuk's actions were motivated by hostility toward Staub's military obligations. There was also evidence that Mulally's and Korenchuk's actions were causal factors underlying Buck's decision to fire Staub. Buck's termination notice expressly stated that Staub was terminated because he had "ignored" the directive in the Corrective Action. Finally, there was evidence that both Mulally and Korenchuk had the specific intent to cause Staub to be terminated. Mulally stated she was trying to " 'get rid of' " Staub, and Korenchuk was aware that Mulally was " 'out to get' " Staub. Moreover, Korenchuk informed Buck, Proctor's personnel officer responsible for terminating employees, of Staub's alleged noncompliance with Mulally's Corrective Action, and Buck fired Staub immediately thereafter; a reasonable jury could infer that Korenchuk intended that Staub be fired. The Seventh Circuit therefore erred in holding that Proctor was entitled to judgment as a matter of law.

It is less clear whether the jury's verdict should be reinstated or whether Proctor is entitled to a new trial. The jury instruction did not hew precisely to the rule we adopt today; it required only that the jury find that "military status was a motivating factor in [Proctor's] decision to discharge him." Whether the variance between the instruction and our rule was harmless error or should mandate a new trial is a matter the Seventh Circuit may consider in the first instance.

NOTES AND QUESTIONS

> *Background Note*
>
> The term "cat's paw" originated from a fable in which a monkey persuades a cat to remove chestnuts from the fire, upon the monkey's promise to divide the chestnuts equally. The cat removes several chestnuts from the fire, burning her paw in the process. The monkey eats all the chestnuts. See The Monkey & the Cat, A Selection of Stories from The Aesop for Children, Library of Congress, www.read.gov/aesop.

Test Your Understanding of the Material

1.   Make a diagram approximating the organizational structure and reporting relationships of the individuals in the *Staub* case. Which individuals were tainted by discriminatory animus? Illustrate how those individuals influenced the ultimate decision to terminate Staub.

2.   Under *Staub*, if the plaintiff can show that someone who had a discriminatory motivation intentionally caused a decisionmaker to make a decision adverse to the plaintiff on a prohibited ground, the employer is liable

for the discrimination. The Court suggests, however, that the plaintiff must prove that the tainted influence was both the cause in fact and the proximate cause of the adverse decision. How does the court define proximate cause? What role does it play in the analysis?

3.   Would a decisionmaker's independent investigation of a supervisor's biased allegations provide a "superseding" cause if the investigation established the validity of the allegations? What if an investigation caused only by the biased allegations uncovered information that provided a basis for the challenged adverse decision that was unrelated to the biased allegations?

Related Issues

4.   *Application to Other Discrimination Statutes.* The Court's analysis in *Staub* has been applied to Title VII cases. See, e.g., McKenna v. City of Philadelphia, 649 F.3d 171, 179–180 (3rd Cir. 2011) (applying *Staub* to Title VII retaliation case). Because the *Staub* analysis presumes a "motivating factor" causation standard, it has been modified for Age Discrimination in Employment Act (ADEA) cases, where the plaintiff must prove "but for" causation. See, e.g., Simmons v. Sykes Enters., Inc., 647 F.3d 943, 949–950 (10th Cir. 2011) (applying *Staub* to ADEA case, but requiring plaintiff to demonstrate that discharge would not have occurred but for subordinate bias).

5.   *Biased Actions Outside the Scope of Employment.* Note the Court's reservations in footnote 4. The Court assumes that Mulally and Korenchuk when they took actions that allegedly caused Staub's discharge were acting within the scope of their employment for Proctor Hospital. What if the biased actions were not within the scope of employment, however, and were not otherwise of the kind that could subject their employer to liability under agency principles? This may be the case, for instance, where employees subject their co-workers to a discriminatory hostile work environment. Reconsider after reading Faragher v. City of Boca Raton, 524 U.S. 775, 118 S.Ct. 2275, 141 L.Ed.2d 662 (1998) at page 374 infra.

C. SYSTEMIC DISPARATE TREATMENT

PRACTITIONER'S PERSPECTIVE: THE EEOC'S ROLE

Gregory Gochanour
Supervisory Trial Attorney, EEOC.

In many respects the work of an EEOC trial attorney is much like that of a lawyer representing private plaintiffs in employment discrimination cases. We engage in written discovery, take and defend depositions, file and respond to motions, engage in settlement negotiations, and, if the case does not get otherwise resolved, try the case to the jury or judge.

In other significant respects, however, the work of an EEOC attorney differs from representing private plaintiffs. Nearly all of these differences flow from the fact that our client is the federal government charged with enforcing the anti-discrimination laws rather than only the individuals who have filed charges.

Accordingly, one difference is that EEOC attorneys spend about 10–15% of their time assisting and directing investigators as they attempt to: (1) identify which charges are meritorious; and (2) determine whether the evidence uncovered during an investigation warrants either expanding an individual charge to include other victims or to include issues or bases of discrimination that were not alleged by the person filing the charge.

Another, related difference, is how the agency decides which cases to pursue in court. Trial attorneys evaluate reasonable cause findings that were not successfully resolved during the conciliation process and recommend a small fraction of them for litigation by the EEOC. This process is focused on finding cases that will potentially have the most impact—change or develop a particular issue, attempt to address a particular employment practice, etc. The amount of money at stake for the victims is certainly important to the individuals involved but does not determine whether we file suit.

Finally, when resolving a case in settlement, it's the EEOC's general policy and practice to insist that the form of settlement be a publicly-filed consent decree (the public is entitled to know how the government has resolved a case) rather than a confidential private settlement agreement. The EEOC's focus in settlement is as much on obtaining programmatic relief or changes from the employer (policy or practice changes, training) and ensuring through an injunction that similar discrimination does not recur at that employer, as it is on obtaining monetary damages for the persons affected by the alleged discrimination.

INTERNATIONAL BROTH. OF TEAMSTERS V. UNITED STATES

Supreme Court of the United States, 1977.
431 U.S. 324, 97 S.Ct. 1843, 52 L.Ed.2d 396.

MR. JUSTICE STEWART delivered the opinion of the Court.

The central claim in [the] lawsuits was that the company had engaged in a pattern or practice of discriminating against minorities in hiring so-called line drivers.[3] Those Negroes and Spanish-surnamed persons who had been hired, the Government alleged, were given lower paying, less

---

[3] *Line drivers,* also known as over-the-road drivers, engage in long-distance hauling between company terminals. They compose a separate bargaining unit at the company. Other distinct bargaining units include *servicemen,* who service trucks, unhook tractors and trailers, and perform similar tasks; and *city operations,* composed of dockmen, hostlers, and city drivers who pick up and deliver freight within the immediate area of a particular terminal. All of these employees were represented by the petitioner union.

desirable jobs as servicemen or local city drivers, and were thereafter discriminated against with respect to promotions and transfers.

* * *

Consideration of the question whether the company engaged in a pattern or practice of discriminatory hiring practices involves controlling legal principles that are relatively clear. The Government's theory of discrimination was simply that the company, in violation of § 703(a) of Title VII, regularly and purposefully treated Negroes and Spanish-surnamed Americans less favorably than white persons. The disparity in treatment allegedly involved the refusal to recruit, hire, transfer, or promote minority group members on an equal basis with white people, particularly with respect to line-driving positions. The ultimate factual issues are thus simply whether there was a pattern or practice of such disparate treatment and, if so, whether the differences were "racially premised." *McDonnell Douglas Corp. v. Green,* 411 U.S. 792, 805 n. 18, 93 S.Ct. 1817, 1825, 36 L.Ed.2d 668.

As the plaintiff, the Government bore the initial burden of making out a prima facie case of discrimination. *Albemarle Paper Co. v. Moody,* 422 U.S. 405, 425, 95 S.Ct. 2362, 2375, 45 L.Ed.2d 280; *McDonnell Douglas Corp. v. Green, supra,* 411 U.S., at 802, 93 S.Ct., at 1824. And, because it alleged a systemwide pattern or practice of resistance to the full enjoyment of Title VII rights, the Government ultimately had to prove more than the mere occurrence of isolated or "accidental" or sporadic discriminatory acts. It had to establish by a preponderance of the evidence that racial discrimination was the company's standard operating procedure—the regular rather than the unusual practice.[16]

We agree with the District Court and the Court of Appeals that the Government carried its burden of proof. As of March 31, 1971, shortly after the Government filed its complaint alleging systemwide discrimination, the company had 6,472 employees. Of these, 314 (5%) were Negroes and 257 (4%) were Spanish-surnamed Americans. Of the 1,828 line drivers, however, there were only 8 (0.4%) Negroes and 5 (0.3%) Spanish-surnamed persons, and all of the Negroes had been hired after the litigation had commenced. With one exception—a man who worked as a line driver at the

---

[16] The "pattern or practice" language in § 707(a) of Title VII was not intended as a term of art, and the words reflect only their usual meaning. Senator Humphrey explained:

"[A] pattern or practice would be present only where the denial of rights consists of something more than an isolated, sporadic incident, but is repeated, routine, or of a generalized nature. There would be a pattern or practice if, for example, a number of companies or persons in the same industry or line of business discriminated, if a chain of motels or restaurants practiced racial discrimination throughout all or a significant part of its system, or if a company repeatedly and regularly engaged in acts prohibited by the statute.

* * *

"The point is that single, insignificant, isolated acts of discrimination by a single business would not justify a finding of a pattern or practice * * * ." 110 Cong.Rec. 14270 (1964).

Chicago terminal from 1950 to 1959—the company and its predecessors *did not employ a Negro on a regular basis as a line driver until 1969*. And, as the Government showed, even in 1971 there were terminals in areas of substantial Negro population where all of the company's line drivers were white.[17] A great majority of the Negroes (83%) and Spanish-surnamed Americans (78%) who did work for the company held the lower paying city operations and serviceman jobs,[18] whereas only 39% of the nonminority employees held jobs in those categories.

anecdotal evidence

The Government bolstered its statistical evidence with the testimony of individuals who recounted over 40 specific instances of discrimination. Upon the basis of this testimony the District Court found that "[n]umerous qualified black and Spanish-surnamed American applicants who sought line driving jobs at the company over the years, either had their requests ignored, were given false or misleading information about requirements, opportunities, and application procedures, or were not considered and hired on the same basis that whites were considered and hired." Minority employees who wanted to transfer to line-driver jobs met with similar difficulties.[19]

The company's principal response to this evidence is that statistics can never in and of themselves prove the existence of a pattern or practice of discrimination, or even establish a prima facie case shifting to the employer the burden of rebutting the inference raised by the figures. But, as even our brief summary of the evidence shows, this was not a case in which the Government relied on "statistics alone." The individuals who testified

---

[17] In Atlanta, for instance, Negroes composed 22.35% of the population in the surrounding metropolitan area and 51.31% of the population in the city proper. The company's Atlanta terminal employed 57 line drivers. All were white. In Los Angeles, 10.84% of the greater metropolitan population and 17.88% of the city population were Negro. But at the company's two Los Angeles terminals there was not a single Negro among the 374 line drivers. The proof showed similar disparities in San Francisco, Denver, Nashville, Chicago, Dallas, and at several other terminals.

[18] Although line-driver jobs pay more than other jobs, and the District Court found them to be "considered the most desirable of the driving jobs," it is by no means clear that all employees, even driver employees, would prefer to be line drivers. Of course, Title VII provides for equal opportunity to compete for *any* job, whether it is thought better or worse than another. See, *e.g., United States v. Hayes Int'l Corp.,* 456 F.2d 112, 118 (CA5); *United States v. National Lead Co.,* 438 F.2d 935, 939 (CA8).

[19] Two examples are illustrative:

George Taylor, a Negro, worked for the company as a city driver in Los Angeles, beginning late in 1966. In 1968, after hearing that a white city driver had transferred to a line-driver job, he told the terminal manager that he also would like to consider line driving. The manager replied that there would be "a lot of problems on the road * * * with different people, Caucasian, et cetera," and stated: "I don't feel that the company is ready for this right now. * * * Give us a little time. It will come around, you know." Mr. Taylor made similar requests some months later and got similar responses. He was never offered a line-driving job or an application.

Feliberto Trujillo worked as a dockman at the company's Denver terminal. When he applied for a line-driver job in 1967, he was told by a personnel officer that he had one strike against him. He asked what that was and was told: "You're a Chicano, and as far as we know, there isn't a Chicano driver in the system."

about their personal experiences with the company brought the cold numbers convincingly to life.

In any event, our cases make it unmistakably clear that "[s]tatistical analyses have served and will continue to serve an important role" in cases in which the existence of discrimination is a disputed issue. *Mayor of Philadelphia v. Educational Equality League,* 415 U.S. 605, 620, 94 S.Ct. 1323, 1333, 39 L.Ed.2d 630. See also *McDonnell Douglas Corp. v. Green,* 411 U.S., at 805, 93 S.Ct., at 1825. Cf. *Washington v. Davis,* 426 U.S. 229, 241–242, 96 S.Ct. 2040, 2048–2049, 48 L.Ed.2d 597. We have repeatedly approved the use of statistical proof, where it reached proportions comparable to those in this case, to establish a prima facie case of racial discrimination in jury selection cases, see, *e.g., Turner v. Fouche,* 396 U.S. 346, 90 S.Ct. 532, 24 L.Ed.2d 567; *Hernandez v. Texas,* 347 U.S. 475, 74 S.Ct. 667, 98 L.Ed. 866; *Norris v. Alabama,* 294 U.S. 587, 55 S.Ct. 579, 79 L.Ed. 1074. Statistics are equally competent in proving employment discrimination.[20] We caution only that statistics are not irrefutable; they come in infinite variety and, like any other kind of evidence, they may be rebutted. In short, their usefulness depends on all of the surrounding facts and circumstances. See, *e.g., Hester v. Southern R. Co.,* 497 F.2d 1374, 1379–1381 (CA5).

In addition to its general protest against the use of statistics in Title VII cases, the company claims that in this case the statistics revealing racial imbalance are misleading because they fail to take into account the company's particular business situation as of the effective date of Title VII. The company concedes that its line drivers were virtually all white in July 1965, but it claims that thereafter business conditions were such that its work force dropped. Its argument is that low personnel turnover, rather than post-Act discrimination, accounts for more recent statistical disparities. It points to substantial minority hiring in later years,

---

[20] Petitioners argue that statistics, at least those comparing the racial composition of an employer's work force to the composition of the population at large, should never be given decisive weight in a Title VII case because to do so would conflict with § 703(j) of the Act, 42 U.S.C. § 2000e–2(j). * * *

The argument fails in this case because the statistical evidence was not offered or used to support an erroneous theory that Title VII requires an employer's work force to be racially balanced. Statistics showing racial or ethnic imbalance are probative in a case such as this one only because such imbalance is often a telltale sign of purposeful discrimination; absent explanation, it is ordinarily to be expected that nondiscriminatory hiring practices will in time result in a work force more or less representative of the racial and ethnic composition of the population in the community from which employees are hired. Evidence of longlasting and gross disparity between the composition of a work force and that of the general population thus may be significant even though § 703(j) makes clear that Title VII imposes no requirement that a work force mirror the general population. See, *e.g., United States v. Sheet Metal Workers Local 36,* 416 F.2d 123, 127 n. 7 (CA8). Considerations such as small sample size may, of course, detract from the value of such evidence, see, *e.g., Mayor of Philadelphia v. Educational Equality League,* 415 U.S. 605, 620–621, 94 S.Ct. 1323, 1333, 39 L.Ed.2d 630, and evidence showing that the figures for the general population might not accurately reflect the pool of qualified job applicants would also be relevant. *Ibid.* * * *

especially after 1971, as showing that any pre-Act patterns of discrimination were broken.

The argument would be a forceful one if this were an employer who, at the time of suit, had done virtually no new hiring since the effective date of Title VII. But it is not. Although the company's total number of employees apparently dropped somewhat during the late 1960's, the record shows that many line drivers continued to be hired throughout this period, and that almost all of them were white.[21] To be sure, there were improvements in the company's hiring practices. The Court of Appeals commented that "T.I.M.E.-D.C.'s recent minority hiring progress stands as a laudable good faith effort to eradicate the effects of past discrimination in the area of hiring and initial assignment."[22] But the District Court and the Court of Appeals found upon substantial evidence that the company had engaged in a course of discrimination that continued well after the effective date of Title VII. The company's later changes in its hiring and promotion policies could be of little comfort to the victims of the earlier post-Act discrimination, and could not erase its previous illegal conduct or its obligation to afford relief to those who suffered because of it. Cf. *Albemarle Paper Co. v. Moody,* 422 U.S., at 413–423, 95 S.Ct., at 2369–2374.[23]

The District Court and the Court of Appeals, on the basis of substantial evidence, held that the Government had proved a prima facie case of systematic and purposeful employment discrimination, continuing well

---

[21] Between July 2, 1965, and January 1, 1969, hundreds of line drivers were hired systemwide, either from the outside or from the ranks of employees filling other jobs within the company. None was a Negro.

[22] For example, in 1971 the company hired 116 new line drivers, of whom 16 were Negro or Spanish-surnamed Americans. Minority employees composed 7.1% of the company's systemwide work force in 1967 and 10.5% in 1972. Minority hiring increased greatly in 1972 and 1973, presumably due at least in part to the existence of the consent decree.

[23] The company's narrower attacks upon the statistical evidence—that there was no precise delineation of the areas referred to in the general population statistics, that the Government did not demonstrate that minority populations were located close to terminals or that transportation was available, that the statistics failed to show what portion of the minority population was suited by age, health, or other qualifications to hold trucking jobs, etc.—are equally lacking in force. At best, these attacks go only to the accuracy of the comparison between the composition of the company's work force at various terminals and the general population of the surrounding communities. They detract little from the Government's further showing that Negroes and Spanish-surnamed Americans who were hired were overwhelmingly excluded from line-driver jobs. Such employees were willing to work, had access to the terminal, were healthy and of working age, and often were at least sufficiently qualified to hold city-driver jobs. Yet they became line drivers with far less frequency than whites. See, *e.g.,* Pretrial Stipulation 14 (of 2,919 whites who held driving jobs in 1971, 1,802 (62%) were line drivers and 1,117 (38%) were city drivers; of 180 Negroes and Spanish-surnamed Americans who held driving jobs, 13 (7%) were line drivers and 167 (93%) were city drivers).

In any event, fine tuning of the statistics could not have obscured the glaring absence of minority line drivers. As the Court of Appeals remarked, the company's inability to rebut the inference of discrimination came not from a misuse of statistics but from "the inexorable zero."

beyond the effective date of Title VII. The company's attempts to rebut that conclusion were * * * inadequate.[24]

NOTES AND QUESTIONS

Test Your Understanding of the Material

1.   How does the Court in *Teamsters* define a "pattern or practice" of intentional discrimination?

2.   What is the statutory source of the "pattern or practice" cause of action?

3.   What was the Government's prima facie showing in *Teamsters*? What was the company's challenge to that showing? How did the Court address the challenge?

4.   What is the effect of a successful prima facie showing? Is the effect the same as the prima-facie case under the *McDonnell Douglas-Burdine* proof methodology?

Related Issues

5.   *Applicant Flow Data.* Why did the Court in *Teamsters* allow the Government to dispense with proving its prima facie case on the basis of actual applicant data? Using proxies for applicant flow data, whether from general population or local labor market figures, does not replicate the employer's actual decision making process, and may not present a good approximation of the pool of individuals qualified for and interested in the particular position. Consider the following:

> If actual applicant data are available and reliable, then selection rates for the groups (e.g., male/female, black/white) should be compared. If actual applicant data are either unavailable or there are questions about the fairness of the process through which applicants are obtained (i.e., recruitment), then an alternative proxy labor pool must be used to estimate the theoretical applicant pool that would have been obtained, absent discrimination, and representation rates should be compared.

Ramona L. Paetzold & Steven L. Willborn, The Statistics of Discrimination (2011–2012 ed.) § 4.10, at 138. In *Teamsters*, however, the Government made a strong showing on the qualifications and availability of drivers for intercity

---

[24]   * * * The company also attempted to show that all of the witnesses who testified to specific instances of discrimination either were not discriminated against or suffered no injury. The Court of Appeals correctly ruled that the trial judge was not bound to accept this testimony and that it committed no error by relying instead on the other overpowering evidence in the case. The Court of Appeals was also correct in the view that individual proof concerning each class member's specific injury was appropriately left to proceedings to determine individual relief. In a suit brought by the Government under § 707(a) of the Act the District Court's initial concern is in deciding whether the Government has proved that the defendant has engaged in a pattern or practice of discriminatory conduct.

jobs based on the prevalence of African-American and Hispanic city drivers for the same company.

Applicant-flow data, if available, generally is highly probative and should be used. There are, however, several sources of possible distortion in applicant flow data. First, the employer may not have compiled reliable data. There may be reasons to believe that actual applicants are not representative of the pool of individuals who would apply under normal labor supply conditions. The actual applicant flow may underrepresent minority-group availability because of the "chilling effect" of the employer's reputation as a discriminator, as is suggested by the facts in *Teamsters*, or because the employer's eligibility requirements in dispute are generally known and nearly automatically disqualify a particular group—a factor present in *Dothard v. Rawlinson*, page 204 infra.

6.   *Can Statistics Alone Establish Systemic Disparate Treatment?* Some lower courts have answered affirmatively. See, e.g., Segar v. Smith, 738 F.2d 1249, 1278 (D.C.Cir.1984) ("when a plaintiff's statistical methodology focuses on the appropriate labor pool and generates evidence of discrimination at a statistically significant level, no sound reason exists for subjecting the plaintiff to the additional requirement of * * * proving anecdotal evidence"). Other courts, however, have held that there must be convincing evidence of individual acts of discrimination where there are weaknesses in the statistical proof. See, e.g., EEOC v. Sears, Roebuck & Co., 839 F.2d 302 (7th Cir.1988).

7.   *Rebuttal of a Prima Facie Case.* The government's prima facie case in *Teamsters* carries much more probative force than the plaintiff's prima facie showing in *McDonnell Douglas*. To the extent that a prima facie case is based on a statistical disparity, how may it be rebutted? In *Teamsters* the Court stated that an employer may attempt to show that the plaintiffs' proof is "inaccurate or insignificant" or that there is a "nondiscriminatory explanation for the apparently discriminatory result", such as the plaintiffs' failure to control for relevant differences in qualifications. Some courts have held that defendants cannot rebut a statistically based inference of discrimination by merely pointing out flaws in the statistical proof. See, e.g., Hemmings v. Tidyman's Inc., 285 F.3d 1174, 1188 (9th Cir. 2002) ("the law does not require the near-impossible standard of eliminating all possible nondiscriminatory factors"); Sobel v. Yeshiva Univ., 839 F.2d 18 (2d Cir.1988) (employer is "free . . . to show that any regression offered by plaintiffs is inadequate for lack of a given variable, but such an attack should be specific and make a showing of relevance for each particular variable it contends plaintiffs ought to include.") See, e.g., Rosenfeld v. Oceania Cruises, Inc., 654 F.3d 1190, 1193 (11th Cir. 2011).

8.   *Relevance of Proof of Differential Interest?* May a defendant rebut a prima facie showing of statistical disparity by demonstrating that members of the plaintiffs' class are not interested in the disputed positions to the same extent as those outside the class? See *EEOC v. Sears, Roebuck & Co., supra* (employer adequately explained disproportionate employment of female salespersons in lower paying but more secure noncommission positions by

testimony of managers on differential female interest as confirmed by general social scientific research). Is this differential interest defense likely to be available in a race discrimination case? Should it be a recognized defense even in a gender case? See generally Vicki Schultz, Telling Stories About Women and Work: Judicial Interpretation of Sex Segregation in the Workplace in Title VII Cases Raising the Lack of Interest Argument, 103 Harv.L.Rev. 1750 (1990).

HAZELWOOD SCHOOL DISTRICT V. UNITED STATES
Supreme Court of the United States, 1977.
433 U.S. 299, 97 S.Ct. 2736, 53 L.Ed.2d 768.

JUSTICE STEWART delivered the opinion of the Court.

The petitioner Hazelwood School District covers 78 square miles in the northern part of St. Louis County, Mo. In 1973 the Attorney General brought this lawsuit against Hazelwood and various of its officials, alleging that they were engaged in a "pattern or practice" of employment discrimination in violation of Title VII of the Civil Rights Act of 1964.

* * *

From the beginning, Hazelwood followed relatively unstructured procedures in hiring its teachers. Every person requesting an application for a teaching position was sent one, and completed applications were submitted to a central personnel office, where they were kept on file.[2] During the early 1960's the personnel office notified all applicants whenever a teaching position became available, but as the number of applications on file increased in the late 1960's and early 1970's, this practice was no longer considered feasible. The personnel office thus began the practice of selecting anywhere from 3 to 10 applicants for interviews at the school where the vacancy existed. * * *

Interviews were conducted by a department chairman, program coordinator, or the principal at the school where the teaching vacancy existed. Although those conducting the interviews did fill out forms rating the applicants in a number of respects, it is undisputed that each school principal possessed virtually unlimited discretion in hiring teachers for his school. * * *

In the early 1960's Hazelwood found it necessary to recruit new teachers, and for that purpose members of its staff visited a number of colleges and universities in Missouri and bordering States. All the institutions visited were predominantly white, and Hazelwood did not seriously recruit at either of the two predominantly Negro four-year

---

[2]   Before 1954 Hazelwood's application forms required designation of race, and those forms were in use as late as the 1962–1963 school year.

colleges in Missouri.[4] As a buyer's market began to develop for public school teachers, Hazelwood curtailed its recruiting efforts. For the 1971–1972 school year, 3,127 persons applied for only 234 teaching vacancies; for the 1972–1973 school year, there were 2,373 applications for 282 vacancies. A number of the applicants who were not hired were Negroes.[5]

Hazelwood hired its first Negro teacher in 1969. The number of Negro faculty members gradually increased in successive years: 6 of 957 in the 1970 school year; 16 of 1,107 by the end of the 1972 school year; 22 of 1,231 in the 1973 school year. By comparison, according to 1970 census figures, of more than 19,000 teachers employed in that year in the St. Louis area, 15.4% were Negro. That percentage figure included the St. Louis City School District, which in recent years has followed a policy of attempting to maintain a 50% Negro teaching staff. Apart from that school district, 5.7% of the teachers in the county were Negro in 1970.

* * *

The District Court ruled that the Government had failed to establish a pattern or practice of discrimination. * * *

The Court of Appeals for the Eighth Circuit reversed. After suggesting that the District Court had assigned inadequate weight to evidence of discriminatory conduct on the part of Hazelwood before the effective date of Title VII,[7] the Court of Appeals rejected the trial court's analysis of the statistical data as resting on an irrelevant comparison of Negro teachers to Negro pupils in Hazelwood. The proper comparison, in the appellate court's view, was one between Negro teachers in Hazelwood and Negro teachers in the relevant labor market area. Selecting St. Louis County and St. Louis City as the relevant area,[8] the Court of Appeals compared the 1970 census figures, showing that 15.4% of teachers in that area were Negro, to the racial composition of Hazelwood's teaching staff. In the 1972–1973 and 1973–1974 school years, only 1.4% and 1.8%, respectively, of Hazelwood's teachers were Negroes. This statistical disparity, particularly when viewed against the background of the teacher-hiring procedures that Hazelwood had followed, was held to constitute a prima facie case of a pattern or practice of racial discrimination.

In addition, the Court of Appeals reasoned that the trial court had erred in failing to measure the 55 instances in which Negro applicants were

[4]   One of those two schools was never visited even though it was located in nearby St. Louis. The second was briefly visited on one occasion, but no potential applicant was interviewed.

[5]   The parties disagree whether it is possible to determine from the present record exactly how many of the job applicants in each of the school years were Negroes.

[7]   * * * The evidence of pre-Act discrimination relied upon by the Court of Appeals included the failure to hire any Negro teachers until 1969, the failure to recruit at predominantly Negro colleges in Missouri, and somewhat inconclusive evidence that Hazelwood was responsible for a 1962 Mississippi newspaper advertisement for teacher applicants that specified "white only."

[8]   The city of St. Louis is surrounded by, but not included in, St. Louis County. Mo.Ann.Stat. § 46.145 (1966).

denied jobs against the four-part standard for establishing a prima facie case of individual discrimination set out in this Court's opinion in *McDonnell Douglas Corp. v. Green,* 411 U.S. 792, 802, 93 S.Ct. 1817, 1824, 36 L.Ed.2d 668. Applying that standard, the appellate court found 16 cases of individual discrimination, which "buttressed" the statistical proof. Because Hazelwood had not rebutted the Government's prima facie case of a pattern or practice of racial discrimination, the Court of Appeals directed judgment for the Government and prescribed the remedial order to be entered.

* * *

There can be no doubt, in light of the *Teamsters* case, that the District Court's comparison of Hazelwood's teacher work force to its student population fundamentally misconceived the role of statistics in employment discrimination cases. The Court of Appeals was correct in the view that a proper comparison was between the racial composition of Hazelwood's teaching staff and the racial composition of the qualified public school teacher population in the relevant labor market.[13] See *Teamsters, supra,* at 337–338, and n. 17, 97 S.Ct., at 1855, and n. 17. The percentage of Negroes on Hazelwood's teaching staff in 1972–1973 was 1.4% and in 1973–1974 it was 1.8%. By contrast, the percentage of qualified Negro teachers in the area was, according to the 1970 census, at least 5.7%.[14] Although these differences were on their face substantial, the Court

---

[13] In *Teamsters,* the comparison between the percentage of Negroes on the employer's work force and the percentage in the general area-wide population was highly probative, because the job skill there involved—the ability to drive a truck—is one that many persons possess or can fairly readily acquire. When special qualifications are required to fill particular jobs, comparisons to the general population (rather than to the smaller group of individuals who possess the necessary qualifications) may have little probative value. The comparative statistics introduced by the Government in the District Court, however, were properly limited to public school teachers, and therefore this is not a case like *Mayor v. Educational Equality League,* 415 U.S. 605, 94 S.Ct. 1323, 39 L.Ed.2d 630, in which the racial-composition comparisons failed to take into account special qualifications for the position in question. *Id.,* at 620–621, 94 S.Ct., at 1333–1334.

Although the petitioners concede as a general matter the probative force of the comparative work-force statistics, they object to the Court of Appeals' heavy reliance on these data on the ground that applicant-flow data, showing the actual percentage of white and Negro applicants for teaching positions at Hazelwood, would be firmer proof. As we have noted, see n. 5, *supra,* there was no clear evidence of such statistics. We leave it to the District Court on remand to determine whether competent proof of those data can be adduced. If so, it would, of course, be very relevant. Cf. *Dothard v. Rawlinson,* 433 U.S., 321, 330, 97 S.Ct. 2720, 2727, 53 L.Ed.2d 786.

[14] As is discussed below, the Government contends that a comparative figure of 15.4%, rather than 5.7%, is the appropriate one. But even assuming, *arguendo,* that the 5.7% figure urged by the petitioners is correct, the disparity between that figure and the percentage of Negroes on Hazelwood's teaching staff would be more than fourfold for the 1972–1973 school year, and threefold for the 1973–1974 school year. A precise method of measuring the significance of such statistical disparities was explained in *Castaneda v. Partida,* 430 U.S. 482, 496–497, n. 17, 97 S.Ct. 1272, 1281, n. 17, 51 L.Ed.2d 498, n. 17. It involves calculation of the "standard deviation" as a measure of predicted fluctuations from the expected value of a sample. Using the 5.7% figure as the basis for calculating the expected value, the expected number of Negroes on the Hazelwood teaching staff would be roughly 63 in 1972–1973 and 70 in 1973–1974. The observed number in those years was 16 and 22, respectively. The difference between the observed and expected values was more than six standard deviations in 1972–1973 and more than five standard deviations in 1973–1974. The Court in *Castaneda* noted that "[a]s a general rule for such large samples, if the

of Appeals erred in substituting its judgment for that of the District Court and holding that the Government had conclusively proved its "pattern or practice" lawsuit.

The Court of Appeals totally disregarded the possibility that this prima facie statistical proof in the record might at the trial court level be rebutted by statistics dealing with Hazelwood's hiring after it became subject to Title VII. Racial discrimination by public employers was not made illegal under Title VII until March 24, 1972. A public employer who from that date forward made all its employment decisions in a wholly nondiscriminatory way would not violate Title VII even if it had formerly maintained an all-white work force by purposefully excluding Negroes.[15] For this reason, the Court cautioned in the *Teamsters* opinion that once a prima facie case has been established by statistical work-force disparities, the employer must be given an opportunity to show that "the claimed discriminatory pattern is a product of pre-Act hiring rather than unlawful post-Act discrimination." 431 U.S., at 360, 97 S.Ct., at 1867.

The record in this case showed that for the 1972–1973 school year, Hazelwood hired 282 new teachers, 10 of whom (3.5%) were Negroes; for the following school year it hired 123 new teachers, 5 of whom (4.1%) were Negroes. Over the two-year period, Negroes constituted a total of 15 of the 405 new teachers hired (3.7%). Although the Court of Appeals briefly mentioned these data in reciting the facts, it wholly ignored them in discussing whether the Government had shown a pattern or practice of discrimination. And it gave no consideration at all to the possibility that post-Act data as to the number of Negroes hired compared to the total number of Negro applicants might tell a totally different story.

What the hiring figures prove obviously depends upon the figures to which they are compared. The Court of Appeals accepted the Government's argument that the relevant comparison was to the labor market area of St. Louis County and the city of St. Louis, in which, according to the 1970 census, 15.4% of all teachers were Negro. The propriety of that comparison was vigorously disputed by the petitioners, who urged that because the city of St. Louis has made special attempts to maintain a 50% Negro teaching staff, inclusion of that school district in the relevant market area distorts the comparison. Were that argument accepted, the percentage of Negro

---

difference between the expected value and the observed number is greater than two or three standard deviations," then the hypothesis that teachers were hired without regard to race would be suspect. 430 U.S., at 497 n. 17, 97 S.Ct., at 1281 n. 17.

[15] This is not to say that evidence of pre-Act discrimination can never have any probative force. Proof that an employer engaged in racial discrimination prior to the effective date of Title VII might in some circumstances support the inference that such discrimination continued, particularly where relevant aspects of the decisionmaking process had undergone little change. Cf. Fed.Rule Evid. 406; *Village of Arlington Heights v. Metropolitan Housing Development Corp.,* 429 U.S., 252, 267, 97 S.Ct. 555, 564, 50 L.Ed.2d 450; 1 J. Wigmore, Evidence § 92 (3d ed. 1940); 2 *id.,* 302–305, 371, 375. And, of course, a public employer even before the extension of Title VII in 1972 was subject to the command of the Fourteenth Amendment not to engage in purposeful racial discrimination.

teachers in the relevant labor market area (St. Louis County alone) as shown in the 1970 census would be 5.7% rather than 15.4%.

The difference between these figures may well be important; the disparity between 3.7% (the percentage of Negro teachers hired by Hazelwood in 1972–1973 and 1973–1974) and 5.7% may be sufficiently small to weaken the Government's other proof, while the disparity between 3.7% and 15.4% may be sufficiently large to reinforce it.[17] In determining which of the two figures—or, very possibly, what intermediate figure—provides the most accurate basis for comparison to the hiring figures at Hazelwood, it will be necessary to evaluate such considerations as (i) whether the racially based hiring policies of the St. Louis City School District were in effect as far back as 1970, the year in which the census figures were taken; (ii) to what extent those policies have changed the racial composition of that district's teaching staff from what it would otherwise have been; (iii) to what extent St. Louis' recruitment policies have diverted to the city, teachers who might otherwise have applied to Hazelwood; (iv) to what extent Negro teachers employed by the city would prefer employment in other districts such as Hazelwood; and (v) what the experience in other school districts in St. Louis County indicates about the validity of excluding the City School District from the relevant labor market.

It is thus clear that a determination of the appropriate comparative figures in this case will depend upon further evaluation by the trial court. As this Court admonished in *Teamsters*: "[S]tatistics * * * come in infinite variety * * * . [T]heir usefulness depends on all of the surrounding facts and circumstances." 431 U.S., at 340, 97 S.Ct., at 1856–1857. Only the trial court is in a position to make the appropriate determination after further findings. And only after such a determination is made can a foundation be established for deciding whether or not Hazelwood engaged in a pattern or

---

[17] Indeed, under the statistical methodology explained in *Castaneda v. Partida, supra,* 430 U.S., at 496–497, n. 17, 97 S.Ct. 1272, at 1281, n. 17, 51 L.Ed.2d 498 n. 17, involving the calculation of the standard deviation as a measure of predicted fluctuations, the difference between using 15.4% and 5.7% as the areawide figure would be significant. If the 15.4% figure is taken as the basis for comparison, the expected number of Negro teachers hired by Hazelwood in 1972–1973 would be 43 (rather than the actual figure of 10) of a total of 282, a difference of more than five standard deviations; the expected number of 1973–1974 would be 19 (rather than the actual figure 5) of a total of 123, a difference of more than three standard deviations. For the two years combined, the difference between the observed number of 15 Negro teachers hired (of a total of 405) would vary from the expected number of 62 by more than six standard deviations. Because a fluctuation of more than two or three standard deviations would undercut the hypothesis that decisions were being made randomly with respect to race, 430 U.S., at 497 n. 17, 97 S.Ct., at 1281 n. 17, each of these statistical comparisons would reinforce rather than rebut the Government's other proof. If, however, the 5.7% areawide figure is used, the expected number of Negro teachers hired in 1972–1973 would be roughly 16, less than two standard deviations from the observed number of 10; for 1973–1974, the expected value would be roughly seven, less than one standard deviation from the observed value of 5; and for the two years combined, the expected value of 23 would be less than two standard deviations from the observed total of 15. A more precise method of analyzing these statistics confirms the results of the standard deviation analysis. See F. Mosteller, R. Rourke, & G. Thomas, Probability with Statistical Applications 494 (2d ed. 1970).

practice of racial discrimination in its employment practices in violation of the law.[21]

JUSTICE BRENNAN, concurring.

* * * It is my understanding, as apparently it is Mr. Justice Stevens', that the statistical inquiry mentioned by the Court, and accompanying text, can be of no help to the Hazelwood School Board in rebutting the Government's evidence of discrimination. Indeed, even if the relative comparison market is found to be 5.7% rather than 15.4% black, the applicable statistical analysis at most will not serve to bolster the Government's case. This obviously is of no aid to Hazelwood in meeting *its* burden of proof. Nonetheless I think that the remand directed by the Court is appropriate and will allow the parties to address these figures and calculations with greater care and precision. I also agree that given the misapplication of governing legal principles by the District Court, Hazelwood reasonably should be given the opportunity to come forward with more focused and specific applicant-flow data in the hope of answering the Government's prima facie case. If, as presently seems likely, reliable applicant data are found to be lacking, the conclusion reached by my Brother Stevens will inevitably be forthcoming.

JUSTICE STEVENS, dissenting.

* * * In this case, since neither party complains that any relevant evidence was excluded, our task is to decide (1) whether the Government's evidence established a prima facie case; and (2), if so, whether the remaining evidence is sufficient to carry Hazelwood's burden of rebutting that prima facie case.

I

The first question is clearly answered by the Government's statistical evidence, its historical evidence, and its evidence relating to specific acts of discrimination.

One-third of the teachers hired by Hazelwood resided in the city of St. Louis at the time of their initial employment. As Mr. Justice Clark explained in his opinion for the Court of Appeals, it was therefore appropriate to treat the city, as well as the county, as part of the relevant labor market. In that market, 15% of the teachers were black. In the Hazelwood District at the time of trial less than 2% of the teachers were black. An even more telling statistic is that after Title VII became applicable to it, only 3.7% of the new teachers hired by Hazelwood were black. Proof of these gross disparities was in itself sufficient to make out a prima facie case of discrimination. See *International Brotherhood of Teamsters v. United States,* 431 U.S. 324, 339, 97 S.Ct. 1843, 1856, 52

---

[21] It will also be open to the District Court on remand to determine whether sufficiently reliable applicant-flow data are available to permit consideration of the petitioners' argument that those data may undercut a statistical analysis dependent upon hirings alone.

L.Ed.2d 396 (1977); *Castaneda v. Partida,* 430 U.S. 482, 494–498, 97 S.Ct. 1272, 1280–1282, 51 L.Ed.2d 498.

As a matter of history, Hazelwood employed no black teachers until 1969. Both before and after the 1972 amendment making the statute applicable to public school districts, petitioner used a standardless and largely subjective hiring procedure. Since "relevant aspects of the decisionmaking process had undergone little change," it is proper to infer that the pre-Act policy of preferring white teachers continued to influence Hazelwood's hiring practices.[3]

The inference of discrimination was corroborated by post-Act evidence that Hazelwood had refused to hire 16 qualified black applicants for racial reasons. Taking the Government's evidence as a whole, there can be no doubt about the sufficiency of its prima facie case.

II

* * *

The petitioners offered no evidence concerning wage differentials, commuting problems, or the relative advantages of teaching in an inner-city school as opposed to a suburban school. Without any such evidence in the record, it is difficult to understand why the simple fact that the city was the source of a third of Hazelwood's faculty should not be sufficient to demonstrate that it is a part of the relevant market. The city's policy of attempting to maintain a 50/50 ratio clearly does not undermine that conclusion, particularly when the record reveals no shortage of qualified black applicants in either Hazelwood or other suburban school districts.[4] Surely not *all* of the 2,000 black teachers employed by the city were unavailable for employment in Hazelwood at the time of their initial hire.

But even if it were proper to exclude the city of St. Louis from the market, the statistical evidence would still tend to prove discrimination. With the city excluded, 5.7% of the teachers in the remaining market were black. On the basis of a random selection, one would therefore expect 5.7% of the 405 teachers hired by Hazelwood in the 1972–1973 and 1973–1974 school years to have been black. But instead of 23 black teachers,

---

[3] Proof that an employer engaged in racial discrimination prior to the effective date of the Act creates the inference that such discrimination continued "particularly where relevant aspects of the decisionmaking process [have] undergone little change". Cf. Fed.Rule Evid. 406; *Village of Arlington Heights v. Metropolitan Housing Development Corp.,* 429 U.S. 252, 267, 97 S.Ct. 555, 50 L.Ed.2d 450; 1 J. Wigmore, Evidence § 92 (3d ed. 1940); 2 *id.,* §§ 302–305, 371, 375. And, of course, a public employer even before the extension of Title VII in 1972 was subject to the command of the Fourteenth Amendment not to engage in purposeful racial discrimination.

Since Hazelwood's hiring before 1972 was so clearly discriminatory, there is some irony in its claim that "Hazelwood continued [after 1972] to select its teachers on the same careful basis that it had relied on before in staffing its growing system."

[4] "Had there been evidence obtainable to contradict and disprove the testimony offered by [the Government], it cannot be assumed that the State would have refrained from introducing it." *Pierre v. Louisiana,* 306 U.S. 354, 361–362, 59 S.Ct. 536, 540, 83 L.Ed. 757.

Hazelwood hired only 15, less than two-thirds of the expected number. Without the benefit of expert testimony, I would hesitate to infer that the disparity between 23 and 15 is great enough, in itself, to prove discrimination.[5] It is perfectly clear, however, that whatever probative force this disparity has, it tends to prove discrimination and does absolutely nothing in the way of carrying Hazelwood's burden of overcoming the Government's prima facie case.

Absolute precision in the analysis of market data is too much to expect. We may fairly assume that a nondiscriminatory selection process would have resulted in the hiring of somewhere between the 15% suggested by the Government and the 5.7% suggested by petitioners, or perhaps 30 or 40 black teachers, instead of the 15 actually hired.[6] On that assumption, the Court of Appeals' determination that there were 16 individual cases of discriminatory refusal to hire black applicants in the post-1972 period seems remarkably accurate.

NOTES AND QUESTIONS

Test Your Understanding of the Material

1.   The parties in *Hazelwood* disagreed about the inclusion of residents of the city of St. Louis in the labor market pool used as a comparator for Hazelwood's hiring statistics. Why does it matter to the case? What are the best arguments for and against including residents of the city of St. Louis in the pool?

2.   Why did the Court not require a comparison to those who actually applied for the disputed positions in both *Teamsters* and *Hazelwood*? Consider the discussion of applicant flow data in Note 5, following the *Teamsters* decision at p. 153, supra.

Related Issues

3.   *Statistical Significance*. As discussed in *Hazelwood*, courts consider whether differences in selection rates for a protected group is statistically significant, meaning that it is very unlikely the differences would result solely from chance.

Suppose for example, that the employer in *Teamsters* hired applicants into the line driver position from its existing employee pool using a roulette wheel. With each spin of the wheel, a new applicant is randomly selected into the line driver position. Where African-Americans make up 5% of the employee population, we would expect the roulette wheel to assign something like 5% of African-Americans to the line driver position.

---

[5]   After I had drafted this opinion, one of my law clerks advised me that, given the size of the two-year sample, there is only about a 5% likelihood that a disparity this large would be produced by a random selection from the labor pool. If his calculation (which was made using the method described in H. Blalock, Social Statistics 151–173 (1972)) is correct, it is easy to understand why Hazelwood offered no expert testimony.

[6]   Some of the other school districts in the county have a 10% ratio of blacks on their faculties.

The statistical significance test measures the likelihood that some number other than 5% (or 91 employees out of 1,828) would arise purely by chance. Thus, it would measure the statistical likelihood that a company would hire only 8 African-Americans (0.4%). As you might imagine, it is very unlikely that such a result would occur by chance (less than 1 in 1,000). If the company were selecting African-American employees into the line driver position on a random basis, as through the spin of a roulette wheel, we would expect the number of African-Americans in the position to be somewhere in the range of 70–110 employees in over 95% of the iterations in which a roulette wheel selected the 1,828 employees.

Where the difference in selection rate would not result by chance in 95% of cases, it is considered "statistically significant." Statistical significance does not prove that difference in selection rate is the result of discrimination; it only discounts chance as an explanation.

4. *Relevant Labor Pool?* Note that the Court in *Hazelwood,* but not in *Teamsters,* requires a comparison to the qualified labor market. What explains the difference? The systemic disparate theory should attempt to model the employer's decisionmaking process, but is it always a defense that there are no or few members of the plaintiff class in the qualified labor market? Cf. Scoggins v. Board of Educ. of Nashville, 853 F.2d 1472, 1478 (8th Cir.1988) (school district with monopoly in area cannot rely on labor market statistics that its discriminatory conduct has created). Should a defendant ever be able to challenge plaintiffs' statistics because the pool compared included workers too qualified to be interested? Cf. EEOC v. Chicago Miniature Lamp Works, 947 F.2d 292, 305 (7th Cir.1991) (government should have considered English fluency requirement for disputed jobs as explanation of low levels of hiring and applications of blacks relative to Hispanics and Asian-Americans in labor market).

Can a defendant challenge plaintiffs' statistics because the pool compared included workers considered too qualified to be interested? Cf. EEOC v. Chicago Miniature Lamp Works, 947 F.2d 292, 305 (7th Cir.1991) (government should have considered English fluency requirement for disputed jobs as explanation of low levels of hiring and applications of blacks relative to Hispanics and Asian-Americans in labor market).

Should the proportion of the protected class in other less desirable jobs with a defendant employer ever be relevant? See footnote 23 in *Teamsters.* See also Wards Cove Packing Co. Inc. v. Atonio p. 216 infra.

5. *Geographical Limits on the Labor Pool?* Some jobs are filled through national searches, while others are filled almost exclusively filled from a surrounding region, metropolitan area, or even town. Should plaintiffs at least be permitted to include qualified workers who live within commuting distance of the disputed jobs, rather than accept an employer's claim that it only hires within a limited radius for jobs located in the midst of effectively segregated housing? Compare *Chicago Miniature Lamp Works*, supra, (government should have used relative commuting distance as part of statistical analysis),

with Abron v. Black & Decker Manufacturing Co., 439 F.Supp. 1095 (D.Md.1977) (boundaries of labor force should be defined by reasonable expectation of commuting).

6. *Nonstatistical Proof of Systemic Discrimination.* What other kinds of proof do *Teamsters* and *Hazelwood* suggest are relevant to proving a pattern or practice of discrimination?

7. *Application.* A cleaning service employing about 100 cleaners is owned by a Korean-American immigrant. Over the past two years 81% of his employees also have been Korean-Americans. Korean-Americans are only 1% of the general population and only 3% of the workforce engaged in cleaning in the metropolitan area in which the service operates. The owner has records showing that 71% of applicants for employment with the service are also Korean-Americans. The owner testifies that this results from the location of the service's offices in a heavily Korean-American neighborhood and from his reliance on word-of-mouth recruiting. He claims this is the cheapest way to fill his jobs and that he does not need to advertise or recruit. Should the service be found to be in violation of Title VII? What more information would you like to have? What if the trier of fact believes that the owner prefers hiring Korean-Americans, but would use word-of-mouth recruiting to save costs even if it did not result in a predominantly Korean-American workforce? Compare EEOC v. Consolidated Service Systems, 989 F.2d 233 (7th Cir.1993), with EEOC v. Metal Service Co. 892 F.2d 341, 350–51 (3d Cir.1990).

NOTE: STATISTICAL ANALYSIS OF DISCRIMINATION

Teamsters and *Hazelwood* highlight the importance of statistical analysis in systemic disparate treatment cases. Both cases utilize the "binomial distribution" technique, which attempts to draw inferences from a comparison between minority-group selection rates actually observed and the rates one would predict on the basis of that group's representation in the work force, applicant pool, or local population, or some other source of availability data. In Bazemore v. Friday, 478 U.S. 385 (1986), the Court approved a somewhat distinct statistical approach, termed "multiple regression analysis." The Court's three decisions, viewed jointly, broadly endorse the use of statistics, subject to the caveat stated in *Teamsters:* they "are not irrefutable; they come in infinite variety and like, any other kind of evidence, they may be rebutted. In short, their usefulness depends on all of the surrounding facts and circumstances." Compare the rather different reception accorded statistical analysis in death penalty litigation. See McCleskey v. Kemp, 481 U.S. 279, 107 S.Ct. 1756, 95 L.Ed.2d 262 (1987).

Although statistical analysis is best undertaken with the aid of experts, lawyers do need to have some familiarity with basic concepts. For good general references, see Michael O. Finkelstein & Bruce A. Levin, Statistics for Lawyers (2001); Ramona L. Paetzold & Steven L. Willborn, The Statistics of Discrimination (2011–2012 ed.); Walter B. Connolly, Jr. & David W. Peterson, Use of Statistics in Equal Employment Opportunity Litigation (1980).

Drawing Inferences from Statistical Disparity

1. *Types of Comparisons.* Since the binomial method involves a comparison between observed outcomes and predicted outcomes, it must first be determined what is an appropriate basis for comparison. *Teamsters* in footnote 17 compared the percentage of minority line drivers in the employer's work force to the percentage of minorities in the local population (disputed position/general local population comparison); the Court also at least implicitly compared the percentage of minority line drivers to the percentage of minorities in the employer's work force (disputed position/work force comparison). *Hazelwood* involved a comparison between the percentage of minority group teachers in the Hazelwood system with the percentage of minority group teachers in the local labor market (disputed position/qualified local population comparison). However, as previously discussed, applicant flow data in most cases represents the best measure of the pool of individuals qualified for and interested in the particular position.

2. *Binomial Distribution.* Once the appropriate basis for comparison has been determined and selection rates—both observed and expected—have been derived, the question arises whether the differences between these percentage comparisons are attributable to chance. We know from coin-tossing experiments that even though the probability of drawing a head on each coin toss is 50%, there is no guarantee even with a flawless coin that any given pair of tosses will yield one head, or that a string of tails is precluded. If, however, after a 1000 coin tosses (or "trials") you ended up with 200 heads and 800 tails, you might suspect that the coin was "rigged" in some fashion. The binomial model provides a statistical means for determining whether the observed outcomes are likely to be the product of chance (the "null hypothesis"). This technique can be applied to any series of events in which there are (i) two possible outcomes for each trial,(ii) fixed, known probabilities for each outcome, and (iii) independence among the trials (the results of one trial will not affect the probability of the event's occurrence in subsequent trials).

Given a sufficiently large number of trials, the results of a binomial experiment should fall into a pattern called a "normal distribution," which may be graphically depicted as a bell-shaped curve. The curve will reach its highest point at the mean or expected value of the distribution (determined by multiplying the number of trials by the probability of the event's occurrence) and will decline symmetrically on either side. The characteristics of the curve are such that outcomes closest to expected value are more probable than those further down on the curve; outcomes equidistant from the expected value on either side have the same probability of occurrence; and probabilities decline faster for outcomes lying past the point on either side where the curve concaves upward.

A measure of the extent to which the actual outcomes are likely to diverge from the expected value is called the "standard deviation"; the larger the number of standard deviations an observed result is from the expected result, the lower the probability of that event's occurrence. In a normal distribution, 68% of all outcomes are plotted between + 1 and − 1 standard deviations from expected value; 5% of the outcomes lie beyond + 1.96 and − 1.96 standard deviations from the expected value; and only 2% of the outcomes lie beyond + 2 and − 2 standard deviations. As a matter of convention, a result is considered to be "statistically significant" if it will occur as a matter of chance in five or fewer tries out of a hundred. Because outcomes more than two standard deviations from the expected value should occur in two or fewer tries out of a hundred, such a result plainly satisfies the .05 significance test. Thus, the Court observed in Castaneda v. Partida, 430 U.S. 482, 497 n. 17, 97 S.Ct. 1272, 1281 n. 17, 51 L.Ed.2d 498 (1977), "if the difference between the expected value and the observed number is greater than two or three standard deviations," the null hypothesis—that the observed results are attributable to chance— "would be suspect to a social scientist" and presumably may be rejected. The Supreme Court did not bother to calculate standard deviations in *Teamsters* because of the virtually complete exclusion of minorities (13 out of 1828) from line driver positions. It did offer the results of such an analysis in *Hazelwood,* see 433 U.S. at 311 n. 17, 97 S.Ct. at 2744 n. 17.

    3.   *Selected Issues.*

    a.   *The Process of Logical Inference.* Even a score of two or more standard deviations from the expected value does not prove discrimination. The most that such an analysis can provide is a basis for excluding the role of chance, but of course no employer would make hiring or promotion decisions as a matter of random distribution. The Court stated in footnote 20 of *Teamsters*:

> Statistics showing racial or ethnic imbalance are probative in a case such as this one because such imbalance is often a telltale sign of purposeful discrimination; absent explanation, it is ordinarily to be expected that nondiscriminatory hiring practices will in time result in a work force more or less representative of the racial and ethnic composition of the population from which employees are hired.

Whether such evidence of statistical disparity properly supports an inference of discriminatory intent will depend on the extent to which expected outcomes—against which observed outcomes are measured—reflect an available, qualified supply of minority-group workers similar in all relevant respects to the white workers actually hired or promoted. Professor Laycock observes:

> The Court explicitly assumes that but for discrimination, the employer's work force would in the long run mirror the racial composition of the labor force from which it was hired. That conclusion requires the further implicit assumption that the black and white populations are substantially the same in all relevant ways, so that any differences in result are attributable to discrimination.

> Some variation of that assumption is critical to all statistical evidence of disparate treatment. It is a powerful and *implausible* assumption: the two populations are assumed to be substantially the same in their distribution of skills, aptitudes, and job preferences. Two hundred

and fifty years of slavery, nearly a century of Jim Crow, and a generation of less virulent discrimination are assumed to have had no effect * * * .

Douglas Laycock, Statistical Proof and Theories of Discrimination, 49 L. & Contemp.Probl. 97, 98 (1986) (emphasis added). See also Daniel Rubinfeld, Econometrics in the Courtroom, 85 Colum.L.Rev. 1048, 1057 n. 29 (1985); Louis J. Braun, Statistics and the Law: Hypothesis Testing and its Application to Title VII Cases, 32 Hastings L.J. 59 (1980); Paul Meier, Jerome Sacks & Sandy L. Zabell, What Happened in *Hazelwood*: Statistics, Employment Discrimination, and the 80% Rule, 1984 Am.B.Found.Res.J. 139.

b.   *"Practical Significance."* Although a finding of statistical significance will often depend on the size of the disparity between the results for the two affected groups, statistical significance should not be equated with practical or legal significance. First, with large samples a relatively small difference in percentage points will be statistically significant yet may be viewed as *de minimis* by the courts. See Paetzold & Willborn, supra, § 4.09, at 130–136. Conversely, large disparities may not pass conventional significance tests because of a small sample size, yet may still be considered probative evidence. Second, practical or legal significance depends on substantive law considerations. The *Castaneda* rule of thumb and the .05 significance test are conventions which arguably may be varied in appropriate circumstances:

> Why apply a five percent significance test before the burden of production can be shifted from the plaintiff to the defendant, particularly where the only possible alternative hypotheses involve discrimination? * * *

> The selection of a significance level should include consideration of broader social issues that go beyond the narrow question of whether an individual defendant should be held liable. For example, the level of significance should be lower in situations where there are higher costs to concluding mistakenly that there is discrimination.

Rubinfeld, supra, at 1062–63. See also D.H. Kaye, Is Proof of Statistical Significance Relevant?, 61 Wash.L.Rev. 1333 (1986).

Note also that the .05 (or 1.96 standard deviations) significance test is known as a "two-tailed" test. With a normal distribution, approximately 2.5% of the distribution lies in each tail of the bell-shaped curve—the area on either side of the expected value before the curve concaves upward. If one uses a "one-tailed" test, which tests only for discrimination *against* the particular group, a disparity of only 1.65 standard deviations will be statistically significant. See Rubinfeld, supra, at 1057 n. 32. The D.C. Circuit in a 1987 opinion, however, announced a preference for the two-tailed test: "After all, the hypothesis to be tested in any disparate treatment claim should generally be that the selection process treated men and women equally, *not* that the selection process treated women at least as well as or better than men. Two-tailed tests are used where the hypothesis to be rejected is that certain proportions are equal and not that one proportion is equal to or greater than the other proportion." Palmer v.

Shultz, 815 F.2d 84, 95 (D.C.Cir.1987). Do you agree with this reasoning? *See also* EEOC v. Federal Reserve Bank of Richmond, 698 F.2d 633, 654–60 (4th Cir.1983) (two-tailed test should be used absent independent evidence of discrimination of the type challenged), reversed on other grounds sub nom. Cooper v. Federal Reserve Bank of Richmond, 467 U.S. 867, 104 S.Ct. 2794, 81 L.Ed.2d 718 (1984).

c.   *Limits of the Binomial Model.* The binomial model provides a limited tool. First, the binomial technique is inappropriate for small sample sizes because "the binomial distribution approximates the normal distribution well only for sample sizes of sufficient magnitude." Thomas J. Sugrue & William B. Fairley, A Case of Unexamined Assumptions: The Use and Misuse of the Statistical Analysis of *Castaneda/Hazelwood* in Discrimination Litigation, 24 Bost.Coll.L.Rev. 925, 958 (1983). Second, this technique may not be used where its requirements—two possible outcomes for each trial, fixed probabilities associated with each outcome, and independence among the trials—are not satisfied. Hence, it may be used only for selection processes which produce dichotomous results, not for cases involving continuous or interval variables, such as salary discrimination. See id. at 936 n. 49. Moreover, in cases where the number to be selected is a substantial percentage of the eligible pool, the fixed-probability and independence requirements are not met. Use of the binomial technique in such circumstances will "understate the statistical significance of the racial disparities observed": "[I]f blacks, for example, are selected at a disproportionately low rate, the percentage of blacks remaining in the eligible pool will tend to increase as selections are made." Id. at 938.

4.   *Other Techniques for Assessing Statistical Disparity.*

a.   *EEOC's 80% or Four-Fifths Rule.* The EEOC applies a shorthand comparison of selection rates known as the 80% test in disparate impact cases. See Note 5 in Chapter 4 at p. 202.

b.   *"Chi-Square" Test.* Whereas the binomial method compares the number of those selected from a given group with an expected number of selections from that group, it is possible to analyze the same data by comparing the selection percentages for each group from among its own eligible population. Thus, if the selection procedure operates independently of race, the proportion of eligible blacks selected should be nearly the same as the proportion of eligible whites selected. A Z-score may be obtained by taking the pass-rate difference between whites and blacks and dividing that difference by the "standard error," which is a uniform measure of the variance or range of scores in a sample. Like the binomial method, this technique requires that there be only two groups, only two possible outcomes for each group, and that selections be independent of one another. However, unlike the binomial technique, it may be used where selections constitute a large proportion of the eligible pool, and is more sensitive to sample-size differences than the four-fifths rule. See Shoben, supra, at 799 ff.; Sugrue & Fairley, supra, at 939–41.

The "chi-square" test is an equivalent test for assessing the statistical significance of an observed difference between two or more proportions. It has received some judicial acceptance. See, e.g., Chance v. Board of Examiners, 330 F.Supp. 203 (S.D.N.Y.1971), affirmed, 458 F.2d 1167 (2d Cir.1972).

c. *Multiple Regression Analysis.* Multiple regression analysis is a powerful tool for assessing the relationship between a set of independent or predictor variables and a dependent or outcome variable. The binomial and other methods discussed above are useful for determining whether observed differences in results for two groups are likely to be due to chance, but they are based on a debatable, often readily rebuttable assumption that the characteristics of the two groups are the same in all other relevant respects save group status. Regression analysis provides a means for controlling for important explanatory factors that are likely sources of differences, and thus generating a measure of the explanatory power of the group status variable. See generally Paetzold & Willborn, supra, ch. 6; David E. Bloom & Mark E. Killingsworth, Pay Discrimination Research and Litigation: The Use of Regression, 21 Ind.Rels. 318 (1982); Michael D. Finkelstein, The Judicial Reception of Multiple Regression Studies in Race and Sex Discrimination Cases, 80 Colum.L.Rev. 737 (1980); Franklin M. Fisher, Multiple Regression in Legal Proceedings, 80 Colum.L.Rev. 702 (1980).

Linear multiple regression analysis is normally used for continuous dependent variables such as salary, and has played a very important role in pay discrimination litigation such as *Bazemore v. Friday*, supra. It is possible in some cases to convert selection processes involving dichotomous outcomes, such as promotions, into a continuous variable by developing a ranking of positions based on, say, the salaries associated with those positions.

Typically, there is no single determinant of salary, and a multivariate analysis considering the impact of several predictor variables is necessary. A model of an employer's wage determination policy positing that wage is a function of experience, age and gender could be expressed in the following regression equation. (This example and some of the discussion that follows is paraphrased from Rubinfeld, 85 Colum.L.Rev. at 1066–68.)

$$W = B1 + B2(E) + B3(A) + B4(S) + e, \text{ where}$$

W is hourly wage rate; B1 is a constant reflecting base wage; B2 is the coefficient associated with years of education; B3 is the coefficient associated with age; B4 is the coefficient associated with gender; S is the predictor variable for gender and is equal to one if the worker is female and zero if a male; and e is a random error term which captures all omitted determinants of wage rate. It is critical, however, that there be no correlation between the omitted variables in the error term and explanatory variables of interest. See Fisher, supra, at 708–11, for a good discussion of the technical requirements for the standard error term. The coefficients describe the slope of the multi-dimensional line which relates differences in wage rate to differences in experience, age and gender. This equation permits evaluation of the wage differences for men and women of equal age and salary. Theoretically, if gender plays no rule, the B4 coefficient should approximate zero and the B4(S) term should drop out of the equation.

A regression equation in a particular case might appear as follows:

$$W = 1.50 + .25E + .02A - .75S \qquad R^2 = .30$$
$$\quad (.50) \quad\quad (.05) \quad\quad (.01) \quad\quad (.25)$$

The coefficient of .25 for the education variable indicates that the average hourly wage of employees in the sample increases by 25 cents for each year of education. The $-.75$ coefficient for gender suggests that the average wage of women is 75 cents lower than for men, after controlling for age and education. The standard errors of the coefficients are given in the parentheticals. A hypothesis-testing approach similar to the binomial method is employed to determine the statistical significance of the coefficients obtained. If the null hypothesis of no discrimination were correct, we would expect a B4 coefficient of zero. The standard error tells us that we should expect as a matter of random distribution variability in the B4 coefficient of $+.25$ or $-.25$ but not as large as .75. A t-statistic, defined as the estimated coefficient divided by its standard error, is sometimes also used; in large samples a t-statistic of approximately 2.0 is considered significant at the .05 level, and a t-statistic of approximately 2.5 is significant at the .01 level. See Fisher, supra, at 717; Rubinfeld, supra, at 1067.

Results of a regression analysis are accompanied by an R-squared (R^2) statistic, which tells us how much of the variance in the dependent variable (here, wages) is explained by the independent variables in the equation (here, education, gender, and age). For example, if an adjusted R-squared statistic is 0.10 or less, it means that 10% of the variance in the observed data is explained by the regression equation. See Thomas Campbell, Regression Analysis in Title VII Cases: Minimum Standards, Comparable Worth, and Other Issues Where Law and Statistics Meet, 36 Stan.L.Rev. 1299, 1310–11 & nn. 37–38 (1984).Because this statistic can be manipulated upwards by, among other things, increasing the number of explanatory variables to observations in the sample, some courts have questioned its utility. See, e.g., Vuyanich v. Republic Nat'l Bank of Dallas, 505 F.Supp. 224, 287 n. 87 (N.D.Tex.1980), vacated & remanded, 723 F.2d 1195 (5th Cir.1984).

Typically, a defendant will attempt to impeach a regression study by suggesting that critical explanatory variables which happen to be correlated with the prohibited characteristic were omitted from the equation. In the above example, an experience variable such as years on the job and a performance measure such as rating scores were omitted. In *Bazemore,* the plaintiffs' regressions included the variables race, education, experience and tenure, but were faulted by the Court of Appeals for not considering other important variables, notably county-by-county pay differences. Although the United States had presented evidence tending to negate the saliency of county-by-county variations, Justice Brennan's concurrence for a unanimous Court plainly states that a plaintiff's *prima facie* case may include less than "all measurable variables" as long as the "major factors" are accounted for:

> While the omission of variables from a regression analysis may render the analysis less probative than it otherwise might be, it can

hardly be said, absent some other infirmity, that an analysis which accounts for the major factors "must be considered unacceptable as evidence of discrimination" * * * . Normally, failure to include variables will affect the analysis' probativeness, not its admissibility.

478 U.S. at 400, 106 S.Ct. at 3009 [citation omitted].

One reason for the Court's seeming leniency may be that the addition of too many variables to a regression equation carries with it certain costs. First, as a general matter, "the more variables in the equation, the larger the population must be," Laycock, supra, at 100, in order to produce statistically significant results. Second, to the extent the added variables are correlated with the group status variable (B4 in the above example), the standard error of the group status coefficient may be inflated, and thus "provides little basis for accurate inference." Paetzold & Willborn, § 6.15, at 303. Finally, "[t]he over-inclusion of variables, or overfitting, can produce multicollinearity, which in turn can affect statistical and legal inferences. It can also alter the overall fit of the model to render it less reliable and can tend to produce nonsignificant coefficients for key predictor variables." Id. at 306, fn. 10.

Aside from these technical problems, defendants may have a difficult time insisting on the addition of particular variables which, despite their important explanatory role, may not be recognized because they depend on subjective judgments, such as job evaluation scores, or are too subject to employer control, such as grade level. See, e.g., James v. Stockham Valves & Fittings Co., 559 F.2d 310, 332 (5th Cir.1977) (subjective merit ratings by white supervisors might conceal supervisory bias); Craik v. Minnesota State University Board, 731 F.2d 465, 475–78 (8th Cir.1984) (evidence of discrimination in rank assignment precluded consideration of rank variable). The question arises whether such variables may be deemed "tainted" simply because of subjectivity or extent of employer control even without proof of actual discrimination. See, e.g., Presseisen v. Swarthmore College, 442 F.Supp. 593, 612–13 (E.D.Pa.1977), affirmed mem., 582 F.2d 1275 (3d Cir.1978) (plaintiff's expert should have included academic rank despite fact that women on the average took longer to achieve a given rank than men because the court had denied claim of discrimination in promotions), criticized in Finkelstein, supra, at 741–42. It has been argued that before requiring consideration of such problematic variables, the defendant should have the burden of persuading the trier of fact of their business necessity. See Barbara A. Norris, Multiple Regression Analysis in Title VII Cases: A Structural Approach to Attacks of "Missing Factors" and "Pre-Act Discrimination," 49 L. & Contemp.Probl. 63, 73, 79–81 (1986). Professor Laycock counters that excluding consideration of subjective performance measures ignores differences between the two relevant groups and overstates the explanatory power of the group status variable:

In disparate treatment cases, proof of differences between the two populations must be admissible. Once admitted, such evidence must not be subjected to a level of scrutiny that makes it futile. Subjective evaluations must be given reasonable weight and, if necessary, reviewed on an individual basis. For large employers, the court might review a random sample of subjective evaluations to see if they were being used to hide discrimination.

Laycock, supra, at 104.

INTERNATIONAL BROTH. OF TEAMSTERS V. UNITED STATES
Supreme Court of the United States, 1977.
431 U.S. 324, 97 S.Ct. 1843, 52 L.Ed.2d 396.

[*Eds.* For additional excerpts from this decision, see pp. 148–153 supra and pp. 247–251 infra.]

JUSTICE STEWART delivered the opinion of the Court.

III

Our conclusion that the seniority system does not violate Title VII will necessarily affect the remedy granted to individual employees on remand of this litigation to the District Court. Those employees who suffered only pre-Act discrimination are not entitled to relief, and no person may be given retroactive seniority to a date earlier than the effective date of the Act. Several other questions relating to the appropriate measure of individual relief remain, however, for our consideration.

The petitioners argue generally that the trial court did not err in tailoring the remedy to the "degree of injury" suffered by each individual employee, and that the Court of Appeals' "qualification date" formula sweeps with too broad a brush by granting a remedy to employees who were not shown to be actual victims of unlawful discrimination. Specifically, the petitioners assert that no employee should be entitled to relief until the Government demonstrates that he was an actual victim of the company's discriminatory practices; that no employee who did not apply for a line-driver job should be granted retroactive competitive seniority; and that no employee should be elevated to a line-driver job ahead of any current line driver on layoff status. We consider each of these contentions separately.

A

* * *

If an employer fails to rebut the inference that arises from the Government's prima facie case, a trial court may then conclude that a violation has occurred and determine the appropriate remedy. Without any further evidence from the Government, a court's finding of a pattern or practice justifies an award of prospective relief. Such relief might take the form of an injunctive order against continuation of the discriminatory practice, an order that the employer keep records of its future employment decisions and file periodic reports with the court, or any other order "necessary to ensure the full enjoyment of the rights" protected by Title VII.

When the Government seeks individual relief for the victims of the discriminatory practice, a district court must usually conduct additional proceedings after the liability phase of the trial to determine the scope of individual relief. The petitioners' contention in this case is that if the Government has not, in the course of proving a pattern or practice, already brought forth specific evidence that each individual was discriminatorily denied an employment opportunity, it must carry that burden at the second, "remedial" stage of trial. That basic contention was rejected in the *Franks* case. As was true of the particular facts in *Franks,* and as is typical of Title VII pattern-or-practice suits, the question of individual relief does not arise until it has been proved that the employer has followed an employment policy of unlawful discrimination. The force of that proof does not dissipate at the remedial stage of the trial. The employer cannot, therefore, claim that there is no reason to believe that its individual employment decisions were discriminatorily based; it has already been shown to have maintained a policy of discriminatory decisionmaking.

The proof of the pattern or practice supports an inference that any particular employment decision, during the period in which the discriminatory policy was in force, was made in pursuit of that policy. The Government need only show that an alleged individual discriminatee unsuccessfully applied for a job and therefore was a potential victim of the proved discrimination. As in *Franks* [*v. Bowman Transportation Co.,* 424 U.S. 747, 96 S.Ct. 1251, 47 L.Ed.2d 444 (1976)], the burden then rests on the employer to demonstrate that the individual applicant was denied an employment opportunity for lawful reasons. See 424 U.S., at 773 n. 32, 96 S.Ct., at 1268.

* * * [W]e have held that the District Court and Court of Appeals were not in error in finding that the Government had proved a systemwide pattern and practice of racial and ethnic discrimination on the part of the company. On remand, therefore, every post-Act minority group applicant[49] for a line-driver position will be presumptively entitled to relief, subject to a showing by the company that its earlier refusal to place the applicant in a line-driver job was not based on its policy of discrimination.[50]

B

* * *

The question whether seniority relief may be awarded to nonapplicants was left open by our decision in *Franks,* since the class at

---

[49] Employees who initially applied for line-driver jobs and were hired in other jobs before the effective date of the Act, and who did not later apply for transfer to line-driver jobs, are part of the group of nonapplicants discussed *infra.*

[50] Any nondiscriminatory justification offered by the company will be subject to further evidence by the Government that the purported reason for an applicant's rejection was in fact a pretext for unlawful discrimination. *McDonnell Douglas Corp. v. Green,* 411 U.S., at 804–806, 93 S.Ct., at 1825–1826.

issue in that case was limited to "identifiable applicants who were denied employment * * * after the effective date * * * of Title VII." 424 U.S., at 750, 96 S.Ct., at 1257. We now decide that an incumbent employee's failure to apply for a job is not an inexorable bar to an award of retroactive seniority. Individual nonapplicants must be given an opportunity to undertake their difficult task of proving that they should be treated as applicants and therefore are presumptively entitled to relief accordingly.

* * * The effects of and the injuries suffered from discriminatory employment practices are not always confined to those who were expressly denied a requested employment opportunity. A consistently enforced discriminatory policy can surely deter job applications from those who are aware of it and are unwilling to subject themselves to the humiliation of explicit and certain rejection.

If an employer should announce his policy of discrimination by a sign reading "Whites Only" on the hiring-office door, his victims would not be limited to the few who ignored the sign and subjected themselves to personal rebuffs. The same message can be communicated to potential applicants more subtly but just as clearly by an employer's actual practices—by his consistent discriminatory treatment of actual applicants, by the manner in which he publicizes vacancies, his recruitment techniques, his responses to casual or tentative inquiries, and even by the racial or ethnic composition of that part of his work force from which he has discriminatorily excluded members of minority groups. When a person's desire for a job is not translated into a formal application solely because of his unwillingness to engage in a futile gesture he is as much a victim of discrimination as is he who goes through the motions of submitting an application.

* * *

The denial of Title VII relief on the ground that the claimant had not formally applied for the job could exclude from the Act's coverage the victims of the most entrenched forms of discrimination. Victims of gross and pervasive discrimination could be denied relief precisely because the unlawful practices had been so successful as totally to deter job applications from members of minority groups.

* * *

To conclude that a person's failure to submit an application for a job does not inevitably and forever foreclose his entitlement to seniority relief under Title VII is a far cry, however, from holding that nonapplicants are always entitled to such relief. A nonapplicant must show that he was a potential victim of unlawful discrimination. Because he is necessarily claiming that he was deterred from applying for the job by the employer's discriminatory practices, his is the not always easy burden of proving that he would have applied for the job had it not been for those practices. Cf.

Mt. Healthy City Board of Education v. Doyle, 429 U.S. 274, 97 S.Ct. 568, 50 L.Ed.2d 471. When this burden is met, the nonapplicant is in a position analogous to that of an applicant * * * .

The Government contends that the evidence it presented in this case at the liability stage of the trial identified all nonapplicants as victims of unlawful discrimination "with a fair degree of specificity," and that the Court of Appeals' determination that qualified nonapplicants are presumptively entitled to an award of seniority should accordingly be affirmed. In support of this contention the Government cites its proof of an extended pattern and practice of discrimination as evidence that an application from a minority employee for a line-driver job would have been a vain and useless act. It further argues that since the class of nonapplicant discriminatees is limited to incumbent employees, it is likely that every class member was aware of the futility of seeking a line-driver job and was therefore deterred from filing both an initial and a followup application.[52]

We cannot agree. While the scope and duration of the company's discriminatory policy can leave little doubt that the futility of seeking line-driver jobs was communicated to the company's minority employees, that in itself is insufficient. The known prospect of discriminatory rejection shows only that employees who wanted line-driving jobs may have been deterred from applying for them. It does not show which of the nonapplicants actually wanted such jobs, or which possessed the requisite qualifications.[53] There are differences between city-and line-driving jobs, for example, but the desirability of the latter is not so self-evident as to warrant a conclusion that all employees would prefer to be line drivers if given a free choice.[55] Indeed, a substantial number of white city drivers

---

[52] * * * The refused applicants in *Franks* had been denied an opportunity they clearly sought, and the only issue to be resolved was whether the denial was pursuant to a proved discriminatory practice. Resolution of the nonapplicant's claim, however, requires two distinct determinations: that he would have applied but for discrimination and that he would have been discriminatorily rejected had he applied. The mere fact of incumbency does not resolve the first issue, although it may tend to support a nonapplicant's claim to the extent that it shows he was willing and competent to work as a driver, that he was familiar with the tasks of line drivers, etc. An incumbent's claim that he would have applied for a line-driver job would certainly be more superficially plausible than a similar claim by a member of the general public who may never have worked in the trucking industry or heard of the company prior to suit.

[53] Inasmuch as the purpose of the nonapplicant's burden of proof will be to establish that his status is similar to that of the applicant, he must bear the burden of coming forward with the basic information about his qualifications that he would have presented in an application. As in *Franks,* * * * the burden then will be on the employer to show that the nonapplicant was nevertheless not a victim of discrimination. For example, the employer might show that there were other, more qualified persons who would have been chosen for a particular vacancy, or that the nonapplicant's stated qualifications were insufficient. See *Franks,* 424 U.S., at 773 n. 32, 96 S.Ct., at 1268.

[55] The company's line drivers generally earned more annually than its city drivers, but the difference varied from under $1,000 to more than $5,000 depending on the terminal and the year. In 1971 city drivers at two California terminals, "LOS" and San Francisco, earned substantially more than the line drivers at those terminals. In addition to earnings, line drivers have the advantage of not being required to load and unload their trucks. City drivers, however, have regular working hours, are not required to spend extended periods away from home and family, and do not face the hazards of long-distance driving at high speeds. As the Government

who were not subjected to the company's discriminatory practices were apparently content to retain their city jobs.

* * * A willingness to accept the job security and bidding power afforded by retroactive seniority says little about what choice an employee would have made had he previously been given the opportunity freely to choose a starting line-driver job. While it may be true that many of the nonapplicant employees desired and would have applied for line-driver jobs but for their knowledge of the company's policy of discrimination, the Government must carry its burden of proof, with respect to each specific individual, at the remedial hearings to be conducted by the District Court on remand.[58]

C

The task remaining for the District Court on remand will not be a simple one. Initially, the court will have to make a substantial number of individual determinations in deciding which of the minority employees were actual victims of the company's discriminatory practices. After the victims have been identified, the court must, as nearly as possible, " 'recreate the conditions and relationships that would have been had there been no' " unlawful discrimination. *Franks,* 424 U.S., at 769, 96 S.Ct., at 1266. This process of recreating the past will necessarily involve a degree of approximation and imprecision. Because the class of victims may include some who did not apply for line-driver jobs as well as those who did, and because more than one minority employee may have been denied each line-driver vacancy, the court will be required to balance the equities of each minority employee's situation in allocating the limited number of vacancies that were discriminatorily refused to class members. * * *

After the evidentiary hearings to be conducted on remand, both the size and the composition of the class of minority employees entitled to relief may be altered substantially. Until those hearings have been conducted and both the number of identifiable victims and the consequent extent of necessary relief have been determined, it is not possible to evaluate abstract claims concerning the equitable balance that should be struck between the statutory rights of victims and the contractual rights of

---

acknowledged at argument, the jobs are in some sense "parallel"—some may prefer one job and some may prefer another.

The District Court found generally that line-driver jobs "are considered the most desirable of the driving jobs." That finding is not challenged here, and we see no reason to disturb it. We observe only that the differences between city and line driving were not such that it can be said with confidence that all minority employees free from the threat of discriminatory treatment would have chosen to give up city for line driving.

[58] While the most convincing proof would be some overt act such as a pre-Act application for a line-driver job, the District Court may find evidence of an employee's informal inquiry, expression of interest, or even unexpressed desire credible and convincing. The question is a factual one for determination by the trial judge.

nonvictim employees.[61] That determination is best left, in the first instance, to the sound equitable discretion of the trial court.[62]

NOTES AND QUESTIONS

Test Your Understanding of the Material

1.   Relying on its decision in Franks v. Bowman Transportation Co., 424 U.S. 747, 96 S.Ct. 1251, 47 L.Ed.2d 444 (1976), the Court in *Teamsters* indicates that systematic disparate treatment litigation may be divided into liability and remediation stages. In the first stage, as explained above, the plaintiffs have the burden of demonstrating the existence of a pattern or practice of discrimination. Once a discriminatory policy has been found, a shift in the burden of persuasion occurs. All applicants (and some nonapplicants) for the disputed positions are presumed to have been victims of that policy. What precisely is the burden that is imposed on employers at the remedial stage? How might employers carry that burden? Consider footnote 53 in *Teamsters*. In *Franks* the Court also stated that in order to be eligible for priority hiring under a remedial order victims of previous discrimination "must be presently qualified."

2.   *Teamsters* expands the class of victims entitled to relief to include some individuals who never actually applied for the jobs in question but can prove that they would have applied but for the employer's discriminatory policy. How might nonapplicant plaintiffs go about proving what they might have done in that hypothetical situation?

3.   *Teamsters* states that certain equitable remedies can be imposed on a defendant in a pattern-or-practice case before any individuals establish their claims for relief. Are any of the remedies listed by the Court likely to be significant?

Related Issues

4.   *Retroactive Seniority Relief.* In *Franks*, supra, the Court held that the seniority provision in § 703(h) does not prevent the grant of retroactive seniority relief to make-whole victims of past discrimination inflicted independently of the seniority system. The *Franks* Court also stated that

---

[61] The petitioners argue that to permit a victim of discrimination to use his rightful-place seniority to bid on a line-driver job before the recall of all employees on layoff would amount to a racial or ethnic preference in violation of § 703(j) of the Act. Section 703(j) provides no support for this argument. It provides only that Title VII does not require an employer to grant preferential treatment to any group in order to rectify an imbalance between the composition of the employer's work force and the makeup of the population at large. To allow identifiable victims of unlawful discrimination to participate in a layoff recall is not the kind of "preference" prohibited by § 703(j). If a discriminatee is ultimately allowed to secure a position before a laid-off line driver, a question we do not now decide, he will do so because of the bidding power inherent in his rightful-place seniority, and not because of a preference based on race. See *Franks,* 424 U.S., at 792, 96 S.Ct., at 1277 (Powell, J., concurring in part and dissenting in part).

[62] Other factors, such as the number of victims, the number of nonvictim employees affected and the alternatives available to them, and the economic circumstances of the industry may also be relevant in the exercise of the District Court's discretion. See *Franks, supra,* at 796 n. 17, 96 S.Ct., at 1362 (Powell, J., concurring in part and dissenting in part).

courts exercising remedial discretion under § 703(g) "ordinarily" will find such retroactive relief "necessary to achieve the 'make-whole' purposes of the Act."

However, the Court in both *Franks* and *Teamsters* indicates that a Title VII court may account for incumbent employees' interests. The lower courts generally have ordered the displacement of incumbent employees only in "extraordinary" circumstances "when a careful balancing of the equities" indicates that absent bumping plaintiffs' relief will be inadequate. See Walters v. City of Atlanta, 803 F.2d 1135, 1149 (11th Cir.1986) (plaintiff, who was frequent victim of discrimination, sought a unique position, and bumped employee could make lateral move). See also Lander v. Lujan, 888 F.2d 153, 156–58 (D.C.Cir.1989) (employer may be required to displace a high-level employee to open a job where there are no reasonable substitutes for victim of discrimination). Courts, however, generally have required that victims of discrimination be given priority only for future openings. See, e.g., Mims v. Wilson, 514 F.2d 106 (5th Cir.1975) (remanding to district court to consider the feasibility of affirmative recruitment efforts).

5. *Manageability of Remediation Stage?* The *Teamsters* Court allows that the task for the "District Court on remand will not be a simple one." Absent settlement, will such a task always be manageable where there is a large class of possible victims? Would the task ever be manageable in a case brought before a jury for compensatory and punitive damages? Recall that before the 1991 Act damages and jury trials were not available in Title VII actions. Few cases seem to have proceeded to the remediation stage without settlement. For treatment of the procedural issues in class actions, see Chapter 21.

D. DISCRIMINATION BY UNIONS

Section 703(c) of Title VII proscribes the same five types of status discrimination (race, color, religion, sex, or national origin) by a labor organization that § 703(a) prohibits by employers. "Labor organization" is defined broadly in § 701(d) to include any kind of group or plan that exists in whole or in part to deal with employers on behalf of employees, and that also is "engaged in an industry affecting commerce". Section 701(e) in turn defines when a labor organization is so engaged. It must operate a hiring hall or have at least fifteen members, and also either be certified as a bargaining representative under federal labor laws, be recognized as such a representative by an employer engaged in an industry affecting commerce, or be formally associated with a body that is or seeks to become such a representative. Since an "industry affecting commerce" is defined by § 701(h) to include any governmental industry, unions representing state and local governmental employees are covered by § 703(c).[2] Unions with fifteen or more employees of course may be covered as private employers,

---

[2]   The coverage of federal employee unions seems more problematic because the federal government is excluded from the definition of employer in § 701(b); and § 717 covers only discrimination in federal "personnel actions", not by federal unions. But see Jennings v. American Postal Workers Union, 672 F.2d 712 (8th Cir.1982).

whether or not their business activity as the representative of the employees of other employers is covered.

Title VII's prohibition of union discrimination in § 703(c) is as comprehensive as its prohibition of employer discrimination in § 703(a). Section 703(c) has been interpreted to proscribe both discrimination in the representation of employees and in the conduct of internal union affairs. Unions thus cannot discriminate in the selection of members, in the dispensation of union benefits and burdens, in helping workers to obtain or retain jobs, or in obtaining and protecting the benefits of employment. See, e.g., Maalik v. International Union of Elevator Constructors, Local 2, 437 F.3d 650 (7th Cir. 2006) (union responsible for a member's discriminatory operation of apprentice program under union's authority). One decision found a union's discriminatory organizational strategies illegal. Gray v. Bartenders, Local 52, 1974 WL 10575 (N.D.Cal.1974). Several courts have entertained disparate impact challenges to union membership and apprenticeship requirements. See, e.g., EEOC v. Steamship Clerks Union, Local 1066, 48 F.3d 594 (1st Cir.1995); United States v. Ironworkers, Local 86, 443 F.2d 544 (9th Cir.1971). Furthermore, § 703(c)(3) expressly prohibits causing or attempting to cause an employer to discriminate in violation of the Act.

The decision that follows, however, raises the difficult issue of whether § 703 imposes affirmative duties on unions to resist an employer's discriminatory practices. The union defendants in this case were the exclusive representatives of the firm's employees within units determined appropriate for bargaining by the National Labor Relations Board. This bargaining authority and the applicable collective bargaining agreement gave the unions exclusive control over when the negotiated grievance system could be invoked. Absent a breach of the union's duty of fair representation, that grievance procedure provided the exclusive means of enforcing employee claims under the labor contract.

GOODMAN V. LUKENS STEEL CO.

Supreme Court of the United States, 1987.
482 U.S. 656, 107 S.Ct. 2617, 96 L.Ed.2d 572.

JUSTICE WHITE delivered the opinion of the Court.

In 1973, individual employees of Lukens Steel Company (Lukens) brought this suit on behalf of themselves and others, asserting racial discrimination claims under Title VII of the Civil Rights Act of 1964, 78 Stat. 253, as amended, 42 U.S.C. § 2000e *et seq.*, and 42 U.S.C. § 1981 against their employer and their collective-bargaining agents, the United Steelworkers of America and two of its local unions (Unions). * * * On the merits, the District Court found that Lukens had discriminated in certain respects, but that in others plaintiffs had not made out a case. The District Court concluded that the Unions were also guilty of discriminatory practices, specifically in failing to challenge discriminatory discharges of probationary employees, failing and refusing to assert instances of racial discrimination as grievances, and in tolerating and tacitly encouraging racial harassment. The District Court entered separate injunctive orders against Lukens and the Unions, reserving damages issues for further proceedings. [*Eds.* The Court of Appeals affirmed the liability judgment against the Unions.]

The Unions contend that the judgment against them rests on the erroneous legal premise that Title VII and § 1981 are violated if a Union passively sits by and does not affirmatively oppose the employer's racially discriminatory employment practices. It is true that the District Court declared that mere Union passivity in the face of employer discrimination renders the Union liable under Title VII and, if racial animus is properly inferable, under § 1981 as well.[10] We need not discuss this rather abstract observation, for the court went on to say that the evidence proves "far more" than mere passivity.[11] As found by the court, the facts were that since 1965, the collective-bargaining contract contained an express clause binding both the employer and the Unions not to discriminate on racial grounds; that the employer was discriminating against blacks in discharging probationary employees, which the Unions were aware of but refused to do anything about by way of filing proffered grievances or otherwise; that the Unions had ignored grievances based on instances of harassment which were indisputably racial in nature; and that the Unions had regularly refused to include assertions of racial discrimination in grievances that also asserted other contract violations.[12]

* * *

The Unions insist that it was error to hold them liable for not including racial discrimination claims in grievances claiming other violations of the

---

[10] The first part of this statement must have been addressed to disparate impact, for discriminatory motive is required in disparate treatment Title VII cases as it is in § 1981 claims. See *Teamsters v. United States,* 431 U.S. 324, 335–336, n. 15, 97 S.Ct. 1843, 1854–1855, n. 15, 52 L.Ed.2d 396 (1977); *General Building Contractors Ass'n Inc. v. Pennsylvania,* 458 U.S. 375, 391, 102 S.Ct. 3141, 3150, 73 L.Ed.2d 835 (1982). Because the District Court eventually found that in each respect the Unions violated both Title VII and § 1981 in exactly the same way, liability did not rest on a claim under Title VII that did not rest on intentional discrimination.

[11] The District Court commented that there was substantial evidence, related to events occurring prior to the statute of limitations period, which "casts serious doubt on the unions' total commitment to racial equality." The District Court noted that it was the company, not the Unions, which pressed for a nondiscrimination clause in the collective-bargaining agreement. The District Court found that the Unions never took any action over the segregated locker facilities at Lukens and did not complain over other discriminatory practices by the company. The District Court found that when one employee approached the president of one of the local unions to complain about the segregated locker facilities in 1962, the president dissuaded him from complaining to the appropriate state agency. The District Court, however, found "inconclusive" the evidence offered in support of the employees' claim that the Unions discriminated against blacks in their overall handling of grievances under the collective-bargaining agreement.

[12] The District Court also found that although the Unions had objected to the company's use of certain tests, they had never done so on racial grounds, even though they "were certainly chargeable with knowledge that many of the tests" had a racially disparate impact.

contract. The Unions followed this practice, it was urged, because these grievances could be resolved without making racial allegations and because the employer would "get its back up" if racial bias was charged, thereby making it much more difficult to prevail. The trial judge, although initially impressed by this seemingly neutral reason for failing to press race discrimination claims, ultimately found the explanation "unacceptable" because the Unions also ignored grievances which involved racial harassment violating the contract covenant against racial discrimination but which did not also violate another provision. The judge also noted that the Unions had refused to complain about racially based terminations of probationary employees, even though the express undertaking not to discriminate protected this group of employees, as well as others, and even though, as the District Court found, the Unions knew that blacks were being discharged at a disproportionately higher rate than whites. In the judgment of the District Court, the virtual failure by the Unions to file any race-bias grievances until after this lawsuit started, knowing that the employer was practicing what the contract prevented, rendered the Unions' explanation for their conduct unconvincing.

As we understand it, there was no suggestion below that the Unions held any racial animus against or denigrated blacks generally. Rather, it was held that a collective-bargaining agent could not, without violating Title VII and § 1981, follow a policy of refusing to file grievable racial discrimination claims however strong they might be and however sure the agent was that the employer was discriminating against blacks. The Unions, in effect, categorized racial grievances as unworthy of pursuit and, while pursuing thousands of other legitimate grievances, ignored racial discrimination claims on behalf of blacks, knowing that the employer was discriminating in violation of the contract. * * *

The courts below, in our view, properly construed and applied Title VII and § 1981. Those provisions do not permit a union to refuse to file any and all grievances presented by a black person on the ground that the employer looks with disfavor on and resents such grievances. It is no less violative of these laws for a union to pursue a policy of rejecting disparate treatment grievances presented by blacks solely because the claims assert racial bias and would be very troublesome to process.

JUSTICE POWELL, with whom JUSTICE SCALIA joins, and with whom JUSTICE O'CONNOR joins [in part], concurring in part and dissenting in part.

Close examination of the findings of the District Court is essential to a proper understanding of this case. The plaintiffs, blacks employed by the Lukens Steel Company, sued the United Steelworkers of America and two of its local unions (Unions) for alleged violations of § 1981 and Title VII. The plaintiffs' allegations were directed primarily at the Unions' handling of grievances on behalf of black members. The District Court found that "[t]he steady increase in grievance filings each year has not produced a corresponding increase in the capacity of the grievance-processing system to handle complaints." Consequently, the court found, the Unions gave priority to "[s]erious grievances"—that is, "those involving more than a four-day suspension, and those involving discharges." In an effort to reduce the backlog of grievances, the Unions disposed of many less serious grievances by simply withdrawing them and reserving the right to seek relief in a later grievance proceeding. The District Court found "no hard evidence to support an inference that these inadequacies disadvantage blacks to a greater extent than whites." The incomplete evidence in the record suggests that the percentage of grievances filed on behalf of black employees was proportional to the number of blacks in the work force. Of the relatively few grievances that proceeded all the way to arbitration, the District Court found that the number asserted on behalf of black members was proportional to the number of blacks in the work force. Moreover, black members had a slightly higher rate of success in arbitration than white members.[1]

* * *

The Unions offered a nondiscriminatory reason for their practice of withdrawing grievances that did not involve a discharge or lengthy suspension. According to the Unions, this policy, that is racially neutral on its face, was motivated by the Unions' nondiscriminatory interest in using the inadequate grievance system to assist members who faced the most serious economic harm. The District Court made no finding that the Unions' explanation was a pretext for racial discrimination. The Unions' policy against pursuing grievances on behalf of probationary employees also permitted the Unions to focus their attention on members with the most to lose. Similarly, the Unions' stated purpose for processing racial grievances on nonracial grounds—to obtain the swiftest and most complete relief possible for the claimant—was not racially invidious. The Unions opposed the use of tests that had a disparate impact on black members, although not on that ground. Their explanation was that more complete relief could be obtained by challenging the tests on nonracial grounds. The District Court made no finding that the Unions' decision to base their opposition on nonracial grounds was motivated by racial animus. Absent a finding that the Unions intended to discriminate against black members, the conclusion that the Unions are liable under § 1981 or the disparate treatment theory of Title VII is unjustified.

* * *

---

[1] The District Court found that black union members "actively participated" in union meetings and affairs. A black member served as chairman of the grievance committee, and other black members served on the committee. The percentage of black shop stewards, the Union's primary representatives in the grievance process, frequently exceeded the percentage of black members in the bargaining unit.

NOTES AND QUESTIONS

Test Your Understanding of the Material

1.   Note the finding of the lower court (summarized by Justice Powell) that the grievance system was administered, in the aggregate, in a manner which benefited blacks equally with whites. Note also the majority's acknowledgement that there was no suggestion that the unions "held any racial animus against or denigrated blacks generally." On what basis then were the unions found to have discriminated on the basis of race?

2.   What is the justification for the *Goodman* Court's apparent requirement that unions raise race discrimination grievances even where other, less incendiary contractual bases are available to assert claims on behalf of particular black employees?

3.   Consider the reasoning in *Goodman,* and assess whether the case would have been decided differently had the labor agreement not contained an express antidiscrimination clause. Does *Goodman* require unions to guard against the *potential* for discrimination by pressing in negotiations for clauses prohibiting and remedying race discrimination?

Related Issues

4.   *Employer Liability for Passive Acceptance of Union Discrimination.* In General Building Contractors Ass'n v. Pennsylvania, 458 U.S. 375, 102 S.Ct. 3141, 73 L.Ed.2d 835 (1982), the Court held that an employer should not be liable under § 1981 for a union's discriminatory operation of a hiring hall that furnished the employer with workers. It stressed that § 1981 is only violated by intentional discrimination and concluded that the employer had no duty to discover and eliminate discrimination at the hiring hall. Why should an employer not be liable for acquiescing in a union's independent discrimination if a union is liable for acquiescing in an employer's independent discrimination?

5.   *Joint and Several Liability for Concerted Discrimination.* The courts generally have made employers and unions jointly and severally liable for all damages caused by discriminatory provisions in collective bargaining agreements and other concerted efforts to discriminate. See, e.g., Russell v. American Tobacco Co., 528 F.2d 357 (4th Cir.1975). In Northwest Airlines, Inc. v. Transport Workers Union, 451 U.S. 77, 101 S.Ct. 1571, 67 L.Ed.2d 750 (1981), the Supreme Court held that if *one* jointly liable party is sued under Title VII and loses, it cannot then bring an *independent* action for contribution from the other party. If both the employer and the union are named as defendants, however, the decision may not foreclose one from making a cross-claim for contribution from the other.

6.   *Coverage of Employment Agencies.* In addition to proscribing discrimination by unions and employers, Title VII also prohibits the same five types of status discrimination by an "employment agency"—defined as "any person regularly undertaking * * * to procure employees for an employer or to

procure for employees opportunities to work for an employer * * * ." See §§ 703(b) and 701(c).

E. OTHER FEDERAL CAUSES OF ACTION AGAINST STATUS DISCRIMINATION

Title VII does not provide the only federal cause of action against status discrimination in employment in general, nor even against race discrimination in particular. The remainder of this chapter presents four additional sources of federal antidiscrimination law—the Constitution, the Reconstruction Era Civil Rights Acts (in particular § 1981), Title VI of the Civil Rights Act of 1964, and the Immigration Control and Reform Act. Subsequent chapters will consider some additional federal status discrimination laws that have raised especially significant and interesting issues.

1. EQUAL PROTECTION

The Fourteenth Amendment's command that no "state" shall "deny to any person within its jurisdiction the equal protection of the laws" has been held to apply to the federal government through the due process clause of the Fifth Amendment. Bolling v. Sharpe, 347 U.S. 497, 74 S.Ct. 693, 98 L.Ed. 884 (1954). The constitutional equal protection principle reaches only governmental action; it does not, as a general matter, reach the decisions of private employers.

The Court has interpreted the equal protection clause with sensitivity to its historical origins in the post-Civil War efforts of our society to eradicate the vestiges of slavery. It has presumed that any racial classification reflects a lack of equal respect or regard for black people, and since World War II has demanded that such a classification be narrowly tailored to serve some compelling state interest. In fact, during the post-War period no Supreme Court opinion has found an intentional racial classification that disadvantages blacks to satisfy this demanding test. But see Korematsu v. United States, 323 U.S. 214, 65 S.Ct. 193, 89 L.Ed. 194 (1944) (compelling state interest justifies war-time internment of Japanese-American citizens).

In Washington v. Davis, 426 U.S. 229, 96 S.Ct. 2040, 48 L.Ed.2d 597 (1976), the Court held that government actions that are not undertaken for a racially discriminatory motive but have a disproportionate adverse impact on blacks do not trigger the "strict scrutiny" that attends race-based classifications. The Court's refusal to interpret equal protection as embodying a *Griggs*-type analysis stemmed in part from prudential concerns about the implications of such a mode of challenge for governmental programs outside of employment, such as "tax, welfare, public service, regulatory, and licensing * * * that may be more burdensome to the poor and to the average black than to the more affluent white." 426 U.S. at 248, 96 S.Ct. at 2051. *Davis* also seems to reflect the view that the intense suspicion of governmental motives that attends an explicit racial classification is not appropriate when government acts on neutral grounds even if blacks, perhaps because of their relative poverty, are adversely affected.

The *Davis* Court's finding that the District of Columbia government did not administer a test for racially discriminatory reasons did not completely resolve the Equal Protection issue in that case, however. The test, though it did not classify along racial lines, nonetheless did classify applicants for employment. Under established equal protection doctrine it was thus necessary for the Court to consider whether the test at least had some minimal "rational basis". Although the Court had no difficulty finding this rational basis in a desire to upgrade the "communicative abilities" of employees, there may be cases where government programs will have greater difficulty satisfying such scrutiny.

The application of government programs also may generate equal protection challenges, but the Court held in Engquist v. Oregon Dept. of Agriculture, 553 U.S. 591, 128 S.Ct. 2146, 170 L.Ed.2d 975 (2008), that a public employee cannot "state a claim under the Equal Protection Clause by alleging that she was arbitrarily treated differently from other similarly situated employees, with no assertion that the different treatment was based on the employee's membership in any particular class."

NOTE: THE ENFORCEMENT OF THE EQUAL PROTECTION COMMAND

Section 1983 of Title 42 of the United States Code, originally enacted as § 1 of the Civil Rights Act of 1871, provides both a legal and equitable cause of action for individuals who have been denied a constitutional (or federal statutory) right by a state or local governmental official. Section 1983 authorizes an action for injunctive relief and damages (including punitive damages) against government officials sued in their personal capacity even when the conduct in question also violates state or local law. All government officials, however, even when not fully immune from civil liability as judges, prosecutors, or legislators, "are shielded from liability for civil damages insofar as their conduct does not violate clearly established statutory or constitutional rights of which a reasonable person would have known." Davis v. Scherer, 468 U.S. 183, 190–91, 104 S.Ct. 3012, 82 L.Ed.2d 139 (1984).

Although suit may be brought against the local government entity itself, the Court has interpreted § 1983 to reject the doctrine of respondeat superior. A § 1983 action lies against a local governmental entity only with respect to actions condoned by official policy or custom. See Monell v. Department of Social Services, 436 U.S. 658, 98 S.Ct. 2018, 56 L.Ed.2d 611 (1978); Pembaur v. Cincinnati, 475 U.S. 469, 106 S.Ct. 1292, 89 L.Ed.2d 452 (1986) (municipality may be held liable only for "acts which the municipality has officially sanctioned or ordered" through an officer with "final policymaking authority"); St. Louis v. Praprotnik, 485 U.S. 112, 108 S.Ct. 915, 99 L.Ed.2d 107 (1988) (plurality opinion holding that municipality could not be held liable for retaliatory transfer because mayor and aldermen—the officials with final policymaking authority—had not enacted an ordinance or otherwise indicated that such retaliatory decisions were permissible). Section 1983 actions against governmental entities are treated differently in other respects as well. See City of Newport v. Fact Concerts, Inc., 453 U.S. 247, 101 S.Ct. 2748, 69 L.Ed.2d 616 (1981) (punitive damages are not recoverable); Owen v. City of Independence, 445 U.S. 622, 100 S.Ct. 1398, 63 L.Ed.2d 673 (1980) (no good-faith defense to municipal § 1983 liability).

State governments are insulated from both legal and equitable suits under § 1983 by the doctrine of sovereign immunity as embodied in the Eleventh Amendment.[2] See Quern v. Jordan, 440 U.S. 332, 99 S.Ct. 1139, 59 L.Ed.2d 358 (1979); Edelman v. Jordan, 415 U.S. 651, 94 S.Ct. 1347, 39 L.Ed.2d 662 (1974). However, even absent a waiver of sovereign immunity, § 1983 may be used to obtain prospective injunctive or declaratory relief and attorney's fees from state officials sued in their official capacities; and also to obtain monetary damages from state (as well as local government) officials sued in their personal capacities, absent an official immunity defense. See Hafer v. Melo, 502 U.S. 21, 112 S.Ct. 358, 116 L.Ed.2d 301 (1991); Scheuer v. Rhodes, 416 U.S. 232, 94 S.Ct. 1683, 40 L.Ed.2d 90 (1974). Section 1983 suits may be brought in state courts where the Eleventh Amendment does not apply. However, in Will v. Michigan Department of State Police, 491 U.S. 58, 109 S.Ct. 2304, 105 L.Ed.2d 45 (1989), the court insured that the same sovereign immunity limits apply to § 1983 actions in state courts by holding that grievants cannot sue for monetary damages under § 1983 states or state officers in their official capacities.

Section 1983 does not create a right of action for decisions made under the authority of federal law. See Wheeldin v. Wheeler, 373 U.S. 647, 650 n. 2, 83 S.Ct. 1441 n. 2, 10 L.Ed.2d 605 (1963). A grievant seeking relief from a discriminatory employment decision made by a federal official might try to sue directly under the due process clause of the Fifth Amendment. In Davis v. Passman, 442 U.S. 228, 99 S.Ct. 2264, 60 L.Ed.2d 846 (1979), however, the Court held that such a cause of action is available only if the federal employee is not covered by Title VII.

Should § 1983 causes of action against state and local governments based on the equal protection clause also be precluded if the discrimination challenged is proscribed by Title VII? A number of court of appeals decisions, relying on the 1972 Title VII legislative history have held that § 1983 constitutional claims against public employers are not precluded. See, e.g., Southard v. Texas Board of Criminal Justice, 114 F.3d 539 (5th Cir.1997); Bradley v. Pittsburgh Bd. of Educ., 913 F.2d 1064, 1079 (3d Cir.1990).

---

[2] The Court has held that the eleventh amendment erects no bar to Title VII actions because Congress, pursuant to its enforcement authority under the fourteenth amendment, qualified the states' immunity from Title VII back pay awards. See Fitzpatrick v. Bitzer, 427 U.S. 445, 96 S.Ct. 2666, 49 L.Ed.2d 614 (1976).

Regardless of the availability of the § 1983 remedy for equal protection violations, the Court's decisions strongly suggest that it cannot be used as a remedy for Title VII violations. The Court in Great American Federal Savings & Loan Assn. v. Novotny, 442 U.S. 366, 99 S.Ct. 2345, 60 L.Ed.2d 957 (1979), held that the post-Civil War anti-conspiracy remedial statute, 42 U.S.C. § 1985(3), did not provide an additional remedy for retaliation proscribed by § 704 of Title VII. See also Middlesex County Sewerage Authority v. National Sea Clammers Ass'n, 453 U.S. 1, 20, 101 S.Ct. 2615, 2626, 69 L.Ed.2d 435 (1981) (inclusion of a comprehensive remedial scheme in a statute "may suffice to demonstrate congressional intent to preclude the remedy of suits under § 1983" for violations of that statute).

2. 42 U.S.C. § 1981

Originally part of § 1 of the Civil Rights Act of 1866, and now codified as § 1981 of Title 42 of the United States Code, this provision guarantees all persons the same right "to make and enforce contracts * * * as is enjoyed by white citizens * * * ." Unlike § 1983, § 1981 not only protects rights deriving from other legal sources such as the constitution. It is itself a source of a right to engage in a range of economic and political activities free of racial discrimination.

Section 1981 reaches all forms of racial discrimination. In McDonald v. Santa Fe Trail Transportation Co., supra, the Court held that whites complaining of racial discrimination could sue under § 1981. Then in Saint Francis College v. Al-Khazraji, 481 U.S. 604, 107 S.Ct. 2022, 95 L.Ed.2d 582 (1987), and Shaare Tefila Congregation v. Cobb, 481 U.S. 615, 107 S.Ct. 2019, 95 L.Ed.2d 594 (1987), the Court held that the Congress that enacted § 1981 intended to proscribe "ancestry or ethnic" discrimination, which it would have viewed as equivalent to racial discrimination. However, "the same right * * * as is enjoyed by white citizens" language of § 1981 has been read to preclude the statute's extension to discrimination on account of sex, religion or age; and *Saint Francis* clarifies that it does not cover discrimination based on "place or nation of * * * origin." The courts of appeals have disagreed on coverage of alienage (citizenship) discrimination. Compare Anderson v. Conboy, 156 F.3d 167 (2d Cir.1998) (coverage), with Bhandari v. First National Bank of Commerce, 887 F.2d 609 (5th Cir.1989) (en banc) (no coverage).

Section 1981 actions generally cannot be brought against federal employers. Brown v. GSA, 425 U.S. 820, 96 S.Ct. 1961, 48 L.Ed.2d 402 (1976), held that Congress intended § 717 of Title VII to provide an exclusive remedy for claims of Title VII-type status discrimination against federal government employers. Moreover, in Jett v. Dallas Independent School District, 491 U.S. 701, 109 S.Ct. 2702, 105 L.Ed.2d 598 (1989), a majority of the Justices concluded that there is no private right of action for damages against state and local government actors under § 1981 that is independent of the remedy provided by § 1983. This conclusion is significant because it makes clear that the limitations governing § 1983 actions cannot be avoided by proceeding under § 1981. *Jett* itself, for instance, held that § 1981 could not be invoked to avoid the *Monell* doctrine, which precludes a local government's damages liability for its employees' violations of § 1983 unless the conduct in question constituted the government's official custom or policy. *Jett's* rationale also would seem to settle that § 1981 does not constitute a congressional override of the Eleventh Amendment's sovereign immunity doctrine. See Edelman v. Jordan, 415 U.S. 651, 94 S.Ct. 1347, 39 L.Ed.2d 662 (1974), (§ 1983 plaintiffs are limited to damages from state governmental officials sued as in their personal capacity, rather than from the state employer itself); Singletary v. Missouri Dept. of Corrections, 423 F.3d 886 (8th Cir. 2005) (§ 1981 does not abrogate sovereign immunity). Most courts of appeals have held that the 1991 amendments to § 1981 did not provide a new independent right of action against state actors. See, e.g., McCormick v. Miami Univ., 693 F.3d 654, 660 (6th Cir. 2012); McGovern v. City of Philadelphia, 554 F.3d 114, 118 (3d Cir. 2009); but cf. Federation of African-American Contractors v. Oakland, 96 F.3d 1204, 1214–15 (9th Cir.1996) (although 1991 Civil Rights Act's addition of new § 1981(c) provides an independent cause of action against state actors, principles drawn from § 1983 such as the *Monell* doctrine apply).

Section 101 of the Civil Rights Act of 1991 expressly confirms Congressional intent to reach "nongovernmental discrimination" through § 1981. 42 U.S.C. § 1981(c). As such, Section 1981 provides an independent cause of action for damages against private employers. Unlike Title VII claims, the § 1981 cause of action does not require exhaustion of administrative procedures at the EEOC or state agencies. Conversely, the filing of a Title VII charge with the EEOC does not toll the running of the § 1981 period of limitation.

Although a few district courts and the Seventh Circuit have asserted that an employment-at-will relationship cannot be the basis for a § 1981 claim, see Gonzalez v. Ingersoll Milling Mach. Co., 133 F.3d 1025 (7th Cir.1998), several other Courts of Appeals and a majority of district courts have recognized that a contractual relationship can exist between employers and employees, even when the relationship can be terminated by any party at any time. See, e.g., Turner v. Arkansas Insurance Dept., 297 F.3d 751 (8th Cir.2002) (dismissing *Gonzalez* as dicta and holding, upon review of cases, that it is "clearly established" that § 1981 protects at-will employees); Lauture v. International Business Machines Corp., 216 F.3d 258 (2d Cir.2000); Spriggs v. Diamond Auto Glass, 165 F.3d 1015 (4th Cir.1999); Fadeyi v. Planned Parenthood Ass'n, 160 F.3d 1048 (5th Cir.1998).

3. TITLE VI OF THE CIVIL RIGHTS ACT OF 1964 AND TITLE IX OF THE EDUCATION AMENDMENTS OF 1972

Title VI of the Civil Rights Act of 1964 provides that no person "shall, on the ground of race, color, or national origin, * * * be subjected to discrimination under any program or activity receiving Federal financial assistance." Title IX of the Education Act Amendments of 1972 provides that no person "shall, on the basis of sex, * * * be subjected to discrimination under any education program or activity receiving Federal financial assistance." In the Civil Rights Restoration Act of 1987, 42 U.S.C. § 2000d–4a, Pub.L. 100–259, 102 Stat. 28, Congress overturned a 1984 Supreme Court opinion, Grove City College v. Bell, 465 U.S. 555, 104 S.Ct. 1211, 79 L.Ed.2d 516 (1984), to make clear (with some exceptions) that the Title VI and Title IX antidiscrimination obligations apply to the entire public or private institution accepting federal funds, not simply the specific program or activity to which the funds are allotted.

The Supreme Court has held that Title IX, as well as Title VI, may be enforced through a private right of action. See Cannon v. University of Chicago, 441 U.S. 677, 99 S.Ct. 1946, 60 L.Ed.2d 560 (1979). Under Franklin v. Gwinnett County Public Schools, 503 U.S. 60, 112 S.Ct. 1028, 117 L.Ed.2d 208 (1992), courts may award private plaintiffs damages for intentional violations of Title IX, as well as Title VI. This doctrine could be helpful for some claimants because Title VI and Title IX, like § 1981, but unlike Title VII, do not require exhaustion of administrative procedures before suit. However, some lower courts have held that private plaintiffs cannot circumvent the Title VII administrative system by suing for damages under Title IX. See, e.g., Lakoski v. James, 66 F.3d 751 (5th Cir. 1995) (relying on Great American Federal Savings & Loan Assn. v. Novotny, 442 U.S. 366, 99 S.Ct. 2345, 60 L.Ed.2d 957 (1979).)

The substantive reach of Title VI and Title IX actions is not coextensive with that of Title VII. First, in Guardians Ass'n v. Civil Serv. Comm'n, 463 U.S. 582, 103 S.Ct. 3221, 77 L.Ed.2d 866 (1983), a majority of Justices held that unlike Title VII, Title VI of its own force reaches only intentional discrimination. Though a different majority in *Guardians* agreed that agency regulations implementing Title VI could require recipients to avoid practices that are discriminatory in effect as well as purpose, five other Justices maintained that private plaintiffs cannot obtain compensatory or any other retroactive relief, including comparative seniority, without proof of discriminatory intent. In Alexander v. Sandoval, 532 U.S. 275, 121 S.Ct. 1511, 149 L.Ed.2d 517 (2001), the Court held that only the Government can enforce agency disparate impact regulations; because those regulations go beyond the reach of Title VI (and presumably Title IX), they are not enforceable through a private action.

Second, in Gebser v. Lago Vista Independent School District, 524 U.S. 274, 118 S.Ct. 1989, 141 L.Ed.2d 277 (1998), the Court held that Title IX plaintiffs could not obtain damages for a teacher's sexual harassment of a student without establishing that some school official with corrective authority had actual notice of and was deliberately indifferent to the misconduct. The holding in *Gebser* was limited to its factual context of teacher-student sexual harassment, but the Court's reasoning (based on ensuring that federal funds recipients have adequate notice that they could be liable) could extend the decision's actual knowledge and deliberate indifference standard to other Title IX and possibly Title VI employment discrimination cases as well. Cf. Davis v. Monroe County Board of Education, 526 U.S. 629, 119 S.Ct. 1661, 143 L.Ed.2d 839 (1999) (applying *Gebser* to student-student sexual harassment). (*Gebser*'s holding should be contrasted with the more liberal agency doctrine for Title VII cases pronounced by the Court in the same term. See pp. 374–388 infra.)

In Barnes v. Gorman, 536 U.S. 181, 122 S.Ct. 2097, 153 L.Ed.2d 230 (2002), the Court held in a disability discrimination case brought in part under § 504 of the Rehabilitation Act of 1964, that punitive damages are not available in private suits to enforce statutes governing federal fund recipients, such as § 504, Title VI, and Title IX.

4. THE IMMIGRATION REFORM AND CONTROL ACT

Although Title VII prohibits discrimination on account of national origin, it does not bar discrimination on account of alienage or lack of citizenship. See Espinoza v. Farah Mfg. Co., 414 U.S. 86, 94 S.Ct. 334, 38 L.Ed.2d 287 (1973) (permitting challenge only where citizenship requirement has disparate impact on national origin minority). This is especially significant because the immigration laws not only have historically utilized national origin categories to determine entry into this country, but also have directly restricted the employment of noncitizens who have not acquired resident alien status. Congress in Title VII presumably sought to bar only that dimension of anti-foreigner discrimination that is based on national origin rather than citizenship status.

The Immigration Reform and Control Act of 1986 (IRCA), Pub.L. 99–603, 8 U.S.C. §§ 1324a–1324b, prohibits the knowing employment, recruitment and referral of "unauthorized aliens," defined as noncitizens who are not resident aliens or otherwise authorized to work in the United States. IRCA also requires employers to obtain documentation of citizenship or authorization to work from all employees, and subjects employers to fines for noncompliance. These provisions raised considerable concern that employers would use the documentation requirement as a device for excluding employees of particular national origins who would be unable to marshal proof of their citizenship or work-authorization.

In part to meet this concern, Congress provided in § 102 of IRCA that it is an "unfair immigration-related employment practice" to discriminate against "any individual (other than an unauthorized alien)" who is an "intending citizen" (either a resident alien or an alien seeking legalization under IRCA's amnesty program or lawfully admitted under the refugee and asylum provisions) because of such individual's national origin or "citizenship status." Expressly excluded from this provision is national origin discrimination covered by Title VII and citizenship requirements required by federal or state law or "which the Attorney General determines to be essential for an employer to do business with" a government agency. An Office of the Special Counsel for Immigration-Related Unfair Unemployment Practices, located within the Justice Department, enforces this provision.

In late 1987, the Justice Department issued a ruling that § 102 of IRCA reaches only intentional citizenship status discrimination. See 28 C.F.R. Part 44. The Department thus will investigate employment barriers like English-only rules, residence requirements, or a preference for certain verification documents, only for the presence of intentional bias. IRCA's prohibition of citizenship status discrimination does not, of course, protect aliens who are not lawfully in the United States or within the "intending citizen" category.

Are workers who are "unauthorized aliens" under the IRCA protected by American employment laws? For instance, should an alien who does not receive a promotion because of his national origin be required to show that he can legally work to establish a prima facie case of discrimination under Title VII? Or should his illegal status under the IRCA be treated, under *McKennon v. Nashville Banner Publishing Co.*, supra p. 135, like any other legitimate reason not to hire of which the employer was not aware, and thus relevant only to the remedy that the worker might obtain from the court? See Egbuna v. Time-Life Libraries, Inc., 153 F.3d 184 (4th Cir.1998) (divided en banc decision holding *McKennon* does not control; alien plaintiff must show legal authorization to work in U.S.).

If unauthorized aliens are protected by Title VII, notwithstanding the IRCA, does the latter statute restrict the award of backpay or reinstatement as remedies? In Hoffman Plastic Compounds, Inc. v. NLRB, 535 U.S. 137, 122 S.Ct. 1275, 152 L.Ed.2d 271 (2002), the Court held that although an employer may violate the National Labor Relations Act by discharging undocumented aliens for supporting a union, the IRCA precludes the Labor Board from ordering backpay or reinstatement. In Rivera v. NIBCO, Inc., 364 F.3d 1057 (9th Cir. 2004), the court refused to allow an employer to conduct discovery on the immigration status of the employee plaintiffs because of the court's concern with chilling the employees' and the public's interest in enforcing Title VII. The court further opined:

> We seriously doubt that *Hoffman* * * * applies in Title VII cases.
> * * * First, the NLRA authorizes only certain limited private

causes of action, while Title VII depends principally upon private causes of action for enforcement. * * * Second, Congress has armed Title VII plaintiffs with remedies designed to punish employers who engage in unlawful discriminatory acts, and to deter future discrimination both by the defendant and by all other employers. Title VII's enforcement regime includes not only traditional remedies for employment law violations, such as backpay, frontpay, and reinstatement, but also full compensatory and punitive damages. Third, under the NLRA, the NLRB may award backpay to workers when it has found that an employer has violated the Act. Under Title VII, a federal court decides whether a statutory violation warrants a backpay award. This difference is significant given that *Hoffman* held that the NLRB possesses only the discretion to "select and fashion remedies for violations of the NLRA," and that this discretion, "though broad, is not unlimited." 535 U.S. at 142–43 (citations omitted). The Court held that, given the strong policies underlying IRCA and the Board's limited power to construe statutes outside of its authority, the NLRB's construction of the NLRA was impermissible. This limitation on the Board's authority says nothing regarding a *federal court's power* to balance IRCA against *Title VII* if the two statutes conflict. * * *

We need not decide the *Hoffman* question in this case, however. Regardless whether *Hoffman* applies in Title VII cases, it is clear that it does not *require* a district court to allow the discovery sought here. No backpay award has been authorized in this litigation. Indeed, the plaintiffs have proposed several options for ensuring that, whether or not *Hoffman* applies, no award of backpay is given to any undocumented alien in this proceeding. * * *

Id. at 1067–69.

CHAPTER 4

DISPARATE IMPACT

■ ■ ■

Introduction

Title VII establishes a second mode of proving discrimination which focuses on the adverse impact of employer policies or practices on a Title VII protected group. Discriminatory motive is not a required element. The gravamen of the offense is the unjustified impact of the policy or action.

A. BASIC THEORY AND METHOD OF PROOF

GRIGGS v. DUKE POWER CO.
Supreme Court of United States, 1971.
401 U.S. 424, 91 S.Ct. 849, 28 L.Ed.2d 158.

CHIEF JUSTICE BURGER delivered the opinion of the Court.

The District Court found that prior to July 2, 1965, the effective date of the Civil Rights Act of 1964, the Company openly discriminated on the basis of race in the hiring and assigning of employees at its Dan River plant. The plant was organized into five operating departments: (1) Labor, (2) Coal Handling, (3) Operations, (4) Maintenance, and (5) Laboratory and Test. Negroes were employed only in the Labor Department where the highest paying jobs paid less than the lowest paying jobs in the other four "operating" departments in which only whites were employed. Promotions were normally made within each department on the basis of job seniority. Transferees into a department usually began in the lowest position.

In 1955 the Company instituted a policy of requiring a high school education for initial assignment to any department except Labor, and for transfer from the Coal Handling to any "inside" department (Operations, Maintenance, or Laboratory). When the Company abandoned its policy of restricting Negroes to the Labor Department in 1965, completion of high school also was made a prerequisite to transfer from Labor to any other department. From the time the high school requirement was instituted to the time of trial, however, white employees hired before the time of the high school education requirement continued to perform satisfactorily and achieve promotions in the "operating" departments. Findings on this score are not challenged.

The Company added a further requirement for new employees on July 2, 1965, the date on which Title VII became effective. To qualify for placement in any but the Labor Department it became necessary to register satisfactory scores on two professionally prepared aptitude tests, as well as to have a high school education. Completion of high school alone continued to render employees eligible for transfer to the four desirable departments from which Negroes had been excluded if the incumbent had been employed prior to the time of the new requirement. In September 1965 the Company began to permit incumbent employees who lacked a high school education to qualify for transfer from Labor or Coal Handling to an "inside" job by passing two tests—the Wonderlic Personnel Test, which purports to measure general intelligence, and the Bennett Mechanical Comprehension Test. Neither was directed or intended to measure the ability to learn to perform a particular job or category of jobs. The requisite scores used for both initial hiring and transfer approximated the national median for high school graduates.[3]

The District Court had found that while the Company previously followed a policy of overt racial discrimination in a period prior to the Act, such conduct had ceased. The District Court also concluded that Title VII was intended to be prospective only and, consequently, the impact of prior inequities was beyond the reach of corrective action authorized by the Act.

* * *

The Court of Appeals reversed the District Court in part, rejecting the holding that residual discrimination arising from prior employment practices was insulated from remedial action.[4] The Court of Appeals noted, however, that the District Court was correct in its conclusion that there was no showing of a racial purpose or invidious intent in the adoption of the high school diploma requirement or general intelligence test and that these standards had been applied fairly to whites and Negroes alike. It held that, in the absence of a discriminatory purpose, use of such requirements was permitted by the Act.

* * *

The objective of Congress in the enactment of Title VII is plain from the language of the statute. It was to achieve equality of employment opportunities and remove barriers that have operated in the past to favor an identifiable group of white employees over other employees. Under the Act, practices, procedures, or tests neutral on their face, and even neutral

---

[3]   The test standards are thus more stringent than the high school requirement, since they would screen out approximately half of all high school graduates.

[4]   The Court of Appeals ruled that Negroes employed in the Labor Department at a time when there was no high school or test requirement for entrance into the higher paying departments could not now be made subject to those requirements, since whites hired contemporaneously into those departments were never subject to them. The Court of Appeals also required that the seniority rights of those Negroes be measured on a plantwide, rather than a departmental, basis. However, the Court of Appeals denied relief to the Negro employees without a high school education or its equivalent who were hired into the Labor Department after institution of the educational requirement.

in terms of intent, cannot be maintained if they operate to "freeze" the status quo of prior discriminatory employment practices.

The Court of Appeals' opinion, and the partial dissent, agreed that, on the record in the present case, "whites register far better on the Company's alternative requirements" than Negroes.[6] This consequence would appear to be directly traceable to race. Basic intelligence must have the means of articulation to manifest itself fairly in a testing process. Because they are Negroes, petitioners have long received inferior education in segregated schools and this Court expressly recognized these differences in *Gaston County v. United States*, 395 U.S. 285, 89 S.Ct. 1720, 23 L.Ed.2d 309 (1969). There, because of the inferior education received by Negroes in North Carolina, this Court barred the institution of a literacy test for voter registration on the ground that the test would abridge the right to vote indirectly on account of race. Congress did not intend by Title VII, however, to guarantee a job to every person regardless of qualifications. In short, the Act does not command that any person be hired simply because he was formerly the subject of discrimination, or because he is a member of a minority group. Discriminatory preference for any group, minority or majority, is precisely and only what Congress has proscribed. What is required by Congress is the removal of artificial, arbitrary, and unnecessary barriers to employment when the barriers operate invidiously to discriminate on the basis of racial or other impermissible classification.

Congress has now provided that tests or criteria for employment or promotion may not provide equality of opportunity merely in the sense of the fabled offer of milk to the stork and the fox. On the contrary, Congress has now required that the posture and condition of the job-seeker be taken into account. It has—to resort again to the fable—provided that the vessel in which the milk is proffered be one all seekers can use. The Act proscribes not only overt discrimination but also practices that are fair in form, but discriminatory in operation. The touchstone is business necessity. If an employment practice which operates to exclude Negroes cannot be shown to be related to job performance, the practice is prohibited.

On the record before us, neither the high school completion requirement nor the general intelligence test is shown to bear a demonstrable relationship to successful performance of the jobs for which it was used. Both were adopted, as the Court of Appeals noted, without meaningful study of their relationship to job-performance ability. Rather, a vice president of the Company testified, the requirements were instituted

---

[6] In North Carolina, 1960 census statistics show that, while 34% of white males had completed high school, only 12% of Negro males had done so. U.S. Bureau of the Census, U.S. Census of Population: 1960, Vol. 1, Characteristics of the Population, pt. 35, Table 47.

Similarly, with respect to standardized tests, the EEOC in one case found that use of a battery of tests, including the Wonderlic and Bennett tests used by the Company in the instant case, resulted in 58% of whites passing the tests, as compared with only 6% of the blacks. Decision of EEOC, CCH Empl.Prac.Guide, ¶ 17,304.53 (Dec. 2, 1966). See also Decision of EEOC 70–552, CCH Empl.Prac.Guide, ¶ 6139 (Feb. 19, 1970).

on the Company's judgment that they generally would improve the overall quality of the work force.

The evidence, however, shows that employees who have not completed high school or taken the tests have continued to perform satisfactorily and make progress in departments for which the high school and test criteria are now used.[7] The promotion record of present employees who would not be able to meet the new criteria thus suggests the possibility that the requirements may not be needed even for the limited purpose of preserving the avowed policy of advancement within the Company. In the context of this case, it is unnecessary to reach the question whether testing requirements that take into account capability for the next succeeding position or related future promotion might be utilized upon a showing that such long-range requirements fulfill a genuine business need. In the present case the Company has made no such showing.

The Court of Appeals held that the Company had adopted the diploma and test requirements without any "intention to discriminate against Negro employees." We do not suggest that either the District Court or the Court of Appeals erred in examining the employer's intent; but good intent or absence of discriminatory intent does not redeem employment procedures or testing mechanisms that operate as "built-in headwinds" for minority groups and are unrelated to measuring job capability.

The Company's lack of discriminatory intent is suggested by special efforts to help the undereducated employees through Company financing of two-thirds the cost of tuition for high school training. But Congress directed the thrust of the Act to the *consequences* of employment practices, not simply the motivation. More than that, Congress has placed on the employer the burden of showing that any given requirement must have a manifest relationship to the employment in question. The facts of this case demonstrate the inadequacy of broad and general testing devices as well as the infirmity of using diplomas or degrees as fixed measures of capability. History is filled with examples of men and women who rendered highly effective performance without the conventional badges of accomplishment in terms of certificates, diplomas, or degrees. Diplomas and tests are useful servants, but Congress has mandated the commonsense proposition that they are not to become masters of reality. The Company contends that its general intelligence tests are specifically permitted by § 703(h) of the Act.[8] That section authorizes the use of "any professionally developed ability test" that is not "designed, intended *or used* to discriminate because of race * * * ." (Emphasis added.)

---

[7] For example, between July 2, 1965, and November 14, 1966, the percentage of white employees who were promoted but who were not high school graduates was nearly identical to the percentage of non-graduates in the entire white work force.

[8] Section 703(h) applies only to tests. It has no applicability to the high school diploma requirement.

The Equal Employment Opportunity Commission, having enforcement responsibility, has issued guidelines interpreting § 703(h) to permit only the use of job-related tests.[9] The administrative interpretation of the Act by the enforcing agency is entitled to great deference. See, *e.g., United States v. City of Chicago*, 400 U.S. 8, 91 S.Ct. 18, 27 L.Ed.2d 9 (1970); *Udall v. Tallman*, 380 U.S. 1, 85 S.Ct. 792, 13 L.Ed.2d 616 (1965); *Power Reactor Development Co. v. Electricians*, 367 U.S. 396, 81 S.Ct. 1529, 6 L.Ed.2d 924 (1961). Since the Act and its legislative history support the Commission's construction, this affords good reason to treat the guidelines as expressing the will of Congress.

NOTES AND QUESTIONS

Continuing Use of Wonderlic Test

The Wonderlic Personnel Test is still in use, though it has since been updated and renamed the Wonderlic Cognitive Ability Test. The National Football League (NFL), for example, administers the Wonderlic test during the NLF Scouting Combine. See Alan Siegel, How a Multiple-Choice Test Became a Fixture of the NFL Draft, FiveThirtyEight Sports, April 30, 2015, http://fivethirtyeight.com/features/how-a-multiple-choice -test-became-a-fixture-of-the-nfl-draft/.

Test Your Understanding of the Material

1.   The Court's opinion in *Griggs* authorizes a Title VII challenge based on the disparate impact of employment practices that are "neutral on their face, and even neutral in terms of intent." What facially neutral rules were at issue in *Griggs*?

2.   How did the Court in *Griggs* determine whether the high school diploma requirement and intelligence tests had an adverse impact on African-Americans?

3.   Although *Griggs* did not require plaintiffs to prove discriminatory intent, was there evidence that the Duke Power Co. had a discriminatory motive in maintaining any of the challenged practices after the effective date of Title VII? Would it be sufficient to establish continuing discriminatory intent

---

[9]   EEOC Guidelines on Employment Testing Procedures, issued August 24, 1966, provide:
"The Commission accordingly interprets 'professionally developed ability test' to mean a test which fairly measures the knowledge or skills required by the particular job or class of jobs which the applicant seeks, or which fairly affords the employer a chance to measure the applicant's ability to perform a particular job or class of jobs. The fact that a test was prepared by an individual or organization claiming expertise in test preparation does not, without more, justify its use within the meaning of Title VII."

The EEOC position has been elaborated in the new Guidelines on Employee Selection Procedures, 29 CFR § 1607, 35 Fed. Reg. 12333 (Aug. 1, 1970). These guidelines demand that employers using tests have available "data demonstrating that the test is predictive of or significantly correlated with important elements of work behavior which comprise or are relevant to the job or jobs for which candidates are being evaluated." *Id.,* at § 1607.4(c).

to demonstrate that some of the incumbent employees received their position as a result of pre-Title VII discriminatory job assignments?

4. What was the statutory basis for adopting the disparate impact mode of proof? What in § 703 supports the approach? What detracts from it? What role does § 703(h) play? See Samuel Estreicher, The Story of Griggs v. Duke Power Co., ch. 5 in Employment Discrimination Stories (Joel Wm. Friedman (2006)). Congress did not expressly authorize the disparate impact methodology until its passage of the Civil Rights Act of 1991. See § 105 of that Act, 105 Stat. 1071, inserting new provision § 703(k) into Title VII, 42 U.S.C. § 2000e–2(k), discussed in detail below at p. 225.

Related Issues

5. *Use of Disparate Impact to Challenge Discriminatory Working Conditions.* Is the disparate impact approach limited to challenges to criteria for hiring and promotions? Both before and after the 1991 Act, some courts have applied *Griggs* to employer policies affecting working conditions even if they are not criteria for selecting employees. See, e.g., Maldonado v. City of Altus, 433 F.3d 1294 (10th Cir. 2006) (challenge to "English only" rule by Hispanic employees); Davey v. City of Omaha, 107 F.3d 587 (8th Cir.1997) (challenge to salary classifications); Fitzpatrick v. City of Atlanta, 2 F.3d 1112 (11th Cir.1993) (challenge to "no-beard" rule because of disparate impact on blacks); Lynch v. Freeman, 817 F.2d 380 (6th Cir.1987) (female plaintiffs' challenge to employer's failure to maintain clean toilets); but cf. Garcia v. Spun Steak Co., 998 F.2d 1480 (9th Cir.1993). Section 703(k) of Title VII, added in the 1991 amendments, authorizes disparate impact challenges to "particular employment practice[s]."

CONNECTICUT V. TEAL

Supreme Court of the United States, 1982.
457 U.S. 440, 102 S.Ct. 2525, 73 L.Ed.2d 130.

JUSTICE BRENNAN delivered the opinion of the Court.

I

Four of the respondents, Winnie Teal, Rose Walker, Edith Latney, and Grace Clark, are black employees of the Department of Income Maintenance of the State of Connecticut. Each was promoted provisionally to the position of Welfare Eligibility Supervisor and served in that capacity for almost two years. To attain permanent status as supervisors, however, respondents had to participate in a selection process that required, as the first step, a passing score on a written examination. This written test was administered on December 2, 1978, to 329 candidates. Of these candidates, 48 identified themselves as black and 259 identified themselves as white. The results of the examination were announced in March 1979. With the passing score set at 65,[3] 54.17 percent of the identified black candidates passed. This was approximately 68 percent of the passing rate for the identified white candidates.[4] The four respondents were among the blacks who failed the examination, and they were thus excluded from further consideration for permanent supervisory positions. * * *

More than a year after this action was instituted, and approximately one month before trial, petitioners made promotions from the eligibility list generated by the written examination. In choosing persons from that list, petitioners considered past work performance, recommendations of the candidates' supervisors and, to a lesser extent, seniority. Petitioners then applied what the Court of Appeals characterized as an affirmative-action program in order to ensure a significant number of minority supervisors. Forty-six persons were promoted to permanent supervisory positions, 11 of whom were black and 35 of whom were white. The overall result of the selection process was that, of the 48 identified black candidates who participated in the selection process, 22.9 percent were promoted and of the 259 identified white candidates, 13.5 percent were promoted.[6] It is this "bottom-line" result, more favorable to blacks than to whites, that petitioners urge should be adjudged to be a complete defense to respondents' suit.

* * *

II

* * *

Petitioners' examination, which barred promotion and had a discriminatory impact on black employees, clearly falls within the literal language of § 703(a)(2), as interpreted by *Griggs*. The statute speaks, not

---

[3] The mean score on the examination was 70.4 percent. However, because the black candidates had a mean score 6.7 percentage points lower than the white candidates, the passing score was set at 65, apparently in an attempt to lessen the disparate impact of the examination.

[4] The following table shows the passing rates of various candidate groups:

Candidate Group	Number	No. Receiving Passing Score	Passing Rate (%)
Black	48	26	54.17
Hispanic	4	3	75.00
Indian	3	2	66.67
White	259	206	79.54
Unidentified	15	9	60.00
Total	329	246	74.77

Petitioners do not contest the District Court's implicit finding that the examination itself resulted in disparate impact under the "eighty percent rule" of the Uniform Guidelines on Employee Selection Procedures adopted by the Equal Employment Opportunity Commission. Those guidelines provide that a selection rate that "is less than [80 percent] of the rate for the group with the highest rate will generally be regarded * * * as evidence of adverse impact." 29 CFR § 1607.4D (1981).

[6] The actual promotion rate of blacks was thus close to 170 percent that of the actual promotion rate of whites.

in terms of jobs and promotions, but in terms of *limitations* and *classifications* that would deprive any individual of employment *opportunities*. A disparate-impact claim reflects the language of § 703(a)(2) and Congress' basic objectives in enacting that statute: "to achieve equality of employment *opportunities* and remove barriers that have operated in the past to favor an identifiable group of white employees over other employees." 401 U.S., at 429–430, 91 S.Ct., at 852–853 (emphasis added). When an employer uses a nonjob-related barrier in order to deny a minority or woman applicant employment or promotion, and that barrier has a significant adverse effect on minorities or women, then the applicant has been deprived of an employment *opportunity* "because of * * * race, color, religion, sex, or national origin." In other words, § 703(a)(2) prohibits discriminatory "artificial, arbitrary, and unnecessary barriers to employment," 401 U.S., at 431, 91 S.Ct., at 853, that "limit * * * or classify * * * applicants for employment * * * in any way which would deprive or tend to deprive any individual of employment *opportunities*." (Emphasis added.)

* * *

The [United States] Government [as amicus curiae] argues that the test administered by the petitioners was not "used to discriminate" [within the meaning of § 703(h)] because it did not actually deprive disproportionate numbers of blacks of promotions. But the Government's reliance on § 703(h) as offering the employer some special haven for discriminatory tests is misplaced. * * * A nonjob-related test that has a disparate racial impact, and is used to "limit" or "classify" employees, is "used to discriminate" within the meaning of Title VII, whether or not it was "designed or intended" to have this effect and despite an employer's efforts to compensate for its discriminatory effect. See *Griggs*, 401 U.S., at 433, 91 S.Ct., at 854.

In sum, respondents' claim of disparate impact from the examination, a pass-fail barrier to employment opportunity, states a prima facie case of employment discrimination under § 703(a)(2), despite their employer's nondiscriminatory "bottom line," and that "bottom line" is no defense to this prima facie case under § 703(h).

* * *

Having determined that respondents' claim comes within the terms of Title VII, we must address the suggestion of petitioners and some *amici curiae* that we recognize an exception, either in the nature of an additional burden on plaintiffs seeking to establish a prima facie case or in the nature of an affirmative defense, for cases in which an employer has compensated for a discriminatory pass-fail barrier by hiring or promoting a sufficient number of black employees to reach a nondiscriminatory "bottom line." We reject this suggestion, which is in essence nothing more than a request that we redefine the protections guaranteed by Title VII.[12]

* * *

In suggesting that the "bottom line" may be a defense to a claim of discrimination against an individual employee, petitioners and *amici* appear to confuse unlawful discrimination with discriminatory intent. The Court has stated that a nondiscriminatory "bottom line" and an employer's good-faith efforts to achieve a nondiscriminatory work force, might in some cases assist an employer in rebutting the inference that particular action had been intentionally discriminatory: "Proof that [a] work force was racially balanced or that it contained a disproportionately high percentage of minority employees is not wholly irrelevant on the issue of intent when that issue is yet to be decided." *Furnco Construction Corp. v. Waters*, 438 U.S. 567, 580, 98 S.Ct. 2943, 2951, 57 L.Ed.2d 957 (1978). See also *Teamsters v. United States*, 431 U.S. 324, 340, n. 20, 97 S.Ct. 1843, 1856–1857, n. 20, 52 L.Ed.2d 396 (1977). But resolution of the factual question of intent is not what is at issue in this case. Rather, petitioners seek simply to justify discrimination against respondents on the basis of their favorable treatment of other members of respondents' racial group.

* * *

It is clear that Congress never intended to give an employer license to discriminate against some employees on the basis of race or sex merely because he favorably treats other members of the employees' group.

JUSTICE POWELL, with whom THE CHIEF JUSTICE, JUSTICE REHNQUIST, and JUSTICE O'CONNOR join, dissenting.

Today's decision takes a long and unhappy step in the direction of confusion. Title VII does not require that employers adopt merit hiring or the procedures most likely to permit the greatest number of minority members to be considered for or to qualify for jobs and promotions. See *Texas Dept. of Community Affairs v. Burdine*, 450 U.S. 248, 258–259, 101 S.Ct. 1089, 1096–1097, 67 L.Ed.2d 207 (1981); *Furnco*, 438 U.S., at 578, 98

---

[12] Petitioners suggest that we should defer to the EEOC Guidelines in this regard. But there is nothing in the Guidelines to which we might defer that would aid petitioners in this case. The most support petitioners could conceivably muster from the Uniform Guidelines on Employee Selection Procedures, 29 CFR pt. 1607 (1981) (now issued jointly by the EEOC, the Office of Personnel Management, the Department of Labor, and the Department of Justice, see 29 CFR § 1607.1A (1981)), is *neutrality* on the question whether a discriminatory barrier that does not result in a discriminatory overall result constitutes a violation of Title VII. Section 1607.4C of the Guidelines, relied upon by petitioners, states that as a matter of "*administrative and prosecutorial discretion, in usual circumstances,*" the agencies will not take enforcement action based upon the disparate impact of any component of a selection process if the total selection process results in no adverse impact. (Emphasis added.) The agencies made clear that the "guidelines do not address the underlying question of law," and that an individual "who is denied the job because of a particular component in a procedure which otherwise meets the 'bottom line' standard * * * retains the right to proceed through the appropriate agencies, and into Federal court." 43 Fed.Reg. 38291 (1978). See 29 CFR § 1607.16I (1981). * * *

S.Ct., at 2950. Employers need not develop tests that accurately reflect the skills of every individual candidate; there are few if any tests that do so. Yet the Court seems unaware of this practical reality, and perhaps oblivious to the likely consequences of its decision. By its holding today, the Court may force employers either to eliminate tests or rely on expensive, job-related, testing procedures, the validity of which may or may not be sustained if challenged. For state and local governmental employers with limited funds, the practical effect of today's decision may well be the adoption of simple quota hiring.[8] This arbitrary method of employment is itself unfair to individual applicants, whether or not they are members of minority groups. And it is not likely to produce a competent work force. Moreover, the Court's decision actually may result in employers employing *fewer* minority members.

NOTES AND QUESTIONS

Test Your Understanding of the Material

1.   What did the Court hold in *Teal* concerning the availability of a "bottom-line" defense? How did the Court justify this holding?

2.   Apply the EEOC's Four-Fifths Rule, see Note 5 infra, to the promotion test results in *Connecticut v. Teal*. Did the test have a sufficiently adverse impact to make out a prima facie violation under the disparate impact approach?

3.   Suppose that you represent an employer that has implemented a testing process that produces a disparate impact based on race or gender. What advice would you give the employer following *Connecticut v. Teal*? Can the selection process be altered so that the test can still be used as one component of a multi-component process? See Note 7 below. On the employer's burden in proving the validity of test instruments having a disparate impact, see pp. 242–245.

4.   Did Connecticut's final promotion of a disproportionate number of blacks substantially negate any inference of discriminatory intent? If so, does this indicate that the disparate impact method of proof is not simply a short cut to proof of discriminatory intent?

Related Issues

5.   *Limits of the EEOC's 80% or Four-Fifths Rule of Thumb*. In disparate-impact challenges, the EEOC and other federal agencies will regard a selection rate for a minority group that is less than 80% of the selection rate for the

---

[8]   Another possibility is that employers may integrate consideration of test results into one overall hiring decision based on that "factor" *and* additional factors. Such a process would not, even under the Court's reasoning, result in a finding of discrimination on the basis of disparate impact unless the actual hiring decisions had a disparate impact on the minority group. But if employers integrate test results into a single-step decision, they will be free to select *only* the number of minority candidates proportional to their representation in the work force. If petitioners had used this approach, they would have been able to hire substantially fewer blacks without liability on the basis of disparate impact. The Court hardly could have intended to encourage this.

group with the highest pass rate as evidence of adverse impact, at least for purposes of deciding whether to take enforcement action. See Uniform Guidelines on Employee Selection Practices ("UGESP"), 29 C.F.R. § 1607.4D. For example, a test passed by only half of the minority group, but ninety percent of other test takers, would fail the rule because fifty percent is less than four fifths of ninety percent. This rule of thumb has been criticized for failing to detect statistically significant disparities in large sample sizes, failing to consider magnitude of difference in pass rates, and sometimes producing different results when comparing fail rates. See, Elaine Shoben, Differential Pass-Fail Rates in Employment Testing: Statistical Proof Under Title VII, 91 Harv.L.Rev. 793, 805–06 ff., 810–11 (1978). The Four-Fifths Rule is principally a guide to the government in determining whether to initiate enforcement actions. Courts tend to give only limited weight to the rule when evaluating whether the plaintiff has established a prima facie case. See, e.g., Jones v. City of Boston, 752 F.3d 38, 49–53 (1st Cir. 2014) (plaintiff may demonstrate actionable disparate impact through showing of "statistical significance" without consideration of four fifths rule or any other test for "practical significance"); Isabel v. City of Memphis, 404 F.3d 404 (6th Cir. 2005) (actionable disparate impact may be demonstrated by alternative statistical analysis even when test complies with four-fifths rule).

6. *Is the Disparate-Impact Approach Limited to Certain Groups?* Do any of the possible justifications for the disparate-impact approach apply to selection criteria that disproportionately impede white males? For example, can whites challenge a municipal residency employment requirement on disparate impact grounds? See Meditz v. City of Newark, 658 F.3d 364 (3rd Cir. 2011). On the use of disparate impact to challenge practices disadvanting females, see Dothard v. Rawlinson, infra.

7. *A "Bottom Line" Defense for Multicomponent Decisionmaking?* Consider footnote 8 in Justice Powell's opinion in *Teal*. He assumes the legality of tests that form one part of a multicomponent decision. Whatever the law at the time of *Teal,* section 105 of the 1991 Act now provides that a plaintiff must "demonstrate that each particular challenged employment practice causes a disparate impact", except that where the plaintiff can demonstrate "that the elements of a respondent's decisionmaking process are not capable of separation for analysis, the decisionmaking process may be analyzed as one employment practice." Does this indicate that where a plaintiff can separate out the disparate impact of certain elements of a multicomponent process, it is sufficient to do so, regardless of any aggregate statistics that an employer can present to show a "good" bottom line? Reconsider after reading *Wards Cove Packing Co. v. Atonio*, infra, p. 216.

8. *Race Norming Prohibition of 1991 Act.* Section 106 of the 1991 Act adds a new subsection (1) to § 703 of Title VII, making it an unlawful employment practice "to adjust the scores of, use different cutoff scores for, or otherwise alter the results of, employment related tests on the basis of race, color, religion, sex, or national origin." Would Connecticut's adjustment of the passing score on its test for all candidates in order "to lessen the disparate

impact of the examination" violate § 703(*l*)? See footnote 3 in the majority opinion in *Teal*. Reconsider these questions after reading *Ricci v. DeStefano*, infra p. 261.

DOTHARD V. RAWLINSON
Supreme Court of the United States, 1977.
433 U.S. 321, 97 S.Ct. 2720, 53 L.Ed.2d 786.

JUSTICE STEWART delivered the opinion of the Court.

I

Appellee Dianne Rawlinson sought employment with the Alabama Board of Corrections as a prison guard, called in Alabama a "correctional counselor." * * *

At the time she applied for a position as correctional counselor trainee, Rawlinson was a 22-year-old college graduate whose major course of study had been correctional psychology. She was refused employment because she failed to meet the minimum 120-pound weight requirement established by an Alabama statute. The statute also establishes a height minimum of 5 feet 2 inches.[2]

* * *

II

* * *

A

The gist of the claim that the statutory height and weight requirements discriminate against women does not involve an assertion of purposeful discriminatory motive. It is asserted, rather, that these facially neutral qualification standards work in fact disproportionately to exclude women from eligibility for employment by the Alabama Board of Corrections. We dealt in *Griggs v. Duke Power Co., supra* and *Albemarle Paper Co. v. Moody*, 422 U.S. 405, 95 S.Ct. 2362, 45 L.Ed.2d 280, with similar allegations that facially neutral employment standards disproportionately excluded Negroes from employment, and those cases guide our approach here.

Those cases make clear that to establish a prima facie case of discrimination, a plaintiff need only show that the facially neutral

---

[2] The statute establishes minimum physical standards for all law enforcement officers. In pertinent part, it provides:

"(d) *Physical qualifications.*—The applicant shall be not less than five feet two inches nor more than six feet ten inches in height, shall weigh not less than 120 pounds nor more than 300 pounds and shall be certified by a licensed physician designated as satisfactory by the appointing authority as in good health and physically fit for the performance of his duties as a law-enforcement officer. The commission may for good cause shown permit variances from the physical qualifications prescribed in this subdivision." Ala.Code, Tit. 55, § 373(109) (Supp.1973).

standards in question select applicants for hire in a significantly discriminatory pattern. Once it is thus shown that the employment standards are discriminatory in effect, the employer must meet "the burden of showing that any given requirement [has] * * * a manifest relationship to the employment in question." *Griggs v. Duke Power Co., supra,* at 432, 91 S.Ct., at 854. If the employer proves that the challenged requirements are job related, the plaintiff may then show that other selection devices without a similar discriminatory effect would also "serve the employer's legitimate interest in 'efficient and trustworthy workmanship.'" *Albemarle Paper Co. v. Moody, supra,* at 425, 95 S.Ct., at 2375, quoting *McDonnell Douglas Corp. v. Green,* 411 U.S. 792, 801, 93 S.Ct. 1817, 1823, 36 L.Ed.2d 668.

Although women 14 years of age or older compose 52.75% of the Alabama population and 36.89% of its total labor force, they hold only 12.9% of its correctional counselor positions. In considering the effect of the minimum height and weight standards on this disparity in rate of hiring between the sexes, the District Court found that the 5'2"-requirement would operate to exclude 33.29% of the women in the United States between the ages of 18–79, while excluding only 1.28% of men between the same ages. The 120-pound weight restriction would exclude 22.29% of the women and 2.35% of the men in this age group. * * * Accordingly, the District Court found that Rawlinson had made out a prima facie case of unlawful sex discrimination.

The appellants argue that a showing of disproportionate impact on women based on generalized national statistics should not suffice to establish a prima facie case. They point in particular to Rawlinson's failure to adduce comparative statistics concerning actual applicants for correctional counselor positions in Alabama. There is no requirement, however, that a statistical showing of disproportionate impact must always be based on analysis of the characteristics of actual applicants. See *Griggs v. Duke Power Co., supra,* 401 U.S., at 430, 91 S.Ct., at 853. The application process might itself not adequately reflect the actual potential applicant pool, since otherwise qualified people might be discouraged from applying because of a self-recognized inability to meet the very standards challenged as being discriminatory. See *International Brotherhood of Teamsters v. United States,* 431 U.S. 324, 365–367, 97 S.Ct. 1843, 1869–1871, 52 L.Ed.2d 396. A potential applicant could easily determine her height and weight and conclude that to make an application would be futile. Moreover, reliance on general population demographic data was not misplaced where there was no reason to suppose that physical height and weight characteristics of Alabama men and women differ markedly from those of the national population.

For these reasons, we cannot say that the District Court was wrong in holding that the statutory height and weight standards had a discriminatory impact on women applicants. The plaintiffs in a case such as this are not required to exhaust every possible source of evidence, if the evidence actually presented on its face conspicuously demonstrates a job requirement's grossly discriminatory impact. If the employer discerns fallacies or deficiencies in the data offered by the plaintiff, he is free to adduce countervailing evidence of his own. In this case no such effort was made.

B

We turn, therefore, to the appellants' argument that they have rebutted the prima facie case of discrimination by showing that the height and weight requirements are job related. These requirements, they say, have a relationship to strength, a sufficient but unspecified amount of which is essential to effective job performance as a correctional counselor. In the District Court, however, the appellants produced no evidence correlating the height and weight requirements with the requisite amount of strength thought essential to good job performance. Indeed, they failed to offer evidence of any kind in specific justification of the statutory standards.

If the job-related quality that the appellants identify is bona fide, their purpose could be achieved by adopting and validating a test for applicants that measures strength directly. Such a test, fairly administered, would fully satisfy the standards of Title VII because it would be one that "measure[s] the person for the job and not the person in the abstract." *Griggs v. Duke Power Co.*, 401 U.S., at 436, 91 S.Ct., at 856. But nothing in the present record even approaches such a measurement.

MR. JUSTICE REHNQUIST, with whom THE CHIEF JUSTICE and MR. JUSTICE BLACKMUN join, concurring in the result and concurring in part.

Appellants, in order to rebut the prima facie case under the statute, had the burden placed on them to advance job-related reasons for the qualification. *McDonnell Douglas Corp. v. Green*, 411 U.S. 792, 802, 93 S.Ct. 1817, 1824, 36 L.Ed.2d 668 (1973). This burden could be shouldered by offering evidence or by making legal arguments not dependent on any new evidence. The District Court was confronted, however, with only one suggested job-related reason for the qualification—that of strength. Appellants argued only the job-relatedness of actual physical strength; they did not urge that an equally job-related qualification for prison guards is the *appearance* of strength. As the Court notes, the primary job of correctional counselor in Alabama prisons "is to maintain security and control of the inmates * * * ," a function that I at least would imagine is aided by the psychological impact on prisoners of the presence of tall and heavy guards. If the appearance of strength had been urged upon the District Court here as a reason for the height and weight minima, I think that the District Court would surely have been entitled to reach a different result than it did. For, even if not perfectly correlated, I would think that

Title VII would not preclude a State from saying that anyone under 5′2″ or 120 pounds, no matter how strong in fact, does not have a sufficient appearance of strength to be a prison guard.

NOTES AND QUESTIONS

Test Your Understanding of the Material

1.   Recall that *Griggs* justified the disparate-impact approach in part as a mechanism to "remove barriers that have operated in the past to favor an identifiable group of white employees over other employees" and to prevent employers from " 'freez[ing]' the status quo of prior discriminatory employment practices." Does *Dothard* indicate that the disparate-impact approach is not limited to the effects of prior intentional discrimination?

2.   *Dothard* permits plaintiffs to demonstrate the disparate impact of Alabama's height and weight requirements on the basis of general population statistics. It does not require evidence of a disparate impact on women who actually applied for jobs as Alabama prison guards. Why? Was there sufficient evidence of female interest in working at the prison given the fact that women filled nearly 13% of the correctional counselor positions?

3.   Justice Rehnquist, in his dissent in *Dothard,* suggests that a prison system might justify minimum size requirements by showing that regardless of their actual strength, small guards are not perceived by many prisoners as strong. What arguments or evidence might plaintiffs advance to respond to such a justification?

NEW YORK CITY TRANSIT AUTHORITY V. BEAZER

Supreme Court of the United States, 1979.
440 U.S. 568, 99 S.Ct. 1355, 59 L.Ed.2d 587.

JUSTICE STEVENS delivered the opinion of the Court.

I

The Transit Authority (TA) operates the subway system and certain bus lines in New York City. It employs about 47,000 persons, of whom many—perhaps most—are employed in positions that involve danger to themselves or to the public. For example, some 12,300 are subway motormen, towermen, conductors, or bus operators. The District Court found that these jobs are attended by unusual hazards and must be performed by "persons of maximum alertness and competence." Certain other jobs, such as operating cranes and handling high-voltage equipment, are also considered "critical" or "safety sensitive," while still others, though classified as "noncritical," have a potentially important impact on the overall operation of the transportation system.

TA enforces a general policy against employing persons who use narcotic drugs. The policy is reflected in Rule 11(b) of TA's Rules and Regulations.

> "Employees must not use, or have in their possession, narcotics, tranquilizers, drugs of the Amphetamine group or barbiturate derivatives or paraphernalia used to administer narcotics or barbiturate derivatives, except with the written permission of the Medical Director—Chief Surgeon of the System."

Methadone is regarded as a narcotic within the meaning of Rule 11(b). No written permission has ever been given by TA's medical director for the employment of a person using methadone.

The District Court found that methadone is a synthetic narcotic and a central nervous system depressant. If injected into the bloodstream with a needle, it produces essentially the same effects as heroin. Methadone has been used legitimately in at least three ways—as a pain killer, in "detoxification units" of hospitals as an immediate means of taking addicts off of heroin, and in long-range "methadone maintenance programs" as part of an intended cure for heroin addiction. See 21 CFR § 310.304(b) (1978). In such programs the methadone is taken orally in regular doses for a prolonged period. As so administered, it does not produce euphoria or any pleasurable effects associated with heroin; on the contrary, it prevents users from experiencing those effects when they inject heroin, and also alleviates the severe and prolonged discomfort otherwise associated with an addict's discontinuance of the use of heroin.

About 40,000 persons receive methadone maintenance treatment in New York City, of whom about 26,000 participate in the five major public or semipublic programs, and 14,000 are involved in about 25 private programs. The sole purpose of all these programs is to treat the addiction of persons who have been using heroin for at least two years.

* * *

The evidence indicates that methadone is an effective cure for the physical aspects of heroin addiction. But the District Court also found "that many persons attempting to overcome heroin addiction have psychological or life-style problems which reach beyond what can be cured by the physical taking of doses of methadone." The crucial indicator of successful methadone maintenance is the patient's abstinence from the illegal or excessive use of drugs and alcohol. The District Court found that the risk of reversion to drug or alcohol abuse declines dramatically after the first few months of treatment. Indeed, "the strong majority" of patients who have been on methadone maintenance for at least a year are free from illicit drug use. But a significant number are not. On this critical point, the evidence relied upon by the District Court reveals that even among participants with more than 12 months' tenure in methadone maintenance programs, the incidence of drug and alcohol abuse may often approach and even exceed 25%.

* * *

The District Court enjoined TA from denying employment to any person solely because of participation in a methadone maintenance program. Recognizing, however, the special responsibility for public safety borne by certain TA employees and the correlation between longevity in a methadone maintenance program and performance capability, the injunction authorized TA to exclude methadone users from specific categories of safety-sensitive positions and also to condition eligibility on satisfactory performance in a methadone program for at least a year. In other words, the court held that TA could lawfully adopt general rules excluding all methadone users from some jobs and a large number of methadone users from all jobs.

* * *

II

The District Court's findings do not support its conclusion that TA's regulation prohibiting the use of narcotics, or its interpretation of that regulation to encompass users of methadone, violated Title VII of the Civil Rights Act.

A prima facie violation of the Act may be established by statistical evidence showing that an employment practice has the effect of denying the members of one race equal access to employment opportunities. Even assuming that respondents have crossed this threshold, when the entire record is examined it is clear that the two statistics on which they and the District Court relied do not prove a violation of Title VII.

First, the District Court noted that 81% of the employees referred to TA's medical director for suspected violation of its narcotics rule were either black or Hispanic. But respondents have only challenged the rule to the extent that it is construed to apply to methadone users, and that statistic tells us nothing about the racial composition of the employees suspected of using methadone. Nor does the record give us any information about the number of black, Hispanic, or white persons who were dismissed for using methadone.

Second, the District Court noted that about 63% of the persons in New York City receiving methadone maintenance in *public* programs—*i.e.,* 63% of the 65% of all New York City methadone users who are in such programs—are black or Hispanic. We do not know, however, how many of these persons ever worked or sought to work for TA. This statistic therefore reveals little if anything about the racial composition of the class of TA job applicants and employees receiving methadone treatment. More particularly, it tells us nothing about the class of otherwise-qualified applicants and employees who have participated in methadone maintenance programs for over a year—the only class improperly excluded by TA's policy under the District Court's analysis. The record demonstrates, in fact, that the figure is virtually irrelevant because a substantial portion of the persons included in it are either unqualified for other reasons—such as the illicit use of drugs and alcohol—or have received successful assistance in finding jobs with employers other than TA.[29] Finally, we have absolutely no data on the 14,000 methadone users in the *private* programs, leaving open the possibility that the percentage of blacks and Hispanics in the class of methadone users is not significantly greater than the percentage of those minorities in the general population of New York City.[30]

At best, respondents' statistical showing is weak; even if it is capable of establishing a prima facie case of discrimination, it is assuredly rebutted by TA's demonstration that its narcotics rule (and the rule's application to methadone users) is "job related."[31] The District Court's express finding that the rule was not motivated by racial animus forecloses any claim in rebuttal that it was merely a pretext for intentional discrimination. We conclude that respondents failed to prove a violation of Title VII.

[*Eds.* Justice White argued in dissent that plaintiffs had established a prima facie impact case by showing that about 63% of methadone users in the New York City area are black or Hispanic, whereas such groups comprise only 20% of the population. Hence, "blacks and Hispanics suffer three times as much from the operation of the challenged rule excluding methadone users as one would expect from a neutral practice." He rejected the majority's seeming insistence on applicant data because defendants had refused to allow discovery of the makeup of the applicant pool. In any case, methadone users do apply for jobs with the Transit Authority and 5%

---

[29] Although "a statistical showing of disproportionate impact [need not] always be based on an analysis of the characteristics of actual applicants," *Dothard v. Rawlinson,* 433 U.S. 321, 330, 97 S.Ct. 2720, 2727, 53 L.Ed.2d 786, "evidence showing that the figures for the general population might not accurately reflect the pool of qualified job applicants" undermines the significance of such figures. *Teamsters v. United States, supra,* 431 U.S., at 340 n. 20, 97 S.Ct., at 1857 n. 20.

[30] If all of the participants in private clinics are white, for example, then only about 40% of all methadone users would be black or Hispanic—compared to the 36.3% of the total population of New York City that was black or Hispanic as of the 1970 census. Assuming instead that the percentage of those minorities in the private programs duplicates their percentage in the population of New York City, the figures would still only show that 50% of all methadone users are black or Hispanic compared to 36.3% of the population in the metropolitan area. (The 20% figure relied upon by the dissent refers to blacks and Hispanics in the work force, rather than in the total population of the New York City metropolitan area. The reason the total-population figure is the appropriate one is because the 63% figure relied upon by respondents refers to methadone users in the population generally and not just those in the work force.)

[31] Respondents recognize, and the findings of the District Court establish, that TA's legitimate employment goals of safety and efficiency require the exclusion of all users of illegal narcotics, barbiturates, and amphetamines, and of a majority of all methadone users. The District Court also held that those goals require the exclusion of all methadone users from the 25% of its positions that are "safety sensitive." Finally, the District Court noted that those goals are significantly served by—even if they do not require—TA's rule as it applies to all methadone users including those who are seeking employment in nonsafety-sensitive positions. The record thus demonstrates that TA's rule bears a "manifest relationship to the employment in question." *Griggs v. Duke Power Co.,* 401 U.S. 424, 432, 91 S.Ct. 849, 854, 28 L.Ed.2d 158. See *Albemarle Paper Co. v. Moody,* 422 U.S. 405, 425, 95 S.Ct. 2362, 2375, 45 L.Ed.2d 280. Whether or not respondents' weak showing was sufficient to establish a prima facie case, it clearly failed to carry respondents' ultimate burden of proving a violation of Title VII.

of all applicants are rejected because of the challenged rule. Justice White thus maintained that in the absence of a convincing showing by defendants, there was no reason to adopt the inference that black or Hispanic methadone users would apply with less frequency, or would be less likely to succeed on methadone, than methadone users generally. Disputing the majority's assertion, the dissent contended that the studies relied upon by the District Court did include public as well as private methadone clinics. Finally, Justice White argued that defendants had failed to demonstrate business necessity:

> "Petitioners had the burden of showing job relatedness. They did not show that the rule results in a higher quality labor force, that such a labor force is necessary, or that the cost of making individual decisions about those on methadone was prohibitive. * * * I think it insufficient that the rule as a whole has some relationship to employment so long as a readily identifiable and severable part of it does not."

440 U.S. at 602.]

NOTES AND QUESTIONS

Test Your Understanding of the Material

1. In what respects did the Court find the plaintiff's evidence of disparate impact in *Beazer* deficient?

2. How might you reconcile *Dothard*, which permitted the use of general population data, with *Beazer*, where the Court discounts plaintiffs' evidence concerning the representation of black and Hispanic patients in methadone treatment programs in New York?

3. Section 105 of the Civil Rights Act of 1991 adds a new provision to Title VII, § 703(k)(3), which limits the use of disparate-impact analysis in challenges to bars to the employment of individuals who "currently and knowingly use" controlled substances. How would this provision apply to the challenge in *Beazer*? See also 42 U.S.C. § 12114 ("employee or applicant who is currently engaging in the illegal use of drugs" not covered by the Americans with Disabilities Act).

Related Issues

4. *EEOC Guidance on Arrest and Conviction Records*. In 2012, the EEOC updated its guidance on the use of arrest and conviction records for employment decisions. EEOC Enforcement Guidance No. 915.002 (April 25, 2012). Relying on Green v. Missouri Pacific Railroad, 549 F.2d 1158 (9th Cir. 1977), this guidance states that employers should provide an individualized assessment that takes into account the nature of the crime, the time elapsed, and the nature of the job. However, the EEOC has not had much success in enforcement actions challenging the use of arrest and conviction records. See

EEOC v. Peoplemark, Inc., 732 F.3d 584 (6th Cir. 2013); EEOC v. Freeman, 778 F.3d 463 (4th Cir. 2015).

A small but growing number of states have prohibited employers from inquiring about arrests or convictions at the initial stage of the employee selection process. For more on this issue, see Chapter 16 at p. 774.

WATSON V. FORT WORTH BANK AND TRUST
Supreme Court of the United States, 1988.
487 U.S. 977, 108 S.Ct. 2777, 101 L.Ed.2d 827.

JUSTICE O'CONNOR delivered the judgment of the Court and the opinion of the Court as to [the part reprinted below:]

This case requires us to decide what evidentiary standards should be applied under Title VII of the Civil Rights Act of 1964, 78 Stat. 253, as amended, 42 U.S.C. § 2000e *et seq.*, in determining whether an employer's practice of committing promotion decisions to the subjective discretion of supervisory employees has led to illegal discrimination.

Petitioner Clara Watson, who is black, was hired by respondent Fort Worth Bank and Trust (the Bank) as a proof operator in August 1973. In January 1976, Watson was promoted to a position as teller in the Bank's drive-in facility. In February 1980, she sought to become supervisor of the tellers in the main lobby; a white male, however, was selected for this job. Watson then sought a position as supervisor of the drive-in bank, but this position was given to a white female. In February 1981, after Watson had served for about a year as a commercial teller in the Bank's main lobby, and informally as assistant to the supervisor of tellers, the man holding that position was promoted. Watson applied for the vacancy, but the white female who was the supervisor of the drive-in bank was selected instead. Watson then applied for the vacancy created at the drive-in; a white male was selected for that job. The Bank, which has about 80 employees, had not developed precise and formal criteria for evaluating candidates for the positions for which Watson unsuccessfully applied. It relied instead on the subjective judgment of supervisors who were acquainted with the candidates and with the nature of the jobs to be filled. All the supervisors involved in denying Watson the four promotions at issue were white.

* * *

The District Court addressed Watson's individual claims under the evidentiary standards that apply in a discriminatory treatment case. See *McDonnell Douglas Corp. v. Green*, 411 U.S. 792, 93 S.Ct. 1817, 36 L.Ed.2d 668 (1973), and *Texas Department of Community Affairs v. Burdine*, 450 U.S. 248, 101 S.Ct. 1089, 67 L.Ed.2d 207 (1981). It concluded, on the evidence presented at trial, that Watson had established a prima facie case of employment discrimination, but that the Bank had met its rebuttal burden by presenting legitimate and nondiscriminatory reasons for each of the challenged promotion decisions. The court also concluded that Watson had failed to show that these reasons were pretexts for racial discrimination. Accordingly, the action was dismissed.

* * *

Watson argued that the District Court had erred in failing to apply "disparate impact" analysis to her claims of discrimination in promotion. Relying on Fifth Circuit precedent, the majority of the Court of Appeals panel held that "a Title VII challenge to an allegedly discretionary promotion system is properly analyzed under the disparate treatment model rather than the disparate impact model." Other Courts of Appeals have held that disparate impact analysis may be applied to hiring or promotion systems that involve the use of "discretionary" or "subjective" criteria.

* * *

We are persuaded that our decisions in *Griggs* and succeeding cases could largely be nullified if disparate impact analysis were applied only to standardized selection practices. However one might distinguish "subjective" from "objective" criteria, it is apparent that selection systems that combine both types would generally have to be considered subjective in nature. Thus, for example, if the employer in *Griggs* had consistently preferred applicants who had a high school diploma and who passed the company's general aptitude test, its selection system could nonetheless have been considered "subjective" if it also included brief interviews with the candidates. So long as an employer refrained from making standardized criteria absolutely determinative, it would remain free to give such tests almost as much weight as it chose without risking a disparate impact challenge. If we announced a rule that allowed employers so easily to insulate themselves from liability under *Griggs*, disparate impact analysis might effectively be abolished.

We are also persuaded that disparate impact analysis is in principle no less applicable to subjective employment criteria than to objective or standardized tests. In either case, a facially neutral practice, adopted without discriminatory intent, may have effects that are indistinguishable from intentionally discriminatory practices. It is true, to be sure, that an employer's policy of leaving promotion decisions to the unchecked discretion of lower level supervisors should itself raise no inference of discriminatory conduct. Especially in relatively small businesses like respondent's, it may be customary and quite reasonable simply to delegate employment decisions to those employees who are most familiar with the jobs to be filled and with the candidates for those jobs. It does not follow, however, that the particular supervisors to whom this discretion is delegated always act without discriminatory intent. Furthermore, even if one assumed that any such discrimination can be adequately policed through disparate treatment analysis, the problem of subconscious stereotypes and prejudices would remain. In this case, for example, petitioner was apparently told at one point that the teller position was a big responsibility with "a lot of money * * * for blacks to have to count." Such remarks may not prove discriminatory intent, but they do suggest a lingering form of the problem that Title VII was enacted to combat. If an employer's undisciplined system of subjective decisionmaking has precisely the same effects as a system pervaded by impermissible intentional discrimination, it is difficult to see why Title VII's proscription against discriminatory actions should not apply. In both circumstances, the employer's practices may be said to "adversely affect [an individual's] status as an employee, because of such individual's race, color, religion, sex, or national origin." 42 U.S.C. § 2000e–2(a)(2). We conclude, accordingly, that subjective or discretionary employment practices may be analyzed under the disparate impact approach in appropriate cases.

[*Eds*. That part of JUSTICE O'CONNOR's opinion that was joined in by only a plurality of the Court, as well as the separate concurring opinions of JUSTICES BLACKMUN and STEVENS, are omitted.]

NOTES AND QUESTIONS

Test Your Understanding of the Material

1. The Court in *Watson* held that "subjective or discretionary employment practices" may be challenged under the disparate-impact approach. What distinguishes such practices from "objective" standards like those challenged in the disparate-impact cases previously decided by the Court? Note that Watson was challenging the process of delegating promotion decisions to the discretion of supervisors, rather than the particular subjective criteria that the supervisors were using in that process. How would the *Watson* case be structured after the enactment of § 703(k)?

2. Is a systemic disparate-treatment challenge, see p. 147, available on the facts in *Watson*? How is the inquiry different than in a disparate-impact case? How could the two modes of analysis be used in the same case?

Related Issues

3. *Can Subjective Decisionmaking Mask Intentional Discrimination?* In EEOC v. Joe's Stone Crab, Inc., 136 F.Supp.2d 1311 (S.D. Fla.2001) (decision on remand affirmed in relevant part, 296 F.3d 1265 (11th Cir.2002)), the court of appeals vacated the trial court's finding in an earlier phase that the employer-restaurant's undirected delegation of hiring authority had an unjustified disparate impact on women, but remanded for reconsideration of whether the manner of implementation of the delegated authority warranted a finding of disparate treatment. The appeals court indicated that if the discretionary hiring policy was in fact tainted by sex-based stereotypes, it should be treated as intentionally discriminatory.

4. *Influence of Implicit Bias on Subjective Decisionmaking.* Drawing on studies by cognitive and social psychologists, commentators have argued that discrimination often results from the subconscious use of stereotypes.

Linda H. Krieger, The Content of Our Categories: A Cognitive Bias Approach to Discrimination and Equal Employment Opportunity, 47 Stan. L.Rev. 1161 (1995); see Symposium on Behavioral Realism, 94 Calif. L. Rev. 945 (2006); Melissa Hart, Subjective Decisionmaking and Unconscious Discrimination, 56 Ala. L. Rev. 741 (2005). The "implicit bias" literature, and the "Implied Associatioin Test" on which is it is based, is challenged in Hart Blanton et al., Strong Claims and Weak Evidence: Reassessing the Predictive Validity of the IA, 94 J. App. Psych. 567 (No. 3, 2009).

5. *Proving Disparate Impact of Subjective Employment Practices on a Classwide Basis*. In *Wal-Mart v. Dukes*, excerpted at 968 to 979 infra, a class of 1.5 million women brought a disparate impact and pattern or practice claim against Wal-Mart for its pay and promotion practices. The lawsuit challenged Wal-Mart's policy of giving local managers discretion over pay and promotions, which was "exercised in a largely subjective manner." The Supreme Court ruled that the case should not have been certified as a class action because the plaintiff did not allege a common policy or practice that affected class members in the same way. Writing for the majority, Justice Scalia reasoned,

> "[L]eft to their own devices most managers in any corporation—and surely most managers in a corporation that forbids sex discrimination—would select sex-neutral, performance-based criteria for hiring and promotion that produce no actionable disparity at all. Others may choose to reward various attributes that produce disparate impact—such as scores on general aptitude tests or educational achievements, see Griggs v. Duke Power Co., 401 U.S. 424, 431–432, 91 S. Ct. 849, 28 L. Ed. 2d 158 (1971). And still other managers may be guilty of intentional discrimination that produces a sex-based disparity."

See generally Elizabeth Tippett, Robbing a Barren Vault: The Implications of Dukes v. Wal-Mart for Cases Challenging Subjective Employment Practices, 29 Hofstra Lab. & Emp. L.J. 433 (2012); Michael C. Harper, Class-Based Adjudication in the Age of the Roberts Court, 95 B. U. L. Rev. 1099 (2015).

6. *Challenge to "Word of Mouth" and Other Informal Hiring Processes*. In EEOC v. Chicago Miniature Lamp Works, 947 F.2d 292, 305 (7th Cir.1991), the court held that the EEOC could not use disparate-impact analysis to challenge an employer's reliance on unsolicited employment applications, apparently generated by word-of-mouth publication of employment opportunities by the predominantly nonblack workforce. The court stressed that the employer had simply been passive and had not actively encouraged its incumbent employees to find other workers. Cf. Gaines v. Boston Herald, Inc., 998 F.Supp. 91 (D.Mass.1998) (distinguishing active nepotism from *Chicago Lamp*). Under 703(k) is an employer's "passive" acceptance of employee recruitment efforts an employment practice subject to disparate impact challenge?

WARDS COVE PACKING CO., INC. V. ATONIO

Supreme Court of the United States, 1989.
490 U.S. 642, 109 S.Ct. 2115, 104 L.Ed.2d 733.

JUSTICE WHITE delivered the opinion of the Court.

I

The claims before us are disparate-impact claims, involving the employment practices of petitioners, two companies that operate salmon canneries in remote and widely separated areas of Alaska. The canneries operate only during the salmon runs in the summer months. They are inoperative and vacant for the rest of the year. * * *

The length and size of salmon runs vary from year to year and hence the number of employees needed at each cannery also varies. Estimates are made as early in the winter as possible; the necessary employees are hired, and when the time comes, they are transported to the canneries. Salmon must be processed soon after they are caught, and the work during the canning season is therefore intense. For this reason, and because the canneries are located in remote regions, all workers are housed at the canneries and have their meals in company-owned mess halls.

Jobs at the canneries are of two general types: "cannery jobs" on the cannery line, which are unskilled positions; and "noncannery jobs," which fall into a variety of classifications. Most noncannery jobs are classified as skilled positions.[3] Cannery jobs are filled predominantly by nonwhites, Filipinos and Alaska Natives. The Filipinos are hired through and dispatched by Local 37 of the International Longshoremen Workers Union pursuant to a hiring hall agreement with the Local. The Alaska Natives primarily reside in villages near the remote cannery locations. Noncannery jobs are filled with predominantly white workers, who are hired during the winter months from the companies' offices in Washington and Oregon. Virtually all of the noncannery jobs pay more than cannery positions. The predominantly white noncannery workers and the predominantly nonwhite cannery employees live in separate dormitories and eat in separate mess halls.

In 1974, respondents, a class of nonwhite cannery workers who were (or had been) employed at the canneries, brought this Title VII action against petitioners. Respondents alleged that a variety of petitioners' hiring/promotion practices—e.g., nepotism, a rehire preference, a lack of objective hiring criteria, separate hiring channels, a practice of not promoting from within—were responsible for the racial stratification of the

---

[3]   The noncannery jobs were described as follows by the Court of Appeals: "Machinists and engineers are hired to maintain the smooth and continuous operation of the canning equipment. Quality control personnel conduct the FDA-required inspections and recordkeeping. Tenders are staffed with a crew necessary to operate the vessel. A variety of support personnel are employed to operate the entire cannery community, including, for example, cooks, carpenters, store-keepers, bookkeepers, beach gangs for dock yard labor and construction, etc."

work force, and had denied them and other nonwhites employment as noncannery workers on the basis of race. Respondents also complained of petitioners' racially segregated housing and dining facilities. All of respondents' claims were advanced under both the disparate-treatment and disparate-impact theories of Title VII liability.

The District Court held a bench trial, after which it entered 172 findings of fact. It then rejected all of respondents' disparate-treatment claims. It also rejected the disparate-impact challenges involving the subjective employment criteria used by petitioners to fill these noncannery positions, on the ground that those criteria were not subject to attack under a disparate-impact theory. Petitioner's "objective" employment practices (*e.g.,* an English language requirement, alleged nepotism in hiring, failure to post noncannery openings, the rehire preference, etc.) were found to be subject to challenge under the disparate-impact theory, but these claims were rejected for failure of proof. Judgment was entered for petitioners.

On appeal, a panel of the Ninth Circuit affirmed, but that decision was vacated when the Court of Appeals agreed to hear the case en banc. * * *

On remand, the panel applied the en banc ruling to the facts of this case. It held that respondents had made out a prima facie case of disparate-impact in hiring for both skilled and unskilled noncannery positions. The panel remanded the case for further proceedings, instructing the District Court that it was the employer's burden to prove that any disparate impact caused by its hiring and employment practices was justified by business necessity. Neither the en banc court nor the panel disturbed the District Court's rejection of the disparate-treatment claims.

* * *

II

In holding that respondents had made out a prima facie case of disparate impact, the court of appeals relied solely on respondents' statistics showing a high percentage of nonwhite workers in the cannery jobs and a low percentage of such workers in the noncannery positions. Although statistical proof can alone make out a prima facie case, see *Teamsters v. United States*, 431 U.S. 324, 339, 97 S.Ct. 1843, 1856, 52 L.Ed.2d 396 (1977); *Hazelwood School Dist. v. United States*, 433 U.S. 299, 307–308, 97 S.Ct. 2736, 2741–2742, 53 L.Ed.2d 768 (1977), the Court of Appeals' ruling here misapprehends our precedents and the purposes of Title VII, and we therefore reverse.

"There can be no doubt," as there was when a similar mistaken analysis had been undertaken by the courts below in *Hazelwood, supra*, at 308, 97 S.Ct., at 2741, "that the * * * comparison * * * fundamentally misconceived the role of statistics in employment discrimination cases." The "proper comparison [is] between the racial composition of [the at-issue jobs] and the racial composition of the qualified * * * population in the relevant labor market." *Ibid.* It is such a comparison—between the racial composition of the qualified persons in the labor market and the persons holding at-issue jobs—that generally forms the proper basis for the initial inquiry in a disparate impact case. Alternatively, in cases where such labor market statistics will be difficult if not impossible to ascertain, we have recognized that certain other statistics—such as measures indicating the racial composition of "otherwise-qualified applicants" for at-issue jobs—are equally probative for this purpose. See, *e.g., New York City Transit Authority v. Beazer*, 440 U.S. 568, 585, 99 S.Ct. 1355, 1366, 59 L.Ed.2d 587 (1979).[6]

It is clear to us that the Court of Appeals' acceptance of the comparison between the racial composition of the cannery work force and that of the noncannery work force, as probative of a prima facie case of disparate impact in the selection of the latter group of workers, was flawed for several reasons. Most obviously, with respect to the skilled noncannery jobs at issue here, the cannery work force in no way reflected "the pool of *qualified* job applicants" or the "*qualified* population in the labor force." Measuring alleged discrimination in the selection of accountants, managers, boat captains, electricians, doctors, and engineers—and the long list of other "skilled" noncannery positions found to exist by the District Court—by comparing the number of nonwhites occupying these jobs to the number of nonwhites filling cannery worker positions is nonsensical. If the absence of minorities holding such skilled positions is due to a dearth of qualified nonwhite applicants (for reasons that are not petitioners' fault),[7] petitioners' selection methods or employment practices cannot be said to have had a "disparate impact" on nonwhites.

* * *

* * * The Court of Appeals' theory, at the very least, would mean that any employer who had a segment of his work force that was—for some reason—racially imbalanced, could be haled into court and forced to engage in the expensive and time-consuming task of defending the "business necessity" of the methods used to select the other members of his work force. The only practicable option for many employers will be to adopt racial quotas, insuring that no portion of his [sic] work force deviates in racial composition from the other portions thereof; this is a result that Congress expressly rejected in drafting Title VII. See 42 U.S.C. § 2000e–2(j). * * *

---

[6] In fact, where "figures for the general population might * * * accurately reflect the pool of qualified job applicants," cf. *Teamsters v. United States*, 431 U.S. 324, 340, n. 20, 97 S.Ct. 1843, 1856 n. 20, 52 L.Ed.2d 396 (1977), we have even permitted plaintiffs to rest their prima facie cases on such statistics as well. See, *e.g., Dothard v. Rawlinson*, 433 U.S. 321, 329–330, 97 S.Ct. 2720, 2726, 53 L.Ed.2d 786 (1977).

[7] Obviously, the analysis would be different if it were found that the dearth of qualified nonwhite applicants was due to practices on petitioner's part which—expressly or implicitly— deterred minority group members from applying for noncannery positions. See, *e.g., Teamsters v. United States, supra*, 431 U.S., at 365, 97 S.Ct., at 1869.

The Court of Appeals also erred with respect to the unskilled noncannery positions. Racial imbalance in one segment of an employer's work force does not, without more, establish a prima facie case of disparate impact with respect to the selection of workers for the employer's other positions, even where workers for the different positions may have somewhat fungible skills (as is arguably the case for cannery and unskilled noncannery workers). As long as there are no barriers or practices deterring qualified nonwhites from applying for noncannery positions, if the percentage of selected applicants who are nonwhite is not significantly less than the percentage of qualified applicants who are nonwhite, the employer's selection mechanism probably does not operate with a disparate impact on minorities.[8] Where this is the case, the percentage of nonwhite workers found in other positions in the employer's labor force is irrelevant to the question of a prima facie statistical case of disparate impact. As noted above, a contrary ruling on this point would almost inexorably lead to the use of numerical quotas in the workplace, a result that Congress and this Court have rejected repeatedly in the past.

* * *

The peculiar facts of this case further illustrate why a comparison between the percentage of nonwhite cannery workers and nonwhite noncannery workers is an improper basis for making out a claim of disparate impact. Here, the District Court found that nonwhites were "overrepresent[ed]" among cannery workers because petitioners had contracted with a predominantly nonwhite union (Local 37) to fill these positions. As a result, if petitioners (for some permissible reason) ceased using Local 37 as its hiring channel for cannery positions, it appears (according to the District Court's findings) that the racial stratification between the cannery and noncannery workers might diminish to statistical insignificance. Under the Court of Appeals' approach, therefore, it is possible that *with no change whatsoever* in their hiring practices for noncannery workers—the jobs at-issue in this lawsuit—petitioners could make respondents' prima facie case of disparate impact "disappear."

* * *

III

Since the statistical disparity relied on by the Court of Appeals did not suffice to make out a prima facie case, any inquiry by us into whether the specific challenged employment practices of petitioners caused that

---

[8]   We qualify this conclusion—observing that it is only "probable" that there has been no disparate impact on minorities in such circumstances—because bottom-line racial balance is not a defense under Title VII. See *Connecticut v. Teal*, 457 U.S. 440, 102 S.Ct. 2525, 73 L.Ed.2d 130 (1982). Thus, even if petitioners could show that the percentage of selected applicants who are nonwhite is not significantly less than the percentage of qualified applicants who are nonwhite, respondents would still have a case under Title VII, if they could prove that some particular hiring practice has a disparate impact on minorities, notwithstanding the bottom-line racial balance in petitioners' workforce. See *Teal, supra*, at 450, 102 S.Ct., at 2532 * * * .

disparity is pretermitted, as is any inquiry into whether the disparate impact that any employment practice may have had was justified by business considerations. Because we remand for further proceedings, however, on whether a prima facie case of disparate impact has been made in defensible fashion in this case, we address two other challenges petitioners have made to the decision of the Court of Appeals.

A

First is the question of causation in a disparate-impact case. The law in this respect was correctly stated by Justice O'Connor's opinion (for a plurality of the Court) last Term in *Watson v. Fort Worth Bank & Trust*, 487 U.S., at 994, 108 S.Ct., at 2788:

> "[W]e note that the plaintiff's burden in establishing a prima facie case goes beyond the need to show that there are statistical disparities in the employer's work force. The plaintiff must begin by identifying the specific employment practice that is challenged * * * . Especially in cases where an employer combines subjective criteria with the use of more rigid standardized rules or tests, the plaintiff is in our view responsible for isolating and identifying the specific employment practices that are allegedly responsible for any observed statistical disparities."

* * *

Our disparate-impact cases have always focused on the impact of *particular* hiring practices on employment opportunities for minorities. Just as an employer cannot escape liability under Title VII by demonstrating that, "at the bottom line," his work force is racially balanced (where particular hiring practices may operate to deprive minorities of employment opportunities), see *Connecticut v. Teal*, 457 U.S., at 450, 102 S.Ct., at 2532, a Title VII plaintiff does not make out a case of disparate impact simply by showing that, "at the bottom line," there is racial *imbalance* in the work force. As a general matter, a plaintiff must demonstrate that it is the application of a specific or particular employment practice that has created the disparate impact under attack. Such a showing is an integral part of the plaintiff's prima facie case in a disparate-impact suit under Title VII.

Here, respondents have alleged that several "objective" employment practices (*e.g.*, nepotism, separate hiring channels, rehire preferences), as well as the use of "subjective decision making" to select noncannery workers, have had a disparate impact on nonwhites. Respondents base this claim on statistics that allegedly show a disproportionately low percentage of nonwhites in the at-issue positions. However, even if on remand respondents can show that nonwhites are underrepresented in the at-issue jobs in a manner that is acceptable under the standards set forth in Part II, *supra*, this alone will *not* suffice to make out a prima facie case of disparate impact. Respondents will also have to demonstrate that the disparity they complain of is the result of one or more of the employment practices that they are attacking here, specifically showing that each challenged practice has a significantly disparate impact on employment opportunities for whites and nonwhites. To hold otherwise would result in employers being potentially liable for "the myriad of innocent causes that may lead to statistical imbalances in the composition of their work forces." *Watson v. Fort Worth Bank & Trust, supra*, 487 U.S., at 992, 108 S.Ct., at 2787 (plurality opinion).

Some will complain that this specific causation requirement is unduly burdensome on Title VII plaintiffs. But liberal civil discovery rules give plaintiffs broad access to employers' records in an effort to document their claims. Also, employers falling within the scope of the Uniform Guidelines on Employee Selection Procedures, 29 CFR § 1607.1 *et seq.* (1988), are required to "maintain * * * records or other information which will disclose the impact which its tests and other selection procedures have upon employment opportunities of persons by identifiable race, sex, or ethnic group[s.]" See § 1607.4(A). This includes records concerning "the individual components of the selection process" where there is a significant disparity in the selection rates of whites and nonwhites. See § 1607.4(C). Plaintiffs as a general matter will have the benefit of these tools to meet their burden of showing a causal link between challenged employment practices and racial imbalances in the work force; respondents presumably took full advantage of these opportunities to build their case before the trial in the District Court was held.[10]

* * *

B

If, on remand, respondents meet the proof burdens outlined above, and establish a prima facie case of disparate impact with respect to any of petitioners' employment practices, the case will shift to any business justification petitioners offer for their use of these practices. This phase of the disparate-impact case contains two components: first, a consideration of the justifications an employer offers for his use of these practices; and second, the availability of alternate practices to achieve the same business ends, with less racial impact. See, *e.g., Albemarle Paper Co. v. Moody*, 422 U.S., [405], 425, 95 S.Ct., [2362,] 2375 [(1975)]. We consider these two components in turn.

(1)

Though we have phrased the query differently in different cases, it is generally well-established that at the justification stage of such a disparate

---

[10] Of course, petitioners' obligation to collect or retain any of these data may be limited by the Guidelines themselves. See 29 CFR § 1602.14(b) (1988) (exempting "seasonal" jobs from certain record-keeping requirements).

impact case, the dispositive issue is whether a challenged practice serves, in a significant way, the legitimate employment goals of the employer. See, *e.g., Watson v. Fort Worth Bank & Trust Co.,* 487 U.S., at 997, 108 S.Ct., at 2790; *New York Transit Authority v. Beazer,* 440 U.S., at 587, n. 31, 99 S.Ct., at 1366, n. 31; *Griggs v. Duke Power Co.,* 401 U.S., at 432, 91 S.Ct., at 854. The touchstone of this inquiry is a reasoned review of the employer's justification for his use of the challenged practice. A mere insubstantial justification in this regard will not suffice, because such a low standard of review would permit discrimination to be practiced through the use of spurious, seemingly neutral employment practices. At the same time, though, there is no requirement that the challenged practice be "essential" or "indispensable" to the employer's business for it to pass muster: this degree of scrutiny would be almost impossible for most employers to meet, and would result in a host of evils we have identified above.

In this phase, the employer carries the burden of producing evidence of a business justification for his employment practice. The burden of persuasion, however, remains with the disparate-impact plaintiff. * * * This rule conforms with the usual method for allocating persuasion and production burdens in the federal courts, see Fed. Rule Evid. 301, and more specifically, it conforms to the rule in disparate-treatment cases that the plaintiff bears the burden of disproving an employer's assertion that the adverse employment action or practice was based solely on a legitimate neutral consideration. See *Texas Dept. of Community Affairs v. Burdine,* 450 U.S. 248, 256–258, 101 S.Ct. 1089, 1095–1096, 67 L.Ed.2d 207 (1981). We acknowledge that some of our earlier decisions can be read as suggesting otherwise. See *Watson, supra,* 487 U.S., at 1001, 108 S.Ct., at 2794 (Blackmun, J., concurring). But to the extent that those cases speak of an employers' "burden of proof" with respect to a legitimate business justification defense, see, *e.g., Dothard v. Rawlinson,* 433 U.S. 321, 329, 97 S.Ct. 2720, 2726, 53 L.Ed.2d 786 (1977), they should have been understood to mean an employer's production—but not persuasion—burden. Cf., *e.g., NLRB v. Transportation Management Corp.,* 462 U.S. 393, 404, n. 7, 103 S.Ct. 2469, 2475, n. 7, 76 L.Ed.2d 667 (1983). The persuasion burden here must remain with the plaintiff, for it is he who must prove that it was "because of such individual's race, color," etc., that he was denied a desired employment opportunity. See 42 U.S.C. § 2000e–2(a).

(2)

Finally, if on remand the case reaches this point, and respondents cannot persuade the trier of fact on the question of petitioners' business necessity defense, respondents may still be able to prevail. To do so, respondents will have to persuade the factfinder that "other tests or selection devices, without a similarly undesirable racial effect, would also serve the employer's legitimate [hiring] interest[s]"; by so demonstrating, respondents would prove that "[petitioners were] using [their] tests merely as a 'pretext' for discrimination." *Albemarle Paper Co., supra,* 422 U.S., at 425, 95 S.Ct., at 2375; see also *Watson,* 487 U.S., at 998, 108 S.Ct., at 2779 (O'Connor, J.); *id.,* at 1003, 108 S.Ct., at 2781 (Blackmun, J.). If respondents, having established a prima facie case, come forward with alternatives to petitioners' hiring practices that reduce the racially-disparate impact of practices currently being used, and petitioners refuse to adopt these alternatives, such a refusal would belie a claim by petitioners that their incumbent practices are being employed for nondiscriminatory reasons.

Of course, any alternative practices which respondents offer up in this respect must be equally effective as petitioners' chosen hiring procedures in achieving petitioners' legitimate employment goals. Moreover, "[f]actors such as the cost or other burdens of proposed alternative selection devices are relevant in determining whether they would be equally as effective as the challenged practice in serving the employer's legitimate business goals." *Watson, supra,* at 998, 108 S.Ct., at 2790 (O'Connor, J.). "Courts are generally less competent than employers to restructure business practices," *Furnco Construction Corp. v. Waters,* 438 U.S. 567, 578, 98 S.Ct. 2943, 2950, 57 L.Ed.2d 957 (1978); consequently, the judiciary should proceed with care before mandating that an employer must adopt a plaintiff's alternate selection or hiring practice in response to a Title VII suit.

JUSTICE STEVENS, with whom JUSTICE BRENNAN, JUSTICE MARSHALL, and JUSTICE BLACKMUN join, dissenting.

* * * [T]he Court announces that our frequent statements that the employer shoulders the burden of proof respecting business necessity "should have been understood to mean an employer's production—but not persuasion—burden." Our opinions always have emphasized that in a disparate impact case the employer's burden is weighty. "The touchstone," the Court said in *Griggs,* "is business necessity." 401 U.S., at 431, 91 S.Ct., at 853. Later, we held that prison administrators had failed to "rebu[t] the prima facie case of discrimination by showing that the height and weight requirements are * * * essential to effective job performance," *Dothard v. Rawlinson,* 433 U.S. 321, 331, 97 S.Ct. 2720, 2727, 53 L.Ed.2d 786 (1977). I am thus astonished to read that the "touchstone of this inquiry is a reasoned review of the employer's justification for his use of the challenged practice * * * . [T]here is no requirement that the challenged practice be * * * 'essential.' " * * *

* * *

Petitioners contend that the relevant labor market in this case is the general population of the " 'external' labor market for the jobs at issue." While they would rely on the District Court's findings in this regard, those findings are ambiguous. At one point the District Court specifies "Alaska, the Pacific Northwest, and California" as "the geographical region from which [petitioners] draw their employees," but its next finding refers to "this relevant geographical area for cannery worker, laborer, and other nonskilled jobs." There is no express finding of the relevant labor market for noncannery jobs.

Even assuming that the District Court properly defined the relevant geographical area, its apparent assumption that the population in that area constituted the "available labor supply," is not adequately founded. An undisputed requirement for employment either as a cannery or noncannery worker is availability for seasonal employment in the far reaches of Alaska. Many noncannery workers, furthermore, must be available for preseason work. Yet the record does not identify the portion of the general population in Alaska, California, and the Pacific Northwest that would accept this type of employment. This deficiency respecting a crucial job qualification diminishes the usefulness of petitioners' statistical evidence. In contrast, respondents' evidence, comparing racial compositions within the work force, identifies a pool of workers willing to work during the relevant times and familiar with the workings of the industry. Surely this is more probative than the untailored general population statistics on which petitioners focus. Cf. *Hazelwood*, 433 U.S., at 308, n. 13, 97 S.Ct., at 2742, n. 13; *Teamsters*, 431 U.S., at 339–340, n. 20, 97 S.Ct., at 1856, n. 20.

Evidence that virtually all the employees in the major categories of at-issue jobs were white, whereas about two-thirds of the cannery workers were nonwhite, may not by itself suffice to establish a prima facie case of discrimination. But such evidence of racial stratification puts the specific employment practices challenged by respondents into perspective. Petitioners recruit employees for at-issue jobs from outside the work force rather than from lower-paying, overwhelmingly nonwhite, cannery worker positions. Information about availability of at-issue positions is conducted by word of mouth; therefore, the maintenance of housing and mess halls that separate the largely white noncannery work force from the cannery workers, coupled with the tendency toward nepotistic hiring, are obvious barriers to employment opportunities for nonwhites. Putting to one side the issue of business justifications, it would be quite wrong to conclude that these practices have no discriminatory consequence. Thus I agree with the Court of Appeals, that when the District Court makes the additional findings prescribed today, it should treat the evidence of racial stratification in the work force as a significant element of respondents' prima facie case.

NOTES AND QUESTIONS

Subsequent Developments in the Wards Cove *Litigation*

The Ninth Circuit ultimately affirmed the trial court's finding that the plaintiffs did not prove any of their disparate-impact claims. Atonio v. Wards Cove Packing Company, Inc., 275 F.3d 797 (9th Cir. 2001). The court of appeals had earlier approved the trial court's acceptance of the defendant's proffered census data (indicating a labor pool approximately 10% nonwhite), and rejection of the plaintiffs' alternative proposals of either the total salmon canning industry work force (48% nonwhite) or those applicants who identified their ethnicity on company application forms (26% nonwhite), to define the relevant labor market for the unskilled noncannery positions. See 10 F.3d 1485 (9th Cir.1993).

Related Issues

1. *Civil Rights Act of 1991.* Congressional dissatisfaction with the *Wards Cove* decision was one of the major reasons for passage of the Civil Rights Act of 1991. Section 105 of that Act rejects some of the analysis of *Wards Cove*, as summarized below.

First, Congress repudiated the *Wards Cove* Court's assignment to plaintiffs of the burden of persuasion at the justification stage of a disparate-impact case. Section 105 adds to § 703 of Title VII a new subsection (k) which states that an unlawful employment practice is established if a complaining party demonstrates a disparate impact "and the respondent fails to demonstrate that the challenged practice is job related for the position in question and consistent with business necessity". Section 104 of the 1991 Act defines "demonstrates" to mean "meets the burdens of production and persuasion".

Second, the "job related" and "business necessity" standards of justification required by § 105 are similar to standards first articulated in *Griggs* and other pre-*Wards Cove* decisions. Furthermore, § 105(b) directs courts to use as legislative history for purposes of "construing or applying, any provision of this Act that relates to Wards Cove", including "(b)usiness necessity", only one interpretive memorandum appearing at 137 Cong.Rec. S 15276 (daily ed. Oct. 25, 1991). This memorandum states the "terms 'business necessity' and 'job related' are intended to reflect the concepts enunciated by the Supreme Court in *Griggs* * * * and in the other Supreme Court decisions prior to *Wards Cove*".

2. *Preserving the Alternative Employment Practice Option.* New §§ 703(k)(1)(A)(ii) and (k)(1)(C) provide that a plaintiff also can establish an unlawful practice by making a demonstration with respect to an "alternative employment practice" "in accordance with the law as it existed on June 4, 1989", the day before *Wards Cove*, if the "respondent refuses to adopt such alternative employment practice." This provision reflects prior Supreme Court

decisions, including *Dothard*, which contemplated a third stage in a disparate-impact case in which plaintiffs could respond to a defendant's demonstration of business necessity by demonstrating that an alternative employment practice could also effectively serve the defendant's legitimate business interests without a similarly undesirable racial effect.

3. *Refusal of an Alternative Practice*. The 1991 Act authorizes a finding of illegality based on the existence of a less discriminatory alternative practice only if the defendant refuses to adopt the practice. Must the employer know not only of the alternative practice but also of its validity before taking the challenged employment actions? See Adams v. City of Chicago, 469 F.3d 609 (7th Cir. 2006) (defendant must have had an opportunity to adopt the alternative practice and must be aware of its validity at the time of making the challenged decisions).

4. *Proving Causation in Disparate-Impact Cases*. New § 703(k)(1)(B)(i), as added by § 105 of the 1991 Act, provides that the plaintiff in a Title VII disparate-impact case must demonstrate that a "particular" employment practice causes a disparate impact, "except that if the complaining party can demonstrate to the court that the elements of a respondent's decisionmaking process are not capable of separation for analysis, the decisionmaking process may be analyzed as one employment practice." Section 703(k)(1)(B)(ii) further provides that if "the respondent demonstrates that a specific employment practice does not cause the disparate impact, the respondent shall not be required to demonstrate that such practice is required by business necessity."

5. *Record Keeping on Adverse Impact*. The EEOC requires all employers to maintain data on the impact of their employment practices. See 29 C.F.R. § 1607.15(a) ("[u]sers of selection procedures * * * should maintain and have available for each job information on adverse impact of the selection process for that job"). Presumably § 703(k) encourages employers to maintain information that separates the impact of each element of their selection processes.

6. *Defining the Relevant Labor Market for Comparison*. It is not difficult to understand why the *Wards Cove* Court rejected the plaintiffs' comparison of the percentage of nonwhite workers in the unskilled cannery jobs with the much lower percentage of nonwhite workers in the relatively skilled noncannery positions. The Court's insistence that the plaintiffs use a pool of only workers who have the special qualifications needed for the various skilled noncannery positions is consistent with *Hazelwood*. But why did the Court also state that the cannery workforce did not provide an appropriate labor pool to determine the relative impact on nonwhites of the employer's methods for filling the unskilled noncannery positions? How should the labor market have been defined on remand in *Wards Cove*?

B. PROVING BUSINESS NECESSITY

Section 105 of the Civil Rights Act of 1991 amends Title VII to endorse the "business necessity" and "job related" defenses to a disparate impact showing. Under Section 105(b), courts are to apply these standards in accordance with pre-*Wards Cove* law. The next case, *Albemarle Paper Co. v. Moody,* is the leading Supreme Court case on "business necessity" pre-*Wards Cove.*

ALBEMARLE PAPER CO. V. MOODY

Supreme Court of the United States, 1975.
422 U.S. 405, 95 S.Ct. 2362, 45 L.Ed.2d 280.

JUSTICE STEWART delivered the opinion of the Court.

Like the employer in *Griggs* [*v. Duke Power Co.*, 401 U.S. 424, 91 S.Ct. 849, 28 L.Ed.2d 158 (1971)], Albemarle uses two general ability tests, the Beta Examination, to test nonverbal intelligence, and the Wonderlic Test (Forms A and B), the purported measure of general verbal facility which was also involved in the *Griggs* case. Applicants for hire into various skilled lines of progression at the plant are required to score 100 on the Beta Exam and 18 on one of the Wonderlic Test's two alternative forms.

The question of job relatedness must be viewed in the context of the plant's operation and the history of the testing program. The plant, which now employs about 650 persons, converts raw wood into paper products. It is organized into a number of functional departments, each with one or more distinct lines of progression, the theory being that workers can move up the line as they acquire the necessary skills. The number and structure of the lines have varied greatly over time. For many years, certain lines were themselves more skilled and paid higher wages than others, and until 1964 these skilled lines were expressly reserved for white workers. In 1968, many of the unskilled "Negro" lines were "end-tailed" onto skilled "white" lines, but it apparently remains true that at least the top jobs in certain lines require greater skills than the top jobs in other lines. In this sense, at least, it is still possible to speak of relatively skilled and relatively unskilled lines.

In the 1950's while the plant was being modernized with new and more sophisticated equipment, the Company introduced a high school diploma requirement for entry into the skilled lines. Though the Company soon concluded that this requirement did not improve the quality of the labor force, the requirement was continued until the District Court enjoined its use. In the late 1950's, the Company began using the Beta Examination and the Bennett Mechanical Comprehension Test (also involved in the *Griggs* case) to screen applicants for entry into the skilled lines. The Bennett Test was dropped several years later, but use of the Beta Test continued. [23]

---

[23] While the Company contends that the Bennett and Beta Tests were "locally validated" when they were introduced, no record of this validation was made. Plant officials could recall only the barest outlines of the alleged validation. Job relatedness cannot be proved through vague and unsubstantiated hearsay.

The Company added the Wonderlic Tests in 1963, for the skilled lines, on the theory that a certain verbal intelligence was called for by the increasing sophistication of the plant's operations. The Company made no attempt to validate the test for job relatedness,[24] and simply adopted the national "norm" score of 18 as a cut-off point for new job applicants. After 1964, when it discontinued overt segregation in the lines of progression, the Company allowed Negro workers to transfer to the skilled lines if they could pass the Beta and Wonderlic Tests, but few succeeded in doing so. Incumbents in the skilled lines, some of whom had been hired before adoption of the tests, were not required to pass them to retain their jobs or their promotion rights. The record shows that a number of white incumbents in high-ranking job groups could not pass the tests.[25]

* * *

Four months before this case went to trial, Albemarle engaged an expert in industrial psychology to "validate" the job relatedness of its testing program. He spent a half day at the plant and devised a "concurrent validation" study, which was conducted by plant officials, without his supervision. The expert then subjected the results to statistical analysis. The study dealt with 10 job groupings, selected from near the top of nine of the lines of progression. Jobs were grouped together solely by their proximity in the line of progression; no attempt was made to analyze jobs in terms of the particular skills they might require. All, or nearly all, employees in the selected groups participated in the study—105 employees in all, but only four Negroes. Within each job grouping the study compared the test scores of each employee with an independent "ranking" of the employee, relative to each of his coworkers, made by two of the employee's supervisors. The supervisors, who did not know the test scores, were asked to

---

[24] As explained by the responsible plant official, the Wonderlic Test was chosen in rather casual fashion:

"I had had experience with using the Wonderlic before, which is a short form Verbal Intelligence Test, and knew that it had, uh, probably more validation studies behind it than any other short form Verbal Intelligence Test. So, after consultation we decided to institute the Wonderlic, in addition to the Beta, in view of the fact that the mill had changed quite a bit and it had become exceedingly more complex in operation * * * . [W]e did not, uh, validate it, uh, locally, primarily, because of the, the expense of conducting such a validation, and there were some other considerations, such as, uh, we didn't know whether we would get the co-operation of the employees that we'd need to validate it against [sic] in taking the test, and we certainly have to have that, so, we used National Norms and on my suggestion after study of the Wonderlic and Norms had been established nationally for skilled jobs, we developed a, uh, cut-off score of eighteen (18)."

[25] In the course of a 1971 validation effort, test scores were accumulated for 105 incumbent employees (101 of whom were white) working in relatively high-ranking jobs. Some of these employees apparently took the tests for the first time as part of this study. The Company's expert testified that the test cut-off scores originally used to screen these incumbents for employment or promotion "couldn't have been * * * very high scores because some of these guys tested very low, as low as 8 in the Wonderlic test, and as low as 95 in the Beta. They couldn't have been using very high cut-off scores or they wouldn't have these low testing employees."

"determine which ones they felt irrespective of the job that they were actually doing, but in their respective jobs, did a better job than the person they were rating against * * * ."

For each job grouping, the expert computed the "Phi coefficient" of statistical correlation between the test scores and an average of the two supervisorial rankings. Consonant with professional conventions, the expert regarded as "statistically significant" any correlation that could have occurred by chance only five times, or fewer, in 100 trials. On the basis of these results, the District Court found that "[t]he personnel test administered at the plant have undergone validation studies and have been proven to be job related." Like the Court of Appeals, we are constrained to disagree.

The EEOC has issued "Guidelines" for employers seeking to determine, through professional validation studies, whether their employment tests are job related. 29 CFR Part 1607. These Guidelines draw upon and make reference to professional standards of test validation established by the American Psychological Association. The EEOC Guidelines are not administrative "regulations" promulgated pursuant to formal procedures established by the Congress. But, as this Court has heretofore noted, they do constitute "[t]he administrative interpretation of the Act by the enforcing agency," and consequently they are "entitled to great deference." *Griggs v. Duke Power Co.*, 401 U.S., at 433–434, 91 S.Ct., at 854. See also *Espinoza v. Farah Mfg. Co.*, 414 U.S. 86, 94, 94 S.Ct. 334, 339, 38 L.Ed.2d 287 (1973).

The message of these Guidelines is the same as that of the *Griggs* case—that discriminatory tests are impermissible unless shown, by professionally acceptable methods, to be "predictive of or significantly correlated with important elements of work behavior which comprise or are relevant to the job or jobs for which candidates are being evaluated." 29 CFR § 1607.4(c).

Measured against the Guidelines, Albemarle's validation study is materially defective in several respects:

(1) Even if it had been otherwise adequate, the study would not have "validated" the Beta and Wonderlic test battery for all of the skilled lines of progression for which the two tests are, apparently, now required. The study showed significant correlations for the Beta Exam in only three of the eight lines. Though the Wonderlic Test's Form A and Form B are in theory identical and interchangeable measures of verbal facility, significant correlations for one form but not for the other were obtained in four job groupings. In two job groupings neither form showed a significant correlation. Within some of the lines of progression, one form was found acceptable for some job groupings but not for others. Even if the study were otherwise reliable, this odd patchwork of results would not entitle Albemarle to impose its testing program under the Guidelines. A test may

be used in jobs other than those for which it has been professionally validated only if there are "no significant differences" between the studied and unstudied jobs. 29 CFR § 1607.4(c)(2). The study in this case involved no analysis of the attributes of, or the particular skills needed in, the studied job groups. There is accordingly no basis for concluding that "no significant differences" exist among the lines of progression, or among distinct job groupings within the studied lines of progression. Indeed, the study's checkered results appear to compel the opposite conclusion.

(2) The study compared test scores with subjective supervisorial rankings. While they allow the use of supervisorial rankings in test validation, the Guidelines quite plainly contemplate that the rankings will be elicited with far more care than was demonstrated here.[30] Albemarle's supervisors were asked to rank employees by a "standard" that was extremely vague and fatally open to divergent interpretations. As previously noted, each "job grouping" contained a number of different jobs, and the supervisors were asked, in each grouping to

> "determine which ones [employees] they felt irrespective of the job that they were actually doing, but in their respective jobs, did a better job than the person they were rating against * * * ."

There is no way of knowing precisely what criteria of job performance the supervisors were considering, whether each of the supervisors was considering the same criteria or whether, indeed, any of the supervisors actually applied a focused and stable body of criteria of any kind.[32] There is, in short, simply no way to determine whether the criteria *actually* considered were sufficiently related to the Company's legitimate interest in job-specific ability to justify a testing system with a racially discriminatory impact.

(3) The Company's study focused, in most cases, on job groups near the top of the various lines of progression. In *Griggs v. Duke Power Co., supra*, the Court left open "the question whether testing requirements that

---

[30] The Guidelines provide, at 29 CFR §§ 1607.5(b)(3) and (4):

"(3)   The work behaviors or other criteria of employee adequacy which the test is intended to predict or identify must be fully described; and, additionally, in the case of rating techniques, the appraisal form(s) and instructions to the rater(s) must be included as a part of the validation evidence. Such criteria may include measures other than actual work proficiency, such as training time, supervisory ratings, regularity of attendance and tenure. Whatever criteria are used they must represent major or critical work behaviors as revealed by careful job analyses.

"(4)   In view of the possibility of bias inherent in subjective evaluations, supervisory rating techniques should be carefully developed, and the ratings should be closely examined for evidence of bias. In addition, minorities might obtain unfairly low performance criterion scores for reasons other than supervisor's prejudice, as when, as new employees, they have had less opportunity to learn job skills. The general point is that all criteria need to be examined to insure freedom from factors which would unfairly depress the scores of minority groups."

[32] It cannot escape notice that Albemarle's study was conducted by plant-officials, without neutral, on-the-scene oversight, at a time when this litigation was about to come to trial. Studies so closely controlled by an interested party in litigation must be examined with great care.

take into account capability for the next succeeding position or related future promotion might be utilized upon a showing that such long-range requirements fulfill a genuine business need." 401 U.S., at 432, 91 S.Ct., at 854. The Guidelines take a sensible approach to this issue, and we now endorse it:

> If job progression structures and seniority provisions are so established that new employees will probably, within a reasonable period of time and in a great majority of cases, progress to a higher level, it may be considered that candidates are being evaluated for jobs at that higher level. However, where job progression is not so nearly automatic, or the time span is such that higher level jobs or employees' potential may be expected to change in significant ways, it shall be considered that candidates are being evaluated for a job at or near the entry level. 29 CFR § 1607.4(c)(1).

The fact that the best of those employees working near the top of a line of progression score well on a test does not necessarily mean that that test, or some particular cutoff score on the test, is a permissible measure of the minimal qualifications of new workers entering lower level jobs. In drawing any such conclusion, detailed consideration must be given to the normal speed of promotion, to the efficacy of on-the-job training in the scheme of promotion, and to the possible use of testing as a promotion device, rather than as a screen for entry into low-level jobs. The District Court made no findings on these issues. The issues take on special importance in a case, such as this one, where incumbent employees are permitted to work at even high-level jobs without passing the company's test battery. See 29 CFR § 1607.11.

(4) Albemarle's validation study dealt only with job-experienced, white workers; but the tests themselves are given to new job applicants, who are younger, largely inexperienced, and in many instances nonwhite. The APA Standards state that it is "essential" that

> "[t]he validity of a test should be determined on subjects who are at the age or in the same educational or vocational situation as the persons for whom the test is recommended in practice."

The EEOC Guidelines likewise provide that "[d]ata must be generated and results separately reported for minority and nonminority groups wherever technically feasible." 29 CFR § 1607.5(b)(5). In the present case, such "differential validation" as to racial groups was very likely not "feasible," because years of discrimination at the plant have insured that nearly all of the upper level employees are white. But there has been no clear showing that differential validation was not feasible for lower level jobs.

* * *

For all these reasons, we agree with the Court of Appeals that the District Court erred in concluding that Albemarle had proved the job relatedness of its testing program and that the respondents were consequently not entitled to equitable relief.

NOTES AND QUESTIONS

Test Your Understanding of the Material

1.   What did Albemarle Paper do wrong in its attempt to validate its challenged tests?

2.   Does *Albemarle* stand for the proposition that the tests in question may not be utilized by other employers or even by Albemarle Paper in its other facilities?

Related Issues

3.   *Flawed Psychological Premise for General Aptitude Tests?* The tests used were scored psychological instruments, which seek to measure an individual's traits or skills—in this case, verbal and mechanical intelligence and problem-solving abilities. They are based on a psychological theory that individuals have certain stable personality traits and skills which are not modified by workplace environment. Some psychologists, however, have suggested that personality characteristics and innate skills are not as good predictors of subsequent behavior as changes in immediate situational conditions. See, e.g., Walter Mischel, Personality and Assessment (1968); Susan T. Fiske, The Limits for the Conventional Science of Personality, 42 J. Personality 1 (1974). For the view that alternative models of behavior cast doubt on the validity of scored personality tests, see Craig Haney, Employment Tests and Employment Discrimination: A Dissenting Psychological Opinion, 5 Indus.Rel.L.J. 1, 48 ff. (1982).

4.   *Criterion Validity. Albemarle* involved a particular mode of establishing business necessity for job testing—criterion-related validation. This was the preferred method under the EEOC Guidelines in effect at the time. 29 CFR Part 1607. Under this approach, a test is "valid" if it can predict successful job performance. Usually measures of job performance or criteria obtained from supervisory ratings of a sample of incumbent employees are compared to test scores achieved by these workers. If there is a sufficient correlation between the performance scores and test scores (termed the "correlation coefficient") and the results satisfy conventions of statistical significance (normally, a five-percent or less probability that the results are the product of chance), the test is considered to have sufficient predictive power to be used notwithstanding its adverse impact on minorities.

5.   *Promotability as a Criterion.* Promotability to higher-level jobs is a criterion previously encountered in *Griggs*. Why has this criterion encountered administrative and judicial scrutiny? Are there circumstances where employers should be able to restrict entry-level positions to individuals who are likely to be promoted to higher levels in the organization? The Uniform Guidelines on Employee Selection Procedures (Uniform Guidelines or UGESP), 29 C.F.R. § 1607.5(I), which were promulgated after *Albemarle*,

would permit testing for promotability where "job progression structures are so stabilized that employees will probably, within a reasonable period of time and in a majority of cases, progress to a higher level," but would not permit such testing where "there is a reason to doubt that the higher level job will continue to require essentially similar skills during the progression period," or where the skills required are expected to develop from training or on-the-job experience.

6.   *Differential Validity.* Albemarle's validation study failed to provide evidence of "differential validity": proof that tests, which may be valid for the tested population overall, are not good predictors of job performance for particular minority subgroups. Are there good reasons for requiring such validation? The concept has been criticized in the psychological literature. See, e.g., Virginia R. Boehm, Differential Prediction: A Methodological Artifact?, 62 J. of Applied Psych. 146 (1977); Frank Schmidt, John G. Berner & John E. Hunter, Racial Differences in Validity of Employment Tests: Reality or Illusion?, 58 J. of Applied Psych. 5 (1973). The Uniform Guidelines "generally" require a differential study only where it is "technically feasible," i.e., where the minority composition of the workforce is large enough to permit separate assessment of validity with respect to that group. 29 C.F.R. § 1607.14(B)(8).

WASHINGTON V. DAVIS
Supreme Court of the United States, 1976.
426 U.S. 229, 96 S.Ct. 2040, 48 L.Ed.2d 597.

JUSTICE WHITE delivered the opinion of the Court.

This case involves the validity of a qualifying test administered to applicants for positions as police officers in the District of Columbia Metropolitan Police Department. The test was sustained by the District Court but invalidated by the Court of Appeals. We are in agreement with the District Court and hence reverse the judgment of the Court of Appeals.

I

* * *

According to the findings and conclusions of the District Court, to be accepted by the Department and to enter an intensive 17-week training program, the police recruit was required to satisfy certain physical and character standards, to be a high school graduate or its equivalent, and to receive a grade of at least 40 out of 80 on "Test 21," which is "an examination that is used generally throughout the federal service," which "was developed by the Civil Service Commission, not the Police Department," and which was "designed to test verbal ability, vocabulary, reading and comprehension."

* * *

III

* * *

The submission of the defendants in the District Court was that Test 21 complied with all applicable statutory as well as constitutional requirements; and they appear not to have disputed that under the statutes and regulations governing their conduct standards similar to those obtaining under Title VII had to be satisfied. The District Court also assumed that Title VII standards were to control the case, identified the determinative issue as whether Test 21 was sufficiently job related and proceeded to uphold use of the test because it was "directly related to a determination of whether the applicant possesses sufficient skills requisite to the demands of the curriculum a recruit must master at the police academy." The Court of Appeals reversed because the relationship between Test 21 and training school success, if demonstrated at all, did not satisfy what it deemed to be the crucial requirement of a direct relationship between performance on Test 21 and performance on the policeman's job.

We agree with petitioners and the federal parties that this was error. The advisability of the police recruit training course informing the recruit about his upcoming job, acquainting him with its demands, and attempting to impart a modicum of required skills seems conceded. It is also apparent to us, as it was to the District Judge, that some minimum verbal and communicative skill would be very useful, if not essential, to satisfactory progress in the training regimen. Based on the evidence before him, the District Judge concluded that Test 21 was directly related to the requirements of the police training program and that a positive relationship between the test and training-course performance was sufficient to validate the former, wholly aside from its possible relationship to actual performance as a police officer. This conclusion of the District Judge that training-program validation may itself be sufficient is supported by regulations of the Civil Service Commission, by the opinion evidence placed before the District Judge, and by the current views of the Civil Service Commissioners who were parties to the case.[16] Nor is the

---

[16] See n. 17, *infra.* Current instructions of the Civil Service Commission on "Examining, Testing, Standards, and Employment Practices" provide in pertinent part:

"S2–2—Use of applicant appraisal procedures

"a. *Policy.* The Commission's staff develops and uses applicant appraisal procedures to assess the knowledges, skills, and abilities of persons for jobs and not persons in the abstract.

"(1) Appraisal procedures are designed to reflect real, reasonable, and necessary qualifications for effective job behavior.

"(2) An appraisal procedure must, among other requirements, have a demonstrable and rational relationship to important job-related performance objectives identified by management, such as:

(a) Effective job performance;

(b) Capability;

(c) Success in training;

conclusion foreclosed by either *Griggs* or *Albemarle Paper Co. v. Moody*, 422 U.S. 405, 95 S.Ct. 2362, 45 L.Ed.2d 280 (1975); and it seems to us the much more sensible construction of the job-relatedness requirement.

The District Court's accompanying conclusion that Test 21 was in fact directly related to the requirements of the police training program was supported by a validation study, as well as by other evidence of record;[17] and we are not convinced that this conclusion was erroneous.

JUSTICE BRENNAN, with whom JUSTICE MARSHALL joins, dissenting.

The [Civil Service Commission (CSC)'s] standards * * * recognize that Test 21 can be validated by a correlation between Test 21 scores and recruits' averages on training examinations only if (1) the training averages predict job performance or (2) the averages are proved to measure performance in job-related training. There is no proof that the recruits' average is correlated with job performance after completion of training. And although a positive relationship to the recruits' average might be sufficient to validate Test 21 if the average were proved to reflect mastery of material on the training curriculum that was in turn demonstrated to be relevant to job performance, the record is devoid of proof in this regard. First, there is no demonstration by petitioners that the training-course examinations measure comprehension of the training curriculum; indeed, these examinations do not even appear in the record. Furthermore, the Futransky study simply designated an average of 85 on the examination as a "good" performance and assumed that a recruit with such an average learned the material taught in the training course.[7] Without any further proof of the significance of a score of 85, and there is none in the record, I cannot agree that Test 21 is predictive of "success in training."

The EEOC regulations require that the validity of a job qualification test be proved by "empirical data demonstrating that the test is predictive

---

(d) Reduced turnover; or

(e) Job satisfaction.

37 Fed.Reg. 21557 (1972). See also Equal Employment Opportunity Commission Guidelines on Employee Selection Procedures, 29 CFR § 1607.5(b)(3) (1975), discussed in *Albemarle Paper Co. v. Moody*, 422 U.S., at 430–435, 95 S.Ct. 2362, 2378–2380, 45 L.Ed.2d 280, 304–307.

[17] The record includes a validation study of Test 21's relationship to performance in the recruit training program. The study was made by D.L. Futransky of the Standards Division, Bureau of Policies and Standards, United States Civil Service Commission. Findings of the study included data "support[ing] the conclusion that T[est] 21 is effective in selecting trainees who can learn the material that is taught at the Recruit School." Opinion evidence, submitted by qualified experts examining the Futransky study and/or conducting their own research, affirmed the correlation between scores on Test 21 and success in the training program. * * *

The Court of Appeals was "willing to assume for purposes of this appeal that appellees have shown that Test 21 is predictive of further progress in Recruit School."

[7] The finding in the Futransky study on which the Court relies, was that Test 21 "is effective in selecting trainees who can learn the material that is taught at the Recruit School," because it predicts averages over 85. On its face, this would appear to be an important finding, but the fact is that *everyone* learns the material included in the training course. The study noted that all recruits pass the training examinations; if a particular recruit has any difficulty, he is given assistance until he passes.

of or significantly correlated with important elements of work behavior which comprise or are relevant to the job or jobs for which candidates are being evaluated." 29 CFR § 1607.4(c) (1975). This construction of Title VII was approved in *Albemarle*, where we quoted this provision and remarked that "[t]he message of these Guidelines is the same as that of the *Griggs* case." 422 U.S., at 431, 95 S.Ct., at 2378, 45 L.Ed.2d, at 304. The regulations also set forth minimum standards for validation and delineate the criteria that may be used for this purpose.

> "The work behaviors or other criteria of employee adequacy which the test is intended to predict or identify must be fully described; and, additionally, in the case of rating techniques, the appraisal form(s) and instructions to the rater(s) must be included as a part of the validation evidence. Such criteria may include measures other than actual work proficiency, such as training time, supervisory ratings, regularity of attendance and tenure. Whatever criteria are used they must represent major or critical work behaviors as revealed by careful job analyses." 29 CFR § 1607.5(b)(3) (1975).

This provision was also approved in *Albemarle*, 422 U.S., at 432, 95 S.Ct., at 2379, 45 L.Ed.2d, at 304, and n. 30.

If we measure the validity of Test 21 by this standard, which I submit we are bound to do, petitioners' proof is deficient in a number of ways similar to those noted above. First, the criterion of final training examination averages does not appear to be "fully described." Although the record contains some general discussion of the training curriculum, the examinations are not in the record, and there is no other evidence completely elucidating the subject matter tested by the training examinations. Without this required description we cannot determine whether the correlation with training examination averages is sufficiently related to petitioners' need to ascertain "job-specific ability." See *Albemarle*, 422 U.S., at 433, 95 S.Ct., at 2379, 45 L.Ed.2d, at 305. Second, the EEOC regulations do not expressly permit validation by correlation to training performance, unlike the CSC instructions. Among the specified criteria the closest to training performance is "training time." All recruits to the Metropolitan Police Department, however, go through the same training course in the same amount of time, including those who experience some difficulty. See n. 7, *supra*. Third, the final requirement of § 1607.5(b)(3) has not been met. There has been no job analysis establishing the significance of scores on training examinations, nor is there any other type of evidence showing that these scores are of "major or critical" importance.

* * *

* * * Sound policy considerations support the view that, at a minimum, petitioners should have been required to prove that the police training examinations either measure job-related skills or predict job performance. Where employers try to validate written qualification tests by proving a correlation with written examinations in a training course, there is a substantial danger that people who have good verbal skills will achieve high scores on both tests due to verbal ability, rather than "job-specific ability." As a result, employers could validate any entrance examination that measures only verbal ability by giving another written test that measures verbal ability at the end of a training course. Any contention that the resulting correlation between examination scores would be evidence that the initial test is "job related" is plainly erroneous. It seems to me, however, that the Court's holding in this case can be read as endorsing this dubious proposition. Today's result will prove particularly unfortunate if it is extended to govern Title VII cases.

UNITED STATES V. STATE OF SOUTH CAROLINA

United States District Court, District of South Carolina, 1977.
445 F.Supp. 1094.

Before HAYNSWORTH and RUSSELL, CIRCUIT JUDGES and SIMONS, DISTRICT JUDGE.

For over thirty years [defendants] have used scores on the [National Teachers' Examinations (NTE)] to make decisions with respect to the certification of teachers and the amount of state aid payable to local school districts. Local school boards within the State use scores on the NTE for selection and compensation of teachers. From 1969 to 1976, a minimum score of 975 was required by the State for its certification and state aid decisions. In June, 1976, after an exhaustive validation study by Educational Testing Service (ETS), and, after a critical review and evaluation of this study by the Board of Education's Committee on Teacher Recruitment, Training and Compensation and the Department Staff, the State established new certification requirements involving different minimum scores in various areas of teaching specialization that range from 940 to 1198.

* * *

Plaintiffs have proved that the use of NTE scores by the State in its certification decisions disqualifies substantially disproportionate numbers of blacks. The burden of proof was thereby shifted to the defendants, and in an effort to meet this burden the State commissioned an extensive validity study by ETS. The design of this study is novel, but consistent with the basic requirements enunciated by the Supreme Court, and we accordingly hold such study sufficient to meet the burden placed on defendants under Title VII.

The study seeks to demonstrate content validity by measuring the degree to which the content of the tests matches the content of the teacher training programs in South Carolina. It also seeks to establish a minimum score requirement by estimating the amount of knowledge (measured by the ability to answer correctly test questions that have been content validated) that a minimally qualified teacher candidate in South Carolina would have.

To conduct the study, all 25 of the teacher training institutions in South Carolina were canvassed for experienced teacher educators in the various specialty fields tested in the NTE program. A group of 456 persons with the requisite professional credentials was assembled including representative numbers from each institution and both races. All were volunteers nominated by the colleges themselves. These 456 participants were divided into two general groups. One group was assigned the task of assessing the content validity of the NTE as compared to the curriculum in South Carolina institutions. The other was assigned the task of establishing the minimum score requirement. The two large groups were then each subdivided into panels of about 10 participants assigned to each test in the Common Examinations and each of the Area Examinations. The panelists were given the questions and answers on two current forms of the NTE and asked to record certain judgments about the tests.

Each content review panel member was asked to decide whether each question on the tests involved subject matter that was a part of the curriculum at his or her teacher training institution, and therefore could be judged to be appropriate for use in South Carolina. Each minimum score panel member was asked to look at each of the questions on the test and estimate the percentage of minimally qualified students in teacher education programs in South Carolina who would know the correct answer. Each test was evaluated by teacher educators specializing in the field or one of the major fields covered by the test. Art education teachers evaluated the test in Art Education; French teachers evaluated the test in French, and so on.

The content review panels determined that from 63% to 98% of the questions on the various tests were content valid for use in South Carolina. The panel members' overview of the tests as a whole also found the NTE to be sufficiently closely related to the curriculum in South Carolina to be an appropriate measure of achievement with respect to that curriculum.

The estimates made by the minimum score panel members (as to the percentage of minimally qualified students who would answer the question correctly) were combined statistically and analyzed to generate scaled scores that reflected, for each test, the level that would be achieved by the minimally knowledgeable candidate. Only test questions that had been determined by a majority of the content review panel members to be content appropriate for use in South Carolina were used in making the minimum score estimates.

* * *

The design of the validity study is adequate for Title VII purposes. The Supreme Court made clear once again in *Washington v. Davis* that a content validity study that satisfies professional standards also satisfies Title VII. 426 U.S. at 247, n. 13, 96 S.Ct. 2040. The defendants called as an expert witness Dr. Robert M. Guion, the principal author of *Standards for Educational and Psychological Tests* published by the American Psychological Association and a nationally recognized authority in the field of testing and measurement who testified in an unqualified fashion that in his expert opinion the ETS study design met all of the requirements of the APA Standards, the Division 14 Principles, and the EEOC Guidelines. Two other experts testified similarly, and ETS sought and obtained favorable opinions on the study design, before its implementation, from another two independent experts. The ETS decision to validate against the academic training program rather than job performance is specifically endorsed in principle in *Davis, supra* * * * .

NATIONAL EDUCATION ASS'N V. SOUTH CAROLINA

Supreme Court of the United States, 1978.
434 U.S. 1026, 98 S.Ct. 756, 54 L.Ed.2d 775.

JUSTICE WHITE, with whom JUSTICE BRENNAN joins, dissenting [from the Court's summary affirmance on appeal].

For many years, South Carolina has used the National Teachers' Examinations (NTE) in hiring and classifying teachers despite the advice of its authors that it should not be used as the State uses it and despite the fact that it serves to disqualify a greater proportion of black applicants than white and to place a greater percentage of black teachers in lower paying classifications. For example, the new test score requirements contained in the 1976 revision of the State's plan will disqualify 83% of black applicants, but only 17.5% of white applicants; and 96% of the newly certified candidates permitted to teach will be white teachers.

This litigation began when the United States brought suit challenging the use of the NTE under both the Constitution and Title VII of the Civil Rights Act of 1964. The District Court upheld the State's use of the test and rejected both claims. Not only had plaintiffs failed to prove a racially discriminatory purpose in the State's uses of the NTE but, in the view of the District Court, the State had carried its burden of justifying the test despite its disparate racial impact.

The State's evidence in this regard consisted of a validation study prepared by the authors of the test at the request of the State. The District Court deemed the study sufficient to validate the NTE, even though the validation was not in relation to job performance and showed at best that the test measured the familiarity of the candidate with the content of certain teacher training courses.

Washington v. Davis, 426 U.S. 229, 96 S.Ct. 2040, 48 L.Ed.2d 597 (1976), was thought by the District Court to have warranted validating the test in terms of the applicant's training rather than against job requirements; but *Washington v. Davis*, in this respect, held only that the test there involved, which sought to ascertain whether the applicant had the minimum communication skills necessary to understand the offerings in a police training course, could be used to measure eligibility to enter that program. The case did not hold that a training course, the completion of which is required for employment, need not itself be validated in terms of job relatedness. Nor did it hold that a test that a job applicant must pass and that is designed to indicate his mastery of the materials or skills taught in the training course can be validated without reference to the job. Tests supposedly measuring an applicant's qualifications for employment, if they have differential racial impact, must bear some "manifest relationship to the employment in question," *Griggs v. Duke Power Co.,* 401 U.S. 424, 432, 91 S.Ct. 849, 854, 28 L.Ed.2d 158 (1971), and it is insufficient for the employer "to demonstrate some rational basis for the challenged practices." *Washington v. Davis, supra,* at 247, 96 S.Ct., at 2051.

The District Court here held that no other measures would satisfy the State's interest in obtaining qualified teachers and paying them fairly. But only two other States use the NTE for initial certification and South Carolina is the *only* State which uses the NTE in determining pay. Furthermore, the authors of the test themselves advise against using it for determining the pay for experienced teachers and believe that the NTE should not be the sole criterion for initial certification.

The question here is not merely whether the District Court, applying correct legal standards, reached the correct conclusion on the record before it, but whether the court was legally correct in holding that the NTE need not be validated against job performance and that the validation requirement was satisfied by a study which demonstrated only that a trained person could pass the test.

I therefore dissent from the Court's summary affirmance and would set the case for oral argument.

NOTES AND QUESTIONS

Test Your Understanding of the Material

1.   The Court in *Washington v. Davis* did not require that the tests used in that case be related to the positions that the employees (D.C. police) would perform. Rather, the Court found it sufficient that the tests were related to success in the police training program. Is this somewhat like using the LSAT

to determine law school admissions because the LSAT is a good predictor of success in the first year of law school? Are LSAT scores a good predictor of success as a lawyer? Do you see any problems with using success in a training program as the criterion for predictive validity? Should it matter how expensive the tests are, that everyone who is admitted to the training program ultimately passes (as was true in *Davis*), and that success on the job will be very difficult to measure?

2.   Did Justice White, who authored the *Davis* opinion, have a convincing basis in his dissent for distinguishing *Davis* from the summary affirmance in *South Carolina?*

Related Issues

3.   *Uniform Guidelines on Employee Selection Procedures (UGESP).* Both *Davis* and *South Carolina* preceded the 1978 Uniform Guidelines on Employee Selection Procedures. The UGESP were jointly endorsed by the four federal agencies with EEO responsibilities—the EEOC, the U.S. Civil Service Commission (now Office of Personnel Management), and the Departments of Justice and Labor, and represented the culmination of an extensive reexamination of testing principles in consultation with industrial psychologists' Division 14 of the American Psychological Association.

On the question of entrance tests, the UGESP takes the same approach as the EEOC Guidelines cited in the dissent—before success on a training examination may be used as the criterion for validating an entrance test, the training test itself must be empirically shown to be related to the job. 29 C.F.R. § 1607.14(B)(3). Given the Court's decision in *Davis*, does this aspect of the UGESP state operative legal requirements or is it to be taken simply as a policy recommendation?

4.   Davis's *Precedential Effect?* The events giving rise to the *Davis* litigation predated the 1972 Amendments which made Title VII applicable to the Federal Government. The litigation proceeded under § 1981, the D.C. Code and the Constitution, rather than under Title VII, and plaintiffs conceded in oral argument that they had not complied with Title VII filing requirements. See 426 U.S. at 238 n. 10, 96 S.Ct. at 2047 n. 10. One could therefore dismiss the *Davis* Court's reference to Title VII as dicta.

The courts of appeals have tended to read *Davis* narrowly. See, e.g., Guardians Ass'n of the New York City Police Dep't v. Civil Service Comm'n, 633 F.2d 232, 247 (2d Cir.1980) (test seeking to do more than screen for minimal requirements for a training program must be job-related); Craig v. County of Los Angeles, 626 F.2d 659, 663 (9th Cir.1980). But cf. Commonwealth of Pennsylvania v. Flaherty, 983 F.2d 1267, 1273–74 (3d Cir.1993) (accepting correlation between scores on challenged pre-training written test and performance in police academy that taught skills "critical" for police work).

5.   *Content Validation. South Carolina* involved a second mode of test validation—content-based validation. Content validity is based not on a statistical correlation of success on the test with some criterion of job

performance, but rather on the extent to which the test is correlated with the content of a job, by assessing a representative sample of important areas of job knowledge or skills required for success. In its simplest, least problematic form, a content-valid test would contain actual work samples from the job. Content validation, like criterion validation, thus must be related to the particular jobs at issue. Compare Williams v. Ford Motor Co., 187 F.3d 533 (6th Cir.1999) (upholding content-validation study for unskilled workers based on analysis of multiple job classifications through which workers could be expected to rotate), with Walston v. County School Bd., 492 F.2d 919 (4th Cir.1974) (National Teacher Examinations valid for some teaching positions may not be valid for others).

In the *South Carolina* case the state sought to show that the test was correlated not with the content of the job of teaching but rather with the content of teacher training programs. Was such an approach justifiable? Could the Court assume that the knowledge transmitted in teachers' colleges is representative of the body of knowledge teachers will need on the job? See Dean Booth & James L. Mackay, Legal Constraints on Employment Testing and Evolving Trends in the Law, 29 Emory L.J. 121, 137 n. 78 (1980).

NOTE: UNIFORM GUIDELINES AND EMPLOYMENT TESTING LITIGATION

1. *Preference for Empirical Demonstration of Validity*. The Uniform Guidelines on Employee Selection Procedures (Uniform Guidelines or UGESP). 29 C.F.R. § 1607 et seq., seem to require employers to undertake complex validation studies to support selection practices that have an adverse impact on the basis of race, gender, or other Title VII protected status group. The Guidelines further articulate what employers must prove to establish "business necessity" for such practices.

In theory, the Uniform Guidelines apply to all employer selection procedures. Id. § 1607.2(B). However, as *Dothard* and *Beazer* illustrate, the courts have permitted a considerably less rigorous, "facial validity" showing for nonscored, objective selection requirements. See e.g. Spurlock v. United Airlines, Inc., 475 F.2d 216, 219 (10th Cir.1972) (sustaining United's requirement of a college degree and 500 prior flight hours for employment as an airline flight officer); Fitzpatrick v. City of Atlanta, 2 F.3d 1112 (11th Cir.1993) (upholding "no-beard" policy for firefighters notwithstanding disparate impact on blacks); Zamlen v. City of Cleveland, 906 F.2d 209 (6th Cir.1990) (upholding physical test for firefighters notwithstanding disparate impact on women). But cf. EEOC v. Dial Corp., 469 F.3d 735 (8th Cir. 2006) (strength test for workers in sausage plant not shown to be necessary to reduce injuries).

Furthermore, courts generally do not go beyond requiring reasonable specificity of standards and minimum procedures, to also require formal validation studies for subjective systems. As noted, the *Watson* plurality suggested formal validation might not be required in all cases:

In the context of subjective or discretionary employment decisions, the employer will often find it easier than in the case of standardized tests to produce evidence of a "manifest relationship to the employment in question." It is self-evident that many jobs, for example those involving managerial responsibilities, require personal qualities that have never been considered amenable to standardized testing.

487 U.S. at 999, 108 S.Ct. at 2791.

2. *The Disparate Impact Predicate.* The Uniform Guidelines do not require test users to develop evidence of validity unless their selection procedures work a disparate impact on a statutorily protected group. However, because such evidence is gathered in any event for the purpose of assessing the usefulness of the testing program and because of the widespread perception that certain minorities do not perform as well as their white counterparts on standardized aptitude tests, see Haney, supra, 5 Indus.Rel.L.J. at 27 n. 131 (collecting authorities), large employers may undertake a validation effort pursuant to the UGESP in advance of any threat of litigation.

3. *Modes of Establishing Validity.* The Uniform Guidelines contemplate three methods for establishing the validity of a scored selection procedure. The two principal approaches—criterion validation and content validation—were previously discussed. Criterion validation refers to whether the test accurately predicts successful job performance. Content validation refers to whether the test mirrors the job itself.

The third, construct validation, is used for tests which measure psychological "constructs," such as intelligence, verbal fluency, mechanical comprehension, and motivation. Test users are required through a job analysis to identify the construct or constructs necessary to successful job performance, and then to demonstrate that the test reliably measures that construct. Due to the complexity of establishing construct validity, this form of testing is infrequently used.

4. *Job Analysis.* Both criterion and content studies require a thorough analysis of the jobs for which tests are being administered (although the job analysis is likely to loom larger in significance in content studies). For criterion studies, the critical knowledge, skills and abilities (KSAs) identified in the job analysis will govern the range of test instruments considered appropriate, and more importantly will dictate the criterion measures that may be utilized. Only certain objective criteria, such as production rate, error rate, tardiness, length of service, etc., may be used without a full-scale job analysis. Otherwise, "[w]hatever criteria are used should represent important or critical work behavior(s) or work outcomes." 29 C.F.R. § 1607.14(B)(3). For example, as both *Griggs* and *Albemarle* illustrate, if promotability is a criterion, the job analysis should confirm that a majority of employees in the tested categories will progress to higher-level positions within a reasonable time.

5. *Criterion Validation.* Criterion validation requires the employer to identify the important or critical work behavior that the test attempts to

predict. *Albemarle* involved what is called the "concurrent" variant of criterion validation. In that case, the tests were administered to incumbents who had been hired without testing and whose job performance scores may have been significantly influenced by on-the-job training and other workplace factors. The theoretically preferred approach—"predictive" criterion validation—would have been to control for these workplace factors by hiring a group of applicants irrespective of test scores, and then comparing subsequent performance against test scores. Practical considerations—such as the size of the group hired for a particular job, the unwillingness of employers to hire individuals deemed unqualified because of their test scores and the difficulties inherent in discharging low-test scorers once the "experiment" is concluded—explain the professional and judicial acceptance of the "concurrent" approach.

The widespread use of the "concurrent" approach, however, raises questions about the results of such studies. The range of scores is likely to be restricted because incumbents tend to be relatively homogenous in their abilities, and this drives down the correlation coefficients that can be expected. Such studies also may confuse the flow of causation—performance scores may be a function of on-the-job experience rather than the innate traits or skills measured by the test. They may also present "false negative" errors, for conceivably individuals denied employment might have performed as well as the incumbents. Finally, again as illustrated by *Albemarle*, the sample of incumbents may not be representative of the minority composition of the applicant pool; such representativeness is required "insofar as feasible" by the UGESP, 29 C.F.R. § 1607.14(B)(4).

As *Albemarle* also illustrates, to the extent the criterion is based on supervisor evaluations, steps must be taken to eliminate excessive subjectivity in performance ratings. The courts generally have insisted that supervisors make a focused evaluation of the employees in terms of the specific skills or work functions identified in the work analysis, rather than generalized assessments of overall job performance.

6.   *Content Validation.* As previously noted, the simplest form of content validation consists of actual work samples from the job. However, content validation can be difficult when trying to translate complex job tasks into a simplified environment. For example, a test for promotion to fire captain involved showing candidates pictures of a large fire and asking them to write down their observations and the orders they would give. In a decision rejecting the validation of the test, the Eighth Circuit observed:

> The fire scene simulation * * * cannot avoid testing the candidate's proficiency in the written exercise of verbal skills which is certainly not a critical or necessary job behavior for a fire captain. The candidates may be very proficient at assessing the scene of a fire and issuing appropriate oral orders but ineffectual in communicating those orders in writing.

Firefighters Institute v. City of St. Louis, 616 F.2d 350, 361 (8th Cir.1980). See also United States v. City of New York, 731 F.Supp.2d 291 (E.D.N.Y. 2010) (city demonstrated that the constructs it wanted to test were related to job of firefighter, but failed to demonstrate that its examination actually tested those constructs).

The extent to which the test is representative of key work behaviors and skills will often be the focus of litigation. In the *Guardians Ass'n* suit, the Second Circuit sustained the test for entry-level police officers despite its failure to measure for human relations skills identified by the job analysis as important:

> [T]he [skills the test] did measure—memory, the ability to fill out forms, and the ability to apply rules to factual situations—are all significant aspects of entry-level police work. To be sure, this conclusion would have been easier to reach if the City had spelled out the relationship between the abilities that were tested for and the job behaviors that had been identified. But the relationship is sufficiently apparent to indicate that the City was not seizing on minor aspects of the police officer's job as the basis for selection of candidates. The inadequate assessment of human relations skill lessens the representativeness of the exam and consequently lessens its degree of content validity, but this deficiency is not fatal, especially in light of the difficulty of measuring such an abstract ability.

630 F.2d at 99. Judge Sifton, concurring separately, was more skeptical on this point:

> While I join in rejecting the argument of the United States as *amicus,* that the requirement of representativeness means that *all* the knowledges, skills and abilities needed for police work must be tested, each in its proper proportions, I disagree with the [majority's] conclusion that an exam which contains omissions as extensive as the present exam meets the "representative requirements to an adequate degree."

* * *

The practical effect of validating a test for New York City police work which does not examine for human relations skills is to leave out of the entry level employment decision an area of qualifications in which minority groups would, one must assume, perform well despite educational and other deprivations.

Id. at 113–14 (emphasis in original).

C. SENIORITY SYSTEMS

Seniority, or length of service, rules provide a basis for dispensing nonexclusive benefits, such as severance pay and sick leave ("benefit seniority" rules), and for allocating scarce or exclusive opportunities or protections, such as choice job assignments, promotions and security against layoffs ("competitive status seniority" rules). *See* Sumner H.

Slichter, James J. Healy & E. Robert Livernash, The Impact of Collective Bargaining on Management 104–06 (1960).

Several reasons explain the widespread use of such rules both in collective bargaining and even in some nonunion settings. First, seniority rules tend to promote long-term commitment to the firm. They encourage workers to acquire job-specific skills, to train newcomers without fear of being replaced, and to continue to work hard to gain deferred benefits. Second, unions traditionally have favored seniority rules because they operate to limit the discretion of management and provide a relatively neutral means of resolving the competing interests of their members. Finally, such rules enjoy legitimacy among many workers because the rules are based on a criterion—length of service—which confirms the worth of past work and which offers greater security to workers who remain with the firm. There is also a documented, apparent psychological preference in our culture for having greater economic benefits later in life. See, e.g., George Loewenstein & Nachum Sicherman, Do Workers Prefer Increasing Wage Profiles?, J. Lab. & Econ. 67, 77–80 (1989).

Despite these advantages, seniority systems pose a major dilemma for statutes like Title VII that seek to promote the integration of previously disadvantaged groups into the larger economy. Because such systems favor incumbency and length of service over new entrants, they necessarily operate to perpetuate the effects of prior exclusion of particular groups from the workplace. This is most true of "competitive status seniority" rules, especially those governing layoffs and promotions. For instance, to the extent that an employer's average black employee, perhaps because of historical discrimination, was hired more recently than the employer's average white employee, competitive status seniority rules may make the black employee more vulnerable to being laid off in an economic downturn and less able to compete for a promotion when a better position is available. Also, many seniority systems seek to encourage long-term commitment to a particular department of the firm by requiring workers who transfer to new departments to forfeit their competitive status seniority. By discouraging black employees and others from transferring to more desirable departments from which they previously had been excluded, such arrangements in effect maintain prior discriminatory barriers.

Congress in § 703(h) of Title VII attempted to resolve the conflict between the legitimate interests advanced by seniority rules and the remedial goals of the statute by providing that differentials created by "bona fide" seniority systems are insulated from challenge if they "are not the result of an intention to discriminate because of race, color, religion, sex, or national origin * * * ." The Supreme Court held in Franks v. Bowman Transportation Co., 424 U.S. 747, 96 S.Ct. 1251, 47 L.Ed.2d 444 (1976), that § 703(h) does not limit the remedies courts may order for discriminatory conduct that is independent of the operation of the seniority system. This decision, however, did not resolve the extent to which § 703(h) protects seniority systems from disparate impact challenges.

The disparate-impact doctrine fashioned by the *Griggs* Court is not readily transferable to seniority systems. Because such systems are in place for reasons other than improving or predicting job performance, there is no easily identifiable objective criterion for being job—or business-related without rendering all seniority systems either valid or invalid. At the root lies a fundamental policy question—whether the legitimate reasons for adopting seniority rules are sufficient to overcome their likely disparate impact on minority workers. In most cases, the critical issue for seniority systems is the weight of the nondiscriminatory goals, not whether particular systems serve those goals.

Finally, even if seniority systems are not invalid simply because they perpetuate past discrimination, and conventional disparate-impact analysis is not available, are there special circumstances that render systems vulnerable to challenge? In particular, the language of § 703(h) raises questions about how courts should otherwise determine whether a seniority system is "bona fide" and whether it is "not the result of an intention to discriminate" on racial or other invidious grounds.

INTERNATIONAL BROTH. OF TEAMSTERS V. UNITED STATES

Supreme Court of the United States, 1977.
431 U.S. 324, 97 S.Ct. 1843, 52 L.Ed.2d 396.

[*Eds.* For additional excerpts, see pp. 148–153 and 172–177 supra.]

MR. JUSTICE STEWART delivered the opinion of the Court.

The District Court and the Court of Appeals also found that the seniority system contained in the collective-bargaining agreements between the company and the union operated to violate Title VII of the Act.

For purposes of calculating benefits, such as vacations, pensions, and other fringe benefits, an employee's seniority under this system runs from the date he joins the company, and takes into account his total service in all jobs and bargaining units. For competitive purposes, however, such as determining the order in which employees may bid for particular jobs, are laid off, or are recalled from layoff, it is bargaining-unit seniority that controls. Thus, a line driver's seniority, for purposes of bidding for particular runs and protection against layoff, takes into account only the length of time he has been a line driver at a particular terminal. The practical effect is that a city driver or serviceman who transfers to a line-driver job must forfeit all the competitive seniority he has accumulated in his previous bargaining unit and start at the bottom of the line drivers' "board."

The vice of this arrangement, as found by the District Court and the Court of Appeals, was that it "locked" minority workers into inferior jobs and perpetuated prior discrimination by discouraging transfers to jobs as line drivers. While the disincentive applied to all workers, including whites, it was Negroes and Spanish-surnamed persons who, those courts found, suffered the most because many of them had been denied the equal opportunity to become line drivers when they were initially hired, whereas whites either had not sought or were refused line-driver positions for reasons unrelated to their race or national origin.

* * *

The union, while acknowledging that the seniority system may in some sense perpetuate the effects of prior discrimination, asserts that the system is immunized from a finding of illegality by reason of § 703(h) of Title VII.

* * *

The Government responds that a seniority system that perpetuates the effects of prior discrimination—pre-Act or post-Act—can never be "bona fide" under § 703(h); at a minimum Title VII prohibits those applications of a seniority system that perpetuate the effects on incumbent employees of prior discriminatory job assignments.

* * *

Because the company discriminated both before and after the enactment of Title VII, the seniority system is said to have operated to perpetuate the effects of both pre-and post-Act discrimination. Post-Act discriminatees, however, may obtain full "make whole" relief, including retroactive seniority under *Franks v. Bowman, supra*, without attacking the legality of the seniority system as applied to them. *Franks* made clear and the union acknowledges that retroactive seniority may be awarded as relief from an employer's discriminatory hiring and assignment policies even if the seniority system agreement itself makes no provision for such relief. 424 U.S., at 778–779, 96 S.Ct., at 1271. Here the Government has proved that the company engaged in a post-Act pattern of discriminatory hiring, assignment, transfer and promotion policies. Any Negro or Spanish-surnamed American injured by those policies may receive all appropriate relief as a direct remedy for this discrimination.[30]

---

[30] The legality of the seniority system insofar as it perpetuates post-Act discrimination nonetheless remains at issue in this case, in light of the injunction entered against the union. Our decision today in *United Air Lines, Inc. v. Evans*, 431 U.S. 553, 97 S.Ct. 1885, 52 L.Ed.2d 571, is largely dispositive of this issue. *Evans* holds that the operation of a seniority system is not unlawful under Title VII even though it perpetuates post-Act discrimination that has not been the subject of a timely charge by the discriminatee. Here, of course, the Government has sued to remedy the post-Act discrimination directly, and there is no claim that any relief would be time barred. But this is simply an additional reason not to hold the seniority system unlawful, since such a holding would in no way enlarge the relief to be awarded. See *Franks v. Bowman, Transportation Co.*, 424 U.S. 747, 778–779, 96 S.Ct. 1251, 1271, 47 L.Ed.2d 444. Section 703(h) on

What remains for review is the judgment that the seniority system unlawfully perpetuated the effects of *pre-Act* discrimination. We must decide, in short, whether § 703(h) validates otherwise bona fide seniority systems that afford no constructive seniority to victims discriminated against prior to the effective date of Title VII, and it is to that issue that we now turn.

* * *

Were it not for § 703(h), the seniority system in this case would seem to fall under the *Griggs* rationale. The heart of the system is its allocation of the choicest jobs, the greatest protection against layoffs, and other advantages to those employees who have been line drivers for the longest time. Where, because of the employer's prior intentional discrimination, the line drivers with the longest tenure are without exception white, the advantages of the seniority system flow disproportionately to them and away from Negro and Spanish-surnamed employees who might by now have enjoyed those advantages had not the employer discriminated before the passage of the Act. This disproportionate distribution of advantages does in a very real sense "operate to 'freeze' the status quo of prior discriminatory employment practices." But both the literal terms of § 703(h) and the legislative history of Title VII demonstrate that Congress considered this very effect of many seniority systems and extended a measure of immunity to them.

Throughout the initial consideration of H.R. 7152, later enacted as the Civil Rights Act of 1964, critics of the bill charged that it would destroy existing seniority rights. The consistent response of Title VII's congressional proponents and of the Justice Department was that seniority rights would not be affected, even where the employer had discriminated prior to the Act. An interpretive memorandum placed in the Congressional Record by Senators Clark and Case stated:

> Title VII would have no effect on established seniority rights. Its effect is prospective and not retrospective. Thus, for example, *if a business has been discriminating in the past and as a result has an all-white working force, when the title comes into effect the employer's obligation would be simply to fill future vacancies on a non-discriminatory basis.* He would not be obliged—or indeed, permitted—to fire whites in order to hire Negroes or to prefer Negroes for future vacancies, or, once Negroes are hired, to give them special seniority rights at the expense of the white workers hired earlier." 110 Cong.Rec. 7213 (1964) (emphasis added).

A Justice Department statement concerning Title VII, placed in the Congressional Record by Senator Clark, voiced the same conclusion:

---

its face immunizes all bona fide seniority systems, and does not distinguish between the perpetuation of pre-and post-Act discrimination.

Title VII would have no effect on seniority rights existing at the time it takes effect. If, for example, a collective bargaining contract provides that in the event of layoffs, those who were hired last must be laid off first, such a provision would not be affected in the least by Title VII. *This would be true even in the case where owing to discrimination prior to the effective date of the title, white workers had more seniority than Negroes." Id.,* at 7207 (emphasis added).

While these statements were made before § 703(h) was added to Title VII, they are authoritative indicators of that section's purpose. Section 703(h) was enacted as part of the Mansfield-Dirksen compromise substitute bill that cleared the way for the passage of Title VII. The drafters of the compromise bill stated that one of its principal goals was to resolve the ambiguities in the House-passed version of H.R. 7152. * * * As the debates indicate, one of those ambiguities concerned Title VII's impact on existing collectively bargained seniority rights.

* * *

To be sure, § 703(h) does not immunize all seniority systems. It refers only to "bona fide" systems, and a proviso requires that any differences in treatment not be "the result of an intention to discriminate because of race * * * or national origin * * * ." But our reading of the legislative history compels us to reject the Government's broad argument that no seniority system that tends to perpetuate pre-Act discrimination can be "bona fide." To accept the argument would require us to hold that a seniority system becomes illegal simply because it allows the full exercise of the pre-Act seniority rights of employees of a company that discriminated before Title VII was enacted. It would place an affirmative obligation on the parties to the seniority agreement to subordinate those rights in favor of the claims of pre-Act discriminatees without seniority. The consequence would be a perversion of the congressional purpose. We cannot accept the invitation to disembowel § 703(h) by reading the words "bona fide" as the Government would have us do. [38] Accordingly, we hold that an otherwise neutral, legitimate seniority system does not become unlawful under Title VII simply because it may perpetuate pre-Act discrimination.

* * *

That conclusion is inescapable even in a case, such as this one, where the pre-Act discriminatees are incumbent employees who accumulated

---

[38] For the same reason, we reject the contention that the proviso in § 703(h), which bars differences in treatment resulting from "an intention to discriminate," applies to any application of a seniority system that may perpetuate past discrimination. In this regard the language of the Justice Department memorandum introduced at the legislative hearings, is especially pertinent: "It is perfectly clear that when a worker is laid off or denied a chance for promotion because under established seniority rules he is 'low man on the totem pole' he is not being discriminated against because of his race. * * * Any differences in treatment based on established seniority rights would not be based on race and would not be forbidden by the title." 110 Cong.Rec. 7207 (1964).

seniority in other bargaining units. Although there seems to be no explicit reference in the legislative history to pre-Act discriminatees already employed in less desirable jobs, there can be no rational basis for distinguishing their claims from those of persons initially denied *any* job but hired later with less seniority than they might have had in the absence of pre-Act discrimination. [41]

The seniority system in this litigation is entirely bona fide. It applies equally to all races and ethnic groups. To the extent that it "locks" employees into non-line-driver jobs, it does so for all. The city drivers and servicemen who are discouraged from transferring to line-driver jobs are not all Negroes or Spanish-surnamed Americans; to the contrary, the overwhelming majority are white. The placing of line drivers in a separate bargaining unit from other employees is rational in accord with the industry practice, and consistent with National Labor Relations Board precedents.[42] It is conceded that the seniority system did not have its genesis in racial discrimination, and that it was negotiated and has been maintained free from any illegal purpose. In these circumstances, the single fact that the system extends no retroactive seniority to pre-Act discriminatees does not make it unlawful.

NOTES AND QUESTIONS

Test Your Understanding of the Material

1. Did *Teamsters* turn on the discrimination perpetuated by the seniority system having occurred before the effective date of Title VII?

2. Does *Teamsters* interpret § 703(h) effectively to establish an irrebuttable presumption that any bona fide seniority system is justified as business-related and that there are no less restrictive alternatives that must be used in its stead?

Related Issues

3. *What Is a "Seniority System"?* What are the distinguishing characteristics of the seniority systems protected by § 703(h)? In California Brewers Ass'n v. Bryant, 444 U.S. 598, 100 S.Ct. 814, 63 L.Ed.2d 55 (1980),

---

[41] In addition, there is no reason to suppose that Congress intended in 1964 to extend less protection to legitimate departmental seniority systems than to plantwide seniority systems. Then, as now, seniority was measured in a number of ways, including length of time with the employer, in a particular plant, in a department, in a job, or in a line of progression. See Aaron, Reflections on the Legal Nature and Enforceability of Seniority Rights, 75 Harv.L.Rev. 1532, 1534 (1962); Cooper & Sobol, Seniority and Testing under Fair Employment Laws: A General Approach to Objective Criteria of Hiring and Promotion, 82 Harv.L.Rev. 1598, 1602 (1969). The legislative history contains no suggestion that any one system was preferred.

[42] See *Georgia Highway Express*, 150 N.L.R.B. 1649, 1651: "The Board has long held that local drivers and over-the-road drivers constitute separate appropriate units where they are shown to be clearly defined, homogeneous, and functionally distinct groups with separate interests which can effectively be represented separately for bargaining purposes. * * * In view of the different duties and functions, separate supervision, and different bases of payment, it is clear that the over-the-road drivers have divergent interests from those of the employees in the [city operations] unit * * * and should not be included in that unit."

the Court considered the scope of § 703(h) in a case involving a clause in a California brewery industry collective-bargaining agreement according greater benefits to "permanent" than to "temporary" employees, and providing that a temporary employee must work at least 45 weeks in a single calendar year before he could become a permanent employee. The Court held that this clause was part of a seniority system protected by § 703(h) from disparate-impact challenge:

> In the area of labor relations, "seniority" is a term that connotes length of employment. A "seniority system" is a scheme that, alone or in tandem with non-"seniority" criteria, allots to employees ever improving employment rights and benefits as their relative lengths of pertinent employment increase. Unlike other methods of allocating employment benefits and opportunities, such as subjective evaluations or educational requirements, the principal feature of any and every "seniority system" is that preferential treatment is dispensed on the basis of some measure of time served in employment.
>
> * * *
>
> What has been said does not mean that § 703(h) is to be given a scope that risks swallowing up Title VII's otherwise broad prohibition of "practices, procedures, or tests" that disproportionately affect members of those groups that the Act protects. Significant freedom must be afforded employers and unions to create differing seniority systems. But that freedom must not be allowed to sweep within the ambit of § 703(h) employment rules that depart fundamentally from commonly accepted notions concerning the acceptable contours of a seniority system, simply because those rules are dubbed "seniority" provisions or have some nexus to an arrangement that concededly operates on the basis of seniority. There can be no doubt, for instance, that a threshold requirement for entering a seniority track that took the form of an educational prerequisite would not be part of a "seniority system" within the intendment of § 703(h).

For lower court decisions applying the *Bryant* decision, see, e.g., Mitchell v. Jefferson County Bd. of Educ., 936 F.2d 539, 545–46 (11th Cir.1991) (pay system that provides for automatic annual increases from a base level set by factors other than length of employment is not a seniority system); Chambers v. Parco Foods, 935 F.2d 902, 904–05 (7th Cir.1991) (absolute hiring preference for those who had served within same department is an aspect of a protected departmental seniority system); Allen v. Prince George's County, 737 F.2d 1299, 1302 (4th Cir.1984) (policy of filling vacancies from within before hiring new employees is a seniority system); Prieto v. City of Miami Beach, 190 F.Supp.2d 1340 (S.D.Fla.2002) (protecting a two-tier wage and pension system under which those hired after a certain date are disfavored).

4. *"Bona Fide" Seniority Systems.* Seniority systems are protected by § 703(h) only if they are "bona fide." Review the Court's discussion of the

reasons why the system in *Teamsters* was considered bona fide. Within a year of the *Teamsters* decision, the Fifth Circuit read this discussion to focus on four factors critical to judging whether a seniority system is bona fide: (1) whether the seniority system operates to discourage all employees equally from transferring between seniority units; (2) whether the seniority units are in the same or separate bargaining units (if the latter, whether that structure is rational and in conformance with industry practice); (3) whether the seniority system had its genesis in racial discrimination; and (4) whether the system was negotiated and has been maintained free from any illegal purpose. James v. Stockham Valves & Fittings Co., 559 F.2d 310, 352 (5th Cir.1977). See generally Mark Brodin, Role of Fault and Motive in Defining Discrimination: The Seniority Question Under Title VII, 62 N.C.L.Rev. 943 (1984).

In Pullman-Standard v. Swint, 456 U.S. 273, 102 S.Ct. 1781, 72 L.Ed.2d 66 (1982), the Court implicitly reaffirmed the relevance of these factors, though it cautioned that its *Teamsters* discussion was not meant to present an exhaustive list. More importantly, the *Swint* Court also confirmed that the determination of whether a seniority system is bona fide ultimately must turn on a finding of fact by the trial court—"a finding of actual intent to discriminate on racial grounds on the part of those who negotiated or maintained the system." Although discriminatory impact may be relevant to determination of intent, it would not be appropriate for a lower court to employ a legal presumption that impact proves intent: "Discriminatory intent here means actual motive; it is not a legal presumption to be drawn from a factual showing of something less than actual motive." Id. at 289–90, 102 S.Ct. at 1790–91.

5. *Does* Teamsters *Apply to Benefit Seniority as Well as Competitive Seniority Rules?* In AT&T Corp. v. Hulteen, 556 U.S. 701, 129 S.Ct. 1962, 173 L.Ed.2d 898 (2009), a case involving a claim of discriminatory allotment of service time for determining pension and disability benefits, the Court further defined the scope of § 703(h)'s seniority clause. Before Title VII's definition of sex discrimination was expanded in 1978 to encompass pregnancy discrimination, see p. 336 infra, AT&T had legally granted retirement credit for medical leave generally, but not for pregnancy leave. After 1978, AT&T amended its benefit plans to grant credit for pregnancy leave, but female employees who had been denied credit for pre-1978 pregnancy leave when later claiming benefits sued alleging discrimination on the basis of sex and pregnancy. Citing *Bryant* the Court treated the suit as a challenge to a seniority system covered by § 703(h): "Benefit differentials produced by a bona fide seniority-based pension plan are permitted unless they are 'the result of an intention to discriminate.'"

6. *Burden of Proof as to the Seniority System's Validity.* In Lorance v. AT&T Technologies, 490 U.S. 900, 109 S.Ct. 2261, 104 L.Ed.2d 961 (1989), see p. 954, the Court made clear that it does not "view § 703(h) as merely providing an affirmative defense." Instead, proof that a system is intentionally discriminatory must be "an element of any Title VII action challenging a seniority system."

UNITED AIR LINES V. EVANS

Supreme Court of the United States, 1977.
431 U.S. 553, 97 S.Ct. 1885, 52 L.Ed.2d 571.

JUSTICE STEVENS delivered the opinion of the Court.

Respondent was employed by United Air Lines as a flight attendant from November 1966 to February 1968. She was rehired in February 1972. Assuming, as she alleges, that her separation from employment in 1968 violated Title VII of the Civil Rights Act of 1964, the question now presented is whether the employer is committing a second violation of Title VII by refusing to credit her with seniority for any period prior to February 1972.

* * *

During respondent's initial period of employment, United maintained a policy of refusing to allow its female flight attendants to be married.[2] When she married in 1968, she was therefore forced to resign. Although it was subsequently decided that such a resignation violated Title VII, *Sprogis v. United Air Lines*, 444 F.2d 1194 (C.A.7 1971), cert. denied, 404 U.S. 991, 92 S.Ct. 536, 30 L.Ed.2d 543, respondent was not a party to that case and did not initiate any proceedings of her own in 1968 by filing a charge with the EEOC within 90 days of her separation.[3] A claim based on that discriminatory act is therefore barred.[4]

In November 1968, United entered into a new collective-bargaining agreement which ended the pre-existing "no marriage" rule and provided for the reinstatement of certain flight attendants who had been terminated pursuant to that rule. Respondent was not covered by that agreement. On several occasions she unsuccessfully sought reinstatement; on February 16, 1972, she was hired as a new employee. Although her personnel file carried the same number as it did in 1968, for seniority purposes she has been treated as though she had no prior service with United. She has not alleged that any other rehired employees were given credit for prior service with United, or that United's administration of the seniority system has violated the collective-bargaining agreement covering her employment.

* * *

---

[2] At that time United required that all flight attendants be female, except on flights between the mainland and Hawaii and on overseas military charter flights. See *Sprogis v. United Air Lines*, 444 F.2d 1194, 1203 (C.A.7 1971) (Stevens, J., dissenting), cert. denied, 404 U.S. 991, 92 S.Ct. 536, 30 L.Ed.2d 543.

[3] Section 706(d), 78 Stat. 260, 42 U.S.C. § 2000e–5(e), then provided in part:

"A charge under subsection (a) shall be filed within ninety days after the alleged unlawful employment practice occurred * * * ." The 1972 amendments to Title VII added a new subsection (a) to § 706. Consequently, subsection (d) was redesignated as subsection (e). At the same time it was amended to enlarge the limitations period to 180 days. See 86 Stat. 105, 42 U.S.C. § 2000e–5(e) (1970 ed., Supp. V).

[4] Timely filing is a prerequisite to the maintenance of a Title VII action. *Alexander v. Gardner-Denver Co.*, 415 U.S. 36, 47, 94 S.Ct. 1011, 1019, 39 L.Ed.2d 147. See *Electrical Workers v. Robbins & Myers, Inc.*, 429 U.S. 229, 239–240, 97 S.Ct. 441, 448–449, 50 L.Ed.2d 427.

Respondent recognizes that it is now too late to obtain relief based on an unlawful employment practice which occurred in 1968. She contends, however, that United is guilty of a present, continuing violation of Title VII and therefore that her claim is timely. She advances two reasons for holding that United's seniority system illegally discriminates against her: First, she is treated less favorably than males who were hired after her termination in 1968 and prior to her re-employment in 1972; second, the seniority system gives present effect to the past illegal act and therefore perpetuates the consequences of forbidden discrimination. Neither argument persuades us that United is presently violating the statute.

It is true that some male employees with less total service than respondent have more seniority than she. But this disparity is not a consequence of their sex, or of her sex. For females hired between 1968 and 1972 also acquired the same preference over respondent as males hired during that period. Moreover, both male and female employees who had service prior to February 1968, who resigned or were terminated for a nondiscriminatory reason (or for an unchallenged discriminatory reason), and who were later re-employed, also were treated as new employees receiving no seniority credit for their prior service. Nothing alleged in the complaint indicates that United's seniority system treats existing female employees differently from existing male employees, or that the failure to credit prior service differentiates in any way between prior service by males and prior service by females. Respondent has failed to allege that United's seniority system differentiates between similarly situated males and females on the basis of sex.

Respondent is correct in pointing out that the seniority system gives present effect to a past act of discrimination. But United was entitled to treat that past act as lawful after respondent failed to file a charge of discrimination within the 90 days then allowed by § 706(d). A discriminatory act which is not made the basis for a timely charge is the legal equivalent of a discriminatory act which occurred before the statute was passed. It may constitute relevant background evidence in a proceeding in which the status of a current practice is at issue, but separately considered, it is merely an unfortunate event in history which has no present legal consequences.

* * * Since respondent does not attack the bona fides of United's seniority system, and since she makes no charge that the system is intentionally designed to discriminate because of race, color, religion, sex, or national origin, § 703(h) provides an additional ground for rejecting her claim.

The Court of Appeals read § 703(h) as intended to bar an attack on a seniority system based on the consequences of discriminatory acts which occurred prior to the effective date of Title VII in 1965, but having no application to such attacks based on acts occurring after 1965. This reading of § 703(h) is too narrow. The statute does not foreclose attacks on the current operation of seniority systems which are subject to challenge as discriminatory. But such a challenge to a neutral system may not be predicated on the mere fact that a past event which has no present legal significance has affected the calculation of seniority credit, even if the past event might at one time have justified a valid claim against the employer. A contrary view would substitute a claim for seniority credit for almost every claim which is barred by limitations. Such a result would contravene the mandate of § 703(h).

AMERICAN TOBACCO CO. v. PATTERSON
Supreme Court of the United States, 1982.
456 U.S. 63, 102 S.Ct. 1534, 71 L.Ed.2d 748.

JUSTICE WHITE delivered the opinion of the Court.

* * * Under § 703(h), the fact that a seniority system has a discriminatory impact is not alone sufficient to invalidate the system; actual intent to discriminate must be proved. The Court of Appeals in this case, however, held that § 703(h) does not apply to seniority systems adopted after the effective date of the Civil Rights Act.

* * *

I

Petitioner American Tobacco Co. operates two plants in Richmond, Va., one which manufactures cigarettes and one which manufactures pipe tobacco. Each plant is divided into a prefabrication department, which blends and prepares tobacco for further processing, and a fabrication department, which manufactures the final product. Petitioner Bakery, Confectionery & Tobacco Workers' International Union and its affiliate Local 182 are the exclusive collective-bargaining agents for hourly paid production workers at both plants.

It is uncontested that prior to 1963 the company and the union engaged in overt race discrimination. The union maintained two segregated locals, and black employees were assigned to jobs in the lower paying prefabrication departments. Higher paying jobs in the fabrication departments were largely reserved for white employees. An employee could transfer from one of the predominately black prefabrication departments to one of the predominately white fabrication departments only by forfeiting his seniority.

In 1963, under pressure from Government procurement agencies enforcing the antidiscrimination obligations of Government contractors, the company abolished departmental seniority in favor of plantwide seniority and the black union local was merged into the white local. However, promotions were no longer based solely on seniority but rather on seniority plus certain qualifications, and employees lost accumulated seniority in the event of a transfer between plants. Between 1963 and 1968, when this promotions policy was in force, virtually all vacancies in the fabrication departments were filled by white employees due to the discretion vested in supervisors to determine who was qualified.

In November 1968, the company proposed the establishment of nine lines of progression, six of which are at issue in this case. The union accepted and ratified the lines of progression in 1969. Each line of progression generally consisted of two jobs. An employee was not eligible for the top job in the line until he had worked in a bottom job. Four of the six lines of progression at issue here consisted of nearly all-white top jobs from the fabrication departments linked with nearly all-white bottom jobs from the fabrication departments; the other two consisted of all-black top jobs from the prefabrication departments linked with all-black bottom jobs from the prefabrication departments. The top jobs in the white lines of progression were among the best paying jobs in the plants.

* * *

II

Petitioners argue that the plain language of § 703(h) applies to post-Act as well as pre-Act seniority systems. The respondent employees claim that the provision "provides a narrow exemption—from the ordinary discriminatory impact test—which was specifically designed to protect bona fide seniority systems which were in existence before the effective date of Title VII." Respondent EEOC supports the judgment below, but urges us to interpret § 703(h) so as to protect the post-Act *application* of a bona fide seniority system but not the post-Act *adoption* of a seniority system or an aspect of a seniority system.

* * *

On its face § 703(h) makes no distinction between pre-and post-Act seniority systems, just as it does not distinguish between pre-and post-Act merit systems or pre-and post-Act ability tests. The section does not take the form of a saving clause or a grandfather clause designed to exclude existing practices from the operation of a new rule.

* * *

Furthermore, for the purpose of construing § 703(h), the proposed distinction between application and adoption on its face makes little sense. The adoption of a seniority system which has not been applied would not give rise to a cause of action. A discriminatory effect would arise only when the system is put into operation and the employer "applies" the system. Such application is not infirm under § 703(h) unless it is accompanied by a discriminatory purpose. An adequate remedy for adopting a discriminatory seniority system would very likely include an injunction against the future application of the system and backpay awards for those harmed by its application. Such an injunction, however, would lie only if the requirement of § 703(h)—that such application be intentionally discriminatory—were satisfied.

* * *

A further result of the EEOC's theory would be to discourage unions and employers from modifying pre-Act seniority systems or post-Act systems whose adoption was not timely challenged. Any modification, if timely challenged, would be subject to the *Griggs* standard—even if it benefited persons covered by Title VII—thereby creating an incentive to retain existing systems which enjoy the protection of § 703(h).[5]

* * *

We have not been informed of and have not found a single statement anywhere in the legislative history saying that § 703(h) does not protect seniority systems adopted or modified after the effective date of Title VII. Nor does the legislative history reveal that Congress intended to distinguish between adoption and application of a bona fide seniority system. The most which can be said for the legislative history of § 703(h) is that it is inconclusive with respect to the issue presented in this case.

* * * Congress was well aware in 1964 that the overall purpose of Title VII, to eliminate discrimination in employment, inevitably would, on occasion, conflict with the policy favoring minimal supervision by courts and other governmental agencies over the substantive terms of collective-bargaining agreements. *California Brewers Assn. v. Bryant,* 444 U.S. 598, 608, 100 S.Ct. 814, 820, 63 L.Ed.2d 55 (1980). Section 703(h) represents the balance Congress struck between the two policies, and it is not this Court's function to upset that balance.[17]

JUSTICE BRENNAN, with whom JUSTICE MARSHALL and JUSTICE BLACKMUN join, dissenting.

* * * [Section] 703(h) should not be construed to further objectives beyond those which Congress expressly wished to serve. As demonstrated by the legislative history * * *, Congress' basic purpose in adding the provision was to protect the *expectations* that employees acquire through the continued operation of a seniority system. A timely challenge to the

---

[5] "Significant freedom must be afforded employers and unions to create differing seniority systems." *California Brewers Assn. v. Bryant,* 444 U.S. 598, 608, 100 S.Ct. 814, 820, 63 L.Ed.2d 55 (1980). Respondents' interpretation of § 703(h) would impinge on that freedom by discouraging modification of existing seniority systems or adoption of new systems.

[17] Justice Brennan's dissent makes no mention of the importance which Congress and this Court have accorded to seniority systems and collective bargaining. It reads the legislative history as showing that Congress' basic purpose in enacting § 703(h) was to protect employee expectations. In doing so, it ignores the policy favoring minimal governmental intervention in collective bargaining.

adoption of a seniority plan may forestall discrimination *before* such legitimate employee expectations have arisen.

* * *

While [the] legislative history does not contain any explicit reference to the distinction between adoption and application urged by the EEOC, it surely contains no suggestion that Congress intended to treat the decision *to adopt* a seniority plan any differently from the decision *to adopt* a discriminatory employment practice unrelated to seniority. Rather, the legislative history indicates that Congress was concerned *only* about protecting the good-faith expectations of employees who rely on the continued *application* of established, bona fide seniority systems.

* * *

JUSTICE STEVENS, dissenting.

It is clear to me that a seniority system that is unlawful at the time it is adopted cannot be "bona fide" within the meaning of § 703(h). Thus, a post-Act seniority system cannot be bona fide if it was adopted in violation of Title VII; such a system would not provide an employer with a defense under § 703(h). Section 703(h) itself does not address the question of how to determine whether the adoption of a post-Act merit or seniority system is unlawful. Since the adoption of a seniority system is in my opinion an employment practice subject to the requirements of Title VII, it is reasonable to infer that the same standard that applies to hiring, promotion, discharge, and compensation practices also applies to the adoption of a merit or seniority system.

This inference is confirmed by the fact that § 703(h) does not merely provide an affirmative defense for seniority systems; it also provides a similar defense for merit systems and professionally developed ability tests. * * *

The Court in this case, however, reads the "specific intent" proviso of § 703(h) as though it were intended to define the proper standard for measuring any challenge to a merit or seniority system. This reading of the proviso is entirely unwarranted. The proviso is a limitation on the scope of the affirmative defense. It addresses the problem created by pre-Act seniority systems, which of course were "lawful" because adopted before the Act became effective and therefore presumptively "bona fide" within the meaning of § 703(h). As the legislative history makes clear, Congress sought to protect seniority rights that had accrued before the effective date of the Act, but it did not want to extend that protection to benefits under seniority systems that were the product of deliberate racial discrimination. The obvious purpose of the proviso was to place a limit on the protection given to pre-Act seniority systems. The Court's broad reading of the proviso ignores both its context in § 703(h) and the historical context in which it was enacted.

The Court's strained reading of the statute may be based on an assumption that if the *Griggs* standard were applied to the adoption of a post-Act seniority system, most post-Act systems would be unlawful since it is virtually impossible to establish a seniority system whose classification of employees will not have a disparate impact on members of some race or sex. Under *Griggs*, however, illegality does not follow automatically from a disparate impact. If the initiation of a new seniority system—or the modification of an existing system—is substantially related to a valid business purpose, the system is lawful. "The touchstone is business necessity." *Griggs, supra*, at 431, 91 S.Ct. at 853; cf. *New York Transit Authority v. Beazer*, 440 U.S. 568, 587, 99 S.Ct. 1355, 1366, 59 L.Ed.2d 587. A reasoned application of *Griggs* would leave ample room for bona fide systems; the adoption of a seniority system often may be justified by the need to induce experienced employees to remain, to establish fair rules for advancement, or to reward continuous, effective service. I can find no provision of Title VII, however, that grants a blanket exemption to the initiation of every seniority system that has not been conceived with a deliberate purpose to discriminate because of race or sex.

NOTES AND QUESTIONS

Test Your Understanding of the Material

1.   How did the facts of *Evans* differ from those in *Teamsters*? Was Congress' concern with the protection of seniority expectations equally applicable in *Evans*?

2.   How does *Patterson* extend the holdings of *Teamsters* and *Evans*? Was Congress' concern with the protection of seniority expectations also applicable in *Patterson*?

3.   Review the statutory language in Section 703(h). Is the Court's interpretation in *Patterson* consistent with the plain meaning of the text? Are the dissents' interpretations?

Related Issues

4.   *Viability of Disparate-Impact Challenges to Aspects of Seniority Systems Not Tied to Rewards for Past Service.* Does *Teamsters'* reading of § 703(h) preclude disparate-impact challenges to all aspects of a seniority system, even aspects that are not closely tied to a policy of rewarding past service for the employer? Note that in *Evans,* rewarding past service probably benefitted women as a group because of the historical exclusion of men from flight attendant positions, but the break-in-service rule probably disproportionately disadvantaged women because of their greater likelihood of leaving the work force for family reasons.

5. *What If the Pre-Act System Was Itself Discriminatory?* In *Evans* and *Patterson*, as in *Teamsters*, the challenged seniority system perpetuated earlier discrimination that was independent of the seniority system. Does it make a difference if the earlier discrimination being perpetuated was part of the seniority system itself? In *AT&T Corp. v. Hulteen*, note 5 at page 253 supra, the Court held that the "differential" assignment of seniority credit that was legal at the time of assignment "did not taint the system" under the terms of § 703(h) as long as the differential was eliminated by the time it became illegal discrimination under Title VII. *Hulteen* involved the differential assignment of service credit for pregnancy leave before discrimination on the basis of pregnancy was made illegal in 1978, see page 336 infra.

6. *Statute of Limitations for Seniority-System Challenges.* In a case determining when Title VII's administrative filing period begins to run, Lorance v. AT&T Technologies, 490 U.S. 900, 109 S.Ct. 2261, 104 L.Ed.2d 961 (1989), see p. 954, the Court held that facially neutral seniority systems can be challenged only within the 180 or 300 day limitation period after their adoption even if they were adopted with a discriminatory intent. The Civil Rights Act of 1991 rejected this holding. Section 112 of that Act amended § 706(e) of Title VII to clarify that an "unlawful employment practice occurs" when an intentionally discriminatory seniority system "is adopted, when an individual becomes subject to the seniority system, or when a person aggrieved is injured by the application of the seniority system". In *Hulteen*, the Court held that this section does not warrant a later challenge to a seniority system tainted by a discriminatory purpose at a time before such a purpose had been made illegal.

D. RECONCILING DISPARATE IMPACT AND DISPARATE TREATMENT

RICCI V. DESTEFANO

Supreme Court of the United States, 2009.
557 U.S. 557, 129 S.Ct. 2658, 174 L.Ed.2d 490.

JUSTICE KENNEDY delivered the opinion of the Court.

In 2003, 118 New Haven firefighters took examinations to qualify for promotion to the rank of lieutenant or captain. Promotion examinations in New Haven (or City) were infrequent, so the stakes were high. The results would determine which firefighters would be considered for promotions during the next two years, and the order in which they would be considered. Many firefighters studied for months, at considerable personal and financial cost.

When the examination results showed that white candidates had outperformed minority candidates, the mayor and other local politicians opened a public debate that turned rancorous. Some firefighters argued the tests should be discarded because the results showed the tests to be discriminatory. They threatened a discrimination lawsuit if the City made promotions based on the tests. Other firefighters said the exams were neutral and fair. And they, in turn, threatened a discrimination lawsuit if the City, relying on the statistical racial disparity, ignored the test results and denied promotions to the candidates who had performed well. In the end the City took the side of those who protested the test results. It threw out the examinations.

Certain white and Hispanic firefighters who likely would have been promoted based on their good test performance sued the City and some of its officials. Theirs is the suit now before us. The suit alleges that, by discarding the test results, the City and the named officials discriminated against the plaintiffs based on their race, in violation of both Title VII of the Civil Rights Act of 1964, 78 Stat. 253, as amended, 42 U.S.C. § 2000e et seq., and the Equal Protection Clause of the Fourteenth Amendment. The City and the officials defended their actions, arguing that if they had certified the results, they could have faced liability under Title VII for adopting a practice that had a disparate impact on the minority firefighters. The District Court granted summary judgment for the defendants, and the Court of Appeals affirmed.

We conclude that race-based action like the City's in this case is impermissible under Title VII unless the employer can demonstrate a strong basis in evidence that, had it not taken the action, it would have been liable under the disparate-impact statute. The respondents, we further determine, cannot meet that threshold standard. As a result, the City's action in discarding the tests was a violation of Title VII. In light of our ruling under the statutes, we need not reach the question whether respondents' actions may have violated the Equal Protection Clause.

I

This litigation comes to us after the parties' cross-motions for summary judgment, so we set out the facts in some detail. As the District Court noted, although "the parties strenuously dispute the relevance and legal import of, and inferences to be drawn from, many aspects of this case, the underlying facts are largely undisputed."

A

When the City of New Haven undertook to fill vacant lieutenant and captain positions in its fire department (Department), the promotion and hiring process was governed by the city charter, in addition to federal and state law. The charter establishes a merit system. That system requires the City to fill vacancies in the classified civil-service ranks with the most qualified individuals, as determined by job-related examinations. After each examination, the New Haven Civil Service Board (CSB) certifies a ranked list of applicants who passed the test. Under the charter's "rule of three," the relevant hiring authority must fill each vacancy by choosing one candidate from the top three scorers on the list. Certified promotional lists remain valid for two years.

The City's contract with the New Haven firefighters' union specifies additional requirements for the promotion process. Under the contract, applicants for lieutenant and captain positions were to be screened using written and oral examinations, with the written exam accounting for 60 percent and the oral exam 40 percent of an applicant's total score. To sit for the examinations, candidates for lieutenant needed 30 months' experience in the Department, a high-school diploma, and certain vocational training courses. Candidates for captain needed one year's service as a lieutenant in the Department, a high-school diploma, and certain vocational training courses.

After reviewing bids from various consultants, the City hired Industrial/Organizational Solutions, Inc. (IOS) to develop and administer the examinations, at a cost to the City of $100,000. IOS is an Illinois company that specializes in designing entry-level and promotional examinations for fire and police departments. In order to fit the examinations to the New Haven Department, IOS began the test-design process by performing job analyses to identify the tasks, knowledge, skills, and abilities that are essential for the lieutenant and captain positions. IOS representatives interviewed incumbent captains and lieutenants and their supervisors. They rode with and observed other on-duty officers. Using information from those interviews and ride-alongs, IOS wrote job-analysis questionnaires and administered them to most of the incumbent battalion chiefs, captains, and lieutenants in the Department. At every stage of the job analyses, IOS, by deliberate choice, oversampled minority firefighters to ensure that the results—which IOS would use to develop the examinations—would not unintentionally favor white candidates.

With the job-analysis information in hand, IOS developed the written examinations to measure the candidates' job-related knowledge. For each test, IOS compiled a list of training manuals, Department procedures, and other materials to use as sources for the test questions. IOS presented the proposed sources to the New Haven fire chief and assistant fire chief for their approval. Then, using the approved sources, IOS drafted a multiple-choice test for each position. Each test had 100 questions, as required by CSB rules, and was written below a 10th-grade reading level. After IOS prepared the tests, the City opened a 3-month study period. It gave candidates a list that identified the source material for the questions, including the specific chapters from which the questions were taken.

IOS developed the oral examinations as well. These concentrated on job skills and abilities. Using the job-analysis information, IOS wrote hypothetical situations to test incident-command skills, firefighting tactics, interpersonal skills, leadership, and management ability, among other things. Candidates would be presented with these hypotheticals and asked to respond before a panel of three assessors.

IOS assembled a pool of 30 assessors who were superior in rank to the positions being tested. At the City's insistence (because of controversy surrounding previous examinations), all the assessors came from outside Connecticut. IOS submitted the assessors' resumes to City officials for approval. They were battalion chiefs, assistant chiefs, and chiefs from departments of similar sizes to New Haven's throughout the country. Sixty-six percent of the panelists were minorities, and each of the nine three-member assessment panels contained two minority members. IOS trained the panelists for several hours on the day before it administered the examinations, teaching them how to score the candidates' responses consistently using checklists of desired criteria.

Candidates took the examinations in November and December 2003. Seventy-seven candidates completed the lieutenant examination—43 whites, 19 blacks, and 15 Hispanics. Of those, 34 candidates passed—25 whites, 6 blacks, and 3 Hispanics. Eight lieutenant positions were vacant at the time of the examination. As the rule of three operated, this meant that the top 10 candidates were eligible for an immediate promotion to lieutenant. All 10 were white. Subsequent vacancies would have allowed at least 3 black candidates to be considered for promotion to lieutenant.

Forty-one candidates completed the captain examination—25 whites, 8 blacks, and 8 Hispanics. Of those, 22 candidates passed—16 whites, 3 blacks, and 3 Hispanics. Seven captain positions were vacant at the time of the examination. Under the rule of three, 9 candidates were eligible for an immediate promotion to captain—7 whites and 2 Hispanics.

B

The City's contract with IOS contemplated that, after the examinations, IOS would prepare a technical report that described the examination processes and methodologies and analyzed the results. But in January 2004, rather than requesting the technical report, City officials, including the City's counsel, Thomas Ude, convened a meeting with IOS Vice President Chad Legel. (Legel was the leader of the IOS team that developed and administered the tests.) Based on the test results, the City officials expressed concern that the tests had discriminated against minority candidates. Legel defended the examinations' validity, stating that any numerical disparity between white and minority candidates was likely due to various external factors and was in line with results of the Department's previous promotional examinations.

Several days after the meeting, Ude sent a letter to the CSB purporting to outline its duties with respect to the examination results. Ude stated that under federal law, "a statistical demonstration of disparate impact," standing alone, "constitutes a sufficiently serious claim of racial discrimination to serve as a predicate for employer-initiated, voluntar[y] remedies—even . . . race-conscious remedies."

* * *

At a * * * meeting, on February 11, Legel addressed the CSB on behalf of IOS. * * *

Legel explained the exam-development process to the CSB. He began by describing the job analyses IOS performed of the captain and lieutenant positions—the interviews, ride-alongs, and questionnaires IOS designed to "generate a list of tasks, knowledge, skills and abilities that are considered essential to performance" of the jobs. He outlined how IOS prepared the written and oral examinations, based on the job-analysis results, to test most heavily those qualities that the results indicated were "critica[l]" or "essentia[l]." And he noted that IOS took the material for each test question directly from the approved source materials. Legel told the CSB that third-party reviewers had scrutinized the examinations to ensure that the written test was drawn from the source material and that the oral test accurately tested real-world situations that captains and lieutenants would face. Legel confirmed that IOS had selected oral-examination panelists so that each three-member assessment panel included one white, one black, and one Hispanic member.

At the next meeting, on March 11, the CSB heard from three witnesses it had selected to "tell us a little bit about their views of the testing, the process, [and] the methodology." The first, Christopher Hornick, spoke to the CSB by telephone. Hornick is an industrial/organizational psychologist from Texas who operates a consulting business that "direct[ly]" competes with IOS. * * * Hornick stated that the "adverse impact on the written exam was somewhat higher but generally in the range that we've seen professionally."

When asked to explain the New Haven test results, Hornick opined in the telephone conversation that the collective-bargaining agreement's requirement of using written and oral examinations with a 60/40 composite score might account for the statistical disparity. * * *

Hornick made clear that he was "not suggesting that [IOS] somehow created a test that had adverse impacts that it should not have had." He described the IOS examinations as "reasonably good test[s]." * *

The second witness was Vincent Lewis, a fire program specialist for the Department of Homeland Security and a retired fire captain from Michigan. Lewis, who is black, had looked "extensively" at the lieutenant exam and "a little less extensively" at the captain exam. He stated that the candidates "should know that material." In Lewis's view, the "questions were relevant for both exams," and the New Haven candidates had an advantage because the study materials identified the particular book chapters from which the questions were taken. * * *

The final witness was Janet Helms, a professor at Boston College whose "primary area of expertise" is "not with firefighters per se" but in "race and culture as they influence performance on tests and other assessment procedures." Helms expressly declined the CSB's offer to review the examinations. At the outset, she noted that "regardless of what kind of written test we give in this country . . . we can just about predict how many people will pass who are members of under-represented groups." * * * Helms closed by stating that no matter what test the City had administered, it would have revealed "a disparity between blacks and whites, Hispanics and whites," particularly on a written test.

* * *

At the close of witness testimony, the CSB voted on a motion to certify the examinations. With one member recused, the CSB deadlocked 2 to 2, resulting in a decision not to certify the results. * * *

C

The CSB's decision not to certify the examination results led to this lawsuit. The plaintiffs—who are the petitioners here—are 17 white firefighters and 1 Hispanic firefighter who passed the examinations but were denied a chance at promotions when the CSB refused to certify the test results. They include the named plaintiff, Frank Ricci, who addressed the CSB at multiple meetings.

* * *

II

Petitioners raise a statutory claim, under the disparate-treatment prohibition of Title VII, and a constitutional claim, under the Equal Protection Clause of the Fourteenth Amendment. A decision for petitioners on their statutory claim would provide the relief sought, so we consider it first. * * *

* * *

B

* * *

Our analysis begins with this premise: The City's actions would violate the disparate-treatment prohibition of Title VII absent some valid defense. All the evidence demonstrates that the City chose not to certify the examination results because of the statistical disparity based on race—*i.e.*, how minority candidates had performed when compared to white candidates. * * * Without some other justification, this express, race-based decisionmaking violates Title VII's command that employers cannot take adverse employment actions because of an individual's race. See § 2000e–2(a)(1).

* * *

We consider, therefore, whether the purpose to avoid disparate-impact liability excuses what otherwise would be prohibited disparate-treatment discrimination. * * *

* * * we turn to the parties' proposed means of reconciling the statutory provisions. Petitioners take a strict approach, arguing that under Title VII, it cannot be permissible for an employer to take race-based adverse employment actions in order to avoid disparate-impact liability— even if the employer knows its practice violates the disparate-impact provision. Petitioners would have us hold that, under Title VII, avoiding unintentional discrimination cannot justify intentional discrimination. That assertion, however, ignores the fact that, by codifying the disparate-impact provision in 1991, Congress has expressly prohibited both types of discrimination. We must interpret the statute to give effect to both provisions where possible. * * *

Petitioners next suggest that an employer in fact must be in violation of the disparate-impact provision before it can use compliance as a defense in a disparate-treatment suit. Again, this is overly simplistic and too restrictive of Title VII's purpose. The rule petitioners offer would run counter to what we have recognized as Congress's intent that "voluntary compliance" be "the preferred means of achieving the objectives of Title VII." *Firefighters v. Cleveland*, 478 U.S. 501, 515, 106 S. Ct. 3063, 92 L. Ed. 2d 405 (1986); see also *Wygant v. Jackson Bd. of Ed.*, 476 U.S. 267, 290, 106 S. Ct. 1842, 90 L. Ed. 2d 260 (1986) (O'Connor, J., concurring in part and concurring in judgment). Forbidding employers to act unless they know, with certainty, that a practice violates the disparate-impact provision would bring compliance efforts to a near standstill. Even in the limited situations when this restricted standard could be met, employers likely would hesitate before taking voluntary action for fear of later being proven wrong in the course of litigation and then held to account for disparate treatment.

At the opposite end of the spectrum, respondents and the Government assert that an employer's good-faith belief that its actions are necessary to comply with Title VII's disparate-impact provision should be enough to justify race-conscious conduct. But the original, foundational prohibition of Title VII bars employers from taking adverse action "because of . . . race." § 2000e–2(a)(1). And when Congress codified the disparate-impact provision in 1991, it made no exception to disparate-treatment liability for actions taken in a good-faith effort to comply with the new disparate-impact provision in subsection (k). Allowing employers to violate the disparate-treatment prohibition based on a mere good-faith fear of disparate-impact liability would encourage race-based action at the slightest hint of disparate impact. A minimal standard could cause employers to discard the results of lawful and beneficial promotional examinations even where there is little if any evidence of disparate-impact discrimination. That would amount to a de facto quota system. . . . Even worse, an employer could discard test results (or other employment practices) with the intent of obtaining the employer's preferred racial balance. That operational principle could not be justified, for Title VII is express in disclaiming any interpretation of its requirements as calling for outright racial balancing. § 2000e–2(j). The purpose of Title VII "is to promote hiring on the basis of job qualifications, rather than on the basis of race or color."

In searching for a standard that strikes a more appropriate balance, we note that this Court has considered cases similar to this one, albeit in the context of the Equal Protection Clause of the Fourteenth Amendment. The Court has held that certain government actions to remedy past racial discrimination—actions that are themselves based on race—are constitutional only where there is a " 'strong basis in evidence' " that the remedial actions were necessary. *Richmond v. J. A. Croson Co.*, 488 U.S. 469, 500, 109 S. Ct. 706, 102 L. Ed. 2d 854 (1989) (quoting *Wygant*, supra, at 277, 106 S. Ct. 1842, 90 L. Ed. 2d 260 (plurality opinion)). This suit does not call on us to consider whether the statutory constraints under Title VII must be parallel in all respects to those under the Constitution. That does not mean the constitutional authorities are irrelevant, however. Our cases discussing constitutional principles can provide helpful guidance in this statutory context.

* * * Applying the strong-basis-in-evidence standard to Title VII gives effect to both the disparate-treatment and disparate-impact provisions, allowing violations of one in the name of compliance with the other only in certain, narrow circumstances. The standard leaves ample room for employers' voluntary compliance efforts, which are essential to the statutory scheme and to Congress's efforts to eradicate workplace discrimination. See *Firefighters*, *supra*, at 515, 106 S. Ct. 3063, 92 L. Ed. 2d 405. And the standard appropriately constrains employers' discretion in making race-based decisions: It limits that discretion to cases in which there is a strong basis in evidence of disparate-impact liability, but it is not so restrictive that it allows employers to act only when there is a provable, actual violation.

Resolving the statutory conflict in this way allows the disparate-impact prohibition to work in a manner that is consistent with other provisions of Title VII, including the prohibition on adjusting employment-related test scores on the basis of race. See § 2000e–2(*l*). Examinations like those administered by the City create legitimate expectations on the part of those who took the tests. As is the case with any promotion exam, some of the firefighters here invested substantial time, money, and personal commitment in preparing for the tests. Employment tests can be an important part of a neutral selection system that safeguards against the very racial animosities Title VII was intended to prevent. Here, however, the firefighters saw their efforts invalidated by the City in sole reliance upon race-based statistics.

If an employer cannot rescore a test based on the candidates' race, § 2000e–2(*l*), then it follows a fortiori that it may not take the greater step of discarding the test altogether to achieve a more desirable racial distribution of promotion-eligible candidates—absent a strong basis in evidence that the test was deficient and that discarding the results is necessary to avoid violating the disparate-impact provision. * * *

For the foregoing reasons, we adopt the strong-basis-in-evidence standard as a matter of statutory construction to resolve any conflict between the disparate-treatment and disparate-impact provisions of Title VII.

Our statutory holding does not address the constitutionality of the measures taken here in purported compliance with Title VII. We also do not hold that meeting the strong-basis-in-evidence standard would satisfy the Equal Protection Clause in a future case. As we explain below, because respondents have not met their burden under Title VII, we need not decide whether a legitimate fear of disparate impact is ever sufficient to justify discriminatory treatment under the Constitution.

Nor do we question an employer's affirmative efforts to ensure that all groups have a fair opportunity to apply for promotions and to participate in the process by which promotions will be made. But once that process has been established and employers have made clear their selection criteria, they may not then invalidate the test results, thus upsetting an employee's legitimate expectation not to be judged on the basis of race. Doing so, absent a strong basis in evidence of an impermissible disparate impact, amounts to the sort of racial preference that Congress has disclaimed, § 2000e–2(j), and is antithetical to the notion of a workplace where individuals are guaranteed equal opportunity regardless of race.

Title VII does not prohibit an employer from considering, before administering a test or practice, how to design that test or practice in order to provide a fair opportunity for all individuals, regardless of their race. And when, during the test-design stage, an employer invites comments to ensure the test is fair, that process can provide a common ground for open discussions toward that end. We hold only that, under Title VII, before an employer can engage in intentional discrimination for the asserted purpose of avoiding or remedying an unintentional disparate impact, the employer must have a strong basis in evidence to believe it will be subject to disparate-impact liability if it fails to take the race-conscious, discriminatory action.

C

The City argues that, even under the strong-basis-in-evidence standard, its decision to discard the examination results was permissible under Title VII. That is incorrect. Even if respondents were motivated as a subjective matter by a desire to avoid committing disparate-impact discrimination, the record makes clear there is no support for the conclusion that respondents had an objective, strong basis in evidence to find the tests inadequate, with some consequent disparate-impact liability in violation of Title VII.

* * *

The racial adverse impact here was significant, and petitioners do not dispute that the City was faced with a prima facie case of disparate-impact liability. * * *

Based on the degree of adverse impact reflected in the results, respondents were compelled to take a hard look at the examinations to determine whether certifying the results would have had an impermissible disparate impact. The problem for respondents is that a prima facie case of disparate-impact liability—essentially, a threshold showing of a significant statistical disparity, *Connecticut v. Teal*, 457 U.S. 440, 446, 102 S. Ct. 2525, 73 L. Ed. 2d 130 (1982), and nothing more—is far from a strong basis in evidence that the City would have been liable under Title VII had it certified the results. That is because the City could be liable for disparate-impact discrimination only if the examinations were not job related and consistent with business necessity, or if there existed an equally valid, less-discriminatory alternative that served the City's needs but that the City refused to adopt. § 2000e–2(k)(1)(A), (C). We conclude there is no strong basis in evidence to establish that the test was deficient in either of these respects. * * *

1

There is no genuine dispute that the examinations were job-related and consistent with business necessity. * * * The CSB heard statements from Chad Legel (the IOS vice president) as well as city officials outlining the detailed steps IOS took to develop and administer the examinations. IOS devised the written examinations, which were the focus of the CSB's inquiry, after painstaking analyses of the captain and lieutenant positions—analyses in which IOS made sure that minorities were overrepresented. And IOS drew the questions from source material approved by the Department. Of the outside witnesses who appeared before the CSB, only one, Vincent Lewis, had reviewed the examinations in any detail, and he was the only one with any firefighting experience. Lewis stated that the "questions were relevant for both exams." The only other witness who had seen any part of the examinations, Christopher Hornick (a competitor of IOS's), criticized the fact that no one within the

Department had reviewed the tests—a condition imposed by the City to protect the integrity of the exams in light of past alleged security breaches. But Hornick stated that the exams "appea[r] to be . . . reasonably good" and recommended that the CSB certify the results.

* * *

2

Respondents also lacked a strong basis in evidence of an equally valid, less-discriminatory testing alternative that the City, by certifying the examination results, would necessarily have refused to adopt. Respondents raise three arguments to the contrary, but each argument fails. First, respondents refer to testimony before the CSB that a different composite-score calculation—weighting the written and oral examination scores 30/70—would have allowed the City to consider two black candidates for then-open lieutenant positions and one black candidate for then-open captain positions. (The City used a 60/40 weighting as required by its contract with the New Haven firefighters' union.) But respondents have produced no evidence to show that the 60/40 weighting was indeed arbitrary. In fact, because that formula was the result of a union-negotiated collective-bargaining agreement, we presume the parties negotiated that weighting for a rational reason. Nor does the record contain any evidence that the 30/70 weighting would be an equally valid way to determine whether candidates possess the proper mix of job knowledge and situational skills to earn promotions. Changing the weighting formula, moreover, could well have violated Title VII's prohibition of altering test scores on the basis of race. See § 2000e–2(*l*). On this record, there is no basis to conclude that a 30/70 weighting was an equally valid alternative the City could have adopted.

Second, respondents argue that the City could have adopted a different interpretation of the "rule of three" that would have produced less discriminatory results. The rule, in the New Haven city charter, requires the City to promote only from "those applicants with the three highest scores" on a promotional examination. New Haven, Conn., Code of Ordinances, Tit. I, Art. XXX, § 160 (1992). A state court has interpreted the charter to prohibit so-called "banding"—the City's previous practice of rounding scores to the nearest whole number and considering all candidates with the same whole-number score as being of one rank. Banding allowed the City to consider three ranks of candidates (with the possibility of multiple candidates filling each rank) for purposes of the rule of three. See *Kelly v. City of New Haven*, No. CV000444614, 2004 WL 114377, *3 (Conn. Super. Ct., Jan. 9, 2004). Respondents claim that employing banding here would have made four black and one Hispanic candidates eligible for then-open lieutenant and captain positions.

A state court's prohibition of banding, as a matter of municipal law under the charter, may not eliminate banding as a valid alternative under Title VII. See 42 U.S.C. § 2000e–7. We need not resolve that point, however. Here, banding was not a valid alternative for this reason: Had the City reviewed the exam results and then adopted banding to make the minority test scores appear higher, it would have violated Title VII's prohibition of adjusting test results on the basis of race. § 2000e–2(*l*); see also *Chicago Firefighters Local 2 v. Chicago*, 249 F.3d 649, 656 (CA7 2001) (Posner, J.) ("We have no doubt that if banding were adopted in order to make lower black scores seem higher, it would indeed be . . . forbidden"). As a matter of law, banding was not an alternative available to the City when it was considering whether to certify the examination results.

Third, and finally, respondents refer to statements by Hornick in his telephone interview with the CSB regarding alternatives to the written examinations. Hornick stated his "belie[f]" that an "assessment center process," which would have evaluated candidates' behavior in typical job tasks, "would have demonstrated less adverse impact." But Hornick's brief mention of alternative testing methods, standing alone, does not raise a genuine issue of material fact that assessment centers were available to the City at the time of the examinations and that they would have produced less adverse impact. Other statements to the CSB indicated that the Department could not have used assessment centers for the 2003 examinations. And although respondents later argued to the CSB that Hornick had pushed the City to reject the test results, the truth is that the essence of Hornick's remarks supported its certifying the test results.

* * *

3

On the record before us, there is no genuine dispute that the City lacked a strong basis in evidence to believe it would face disparate-impact liability if it certified the examination results. In other words, there is no evidence—let alone the required strong basis in evidence—that the tests were flawed because they were not job-related or because other, equally valid and less discriminatory tests were available to the City. Fear of litigation alone cannot justify an employer's reliance on race to the detriment of individuals who passed the examinations and qualified for promotions. The City's discarding the test results was impermissible under Title VII, and summary judgment is appropriate for petitioners on their disparate-treatment claim.

* * *

Our holding today clarifies how Title VII applies to resolve competing expectations under the disparate-treatment and disparate-impact provisions. If, after it certifies the test results, the City faces a disparate-impact suit, then in light of our holding today it should be clear that the

City would avoid disparate-impact liability based on the strong basis in evidence that, had it not certified the results, it would have been subject to disparate-treatment liability.

JUSTICE SCALIA, concurring. [*Eds.*—This opinion is included at pages 320–321 infra.]

JUSTICE GINSBURG, with whom JUSTICE STEVENS, JUSTICE SOUTER, and JUSTICE BREYER join, dissenting.

* * *

In codifying the Griggs and Albemarle instructions, Congress declared unambiguously that selection criteria operating to the disadvantage of minority group members can be retained only if justified by business necessity.[5] In keeping with Congress' design, employers who reject such criteria due to reasonable doubts about their reliability can hardly be held to have engaged in discrimination "because of" race. A reasonable endeavor to comply with the law and to ensure that qualified candidates of all races have a fair opportunity to compete is simply not what Congress meant to interdict. I would therefore hold that an employer who jettisons a selection device when its disproportionate racial impact becomes apparent does not violate Title VII's disparate-treatment bar automatically or at all, subject to this key condition: The employer must have good cause to believe the device would not withstand examination for business necessity.

* * *

The City, all agree, "was faced with a prima facie case of disparate-impact liability": The pass rate for minority candidates was half the rate for nonminority candidates, and virtually no minority candidates would have been eligible for promotion had the exam results been certified. Alerted to this stark disparity, the CSB heard expert and lay testimony, presented at public hearings, in an endeavor to ascertain whether the exams were fair and consistent with business necessity. Its investigation revealed grave cause for concern about the exam process itself and the City's failure to consider alternative selection devices.

Chief among the City's problems was the very nature of the tests for promotion. In choosing to use written and oral exams with a 60/40 weighting, the City simply adhered to the union's preference and apparently gave no consideration to whether the weighting was likely to identify the most qualified fire-officer candidates.[11] There is strong reason to think it was not.

---

[5] What was the "business necessity" for the tests New Haven used? How could one justify, e.g., the 60/40 written/oral ratio under that standard? Neither the Court nor the concurring opinions attempt to defend the ratio.

[11] This alone would have posed a substantial problem for New Haven in a disparate-impact suit, particularly in light of the disparate results the City's scheme had produced in the past. Under the Uniform Guidelines on Employee Selection Procedures (Uniform Guidelines), employers

Relying heavily on written tests to select fire officers is a questionable practice, to say the least. Successful fire officers, the City's description of the position makes clear, must have the "[a]bility to lead personnel effectively, maintain discipline, promote harmony, exercise sound judgment, and cooperate with other officials." These qualities are not well measured by written tests. Testifying before the CSB, Christopher Hornick, an exam-design expert with more than two decades of relevant experience, was emphatic on this point: Leadership skills, command presence, and the like "could have been identified and evaluated in a much more appropriate way."

Hornick's commonsense observation is mirrored in case law and in Title VII's administrative guidelines. Courts have long criticized written firefighter promotion exams for being "more probative of the test-taker's ability to recall what a particular text stated on a given topic than of his firefighting or supervisory knowledge and abilities." *Vulcan Pioneers, Inc. v. New Jersey Dep't of Civil Serv.*, 625 F. Supp. 527, 539 (NJ 1985). A fire officer's job, courts have observed, "involves complex behaviors, good interpersonal skills, the ability to make decisions under tremendous pressure, and a host of other abilities—none of which is easily measured by a written, multiple choice test." *Firefighters Inst. for Racial Equality v. St. Louis*, 616 F.2d 350, 359 (CA8 1980). Interpreting the Uniform Guidelines, EEOC and other federal agencies responsible for enforcing equal opportunity employment laws have similarly recognized that, as measures of "interpersonal relations" or "ability to function under danger (e.g., firefighters)," "[p]encil-and-paper tests . . . generally are not close enough approximations of work behaviors to show content validity." 44 Fed. Reg. 12007 (1979). See also 29 CFR § 1607.15(C)(4).

Given these unfavorable appraisals, it is unsurprising that most municipal employers do not evaluate their fire-officer candidates as New Haven does. Although comprehensive statistics are scarce, a 1996 study found that nearly two-thirds of surveyed municipalities used assessment centers ("simulations of the real world of work") as part of their promotion processes. P. Lowry, A Survey of the Assessment Center Process in the Public Sector, 25 Public Personnel Management 307, 315 (1996). That figure represented a marked increase over the previous decade, see *ibid.*, so the percentage today may well be even higher. Among municipalities still relying in part on written exams, the median weight assigned to them

---

must conduct "an investigation of suitable alternative selection procedures." 29 CFR § 1607.3(B). See also *Officers for Justice v. Civil Serv. Comm'n*, 979 F.2d 721, 728 (CA9 1992) ("before utilizing a procedure that has an adverse impact on minorities, the City has an obligation pursuant to the Uniform Guidelines to explore alternative procedures and to implement them if they have less adverse impact and are substantially equally valid"). It is no answer to "presume" that the two-decades-old 60/40 formula was adopted for a "rational reason" because it "was the result of a union-negotiated collective bargaining agreement." That the parties may have been "rational" says nothing about whether their agreed-upon selection process was consistent with business necessity.
* * *

was 30 percent—half the weight given to New Haven's written exam. Id., at 309.

Testimony before the CSB indicated that these alternative methods were both more reliable and notably less discriminatory in operation. According to Donald Day of the International Association of Black Professional Firefighters, nearby Bridgeport saw less skewed results after switching to a selection process that placed primary weight on an oral exam. And Hornick described assessment centers as "demonstrat[ing] dramatically less adverse impacts" than written exams. CA2 App. A1040. Considering the prevalence of these proven alternatives, New Haven was poorly positioned to argue that promotions based on its outmoded and exclusionary selection process qualified as a business necessity. Cf. *Robinson v. Lorillard Corp.*, 444 F.2d 791, 798, n. 7 (CA4 1971) ("It should go without saying that a practice is hardly 'necessary' if an alternative practice better effectuates its intended purpose or is equally effective but less discriminatory.").[15]

Ignoring the conceptual and other defects in New Haven's selection process, the Court describes the exams as "painstaking[ly]" developed to test "relevant" material and on that basis finds no substantial risk of disparate-impact liability. Perhaps such reasoning would have sufficed under *Wards Cove* [*Packing Co., Inc. v. Atonio*, 490 U.S. 642, 109 S. Ct. 2115, 104 L. Ed. 2d 733 (1989)], which permitted exclusionary practices as long as they advanced an employer's "legitimate" goals. 490 U.S., at 659, 109 S. Ct. 2115, 104 L. Ed. 2d 733. But Congress repudiated *Wards Cove* and reinstated the "business necessity" rule attended by a "manifest relationship" requirement. See *Griggs*, 401 U.S., at 431–432, 91 S. Ct. 849, 28 L. Ed. 2d 158. * * *

In addition to the highly questionable character of the exams and the neglect of available alternatives, the City had other reasons to worry about its vulnerability to disparate-impact liability. Under the City's ground rules, IOS was not allowed to show the exams to anyone in the New Haven Fire Department prior to their administration. This "precluded [IOS] from being able to engage in [its] normal subject matter expert review process"— something Legel described as "very critical." As a result, some of the exam questions were confusing or irrelevant, and the exams may have over-

---

[15] Finding the evidence concerning these alternatives insufficiently developed to "create a genuine issue of fact," the Court effectively confirms that an employer cannot prevail under its strong-basis-in-evidence standard unless the employer decisively proves a disparate-impact violation against itself. The Court's specific arguments are unavailing. First, the Court suggests, changing the oral/written weighting may have violated Title VII's prohibition on altering test scores. No one is arguing, however, that the results of the exams given should have been altered. Rather, the argument is that the City could have availed itself of a better option when it initially decided what selection process to use. Second, with respect to assessment centers, the Court identifies "statements to the CSB indicat[ing] that the Department could not have used [them] for the 2003 examinations." * * * Given the large number of municipalities that regularly use assessment centers, it is impossible to fathom why the City, with proper planning, could not have done so as well.

tested some subject-matter areas while missing others. Testimony before the CSB also raised questions concerning unequal access to study materials, and the potential bias introduced by relying principally on job analyses from nonminority fire officers to develop the exams. * * *

NOTES AND QUESTIONS

Test Your Understanding of the Material

1. What must an employer demonstrate to satisfy the Court's strong-basis-in-evidence test? How does the Court's test differ in application from the good-cause test offered by Justice Ginsburg?

2. To what extent does the *Ricci* decision turn on the fact that the defendants discarded the results of an employment test that had already been administered? After *Ricci*, can New Haven hire Dr. Hornick to develop for future promotions a new test that is not likely to have a significant disparate impact?

3. What does the Court's opinion in *Ricci* indicate about the meaning of § 703(*l*), (codified at 42 U.S.C. § 2000e-2(*l*))? Does this provison prohibit changing the use of test results because of race-based considerations even if the test scores are not themselves altered? What if the test has not been validated?

Related Issues

4. *Dicta for a Symmetrical Rule?* Consider the last sentence in the *Ricci* majority opinion excerpted above. Can a defendant escape disparate-impact liability by presenting a strong basis in evidence that it would be subject to disparate-treatment liability had it not continued the practice having a disparate impact? See Joseph A. Seiner and Benjamin N. Gutman, Does *Ricci* Herald a New Disparate Impact?, 90 B.U. L.Rev. 2181, 2204–09 (2010).

After the *Ricci* decision, Briscoe, an unsuccessful African-American candidate for promotion brought a disparate-impact claim against New Haven for its 60–40 weighting of the written and oral examination results. Briscoe argued he would have been promotable to lieutenant had the city weighted the results 30–70 as was the "industry norm." Briscoe asked that he be considered for a future promotion without displacing the *Ricci* plaintiffs and that the city be enjoined from using the 60–40 weighting. See Briscoe v. City of New Haven, 654 F.3d 200 (2d Cir. 2011). New Haven relied on the last sentence in the *Ricci* majority opinion excerpt to argue that Briscoe's claim had to be dismissed because of the Court's holding on Ricci's disparate treatment claim. The *Briscoe* court, however, held that the final sentence was unconsidered dicta that was not intended by the Court to modify disparate-impact law. Id. at 205–209. The court allowed Briscoe, who was not a party to the *Ricci* litigation, to proceed with his case.

CHAPTER 5

AFFIRMATIVE ACTION

■ ■ ■

Introduction

Sometimes employers make take affirmative action to improve their utilization of individuals from underrepresented groups in the workplace. This is sometimes due to legal compulsion, whether to minimize the defense burdens or the uncertainty of potential litigation or to meet the obligations of government contractors. Employers also may engage in entirely voluntary actions to take advantage of the benefits of a diverse workforce. This chapter considers the extent to which the law requires, permits, or prohibits such affirmative action.

A. JUDICIALLY ORDERED AFFIRMATIVE ACTION

LOCAL 28, SHEET METAL WORKERS V. EEOC
Supreme Court of the United States, 1986.
478 U.S. 421, 106 S.Ct. 3019, 92 L.Ed.2d 344.

JUSTICE BRENNAN announced the judgment of the Court and delivered the opinion of the Court with respect to Parts I, II, III, and VI, and an opinion with respect to Parts IV, V, and VII in which JUSTICE MARSHALL, JUSTICE BLACKMUN, and JUSTICE STEVENS join.

Following a trial in 1975, the District Court concluded that petitioners had violated both Title VII and New York law by discriminating against nonwhite workers in recruitment, selection, training, and admission to the union. Noting that as of July 1, 1974, only 3.19% of the union's total membership, including apprentices and journeymen, was nonwhite, the court found that petitioners had denied qualified nonwhites access to union membership through a variety of discriminatory practices. First, the court found that petitioners had adopted discriminatory procedures and standards for admission into the apprenticeship program. The court examined some of the factors used to select apprentices, including the entrance examination and high-school diploma requirement, and determined that these criteria had an adverse discriminatory impact on nonwhites, and were not related to job performance. The court also observed that petitioners had used union funds to subsidize special training sessions for friends and relatives of union members taking the apprenticeship examination.

Second, the court determined that Local 28 had restricted the size of its membership in order to deny access to nonwhites. The court found that Local 28 had refused to administer yearly journeymen's examinations despite a growing demand for members' services. Rather, to meet this increase in demand, Local 28 recalled pensioners who obtained doctors' certificates that they were able to work, and issued hundreds of temporary work permits to nonmembers; only one of these permits was issued to a nonwhite.

* * *

Third, the District Court determined that Local 28 had selectively organized non-union sheet metal shops with few, if any, minority employees, and admitted to membership only white employees from those shops. * * *

Finally, the court found that Local 28 had discriminated in favor of white applicants seeking to transfer from sister locals. * * *

The District Court entered an order and judgment (O & J) enjoining petitioners from discriminating against nonwhites, and enjoining the specific practices the court had found to be discriminatory. Recognizing that "the record in both state and federal court against these defendants is replete with instances of . . . bad faith attempts to prevent or delay affirmative action," the court concluded that "the imposition of a remedial racial goal in conjunction with an admission preference in favor of non-whites is essential to place the defendants in a position of compliance with Title VII." The court established a 29% nonwhite membership goal, based on the percentage of nonwhites in the relevant labor pool in New York City, for the union to achieve by July 1, 1981. The parties were ordered to devise and to implement recruitment and admission procedures designed to achieve this goal under the supervision of a court-appointed administrator.

* * *

The Court of Appeals for the Second Circuit affirmed the District Court's determination of liability, finding that petitioners had "consistently and egregiously violated Title VII." The court upheld the 29% nonwhite membership goal as a temporary remedy, justified by a "long and persistent pattern of discrimination," and concluded that the appointment of an administrator with broad powers was clearly appropriate, given petitioners' refusal to change their membership practices in the face of prior state and federal court orders. However, the court modified the District Court's order to permit the use of a white-nonwhite ratio for the apprenticeship program only pending implementation of valid, job-related entrance tests. Local 28 did not seek certiorari in this Court to review the Court of Appeals' judgment.

On remand, the District Court adopted a Revised Affirmative Action Program and Order (RAAPO) to incorporate the Court of Appeals' mandate. RAAPO also modified the original Affirmative Action Program to accommodate petitioners' claim that economic problems facing the construction industry had made it difficult for them to comply with the court's orders. Petitioners were given an additional year to meet the 29% membership goal. RAAPO also established interim membership goals designed to "afford the parties and the Administrator with some device to measure progress so that, if warranted, other provisions of the program could be modified to reflect change (sic) circumstances." The Local 28 Joint Apprenticeship Committee (JAC) was directed to indenture at least 36 apprentices by February 1977, and to determine the size of future apprenticeship classes subject to review by the administrator. A divided panel of the Court of Appeals affirmed RAAPO in its entirety, including the 29% nonwhite membership goal. Petitioners again chose not to seek certiorari from this Court to review the Court of Appeals' judgment.

In April 1982, the City and State moved in the District Court for an order holding petitioners in contempt. They alleged that petitioners had not achieved RAAPO's 29% nonwhite membership goal, and that this failure was due to petitioners' numerous violations of the O & J, RAAPO, and orders of the administrator. The District Court, after receiving detailed evidence of how the O & J and RAAPO had operated over the previous six years, held petitioners in civil contempt. The court did not rest its contempt finding on petitioners' failure to meet the 29% membership goal, although nonwhite membership in Local 28 was only 10.8% at the time of the hearing. Instead, the court found that petitioners had "failed to comply with RAAPO * * * almost from its date of entry," identifying six "separate actions or omissions on the part of the defendants [that] have impeded the entry of non-whites into Local 28 in contravention of the prior orders of this court."

* * *

In 1983, the City brought a second contempt proceeding before the administrator, charging petitioners with additional violations of the O & J, RAAPO, and various administrative orders. The administrator found that the JAC had violated RAAPO [with respect to certain reporting and record keeping requirements].

The District Court adopted the administrator's findings and once again adjudicated petitioners guilty of civil contempt. The court ordered petitioners to pay for a computerized recordkeeping system to be maintained by outside consultants, but deferred ruling on additional contempt fines pending submission of the administrator's fund proposal. The court subsequently adopted the administrator's proposed Employment, Training, Education, and Recruitment Fund (Fund) to "be used for the purpose of remedying discrimination." The Fund was used for a variety of purposes. In order to increase the pool of qualified nonwhite applicants for the apprenticeship program, the Fund paid for nonwhite union members to serve as liaisons to vocational and technical schools with sheet metal programs, created part-time and summer sheet metal jobs for qualified nonwhite youths, and extended financial assistance to needy apprentices. The Fund also extended counseling and tutorial services to nonwhite apprentices, giving them the benefits that had traditionally been available to white apprentices from family and friends. Finally, in an effort to maximize employment opportunities for all apprentices, the Fund provided financial support to employers otherwise unable to hire a sufficient number of apprentices, as well as matching funds to attract additional funding for job training programs.[1]

The District Court also entered an Amended Affirmative Action Plan and Order (AAAPO) which modified RAAPO in several respects. AAAPO established a 29.23% minority membership goal to be met by August 31, 1987. The new goal was based on the labor pool in the area covered by the newly expanded union. The court abolished the apprenticeship examination, concluding that "the violations that have occurred in the past have been so egregious that a new approach must be taken to solve the apprentice selection problem." Apprentices were to be selected by a three-member Board, which would select one minority apprentice for each white apprentice indentured. Finally, to prevent petitioners from underutilizing the apprenticeship program, the JAC was required to assign to Local 28 contractors one apprentice for every four journeymen, unless the contractor obtained a written waiver from respondents.

Petitioners appealed the District Court's contempt orders, the Fund order, and the order adopting AAAPO. A panel of the Court of Appeals [largely] affirmed the District Court's contempt findings * * * . * * * The court also affirmed the District Court's contempt remedies, including the Fund order, and affirmed AAAPO with two modifications: it set aside the requirement that one minority apprentice be indentured for every white apprentice,[18] and clarified the District Court's orders to allow petitioners to implement objective, nondiscriminatory apprentice selection procedures.

* * *

---

[1] The Fund was to be financed by the $150,000 fine from the first contempt proceeding, plus an additional payment of $0.02 per hour for each hour worked by a journeyman or apprentice. The Fund would remain in existence until the union achieved its nonwhite membership goal, and the District Court determined that the Fund was no longer necessary.

[18] The court recognized that "temporary hiring ratios may be necessary in order to achieve integration of a work force from which minorities have been unlawfully barred," but cautioned that "such race-conscious ratios are extreme remedies that must be used sparingly and 'carefully tailored to fit the violations found.'" Noting that petitioners had voluntarily indentured 45% nonwhites since January of 1981, the court concluded that a strict one-to-one hiring requirement was not needed to insure that a sufficient number of nonwhites were selected for the apprenticeship program.

IV

Petitioners, joined by the Solicitor General, argue that the membership goal, the Fund order, and other orders which require petitioners to grant membership preferences to nonwhites are expressly prohibited by § 706(g), 42 U.S.C. § 2000e–5(g), which defines the remedies available under Title VII. Petitioners and the Solicitor General maintain that § 706(g) authorizes a district court to award preferential relief only to the actual victims of unlawful discrimination.[25]

A

* * *

The last sentence of § 706(g) prohibits a court from ordering a union to admit an individual who was "refused admission * * * for any reason other than discrimination." It does not, as petitioners and the Solicitor General suggest, say that a court may order relief only for the actual victims of past discrimination. The sentence on its face addresses only the situation where a plaintiff demonstrates that a union (or an employer) has engaged in unlawful discrimination, but the union can show that a particular individual would have been refused admission even in the absence of discrimination, for example because that individual was unqualified. In these circumstances, § 706(g) confirms that a court could not order the union to admit the unqualified individual. * * * In this case, neither the membership goal nor the Fund order required petitioners to admit to membership individuals who had been refused admission for reasons unrelated to discrimination. Thus, we do not read § 706(g) to prohibit a court from ordering the kind of affirmative relief the District Court awarded in this case.

B

The availability of race-conscious affirmative relief under § 706(g) as a remedy for a violation of Title VII also furthers the broad purposes underlying the statute. * * *

In most cases, the court need only order the employer or union to cease engaging in discriminatory practices, and award make-whole relief to the

---

[25] The last sentence of § 706(g) addresses only court orders requiring the "admission or reinstatement of an individual as a member of a union." 42 U.S.C. § 2000e–5(g). Thus, even under petitioners' reading of § 706(g), that provision would not apply to several of the benefits conferred by the Fund, to wit, the tutorial, liaison, counseling, stipend, and loan programs extended to nonwhites. Moreover, the District Court established the Fund in the exercise of its contempt powers. Thus, even assuming that petitioners correctly read § 706(g) to limit the remedies a court may impose *for a violation of Title VII*, that provision would not necessarily limit the District Court's authority to order petitioners to implement the Fund. The Solicitor General, without citing any authority, maintains that "contempt sanctions imposed to enforce Title VII must not themselves violate the statute's policy of providing relief only to the actual victims of discrimination." We need not decide whether § 706(g) restricts a court's contempt powers, since we reject the proposition that § 706(g) always prohibits a court from ordering affirmative race-conscious relief which might incidentally benefit individuals who were not the actual victims of discrimination.

individuals victimized by those practices. In some instances, however, it may be necessary to require the employer or union to take affirmative steps to end discrimination effectively to enforce Title VII. Where an employer or union has engaged in particularly longstanding or egregious discrimination, an injunction simply reiterating Title VII's prohibition against discrimination will often prove useless and will only result in endless enforcement litigation. In such cases, requiring recalcitrant employers or unions to hire and to admit qualified minorities roughly in proportion to the number of qualified minorities in the work force may be the only effective way to ensure the full enjoyment of the rights protected by Title VII.

* * *

Further, even where the employer or union formally ceases to engage in discrimination, informal mechanisms may obstruct equal employment opportunities. An employer's reputation for discrimination may discourage minorities from seeking available employment.

* * *

Finally, a district court may find it necessary to order interim hiring or promotional goals pending the development of nondiscriminatory hiring or promotion procedures. In these cases, the use of numerical goals provides a compromise between two unacceptable alternatives: an outright ban on hiring or promotions, or continued use of a discriminatory selection procedure.

C

[*Eds.* The Court's discussion of the legislative history and administrative interpretation is omitted.]

D

* * *

Petitioners claim to find their strongest support in *Firefighters v. Stotts*, 467 U.S. 561, 104 S.Ct. 2576, 81 L.Ed.2d 483 (1984). In *Stotts*, the city of Memphis, Tennessee had entered into a consent decree requiring affirmative steps to increase the proportion of minority employees in its Fire Department. Budgetary cuts subsequently forced the city to lay off employees; under the city's last-hired, first-fired seniority system, many of the black employees who had been hired pursuant to the consent decree would have been laid off first. These employees sought relief, and the District Court, concluding that the proposed layoffs would have a racially discriminatory effect, enjoined the city from applying its seniority policy "insofar as it will decrease the percentage of black[s] that are presently employed." *Id.,* at 567, 104 S.Ct., at 2582. We held that the District Court exceeded its authority.

First, we rejected the claim that the District Court was merely enforcing the terms of the consent decree since the parties had expressed no intention to depart from the existing seniority system in the event of layoffs. Second, we concluded that the District Court's order conflicted with § 703(h) of Title VII, which "permits the routine application of a seniority system absent proof of an intention to discriminate." *Id.,* at 577. Since the District Court had found that the proposed layoffs were not motivated by a discriminatory purpose, we held that the court erred in enjoining the city from applying its seniority system in making the layoffs.

We also rejected the Court of Appeals' suggestion that the District Court's order was justified by the fact that, had plaintiffs prevailed at trial, the court could have entered an order overriding the city's seniority system. Relying on *Teamsters* [*v. United States*, 431 U.S. 324, 97 S.Ct. 1843, 52 L.Ed.2d 396 (1977)], we observed that a court may abridge a bona fide seniority system in fashioning a Title VII remedy only to make victims of intentional discrimination whole, that is, a court may award competitive seniority to individuals who show that they had been discriminated against. However, because none of the firefighters protected by the court's order was a proven victim of illegal discrimination, we reasoned that at trial the District Court would have been without authority to override the city's seniority system, and therefore the court could not enter such an order merely to effectuate the purposes of the consent decree.

While not strictly necessary to the result, we went on to comment that "[o]ur ruling in *Teamsters* that a court can award competitive seniority only when the beneficiary of the award has actually been a victim of illegal discrimination is consistent with the policy behind § 706(g)" which, we noted, "is to provide 'make-whole' relief only to those who have been actual victims of illegal discrimination." *Id.,* at 579–580. Relying on this language, petitioners, joined by the Solicitor General, argue that both the membership goal and the Fund order contravene the policy behind § 706(g) since they extend preferential relief to individuals who were not the actual victims of illegal discrimination. We think this argument both reads *Stotts* too broadly and ignores the important differences between *Stotts* and this case.

Stotts discussed the "policy" behind § 706(g) in order to supplement the holding that the District Court could not have interfered with the city's seniority system in fashioning a Title VII remedy. This "policy" was read to prohibit a court from awarding make-whole relief, such as competitive seniority, back pay, or promotion, to individuals who were denied employment opportunities for reasons unrelated to discrimination. The District Court's injunction was considered to be inconsistent with this "policy" because it was tantamount to an award of make-whole relief (in the form of competitive seniority) to individual black firefighters who had not shown that the proposed layoffs were motivated by racial discrimination.[44] However, this limitation on *individual* make-whole relief does not affect a court's authority to order race-conscious affirmative action. The purpose of affirmative action is not to make identified victims whole, but rather to dismantle prior patterns of employment discrimination and to prevent discrimination in the future. Such relief is provided to the class as a whole rather than to individual members; no individual is entitled to relief, and beneficiaries need not show that they were themselves victims of discrimination. In this case, neither the membership goal nor the Fund order required the petitioners to indenture or train particular individuals, and neither required them to admit to membership individuals who were refused admission for reasons unrelated to discrimination. We decline petitioners' invitation to read *Stotts* to prohibit a court from ordering any kind of race-conscious affirmative relief that might benefit nonvictims. This reading would distort the language of § 706(g), and would deprive the courts of an important means of enforcing Title VII's guarantee of equal employment opportunity.

E

Although we conclude that § 706(g) does not foreclose a district court from instituting some sorts of racial preferences where necessary to remedy past discrimination, we do not mean to suggest that such relief is always proper. While the fashioning of "appropriate" remedies for a particular Title VII violation invokes the "equitable discretion of the district courts," *Franks* [*v. Bowman Transportation Co.*, 424 U.S. 747, 770 96 S.Ct. 1251, 1267, 47 L.Ed.2d 444 (1976),] we emphasize that a court's judgment should be guided by sound legal principles. In particular, the court should exercise its discretion with an eye towards Congress' concern that race-conscious affirmative measures not be invoked simply to create a racially balanced work force. * * * We note * * * that a court should consider whether affirmative action is necessary to remedy past discrimination in a particular case before imposing such measures, and that the court should also take care to tailor its orders to fit the nature of the violation it seeks to correct. In this case, several factors lead us to conclude that the relief ordered by the District Court was proper.

First, both the District Court and the Court of Appeals agreed that the membership goal and Fund order were necessary to remedy petitioners' pervasive and egregious discrimination. * * *

Both the membership goal and Fund order were similarly necessary to combat the lingering effects of past discrimination. In light of the District Court's determination that the union's reputation for discrimination operated to discourage nonwhites from even applying for membership, it is unlikely that an injunction would have been sufficient to extend to

---

[44] We note that, consistent with *Stotts*, the District Court in this case properly limited make-whole relief to the actual victims of discrimination. The court awarded back pay, for example, only to those class members who could establish that they were discriminated against.

nonwhites equal opportunities for employment. Rather, because access to admission, membership, training, and employment in the industry had traditionally been obtained through informal contacts with union members, it was necessary for a substantial number of nonwhite workers to become members of the union in order for the effects of discrimination to cease. The Fund, in particular, was designed to insure that nonwhites would receive the kind of assistance that white apprentices and applicants had traditionally received through informal sources. * * *

Second, the District Court's flexible application of the membership goal gives strong indication that it is not being used simply to achieve and maintain racial balance, but rather as a benchmark against which the court could gauge petitioners' efforts to remedy past discrimination. The court has twice adjusted the deadline for achieving the goal, and has continually approved of changes in the size of the apprenticeship classes to account for the fact that economic conditions prevented petitioners from meeting their membership targets; there is every reason to believe that both the court and the administrator will continue to accommodate *legitimate* explanations for the petitioners' failure to comply with the court's orders. Moreover, the District Court expressly disavowed any reliance on petitioners' failure to meet the goal as a basis for the contempt finding, but instead viewed this failure as symptomatic of petitioners' refusal to comply with various subsidiary provisions of RAAPO. In sum, the District Court has implemented the membership goal as a means by which it can measure petitioners' compliance with its orders, rather than as a strict racial quota.

Third, both the membership goal and the Fund order are temporary measures. Under AAAPO "[p]referential selection of union members [w]ill end as soon as the percentage of [minority union members] approximates the percentage of [minorities] in the local labor force." [*United Steelworkers v. Weber*, 443 U.S. 193, 208–209, 99 S.Ct. 2721, 2730 (1979).] * * * Similarly, the Fund is scheduled to terminate when petitioners achieve the membership goal, and the court determines that it is no longer needed to remedy past discrimination. * * *

Finally, we think it significant that neither the membership goal nor the Fund order "unnecessarily trammel the interests of white employees." *Id.*, 443 U.S., at 208, 99 S.Ct., at 2730; *Teamsters*, 431 U.S., at 352–353, 97 S.Ct., at 1863–1864. Petitioners concede that the District Court's orders did not require any member of the union to be laid off, and did not discriminate against *existing* union members. See *Weber, supra*, 443 U.S., at 208, 99 S.Ct., at 2729–2730. While whites seeking admission into the union may be denied benefits extended to their nonwhite counterparts, the court's orders do not stand as an absolute bar to such individuals; indeed, a majority of new union members have been white. Many provisions of the court's orders are race-neutral (for example, the requirement that the JAC assign one apprentice for every four journeymen workers), and petitioners remain free to adopt the provisions of AAAPO and the Fund Order for the benefit of white members and applicants.

V

Petitioners also allege that the membership goal and Fund order contravene the equal protection component of the Due Process Clause of the Fifth Amendment because they deny benefits to white individuals based on race. We have consistently recognized that government bodies constitutionally may adopt racial classifications as a remedy for past discrimination. See *Wygant v. Jackson Board of Education*, 476 U.S. 267, 106 S.Ct. 1842, 90 L.Ed.2d 260 (1986); *Fullilove v. Klutznick*, 448 U.S. 448, 100 S.Ct. 2758, 65 L.Ed.2d 902 (1980); *University of California Regents v. Bakke*, 438 U.S. 265, 98 S.Ct. 2733, 57 L.Ed.2d 750 (1978); *Swann v. Charlotte-Mecklenburg Board of Education*, 402 U.S. 1, 91 S.Ct. 1267, 28 L.Ed.2d 554 (1971). We have not agreed, however, on the proper test to be applied in analyzing the constitutionality of race-conscious remedial measures. * * * We need not resolve this dispute here, since we conclude that the relief ordered in this case passes even the most rigorous test—it is narrowly tailored to further the Government's compelling interest in remedying past discrimination.

JUSTICE POWELL, concurring in part and concurring in the judgment.

I join Parts I, II, III, and VI of Justice Brennan's opinion. * * * I write separately with respect to the issues raised in parts IV and V to explain why I think the remedy ordered under the circumstances of this case violated neither Title VII nor the Constitution.

* * *

The history of petitioners' contemptuous racial discrimination and their successive attempts to evade all efforts to end that discrimination is well stated in part I of the Court's opinion. Under these circumstances the District Court acted within the remedial authority granted by § 706(g) in establishing the Fund order and numerical goal at issue in this case. * * *

There remains for consideration the question whether the Fund order and membership goal contravene the equal protection component of the Due Process Clause of the Fifth Amendment because they may deny benefits to white individuals based on race. * * *

The finding by the District Court and the Court of Appeals that petitioners have engaged in egregious violations of Title VII establishes, without doubt, a compelling governmental interest sufficient to justify the imposition of a racially classified remedy. It would be difficult to find defendants more determined to discriminate against minorities. My inquiry, therefore, focuses on whether the District Court's remedy is "narrowly tailored" to the goal of eradicating the discrimination engaged in by petitioners. I believe it is.

The Fund order is supported not only by the governmental interest in eradicating petitioners' discriminatory practices, it also is supported by the societal interest in compliance with the judgments of federal courts. Cf. *United States v. Mine Workers*, 330 U.S. 258, 303, 67 S.Ct. 677, 701, 91 L.Ed. 884 (1947). The Fund order was not imposed until *after* petitioners were held in contempt. In requiring the Union to create the Fund, the District Court expressly considered " 'the consequent seriousness of the burden' to the defendants." Moreover, the focus of the Fund order was to give minorities opportunities that for years had been available informally only to nonminorities. The burden this imposes on nonminorities is slight. Under these circumstances, I have little difficulty concluding that the Fund order was carefully structured to vindicate the compelling governmental interests present in this case.

The percentage goal raises a different question. * * *

First, it is doubtful, given petitioners' history in this litigation, that the District Court had available to it any other effective remedy. * * * Second, the goal was not imposed as a permanent requirement, but is of limited duration. Third, the goal is directly related to the percentage of nonwhites in the relevant workforce.

* * *

[Fourth, the] flexible application of the goal requirement in this case demonstrates that it is not a means to achieve racial balance. * * *

It is also important to emphasize that on the record before us, it does not appear that nonminorities will be burdened directly, if at all. * * *

JUSTICE O'CONNOR, concurring in part and dissenting in part.

* * * I would reverse the judgment of the Court of Appeals on statutory grounds insofar as the membership "goal" and the Fund order are concerned, and I would not reach petitioners' constitutional claims. I agree with Justice White, however, that the membership "goal" in this case operates as a rigid racial quota that cannot feasibly be met through good-faith efforts by Local 28. In my view, § 703(j), 42 U.S.C. § 2000e–2(j), and § 706(g), 42 U.S.C. § 2000e–5(g), read together, preclude courts from ordering racial quotas such as this. I therefore dissent from the Court's judgment insofar as it affirms the use of these mandatory quotas.

* * *

To be consistent with § 703(j), a racial hiring or membership goal must be intended to serve merely as a benchmark for measuring compliance with Title VII and eliminating the lingering effects of past discrimination, rather than as a rigid numerical requirement that must unconditionally be met on pain of sanctions. To hold an employer or union to achievement of a particular percentage of minority employment or membership, and to do so regardless of circumstances such as economic conditions or the number of available qualified minority applicants, is to impose an impermissible quota. By contrast, a permissible goal should require only a good faith effort on the employer's or union's part to come within a range demarcated by the goal itself.

* * *

In this case, I agree with Justice White that the membership "goal" established by the District Court's successive orders in this case has been administered and will continue to operate "not just [as] a minority membership goal but also [as] a strict racial quota that the union was required to attain." It is important to realize that the membership "goal" ordered by the District Court goes well beyond a requirement, such as the ones the plurality discusses approvingly, that a union "admit qualified minorities roughly in proportion to the number of qualified minorities in the work force." The "goal" here requires that the racial composition of Local 28's entire membership mirror that of the relevant labor pool by August 31, 1987, without regard to variables such as the number of qualified minority applicants available or the number of new apprentices needed. The District Court plainly stated that "[i]f the goal is not attained by that date, defendants will face fines that will threaten their very existence."

* * * For similar reasons, I believe that the Fund order, which created benefits for minority apprentices that nonminority apprentices were precluded from enjoying, operated as a form of racial quota.

NOTES AND QUESTIONS

Test Your Understanding of the Material

1. A majority of the Court in *Sheet Metal Workers* (the four-Justice plurality and Justice Powell) endorsed the proposition that in appropriate circumstances Title VII courts may order race-conscious relief that benefits individuals other than those who have been judged victims of a defendant's discrimination. What purposes does the plurality opinion suggest such orders may appropriately serve? Which of these purposes, if any, do you think were served by the challenged order in *Sheet Metal Workers*?

2. Assuming acceptable purposes, what limitations does the *Sheet Metal Workers* plurality suggest should be placed on orders for race-conscious relief for Title VII violations? What limitations would Justice Powell impose?

3. Consider the *Sheet Metal Workers* decision's treatment of Firefighters v. Stotts, 467 U.S. 561, 104 S.Ct. 2576, 81 L.Ed.2d 483 (1984). Why was race-conscious relief held not acceptable in *Stotts*? Note that the trial court in *Stotts* framed its decree to provide "make-whole relief" to particular laid-off black

employees who were not actual direct victims of the defendant's past discrimination, rather than as "forward looking" affirmative action "to dismantle prior patterns of employment discrimination and to prevent discrimination in the future." Could the trial court in *Stotts* have justified ordering a suspension of the normal operation of the fire department's bona fide seniority system as necessary to dismantle a system of discrimination?

Related Issues

4. *Justice O'Connor and the Distinction Between Goals and Quotas.* Consider how Justice O'Connor contrasted quotas and goals seventeen years later in her opinion for the Court in Grutter v. Bollinger, 539 U.S. 306, 123 S.Ct. 2325, 156 L.Ed.2d 304 (2003), upholding the University of Michigan Law School's affirmative action plan for student admissions:

> Properly understood, a quota is a program in which a certain fixed number or proportion of opportunities are reserved exclusively for certain minority groups. Quotas impose a fixed number or percentage which must be attained, or which cannot be exceeded, and insulate the individual from comparison with all other candidates for the available seats. In contrast, a permissible goal requires only a good-faith effort . . . to come within a range demarcated by the goal itself, and permits consideration of race as a plus factor in any given case while still ensuring that each candidate competes with all other qualified applicants. . . .

539 U.S. at 336 [citations and quotations omitted]. See also Gratz v. Bollinger, 539 U.S. 244, 123 S.Ct. 2411, 156 L.Ed.2d 257 (2003) (stressing the importance of each candidate being given individualized consideration).

5. *Constitutional vs. Title VII Standard.* What standards for judging the constitutionality of affirmative action relief are suggested by the plurality opinion and Justice Powell's concurring opinion in *Sheet Metal Workers*? Do these differ from the Title VII standards as applied in *Sheet Metal Workers*?

6. *Race-Conscious Remedies in Consent Decrees.* Local No. 93, International Assn. of Firefighters v. Cleveland, 478 U.S. 501, 106 S.Ct. 3063, 92 L.Ed.2d 405 (1986) involved a Title VII court's authority to approve race-conscious classwide remedies as part of a consent decree. In *Firefighters*, the Court held that consent decrees are to be judged only under § 703 and not § 706(g) standards. In an opinion for six Justices, Justice Brennan explained that the congressional preference for voluntary compliance in Title VII required that consent decrees not be evaluated in the same terms as judicially mandated action under § 706(g). In doing so, Justice Brennan discounted the fact that consent decrees, unlike other voluntary agreements, can be enforced through judicial contempt proceedings: "For the choice of an enforcement scheme—whether to rely on contractual remedies or to have an agreement entered as a consent decree—is itself made voluntarily by the parties." Id. at 523, 106 S.Ct. at 3076.

7. *Section 108 of the 1991 Civil Rights Act.* In Martin v. Wilks, 490 U.S. 755, 109 S.Ct. 2180, 104 L.Ed.2d 835 (1989), the Court held that white

employees who were disadvantaged by an affirmative action consent decree established in litigation in which they did not intervene, but of which they had notice, could challenge under Title VII decisions made pursuant to that decree. However, the *Wilks* decision was substantially modified by § 108 of the Civil Rights Act of 1991, 105 Stat. 1071. This section added a new § 703(n) to Title VII, 42 U,S.C. § 2000e–2(n), which provides that a litigated or consent judgment that resolves federal claims of employment discrimination cannot be challenged "in a claim under the Constitution or Federal civil rights laws", either by persons with actual notice of the judgment and with an opportunity to present objections prior to the judgment's entry, or by persons "whose interests were adequately represented by another person who had previously challenged the judgment or order on the same legal grounds and with a similar factual situation, unless there has been an intervening change in law or fact."

B. VOLUNTARY AFFIRMATIVE ACTION

1. THE CONSTITUTIONAL STANDARD

WYGANT V. JACKSON BOARD OF EDUCATION

Supreme Court of the United States, 1986.
476 U.S. 267, 106 S.Ct. 1842, 90 L.Ed.2d 260.

JUSTICE POWELL announced the judgment of the Court and delivered an opinion in which THE CHIEF JUSTICE and JUSTICE REHNQUIST joined, and which JUSTICE O'CONNOR joined in parts I, II, III-A, III-B, and V.

I

In 1972 the Jackson Board of Education, because of racial tension in the community that extended to its schools, considered adding a layoff provision to the Collective Bargaining Agreement (CBA) between the Board and the Jackson Education Association (the Union) that would protect employees who were members of certain minority groups against layoffs.[1] The Board and the Union eventually approved a new provision, Article XII of the CBA, covering layoffs. It stated:

> "In the event that it becomes necessary to reduce the number of teachers through layoff from employment by the Board, teachers with the most seniority in the district shall be retained, except that at no time will there be a greater percentage of minority personnel laid off than the current percentage of minority personnel employed at the time of the layoff. In no event will the number given notice of possible layoff be greater than the number

---

[1] Prior to bargaining on this subject, the Minority Affairs Office of the Jackson Public Schools sent a questionnaire to all teachers, soliciting their views as to a layoff policy. The questionnaire proposed two alternatives: continuation of the existing straight seniority system, or a freeze of minority layoffs to ensure retention of minority teachers in exact proportion to the minority student population. Ninety-six percent of the teachers who responded to the questionnaire expressed a preference for the straight seniority system.

of positions to be eliminated. Each teacher so affected will be called back in reverse order for positions for which he is certificated maintaining the above minority balance."[2]

As a result, during the 1976–1977 and 1981–1982 school years, nonminority teachers were laid off, while minority teachers with less seniority were retained. The displaced nonminority teachers, petitioners here, brought suit in Federal District Court, alleging violations of the Equal Protection Clause, Title VII, 42 U.S.C. § 1983, and other federal and state statutes.

* * *

II

Petitioners' central claim is that they were laid off because of their race in violation of the Equal Protection Clause of the Fourteenth Amendment. * * *

The Court has recognized that the level of scrutiny does not change merely because the challenged classification operates against a group that historically has not been subject to governmental discrimination. * * * "Any preference based on racial or ethnic criteria must necessarily receive a most searching examination to make sure that it does not conflict with constitutional guarantees." *Fullilove v. Klutznick*, 448 U.S. 448, 491, 100 S.Ct. 2758, 2781, 65 L.Ed.2d 902 (1980) (opinion of Burger, C.J.). There are two prongs to this examination. First, any racial classification "must be justified by a compelling governmental interest." *Palmore v. Sidoti*, 466 U.S. 429, 432, 104 S.Ct. 1879, 1882, 80 L.Ed.2d 421 (1984). * * * Second, the means chosen by the State to effectuate its purpose must be "narrowly tailored to the achievement of that goal." *Fullilove*, 448 U.S., at 480, 100 S.Ct., at 2776. We must decide whether the layoff provision is supported by a compelling state purpose and whether the means chosen to accomplish that purpose are narrowly tailored.

III

A

The Court of Appeals, relying on the reasoning and language of the District Court's opinion, held that the Board's interest in providing minority role models for its minority students, as an attempt to alleviate the effects of societal discrimination, was sufficiently important to justify the racial classification embodied in the layoff provision. The court discerned a need for more minority faculty role models by finding that the percentage of minority teachers was less than the percentage of minority students.

This Court never has held that societal discrimination alone is sufficient to justify a racial classification. Rather, the Court has insisted

---

[2]   Article VII of the CBA defined "minority group personnel" as "those employees who are Black, American Indian, Oriental, or of Spanish descendancy."

upon some showing of prior discrimination by the governmental unit involved before allowing limited use of racial classifications in order to remedy such discrimination. This Court's reasoning in *Hazelwood School District v. United States*, 433 U.S. 299, 97 S.Ct. 2736, 53 L.Ed.2d 768 (1977), illustrates that the relevant analysis in cases involving proof of discrimination by statistical disparity focuses on those disparities that demonstrate such prior governmental discrimination. In *Hazelwood* the Court concluded that, absent employment discrimination by the school board, " 'nondiscriminatory hiring practices will in time result in a work force more or less representative of the racial and ethnic composition of the population in the community from which the employees are hired.' " *Id.,* at 307, 97 S.Ct., at 2741, quoting *Teamsters v. United States*, 431 U.S. 324, 340, n. 20.

* * *

Unlike the analysis in *Hazelwood*, the role model theory employed by the District Court has no logical stopping point. The role model theory allows the Board to engage in discriminatory hiring and layoff practices long past the point required by any legitimate remedial purpose.

* * *

Societal discrimination, without more, is too amorphous a basis for imposing a racially classified remedy. The role model theory announced by the District Court and the resultant holding typify this indefiniteness. There are numerous explanations for a disparity between the percentage of minority students and the percentage of minority faculty, many of them completely unrelated to discrimination of any kind. In fact, there is no apparent connection between the two groups. Nevertheless, the District Court combined irrelevant comparisons between these two groups with an indisputable statement that there has been societal discrimination, and upheld state action predicated upon racial classifications. No one doubts that there has been serious racial discrimination in this country. But as the basis for imposing discriminatory *legal* remedies that work against innocent people, societal discrimination is insufficient and over expansive. In the absence of particularized findings, a court could uphold remedies that are ageless in their reach into the past, and timeless in their ability to affect the future.

B

Respondents also now argue that their purpose in adopting the layoff provision was to remedy prior discrimination against minorities by the Jackson School District in hiring teachers. Public schools, like other public employers, operate under two interrelated constitutional duties. They are under a clear command from this Court, starting with *Brown v. Board of Education*, 349 U.S. 294, 75 S.Ct. 753, 99 L.Ed. 1083 (1955), to eliminate every vestige of racial segregation and discrimination in the schools.

Pursuant to that goal, race-conscious remedial action may be necessary. *North Carolina State Board of Education v. Swann*, 402 U.S. 43, 46, 91 S.Ct. 1284, 1286, 28 L.Ed.2d 586 (1971). On the other hand, public employers, including public schools, also must act in accordance with a "core purpose of the Fourteenth Amendment" which is to "do away with all governmentally imposed distinctions based on race." *Palmore v. Sidoti*, 466 U.S., at 432, 104 S.Ct., at 1881–1882. These related constitutional duties are not always harmonious; reconciling them requires public employers to act with extraordinary care. In particular, a public employer like the Board must ensure that, before it embarks on an affirmative action program, it has convincing evidence that remedial action is warranted. That is, it must have sufficient evidence to justify the conclusion that there has been prior discrimination.

Evidentiary support for the conclusion that remedial action is warranted becomes crucial when the remedial program is challenged in court by nonminority employees. In this case, for example, petitioners contended at trial that the remedial program—Article XII—had the purpose and effect of instituting a racial classification that was not justified by a remedial purpose. In such a case, the trial court must make a factual determination that the employer had a strong basis in evidence for its conclusion that remedial action was necessary. The ultimate burden remains with the employees to demonstrate the unconstitutionality of an affirmative action program. But unless such a determination is made, an appellate court reviewing a challenge to remedial action by nonminority employees cannot determine whether the race-based action is justified as a remedy for prior discrimination.

Despite the fact that Article XII has spawned years of litigation and three separate lawsuits, no such determination ever has been made. Although its litigation position was different, the Board in [two prior suits brought to compel the Board's adherence to its Article XII obligations] denied the existence of prior discriminatory hiring practices. * * * Both courts concluded that any statistical disparities were the result of general societal discrimination, not of prior discrimination by the Board. The Board now contends that, given another opportunity, it could establish the existence of prior discrimination. Although this argument seems belated at this point in the proceedings, we need not consider the question since we conclude below that the layoff provision was not a legally appropriate means of achieving even a compelling purpose.[5]

---

[5]   * * * The real dispute * * * is not over the state of the record. It is disagreement as to what constitutes a "legitimate factual predicate." If the necessary factual predicate is *prior discrimination*—that is, that race-based state action is taken to remedy prior discrimination by the governmental unit involved—then the very nature of appellate review requires that a factfinder determine whether the employer was justified in instituting a remedial plan. Nor can the respondent unilaterally insulate itself from this key constitutional question by conceding that it has discriminated in the past, now that it is in its interest to make such a concession. Contrary to the dissent's assertion, the requirement of such a determination by the trial court is not some

IV

The Court of Appeals examined the means chosen to accomplish the Board's race-conscious purposes under a test of "reasonableness." That standard has no support in the decisions of this Court. As demonstrated in Part II above, our decisions always have employed a more stringent standard—however articulated—to test the validity of the means chosen by a state to accomplish its race-conscious purposes. See, *e.g., Palmore*, 466 U.S., at 432, 104 S.Ct., at 1882 ("to pass constitutional muster, [racial classifications] must be necessary * * * to the accomplishment of their legitimate purpose") (quoting *McLaughlin v. Florida*, 379 U.S. 184, 196, 85 S.Ct. 283, 290, 13 L.Ed.2d 222 (1964); *Fullilove*, 448 U.S., at 480, 100 S.Ct., at 2775 (opinion of Burger, C.J.) * * * . "Racial classifications are simply too pernicious to permit any but the most exact connection between justification and classification." *Id.,* at 537, 100 S.Ct., at 2805 (Stevens, J., dissenting).

We have recognized, however, that in order to remedy the effects of prior discrimination, it may be necessary to take race into account. As part of this Nation's dedication to eradicating racial discrimination, innocent persons may be called upon to bear some of the burden of the remedy. "When effectuating a limited and properly tailored remedy to cure the effects of prior discrimination, such a 'sharing of the burden' by innocent parties is not impermissible." *Id.,* at 484, 100 S.Ct., at 2778, quoting *Franks v. Bowman Transportation Co.,* 424 U.S. 747.[8]

Significantly, none of the cases discussed above involved layoffs. Here, by contrast, the means chosen to achieve the Board's asserted purposes is that of laying off nonminority teachers with greater seniority in order to retain minority teachers with less seniority. We have previously expressed concern over the burden that a preferential layoffs scheme imposes on

---

arbitrary barrier set up by today's opinion. Rather, it is a necessary result of the requirement that race-based state action be remedial. * * *

    [8]   Of course, when a state implements a race-based plan that requires such a sharing of the burden, it cannot justify the discriminatory effect on some individuals because other individuals had approved the plan. Any "waiver" of the right not to be dealt with by the government on the basis of one's race must be made by those affected. Yet Justice Marshall repeatedly contends that the fact that Article XII was approved by a majority vote of the Union somehow validates this plan. He sees this case not in terms of individual constitutional rights, but as an allocation of burdens "between two racial groups." * * * Thus, Article XII becomes a political compromise that "avoided placing the entire burden of layoffs on either the white teachers as a group or the minority teachers as a group." * * * But the petitioners before us today are not "the white teachers as a group." They are Wendy Wygant and other individuals who claim that they were fired from their jobs because of their race. That claim cannot be waived by petitioners' more senior colleagues. In view of the way union seniority works, it is not surprising that while a straight freeze on minority layoffs was overwhelmingly rejected, a "compromise" eventually was reached that placed the entire burden of the compromise on the most junior union members. The more senior union members simply had nothing to lose from such a compromise. * * * ("To petitioners, at the bottom of the seniority scale among white teachers, fell the lot of bearing the white group's proportionate share of layoffs that became necessary in 1982.") The fact that such a painless accommodation was approved by the more senior union members six times since 1972 is irrelevant. The Constitution does not allocate constitutional rights to be distributed like bloc grants within discrete racial groups; and until it does, petitioners' more senior union colleagues cannot vote away petitioners' rights. * * *

innocent parties. See *Firefighters v. Stotts*, 467 U.S. 561, 574–576, 578–579, 104 S.Ct. 2576, 81 L.Ed.2d 483 (1984) * * * . In cases involving valid *hiring* goals, the burden to be borne by innocent individuals is diffused to a considerable extent among society generally. Though hiring goals may burden some innocent individuals, they simply do not impose the same kind of injury that layoffs impose. Denial of a future employment opportunity is not as intrusive as loss of an existing job.

* * *

While hiring goals impose a diffuse burden, often foreclosing only one of several opportunities, layoffs impose the entire burden of achieving racial equality on particular individuals, often resulting in serious disruption of their lives. That burden is too intrusive. We therefore hold that, as a means of accomplishing purposes that otherwise may be legitimate, the Board's layoff plan is not sufficiently narrowly tailored. Other, less intrusive means of accomplishing similar purposes—such as the adoption of hiring goals—are available. For these reasons, the Board's selection of layoffs as the means to accomplish even a valid purpose cannot satisfy the demands of the Equal Protection Clause.[13]

JUSTICE O'CONNOR, concurring in part and concurring in the judgment.

I agree with the Court that a governmental agency's interest in remedying "societal" discrimination, that is, discrimination not traceable to its own actions, cannot be deemed sufficiently compelling to pass constitutional muster under strict scrutiny. * * * I also concur in the Court's assessment that use by the courts below of a "role model" theory to justify the conclusion that this plan had a legitimate remedial purpose was in error. * * * Thus, in my view, the District Court and the Court of Appeals clearly erred in relying on these purposes and in failing to give greater attention to the School Board's asserted purpose of rectifying its own apparent discrimination.

* * *

The courts below ruled that a particularized, contemporaneous finding of discrimination was not necessary and upheld the plan as a remedy for "societal" discrimination, apparently on the assumption that in the absence of a specific, contemporaneous finding, any discrimination addressed by an affirmative action plan could only be termed "societal." I believe that this assumption is false and therefore agree with the Court that a contemporaneous or antecedent finding of past discrimination by a court or

---

[13] The Board's definition of minority to include blacks, Orientals, American Indians, and persons of Spanish descent, further illustrates the undifferentiated nature of the plan. There is no explanation of why the Board chose to favor these particular minorities or how in fact members of some of the categories can be identified. Moreover, respondents have never suggested—much less formally found—that they have engaged in prior, purposeful discrimination against members of each of these minority groups.

other competent body is not a constitutional prerequisite to a public employer's voluntary agreement to an affirmative action plan.

* * *

The imposition of a requirement that public employers make findings that they have engaged in illegal discrimination before they engage in affirmative action programs would severely undermine public employers' incentive to meet voluntarily their civil rights obligations. * * * This result would clearly be at odds with this Court's and Congress' consistent emphasis on "the value of voluntary efforts to further the objectives of the law." * * * The value of voluntary compliance is doubly important when it is a public employer that acts, both because of the example its voluntary assumption of responsibility sets and because the remediation of governmental discrimination is of unique importance. See S.Rep. No. 92–415, p. 10 (1971) (accompanying the amendments extending coverage of Title VII to the States) ("Discrimination by government * * * serves a doubly destructive purpose. The exclusion of minorities from effective participation in the bureaucracy not only promotes ignorance of minority problems in that particular community, but also creates mistrust, alienation, and all too often hostility toward the entire process of government"). * * *

Such results cannot, in my view, be justified by reference to the incremental value a contemporaneous findings requirement would have as an evidentiary safeguard. As is illustrated by this case, public employers are trapped between the competing hazards of liability to minorities if affirmative action *is not* taken to remedy apparent employment discrimination and liability to nonminorities if affirmative action *is* taken. Where these employers, who are presumably fully aware both of their duty under federal law to respect the rights of *all* their employees and of their potential liability for failing to do so, act on the basis of information which gives them a sufficient basis for concluding that remedial action is necessary, a contemporaneous findings requirement should not be necessary.

* * *

There is, however, no need to inquire whether the provision actually had a legitimate remedial purpose based on the record, such as it is, because the judgment is vulnerable on yet another ground: the courts below applied a "reasonableness" test in evaluating the relationship between the ends pursued and the means employed to achieve them that is plainly incorrect under any of the standards articulated by this Court. Nor is it necessary, in my view, to resolve the troubling questions of whether any layoff provision could survive strict scrutiny or whether this particular layoff provision could, when considered without reference to the hiring goal it was intended to further, pass the onerous "narrowly tailored" requirement. Petitioners have met their burden of establishing that this layoff provision is not "narrowly tailored" to achieve its asserted remedial purpose by demonstrating that the provision is keyed to a hiring goal that itself has no relation to the remedying of employment discrimination.

Although the constitutionality of the hiring goal as such is not before us, it is impossible to evaluate the necessity of the layoff provision as a remedy for the apparent prior employment discrimination absent reference to that goal. * * * In this case, the hiring goal that the layoff provision was designed to safeguard was tied to the percentage of minority students in the school district, not to the percentage of qualified minority teachers within the relevant labor pool. The disparity between the percentage of minorities on the teaching staff and the percentage of minorities in the student body is not probative of employment discrimination; it is only when it is established that the availability of minorities in the relevant labor pool substantially exceeded those hired that one may draw an inference of deliberate discrimination in employment. See *Hazelwood School District v. United States*, 433 U.S. 299, 308, 97 S.Ct. 2736, 2741, 53 L.Ed.2d 768 (1977) (Title VII context). Because the layoff provision here acts to maintain levels of minority hiring that have no relation to remedying employment discrimination, it cannot be adjudged "narrowly tailored" to effectuate its asserted remedial purpose.

JUSTICE WHITE, concurring in the judgment.

The school board's policy when layoffs are necessary is to maintain a certain proportion of minority teachers. This policy requires laying off non-minority teachers solely on the basis of their race, including teachers with seniority, and retaining other teachers solely because they are black, even though some of them are in probationary status. None of the interests asserted by the board, singly or together, justify this racially discriminatory layoff policy and save it from the strictures of the Equal Protection Clause. Whatever the legitimacy of hiring goals or quotas may be, the discharge of white teachers to make room for blacks, none of whom has been shown to be a victim of any racial discrimination, is quite a different matter. I cannot believe that in order to integrate a work force, it would be permissible to discharge whites and hire blacks until the latter comprised a suitable percentage of the work force. None of our cases suggest that this would be permissible under the Equal Protection Clause. Indeed, our cases look quite the other way. The layoff policy in this case—laying off whites who would otherwise be retained in order to keep blacks on the job—has the same effect and is equally violative of the Equal Protection Clause. I agree with the plurality that this official policy is unconstitutional and hence concur in the judgment.

JUSTICE MARSHALL, with whom JUSTICE BRENNAN and JUSTICE BLACKMUN join, dissenting.

* * *

The principal state purpose supporting Article XII is the need to preserve the levels of faculty integration achieved through the affirmative hiring policy adopted in the early 1970's. Justification for the hiring policy itself is found in the turbulent history of the effort to integrate the Jackson Public Schools—not even mentioned in the majority opinion—which attests to the bona fides of the Board's current employment practices.

The record and lodgings indicate that the [Michigan Civil Rights] Commission, endowed by the State Constitution with the power to investigate complaints of discrimination and the duty to secure the equal protection of the laws, Mich. Const., Art. V, § 29, prompted and oversaw the remedial steps now under attack. When the Board agreed to take specified remedial action, including the hiring and promotion of minority teachers, the Commission did not pursue its investigation of the apparent violations to the point of rendering formal findings of discrimination.

Instead of subjecting an already volatile school system to the further disruption of formal accusations and trials, it appears that the Board set about achieving the goals articulated in the settlement.

* * *

Testimony of both Union and school officials illustrates that the Board's obligation to integrate its faculty could not have been fulfilled meaningfully as long as layoffs continued to eliminate the last hired. In addition, qualified minority teachers from other States were reluctant to uproot their lives and move to Michigan without any promise of protection from imminent layoff. The testimony suggests that the lack of some layoff protection would have crippled the efforts to recruit minority applicants. Adjustment of the layoff hierarchy under these circumstances was a necessary corollary of an affirmative hiring policy.

Under Justice Powell's approach, the community of Jackson, having painfully watched the hard-won benefits of its integration efforts vanish as a result of massive layoffs, would be informed today, simply, that preferential layoff protection is never permissible because hiring policies serve the same purpose at a lesser cost. * * * As a matter of logic as well as fact, a hiring policy achieves no purpose at all if it is eviscerated by layoffs. Justice Powell's position is untenable.

* * *

The Board's goal of preserving minority proportions could have been achieved, perhaps, in a different way. For example, if layoffs had been determined by lottery, the ultimate effect would have been retention of current racial percentages. A random system, however, would place every teacher in equal jeopardy, working a much greater upheaval of the seniority hierarchy than that occasioned by Article XII; it is not at all a less restrictive means of achieving the Board's goal.

JUSTICE STEVENS, dissenting.

In the context of public education, it is quite obvious that a school board may reasonably conclude that an integrated faculty will be able to provide benefits to the student body that could not be provided by an all white, or nearly all white, faculty. For one of the most important lessons that the American public schools teach is that the diverse ethnic, cultural, and national backgrounds that have been brought together in our famous "melting pot" do not identify essential differences among the human beings that inhabit our land. It is one thing for a white child to be taught by a white teacher that color, like beauty, is only "skin deep"; it is far more convincing to experience that truth on a day to day basis during the routine, ongoing learning process.

* * *

Even if there is a valid purpose to the race consciousness, however, the question that remains is whether that public purpose transcends the harm to the white teachers who are disadvantaged by the special preference the Board has given to its most recently hired minority teachers. In my view, there are two important inquiries in assessing the harm to the disadvantaged teacher. The first is an assessment of the procedures that were used to adopt, and implement, the race-conscious action. The second is an evaluation of the nature of the harm itself.

In this case, there can be no question about either the fairness of the procedures used to adopt the race-conscious provision, or the propriety of its breadth. As Justice Marshall has demonstrated, the procedures for adopting this provision were scrupulously fair. The Union that represents the petitioners negotiated the provision and agreed to it; the agreement was put to a vote of the membership, and overwhelmingly approved. Again, not a shred of evidence in the record suggests *any* procedural unfairness in the adoption of the agreement. Similarly, the provision is specifically designed to achieve its objective—retaining the minority teachers that have been specially recruited to give the Jackson schools, after a period of racial unrest, an integrated faculty. * * *

Finally, we must consider the harm to the petitioners. Every layoff, like every refusal to employ a qualified applicant, is a grave loss to the affected individual. However, the undisputed facts in this case demonstrate that this serious consequence to the petitioners is not based on any lack of respect for their race, or on blind habit and stereotype. Rather, petitioners have been laid off for a combination of two reasons: the economic conditions that have led Jackson to lay off some teachers, and the special contractual protections intended to preserve the newly integrated character of the faculty in the Jackson schools. Thus, the same harm might occur if a number of gifted young teachers had been given special contractual protection because their specialties were in short supply and if the Jackson Board of Education faced a fiscal need for layoffs. * * * [14]

NOTE: RICHMOND V. J.A. CROSON CO. AND THE AFFIRMATION OF WYGANT

Several important positions taken by Justice Powell in his opinion in *Wygant* did not command the explicit concurrence of a majority of the Court. However, a decision rendered a year after Justice Powell's retirement, City of Richmond v. J.A. Croson Co., 488 U.S. 469, 109 S.Ct. 706, 102 L.Ed.2d 854 (1989), indicates that these positions were soon embraced by a majority of the Justices.

In *Croson* the Court struck down a plan of the city of Richmond that required prime contractors awarded construction contracts to subcontract at least 30% of the value of each contract to "minority business enterprises," defined to include any business at least 51% of which is owned by black, Spanish-speaking, Oriental, Indian, Eskimo, or Aleut citizens. The Richmond City Council, a majority of whose members were black, adopted the plan after expressing its view that there had been past discrimination in the local construction industry and noting that minority businesses received only .67% of contracts from the city while constituting 50% of the city's population.

Writing for four Justices (herself, Rehnquist, White and Kennedy), Justice O'Connor stated that the equal protection clause requires heightened or strict scrutiny of any racial classification, regardless of "the race of those burdened or benefitted * * * ." 109 S.Ct. at 721. In a concurring opinion Justice Scalia agreed. Justice O'Connor also cautioned that such scrutiny could not be satisfied by an asserted governmental interest in the remedying of general "societal discrimination." Rather, the government must be attempting to "rectify the effects of identified discrimination within its jurisdiction", with "a strong basis in evidence" that remedial action is necessary. Justice O'Connor stated that only in "the extreme case" might "some form of narrowly tailored racial preference * * * be necessary to break down patterns of deliberate exclusion." Justice Scalia would be even more restrictive of state power, allowing the states to use race to undo the effects of past discrimination only "where that is necessary to eliminate their own maintenance" of a racially discriminatory system. Justices Stevens and Kennedy, in separate concurring

---

[14] The fact that the issue arises in a layoff context, rather than a hiring context, has no bearing on the equal protection question. For if the Board's interest in employing more minority teachers is sufficient to justify providing them with an extra incentive to accept jobs in Jackson, Michigan, it is also sufficient to justify their retention when the number of available jobs is reduced. Justice Powell's suggestion, * * * that there is a distinction of constitutional significance under the Equal Protection Clause between a racial preference at the time of hiring and an identical preference at the time of discharge is thus wholly unpersuasive. He seems to assume that a teacher who has been working for a few years suffers a greater harm when he is laid off than the harm suffered by an unemployed teacher who is refused a job for which he is qualified. In either event, the adverse decision forecloses "only one of several opportunities" that may be available, * * * to the disappointed teacher. Moreover, the distinction is artificial, for the layoff provision at issue in this case was included as part of the terms of the *hiring* of minority and other teachers under the collective-bargaining agreement.

opinions, agreed that broad quota plans like that of Richmond's cannot be justified as a remedy for past discrimination.

NOTES AND QUESTIONS

Test Your Understanding of the Material

1.   Consider Justice Powell's position for the *Wygant* plurality—endorsed in *Croson* as well as later decisions, by a majority of the Court—that preferences for racial groups historically subject to discrimination must withstand the same "strict scrutiny" as race-based classifications that disadvantage such groups. This equal protection standard operates as a rule of presumptive invalidity that first emerged because of suspicion about the legitimacy of the government's motives when racial minorities were disadvantaged by government action. Is such a presumption appropriate in the affirmative action context?

2.   Justice Powell's opinion in *Wygant* draws a distinction between race-conscious hiring goals and race-conscious layoff plans. Are you persuaded by this distinction? Why or why not?

Related Issues

3.   *Intermediate Scrutiny for Gender-Based Classifications.* Should affirmative action programs for women be reviewed under a less demanding standard in accordance with the way the Court generally treats gender classifications? See, e.g., Mississippi Univ. for Women v. Hogan, 458 U.S. 718, 102 S.Ct. 3331, 73 L.Ed.2d 1090 (1982) (intermediate scrutiny). Compare Danskine v. Miami Dade Fire Dept., 253 F.3d 1288 (11th Cir.2001), with Brunet v. City of Columbus, 1 F.3d 390, 403–04 (6th Cir.1993).

4.   *Prima Facie Case Showing for Voluntary Affirmative Action?* Do *Wygant* and *Croson* require the public employer to demonstrate a prima facie case of its own past discrimination as justification for the utilization of a race-conscious voluntary affirmative action plan? See, e.g., Maryland Troopers Ass'n, Inc. v. Evans, 993 F.2d 1072, 1074 (4th Cir.1993) (applying this standard); Cotter v. City of Boston, 323 F.3d 160, 169–170 (1st Cir. 2003) (holding sufficient "evidence approaching a prima facie case of a constitutional or statutory violation", including "a statistical disparity between the racial composition of the workforce and the relevant, qualified employment pool.") Consider also the Court's opinion in *Ricci*, supra page 261. Are many public employees likely to want to make this demonstration?

5.   *Is Remedying "Societal Discrimination" a Compelling Purpose?* Why is the elimination of societal discrimination not as compelling a state interest as remedying a particular employer's wrongdoing? Is it because the former objective—in the words of Justice Powell—has "no logical stopping point?" Is this true as well of other forward-looking justifications, such as a public school's interest in providing affirmative role models for school children?

6.   *Implications of Political Representation Theory.* Professor John Hart Ely argued that heightened judicial scrutiny is inappropriate in the affirmative

action context because the normal majoritarian political process can be counted on to take account of the interests of the burdened or nonbenefitted majority group. See John H. Ely, Democracy and Distrust 170 (1980). Justice O'Connor invoked this political representation theory in support of applying strict scrutiny in *Croson*, noting that blacks comprised a majority of the Richmond City Council—an approach Ely presumably would favor, see Ely, The Constitutionality of Reverse Racial Discrimination, 41 U.Chi.L.Rev. 723, 739 n. 58 (1974). In *Wygant*, Justice Powell's plurality opinion and Justice Marshall's and Justice Stevens's dissents take different views of whether the negotiation of the layoff quota with the union representative of a bargaining unit that included the affected workers provided a sufficient guarantee that the interests of the burdened group were adequately taken into account.

NOTE: GRUTTER V. BOLLINGER *AND DIVERSITY AS A COMPELLING JUSTIFICATION*

The Supreme Court's 2003 decision upholding against equal protection challenge the University of Michigan Law School's race conscious admissions system, Grutter v. Bollinger, 539 U.S. 306, 123 S.Ct. 2325, 156 L.Ed.2d 304 (2003), qualifies one principle suggested by the *Wygant* and *Croson* decisions— "that remedying past discrimination is the only permissible justification for race-based governmental action", 123 S.Ct. at 2338. The *Grutter* Court's acceptance of the Law School's plan was premised on its holding that the Law School "has a compelling interest in attaining a diverse student body." The Court deferred to the "Law School's educational judgment[s] that such diversity is essential to its educational mission," and that the "educational benefits that diversity is designed to produce" require the presence of a "critical mass" of minority students. Id. at 2339. Justice O'Connor, writing for the five-Justice majority, asserted:

> These benefits are substantial. As the District Court emphasized, the Law School's admissions policy promotes "cross-racial understanding," helps to break down racial stereotypes, and "enables [students] to better understand persons of different races." These benefits are "important and laudable," because "classroom discussion is livelier, more spirited, and simply more enlightening and interesting" when the students have "the greatest possible variety of backgrounds." * * *

> The Law School does not premise its need for critical mass on "any belief that minority students always (or even consistently) express some characteristic minority viewpoint on any issue." To the contrary, diminishing the force of such stereotypes is both a crucial part of the Law School's mission, and one that it cannot accomplish with only token numbers of minority students.

Id. at 2339–41. See also Fisher v. University of Texas at Austin, 133 S.Ct. 2411, 570 U.S. ___, 186 L.Ed.2d 474 (2013) (stating that "a diverse student body . . . serves values beyond race alone including enhanced classroom dialogue and the lessening of racial isolation and stereotypes", which can support a compelling state interest).

Grutter does not purport to address affirmative action plans for employment. Moreover, the opinion is tailored to underscore "education as pivotal to 'sustaining our political and cultural heritage' with a fundamental role in maintaining the fabric of society." The Court's acceptance of the goal of diversity as compelling for admissions programs in public higher education would seem to leave the door ajar for arguments that a similar goal could be compelling for certain public sector jobs.

Could a police force, for instance, concerned about understanding the needs of all of it constituents, lawfully use diversity to justify a hiring and promotion preference for African-American or Hispanic candidates? Note that Justice O'Connor in a footnote in her concurring opinion in *Wygant* distinguished the rejected "role-models" justification from "the very different goal of promoting racial diversity among the faculty", which was not advanced by the employer there and thus was not "necessary to discuss". Compare Lomack v. City of Newark, 463 F.3d 303 (3d Cir. 2006) (diversity not a compelling justification for use of race in assigning firefighters), with Petit v. City of Chicago, 352 F.3d 1111, 1114 (7th Cir. 2003) (diversity provides a compelling justification for consideration of race in promotions in large urban police department). But see Lutheran Church-Missouri Synod v. Federal Communications Commission, 141 F.3d 344 (D.C.Cir. 1998) (doubting that broadcast program diversity can provide a compelling justification for race-conscious hiring goals); Taxman v. Board of Education of Township of Piscataway, 91 F.3d 1547 (3d Cir. 1996) (holding that achieving racial "diversity" in teaching staff does not justify race-based layoff of teacher).

2. THE TITLE VII STANDARD

JOHNSON V. TRANSPORTATION AGENCY, SANTA CLARA COUNTY

Supreme Court of the United States, 1987.
480 U.S. 616, 107 S.Ct. 1442, 94 L.Ed.2d 615.

JUSTICE BRENNAN delivered the opinion of the Court.

I

A

In December 1978, the Santa Clara County Transit District Board of Supervisors adopted an Affirmative Action Plan (Plan) for the County Transportation Agency. The Plan implemented a County Affirmative Action Plan, which had been adopted, declared the County, because "mere prohibition of discriminatory practices is not enough to remedy the effects of past practices and to permit attainment of an equitable representation of minorities, women and handicapped persons." Relevant to this case, the Agency Plan provides that, in making promotions to positions within a traditionally segregated job classification in which women have been significantly underrepresented, the Agency is authorized to consider as one factor the sex of a qualified applicant.

In reviewing the composition of its work force, the Agency noted in its Plan that women were represented in numbers far less than their proportion of the county labor force in both the Agency as a whole and in five of seven job categories. Specifically, while women constituted 36.4% of the area labor market, they composed only 22.4% of Agency employees. Furthermore, women working at the Agency were concentrated largely in EEOC job categories traditionally held by women: women made up 76% of Office and Clerical Workers, but only 7.1% of Agency Officials and Administrators, 8.6% of Professionals, 9.7% of Technicians, and 22% of Service and Maintenance workers. As for the job classification relevant to this case, none of the 238 Skilled Craft Worker positions was held by a woman. The Plan noted that this underrepresentation of women in part reflected the fact that women had not traditionally been employed in these positions, and that they had not been strongly motivated to seek training or employment in them "because of the limited opportunities that have existed in the past for them to work in such classifications." The Plan also observed that, while the proportion of ethnic minorities in the Agency as a whole exceeded the proportion of such minorities in the county work force, a smaller percentage of minority employees held management, professional, and technical positions.

The Agency stated that its Plan was intended to achieve "a statistically measurable yearly improvement in hiring, training and promotion of minorities and women throughout the Agency in all major job classifications where they are underrepresented." As a benchmark by which to evaluate progress, the Agency stated that its long-term goal was to attain a work force whose composition reflected the proportion of minorities and women in the area labor force. Thus, for the Skilled Craft category in which the road dispatcher position at issue here was classified, the Agency's aspiration was that eventually about 36% of the jobs would be occupied by women.

The Plan acknowledged that a number of factors might make it unrealistic to rely on the Agency's long-term goals in evaluating the Agency's progress in expanding job opportunities for minorities and women. Among the factors identified were low turnover rates in some classifications, the fact that some jobs involved heavy labor, the small number of positions within some job categories, the limited number of entry positions leading to the Technical and Skilled Craft classifications, and the limited number of minorities and women qualified for positions requiring specialized training and experience. As a result, the Plan counselled that short-range goals be established and annually adjusted to serve as the most realistic guide for actual employment decisions.

* * *

The Agency's Plan thus set aside no specific number of positions for minorities or women, but authorized the consideration of ethnicity or sex as a factor when evaluating qualified candidates for jobs in which members of such groups were poorly represented. One such job was the road dispatcher position that is the subject of the dispute in this case.[2]

B

On December 12, 1979, the Agency announced a vacancy for the promotional position of road dispatcher in the Agency's Roads Division. Dispatchers assign road crews, equipment, and materials, and maintain records pertaining to road maintenance jobs. The position requires at minimum four years of dispatch or road maintenance work experience for Santa Clara County. The EEOC job classification scheme designates a road dispatcher as a Skilled Craft worker.

Twelve County employees applied for the promotion, including Joyce and Johnson. Joyce had worked for the County since 1970, serving as an account clerk until 1975. She had applied for a road dispatcher position in 1974, but was deemed ineligible because she had not served as a road maintenance worker. In 1975, Joyce transferred from a senior account clerk position to a road maintenance worker position, becoming the first woman to fill such a job. During her four years in that position, she occasionally worked out of class as a road dispatcher.

* * *

Nine of the applicants, including Joyce and Johnson, were deemed qualified for the job, and were interviewed by a two-person board. Seven of the applicants scored above 70 on this interview, which meant that they were certified as eligible for selection by the appointing authority. The scores awarded ranged from 70 to 80. Johnson was tied for second with a score of 75, while Joyce ranked next with a score of 73. A second interview was conducted by three Agency supervisors, who ultimately recommended that Johnson be promoted. Prior to the second interview, Joyce had contacted the County's Affirmative Action Office because she feared that her application might not receive disinterested review.[5] The Office in turn

---

[2]   No constitutional issue was either raised or addressed in the litigation below. We therefore decide in this case only the issue of the prohibitory scope of Title VII. Of course, where the issue is properly raised, public employers must justify the adoption and implementation of a voluntary affirmative action plan under the Equal Protection Clause. See *Wygant v. Jackson Board of Education,* 476 U.S. 267, 106 S.Ct. 1842, 90 L.Ed.2d 260 (1986).

[5]   Joyce testified that she had had disagreements with two of the three members of the second interview panel. One had been her first supervisor when she began work as a road maintenance worker. In performing arduous work in this job, she had not been issued coveralls, although her male co-workers had received them. After ruining her pants, she complained to her supervisor, to no avail. After three other similar incidents, ruining clothes on each occasion, she filed a grievance, and was issued four pair of coveralls the next day. Joyce had dealt with a second member of the panel for a year and a half in her capacity as chair of the Roads Operations Safety Committee, where she and he "had several differences of opinion on how safety should be implemented." In

contacted the Agency's Affirmative Action Coordinator, whom the Agency's Plan makes responsible for, *inter alia*, keeping the Director informed of opportunities for the Agency to accomplish its objectives under the Plan. At the time, the Agency employed no women in any Skilled Craft position, and had never employed a woman as a road dispatcher. The Coordinator recommended to the Director of the Agency, James Graebner, that Joyce be promoted.

Graebner, authorized to choose any of the seven persons deemed eligible, thus had the benefit of suggestions by the second interview panel and by the Agency Coordinator in arriving at his decision. After deliberation, Graebner concluded that the promotion should be given to Joyce. As he testified: "I tried to look at the whole picture, the combination of her qualifications and Mr. Johnson's qualifications, their test scores, their expertise, their background, affirmative action matters, things like that * * * I believe it was a combination of all those."

The certification form naming Joyce as the person promoted to the dispatcher position stated that both she and Johnson were rated as well-qualified for the job.

* * *

II

As a preliminary matter, we note that petitioner bears the burden of establishing the invalidity of the Agency's Plan. Only last term in *Wygant v. Jackson Board of Education*, 476 U.S. 267, 277–78, 106 S.Ct. 1842, 1849, 90 L.Ed.2d 260 (1986), we held that "[t]he ultimate burden remains with the employees to demonstrate the unconstitutionality of an affirmative-action program," and we see no basis for a different rule regarding a plan's alleged violation of Title VII. This case also fits readily within the analytical framework set forth in *McDonnell Douglas Corp. v. Green*, 411 U.S. 792, 93 S.Ct. 1817, 36 L.Ed.2d 668 (1973). Once a plaintiff establishes a prima facie case that race or sex has been taken into account in an employer's employment decision, the burden shifts to the employer to articulate a nondiscriminatory rationale for its decision. The existence of an affirmative action plan provides such a rationale. If such a plan is articulated as the basis for the employer's decision, the burden shifts to the plaintiff to prove that the employer's justification is pretextual and the plan is invalid. As a practical matter, of course, an employer will generally seek to avoid a charge of pretext by presenting evidence in support of its plan. That does not mean, however, as petitioner suggests, that reliance on an

---

addition, Joyce testified that she had informed the person responsible for arranging her second interview that she had a disaster preparedness class on a certain day the following week. By this time about ten days had passed since she had notified this person of her availability, and no date had yet been set for the interview. Within a day or two after this conversation, however, she received a notice setting her interview at a time directly in the middle of her disaster preparedness class. This same panel member had earlier described Joyce as a "rebel-rousing, skirt-wearing person."

affirmative action plan is to be treated as an affirmative defense requiring the employer to carry the burden of proving the validity of the plan. The burden of proving its invalidity remains on the plaintiff.

The assessment of the legality of the Agency Plan must be guided by our decision in [*United Steelworkers v. Weber*, 443 U.S. 193, 99 S.Ct. 2721, 61 L.Ed.2d 480 (1979)]. In that case, the Court addressed the question whether the employer violated Title VII by adopting a voluntary affirmative action plan designed to "eliminate manifest racial imbalances in traditionally segregated job categories." *Id.*, at 197, 99 S.Ct., at 2724. The respondent employee in that case challenged the employer's denial of his application for a position in a newly established craft training program, contending that the employer's selection process impermissibly took into account the race of the applicants. The selection process was guided by an affirmative action plan, which provided that 50% of the new trainees were to be black until the percentage of black skilled craftworkers in the employer's plant approximated the percentage of blacks in the local labor force. Adoption of the plan had been prompted by the fact that only 5 of 273, or 1.83%, of skilled craftworkers at the plant were black, even though the work force in the area was approximately 39% black. Because of the historical exclusion of blacks from craft positions, the employer regarded its former policy of hiring trained outsiders as inadequate to redress the imbalance in its work force.

We upheld the employer's decision to select less senior black applicants over the white respondent, for we found that taking race into account was consistent with Title VII's objective of "break[ing] down old patterns of racial segregation and hierarchy." *Id.*, at 208, 99 S.Ct., at 2730.

* * *

We noted that the plan did not "unnecessarily trammel the interests of the white employees," since it did not require "the discharge of white workers and their replacement with new black hirees." *Ibid.* Nor did the plan create "an absolute bar to the advancement of white employees," since half of those trained in the new program were to be white. *Ibid.* Finally, we observed that the plan was a temporary measure, not designed to maintain racial balance, but to "eliminate a manifest racial imbalance." *Ibid.* As Justice Blackmun's concurrence made clear, *Weber* held that an employer seeking to justify the adoption of a plan need not point to its own prior discriminatory practices, nor even to evidence of an "arguable violation" on its part. *Id.*, at 212, 99 S.Ct., at 2731. Rather, it need point only to a "conspicuous * * * imbalance in traditionally segregated job categories." *Id.*, at 209, 99 S.Ct., at 2730. Our decision was grounded in the recognition that voluntary employer action can play a crucial role in furthering Title VII's purpose of eliminating the effects of discrimination in the workplace, and that Title VII should not be read to thwart such efforts. *Id.,* at 204, 99 S.Ct., at 2727–28.[8]

In reviewing the employment decision at issue in this case, we must first examine whether that decision was made pursuant to a plan prompted by concerns similar to those of the employer in *Weber.* Next, we must determine whether the effect of the plan on males and non-minorities is comparable to the effect of the plan in that case.

The first issue is therefore whether consideration of the sex of applicants for skilled craft jobs was justified by the existence of a "manifest imbalance" that reflected underrepresentation of women in "traditionally segregated job categories." *Id.,* at 197, 99 S.Ct., at 2724. In determining whether an imbalance exists that would justify taking sex or race into account, a comparison of the percentage of minorities or women in the employer's work force with the percentage in the area labor market or general population is appropriate in analyzing jobs that require no special expertise, see *Teamsters v. United States,* 431 U.S. 324, 97 S.Ct. 1843, 52 L.Ed.2d 396 (1977). * * * Where a job requires special training, however, the comparison should be with those in the labor force who possess the relevant qualifications. See *Hazelwood School District v. United States,* 433 U.S. 299, 97 S.Ct. 2736, 53 L.Ed.2d 768 (1977). * * * The requirement that the "manifest imbalance" relate to a "traditionally segregated job category" provides assurance both that sex or race will be taken into account in a manner consistent with Title VII's purpose of eliminating the effects of employment discrimination, and that the interests of those employees not benefitting from the plan will not be unduly infringed.

A manifest imbalance need not be such that it would support a prima facie case against the employer, as suggested in Justice O'Connor's concurrence, since we do not regard as identical the constraints of Title VII and the federal constitution on voluntarily adopted affirmative action plans. Application of the "prima facie" standard in Title VII cases would be inconsistent with *Weber*'s focus on statistical imbalance,[9] and could

---

[8]   * * * The dissent's suggestion that an affirmative action program may be adopted only to redress an employer's past discrimination was rejected in *Steelworkers v. Weber,* 443 U.S. 193, 99 S.Ct. 2721, 61 L.Ed.2d 480 (1979), because the prospect of liability created by such an admission would create a significant disincentive for voluntary action. As Justice Blackmun's concurrence in that case pointed out, such a standard would "plac[e] voluntary compliance with Title VII in profound jeopardy. The only way for the employer and the union to keep their footing on the 'tightrope' it creates would be to eschew all forms of voluntary affirmative action." 443 U.S., at 210, 99 S.Ct., at 2731. Similarly, Justice O'Connor has observed in the constitutional context that "[t]he imposition of a requirement that public employers make findings that they have engaged in illegal discrimination before they engage in affirmative action programs would severely undermine public employers' incentive to meet voluntarily their civil rights obligations." *Wygant, supra,* at 290, 106 S.Ct., at 1855 (O'Connor, J., concurring in part and concurring in the judgment).

[9]   The difference between the "manifest imbalance" and "prima facie" standards is illuminated by *Weber.* Had the Court in that case been concerned with past discrimination by the employer, it would have focused on discrimination in hiring skilled, not unskilled, workers, since only the scarcity of the former in Kaiser's work force would have made it vulnerable to a Title VII suit. In order to make out a prima facie case on such a claim, a plaintiff would be required to

inappropriately create a significant disincentive for employers to adopt an affirmative action plan. See *Weber, supra*, 443 U.S., at 204, 99 S.Ct., at 2727–28 (Title VII intended as a "catalyst" for employer efforts to eliminate vestiges of discrimination). A corporation concerned with maximizing return on investment, for instance, is hardly likely to adopt a plan if in order to do so it must compile evidence that could be used to subject it to a colorable Title VII suit.

It is clear that the decision to hire Joyce was made pursuant to an Agency plan that directed that sex or race be taken into account for the purpose of remedying underrepresentation.

* * *

As an initial matter, the Agency adopted as a benchmark for measuring progress in eliminating underrepresentation the long-term goal of a work force that mirrored in its major job classifications the percentage of women in the area labor market. Even as it did so, however, the Agency acknowledged that such a figure could not by itself necessarily justify taking into account the sex of applicants for positions in all job categories. For positions requiring specialized training and experience, the Plan observed that the number of minorities and women "who possess the qualifications required for entry into such job classifications is limited." The Plan therefore directed that annual short-term goals be formulated that would provide a more realistic indication of the degree to which sex should be taken into account in filling particular positions.

* * *

As the Agency Plan recognized, women were most egregiously underrepresented in the Skilled Craft job category, since *none* of the 238 positions was occupied by a woman. In mid-1980, when Joyce was selected for the road dispatcher position, the Agency was still in the process of refining its short-term goals for Skilled Craft Workers in accordance with the directive of the Plan. This process did not reach fruition until 1982, when the Agency established a short-term goal for that year of three

---

compare the percentage of black skilled workers in the Kaiser work force with the percentage of black skilled craft workers in the area labor market.

Weber obviously did not make such a comparison. Instead, it focused on the disparity between the percentage of black skilled craft workers in Kaiser's ranks and the percentage of blacks in the area labor force. 443 U.S., at 198–199, 99 S.Ct., at 2724–2725. Such an approach reflected a recognition that the proportion of black craft workers in the local labor force was likely [to be] as miniscule as the proportion in Kaiser's work force. The Court realized that the lack of imbalance between these figures would mean that employers in precisely those industries in which discrimination has been most effective would be precluded from adopting training programs to increase the percentage of qualified minorities. Thus, in cases such as *Weber,* where the employment decision at issue involves the selection of unskilled persons for a training program, the "manifest imbalance" standard permits comparison with the general labor force. By contrast, the "prima facie" standard would require comparison with the percentage of minorities or women qualified for the job for which the trainees are being trained, a standard that would have invalidated the plan in *Weber* itself.

women for the 55 expected openings in that job category—a modest goal of about 6% for that category.

* * *

We reject petitioner's argument that, since only the long-term goal was in place for Skilled Craft positions at the time of Joyce's promotion, it was inappropriate for the Director to take into account affirmative action considerations in filling the road dispatcher position. The Agency's Plan emphasized that the long-term goals were not to be taken as guides for actual hiring decisions, but that supervisors were to consider a host of practical factors in seeking to meet affirmative action objectives, including the fact that in some job categories women were not qualified in numbers comparable to their representation in the labor force.

By contrast, had the Plan simply calculated imbalances in all categories according to the proportion of women in the area labor pool, and then directed that hiring be governed solely by those figures, its validity fairly could be called into question. This is because analysis of a more specialized labor pool normally is necessary in determining underrepresentation in some positions. If a plan failed to take distinctions in qualifications into account in providing guidance for actual employment decisions, it would dictate mere blind hiring by the numbers, for it would hold supervisors to "achievement of a particular percentage of minority employment or membership * * * regardless of circumstances such as economic conditions or the number of qualified minority applicants * * * ," *Sheet Metal Workers v. EEOC*, 478 U.S. 421, 106 S.Ct. 3019, 92 L.Ed.2d 344 (1986) (O'Connor, J., concurring in part and dissenting in part).

The Agency's Plan emphatically did *not* authorize such blind hiring. It expressly directed that numerous factors be taken into account in making hiring decisions, including specifically the qualifications of female applicants for particular jobs. Thus, despite the fact that no precise short-term goal was yet in place for the Skilled Craft category in mid-1980, the Agency's management nevertheless had been clearly instructed that they were not to hire solely by reference to statistics. The fact that only the long-term goal had been established for this category posed no danger that personnel decisions would be made by reflexive adherence to a numerical standard.

* * *

We next consider whether the Agency Plan unnecessarily trammeled the rights of male employees or created an absolute bar to their advancement. In contrast to the plan in *Weber*, which provided that 50% of the positions in the craft training program were exclusively for blacks, and to the consent decree upheld last term in *Firefighters v. Cleveland*, 478 U.S. 501, 106 S.Ct. 3063, 92 L.Ed.2d 405 (1986), which required the promotion of specific numbers of minorities, the Plan sets aside no positions for women. The Plan expressly states that "[t]he 'goals' established for each Division should not be construed as 'quotas' that must be met." Rather, the Plan merely authorizes that consideration be given to affirmative action concerns when evaluating qualified applicants. As the Agency Director testified, the sex of Joyce was but one of numerous factors he took into account in arriving at his decision. The Plan thus resembles the "Harvard Plan" approvingly noted by Justice Powell in *University of California Regents v. Bakke*, 438 U.S. 265, 316–319, 98 S.Ct. 2733, 2761–63, 57 L.Ed.2d 750 (1978), which considers race along with other criteria in determining admission to the college.

* * *

In addition, petitioner had no absolute entitlement to the road dispatcher position. Seven of the applicants were classified as qualified and eligible, and the Agency Director was authorized to promote any of the seven. Thus, denial of the promotion unsettled no legitimate firmly rooted expectation on the part of the petitioner. Furthermore, while the petitioner in this case was denied a promotion, he retained his employment with the Agency, at the same salary and with the same seniority, and remained eligible for other promotions.

Finally, the Agency's Plan was intended to *attain* a balanced work force, not to maintain one. The Plan contains ten references to the Agency's desire to "attain" such a balance, but no reference whatsoever to a goal of maintaining it. The Director testified that, while the "broader goal" of affirmative action, defined as "the desire to hire, to promote, to give opportunity and training on an equitable, non-discriminatory basis," is something that is "a permanent part" of "the Agency's operating philosophy," that broader goal "is divorced, if you will, from specific numbers or percentages."

The Agency acknowledged the difficulties that it would confront in remedying the imbalance in its work force, and it anticipated only gradual increases in the representation of minorities and women. It is thus unsurprising that the Plan contains no explicit end date, for the Agency's flexible, case-by-case approach was not expected to yield success in a brief period of time. * * *

JUSTICE STEVENS, concurring. [omitted]

JUSTICE O'CONNOR, concurring in the judgment.

In my view, the proper initial inquiry in evaluating the legality of an affirmative action plan by a public employer under Title VII is no different from that required by the Equal Protection Clause. In either case, consistent with the congressional intent to provide some measure of protection to the interests of the employer's nonminority employees, the employer must have had a firm basis for believing that remedial action was required. An employer would have such a firm basis if it can point to a statistical disparity sufficient to support a prima facie claim under Title VII by the employee beneficiaries of the affirmative action plan of a pattern or practice claim of discrimination.

* * *

In this case, I am also satisfied that the respondent had a firm basis for adopting an affirmative action program. Although the District Court found no discrimination against women in fact, at the time the affirmative action plan was adopted, there were *no* women in its skilled craft positions. The petitioner concedes that women constituted approximately 5% of the local labor pool of skilled craft workers in 1970. Thus, when compared to the percentage of women in the qualified work force, the statistical disparity would have been sufficient for a prima facie Title VII case brought by unsuccessful women job applicants.

JUSTICE WHITE, dissenting. [omitted]

JUSTICE SCALIA, with whom THE CHIEF JUSTICE joins, and with whom JUSTICE WHITE joins in Parts I and II, dissenting.

* * * today's decision goes well beyond merely allowing racial or sexual discrimination in order to eliminate the effects of prior societal *discrimination*. The majority opinion often uses the phrase "traditionally segregated job category" to describe the evil against which the plan is legitimately (according to the majority) directed. As originally used in *Steelworkers v. Weber*, 443 U.S. 193, 99 S.Ct. 2721, 61 L.Ed.2d 480 (1979), that phrase described skilled jobs from which employers and unions had systematically and intentionally excluded black workers—traditionally segregated jobs, that is, in the sense of conscious, exclusionary discrimination. See *id.,* at 197–198, 99 S.Ct., at 2724–2725. But that is assuredly not the sense in which the phrase is used here. It is absurd to think that the nationwide failure of road maintenance crews, for example, to achieve the Agency's ambition of 36.4% female representation is attributable primarily, if even substantially, to systematic exclusion of women eager to shoulder pick and shovel. It is a "traditionally segregated job category" *not* in the *Weber* sense, but in the sense that, because of longstanding social attitudes, it has not been regarded *by women themselves* as desirable work. * * * There are, of course, those who believe that the social attitudes which cause women themselves to avoid certain jobs and to favor others are as nefarious as conscious, exclusionary discrimination. Whether or not that is so (and there is assuredly no consensus on the point equivalent to our national consensus against intentional discrimination), the two phenomena are certainly distinct. And it is the alteration of social attitudes, rather than the elimination of discrimination, which today's decision approves as justification for state-enforced discrimination. This is an enormous expansion, undertaken without the slightest justification or analysis.

NOTES AND QUESTIONS

Test Your Understanding of the Material

1.   Compare the constitutional standard adopted by the plurality in *Wygant* with the Title VII standard adopted in *Johnson*. In what ways do these standards differ? (While the *Johnson* case involved a public employer, no constitutional issue was raised in that litigation.)

2.   Compare the standards for judging affirmative action relief in *Sheet Metal Workers* (applying Title VII § 706(g)) with the standards for judging voluntary affirmative action plans in *Johnson* (applying § 703). What is the justification for permitting a voluntary affirmative action plan in circumstances that would not support a judicial order of a similar plan?

3.   In his dissent in *Johnson*, Justice Scalia contends that the majority opinion effectively approves affirmative action plans designed simply to facilitate the "alteration of social attitudes" shared by most women concerning what jobs are most appropriate for them. Is this an accurate depiction of the Court's opinion?

Related Issues

4.   *Effect of* Ricci. Does the Court's decision in Ricci v. DeStefano, 557 U.S. 557, 129 S.Ct. 2658, 174 L.Ed.2d 490 (2009), p. 261 supra, supplant the *Johnson-Weber* Title VII standard for reviewing affirmative action plans with the "strong-basis-in-evidence" equal protection standard? Reviewing a voluntary settlement of a suit challenging the disparate impact of a city's methods for selection of custodial engineers, the appeals court in United States v. Brennan, 650 F.3d 65 (2d Cir. 2011) (Calabresi, J.) held that the *Ricci* standard, rather than the *Johnson-Weber* standard, applied to a Title VII reverse discrimination challenge to a settlement granting instatement and retroactive seniority to alleged victims of allegedly discriminatory selection criteria.

5.   *Who Bears the Burden of Persuasion?* Who bears the burden of proving the validity, or invalidity, of an affirmative action plan: the nonminority plaintiff or the defendant employer? Note that the *McDonnell Douglas* approach is intended to determine whether the defendant was motivated by considerations of race or sex, while the issue in affirmative action cases is the very different one of whether such considerations are justified. Note also that *McDonald v. Santa Fe Trail Transp. Co.*, discussed at p. 109 supra, indicates that any race-conscious plan would violate § 703 absent sufficient affirmative action justifications.

6.   *Voluntary Employer Alteration of Objective Test Scores.* In light of § 703(*l*) of Title VII, as added by § 106 of the Civil Rights Act of 1991, may an employer dissatisfied with the pass rate of minority applicants on an employment test, as part of an affirmative action plan, now rescore the examination results so as to reduce adverse impact on blacks and women? See Dean v. City of Shreveport, 438 F.3d 448 (5th Cir. 2006) (no). Does it depend on whether the test has been validated? See also *Ricci*, p. 261 supra.

NOTE: *GRATZ V. BOLLINGER* AND THE REQUIREMENT OF INDIVIDUALIZED CONSIDERATION

On the same day that it sustained the University of Michigan Law School's admissions system from a constitutional challenge in *Grutter v. Bollinger*, supra, the Supreme Court held in Gratz v. Bollinger, 539 U.S. 244, 123 S.Ct. 2411, 156 L.Ed.2d 257 (2003), that the University's use of racial preferences in undergraduate admissions violated the equal protection clause. The *Gratz* Court concluded that the undergraduate admissions system was not "narrowly tailored to achieve the interest in educational diversity" that the University claimed as a justification. The Court rested this conclusion on its finding that the undergraduate system did not consider "each particular applicant as an individual, assessing all of the qualities that individual possesses, and in turn, evaluating that individual ability's to contribute to the unique setting of higher education." Rather than provide this "individualized consideration" to each applicant, the undergraduate admissions plan "automatically" distributed 20 extra points on a 150 point scale to every single applicant from an "underrepresented minority" group, as defined by the University. Justice Rehnquist, writing for the Court, stressed that these 20 points had "the effect of making 'the factor of race * * * decisive' for virtually every minimally qualified underrepresented minority applicant."

Justice O'Connor, by joining in the Court's *Gratz* opinion as well as through a separate concurring opinion in *Gratz* and her majority opinion in *Grutter*, made clear her view that individualized consideration of each applicant is necessary to ensure that an affirmative action program for admissions to higher education is narrowly tailored to achieve an acceptable goal of diversity. In her concurring opinion in *Gratz*, she contrasted the law school's admissions system upheld in *Grutter*; the latter "enables admissions officers to make nuanced judgments with respect to the contributions each applicant is likely to make to the diversity of the incoming class." 539 U.S. at 279. In *Grutter* she stressed that "the Law School engages in a highly individualized, holistic review of each applicant's file, giving serious consideration to all the ways an applicant might contribute to a diverse educational environment." 539 U.S. at 338.

The Supreme Court also stressed the importance of "individualized" review to the "narrow tailoring" prong of strict scrutiny again in its decision finding unconstitutional two school districts' use of race in assigning children to particular schools. See Parents Involved in Community Schools v. Seattle School District No. 1, 551 U.S. 701, 127 S.Ct. 2738, 168 L.Ed.2d 508 (2007). In a part of his opinion supported by a majority of the Court, Chief Justice Roberts acknowledged the Court's recognition as "compelling" justifications for racial classifications "in the school context" not only "remedying the effects of past intentional discrimination", but also an "interest in diversity in higher education". Without deciding that the latter justification could extend to the government's consideration of race in other contexts, including less advanced education, the majority held that the school districts had used race as the University of Michigan had for its undergraduate admissions, not as "one factor weighed with others" "to achieve exposure to widely diverse people, culture, ideas and viewpoints", but rather as "*the* factor" "decisive by itself", in a "nonindividualized, mechanical" manner. 127 S.Ct. at 2753–54. See also Samuel Estreicher, The Non-Preferment Principle, 2006–07 Cato. Sup.Ct.Rev. 239.

C. EXECUTIVE OR CONGRESSIONALLY ORDERED AFFIRMATIVE ACTION

Thus far, this chapter has considered standards for judging affirmative action plans developed free of external governmental coercion (whether or not prompted by an administrative agency investigation) and affirmative action plans required by judicial orders. Such plans also may be mandated by the nonjudicial branches of the federal government. Most importantly, the President through Executive Order 11246 has required all government contractors to analyze the extent to which they utilize available minority and women workers and, if there is underutilization, to develop an appropriate affirmative action plan, subject to oversight by the Office of Federal Contract Compliance Programs (OFCCP) in the Department of Labor.

In Adarand Constructors, Inc. v. Pena, 515 U.S. 200, 115 S.Ct. 2097, 132 L.Ed2d 158 (1995), in a review of a partially race-based and sex-based appropriation bill preference for "socially and economically disadvantaged" small businesses, a majority of the Court took the position that review of federal action must be the same—"congruence"—under the Fifth Amendment as that of state action under the Fourteenth Amendment. This meant, as stated in Justice O'Connor's plurality opinion, "that any person, of whatever race, has the right to demand that any governmental actor subject to the Constitution justify any racial classification subjecting that person to unequal treatment under the strictest scrutiny." In other words, the teachings of *Wygant*, as confirmed by the Court in *Croson* and later cases, apply in challenges to federal as well as state employment actions.

NOTE: EXECUTIVE ORDER 11246

What are the implications of *Adarand* for the affirmative action obligations of federal contractors under Executive Order 11246? Consider the following.

Beginning in 1941 during President Roosevelt's tenure and through the two Eisenhower administrations, executive orders were promulgated barring discrimination on account of race, religion, creed or national origin by firms performing procurement contracts for the federal government. Then in 1961, President Kennedy imposed an "affirmative action" obligation on such contractors through Executive Order 10925. In 1963, Executive Order 11114 extended these obligations to federal construction contractors. Finally, in 1965, President Johnson promulgated Executive Order 11246—in effect to this day—

which carried forward the expanded obligations of the Kennedy administration orders and transferred enforcement authority from what had been the President's Committee on Equal Employment Opportunity to the Secretary of Labor.

Executive Order 11246 requires "all Government contracting agencies" to include "in every Government contract," except where exempted by regulation, provisions pledging the contractor to not discriminate and to "take affirmative action to ensure that applicants are employed, and that employees are treated during employment, without regard to their race, color, religion, sex or national origin." On July 21, 2014, through Executive Order 13672, President Obama extended these categories to included "sexual orientation" and "gender identity." Contractors are required to include similar pledges in their contracts with subcontractors and vendors. The Order assigns responsibility for its enforcement and administration to the Secretary of Labor. Pursuant to the Secretary's authority, the Department's Office of Federal Contract Compliance Programs (OFCCP) has promulgated extensive regulations. These regulations include some narrow exemptions. For instance, most contractors and subcontractors whose contracts with the federal government totalled $10,000 or less over a 12-month period are altogether exempt from the Order. 41 C.F.R. § 60–1.5(a)(1).

The OFCCP regulations implementing the Order for nonconstruction contractors or subcontractors were revised in 2000 for the first time in thirty years. These regulations now require any such contractor or subcontractor that employs more than 50 workers and has a contract for at least $50,000 to analyze its utilization of minorities and women workers, and "[w]hen the percentage of minorities or women employed in a particular job group is less than would reasonably be expected given their availability percentage in [a] particular job group," to establish "a percentage annual placement goal at least equal to the availability figure derived for women or minorities, as appropriate, for that job group." Id. § 60–2.15(b), 2.16(c). "In determining availability, the contractor must consider at least * * * [t]he percentage of minorities and women with requisite skills in the reasonable recruitment area [and] [t]he percentage of minorities or women among those promotable, transferable, and trainable within the contractor's organization." Id. § 60–2.14(c). "Placement goals serve as objectives or targets reasonably attainable by means of applying every good faith effort to make all aspects of the entire affirmative action program work." Id. § 60–2.16(a). Thus, the basis for affirmative action obligations under the Executive Order is not a finding of intentional or adverse-impact discrimination, but rather a finding that the contractor has failed to utilize an available, qualified minority or female workforce.

The current regulations attempt to protect the program from any equal protection challenge. "Placement goals may not be rigid and inflexible quotas, which must be met, nor are they to be considered as either a ceiling or a floor for the employment of particular groups. Quotas are expressly forbidden." Id. § 2.16(e)(1). Furthermore, "[p]lacement goals do not provide the contractor with a justification to extend a preference to any individual, select an individual, or adversely affect an individual's employment status, on the basis of that person's race, color, religion, sex, or national origin." Id. § 2.16(e)(2). And "[p]lacement goals do not create set-asides for specific group, nor are they intended to achieve proportional representation or equal results." Id. § 2.16(e)(3). In addition, "[n]o contractor's compliance status shall be judged alone by whether or not it reaches its goals." Rather, OFCCP will review "the nature and extent of the contractor's good faith affirmative action activities * * * and the appropriateness of those activities to identified equal employment opportunity problems." Id. § 60–2.35.

Construction contractors, whether dealing directly with the federal government or receiving federal monies through state, local or private agencies, are covered by a different set of regulations which also impose specific affirmative obligations. These obligations include the validation of selection criteria and the development of on-the-job training and apprenticeship programs that can benefit minorities and women. Id. § 60–4.3. Construction contractors do not develop their own goals and timetables. The OFCCP periodically issues goals and timetables for minority employment in specific geographical areas. Id. § 60–4.6. The agency has also approved several cooperative or "Hometown Plan" agreements among local construction contractors, unions, and minority groups, that set goals and timetables for a particular metropolitan area. Id. §§ 60–4.4 to –4.5.

Initially, the OFCCP attempts to respond to problems uncovered by compliance reviews or meritorious complaints of discrimination by informal conciliation and persuasion of the contractor. If such efforts are unsuccessful, the OFCCP will issue a notice to the contractor to show cause why it should not be subject to enforcement proceedings. It may then refer the case to the Labor Department's Solicitor to initiate administrative enforcement proceedings. The Department of Justice, on its own initiative or after a request from the OFCCP, and without waiting for the completion of any administrative action, may also investigate and bring judicial proceedings against a delinquent contractor. 41 C.F.R. § 60–1.26. If administrative or judicial proceedings result in a finding that the Executive Order has been violated, the violator may not only be placed under a prospective compliance order, but also may have its contract cancelled, or even be placed on a list of employers debarred from eligibility for future contracts, § 209, Exec. Order No. 11246. A debarred contractor must demonstrate its full compliance with the Order in order to achieve reinstatement. In addition, the OFCCP or the Department of Justice may seek compensation for victims of discrimination through an order for back pay or other equitable relief. 41 C.F.R. § 60–1.26(a)(2), (d).

PRACTITIONER'S PERSPECTIVE

Fred Alvarez
Partner, Jones Day.
Former EEOC Commissioner and Assistant Secretary of Labor.

I enjoy advising on affirmative action compliance issues because the practice is equal opportunity law with a dynamic extra gear. Fifty years ago President Johnson signed Executive Order 11246 directing all who did business with the federal government "take affirmative action" to ensure equal opportunity. Those few words led to the establishment of a federal agency—the Office of Federal Contract Compliance Programs housed in the Department of Labor—and the development of a unique creature called an "Affirmative Action Plan" (AAP). Over the years this distinctive approach to the equal opportunity obligation (with some variation) has been extended by either Executive Order or by statute to ensure equal opportunity on the basis of race, national origin, gender, disability, Veteran status and sexual orientation.

What is so engaging about this area of practice is that the AAP process focuses on three core inquiries: equal opportunity problem identification, solution development and ongoing monitoring of outcomes of those solutions. Moreover, these inquiries are ongoing and need to be updated at least once a year. Quantitative and analytical statistics are integral to how those inquiries are addressed. While the regulations make clear that quotas are never permissible, statistical outcomes are used to trigger further examination into whether good-faith efforts to ensure equal opportunity are being taken.

When the outcomes of any selection processes—recruiting, interviewing, hiring, promoting, compensating or terminating—suggest an unusually disparate outcome based on any of the protected characteristics, lawyers draw upon multiple skills. They are part-time amateur diagnosticians of how employment processes work, part-time amateur industrial organizational psychologists, part-time amateur users of statistics, and full-time advocates before the OFCCP. Oftentimes the lawyer can directly participate in the onsite audits performed by the OFCCP and work collaboratively with the client and the OFCCP to identify how selection systems actually perform and how solution-oriented efforts are working. More often than not, those collaborative efforts yield mutually agreed-upon approaches to problems rather than adversarial disputes between the employer and the OFCCP. Certainly, proactive negotiations between the OFCCP and the employer, based on a shared interest in equal opportunity, are frequently required.

Sometimes disputes are not resolved. On occasion, unresolved disputes with the OFCCP can lead to enforcement proceedings in DOL administrative adjudication before an Administrative Law Judge.

A final distinctive feature of practice in this area is that substantive policy is normally determined by Executive Orders rather than by acts of Congress. Thus, swings in focus by different Administrations can swiftly bring changes to the affirmative action arena. Because the affirmative-action obligation is essentially contractual in nature, each new Administration can determine the terms upon which those who hope to do business with the federal government must agree. While Congress takes an active interest in the affirmative action area, its role is primarily an oversight one as each new President can determine how this contractual obligation will be enforced and, indeed, what the content of the "contract" will be.

NOTE: CONSTITUTIONALITY OF
EXECUTIVE ORDER OBLIGATIONS

Can a serious challenge be posed to the constitutionality of the Executive Order and its implementing regulations? Or would such a challenge necessarily fail because of the flexibility and reasonableness of the goals that contractors must establish to address "underutilization" of minorities? Must not any race-or sex-conscious goals, no matter how reasonable, have a compelling justification? See Lutheran Church-Missouri Synod v. Federal Communications Commission, 141 F.3d 344 (D.C.Cir. 1998) (holding that any technique that "induces an employer to hire with an eye toward meeting the numerical target" must "serve a compelling state interest"). Is a finding of underutilization adequate as a factual predicate for the remedying of past discrimination? If not, are there other possible compelling justifications for the Executive Order and accompanying regulations? Is the goal of diversity, as recognized in *Grutter*, relevant to most jobs covered by the Order? Can the Order and accompanying regulations be justified as helping to insure that the federal government does not support future discrimination? Or as an encouragement of an efficient enlargement of the utilized labor market? Cf. United States v. New Orleans Public Service, Inc., 553 F.2d 459, 466 (5th Cir.1977), vacated and remanded on other grounds, 436 U.S. 942, 98 S.Ct. 2841, 56 L.Ed.2d 783 (1978); Rossetti Contracting Co. v. Brennan, 508 F.2d 1039, 1045 n. 18 (7th Cir.1974) (finding Presidential power to issue Executive Order delegated from Congress by the Federal Property and Administrative Services Act, 40 U.S.C. § 471 et seq., which empowers the President to provide an "economical and efficient system" for the procurement of services by the federal government).

In a pre-*Grutter* decision potentially relevant to the Executive Order, the D.C. Circuit held unconstitutional an FCC rule framed to encourage regulated broadcasters to expand their applicant pool for jobs beyond that which resulted from traditional "word-of-mouth" recruiting. District of Columbia MD/DC/DE Broadcasters Assn. v. Federal Communications Commission, 236 F.3d 13 (D.C.Cir. 2001). The court focused on one of the options afforded to broadcasters, which required reporting on the race, sex, and source of referral of each applicant and a modification of recruitment practices if "the data collected does [sic] not confirm that notifications are reaching the entire community". Recognizing that the rule treated recruitment into an applicant pool rather than actual hiring, the court nonetheless found this option was subject to strict scrutiny because it created "pressure" "to recruit minorities" and the probable nonrecruitment of "some prospective nonminority applicants who [otherwise] would have learned of job opportunities". The court further found that this option was not narrowly tailored to further any compelling governmental interest, because it placed "pressure upon each broadcaster to recruit minorities without a predicate finding that the particular broadcaster discriminated in the past or reasonably could be expected to do so in the future." Id. at 22. Would the decision in *MC/DC/DE* be upheld by the Supreme Court?

NOTE: DISPARATE-IMPACT ANALYSIS AS A FORM OF AFFIRMATIVE ACTION?

Does the Court's equal protection review of government affirmative action programs call into question the disparate-impact provisions of Title VII? Review the Court's decision in *Ricci v. DeStefano* at page 261 above, and consider Justice Scalia's concurring opinion:

> I join the Court's opinion in full, but write separately to observe that its resolution of this dispute merely postpones the evil day on which the Court will have to confront the question: Whether, or to what extent, are the disparate-impact provisions of Title VII of the Civil Rights Act of 1964 consistent with the Constitution's guarantee of equal protection? The question is not an easy one. See generally Primus, Equal Protection and Disparate Impact: Round Three, 117 Harv. L. Rev. 493 (2003).
>
> The difficulty is this: Whether or not Title VII's disparate-treatment provisions forbid "remedial" race-based actions when a disparate-impact violation would not otherwise result—the question resolved by the Court today—it is clear that Title VII not only permits but affirmatively requires such actions when a disparate-impact violation would otherwise result. But if the Federal Government is prohibited from discriminating on the basis of race, *Bolling v. Sharpe*, 347 U.S. 497, 500, 74 S.Ct. 693, 98 L.Ed. 884 (1954), then surely it is also prohibited from enacting laws mandating that third parties— e.g., employers, whether private, State, or municipal—discriminate on the basis of race. See *Buchanan v. Warley*, 245 U.S. 60, 78–82, 38 S.Ct. 16, 62 L.Ed. 149 (1917). As the facts of these cases illustrate, Title VII's disparate-impact provisions place a racial thumb on the scales, often requiring employers to evaluate the racial outcomes of their policies, and to make decisions based on (because of) those racial outcomes. That type of racial decisionmaking is, as the Court explains, discriminatory. See *Personnel Administrator of Mass. v. Feeney*, 442 U.S. 256, 279, 99 S.Ct. 2282, 60 L.Ed.2d 870 (1979).

To be sure, the disparate-impact laws do not mandate imposition of quotas, but it is not clear why that should provide a safe harbor. Would a private employer not be guilty of unlawful discrimination if he refrained from establishing a racial hiring quota but intentionally designed his hiring practices to achieve the same end? Surely he would. Intentional discrimination is still occurring, just one step up the chain. Government compulsion of such design would therefore seemingly violate equal protection principles. Nor would it matter that Title VII requires consideration of race on a wholesale, rather than retail, level. "[T]he Government must treat citizens as individuals, not as simply components of a racial, religious, sexual or national class." *Miller v. Johnson*, 515 U.S. 900, 911, 115 S.Ct. 2475, 132 L.Ed.2d 762 (1995) (internal quotation marks omitted). And of course the purportedly benign motive for the disparate-impact provisions cannot save the statute. See *Adarand Constructors, Inc. v. Pena*, 515 U.S. 200, 227, 115 S.Ct. 2097, 132 L.Ed.2d 158 (1995).

It might be possible to defend the law by framing it as simply an evidentiary tool used to identify genuine, intentional discrimination—to "smoke out," as it were, disparate treatment. See Primus, supra, at 498–499, 520–521. Disparate impact is sometimes (though not always, see *Watson v. Fort Worth Bank & Trust*, 487 U.S. 977, 992, 108 S.Ct. 2777, 101 L.Ed.2d 827 (1988) (plurality opinion)) a signal of something illicit, so a regulator might allow statistical disparities to play some role in the evidentiary process. Cf. *McDonnell Douglas Corp. v. Green*, 411 U.S. 792, 802–803, 93 S.Ct. 1817, 36 L.Ed.2d 668 (1973). But arguably the disparate-impact provisions sweep too broadly to be fairly characterized in such a fashion—since they fail to provide an affirmative defense for good-faith (i.e., nonracially motivated) conduct, or perhaps even for good faith plus hiring standards that are entirely reasonable. This is a question that this Court will have to consider in due course. It is one thing to free plaintiffs from proving an employer's illicit intent, but quite another to preclude the employer from proving that its motives were pure and its actions reasonable.

The Court's resolution of these cases makes it unnecessary to resolve these matters today. But the war between disparate impact and equal protection will be waged sooner or later, and it behooves us to begin thinking about how—and on what terms—to make peace between them.

* * *

Is Justice Scalia right that a federal statute requiring employers to consider the race-based effects of employment tests before adopting the tests is problematic under the equal protection clause? That requiring an employer to avoid employment practices with unnecessary disparate impacts is tantamount to requiring prohibited intentional discrimination? If an employer is going to be held liable for disparate impacts that cannot be adequately justified, can it be unconstitutional for public employers to monitor the impact of their practices before they are sued? See generally Eang L. Ngov, When the Evil Day Comes, Will Title VII's Disparate Impact Provision Be Narrowly Tailored to Survive an Equal Protection Clause Challenge, 60 Amer. L. Rev. 535 (2011).

CHAPTER 6

SEX DISCRIMINATION

∎ ∎ ∎

Introduction

The basic principles we have encountered in connection with Title VII's prohibition of race discrimination generally apply with equal force to Title VII's prohibition of sex discrimination. This chapter focuses on some of the special issues that have been presented by sex discrimination claims and litigation.

A. SEX-BASED PENSION FUNDING

ARIZONA GOVERNING COMMITTEE v. NORRIS

Supreme Court of the United States, 1983.
463 U.S. 1073, 103 S.Ct. 3492, 77 L.Ed.2d 1236.

JUSTICE MARSHALL, with whom JUSTICE BRENNAN, JUSTICE WHITE, and JUSTICE STEVENS join, and with whom JUSTICE O'CONNOR joins as to Parts I, II, and III, concurring in the judgment in part.

I

Since 1974 the State of Arizona has offered its employees the opportunity to enroll in a deferred compensation plan administered by the Arizona Governing Committee for Tax Deferred Annuity and Deferred Compensation Plans (Governing Committee). Ariz.Rev.Stat.Ann. § 38–871 *et seq.* (1974 and Supp.1982–1983); Ariz.Regs. 2–9–01 *et seq.* (1975). Employees who participate in the plan may thereby postpone the receipt of a portion of their wages until retirement. By doing so, they postpone paying federal income tax on the amounts deferred until after retirement, when they receive those amounts and any earnings thereon.

After inviting private companies to submit bids outlining the investment opportunities that they were willing to offer state employees, the State selected several companies to participate in its deferred compensation plan. Many of the companies selected offer three basic retirement options: (1) a single lump-sum payment upon retirement, (2) periodic payments of a fixed sum for a fixed period of time, and (3) monthly annuity payments for the remainder of the employee's life. When an employee decides to take part in the deferred compensation plan, he must designate the company in which he wishes to invest his deferred wages. Employees must choose one of the companies selected by the State

323

to participate in the plan; they are not free to invest their deferred compensation in any other way. At the time an employee enrolls in the plan, he may also select one of the payout options offered by the company that he has chosen, but when he reaches retirement age he is free to switch to one of the company's other options. If at retirement the employee decides to receive a lump-sum payment, he may also purchase any of the options then being offered by the other companies participating in the plan. Many employees find an annuity contract to be the most attractive option, since receipt of a lump sum upon retirement requires payment of taxes on the entire sum in one year, and the choice of a fixed sum for a fixed period requires an employee to speculate as to how long he will live.

Once an employee chooses the company in which he wishes to invest and decides the amount of compensation to be deferred each month, the State is responsible for withholding the appropriate sums from the employee's wages and channelling those sums to the company designated by the employee. The State bears the cost of making the necessary payroll deductions and of giving employees time off to attend group meetings to learn about the plan, but it does not contribute any moneys to supplement the employees' deferred wages.

For an employee who elects to receive a monthly annuity following retirement, the amount of the employee's monthly benefits depends upon the amount of compensation that the employee deferred (and any earnings thereon), the employee's age at retirement, and the employee's sex. All of the companies selected by the State to participate in the plan use sex-based mortality tables to calculate monthly retirement benefits. Under these tables a man receives larger monthly payments than a woman who deferred the same amount of compensation and retired at the same age, because the tables classify annuitants on the basis of sex and women on average live longer than men.[1] Sex is the only factor that the tables use to classify individuals of the same age; the tables do not incorporate other factors correlating with longevity such as smoking habits, alcohol consumption, weight, medical history, or family history.

* * *

II

We consider first whether petitioners would have violated Title VII if they had run the entire deferred compensation plan themselves, without the participation of any insurance companies. Title VII makes it an unlawful employment practice "to discriminate against any individual with respect to his compensation, terms, conditions, or privileges of

---

[1]   Different insurance companies participating in the plan use different means of classifying individuals on the basis of sex. Several companies use separate tables for men and women. Another company uses a single actuarial table based on male mortality rates, but calculates the annuities to be paid to women by using a 6-year "setback," *i.e.,* by treating a woman as if she were a man six years younger and had the life expectancy of a man that age.

employment, because of such individual's race, color, religion, sex or national origin." 42 U.S.C. § 2000e–2(a)(1). There is no question that the opportunity to participate in a deferred compensation plan constitutes a "conditio[n] or privileg[e] of employment," and that retirement benefits constitute a form of "compensation." The issue we must decide is whether it is discrimination "because of * * * sex" to pay a retired woman lower monthly benefits than a man who deferred the same amount of compensation.

In *Los Angeles Dept. of Water & Power v. Manhart,* 435 U.S. 702, 98 S.Ct. 1370, 55 L.Ed.2d 657 (1978), we held that an employer had violated Title VII by requiring its female employees to make larger contributions to a pension fund than male employees in order to obtain the same monthly benefits upon retirement. Noting that Title VII's "focus on the individual is unambiguous," *id.,* at 708, 98 S.Ct., at 1375, we emphasized that the statute prohibits an employer from treating some employees less favorably than others because of their race, religion, sex, or national origin. *Id.,* at 708–709, 98 S.Ct., at 1375–1376. While women as a class live longer than men, *id.,* at 704, 98 S.Ct., at 1373, we rejected the argument that the exaction of greater contributions from women was based on a "factor other than sex"—*i.e.,* longevity—and was therefore permissible under the Equal Pay Act[.][8] * * * We concluded that a plan requiring women to make greater contributions than men discriminates "because of * * * sex" for the simple reason that it treats each woman " 'in a manner which but for [her] sex would [have been] different.' " 435 U.S., at 711, 98 S.Ct., at 1377, * * * .

We have no hesitation in holding, as have all but one of the lower courts that have considered the question, that the classification of employees on the basis of sex is no more permissible at the pay-out stage of a retirement plan than at the pay-in stage.[10] We reject petitioners' contention that the Arizona plan does not discriminate on the basis of sex because a woman and a man who defer the same amount of compensation will obtain upon retirement annuity policies having approximately the same present actuarial value. Arizona has simply offered its employees a

---

[8]   Section 703(h) of Title VII, the so-called Bennett Amendment, provides that Title VII does not prohibit an employer from "differentiat[ing] upon the basis of sex in determining the amount of the wages or compensation paid or to be paid to employees of such employer if such differentiation is authorized by [the Equal Pay Act]." 78 Stat. 257, 42 U.S.C. § 2000e–2(h). As in *Manhart, supra,* at 712, n. 23, 98 S.Ct., at 1377, n. 23, we need not decide whether retirement benefits constitute "wages" under the Equal Pay Act, because the Bennett Amendment extends the four exceptions recognized in the Act to all forms of "compensation" covered by Title VII.

[10]   It is irrelevant that female employees in *Manhart* were required to participate in the pension plan, whereas participation in the Arizona deferred compensation plan is voluntary. Title VII forbids all discrimination concerning "compensation, terms, conditions, or privileges of employment," not just discrimination concerning those aspects of the employment relationship as to which the employee has no choice. It is likewise irrelevant that the Arizona plan includes two options—the lump-sum option and the fixed-sum-for-a-fixed-period option—that are provided on equal terms to men and women. An employer that offers one fringe benefit on a discriminatory basis cannot escape liability because he also offers other benefits on a nondiscriminatory basis. Cf. *Mississippi University for Women v. Hogan,* 458 U.S. 718, 723–724, n. 8, 102 S.Ct. 3331, 3336, n. 8, 73 L.Ed.2d 1090 (1982).

choice among different levels of annuity benefits, any one of which, if offered alone, would be equivalent to the plan at issue in *Manhart,* where the employer determined both the monthly contributions employees were required to make and the level of benefits that they were paid. If a woman participating in the Arizona plan wishes to obtain monthly benefits equal to those obtained by a man, she must make greater monthly contributions than he, just as the female employees in *Manhart* had to make greater contributions to obtain equal benefits. For any particular level of benefits that a woman might wish to receive, she will have to make greater monthly contributions to obtain that level of benefits than a man would have to make. The fact that Arizona has offered a range of discriminatory benefit levels, rather than only one such level, obviously provides no basis whatsoever for distinguishing *Manhart.*

* * *

[The] underlying assumption—that sex may properly be used to predict longevity—is flatly inconsistent with the basic teaching of *Manhart:* that Title VII requires employers to treat their employees as *individuals,* not "as simply components of a racial, religious, sexual, or national class." 435 U.S., at 708, 98 S.Ct., at 1375. *Manhart* squarely rejected the notion that, because women as a class live longer than men, an employer may adopt a retirement plan that treats every individual woman less favorably than every individual man. *Id.,* at 716–717, 98 S.Ct., at 1379–1380.

As we observed in *Manhart,* "[a]ctuarial studies could unquestionably identify differences in life expectancy based on race or national origin, as well as sex." *Id.,* at 709, 98 S.Ct., at 1376 (footnote omitted). If petitioners' interpretation of the statute were correct, such studies could be used as a justification for paying employees of one race lower monthly benefits than employees of another race. We continue to believe that "a statute that was designed to make race irrelevant in the employment market," *ibid.,* citing *Griggs v. Duke Power Co.,* 401 U.S. 424, 436, 91 S.Ct. 849, 856, 28 L.Ed.2d 158 (1971), could not reasonably be construed to permit such a racial classification. And if it would be unlawful to use race-based actuarial tables, it must also be unlawful to use sex-based tables, for under Title VII a distinction based on sex stands on the same footing as a distinction based on race unless it falls within one of a few narrow exceptions that are plainly inapplicable here.[13]

---

[13] The exception for bona fide occupational qualifications, 42 U.S.C. § 2000e–2(e), is inapplicable since the terms of a retirement plan have nothing to do with occupational qualifications. The only possible relevant exception recognized in the Bennett Amendment, see n. 8, *supra,* is inapplicable in this case for the same reason it was inapplicable in *Manhart:* a scheme that uses sex to predict longevity is based on sex; it is not based on "any other factor other than sex." See 435 U.S., at 712, 98 S.Ct., at 1377 ("any individual's life expectancy is based on any number of factors, of which sex is only one").

What we said in *Manhart* bears repeating: "Congress has decided that classifications based on sex, like those based on national origin or race, are unlawful." 435 U.S., at 709, 98 S.Ct., at 1376. The use of sex-segregated actuarial tables to calculate retirement benefits violates Title VII whether or not the tables reflect an accurate prediction of the longevity of women as a class, for under the statute "[e]ven a true generalization about [a] class" cannot justify class-based treatment. *Id.,* at 708, 98 S.Ct., at 1375. An individual woman may not be paid lower monthly benefits simply because women as a class live longer than men.[15] Cf. *Connecticut v. Teal,* 457 U.S. 440, 102 S.Ct. 2525, 73 L.Ed.2d 130 (1982) (an individual may object that an employment test used in making promotion decisions has a discriminatory impact even if the class of which he is a member has not been disproportionately denied promotion).

We conclude that it is just as much discrimination "because of * * * sex" to pay a woman lower benefits when she has made the same contributions as a man as it is to make her pay larger contributions to obtain the same benefits.

III

Since petitioners plainly would have violated Title VII if they had run the entire deferred compensation plan themselves, the only remaining question as to liability is whether their conduct is beyond the reach of the statute because it is the companies chosen by petitioners to participate in the plan that calculate and pay the retirement benefits.

* * * [T]he State provided the opportunity to obtain an annuity as part of its own deferred compensation plan. It invited insurance companies to submit bids outlining the terms on which they would supply retirement benefits and selected the companies that were permitted to participate in the plan. Once the State selected these companies, it entered into contracts with them governing the terms on which benefits were to be provided to

---

[15] As we noted in *Manhart,* "insurance is concerned with events that are individually unpredictable, but that is characteristic of many employment decisions" and has never been deemed a justification for "resort to classifications proscribed by Title VII." 435 U.S., at 710, 98 S.Ct., at 1376. It is true that properly designed tests can identify many job qualifications before employment, whereas it cannot be determined in advance when a particular employee will die. See *id.,* 435 U.S., at 724, 98 S.Ct., at 1383 (Blackmun, J., concurring in part and concurring in the judgment). For some jobs, however, there may be relevant skills that cannot be identified by testing. Yet Title VII clearly would not permit use of race, national origin, sex, or religion as a proxy for such an employment qualification, regardless of whether a statistical correlation could be established.

There is no support in either logic or experience for the view, referred to by Justice Powell, that an annuity plan must classify on the basis of sex to be actuarially sound. Neither Title VII nor the Equal Pay Act "makes it unlawful to determine the funding requirements for an establishment's benefit plan by considering the [sexual] composition of the entire force," *Manhart,* 435 U.S., at 718, n. 34, 98 S.Ct., at 1380, n. 34, and it is simply not necessary either to exact greater contributions from women than from men or to pay women lower benefits than men. For example, the Minnesota Mutual Life Insurance Co. and the Northwestern National Life Insurance Co. have offered an annuity plan that treats men and women equally. See The Chronicle of Higher Education, Vol. 25, No. 7, Oct. 13, 1982, pp. 25–26.

employees. Employees enrolling in the plan could obtain retirement benefits only from one of those companies, and no employee could be contacted by a company except as permitted by the State. Ariz.Regs. 2–9–06.A, 2–9–20.A (1975).

Under these circumstances there can be no serious question that petitioners are legally responsible for the discriminatory terms on which annuities are offered by the companies chosen to participate in the plan. Having created a plan whereby employees can obtain the advantages of using deferred compensation to purchase an annuity only if they invest in one of the companies specifically selected by the State, the State cannot disclaim responsibility for the discriminatory features of the insurers' options. * * * It would be inconsistent with the broad remedial purposes of Title VII to hold that an employer who adopts a discriminatory fringe-benefit plan can avoid liability on the ground that he could not find a third party willing to treat his employees on a nondiscriminatory basis. An employer who confronts such a situation must either supply the fringe benefit himself, without the assistance of any third party, or not provide it at all.

JUSTICE POWELL, with whom THE CHIEF JUSTICE, JUSTICE BLACKMUN, and JUSTICE REHNQUIST join, dissenting in part and concurring in part.

* * *

The accuracy with which an insurance company predicts the rate of mortality depends on its ability to identify groups with similar mortality rates. The writing of annuities thus requires that an insurance company group individuals according to attributes that have a significant correlation with mortality. The most accurate classification system would be to identify all attributes that have some verifiable correlation with mortality and divide people into groups accordingly, but the administrative cost of such an undertaking would be prohibitive. Instead of identifying all relevant attributes, most insurance companies classify individuals according to criteria that provide both an accurate and efficient measure of longevity, including a person's age and sex. These particular criteria are readily identifiable, stable, and easily verifiable. See Benston, The Economics of Gender Discrimination in Employee Fringe Benefits: *Manhart* Revisited, 49 U.Chi.L.Rev. 489, 499–501 (1982).

It is this practice—the use of a sex-based group classification—that the majority ultimately condemns. * * * The policies underlying Title VII, rather than supporting the majority's decision, strongly suggest—at least for me—the opposite conclusion. This remedial statute was enacted to eradicate the types of discrimination in employment that then were pervasive in our society. The entire thrust of Title VII is directed against *discrimination*—disparate treatment on the basis of race or sex that intentionally or arbitrarily affects an individual. But as Justice Blackmun has stated, life expectancy is a "nonstigmatizing factor that demonstrably differentiates females from males and that is not measurable on an individual basis * * * . [T]here is nothing arbitrary, irrational, or 'discriminatory' about recognizing the objective and accepted * * * disparity in female-male life expectancies in computing rates for retirement plans." *Manhart,* 435 U.S., at 724, 98 S.Ct., at 1383 (concurring in part and concurring in judgment). Explicit sexual classifications, to be sure, require close examination, but they are not automatically invalid. Sex-based mortality tables reflect objective actuarial experience. Because their use does not entail discrimination in any normal understanding of that term,[9] a court should hesitate to invalidate this long-approved practice on the basis of its own policy judgment.

NOTES AND QUESTIONS

Test Your Understanding of the Material

    1.   On the assumption that sex-based actuarial tables on the mortality of men and women are accurate, does the use of such tables mean that women as a group will receive lower annuity benefits proportionate to their contributions than will men? Would the use of unisex tables mean that men as a group would receive lower annuity benefits proportionate to their contributions?

    2.   Review footnote 8 and footnote 13 of *Norris.* The Bennett Amendment (§ 703(h)) to Title VII permits employers to differentiate in compensation on the basis of sex where such differentiation would be authorized under the Equal Pay Act, 29 U.S.C. § 206(d). The Equal Pay Act recognizes an affirmative defense for compensation differentials based on:

> (i)   a seniority system; (ii) a merit system; (iii) a system which measures earnings by quantity or quality of production; or (iv) a differential based on any other factor other than sex.

Do any of these exceptions apply to the benefit scheme in *Norris*?

Related Issues

    3.   *Rationale for Proscribing Sex-Based Tables?* In light of your answers to the questions in the first note, why would policy makers concerned about achieving equality for women want to proscribe sex-based tables? Note that *Norris* helps insure that women do not need to save more to have the same expectations as men of a given post-retirement living standard over a longer life span.

    4.   *Would Accepting Sex-Based Tables Require Accepting All Rational "Statistical Discrimination"?* Consider an employer that attempted to justify its refusal to hire any women for certain jobs by offering evidence that women are more likely to withdraw from the labor market after a few years before the

---

[9] Indeed, if employers and insurance carriers offer annuities based on unisex mortality tables, men as a class will receive less aggregate benefits than similarly situated women.

recoupment of training costs could occur, and that there is no cost-effective way to determine which women are exceptions to this profile. Is this use of what labor economists call "statistical discrimination" different from the use of sex-based actuarial tables? If so, how?

　　5.　*Insurance Industry Reaction to* Norris. The insurance industry adjusted to *Norris* by offering unisex annuity options. See Mary Gray & Sana F. Shtasel, Insurers Are Surviving Without Sex, 71 A.B.A.Journal 89–90 (Feb. 1985) (Arizona itself reinstated the unisex annuity option after the *Norris* decision); Graham v. State of N.Y., Dept. of Civil Service, 907 F.2d 324 (2d Cir. 1990) (also true of New York). Is there any reason why insurers cannot derive the same profits from unisex as from sex-based annuities without imposing extra costs on employers? Does anything in *Norris* prohibit insurers from adjusting their annuity pay outs to reflect the proportion of women in their annuity pool? See McDaniel v. Corp, 203 F.3d 1099 (9th Cir. 2000) (ERISA case where employer used unisex tables to calculate payout, but failed to disclose that payouts were adjusted for female representation in insurance pool; employees did not bring Title VII claim). Such an adjustment may result in the reduction of annuities for men as well as the raising of annuities for women, but does it result in employers having any incentive not to hire women?

B.　PREGNANCY AND FERTILITY

GENERAL ELECTRIC CO. v. GILBERT

Supreme Court of the United States, 1976.
429 U.S. 125, 97 S.Ct. 401, 50 L.Ed.2d 343.

MR. JUSTICE REHNQUIST delivered the opinion of the Court.

Petitioner, General Electric Co., provides for all of its employees a disability plan which pays weekly nonoccupational sickness and accident benefits. Excluded from the plan's coverage, however, are disabilities arising from pregnancy.

* * *

Following trial, the District Court made findings of fact and conclusions of law, and entered an order in which it determined that General Electric, by excluding pregnancy disabilities from the coverage of the Plan, had engaged in sex discrimination in violation of § 703(a)(1) of Title VII.

* * *

　　Between the date on which the District Court's judgment was rendered and the time this case was decided by the Court of Appeals, we decided *Geduldig v. Aiello,* 417 U.S. 484, 94 S.Ct. 2485, 41 L.Ed.2d 256 (1974), where we rejected a claim that a very similar disability program established under California law violated the Equal Protection Clause of the Fourteenth Amendment because that plan's exclusion of pregnancy disabilities represented sex discrimination.

* * *

There is no more showing in this case than there was in *Geduldig* that the exclusion of pregnancy benefits is a mere "pretex[t] designed to effect an invidious discrimination against the members of one sex or the other." The Court of Appeals expressed the view that the decision in *Geduldig* had actually turned on whether or not a conceded discrimination was "invidious" but we think that in so doing it misread the quoted language from our opinion. As we noted in that opinion, a distinction which on its face is not sex related might nonetheless violate the Equal Protection Clause if it were in fact a subterfuge to accomplish a forbidden discrimination. But we have here no question of excluding a disease or disability comparable in all other respects to covered diseases or disabilities and yet confined to the members of one race or sex. Pregnancy is, of course, confined to women, but it is in other ways significantly different from the typical covered disease or disability. The District Court found that it is not a "disease" at all, and is often a voluntarily undertaken and desired condition. We do not therefore infer that the exclusion of pregnancy disability benefits from petitioner's plan is a simple pretext for discriminating against women. * * *

The instant suit was grounded on Title VII rather than the Equal Protection Clause, and our cases recognize that a prima facie violation of Title VII can be established in some circumstances upon proof that the *effect* of an otherwise facially neutral plan or classification is to discriminate against members of one class or another. See *Washington v. Davis,* 426 U.S. 229, 246–248, 96 S.Ct. 2040, 2051, 48 L.Ed.2d 597 (1976). For example, in the context of a challenge, under the provisions of § 703(a)(2), to a facially neutral employment test, this Court held that a prima facie case of discrimination would be established if, even absent proof of intent, the consequences of the test were "invidiously to discriminate on the basis of racial or other impermissible classification," *Griggs v. Duke Power Co.,* 401 U.S. 424, 431, 91 S.Ct. 849, 853, 28 L.Ed.2d 158 (1971). Even assuming that it is not necessary in this case to prove intent to establish a prima facie violation of § 703(a)(1), but cf. *McDonnell Douglas Corp. v. Green,* 411 U.S. 792, 802–806, 93 S.Ct. 1817, 1824–1826, 36 L.Ed.2d 668 (1973), the respondents have not made the requisite showing of gender-based effect.

As in *Geduldig,* respondents have not attempted to meet the burden of demonstrating a gender-based discriminatory effect resulting from the exclusion of pregnancy-related disabilities from coverage. Whatever the ultimate probative value of the evidence introduced before the District Court on this subject in the instant case, at the very least it tended to illustrate that the selection of risks covered by the Plan did not operate, in fact, to discriminate against women. As in *Geduldig,* we start from the indisputable baseline that "[t]he fiscal and actuarial benefits of the program * * * accrue to members of both sexes," 417 U.S., at 497 n. 20, 94 S.Ct., at 2492 n. 20. We need not disturb the findings of the District Court to note that neither is there a finding, nor was there any evidence which would support a finding, that the financial benefits of the Plan "worked to discriminate against any definable group or class in terms of the aggregate risk protection derived by that group or class from the program," *id.,* at 496, 94 S.Ct., at 2492. The Plan, in effect (and for all that appears), is nothing more than an insurance package, which covers some risks, but excludes others, see *id.,* at 494, 496–497, 94 S.Ct., at 2491–2492. The "package" going to relevant identifiable groups we are presently concerned with—General Electric's male and female employees—covers exactly the same categories of risk, and is facially nondiscriminatory in the sense that "[t]here is no risk from which men are protected and women are not. Likewise, there is no risk from which women are protected and men are not." *Id.,* at 496–497, 94 S.Ct., at 2492. As there is no proof that the package is in fact worth more to men than to women, it is impossible to find any gender-based discriminatory effect in this scheme simply because women disabled as a result of pregnancy do not receive benefits; that is to say, gender-based discrimination does not result simply because an employer's disability-benefits plan is less than all-inclusive.[17] For all that appears, pregnancy-related disabilities constitute an *additional* risk, unique to women, and the failure to compensate them for this risk does not destroy the presumed parity of the benefits, accruing to men and women alike, which results from the facially evenhanded *inclusion* of risks. To hold otherwise would endanger the commonsense notion that an employer who has no disability benefits program at all does not violate Title VII even though the "underinclusion" of risks impacts, as a result of pregnancy-related disabilities, more heavily upon one gender than upon the other.

NASHVILLE GAS CO. v. SATTY
Supreme Court of the United States, 1977.
434 U.S. 136, 98 S.Ct. 347, 54 L.Ed.2d 356.

MR. JUSTICE REHNQUIST delivered the opinion of the Court.

Two separate policies are at issue in this case. The first is petitioner's practice of giving sick pay to employees disabled by reason of nonoccupational sickness or injury but not to those disabled by pregnancy. The second is petitioner's practice of denying accumulated seniority to

---

[17]   Absent proof of different values, the cost to "insure" against the risks is, in essence, nothing more than extra compensation to the employees, in the form of fringe benefits. If the employer were to remove the insurance fringe benefits and, instead, increase wages by an amount equal to the cost of the "insurance," there would clearly be no gender-based discrimination, even though a female employee who wished to purchase disability insurance that covered all risks would have to pay more than would a male employee who purchased identical disability insurance, due to the fact that her insurance had to cover the "extra" disabilities due to pregnancy. * * *

female employees returning to work following disability caused by childbirth. We shall discuss them in reversed order.

I

Petitioner requires an employee who is about to give birth to take a pregnancy leave of indeterminate length. Such an employee does not accumulate seniority while absent, but instead actually loses any job seniority accrued before the leave commenced. Petitioner will not hold the employee's job open for her awaiting her return from pregnancy leave. An employee who wishes to return to work from such leave will be placed in any open position for which she is qualified and for which no individual currently employed is bidding; before such time as a permanent position becomes available, the company attempts to find temporary work for the employee. If and when the employee acquires a permanent position, she regains previously accumulated seniority for purposes of pension, vacation, and the like, but does not regain it for the purpose of bidding on future job openings.

* * *

We conclude that petitioner's policy of denying accumulated seniority to female employees returning from pregnancy leave violates § 703(a)(2) of Title VII.

* * *

On its face, petitioner's seniority policy appears to be neutral in its treatment of male and female employees. If an employee is forced to take a leave of absence from his or her job because of disease or any disability other than pregnancy, the employee, whether male or female, retains accumulated seniority and, indeed, continues to accrue seniority while on leave. If the employee takes a leave of absence for any other reason, including pregnancy, accumulated seniority is divested. Petitioner's decision not to treat pregnancy as a disease or disability for purposes of seniority retention is not on its face a discriminatory policy. "Pregnancy is, of course, confined to women, but it is in other ways significantly different from the typical covered disease or disability." *Gilbert,* 429 U.S., at 136, 97 S.Ct., at 408.

We have recognized, however, that both intentional discrimination and policies neutral on their face but having a discriminatory effect may run afoul of § 703(a)(2). *Griggs v. Duke Power Co.,* 401 U.S. 424, 431, 91 S.Ct. 849, 854, 28 L.Ed.2d 158 (1971). It is beyond dispute that petitioner's policy of depriving employees returning from pregnancy leave of their accumulated seniority acts both to deprive them "of employment opportunities" and to "adversely affect [their] status as an employee." It is apparent from the previous recitation of the events which occurred following respondent's return from pregnancy leave that petitioner's policy denied her specific employment opportunities that she otherwise would have obtained. Even if she had ultimately been able to regain a permanent position with petitioner, she would have felt the effects of a lower seniority level, with its attendant relegation to less desirable and lower paying jobs, for the remainder of her career with petitioner.

In *Gilbert, supra,* there was no showing that General Electric's policy of compensating for all non-job-related disabilities except pregnancy favored men over women. No evidence was produced to suggest that men received more benefits from General Electric's disability insurance fund than did women; both men and women were subject generally to the disabilities covered and presumably drew similar amounts from the insurance fund.

* * *

Here, by comparison, petitioner has not merely refused to extend to women a benefit that men cannot and do not receive, but has imposed on women a substantial burden that men need not suffer. The distinction between benefits and burdens is more than one of semantics. We held in *Gilbert* that § 703(a)(1) did not require that greater economic benefits be paid to one sex or the other "because of their differing roles in 'the scheme of human existence,'" 429 U.S., at 139 n. 17, 97 S.Ct., at 410 n. 17. But that holding does not allow us to read § 703(a)(2) to permit an employer to burden female employees in such a way as to deprive them of employment opportunities because of their different role.

Recognition that petitioner's facially neutral seniority system does deprive women of employment opportunities because of their sex does not end the inquiry under § 703(a)(2) of Title VII. * * * But we agree with the District Court in this case that since there was no proof of any business necessity adduced with respect to the policies in question, that court was entitled to "assume no justification exists."[5]

II

On the basis of the evidence presented to the District Court, petitioner's policy of not awarding sick-leave pay to pregnant employees is legally indistinguishable from the disability-insurance program upheld in *Gilbert.* As in *Gilbert,* petitioner compensates employees for limited periods of time during which the employee must miss work because of a non-job-related illness or disability. As in *Gilbert,* the compensation is not extended to pregnancy-related absences.

---

[5] Indeed, petitioner's policy of denying accumulated seniority to employees returning from pregnancy leave might easily conflict with its own economic and efficiency interests. In particular, as a result of petitioner's policy, inexperienced employees are favored over experienced employees; employees who have spent lengthy periods with petitioner and might be expected to be more loyal to the company are displaced by relatively new employees. Female employees may also be less motivated to perform efficiently in their jobs because of the greater difficulty of advancing through the firm.

* * *

We again need not decide whether, when confronted by a facially neutral plan, it is necessary to prove intent to establish a prima facie violation of § 703(a)(1).

MR. JUSTICE STEVENS, concurring in the judgment.

The general problem is to decide when a company policy which attaches a special burden to the risk of absenteeism caused by pregnancy is a prima facie violation of the statutory prohibition against sex discrimination. The answer "always," which I had thought quite plainly correct, is foreclosed by the Court's holding in *Gilbert*. The answer "never" would seem to be dictated by the Court's view that a discrimination against pregnancy is "not a gender-based discrimination at all." The Court has, however, made it clear that the correct answer is "sometimes." Even though a plan which frankly and unambiguously discriminates against pregnancy is "facially neutral," the Court will find it unlawful if it has a "discriminatory effect." The question, then, is how to identify this discriminatory effect. Two possible answers are suggested by the Court. The Court seems to rely on (a) the difference between a benefit and a burden, and (b) the difference between § 703(a)(2) and § 703(a)(1). In my judgment, both of these differences are illusory.[4] I agree with the Court that the effect of the respondent's seniority plan is significantly different from that of the General Electric disability plan in *Gilbert,* but I suggest that the difference may be described in this way: Although the *Gilbert* Court was unwilling to hold that discrimination against pregnancy—as compared with other physical disabilities—is discrimination on account of sex, it may nevertheless be true that discrimination against pregnant or formerly pregnant employees—as compared with other employees—does constitute sex discrimination. This distinction may be pragmatically expressed in terms of whether the employer has a policy which adversely affects a woman beyond the term of her pregnancy leave.

---

[4] Differences between benefits and burdens cannot provide a meaningful test of discrimination since, by hypothesis, the favored class is always benefited and the disfavored class is equally burdened. The grant of seniority is a benefit which is not shared by the burdened class; conversely, the denial of sick pay is a burden which the benefited class need not bear.

The Court's second apparent ground of distinction is equally unsatisfactory. The Court suggests that its analysis of the seniority plan is different because that plan was attacked under § 703(a)(2) of Title VII not § 703(a)(1). Again, I must confess that I do not understand the relevance of this distinction. It is true that § 703(a)(1) refers to "discrimination" and § 703(a)(2) does not. But the Court itself recognizes that this is not significant since a violation of § 703(a)(2) occurs when a facially neutral policy has a "*discriminatory effect.*" The Court also suggests that § 703(a)(1) may contain a requirement of intent not present in § 703(a)(2). Whatever the merits of that suggestion, it is apparent that it does not form the basis for any differentiation between the two subparagraphs of § 703 in this case, since the Court expressly refuses to decide the issue.

NOTE: PREGNANCY DISCRIMINATION ACT OF 1978

In 1978 Congress rejected at least the specific holding of *Gilbert* by passing the Pregnancy Discrimination Act (PDA), 92 Stat. 2076, 42 U.S.C. § 2000(e)(k), which added a new definitional section to Title VII. This section, 701(k), provides:

> The terms "because of sex" or "on the basis of sex" include, but are not limited to, because of or on the basis of pregnancy, childbirth, or related medical conditions; and women affected by pregnancy, childbirth, or related medical conditions shall be treated the same for all employment-related purposes, including receipt of benefits under fringe benefit programs, as other persons not so affected but similar in their ability or inability to work, and nothing in section 703(h) of this title shall be interpreted to permit otherwise * * * .

The Supreme Court has interpreted this provision on several occasions. First, in Newport News Shipbuilding and Dry Dock Co. v. EEOC, 462 U.S. 669, 103 S.Ct. 2622, 77 L.Ed.2d 89 (1983), the Court held that § 701(k) prohibited an employer from providing less health insurance coverage for the pregnancy-related medical expenses of the spouses of its male employees than it provided for either the pregnancy-related expenses of its female employees or for nonpregnancy-related medical expenses of its employees' spouses. The Court took pains to make clear that employers are under no Title VII obligation to provide dependent benefits, and would not violate § 701(k) by providing benefits only for employees and not their spouses. 462 U.S. at 675.

In its second interpretation of the PDA, California Federal Savings & Loan Association v. Guerra, 479 U.S. 272, 107 S.Ct. 683, 93 L.Ed.2d 613 (1987), the Court held that the PDA does not preempt a California law that required employers to provide leave and reinstatement to employees disabled by pregnancy regardless of the employer's provision of other disability benefits. Even though the PDA does not *require* coverage of pregnancy benefits when other disability benefits are not granted, the states are not barred from giving special protection to disability due to pregnancy because "Congress [intended the PDA to be] a 'floor beneath which pregnancy disability benefits may not drop—not a ceiling above which they may not rise.' " Id. at 280, 107 S.Ct. at 689. The Court further noted that the California statute was "narrowly drawn to cover only the period of *actual physical disability*," and thus "does not reflect archaic or stereotypical notions about pregnancy and the abilities of pregnant workers." Id. at 290, 107 S.Ct. at 694 (emphasis in original).

In a third interpretation of the PDA, AT&T v. Hulteen, 556 U.S. 701, 129 S.Ct. 1962, 173 L.Ed.2d 898 (2009), the Court held that the PDA has no retroactive effect, and employees thus cannot claim illegal discrimination for the denial of seniority credits for pregnancy leave taken before the effective date of the Act. The Court's fourth interpretation of the PDA is presented after the following notes and questions.

NOTES AND QUESTIONS

Test Your Understanding of the Material

1. Why wasn't General Electric's exclusion of pregnancy from its otherwise comprehensive disability plan treated as sex-based discrimination against a subset of women, even before the PDA? In Phillips v. Martin Marietta, 400 U.S. 542, 91 S.Ct. 496, 27 L.Ed.2d 613 (1971), the Court had ruled that an employer discriminates on the basis of sex by implementing an employment policy that discriminates against a subset of all women—in that case, hiring men but not women with preschool children. Was *Phillips* distinguishable?

2. Why didn't the plaintiffs in *Gilbert* at least succeed on a disparate-impact theory?

3. Why was the denial of accumulated seniority to women returning from pregnancy leave held vulnerable under disparate impact analysis when the exclusion of pregnancy benefits in *Gilbert* was not?

Related Issues

4. *Special Needs and Equality.* Note Justice Rehnquist's distinction between (i) disability payments as a "benefit" and (ii) the divestment of accumulated seniority as a "burden". Might Justice Rehnquist have been concerned that protected classes with special needs could use antidiscrimination law to demand extra support from employers? Does the PDA in part reflect a judgment by Congress that pregnant women should be granted such support in order to achieve greater workplace equality? Does the Court's opinion in *Gilbert* have implications for compensation cases not involving pregnancy even after the PDA (and the Civil Rights Act of 1991)? Consider, for instance, an employer's adoption of a health insurance plan that excluded coverage of the costs of treating AIDS, a disease that has disproportionately afflicted males and African-Americans. (Consider also the treatment of such an exclusion under the Americans with Disabilities Act, see pp. 560–561.)

5. *Pregnancy Disability vs. Maternity Leave.* Can an employer grant maternity leave beyond the period of a new mother's physical disability without also granting comparable paternity leave? See Schafer v. Board of Public Educ. of School Dist. of Pittsburgh, 903 F.2d 243 (3d Cir.1990) (holding that equal leave must be granted to both sexes notwithstanding PDA); but cf. Johnson v. University of Iowa, 431 F.3d 325 (8th Cir. 2005) (university may establish "a period of presumptive disability" for pregnancy). The EEOC's position is in accord with that of the *Schafer* court. See EEOC Enforcement Guidance on Pregnancy Discrimination and Related Issues, Notice 915.003 (June 25, 2015) ("leave related to pregnancy, childbirth, or related medical conditions can be limited to women affected by those conditions. However, parental leave must be provided to similarly situated men and women on the same terms). See also the discussion of the Family Medical Leave Act at pp. 897–899 below.

6. *Applications of* Gilbert *and* Satty *to Post-PDA Litigation?*

a.   A school district provides teachers with three different types of leave: (i) paid sick leave, with continuing unpaid illness leave, (ii) unpaid maternity or paternity leave, and (iii) an unpaid leave of absence. The district bars employees from combining any of these leaves. Hence, a pregnant teacher can use her accumulated paid sick leave for the period of her disability, but must return to work when her disability ends. She may not combine paid sick leave with an unpaid maternity leave. Has the school district violated the PDA, even though pregnancy is not treated differently from other disabilities under this plan? If, as most courts have held, disparate-impact analysis is available under the PDA, can the employer defend by using Justice Rehnquist's aggregation of benefits analysis? See Scherr v. Woodland School Community Consolidated District No. 50, 867 F.2d 974 (7th Cir.1988).

b.   Can an employer fire or refuse to hire a woman because she became pregnant without being married? What if the employer cited a formal policy against employing any parents of children conceived out of wedlock? See Chambers v. Omaha Girls Club, 834 F.2d 697 (8th Cir.1987).

7. *Lactation Breaks.* The Affordable Care Act, 124 Stat. 119 (2010), amended § 7 of the Fair Labor Standards Act, 29 U.S.C. § 207, to require employers to provide unpaid break time for breastfeeding mothers to express milk until a child's first birthday. It also requires employers to provide "a place, other than a bathroom, that is shielded from view and free from intrusion from coworkers and the public, which may be used by an employee to express breast milk." 29 U.S.C. § 207(r).

8. *Contraception.* Many state laws require health insurance plans providing coverage for prescription medicines also to provide coverage for all FDA-approved prescription methods of contraception. The Affordable Care Act requires such coverage without cost sharing.

9. *Infertility.* Does an employer's denial of health insurance coverage for fertility treatments violate the PDA? Title VII generally? See Krauel v. Iowa Methodist Medical Center, 95 F.3d 674 (8th Cir.1996) (infertility not a "related medical condition" and no showing of a disparate impact on women). What if an employer's plan includes coverage for most infertility treatments, but excludes coverage for surgical impregnation procedures, which of course would only be performed on women? See Saks v. Franklin Covey Co., 316 F.3d 337, 346–47 (2d Cir.2003); see also Hall v. Nalco, 534 F.3d 644, 647 (7th Cir. 2008) (termination of employee for undergoing in vitro fertilization constitutes sex discrimination because based on childbearing capacity).

10. *The PDA and Abortion Funding.* The last sentence in § 701(k) provides:

This subsection shall not require an employer to pay for health insurance benefits for abortion, except where the life of the mother would be endangered if the fetus were carried to term, or except where medical complications have arisen from an abortion: Provided, That nothing herein shall preclude an employer from providing abortion benefits or otherwise affect bargaining agreements in regard to abortion.

In light of this language, does § 701(k) prevent an employer from discharging a woman because she had an elective or optional abortion? See Doe v. C.A.R.S. Protection Plus Inc., 527 F.3d 358 (3d Cir. 2008); Turic v. Holland Hospitality Inc., 85 F.3d 1211 (6th Cir. 1996) (holding the PDA protects women from discrimination for having or considering an abortion). Does it permit employers to exclude the costs of such abortions from their health insurance coverage? Does it permit employers who pay sick leave benefits generally to not pay such benefits for elective abortions? See EEOC, Questions and Answers on Pregnancy Discrimination, 29 C.F.R. § 1604, App. Q&A 34–36 (Apr. 20, 1979).

YOUNG V. UNITED PARCEL SERVICE, INC.

Supreme Court of the United States, 2015.
575 U.S. ___, 135 S.Ct. 1338, 191 L.Ed.2d 279.

JUSTICE BREYER delivered the opinion of the Court.

The Pregnancy Discrimination Act makes clear that Title VII's prohibition against sex discrimination applies to discrimination based on pregnancy. It also says that employers must treat "women affected by pregnancy . . . the same for all employment-related purposes . . . as other persons not so affected but similar in their ability or inability to work." 42 U.S.C. § 2000e(k). We must decide how this latter provision applies in the context of an employer's policy that accommodates many, but not all, workers with nonpregnancy-related disabilities.

In our view, the Act requires courts to consider the extent to which an employer's policy treats pregnant workers less favorably than it treats nonpregnant workers similar in their ability or inability to work. And here—as in all cases in which an individual plaintiff seeks to show disparate treatment through indirect evidence—it requires courts to consider any legitimate, nondiscriminatory, nonpretextual justification for these differences in treatment. See *McDonnell Douglas Corp. v. Green,* 411 U.S. 792, 802, 93 S.Ct. 1817, 36 L.Ed.2d 668 (1973). Ultimately the court must determine whether the nature of the employer's policy and the way in which it burdens pregnant women shows that the employer has engaged in intentional discrimination. The Court of Appeals here affirmed a grant of summary judgment in favor of the employer. Given our view of the law, we must vacate that court's judgment.

I

A

We begin with a summary of the facts. The petitioner, Peggy Young, worked as a part-time driver for the respondent, United Parcel Service (UPS). Her responsibilities included pickup and delivery of packages that had arrived by air carrier the previous night. In 2006, after suffering several miscarriages, she became pregnant. Her doctor told her that she should not lift more than 20 pounds during the first 20 weeks of her pregnancy or more than 10 pounds thereafter. UPS required drivers like Young to be able to lift parcels weighing up to 70 pounds (and up to 150 pounds with assistance). UPS told Young she could not work while under a lifting restriction. Young consequently stayed home without pay during most of the time she was pregnant and eventually lost her employee medical coverage.

Young subsequently brought this federal lawsuit. We focus here on her claim that UPS acted unlawfully in refusing to accommodate her pregnancy-related lifting restriction. Young said that her co-workers were willing to help her with heavy packages. She also said that UPS accommodated other drivers who were "similar in their . . . inability to work." She accordingly concluded that UPS must accommodate her as well.

UPS responded that the "other persons" whom it had accommodated were (1) drivers who had become disabled on the job, (2) those who had lost their Department of Transportation (DOT) certifications, and (3) those who suffered from a disability covered by the Americans with Disabilities Act of 1990 (ADA), 104 Stat. 327, 42 U.S.C. § 12101 *et seq.* UPS said that, since Young did not fall within any of those categories, it had not discriminated against Young on the basis of pregnancy but had treated her just as it treated all "other" relevant "persons."

B * * *

This case requires us to consider the application of the second clause [of the PDA] to a "disparate-treatment" claim—a claim that an employer intentionally treated a complainant less favorably than employees with the "complainant's qualifications" but outside the complainant's protected class. * * * Young has not alleged a disparate-impact claim. * * *

C * * *

Young introduced . . . evidence indicating that UPS had accommodated several individuals when they suffered disabilities that created work restrictions similar to hers. UPS contests the correctness of some of these facts and the relevance of others. But because we are at the summary judgment stage, and because there is a genuine dispute as to these facts, we view this evidence in the light most favorable to Young, the nonmoving party:

— Several employees received accommodations while suffering various similar or more serious disabilities incurred on the job. See App. 400–401* (10-pound lifting limitation); *id.,* at 635 (foot injury); *id.,* at 637 (arm injury).

— Several employees received accommodations following injury, where the record is unclear as to whether the injury was incurred on or off the job. See *id.,* at 381 (recurring knee injury); *id.,* at 655 (ankle injury); *id.,* at 655 (knee injury); *id.,* at 394 & 398 (stroke); *id.,* at 425, 636–637 (leg injury).

— Several employees received "inside" jobs after losing their DOT certifications. See *id.,* at 372 (DOT certification suspended after conviction for driving under the influence); *id.,* at 636, 647 (failed DOT test due to high blood pressure); *id.,* at 640–641 (DOT certification lost due to sleep apnea diagnosis).

— Some employees were accommodated despite the fact that their disabilities had been incurred off the job. See *id.,* at 446 (ankle injury); *id.,* at 433, 635–636 (cancer).

— According to a deposition of a UPS shop steward who had worked for UPS for roughly a decade, *id.,* at 461, 463, "the only light duty requested [due to physical] restrictions that became an issue" at UPS "were with women who were pregnant," *id.,* at 504.

The District Court granted UPS' motion for summary judgment. * * *

On appeal, the Fourth Circuit affirmed. It wrote that "UPS has crafted a pregnancy-blind policy" that is "at least facially a 'neutral and legitimate business practice,' and not evidence of UPS's discriminatory animus toward pregnant workers." It also agreed with the District Court that Young could not show that "similarly-situated employees outside the protected class received more favorable treatment than Young. Specifically, it believed that Young was different from those workers who were "disabled under the ADA" (which then protected only those with permanent disabilities) because Young was "not disabled"; her lifting limitation was only "temporary and not a significant restriction on her ability to perform major life activities." Young was also different from those workers who had lost their DOT certifications because "no legal obstacle stands between her and her work" and because many with lost DOT certifications retained physical (*i.e.,* lifting) capacity that Young lacked. And Young was different from those "injured on the job because, quite

---

*   [Eds – Refers to Appendix filed with the Court but not reproduced here.]

simply, her inability to work [did] not arise from an on-the-job injury. Rather, Young more closely resembled "an employee who injured his back while picking up his infant child or . . . an employee whose lifting limitation arose from her off-the-job work as a volunteer firefighter," neither of whom would have been eligible for accommodation under UPS' policies. * * *

D

We note that statutory changes made after the time of Young's pregnancy may limit the future significance of our interpretation of the Act. In 2008, Congress expanded the definition of "disability" under the ADA to make clear that "physical or mental impairment[s] that substantially limi[t]" an individual's ability to lift, stand, or bend are ADA-covered disabilities. ADA Amendments Act of 2008, 122 Stat. 3555, codified at 42 U.S.C. §§ 12102(1)–(2). As interpreted by the EEOC, the new statutory definition requires employers to accommodate employees whose temporary lifting restrictions originate off the job. See 29 CFR pt. 1630, App., § 1630.2(j)(1)(ix). We express no view on these statutory and regulatory changes.

II

The parties disagree about the interpretation of the Pregnancy Discrimination Act's second clause. * * *

Young and the United States believe that the second clause of the Pregnancy Discrimination Act "requires an employer to provide the same accommodations to workplace disabilities caused by pregnancy that it provides to workplace disabilities that have other causes but have a similar effect on the ability to work." In other words, Young contends that the second clause means that whenever "an employer accommodates only a subset of workers with disabling conditions," a court should find a Title VII violation if "pregnant workers who are similar in the ability to work" do not "receive the same [accommodation] even if still other non-pregnant workers do not receive accommodations."

UPS takes an almost polar opposite view. It contends that the second clause does no more than define sex discrimination to include pregnancy discrimination. Under this view, courts would compare the accommodations an employer provides to pregnant women with the accommodations it provides to others *within* a facially neutral category (such as those with off-the-job injuries) to determine whether the employer has violated Title VII.

A

We cannot accept either of these interpretations. * * *

The problem with Young's approach is that it proves too much. It seems to say that the statute grants pregnant workers a "most-favored-nation" status. As long as an employer provides one or two workers with an accommodation—say, those with particularly hazardous jobs, or those whose workplace presence is particularly needed, or those who have worked at the company for many years, or those who are over the age of 55—then it must provide similar accommodations to *all* pregnant workers (with comparable physical limitations), irrespective of the nature of their jobs, the employer's need to keep them working, their ages, or any other criteria. * * *

C

We find it similarly difficult to accept the opposite interpretation of the Act's second clause. UPS says that the second clause simply defines sex discrimination to include pregnancy discrimination. But that cannot be so. * * *

* * * [T]he second clause was intended to do more than that—it "was intended to overrule the holding in [*General Electric Co. v. Gilbert,* 429 U.S. 125, 97 S.Ct. 401, 50 L.Ed.2d 343 (1976)] and to illustrate how discrimination against pregnancy is to be remedied." *Id.,* at 285, 107 S.Ct. 683. The dissent's view, like that of UPS', ignores this precedent.

III

The statute lends itself to an interpretation other than those that the parties advocate. . . . Our interpretation minimizes the problems we have discussed, responds directly to *Gilbert*, and is consistent with longstanding interpretations of Title VII.

In our view, an individual pregnant worker who seeks to show disparate treatment through indirect evidence may do so through application of the *McDonnell Douglas* framework. * * *

[T]hus, a plaintiff alleging that the denial of an accommodation constituted disparate treatment under the Pregnancy Discrimination Act's second clause may make out a prima facie case by showing, as in *McDonnell Douglas*, that she belongs to the protected class, that she sought accommodation, that the employer did not accommodate her, and that the employer did accommodate others "similar in their ability or inability to work."

The employer may then seek to justify its refusal to accommodate the plaintiff by relying on "legitimate, nondiscriminatory" reasons for denying her accommodation. But, consistent with the Act's basic objective, that reason normally cannot consist simply of a claim that it is more expensive or less convenient to add pregnant women to the category of those ("similar in their ability or inability to work") whom the employer accommodates. After all, the employer in *Gilbert* could in all likelihood have made just such a claim.

If the employer offers an apparently "legitimate, non-discriminatory" reason for its actions, the plaintiff may in turn show that the employer's proffered reasons are in fact pretextual. We believe that the plaintiff may reach a jury on this issue by providing sufficient evidence that the employer's policies impose a significant burden on pregnant workers, and that the employer's "legitimate, nondiscriminatory" reasons are not sufficiently strong to justify the burden, but rather—when considered along with the burden imposed—give rise to an inference of intentional discrimination.

The plaintiff can create a genuine issue of material fact as to whether a significant burden exists by providing evidence that the employer accommodates a large percentage of nonpregnant workers while failing to accommodate a large percentage of pregnant workers. Here, for example, if the facts are as Young says they are, she can show that UPS accommodates most nonpregnant employees with lifting limitations while categorically failing to accommodate pregnant employees with lifting limitations. Young might also add that the fact that UPS has multiple policies that accommodate nonpregnant employees with lifting restrictions suggests that its reasons for failing to accommodate pregnant employees with lifting restrictions are not sufficiently strong—to the point that a jury could find that its reasons for failing to accommodate pregnant employees give rise to an inference of intentional discrimination. * * *

IV

Under this interpretation of the Act, the judgment of the Fourth Circuit must be vacated. * * * Viewing the record in the light most favorable to Young, there is a genuine dispute as to whether UPS provided more favorable treatment to at least some employees whose situation cannot reasonably be distinguished from Young's. In other words, Young created a genuine dispute of material fact as to the fourth prong of the *McDonnell Douglas* analysis.

Young also introduced evidence that UPS had three separate accommodation policies (on-the-job, ADA, DOT). Taken together, Young argued, these policies significantly burdened pregnant women. The Fourth Circuit did not consider the combined effects of these policies, nor did it consider the strength of UPS' justifications for each when combined. That is, why, when the employer accommodated so many, could it not accommodate pregnant women as well?

We do not determine whether Young created a genuine issue of material fact as to whether UPS' reasons for having treated Young less favorably than it treated these other nonpregnant employees were pretextual. We leave a final determination of that question for the Fourth Circuit to make on remand, in light of the interpretation of the Pregnancy Discrimination Act that we have set out above.

JUSTICE ALITO, concurring in the judgment. * * *

It is obvious that respondent had a neutral reason for providing an accommodation when that was required by the ADA. Respondent also had neutral grounds for providing special accommodations for employees who were injured on the job. If these employees had not been permitted to work at all, it appears that they would have been eligible for workers' compensation benefits. See Md. Lab. & Empl. Code Ann. § 9–614 (2008).

The accommodations that are provided to drivers who lost their DOT certifications, however, are another matter. A driver may lose DOT certification for a variety of reasons, including medical conditions or injuries incurred off the job that impair the driver's ability to operate a motor vehicle. Such drivers may then be transferred to jobs that do not require physical tasks incompatible with their illness or injury. It does not appear that respondent has provided any plausible justification for treating these drivers more favorably than drivers who were pregnant.

JUSTICE SCALIA, with whom JUSTICE KENNEDY and JUSTICE THOMAS join, dissenting.

Faced with two conceivable readings of the Pregnancy Discrimination Act, the Court chooses neither. It crafts instead a new law that is splendidly unconnected with the text and even the legislative history of the Act. * * *

* * * The point of Title VII's bans on discrimination is to prohibit employers from treating one worker differently from another *because of a protected trait*. It is not to prohibit employers from treating workers differently for reasons that have nothing to do with protected traits. See *Texas Dept. of Community Affairs v. Burdine,* 450 U.S. 248, 259, 101 S.Ct. 1089, 67 L.Ed.2d 207 (1981). Against that backdrop, a requirement that pregnant women and other workers be treated the same is sensibly read to forbid distinctions that discriminate against pregnancy, not all distinctions whatsoever.

Prohibiting employers from making *any* distinctions between pregnant workers and others of similar ability would elevate pregnant workers to most favored employees. If Boeing offered chauffeurs to injured directors, it would have to offer chauffeurs to pregnant mechanics. And if Disney paid pensions to workers who can no longer work because of old age, it would have to pay pensions to workers who can no longer work because of childbirth. It is implausible that Title VII, which elsewhere creates guarantees of *equal* treatment, here alone creates a guarantee of *favored* treatment. * * *

The Court agrees that the same-treatment clause is not a most-favored-employee law, but at the same time refuses to adopt the reading I propose—which is the only other reading the clause could conceivably bear. The Court's reasons for resisting this reading fail to persuade.

The Court starts by arguing that the same-treatment clause must do more than ban distinctions on the basis of pregnancy, lest it add nothing to the part of the Act defining pregnancy discrimination as sex discrimination. Even so read, however, the same-treatment clause *does* add something: clarity. * * *

That brings me to the Court's remaining argument: the claim that the reading I have set forth would not suffice to overturn our decision in *Gilbert.* Wrong. *Gilbert* upheld an otherwise comprehensive disability-benefits plan that singled pregnancy out for disfavor. The most natural reading of the Act overturns that decision, because it prohibits singling pregnancy out for disfavor.

The Court goes astray here because it mistakenly assumes that the *Gilbert* plan excluded pregnancy on "a neutral ground"—covering sicknesses and accidents but nothing else. In reality, the plan in *Gilbert* was not neutral toward pregnancy. It "place[d] . . . pregnancy in a class by itself," treating it differently from "any other kind" of condition. At the same time that it denied coverage for pregnancy, it provided coverage for a comprehensive range of other conditions, including many that one would not necessarily call sicknesses or accidents—like "sport injuries, attempted suicides . . . disabilities incurred in the commission of a crime or during a fight, and elective cosmetic surgery." What is more, the plan denied coverage even to sicknesses, if they were related to pregnancy or childbirth. *Ibid.* For that matter, the plan denied coverage to sicknesses that were *unrelated* to pregnancy or childbirth, if they were suffered during recovery from the birth of a child. *Gilbert,* there can be no doubt, involved "the lone exclusion of pregnancy from [a] program." The most natural interpretation of the Act easily suffices to make that unlawful.

NOTES AND QUESTIONS

Test Your Understanding of the Material

1.   Despite the views of the Court, is the better view of the text of the PDA that women are to be treated as well when disabled by pregnancy as any other comparable worker disabled for other causes? See generally Michael C. Harper, Confusion on the Court: Distinguishing Disparate Treatment from Disparate Impact in Young v. UPS and EEOC v. Abercrombie & Fitch, Inc., 96 B.U. L. Rev. 541, 561 (2016) (antidiscrimination law generally requires protected groups to be given most favored nation status).

2.   Justice Breyer's opinion for the Court in *Young* purports to reject UPS's argument that "the second clause simply defines sex discrimination to include pregnancy discrimination." How does the Court's test differ from UPS's interpretation?

3.   The Court states that it does "not determine whether Young created a genuine issue of material fact as to whether UPS' reasons for having treated Young less favorably than it treated . . . other nonpregnant employees were pretextual. . . ." How does the lower court conduct this inquiry?

Related Issues

4. *Implicit Rejection of* Guerra*?* Can the Court's treatment of Young's disparate treatment claim best be explained by a concern that requiring the employer to treat a pregnancy disability as well as its most favored disabilities would also require the employer to treat all other disabilities equally well? If so, does this suggest that the Court no longer assumes the PDA sets only a "floor" and not a "ceiling" for pregnancy benefits, contrary to what the Court held in *Guerra*? See Harper, supra, at 565-566.

5. *Effect of* Young *on Future Cases?* Note that the Court acknowledges that the 2008 amendments to the Americans with Disabilities Act (ADA), discussed infra at pp. 517–519, may limit the significance of its interpretation of the PDA. This is because the ADA now requires employers to accommodate reasonably the kind of temporary but limiting disabilities, such as Young's, often caused by pregnancy.

6. *State and Local Legislation.* A growing number of states and cities have passed legislation, like the California legislation upheld in *Guerra*, that requires employers to provide reasonable accommodations to pregnant employees, regardless of the accommodations made to other employees for other reasons. For instance, Illinois enacted legislation, effective January 1, 2015, that suggests such accommodations can include not only temporary transfers to light duty, but also bathroom breaks, providing stools for workers needing to stand during their shifts, and lactation breaks. 775 Ill. Comp. Stat. 5/2–102(H)–(J).

C. THE BONA FIDE OCCUPATIONAL QUALIFICATION DEFENSE

INTERNATIONAL UNION, UAW v. JOHNSON CONTROLS, INC.

Supreme Court of the United States, 1991.
499 U.S. 187, 111 S.Ct. 1196, 113 L.Ed.2d 158.

JUSTICE BLACKMUN delivered the opinion of the Court.

In this case we are concerned with an employer's gender-based fetal-protection policy. May an employer exclude a fertile female employee from certain jobs because of its concern for the health of the fetus the woman might conceive?

* * *

Respondent Johnson Controls, Inc., manufactures batteries. In the manufacturing process, the element lead is a primary ingredient. Occupational exposure to lead entails health risks, including the risk of harm to any fetus carried by a female employee.

Before the Civil Rights Act of 1964 became law, Johnson Controls did not employ any woman in a battery-manufacturing job. In June 1977, however, it announced its first official policy concerning its employment of women in lead-exposure work:

> "[P]rotection of the health of the unborn child is the immediate and direct responsibility of the prospective parents. While the medical profession and the company can support them in the exercise of this responsibility, it cannot assume it for them without simultaneously infringing their rights as persons.

* * *

> " * * * Since not all women who can become mothers wish to become mothers (or will become mothers), it would appear to be illegal discrimination to treat all who are capable of pregnancy as though they will become pregnant."

Consistent with that view, Johnson Controls "stopped short of excluding women capable of bearing children from lead exposure," but emphasized that a woman who expected to have a child should not choose a job in which she would have such exposure. The company also required a woman who wished to be considered for employment to sign a statement that she had been advised of the risk of having a child while she was exposed to lead. The statement informed the woman that although there was evidence "that women exposed to lead have a higher rate of abortion," this evidence was "not as clear * * * as the relationship between cigarette smoking and cancer," but that it was, "medically speaking, just good sense not to run that risk if you want children and do not want to expose the unborn child to risk, however small. * * * "

Five years later, in 1982, Johnson Controls shifted from a policy of warning to a policy of exclusion. Between 1979 and 1983, eight employees became pregnant while maintaining blood lead levels in excess of 30 micrograms per deciliter. This appeared to be the critical level noted by the Occupational Health and Safety Administration (OSHA) for a worker who was planning to have a family. See 29 CFR § 1910.1025 (1989). The company responded by announcing a broad exclusion of women from jobs that exposed them to lead:

> " * * * [I]t is [Johnson Controls'] policy that women who are pregnant or who are capable of bearing children will not be placed into jobs involving lead exposure or which could expose them to lead through the exercise of job bidding, bumping, transfer or promotion rights."

The policy defined "women * * * capable of bearing children" as "[a]ll women except those whose inability to bear children is medically documented." It further stated that an unacceptable work station was one where, "over the past year," an employee had recorded a blood lead level of more than 30 micrograms per deciliter or the work site had yielded an air sample containing a lead level in excess of 30 micrograms per cubic meter.

* * *

The bias in Johnson Controls' policy is obvious. Fertile men, but not fertile women, are given a choice as to whether they wish to risk their reproductive health for a particular job. Section 703(a) of the Civil Rights Act of 1964, prohibits sex-based classifications in terms and conditions of employment, in hiring and discharging decisions, and in other employment decisions that adversely affect an employee's status. Respondent's fetal-protection policy explicitly discriminates against women on the basis of their sex. The policy excludes women with childbearing capacity from lead-exposed jobs and so creates a facial classification based on gender.

* * *

* * * Johnson Controls' policy classifies on the basis of gender and childbearing capacity, rather than fertility alone. Respondent does not seek to protect the unconceived children of all its employees. Despite evidence in the record about the debilitating effect of lead exposure on the male reproductive system, Johnson Controls is concerned only with the harms that may befall the unborn offspring of its female employees. * * * This Court faced a conceptually similar situation in *Phillips v. Martin Marietta Corp.*, 400 U.S. 542, 91 S.Ct. 496, 27 L.Ed.2d 613 (1971), and found sex discrimination because the policy established "one hiring policy for women and another for men—each having pre-school-age children." Id., at 544, 91 S.Ct., at 498. Johnson Controls' policy is facially discriminatory because it requires only a female employee to produce proof that she is not capable of reproducing.

Our conclusion is bolstered by the Pregnancy Discrimination Act of 1978 (PDA), in which Congress explicitly provided that, for purposes of Title VII, discrimination "on the basis of sex" includes discrimination "because of or on the basis of pregnancy, childbirth, or related medical conditions." "The Pregnancy Discrimination Act has now made clear that, for all Title VII purposes, discrimination based on a woman's pregnancy is, on its face, discrimination because of her sex." *Newport News Shipbuilding & Dry Dock Co. v. EEOC,* 462 U.S. 669, 684, 103 S.Ct. 2622, 2631, 77 L.Ed.2d 89 (1983). In its use of the words "capable of bearing children" in the 1982 policy statement as the criterion for exclusion, Johnson Controls explicitly classifies on the basis of potential for pregnancy. Under the PDA, such a classification must be regarded, for Title VII purposes, in the same light as explicit sex discrimination. Respondent has chosen to treat all its female employees as potentially pregnant; that choice evinces discrimination on the basis of sex.

* * * [T]he absence of a malevolent motive does not convert a facially discriminatory policy into a neutral policy with a discriminatory effect. Whether an employment practice involves disparate treatment through explicit facial discrimination does not depend on why the employer

discriminates but rather on the explicit terms of the discrimination. * * * The beneficence of an employer's purpose does not undermine the conclusion that an explicit gender-based policy is sex discrimination under § 703(a) and thus may be defended only as a BFOQ.

* * *

The BFOQ defense is written narrowly, and this Court has read it narrowly. See, e.g., *Dothard v. Rawlinson*, 433 U.S. 321, 332–337, 97 S.Ct. 2720, 2728–2731, 53 L.Ed.2d 786 (1977); *Trans World Airlines, Inc. v. Thurston*, 469 U.S. 111, 122–125, 105 S.Ct. 613, 622–624, 83 L.Ed.2d 523 (1985). We have read the BFOQ language of § 4(f) of the Age Discrimination in Employment Act of 1967 (ADEA), as amended, which tracks the BFOQ provision in Title VII just as narrowly. See *Western Air Lines, Inc. v. Criswell*, 472 U.S. 400, 105 S.Ct. 2743, 86 L.Ed.2d 321 (1985). Our emphasis on the restrictive scope of the BFOQ defense is grounded on both the language and the legislative history of § 703.

The wording of the BFOQ defense contains several terms of restriction that indicate that the exception reaches only special situations. The statute thus limits the situations in which discrimination is permissible to "certain instances" where sex discrimination is "reasonably necessary" to the "normal operation" of the "particular" business. Each one of these terms— certain, normal, particular—prevents the use of general subjective standards and favors an objective, verifiable requirement. But the most telling term is "occupational"; this indicates that these objective, verifiable requirements must concern job-related skills and aptitudes.

The concurrence defines "occupational" as meaning related to a job. According to the concurrence, any discriminatory requirement imposed by an employer is "job-related" simply because the employer has chosen to make the requirement a condition of employment. In effect, the concurrence argues that sterility may be an occupational qualification for women because Johnson Controls has chosen to require it. This reading of "occupational" renders the word mere surplusage. "Qualification" by itself would encompass an employer's idiosyncratic requirements. By modifying "qualification" with "occupational," Congress narrowed the term to qualifications that affect an employee's ability to do the job.

Johnson Controls argues that its fetal-protection policy falls within the so-called safety exception to the BFOQ. Our cases have stressed that discrimination on the basis of sex because of safety concerns is allowed only in narrow circumstances. In *Dothard v. Rawlinson,* this Court indicated that danger to a woman herself does not justify discrimination. 433 U.S., at 335, 97 S.Ct., at 2729–2730. We there allowed the employer to hire only male guards in contact areas of maximum-security male penitentiaries only because more was at stake than the "individual woman's decision to weigh and accept the risks of employment." Ibid. We found sex to be a

BFOQ inasmuch as the employment of a female guard would create real risks of safety to others if violence broke out because the guard was a woman. Sex discrimination was tolerated because sex was related to the guard's ability to do the job—maintaining prison security. We also required in *Dothard* a high correlation between sex and ability to perform job functions and refused to allow employers to use sex as a proxy for strength although it might be a fairly accurate one.

Similarly, some courts have approved airlines' layoffs of pregnant flight attendants at different points during the first five months of pregnancy on the ground that the employer's policy was necessary to ensure the safety of passengers. See *Harriss v. Pan American World Airways, Inc.,* 649 F.2d 670 (C.A.9 1980); *Burwell v. Eastern Air Lines, Inc.,* 633 F.2d 361 (C.A.4 1980), cert. denied, 450 U.S. 965, 101 S.Ct. 1480, 67 L.Ed.2d 613 (1981); *Condit v. United Air Lines, Inc.,* 558 F.2d 1176 (C.A.4 1977), cert. denied, 435 U.S. 934, 98 S.Ct. 1510, 55 L.Ed.2d 531 (1978); *In re National Airlines, Inc.,* 434 F.Supp. 249 (S.D.Fla.1977). In two of these cases, the courts pointedly indicated that fetal, as opposed to passenger, safety was best left to the mother. *Burwell,* 633 F.2d, at 371; *National Airlines,* 434 F.Supp., at 259.

We considered safety to third parties in *Western Airlines, Inc. v. Criswell,* supra, in the context of the ADEA. We focused upon "the nature of the flight engineer's tasks," and the "actual capabilities of persons over age 60" in relation to those tasks. 472 U.S., at 406, 105 S.Ct., at 2747. Our safety concerns were not independent of the individual's ability to perform the assigned tasks, but rather involved the possibility that, because of age-connected debility, a flight engineer might not properly assist the pilot, and might thereby cause a safety emergency. Furthermore, although we considered the safety of third parties in *Dothard* and *Criswell,* those third parties were indispensable to the particular business at issue. In *Dothard,* the third parties were the inmates; in *Criswell,* the third parties were the passengers on the plane. We stressed that in order to qualify as a BFOQ, a job qualification must relate to the "essence," *Dothard,* 433 U.S., at 333, 97 S.Ct., at 2751, or to the "central mission of the employer's business," *Criswell,* 472 U.S., at 413, 105 S.Ct., at 2751.

The concurrence ignores the "essence of the business" test and so concludes that "the safety to fetuses in carrying out the duties of battery manufacturing is as much a legitimate concern as is safety to third parties in guarding prisons (*Dothard*) or flying airplanes (*Criswell*)." * * * Third-party safety considerations properly entered into the BFOQ analysis in *Dothard* and *Criswell* because they went to the core of the employee's job performance. Moreover, that performance involved the central purpose of the enterprise. *Dothard,* 433 U.S., at 335, 97 S.Ct., at 2729–2730 ("The essence of a correctional counselor's job is to maintain prison security"); *Criswell,* 472 U.S., at 413, 105 S.Ct., at 2751 (the central mission of the airline's business was the safe transportation of its passengers). The concurrence attempts to transform this case into one of customer safety. The unconceived fetuses of Johnson Controls' female employees, however, are neither customers nor third parties whose safety is essential to the business of battery manufacturing. No one can disregard the possibility of injury to future children; the BFOQ, however, is not so broad that it transforms this deep social concern into an essential aspect of batterymaking.

Our case law, therefore, makes clear that the safety exception is limited to instances in which sex or pregnancy actually interferes with the employee's ability to perform the job. * * *4

* * *

We have no difficulty concluding that Johnson Controls cannot establish a BFOQ. Fertile women, as far as appears in the record, participate in the manufacture of batteries as efficiently as anyone else. Johnson Controls' professed moral and ethical concerns about the welfare of the next generation do not suffice to establish a BFOQ of female sterility. Decisions about the welfare of future children must be left to the parents who conceive, bear, support, and raise them rather than to the employers who hire those parents.

* * *

Johnson Controls argues that it must exclude all fertile women because it is impossible to tell which women will become pregnant while working with lead. This argument is somewhat academic in light of our conclusion that the company may not exclude fertile women at all; it perhaps is worth noting, however, that Johnson Controls has shown no "factual basis for believing that all or substantially all women would be unable to perform safely and efficiently the duties of the job involved." *Weeks v. Southern Bell Tel. & Tel. Co.,* 408 F.2d 228, 235 (C.A.5 1969), quoted with approval in *Dothard,* 433 U.S., at 333, 97 S.Ct., at 2751. Even on this sparse record, it is apparent that Johnson Controls is concerned about only a small minority of women. Of eight pregnancies reported among the female employees, it has not been shown that any of the babies have birth defects or other abnormalities. The record does not reveal the birth rate for Johnson Controls' female workers but national statistics show that approximately nine percent of all fertile women become pregnant each year. The birthrate drops to two percent for blue collar workers over

---

4   The concurrence predicts that our reaffirmation of the narrowness of the BFOQ defense will preclude considerations of privacy as a basis for sex-based discrimination. We have never addressed privacy-based sex discrimination and shall not do so here because the sex-based discrimination at issue today does not involve the privacy interests of Johnson Controls' customers. Nothing in our discussion of the "essence of the business test," however, suggests that sex could not constitute a BFOQ when privacy interests are implicated. See, e.g., *Backus v. Baptist Medical Center,* 510 F.Supp. 1191 (E.D.Ark.1981), vacated as moot, 671 F.2d 1100 (C.A.8 1982) (essence of obstetrics nurse's business is to provide sensitive care for patient's intimate and private concerns).

age 30. * * * Johnson Controls' fear of prenatal injury, no matter how sincere, does not begin to show that substantially all of its fertile women employees are incapable of doing their jobs.

* * *

A word about tort liability and the increased cost of fertile women in the workplace is perhaps necessary. One of the dissenting judges in this case expressed concern about an employer's tort liability and concluded that liability for a potential injury to a fetus is a social cost that Title VII does not require a company to ignore. It is correct to say that Title VII does not prevent the employer from having a conscience. The statute, however, does prevent sex-specific fetal-protection policies. These two aspects of Title VII do not conflict.

More than 40 States currently recognize a right to recover for a prenatal injury based either on negligence or on wrongful death. See, e.g., *Wolfe v. Isbell,* 291 Ala. 327, 333–334, 280 So.2d 758, 763 (1973); *Simon v. Mullin,* 34 Conn.Sup. 139, 147, 380 A.2d 1353, 1357 (1977). See also Note, 22 Suffolk U.L.Rev. 747, 754–756, and nn. 54, 57, and 58 (1988) (listing cases). According to Johnson Controls, however, the company complies with the lead standard developed by OSHA and warns its female employees about the damaging effects of lead. It is worth noting that OSHA gave the problem of lead lengthy consideration and concluded that "there is no basis whatsoever for the claim that women of childbearing age should be excluded from the workplace in order to protect the fetus or the course of pregnancy." 43 Fed.Reg. 52952, 52966 (1978). See also *id.,* at 54354, 54398. Instead, OSHA established a series of mandatory protections which, taken together, "should effectively minimize any risk to the fetus and newborn child." Id., at 52966. See 29 CFR § 1910.125(k)(ii) (1989). Without negligence, it would be difficult for a court to find liability on the part of the employer. If, under general tort principles, Title VII bans sex-specific fetal-protection policies, the employer fully informs the woman of the risk, and the employer has not acted negligently, the basis for holding an employer liable seems remote at best.

Although the issue is not before us, the concurrence observes that "it is far from clear that compliance with Title VII will preempt state tort liability." The cases relied upon by the concurrence to support its prediction, however, are inapposite. For example, in *California Federal S. & L. Ass'n. v. Guerra,* 479 U.S. 272, 107 S.Ct. 683, 93 L.Ed.2d 613 (1987), we considered a California statute that expanded upon the requirements of the PDA and concluded that the statute was not pre-empted by Title VII because it was not inconsistent with the purposes of the federal statute and did not require an act that was unlawful under Title VII. Id., at 291–292, 107 S.Ct., at 694–695. Here, in contrast, the tort liability that the concurrence fears will punish employers for complying with Title VII's clear command. When it is impossible for an employer to comply with both state and federal requirements, this Court has ruled that federal law pre-empts that of the States. See, e.g., *Florida Lime & Avocado Growers, Inc. v. Paul,* 373 U.S. 132, 142–143, 83 S.Ct. 1210, 1217–1218, 10 L.Ed.2d 248 (1963).

* * *

If state tort law furthers discrimination in the workplace and prevents employers from hiring women who are capable of manufacturing the product as efficiently as men, then it will impede the accomplishment of Congress' goals in enacting Title VII. Because Johnson Controls has not argued that it faces any costs from tort liability, not to mention crippling ones, the pre-emption question is not before us. We therefore say no more than that the concurrence's speculation appears unfounded as well as premature.

* * * [T]he spectre of an award of damages reflects a fear that hiring fertile women will cost more. The extra cost of employing members of one sex, however, does not provide an affirmative Title VII defense for a discriminatory refusal to hire members of that gender. See *Manhart,* 435 U.S., at 716–718, and n. 32, 98 S.Ct., at 1379–1380, and n. 32. Indeed, in passing the PDA, Congress considered at length the considerable cost of providing equal treatment of pregnancy and related conditions, but made the "decision to forbid special treatment of pregnancy despite the social costs associated therewith." *Arizona Governing Committee v. Norris,* 463 U.S. 1073, 1084, n. 14, 103 S.Ct. 3492, 3499, n. 14, 77 L.Ed.2d 1236 (1983) (opinion of Marshall, J.).

We, of course, are not presented with, nor do we decide, a case in which costs would be so prohibitive as to threaten the survival of the employer's business. We merely reiterate our prior holdings that the incremental cost of hiring women cannot justify discriminating against them.

JUSTICE WHITE, with whom THE CHIEF JUSTICE and JUSTICE KENNEDY join, concurring in part and concurring in the judgment.

* * *

Dothard and *Criswell* make clear that avoidance of substantial safety risks to third parties is *inherently* part of both an employee's ability to perform a job and an employer's "normal operation" of its business. Indeed, in both cases, the Court approved the statement in *Weeks v. Southern Bell Telephone & Telegraph Co.,* 408 F.2d 228 (C.A.5 1969), that an employer could establish a BFOQ defense by showing that "all or substantially all women would be unable to perform *safely and efficiently* the duties of the job involved." Id., at 235 (emphasis added). See *Criswell,* 472 U.S., at 414, 105 S.Ct., at 2751–52; *Dothard,* supra, 433 U.S., at 333, 97 S.Ct., at 2728–29. The Court's statement in this case that "the safety exception is limited to instances in which sex or pregnancy actually interferes with the employee's ability to perform the job," therefore adds no support to its conclusion that a fetal protection policy could never be justified as a BFOQ. On the facts of this case, for example, protecting fetal safety while carrying out the duties of battery manufacturing is as much a legitimate concern as is safety to third parties in guarding prisons (*Dothard*) or flying airplanes (*Criswell*).[5]

Dothard and *Criswell* also confirm that costs are relevant in determining whether a discriminatory policy is reasonably necessary for the normal operation of a business. In *Dothard,* the safety problem that justified exclusion of women from the prison guard positions was largely a result of inadequate staff and facilities. See 433 U.S., at 335, 97 S.Ct., at 2729–30. If the cost of employing women could not be considered, the employer there should have been required to hire more staff and restructure the prison environment rather than exclude women. Similarly, in *Criswell* the airline could have been required to hire more pilots and install expensive monitoring devices rather than discriminate against older employees. The BFOQ statute, however, reflects "Congress' unwillingness to require employers to change the very nature of their operations." *Price Waterhouse v. Hopkins,* 490 U.S. 228, 242, 109 S.Ct. 1775, 1786, 104 L.Ed.2d 268 (1989) (plurality opinion).

* * *

Despite my disagreement with the Court concerning the scope of the BFOQ defense, I concur in reversing the Court of Appeals because that court erred in affirming the District Court's grant of summary judgment in favor of Johnson Controls. First, the Court of Appeals erred in failing to consider the level of risk-avoidance that was part of Johnson Controls' "normal operation." * * *

Second, even without more information about the normal level of risk at Johnson Controls, the fetal protection policy at issue here reaches too far. This is evident both in its presumption that, absent medical documentation to the contrary, all women are fertile regardless of their age, and in its exclusion of presumptively fertile women from positions that might result in a promotion to a position involving high lead exposure. * * *

Third, it should be recalled that until 1982 Johnson Controls operated without an exclusionary policy, and it has not identified any grounds for believing that its current policy is reasonably necessary to its normal operations. * * *

Finally, the Court of Appeals failed to consider properly petitioners evidence of harm to offspring caused by lead exposure in males. * * *

---

[5] I do not, as the Court asserts, reject the "essence of the business" test. Rather, I merely reaffirm the obvious—that safety to third parties is part of the "essence" of most if not all businesses. * * *

JUSTICE SCALIA, concurring in the judgment.

* * * I am willing to assume, as the Court intimates, that any action required by Title VII cannot give rise to liability under state tort law. That assumption, however, does not answer the question whether an action *is* required by Title VII (including the BFOQ provision) even if it is subject to liability under state tort law. It is perfectly reasonable to believe that Title VII has *accommodated* state tort law through the BFOQ exception. However, all that need be said in the present case is that Johnson has not demonstrated a substantial risk of tort liability—which is alone enough to defeat a tort-based assertion of the BFOQ exception.

[T]he Court [also] goes far afield, it seems to me, in suggesting that increased cost alone—short of "costs * * * so prohibitive as to threaten survival of the employer's business"—cannot support a BFOQ defense. I agree with Justice White's concurrence that nothing in our prior cases suggests this, and in my view it is wrong. I think, for example, that a shipping company may refuse to hire pregnant women as crew members on long voyages because the on-board facilities for foreseeable emergencies, though quite feasible, would be inordinately expensive. In the present case, however, Johnson has not asserted a cost-based BFOQ.

NOTES AND QUESTIONS

Test Your Understanding of the Material

1.   In deciding that maintaining a safe workplace is not "reasonably necessary" to the normal operation of all businesses, how did the Court distinguish *Dothard* and *Criswell*?

2.   Does *Johnson Controls* permit an employer to adopt a sex-neutral fetal protection policy that excludes any fertile worker (male or female) from a job that poses a significant threat to his or her unborn children? Would such a policy be vulnerable to a disparate-impact challenge?

3.   Note the *Johnson Controls* Court's statement that the absence of a "malevolent motive does not convert a facially discriminatory policy into a neutral policy with a discriminatory effect." Similarly, in *Norris* and *Manhart*, the Court found disparate treatment in the absence of any malice or animus toward a disfavored group.

Related Issues

4.   *No BFOQ Defense for Race.* Why did Congress provide that sex but not race may be shown to be a bona fide occupational qualification (BFOQ)? Are there any jobs for which race or skin color ought to be a qualification?

5.   *The* Weeks *"All or Substantially All" Test.* Note that the Court in *Johnson Controls*, after defining the "essence" of the business to exclude the protection of workers' unborn children, also relies on *Dothard*, discussed p. 204 supra, to stress that "Johnson Controls has shown no 'factual basis for believing that all or substantially all women would be unable to perform safely

and efficiently the duties of the job involved.'" The Court drew this "all or substantially all" test from Weeks v. Southern Bell Tel. & Tel. Co., 408 F.2d 228 (5th Cir.1969).

In Western Air Lines v. Criswell, 427 U.S. 400, 105 S.Ct. 2743, 86 L.Ed.2d 321 (1985) excerpted p. 454, infra. a post-*Dothard* ruling interpreting a similar BFOQ defense under the ADEA, the Court quoted favorably from Usery v. Tamiami Trail Tours, Inc., 531 F.2d 224, 235 (5th Cir.1976), which suggested that an employer could satisfy the *Weeks* test in one of two ways. First, the employer could show that it " 'had reasonable cause to believe, that is, a factual basis for believing, that all or substantially all [persons over the age qualification] would be unable to perform safely and efficiently the duties of the job involved.'" Second, in the alternative, the employer could establish that age was a legitimate proxy for safety-related qualifications by proving that it is " 'impossible or highly impractical'" to make individualized assessments of the qualification of the older worker:

> One method by which the employer can carry this burden is to establish that some members of the discriminated against class possess a trait precluding safe and efficient job performance that cannot be ascertained by means other than knowledge of the applicant's membership in the class. 427 U.S. at 414–415.

Is the *Johnson Controls* Court's statement that the company could have been concerned with only the "small minority of women" who could have been affected by lead exposure consistent with this approach?

6. *Increased Costs as a BFOQ Defense?* The *Johnson Controls* Court concludes that "the extra costs of employing members of one sex" cannot justify refusing to hire that sex, unless perhaps the costs would "threaten the survival of the employer's business." Do costs of compliance provide a defense to intentional discrimination on account of a person's sex? If not, can costs be a factor informing the availability of a BFOQ? Consider Justice White's description in his concurrence in *Johnson Controls* of the *Dothard* and *Criswell* cases as ultimately turning on costs. Are those cases distinguishable?

7. *Tort Liability as a BFOQ Defense? After Johnson Controls,* do employers still face potential liability in state law tort actions for injuries to an unborn offspring that could have been prevented by the exclusion of the mother from a hazardous workplace? See Asad v. Continental Airlines, Inc., 328 F.Supp.2d 772 (N.D. 2004) (tort against employer for fetal defects not preempted by Title VII because it would not have been "impossible for [employer] to comply with the mandates of Title VII and state tort law"; employer could have granted pregnant employee's request for a temporary transfer "for the protection of her fetus"); Ransburg Indus. v. Brown, 659 N.E.2d 1081 (Ind. Ct. App. 1995) (wrongful death claim based on in vitro exposure to paint fumes in the workplace not preempted by Title VII).

WILSON v. SOUTHWEST AIRLINES CO.

United States District Court, Northern District of Texas, 1981.
517 F.Supp. 292.

HIGGINBOTHAM, J.

* * * [I] in early 1971, called upon a Dallas advertising agency, the Bloom Agency, to develop a winning marketing strategy. Planning to initiate service quickly, Southwest needed instant recognition and a "catchy" image to distinguish it from its competitors.

The Bloom Agency evaluated both the images of the incumbent competitor airlines as well as the characteristics of passengers to be served by a commuter airline. Bloom determined that the other carriers serving the Texas market tended to project an image of conservatism. The agency also determined that the relatively short haul commuter market which Southwest hoped to serve was comprised of predominantly male businessmen. Based on these factors, Bloom suggested that Southwest break away from the conservative image of other airlines and project to the traveling public an airline personification of feminine youth and vitality. A specific female personality description was recommended and adopted by Southwest for its corporate image:

> This lady is young and vital * * * she is charming and goes through life with great flair and exuberance * * * you notice first her exciting smile, friendly air, her wit * * * yet she is quite efficient and approaches all her tasks with care and attention * * * .

From the personality description suggested by The Bloom Agency, Southwest developed its now famous "Love" personality. Southwest projects an image of feminine spirit, fun and sex appeal. Its ads promise to provide "tender loving care" to its predominantly male, business passengers. The first advertisements run by the airline featured the slogan, "AT LAST THERE IS SOMEBODY ELSE UP THERE WHO LOVES YOU." Variations on this theme have continued through newspaper, billboard, magazine and television advertisements during the past ten years.

* * *

As an integral part of its youthful, feminine image, Southwest has employed only females in the high customer contact positions of ticket agent and flight attendant. From the start, Southwest's attractive personnel, dressed in high boots and hot-pants, generated public interest and "free ink." Their sex appeal has been used to attract male customers to the airline. Southwest's flight attendants, and to a lesser degree its ticket agents, have been featured in newspaper, magazine, billboard and television advertisements during the past ten years. * * * The airline also encourages its attendants to entertain the passengers and maintain an atmosphere of informality and "fun" during flights. According to Southwest, its female flight attendants have come to "personify" Southwest's public image.

Southwest has enjoyed enormous success in recent years. This is in no small part due to its marketing image.

* * *

Less certain, however, is Southwest's assertion that its females-only hiring policy is necessary for the continued success of its image and its business. Based on two onboard surveys, one conducted in October, 1979, before this suit was filed, and another in August, 1980, when the suit was pending, Southwest contends its attractive flight attendants are the "largest single component" of its success. In the 1979 survey, however, of the attributes considered most important by passengers, the category "courteous and attentive hostesses" ranked fifth in importance behind (1) on time departures, (2) frequently scheduled departures, (3) friendly and helpful reservations and ground personnel, and (4) convenient departure times. Apparently, one of the remaining eight alternative categories, "attractive hostesses," was not selected with sufficient frequency to warrant being included in the reported survey results.

* * *

The 1980 survey proves nothing more. Indeed, rather than Southwest's female personnel being the "sole factor" distinguishing the airline from its competitors, as Defendant contends, the 1980 survey lists Southwest's "personnel" as only one among five characteristics contributing to Southwest's public image. Accordingly, there is no persuasive proof that Southwest's passengers prefer female over male flight attendants and ticket agents, or, of greater importance, that they would be less likely to fly Southwest if males were hired.

In evaluating Southwest's BFOQ defense, therefore, the Court proceeds on the basis that "love," while important, is not everything in the relationship between Defendant and its passengers. Still, it is proper to infer from the airline's competitive successes that Southwest's overall "love image" has enhanced its ability to attract passengers. To the extent the airline has successfully feminized its image and made attractive females an integral part of its public face, it also follows that femininity and sex appeal are qualities related to successful job performance by Southwest's flight attendants and ticket agents. The strength of this relationship has not been proved. It is with this factual orientation that the Court turns to examine Southwest's BFOQ defense.

* * *

Congress provided sparse evidence of its intent when enacting the BFOQ exception to Title VII.[12] The only relevant remarks from the floor of the House were those of Representative Goodell of New York who proposed adding "sex" as a BFOQ category after sex was designated a prohibited classification under Title VII. [He] stated:

> There are so many instances where the matter of sex is a bona fide occupational qualification. For instance, I think of an elderly woman who wants a female nurse. There are many things of this nature which are bona fide occupational qualifications, and it seems to me they would be properly considered here as an exception.

110 Cong.Rec. 2718 (1964).

Most often relied upon as a source of legislative intent is the Interpretative Memorandum of Title VII submitted by the Senate Floor Managers of the Civil Rights Bill. 110 Cong.Rec. 7212 (1964). The Memorandum referred to the BFOQ as a "limited exception" to the Act's prohibition against discrimination, conferring upon employers a "limited right to discriminate on the basis of religion, sex, or national origin where the reason for the discrimination is a bona fide occupational qualification." *Id.* at 7213. As examples of "legitimate discrimination," the memorandum cited "the preference of a French restaurant for a French cook, the preference of a professional baseball team for male players, and the preference of a business which seeks the patronage of members of particular religious groups for a salesman of that religion * * * ." *Id.* In *Dothard v. Rawlinson,* 433 U.S [321, 334, 97 S.Ct. 2720, 2729 53 L.Ed.2d 786], the Court cited the Memorandum in support of its conclusion that Congress intended the BFOQ as an "extremely narrow exception" to Title VII's prohibition against sex discrimination, ignoring Representative Goodell's broader construction.

* * *

[As the Fifth Circuit stated:]

[T]he use of the word "necessary" in Section 703(e) requires that we apply a business *necessity* test, not a business *convenience* test. That is to say, discrimination based on sex is valid only when the *essence* of the business operation would be undermined by not hiring members of one sex exclusively.

---

[12] Because sex was added as a prohibited classification in a last minute attempt by opponents to block passage of the Civil Rights Bill, House consideration of the BFOQ exception for sex was limited to the final day for House debate on the Bill. *See* 110 Cong.Rec. 2577 (remarks of Rep. Smith), 2581–82 (remarks of Rep. Green) (1964). *See also Barnes v. Costle,* 561 F.2d 983, 987 (D.C.Cir.1977); Sirota, "Sex Discrimination Title VII and the Bona Fide Occupational Qualification," 55 Tex.L.Rev. 1025, 1027 (1977).

[*Diaz v. Pan American World Airways*, 442 F.2d 385, 388 (5th Cir.1971), cert. denied, 404 U.S. 950, 92 S.Ct. 275, 30 L.Ed.2d 267 (1971) (original emphasis)].

Southwest concedes with respect to the test [of *Weeks v. Southern Bell Tel. & Tel. Co.*, 408 F.2d 228 (5th Cir.1969),] that males are able to perform safely and efficiently all the basic, mechanical functions required of flight attendants and ticket agents. * * *

A similar, though not identical, argument [to Southwest's] that females could better perform certain non-mechanical functions required of flight attendants was rejected in *Diaz*. There, the airline argued and the trial court found that being female was a BFOQ because women were superior in "providing reassurance to anxious passengers, giving courteous personalized service and, in general, making flights as pleasurable as possible within the limitations imposed by aircraft operations." Although it accepted the trial court findings, the Court of Appeals reversed, holding that femininity was not a BFOQ, because catering to passengers psychological needs was only "tangential" to what was "reasonably *necessary*" for the business involved (original emphasis). [442 F.2d] at 388.

* * *

Diaz and its progeny establish that to recognize a BFOQ for jobs requiring multiple abilities, some sex-linked and some sex-neutral, the sex-linked aspects of the job must predominate. Only then will an employer have satisfied *Weeks'* requirement that sex be so essential to successful job performance that a member of the opposite sex could not perform the job. An illustration of such dominance in sex cases is the exception recognized by the EEOC for authenticity and genuineness. * * * In the example given in [the EEOC Guidelines] § 1604.2(a)(2), that of an actor or actress, the primary function of the position, its essence, is to fulfill the audience's expectation and desire for a particular role, characterized by particular physical or emotional traits. Generally, a male could not supply the authenticity required to perform a female role. Similarly, in jobs where sex or vicarious sexual recreation is the primary service provided, *e.g.* a social escort or topless dancer, the job automatically calls for one sex exclusively; the employee's sex and the service provided are inseparable. Thus, being female has been deemed a BFOQ for the position of a Playboy Bunny, female sexuality being reasonably necessary to perform the dominant purpose of the job which is forthrightly to titillate and entice male customers. *See St. Cross v. Playboy Club,* Appeal No. 773, Case No. CFS 22618–70 (New York Human Rights Appeal Board, 1971) (dicta); *Weber v. Playboy Club,* Appeal No. 774, Case No. CFS 22619–70 (New York Human Rights Appeal Board, 1971) (dicta). One court has also suggested, without holding, that the authenticity exception would give rise to a BFOQ for Chinese nationality where necessary to maintain the authentic atmosphere of an ethnic Chinese restaurant, *Utility Workers v. Southern*

California Edison, 320 F.Supp. 1262, 1265 (C.D.Cal.1970). Consistent with the language of *Diaz,* customer preference for one sex only in such a case would logically be so strong that the employer's ability to perform the primary function or service offered would be undermined by not hiring members of the authentic sex or group exclusively.

The Court is aware of only one decision where sex was held to be a BFOQ for an occupation not providing primarily sex oriented services. In *Fernandez v. Wynn Oil Co.,* 20 FEP Cases 1162 (C.D.Cal.1979), the court approved restricting to males the job of international marketing director for a company with extensive overseas operations. The position involved primarily attracting and transacting business with Latin American and Southeast Asian customers who would not feel comfortable doing business with a woman. The court found that the customers' attitudes, customs, and mores relating to the proper business roles of the sexes created formidable obstacles to successful job performance by a woman. South American distributors and customers, for example, would have been offended by a woman conducting business meetings in her hotel room. Applying the *Diaz* test, the court concluded that hiring a female as international marketing director "would have totally subverted any business [defendant] hoped to accomplish in those areas of the world." *Id.* at 1165. Because hiring a male was *necessary* to the Defendant's ability to continue its foreign operations, sex was deemed a BFOQ for the marketing position.

* * *

While possession of female allure and sex appeal have been made qualifications for Southwest's contact personnel by virtue of the "love" campaign, the functions served by employee sexuality in Southwest's operations are not dominant ones. According to Southwest, female sex appeal serves two purposes: (1) attracting and entertaining male passengers and (2) fulfilling customer expectations for female service engendered by Southwest's advertising which features female personnel. As in *Diaz,* these non-mechanical, sex-linked job functions are only "tangential" to the essence of the occupations and business involved. Southwest is not a business where vicarious sex entertainment is the primary service provided. Accordingly, the ability of the airline to perform its primary business function, the transportation of passengers, would not be jeopardized by hiring males.

* * *

It is also relevant that Southwest's female image was adopted at its discretion, to promote a business unrelated to sex.

* * *

* * * Similarly, a potential loss of profits or possible loss of competitive advantage following a shift to non-discriminatory hiring does not establish business necessity under *Diaz*. To hold otherwise would permit employers within the same industry to establish different hiring standards based on the financial condition of their respective businesses. A rule prohibiting only financially successful enterprises from discriminating under Title VII, while allowing their less successful competitors to ignore the law, has no merit.

NOTES AND QUESTIONS

Test Your Understanding of the Material

1.   Under what conditions, if any, can an employer successfully assert a BFOQ based on the sexual appeal of persons of one sex rather the other? Would *Wilson* have been decided differently if the airline's marketing research had demonstrated that female flight attendants continued to be very important to the company's success? Consider also litigation challenging the female-only table attendant policy of the Hooters restaurant chain. Latuga v. Hooters, Inc., Case No. 93 C7709, 1996 WL 164427 (N.D. Ill. March 29, 1996).

Related Issues

2.   *Customer Privacy BFOQ.* The courts have accepted in limited settings customer preferences based on privacy concerns as justifications for sex-based hiring or job assignments. See, e.g., Everson v. Michigan Dept. of Corrections, 391 F.3d 737 (6th Cir. 2004) (the privacy and security of female inmates justifies hiring only female guards for prison housing units); Jennings v. New York State Office of Mental Health, 786 F.Supp. 376, 380 (S.D.N.Y.1992) (sex-based staffing assignments to protect privacy of patients in a mental hospital); Brooks v. ACF Industries, Inc., 537 F.Supp. 1122 (S.D.W.Va.1982) (sex-based hiring of attendants in bath and changing rooms); but cf. Henry v. Milwaukee County, 539 F.3d 573 (7th Cir. 2008) (county failed to establish the reasonable necessity of its policy requiring each unit of juvenile detention center to be staffed at all times by at least one officer of the same sex). See 29 C.F.R. § 1604.2(a)(1)(iii).

3.   *National Origin BFOQ.* The BFOQ defense is also available for national origin-based discrimination. Should a Chinese restaurant be able to employ as table attendants only those of Chinese descent to preserve an "authentic atmosphere"? If so, should an employer be able to replace female waitresses with male waiters in order to "upgrade" its reputation? Are these two cases distinguishable? What if the second restaurant claims that it wants to effect the authentic atmosphere of an expensive Parisian eatery where all the table attendants are male? See Levendos v. Stern Entertainment, Inc., 723 F.Supp. 1104, 1107 (W.D.Pa.1989), reversed on other grounds, 909 F.2d 747 (3d Cir.1990) (sex is not a BFOQ for server at high-class restaurant). See also EEOC v. Joe's Stone Crab, Inc., 136 F.Supp.2d 1311 (S.D. Fla.2001), affirmed in relevant part, 296 F.3d 1265 (11th Cir. 2002) (Title VII violated by restaurant's preference for male table attendants to effect a European style).

4.   *Documented Customer Preferences as Grounds for a BFOQ Defense?* Even if a marketing survey would have been insufficient in the *Southwest* case,

might market research provide justification in other cases? Consider, for instance, a ratings-conscious television station's decision to replace an older female coanchor with a younger woman while retaining its equally old male coanchor. Ostensibly, this seems to be both sex-plus and age-plus discrimination because the station seems to have treated the incumbent male coanchor differently on the basis of sex and the new female coanchor differently on the basis of age. Could the station nonetheless justify its decision by market research that demonstrated the unpopularity of the discharged older female? Cf. Craft v. Metromedia, 766 F.2d 1205 (8th Cir.1985) (partial reliance on market survey to find no discrimination).

5. *Psychological Needs or Problems of Customers as Grounds for a BFOQ Defense.* If customer preferences based on sex-based stereotypes or even sexual drives normally cannot provide a basis for a BFOQ defense, can sexually-charged psychological problems? For instance, should a psychiatric hospital housing emotionally disturbed patients, some of whom had been sexually abused, be able to make shift assignments on the basis of gender in order to provide both male and female "role models" and confidants for patients of both sexes? See Healey v. Southwood Psychiatric Hospital, 78 F.3d 128 (3d Cir.1996) (accepting BFOQ defense). Should a maximum security women's prison be able to hire only female correctional officers because of expert opinion that the power relationship between male guards and female prisoners could hamper the rehabilitation of prisoners who have suffered unhealthy domination by males? See Torres v. Wisconsin Dept. of Health & Social Services, 859 F.2d 1523 (7th Cir.1988) (en banc; accepting BFOQ defense), with Ambat v. City & County of San Francisco, 757 F.3d 1017 (9th Cir. 2014) (denying sheriff department summary judgment based on BFOQ defense for not allowing male guards to supervise female jail inmates).

D. HARASSMENT

HARRIS V. FORKLIFT SYSTEMS, INC.

Supreme Court of the United States, 1993.
510 U.S. 17, 114 S.Ct. 367, 126 L.Ed.2d 295.

JUSTICE O'CONNOR delivered the opinion of the Court.

In this case we consider the definition of a discriminatorily "abusive work environment" (also known as a "hostile work environment") under Title VII of the Civil Rights Act of 1964.

I

Teresa Harris worked as a manager at Forklift Systems, Inc., an equipment rental company, from April 1985 until October 1987. Charles Hardy was Forklift's president.

The Magistrate found that, throughout Harris' time at Forklift, Hardy often insulted her because of her gender and often made her the target of unwanted sexual innuendos. Hardy told Harris on several occasions, in the presence of other employees, "You're a woman, what do you know" and "We need a man as the rental manager"; at least once, he told her she was "a dumb ass woman." Again in front of others, he suggested that the two of them "go to the Holiday Inn to negotiate [Harris'] raise." Hardy occasionally asked Harris and other female employees to get coins from his front pants pocket. He threw objects on the ground in front of Harris and other women, and asked them to pick the objects up. He made sexual innuendos about Harris' and other women's clothing.

In mid-August 1987, Harris complained to Hardy about his conduct. Hardy said he was surprised that Harris was offended, claimed he was only joking, and apologized. He also promised he would stop, and based on this assurance Harris stayed on the job. Ibid. But in early September, Hardy began anew: While Harris was arranging a deal with one of Forklift's customers, he asked her, again in front of other employees, "What did you do, promise the guy * * * some [sex] Saturday night?" On October 1, Harris collected her paycheck and quit.

Harris then sued Forklift, claiming that Hardy's conduct had created an abusive work environment for her because of her gender. The United States District Court for the Middle District of Tennessee, adopting the report and recommendation of the Magistrate, found this to be "a close case," but held that Hardy's conduct did not create an abusive environment. The court found that some of Hardy's comments "offended [Harris], and would offend the reasonable woman," but that they were not "so severe as to be expected to seriously affect [Harris'] psychological well-being." A reasonable woman manager under like circumstances would have been offended by Hardy, but his conduct would not have risen to the level of interfering with that person's work performance. "Neither do I believe that [Harris] was subjectively so offended that she suffered injury * * *. Although Hardy may at times have genuinely offended [Harris], I do not believe that he created a working environment so poisoned as to be intimidating or abusive to [Harris]."

In focusing on the employee's psychological well-being, the District Court was following Circuit precedent. See *Rabidue v. Osceola Refining Co.*, 805 F.2d 611, 620 (C.A.6 1986), cert. denied, 481 U.S. 1041, 107 S.Ct. 1983, 95 L.Ed.2d 823 (1987). The United States Court of Appeals for the Sixth Circuit affirmed.

* * *

II

Title VII of the Civil Rights Act of 1964 makes it "an unlawful employment practice for an employer * * * to discriminate against any individual with respect to his compensation, terms, conditions, or privileges of employment, because of such individual's race, color, religion, sex, or national origin." 42 U.S.C. § 2000e–2(a)(1). As we made clear in

Meritor Savings Bank v. Vinson, 477 U.S. 57 (1986), this language "is not limited to 'economic' or 'tangible' discrimination. The phrase 'terms, conditions, or privileges of employment' evinces a congressional intent 'to strike at the entire spectrum of disparate treatment of men and women' in employment," which includes requiring people to work in a discriminatorily hostile or abusive environment. *Id.,* at 64. When the workplace is permeated with "discriminatory intimidation, ridicule, and insult," 477 U.S., at 65, that is "sufficiently severe or pervasive to alter the conditions of the victim's employment and create an abusive working environment," *id.,* at 67, Title VII is violated.

This standard, which we reaffirm today, takes a middle path between making actionable any conduct that is merely offensive and requiring the conduct to cause a tangible psychological injury. As we pointed out in *Meritor,* "mere utterance of an * * * epithet which engenders offensive feelings in an employee" * * * does not sufficiently affect the conditions of employment to implicate Title VII. Conduct that is not severe or pervasive enough to create an objectively hostile or abusive work environment—an environment that a reasonable person would find hostile or abusive—is beyond Title VII's purview. Likewise, if the victim does not subjectively perceive the environment to be abusive, the conduct has not actually altered the conditions of the victim's employment, and there is no Title VII violation.

But Title VII comes into play before the harassing conduct leads to a nervous breakdown. A discriminatorily abusive work environment, even one that does not seriously affect employees' psychological well-being, can and often will detract from employees' job performance, discourage employees from remaining on the job, or keep them from advancing in their careers. Moreover, even without regard to these tangible effects, the very fact that the discriminatory conduct was so severe or pervasive that it created a work environment abusive to employees because of their race, gender, religion, or national origin offends Title VII's broad rule of workplace equality. The appalling conduct alleged in *Meritor,* and the reference in that case to environments " 'so heavily polluted with discrimination as to destroy completely the emotional and psychological stability of minority group workers,' " *supra,* at 66, merely present some especially egregious examples of harassment. They do not mark the boundary of what is actionable.

We therefore believe the District Court erred in relying on whether the conduct "seriously affect[ed] plaintiff's psychological well-being" or led her to "suffe[r] injury." Such an inquiry may needlessly focus the factfinder's attention on concrete psychological harm, an element Title VII does not require. Certainly Title VII bars conduct that would seriously affect a reasonable person's psychological well-being, but the statute is not limited to such conduct. So long as the environment would reasonably be perceived, and is perceived, as hostile or abusive, *Meritor*, supra, 477 U.S., at 67, there is no need for it also to be psychologically injurious.

This is not, and by its nature cannot be, a mathematically precise test. We need not answer today all the potential questions it raises, nor specifically address the EEOC's new regulations on this subject, see 58 Fed.Reg. 51266 (1993) (proposed 29 CFR §§ 1609.1, 1609.2); see also 29 CFR § 1604.11 (1993). But we can say that whether an environment is "hostile" or "abusive" can be determined only by looking at all the circumstances. These may include the frequency of the discriminatory conduct; its severity; whether it is physically threatening or humiliating, or a mere offensive utterance; and whether it unreasonably interferes with an employee's work performance. The effect on the employee's psychological well-being is, of course, relevant to determining whether the plaintiff actually found the environment abusive. But while psychological harm, like any other relevant factor, may be taken into account, no single factor is required.

III

Forklift, while conceding that a requirement that the conduct seriously affect psychological well-being is unfounded, argues that the District Court nonetheless correctly applied the *Meritor* standard. We disagree. Though the District Court did conclude that the work environment was not "intimidating or abusive to [Harris]," it did so only after finding that the conduct was not "so severe as to be expected to seriously affect plaintiff's psychological well-being," and that Harris was not "subjectively so offended that she suffered injury." The District Court's application of these incorrect standards may well have influenced its ultimate conclusion, especially given that the court found this to be a "close case."

We therefore reverse the judgment of the Court of Appeals, and remand the case for further proceedings consistent with this opinion.

JUSTICE GINSBURG, concurring.

The critical issue, Title VII's text indicates, is whether members of one sex are exposed to disadvantageous terms or conditions of employment to which members of the other sex are not exposed. * * * [T]he adjudicator's inquiry should center, dominantly, on whether the discriminatory conduct has unreasonably interfered with the plaintiff's work performance. To show such interference, "the plaintiff need not prove that his or her tangible productivity has declined as a result of the harassment." *Davis v. Monsanto Chemical Co.*, 858 F.2d 345, 349 (C.A.6 1988). It suffices to prove that a reasonable person subjected to the discriminatory conduct would find, as the plaintiff did, that the harassment so altered working conditions as to "make it more difficult to do the job." See *ibid.*

ONCALE V. SUNDOWNER OFFSHORE SERVICES, INC.

Supreme Court of the United States, 1998.
523 U.S. 75, 118 S.Ct. 998, 140 L.Ed.2d 201.

JUSTICE SCALIA delivered the opinion of the Court.

This case presents the question whether workplace harassment can violate Title VII's prohibition against "discriminat[ion] * * * because of * * * sex," 42 U.S.C. § 2000e–2(a)(1), when the harasser and the harassed employee are of the same sex.

I

The District Court having granted summary judgment for respondent, we must assume the facts to be as alleged by petitioner Joseph Oncale. The precise details are irrelevant to the legal point we must decide, and in the interest of both brevity and dignity we shall describe them only generally. In late October 1991, Oncale was working for respondent Sundowner Offshore Services on a Chevron U.S.A., Inc., oil platform in the Gulf of Mexico. He was employed as a roustabout on an eight-man crew which included respondents John Lyons, Danny Pippen, and Brandon Johnson. Lyons, the crane operator, and Pippen, the driller, had supervisory authority. On several occasions, Oncale was forcibly subjected to sex-related, humiliating actions against him by Lyons, Pippen and Johnson in the presence of the rest of the crew. Pippen and Lyons also physically assaulted Oncale in a sexual manner, and Lyons threatened him with rape.

Oncale's complaints to supervisory personnel produced no remedial action; in fact, the company's Safety Compliance Clerk, Valent Hohen, told Oncale that Lyons and Pippen "picked [on] him all the time too," and called him a name suggesting homosexuality. Oncale eventually quit—asking that his pink slip reflect that he "voluntarily left due to sexual harassment and verbal abuse." When asked at his deposition why he left Sundowner, Oncale stated "I felt that if I didn't leave my job, that I would be raped or forced to have sex."

Oncale filed a complaint against Sundowner in the United States District Court for the Eastern District of Louisiana, alleging that he was discriminated against in his employment because of his sex. Relying on the Fifth Circuit's decision in *Garcia v. Elf Atochem North America*, 28 F.3d 446, 451–452 (C.A.5 1994), the district court held that "Mr. Oncale, a male, has no cause of action under Title VII for harassment by male co-workers." On appeal, a panel of the Fifth Circuit concluded that Garcia was binding Circuit precedent, and affirmed. We granted certiorari.

II

* * *

Title VII's prohibition of discrimination "because of * * * sex" protects men as well as women, *Newport News Shipbuilding & Dry Dock Co. v.*

EEOC, 462 U.S. 669, 682, 103 S.Ct. 2622, 2630, 77 L.Ed.2d 89 (1983), and in the related context of racial discrimination in the workplace we have rejected any conclusive presumption that an employer will not discriminate against members of his own race. "Because of the many facets of human motivation, it would be unwise to presume as a matter of law that human beings of one definable group will not discriminate against other members of that group." *Castaneda v. Partida*, 430 U.S. 482, 499, 97 S.Ct. 1272, 1282, 51 L.Ed.2d 498 (1977). * * * In *Johnson v. Transportation Agency, Santa Clara Cty.*, 480 U.S. 616, 107 S.Ct. 1442, 94 L.Ed.2d 615 (1987), a male employee claimed that his employer discriminated against him because of his sex when it preferred a female employee for promotion. Although we ultimately rejected the claim on other grounds, we did not consider it significant that the supervisor who made that decision was also a man. See *id.*, at 624–625, 107 S.Ct., at 1447–1448. If our precedents leave any doubt on the question, we hold today that nothing in Title VII necessarily bars a claim of discrimination "because of * * * sex" merely because the plaintiff and the defendant (or the person charged with acting on behalf of the defendant) are of the same sex.

* * *

We see no justification in the statutory language or our precedents for a categorical rule excluding same-sex harassment claims from the coverage of Title VII. As some courts have observed, male-on-male sexual harassment in the workplace was assuredly not the principal evil Congress was concerned with when it enacted Title VII. But statutory prohibitions often go beyond the principal evil to cover reasonably comparable evils, and it is ultimately the provisions of our laws rather than the principal concerns of our legislators by which we are governed. Title VII prohibits "discriminat[ion] * * * because of * * * sex" in the "terms" or "conditions" of employment. Our holding that this includes sexual harassment must extend to sexual harassment of any kind that meets the statutory requirements.

Respondents and their amici contend that recognizing liability for same-sex harassment will transform Title VII into a general civility code for the American workplace. But that risk is no greater for same-sex than for opposite-sex harassment, and is adequately met by careful attention to the requirements of the statute. Title VII does not prohibit all verbal or physical harassment in the workplace; it is directed only at "discriminat[ion] * * * because of * * * sex." We have never held that workplace harassment, even harassment between men and women, is automatically discrimination because of sex merely because the words used have sexual content or connotations. "The critical issue, Title VII's text indicates, is whether members of one sex are exposed to disadvantageous terms or conditions of employment to which members of the other sex are not exposed." *Harris*, supra, at 25, 114 S.Ct., at 372 (Ginsburg, J., concurring).

Courts and juries have found the inference of discrimination easy to draw in most male-female sexual harassment situations, because the challenged conduct typically involves explicit or implicit proposals of sexual activity; it is reasonable to assume those proposals would not have been made to someone of the same sex. The same chain of inference would be available to a plaintiff alleging same-sex harassment, if there were credible evidence that the harasser was homosexual. But harassing conduct need not be motivated by sexual desire to support an inference of discrimination on the basis of sex. A trier of fact might reasonably find such discrimination, for example, if a female victim is harassed in such sex-specific and derogatory terms by another woman as to make it clear that the harasser is motivated by general hostility to the presence of women in the workplace. A same-sex harassment plaintiff may also, of course, offer direct comparative evidence about how the alleged harasser treated members of both sexes in a mixed-sex workplace. Whatever evidentiary route the plaintiff chooses to follow, he or she must always prove that the conduct at issue was not merely tinged with offensive sexual connotations, but actually constituted "discrimina[tion] * * * because of * * * sex."

And there is another requirement that prevents Title VII from expanding into a general civility code: As we emphasized in *Meritor* and *Harris*, the statute does not reach genuine but innocuous differences in the ways men and women routinely interact with members of the same sex and of the opposite sex. The prohibition of harassment on the basis of sex requires neither asexuality nor androgyny in the workplace; it forbids only behavior so objectively offensive as to alter the "conditions" of the victim's employment. "Conduct that is not severe or pervasive enough to create an objectively hostile or abusive work environment—an environment that a reasonable person would find hostile or abusive—is beyond Title VII's purview." *Harris*, 510 U.S., at 21, 114 S.Ct., at 370, citing *Meritor*, 477 U.S., at 67, 106 S.Ct., at 2405–2406. We have always regarded that requirement as crucial, and as sufficient to ensure that courts and juries do not mistake ordinary socializing in the workplace—such as male-on-male horseplay or intersexual flirtation—for discriminatory "conditions of employment."

We have emphasized, moreover, that the objective severity of harassment should be judged from the perspective of a reasonable person in the plaintiff's position, considering "all the circumstances." *Harris*, supra, at 23, 114 S.Ct., at 371. In same-sex (as in all) harassment cases, that inquiry requires careful consideration of the social context in which particular behavior occurs and is experienced by its target. A professional football player's working environment is not severely or pervasively abusive, for example, if the coach smacks him on the buttocks as he heads onto the field—even if the same behavior would reasonably be experienced as abusive by the coach's secretary (male or female) back at the office. The real social impact of workplace behavior often depends on a constellation of surrounding circumstances, expectations, and relationships which are not fully captured by a simple recitation of the words used or the physical acts performed. Common sense, and an appropriate sensitivity to social context, will enable courts and juries to distinguish between simple teasing or roughhousing among members of the same sex, and conduct which a reasonable person in the plaintiff's position would find severely hostile or abusive.

NOTES AND QUESTIONS

Test Your Understanding of the Material

1. *Harris* and *Oncale* are both sex discrimination cases. Review the statutory language of Title VII. What language in Section 703 provides support for treating harassment as a form of discrimination?

2. What elements must a plaintiff prove under *Harris* and *Oncale* to establish a sex-based harassment claim?

3. Prior to the *Harris* decision, the EEOC's proposed guidelines on harassment advised that the "reasonable person" standard include "consideration of the perspective of persons of the alleged victim's race, color, religion, gender, national origin, age, or disability." 58 Fed. Reg. 51266 (Oct. 1, 1993). (These guidelines have since been withdrawn.) Does *Harris* provide support for the EEOC's previous position? Does *Oncale*?

Related Issues

4. *Racial, Religious, and National Origin Harassment.* The Court's decisions on sexual harassment are instructive for the other types of discrimination covered by Title VII. See, e.g., Kang v. U. Lim America, Inc., 296 F.3d 810 (9th Cir.2002) (Korean employer's abusive treatment of Korean employee actionable national origin discrimination because employer demanded more of Korean workers); Whidbee v. Garzarelli Food Specialties, Inc., 223 F.3d 62 (2d Cir.2000) (§ 1981 racial harassment claim). See also Pat K. Chew & Robert E. Kelley, Unwrapping Racial Harassment Law, 27 Berk. J. of Emp. & Lab. L. 49 (2006).

5. *"Severe or Pervasive".* Does this phrase mean that some conduct that would be actionable if engaged in repeatedly is not actionable if only represented in isolated incidents? See, e.g., Clark County Sch. Dist. v. Breeden, 532 U.S. 268, 121 S.Ct. 1508, 149 L.Ed.2d 509 (2001) (plaintiff could not reasonably believe that isolated joke at a group meeting could be actionable harassment); Douglass v. Rochester City Sch. Dist., 522 F. Appx. 5, 8 (2d Cir. 2013) (single demeaning reference to parts of plaintiff's anatomy not actionable); Chamberlin v. 101 Realty, Inc., 915 F.2d 777 (1st Cir.1990) (individual sexual proposition not actionable). On the other hand, does the use of the disjunctive word "or" in this phrase indicate that some conduct can be sufficiently hostile even if only one or two incidents occur? See, e.g., Boyer-

Liberto v. Fontainebleau Corp., 786 F.3d 264, 280 (4th Cir. 2015) ("a reasonable jury could find that [ ] two uses of the 'porch monkey' epithet . . . were severe enough to engender a hostile work environment"); Little v. Windermere Relocation, Inc., 301 F.3d 958 (9th Cir.2002) (single incident of rape sufficient); Howley v. Town of Stratford, 217 F.3d 141 (2d Cir.2000) (single verbal sexual harassment could be sufficiently severe); Vance v. Southern Bell Tel. & Tel. Co., 863 F.2d 1503 (11th Cir.1989) (noose hung twice over plaintiff's work station may have created racially hostile work environment). But cf. Ann Juliano & Stewart J. Schwab, The Sweep of Sexual Harassment Cases, 86 Corn. L.Rev. 548 (2001) (empirical study finding only small percentage of reported decisions involving a single incident).

6. *"Unwelcome"*. In Meritor Savings Bank v. Vinson, 477 U.S. 57 (1986), a bank employee alleged that she was pressured to engage in sexual relations with her supervisor, a branch office manager. The Court held that the plaintiff's "voluntary" participation in sexual activity would not insulate that activity from being actionable if the plaintiff nonetheless could demonstrate that the activity was "unwelcome." The *Meritor* Court stated that "a complainant's sexually provocative speech or dress" is relevant "in determining whether he or she found particular sexual advances unwelcome." Do you agree? Should a woman who dresses in a certain fashion and talks openly about her sexual desires have to say "No" more often and more forcefully to establish that particular sexual advances are unwelcome? See generally Henry L. Chambers, Jr., (Un)Welcome Conduct and the Sexually Hostile Environment, 53 Ala. L.Rev. 733 (2002).

7. *"Equal Opportunity Harassment"?* The *Oncale* Court stresses that to be actionable under Title VII workplace harassment also must be "discrimination because of sex", or because of some other protected status category. Does this mean that if Oncale's sister had worked with him on the oil platform and also had been subjected to sexual taunts, threats, and assaults, neither would have a cause of action under Title VII? See Holman v. Indiana, 211 F.3d 399 (7th Cir. 2000) (sexual harassment of both husband and wife not actionable because not discriminatory); Smith v. Hy-Vee, 622 F.3d 904 (8th Cir. 2010) (female employee's "rude, vulgar, sexually-charged behavior" not actionable because directed at both men and women).

8. *Sexual Conduct vs. Sex-Based Harassment.* Evidence of sexual conduct may be sufficient, but is not necessary to establish a harassment claim post-*Oncale*. Nevertheless, some courts continue to attach particular significance to sexual propositions and conduct motivated by sexual attraction. See Pedroza v. Cintas Corp. No. 2, 397 F.3d 1063 (8th Cir. 2005) (sexual propositioning of female employee by female coworker not actionable discrimination in absence of proof of harasser's homosexuality); EEOC v. Harbert-Yeargin, Inc., 266 F.3d 498 (6th Cir.2001) (refusing to find workplace "goosing" of only male employees actionable where not done to initiate sex or to discourage employment of class or subclass of males); Rene v. MGM Grand Hotel, Inc., 305 F.3d 1061 (9th Cir.2002) (plurality of *en banc* panel holds that under *Oncale* it is enough to show "physical conduct of a sexual nature" and

discrimination in comparison to others of the plaintiff's own sex); David S. Schwartz, When Is Sex Because of Sex? The Causation Problem in Sexual Harassment Law, 150 Penn. L.Rev. 1697 (2002) (arguing for a per se causation rule when sexual contact is involved); Vicki Schultz, Reconceptualizing Sexual Harassment, 107 Yale L.J. 1683 (1998).

9. *Relevance of "Sexualized" Common Workplace Environment.* The open display of sexually-oriented pictures or paraphernalia, or permitting male and female workers to engage openly in sexual horseplay or affairs, can form the basis for a harassment claim, even absent evidence that female or male employees were disproportionately targeted. In Reeves v. C.H. Robinson Worldwide, Inc., 594 F.3d 798 (11th Cir. 2010) (en banc) a unanimous appeals court held that sexist office talk and radio programming that was particularly offensive to women need not be targeted at particular women to be actionable disparate treatment. See also, e.g., Petrosino v. Bell Atlantic, 385 F.3d 210 (2d Cir. 2004) (sexually offensive material may be actionable because "disproportionately demeaning" of women); Robinson v. Jacksonville Shipyards, Inc., 760 F.Supp. 1486 (M.D.Fla.1991) (finding disparate impact based on expert testimony that "sexualize[d] work environment" disadvantaged female employees). But cf. Lyle v. Warner Bros. Television Productions, 38 Cal.4th 264, 42 Cal.Rptr.3d 2, 132 P.3d 211 (Cal. S.Ct. 2006) (sexually vulgar language not harassment because part of comedy writers' common workplace).

10. *"Quid Pro Quo" Harassment.* In addition to hostile work environment harassment, the courts have recognized as a form of sex discrimination an employer's denial of some economic benefit of employment because of an employee's refusal to submit to the advances of a fellow employee, usually one of her supervisors. This form of actionable sexual discrimination, which was first described as "quid pro quo" harassment, usually is also an example of "sex plus" discrimination, as some targeted women are asked to do more than similarly situated men to achieve some employment benefit.

11. *Favoritism Toward Lovers.* The courts generally hold that a supervisor's favoritism toward a subordinate with whom he has or had a consensual romantic relationship does not violate Title VII. See, e.g., Clark v. Cache Valley Elec. Co., 573 F.Appx. 693 (10th Cir. 2014); Womack v. Runyon, 147 F.3d 1298 (11th Cir.1998); DeCintio v. Westchester County Medical Ctr., 807 F.2d 304 (2d Cir.1986). In upholding summary judgment against a male employee claiming he was disadvantaged by an alleged romantic relationship between a supervisor and subordinate, the Tenth Circuit reasoned, "[the plaintiff] presented no evidence that [the employer] treated women more favorably than men . . . [he] merely provided evidence that [the supervisor] extended preferential treatment to *one* female employee . . . favoritism of a paramour is not gender discrimination". Clark, 573 F.Appx. at 697. The courts thus treat motivation based on a particular personal relationship differently than motivation based more generally on sex. Cf. Nelson v. James H. Knight DDS, 834 N.W.2d 64 (Ia. S.Ct. 2013) (holding it was not sex-based discrimination for dentist to discharge his assistant because his wife was

concerned about the assistant's potential romantic relationship with her husband).

The EEOC takes the position that "widespread sexual favoritism" at a workplace may create an actionable "demeaning" hostile work environment. See EEOC Policy Guidance on Employer Liability Under Title VII for Sexual Favoritism (Feb. 15, 1990). There is limited decisional support for this position. See Tenge v. Phillips Modern Ag Co., 446 F.3d 903 (8th Cir. 2006) (accepting EEOC's view in dicta); Miller v. Department of Corrections, 36 Cal.4th 446, 30 Cal.Rptr.3d 797, 115 P.3d 77 (2005) (adopting as a matter of California law EEOC's view on "widespread" favoritism).

FARAGHER V. CITY OF BOCA RATON

Supreme Court of the United States, 1998.
524 U.S. 775, 118 S.Ct. 2275, 141 L.Ed.2d 662.

JUSTICE SOUTER delivered the opinion of the Court.

This case calls for identification of the circumstances under which an employer may be held liable under Title VII of the Civil Rights Act of 1964, 78 Stat. 253, as amended, 42 U.S.C. § 2000e et seq., for the acts of a supervisory employee whose sexual harassment of subordinates has created a hostile work environment amounting to employment discrimination. We hold that an employer is vicariously liable for actionable discrimination caused by a supervisor, but subject to an affirmative defense looking to the reasonableness of the employer's conduct as well as that of a plaintiff victim.

I

Between 1985 and 1990, while attending college, petitioner Beth Ann Faragher worked part time and during the summers as an ocean lifeguard for the Marine Safety Section of the Parks and Recreation Department of respondent, the City of Boca Raton, Florida (City). During this period, Faragher's immediate supervisors were Bill Terry, David Silverman, and Robert Gordon. In June 1990, Faragher resigned.

In 1992, Faragher brought an action against Terry, Silverman, and the City, asserting claims under Title VII, 42 U.S.C. § 1983, and Florida law. So far as it concerns the Title VII claim, the complaint alleged that Terry and Silverman created a "sexually hostile atmosphere" at the beach by repeatedly subjecting Faragher and other female lifeguards to "uninvited and offensive touching," by making lewd remarks, and by speaking of women in offensive terms. The complaint contained specific allegations that Terry once said that he would never promote a woman to the rank of lieutenant, and that Silverman had said to Faragher, "Date me or clean the toilets for a year." Asserting that Terry and Silverman were agents of the City, and that their conduct amounted to discrimination in the "terms, conditions, and privileges" of her employment, 42 U.S.C. § 2000e–2(a)(1),

Faragher sought a judgment against the City for nominal damages, costs, and attorney's fees.

Following a bench trial, the United States District Court for the Southern District of Florida found that throughout Faragher's employment with the City, Terry served as Chief of the Marine Safety Division, with authority to hire new lifeguards (subject to the approval of higher management), to supervise all aspects of the lifeguards' work assignments, to engage in counseling, to deliver oral reprimands, and to make a record of any such discipline. Silverman was a Marine Safety lieutenant from 1985 until June 1989, when he became a captain. Gordon began the employment period as a lieutenant and at some point was promoted to the position of training captain. In these positions, Silverman and Gordon were responsible for making the lifeguards' daily assignments, and for supervising their work and fitness training.

The lifeguards and supervisors were stationed at the city beach and worked out of the Marine Safety Headquarters, a small one-story building containing an office, a meeting room, and a single, unisex locker room with a shower. Their work routine was structured in a "paramilitary configuration," with a clear chain of command. Lifeguards reported to lieutenants and captains, who reported to Terry. He was supervised by the Recreation Superintendent, who in turn reported to a Director of Parks and Recreation, answerable to the City Manager. The lifeguards had no significant contact with higher city officials like the Recreation Superintendent.

In February 1986, the City adopted a sexual harassment policy, which it stated in a memorandum from the City Manager addressed to all employees. In May 1990, the City revised the policy and reissued a statement of it. Although the City may actually have circulated the memos and statements to some employees, it completely failed to disseminate its policy among employees of the Marine Safety Section, with the result that Terry, Silverman, Gordon, and many lifeguards were unaware of it.

From time to time over the course of Faragher's tenure at the Marine Safety Section, between 4 and 6 of the 40 to 50 lifeguards were women. During that 5-year period, Terry repeatedly touched the bodies of female employees without invitation, would put his arm around Faragher, with his hand on her buttocks, and once made contact with another female lifeguard in a motion of sexual simulation. He made crudely demeaning references to women generally, and once commented disparagingly on Faragher's shape. During a job interview with a woman he hired as a lifeguard, Terry said that the female lifeguards had sex with their male counterparts and asked whether she would do the same.

Silverman behaved in similar ways. He once tackled Faragher and remarked that, but for a physical characteristic he found unattractive, he would readily have had sexual relations with her. Another time, he pantomimed an act of oral sex. Within earshot of the female lifeguards, Silverman made frequent, vulgar references to women and sexual matters, commented on the bodies of female lifeguards and beachgoers, and at least twice told female lifeguards that he would like to engage in sex with them.

Faragher did not complain to higher management about Terry or Silverman. Although she spoke of their behavior to Gordon, she did not regard these discussions as formal complaints to a supervisor but as conversations with a person she held in high esteem. Other female lifeguards had similarly informal talks with Gordon, but because Gordon did not feel that it was his place to do so, he did not report these complaints to Terry, his own supervisor, or to any other city official. Gordon responded to the complaints of one lifeguard by saying that "the City just [doesn't] care."

In April 1990, however, two months before Faragher's resignation, Nancy Ewanchew, a former lifeguard, wrote to Richard Bender, the City's Personnel Director, complaining that Terry and Silverman had harassed her and other female lifeguards. Following investigation of this complaint, the City found that Terry and Silverman had behaved improperly, reprimanded them, and required them to choose between a suspension without pay or the forfeiture of annual leave.

On the basis of these findings, the District Court concluded that the conduct of Terry and Silverman was discriminatory harassment sufficiently serious to alter the conditions of Faragher's employment and constitute an abusive working environment. The District Court then ruled that there were three justifications for holding the City liable for the harassment of its supervisory employees. First, the court noted that the harassment was pervasive enough to support an inference that the City had "knowledge, or constructive knowledge" of it. Next, it ruled that the City was liable under traditional agency principles because Terry and Silverman were acting as its agents when they committed the harassing acts. Finally, the court observed that Gordon's knowledge of the harassment, combined with his inaction, "provides a further basis for imputing liability on [sic] the City." The District Court then awarded Faragher one dollar in nominal damages on her Title VII claim.

A panel of the Court of Appeals for the Eleventh Circuit reversed the judgment against the City. Although the panel had "no trouble concluding that Terry's and Silverman's conduct * * * was severe and pervasive enough to create an objectively abusive work environment," it overturned the District Court's conclusion that the City was liable. The panel ruled that Terry and Silverman were not acting within the scope of their employment when they engaged in the harassment, that they were not aided in their actions by the agency relationship, and that the City had no constructive knowledge of the harassment by virtue of its pervasiveness or Gordon's actual knowledge.

In a 7-to-5 decision, the full Court of Appeals, sitting en banc, adopted the panel's conclusion. * * *

II

A

* * *

While indicating the substantive contours of the hostile environments forbidden by Title VII, our cases have established few definite rules for determining when an employer will be liable for a discriminatory environment that is otherwise actionably abusive. Given the circumstances of many of the litigated cases, including some that have come to us, it is not surprising that in many of them, the issue has been joined over the sufficiency of the abusive conditions, not the standards for determining an employer's liability for them. * * *

[T]here is also nothing remarkable in the fact that claims against employers for discriminatory employment actions with tangible results, like hiring, firing, promotion, compensation, and work assignment, have resulted in employer liability once the discrimination was shown. See *Meritor* [*Savings Bank, FSB v. Vinson,* 477 U.S. 57, 70–71, 106 S.Ct. 2399, 2407–2408, 91 L.Ed.2d 49] (noting that "courts have consistently held employers liable for the discriminatory discharges of employees by supervisory personnel, whether or not the employer knew, should have known, or approved of the supervisor's actions"); *id.,* at 75, 106 S.Ct., at 2409–2410 (Marshall, J., concurring in judgment) ("[W]hen a supervisor discriminatorily fires or refuses to promote a black employee, that act is, without more, considered the act of the employer"); see also *Anderson v. Methodist Evangelical Hospital, Inc.,* 464 F.2d 723, 725 (C.A.6 1972) (imposing liability on employer for racially motivated discharge by low-level supervisor, although the "record clearly shows that [its] record in race relations * * * is exemplary").

* * *

The soundness of the results in these cases (and their continuing vitality), in light of basic agency principles, was confirmed by this Court's only discussion to date of standards of employer liability, in *Meritor, supra,* which involved a claim of discrimination by a supervisor's sexual harassment of a subordinate over an extended period. In affirming the Court of Appeals's holding that a hostile atmosphere resulting from sex discrimination is actionable under Title VII, we also anticipated proceedings on remand by holding agency principles relevant in assigning employer liability and by rejecting three per se rules of liability or immunity. 477 U.S., at 70–72, 106 S.Ct., at 2407–2408. We observed that the very definition of employer in Title VII, as including an "agent," *id.,* at 72, 106 S.Ct., at 2408, expressed Congress's intent that courts look to traditional principles of the law of agency in devising standards of employer liability in those instances where liability for the actions of a supervisory employee was not otherwise obvious, ibid., and although we cautioned that "common-law principles may not be transferable in all their particulars to Title VII," we cited the Restatement [(Second) of Torts] §§ 219–237, with general approval. *Ibid.*

We then proceeded to reject two limitations on employer liability, while establishing the rule that some limitation was intended. We held that neither the existence of a company grievance procedure nor the absence of actual notice of the harassment on the part of upper management would be dispositive of such a claim; while either might be relevant to the liability, neither would result automatically in employer immunity. *Ibid.* Conversely, we held that Title VII placed some limit on employer responsibility for the creation of a discriminatory environment by a supervisor, and we held that Title VII does not make employers "always automatically liable for sexual harassment by their supervisors," *ibid.*, contrary to the view of the Court of Appeals, which had held that "an employer is strictly liable for a hostile environment created by a supervisor's sexual advances, even though the employer neither knew nor reasonably could have known of the alleged misconduct," *id.*, at 69–70, 106 S.Ct., at 2406–2407.

Meritor's statement of the law is the foundation on which we build today. Neither party before us has urged us to depart from our customary adherence to stare decisis in statutory interpretation, * * * .

B

* * *

1

A "master is subject to liability for the torts of his servants committed while acting in the scope of their employment." Restatement § 219(1). This doctrine has traditionally defined the "scope of employment" as including conduct "of the kind [a servant] is employed to perform," occurring "substantially within the authorized time and space limits," and "actuated, at least in part, by a purpose to serve the master," but as excluding an intentional use of force "unexpectable by the master." *Id.*, § 228(1).

Courts of Appeals have typically held, or assumed, that conduct similar to the subject of this complaint falls outside the scope of employment [citations omitted]. In so doing, the courts have emphasized that harassment consisting of unwelcome remarks and touching is motivated solely by individual desires and serves no purpose of the employer. For this reason, courts have likened hostile environment sexual harassment to the classic "frolic and detour" for which an employer has no vicarious liability.

These cases ostensibly stand in some tension with others arising outside Title VII, where the scope of employment has been defined broadly enough to hold employers vicariously liable for intentional torts that were in no sense inspired by any purpose to serve the employer. In *Ira S. Bushey & Sons, Inc. v. United States*, 398 F.2d 167 (C.A.2 1968), for example, the Second Circuit charged the Government with vicarious liability for the depredation of a drunken sailor returning to his ship after a night's carouse, who inexplicably opened valves that flooded a drydock, damaging both the drydock and the ship. Judge Friendly acknowledged that the sailor's conduct was not remotely motivated by a purpose to serve his employer, but relied on the "deeply rooted sentiment that a business enterprise cannot justly disclaim responsibility for accidents which may fairly be said to be characteristic of its activities," and imposed vicarious liability on the ground that the sailor's conduct "was not so 'unforeseeable' as to make it unfair to charge the Government with responsibility." *Id.*, at 171. Other examples of an expansive sense of scope of employment are readily found, see, e.g., *Leonbruno v. Champlain Silk Mills,* 229 N.Y. 470, 128 N.E. 711 (1920) (opinion of Cardozo, J.) (employer was liable under worker's compensation statute for eye injury sustained when employee threw an apple at another; the accident arose "in the course of employment" because such horseplay should be expected); *Carr v. Wm. C. Crowell Co.*, 28 Cal.2d 652, 171 P.2d 5 (1946) (employer liable for actions of carpenter who attacked a co-employee with a hammer). Courts, in fact, have treated scope of employment generously enough to include sexual assaults. See, e.g., *Primeaux v. United States*, 102 F.3d 1458, 1462–1463 (C.A.8 1996) (federal police officer on limited duty sexually assaulted stranded motorist); *Mary M. v. Los Angeles*, 54 Cal.3d 202, 216–221, 285 Cal.Rptr. 99, 107–111, 814 P.2d 1341, 1349–1352 (1991) (en banc) (police officer raped motorist after placing her under arrest); *Doe v. Samaritan Counseling Ctr.*, 791 P.2d 344, 348–349 (Alaska 1990) (therapist had sexual relations with patient); *Turner v. State*, 494 So.2d 1292, 1296 (La.App.1986) (National Guard recruiting officer committed sexual battery during sham physical examinations); *Lyon v. Carey*, 533 F.2d 649, 655 (C.A.D.C.1976) (furniture deliveryman raped recipient of furniture); *Samuels v. Southern Baptist Hospital*, 594 So.2d 571, 574 (La.App.1992) (nursing assistant raped patient). The rationales for these decisions have varied, with some courts echoing *Bushey* in explaining that the employees' acts were foreseeable and that the employer should in fairness bear the resulting costs of doing business, see, e.g., *Mary M., supra*, at 218, 285 Cal.Rptr., at 108, 814 P.2d., at 1350, and others finding that the employee's sexual misconduct arose from or was in some way related to the employee's essential duties. *See, e.g., Samuels, supra,* at 574 (tortious conduct was "reasonably incidental" to the performance of the nursing assistant's duties in caring for a "helpless" patient in a "locked environment").

An assignment to reconcile the run of the Title VII cases with those just cited would be a taxing one. Here it is enough to recognize that their disparate results do not necessarily reflect wildly varying terms of the particular employment contracts involved, but represent differing judgments about the desirability of holding an employer liable for his subordinates' wayward behavior. * * *

The proper analysis * * * calls not for a mechanical application of indefinite and malleable factors set forth in the Restatement, see, e.g., §§ 219, 228, 229, but rather an inquiry into the reasons that would support a conclusion that harassing behavior ought to be held within the scope of a supervisor's employment, and the reasons for the opposite view. The Restatement itself points to such an approach, as in the commentary that the "ultimate question" in determining the scope of employment is "whether or not it is just that the loss resulting from the servant's acts should be considered as one of the normal risks to be borne by the business in which the servant is employed." Id., § 229, Comment a. See generally *Taber v. Maine*, 67 F.3d 1029, 1037 (C.A.2 1995) ("As the leading Torts treatise has put it, 'the integrating principle' of respondeat superior is 'that the employer should be liable for those faults that may be fairly regarded as risks of his business, whether they are committed in furthering it or not' ") (quoting 5 F. Harper, F. James & O. Gray, Law of Torts § 26.8, pp. 40–41 (2d ed.1986)).

In the case before us, a justification for holding the offensive behavior within the scope of Terry's and Silverman's employment was well put in Judge Barkett's dissent: "[A] pervasively hostile work environment of sexual harassment is never (one would hope) authorized, but the supervisor is clearly charged with maintaining a productive, safe work environment. The supervisor directs and controls the conduct of the employees, and the manner of doing so may inure to the employer's benefit or detriment, including subjecting the employer to Title VII liability." It is by now well recognized that hostile environment sexual harassment by supervisors (and, for that matter, co-employees) is a persistent problem in the workplace [citations omitted]. An employer can, in a general sense, reasonably anticipate the possibility of such conduct occurring in its workplace, and one might justify the assignment of the burden of the untoward behavior to the employer as one of the costs of doing business, to be charged to the enterprise rather than the victim. * * *

Two things counsel us to draw the contrary conclusion. First, there is no reason to suppose that Congress wished courts to ignore the traditional distinction between acts falling within the scope and acts amounting to what the older law called frolics or detours from the course of employment. * * *

The second reason goes to an even broader unanimity of views among the holdings of District Courts and Courts of Appeals thus far. Those courts have held not only that the sort of harassment at issue here was outside the scope of supervisors' authority, but, by uniformly judging employer liability for co-worker harassment under a negligence standard, they have also implicitly treated such harassment as outside the scope of common employees' duties as well [citations omitted]; see also 29 CFR § 1604.11(d) (1997) (employer is liable for co-worker harassment if it "knows or should have known of the conduct, unless it can show that it took immediate and appropriate corrective action"); 3 L. Larson & A. Larson, Employment Discrimination § 46.07[4][a], p. 46–101 (2d ed.1998) (courts "uniformly" apply EEOC rule; "[i]t is not a controversial area"). If, indeed, the cases did not rest, at least implicitly, on the notion that such harassment falls outside the scope of employment, their liability issues would have turned simply on the application of the scope-of-employment rule. Cf. *Hunter v. Allis-Chalmers, Corp.*, 797 F.2d 1417, 1422 (C.A.7 1986) (noting that employer will not usually be liable under respondeat superior for employee's racial harassment because it "would be the rare case where racial harassment * * * could be thought by the author of the harassment to help the employer's business").

It is quite unlikely that these cases would escape efforts to render them obsolete if we were to hold that supervisors who engage in discriminatory harassment are necessarily acting within the scope of their employment. The rationale for placing harassment within the scope of supervisory authority would be the fairness of requiring the employer to bear the burden of foreseeable social behavior, and the same rationale would apply when the behavior was that of co-employees. The employer generally benefits just as obviously from the work of common employees as from the work of supervisors; they simply have different jobs to do, all aimed at the success of the enterprise. As between an innocent employer and an innocent employee, if we use scope of employment reasoning to require the employer to bear the cost of an actionably hostile workplace created by one class of employees (i.e., supervisors), it could appear just as appropriate to do the same when the environment was created by another class (i.e., co-workers).

* * *

2

* * *

We * * * agree with Faragher that in implementing Title VII it makes sense to hold an employer vicariously liable for some tortious conduct of a supervisor made possible by abuse of his supervisory authority, * * *. Several courts, indeed, have noted what Faragher has argued, that there is a sense in which a harassing supervisor is always assisted in his misconduct by the supervisory relationship [citations omitted]. The agency relationship affords contact with an employee subjected to a supervisor's sexual harassment, and the victim may well be reluctant to accept the risks of blowing the whistle on a superior. When a person with supervisory authority discriminates in the terms and conditions of subordinates' employment, his actions necessarily draw upon his superior position over the people who report to him, or those under them, whereas an employee generally cannot check a supervisor's abusive conduct the same way that she might deal with abuse from a co-worker. When a fellow employee harasses, the victim can walk away or tell the offender where to go, but it may be difficult to offer such responses to a supervisor, whose "power to supervise—[which may be] to hire and fire, and to set work schedules and pay rates—does not disappear * * * when he chooses to harass through insults and offensive gestures rather than directly with threats of firing or promises of promotion." Estrich, Sex at Work, 43 Stan. L.Rev. 813, 854 (1991). Recognition of employer liability when discriminatory misuse of supervisory authority alters the terms and conditions of a victim's employment is underscored by the fact that the employer has a greater opportunity to guard against misconduct by supervisors than by common workers; employers have greater opportunity and incentive to screen them, train them, and monitor their performance.

In sum, there are good reasons for vicarious liability for misuse of supervisory authority. That rationale must, however, satisfy one more condition. We are not entitled to recognize this theory under Title VII unless we can square it with *Meritor*'s holding that an employer is not "automatically" liable for harassment by a supervisor who creates the requisite degree of discrimination, and there is obviously some tension between that holding and the position that a supervisor's misconduct aided by supervisory authority subjects the employer to liability vicariously; if the "aid" may be the unspoken suggestion of retaliation by misuse of supervisory authority, the risk of automatic liability is high. To counter it, we think there are two basic alternatives, one being to require proof of some affirmative invocation of that authority by the harassing supervisor, the other to recognize an affirmative defense to liability in some circumstances, even when a supervisor has created the actionable environment.

There is certainly some authority for requiring active or affirmative, as distinct from passive or implicit, misuse of supervisory authority before liability may be imputed. * * *

But neat examples illustrating the line between the affirmative and merely implicit uses of power are not easy to come by in considering management behavior. Supervisors do not make speeches threatening sanctions whenever they make requests in the legitimate exercise of managerial authority, and yet every subordinate employee knows the sanctions exist; this is the reason that courts have consistently held that acts of supervisors have greater power to alter the environment than acts of co-employees generally. How far from the course of ostensible supervisory behavior would a company officer have to step before his orders would not reasonably be seen as actively using authority? Judgment calls would often be close, the results would often seem disparate even if not demonstrably contradictory, and the temptation to litigate would be hard to resist. We think plaintiffs and defendants alike would be poorly served by an active-use rule.

The other basic alternative to automatic liability would avoid this particular temptation to litigate, but allow an employer to show as an affirmative defense to liability that the employer had exercised reasonable care to avoid harassment and to eliminate it when it might occur, and that the complaining employee had failed to act with like reasonable care to take advantage of the employer's safeguards and otherwise to prevent harm that could have been avoided. This composite defense would, we think, implement the statute sensibly, for reasons that are not hard to fathom.

* * *

The requirement to show that the employee has failed in a coordinate duty to avoid or mitigate harm reflects an equally obvious policy imported from the general theory of damages, that a victim has a duty "to use such means as are reasonable under the circumstances to avoid or minimize the damages" that result from violations of the statute. *Ford Motor Co. v. EEOC*, 458 U.S. 219, 231, n. 15, 102 S.Ct. 3057, 3065, n. 15, 73 L.Ed.2d 721 (1982) (quoting C. McCormick, Law of Damages 127 (1935) (internal quotation marks omitted)). An employer may, for example, have provided a proven, effective mechanism for reporting and resolving complaints of sexual harassment, available to the employee without undue risk or expense. If the plaintiff unreasonably failed to avail herself of the employer's preventive or remedial apparatus, she should not recover damages that could have been avoided if she had done so. If the victim could have avoided harm, no liability should be found against the employer who had taken reasonable care, and if damages could reasonably have been mitigated no award against a liable employer should reward a plaintiff for what her own efforts could have avoided.

In order to accommodate the principle of vicarious liability for harm caused by misuse of supervisory authority, as well as Title VII's equally basic policies of encouraging forethought by employers and saving action by objecting employees, we adopt the following holding in this case and in *Burlington Industries, Inc. v. Ellerth*, [524 U.S. 742, 118 S.Ct. 2257,] also decided today. An employer is subject to vicarious liability to a victimized employee for an actionable hostile environment created by a supervisor with immediate (or successively higher) authority over the employee. When no tangible employment action is taken, a defending employer may raise an affirmative defense to liability or damages, subject to proof by a preponderance of the evidence, see Fed. Rule. Civ. Proc. 8(c). The defense comprises two necessary elements: (a) that the employer exercised reasonable care to prevent and correct promptly any sexually harassing behavior, and (b) that the plaintiff employee unreasonably failed to take advantage of any preventive or corrective opportunities provided by the employer or to avoid harm otherwise. While proof that an employer had promulgated an antiharassment policy with complaint procedure is not necessary in every instance as a matter of law, the need for a stated policy suitable to the employment circumstances may appropriately be addressed in any case when litigating the first element of the defense. And while proof that an employee failed to fulfill the corresponding obligation of reasonable care to avoid harm is not limited to showing an unreasonable failure to use any complaint procedure provided by the employer, a demonstration of such failure will normally suffice to satisfy the employer's burden under the second element of the defense. No affirmative defense is available, however, when the supervisor's harassment culminates in a tangible employment action, such as discharge, demotion, or undesirable reassignment.

Applying these rules here, we believe that the judgment of the Court of Appeals must be reversed. The District Court found that the degree of hostility in the work environment rose to the actionable level and was attributable to Silverman and Terry. It is undisputed that these supervisors "were granted virtually unchecked authority" over their subordinates, "directly controll[ing] and supervis[ing] all aspects of [Faragher's] day-to-day activities." It is also clear that Faragher and her colleagues were "completely isolated from the City's higher management." The City did not seek review of these findings.

While the City would have an opportunity to raise an affirmative defense if there were any serious prospect of its presenting one, it appears from the record that any such avenue is closed. The District Court found that the City had entirely failed to disseminate its policy against sexual harassment among the beach employees and that its officials made no attempt to keep track of the conduct of supervisors like Terry and Silverman. The record also makes clear that the City's policy did not include any assurance that the harassing supervisors could be bypassed in registering complaints. Under such circumstances, we hold as a matter of law that the City could not be found to have exercised reasonable care to prevent the supervisors' harassing conduct. Unlike the employer of a small workforce, who might expect that sufficient care to prevent tortious behavior could be exercised informally, those responsible for city operations could not reasonably have thought that precautions against hostile environments in any one of many departments in far-flung locations could be effective without communicating some formal policy against harassment, with a sensible complaint procedure.

* * *

The City points to nothing that might justify a conclusion by the District Court on remand that the City had exercised reasonable care. Nor is there any reason to remand for consideration of Faragher's efforts to mitigate her own damages, since the award to her was solely nominal.

3

The Court of Appeals also rejected the possibility that it could hold the City liable for the reason that it knew of the harassment vicariously through the knowledge of its supervisors. We have no occasion to consider whether this was error, however. We are satisfied that liability on the ground of vicarious knowledge could not be determined without further factfinding on remand, whereas the reversal necessary on the theory of supervisory harassment renders any remand for consideration of imputed knowledge entirely unjustifiable (as would be any consideration of negligence as an alternative to a theory of vicarious liability here).

JUSTICE THOMAS, with whom JUSTICE SCALIA joins, dissenting.

* * *

Petitioner suffered no adverse employment consequence; thus the Court of Appeals was correct to hold that the City is not vicariously liable for the conduct of Chief Terry and Lieutenant Silverman. Because the Court reverses this judgment, I dissent.

As for petitioner's negligence claim, the District Court made no finding as to the City's negligence, and the Court of Appeals did not directly consider the issue. I would therefore remand the case to the District Court for further proceedings on this question alone. I disagree with the Court's conclusion that merely because the City did not disseminate its sexual harassment policy, it should be liable as a matter of law. The City should be allowed to show either that: (1) there was a reasonably available avenue through which petitioner could have complained to a City official who supervised both Chief Terry and Lieutenant Silverman, or (2) it would not have learned of the harassment even if the policy had been distributed. Petitioner, as the plaintiff, would of course bear the burden of proving the City's negligence.

NOTES AND QUESTIONS

Note on Burlington Industries, Inc. v. Ellerth

In a separate decision issued on the same day as that in *Faragher*, the Court in *Ellerth*, through a similar analysis provided by Justice Kennedy, articulated the identical standard as in *Faragher* for qualified vicarious employer liability under Title VII where supervisors have created an actionable hostile work environment. Unlike *Faragher*, *Ellerth* involved alleged threats by a supervisor to take an adverse employment action against an employee who declined the supervisor's sexual advances. Since the "quid pro quo" threats were not carried out, however, the case did not involve tangible employment decisions on which to base direct employer liablity.

Test Your Understanding of the Material

1.   How does the employer liability standard adopted in *Faragher* and *Ellerth* differ from the Restatement of Tort's "scope of employment" standard?

2.   Why did the Court hold that Boca Raton would not be able to prove an affirmative defense?

3.   What would you advise employers to include in their anti-harassment policies? Consider, in particular, how an employer could provide effective assurances to potential victims that they would not be retaliated against for reporting on their superiors.

Related Issues

4.   *Least-Cost Avoider?* Professor, now Judge, Calabresi argued that where general deterrence is the primary goal, liability for an accident should be placed on that party who would have been the accident's "cheapest cost avoider". See Guido Calabresi & Jon T. Hirschoff, Toward a Test for Strict Liability in Torts, 81 Yale L.J. 1055 (1972); Guido Calabresi, The Costs of Accidents, (1970), esp. chs. 7 and 10. In what respects is the Faragher-Ellerth liability standard consistent with the "least cost avoider" principle? See Michael C. Harper, Employer Liability for Harassment Under Title VII: A Functional Rationale for *Faragher* and *Ellerth*, 6 San Diego L. Rev. 101 (1999).

5.   *Employee's Failure to Report.* Generally, an employee's failure to utilize a fair, reasonable internal procedure to report harassment will be fatal to a harassment claim. But see Monteagudo v. Asociacion de Empleados del Estado Libre Asociado, 554 F.3d 164 (1st Cir. 2009) (young employee may have reasonably failed to report on senior employee who was friends with those to whom she was directed to report); Johnson v. West, 218 F.3d 725 (7th Cir.2000) (reasonable employer may still be liable if employee reasonably did not take advantage of corrective system because of intimidation and threats from harasser).

6. *Employer Liability Where the Employee Reports the Harassment.* Under a strict application of the *Faragher-Ellerth* affirmative defense, an employer cannot satisfy the second prong of the affirmative defense when the employee promptly uses the employer's complaint system. In most cases, employers nonetheless can avoid liability by stopping the harassment through an adequate response to the employee's prompt report. See, e.g., Indest v. Freeman Decorating, Inc., 164 F.3d 258, 265–66 (5th Cir.1999) (no employer liability if "swift and appropriate remedial response").

7. *Appropriate Corrective Action to Prevent Reoccurrence.* Employers must decide how to respond after determining that an employee has engaged in sexual or other unlawful harassment. Does Title VII demand punishment commensurate with the degree of harassment, or only a response sufficient to avoid a reoccurrence? See, e.g., Tutman v. WBBM-TV, 209 F.3d 1044 (7th Cir.2000).

8. *Manner of Response After Reasonable Investigation?* How would you advise employers to respond when their investigations of alleged surreptitious discriminatory harassment are inconclusive? If the employer takes no action to separate a supervisor and a complaining assistant, can the assistant in a Title VII action potentially collect damages from the employer for the impact of any actionable comments or harassment from the supervisor? Alternatively, what if the employer after its serious, but inconclusive investigation, transfers the assistant to another position under different supervision? Does the assistant have a claim for retaliation under § 704(a) of the Act if the new position is of lesser responsibility or requires a longer commute? Cf. Hostetler v. Quality Dining, 218 F.3d 798 (7th Cir.2000).

9. *Individual Liability for the Harassing Supervisor.* Title VII does not authorize victims of sexual harassment, or of other forms of illegal discrimination, to recover damages from the supervisor or other employer agent who actually perpetrates the discrimination. Most courts interpret Congress's use of the word "agent" in the definition of employer in the Act, see § 701(b), to incorporate vicarious liability principles, but not to provide a direct action against the offending supervisor. See, e.g., Wathen v. General Elec. Co., 115 F.3d 400 (6th Cir.1997); Williams v. Banning, 72 F.3d 552 (7th Cir.1995); Tomka v. Seiler Corp., 66 F.3d 1295 (2d Cir.1995).

Victims of some forms of discrimination, including sexual harassment, however, may be able to recover against responsible individual employees, as well as their employer, under state or local civil rights statutes or through state common law tort actions (such as intentional infliction of emotional distress, assault and battery, or negligent supervision), or if public employees, § 1983. See, e.g., Badia v. City of Miami, 133 F.3d 1443 (11th Cir.1998) (city employee's § 1983 action not barred by supervisor's official immunity because right to be free of sexual harassment is clearly established). In addition, the lower courts have held that racial harassment claims may be brought under § 1981. See, e.g., Whidbee v. Garzarelli Food Specialties, Inc., supra; Allen v. Denver Pub. Sch. Bd., 928 F.2d 978, 983 (10th Cir.1991) (both finding individual liability where there is "some affirmative link to causally connect the actor with the discriminatory action"). See Restatement of Employment Law § 4.06(c) and § 6.04 (2015).

10. *Are Constructive Discharges Tangible Employment Actions?* In Pennsylvania State Police v. Suders, 542 U.S. 129, 124 S.Ct. 2342, 159 L.Ed.2d 204 (2004), the Court held that the *Faragher-Ellerth* affirmative defense is available in some cases even where a supervisor's misconduct warranted the plaintiff's resignation and thus constituted a constructive discharge. A finding of constructive discharge, the Court explained, turns on the degree of severity of the harassment, a showing of working conditions so intolerable that a reasonable person would have felt compelled to resign.

The availability of the affirmative defense, by contrast, turns not on the degree of severity of the harassment, but on whether the harassment constituted a "tangible employment action," or as the *Suders* Court stated, quoting from *Ellerth* (524 U.S. at 762), "an official act of the enterprise, a company act":

> Unlike injuries that could equally be inflicted by a co-worker, * * * tangible employment actions "fall within the special province of the supervisor," who "has been empowered by the company as . . . [an] agent to make economic decisions affecting other employees under his or her control." . . . Often, the supervisor will "use [the company's] internal processes" and thereby "obtain the imprimatur of the enterprise." Ordinarily, the tangible employment decision is documented in official company records, and may be subject to review by higher level supervisors.

542 U.S. at 144–45.

The Court explained that harassment so intolerable as to cause a resignation may be effected through co-worker conduct, unofficial supervisory conduct, or official company acts. The Court provided as an example of a constructive discharge with no official conduct, for which the affirmative defense would be available, a supervisor's repeated sexual comments and an incident in which he sexually assaulted the employee-victim. See Reed v. MBNA Marketing Systems, Inc., 333 F.3d 27 (1st Cir. 2003). As an example of a constructive discharge based on official conduct, for which the affirmative defense would not be available, the Court noted a case involving the transfer of a harassment victim to a less desirable position. See Robinson v. Sappington, 351 F.3d 317 (7th Cir. 2003). While most of Suders' allegations unofficial conduct, her supervisors' failure to forward her computer-skill exams for grading and their false statements that she had failed the exams, were less obviously unofficial.

VANCE v. BALL STATE UNIVERSITY

Supreme Court of the United States, 2013.
570 U.S. ___, 133 S.Ct. 2434, 286 L.Ed.2d 565.

JUSTICE ALITO delivered the opinion of the Court.

I

Maetta Vance, an African-American woman, began working for Ball State University (BSU) in 1989 as a substitute server in the University Banquet and Catering division of Dining Services. In 1991, BSU promoted Vance to a part-time catering assistant position, and in 2007 she applied and was selected for a position as a full-time catering assistant. * * *

During the time in question, Davis, a white woman, was employed as a catering specialist in the Banquet and Catering division. The parties vigorously dispute the precise nature and scope of Davis' duties, but they agree that Davis did not have the power to hire, fire, demote, promote, transfer, or discipline Vance. * * *

In late 2005 and early 2006, Vance filed internal complaints with BSU and charges with the Equal Employment Opportunity Commission (EEOC), alleging racial harassment and discrimination, and many of these complaints and charges pertained to Davis. Vance complained that Davis "gave her a hard time at work by glaring at her, slamming pots and pans around her, and intimidating her." She alleged that she was "left alone in the kitchen with Davis, who smiled at her"; that Davis "blocked" her on an elevator and "stood there with her cart smiling"; and that Davis often gave her "weird" looks.

Vance's workplace strife persisted despite BSU's attempts to address the problem. As a result, Vance filed this lawsuit in 2006 in the United States District Court for the Southern District of Indiana, claiming, among other things, that she had been subjected to a racially hostile work environment in violation of Title VII. In her complaint, she alleged that Davis was her supervisor and that BSU was liable for Davis' creation of a racially hostile work environment.

Both parties moved for summary judgment, and the District Court entered summary judgment in favor of BSU. The court explained that BSU could not be held vicariously liable for Davis' alleged racial harassment because Davis could not " 'hire, fire, demote, promote, transfer, or discipline' " Vance and, as a result, was not Vance's supervisor under the Seventh Circuit's interpretation of that concept. The court further held that BSU could not be liable in negligence because it responded reasonably to the incidents of which it was aware.

The Seventh Circuit affirmed. 646 F.3d 461. * * *

II

* * *

III

We hold that an employer may be vicariously liable for an employee's unlawful harassment only when the employer has empowered that employee to take tangible employment actions against the victim, *i.e.*, to effect a "significant change in employment status, such as hiring, firing, failing to promote, reassignment with significantly different responsibilities, or a decision causing a significant change in benefits." *Ellerth*, supra, at 761, 118 S. Ct. 2257, 141 L. Ed. 2d 633. * * *

* * * In *Ellerth*, it was clear that the alleged harasser was a supervisor under any definition of the term: He hired his victim, and he promoted her (subject only to the ministerial approval of his supervisor, who merely signed the paperwork). 524 U.S., at 747, 118 S. Ct. 2257, 141 L. Ed. 2d 633. *Ellerth* was a case from the Seventh Circuit, and at the time of its decision in that case, that court had already adopted its current definition of a supervisor. * * *

The same is true with respect to *Faragher*. In that case, Faragher, a female lifeguard, sued her employer, the city of Boca Raton, for sexual harassment based on the conduct of two other lifeguards, Bill Terry and David Silverman, and we held that the city was vicariously liable for Terry's and Silverman's harassment. Although it is clear that Terry had authority to take tangible employment actions affecting the victim,[8] see 524 U.S., at 781, 118 S. Ct. 2275, 141 L. Ed. 2d 662 (explaining that Terry could hire new lifeguards, supervise their work assignments, counsel, and discipline them), Silverman may have wielded less authority, *ibid.* (noting that Silverman was "responsible for making the lifeguards' daily assignments, and for supervising their work and fitness training"). Nevertheless, the city never disputed Faragher's characterization of both men as her "supervisors."[9]

---

[8]   The dissent suggests that it is unclear whether Terry would qualify as a supervisor under the test we adopt because his hiring decisions were subject to approval by higher management. * * * But we have assumed that tangible employment actions can be subject to such approval. See *Ellerth*, 524 U.S., at 762, 118 S. Ct. 2257, 141 L. Ed. 2d 633. * * *

[9]   Moreover, it is by no means certain that Silverman lacked the authority to take tangible employment actions against Faragher. In her merits brief, Faragher stated that, as a lieutenant, Silverman "made supervisory and disciplinary decisions and had input on the evaluations as well." *Id.*, at 9–10. If that discipline had economic consequences (such as suspension without pay), then Silverman might qualify as a supervisor under the definition we adopt today.

Silverman's ability to assign Faragher significantly different work responsibilities also may have constituted a tangible employment action. Silverman told Faragher, " 'Date me or clean the toilets for a year.' " *Faragher*, supra, at 780, 118 S. Ct. 2275, 141 L. Ed. 2d 662. That threatened reassignment of duties likely would have constituted significantly different responsibilities for a lifeguard, whose job typically is to guard the beach. If that reassignment had economic consequences, such as foreclosing Faragher's eligibility for promotion, then it might constitute a tangible employment action.

In light of the parties' undisputed characterization of the alleged harassers, this Court simply was not presented with the question of the degree of authority that an employee must have in order to be classified as a supervisor. * * *

The dissent acknowledges that our prior cases do "not squarely resolve whether an employee without power to take tangible employment actions may nonetheless qualify as a supervisor," but accuses us of ignoring the "all-too-plain reality" that employees with authority to control their subordinates' daily work are aided by that authority in perpetuating a discriminatory work environment. As *Ellerth* recognized, however, "most workplace tortfeasors are aided in accomplishing their tortious objective by the existence of the agency relation," and consequently "something more" is required in order to warrant vicarious liability. 524 U.S., at 760, 118 S. Ct. 2257, 141 L. Ed. 2d 633. The ability to direct another employee's tasks is simply not sufficient. Employees with such powers are certainly capable of creating intolerable work environments, but so are many other co-workers. Negligence provides the better framework for evaluating an employer's liability when a harassing employee lacks the power to take tangible employment actions.

C

* * * The *Ellerth/Faragher* framework draws a sharp line between co-workers and supervisors. Co-workers, the Court noted, "can inflict psychological injuries" by creating a hostile work environment, but they "cannot dock another's pay, nor can one co-worker demote another." *Ellerth*, 524 U.S., at 762, 118 S. Ct. 2257, 141 L. Ed. 2d 633. Only a supervisor has the power to cause "direct economic harm" by taking a tangible employment action. *Ibid.* "Tangible employment actions fall within the special province of the supervisor. The supervisor has been empowered by the company *as a distinct class* of agent to make economic decisions affecting other employees under his or her control. . . . Tangible employment actions are the means by which the supervisor brings the official power of the enterprise to bear on subordinates." *Ibid.* (emphasis added). The strong implication of this passage is that the authority to take tangible employment actions is the defining characteristic of a supervisor, not simply a characteristic of a subset of an ill-defined class of employees who qualify as supervisors. * * *

The interpretation of the concept of a supervisor that we adopt today is one that can be readily applied. In a great many cases, it will be known even before litigation is commenced whether an alleged harasser was a supervisor, and in others, the alleged harasser's status will become clear to both sides after discovery. And once this is known, the parties will be in a position to assess the strength of a case and to explore the possibility of resolving the dispute. Where this does not occur, supervisor status will generally be capable of resolution at summary judgment. * * * . In its

Enforcement Guidance, the EEOC takes the position that an employee, in order to be classified as a supervisor, must wield authority " 'of sufficient magnitude so as to assist the harasser explicitly or implicitly in carrying out the harassment.' " But *any* authority over the work of another employee provides at least some assistance, and that is not what the United States interprets the Guidance to mean. Rather, it informs us, the authority must exceed both an ill-defined temporal requirement (it must be more than "occasiona[l]") and an ill-defined substantive requirement ("an employee who directs 'only a limited number of tasks or assignments' for another employee . . . would not have sufficient authority to qualify as a supervisor." * * *

Contrary to the dissent's suggestions, this approach will not leave employees unprotected against harassment by co-workers who possess the authority to inflict psychological injury by assigning unpleasant tasks or by altering the work environment in objectionable ways. In such cases, the victims will be able to prevail simply by showing that the employer was negligent in permitting this harassment to occur, and the jury should be instructed that the nature and degree of authority wielded by the harasser is an important factor to be considered in determining whether the employer was negligent. * * *

IV * * *

Turning to the "specific facts" of petitioner's and Davis' working relationship, there is simply no evidence that Davis directed petitioner's day-to-day activities. The record indicates that Bill Kimes (the general manager of the Catering Division) and the chef assigned petitioner's daily tasks, which were given to her on "prep lists." The fact that Davis sometimes may have handed prep lists to petitioner is insufficient to confer supervisor status. And Kimes—*not* Davis—set petitioner's work schedule.

We hold that an employee is a "supervisor" for purposes of vicarious liability under Title VII if he or she is empowered by the employer to take tangible employment actions against the victim. Because there is no evidence that BSU empowered Davis to take any tangible employment actions against Vance, the judgment of the Seventh Circuit is affirmed.

Jᴜsᴛɪᴄᴇ Gɪɴsʙᴜʀɢ, with whom Jᴜsᴛɪᴄᴇ Bʀᴇʏᴇʀ, Jᴜsᴛɪᴄᴇ Sᴏᴛᴏᴍᴀʏᴏʀ, and Jᴜsᴛɪᴄᴇ Kᴀɢᴀɴ join, dissenting. * * *

The Court today strikes from the supervisory category employees who control the day-to-day schedules and assignments of others, confining the category to those formally empowered to take tangible employment actions. * * *

The distinction *Faragher* and *Ellerth* drew between supervisors and co-workers corresponds to the realities of the workplace. Exposed to a fellow employee's harassment, one can walk away or tell the offender to "buzz off." A supervisor's slings and arrows, however, are not so easily avoided. An employee who confronts her harassing supervisor risks, for example, receiving an undesirable or unsafe work assignment or an unwanted transfer. She may be saddled with an excessive workload or with placement on a shift spanning hours disruptive of her family life. And she may be demoted or fired. Facing such dangers, she may be reluctant to blow the whistle on her superior, whose "power and authority invests his or her harassing conduct with a particular threatening character." *Ellerth*, 524 U.S., at 763, 118 S. Ct. 2257, 141 L. Ed. 2d 633. * * * In short, as *Faragher* and *Ellerth* recognized, harassment by supervisors is more likely to cause palpable harm and to persist unabated than similar conduct by fellow employees.

* * *

* * * That the Court has adopted a standard, rather than a clear rule, is not surprising, for no crisp definition of supervisor could supply the unwavering line the Court desires. Supervisors, like the workplaces they manage, come in all shapes and sizes. Whether a pitching coach supervises his pitchers (can he demote them?), or an artistic director supervises her opera star (can she impose significantly different responsibilities?), or a law firm associate supervises the firm's paralegals (can she fire them?) are matters not susceptible to mechanical rules and on-off switches. One cannot know whether an employer has vested supervisory authority in an employee, and whether harassment is aided by that authority, without looking to the particular working relationship between the harasser and the victim. That is why *Faragher* and *Ellerth* crafted an employer liability standard embracive of all whose authority significantly aids in the creation and perpetuation of harassment.

* * *

The negligence standard allowed by the Court scarcely affords the protection the *Faragher* and *Ellerth* framework gave victims harassed by those in control of their lives at work. Recall that an employer is negligent with regard to harassment only if it knew or should have known of the conduct but failed to take appropriate corrective action. See 29 C.F.R. § 1604.11(d); EEOC Guidance 405:7652 to 405:7653. It is not uncommon for employers to lack actual or constructive notice of a harassing employee's conduct. * * * An employee may have a reputation as a harasser among those in his vicinity, but if no complaint makes its way up to management, the employer will escape liability under a negligence standard. *Id.*, at 1378.

Faragher is illustrative. After enduring unrelenting harassment, Faragher reported Terry's and Silverman's conduct informally to Robert Gordon, another immediate supervisor. 524 U.S., at 782–783, 118 S. Ct. 2275, 141 L. Ed. 2d 662. But the lifeguards were "completely isolated from the City's higher management," and it did not occur to Faragher to pursue the matter with higher ranking city officials distant from the beach. *Id.*, at 783, 808, 118 S. Ct. 2275, 141 L. Ed. 2d 662 (internal quotation marks omitted). Applying a negligence standard, the Eleventh Circuit held that, despite the pervasiveness of the harassment, and despite Gordon's awareness of it, Boca Raton lacked constructive notice and therefore escaped liability. *Id.*, at 784–785, 118 S. Ct. 2275, 141 L. Ed. 2d 662. Under the vicarious liability standard, however, Boca Raton could not make out the affirmative defense, for it had failed to disseminate a policy against sexual harassment. *Id.*, at 808–809, 118 S. Ct. 2275, 141 L. Ed. 2d 662.

NOTES AND QUESTIONS

Test Your Understanding of the Material

1.   How does the Court's definition of supervisor differ from that of the EEOC which it rejected? What are the respective merits (or demerits) of the two approaches?

2.   What constitutes a "tangible employment action"? Is a work assignment, such as Silberman's assignment of Faragher to toilet duty, tangible because it might have significant economic consequences, even if not an "official" act that is reported or recorded for potential review?

3.   How would you decide the pitching coach, opera director, and law firm associate examples in Justice Ginsburg's dissent?

Related Issues

4.   *Applicability to Racial as Well as Sexual Harassment.* Note that *Vance* involved racial rather than sexual harassment. In a footnote, the Court noted that lower court decisions had applied the *Faragher-Ellerth* affirmative defense to racial harassment, and assumed, without directly deciding, that these decisions were correct. Is there basis in the text of Title VII to distinguish racial harassment for purposes of defining employer liability?

5.   *Harassment by Coworkers.* As the Court in *Faragher-Ellerth* assumed, and *Vance* affirms, a negligence standard applies to coworker harassment. See, e.g., Swinton v. Potomac Corp. 270 F.3d 794 (9th Cir. 2001) (if "harasser is merely a co-worker, the plaintiff must prove that the employer . . . knew or should have known of the harassment but did not take adequate steps to address it"); Ocheltree v. Scollon Productions, Inc., 335 F.3d 325 (4th Cir. 2003) (failure to provide adequate complaint mechanism could support jury finding of negligence for coworker harassment); 29 C.F.R. 1604.11(d) (employer negligent where it "knows or should have known of the conduct, unless it can show that it took immediate and appropriate corrective action"). How does the negligence standard differ from the standard for employer liability set forth in *Faragher-Ellerth*? Note the different treatment in the majority and dissenting opinions in *Faragher* of the City of Boca Raton's failure to distribute its anti-harassment policy.

6. *Harassment by Customers or Other Nonemployees.* Employer liability for harassment by customers or other nonemployees is treated under the negligence standard applicable to coworker harassment. See, e.g., Freeman v. Dal-Tile Corp., 750 F.3d 413, 423–24 (4th Cir. 2014) (negligence standard for harassment by independent sales representative); Beckford v. Department of Corr., 605 F.3d 951 (11th Cir. 2010) (prison may be liable for failing to remedy hostile work environment that prisoners created for female employees); Freitag v. Ayers, 463 F.3d 838 (9th Cir. 2006) (prison liable for failure "to take prompt and effective remedial action to address" sexual harassment of female guards by prisoners); Dunn v. Washington County Hosp., 429 F.3d 689 (7th Cir. 2005) (employer may be directly liable for harassment by independent contractor because of failure to take "reasonable care" to provide nondiscriminatory work environment).

7. *Harassment by Senior Executives and Controlling Owners. Faragher* instructs that employers are strictly liable for harassment committed by high level executives "who may be treated as the organization's proxy." 524 U.S. 789. In such cases, the *Faragher-Ellerth* defense is unavailable. See, e.g., Townsend v. Benjamin Enters, Inc. 679 F.3d 41 (2d Cir. 2012) (defense not available when harasser is the sole vice president and husband of president and immediate family owned all of company stock); Passantino v. Johnson & Johnson Consumer Products, 212 F.3d 493, 517 (9th Cir. 2000) ("an individual sufficiently senior in the corporation must be treated as the corporation's proxy for purposes of liability"). See also Clackamas Gastroenterology Associates, P.C. v. Wells, 538 U.S. 440 (2003), page 34 supra; Restatement of Employment Law §§ 1.03 and 4.02 (2015).

E. COMPENSATION DISPARITIES

1. THE EQUAL PAY ACT

CORNING GLASS WORKS V. BRENNAN

Supreme Court of the United States, 1974.
417 U.S. 188, 94 S.Ct. 2223, 41 L.Ed.2d 1.

JUSTICE MARSHALL delivered the opinion of the Court.

I

Prior to 1925, Corning operated its plants in Wellsboro and Corning only during the day, and all inspection work was performed by women. Between 1925 and 1930, the company began to introduce automatic production equipment which made it desirable to institute a night shift. During this period, however, both New York and Pennsylvania law prohibited women from working at night. As a result, in order to fill inspector positions on the new night shift, the company had to recruit male employees from among its male dayworkers. The male employees so transferred demanded and received wages substantially higher than those paid to women inspectors engaged on the two day shifts.[3] During this same period, however, no plant-wide shift differential existed and male employees working at night, other than inspectors, received the same wages as their day shift counterparts. Thus a situation developed where the night inspectors were all male,[4] the day inspectors all female, and the male inspectors received significantly higher wages.

In 1944, Corning plants at both locations were organized by a labor union and a collective-bargaining agreement was negotiated for all production and maintenance employees. This agreement for the first time established a plant-wide shift differential, but this change did not eliminate the higher base wage paid to male night inspectors. Rather, the shift differential was superimposed on the existing difference in base wages between male night inspectors and female day inspectors.

Prior to June 11, 1964, the effective date of the Equal Pay Act, the law in both Pennsylvania and New York was amended to permit women to work at night. It was not until some time after the effective date of the Act, however, that Corning initiated efforts to eliminate the differential rates for male and female inspectors. Beginning in June 1966, Corning started to open up jobs on the night shift to women. Previously separate male and female seniority lists were consolidated and women became eligible to exercise their seniority, on the same basis as men, to bid for the higher paid night inspection jobs as vacancies occurred.

On January 20, 1969, a new collective-bargaining agreement went into effect, establishing a new "job evaluation" system for setting wage rates. The new agreement abolished for the future the separate base wages for day and night shift inspectors and imposed a uniform base wage for inspectors exceeding the wage rate for the night shift previously in effect. All inspectors hired after January 20, 1969, were to receive the same base wage, whatever their sex or shift. The collective-bargaining agreement further provided, however, for a higher "red circle" rate for employees hired prior to January 20, 1969, when working as inspectors on the night shift. This "red circle" rate served essentially to perpetuate the differential in base wages between day and night inspectors.

---

[3]   Higher wages were demanded in part because the men had been earning more money on their day shift jobs than women were paid for inspection work. Thus, at the time of the creation of the new night shift, female day shift inspectors received wages ranging from 20 to 30 cents per hour. Most of the men designated to fill the newly created night shift positions had been working in the blowing room where the lowest wage rate was 48 cents per hour and where additional incentive pay could be earned. As night shift inspectors these men received 53 cents per hour. There is also some evidence in the record that additional compensation was necessary because the men viewed inspection jobs as "demeaning" and as "women's work."

[4]   A temporary exception was made during World War II when manpower shortages caused Corning to be permitted to employ women on the steady night shift inspection jobs at both locations. It appears that women night inspectors during this period were paid the same higher night shift wages earned by the men.

The Secretary of Labor brought these cases to enjoin Corning from violating the Equal Pay Act and to collect back wages allegedly due female employees because of past violations. Three distinct questions are presented: (1) Did Corning ever violate the Equal Pay Act by paying male night shift inspectors more than female day shift inspectors? (2) If so, did Corning cure its violation of the Act in 1966 by permitting women to work as night shift inspectors? (3) Finally, if the violation was not remedied in 1966, did Corning cure its violation in 1969 by equalizing day and night inspector wage rates but establishing higher "red circle" rates for existing employees working on the night shift?

II

Congress' purpose in enacting the Equal Pay Act was to remedy what was perceived to be a serious and endemic problem of employment discrimination in private industry—the fact that the wage structure of "many segments of American industry has been based on an ancient but outmoded belief that a man, because of his role in society, should be paid more than a woman even though his duties are the same." S.Rep. No. 176, 88th Cong., 1st Sess., 1 (1963). The solution adopted was quite simple in principle: to require that "equal work will be rewarded by equal wages." *Ibid.*

The Act's basic structure and operation are similarly straightforward. In order to make out a case under the Act, the Secretary must show that an employer pays different wages to employees of opposite sexes "for equal work on jobs the performance of which requires equal skill, effort, and responsibility, and which are performed under similar working conditions." Although the Act is silent on this point, its legislative history makes plain that the Secretary has the burden of proof on this issue, as both of the courts below recognized.

The Act also establishes four exceptions—three specific and one a general catchall provision—where different payment to employees of opposite sexes "is made pursuant to (i) a seniority system; (ii) a merit system; (iii) a system which measures earnings by quantity or quality of production; or (iv) a differential based on any other factor other than sex." Again, while the Act is silent on this question, its structure and history also suggest that once the Secretary has carried his burden of showing that the employer pays workers of one sex more than workers of the opposite sex for equal work, the burden shifts to the employer to show that the differential is justified under one of the Act's four exceptions. All of the many lower courts that have considered this question have so held, and this view is consistent with the general rule that the application of an exemption under the Fair Labor Standards Act is a matter of affirmative defense on which the employer has the burden of proof.

The contentions of the parties in this case reflect the Act's underlying framework. Corning argues that the Secretary has failed to prove that Corning ever violated the Act because day shift work is not "performed under similar working conditions" as night shift work. The Secretary maintains that day shift and night shift work are performed under "similar working conditions" within the meaning of the Act.[13] Although the Secretary recognizes that higher wages may be paid for night shift work, the Secretary contends that such a shift differential would be based upon a "factor other than sex" within the catch-all exception to the Act and that Corning has failed to carry its burden of proof that its higher base wage for male night inspectors was in fact based on any factor other than sex.

* * *

The most notable feature of the history of the Equal Pay Act is that Congress recognized early in the legislative process that the concept of equal pay for equal work was more readily stated in principle than reduced to statutory language which would be meaningful to employers and workable across the broad range of industries covered by the Act. As originally introduced, the Equal Pay bill required equal pay for "equal work on jobs the performance of which requires equal skills." There were only two exceptions—for differentials "made pursuant to a seniority or merit increase system which does not discriminate on the basis of sex. * * * "

In both the House and Senate committee hearings, witnesses were highly critical of the Act's definition of equal work and of its exemptions. Many noted that most of American industry used formal, systematic job evaluation plans to establish equitable wage structures in their plants. Such systems, as explained coincidentally by a representative of Corning Glass Works who testified at both hearings, took into consideration four separate factors in determining job value—skill, effort, responsibility and working conditions—and each of these four components was further systematically divided into various subcomponents. Under a job evaluation plan, point values are assigned to each of the subcomponents of a given job, resulting in a total point figure representing a relatively objective measure of the job's value.

* * *

Indeed, the most telling evidence of congressional intent is the fact that the Act's amended definition of equal work incorporated the specific language of the job evaluation plan described at the hearings by Corning's

---

[13] The Secretary also advances an argument that even if night and day inspection work is assumed not to be performed under similar working conditions, the differential in base wages is nevertheless unlawful under the Act. The additional burden of working at night, the argument goes, was already fully reflected in the plant-wide shift differential, and the shifts were made "similar" by payment of the shift differential. This argument does not appear to have been presented to either [of] the [courts below], as the opinions in both cases reflect an assumption on the part of all concerned that the Secretary's case would fail unless night and day inspection work was found to be performed under similar working conditions. For this reason, and in view of our resolution of the "working condition" issue, we have no occasion to consider and intimate no views on this aspect of the Secretary's argument.

own representative—that is, the concepts of "skill," "effort," "responsibility," and "working conditions."

* * *

While a layman might well assume that time of day worked reflects one aspect of a job's "working conditions," the term has a different and much more specific meaning in the language of industrial relations. As Corning's own representative testified at the hearings, the element of working conditions encompasses two subfactors: "surroundings" and "hazards." "Surroundings" measures the elements, such as toxic chemicals or fumes, regularly encountered by a worker, their intensity, and their frequency. "Hazards" takes into account the physical hazards regularly encountered, their frequency, and the severity of injury they can cause. This definition of "working conditions" is not only manifested in Corning's own job evaluation plans but is also well accepted across a wide range of American industry.

Nowhere in any of these definitions is time of day worked mentioned as a relevant criterion. The fact of the matter is that the concept of "working conditions," as used in the specialized language of job evaluation systems, simply does not encompass shift differentials. Indeed, while Corning now argues that night inspection work is not equal to day inspection work, all of its own job evaluation plans, including the one now in effect, have consistently treated them as equal in all respects, including working conditions.

* * *

This does not mean, of course, that there is no room in the Equal Pay Act for nondiscriminatory shift differentials. Work on a steady night shift no doubt has psychological and physiological impacts making it less attractive than work on a day shift. The Act contemplates that a male night worker may receive a higher wage than a female day worker, just as it contemplates that a male employee with 20 years' seniority can receive a higher wage than a woman with two years' seniority. Factors such as these play a role under the Act's * * * exceptions—the seniority differential under the specific seniority exception, the shift differential under the catch-all exception for differentials "based on any other factor other than sex."

The question remains, however, whether Corning carried its burden of proving that the higher rate paid for night inspection work, until 1966 performed solely by men, was in fact intended to serve as compensation for night work, or rather constituted an added payment based upon sex. We agree that the record amply supports the District Court's conclusion that Corning had not sustained its burden of proof. As its history revealed, "the higher night rate was in large part the product of the generally higher wage level of male workers and the need to compensate them for performing what were regarded as demeaning tasks." The differential in base wages originated at a time when no other night employees received higher pay than corresponding day workers, and it was maintained long after the company instituted a separate plant-wide shift differential which was thought to compensate adequately for the additional burdens of night work. The differential arose simply because men would not work at the low rates paid women inspectors, and it reflected a job market in which Corning could pay women less than men for the same work. That the company took advantage of such a situation may be understandable as a matter of economics, but its differential nevertheless became illegal once Congress enacted into law the principle of equal pay for equal work.

* * *

We now must consider whether Corning continued to remain in violation of the Act after 1966 when, without changing the base wage rates for day and night inspectors, it began to permit women to bid for jobs on the night shift as vacancies occurred. It is evident that this was more than a token gesture to end discrimination, as turnover in the night shift inspection jobs was rapid. The record * * * shows * * * that during the two-year period after June 1, 1966, the date women were first permitted to bid for night inspection jobs, women took 152 of the 278 openings, and women with very little seniority were able to obtain positions on the night shift. Relying on these facts, the company argues that it ceased discriminating against women in 1966, and was no longer in violation of the Equal Pay Act.

But the issue before us is not whether the company, in some abstract sense, can be said to have treated men the same as women after 1966. Rather, the question is whether the company remedied the specific violation of the Act which the Secretary proved. We agree with the Second Circuit, as well as with all other circuits that have had occasion to consider this issue, that the company could not cure its violation except by equalizing the base wages of female day inspectors with the higher rates paid the night inspectors. This result is implicit in the Act's language, its statement of purpose, and its legislative history.

NOTES AND QUESTIONS

Test Your Understanding of the Material

    1.   How does the Court in *Corning Glass* interpret the Equal Pay Act (EPA) phrase "similar working conditions"? Does it mean that if Corning Glass had always paid its night shift more than its day shift and had always employed women at night as well as the day, Corning still would be compelled to justify paying a female day worker less than a male night worker? In view of the defenses available to an employer, does this present a significant problem?

    2.   How does the *Corning* Court treat the argument that paying men more than women because men will not work for as low a wage as will women

constitutes basing pay on a neutral factor other than sex—payment of the wage necessary to secure the available labor?

3.   Note that *Corning* assigned the burden of persuasion to the employer to show it relied on a "factor other than sex." Is this consistent with the way the Court has allocated burdens in disparate treatment cases under Title VII? What supports this aspect of the *Corning* decision?

4.   Consider the facts of the following cases, and assess whether the employer violated the EPA:

a.   A department store bases the salary of each of its sales personnel in part on the gross markup of that individual's total sales. Because of the appreciably greater markup on most men's clothing, this policy results in the men selling men's clothing making substantially more on average for each hour of work than the women assigned to selling women's clothing. Assume no discriminatory job assignments, but that men gravitated to the men's clothing department, and females gravitated to the women's clothing department. Are the women being paid at a lower rate than the men? Would the women be paid at a lower rate if their average hourly wages were equal to those of the men because the greater volume of sales of women's clothing compensated for the higher markups on men's clothing? See Hodgson v. Robert Hall Clothes, Inc., 473 F.2d 589 (3d Cir.1973), criticized in Paul N. Cox, Equal Work, Comparable Worth and Disparate Treatment: An Argument for Narrowly Construing *County of Washington v. Gunther,* 22 Duq.L.Rev. 65, 77–78 (1983).

b.   A chain of unisex health clubs bases the salary of its managers on the number of new memberships they sell. It assigns female managers to manage female clubs and male managers to manage male clubs. The chain has determined that six new female memberships can be sold with the same effort and in the same time that it takes to sell four new male memberships. The chain therefore gives male managers fifty percent more credit for the sale of a male membership than it gives female managers for the sale of a female membership. This has resulted in the average earnings of male and female managers being equal. Can the female managers present a prima facie EPA case? If so, does the employer have an adequate defense? See Bence v. Detroit Health Corp., 712 F.2d 1024 (6th Cir.1983).

Related Issues

5.   *"Equal Skill, Effort, and Responsibility".* The EPA does not provide a cause of action to challenge disparate pay in different jobs. A plaintiff's job does not have to be identical to more highly compensated jobs filled by males, however. The jobs have to have a substantially common core of functions and responsibilities. See, e.g., Beck-Wilson v. Principi, 441 F.3d 353 (6th Cir. 2006); Tomka v. Seiler Corp., 66 F.3d 1295, 1312 (2d Cir.1995); Mulhall v. Advance

Security, Inc., 19 F.3d 586, 592 (11th Cir.1994); Thompson v. Sawyer, 678 F.2d 257, 271–72 (D.C.Cir.1982). See generally Mayer Freed & Daniel Polsby, Comparable Worth in the Equal Pay Act, 51 U.Chi.L.Rev. 1078 (1984) and Mary Becker, Comparable Worth In Antidiscrimination Legislation: A Reply to Freed and Polsby, 51 U.Chi.L.Rev. 1112 (1984).

6. *Reliance on "Market Rate" or Prior Salary as a "Factor Other than Sex"*. Suppose an employer calculates pay based in part on prior salary. Would the use of prior salary to set opening pay provide a defense for resulting pay disparities as a "factor other than sex?" Does the EPA prevent an employer from securing the best available employees by matching a candidate's prior salary or a salary offer from another company? Most courts considering prior salary standards have distinguished *Corning*. See, e.g., Price v. Northern States Power Co., 664 F.3d 1186, 1192 (8th Cir. 2011) (affirming validity of company policy that allowed employees to retain same salary after transferring); Wernsing v. Department of Human Services, 427 F.3d 466 (7th Cir. 2005) (prior salary is factor other than sex for calculating starting salary); Taylor v. White, 321 F.3d 710 (8th Cir.2003) (employer may rely on "salary retention" policy unless used for purpose of taking advantage of women's "market" position as in *Corning*). But cf. Kouba v. Allstate Ins. Co., 691 F.2d 873 (9th Cir. 1982) (employer must justify use of prior salary as one basis for minimum starting salary).

7. *Workload Discrimination*. Does the EPA proscribe requiring a woman to work longer hours than a man to earn the same salary in an otherwise substantially equal job? Can an EPA court consider an imputed hourly rate of pay for salaried jobs? Or can the court at least take into account whether the man's lighter workload permits him more easily to supplement his income through another job? See Berry v. Board of Supervisors of L.S.U., 715 F.2d 971 (5th Cir.1983) (recognizing the claim of a female professor required to teach at least twice as many hours as her male peers).

NOTE: EQUAL PAY ACT OF 1963

The EPA was to some extent eclipsed by the passage of Title VII only a year later. The latter statute is, of course, much broader in scope. Unlike Title VII, the EPA is limited to sex discrimination and only reaches compensation. Furthermore, the EPA proscribes only discrimination within an "establishment." This makes difficult a company-wide challenge or a challenge requiring comparisons among different plants in the same area owned by the same employer. But see Brennan v. Goose Creek Consol. Ind. Sch. Dist., 519 F.2d 53 (5th Cir.1975) (attack on common hiring and compensation plan for school system).

An understanding of the EPA nonetheless remains important for the employment discrimination lawyer for several reasons. First, Title VII incorporates the special EPA defenses for those Title VII cases involving the disparate treatment of women in compensation. See Kouba v. Allstate Ins. Co., 691 F.2d 873 (9th Cir. 1982). When a woman brings a Title VII claim alleging disparate pay for equal work, some courts hold that the burden of persuasion shifts to the employer to show that the disparity resulted from a factor other than sex. Id. (For all other Title VII cases, the burden of persuasion remains with the plaintiff throughout. See Texas Dept. of Community Affairs v. Burdine, 450 U.S. 248 (1981)).

Second, the employer and employees covered by the two Acts are not identical; and some employment decisions reached by the EPA are not reached by Title VII. The EPA was passed as an amendment to the Fair Labor Standards Act (FLSA), which covers all companies engaged in interstate commerce. By contrast, Title VII only covers employers with 15 or more employees. See generally Mack Player, Enterprise Coverage under the Fair Labor Standards Act: An Assessment of the First Generation, 28 Vand.L.Rev. 283 (1975).

Third, plaintiffs may prefer to invoke the EPA for wage discrimination claims because it provides a different procedural-remedial scheme than that of Title VII. The EPA is enforced through the FLSA procedural scheme. Unlike Title VII, this scheme permits aggrieved employees to proceed directly to state or federal court without filing an administrative complaint or waiting for an administrative investigation or mediation. The private right of action afforded by § 16(b) of the FLSA is terminated if the Labor Department (now the EEOC) first brings a suit on the same complaint, but an employee need not wait any minimum period before filing a private suit.

The EPA remedial scheme differs from Title VII's in other respects. First, although general compensatory and punitive damages appear to be unavailable, the EPA offers the possibility of "liquidated damages", set at doubled back pay. The trial court has discretion to award less than full or even no liquidated damages where the employer shows that its violation was "in good faith" and it "had reasonable grounds" for believing it was not in violation of the EPA. Second, the FLSA's two-year statute of limitations (three years if a "willful" violation) imposes different time constraints than those for the filing periods under Title VII. See Holt v. KMI-Continental, Inc., 95 F.3d 123, 131–32 (2d Cir.1996) (EPA's statute of limitations do not apply to Title VII.)

A final possible advantage of the Equal Pay Act's remedial scheme may be reflected in the proviso to that Act's basic prohibition of wage discrimination. This proviso requires an employer who is paying unlawfully discriminatory wages to equalize them only by "topping up" the compensation of the lower paid group to the level of the higher paid group. By contrast, Title VII does not include a no-wage reduction clause.

2. TITLE VII AND COMPARABLE WORTH

According to the U.S. Department of Labor's Bureau of Labor Statistics, in 2013 women who usually worked full time had median weekly earnings of about 82% of the median weekly earnings of men.

There has been substantial improvement over the last 35 years, much of which occurred during the 1980s and early 1990s. One study attributes the trend in the 80s and 90s to increased female experience and education, a decline in unionization for males, and the fact that women are spending more time working outside the home than before. There has also been a shift in female representation in different occupational categories. For instance, managers and professionals were more likely to be women, while clerical and service workers were somewhat less likely to be female. See Francine D. Blau and Lawrence M. Kahn, Gender Differences in Pay, 14 J. of Econ. Persp. 75 (2000); Francine D. Blau, M. Ferber, and Anne E. Winkler, The Economics of Women, Men, and Work 237–39 (3d ed. 1998); Francine D. Blau and Lawrence M. Kahn, Swimming Upstream: Trends in the Gender Wage Differential in the 1980s, 15 J. of Lab. Econ. 1, 30–32 (1997).

A 2014 study concluded that the tendency of women to be concentrated in certain occupations and disparities in working hours are the two principal causes of the remaining pay gap in the twenty-first century. See Hadas Mandel and Moshe Semyonov, Gender Pay Gap and Employment Sector Sources of Earnings Disparities in the United states, 1970–2010, 51 Demography 1597 (2014); Asaf Levanon, Paula England, and Paul Allison, Occupational feminization and pay: assessing causal dynamics using 1960-2000 U.S. Census Data, 88 Social Forces 865 (2009) (longitudinal study finding a relative reduction in wage rates as female workers predominate in an occupation). Because the EPA proscribes only pay discrimination between jobs that are equal in skill, effort, and responsibility, it cannot remedy lower pay in predominantly female occupational categories.

Is there an approach available under Title VII to challenge employer decisions to pay more for jobs predominantly filled with males than for jobs of "comparable worth" predominantly filled with females, even though the two jobs could not be considered "equal" under EPA standards? This "comparable worth" approach has confronted significant legal hurdles.

COUNTY OF WASHINGTON V. GUNTHER
Supreme Court of the United States, 1981.
452 U.S. 161, 101 S.Ct. 2242, 68 L.Ed.2d 751.

JUSTICE BRENNAN delivered the opinion of the Court.

The question presented is whether § 703(h) of Title VII of the Civil Rights Act of 1964, 78 Stat. 257, 42 U.S.C. § 2000e–2(h), restricts Title VII's prohibition of sex-based wage discrimination to claims of equal pay for equal work.

I

This case arises over the payment by petitioner, County of Washington, Ore., of substantially lower wages to female guards in the female section of the county jail than it paid to male guards in the male section of the jail.[1] Respondents are four women who were employed to

---

[1] Prior to February 1, 1973, the female guards were paid between $476 and $606 per month, while the male guards were paid between $668 and $853. Effective February 1, 1973, the female

guard female prisoners and to carry out certain other functions in the jail.[2] In January 1974, the county eliminated the female section of the jail, transferred the female prisoners to the jail of a nearby county, and discharged respondents.

Respondents filed suit against petitioners in Federal District Court under Title VII, 42 U.S.C. § 2000e *et seq.,* seeking backpay and other relief.[3] They alleged that they were paid unequal wages for work substantially equal to that performed by male guards, and in the alternative, that part of the pay differential was attributable to intentional sex discrimination. The latter allegation was based on a claim that, because of intentional discrimination, the county set the pay scale for female guards, but not for male guards, at a level lower than that warranted by its own survey of outside markets and the worth of the jobs.

* * *

We emphasize at the outset the narrowness of the question before us in this case. Respondents' claim is not based on the controversial concept of "comparable worth," under which plaintiffs might claim increased compensation on the basis of a comparison of the intrinsic worth or difficulty of their job with that of other jobs in the same organization or community. Rather, respondents seek to prove, by direct evidence, that their wages were depressed because of intentional sex discrimination, consisting of setting the wage scale for female guards, but not for male guards, at a level lower than its own survey of outside markets and the worth of the jobs warranted. The narrow question in this case is whether such a claim is precluded by the last sentence of § 703(h) of Title VII, called the "Bennett Amendment."

II

* * * The Bennett Amendment to Title VII, however, provides:

"It shall not be an unlawful employment practice under this subchapter for any employer to differentiate upon the basis of sex in determining the amount of the wages or compensation paid or to be paid to employees of such employer if such differentiation is authorized by the provisions of section 206(d) of title 29." 42 U.S.C. § 2000e–2(h).

---

guards were paid between $525 and $668, while salaries for male guards ranged from $701 to $940.

  [2] Oregon requires that female inmates be guarded solely by women, Or.Rev.Stat. §§ 137.350, 137.360 (1979), and the District Court opinion indicates that women had not been employed to guard male prisoners. For purposes of this litigation, respondents concede that gender is a bona fide occupational qualification for some of the female guard positions. See 42 U.S.C. § 2000e–2(e)(1); *Dothard v. Rawlinson,* 433 U.S. 321, 97 S.Ct. 2720, 53 L.Ed.2d 786 (1977).

  [3] Respondents could not sue under the Equal Pay Act because the Equal Pay Act did not apply to municipal employees until passage of the Fair Labor Standards Amendments of 1974, 88 Stat. 55, 58–62. Title VII has applied to such employees since passage of the Equal Employment Opportunity Act of 1972, § 2(1), 86 Stat. 103.

To discover what practices are exempted from Title VII's prohibitions by the Bennett Amendment, we must turn to § 206(d)—the Equal Pay Act—which provides in relevant part:

> "No employer having employees subject to any provisions of this section shall discriminate, within any establishment in which such employees are employed, between employees on the basis of sex by paying wages to employees in such establishment at a rate less than the rate at which he pays wages to employees of the opposite sex in such establishment for equal work on jobs the performance of which requires equal skill, effort, and responsibility, and which are performed under similar working conditions, except where such payment is made pursuant to (i) a seniority system; (ii) a merit system; (iii) a system which measures earnings by quantity or quality of production; or (iv) a differential based on any other factor other than sex." 77 Stat. 56, 29 U.S.C. § 206(d)(1).

On its face, the Equal Pay Act contains three restrictions pertinent to this case. First, its coverage is limited to those employers subject to the Fair Labor Standards Act. S.Rep. No. 176, 88th Cong., 1st Sess., 2 (1963). Thus, the Act does not apply, for example, to certain businesses engaged in retail sales, fishing, agriculture, and newspaper publishing. See 29 U.S.C. §§ 203(s), 213(a) (1976 ed. and Supp. III). Second, the Act is restricted to cases involving "equal work on jobs the performance of which requires equal skill, effort, and responsibility, and which are performed under similar working conditions." 29 U.S.C. § 206(d)(1). Third, the Act's four affirmative defenses exempt any wage differentials attributable to seniority, merit, quantity or quality of production, or "any other factor other than sex." *Ibid.*

* * *

The language of the Bennett Amendment suggests an intention to incorporate only the affirmative defenses of the Equal Pay Act into Title VII. The Amendment bars sex-based wage discrimination claims under Title VII where the pay differential is "authorized" by the Equal Pay Act. Although the word "authorize" sometimes means simply "to permit," it ordinarily denotes affirmative enabling action. Black's Law Dictionary 122 (5th ed. 1979) defines "authorize" as "[t]o empower; to give a right or authority to act." Cf. 18 U.S.C. § 1905 (prohibiting the release by federal employees of certain information "to any extent not authorized by law"); 28 U.S.C. § 1343 (1976 ed., Supp. III) (granting district courts jurisdiction over "any civil action authorized by law"). The question, then, is what wage practices have been affirmatively authorized by the Equal Pay Act.

The Equal Pay Act is divided into two parts: a definition of the violation, followed by four affirmative defenses. The first part can hardly be said to "authorize" anything at all: it is purely prohibitory. The second part, however, in essence "authorizes" employers to differentiate in pay on the basis of seniority, merit, quantity or quality of production, or any other factor other than sex, even though such differentiation might otherwise violate the Act. It is to these provisions, therefore, that the Bennett Amendment must refer.

Petitioners argue that this construction of the Bennett Amendment would render it superfluous. Petitioners claim that the first three affirmative defenses are simply redundant of the provisions elsewhere in § 703(h) of Title VII that already exempt bona fide seniority and merit systems and systems measuring earnings by quantity or quality of production, and that the fourth defense—"any other factor other than sex"—is implicit in Title VII's general prohibition of sex-based discrimination.

We cannot agree. The Bennett Amendment was offered as a "technical amendment" designed to resolve any potential conflicts between Title VII and the Equal Pay Act. Thus, with respect to the first three defenses, the Bennett Amendment has the effect of guaranteeing that courts and administrative agencies adopt a consistent interpretation of like provisions in both statutes. Otherwise, they might develop inconsistent bodies of case law interpreting two sets of nearly identical language.

More importantly, incorporation of the fourth affirmative defense could have significant consequences for Title VII litigation. Title VII's prohibition of discriminatory employment practices was intended to be broadly inclusive, proscribing "not only overt discrimination but also practices that are fair in form, but discriminatory in operation." *Griggs v. Duke Power Co.,* 401 U.S. 424, 431, 91 S.Ct. 849, 853, 28 L.Ed.2d 158 (1971). The structure of Title VII litigation, including presumptions, burdens of proof, and defenses, has been designed to reflect this approach. The fourth affirmative defense of the Equal Pay Act, however, was designed differently, to confine the application of the Act to wage differentials attributable to sex discrimination. H.R.Rep. No. 309, 88th Cong., 1st Sess. 3 (1963), U.S.Code Cong. & Admin.News 1963, p. 687. Equal Pay Act litigation, therefore, has been structured to permit employers to defend against charges of discrimination where their pay differentials are based on a bona fide use of "other factors other than sex." Under the Equal Pay Act, the courts and administrative agencies are not permitted to "substitute their judgment for the judgment of the employer * * * who [has] established and applied a bona fide job rating system," so long as it does not discriminate on the basis of sex. 109 Cong.Rec. 9209 (1963) (statement of Rep. Goodell, principal exponent of the Act). Although we do not decide in this case how sex-based wage discrimination litigation under Title VII should be structured to accommodate the fourth affirmative defense of the Equal Pay Act, we consider it clear that the Bennett Amendment, under this interpretation, is not rendered superfluous.

* * *

Under petitioners' reading of the Bennett Amendment, only those sex-based wage discrimination claims that satisfy the "equal work" standard of the Equal Pay Act could be brought under Title VII. In practical terms, this means that a woman who is discriminatorily underpaid could obtain no relief—no matter how egregious the discrimination might be—unless her employer also employed a man in an equal job in the same establishment, at a higher rate of pay. Thus, if an employer hired a woman for a unique position in the company and then admitted that her salary would have been higher had she been male, the woman would be unable to obtain legal redress under petitioners' interpretation. Similarly, if an employer used a transparently sex-biased system for wage determination, women holding jobs not equal to those held by men would be denied the right to prove that the system is a pretext for discrimination. Moreover, to cite an example arising from a recent case, *Los Angeles, Dept. of Water & Power v. Manhart*, 435 U.S. 702, 98 S.Ct. 1370, 55 L.Ed.2d 657 (1978), if the employer required its female workers to pay more into its pension program than male workers were required to pay, the only women who could bring a Title VII action under petitioners' interpretation would be those who could establish that a man performed equal work: a female auditor thus might have a cause of action while a female secretary might not. Congress surely did not intend the Bennett Amendment to insulate such blatantly discriminatory practices from judicial redress under Title VII.[19]

Moreover, petitioners' interpretation would have other far-reaching consequences. Since it rests on the proposition that any wage differentials not prohibited by the Equal Pay Act are "authorized" by it, petitioners' interpretation would lead to the conclusion that discriminatory compensation by employers not covered by the Fair Labor Standards Act is "authorized"—since not prohibited—by the Equal Pay Act. Thus it would deny Title VII protection against sex-based wage discrimination by those employers not subject to the Fair Labor Standards Act but covered by Title VII. There is no persuasive evidence that Congress intended such a result, and the EEOC has rejected it since at least 1965. See 29 CFR § 1604.7.

* * *

III

Petitioners argue strenuously that the approach of the Court of Appeals places "the pay structure of virtually every employer and the

---

[19] The dissent attempts to minimize the significance of the Title VII remedy in these cases on the ground that the Equal Pay Act already provides an action for sex-biased wage discrimination by women who hold jobs not *currently* held by men. But the dissent's position would still leave remediless all victims of discrimination who hold jobs *never* held by men.

entire economy * * * at risk and subject to scrutiny by the federal courts." They raise the specter that "Title VII plaintiffs could draw any type of comparison imaginable concerning job duties and pay between any job predominantly performed by women and any job predominantly performed by men." But whatever the merit of petitioners' arguments in other contexts, they are inapplicable here, for claims based on the type of job comparisons petitioners describe are manifestly different from respondents' claim. Respondents contend that the County of Washington evaluated the worth of their jobs; that the county determined that they should be paid approximately 95% as much as the male correctional officers; that it paid them only about 70% as much, while paying the male officers the full evaluated worth of their jobs; and that the failure of the county to pay respondents the full evaluated worth of their jobs can be proved to be attributable to intentional sex discrimination. Thus, respondents' suit does not require a court to make its own subjective assessment of the value of the male and female guard jobs, or to attempt by statistical technique or other method to quantify the effect of sex discrimination on the wage rates.

We do not decide in this case the precise contours of lawsuits challenging sex discrimination in compensation under Title VII. It is sufficient to note that respondents' claims of discriminatory undercompensation are not barred by § 703(h) of Title VII merely because respondents do not perform work equal to that of male jail guards. The judgment of the Court of Appeals is therefore affirmed.

JUSTICE REHNQUIST, with whom THE CHIEF JUSTICE, JUSTICE STEWART, and JUSTICE POWELL join, dissenting. [omitted]

NOTES AND QUESTIONS

Test Your Understanding of the Material

1.   How did the *Gunther* Court account for the Bennett Amendment without rendering it superfluous?

2.   Suppose the plaintiffs in *Gunther* had asserted a disparate-impact claim. Are the affirmative defenses imported from the EPA easier or harder to prove than the business necessity defense to disparate impact claims? What does the Court suggest on this point?

3.   The EPA was not invoked in *Gunther* because the statute did not apply to state and local governments at the time. Had the statute applied, would the plaintiffs have a viable EPA case? Consider the district court's finding that male guards supervised more than ten times as many prisoners as did the female guards, but that the female guards performed clerical duties that the male guards did not.

Related Issues

4.   *What Proof of Discriminatory Intent Is Adequate in Job Comparison Cases?* Absent a facially discriminatory policy or inculpatory admission, how would plaintiffs in a case like *Gunther* go about proving that intentional sex discrimination was at work in a pay structure? *Gunther* involved a case where the jobs compared shared a substantial common core of duties. In such cases, where jobs are not sufficiently equal to establish a prima facie EPA case, some courts have adapted the *McDonnell Douglas-Burdine* methodology to accept a prima facie case based on unequal pay in "substantially similar" jobs and pretext proof directed at the employer's proffered explanation. See, e.g., Conti v. Universal Enterprises, Inc., 50 Fed.Appx. 690 (6th Cir.2002) (unpulished); Mulhall v. Advance Sec., Inc., 19 F.3d 586, 597–98 (11th Cir.1994) (also explaining that the "substantially similar" standard is somewhat more relaxed than the equality standard under the EPA). Proof of pretext under the *McDonnell Douglas* framework presumably would not be available in cases dependent on comparisons of entirely dissimilar jobs, however.

5.   *Who Has the Burden of Proof in Title VII Pay Discrimination Cases? Corning* confirms that a plaintiff can establish an EPA prima facie case without showing discriminatory intent. Under the EPA, the employer thus has the burden of proving a non-discriminatory motive through its factor other than sex defense. Does the same burden shifting apply to Title VII compensation cases? The EEOC has taken the position that it does. 29 C.F.R. § 1620.27. See also Korte v. Diemer, 909 F.2d 954, 959 (6th Cir. 1990); McKee v. Bi-State Dev. Agency, 801 F.2d 1014, 1019 (8th Cir.1986): Kouba v. Allstate Ins. Co., 691 F.2d 873 (9th Cir. 1982) (all agreeing with EEOC that EPA liability necessarily entails Title VII liability). Other Courts of Appeals, however, have held that plaintiffs must prove discriminatory intent to establish a Title VII case and thus can lose such a case even while being successful on a cognate EPA claim on which the defendant employer has not demonstrated an affirmative defense. See, e.g., Brinkley-Obu v. Hughes Training, Inc., 36 F.3d 336, 343–344 & n. 17 (4th Cir.1994); Meeks v. Computer Assocs. Intl., 15 F.3d 1013 (11th Cir.1994); Fallon v. Illinois, 882 F.2d 1206, 1217 (7th Cir.1989).

AMERICAN FEDERATION OF STATE, COUNTY, AND MUNICIPAL EMPLOYEES, AFL-CIO V. STATE OF WASHINGTON

United States Court of Appeals, Ninth Circuit, 1985.
770 F.2d 1401.

KENNEDY, J.

In this class action affecting approximately 15,500 of its employees, the State of Washington was sued in the United States District Court for the Western District of Washington. The class comprises state employees who have worked or do work in job categories that are or have been at least seventy percent female. The action was commenced for the class members by two unions, the American Federation of State, County, and Municipal Employees (AFSCME) and the Washington Federation of State Employees (WFSE). In all of the proceedings to date and in the opinion that follows, the plaintiffs are referred to as AFSCME. The district court found the State discriminated on the basis of sex in violation of Title VII of the Civil Rights Act of 1964, 42 U.S.C. § 2000e–2(a) (1982), by compensating employees in jobs where females predominate at lower rates than employees in jobs where males predominate, if these jobs, though dissimilar, were identified by certain studies to be of comparable worth. The State appeals. We conclude a violation of Title VII was not established here, and we reverse.

* * *

In 1974 the State commissioned a study by management consultant Norman Willis to determine whether a wage disparity existed between employees in jobs held predominantly by women and jobs held predominantly by men. The study examined sixty-two classifications in which at least seventy percent of the employees were women, and fifty-nine job classifications in which at least seventy percent of the employees were men. It found a wage disparity of about twenty percent, to the disadvantage of employees in jobs held mostly by women, for jobs considered of comparable worth. Comparable worth was calculated by evaluating jobs under four criteria: knowledge and skills, mental demands, accountability, and working conditions. A maximum number of points was allotted to each category: 280 for knowledge and skills, 140 for mental demands, 160 for accountability, and 20 for working conditions. Every job was assigned a numerical value under each of the four criteria. The State of Washington conducted similar studies in 1976 and 1980, and in 1983 the State enacted legislation providing for a compensation scheme based on comparable worth. The scheme is to take effect over a ten-year period. Act of June 15, 1983, ch. 75, 1983 Wash.Laws 1st Ex.Sess. 2071.

* * *

AFSCME alleges sex-based wage discrimination throughout the state system, but its explanation and proof of the violation is, in essence, Washington's failure as early as 1979 to adopt and implement at once a comparable worth compensation program. The trial court adopted this theory as well. The comparable worth theory, as developed in the case before us, postulates that sex-based wage discrimination exists if employees in job classifications occupied primarily by women are paid less than employees in job classifications filled primarily by men, if the jobs are of equal value to the employer, though otherwise dissimilar. We must determine whether comparable worth, as presented in this case, affords AFSCME a basis for recovery under Title VII.

* * *

The trial court erred in ruling that liability was established under a disparate impact analysis. The precedents do not permit the case to proceed upon that premise. AFSCME's disparate impact argument is based on the contention that the State of Washington's practice of taking prevailing market rates into account in setting wages has an adverse impact on women, who, historically, have received lower wages than men in the labor market. Disparate impact analysis is confined to cases that challenge a specific, clearly delineated employment practice applied at a single point in the job selection process. *Atonio v. Wards Cove Packing Co.,* 768 F.2d 1120, 1130 (9th Cir.1985); * * * . The instant case does not involve an employment practice that yields to disparate impact analysis. [T]he decision to base compensation on the competitive market, rather than on a theory of comparable worth, involves the assessment of a number of complex factors not easily ascertainable, an assessment too multifaceted to be appropriate for disparate impact analysis. In the case before us, the compensation system in question resulted from surveys, agency hearings, administrative recommendations, budget proposals, executive actions, and legislative enactments. A compensation system that is responsive to supply and demand and other market forces * * * does not constitute a single practice that suffices to support a claim under disparate impact theory. We consider next the allegations of disparate treatment. Under the disparate treatment theory, AFSCME was required to prove a prima facie case of sex discrimination by a preponderance of the evidence. * * * Our review of the record, however, indicates failure by AFSCME to establish the requisite element of intent by either circumstantial or direct evidence.

AFSCME contends discriminatory motive may be inferred from the Willis study, which finds the State's practice of setting salaries in reliance on market rates creates a sex-based wage disparity for jobs deemed of comparable worth. AFSCME argues from the study that the market reflects a historical pattern of lower wages to employees in positions staffed predominantly by women; and it contends the State of Washington perpetuates that disparity, in violation of Title VII, by using market rates in the compensation system. The inference of discriminatory motive which AFSCME seeks to draw from the State's participation in the market system fails, as the State did not create the market disparity and has not been shown to have been motivated by impermissible sex-based considerations in setting salaries.

NOTES AND QUESTIONS

Test Your Understanding of the Material

1.   Was the *AFSCME* court's acceptance of Washington's reliance on prevailing labor market rates consistent with *Corning*?

2.   Should the plaintiffs have been able to proceed with their disparate-impact claim? What would have been the likelihood of such a lawsuit being successful?

Related Issues

3.   *The Limitations of Comparable Worth Litigation.* Note that the comparable worth theory advanced by the plaintiffs in the *AFSCME* case could not be used to challenge pay disparities between the female dominated jobs of one employer and the male dominated jobs of another. Furthermore, the plaintiffs' case was dependent upon the State of Washington's comparable worth study evaluating variant jobs under ostensibly objective criteria. Few employers, especially in the private sector, attempt to set pay in this fashion, rather than through job market analysis. Not surprisingly, the comparable worth theory has not provided an effective litigation tool to narrow the pay gap. See generally Paul C. Weiler, The Wages of Sex: The Uses and Limits of Comparable Worth, 99 Harv. L. Rev. 1728 (1986).

4.   *Proposed Paycheck Fairness Act and California Fair Pay Act.* The proposed Paycheck Fairness Act, which passed the House of Representatives in January 2009 and has been reintroduced in similar form in several sessions of Congres, would amend the EPA to provide in effect a disparate-impact cause of action against pay disparities in equal jobs. The proposed law would, inter alia, limit a factor other than sex to "a bona fide factor, such as education, training, or experience," and would require the factor to be "job-related" and "consistent with business necessity" and not avoidable by "an alternative practice" that "would serve the same business purpose without producing" the same differential wage rate.

California has enacted a Fair Pay Act, effective January, 2016, that adopts the same defenses to pay disparities proposed in the federal Paycheck Fairness Act. See California Labor Code § 1197.5. The California legislation also takes a further step toward providing a comparable worth cause of action by expanding the jobs for which employers must justify pay disparities from those "in the same establishment" with "equal work" to jobs that are "substantially similar" regardless of location. Id.

5.   *Protecting Employee Communications Concerning Pay.* Some believe that women could better challenge pay disparities if their efforts to determine their relative pay were protected from discrimination. In April, 2014, President Obama signed Executive Order 13665, which amends Executive Order 11246 to require federal contractors to not discharge or discriminate against employees or applicants for employment because they have "inquired about, discussed, or disclosed" their own compensation or the compensation of another employee or applicant. Furthermore, the most recent version of the Paycheck Fairness Act, see Note 4 supra, would amend the Fair Labor Standards Act to protect from retaliation an employee who "has inquired about, discussed or disclosed the wages of the employee or another employee." The California Fair Pay Act includes a similar provision.

An employee's disclosure of his/her pay to other employees may also be protected by the National Labor Relations Act, 29 U.S.C. § 157. The NLRB has taken the position that discussions among employees about improving their pay qualify as protected "concerted activity" under Section 7 of the NLRA. See e.g. Flex Frac Logistics, LLC v. NLRB, 746 F.3d 205 (5th Cir. 2014) (employer policy that prohibited discussion of "personnel information outside the company" violated Section 7 rights to discuss "terms and conditions of employment, including wages"); NLRB v. Brookshire Grocery Co., 919 F.2d 359 (5th Cir. 1990) ("a workplace rule that forbade the discussion of confidential wage information between employees . . . patently violated" the NLRA).

6.   *Effect of Marriage and Family Responsibilities?* According to the Bureau of Labor Statisitcs, in 2010 the median wage of unmarried women working full time and without children was almost 94% of the median wage of unmarried men working full time and without children. What governmental or employer policies might lessen the impact of marriage and children on the male-female wage gap? Note the treatment of family leave legislation in Chapter 19 infra. See generally Jane Waldfogel, Understanding the "Family Gap" in Pay for Women with Children, 12 J. Econ. Persp. Winter 1998.

CHAPTER 7

SEXUAL ORIENTATION AND GENDER IDENTITY DISCRIMINATION

■ ■ ■

Introduction

Protection against employment discrimination on account of one's sexual orientation or gender identity is an emerging area. As of this writing, Title VII has not been interpreted by courts to prohibit such discrimination, except where it can be tied to a theory of gender discrimination based on stereotypes of male and female roles and styles. Such discrimination is increasingly the subject of legislation and civil rights litigation.

A. AN EMERGING AREA OF ANTIDISCRIMINATION LAW

Despite vigorous political efforts, Title VII's express categories of prohibited discrimination do not yet include sexual orientation or gender identity. Legislative proposals to ban sexual orientation discrimination by statue were first introduced in congress in the 1970s. In 1993, legislation containing the same language set forth in § 703(a)(1) and (2) was introduced to prohibit intentional discrimination in a bill titled The Employment Non-Discrimination Act (ENDA). Disparate impact claims were expressly excluded. ENDA was approved by the House of Representatives, but not the Senate, in 2007. H.R. 3685, 110th Cong., 1st Sess. In 2013, the Senate approved a revised version of ENDA that would prohibit discrimination because of gender identity as well as sexual orientation. S.185. 113th Cong., 1st Sess. This version, however, also included a broadly worded exemption from compliance by religiously affiliated organizations that caused proponents to withdraw support before any vote in the House of Representatives.

A substantial part of the gay and lesbian population nonetheless is protected from employment discrimination by express provisions in state and local statutes. Most major cities and twenty-two states provide protection against sexual orientation discrimination in private as well as public employment.[1] The District of Columbia and most major American

---

[1] California, Colorado, Connecticut, Delaware, Hawaii, Illinois, Iowa, Maine, Maryland, Massachusetts, Minnesota, Nevada, New Hampshire, New Jersey, New Mexico, New York, Oregon, Rhode Island, Utah, Vermont, Washington, and Wisconsin.

cities also have passed prohibitions against sexual orientation discrimination. Ten other states[2] through an executive or administrative order have prohibited sexual orientation discrimination in public employment.

Most of the states and cities that have enacted prohibitions of sexual orientation discrimination also prohibit gender identity discrimination in private and public employment.[3] Eight other states and the District of Columbia prohibit gender identity discrimination in public employment.

Furthermore, Presidents Clinton and Obama have issued executive orders to reduce sexual orientation and gender identity discrimination. In 1998, through Executive Order 13087, President Clinton added "sexual orientation" to the categories of discrimination forbidden in the federal civilian workforce under Executive Order 11478. On July 21, 2014, through Executive Order 13762, President Obama further amended Executive Order 11478 to add "gender identity" as an additional category of forbidden discrimination in federal employment, and also amended Executive Order 11246 to add both "sexual orientation" and "gender identity" to the list of bases of prohibited discrimination applicable to federal contractors. See pages 315–317 supra.

Finally, the EEOC in 2015 announced in a decision issued under its § 717 authority over the federal sector, that it would treat all allegations of discrimination on the basis of sexual orientation as allegations of illegal discrimination on the basis of sex under Title VII. See EEOC, Federal Sector Appellate Decision, Baldwin v. Department of Transportation, EEOC Appeal No. 0120133080, 2015 BL 229966 (July 15, 2015).

Individuals seeking protection against sexual orientation or gender identity employment discrimination by employers not reached by state or local law or by the Executive Order or the EEOC's ruling also may press claims under Title VII's prohibition of stereotype-based sex discrimination, or, for public sector workers, under the equal protection clause. The remainder of this chapter treats the bases for such claims.

PRACTITIONER'S PERSPECTIVE
Chai R. Feldblum
Commissioner, EEOC.

Enacting lasting social change requires a series of events and actors—advocates on the ground pushing for legislative change, the legislative

---

[2] Alaska, Arizona, Indiana, Kentucky, Michigan, Missouri, Montana, Ohio, Pennsylvania, and Virginia.

[3] California, Connecticut, Colorado, Delaware, Hawaii, Illinois, Iowa, Maine, Maryland, Massachusetts, Minnesota, Nevada, New Jersey, New Mexico, Oregon, Rhode Island, Utah, Vermont, and Washington.

change itself, advocates pushing for effective implementation of the law, the administrative and judicial implementation of the law, and normative change in the culture such that a vast majority of the public accepts the goals of the legislative change. This is not a linear set of events; there is a dialectical movement between them. Some level of cultural change is necessary before legislative change can occur and administrative implementation of law may shape the course advocates will take.

In my work, I have focused particularly on the rights of people with disabilities and LGBT people. As an advocate, I was the lead drafter and negotiator for the Americans with Disabilities Act in 1990 (ADA), working with a talented and tenacious group of advocates. I played the same role in 2008 during passage of the ADA Amendments Act (ADAAA) that restored the broad definition of "disability" under the law. I then became a Commissioner on the EEOC, the agency charged with implementing employment anti-discrimination laws, including the ADA.

In the area of LGBT rights, cultural change has been happening throughout my adult life, but federal legislative protection has not.

But something interesting happened. I call it: "A Funny Thing Happened on the Way to Non-Passage." An older law, passed in 1964, is now being applied to protect LGBT people. I feel fortunate to have been part of that effort, this time not as an advocate, but as a Commissioner.

I am talking, of course, about the prohibition on sex discrimination passed as part of Title VII of the Civil Rights Act of 1964. In the early 1970s, gay people and transgender people brought charges to the EEOC and the courts, claiming that they had been subjected to sex discrimination. Both the EEOC and the courts blew those claims out of the water on the grounds that sexual orientation and gender identity discrimination had nothing to do with sex discrimination.

When I came to the EEOC in 2010, however, it was time to take another look at the legal basis for those claims. From 2012 to 2015, the EEOC issued decisions holding that gender identity and sexual orientation discrimination are indeed forms of sex discrimination.[4] The agency's position has also rejuvenated efforts by advocates to bring cases in court for LGBT people using Title VII and some courts have begun to agree with those arguments. Sometimes one doesn't need a new law. Rather, one needs an existing law to be given its full due.

---

[4] See Mia Macy v. Eric Holder, Attorney General, Department of Justice, EEOC DOC 0120120821, 2012 WL 1435995 (Apr. 20, 2012); Baldwin v. Department of Transportation, EEOC Appeal No. 0120133080, 2015 BL 229966 (July 15, 2015).

B. TITLE VII PROHIBITION OF STEREOTYPE-BASED SEX DISCRIMINATION

PRICE WATERHOUSE V. HOPKINS

Supreme Court of the United States, 1989.
490 U.S. 228, 109 S.Ct. 1775, 104 L.Ed.2d 268.

JUSTICE BRENNAN announced the judgment of the Court and delivered an opinion, in which JUSTICE MARSHALL, JUSTICE BLACKMUN, and JUSTICE STEVENS join.

* * *

Ann Hopkins had worked at Price Waterhouse's Office of Government Services in Washington, D.C., for five years when the partners in that office proposed her as a candidate for partnership. Of the 662 partners at the firm at that time, 7 were women. Of the 88 persons proposed for partnership that year, only 1—Hopkins—was a woman. Forty-seven of these candidates were admitted to the partnership, 21 were rejected, and 20—including Hopkins—were "held" for reconsideration the following year. Thirteen of the 32 partners who had submitted comments on Hopkins supported her bid for partnership. Three partners recommended that her candidacy be placed on hold, eight stated that they did not have an informed opinion about her, and eight recommended that she be denied partnership.

In a jointly prepared statement supporting her candidacy, the partners in Hopkins' office showcased her successful 2-year effort to secure a $25 million contract with the Department of State, labeling it "an outstanding performance" and one that Hopkins carried out "virtually at the partner level." Despite Price Waterhouse's attempt at trial to minimize her contribution to this project, Judge Gesell specifically found that Hopkins had "played a key role in Price Waterhouse's successful effort to win a multi-million dollar contract with the Department of State." Indeed, he went on, "[n]one of the other partnership candidates at Price Waterhouse that year had a comparable record in terms of successfully securing major contracts for the partnership."

The partners in Hopkins' office praised her character as well as her accomplishments, describing her in their joint statement as "an outstanding professional" who had a "deft touch," a "strong character, independence and integrity." Clients appear to have agreed with these assessments. At trial, one official from the State Department described her as "extremely competent, intelligent," "strong and forthright, very productive, energetic and creative." Another high-ranking official praised Hopkins' decisiveness, broadmindedness, and "intellectual clarity"; she was, in his words, "a stimulating conversationalist." Evaluations such as these led Judge Gesell to conclude that Hopkins "had no difficulty dealing with clients and her clients appear to have been very pleased with her work" and that she "was generally viewed as a highly competent project leader who worked long hours, pushed vigorously to meet deadlines and demanded much from the multidisciplinary staffs with which she worked."

On too many occasions, however, Hopkins' aggressiveness apparently spilled over into abrasiveness. Staff members seem to have borne the brunt of Hopkins' brusqueness. Long before her bid for partnership, partners evaluating her work had counseled her to improve her relations with staff members. Although later evaluations indicate an improvement, Hopkins' perceived shortcomings in this important area eventually doomed her bid for partnership. Virtually all of the partners' negative remarks about Hopkins—even those of partners supporting her—had to do with her "interpersonal skills." Both "[s]upporters and opponents of her candidacy," stressed Judge Gesell, "indicated that she was sometimes overly aggressive, unduly harsh, difficult to work with and impatient with staff."

There were clear signs, though, that some of the partners reacted negatively to Hopkins' personality because she was a woman. One partner described her as "macho"; another suggested that she "overcompensated for being a woman"; a third advised her to take "a course at charm school." Several partners criticized her use of profanity; in response, one partner suggested that those partners objected to her swearing only "because it[']s a lady using foul language." Another supporter explained that Hopkins "ha[d] matured from a tough-talking somewhat masculine hardnosed mgr to an authoritative, formidable, but much more appealing lady ptr candidate." But it was the man who, as Judge Gesell found, bore responsibility for explaining to Hopkins the reasons for the Policy Board's decision to place her candidacy on hold who delivered the *coup de grace:* in order to improve her chances for partnership, Thomas Beyer advised, Hopkins should "walk more femininely, talk more femininely, dress more femininely, wear make-up, have her hair styled, and wear jewelry."

* * *

Judge Gesell found that Price Waterhouse legitimately emphasized interpersonal skills in its partnership decisions, and also found that the firm had not fabricated its complaints about Hopkins' interpersonal skills as a pretext for discrimination. Moreover, he concluded, the firm did not give decisive emphasis to such traits only because Hopkins was a woman; although there were male candidates who lacked these skills but who were admitted to partnership, the judge found that these candidates possessed other, positive traits that Hopkins lacked.

The judge went on to decide, however, that some of the partners' remarks about Hopkins stemmed from an impermissibly cabined view of the proper behavior of women, and that Price Waterhouse had done nothing to disavow reliance on such comments. He held that Price

Waterhouse had unlawfully discriminated against Hopkins on the basis of sex by consciously giving credence and effect to partners' comments that resulted from sex stereotyping. Noting that Price Waterhouse could avoid equitable relief by proving by clear and convincing evidence that it would have placed Hopkins' candidacy on hold even absent this discrimination, the judge decided that the firm had not carried this heavy burden.

The Court of Appeals affirmed the District Court's ultimate conclusion, but departed from its analysis in one particular: it held that even if a plaintiff proves that discrimination played a role in an employment decision, the defendant will not be found liable if it proves, by clear and convincing evidence, that it would have made the same decision in the absence of discrimination. * * *

[*Eds*. The plurality's treatment of the causation issue, see Desert Palace, Inc. v. Costa, 539 U.S. 90, 123 S.Ct. 2148, 156 L.Ed.2d 84 (2003), pp. 126–131 supra, is omitted here.]

In saying that gender played a motivating part in an employment decision, we mean that, if we asked the employer at the moment of the decision what its reasons were and if we received a truthful response, one of those reasons would be that the applicant or employee was a woman. In the specific context of sex stereotyping, an employer who acts on the basis of a belief that a woman cannot be aggressive, or that she must not be, has acted on the basis of gender. * * * An employer who objects to aggressiveness in women but whose positions require this trait places women in an intolerable and impermissible Catch-22: out of a job if they behave aggressively and out of a job if they don't. Title VII lifts women out of this bind.

Remarks at work that are based on sex stereotypes do not inevitably prove that gender played a part in a particular employment decision. The plaintiff must show that the employer actually relied on her gender in making its decision. In making this showing, stereotyped remarks can certainly be *evidence* that gender played a part. In any event, the stereotyping in this case did not simply consist of stray remarks. On the contrary, Hopkins proved that Price Waterhouse invited partners to submit comments; that some of the comments stemmed from sex stereotypes; that an important part of the Policy Board's decision on Hopkins was an assessment of the submitted comments; and that Price Waterhouse in no way disclaimed reliance on the sex-linked evaluation. This is not, as Price Waterhouse suggests, "discrimination in the air"; rather, it is, as Hopkins puts it, "discrimination brought to ground and visited upon" an employee. By focusing on Hopkins' specific proof, however, we do not suggest a limitation on the possible ways of proving that stereotyping played a motivating role in an employment decision, and we refrain from deciding here which specific facts, "standing alone," would or would not establish a plaintiff's case, since such a decision is unnecessary in this case. * * *

The District Court found that sex stereotyping "was permitted to play a part" in the evaluation of Hopkins as a candidate for partnership. Price Waterhouse disputes both that stereotyping occurred and that it played any part in the decision to place Hopkins' candidacy on hold. In the firm's view, in other words, the District Court's factual conclusions are clearly erroneous. We do not agree. * * * It takes no special training to discern sex stereotyping in a description of an aggressive female employee as requiring "a course at charm school." Nor, turning to Thomas Beyer's memorable advice to Hopkins, does it require expertise in psychology to know that, if an employee's flawed "interpersonal skills" can be corrected by a soft-hued suit or a new shade of lipstick, perhaps it is the employee's sex and not her interpersonal skills that has drawn the criticism.

* * *

Nor is the finding that sex stereotyping played a part in the Policy Board's decision undermined by the fact that many of the suspect comments were made by supporters rather than detractors of Hopkins. A negative comment, even when made in the context of a generally favorable review, nevertheless may influence the decisionmaker to think less highly of the candidate; the Policy Board, in fact, did not simply tally the "yes's" and "no's" regarding a candidate, but carefully reviewed the content of the submitted comments. The additional suggestion that the comments were made by "persons outside the decisionmaking chain"—and therefore could not have harmed Hopkins—simply ignores the critical role that partners' comments played in the Policy Board's partnership decisions.

* * * It is not our job to review the evidence and decide that the negative reactions to Hopkins were based on reality; our perception of Hopkins' character is irrelevant. We sit not to determine whether Ms. Hopkins is nice, but to decide whether the partners reacted negatively to her personality because she is a woman.

JUSTICE KENNEDY, with whom the CHIEF JUSTICE and JUSTICE SCALIA join, dissenting.

Although the District Court's version of Title VII liability is improper under any of today's opinions, I think it important to stress that Title VII creates no independent cause of action for sex stereotyping. Evidence of use by decisionmakers of sex stereotypes is, of course, quite relevant to the question of discriminatory intent. The ultimate question, however, is whether discrimination caused the plaintiff's harm. Our cases do not support the suggestion that failure to "disclaim reliance" on stereotypical comments itself violates Title VII. Neither do they support creation of a "duty to sensitize." As the dissenting judge in the Court of Appeals observed, acceptance of such theories would turn Title VII "from a prohibition of discriminatory conduct into an engine for rooting out sexist thoughts."

NOTES AND QUESTIONS

Test Your Understanding of the Material

1.   *Predictive vs. Normative Stereotypes.* Justice Brennan's plurality opinion states that "an employer who acts on the basis of a belief that a woman cannot be aggressive, or that she must not be, has acted on the basis of gender." What type of stereotype did the trial judge find to have influenced the Price Waterhouse partners: a predictive stereotype ("women are not likely to be sufficiently aggressive") or a normative stereotype ("women should not conduct themselves in an aggressive manner")?

2.   Justice Kennedy's dissent asserts that a stereotype must be proven to have caused an adverse decision. What evidence was there that the sex stereotyping caused the employer's decision in this case?

3.   Apply the mixed-motive standard of causation to the facts of *Price Waterhouse.* See *Desert Palace v. Costa, supra* at 126. Did Hopkins satisfy the "motivating factor" standard? Would Price Waterhouse be able to prove the "same decision" affirmative defense? What would be remedial consequences of proving that defense?

Related Issues

4.   *Grooming Codes.* Many employers either expressly or in practice require employees to conform to different standards of grooming for men and women. Most of the standards, such as hair length for men and dresses for women, conform to general social standards for male and female appearance. The courts have held after *Price Waterhouse* that general grooming codes do not violate Title VII as long as they impose roughly the same aggregate burden on women and men. See, e.g., Jespersen v. Harrah's Operating Co., 444 F.3d 1104 (9th Cir. 2006) (en banc) (requiring only female bartenders to wear makeup not actionable where plaintiff did not present evidence that policy was "more burdensome for women than for men" or required her "to conform to a stereotypical image that would objectively impede her ability to perform her job"); Frank v. United Airlines, Inc., 216 F.3d 845 (9th Cir. 2000); Harper v. Blockbuster Entertainment Corp., 139 F.3d 1385 (11th Cir. 1998); Tavora v. New York Mercantile Exchange, 101 F.3d 907, 908 (2d Cir.1996). But cf. Lewis v. Heartland Inns of Am., LLC, 591 F.3d 1033 (8th Cir. 2010) (finding actionable discharge of desk clerk after company executive complained she did not conform to "Midwestern girl look"). Do grooming standards that are even equally burdensome on men and women perpetuate stereotypes that may impede the economic advancement of women? See generally Karl E. Klare, Power/Dressing: Regulation of Employee Appearance, 26 New Eng. L. Rev. 1395 (1992).

5.   *Different Weight or Height Standards. Dothard v. Rawlinson*, supra page 204, held that an employer cannot impose the same height and weight

requirements on men and women if those requirements have a disparate impact on women that cannot be justified as a business necessity. Can an employer, such as an airline, impose different height or body size standards on women and men if the standards place comparable burdens on members of each sex? In Frank v. United Airlines, Inc., 216 F.3d 845, 855 (9th Cir.2000), the court held that an airline "may not impose different *and more burdensome* weight standards" on female flight attendants "without justifying those standards as BFOQs." (Emphasis in original) United had chosen weight maximums for women that generally corresponded to the medium frame category in life insurance tables, while choosing maximums for men that corresponded with the large frame category. The court did not decide whether United could have used large frame standards for both men and women. See also Gerdom v. Continental Airlines, 692 F.2d 602 (9th Cir.1982) (illegal to have weight requirement only for women); Laffey v. Northwest Airlines, Inc., 567 F.2d 429 (D.C.Cir.1976) (upholding injunction against discriminatory weight differential).

6. *Sexual Orientation and Gender Identity Discrimination as Sex-Based Stereotyping.* The lower courts have not read *Price Waterhouse* to reach sexual orientation or gender identity discrimination as sex discrimination under Title VII, see, e.g., Vickers v. Fairfield Med. Ctr., 453 F.3d 757 (6th Cir. 2006); Dawson v. Bumble & Bumble, 398 F.3d 211 (2d Cir. 2005); Higgins v. New Balance Athletic Shoe, Inc., 194 F.3d 252 (1st Cir. 1999).

One challenge in treating sexual orientation discrimination as a form of disparate treatment on the basis of sex is that such discrimination, at least as a formal matter, treats men and women the same (it expects women to be sexually oriented to men, and men to be sexually oriented to women). However, such formal equality was also true of discrimination against individuals in interracial relationships, which has been held to violate Title VII as race discrimination. See, e.g., Holcomb v. Iona College, 521 F.3d 130 (2d Cir. 2008) ("an employer may violate Title VII if it takes action against an employee because of the employee's association with a person of another race," including because of interracial marriage); Deffenbaugh-Williams v. Wal-Mart Stores, Inc., 156 F.3d 581, 589 (5th Cir.1998) (a "reasonable juror could find that [the plaintiff] was discriminated against because of her race (white), if that discrimination was premised on the fact that she, a white person, had a relationship with a black person").

Consider the reasoning set forth in Parr v. Woodmen of the World Life Ins. Co., 791 F.2d 888, 891–92 (11th Cir.1986):

> Woodmen contends that Parr cannot state a claim based upon discrimination due to an interracial relationship because he also claimed that Woodmen discriminated against blacks. Woodmen argues that if Parr's allegations are true, had Parr been black, he still would not have been hired. Consequently, in Woodmen's view, Parr's race was of no significance in the hiring decision, and thus his claim should not be cognizable. Woodmen's contentions are not persuasive. Had Parr been black, he would not have been hired, but that is a

lawsuit for another day. Parr alleged that he was discriminated against because of his interracial marriage. Title VII proscribes race-conscious discriminatory practices. It would be folly for this court to hold that a plaintiff cannot state a claim under Title VII for discrimination based on an interracial marriage because, had the plaintiff been a member of the spouse's race, the plaintiff would still not have been hired. 791 F.22d at 892.

See also EEOC, Federal Sector Appellate Decision, Complainant v. Department of Transportation, EEOC Appeal No. 0120133080, EEOC DOC 0120133080, 2015 BL 229966 (July 15, 2015) (treating sexual orientation discrimination as sex discrimination for the same reason that discrimination against interracial relationships is discrimination on the basis of sex).

Several courts of appeals have interpreted *Price Waterhouse* to proscribe discriminatory harassment of employees that is caused not by the victim's sexual orientation, but rather by the perception of the victim's general behavior as more closely fitting stereotypes of homosexuals or of members of the opposite sex rather than the stereotypes of heterosexuals of their sex. Compare, e.g., EEOC v. Boh Bros. Constr. Co., LLC, 731 F.3d 444, 457 (5th Cir. 2013) (case for the jury where the "EEOC offered evidence that . . . the crew superintendent thought that [plaintiff] was not a manly-enough man and taunted him tirelessly" and "admitted that epithets were directed at [plaintiff's] masculinity"); Nichols v. Azteca Restaurant Enterprises, Inc., 256 F.3d 864, 875 (9th Cir.2001) ("Sanchez was attacked for walking and carrying his tray "like a woman"—i.e. for having feminine mannerisms. . . . And the most vulgar name-calling directed at Sanchez was cast in feminine terms."), with Bibby v. Philadelphia Coca Cola Bottling Co., 260 F.3d 257, 264 (3d Cir. 2001) ("There was no allegation that . . . [plaintiff] was harassed because he failed to comply with societal stereotypes of how men ought to appear or behave." Plaintiff's "claim was, pure and simple, that he was discriminated against because of his sexual orientation."); Spearman v. Ford Motor Co., 231 F.3d 1080, 1085 (7th Cir. 2000) (finding that gay male automobile worker was subjected to harassment by fellow employees because of sexual orientation, not because "co-workers perceived him to be too feminine to fit the male image").

PROWEL V. WISE BUSINESS FORMS, INC.

United States Court of Appeals, Third Circuit, 2009.
579 F.3d 285.

HARDIMAN, J.

Brian Prowel appeals the District Court's summary judgment in favor of his former employer, Wise Business Forms, Inc. Prowel sued under Title VII of the Civil Rights Act of 1964 and the Pennsylvania Human Relations Act, alleging that Wise harassed and retaliated against him because of sex. . . . The principal issue on appeal is whether Prowel has marshaled sufficient facts for his claim of "gender stereotyping" discrimination to be submitted to a jury. * * *

Prowel began working for Wise in July 1991. A producer and distributor of business forms, Wise employed approximately 145 workers at its facility in Butler, Pennsylvania. From 1997 until his termination, Prowel operated a machine called a nale encoder, which encodes numbers and organizes business forms. On December 13, 2004, after 13 years with the company, Wise informed Prowel that it was laying him off for lack of work.

Prowel's most substantial claim is that Wise harassed and retaliated against him because of sex. The theory of sex discrimination Prowel advances is known as a "gender stereotyping" claim, which was first recognized by the Supreme Court as a viable cause of action in *Price Waterhouse v. Hopkins,* 490 U.S. 228, 109 S.Ct. 1775, 104 L.Ed.2d 268 (1989).

Prowel identifies himself as an effeminate man and believes that his mannerisms caused him not to "fit in" with the other men at Wise. Prowel described the "genuine stereotypical male" at the plant as follows:

[B]lue jeans, t-shirt, blue collar worker, very rough around the edges. Most of the guys there hunted. Most of the guys there fished. If they drank, they drank beer, they didn't drink gin and tonic. Just you know, all into football, sports, all that kind of stuff, everything I wasn't.

In stark contrast to the other men at Wise, Prowel testified that he had a high voice and did not curse; was very well-groomed; wore what others would consider dressy clothes; was neat; filed his nails instead of ripping them off with a utility knife; crossed his legs and had a tendency to shake his foot "the way a woman would sit"; walked and carried himself in an effeminate manner; drove a clean car; had a rainbow decal on the trunk of his car; talked about things like art, music, interior design, and decor; and pushed the buttons on the nale encoder with "pizzazz."

Some of Prowel's co-workers reacted negatively to his demeanor and appearance. During the last two years of his employment at Wise, a female co-worker frequently called Prowel "Princess." In a similar vein, co-workers made comments such as: "Did you see what Rosebud was wearing?"; "Did you see Rosebud sitting there with his legs crossed, filing his nails?"; and "Look at the way he walks."

Prowel also testified that he is homosexual. At some point prior to November 1997, Prowel was "outed" at work when a newspaper clipping of a "man-seeking-man" ad was left at his workstation with a note that read: "Why don't you give him a call, big boy." Prowel reported the incident to two management-level personnel and asked that something be done. The culprit was never identified, however.

After Prowel was outed, some of his co-workers began causing problems for him, subjecting him to verbal and written attacks during the last seven years of his tenure at Wise. In addition to the nicknames "Princess" and "Rosebud," a female co-worker called him "fag" and said: "Listen, faggot, I don't have to put up with this from you." Prowel reported this to his shift supervisor but received no response.

At some point during the last two years of Prowel's employment, a pink, light-up, feather tiara with a package of lubricant jelly was left on his nale encoder. The items were removed after Prowel complained to Henry Nolan, the shift supervisor at that time. On March 24, 2004, as Prowel entered the plant, he overheard a co-worker state: "I hate him. They should shoot all the fags." Prowel reported this remark to Nolan, who said he would look into it. Prowel also overheard conversations between co-workers, one of whom was a supervisor, who disapproved of how he lived his life. Finally, messages began to appear on the wall of the men's bathroom, claiming Prowel had AIDS and engaged in sexual relations with male co-workers. After Prowel complained, the company repainted the restroom. * * *

Prowel alleges that his co-workers shunned him and his work environment became so stressful that he had to stop his car on the way to work to vomit. At some point in 2004, Prowel became increasingly dissatisfied with his work assignments and pay. Prowel believed he was asked to perform more varied tasks than other nale encoder operators, but was not compensated fairly for these extra tasks, even though work piled up on his nale encoder.

In April 2004, Prowel considered suing Wise and stated his intentions to four non-management personnel, asking them to testify on his behalf. Prowel allegedly told his colleagues that the lawsuit would be based on harassment for not "fitting in"; he did not say anything about being harassed because of his homosexuality. These four colleagues complained to management that Prowel was bothering them.

On May 6, 2004, General Manager Jeff Straub convened a meeting with Prowel and supervisors Nolan and John Hodak to discuss Prowel's concern that he was doing more work for less money than other nale encoder operators. Prowel's compensation and workload were discussed, but the parties did not reach agreement on those issues. Straub then asked Prowel if he had approached employees to testify for him in a lawsuit, and Prowel replied that he had not done so. Prowel has since conceded that he did approach other employees in this regard.

On December 13, 2004, Prowel was summoned to meet with his supervisors, who informed him that he was terminated effective immediately for lack of work. * * *

After exhausting his administrative remedies before the Equal Employment Opportunity Commission, Prowel sued Wise in the United States District Court for the Western District of Pennsylvania, alleging claims under Title VII of the Civil Rights Act of 1964, 42 U.S.C. § 2000e, *et seq.*, and the Pennsylvania Human Relations Act, 43 Pa. Cons.Stat. § 951, *et seq.* (PHRA). * * * Following discovery, Wise moved for summary judgment and the District Court granted the company's motion in its entirety. As relevant to this appeal, the District Court held that Prowel's suit was merely a claim for sexual orientation discrimination—which is not cognizable under Title VII—that he repackaged as a gender stereotyping claim in an attempt to avoid summary judgment. * * *

In evaluating Wise's motion for summary judgment, the District Court properly focused on our decision in *Bibby v. Philadelphia Coca Cola Bottling Co.*, 260 F.3d 257 (3d Cir.2001), wherein we stated: "Title VII does not prohibit discrimination based on sexual orientation. * * * As the District Court noted, "once a plaintiff shows that harassment is motivated by sex, it is no defense that it may also have been motivated by anti-gay animus." ... In sum, "[w]hatever the sexual orientation of a plaintiff bringing a same-sex sexual harassment claim, that plaintiff is required to demonstrate that the harassment was directed at him or her because of his or her sex." *Bibby*, 260 F.3d at 265.

Both Prowel and Wise rely heavily upon *Bibby*. Wise claims this appeal is indistinguishable from *Bibby* and therefore we should affirm its summary judgment for the same reason we affirmed summary judgment in *Bibby*. Prowel counters that reversal is required here because gender stereotyping was not at issue in *Bibby*. As we shall explain, *Bibby* does not dictate the result in this appeal. Because it guides our analysis, however, we shall review it in some detail.

John Bibby, a homosexual man, was a long-time employee of the Philadelphia Coca Cola Bottling Company. [260 F.3d] at 259. The company terminated Bibby after he sought sick leave, but ultimately reinstated him. *Id.* After Bibby's reinstatement, he alleged that he was assaulted and harmed by co-workers and supervisors when he was subjected to crude remarks and derogatory sexual graffiti in the bathrooms. *Id.* at 260. * * *

On appeal, this Court [held] that Bibby presented insufficient evidence to support a claim of same-sex harassment under Title VII. Despite acknowledging that harassment based on sexual orientation has no place in a just society, we explained that Congress chose not to include sexual orientation harassment in Title VII. *Id.* at 261, 265. Nevertheless, we stated that employees may—consistent with the Supreme Court's decision in *Price Waterhouse*—raise a Title VII *gender stereotyping* claim, provided they can demonstrate that "the[ir] harasser was acting to punish [their] noncompliance with gender stereotypes." *Id.* at 264; *accord Vickers v. Fairfield Med. Ctr.*, 453 F.3d 757, 762 (6th Cir.2006); *Nichols v. Azteca Rest. Enters., Inc.*, 256 F.3d 864, 874 (9th Cir.2001); *Higgins v. New Balance Athletic Shoe, Inc.*, 194 F.3d 252, 259 (1st Cir.1999). Because Bibby did not claim gender stereotyping, however, he could not prevail on that theory.

We also concluded, in dicta, that even had we construed Bibby's claim to involve gender stereotyping, he did not marshal sufficient evidence to withstand summary judgment on that claim. *Bibby,* 260 F.3d at 264–65.

In light of the foregoing discussion, we disagree with both parties' arguments that *Bibby* dictates the outcome of this case. *Bibby* does not carry the day for Wise because in that case, the plaintiff failed to raise a gender stereotyping claim as Prowel has done here. * * *

The record demonstrates that Prowel has adduced evidence of harassment based on gender stereotypes. He acknowledged that he has a high voice and walks in an effeminate manner. In contrast with the typical male at Wise, Prowel testified that he: did not curse and was very well-groomed; filed his nails instead of ripping them off with a utility knife; crossed his legs and had a tendency to shake his foot "the way a woman would sit." Prowel also discussed things like art, music, interior design, and decor, and pushed the buttons on his nale encoder with "pizzazz." Prowel's effeminate traits did not go unnoticed by his co-workers, who commented: "Did you see what Rosebud was wearing?"; "Did you see Rosebud sitting there with his legs crossed, filing his nails?"; and "Look at the way he walks." Finally, a co-worker deposited a feathered, pink tiara at Prowel's workstation. When the aforementioned facts are considered in the light most favorable to Prowel, they constitute sufficient evidence of gender stereotyping harassment-namely, Prowel was harassed because he did not conform to Wise's vision of how a man should look, speak, and act-rather than harassment based solely on his sexual orientation.

To be sure, the District Court correctly noted that the record is replete with evidence of harassment motivated by Prowel's sexual orientation. Thus, it is possible that the harassment Prowel alleges was because of his sexual orientation, not his effeminacy. Nevertheless, this does not vitiate the possibility that Prowel was also harassed for his failure to conform to gender stereotypes. *See* 42 U.S.C. § 2000e–2(m) ("[A]n unlawful employment practice is established when the complaining party demonstrates that . . . sex . . . was a motivating factor for any employment practice, even though other factors also motivated the practice."). Because both scenarios are plausible, the case presents a question of fact for the jury and is not appropriate for summary judgment.

* * * Wise cannot persuasively argue that *because* Prowel is homosexual, he is precluded from bringing a gender stereotyping claim. There is no basis in the statutory or case law to support the notion that an effeminate *heterosexual* man can bring a gender stereotyping claim while an effeminate *homosexual* man may not. As long as the employee-regardless of his or her sexual orientation-marshals sufficient evidence such that a reasonable jury could conclude that harassment or discrimination occurred "because of sex," the case is not appropriate for

summary judgment. For the reasons we have articulated, Prowel has adduced sufficient evidence to submit this claim to a jury.

NOTES AND QUESTIONS

Test Your Understanding of the Material

1.   What is the basis for the court's interpretation of Title VII to prohibit harassment of Prowel based on "effeminacy" but not harassment based on sexual orientation? Does the text or purpose of Title VII, as developed in Supreme Court decisions, support the drawing of a line protecting the former but not the latter?

2.   *Relevance of 703(m)?* Note the court's citation of the "motivating" causation standard, as confirmed in *Desert Palace*, page 126 supra, for Title VII discrimination claims. Based on the facts as presented in the opinion, is it likely that Prowel would have suffered the same level of severe and pervasive harassment but for his being perceived as effeminate?

Related Issues

3.   *Gender Identity Discrimination Cases.* The lower courts also have recognized stereotype-based sex discrimination in Title VII cases brought by transgender individuals. For instance, in Smith v. Salem, 378 F.3d 566 (6th Cir. 2004) (rehearing en banc denied), the court held actionable a fire department's suspension of a biologically male employee with a female gender identity because of the employee's feminine appearance and mannerisms:

> After *Price Waterhouse*, an employer who discriminates against women because, for instance, they do not wear dresses or makeup, is engaging in sex discrimination because the discrimination would not occur but for the victim's sex. It follows that employers who discriminate against men because they *do* wear dresses and makeup, or otherwise act femininely, are also engaging in sex discrimination, because the discrimination would not occur but for the victim's sex. . . . [D]iscrimination against a plaintiff who is a transsexual—and therefore fails to act and/or identify with his or her gender—is no different from the discrimination directed against Ann Hopkins in *Price Waterhouse*, who, in sex-stereotypical terms, did not act like a woman. Sex stereotyping based on a person's gender non-conforming behavior is impermissible discrimination, irrespective of the cause of that behavior; a label, such as "transsexual," is not fatal to a sex discrimination claim where the victim has suffered discrimination because of his or her gender non-conformity.

Id. at 574–75. Accord, Barnes v. City of Cincinnati, 401 F.3d 729 (6th Cir. 2005) (transgendered police officer had Title VII cause of action for being demoted because lack of conformity to male norms, including dressing like a female outside of work).

However, some courts have ruled that Title VII does not cover discrimination against a transgender individual's status rather than the individual's nonconforming behavior. See, e.g., Etsitty v. Utah Transit Auth., 502 F.3d 1215, 1222 (10th Cir. 2007) ("discrimination against a transsexual because she is a transsexual is not discrimination because of sex"); Ulane v. Eastern Airlines, 742 F.2d 1081, 1087 (7th Cir.1984) ("if the term 'sex' as it is used in Title VII is to mean more than biological male or biological female, the new definition must come from Congress"); but cf. Schroer v. Billington, 577 F.Supp.2d 293, 307 (D.D.C. 2008) (discrimination because of sex also includes discrimination because of a change in sex); Enriquez v. W. Jersey Health Sys., 342 N.J. Super. 501, 515–16, 777 A.2d 365, 373 (Super. Ct. App. Div. 2001) (interpreting New Jersey Law Against Discrimination); Maffei v. Kolaeton Industry, Inc., 164 Misc.2d 547, 626 N.Y.S.2d 391 (1995) (interpreting Administrative Code of City of New York).

The EEOC has rejected the distinction between allowable discrimination on the basis of status and illegal discrimination on the basis of nonconforming behavior for transgender complainants. In an administrative decision rendered under its § 717 authority over federal employment, Macy v. Holder, 2012 WL 1435995 (April 20, 2012), the Commission held that a federal agency's reversal of a decision to hire an employment applicant because the applicant was in the process of transitioning from male to female would be a form of sex discrimination regardless of whether the decision maker "was engaging in gender stereotyping." The Commission explained that if the agency's director "was willing to hire her when he thought she was a man, but was not willing to hire her once he found out that she was now a woman—she will have proven that the Director discriminated on the basis of sex." Id.

C. CONSTITUTIONAL PROTECTION FOR PUBLIC SECTOR EMPLOYEES

NOTE: EQUAL PROTECTION SCRUTINY OF SEXUAL ORIENTATION AND GENDER IDENTITY DISCRIMINATION

The Supreme Court has never held directly that some level of heightened scrutiny should be given to governmental classifications based on sexual orientation or gender identity. In Obergefell v. Hodges, 576 U.S. ___, 135 S. Ct. 2584, 192 L.Ed.2d 609 (2015), the Court held that a state's denial to same-sex couples of the "fundamental right" to marry violated the equal protection clause as well as the due process clause of the Fourteenth Amendment. "The imposition of this disability on gays and lesbians serves to disrespect and subordinate them. And the Equal Protection clause, like the Due Process Clause, prohibits this unjustified infringement of the fundamental right to marry." Id. at 2604. The Obergefell Court's analysis, however, did not assert a particular level of equal protection review for all forms of sexual orientation discrimination; it instead stressed the importance of the right to marry as a fundamental liberty to be granted equally to all citizens.

The Court's stress on the denial of a fundamental liberty interest in Obergefell was preceded by its decision in Lawrence v. Texas, 539 U.S. 558, 123

S.Ct. 2472, 156 L.Ed.2d 508 (2003), striking down a state criminal statute's ban on sodomy. The *Lawrence* Court held that the statute denied a right of liberty guaranteed by the due process clause of the Fourteenth Amendment by intruding "into the personal and private life of the individual" without any "legitimate state interest." In *Lawrence* the Court also did not define the level of review it applied.

Two terms before *Obergefell*, in United States v. Windsor, 133 S. Ct. 2675 (2013), the Court (5–4) held unconstitutional § 3 of the Defense of Marriage Act (DOMA), 110 Stat. 2419, which defined "marriage" and "spouse" to exclude same-sex marriages for purposes of federal law. The Court held DOMA unconstitutional as a deprivation of an "essential part of the liberty of persons that is protected by the Fifth Amendment." The Court stressed that the purpose and effect of the DOMA was to interfere with the equal dignity of same-sex marriages that had been recognized by states in the exercise of their sovereign power. The Court in *Windsor* also stopped short of defining any particular level of equal protection review for sexual orientation discrimination cases. However, in SmithKline Beechham Corp. v. Abbott Labs., 740 F.3d 471, 480–484 (9th Cir. 2014), a case challenging a discriminatory peremptory challenge in jury selection, the Court of Appeals read the *Windsor* Court's lack of deference to the asserted governmental justifications for DOMA and the balancing of the harms of the Act on gays and lesbians to support a heightened scrutiny review of all government discrimination on the basis of sexual orientation.

How should lower courts decide what level of scrutiny to give to a public sector employment discrimination claim based on sexual orientation or gender identity? Should they attempt to infer appropriate analysis from the Court's dicta, as did the *SmithKline* court?

In another decision involving state action adverse to homosexuals and relied on by the Court in *Lawrence*, Romer v. Evans, 517 U.S. 620, 116 S.Ct. 1620, 134 L.Ed.2d 855 (1996), the Court indicated that governmental classifications sometimes can fail even rational basis review. In *Romer* Colorado voters through a statewide referendum had adopted a state constitutional amendment which precluded all legislative, executive, or judicial action at any level of state or local government designed to protect any person or class of persons on the basis of "homosexual, lesbian or bisexual orientation, conduct, practices or relationships." Though it professed to apply only rational basis review, the Court held that the state constitutional amendment denied homosexuals equal protection of the laws. The Court stressed that the amendment had "the peculiar property of imposing a broad and undifferentiated disability" on one group of citizens to seek aid from the government. Id. at 632. The Court found that this preclusion could not be justified by any interest asserted by Colorado, and thus raised "the inevitable inference that the disadvantage imposed is born of animosity toward the class of persons affected." Id. at 634.

At least before the Court's decisions in *Lawrence, Windsor,* and *Obergefell,* lower courts had not read *Romer* expansively to strike down all governmental classifications that intentionally disadvantage homosexuals. Until its reversal by the Obama Administration in July 2011, for instance, the military's "don't ask/don't tell" policy under which the armed services did not accept persons who demonstrated a propensity or intent to engage in homosexual acts generally was upheld by the lower courts. See, e.g., Able v. United States, 155 F.3d 628 (2d Cir.1998); Holmes v. California Army National Guard, 124 F.3d 1126 (9th Cir.1997).

Outside the context of military and national security, however, are governmental employers now likely to be able to convince courts they have even rational reasons for not granting equal treatment to homosexuals or transgender individuals? Even before the Court's most recent decisions protecting the rights of gays and lesbians, public sector employers generally were not able to justify sexual orientation discrimination. See, e.g., Quinn v. Nassau County Police Dept., 53 F.Supp.2d 347 (E.D.N.Y.1999) (police officer could not be subjected to harassment because of his sexual orientation); Weaver v. Nebo School Dist., 29 F.Supp.2d 1279 (D.Utah 1998) (finding no rational, job-related reason to not assign lesbian as volleyball coach); Glover v. Williamsburg Local School Dist. Bd. of Educ., 20 F.Supp.2d 1160 (S.D.Ohio 1998) (non-renewal of teaching contract because of sexual orientation held denial of equal protection); Jantz v. Muci, 759 F.Supp. 1543 (D.Kan.1991), reversed on other grounds, 976 F.2d 623 (10th Cir.1992) (teacher could not be rejected merely because of "homosexual tendencies").

GLENN V. BRUMBY

United States Court of Appeals, Eleventh Circuit, 2011.
663 F.3d 1312.

BARKETT, J.

Sewell R. Brumby appeals from an adverse summary judgment in favor of Vandiver Elizabeth Glenn on her complaint seeking declaratory and injunctive relief pursuant to 42 U.S.C. § 1983 for alleged violations of her rights under the Equal Protection Clause of the Fourteenth Amendment of the U.S. Constitution. Glenn claimed that Brumby fired her from her job as an editor in the Georgia General Assembly's Office of Legislative Counsel ("OLC") because of sex discrimination, thus violating the Equal Protection Clause. The district court granted summary judgment in Glenn's favor on this claim.

* * * Vandiver Elizabeth Glenn was born a biological male. Since puberty, Glenn has felt that she is a woman, and in 2005, she was diagnosed with GID (Gender Identity Disorder), a diagnosis listed in the American Psychiatric Association's Diagnostic and Statistical Manual of Mental Disorders.

Starting in 2005, Glenn began to take steps to transition from male to female under the supervision of health care providers. This process included living as a woman outside of the workplace, which is a prerequisite to sex reassignment surgery. In October 2005, then known as Glenn Morrison and presenting as a man, Glenn was hired as an editor by the Georgia General Assembly's OLC. Sewell Brumby is the head of the OLC and is responsible for OLC personnel decisions, including the decision to fire Glenn.

In 2006, Glenn informed her direct supervisor, Beth Yinger, that she was a transsexual and was in the process of becoming a woman. On Halloween in 2006, when OLC employees were permitted to come to work wearing costumes, Glenn came to work presenting as a woman. When Brumby saw her, he told her that her appearance was not appropriate and asked her to leave the office. Brumby deemed her appearance inappropriate "[b]ecause he was a man dressed as a woman and made up as a woman." Brumby stated that "it's unsettling to think of someone dressed in women's clothing with male sexual organs inside that clothing," and that a male in women's clothing is "unnatural." Following this incident, Brumby met with Yinger to discuss Glenn's appearance on Halloween of 2006 and was informed by Yinger that Glenn intended to undergo a gender transition.

In the fall of 2007, Glenn informed Yinger that she was ready to proceed with gender transition and would begin coming to work as a woman and was also changing her legal name. Yinger notified Brumby, who subsequently terminated Glenn because "Glenn's intended gender transition was inappropriate, that it would be disruptive, that some people would view it as a moral issue, and that it would make Glenn's coworkers uncomfortable."

Glenn sued, alleging two claims of discrimination under the Equal Protection Clause. First, Glenn alleged that Brumby "discriminat[ed] against her because of her sex, including her female gender identity and her failure to conform to the sex stereotypes associated with the sex Defendant[ ] perceived her to be." Second, Glenn alleged that Brumby "discriminat[ed] against her because of her medical condition, GID[,]" because "[r]eceiving necessary treatment for a medical condition is an integral component of living with such a condition, and blocking that treatment is a form of discrimination based on the underlying medical condition."

Glenn and Brumby filed cross-motions for summary judgment. The District Court granted summary judgment to Glenn on her sex discrimination claim, and granted summary judgment to Brumby on Glenn's medical discrimination claim. Both sides timely appealed to this Court. We first address Glenn's sex discrimination claim.

* * * The question here is whether discriminating against someone on the basis of his or her gender non-conformity constitutes sex-based discrimination under the Equal Protection Clause. For the reasons discussed below, we hold that it does.

In *Price Waterhouse v. Hopkins*, 490 U.S. 228, 109 S.Ct. 1775, 104 L.Ed.2d 268 (1989), the Supreme Court held that discrimination on the basis of gender stereotype is sex-based discrimination. * * *

A person is defined as transgender precisely because of the perception that his or her behavior transgresses gender stereotypes. "[T]he very acts that define transgender people as transgender are those that contradict stereotypes of gender-appropriate appearance and behavior." Ilona M. Turner, *Sex Stereotyping Per Se: Transgender Employees and Title VII*, 95 Cal. L. Rev. 561, 563 (2007); *see also* Taylor Flinn, *Transforming the Debate: Why We Need to Include Transgender Rights in the Struggles for Sex and Sexual Orientation Equality*, 101 Colum. L.Rev. 392, 392 (2001) (defining transgender persons as those whose "appearance, behavior, or other personal characteristics differ from traditional gender norms"). There is thus a congruence between discriminating against transgender and transsexual individuals and discrimination on the basis of gender-based behavioral norms.

Accordingly, discrimination against a transgender individual because of her gender-nonconformity is sex discrimination, whether it's described as being on the basis of sex or gender. Indeed, several circuits have so held. For example, in *Schwenk v. Hartford*, the Ninth Circuit concluded that a male-to-female transgender plaintiff who was singled out for harassment because he presented and defined himself as a woman had stated an actionable claim for sex discrimination under the Gender Motivated Violence Act because "the perpetrator's actions stem from the fact that he believed that the victim was a man who 'failed to act like one.'" 204 F.3d 1187, 1198–1203 (9th Cir.2000). The First Circuit echoed this reasoning in *Rosa v. Park West Bank & Trust Co.*, where it held that a transgender plaintiff stated a claim by alleging that he "did not receive [a] loan application because he was a man, whereas a similarly situated woman would have received [a] loan application. That is, the Bank . . . treat[s] . . . a woman who dresses like a man differently than a man who dresses like a woman." 214 F.3d 213, 215–16 (1st Cir.2000). These instances of discrimination against plaintiffs because they fail to act according to socially prescribed gender roles constitute discrimination under Title VII according to the rationale of *Price Waterhouse*.

The Sixth Circuit likewise recognized that discrimination against a transgender individual because of his or her gender non-conformity is gender stereotyping prohibited by Title VII and the Equal Protection Clause. *See Smith v. City of Salem*, 378 F.3d 566 (6th Cir.2004). The court concluded that a transsexual firefighter could not be suspended because of "his transsexualism and its manifestations," *id.* at 569, because to do so was discrimination against him "based on his failure to conform to sex stereotypes by expressing less masculine, and more feminine mannerisms and appearance." *Id.* at 572; *see Barnes v. City of Cincinnati*, 401 F.3d 729

(6th Cir.2005) (holding that transsexual plaintiff stated a claim for sex discrimination "by alleging discrimination . . . for his failure to conform to sex stereotypes"). * * *

All persons, whether transgender or not, are protected from discrimination on the basis of gender stereotype. For example, courts have held that plaintiffs cannot be discriminated against for wearing jewelry that was considered too effeminate, carrying a serving tray too gracefully, or taking too active a role in child-rearing. An individual cannot be punished because of his or her perceived gender-nonconformity. Because these protections are afforded to everyone, they cannot be denied to a transgender individual. The nature of the discrimination is the same; it may differ in degree but not in kind, and discrimination on this basis is a form of sex-based discrimination that is subject to heightened scrutiny under the Equal Protection Clause. Ever since the Supreme Court began to apply heightened scrutiny to sex-based classifications, its consistent purpose has been to eliminate discrimination on the basis of gender stereotypes. * * *

We now turn to whether Glenn was fired on the basis of gender stereotyping. The first inquiry is whether Brumby acted on the basis of Glenn's gender-nonconformity. * * * In this case, Brumby testified at his deposition that he fired Glenn because he considered it "inappropriate" for her to appear at work dressed as a woman and that he found it "unsettling" and "unnatural" that Glenn would appear wearing women's clothing. Brumby testified that his decision to dismiss Glenn was based on his perception of Glenn as "a man dressed as a woman and made up as a woman," and Brumby admitted that his decision to fire Glenn was based on "the sheer fact of the transition." Brumby's testimony provides ample direct evidence to support the district court's conclusion that Brumby acted on the basis of Glenn's gender non-conformity.

If this were a Title VII case, the analysis would end here. . . . However, because Glenn's claim is based on the Equal Protection Clause, we must, under heightened scrutiny, consider whether Brumby succeeded in showing an "exceedingly persuasive justification," [*United States v. Virginia*, 518 U.S. 515, 546, 116 S.Ct. 2264, 135 L.Ed.2d 735 (1996)] (internal quotation marks omitted), that is, that there was a "sufficiently important governmental interest" for his discriminatory conduct, *Cleburne*, 473 U.S. at 441, 105 S.Ct. 3249. This burden "is demanding and it rests entirely on the State." *Virginia*, 518 U.S. at 533, 116 S.Ct. 2264. The defendant's burden cannot be met by relying on a justification that is "hypothesized or invented post hoc in response to litigation." *Id.*

On appeal, Brumby advances only one putative justification for Glenn's firing: his purported concern that other women might object to Glenn's restroom use. However, Brumby presented insufficient evidence to show that he was actually motivated by concern over litigation regarding

Glenn's restroom use. * * * The fact that such a hypothetical justification may have been sufficient to withstand rational-basis scrutiny, however, is wholly irrelevant to the heightened scrutiny analysis that is required here.

NOTES AND QUESTIONS

Test Your Understanding of the Material

1.   How does the *Glenn* court explain its application of heightened scrutiny to Bumbry's discharge of Glenn? For purposes of discrimination against the transgendered, does this explanation accept the distinction drawn by Title VII courts between stereotyped-based sex discrimination based on nonconformity to gender norms and discrimination against a sexual minority based on status? Note that the court states that its analysis under Title VII could end based on its finding of discrimination without any consideration of the employer's justification.

2.   Would the court have affirmed the district court's grant of summary judgment if Brumby had never expressed any discomfort with Glenn's dressing as a woman, but instead had stated in his deposition that he fired Glenn only because of her announced intent to transition from her biological birth sex?

Related Issues

3.   *Justifications for Gender Identity Employment Discrimination.* The *Glenn* court finds that Bumbry offered "insufficient evidence to show he was actually motivated by concern over . . . restroom use." Could a concern with restroom use and the sensibilities of other employees, when well documented, provide a justification for at least the restriction of bathroom use in a case like *Glenn* involving a pre-operative transgendered employee? But cf. Lusardi v. McHugh, 2015 WL 1607756 (EEOC) (restricting transgender female's use of women's bathroom before "final surgery" may be actionable disparate treatment, not justified by coworker anxiety).

CHAPTER 8

AGE DISCRIMINATION

■ ■ ■

Introduction

This chapter deals with the subject of employment discrimination on the basis of age as addressed in the Age Discrimination in Employment Act of 1967 (ADEA), 29 U.S.C. §§ 621–34, as well as similar state laws. During consideration of Title VII of the 1964 Civil Rights Act, Congress decided to defer enactment of a federal measure to bar age bias. It directed the Secretary of Labor to investigate the problem and report on whether legislation was needed. Labor Secretary Wirtz's report, The Older American Worker—Age Discrimination in Employment, Report of the Secretary of Labor to Congress Under Section 715 of the Civil Rights Act of 1964 (June 1965), led to the enactment of ADEA.

A. JUSTIFICATIONS FOR AGE DISCRIMINATION REGULATION

What are the justifications for regulating age discrimination? The reasons, while similar, are not identical to those that may explain regulation of race and sex discrimination.

1. *Prejudice.* Unlike race and sex, age is a changing status. Most youths hope to achieve middle and old age. Most also have close members of their families who have achieved that status. It therefore seems less likely that older workers will be the object of antagonistic social prejudice. At least up to some point in middle age, average earnings increase rather than decline with age; and white, male older workers largely comprise the managerial and supervisory ranks of American firms. It is not clear that older Americans as a class share the economic disadvantages of many African Americans or confront the same occupational and other barriers as minority and female workers.

Nevertheless, the anticipation of aging and close association with the elderly does not exclude the possibility of some prejudice against older workers. Prejudice is a complicated phenomenon and need not be dependent on lack of contact, as attested by the presence of sex-based prejudice despite the close intrafamily association of men and women. Both the high value placed on novelty and youth in our culture and the force of intergenerational conflict may engender age bias.

The role of employee and customer prejudice in reinforcing the use of age stereotypes by employers is probably less significant than for race and sex stereotyping. There will certainly be situations where employers accede to the associational preferences of coworkers or customers to deal with younger people, but it is questionable whether this is more than a marginal phenomenon.

2. *Statistical Discrimination.* More important than any form of antagonistic prejudice, however, may be the use of stereotyping presumptions about the capabilities of older workers. Similar observations can be found in § 2 of ADEA, 29 U.S.C. § 621 ("Congressional Statement of Findings and Purpose").

The use of age stereotypes may be efficient for reasons not traceable to, and not sustained by, social prejudice, and hence likely to persist in the absence of regulation. In many settings, age may be a relatively good proxy for difficult predictive judgments and cheaper to use than any direct individualized test of present or future capabilities. A rational employer may find it irrelevant that many older workers can efficiently perform a particular job if these capable workers cannot be cheaply segregated from the greater number of less efficient older workers.

The probability of such "statistical discrimination" against older workers seems especially strong when those workers apply for a new job. An employer sifting through new job applications must make difficult decisions on the basis of imperfect and indirect information. The employer also might have to train any worker it hires for a period during which the worker may have to be paid more than his or her productivity. All in all, age might well help personnel officers predict which applicants will be the most productive for the longest period. See Robert M. Hutchens, Delayed Payment Contracts and a Firm's Propensity to Hire Older Workers, 4 J.Lab.Econ. 439 (1986) (firms which continue to employ older workers also tend not to hire new older workers).

ADEA's regulations extend, of course, beyond the hiring stage to reach, in a manner akin to Title VII, all personnel decisions affecting the terms and conditions of employment. There may be less reason to suspect that employers engage in statistical discrimination against older incumbent workers. "Yet, promotions to new positions also may require new skills and training and predictions about future returns; and employers may rationally decide to displace older satisfactorily performing employees, rather than younger ones, during an economic downturn because of predictions about future productivity and likely retirement dates." Michael C. Harper, A Gap in the Agenda: Enhancing the Regulation of Age Discrimination, in Labor and Employment Law Initiatives and Proposals Under the Obama Administration, ch. 14, 606 (Eigen ed. 2011).

The fact that statistical discrimination may be efficient for individual employers, however, need not make it acceptable as social policy. We may be concerned about many individual older workers losing jobs for which they are capable both because we want to extend the opportunity for dignified work to as many citizens as possible, and because of the social costs of supporting potentially productive older workers assigned to an unproductive status.

3. *Employer Opportunism.* A possible justification for using an age discrimination statute to protect the job security of even those older workers whose pay exceeds their present productivity might be the avoidance of what some economists call "opportunistic" behavior on the part of employers against older employees. It has been suggested that employers pay junior employees less than their marginal product on the implicit promise that they will be paid more than their marginal product as their productivity declines towards the twilight of their careers. See, e.g., Edward P. Lazear, Agency, Earning Profiles, Productivity and Hours Restrictions, 71 Am.Econ.Rev. 606 (1981); Robert M. Hutchens, supra.

Presumably, these implicit arrangements work without any formal contractual remedy because younger employees see their employer paying older employees in accord with the promise. However, certain situations such as business contractions, when new employees are not being hired or a firm is withdrawing from a particular line of business, may provide opportunities for employers to take advantage of current older employees without demoralizing new employees. See Samuel Estreicher, Employer Reputation at Work, 27 Hofstra Lab. & Empl. L.J. 1 (2009). Conceivably, age discrimination laws like ADEA help compel compliance with these implicit relational contracts.

Whatever its justifications, ADEA is one of the most significant areas of federal employment law, accounting for a significant portion of the charges filed with the EEOC. Studies of the profiles of ADEA claimants suggest a predominantly white, relatively well-educated, professional or middle-management plaintiff class. See Michael Schuster & Christopher S. Miller, An Empirical Assessment of the Age Discrimination in Employment Act, 38 Ind. & Lab.Rel.Rev. 64 (1984). Except in states where the courts have recognized major departures from the American rule of "at will" employment, ADEA provides the principal means for white male nonunion private employees to challenge termination from employment.

NOTE: THE ADEA STATUTORY SCHEME

ADEA applies to all employers engaged in an industry affecting commerce having twenty or more employees for each working day in each of twenty or more weeks in the current or preceding calendar year. Like Title VII, ADEA also covers labor organizations and employment agencies. The ADEA protected class now includes all individuals over the age of 40 no matter how old. Under some state laws, protection may extend to even earlier ages. See, e.g., Bergen Commercial Bank v. Sisler, 157 N.J. 188, 723 A.2d 944 (1999).

Congress created in ADEA a hybrid: borrowing the substantive law from Title VII, while incorporating the remedial provisions of the Fair Labor Standards Act of 1938 (FLSA), 29 U.S.C. §§ 211, 216–17, 255, 259. The Secretary of Labor administered ADEA until the 1977 Reorganization Act authorized President Carter to transfer authority to the EEOC.

Generally, an ADEA court has the same range of remedial authority as a Title VII court. Under § 7(c)(1), 29 U.S.C. § 626(c)(1), "[a]ny person aggrieved may bring a civil action * * * for such legal or equitable relief as will effectuate" the statute. Moreover, a right to a jury trial "of any issue of fact * * * for recovery of amounts owing as a result of a violation of this Act" is guaranteed by § 7(c)(2), a result of 1978 amendments. Where the court, in its equitable discretion, declines to award reinstatement, the decisions authorize an award of "front pay" relief—a development which has carried over to Title VII cases. See pp. 914–915 infra.

Because ADEA incorporates certain FLSA remedial provisions, plaintiffs can also seek to recover an amount equal to their damages as "liquidated damages." However, ADEA permits recovery of such extra damages "only in cases of willful violations." ADEA § 7(b), 29 U.S.C. § 626(b). In Trans World Airlines, Inc. v. Thurston, 469 U.S. 111, 105 S.Ct. 613, 83 L.Ed.2d 523 (1985), the Supreme Court held that a "willful" violation requires proof that the defendant acted in knowing or "reckless disregard" of ADEA requirements.

B. DISPARATE TREATMENT

1. APPLICABILITY OF TITLE VII MODE OF PROOF

O'CONNOR V. CONSOLIDATED COIN CATERERS CORP.
Supreme Court of the United States, 1996.
517 U.S. 308, 116 S.Ct. 1307, 134 L.Ed.2d 433.

JUSTICE SCALIA delivered the opinion of the Court.

This case presents the question whether a plaintiff alleging that he was discharged in violation of the Age Discrimination in Employment Act of 1967 (ADEA), 81 Stat. 602, as amended, 29 U.S.C. § 621 et seq., must show that he was replaced by someone outside the age group protected by the ADEA to make out a prima facie case under the framework established by McDonnell Douglas Corp. v. Green, 411 U.S. 792, 36 L. Ed. 2d 668, 93 S. Ct. 1817 (1973).

Petitioner James O'Connor was employed by respondent Consolidated Coin Caterers Corporation from 1978 until August 10, 1990, when, at age 56, he was fired. Claiming that he had been dismissed because of his age in violation of the ADEA, petitioner brought suit in the United States District Court for the Western District of North Carolina. After discovery, the District Court granted respondent's motion for summary judgment, and petitioner appealed. The Court of Appeals for the Fourth Circuit stated that petitioner could establish a prima facie case under *McDonnell Douglas* only if he could prove that (1) he was in the age group protected by the ADEA; (2) he was discharged or demoted; (3) at the time of his discharge or demotion, he was performing his job at a level that met his employer's legitimate expectations; and (4) following his discharge or demotion, he was replaced by someone of comparable qualifications outside the protected class. Since petitioner's replacement was 40 years old, the Court of Appeals concluded that the last element of the prima facie case had not been made out. Finding that petitioner's claim could not survive a motion for summary judgment without benefit of the *McDonnell Douglas* presumption (i.e., "under the ordinary standards of proof used in civil cases,") the Court of Appeals affirmed the judgment of dismissal. * * *

In assessing claims of age discrimination brought under the ADEA, the Fourth Circuit, like others, has applied some variant of the basic evidentiary framework set forth in *McDonnell Douglas*. We have never had occasion to decide whether that application of the Title VII rule to the ADEA context is correct, but since the parties do not contest that point, we shall assume it. On that assumption, the question presented for our determination is what elements must be shown in an ADEA case to establish the prima facie case that triggers the employer's burden of production.

As the very name "prima facie case" suggests, there must be at least a logical connection between each element of the prima facie case and the illegal discrimination for which it establishes a "legally mandatory, rebuttable presumption," [*Texas Dept. of Community Affairs v. Burdine*, 450 U.S. 248, 254 n. 7, 101 S. Ct. 1089, 67 L. Ed. 2d 207 (1981).] The element of replacement by someone under 40 fails this requirement. The discrimination prohibited by the ADEA is discrimination "because of [an] individual's age," 29 U.S.C. § 623(a)(1), though the prohibition is "limited to individuals who are at least 40 years of age," § 631(a). This language does not ban discrimination against employees because they are aged 40 or older; it bans discrimination against employees because of their age, but limits the protected class to those who are 40 or older. The fact that one person in the protected class has lost out to another person in the protected class is thus irrelevant, so long as he has lost out because of his age. Or to put the point more concretely, there can be no greater inference of age discrimination (as opposed to "40 or over" discrimination) when a 40 year-old is replaced by a 39 year-old than when a 56 year-old is replaced by a 40 year-old. Because it lacks probative value, the fact that an ADEA plaintiff was replaced by someone outside the protected class is not a proper element of the *McDonnell Douglas* prima facie case.

Perhaps some courts have been induced to adopt the principle urged by respondent in order to avoid creating a prima facie case on the basis of very thin evidence—for example, the replacement of a 68 year-old by a 65 year-old. While the respondent's principle theoretically permits such thin evidence (consider the example above of a 40 year-old replaced by a 39 year-old), as a practical matter it will rarely do so, since the vast majority of age-discrimination claims come from older employees. In our view, however, the proper solution to the problem lies not in making an utterly irrelevant factor an element of the prima facie case, but rather in recognizing that the prima facie case requires "evidence adequate to create an inference that an employment decision was based on an [illegal] discriminatory criterion. * * * " *Teamsters v. United States*, 431 U.S. 324, 358, 52 L. Ed. 2d 396, 97 S. Ct. 1843 (1977). In the age-discrimination context, such an inference can not be drawn from the replacement of one worker with another worker insignificantly younger. Because the ADEA prohibits discrimination on the basis of age and not class membership, the fact that a replacement is substantially younger than the plaintiff is a far more reliable indicator of age discrimination than is the fact that the plaintiff was replaced by someone outside the protected class. The judgment of the Fourth Circuit is reversed, and the case is remanded for proceedings consistent with this opinion.

NOTES AND QUESTIONS

Test Your Understanding of the Material

1.   Under *O'Connor*, is the multi-factor fomula for a prima facie case stated in *McDonnell Douglas* for Title VII cases equally applicable in most ADEA cases? If not, how does it need to be adjusted? Does it need to be adjusted for reduction-in-force cases where there may be no obvious replacement for those let go?

Related Issues

2.   *"Insignificantly Younger."* For decisions applying the Court's statement that replacement by "insignificantly younger" workers does not establish an ADEA prima facie case, compare Grosjean v. First Energy Corp., 349 F.3d 332, 340 (6th Cir. 2003) (age difference of six years or less "not significant"); Cianci v. Pettibone Corp., 152 F.3d 723, 728 (7th Cir. 1998) ("age disparity of less than ten years is presumptively insubstantial"), with Whittington v. Nordam Group Inc., 429 F.3d 986, 996 (10th Cir. 2005) (rejecting any firm age-disparity "outside context of the case").

3.   *Discrimination Against Younger Worker Age 40 or More.* In General Dynamics Land Systems, Inc. v. Cline, 540 U.S. 581, 591–92, 124 S.Ct. 1236, 157 L.Ed.2d 1094 (2004), the Supreme Court held that the ADEA does not prohibit favoring older over younger workers. Justice Souter, for a six-Justice majority, explained:

> If Congress had been worrying about protecting the younger against the older, it would not likely have ignored everyone under 40. The youthful deficiencies of inexperience and unsteadiness invite stereotypical and discriminatory thinking about those a lot younger

than 40, and prejudice suffered by a 40-year-old is not typically owing to youth, as 40-year-olds sadly tend to find out. . . . Thus, the 40-year threshold makes sense as identifying a class requiring protection against preference for their juniors, not as defining a class that might be threatened by favoritism toward seniors.

Some state age discrimination laws define the protected class at age 18 and above and protect younger workers from discrimination because they are "too young" for the job. See, e.g., Bergen Commercial Bank v. Sisler, 157 N.J. 188 (1999). A few courts have found actionable discrimination against younger workers even if older workers within the protected class are benefited by the challenged practice. See, e.g., Ace Electrical Contractors, Inc. v. International Brotherhood of Electrical Workers, 414 F.3d 896 (8th Cir. 2005) (negotiated employee age ratio in collective bargaining agreement requiring that 1 out of every 5 electrical workers be age 50 or older violates public policy articulated in § 363A.03 of the Minnesota Human Rights Act).

4. *When Decisionmaker Is the Same Age or Older than the Plaintiff.* Is an ADEA prima facie case precluded when the decisionamker is older than the plaintiff? In the ADEA context, as in Title VII case, the question is the weight to be given this fact. It is not implausible that managers of the same age or older than the plaintiff may still harbor a preference for younger workers. See, e.g., Kadas v. MCI Systemhouse Corp., 255 F.3d 359, 361–362 (7th Cir.2001), Wexler v. White's Fine Furniture, Inc., 317 F.3d 564 (6th Cir.2003) (en banc).

5. *"Same Actor" Inference.* "[I]n cases where the hirer and the firer are the same individual and the termination occurs within a relatively short time space following the hiring," some courts will infer that discrimination was not a determining factor for the adverse action. See Proud v. Stone, 945 F.2d 796, 798 (4th Cir.1991); Brown v. CSC Logic, Inc., 82 F.3d 651 (5th Cir.1996) (invoking same-actor inference to the dismissal of a 58 year-old employee who was hired four years earlier by the same man who fired him); *Kadas v. MCI Systemhouse Corp.*, supra, at 361–62 ("it is eminently reasonable to doubt that, as in this case, a worker hired * * * and terminated *within months*, that is, before he is appreciably older, was a victim of age discrimination"). But see *Wexler v. White's Fine Furniture, Inc.*, supra.

6. *Prima Facie Showing in Workforce Reduction Cases.* Age discrimination often has been alleged in cases where the employer does not fill the position from which the alleged victim is laid off or discharged, either because the job function has been entirely eliminated or because aspects of the function have been distributed among several incumbent employees. How should the "prima facie" case be framed for reduction-in-force (RIF) cases?

Consider the Fourth Circuit's position in Blistein v. St. John's College, 74 F.3d 1459, 1470 (1996):

A plaintiff in such circumstances [cannot point to a replacement] but can establish this element of his prima facie case "either by showing that (comparably qualified) persons outside the protected class were retained in the same position *or* by producing some other evidence indicating that the employer did not treat age neutrally (in deciding to dismiss the plaintiff)."

Where relative qualification is asserted as the basis of selection for the force reduction, the *Blistein* court would require proof that "the plaintiff was performing at a level substantially equivalent to the lowest level of those retained" and that "the process of selection produced a residual work force with some unprotected persons who were performing at a level lower than that at which the plaintiff was performing." Id. at 1470–1471 n.13. For another approach, see Radue v. Kimberly-Clark Corp., 219 F.3d 612, 617 (7th Cir.2000) (plaintiff may show as fourth prong of prima facie case that "other similarly situated employees who were substantially younger than him were treated more favorably"). On the difficulty of proving discrimination in reduction in force cases, see Daniel B. Kohrman & Mark Stewart Hayes, Employers Who Cry "RIF" and the Courts That Believe Them, 23 Hof. L. & Emp.L.J. 153 (2005).

7. *Age-Based Harassment.* Title VII harassment jurisprudence generally has been applied to the ADEA. See, e.g., Dediol v. Best Chevrolet, Inc., 655 F.3d 435 (5th Cir. 2011); Crawford v. Medina General Hospital, 96 F.3d 830 (6th Cir.1996).

PRACTITIONER'S PERSPECTIVE

Zachary Fasman
Partner, Proskauer.

Trying an age discrimination claim before a jury is among the more daunting tasks a defense lawyer faces. Jurors often identify with age discrimination plaintiffs because we all know or remember older relatives or friends, and instinctively don't want to see them mistreated. Jurors also know that unless they pass away prematurely, they also will grow older, and can envision themselves in the plaintiff's shoes.

Advocates therefore need to evaluate an age discrimination case realistically before advising a client to go to trial. Wholly apart from legal issues, it is essential to make sure that your client's treatment of the plaintiff is fair in the abstract. Is this the way you would like to have your parent treated? Basing an age discrimination trial defense on abstract legal issues is dangerous; some juries will listen to arguments about burdens of proof and legal requirements, while others will ignore the law and react emotionally to "fairness" concerns. Test your arguments out before a mock jury to make sure your assessment is not overly optimistic. Even if you are convinced that your arguments are sound and appealing, consider who your witnesses will be and how a jury is likely to react to them in comparison to the plaintiff.

If you are convinced you have a persuasive story to tell and appealing witnesses to tell it, it is essential at trial to prevent a sympathy verdict. This requires, first, doing everything you can to make the plaintiff less sympathetic to jurors. Has the plaintiff changed his or her story during the course of the proceedings? Are there issues in the case that reveal attempts to tell less than the entire truth? It is vital to take a thorough and well-planned deposition, and to videotape the plaintiff's deposition. If done properly, on cross examination the jury can see the plaintiff in person, during the deposition, testifying under oath contradicting his or her testimony in open court.

Second, jurors must be instructed by the court, at the start of the trial and following presentation of the evidence, that sympathy for the plaintiff is not proof of age discrimination. Under federal law, an age discrimination plaintiff must prove that his or her age caused the termination, layoff, or denial of promotion. Merely being older and having worked for the employer for many years does not prove discrimination, and the court must instruct the jury to this effect. The jury must be directed to consider carefully the evidence of age discrimination the plaintiff has supplied, and defense lawyers must reinforce this legal issue without admitting, even implicitly, that the plaintiff was treated unfairly. Has plaintiff proven that that his or her treatment was a direct result of age? How have other individuals in comparable circumstances been treated? Is there any reason to believe that if the plaintiff was 40 years old instead of 60 the result would have been different?

One related and recurring problem in many age discrimination cases is what courts call "stray remarks"—that is, remarks making some reference to age that are remote in time or uttered by someone who is not the decision-maker. These are not relevant and should not be admitted, but unless the court precludes introduction of such remarks you cannot assume that the jury will appropriately discount such remarks. Juries may seize upon those remarks as proof that the employer was considering age, and "unringing" that bell may be difficult. Pre-trial motion practice designed to prevent the introduction of irrelevant but potentially prejudicial evidence is absolutely vital to ensuring a successful result in an age discrimination trial.

---

2. CAUSATION UNDER THE ADEA

GROSS V. FBL FINANCIAL SERVICES, INC.

Supreme Court of the United States, 2009.
557 U.S. 167, 129 S.Ct. 2343, 174 L.Ed.2d 119.

JUSTICE THOMAS delivered the opinion of the Court.

The question presented by the petitioner in this case is whether a plaintiff must present direct evidence of age discrimination in order to obtain a mixed-motives jury instruction in a suit brought under the Age Discrimination in Employment Act of 1967 (ADEA), 81 Stat. 602, as amended, 29 U.S.C. § 621 et seq. Because we hold that such a jury instruction is never proper in an ADEA case, we vacate the decision below.

I

Petitioner Jack Gross began working for respondent FBL Financial Group, Inc. (FBL), in 1971. As of 2001, Gross held the position of claims administration director. But in 2003, when he was 54 years old, Gross was reassigned to the position of claims project coordinator. At that same time, FBL transferred many of Gross' job responsibilities to a newly created position—claims administration manager. That position was given to Lisa Kneeskern, who had previously been supervised by Gross and who was then in her early forties. Although Gross (in his new position) and Kneeskern received the same compensation, Gross considered the reassignment a demotion because of FBL's reallocation of his former job responsibilities to Kneeskern.

In April 2004, Gross filed suit in District Court, alleging that his reassignment to the position of claims project coordinator violated the ADEA, which makes it unlawful for an employer to take adverse action against an employee "because of such individual's age." 29 U.S.C. § 623(a). The case proceeded to trial, where Gross introduced evidence suggesting that his reassignment was based at least in part on his age. FBL defended its decision on the grounds that Gross' reassignment was part of a corporate restructuring and that Gross' new position was better suited to his skills.

At the close of trial, and over FBL's objections, the District Court instructed the jury that it must return a verdict for Gross if he proved, by a preponderance of the evidence, that FBL "demoted [him] to claims projec[t] coordinator" and that his "age was a motivating factor" in FBL's decision to demote him. The jury was further instructed that Gross' age would qualify as a " 'motivating factor,' if [it] played a part or a role in [FBL]'s decision to demote [him]." The jury was also instructed regarding FBL's burden of proof. According to the District Court, the "verdict must be for [FBL] . . . if it has been proved by the preponderance of the evidence that [FBL] would have demoted [Gross] regardless of his age." The jury returned a verdict for Gross, awarding him $46,945 in lost compensation.

FBL challenged the jury instructions on appeal. The United States Court of Appeals for the Eighth Circuit reversed and remanded for a new trial, holding that the jury had been incorrectly instructed under the standard established in *Price Waterhouse v. Hopkins*, 490 U.S. 228, 109 S. Ct. 1775, 104 L. Ed. 2d 268 (1989). In *Price Waterhouse*, this Court addressed the proper allocation of the burden of persuasion in cases brought under Title VII of the Civil Rights Act of 1964, 78 Stat. 253, as amended, 42 U.S.C. § 2000e et seq., when an employee alleges that he suffered an adverse employment action because of both permissible and impermissible considerations—i.e., a "mixed-motives" case. 490 U.S., at 232, 244–247, 109 S. Ct. 1775, 104 L. Ed. 2d 268 (plurality opinion). The *Price Waterhouse* decision was splintered. Four Justices joined a plurality opinion, see id., at 231–258, 109 S. Ct. 1775, 104 L. Ed. 2d 268, Justices White and O'Connor separately concurred in the judgment, see id., at 258–261, 109 S. Ct. 1775, 104 L. Ed. 2d 268 (opinion of White, J.); id., at 261–279, 109 S. Ct. 1775, 104 L. Ed. 2d 268 (opinion of O'Connor, J.), and three Justices dissented, see id., at 279–295, 109 S. Ct. 1775, 104 L. Ed. 2d 268 (opinion of Kennedy, J.). Six Justices ultimately agreed that if a Title VII plaintiff shows that discrimination was a "motivating" or a " 'substantial' " factor in the employer's action, the burden of persuasion should shift to the employer to show that it would have taken the same action regardless of that impermissible consideration. See id., at 258, 109 S. Ct. 1775, 104 L. Ed. 2d 268 (plurality opinion); id., at 259–260, 109 S. Ct. 1775, 104 L. Ed. 2d 268 (opinion of White, J.); id., at 276, 109 S. Ct. 1775, 104 L. Ed. 2d 268 (opinion of O'Connor, J.). Justice O'Connor further found that to shift the burden of persuasion to the employer, the employee must present "direct evidence that an illegitimate criterion was a substantial factor in the [employment] decision." Id., at 276, 109 S. Ct. 1775, 104 L. Ed. 2d 268.

In accordance with Circuit precedent, the Court of Appeals identified Justice O'Connor's opinion as controlling. * * *

The Court of Appeals thus concluded that the District Court's jury instructions were flawed because they allowed the burden to shift to FBL upon a presentation of a preponderance of any category of evidence showing that age was a motivating factor—not just "direct evidence" related to FBL's alleged consideration of age. Because Gross conceded that he had not presented direct evidence of discrimination, the Court of Appeals held that the District Court should not have given the mixed-motives instruction. Rather, Gross should have been held to the burden of persuasion applicable to typical, non-mixed-motives claims; the jury thus should have been instructed only to determine whether Gross had carried his burden of "prov[ing] that age was the determining factor in FBL's employment action."

We granted certiorari, and now vacate the decision of the Court of Appeals.

II

The parties have asked us to decide whether a plaintiff must "present direct evidence of discrimination in order to obtain a mixed-motive instruction in a non-Title VII discrimination case." Before reaching this question, however, we must first determine whether the burden of persuasion ever shifts to the party defending an alleged mixed-motives discrimination claim brought under the ADEA. We hold that it does not.

A

Petitioner relies on this Court's decisions construing Title VII for his interpretation of the ADEA. Because Title VII is materially different with respect to the relevant burden of persuasion, however, these decisions do not control our construction of the ADEA.

In *Price Waterhouse*, a plurality of the Court and two Justices concurring in the judgment determined that once a "plaintiff in a Title VII case proves that [the plaintiff's membership in a protected class] played a motivating part in an employment decision, the defendant may avoid a finding of liability only by proving by a preponderance of the evidence that it would have made the same decision even if it had not taken [that factor] into account." 490 U.S., at 258, 109 S. Ct. 1775, 104 L. Ed. 2d 268; see also id., at 259–260, 109 S. Ct. 1775, 104 L. Ed. 2d 268 (opinion of White, J.); id., at 276, 109 S. Ct. 1775, 104 L. Ed. 2d 268 (opinion of O'Connor, J.). But as we explained in *Desert Palace, Inc. v. Costa*, 539 U.S. 90, 94–95, 123 S. Ct. 2148, 156 L. Ed. 2d 84 (2003), Congress has since amended Title VII by explicitly authorizing discrimination claims in which an improper consideration was "a motivating factor" for an adverse employment decision. See 42 U.S.C. § 2000e–2(m) (providing that "an unlawful employment practice is established when the complaining party demonstrates that race, color, religion, sex, or national origin was *a motivating factor* for any employment practice, even though other factors also motivated the practice" (emphasis added)); § 2000e–5(g)(2)(B) (restricting the remedies available to plaintiffs proving violations of § 2000e–2(m)).

This Court has never held that this burden-shifting framework applies to ADEA claims. And, we decline to do so now. When conducting statutory interpretation, we "must be careful not to apply rules applicable under one statute to a different statute without careful and critical examination." *Fed. Express Corp. v. Holowecki*, 552 U.S. 389, 128 S. Ct. 1147, 1153, 170 L. Ed. 2d 10, 17 (2008). Unlike Title VII, the ADEA's text does not provide that a plaintiff may establish discrimination by showing that age was simply a motivating factor. Moreover, Congress neglected to add such a provision to the ADEA when it amended Title VII to add §§ 2000e–2(m) and 2000e–5(g)(2)(B), even though it contemporaneously amended the ADEA in several ways, see Civil Rights Act of 1991, § 115, 105 Stat. 1079; id., § 302, at 1088.

We cannot ignore Congress' decision to amend Title VII's relevant provisions but not make similar changes to the ADEA. When Congress amends one statutory provision but not another, it is presumed to have acted intentionally. See *EEOC v. Arabian American Oil Co.*, 499 U.S. 244, 256, 111 S. Ct. 1227, 113 L. Ed. 2d 274 (1991). Furthermore, as the Court has explained, "negative implications raised by disparate provisions are strongest" when the provisions were "considered simultaneously when the language raising the implication was inserted." *Lindh v. Murphy*, 521 U.S. 320, 330, 117 S. Ct. 2059, 138 L. Ed. 2d 481 (1997). As a result, the Court's interpretation of the ADEA is not governed by Title VII decisions such as *Desert Palace* and *Price Waterhouse*.

B

Our inquiry therefore must focus on the text of the ADEA to decide whether it authorizes a mixed-motives age discrimination claim. It does not. "Statutory construction must begin with the language employed by Congress and the assumption that the ordinary meaning of that language accurately expresses the legislative purpose." *Engine Mfrs. Assn. v. South Coast Air Quality* Management Dist., 541 U.S. 246, 252, 124 S. Ct. 1756, 158 L. Ed. 2d 529 (2004) (internal quotation marks omitted). The ADEA provides, in relevant part, that "[i]t shall be unlawful for an employer . . . to fail or refuse to hire or to discharge any individual or otherwise discriminate against any individual with respect to his compensation, terms, conditions, or privileges of employment, *because of* such individual's age." 29 U.S.C. § 623(a)(1) (emphasis added).

The words "because of" mean "by reason of: on account of." 1 Webster's Third New International Dictionary 194 (1966); see also 1 Oxford English Dictionary 746 (1933) (defining "because of" to mean "By reason *of*, on account *of*" (italics in original)); The Random House Dictionary of the English Language 132 (1966) (defining "because" to mean "by reason; on account"). Thus, the ordinary meaning of the ADEA's requirement that an employer took adverse action "because of" age is that age was the "reason" that the employer decided to act. See *Hazen Paper Co. v. Biggins*, 507 U.S. 604, 610, 113 S. Ct. 1701, 123 L. Ed. 2d 338 (1993) (explaining that the claim "cannot succeed unless the employee's protected trait actually played a role in [the employer's decisionmaking] process *and had a determinative influence on the outcome*" (emphasis added)). To establish a disparate-treatment claim under the plain language of the ADEA, therefore, a plaintiff must prove that age was the "but-for" cause of the employer's adverse decision. See *Bridge v. Phoenix Bond & Indem. Co.*, 553 U.S. 639, 128 S. Ct. 2131, 2141, 170 L. Ed. 2d 1012, 1024 (2008) (recognizing that the phrase, "by reason of," requires at least a showing of "but for" causation (internal quotation marks omitted)); *Safeco Ins. Co. of America v. Burr,* 551 U.S. 47, 63–64, 127 S. Ct. 2201, 167 L. Ed. 2d 1045, and n. 14 (2007) (observing that "[i]n common talk, the phrase 'based on' indicates a but-for causal relationship and thus a necessary logical condition" and that the statutory phrase, "based on," has the same meaning as the phrase, "because of" (internal quotation marks omitted)); cf. W. Keeton, D. Dobbs, R. Keeton, & D. Owen, Prosser and Keeton on Law of Torts 265 (5th ed. 1984) ("An act or omission is not regarded as a cause of an event if the particular event would have occurred without it").

* * *

Hence, the burden of persuasion necessary to establish employer liability is the same in alleged mixed-motives cases as in any other ADEA disparate-treatment action. A plaintiff must prove by a preponderance of the evidence (which may be direct or circumstantial), that age was the "but-for" cause of the challenged employer decision.

III

* * *

Whatever the deficiencies of *Price Waterhouse* in retrospect, it has become evident in the years since that case was decided that its burden-shifting framework is difficult to apply. For example, in cases tried to a jury, courts have found it particularly difficult to craft an instruction to explain its burden-shifting framework. * * * Thus, even if *Price Waterhouse* was doctrinally sound, the problems associated with its application have eliminated any perceivable benefit to extending its framework to ADEA claims. * * *

IV

We hold that a plaintiff bringing a disparate-treatment claim pursuant to the ADEA must prove, by a preponderance of the evidence, that age was the "but-for" cause of the challenged adverse employment action. The burden of persuasion does not shift to the employer to show that it would have taken the action regardless of age, even when a plaintiff has produced some evidence that age was one motivating factor in that decision. Accordingly, we vacate the judgment of the Court of Appeals and remand the case for further proceedings consistent with this opinion.

JUSTICE STEVENS, with whom JUSTICE SOUTER, JUSTICE GINSBURG, and JUSTICE BREYER join, dissenting.

* * * The most natural reading of th[e] statutory text prohibits adverse employment actions motivated in whole or in part by the age of the employee. The "but-for" causation standard endorsed by the Court today was advanced in Justice Kennedy's dissenting opinion in *Price Waterhouse v. Hopkins,* 490 U.S. 228, 279, 109 S. Ct. 1775, 104 L. Ed. 2d 268 (1989), a case construing identical language in Title VII of the Civil Rights Act of

1964, 42 U.S.C. § 2000e–2(a)(1). Not only did the Court reject the but-for standard in that case, but so too did Congress when it amended Title VII in 1991. Given this unambiguous history, it is particularly inappropriate for the Court, on its own initiative, to adopt an interpretation of the causation requirement in the ADEA that differs from the established reading of Title VII. I disagree not only with the Court's interpretation of the statute, but also with its decision to engage in unnecessary lawmaking. I would simply answer the question presented by the certiorari petition and hold that a plaintiff need not present direct evidence of age discrimination to obtain a mixed-motives instruction.

* * * That the Court is construing the ADEA rather than Title VII does not justify this departure from precedent. The relevant language in the two statutes is identical, and we have long recognized that our interpretations of Title VII's language apply "with equal force in the context of age discrimination, for the substantive provisions of the ADEA 'were derived in haec verba from Title VII.'" *Trans World Airlines, Inc. v. Thurston*, 469 U.S. 111, 121, 105 S. Ct. 613, 83 L. Ed. 2d 523 (1985) (quoting *Lorillard v. Pons*, 434 U.S. 575, 584, 98 S. Ct. 866, 55 L. Ed. 2d 40 (1978)). See generally *Northcross v. Board of Ed. of Memphis City Schools*, 412 U.S. 427, 428, 93 S. Ct. 2201, 37 L. Ed. 2d 48 (1973) (per curiam). For this reason, Justice Kennedy's dissent in *Price Waterhouse* assumed the plurality's mixed-motives framework extended to the ADEA, see 490 U.S., at 292, 109 S. Ct. 1775, 104 L. Ed. 2d 268, and the Courts of Appeals to have considered the issue unanimously have applied *Price Waterhouse* to ADEA claims. * * *

Because the 1991 Act amended only Title VII and not the ADEA with respect to mixed-motives claims, the Court reasonably declines to apply the amended provisions to the ADEA. But it proceeds to ignore the conclusion compelled by this interpretation of the Act: *Price Waterhouse*'s construction of "because of" remains the governing law for ADEA claims.

Our recent decision in *Smith v. City of Jackson*, 544 U.S. 228, 240, 125 S. Ct. 1536, 161 L. Ed. 2d 410 (2005), is precisely on point, as we considered in that case the effect of Congress' failure to amend the disparate-impact provisions of the ADEA when it amended the corresponding Title VII provisions in the 1991 Act. Noting that "the relevant 1991 amendments expanded the coverage of Title VII [but] did not amend the ADEA or speak to the subject of age discrimination," we held that "*Wards Cove*'s pre-1991 interpretation of Title VII's identical language remains applicable to the ADEA." 544 U.S., at 240, 125 S. Ct. 1536, 161 L. Ed. 2d 410 (discussing *Wards Cove Packing Co. v. Atonio*, 490 U.S. 642, 109 S. Ct. 2115, 104 L. Ed. 2d 733 (1989)). If the *Wards Cove* disparate-impact framework that Congress flatly repudiated in the Title VII context continues to apply to ADEA claims, the mixed-motives framework that Congress substantially endorsed surely applies. * * *

The 1991 amendments to Title VII also provide the answer to the majority's argument that the mixed-motives approach has proved unworkable. Because Congress has codified a mixed-motives framework for Title VII cases—the vast majority of antidiscrimination lawsuits—the Court's concerns about that framework are of no moment. Were the Court truly worried about difficulties faced by trial courts and juries, moreover, it would not reach today's decision, which will further complicate every case in which a plaintiff raises both ADEA and Title VII claims. * * *

Although the Court declines to address the question we granted certiorari to decide, I would answer that question by following our unanimous opinion in *Desert Palace, Inc. v. Costa*, 539 U.S. 90, 123 S. Ct. 2148, 156 L. Ed. 2d 84 (2003). I would accordingly hold that a plaintiff need not present direct evidence of age discrimination to obtain a mixed-motives instruction. * * *

JUSTICE BREYER, with whom JUSTICE SOUTER and JUSTICE GINSBURG join, dissenting.

* * * The words "because of" do not inherently require a showing of "but-for" causation, and I see no reason to read them to require such a showing.

It is one thing to require a typical tort plaintiff to show "but-for" causation. In that context, reasonably objective scientific or commonsense theories of physical causation make the concept of "but-for" causation comparatively easy to understand and relatively easy to apply. But it is an entirely different matter to determine a "but-for" relation when we consider, not physical forces, but the mind-related characterizations that constitute motive. * * *

All that a plaintiff can know for certain in such a context is that the forbidden motive did play a role in the employer's decision. And the fact that a jury has found that age did play a role in the decision justifies the use of the word "because," i.e., the employer dismissed the employee because of his age (and other things). * * * But the law need not automatically assess liability in these circumstances. In *Price Waterhouse* [*v. Hopkins*, 490 U.S. 228, 109 S. Ct. 1775, 104 L.Ed. 2d 268 (1989)], the plurality recognized an affirmative defense where the defendant could show that the employee would have been dismissed regardless. The law permits the employer this defense, not because the forbidden motive, age, had no role in the actual decision, but because the employer can show that he would have dismissed the employee anyway in the hypothetical circumstance in which his age-related motive was absent. And it makes sense that this would be an affirmative defense, rather than part of the showing of a violation, precisely because the defendant is in a better position than the plaintiff to establish how he would have acted in this hypothetical situation. See id., at 242, 109 S. Ct. 1775, 104 L. Ed. 2d

268; * * * . I can see nothing unfair or impractical about allocating the burdens of proof in this way.

NOTES AND QUESTIONS

Test Your Understanding of the Material

1. Suppose an employer engages in "age plus" discrimination by imposing higher performance standards on employees over 40 than on younger employees. An older employee who fails to meet those higher performance standards is terminated for performance. Would this constitute "but for" causation under *Gross*?

2. How can plaintiffs demonstrate but-for causation? Absent the rare inculpatory statement from a decionmaker, will plaintiffs invariably have to point to a significantly younger comparator who has been treated more favorably?

Related Issues

3. *Causation Standard for Other Statutes*. *Gross* has provided a default causation standard for other federal statutes. See, e.g. Lewis v. Humboldt Acquisition Corp., 681 F.3d 312 (6th Cir 2012) (*en banc*) (Americans with Disabilities Act). Furthermore, in University of Texas Southwestern Medical Center v. Nassar, 133 S.Ct. 2517 (2013), the Court held that Title VII retaliation claims brought under § 704(a), unlike discrimination claims brought under § 703, must meet the "but-for" cause standard adopted in *Gross*. The Court concluded that the but-for standard should be used in the absence of any contrary statutory directive. But cf. Ford v. Mabus, 629 F.3d 198 (D.C. Cir. 2010) (interpreting "shall be made free from any discrimination based on age" in § 633a of the ADEA to create a motivating-factor causation standard for age discrimination by the federal government). Is *Mabus* still good law after *Gross* and *Nassar*? For the standard in constitutional cases under 42 U.S.C. § 1983, see Mt. Healthy City Board of Ed. v. Doyle, 429 U.S. 274, 97 S.Ct. 568, 50 L.Ed.2d 471 (1977).

4. For criticism of *Gross*, see Michael C. Harper, The Causation Standard in Federal Employment Law; *Gross v. FBL Services*, and the Unfulfilled Promise of the Civil Rights Act of 1991, 58 Buffalo L. Rev. 69, 105–111 (2010).

3.   AGE AS A BONA FIDE OCCUPATIONAL QUALIFICATION (BFOQ)

WESTERN AIR LINES V. CRISWELL

Supreme Court of the United States, 1985.
472 U.S. 400, 105 S.Ct. 2743, 86 L.Ed.2d 321.

JUSTICE STEVENS delivered the opinion of the Court.

The petitioner, Western Air Lines, Inc., requires that its flight engineers retire at age 60. Although the Age Discrimination in Employment Act of 1967 (ADEA), 29 U.S.C. §§ 621–634, generally prohibits mandatory retirement before age 70, the Act provides an exception "where age is a bona fide occupational qualification [BFOQ] reasonably necessary to the normal operation of the particular business." A jury concluded that Western's mandatory retirement rule did not qualify as a BFOQ even though it purportedly was adopted for safety reasons. The question here is whether the jury was properly instructed on the elements of the BFOQ defense.

In its commercial airline operations, Western operates a variety of aircraft, including the Boeing 727 and the McDonnell-Douglas DC-10. These aircraft require three crew members in the cockpit: a captain, a first officer, and a flight engineer. "The 'captain' is the pilot and controls the aircraft. He is responsible for all phases of its operation. The 'first officer' is the copilot and assists the captain. The 'flight engineer' usually monitors a side-facing instrument panel. He does not operate the flight controls unless the captain and the first officer become incapacitated." *Trans World Airlines, Inc. v. Thurston,* 469 U.S. 111, 114, 105 S.Ct. 613, 618, 83 L.Ed.2d 523 (1985).

A regulation of the Federal Aviation Administration [(FAA)] prohibits any person from serving as a pilot or first officer on a commercial flight "if that person has reached his 60th birthday." 14 CFR § 121.383(c) (1985). The FAA has justified the retention of mandatory retirement for pilots on the theory that "incapacitating medical events" and "adverse psychological, emotional, and physical changes" occur as a consequence of aging. "The inability to detect or predict with precision an individual's risk of sudden or subtle incapacitation, in the face of known age-related risks, counsels against relaxation of the rule." 49 Fed.Reg. 14695 (1984). See also 24 Fed.Reg. 9776 (1959).

At the same time, the FAA has refused to establish a mandatory retirement age for flight engineers. "While a flight engineer has important duties which contribute to the safe operation of the airplane, he or she may not assume the responsibilities of the pilot in command." 49 Fed.Reg., at 14694. Moreover, available statistics establish that flight engineers have rarely been a contributing cause or factor in commercial aircraft "accidents" or "incidents." *Ibid.*

In 1978, respondents Criswell and Starley were Captains operating DC-10s for Western. Both men celebrated their 60th birthdays in July 1978. Under the collective-bargaining agreement in effect between Western and the union, cockpit crew members could obtain open positions by bidding in order of seniority. In order to avoid mandatory retirement under the FAA's under-age-60 rule for pilots, Criswell and Starley applied for reassignment as flight engineers. Western denied both requests, ostensibly on the ground that both employees were members of the company's retirement plan which required all crew members to retire at age 60.[1] For the same reason, respondent Ron, a career flight engineer, was also retired in 1978 after his 60th birthday.

Mandatory retirement provisions similar to those contained in Western's pension plan had previously been upheld under the ADEA. *United Air Lines, Inc. v. McMann,* 434 U.S. 192, 98 S.Ct. 444, 54 L.Ed.2d 402 (1977). As originally enacted in 1967, the Act provided an exception to its general proscription of age discrimination for any actions undertaken "to observe the terms of a * * * bona fide employee benefit plan such as a retirement, pension, or insurance plan, which is not a subterfuge to evade the purposes of this Act." In April 1978, however, Congress amended the statute to prohibit employee benefit plans from requiring the involuntary retirement of any employee because of age.

* * *

As the District Court summarized, the evidence at trial established that the flight engineer's "normal duties are less critical to the safety of flight than those of a pilot." The flight engineer, however, does have critical functions in emergency situations and, of course, might cause considerable disruption in the event of his own medical emergency.

The actual capabilities of persons over age 60, and the ability to detect disease or a precipitous decline in their faculties, were the subject of conflicting medical testimony. Western's expert witness, a former FAA Deputy Federal Air Surgeon, was especially concerned about the possibility of a "cardiovascular event" such as a heart attack. He testified that "with advancing age the likelihood of onset of disease increases and that in persons over age 60 it could not be predicted whether and when such diseases would occur."

The plaintiffs' experts, on the other hand, testified that physiological deterioration is caused by disease, not aging, and that "it was feasible to

---

[1]   The Western official who was responsible for the decision to retire the plaintiffs conceded that "the sole basis" for the denial of the applications of Criswell, Starley and Ron was the same: "the provision in the pension plan regarding retirement at age 60." In addition, he admitted that he had "no personal knowledge" of any safety rationale for the under-age-60 rule for flight engineers, nor had it played any significant role in his decision to retire them.

determine on the basis of individual medical examinations whether flight deck crew members, including those over age 60, were physically qualified to continue to fly." These conclusions were corroborated by the nonmedical evidence:

> "The record also reveals that both the FAA and the airlines have been able to deal with the health problems of pilots on an individualized basis. Pilots who have been grounded because of alcoholism or cardiovascular disease have been recertified by the FAA and allowed to resume flying. Pilots who were unable to pass the necessary examination to maintain their FAA first class medical certificates, but who continued to qualify for second class medical certificates were allowed to 'down-grade' from pilot to [flight engineer]. There is nothing in the record to indicate that these flight deck crew members are physically better able to perform their duties than flight engineers over age 60 who have not experienced such events or that they are less likely to become incapacitated."

Moreover, several large commercial airlines have flight engineers over age 60 "flying the line" without any reduction in their safety record.

The jury was instructed that the "BFOQ defense is available only if it is reasonably necessary to the normal operation or essence of defendant's business." The jury was informed that "the essence of Western's business is the safe transportation of their passengers." * * * The jury rendered a verdict for the plaintiffs, and awarded damages. After trial, the District Court granted equitable relief, explaining in a written opinion why he found no merit in Western's BFOQ defense to the mandatory retirement rule.

On appeal, Western made various arguments attacking the verdict and judgment below, but the Court of Appeals affirmed in all respects.

* * *

II

Throughout the legislative history of the ADEA, one empirical fact is repeatedly emphasized: the process of psychological and physiological degeneration caused by aging varies with each individual. "The basic research in the field of aging has established that there is a wide range of individual physical ability regardless of age." As a result, many older American workers perform at levels equal or superior to their younger colleagues.

* * *

III

In *Usery v. Tamiami Trail Tours, Inc.*, 531 F.2d 224 (1976), the Court of Appeals for the Fifth Circuit was called upon to evaluate the merits of a BFOQ defense to a claim of age discrimination. Tamiami Trail Tours, Inc. had a policy of refusing to hire persons over age 40 as intercity bus drivers. At trial, the bus company introduced testimony supporting its theory that the hiring policy was a BFOQ based upon safety considerations—the need to employ persons who have a low risk of accidents. In evaluating this contention, the Court of Appeals drew on its Title VII precedents, and concluded that two inquiries were relevant.

First, the court recognized that some job qualifications may be so peripheral to the central mission of the employer's business that *no* age discrimination can be "reasonably *necessary* to the normal operation of the particular business." 29 U.S.C. § 623(f)(1). The bus company justified the age qualification for hiring its drivers on safety considerations, but the court concluded that this claim was to be evaluated under an objective standard:

> "[T]he job qualifications which the employer invokes to justify his discrimination must be *reasonably necessary* to the essence of his business—here, the *safe* transportation of bus passengers from one point to another. The greater the safety factor, measured by the likelihood of harm and the probable severity of that harm in case of an accident, the more stringent may be the job qualifications designed to insure safe driving." 531 F.2d, at 236.

This inquiry "adjusts to the safety factor" by ensuring that the employer's restrictive job qualifications are "reasonably necessary" to further the overriding interest in public safety. *Ibid.* In *Tamiami,* the court noted that no one had seriously challenged the bus company's safety justification for hiring drivers with a low risk of having accidents.

Second, the court recognized that the ADEA requires that age qualifications be something more than "convenient" or "reasonable"; they must be "reasonably necessary * * * to the particular business," and this is only so when the employer is compelled to rely on age as a proxy for the safety-related job qualifications validated in the first inquiry. This showing could be made in two ways. The employer could establish that it " 'had reasonable cause to believe, that is, a factual basis for believing, that all or substantially all (persons over the age qualifications) would be unable to perform safely and efficiently the duties of the job involved.' " In *Tamiami,* the employer did not seek to justify its hiring qualification under this standard.

Alternatively, the employer could establish that age was a legitimate proxy for the safety-related job qualifications by proving that it is " 'impossible or highly impractical' " to deal with the older employees on an individualized basis. "One method by which the employer can carry this burden is to establish that some members of the discriminated-against class possess a trait precluding safe and efficient job performance that cannot be ascertained by means other than knowledge of the applicant's membership in the class." *Id.,* at 235. In *Tamiami,* the medical evidence on this point was conflicting, but the District Court had found that individual examinations could not determine which individuals over the age of 40 would be unable to operate the buses safely. The Court of Appeals found that this finding of fact was not "clearly erroneous," and affirmed the District Court's judgment for the bus company on the BFOQ defense. *Id.,* at 238.

* * *

Every Court of Appeals that has confronted a BFOQ defense based on safety considerations has analyzed the problem consistently with the *Tamiami* standard. An EEOC regulation embraces the same criteria. Considering the narrow language of the BFOQ exception, the parallel treatment of such questions under Title VII, and the uniform application of the standard by the federal courts, the EEOC and Congress, we conclude that this two-part inquiry properly identifies the relevant considerations for resolving a BFOQ defense to an age-based qualification purportedly justified by considerations of safety.

IV

* * *

On a more specific level, Western argues that flight engineers must meet the same stringent qualifications as pilots, and that it was therefore quite logical to extend to flight engineers the FAA's age-60 retirement rule for pilots. Although the FAA's rule for pilots, adopted for safety reasons, is relevant evidence in the airline's BFOQ defense, it is not to be accorded conclusive weight. *Johnson v. Mayor and City Council of Baltimore,* 472 U.S. 353, 105 S.Ct. 2717, 86 L.Ed.2d 286. The extent to which the rule is probative varies with the weight of the evidence supporting its safety rationale and "the congruity between the * * * occupations at issue." In this case, the evidence clearly established that the FAA, Western, and other airlines all recognized that the qualifications for a flight engineer were less rigorous than those required for a pilot.[28]

In the absence of persuasive evidence supporting its position, Western nevertheless argues that the jury should have been instructed to defer to "Western's selection of job qualifications for the position of [flight engineer]

---

[28] As the Court of Appeals noted, the "jury heard testimony that Western itself allows a captain under the age of sixty who cannot, for health reasons, continue to fly as a captain or co-pilot to downbid to a position as second officer. (In addition,) half the pilots flying in the United States are flying for major airlines which do not require second officers to retire at the age of sixty, and * * * there are over 200 such second officers currently flying on wide-bodied aircraft."

that are reasonable in light of the safety risks." This proposal is plainly at odds with Congress' decision, in adopting the ADEA, to subject such management decisions to a test of objective justification in a court of law. The BFOQ standard adopted in the statute is one of "reasonable necessity," not reasonableness.

In adopting that standard, Congress did not ignore the public interest in safety. That interest is adequately reflected in instructions that track the language of the statute. When an employer establishes that a job qualification has been carefully formulated to respond to documented concerns for public safety, it will not be overly burdensome to persuade a trier of fact that the qualification is "reasonably necessary" to safe operation of the business. The uncertainty implicit in the concept of managing safety risks always makes it "reasonably necessary" to err on the side of caution in a close case. The employer cannot be expected to establish the risk of an airline accident "to a certainty, for certainty would require running the risk until a tragic accident would prove that the judgment was sound." *Usery v. Tamiami Trail Tours, Inc.,* 531 F.2d, at 238. When the employer's argument has a credible basis in the record, it is difficult to believe that a jury of lay persons—many of whom no doubt have flown or could expect to fly on commercial air carriers—would not defer in a close case to the airline's judgment. Since the instructions in this case would not have prevented the airline from raising this contention to the jury in closing argument, we are satisfied that the verdict is a consequence of a defect in Western's proof rather than a defect in the trial court's instructions.

* * *

* * * It might well be "rational" to require mandatory retirement at *any* age less than 70, but that result would not comply with Congress' direction that employers must justify the rationale for the age chosen. Unless an employer can establish a substantial basis for believing that all or nearly all employees above an age lack the qualifications required for the position, the age selected for mandatory retirement less than 70 must be an age at which it is highly impractical for the employer to insure by individual testing that its employees will have the necessary qualifications for the job.

* * *

When an employee covered by the Act is able to point to reputable businesses in the same industry that choose to eschew reliance on mandatory retirement earlier than age 70, when the employer itself relies on individualized testing in similar circumstances, and when the administrative agency with primary responsibility for maintaining airline safety has determined that individualized testing is not impractical for the relevant position, the employer's attempt to justify its decision on the basis of the contrary opinion of experts—solicited for the purposes of litigation—is hardly convincing on any objective standard short of complete deference. Even in cases involving public safety, the ADEA plainly does not permit the trier of fact to give complete deference to the employer's decision.

NOTES AND QUESTIONS

> *Mandatory Retirement of Pilots over the Age of 65*
>
> Congress acted in response to the FAA's announcement that it would begin a rulemaking procedure to consider raising the pilots' mandatory retirement age to 65. On December 13, 2007, President George W. Bush signed legislation that allows commercial pilots in the United States to fly until age 65. 121 Stat. 1450, P.L. 110–135, codified at 49 U.S.C. § 40101.

Test Your Understanding of the Material

1. How did Western Air Lines' retirement rule for flight engineers differ from the FAA rules?

2. Following *Criswell*, what must an employer prove to establish a safety-related BFOQ defense in an ADEA case?

3. Do you share the Supreme Court's confidence that lay juries will weigh appropriately safety arguments which have "a credible basis in the record," when faced with real-life plaintiffs who have no documented medical problems and are armed with their own expert witnesses? Should these judgments be made in case-by-case adjudication or should the EEOC (or the Federal Aviation Administration) engage in rulemaking on the issue, so that available data can be dispassionately assessed and generic, across-the-board determinations can be made for particular industries?

Related Issues

4. *Permissible Statistical Discrimination to Avoid Safety Risks?* The *Criswell* Court's adoption of the *Tamiami* modification of the two-prong *Diaz* and *Weeks* BFOQ test would seem to permit some degree of statistical discrimination, at least where necessary to protect public safety. The predicate showing required of employers is a demonstration that it is "impossible or highly impractical" to assess risk on an individualized basis.

Might *Criswell* and *Tamiami* be read to permit employers in some cases to use an age cut-off for *hiring* that is many years short of the average age at which motor coordination skills, attention span, and other characteristics related to safe operation of vehicles begin to decline? In Hodgson v. Greyhound Lines, Inc., 499 F.2d 859 (7th Cir.1974), for instance, the employer defended a 35 year age cut-off for hiring drivers with evidence that average safety records improved with 15 to 20 years of experience, but started to decline on the average at age 55. The employer contended that it could not get the benefit of driver experience if it hired post-40 year old drivers and waited until they reached 55 to determine which of them might be exceptions to the average. Is this a form of statistical discrimination based on average group characteristics that is any different from the maximum-age limitations criticized in Secretary Wirtz's report?

5.   *Exception for Firefighters and Law Enforcement Officers.* ADEA permits state and local governments under certain conditions to engage in age-based hiring or mandatory retirement of firefighters and law enforcement officers. The hiring or retirement action must be based on a state or local law in effect on March 3, 1983 (the date that the Supreme Court upheld application of the ADEA to state governments), or on an age cut-off set by applicable state or local law if that law was enacted after September 30, 1996 (the date of enactment of the ADEA amendments of 1996). If the action is a retirement under a law enacted after September 30, 1996, the terminated individual also must be at least 55. See 29 U.S.C. § 623(j).

6.   *Appearance/Customer Preference BFOQ—The Case of Broadcasting.* Assume that a broadcasting station's market research shows that local viewers prefer younger sportscasters. Could the station use this research to justify replacing an older sportscaster? Cf. *Craft v. Metromedia, Inc.,* 766 F.2d 1205 (8th Cir.1985); *Wilson v. Southwest Airlines Co.,* pp. 358–363 supra. What if the research showed that a particular older sportscaster was not as popular as his younger rival on another station? Should the reason for his relative popularity matter? Cf. *Ryther v. KARE 11,* 108 F.3d 832 (8th Cir.1997) (en banc) (market research found to be pretext for age-based termination).

7.   *Seniority and ADEA.* Section 4(f)(2) of the ADEA also provides a defense for employers who "observe the terms of a bona fide seniority system." Because seniority systems generally favor older workers, ADEA issues in this context rarely arise. The 1978 amendments add the proviso that such systems may not "require or permit" involuntary retirement on account of age.

In *Trans World Airlines, Inc. v. Thurston,* supra, the Court held that the carrier's rule preventing pilots over the age of 60 from bumping less senior flight engineers was an age-based classification and not protected by § 4(f)(2). EEOC regulations require that to be bona fide, a seniority system must treat length of service as "the primary criterion for the equitable allocation of available employment opportunities and prerogatives." 29 C.F.R. § 1625.8 (1986).

4.   SYSTEMIC DISPARATE TREATMENT AND STATISTICAL PROOF

Private ADEA suits alleging a pattern and practice of age discrimination are relatively rare. The next case, *Mistretta v. Sandia Corp.,* represents one such case. See also *Barnes v. GenCorp Inc.,* 896 F.2d 1457 (6th Cir.1990); *Mangold v. California Public Utilities Commission,* 67 F.3d 1470 (9th Cir.1995).

MISTRETTA V. SANDIA CORP.

United States District Court, District of New Mexico, 1977.
15 EPD ¶ 7902, affirmed, 639 F.2d 600 (10th Cir.1980).

MECHEM, J.

What is presently Sandia Corporation began as an engineering support division of Los Alamos Scientific Laboratory in 1946. In response to a request by the United States Government, Sandia was incorporated as a Delaware corporation in 1949 by Western Electric Company, Incorporated, and its wholly owned subsidiary. Sandia is a prime contractor to the Atomic Energy Commission (AEC), now Energy Research and Development Administration (ERDA).

AEC, and its successor ERDA, review the personnel policies and practices of Sandia, including salary administration, for the purpose of ascertaining compliance with applicable Federal statutes, regulations and executive orders. Sandia's personnel policies are derived from Bell system personnel policies.

The contract between Western Electric and ERDA specifies that there shall be no fee or profit for Western Electric or Sandia, and that all costs incurred under the contract are reimbursable and are funded by the Federal Government. Sandia is a "level of effort" laboratory. It is the responsibility of Sandia's management to staff to the level necessary within its overall budget to accomplish the tasks assigned to it by ERDA.

* * *

Since the early 1950's defendant's scientists and engineers involved in the laboratory's primary research and development activities have been classified as Members of Technical Staff (MTS). Since 1960 other employees involved primarily in various technical and non-technical support activities have been employed under defendant's Position Evaluation Plan (PEP). Prior to April, 1973, PEP employees involved in either technical staff or laboratory staff functions were in the following employee classifications:

1) Technical

(a) *Technical Staff Associate* (TSA)—Professional level, non-degree employees who work with MTS, level obtained by experience or technical school background.

(b) *Staff Assistant Technical* (SAT)—Employees who through experience or education have obtained Technical Institute degree level. They work either in direct assistance to MTS and TSA or work independently in testing, maintenance and assembly operations.

2)   Administrative

(a) *Member   Laboratory   Staff*   (MLS)—Professional   level administrative employees, non-MTS supervisors and professional level technical employees performing non-MTS functions such as plant engineering.

(b) *Laboratory   Staff   Associate*   (LSA)—Professional   level employees who work with administrative MLS. They obtained their level by experience in administrative work.

(c) *Staff Assistant Laboratory* (SAL)—Employees who either provide assistance to MLS in administrative work, provide drafting and routine design work for MTS, or are high level clerical employees.

* * *

Sandia admits that it concentrates on college recruiting to assure continuity and gradual turnover. [Sandia's officials] do not actively recruit in the protected age group because older applicants, they say, are not available in significant numbers. Sandia also considers recent academic training to provide broader knowledge than field experience. Sandia does not close the door in an older applicant's face. An older or experienced applicant would normally come to Sandia to fill a specific vacancy rather than being hired at the bottom to be trained into a position.

* * *

There is nothing inherently suspicious about on-campus recruiting programs. The available labor market for Sandia technical staff would be expected to come from recent graduates at all degree levels, in addition to the most recent exposure to advanced education, new techniques and new discoveries in the fields of science, this group would be job hunting while those in the protected age group normally would be established in more permanent positions and advanced to positions attributable to their age and experience. Age discrimination cannot be inferred from facts which show that 90% of new hires are younger than the protected age group. This pattern does not show a significant disparity from what would normally be expected in the market place. No evidence was presented to show whether applicants in the protected age group had less success in finding employment at Sandia than applicants generally. Considering all this evidence together, I hold that plaintiffs have not established by a preponderance of the evidence that Sandia has discriminated against individuals from forty to sixty-five years of age in recruiting and hiring policies and practices.

The next area of inquiry, promotions and educational opportunity, is presented only for its evidentiary value. The Secretary of Labor presents this in support of his contention that age discrimination is present in all major areas of Sandia.

* * *

Plaintiff's expert, Dr. Spalding, divided individuals promoted into MTS and PEP categories by year from 1964 to 1974. He compared the mean age of those on [the] roll to the mean age of those promoted and then tested to determine whether it was improbable that the difference could occur by chance. One of the few things plaintiffs' and defendants' experts agreed upon was that the probability of a chance occurrence had to be less than 5% before it could be considered statistically significant.

Dr. Spalding found no statistical significance in the PEP classification, but he did find statistically significant differences in the MTS category in seven of the eleven years analyzed. Once again, however, all Dr. Spalding was saying was that something was causing the difference, but he could not testify as to the cause on the basis of his tests.

If I read Dr. Spalding's summary of MTS promotions, plaintiff's exhibit 89, vertically rather than horizontally, it shows a trend. The mean age of those on [the] roll increased from 36.1 in 1964 to a mean age of 41.4 in 1974. The mean age of those promoted decreases from 36.3 in 1965 to 34.9 in 1974 with a low of 32.1 in 1971.

Defendant criticizes this study as distorted because it assumes that all MTS were eligible for promotion to a supervisory position. It is true that there are considerable restrictions to mobility between divisions or departments and Dr. Spalding did not analyze the positions being filled and those who might be eligible. This evidence, however, was not intended to present a full blown promotion policy case, but was merely intended to show that there was some age bias in the promotion area. There are approximately 250 MTS division supervisors. The evidence is sufficient to cause a reasonable suspicion that age is a factor in MTS promotion to the first level of supervision.

* * *

As noted before, Sandia's budget is determined by the size of the federal government's appropriation to AEC/ERDA. Sandia's growth period ended in 1968. Sandia entered a period of monetary restrictions and reductions with no change in its general mission or scope of operations beginning with Fiscal Year 1971. These restrictions resulted in voluntary and involuntary reductions in force (R.I.F.) in calendar years 1970 and 1971, amounting to 12 percent of the staff. Sandia's population declined from 8,182 on January 31, 1970 to 7,177 as of December, 1972.

The criteria used as the basis for the selection of employees for involuntary termination in 1970 were "contribution to the mission of the laboratory" and "job elimination". Following the reduction in force in 1970, for a period of one week, a compliance officer of the Department of Labor reviewed the layoff for possible age discrimination. No action was taken against Sandia because the compliance officer's report was favorable to defendant.

* * *

The defendant identified some individuals for involuntary layoff by determining which jobs could be eliminated. Actually, many cases of job elimination were cases of reassigning duties of the individual to others. Other candidates were selected by identifying what Sandia termed "least contributors to the mission of the Company." This was determined by an individual's performance rating and a job importance evaluation.

* * *

Following the close of the voluntary termination option on March 2, 1973. Sandia realized it had under-estimated the number of volunteers. Sandia offered forty-one of the employees on the involuntary list a chance to remain on the [roll] and 39 accepted the offer. All but one were in the protected age group. In the Sandian dialect, these individuals are referred to as "Saved by the Sunday exercise".

* * *

[Eds. The court proceeded to describe the study conducted by the Secretary's expert, Dr. Spalding.] The variable in the study was age on an ordinal scale of 18 to 64. Dr. Spalding made an assumption called a "null hypothesis", which is a conjecture that any differences in the expected and observed data are due to random sampling chance or, in other words, "that selection for layoff was independent of age". Also included in the null hypothesis is the assumption that all other factors are equal. This analysis was portrayed on a * * * chart which displays graphically the cumulative frequencies of the expected and observed groups.

The next step in the analysis is to measure the difference between the observed and expected frequencies and then use statistical tables to make a statement of the probability that the difference occurs by chance. Statisticians on this case agree that when the probability of a distribution happening by random chance is less than 5%, the result is statistically significant. When the probability of a chance occurrence is less than 5%, the statistician rejects his null hypothesis or conjecture. Dr. Spalding rejected his null hypothesis in 34 of his 36 studies.

* * *

I will not discuss Dr. Spalding's various combination studies in detail. His analysis of all PEP and MTS, supervisors included, is the Lab-wide study (graded employees excluded). It helps normalize or generalize some of this data and shows 33% of those terminated involuntarily were between the ages of 54 and 64, while only 15% of the Lab population falls into this age group.

The Secretary introduced numerous exhibits showing that Sandia's management and lower line supervision tended toward stereotyping older non-supervisory employees as unproductive and becoming technically obsolete. Management also believed that the future of the Lab depended upon "new blood", that is, young Ph'd's. There is a factual explanation for this belief in the rapid changes in technology taking place at that time. The end result was an arbitrary generalization that older employees did not have the ability to keep pace with new developments. This "attitude" evidence corroborates the statistical evidence and supports an inference that age was a factor in selection for layoff.

Sandia contends Dr. Spalding's layoff analysis is misleading and insignificant because he assumed all factors other than age were equal and he cannot testify that any individual was laid off because of his age, i.e., a causal relationship between age and layoff. The latter criticism is misplaced because *Teamsters* [*v. United States*, 431 U.S. 324, 97 S.Ct. 1843, 52 L.Ed.2d 396 (1977),] does not require direct proof of discrimination. The assumption in Dr. Spalding's study that all other factors were equal does not significantly undermine the weight. The strength of Dr. Spalding's analysis does not lie in his methods, probability statements, or rejection of a null hypothesis. The value of his testimony lies in the presentation of the data which I have analyzed by a simple numerical and percentage method.

Although it may be technically improper to discuss defendant's evidence before determining whether plaintiff has proved a prima facie case, it is more convenient to discuss Dr. Prairie's statistical tests at this time.

To rebut Dr. Spalding's testimony, defendant's expert, Dr. Prairie, testified that performance was the most significant factor in selection for layoff. The first step in Dr. Prairie's analysis was to prepare contingency tables by job classification and age. The purpose of a contingency analysis is to determine whether two percentages or proportion[s] can be considered statistically equal. * * * He found a significant age-layoff correlation only in the MLS and SAT classifications. Finding a significant correlation in this analysis does not provide evidence of causality. It indicates that further tests must be performed.

Dr. Prairie then divided MTS and non-supervisory MTS into three sub-groups; low performers, middle performers, and high performers. This * * * analysis formed the basis of his opinion that: 1) age was not a factor in determining whether a low performer was to be laid off; 2) among middle performers the impact was on individuals less than age 40; 3) there were no layoffs among high performers.

Dr. Prairie found a significant correlation between performance and age, i.e., those under 40 tended to get higher ratings. He divided the MTS population into two groups; high education (Master's degree level or above), low education (less than a Master's degree), to determine whether education might explain the difference. Dr. Prairie concludes that education level explains a substantial part of the performance-age relationship in the MTS category with supervisors included. But, with supervision excluded, the explanation is weakened. Dr. Prairie finds that the relationship between education and performance is strong and that the under 40 age group tends to account for a greater percentage of those with high education level.

The next analysis is called a discriminant analysis, the purpose of which, according to Dr. Prairie, is "to determine which of the factors or combination of factors * * * is important in properly assigning * * * people to layoff or non-layoff category." This analysis uses actual ages and a numerical value for education that Sandia uses in the personnel area. The layoff group of 123 MTS's was compared against a random sample of 123 employees not laid off to determine whether the selected factors were valuable in predicting who would be laid off. Dr. Prairie concludes that performance is the key factor in predicting who would be laid off.

* * *

Dr. Prairie's discriminant factors analysis leads to his overall opinion that performance was the decisive factor in the 1973 layoff. This explanation will fail if performance ratings contain age bias. In fact, the discriminant analysis depends on the purity of the performance factor as an appropriate classification.

* * *

An age discrimination case is different from a Title VII case. When Title VII type discrimination is present, it is normally a clear cut pattern or practice against a protected group as a whole. Here the pattern and practice has not been shown to affect the whole protected age group. The evidence establishes a prima facie case that at age 52, age is beginning to appear as a factor in layoff decisions. After age 55, the inference that age was a factor in [the] selection process becomes stronger and this trend continues up to about age 58, and then it appears to remain at the same strength up to age 64. * * * This comes as no surprise because a large number of layoff decisions were made by supervisors who were in the lower half of the protected age group. They did not consider themselves or their peers to be "over the hill".

After examining Dr. Prairie's analysis, I find it insufficient to defeat plaintiff's prima facie showing that individuals aged 52 to 64 were adversely affected by layoff decisions in a pattern significantly different from other employees.

Sandia must shoulder the burden of going forward with evidence of its defense. Defendant's evidence can be designed to defeat plaintiff's prima facie case or to show a non-discriminatory reason for its actions.

* * *

The theme of Sandia's defense is that performance ratings were the main ingredient in layoff decisions. The rating system has been described in a preceding section of this opinion. The system is extremely subjective and has never been validated. Supervisors were not told to consider specific criteria in their ratings. Like the system criticized in *Brito v. Zia Co.*, 478 F.2d 1200, 1206 [(10th Cir.1973)], the evaluations were based on [the] best judgment and opinion of the evaluators, but were not based on any definite identifiable criteria based on quality or quantity of work or specific performances that were supported by some kind of record. Courts have condemned subjective standards as fostering discrimination. Thus, they have declined to give much weight to testimony when a company's justification of its decision or policy is based on subjective criteria. *Muller v. U.S. Steel* [*Corp.*, 509 F.2d 923, 929 (10th Cir.), cert. denied, 423 U.S. 825, 96 S.Ct. 39, 46 L.Ed.2d 41 (1975)]; *Rich v. Martin-Marietta* [*Corp.*], 522 F.2d [333, 350 (10th Cir.1975)] * * * .

[Defendant's experts testified that it would] be very difficult to define goals, (and to) develop objective criteria for evaluating engineers and scientists engaged in research. [They] agree that the value of a person is affected by the importance of his assignments and they observe a tendency in other companies to give more challenging assignments to the young Ph'd's. Defendant's experts * * * see a performance level being identified in about ten years and remaining constant for the rest of an individual's career. It would appear, however, that the problems of stating specific objective rating criteria applies [sic] only to a portion of Sandia's work force—those scientists or engineers engaged in research. It would appear to be a relatively simple task to define objective rating criteria for draftsmen, machinists, computer operators and administrative personnel. * * *

Management's concern about the increasing age of its staff, reduced hiring, new technical developments, and emphasis on recruiting and advancing young Ph'd's might not violate ADEA in themselves, but these policies and attitudes could easily be reflected in subjective performance ratings.

* * * Sandia's experts agree that challenging job assignments at other companies go to younger Ph'd's. In this case there were employees who were laid off because they had been in one line of research too long and were considered less versatile than younger employees. The evidence presented is not sufficient to prove or disprove the contention that at Sandia performance declines with age, but there is sufficient circumstantial evidence to indicate that age bias and age based policies

appear throughout the performance rating process to the detriment of the protected age group. This constitutes sufficient reason to reject Dr. Prairie's analyses.

Considering all of defendant's evidence, Sandia's defense does not show: that its actions are nondiscriminatory; that its policies are necessary to the safe and efficient operation of its business; or that its subjective rating system is necessary throughout all of its employee classifications. Sandia has failed to rebut the plaintiff's prima facie case.

I hold that the plaintiffs have established by a preponderance of the evidence that individuals in the 52 to 64 age range were selected for layoff in a pattern which proves that Sandia has engaged in discriminatory conduct.

NOTES AND QUESTIONS

Organizational Theory Note

Organizational theorists have observed the operation of a "Peter Principle": "In an organization consisting of many job levels, each the main source of candidates for filling vacancies in the next higher level, there may be a tendency for individuals to rise in the organization to a level at which they are barely able to perform." See W. Connolly & D. Peterson, Use of Statistics in Equal Employment Opportunity Litigation § 10.05 (1985). Might this "Peter Principle" provide a benign explanation for the arguably suspicious promotion statistics noted by the *Mistretta* court?

Test Your Understanding of the Material

1.   What adverse employment actions formed the basis of plaintiffs' claims? What conclusion did the court reach as to each type of adverse action?

2.   The *Mistretta* court asserts that the hiring of a very high proportion (90%) of new employees from outside the protected ADEA class does not suggest age bias in hiring absent evidence about the relative numbers of members of the protected class in the qualified applicant pool. Would age-based hiring be suggested by proof that individuals over the age of 40 constituted significantly more than 10% of the pool of qualified workers in the external labor market?

Related Issues

3.   *"Me Too" Evidence.* Under what conditions should an employee complaining of a particular personnel decision be allowed to introduce evidence of age bias from supervisors other than the one making the decision? Consider, for instance, an employee claiming that he was selected by a supervisor on the basis of his age for being laid off in a reduction-in-force. Should the introduction of evidence of age bias by other supervisors be dependent upon

the employee introducing statistical or other evidence of a company-wide policy connecting the age bias of various supervisors? Cf. Sprint/United Management Co. v. Mendelsohn, 552 U.S. 379, 128 S.Ct. 1140, 170 L.Ed.2d 1 (2008) ("The question whether evidence of discrimination by other supervisors is relevant in an individual ADEA case is fact based and depends on many factors, including how closely related the evidence is to the plaintiff's circumstances and theory of the case . . . Rules 401 and 403 do not make such evidence per se admissible or per se inadmissible").

4. *Age-Correlated Decline in Research Productivity.* Sandia was not able to counter the government's showing of a correlation between older age with the incidence of involuntary layoff by proving that it selected individuals on the basis of their relative productivity. However, a correlation between age and declining productivity of those engaged in research seems especially plausible for at least two reasons: (i) the increasing obsolescence of any scientific education and (ii) the risks of increasing specialization in particular research. If such explanations were adequately proven, how might a plaintiff respond? What if the plaintiff could establish that the employer never counseled relatively low performers that they needed to improve their technological knowledge or research skills?

5. *Relevance of Intraclass Statistics.* Note that the *Mistretta* court's assumption that age discrimination may present issues of intraclass discrimination is confirmed by the Supreme Court's later decision in *O'Connor*. The *Mistretta* court stressed that the plaintiff's evidence suggested age bias against those in the protected class between the ages of 52 and 64, but not those between the ages of 40 and 52. The court also criticized the defendant's expert for analyzing the impact of involuntary layoffs on those over age 40 as compared with those under age 40, thus possibly "obscur[ing] an impact somewhere inside the protected age group." Assume that the evidence had shown that individuals between the ages of 52 and 58 comprised 30% of the laid-off group and only 10% of the relevant workforce, but that individuals between the ages of 58 and 65 comprised only 5% of the laid-off group and 10% of the relevant workforce. Are such statistics consistent with a plausible account of a discriminatorily motivated employer?

C. DISPARATE IMPACT

HAZEN PAPER COMPANY V. BIGGINS

Supreme Court of the United States, 1993.
507 U.S. 604, 113 S.Ct. 1701, 123 L.Ed.2d 338.

JUSTICE O'CONNOR delivered the opinion of the Court.

* * * Petitioner Hazen Paper Company manufactures coated, laminated, and printed paper and paperboard. The company is owned and operated by two cousins, petitioners Robert Hazen and Thomas N. Hazen. The Hazens hired respondent Walter F. Biggins as their technical director in 1977. They fired him in 1986, when he was 62 years old.

Respondent brought suit against petitioners in the United States District Court for the District of Massachusetts, alleging a violation of the ADEA. He claimed that age had been a determinative factor in petitioners' decision to fire him. Petitioners contested this claim, asserting instead that respondent had been fired for doing business with competitors of Hazen Paper. The case was tried before a jury, which rendered a verdict for respondent on his ADEA claim and also found violations of the Employee Retirement Income Security Act of 1974 (ERISA), 88 Stat. 895, § 510, 29 U.S.C. § 1140, and state law. On the ADEA count, the jury specifically found that petitioners "willfully" violated the statute. Under § 7(b) of the ADEA, 29 U.S.C. § 626(b), a "willful" violation gives rise to liquidated damages.

Petitioners moved for judgment notwithstanding the verdict. The District Court granted the motion with respect to a state-law claim and the finding of "willfulness" but otherwise denied it. An appeal ensued. The United States Court of Appeals for the First Circuit affirmed judgment for respondent on both the ADEA and ERISA counts, and reversed judgment notwithstanding the verdict for petitioners as to "willfulness."

In affirming the judgments of liability, the Court of Appeals relied heavily on the evidence that petitioners had fired respondent in order to prevent his pension benefits from vesting. That evidence, as construed most favorably to respondent by the court, showed that the Hazen Paper pension plan had a 10-year vesting period and that respondent would have reached the 10-year mark had he worked "a few more weeks" after being fired. There was also testimony that petitioners had offered to retain respondent as a consultant to Hazen Paper, in which capacity he would not have been entitled to receive pension benefits. The Court of Appeals found this evidence of pension interference to be sufficient for ERISA liability, and also gave it considerable emphasis in upholding ADEA liability.

* * *

In a disparate treatment case, liability depends on whether the protected trait (under the ADEA, age) actually motivated the employer's decision. The employer may have relied upon a formal, facially discriminatory policy requiring adverse treatment of employees with that trait. Or the employer may have been motivated by the protected trait on an ad hoc, informal basis. Whatever the employer's decisionmaking process, a disparate treatment claim cannot succeed unless the employee's protected trait actually played a role in that process and had a determinative influence on the outcome.

Disparate treatment, thus defined, captures the essence of what Congress sought to prohibit in the ADEA. It is the very essence of age discrimination for an older employee to be fired because the employer believes that productivity and competence decline with old age. As we explained in *EEOC v. Wyoming*, 460 U.S. 226, 75 L. Ed. 2d 18, 103 S. Ct. 1054 (1983), Congress' promulgation of the ADEA was prompted by its concern that older workers were being deprived of employment on the basis of inaccurate and stigmatizing stereotypes. * * * Thus the ADEA commands that "employers are to evaluate [older] employees * * * on their merits and not their age." *Western Air Lines, Inc. v. Criswell*, 472 U.S. 400, 422, 86 L. Ed. 2d 321, 105 S. Ct. 2743 (1985). The employer cannot rely on age as a proxy for an employee's remaining characteristics, such as productivity, but must instead focus on those factors directly.

When the employer's decision is wholly motivated by factors other than age, the problem of inaccurate and stigmatizing stereotypes disappears. This is true even if the motivating factor is correlated with age, as pension status typically is. Pension plans typically provide that an employee's accrued benefits will become nonforfeitable, or "vested," once the employee completes a certain number of years of service with the employer. See 1 J. Mamorsky, Employee Benefits Law § 5.03 (1992). On average, an older employee has had more years in the work force than a younger employee, and thus may well have accumulated more years of service with a particular employer. Yet an employee's age is analytically distinct from his years of service. An employee who is younger than 40, and therefore outside the class of older workers as defined by the ADEA, see 29 U.S.C. § 631(a), may have worked for a particular employer his entire career, while an older worker may have been newly hired. Because age and years of service are analytically distinct, an employer can take account of one while ignoring the other, and thus it is incorrect to say that a decision based on years of service is necessarily "age-based."

The instant case is illustrative. Under the Hazen Paper pension plan, as construed by the Court of Appeals, an employee's pension benefits vest after the employee completes 10 years of service with the company. Perhaps it is true that older employees of Hazen Paper are more likely to be "close to vesting" than younger employees. Yet a decision by the company to fire an older employee solely because he has nine-plus years of service and therefore is "close to vesting" would not constitute discriminatory treatment on the basis of age. The prohibited stereotype ("Older employees are likely to be _____") would not have figured in this decision, and the attendant stigma would not ensue. The decision would not be the result of an inaccurate and denigrating generalization about age, but would rather represent an accurate judgment about the employee— that he indeed is "close to vesting."

We do not mean to suggest that an employer lawfully could fire an employee in order to prevent his pension benefits from vesting. Such conduct is actionable under § 510 of ERISA, as the Court of Appeals rightly found in affirming judgment for respondent under that statute. See *Ingersoll-Rand Co. v. McClendon*, 498 U.S. 133, 142–143, 112 L. Ed. 2d

474, 111 S. Ct. 478 (1990). But it would not, without more, violate the ADEA. * * *

We do not preclude the possibility that an employer who targets employees with a particular pension status on the assumption that these employees are likely to be older thereby engages in age discrimination. Pension status may be a proxy for age, not in the sense that the ADEA makes the two factors equivalent, cf. *Metz* [*v. Transit Mix, Inc.*, 828 F.2d 1202, 1208 (7th Cir., 1987)] (using "proxy" to mean statutory equivalence), but in the sense that the employer may suppose a correlation between the two factors and act accordingly. Nor do we rule out the possibility of dual liability under ERISA and the ADEA where the decision to fire the employee was motivated both by the employee's age and by his pension status. Finally, we do not consider the special case where an employee is about to vest in pension benefits as a result of his age, rather than years of service, see 1 Mamorsky, *supra*, at § 5.02[2], and the employer fires the employee in order to prevent vesting. That case is not presented here. Our holding is simply that an employer does not violate the ADEA just by interfering with an older employee's pension benefits that would have vested by virtue of the employee's years of service.

[*Eds.*: The Court's discussion of the standard for "willful" violations under § 7(b) of ADEA is omitted.]

NOTES AND QUESTIONS

Test Your Understanding of the Material

1.   Does *Hazen Paper* foreclose ADEA challenges to termination decisions based on factors like length of service that are highly correlated with age? Is it significant that the case involved a 10-year vesting period requirement rather than a more continuous length of service crieterion? Is it significant that Congress already provided protection against interference with pension vesting in § 510 of ERISA?

Related Issues

2.   *Irrelevance of Higher Cost of Hiring or Retaining Older Workers?* Does *Hazen Paper* hinder the statutory objective of encouraging the employment of older workers by allowing employers to refuse to hire or to fire employees because of rising wages associated with length of service? See Harper, ADEA Doctrinal Impediments, supra, at 779–790; Christine Jolls, Hands-Tying and the Age Discrimination in Employment Act, 74 Tex. L. Rev. 1813 (1996). In *Metz v. Transit Mix, Inc.*, which was cited cited in *Hazen Paper*, the Seventh Circuit held that the employer could not advance cost saving as a justification for replacing an older worker when the employer's pay structure rewarded length of service in general. Is *Metz* still good law after *Hazen Paper*?

3.   *"Safe Harbor to Encourage the Employment of Older Workers?* For a proposal to encourage the hiring of older workers through mitigation of the disincentive effects of the threat of age-based discrimination litigation, see

Michael C. Harper, A Gap in the Agenda, supra. Professor Harper argues that providing "employers with a period of insulation from being sued for age discrimination by an employee after being hired initially after a high cut-off age," such as 55 or older, would enable employers to "escape their dependence on generalizations by gaining knowledge of older hirees as individuals." Id. at 633.

———————

The *Hazen* Court expressly reserved judgment on whether disparate impact claims are available under the ADEA. Twelve years later, the Court decided the issue.

SMITH V. CITY OF JACKSON, MISSISSIPPI
Supreme Court of the United States, 2005.
544 U.S. 228, 125 S.Ct. 1536, 161 L.Ed.2d 410.

JUSTICE STEVENS announced the judgment of the Court and delivered the opinion of the Court with respect to Parts I, II, and IV, and an opinion with respect to Part III, in which JUSTICE SOUTER, JUSTICE GINSBURG, and JUSTICE BREYER join.

* * *

I

On October 1, 1998, the City adopted a pay plan granting raises to all City employees. The stated purpose of the plan was to "attract and retain qualified people, provide incentive for performance, maintain competitiveness with other public sector agencies and ensure equitable compensation to all employees regardless of age, sex, race and/or disability." On May 1, 1999, a revision of the plan, which was motivated, at least in part, by the City's desire to bring the starting salaries of police officers up to the regional average, granted raises to all police officers and police dispatchers. Those who had less than five years of tenure received proportionately greater raises when compared to their former pay than those with more seniority. Although some officers over the age of 40 had less than five years of service, most of the older officers had more.

Petitioners are a group of older officers who filed suit under the ADEA claiming both that the City deliberately discriminated against them because of their age (the "disparate-treatment" claim) and that they were "adversely affected" by the plan because of their age (the "disparate-impact" claim). The District Court granted summary judgment to the City on both claims. The Court of Appeals held that the ruling on the former claim was premature because petitioners were entitled to further discovery on the issue of intent, but it affirmed the dismissal of the disparate-impact claim. 351 F.3d 183 (CA5 2003). Over one judge's dissent, the majority concluded that disparate-impact claims are categorically unavailable under the ADEA. Both the majority and the dissent assumed that the facts alleged by petitioners would entitle them to relief under the reasoning of *Griggs* [*v. Duke Power Co.*, 401 U.S. 424, 28 L.Ed. 2d 158, 91 S.Ct. 849 (1971)].

* * *

As enacted in 1967, § 4(a)(2) of the ADEA, now codified as 29 U. S. C. § 623(a)(2), provided that it shall be unlawful for an employer "to limit, segregate, or classify his employees in any way which would deprive or tend to deprive any individual of employment opportunities or otherwise adversely affect his status as an employee, because of such individual's age. . . ." 81 Stat. 603. Except for substitution of the word "age" for the words "race, color, religion, sex, or national origin," the language of that provision in the ADEA is identical to that found in § 703(a)(2) of the Civil Rights Act of 1964 (Title VII). Other provisions of the ADEA also parallel the earlier statute. Unlike Title VII, however, § 4(f)(1) of the ADEA, 81 Stat. 603, contains language that significantly narrows its coverage by permitting any "otherwise prohibited" action "where the differentiation is based on reasonable factors other than age" (hereinafter RFOA provision).

III

In determining whether the ADEA authorizes disparate-impact claims, we begin with the premise that when Congress uses the same language in two statutes having similar purposes, particularly when one is enacted shortly after the other, it is appropriate to presume that Congress intended that text to have the same meaning in both statutes. *Northcross v. Board of Ed. of Memphis City Schools*, 412 U.S. 427, 428, 37 L. Ed. 2d 48, 93 S. Ct. 2201 (1973) (per curiam). We have consistently applied that presumption to language in the ADEA that was "derived in haec verba from Title VII." *Lorillard v. Pons*, 434 U.S. 575, 584, 55 L. Ed. 2d 40, 98 S. Ct. 866 (1978). Our unanimous interpretation of § 703(a)(2) of the Title VII in Griggs is therefore a precedent of compelling importance.

In *Griggs*, * * * [w]e explained that Congress had "directed the thrust of the Act to the consequences of employment practices, not simply the motivation." Ibid. We relied on the fact that history is "filled with examples of men and women who rendered highly effective performance without the conventional badges of accomplishment in terms of certificates, diplomas, or degrees. Diplomas and tests are useful servants, but Congress has mandated the commonsense proposition that they are not to become masters of reality." Id., at 433, 28 L. Ed. 2d 158, 91 S. Ct. 849. And we noted that the Equal Employment Opportunity Commission (EEOC), which had enforcement responsibility, had issued guidelines that accorded with our view. Id., at 433–434, 28 L. Ed. 2d 158, 91 S. Ct. 849. We thus squarely held that § 703(a)(2) of Title VII did not require a showing of discriminatory intent.

While our opinion in *Griggs* relied primarily on the purposes of the Act, buttressed by the fact that the EEOC had endorsed the same view, we have subsequently noted that our holding represented the better reading of the statutory text as well. See *Watson v. Fort Worth Bank & Trust*, 487 U.S. 977, 991, 101 L. Ed. 2d 827, 108 S. Ct. 2777 (1988), Neither § 703(a)(2) nor the comparable language in the ADEA simply prohibits actions that "limit, segregate, or classify" persons; rather the language prohibits such actions that "deprive any individual of employment opportunities or *otherwise adversely affect* his status as an employee, because of such individual's" race or age. Ibid. (explaining that in disparate-impact cases, "the employer's practices may be said to 'adversely affect [an individual's status] as an employee'" (alteration in original) (quoting 42 U.S.C. § 2000e–2(a)(2))). Thus the text focuses on the effects of the action on the employee rather than the motivation for the action of the employer.[6]

Griggs, which interpreted the identical text at issue here, thus strongly suggests that a disparate-impact theory should be cognizable under the ADEA. Indeed, for over two decades after our decision in *Griggs*, the Courts of Appeal uniformly interpreted the ADEA as authorizing recovery on a "disparate-impact" theory in appropriate cases. It was only after our decision in *Hazen Paper Co. v. Biggins*, 507 U.S. 604, 123 L. Ed. 2d 338, 113 S. Ct. 1701 (1993), that some of those courts concluded that the ADEA did not authorize a disparate-impact theory of liability. Our opinion in *Hazen Paper*, however, did not address or comment on the issue we decide today. * * *

The Court of Appeals' categorical rejection of disparate-impact liability, like Justice O'Connor's, rested primarily on the RFOA provision and the majority's analysis of legislative history. [W]e think the history of the enactment of the ADEA, with particular reference to the Wirtz Report, supports the pre-Hazen Paper consensus concerning disparate-impact liability. And *Hazen Paper* itself contains the response to the concern over the RFOA provision.

The RFOA provision provides that it shall not be unlawful for an employer "to take any action otherwise prohibited under subsectio[n] (a)

---

[6]   In reaching a contrary conclusion, Justice O'Connor ignores key textual differences between § 4(a)(1), which does not encompass-disparate-impact liability, and § 4(a)(2). Section 4(a)(1) makes it unlawful for an employer "to fail or refuse to hire . . . *any individual* . . . because of *such individual's* age." (Emphasis added.) The focus of the section is on the employer's actions with respect to the targeted individual. Paragraph (a)(2), however, makes it unlawful for an employer "to limit . . . his *employees* in any way that would deprive or tend to deprive *any individual* of employment opportunities or otherwise adversely affect his status as an employee, because of *such individual's* age." (Emphasis added.) Unlike in paragraph (a)(1), there is thus an incongruity between the employer's actions—which are focused on his employees generally—and the individual employee who adversely suffers because of those actions. Thus, an employer who classifies his employees without respect to age may still be liable under the terms of this paragraph if such classification adversely affects the employee because of that employee's age—the very definition of disparate impact. Justice O'Connor is therefore quite wrong to suggest that the textual differences between the two paragraphs are unimportant.

. . . where the differentiation is based on reasonable factors other than age discrimination. . . ." 81 Stat. 603. In most disparate-treatment cases, if an employer in fact acted on a factor other than age, the action would not be prohibited under subsection (a) in the first place. See *Hazen Paper*, 507 U.S., at 609, 123 L. Ed. 2d 338, 113 S. Ct. 1701 ("[T]here is no disparate treatment under the ADEA when the factor motivating the employer is some feature other than the employee's age."). In those disparate-treatment cases, such as in *Hazen Paper* itself, the RFOA provision is simply unnecessary to avoid liability under the ADEA, since there was no prohibited action in the first place. The RFOA provision is not, as Justice O'Connor suggests, a "safe harbor from liability," since there would be no liability under § 4(a). See *Texas Dep't of Community Affairs v. Burdine*, 450 U.S. 248, 254, 67 L. Ed. 2d 207, 101 S. Ct. 1089 (1981) (noting, in a Title VII case, that an employer can defeat liability by showing that the employee was rejected for "a legitimate, nondiscriminatory reason" without reference to an RFOA provision).

In disparate-impact cases, however, the allegedly "otherwise prohibited" activity is not based on age. Ibid. (" '[C]laims that stress "disparate impact" [by contrast] involve employment practices that are facially neutral in their treatment of different groups but that in fact fall more harshly on one group than another . . . ' " (quoting *Teamsters v. United States*, 431 U.S. 324, 335–336, n. 15, 52 L. Ed. 2d 396, 97 S. Ct. 1843 (1977))). It is, accordingly, in cases involving disparate-impact claims that the RFOA provision plays its principal role by precluding liability if the adverse impact was attributable to a nonage factor that was "reasonable." Rather than support an argument that disparate impact is unavailable under the ADEA, the RFOA provision actually supports the contrary conclusion.[11]

Finally, we note that both the Department of Labor, which initially drafted the legislation, and the EEOC, which is the agency charged by Congress with responsibility for implementing the statute, 29 U.S.C. § 628 [29 USCS § 628], have consistently interpreted the ADEA to authorize relief on a disparate-impact theory. The initial regulations, while not mentioning disparate impact by name, nevertheless permitted such claims if the employer relied on a factor that was not related to age. 29 CFR § 860.103(f)(1)(i) (1970) (barring physical fitness requirements that were not "reasonably necessary for the specific work to be performed"). See also § 1625.7 (2004) (setting forth the standards for a disparate-impact claim).

The text of the statute, as interpreted in *Griggs*, the RFOA provision, and the EEOC regulations all support petitioners' view. We therefore

---

[11] We note that if Congress intended to prohibit all disparate-impact claims, it certainly could have done so. For instance, in the Equal Pay Act of 1963, 29 U.S.C. § 206(d)(1), Congress barred recovery if a pay differential was based "on any other factor"—reasonable or unreasonable—"other than sex." The fact that Congress provided that employees could use only *reasonable* factors in defending a suit under the ADEA is therefore instructive.

conclude that it was error for the Court of Appeals to hold that the disparate-impact theory of liability is categorically unavailable under the ADEA.

IV

Two textual differences between the ADEA and Title VII make it clear that even though both statutes authorize recovery on a disparate-impact theory, the scope of disparate-impact liability under ADEA is narrower than under Title VII. The first is the RFOA provision, which we have already identified. The second is the amendment to Title VII contained in the Civil Rights Act of 1991, 105 Stat. 1071. One of the purposes of that amendment was to modify the Court's holding in *Wards Cove Packing Co. v. Atonio*, 490 U.S. 642, 104 L. Ed. 2d 733, 109 S. Ct. 2115 (1989), a case in which we narrowly construed the employer's exposure to liability on a disparate-impact theory. See Civil Rights Act of 1991, § 2, 105 Stat. 1071. While the relevant 1991 amendments expanded the coverage of Title VII, they did not amend the ADEA or speak to the subject of age discrimination. Hence, *Wards Cove's* pre-1991 interpretation of Title VII's identical language remains applicable to the ADEA.

Congress' decision to limit the coverage of the ADEA by including the RFOA provision is consistent with the fact that age, unlike race or other classifications protected by Title VII, not uncommonly has relevance to an individual's capacity to engage in certain types of employment. To be sure, Congress recognized that this is not always the case, and that society may perceive those differences to be larger or more consequential than they are in fact. However, as Secretary Wirtz noted in his report, "certain circumstances . . . unquestionably affect older workers more strongly, as a group, than they do younger workers." Wirtz Report 28. Thus, it is not surprising that certain employment criteria that are routinely used may be reasonable despite their adverse impact on older workers as a group. Moreover, intentional discrimination on the basis of age has not occurred at the same levels as discrimination against those protected by Title VII. While the ADEA reflects Congress' intent to give older workers employment opportunities whenever possible, the RFOA provision reflects this historical difference.

Turning to the case before us, we initially note that petitioners have done little more than point out that the pay plan at issue is relatively less generous to older workers than to younger workers. They have not identified any specific test, requirement, or practice within the pay plan that has an adverse impact on older workers. As we held in *Wards Cove*, it is not enough to simply allege that there is a disparate impact on workers, or point to a generalized policy that leads to such an impact. Rather, the employee is " 'responsible for isolating and identifying the *specific* employment practices that are allegedly responsible for any observed statistical disparities.' " 490 U.S., at 656, 104 L. Ed. 2d 733, 109 S. Ct. 2115 (emphasis added) (quoting *Watson*, 487 U.S., at 994, 101 L. Ed. 2d 827, 108 S. Ct. 2777). Petitioners have failed to do so. Their failure to identify the specific practice being challenged is the sort of omission that could "result in employers being potentially liable for 'the myriad of innocent causes that may lead to statistical imbalances. . . .'" 490 U.S., at 657, 104 L. Ed. 2d 733, 109 S. Ct. 2115. In this case not only did petitioners thus err by failing to identify the relevant practice, but it is also clear from the record that the City's plan was based on reasonable factors other than age.

The plan divided each of five basic positions—police officer, master police officer, police sergeant, police lieutenant, and deputy police chief—into a series of steps and half-steps. The wage for each range was based on a survey of comparable communities in the Southeast. Employees were then assigned a step (or half-step) within their position that corresponded to the lowest step that would still give the individual a 2% raise. Most of the officers were in the three lowest ranks; in each of those ranks there were officers under age 40 and officers over 40. In none did their age affect their compensation. The few officers in the two highest ranks are all over 40. Their raises, though higher in dollar amount than the raises given to junior officers, represented a smaller percentage of their salaries, which of course are higher than the salaries paid to their juniors. They are members of the class complaining of the "disparate impact" of the award.

Petitioners' evidence established two principal facts: First, almost two-thirds (66.2%) of the officers under 40 received raises of more than 10% while less than half (45.3%) of those over 40 did. Second, the average percentage increase for the entire class of officers with less than five years of tenure was somewhat higher than the percentage for those with more seniority. Because older officers tended to occupy more senior positions, on average they received smaller increases when measured as a percentage of their salary. The basic explanation for the differential was the City's perceived need to raise the salaries of junior officers to make them competitive with comparable positions in the market.

Thus, the disparate impact is attributable to the City's decision to give raises based on seniority and position. Reliance on seniority and rank is unquestionably reasonable given the City's goal of raising employees' salaries to match those in surrounding communities. In sum, we hold that the City's decision to grant a larger raise to lower echelon employees for the purpose of bringing salaries in line with that of surrounding police forces was a decision based on a "reasonable factor other than age" that responded to the City's legitimate goal of retaining police officers. Cf. *MacPherson v. University of Montevallo*, 922 F.2d 766, 772 (CA11 1991).

While there may have been other reasonable ways for the City to achieve its goals, the one selected was not unreasonable. Unlike the business necessity test, which asks whether there are other ways for the employer to achieve its goals that do not result in a disparate impact on a protected class, the reasonableness inquiry includes no such requirement.

THE CHIEF JUSTICE took no part in the decision of this case.

JUSTICE SCALIA, concurring in part and concurring in the judgment.

* * *

This is an absolutely classic case for deference to agency interpretation. The Age Discrimination in Employment Act of 1967 (ADEA), 29 U.S.C. § 621 et seq., confers upon the EEOC authority to issue "such rules and regulations as it may consider necessary or appropriate for carrying out the" ADEA. § 628. Pursuant to this authority, the EEOC promulgated, after notice-and-comment rulemaking, see 46 Fed. Reg. 47724, 47727 (1981), a regulation that reads as follows:

"When an employment practice, including a test, is claimed as a basis for different treatment of employees or applicants for employment on the grounds that it is a 'factor other than' age, and such a practice has an adverse impact on individuals within the protected age group, it can only be justified as a business necessity." 29 CFR § 1625.7(d) (2004).

The statement of the EEOC which accompanied publication of the agency's final interpretation of the ADEA said the following regarding this regulation: "Paragraph (d) of § 1625.7 has been rewritten to make it clear that employment criteria that are age-neutral on their face but which nevertheless have a disparate impact on members of the protected age group must be justified as a business necessity. See *Laugesen v. Anaconda Co.*, 510 F.2d 307 (6th Cir. 1975); *Griggs v. Duke Power Co.*, 401 U.S. 424 [28 L. Ed. 2d 158, 91 S. Ct. 849] (1971)." 46 Fed. Reg., at 47725. The regulation affirmed, moreover, what had been the longstanding position of the Department of Labor, the agency that previously administered the ADEA. * * *

JUSTICE O'CONNOR, with whom JUSTICE KENNEDY and JUSTICE THOMAS join, concurring in the judgment.

* * *

Congress' decision not to authorize disparate impact claims is understandable in light of the questionable utility of such claims in the age-discrimination context. No one would argue that older workers have suffered disadvantages as a result of entrenched historical patterns of discrimination, like racial minorities have. See *Massachusetts Bd. of Retirement v. Murgia*, 427 U.S. 307, 313–314, 49 L. Ed. 2d 520, 96 S. Ct. 2562 (1976) (per curiam); see also Wirtz Report 5–6. Accordingly, disparate impact liability under the ADEA cannot be justified, and is not necessary, as a means of redressing the cumulative results of past discrimination. Cf. *Griggs*, 401 U.S., at 430, 28 L. Ed. 2d 158, 91 S. Ct. 849 (reasoning that disparate impact liability is necessary under Title VII to prevent perpetuation of the results of past racial discrimination).

Moreover, the Wirtz Report correctly concluded that—unlike the classifications protected by Title VII—there often is a correlation between an individual's age and her ability to perform a job. Wirtz Report 2, 11–15. That is to be expected, for "physical ability generally declines with age," *Murgia*, supra, at 315, 49 L. Ed. 2d 520, 96 S. Ct. 2562, and in some cases, so does mental capacity, see *Gregory v. Ashcroft*, 501 U.S. 452, 472, 115 L. Ed. 2d 410, 111 S. Ct. 2395 (1991). Perhaps more importantly, advances in technology and increasing access to formal education often leave older workers at a competitive disadvantage vis-a-vis younger workers. Wirtz Report 11–15. Beyond these performance-affecting factors, there is also the fact that many employment benefits, such as salary, vacation time, and so forth, increase as an employee gains experience and seniority. See, e.g., *Finnegan v. Trans World Airlines, Inc.*, 967 F.2d 1161, 1164 (CA7 1992) ("[V]irtually all elements of a standard compensation package are positively correlated with age"). Accordingly, many employer decisions that are intended to cut costs or respond to market forces will likely have a disproportionate effect on older workers. Given the myriad ways in which legitimate business practices can have a disparate impact on older workers, it is hardly surprising that Congress declined to subject employers to civil liability based solely on such effects.

NOTES AND QUESTIONS

Test Your Understanding of the Material

1. In what ways does disparate-impact analysis under ADEA differ from disparate-impact analysis under Title VII? Did any of these differences affect the outcome in *Smith*?

2. Some lower court decisions before *Smith* held that companies could not justify policies limiting the retention of senior or tenured employees who had to be paid higher salaries or the hiring of experienced workers on the ground that such measures would cut labor costs. See, e.g., Leftwich v. Harris-Stowe State College, 702 F.2d 686 (8th Cir. 1983) (policy for reducing full-time higher-paid faculty by limiting number of tenured positions); Geller v. Markham, 635 F.2d 1027 (2d Cir. 1980) (policy against recruitment of teachers with more than five years of experience paid at high salary grade). Are these decisions still good law after *Hazen Paper* and *Smith*?

Related Issues

3. *Does the ADEA Require Individualized Assessments?* Title VII disparate impact cases arguably can be read to require employers to provide at least as much individualized assessment as is consistent with the economic value of the position in question. See, e.g., *Dothard v. Rawlinson*, supra, where the Court rejected the prison system's reliance on size as a proxy for strength.

The Court in *Smith* seems to reject such a requirement for the ADEA by holding the Act does not "ask[ ] whether there are other ways for the employer to achieve its goals that do not result in a disparate impact. . . ." After *Smith*, can an employer thus use a weight-height ratio requirement as a proxy for physical agility, despite the requirement's disparate impact on older workers? Cf. Ellis v. United Airlines, Inc., 73 F.3d 999 (10th Cir. 1996) (airline's weight standards challenged because of their disparate impact on older workers). For the case for legislative reform of ADEA, see Harper, A Gap in the Agenda, supra, at 616–620.

4. *Use of Disparate Impact in ADEA Cases Challenging Subjective Decisionmaking.* Can older workers use disparate-impact proof to challenge an employer for allowing managers to make termination or promotion decisions on the basis of unguided subjective assessments? If so, are such challenges likely to be successful after *Smith*?

5. *Burden of Persuasion on Reasonable Justification.* In Meacham v. Knolls Atomic Power Laboratory, 554 U.S. 84, 128 S.Ct. 2395, 171 L.Ed.2d 283 (2008), the Court held that the "reasonable factors other than age" provision in the ADEA assigned the burden of proving reasonableness to an employer facing an ADEA disparate-impact claim. The EEOC has issued a regulation, 29 C.F.R. § 1625.7, to define an employer's burden in RFOA cases after *Meacham*.

NOTE: EMPLOYEE BENEFIT PLANS AND THE OLDER WORKERS PROTECTION ACT OF 1990

In 1974 Congress enacted the Employee Retirement Income Security Act (ERISA), Pub.L. No. 93–406, 88 Stat. 829, codified at various places in the Internal Revenue Code (Code) and at 29 U.S.C. § 1000 et seq. Congress entered the retirement benefits area in the belief that state laws governing contracts and pension trusts had proven incapable of protecting the pension benefits of workers who lost their jobs prior to retirement age or who learned upon retirement that their employer lacked sufficient assets to satisfy its pension obligations. See generally Richard Ippolito, Pensions, Economics, and Public Policy (1986).

There are two basic types of ERISA pension plans: "defined contribution" plans that provide for an individual account for each participant and for benefits based solely upon the amount contributed to that account plus any income or other gain; and "defined benefit" plans which are defined as any other pension plan but generally involve plans where the employer promises to pay a specific or definitely determinable benefit. Once vesting has occurred (normally after five years of employment), employees have a nonforfeitable right to their accrued retirement benefits. In addition to "employee pension benefit" plans, ERISA also covers "employee welfare benefit" plans, defined in 29 U.S.C. § 1002(1). Welfare benefit plans are not subject to an ERISA vesting requirement, however. ERISA issues are treated at length in Chapter 19.

In 1979, the Department of Labor, acting pursuant to § 4(f)(2) of ADEA, 29 U.S.C. § 623(f)(2), issued an "Interpretative Bulletin," 29 C.F.R. § 660.120, 44 Fed.Reg. 30648 (May 25, 1979), which permitted employers to cease contributions and accruals for employees working beyond normal retirement age. Responding to pressure from the courts, see American Ass'n of Retired Persons v. EEOC, 823 F.2d 600 (D.C.Cir.1987), the EEOC initiated a rulemaking proceeding to reverse this policy. Then in 1986, by adding a new section § 4(i) to ADEA (and amending related sections of the Code and ERISA), Congress required all pension plans to continue contributions and accruals regardless of an employee's age, for plan years commencing on or after January 1, 1988. See Omnibus Budget Reconciliation Act of 1986 (OBRA), Pub.L. 99–509, 100 Stat. 1973–80. Congress expressly provided, however, that employers may limit the "amount of benefits that [a] plan provides" or limit "the number of years which are taken into account for purposes of determining benefit accrual under the plan." 29 U.S.C. § 623(i)(2).

Prior to 1990, § 4(f)(2) of ADEA permitted age-based classifications in "any bona fide employee benefit plan such as a retirement, pension, or insurance plan, which is not a subterfuge to evade the purposes" of the statute. In Public Employees Retirement System of Ohio v. Betts, 492 U.S. 158, 109 S.Ct. 2854, 106 L.d.2d 134 (1989), the Supreme Court held that Congress in this provision intended broadly to shield the use of age classifications in benefit plans, even if the plans provided less valuable benefits for older workers than their younger counterparts and the difference in benefits could not be justified in terms of the higher costs of providing the same level of benefits for the older workers. Justice Kennedy's opinion for the majority read the reference to "subterfuge" in § 4(f)(2) to require proof of an intent to discriminate in other, nonfringe-benefits aspects of the employment relationship. For example, an employer's decision to reduce salaries of all employees while substantially increasing benefits for younger workers might be challenged as a subterfuge to accomplish pay discrimination in violation of § 4(a)(1) of ADEA.

On October 16, 1990, Congress passed the Older Workers Benefit Protection Act (OWBPA), Public L. No. 101–433, 104 Stat. 978. Title I overturns *Betts* in its entirety. OWBPA amends § 4(f)(2) of ADEA: (i) to clarify that benefit plans may be illegally discriminatory; (ii) to remove the "subterfuge" requirement as a condition of illegality; and (iii) to place the burden of proof of justification of a discriminatory plan on the employer.

OWBPA also imposes an equal benefit/equal cost rule—it requires that "for each benefit or benefit package, the actual amount of payment made or cost incurred on behalf of an older worker is no less than that made or incurred on behalf of the younger worker, as permissible under section 1625.10, title 29, Code of Federal Regulations (as in effect on June 22, 1989) * * * ." See, e.g., Quinones v. Evanston, 58 F.3d 275 (7th Cir.1995) (defined benefit plan may provide lower benefits to those hired at older age, but only to the extent necessary to equalize costs). (As provided in the EEOC regulations, cost justification for age-based benefit reductions may be made on either a "benefit-by-benefit" or a "benefit package" basis and by placing employees into five-year age brackets.) OWBPA allows certain exceptions from the equal benefit/equal cost rule.[1]

The OWBPA further amended the ADEA to clarify that an employee pension benefit plan, as defined by ERISA, may specify "a minimum age as a condition of eligibility for normal or early retirement." 29 U.S.C. § 623(*l*)(1)(A). As noted, ADEA and ERISA had already been amended in 1986 to require all pension plans to continue contributions and accruals regardless of an employee's age. 29 U.S.C. § 623(i)(1). This earlier amendment, however, also provided that employers may limit the "amount of benefits that [a] plan provides" or limit "the number of years which are taken into account for purposes of determining benefit accrual under the plan." 29 U.S.C. § 623(i)(2). See, e.g., Atkins v. Northwest Airlines, Inc., 967 F.2d 1197 (8th Cir.1992) (employer may cap benefit accrual for employees who have completed a specified number of years of service even where it lowers retirement benefits for workers who retire before a "normal" retirement age).

In Kentucky Retirement Systems v. EEOC, 554 U.S. 135. 128 S. Ct. 2361, 171 L.Ed.2d 322 (2008), a closely divided Court held that the ADEA does not prevent a state from providing retirement benefits to those who have become severely disabled before full pension eligibility defined in part by age. The Court acknowledged that this could result in some younger disabled individuals being treated more generously than older workers who become eligible for retirement in part on the basis of their age. Relying on *Hazen Paper*, supra, the Court nonetheless held that when an employer "adopts a pension plan that includes age as a factor, and that employer then treats employees differently based on pension status, a plaintiff, to state a disparate treatment claim under the ADEA, must adduce sufficient evidence to show that the differential treatment was 'actually motivated' by age, not pension status."

Title II of the statute requires certain minimum safeguards for ADEA waiver agreements; these are discussed at pp. 495–497 infra.

D. RETIREMENT

NOTE: MANDATORY RETIREMENT

ADEA and analogous state laws take a very restrictive position on mandatory retirement. Congress in 1978 rejected the Court's holding in United Air Lines, Inc. v. McMann, 434 U.S. 192, 98 S.Ct. 444, 54 L.Ed.2d 402 (1977),

---

[1] These exceptions include (i) minimum-age conditions for eligibility for normal or early retirement; (ii) subsidized early retirement benefits under defined-benefit pension plans; (iii) defined-benefit pension plan "bridge payments" that do not exceed Social Security benefits and that terminate with Social Security eligibility; (iv) reduction of long-term disability benefits by the amount of employer-funded pension funds; and (v) limited benefit coordination by which employers can offset against severance pay obligations triggered by a "contingent event unrelated to age" (e.g., a plant closing or staff reduction) the value of retiree health benefits, and if the employees are eligible for not less than an immediate and unreduced pension, any additional pension benefits triggered by the contingent event.

Title I of OWBPA also permits some departure from the equal benefit/equal cost rule in the structuring of voluntary early retirement plans; this is discussed at pp. 486–487 infra.

that mandatory retirement provisions in bona fide employee retirement plans were lawful under § 4(f)(2). In light of the 1978 amendments, involuntary terminations pursuant to a retirement plan are to be treated by the Act like any other involuntary terminations. With the removal of the age 70 cap on protected workers in 1986, and similar movement in the states, age-based mandatory retirement policies are now generally prohibited. Individuals within the protected class may be severed from their employment only for performance or other legitimate business reasons not because of the arrival of a particular birthday. Generally, ADEA imposes no obligation to renew employment contracts, although presumably age cannot be a factor in the non-renewal decision. For an interesting case involving a contract that provided for termination upon the employee's reaching the age of 70—at a time prior to the 1986 ADEA amendments—see Harrington v. Aetna-Bearing Co., 921 F.2d 717 (7th Cir.1991).

After the 1986 amendments, the ADEA contained four limited exceptions to the no-mandatory retirement rule. The most general, the BFOQ, is considered at pp. 454–460. A second, for firefighters and law enforcement officers, was later modified by Congress and is discussed in note 5 on page 461 supra. A third, for employees who attained the age of 70 "serving under a contract of unlimited tenure * * * at an institution of higher education," expired in 1994. The 1986 amendments required the EEOC to commission the National Academy of Sciences (NAS) to study the potential consequences of the elimination of mandatory retirement for institutions of higher education. Predicting that few faculty members will work beyond the age of 70, the NAS-appointed panel concluded that mandatory retirement for tenured university faculty should be ended. See National Research Council, Ending Mandatory Retirement For Tenured Faculty: The Consequences for Higher Education (P.B. Hammond & H.P. Morgan eds. 1991); Richard A. Epstein & Saunders MacLane, Keep Mandatory Retirement for Tenured Faculty, 14 Regulation (Spring 1991), pp. 85–96. The problem of applying performance standards to employees who work past the age of 70 is usefully surveyed in Charles Craver, The Application of the Age Discrimination in Employment Act to Persons Over Seventy, 58 Geo.Wash.L.Rev. 52 (1989).

A fourth exception, § 12(c)(1), permits the mandatory retirement of employees who have attained the age of 65, who are entitled to a specified level of nonforfeitable annual retirement benefit from their employers' plans—raised from $27,000 to $44,000 in 1985—and who for two years prior to retirement were "employed in a bona fide executive or high policy making position * * * ." 29 U.S.C. § 631(c)(1). This exemption is narrowly construed in the EEOC regulations, 29 C.F.R. § 1625.12. "Bona fide executive" status applies "only to a very few top level employees who exercise substantial executive authority over a significant number of employees and a large volume of business," such as heads of major divisions in a corporate headquarters operation. Id. § 1625(d)(2). Similarly, "high policy making" status is limited to "certain top level employees * * * 'whose position and responsibility are such that they play a significant role in the development of corporate policy and effectively recommend the implementation thereof,' " such as a company's chief economist or research scientist who effectively recommends policy direction to the top corporate officers. Id. § 1625.12(e), quoting H.R.Rep. 950, 95th Cong., 2d Sess. 10 (1978). The EEOC's view has received judicial approval. Compare, e.g., Passer v. American Chem. Society, 935 F.2d 322 (D.C.Cir.1991) (exemption applies to head of division with 25 employees and $4 million budget); Colby v. The Graniteville Company, 635 F.Supp. 381 (S.D.N.Y.1986) (exemption applies to company's senior vice president of finance and administration), with Whittlesey v. Union Carbide Corp., 567 F.Supp. 1320 (S.D.N.Y.1983), affirmed, 742 F.2d 724 (2d Cir.1984) (exemption inapplicable to company's chief labor counsel because of minimal contribution to policy making).

Of course, mandatory retirement is not restricted by ADEA for employees excluded from the Act's coverage. State and local elected officials and appointed policymakers, for instance, are expressly excluded from the Act's coverage by the definition of employee in § 11(f) (excluding "any person elected to public office in any State or political subdivision of any State by the qualified voters thereof * * * or an appointee on the policymaking level"). In Gregory v. Ashcroft, 501 U.S. 452, 111 S.Ct. 2395, 115 L.Ed.2d 410 (1991), the Supreme Court held that this exclusion was sufficiently broad to insulate Missouri's constitutional provision requiring mandatory retirement of appointed judges at age 70. Although the appointed judges in that state were subject to periodic unopposed retention elections, the Court's rationale appears to reach all appointed state judges.

NOTE: EARLY RETIREMENT INCENTIVE PROGRAMS

Early retirement normally means retirement at reduced benefit levels because defined-benefit pension plans typically require some combination of age and years of service for eligibility for a full pension benefit. In general, defined-benefit plans provide larger pension benefits with increased length of service. This tends to discourage employees from retiring. To change these incentives in periods of business contraction, some early retirement plans provide a "window" period during which eligibility requirements for full benefits are relaxed or early retirees are given benefits which would have required additional years of service. Under such plans, early retirees can obtain the equivalent (or a pro rata adjustment) of the full pension benefits they would have obtained had they worked to normal retirement age. Other plans offer employees within a certain age range the opportunity to receive benefits exceeding what they would have otherwise received (regardless of their length of service), provided they retire during a limited "window" period.

Age Bias in the Structure of the Incentives?

ADEA has been the basis for two types of challenges to early-retirement incentive plans. The first has been to age-based plans that offer a less valuable retirement incentive to older workers than is offered to their younger counterparts, or that exclude some older workers from the incentive program entirely.

The OWBPA expressly excludes "voluntary early retirement plan[s]" from the equal cost/equal benefit principle, provided such plans are "consistent with the relevant purpose or purposes of the Act." Apparently, Congress meant by the latter clause to prohibit "arbitrary" age distinctions in early-retirement incentive plans, but without defining what would constitute an arbitrary distinction. Consider the following language from the OWBPA Statement of Managers:

1.   * * * Early retirement incentive plans that withhold benefits to older workers above a specific age while continuing to make them available to younger workers may conflict with the purpose of prohibiting arbitrary age discrimination in employment. The purpose of prohibiting arbitrary age discrimination is also undermined by denying or reducing benefits to older workers based on age-related stereotypes. For example, it would be unlawful under this substitute to exclude older workers from an early retirement incentive plan based on stereotypical assumptions that "older workers would be retiring anyway."

2.   It is also clear that a wide variety of voluntary early retirement incentive plans would be lawful under the ADEA. For example, early retirement incentives that provide a flat dollar amount (e.g., $20,000), service-based benefits (e.g., $1000 multiplied by the number of years of service) or a percentage of all salary to all employees above a certain age * * * would remain lawful. * * * Finally, early retirement incentives that impute years of service and/or age would satisfy the ADEA. For example, a plan that gives employees who have attained the age of 55 and who retire during a specified window period credit for 5 additional years of service and/or age would be lawful.

S. 1511, Final Substitute of the Managers, 53 (BNA) FEP Decisions Special Supplement, October 15, 1990 at S–12.

Since passage of the OWBPA, some courts have struck down retirement plans that offered greater benefits to younger workers than those offered to older workers. See, e.g., Jankovitz v. Des Moines Independent Community School Dist., 421 F.3d 649 (8th Cir. 2005); Solon v. Gary Community School Corp., 180 F.3d 844 (7th Cir.1999); EEOC v. Hickman Mills Consolidated School Dist. No. 1, 99 F.Supp.2d 1070 (W.D.Mo. 2000). But see Auerbach v. Board of Educ. of Harborfields Central School Dist. of Greenlawn, 136 F.3d 104 (2d Cir.1998) (employer can provide extra benefits to those retiring when they are first eligible for retirement, even though eligibility is in part based on age); Lyon v. Ohio Educ. Ass'n, 53 F.3d 135 (6th Cir.1995) (employer can give more encouragement to younger workers to retire by granting them greater benefits through imputation of more years of foregone service).

Voluntariness?

The other type of ADEA attack on retirement resignation incentives has been made against plans offering benefits only to older employees on the ground that they place undue pressure on such employees to exit the workforce. This litigation has been brought by those who have been offered and accepted incentives, but who later decide to sue to challenge the circumstances of their retirement. The following case is an example.

HENN V. NATIONAL GEOGRAPHIC SOCIETY

United States Court of Appeals, Seventh Circuit, 1987.
819 F.2d 824.

EASTERBROOK, J.

Experiencing a decline in advertising, the National Geographic Society decided to reduce the number of employees selling ads. The Society offered every ad salesman over age 55 the option of early retirement. The Society made the offer in June 1983; the recipients had more than two months to think it over. The Society offered: a severance payment of one year's salary, retirement benefits calculated as if the retiree had quit at 65, medical coverage for life as if the employee were still on the payroll, and some supplemental life insurance coverage. The letter extending the offer stated that this was a one-time opportunity. Twelve of the fifteen recipients took the offer; the three who declined are still employed by the Society. All twelve have received the promised benefits. Four of the twelve filed this suit, contending that their separation violated the Age Discrimination in Employment Act, 29 U.S.C. §§ 621–34.

The district court granted summary judgment to the Society. It concluded that early retirement violates the ADEA only if the alternative is "constructive discharge"—that is, working conditions so onerous or demeaning that the employee has effectively been fired in place and compelled to leave. See *Bartman v. Allis-Chalmers Corp.,* 799 F.2d 311, 314 (7th Cir.1986); *Brown v. Brienen,* 722 F.2d 360, 365 (7th Cir.1983). The court thought it undisputed that plaintiffs' working conditions were unchanged from what they had always been; there was pressure to perform and dark hints that failure to sell more ads would have unpleasant consequences, but the judge concluded that these went with the territory. Each person's decision to retire was his own, and any pressure he felt was the product of the downturn in sales and the risks of a salesman's job.

The plaintiffs' brief on appeal is principally devoted to insisting that there was enough evidence of constructive discharge to require a trial. The case has been complicated, however, by *Paolillo v. Dresser Industries, Inc.,* 813 F.2d 583 (2d Cir.1987), which holds that *every* retirement under an early retirement plan creates a prima facie case of age discrimination, and that the employer must show both that the details of the plan have solid business justification and that each decision to retire is "voluntary"—by which the Second Circuit apparently meant "without undue strain". If *Paolillo* correctly interprets the ADEA, this case must be tried. We conclude, however, that the parties and the district court, rather than

Paolillo, took the right approach. Only a constructive discharge, where an actual discharge would violate the ADEA, supports a claim of the sort plaintiffs pursue.

* * *

In characterizing retirement under an early retirement program as presumptively discriminatory, *Paolillo* overlooked the regulation governing early retirement plans, 29 C.F.R. § 1625.9(f). This provides: "Neither section 4(f)(2) nor any other provision of the Act makes it unlawful for a plan to permit individuals to elect early retirement at a specified age at their own option." This plausible construction of the ADEA is entitled to considerable weight where, as here, Congress never considered the matter. *Chevron U.S.A., Inc. v. Natural Resources Defense Council, Inc.,* 467 U.S. 837, 843, 104 S.Ct. 2778, 2781, 81 L.Ed.2d 694 (1984). The legislative history of the ADEA is unilluminating about early retirement plans. Given that, § 1625.9(f), and the fact that the offer of early retirement is beneficial to the recipient, there is no reason to treat every early retirement as presumptively an act of age discrimination.

* * * Retirement is an innocuous event, coming once to many employees and more than once to some. Retirement is not itself a prima facie case of age discrimination, not unless all separations from employment are. And * * * an offer of incentives to retire early is a benefit to the recipient, not a sign of discrimination. Taken together, these two events—one neutral, one beneficial to the older employee—do not support an inference of age discrimination.

What distinguishes early retirement from discharge is the power of the employee to choose to keep working. This must mean a "voluntary" choice. But what does "voluntary" mean? We could ask, as the court did in *Paolillo,* whether the employee had enough time to mull over the offer and whether the choice was free from "pressure". (In *Paolillo* the employees had less than a week, which the court thought suspiciously short.) Yet the need to make a decision in a short time, under pressure, is an unusual definition of "involuntary". A criminal defendant may be offered a plea bargain on a take-it-or-leave-it basis, knowing that if he does not act quickly the prosecutor may strike a deal with another defendant instead; the need to act in haste does not make the plea "involuntary" if the defendant knows and accepts the terms of the offer.

* * *

The "voluntariness" question in these and many more examples of important choices turns on such things as: did the person receive information about what would happen in response to the choice? was the choice free from fraud or other misconduct? did the person have an opportunity to say no? A very short period to make a complex choice may show that the person could not digest the information necessary to the decision. This would show that the offer of information was illusory and there was no informed choice. But when the employee has time to consult spouse and financial adviser, the fact that he still found the decision hard cannot be decisive. * * *

The plaintiffs in this case do not say that they lacked information about the terms of the offer. All had time to discuss the offer with families and financial advisers. They complain that they felt pressure and perceived the choice to be excruciating, but that is not important. They could prevail only by showing that the Society manipulated the options so that they were driven to early retirement not by its attractions but by the terror of the alternative. If the terms on which they would have remained at the Society were themselves violations of the ADEA, then taking the offer of early retirement was making the best of things, a form of minimization of damages.

* * *

The plaintiffs complain of two things that made their positions untenable: the "silent treatment" and threats (real and implied) of unpleasant consequences if they did not start selling more ads. The "silent treatment" was principally that no one in the Society would tell them whether they ought to take the offer of early retirement; the Society says this was caused by its policy of sticking to the facts (doubtless to avoid charges of placing undue pressure on the employees), while the plaintiffs say that their inability to get straight answers about whether they should take the offer led them to fear the worst. The threats came about because all four plaintiffs had experienced bad years, and their supervisors told them they needed to sell more ads; this led them to fear for their jobs.

The record contains extensive admissions by the plaintiffs tending to support the district judge's conclusion that any threats made to these plaintiffs while they were considering the offer were no greater than justified by their lack of sales. Selling is a risky profession, and it does not make a salesman's job unbearable to remind him that he must produce and that there are penalties for failure. The plaintiffs say, however, that the Society's warnings were not justified on a more complete review of their performance. They also believe that the Society hassled them more than their sluggish sales performance warranted. To support this belief Henn states that Bill Hughes, his supervisor, said to him early in 1983: "[s]ome of you older guys will not be around at the end of the year". All four plaintiffs rely on a passage in a memorandum that was part of the bureaucratic process that ended in the offer of early retirement: "Of the total twenty sales members one out of two are over 55 years, six are over age 62 and four are presently over age 65. (sic: actually 5 under 55; 5 between 55–61; 6 from 62–65; 4 over 65) Only one sales person over 65 plans to retire this year and an undetermined number desire to continue toward age 70. If an age balance is not struck soon our average age will obviously increase. Serious repercussions will result if younger sales personnel are not available to cultivate clients in new growth industries and insure future sales. To attract youthful qualified sales personnel we must be cognizant of industry practices and offer required incentives." The author of the memo recommended that salesmen be fired; the Society did not take that advice. It maintains that neither comment supports an inference that it acted or would have acted improperly to any person on the payroll.

The district court concluded that neither these nor other comments and incidents added up to constructive discharge or supported a reasonable belief by the plaintiffs that, had they remained at the Society, they would have been fired unlawfully. They were at risk of discipline or discharge for their performance (or lack of performance), and all four were producing less than their quota. The Society turned down the recommendation that it fire people, so the author of the memorandum did not speak for the Society. And although the record may well support an inference that the Society wanted to reduce the average age of its sales staff, this does not show that it used illegal means. Any early retirement program reduces average age, because only older employees are eligible to retire. That the Society favored the results of its program does not condemn the program. * * *

The argument based on constructive discharge depends not on the Society's beliefs about the effects of retirements but on what it communicated to the employees. The district court properly concluded that salesmen must endure adverse reactions and other signs of displeasure when their productivity falls off. An employer's communication of the risks of the job does not spoil the employee's decision to avoid those risks by quitting. Were it otherwise, any employee about whom there was dissatisfaction would have a jury case under the ADEA, even if the dissatisfaction were supported by objective indicators (such as low productivity). In passing on a motion for summary judgment, a court must indulge inferences in favor of the non-moving party, but it need not indulge all possible inferences. The reasonable inferences from this record would not allow a jury to infer that the plaintiffs would have been fired (in violation of the ADEA) had they turned down the offer of early retirement, and without such a constructive discharge they cannot undo their choice to retire.

NOTES AND QUESTIONS

Test Your Understanding of the Material

1. The Seventh Circuit's affirmation of the district court's grant of summary judgment to the Society was not based on a conclusion that the plaintiffs did not advance adequate proof of age bias. The decision instead was based on the plaintiffs' failure to show that they or other members of their age-defined class of offerees were coerced to retire. Do you agree with Judge

Easterbrook that a "prima facie" case of age bias was not made out by plaintiffs' evidence of coercion? Consider in particular the following allegations, taken as true for summary judgment purposes: (i) the plaintiffs had insufficient time to consider their options, (ii) had been led to fear the worst by the firm's "silent treatment", and (iii) had shortly before been criticized for poor sales performance, coupled with (iv) the employer's written statement identifying a need to reduce the average age of its sales staff.

Related Issues

2. *"Take Early Retirement or Be Discharged."* If an employee is given an explicit choice between forced termination and early retirement at enhanced benefits, should the *Henn* presumption of a knowing, voluntary decision apply? In Ackerman v. Diamond Shamrock Corp., 670 F.2d 66 (6th Cir.1982), an ADEA claim was dismissed on a motion for summary judgment in such a situation. *Ackerman* was narrowly distinguished by the Sixth Circuit in Ruane v. G.F. Business Equipment, Inc., 828 F.2d 20 (6th Cir.1987), as a case where the employee was represented by counsel, given 30 days to make up his mind, received $100,000 in additional consideration, and "was not otherwise distinctly informed that he had no right to remain in his present employment [.]" See also Hebert v. Mohawk Rubber Co., 872 F.2d 1104, 1112–13 (1st Cir.1989):

> In our view, to accept the reasoning of the Sixth Circuit [in *Ackerman*] that a person's acceptance of an early retirement package is voluntary when faced with the "choice" between the Scylla of forced retirement and the Charybdis of discharge * * * is to turn a blind eye upon the "take-it-or-leave-it" nature of such an "offer". * * * Absent the right to decline an employer's offer of early retirement and keep working under lawful conditions, the "decision" to take the early retirement "option" is no decision at all. A "choice" between not working with benefits and not working without benefits amounts to, in effect, compulsory retirement.

See also Adams v. Ameritech Services, Inc., 231 F.3d 414 (7th Cir.2000) (holding that coercing employees into accepting positions with lower pay by threatening them with discriminatory reduction in force would constitute illegal "constructive demotion").

3. *"Take Early Retirement or a Position at Lower Pay or Reduced Responsibilities."* Is an employee's retirement decision coerced when an employer states that it will significantly reduce the pay and responsibilities of an older employee if he does not accept an offer of early-retirement incentives? See Vega v. Kodak Caribbean, Ltd., 3 F.3d 476, 480 (1st Cir.1993) ("the law regards as the functional equivalent of a discharge those offers of early retirement which, if refused, will result in work so arduous or unappealing, or working conditions so intolerable, that a reasonable person would feel compelled to forsake his job rather than to submit to looming indignities"). Is it sufficient that an offeree who declines the offer will be placed in a position that is to any extent worse than the status quo? See Mitchell v. Mobil Oil Corp.,

896 F.2d 463, 467 (10th Cir.1990) (adopting this standard). Has the offeree necessarily established an ADEA prima facie violation if the retirement decision is voided on account of coercion?

4. *Effect of the OWBPA.* Does the Seventh Circuit's approach in *Henn* survive the OWBPA? The OWBPA requires that the early retirement be "voluntary," but without defining the term. According to the Senate Labor Committee Report, "window" periods are permitted, provided—

> [e]mployees eligible for these programs [are] given sufficient time to consider their options, particularly in circumstances when no previous retirement counseling has been provided. * * * The critical question involving allegations of involuntary retirement is whether, under the circumstances, a reasonable person would have concluded that there was no choice but to accept the offer. See Paolillo v. Dresser Industries, Inc., 821 F.2d 81, 84 (2d Cir.1987). Thus, threats of imminent layoffs, intimidation or subtle coercion may, either individually or collectively, "require or permit" involuntary retirement in any particular case.

S.Rep. No. 101–263, 101st Cong., 2d Sess. 27 (1990).

For an analysis of the OWBPA and its legislative history, see Michael C. Harper, Age-Based Exit Incentives, Coercion, and the Prospective Waiver of ADEA Rights: The Failure of the Older Workers Benefit Protection Act, 79 Va. L. Rev. 1271, 1309–1328 (1993) (concluding that Congress intended to endorse both the *Henn* constructive-discharge standard and a fair-process approach suggested in the *Paolillo* decision). Courts have continued to apply *Henn's* constructive-discharge and fair-process standards to resignations in response to early-retirement offers. See, e.g., Aliotta v. Bair, 614 F.3d 556, 563–566 (D.C. Cir. 2010).

5. *Do Conditional Retirement Incentives and Threats Together Enable Employers to Circumvent the ADEA?* Should the law, contrary to the analysis in *Henn*, take into account the interaction between the incentives of early-retirement offers and implied employer threats, when assessing whether a retirement is truly voluntary? Consider the following:

> A post-fifty-five-year-old offeree in this typical exit window scenario might well rationally accept early retirement even though she prefers continuing employment. The reason is that the offeree must include in her calculations the chance that she will be terminated without the extra benefits offered for voluntary retirement. Thus, an offeree who prefers employment to retirement with increased benefits might prefer the latter to the perceived chance of continued employment plus the perceived chance of termination without enhanced benefits. Clearly it is the conditional nature of the retirement incentive that makes the two preferences consistent, that, in other words, makes it rational for an offeree to accept the incentive even though she prefers continued employment.

This is highly significant for an employer wanting to rid itself of more older workers than could be justified by individualized comparisons of the productivity of all its workers. For instance, assume an employer wanted to cut a section of its workforce in half and that one half of the employees in this section were over fifty. Assume further that the employer could eliminate half of these post-fifty-year-old employees on the basis of individualized analyses of relative productivity. Also, assume that by offering a conditional incentive, the employer could convince three-fourths of the post-fifty-year-olds to accept retirement, even though many of these employees would prefer continuing to work. Even if none of the other one-fourth that declined retirement were vulnerable to discharge, the employer increased by 50% (from 50% to 75%) the proportion of its older workforce that it could displace. * * *

An employer is thus able to use an age-based retirement plan to eliminate significantly more older workers than it could terminate by individualized consideration of their productivity, despite the fact that many of these older workers prefer continued employment. * * *

Harper, Age-Based Exit Incentives, supra, at 1277–79.

E. WAIVER

The extent to which waiver agreements between employers and employees are enforceable is an issue that arises under Title VII as well as the ADEA. In Alexander v. Gardner-Denver Co., 415 U.S. 36, 52 n. 15, 94 S.Ct. 1011, 1022 n. 15, 39 L.Ed.2d 147 (1974), the Court endorsed the "voluntary and knowing" test applied by the lower courts to agreements of individual employees to waive Title VII claims against their employers for any discrimination that may have already occurred. Title VII courts continue to apply this test, considering either "ordinary contract principles", see, e.g., O'Shea v. Commercial Credit Corp., 930 F.2d 358 (4th Cir.1991), or the "totality of circumstances" under which the agreement was signed, see, e.g., Riley v. American Family Mut. Ins. Co., 881 F.2d 368 (7th Cir.1989). These circumstances include: the plaintiff's business experience and education, the amount of time the employee had to consider the agreement before signing, whether the employee was given additional consideration beyond that to which she was already entitled, the clarity of the agreement, whether the employee was encouraged or discouraged to consult with an attorney, and whether the employee had a fair opportunity to do so. See, e.g., Puentes v. United Parcel Service, Inc., 86 F.3d 196 (11th Cir.1996) (a day was inadequate period for consideration). Even those courts that have applied "ordinary contract principles" have considered some of these factors. See, e.g., Pilon v. University of Minn., 710 F.2d 466 (8th Cir.1983) (representation by attorney and clarity of language).

For a number of reasons, however, the waiver issue in ADEA litigation engaged the particular attention of Congress. First, because the ADEA borrows enforcement procedures from the Fair Labor Standards Act (FLSA), the courts had to distinguish Supreme Court decisions interpreting the FLSA as not allowing waivers unsupervised by the government. See D.A. Schulte, Inc. v. Gangi, 328 U.S. 108, 66 S.Ct. 925, 90 L.Ed. 1114 (1946); Brooklyn Savings Bank v. O'Neil, 324 U.S. 697, 65 S.Ct. 895, 89 L.Ed. 1296 (1945). The FLSA analogy created a hurdle both for ADEA courts professing to apply "ordinary contract principles", see, e.g., Runyan v. National Cash Register Corp., 787 F.2d 1039 (6th Cir.1986), and for those considering the "totality of circumstances", see, e.g., Coventry v. United States Steel Corp., 856 F.2d 514 (3d Cir.1988).

More importantly, the waiver issue has arisen frequently in ADEA litigation, perhaps because employers are likely to offer extra benefits to retiring older workers who have rendered considerable past service, but only if those employees are willing to waive any possible legal claims. Title II of the OWBPA Congress specifies minimum conditions for the waiver of rights under the ADEA.

NOTE: WAIVER AGREEMENTS UNDER THE OWBPA AMENDMENTS TO ADEA

Title II of the OWBPA provides that an individual "may not waive any right or claim under" ADEA unless the waiver is "knowing and voluntary", and stipulates that a waiver may not be considered knowing and voluntary unless it satisfies certain minimum conditions. The party asserting the validity of a waiver has the burden of proof on the "knowing and voluntary" issue.

Individual ADEA Waiver Agreements

For individual waiver agreements, seven minimum conditions must be satisfied: (i) the waiver must be part of an intelligible written agreement; (ii) it must specifically refer to waiver of ADEA rights or claims; (iii) it may not waive rights or claims arising after the date of the agreement; (iv) it must be "in exchange for consideration in addition to anything of value to which the individual already is entitled"; (v) the individual must be advised in writing to consult with an attorney prior to executing the agreement; (vi) the individual must be given at least 21 days to consider the agreement; and (vii) the individual must be given at least seven days following execution to revoke the agreement.

The EEOC elaborated on these conditions in subsequent regulations. See 14 C.F.R. Part 1625. For instance, "the entire waiver agreement must be in writing" in "plain language geared to the level of understanding of the individual party to the agreement or individuals eligible to participate." § 1625.22(b)(2) and (3). The bar to waiver of rights or claims arising after the date of the agreement does not preclude "agreements to perform future employment-related actions such as * * * to retire or otherwise terminate employment at a future date." § 1625.22(c)(2).

The regulations also clarify that an employer is not required to provide workers in the ADEA protected class consideration for the waiver beyond that provided to workers outside this class, but only "consideration in addition" to that which the protected worker is already entitled. § 1625.22(d)(4). Accord, DiBiase v. SmithKline Beecham Corp., 48 F.3d 719 (3d Cir.1995). The extra consideration does not have to be of any particular kind or level, but it cannot be the return of some benefit that "was eliminated in contravention of law or contract, express or implied." § 1625.22(d)(3).

The 21-day mandatory consideration period begins to run from the date of the employer's final offer and is not restarted by changes that are not "material." § 1625.22(e)(4). Furthermore, the parties may agree that even material changes to the offer do not restart the period, and an employee may sign the agreement before the end of the period as long as his doing so is knowing and voluntary and is not induced by fraud, misrepresentation, a threat to alter the offer before the end of the period, or by the provision of different terms to employees who sign early. § 1625.22(e)(4) and (6). The seven-day revocation period, however "cannot be shortened by the parties, by agreement or otherwise." § 1625.22(e)(5).

Waivers in Connection with Group Terminations

Title II treats somewhat differently waivers "requested in connection with an exit incentive or other employment termination program offered to a group or class of employees * * * ." To be effective, such waivers require a longer consideration period (45 days instead of 21 days). The regulations state that a covered "program" exists "when an employer offers additional consideration for the signing of a waiver pursuant to an exit incentive or other employment termination (e.g., a reduction in force) to two or more employees." § 1625.22(f)(1)(iii)(B).

In addition, employers must disclose any eligibility factors for individuals covered by the program and "the job titles and ages of all individuals eligible or selected for the program, and the ages of all individuals in the same job classification or organizational unit who are not eligible or selected for the program." Thus, the employer must disclose the criteria used to select employees for the layoff, along with a list of the positions and ages of employees in that "job classification or organizational unit" selected (and not selected) for the layoff.

The regulations also attempt to clarify the meaning of "job classification or organizational unit", by stating that such a "decisional unit" is "that portion of the employer's organization structure from which the employer chose the persons who would be offered consideration for the signing of a waiver and those who would not be offered consideration for the signing of a waiver." § 1625.22(f)(3)(i)(B). For instance, if the employer intends to reduce its force of accountants by ten percent, then the ages of all its accountants must be provided. § 1625.22(f)(iii)(E) and (iv)(E). This applies even if the "terminees" are to be "selected from a subset of a decisional unit", such as where the employer intends that the ten-percent reduction in accountants "will come from the accountants whose performance is in the bottom one-third" of all accountants. § 1625.22(f)(3)(v). For analysis of these disclosure requirements, *see, e.g.* Burlison v. McDonald's Corp., 455 F.3d 1242 (11th Cir. 2006); Kruchowski v. Weyerhauser Co., 446 F.3d 1090 (10th Cir. 2006).

Settlements of Charges Filed with the EEOC or in Court

Title II also requires that effective settlements of charges already filed with a governmental authority are to be knowing and voluntary, and provides that the first five minimum conditions must be met to satisfy this standard. For such claims, however, the minimum 21- or 45-day consideration period and the seven-day revocation period do not apply; the Act instead only requires that the charging party be "given a reasonable period of time within which to consider the settlement agreement." The regulations provide that what is a "reasonable period" is based in part on whether the charging "individual is represented by counsel". § 1625.22(g)(4).

NOTES AND QUESTIONS

Test Your Understanding of the Material

1. What is the legal significance of a waiver deemed ineffective under the OWBPA standards? Does the employer who requires such a waiver violate ADEA, without more, or must employees who signed the ineffective waiver still prove that the exit incentive plan, or their individual discharges, were otherwise unlawful?

2. Suppose an employer offered its employees a "Voluntary Big Ticket Severance Allowance Plan," under which employees were given only five days to decide whether to participate in the Plan or to remain employed at reduced wages. Employees who decided to resign under the Plan could earn greater severance benefits if they agreed to waive all their claims under the ADEA, including those unrelated to their termination. Did the employer violate the ADEA if it gave the employees only five days to sign the waiver to receive enhanced benefits? What if it provided 45 days to decide whether to sign the waiver, but only five days to decide whether to resign to receive any benefits under the Plan? See EEOC v. Sears, Roebuck & Co., 857 F.Supp. 1233 (N.D.Ill.1994).

3. Would employer misrepresentations invalidate a waiver that otherwise meets the OWBPA minimum conditions?

Related Issues

4. *Right to File an EEOC Charge.* Under Title II, employees cannot waive their right to file a charge with the EEOC or to otherwise cooperate with an EEOC investigation. Cf. EEOC v. Cosmair, Inc., L'Oreal Hair Care Div., 821 F.2d 1085 (5th Cir.1987) (finding such a waiver to be against public policy); EEOC v. Astra, 94 F.3d 738 (1st Cir.1996) (upholding injunction of enforcement of promises in settlement agreements to not assist EEOC in investigation of Title VII charges).

    5. *Must an Employee Return the Consideration for an Ineffective Waiver Before Suit?* In Oubre v. Entergy Operations, Inc., 522 U.S. 422, 118 S.Ct. 838, 139 L.Ed.2d 849 (1998), the Supreme Court held that an employee's ADEA suit against her employer was not barred by her retention of monies that she took from her employer in exchange for a release that was claimed to not satisfy the OWBPA. The Court stressed that the retention, like the release itself, did not constitute an effective waiver of her ADEA claims because it did not comply with the OWBPA mandates. The Court also noted that many employees already will have spent any monies received and that barring suit because of retention thus would tempt employers to evade the requirements of the OWBPA. The Court did allow, however, that "courts may need to inquire whether the employer has claims for restitution, recoupment, or setoff against the employee, and these questions may be more complex where a release is effective as to some claims but not as to ADEA claims." 522 U.S. at 428.

    The EEOC has issued a final legislative rule amending its regulations on ADEA waivers in light of *Oubre*. See 29 C.F.R. § 1625.22. The amendment takes the following positions. First, the *Oubre* Court's rejection of application of the common law ratification and tender back doctrines applies to waivers that are not knowing and voluntary because of common law principles like fraud, duress, coercion, or mistake of material fact, not just to waivers that do not meet the minimum OWBPA conditions. Accord, Bennett v. Coors Brewing Co., 189 F.3d 1221 (10th Cir. 1999).

    Second, "tender back" clauses in waiver agreements are ineffective so that the holding of *Oubre* cannot be circumvented by contract. Third, also to prevent a contractual circumvention of *Oubre*, a "covenant not to sue, or other equivalent arrangement", as well as a waiver agreement, is included under the no "tender back" rule. This means that an employer cannot enforce a "covenant not to sue" that does not meet the OWBPA minimum standards. Fourth, the new rule prohibits and renders ineffective any ADEA waiver agreement, covenant not to sue, or other equivalent arrangement that imposes any condition precedent or penalty or any other limitation, beyond attorney's fees and costs specifically authorized under law, that would discourage challenging the waiver agreement or covenant not to sue under the OWBPA.

    Fifth, where an employee successfully challenges a waiver or covenant not to sue, and prevails on the merits of the ADEA claim, courts have the discretion to determine whether the employer is entitled to restitution, recoupment or setoff against the employee's monetary award. But a reduction cannot exceed the lesser of the amount the employee recovered, on the one hand, and the consideration the employee received for signing the waiver or covenant, on the other. Finally, an employer may not abrogate its duties to any signatory under a waiver agreement or covenant, even if one or more of the signatories or the EEOC successfully challenges the validity of the agreement. The last position is supported by Justice Breyer's concurring opinion in *Oubre*, arguing that the Court's decision makes waiver agreements voidable, but not void, as well as the holding of a district court, Butcher v. Gerber Prods. Co., 8 F.Supp.2d 307 (S.D.N.Y. 1998). For an application of *Oubre* to an ineffective prospective waiver of Title VII claims, see Richardson v. Sugg, 448 F.3d 1046 (8th Cir. 2006).

6. *Time Periods for Settlements.* Why does the OWBPA not demand the same set minimum periods for consideration and revocation of waivers of charges that already have been filed with the EEOC or a court?

7. *Prohibition on Prospective Waivers.* The OWBPA's prohibition of the waiver of rights or claims arising after the date of the agreement is consistent with the analysis of the Supreme Court in *Alexander v. Gardner-Denver*, supra. In that case the Court asserted the "clear" proposition "that there can be no prospective waiver of an employee's rights under Title VII." 415 U.S. at 51, 94 S.Ct. at 1021. This means that an employee cannot agree to trade being protected against discrimination in the future for a higher salary or other enhanced benefits. Do you understand why employees should be able to waive Title VII or ADEA claims against discrimination that has already occurred, but not against future discrimination?

CHAPTER 9

DISABILITY DISCRIMINATION

■ ■ ■

Introduction

This chapter introduces another area of employment discrimination law—protection of individuals from discrimination on account of a disability. In addition to the intentional discrimination and disparate impact approaches we have encountered previously, the legislation in this area defines discrimination on account of disability to include refusal to make reasonable accommodations that would enable disabled job applicants and employees to perform their jobs.

A. JUSTIFICATIONS FOR REGULATING DISABILITY DISCRIMINATION

In the aggregate, individuals with disabilities have occupied an inferior economic position in American society. As highlighted in the House Report on the legislation that became the Americans with Disabilities Act of 1990 (ADA), Pub. L. No. 101–336, 104 Stat. 327, codified at 42 U.S.C. §§ 12101 et seq., before passage of the ADA, two out of every three disabled Americans of working-age were not employed and two of three who were not working wanted to be. The income of disabled workers was about thirty six percent less than that of their nondisabled counterparts. In 1984, fifty percent of adults with disabilities had household incomes of $15,000 or less, compared to only twenty-five percent of nondisabled adults. See H.R. Rep. No. 485, 101st Cong., 2d sess., pt. 2, at 32 (1990). See also Jane West, The Social and Policy Context of the Act, in The Americans with Disabilities Act: From Policy to Practice 5 (Jane West, ed. 1991).

1. SOURCES OF THE PROBLEMS CONFRONTING DISABLED WORKERS

a. Prejudice

The relative economic position of the disabled has been due in part to social prejudice. See generally United States Commission on Civil Rights, Accommodating the Spectrum of Individual Abilities (1983); Jacobus tenBroek & Floyd W. Matson, The Disabled and the Law of Welfare, 54 Cal.L.Rev. 809, 814 & nn. 21–22 (1966). Impairments which are physically disfiguring or socially stigmatizing, such as epilepsy and Down syndrome, may provoke prejudice in the form of unreasoned dislike and a preference for nonassociation. See Harold E. Yuker, The Measurement of Attitudes Toward Disabled Persons (1966); Frank Bowe, Handicapping America (1978); Harlan Hahn, Paternalism and Public Policy, 20 Society 36 (March/April 1983). Employers that lack familiarity with certain disabilities may engage in false stereotyping—overestimating the limiting effects of impairment, the difficulties of shifting impaired workers among tasks, and the costs of supervision and training. See Jean Ruth Schroedel, Employer Attitudes Towards Hiring Persons with Disabilities (1978).

b. Statistical Discrimination

Even if employers harbor no prejudice, they may have economic incentives to not hire or promote the disabled. For particular individuals or disabilities, it may make sense for an employer to avoid the costs of obtaining more information. The likelihood of such "statistical discrimination" against individuals with disabilities is particularly great because employers confront a wide variety of both types and severities of disabilities. Furthermore, just as retirement pensions and the increasing costs of insurance with age may discourage the employment of older workers, benefit programs, however desirable for other reasons, may make the employment of certain types of disabled workers more expensive than workers without disabilities.

c. Need for Workplace Accommodations

The relatively poor experience of the disabled in the employment market, however, cannot be explained fully by employer discrimination. Many disabilities are sufficiently serious to prevent the effective performance of a broad range of jobs. Moreover, employers may find it efficient to refuse to hire anyone with particular disabilities, regardless of their ability to perform the basic jobs they seek, because employers have structured their work processes and physical facilities for the average nondisabled worker.

The lowering of this last kind of barrier to the equal participation of disabled individuals in the workforce warrants regulation beyond the prohibition of unequal treatment on the basis of disability as a suspect, protected classification. It requires asking difficult questions about the extent to which employers must provide equal opportunities for the disabled, not simply formally equal treatment. Should the law compel employers to modify their work processes and physical facilities to accommodate the disabled, even where this involves increased costs for the employer and the economy? Will the costs of accommodation be repaid to society in the long run by enabling more citizens to reach their full productive potential? Even if these costs are not fully repaid, are they well spent in giving these citizens an opportunity to achieve the dignity of productive work? If the social judgment is made that the benefits of enhancing the employability of impaired workers outweigh the costs of accommodation, should the costs be spread through taxation and subsidization by the government or through price increases caused by extra regulations on all private employers?

2. EVOLUTION OF FEDERAL LEGISLATIVE RESPONSE

a. The Rehabilitation Act of 1973

The Rehabilitation Act, 87 Stat. 355, 29 U.S.C. §§ 701–795(i), preceded the ADA. The Rehabilitation Act applies only to the federal government, federal contractors, and employers receiving federal financial assistance. In addition to increasing funding for vocational rehabilitation, the Rehabilitation Act sought to eradicate discriminatory and other barriers to the hiring of disabled workers. Section 501 imposes affirmative action obligations on federal agencies. Section 502 seeks to remove physical access barriers in federal buildings. Section 503 levies affirmative action duties on all federal contractors with contracts in excess of $10,000. Finally, § 504 prohibits federal programs and any program or activity receiving federal financial assistance from discriminating against "otherwise qualified individual[s] with a disability * * * solely by reason of [their] disability * * * ." 42 U.S.C. § 794(a).

b. The Americans with Disabilities Act of 1990 (ADA)

The Americans with Disabilities Act of 1990 (ADA), 104 Stat. 327, 42 U.S.C. § 12101 et seq. applies to all employers subject to Title VII. Title I of the ADA prohibits discrimination against any "qualified individual with a disability" (§ 102(a)), defined as "an individual with a disability who, with or without reasonable accommodation, can perform the essential functions" of the job. (§ 101(8)) Beyond its prohibition of discrimination, the ADA also imposes a duty of reasonable accommodation for "the known physical or mental limitations of an otherwise qualified individual with a disability." (§ 102(b)(5)(A)).

In part because of its broader goals—the statute imposes a reasonable-accommodation requirement on employers with 15 or more employees, whether or not they have the ability, as do covered entities under the Rehabilitation Act to shift costs to the federal government—the ADA has proven to be a controversial statute. See generally, Samuel R. Bagenstos, The Americans with Disabilities Act as Welfare Reform, 44 Wm. & Mary L. Rev. 921,1017–18 (2003); Susan Schwochau & Peter David Blanck, The Economics of the Americans with Disabilities Act, Part III: Does the ADA Disable the Disabled, 21 Berk. J. Emp. & Lab.L. 271 (2000). The ADA's broad and sometimes confusing provisions have generated a great deal of litigation.

NOTE: THE REHABILITATION ACT OF 1973

The Rehabilitation Act continues to be relevant, notwithstanding its narrower coverage and its adoption of the ADA's employment discrimination standards, see 29 U.S.C. §§ 791(g), 794(d). First, § 501 of the Rehabilitation Act covers one very important employer not reached by the ADA: the federal government. Second, the Rehabilitation Act's enforcement procedures and remedies differ somewhat from those provided by the ADA. Section 503's duties on federal contractors, for instance, are enforced by the Office of Federal Contract Compliance Programs (OFFCP) of the Department of Labor through promulgated regulations, which now include a seven percent utilization goal for the employment of workers with disabilities. See 41 C.F.R. Part 60–741.

1. *Employers Receiving Federal Financial Assistance.* Perhaps most importantly, the Rehabilitation Act's prohibition in § 504(a) of disability discrimination "under any program or activity receiving Federal financial assistance" can be enforced directly in court through a private right of action without exhausting the administrative procedure mandated for the ADA. See ADA, § 107(a) (incorporating Title VII's "remedies and procedures"); Consolidated Rail Corp. v. Darrone, 465 U.S. 624, 626, 104 S.Ct. 1248, 79 L.Ed.2d 568 (1984). The courts of appeals have allowed private damages actions under § 504, even after passage of the ADA. See, e.g., Freed v. Consolidated Rail Corp., 201 F.3d 188 (3d Cir.2000). For firms receiving federal financial assistance, coverage extends beyond the specific program or activity to which the federal funds are allotted. See Civil Rights Restoration Act of 1987, Pub.L. 100–259, 102 Stat. 28. For companies not "principally engaged in the business of providing education, health care, housing, social services, or parks and recreation" (§ 504(b)(3)(A)(ii)), the Rehabilitation Act reaches "the entire plant or other comparable, geographically separate facility" to which assistance is extended (§ 504(b)(3)(B)). For other recipients, it reaches their entire institution. But see United States Dept. of Transp. v. Paralyzed Veterans of America, 477 U.S. 597, 605–06, 106 S.Ct. 2705, 91 L.Ed.2d 494 (1986) (§ 504 covers only employers who are the direct recipients of federal assistance, and not simply the ultimate beneficiaries of such assistance). See also Schrader v. Fred A. Ray, M.D., P.C., 296 F.3d 968 (10th Cir.2002) (coverage of federal fund recipients under § 504, in contrast to ADA, not dependent on having 15 employees).

2. *Federal Employees.* Federal employees alleging disability discrimination under the Rehabilitation Act do not have a private right of action. See, e.g., Spence v. Straw, 54 F.3d 196 (3d Cir.1995). They can invoke administrative adjudication under EEOC auspices; if unsuccessful in that forum, they can seek de novo review in federal court. See § 505(a); see also Civil Service Reform Act of 1978, 5 U.S.C. § 2302(b)(1)(D).

3. *Federal Contractors.* Employees of federal contractors also do not have a private right of action. Section 503(b) directs the Department of Labor to investigate promptly and take action on any complaints filed by disabled workers of a federal contractor's failure to comply with its contractual obligations. Under regulations issued by the Labor Department's Office of

Federal Contract Compliance, see 41 C.F.R. pt. 60–741, such action may include equitable relief for the discriminatee, as well as contract termination and disbarment.

PRACTITIONER'S PERSPECTIVE

Jinny Kim
Director, Disability Rights Program.
Senior Staff Attorney, Legal Aid Society—Employment Law Center.

The Disability Rights Program specializes in assisting and representing low-wage workers with disabilities. We regularly receive calls from workers with questions about reasonable accommodations and the process for requesting an accommodation for a disability. Common questions include the timing of an accommodation request, the pros and cons of disclosing a disability, and the documentation required to request an accommodation. We also receive specific questions about common accommodation requests such as a modified work schedule, reassignment to a vacant position, the provision of sign language interpreters or the acquisition or modification of equipment.

Our clients commonly require a leave of absence for treatment and recovery, especially those with cancer, psychiatric conditions, mobility disabilities, and on-the-job orthopedic injuries. Leaves beyond the 12-week leave guaranteed by the Family and Medical Leave Act [29 U.S.C. § 2601 et seq.] may be required as a reasonable accommodation under the ADA or state laws.

Leaves of absence are critical for retaining countless numbers of people with disabilities within the workforce. The purpose of a reasonable accommodation leave of absence is to enable the employee to receive treatment, recover and return to work. That is the essence of an effective accommodation. The entire purpose of the leave is vitiated if the employee recovers but is terminated or otherwise barred from returning to work.

A few clients we have represented include:

- A janitor for a department store who took a leave to receive treatment for colon cancer, but was terminated when she was released by her doctor to return to work.

- A mailroom worker with an anxiety disorder who required a leave of absence for treatment following an adverse reaction to a new medication but was terminated instead.

- A cook with 16 years' seniority who took leave for breast cancer treatment and was terminated at the expiration of her FMLA leave even though she only required two additional weeks of leave.

- A construction worker who needed a leave to recover from an on-the-job back injury, but who was terminated when he tried to return to work.

In these situations, we have written demand letters to employers to advocate on our client's behalf. Sometimes, in response to a demand letter, employers will agree to return our clients to work. On other occasions, we have litigated in court for disability discrimination and failure to accommodate under the ADA and parallel state laws.

B. DEFINITION OF "DISABILITY"

The definition of "disability" in the ADA is included in the preliminary provisions applicable to all Titles of the Act, including Title I, governing employment, Title II, governing activities, services, and programs of public entities, and Title III, governing public accommodations.

The ADA defines disability as:

(A) a physical or mental impairment that substantially limits one or more major life activities of such individual;

(B) a record of such an impairment; or

(C) being regarded as having such an impairment[.]

In Bragdon v. Abbott, 524 U.S. 624, 118 S.Ct. 2196, 141 L.Ed.2d 540 (1998), a Title III case involving a patient with an HIV infection who was denied dental services, the Court confirmed that this definition required those who claim a disability to demonstrate three things: an "impairment"; an impact on one or more "major life activities"; and a degree of impact at least equal to "substantially limits." The *Bragdon* Court first held that an HIV infection is an impairment, even before it progresses to a stage with overt symptoms. The Court relied on a regulation first promulgated by the Department of Health, Education, and Welfare (HEW) for the Rehabilitation Act of 1973, and now adopted by the EEOC for the ADA, see 29 C.F.R. § 1630.2(h), which defines an impairment to include a "disorder or condition . . . affecting one or more body systems" such as the "hemic" and "lymphatic" systems infected by HIV. The Court then accepted the plaintiff's claim that reproduction is a major life activity, "central to the life process itself," even though not among those activities listed in the HEW's Rehabilitation Act regulations. Finally, the *Bragdon* Court determined that the plaintiff's HIV infection substantially limited her ability to reproduce, because of the risk of her sexual partner being infected and the risk of her child being infected during gestation and childbirth.

Subsequent Supreme Court decisions, including Sutton v. United Air Lines, Inc., 527 U.S. 471, 119 S.Ct. 2139, 144 L.Ed.2d 450 (1999), and

Toyota Motor Mfg. v. Williams, 534 U.S. 184, 122 S.Ct. 681, 151 L.Ed.2d 615 (2002), narrowed the ADA's scope. Congress, in turn, overturned those decisions through the ADA Amendments Act of 2008, 122 Stat. 3553 (ADAAA). The ADAAA is described below after the following excerpts from the Court's decisions in *Sutton* and *Toyota*.

SUTTON V. UNITED AIR LINES, INC.

Supreme Court of the United States, 1999.
527 U.S. 471, 119 S.Ct. 2139, 144 L.Ed.2d 450.

JUSTICE O'CONNOR delivered the opinion of the Court.

I

* * *

Petitioners are twin sisters, both of whom have severe myopia. Each petitioner's uncorrected visual acuity is 20/200 or worse in her right eye and 20/400 or worse in her left eye, but "[w]ith the use of corrective lenses, each * * * has vision that is 20/20 or better." Consequently, without corrective lenses, each "effectively cannot see to conduct numerous activities such as driving a vehicle, watching television or shopping in public stores," but with corrective measures, such as glasses or contact lenses, both "function identically to individuals without a similar impairment."

In 1992, petitioners applied to respondent for employment as commercial airline pilots. They met respondent's basic age, education, experience, and FAA certification qualifications. After submitting their applications for employment, both petitioners were invited by respondent to an interview and to flight simulator tests. Both were told during their interviews, however, that a mistake had been made in inviting them to interview because petitioners did not meet respondent's minimum vision requirement, which was uncorrected visual acuity of 20/100 or better. Due to their failure to meet this requirement, petitioners' interviews were terminated, and neither was offered a pilot position.

In light of respondent's proffered reason for rejecting them, petitioners filed a charge of disability discrimination under the ADA with the Equal Employment Opportunity Commission (EEOC). After receiving a right to sue letter, petitioners filed suit in the United States District Court for the District of Colorado, alleging that respondent had discriminated against them "on the basis of their disability, or because [respondent] regarded [petitioners] as having a disability" in violation of the ADA. Specifically, petitioners alleged that due to their severe myopia they actually have a substantially limiting impairment or are regarded as having such an impairment, and are thus disabled under the Act.

* * *

III

* * *

We conclude that respondent is correct that the approach adopted by the agency guidelines—that persons are to be evaluated in their hypothetical uncorrected state—is an impermissible interpretation of the ADA. Looking at the Act as a whole, it is apparent that if a person is taking measures to correct for, or mitigate, a physical or mental impairment, the effects of those measures—both positive and negative—must be taken into account when judging whether that person is "substantially limited" in a major life activity and thus "disabled" under the Act. * * *

* * *

The definition of disability . . . requires that disabilities be evaluated "with respect to an individual" and be determined based on whether an impairment substantially limits the "major life activities of such individual." § 12102(2). Thus, whether a person has a disability under the ADA is an individualized inquiry. See *Bragdon v. Abbott*, 524 U.S. 624, 118 S.Ct. 2196, 141 L.Ed.2d 540 (1998) (declining to consider whether HIV infection is a per se disability under the ADA); 29 CFR pt. 1630, App. § 1630.2(j) ("The determination of whether an individual has a disability is not necessarily based on the name or diagnosis of the impairment the person has, but rather on the effect of that impairment on the life of the individual"). * * *

The agency guidelines' directive that persons be judged in their uncorrected or unmitigated state runs directly counter to the individualized inquiry mandated by the ADA. The agency approach would often require courts and employers to speculate about a person's condition and would, in many cases, force them to make a disability determination based on general information about how an uncorrected impairment usually affects individuals, rather than on the individual's actual condition. For instance, under this view, courts would almost certainly find all diabetics to be disabled, because if they failed to monitor their blood sugar levels and administer insulin, they would almost certainly be substantially limited in one or more major life activities. A diabetic whose illness does not impair his or her daily activities would therefore be considered disabled simply because he or she has diabetes. Thus, the guidelines approach would create a system in which persons often must be treated as members of a group of people with similar impairments, rather than as individuals. This is contrary to both the letter and the spirit of the ADA.

The guidelines approach could also lead to the anomalous result that in determining whether an individual is disabled, courts and employers could not consider any negative side effects suffered by an individual resulting from the use of mitigating measures, even when those side effects are very severe. * * *

* * *

* * * The use of a corrective device does not, by itself, relieve one's disability. Rather, one has a disability under subsection A if, notwithstanding the use of a corrective device, that individual is substantially limited in a major life activity. For example, individuals who use prosthetic limbs or wheelchairs may be mobile and capable of functioning in society but still be disabled because of a substantial limitation on their ability to walk or run. The same may be true of individuals who take medicine to lessen the symptoms of an impairment so that they can function but nevertheless remain substantially limited. Alternatively, one whose high blood pressure is "cured" by medication may be regarded as disabled by a covered entity, and thus disabled under subsection C of the definition. The use or nonuse of a corrective device does not determine whether an individual is disabled; that determination depends on whether the limitations an individual with an impairment actually faces are in fact substantially limiting.

Applying this reading of the Act to the case at hand, we conclude that the Court of Appeals correctly resolved the issue of disability in respondent's favor. As noted above, petitioners allege that with corrective measures, their visual acuity is 20/20, and that they "function identically to individuals without a similar impairment." In addition, petitioners concede that they "do not argue that the use of corrective lenses in itself demonstrates a substantially limiting impairment." Accordingly, because we decide that disability under the Act is to be determined with reference to corrective measures, we agree with the courts below that petitioners have not stated a claim that they are substantially limited in any major life activity.

IV

Our conclusion that petitioners have failed to state a claim that they are actually disabled under subsection (A) of the disability definition does not end our inquiry. Under subsection (C), individuals who are "regarded as" having a disability are disabled within the meaning of the ADA. See § 12102(2)(C). Subsection (C) provides that having a disability includes "being regarded as having," § 12102(2)(C), "a physical or mental impairment that substantially limits one or more of the major life activities of such individual," § 12102(2)(A). There are two apparent ways in which individuals may fall within this statutory definition: (1) a covered entity mistakenly believes that a person has a physical impairment that substantially limits one or more major life activities, or (2) a covered entity mistakenly believes that an actual, nonlimiting impairment substantially limits one or more major life activities. In both cases, it is necessary that a covered entity entertain misperceptions about the individual—it must believe either that one has a substantially limiting impairment that one does not have or that one has a substantially limiting impairment when, in fact, the impairment is not so limiting. These misperceptions often "resul[t] from stereotypic assumptions not truly indicative of * * * individual ability." See 42 U.S.C. § 12101(7). * * *

There is no dispute that petitioners are physically impaired. Petitioners do not make the obvious argument that they are regarded due to their impairments as substantially limited in the major life activity of seeing. They contend only that respondent mistakenly believes their physical impairments substantially limit them in the major life activity of working. To support this claim, petitioners allege that respondent has a vision requirement, which is allegedly based on myth and stereotype. Further, this requirement substantially limits their ability to engage in the major life activity of working by precluding them from obtaining the job of global airline pilot, which they argue is a "class of employment." In reply, respondent argues that the position of global airline pilot is not a class of jobs and therefore petitioners have not stated a claim that they are regarded as substantially limited in the major life activity of working.

Standing alone, the allegation that respondent has a vision requirement in place does not establish a claim that respondent regards petitioners as substantially limited in the major life activity of working. By its terms, the ADA allows employers to prefer some physical attributes over others and to establish physical criteria. An employer runs afoul of the ADA when it makes an employment decision based on a physical or mental impairment, real or imagined, that is regarded as substantially limiting a major life activity. Accordingly, an employer is free to decide that physical characteristics or medical conditions that do not rise to the level of an impairment—such as one's height, build, or singing voice—are preferable to others, just as it is free to decide that some limiting, but not *substantially* limiting, impairments make individuals less than ideally suited for a job.

* * *

When the major life activity under consideration is that of working, the statutory phrase "substantially limits" requires, at a minimum, that plaintiffs allege they are unable to work in a broad class of jobs. Reflecting this requirement, the EEOC uses a specialized definition of the term "substantially limits" when referring to the major life activity of working:

> "significantly restricted in the ability to perform either a class of jobs or a broad range of jobs in various classes as compared to the average person having comparable training, skills and abilities. The inability to perform a single, particular job does not constitute a substantial limitation in the major life activity of working." § 1630.2(j)(3)(i).

The EEOC further identifies several factors that courts should consider when determining whether an individual is substantially limited in the major life activity of working, including the geographic area to which the individual has reasonable access, and "the number and types of jobs utilizing similar training, knowledge, skills or abilities, within the geographical area, from which the individual is also disqualified." §§ 1630.2(j)(3)(ii)(A), (B). To be substantially limited in the major life activity of working, then, one must be precluded from more than one type of job, a specialized job, or a particular job of choice. If jobs utilizing an individual's skills (but perhaps not his or her unique talents) are available, one is not precluded from a substantial class of jobs. Similarly, if a host of different types of jobs are available, one is not precluded from a broad range of jobs.

* * *

Assuming without deciding that working is a major life activity and that the EEOC regulations interpreting the term "substantially limits" are reasonable, petitioners have failed to allege adequately that their poor eyesight is regarded as an impairment that substantially limits them in the major life activity of working. They allege only that respondent regards their poor vision as precluding them from holding positions as a "global airline pilot." Because the position of global airline pilot is a single job, this allegation does not support the claim that respondent regards petitioners as having a substantially limiting impairment. See 29 CFR § 1630.2(j)(3)(i) ("The inability to perform a single, particular job does not constitute a substantial limitation in the major life activity of working"). Indeed, there are a number of other positions utilizing petitioners' skills, such as regional pilot and pilot instructor to name a few, that are available to them. Even under the EEOC's Interpretative Guidance, to which petitioners ask us to defer, "an individual who cannot be a commercial airline pilot because of a minor vision impairment, but who can be a commercial airline co-pilot or a pilot for a courier service, would not be substantially limited in the major life activity of working." 29 CFR pt. 1630, App. § 1630.2.

[Eds. The concurring opinion of JUSTICE GINSBURG and dissenting opinions of JUSTICE STEVENS and JUSTICE BREYER are omitted.]

TOYOTA MOTOR MFG. V. WILLIAMS
Supreme Court of the United States, 2002.
534 U.S. 184, 122 S.Ct. 681, 151 L.Ed.2d 615.

JUSTICE O'CONNOR delivered the opinion of the Court.

I

Respondent began working at petitioner's automobile manufacturing plant in Georgetown, Kentucky, in August 1990. She was soon placed on an engine fabrication assembly line, where her duties included work with pneumatic tools. Use of these tools eventually caused pain in respondent's hands, wrists, and arms. She sought treatment at petitioner's in-house medical service, where she was diagnosed with bilateral carpal tunnel syndrome and bilateral tendinitis. Respondent consulted a personal physician who placed her on permanent work restrictions that precluded her from lifting more than 20 pounds or from "frequently lifting or carrying of objects weighing up to 10 pounds," engaging in "constant repetitive . . . flexion or extension of [her] wrists or elbows," performing "overhead work," or using "vibratory or pneumatic tools."

work restrictions

In light of these restrictions, for the next two years petitioner assigned respondent to various modified duty jobs. Nonetheless, respondent missed some work for medical leave, and eventually filed a claim under the Kentucky Workers' Compensation Act. The parties settled this claim, and respondent returned to work. She was unsatisfied by petitioner's efforts to accommodate her work restrictions, however, and responded by bringing an action in the United States District Court for the Eastern District of Kentucky alleging that petitioner had violated the ADA by refusing to accommodate her disability. That suit was also settled, and as part of the settlement, respondent returned to work in December 1993.

Upon her return, petitioner placed respondent on a team in Quality Control Inspection Operations (QCIO). QCIO is responsible for four tasks: (1) "assembly paint"; (2) "paint second inspection"; (3) "shell body audit"; and (4) "ED surface repair." Respondent was initially placed on a team that performed only the first two of these tasks, and for a couple of years, she rotated on a weekly basis between them. In assembly paint, respondent visually inspected painted cars moving slowly down a conveyor. She scanned for scratches, dents, chips, or any other flaws that may have occurred during the assembly or painting process, at a rate of one car every 54 seconds. When respondent began working in assembly paint, inspection team members were required to open and shut the doors, trunk, and/or hood of each passing car. Sometime during respondent's tenure, however, the position was modified to include only visual inspection with few or no manual tasks. Paint second inspection required team members to use their hands to wipe each painted car with a glove as it moved along a conveyor. The parties agree that respondent was physically capable of performing both of these jobs and that her performance was satisfactory.

During the fall of 1996, petitioner announced that it wanted QCIO employees to be able to rotate through all four of the QCIO processes. Respondent therefore received training for the shell body audit job, in which team members apply a highlight oil to the hood, fender, doors, rear quarter panel, and trunk of passing cars at a rate of approximately one car per minute. The highlight oil has the viscosity of salad oil, and employees spread it on cars with a sponge attached to a block of wood. After they wipe each car with the oil, the employees visually inspect it for flaws. Wiping the cars required respondent to hold her hands and arms up around shoulder height for several hours at a time.

A short while after the shell body audit job was added to respondent's rotations, she began to experience pain in her neck and shoulders. Respondent again sought care at petitioner's in-house medical service, where she was diagnosed with myotendinitis bilateral periscapular, an inflammation of the muscles and tendons around both of her shoulder blades; myotendinitis and myositis bilateral forearms with nerve compression causing median nerve irritation; and thoracic outlet compression, a condition that causes pain in the nerves that lead to the upper extremities. Respondent requested that petitioner accommodate her medical conditions by allowing her to return to doing only her original two jobs in QCIO, which respondent claimed she could still perform without difficulty.

The parties disagree about what happened next. According to respondent, petitioner refused her request and forced her to continue working in the shell body audit job, which caused her even greater physical injury. According to petitioner, respondent simply began missing work on a regular basis. Regardless, it is clear that on December 6, 1996, the last day respondent worked at petitioner's plant, she was placed under a no-work-of-any-kind restriction by her treating physicians. On January 27, 1997, respondent received a letter from petitioner that terminated her employment, citing her poor attendance record.

Respondent filed a charge of disability discrimination with the Equal Employment Opportunity Commission (EEOC). After receiving a right to sue letter, respondent filed suit against petitioner in the United States District Court for the Eastern District of Kentucky. Her complaint alleged that petitioner had violated the ADA and the Kentucky Civil Rights Act, Ky. Rev. Stat. Ann. §§ 344.010 et seq. (1997 and Supp. 2000), by failing to reasonably accommodate her disability and by terminating her employment. * * *

Respondent based her claim that she was "disabled" under the ADA on the ground that her physical impairments substantially limited her in (1) manual tasks; (2) housework; (3) gardening; (4) playing with her children; (5) lifting; and (6) working, all of which, she argued, constituted major life activities under the Act. Respondent also argued, in the alternative, that she was disabled under the ADA because she had a record of a substantially limiting impairment and because she was regarded as having such an impairment. See 42 U.S.C. §§ 12102(2)(B–C) (1994 ed.).

After petitioner filed a motion for summary judgment and respondent filed a motion for partial summary judgment on her disability claims, the District Court granted summary judgment to petitioner. The court found that respondent had not been disabled, as defined by the ADA, at the time of petitioner's alleged refusal to accommodate her, and that she had therefore not been covered by the Act's protections or by the Kentucky Civil Rights Act, which is construed consistently with the ADA. * * *

* * * The Court of Appeals for the Sixth Circuit reversed the District Court's ruling on whether respondent was disabled at the time she sought an accommodation * * *. The Court of Appeals held that in order for respondent to demonstrate that she was disabled due to a substantial limitation in the ability to perform manual tasks at the time of her accommodation request, she had to "show that her manual disability involved a 'class' of manual activities affecting the ability to perform tasks at work." Respondent satisfied this test, according to the Court of Appeals, because her ailments "prevented her from doing the tasks associated with certain types of manual assembly line jobs, manual product handling jobs and manual building trade jobs (painting, plumbing, roofing, etc.) that require the gripping of tools and repetitive work with hands and arms extended at or above shoulder levels for extended periods of time." * * * Because the Court of Appeals concluded that respondent had been substantially limited in performing manual tasks and, for that reason, was entitled to partial summary judgment on the issue of whether she was disabled under the Act, it found that it did not need to determine whether respondent had been substantially limited in the major life activities of lifting or working, or whether she had had a "record of" a disability or had been "regarded as" disabled.

* * *

III

The question presented by this case is whether the Sixth Circuit properly determined that respondent was disabled under subsection (A) of the ADA's disability definition at the time that she sought an accommodation from petitioner. 42 U.S.C. § 12102(2)(A). The parties do not dispute that respondent's medical conditions, which include carpal tunnel syndrome, myotendinitis, and thoracic outlet compression, amount to physical impairments. The relevant question, therefore, is whether the Sixth Circuit correctly analyzed whether these impairments substantially limited respondent in the major life activity of performing manual tasks. Answering this requires us to address an issue about which the EEOC regulations are silent: what a plaintiff must demonstrate to establish a substantial limitation in the specific major life activity of performing manual tasks.

Our consideration of this issue is guided first and foremost by the words of the disability definition itself. "Substantially" in the phrase "substantially limits" suggests "considerable" or "to a large degree." See Webster's Third New International Dictionary 2280 (1976) (defining "substantially" as "in a substantial manner" and "substantial" as "considerable in amount, value, or worth" and "being that specified to a large degree or in the main"); see also 17 Oxford English Dictionary 66–67 (2d ed. 1989) ("substantial": "relating to or proceeding from the essence of a thing; essential"; "of ample or considerable amount, quantity, or dimensions"). The word "substantial" thus clearly precludes impairments that interfere in only a minor way with the performance of manual tasks from qualifying as disabilities. Cf. *Albertson's, Inc. v. Kirkingburg*, 527 U.S. [555,] 565 [(1999)] (explaining that a "mere difference" does not amount to a "significant restriction" and therefore does not satisfy the EEOC's interpretation of "substantially limits").

"Major" in the phrase "major life activities" means important. See Webster's, *supra*, at 1363 (defining "major" as "greater in dignity, rank, importance, or interest"). "Major life activities" thus refers to those activities that are of central importance to daily life. In order for performing manual tasks to fit into this category—a category that includes such basic abilities as walking, seeing, and hearing—the manual tasks in question must be central to daily life. If each of the tasks included in the major life activity of performing manual tasks does not independently qualify as a major life activity, then together they must do so.

That these terms need to be interpreted strictly to create a demanding standard for qualifying as disabled is confirmed by the first section of the ADA, which lays out the legislative findings and purposes that motivate the Act. See 42 U. S. C. § 12101. When it enacted the ADA in 1990, Congress found that "some 43,000,000 Americans have one or more physical or mental disabilities." § 12101(a)(1). If Congress intended everyone with a physical impairment that precluded the performance of some isolated, unimportant, or particularly difficult manual task to qualify as disabled, the number of disabled Americans would surely have been much higher. Cf. *Sutton v. United Air Lines, Inc.*, 527 U. S., at 487 (finding that because more than 100 million people need corrective lenses to see properly, "[h]ad Congress intended to include all persons with corrected physical limitations among those covered by the Act, it undoubtedly would have cited a much higher number [than 43 million] disabled persons in the findings").

We therefore hold that to be substantially limited in performing manual tasks, an individual must have an impairment that prevents or severely restricts the individual from doing activities that are of central importance to most people's daily lives. The impairment's impact must also be permanent or long-term. See 29 CFR §§ 1630.2(j)(2)(ii)–(iii) (2001).

* * *

An individualized assessment of the effect of an impairment is particularly necessary when the impairment is one whose symptoms vary widely from person to person. Carpal tunnel syndrome, one of respondent's impairments, is just such a condition. While cases of severe carpal tunnel syndrome are characterized by muscle atrophy and extreme sensory deficits, mild cases generally do not have either of these effects and create only intermittent symptoms of numbness and tingling. Carniero, Carpal

Tunnel Syndrome: The Cause Dictates the Treatment 66 Cleveland Clinic J. Medicine 159, 161–162 (1999). Studies have further shown that, even without surgical treatment, one quarter of carpal tunnel cases resolve in one month, but that in 22 percent of cases, symptoms last for eight years or longer. See DeStefano, Nordstrom, & Uierkant, Long-term Symptom Outcomes of Carpal Tunnel Syndrome and its Treatment, 22A J. Hand Surgery 200, 204–205 (1997). When pregnancy is the cause of carpal tunnel syndrome, in contrast, the symptoms normally resolve within two weeks of delivery. See Ouellette, Nerve Compression Syndromes of the Upper Extremity in Women, 17 Journal of Musculoskeletal Medicine 536 (2000). Given these large potential differences in the severity and duration of the effects of carpal tunnel syndrome, an individual's carpal tunnel syndrome diagnosis, on its own, does not indicate whether the individual has a disability within the meaning of the ADA.

IV

* * *

The Court of Appeals relied on our opinion in *Sutton v. United Air Lines, Inc.*, for the idea that a "class" of manual activities must be implicated for an impairment to substantially limit the major life activity of performing manual tasks. But *Sutton* said only that "when the major life activity under consideration is that of working, the statutory phrase 'substantially limits' requires . . . that plaintiffs allege that they are unable to work in a broad class of jobs." 527 U.S. 471 at 491. * * *

While the Court of Appeals in this case addressed the different major life activity of performing manual tasks, its analysis circumvented *Sutton* by focusing on respondent's inability to perform manual tasks associated only with her job. This was error. When addressing the major life activity of performing manual tasks, the central inquiry must be whether the claimant is unable to perform the variety of tasks central to most people's daily lives, not whether the claimant is unable to perform the tasks associated with her specific job. Otherwise, *Sutton*'s restriction on claims of disability based on a substantial limitation in working will be rendered meaningless because an inability to perform a specific job always can be recast as an inability to perform a "class" of tasks associated with that specific job.

There is also no support in the Act, our previous opinions, or the regulations for the Court of Appeals' idea that the question of whether an impairment constitutes a disability is to be answered only by analyzing the effect of the impairment in the workplace. Indeed, the fact that the Act's definition of "disability" applies not only to Title I of the Act, 42 U.S.C. §§ 12111–12117 (1994 ed.), which deals with employment, but also to the other portions of the Act, which deal with subjects such as public transportation, §§ 12141–12150, 42 U.S.C. §§ 12161–12165 (1994 ed. and

Supp. V), and privately provided public accommodations, §§ 12181–12189, demonstrates that the definition is intended to cover individuals with disabling impairments regardless of whether the individuals have any connection to a workplace.

Even more critically, the manual tasks unique to any particular job are not necessarily important parts of most people's lives. As a result, occupation-specific tasks may have only limited relevance to the manual task inquiry. In this case, "repetitive work with hands and arms extended at or above shoulder levels for extended periods of time," the manual task on which the Court of Appeals relied, is not an important part of most people's daily lives. The court, therefore, should not have considered respondent's inability to do such manual work in her specialized assembly line job as sufficient proof that she was substantially limited in performing manual tasks.

At the same time, the Court of Appeals appears to have disregarded the very type of evidence that it should have focused upon. It treated as irrelevant "the fact that [respondent] can . . . tend to her personal hygiene [and] carry out personal or household chores." Yet household chores, bathing, and brushing one's teeth are among the types of manual tasks of central importance to people's daily lives, and should have been part of the assessment of whether respondent was substantially limited in performing manual tasks.

The District Court noted that at the time respondent sought an accommodation from petitioner, she admitted that she was able to do the manual tasks required by her original two jobs in QCIO. In addition, according to respondent's deposition testimony, even after her condition worsened, she could still brush her teeth, wash her face, bathe, tend her flower garden, fix breakfast, do laundry, and pick up around the house. The record also indicates that her medical conditions caused her to avoid sweeping, to quit dancing, to occasionally seek help dressing, and to reduce how often she plays with her children, gardens, and drives long distances. But these changes in her life did not amount to such severe restrictions in the activities that are of central importance to most people's daily lives that they establish a manual-task disability as a matter of law. On this record, it was therefore inappropriate for the Court of Appeals to grant partial summary judgment to respondent on the issue whether she was substantially limited in performing manual tasks, and its decision to do so must be reversed. * * *

NOTE: THE ADA AMENDMENTS ACT OF 2008

The ADA Amendments Act of 2008 (ADAAA) modified the ADA in two fundamental ways. First, the ADAAA expanded the class of individuals protected by the ADA. It did so in part by rejecting much of the analysis in *Sutton* and *Toyota*. Second, the ADAAA established a two-tier system of protection, under which the class of individuals protected from discrimination may be much larger than a subclass of individuals also due reasonable accommodation.

The ADAAA expands the class of individuals protected from discrimination by modifying the definition of "regarded as" having an impairment, the third prong of the ADA's definition of disability. ADAAA § 3(3)(A); 42 U.S.C. § 12102(3). The new definition does not require that an actual or perceived impairment "limit" or "be perceived to limit a major life activity." It excludes impairments that are "minor and transitory." Id. at § 3(3)(B) ("transitory" is "with an actual or expected duration of 6 months or less"). Employees "regarded as" impaired are protected from discrimination under the ADA but are not entitled to reasonable accommodation unless they meet one of the other prongs of the definition of "disabled." ADA § 501; 42 U.S.C. § 12201(h).

The ADAAA also enlarges the class of individuals who may claim reasonable accommodations as well as protection from discrimination because they qualify as disabled under the first or second prongs of § 3(1), 42 U.S.C. § 12102(1). The ADAAA does so by providing several clarifications to the meaning of "substantially limits one or more major life activities". First, new § 3(2)(A), 42 U.S.C. § 12102(2)(A) provides an expansive list of major life activities, including, "but [ ] not limited to caring for oneself, performing manual tasks, seeing, hearing, eating, sleeping, walking, standing, lifting, bending, speaking, breathing, learning, reading, concentrating, thinking, communicating, and working." Some of these activities were not established as "major" in lower-court opinions prior to the ADAAA. The inclusion of "working" in the list is particularly significant because the Supreme Court had "been hesitant to hold as much." *Toyota*, 534 U.S. at 200. New § 3(2)(B), 42 U.S.C. § 12102(2)(B) also defines as major life activities, major bodily functions, "including but not limited to functions of the immune system, normal cell growth, digestive, bowel, bladder, neurological, brain, respiratory, circulatory, endocrine, and reproductive functions."

Second, the ADAAA also expands the class of individuals who can claim reasonable accommodations by rejecting, in new § 3(4)(E)(i), 42 U.S.C. § 12102(4)(E)(i) the general teaching of *Sutton* on the relevance of mitigation to whether an impairment substantially limits a major life activity. Section 3(4)(E)(i) provides that the substantially-limits determination "shall be made without regard to the ameliorative effects of mitigating measures." This new provision lists a range of mitigating measures, such as medication, equipment, prosthetics and hearing aids. Ordinary eyeglasses and contact lenses can still "be considered in determining whether an impairment substantially limits a major life activity." ADAAA § 3(4)(E)(ii); 42 U.S.C. § 12102(4)(E)(ii).

Third, the ADAAA clarifies, at new § 3(4)(D), 42 U.S.C. § 12102(4)(D) that an "impairment that is episodic or in remission is a disability if it would substantially limit a major life activity when active." This provision, in tension with some language used in *Sutton* and *Toyota*, may be significant for many potential plaintiffs.

The ADAAA includes a new rule of construction at § 3(4)(A), 42 U.S.C. § 12102(4)(A) stating that the "definition of disability in this Act shall be construed in favor of broad coverage . . . to the maximum extent permitted by the terms of this Act." In addition, the Findings and Purposes in § 2(b)(6) of the ADAAA "express Congress' expectation" that the EEOC "will revise that portion of its current regulations that defines the term 'substantially limits' as 'significantly restricted' to be consistent" with the ADAAA amendments. The EEOC has issued these revised regulations, which are included in the Statutory Supplement and are further discussed in the notes below.

NOTES AND QUESTIONS

Test Your Understanding of the Material

1.   How would the *Sutton* case be decided under the ADAAA? Note that § 5(b) adds a new subsection to § 103 of the ADA, 42 U.S.C. § 12113, which provides that an employer "shall not use qualification standards, employment tests, or other selection criteria based on an individual's uncorrected vision unless the standard, test, or other selection criteria, as used by the covered entity, is shown to be job-related for the position in question and consistent with business necessity."

2.   On the same day that it announced its decision in *Sutton*, the Court also issued decisions in two other cases to which the analysis of *Sutton* was relevant. In Murphy v. United Parcel Service, Inc., 527 U.S. 516, 119 S.Ct. 2133, 144 L.Ed.2d 484 (1999), the Court held that for purposes of assessing "disability" under the first prong of the ADA definition, Murphy's high blood pressure, like the severe myopia of the Sutton sisters, must be considered in its mitigated, medicated state. How would *Murphy* be decided under the ADAAA?

3.   How would the *Toyota* case be decided under the ADAAA? The lower courts generally have treated carpel tunnel syndrome and other limitations on the activity of "performing manual tasks" as disabilities after the passage of the ADAAA. See, e.g., Gregor v. Solar Semiconductor, Inc., 2013 WL 588743 (D.Minn. 2013); Gibbs v. ADS Alliance Data Systems, Inc., 2011 WL 3205779 (D.Kan. 2011). See generally Stephen F. Befort, An Empirical Examination of Case Outcomes Under the ADA Amendments Act, 70 Wash. & Lee L. Rev. 2027 (2013).

Related Issues

4.   *Expansion of Major Life Activities*. The EEOC's accompanying regulations, at 29 C.F.R. § 1630.2(i)(1), present a somewhat larger list of major life activities, including "sitting" and "interacting with others". Section 1630.2(i) also iterates that major life activities are not "limited" to those specified.

5.   *Working as a Major Life Activity*. The ADAAA does not directly address the Supreme Court language in *Sutton* that to be substantially limited in the life activity of working an individual must be "unable to work in a broad

class of jobs." 527 U.S. at 491. See also 29 C.F.R. 1630, App. (noting that "[t]he Commission has removed from the text of the regulations a discussion of the major life activity of working"). In its Interpretive Guidance on its regulations, also included in the Statutory Supplement, the EEOC states that "[i]n the rare cases where an individual has a need to demonstrate that an impairment substantially limits him or her in working, the individual can do so by showing that the impairment substantially limits his or her ability to perform a class of jobs or broad range of jobs in various classes as compared to most people having comparable training, skills, and abilities. In keeping with the findings and purposes of the Amendments Act, the determination of coverage under the law should not require extensive and elaborate assessment, and the EEOC and the courts are to apply a lower standard in determining when an impairment substantially limits a major life activity, including the major life activity of working, than they applied prior to the Amendments Act." Appendix to Part 1630, Interpretive Guidance on Title I of the ADA, § 1630.2(j), Substantially Limited in Working; 29 C.F.R. § 1630, App.

6. *Standard for Substantially Limits*. The EEOC's post-ADAAA regulations state that an "impairment is a disability . . . if it substantially limits the ability of an individual to perform a major life activity as compared to most people in the general population." See 29 C.F.R. § 1630.2 (j)(ii). Should the EEOC establish more definite guidelines for when an impairment places substantial limits on certain major life activities, such as seeing, hearing, and thinking, that can be described along a continuum? For instance, could the EEOC establish, based on scientific evidence, 20/200 vision as a cut-off point for a visual impairment that substantially limits the major life activity of seeing? Cf. Chandler v. City of Dallas, 2 F.3d 1385, 1390 (5th Cir.1993) (vision that can be corrected to 20/200 is not a handicap under Rehabilitation Act).

7. *Coverage of Non-Permanent Conditions*. Before the ADAAA, courts generally held that temporary conditions were not disabilities. See, e.g., Pollard v. High's of Baltimore, Inc., 281 F.3d 462 (4th Cir. 2002) (temporary back injury not a disability). The ADAAA, however, appears to reject such decisions. Section 3(4)(D); 42 U.S.C. § 12102(4)(D) provides that an "impairment that is episodic or in remission is a disability if it would substantially limit a major life activity when active." Section 3(3)(B), moreover, states that the "regarded as" prong of the definition of disability shall not apply to an impairment that is both transitory and minor. The EEOC takes the view that a transitory actual or perceived impairment that is more than minor is covered by the "regarded as" prong; and that impairments that substantially limit a major life activity may be covered by one of the other prongs, even if transitory and minor. Both of these suggestions are confirmed by the EEOC's new regulations. See §§ 1630.2(g)(iii) and 1630.2(j)(ix). See also e.g., Summers v. Altarum Institute Corp., 740 F.3d 325 (4th Cir.2014) (temporary serious injury is a disability under new EEOC regulations).

8. *"Record" of a Substantially Limiting Impairment*. Is the "record" of prong in the definition of disability made unnecessary by the ADAAA rule of construction, at § 3(4)(D), stating that an "impairment that is episodic or in

remission is a disability if it would substantially limit a major life activity when active?" Or might there be cases where an employer discriminates against an employee because of a past condition that is not just in remission, but is permanently eliminated? See, e.g., Eshelman v. Agere Sys., Inc., 554 F.3d 426 (3d Cir. 2009) ("it is immaterial for the purposes of her 'record of' claim whether Eshelman was actually disabled at the time Agere terminated her"). Note that the requirement of reasonable accommodation continues to apply for those with a record of an impairment that once significantly limited a major life activity.

9. *Per Se Disabilities Limiting Major Bodily Functions.* The EEOC's post-ADAAA regulations provide examples of impairments that will "in virtually all cases." 29 C.F.R. § 1630.2(j)(3)(ii), substantially limit at least some bodily function which the amended ADA treats as a major life activity:

> Deafness substantially limits hearing; blindness substantially limits seeing; an intellectual disability (formerly termed mental retardation) substantially limits brain function; partially or completely missing limbs or mobility impairments requiring the use of a wheelchair substantially limit musculoskeletal function; autism substantially limits brain function; cancer substantially limits normal cell growth; cerebral palsy substantially limits brain function; diabetes substantially limits endocrine function; epilepsy substantially limits neurological function; Human Immunodeficiency Virus (HIV) infection substantially limits immune function; multiple sclerosis substantially limits neurological function; muscular dystrophy substantially limits neurological function; and major depressive disorder, bipolar disorder, post-traumatic stress disorder, obsessive compulsive disorder, and schizophrenia substantially limit brain function.

For post-ADAAA decisions, see, e.g., Meinelt v. P.F. Chang's China Bistro, Inc., 787 F.Supp.2d 643, 651–52 (S.D.Tex. 2011) (operable brain tumor substantially limits normal cell growth); Norton v. Assisted Living Concepts, Inc., 786 F.Supp.2d 1173, 1185–1186 (E.D.Tex. 2011) (renal cancer could substantially limit normal cell growth); Horgan v. Simmons, 704 F.Supp.2d 814, 818–819 (N.D.Ill. 2010) (HIV infection substantially limited functioning of immune system).

10. *Defining "Impairment."* By protecting the impaired from "regarded as" discrimination under § 3(3), even if the impairment does not limit a major life activity, the ADAAA makes particularly salient the question of what is an "impairment." The term is not defined in the statute, but only in the regulations. This definition includes "[a]ny physiological disorder or condition, cosmetic disfigurement, or anatomical loss affecting one or more body systems" or "[a]ny mental or psychological disorder." See 29 C.F.R. § 1630.2(h). The EEOC's Interpretive Guidance also states that "the term "impairment" does not include physical characteristics such as eye color, hair color, left-handedness, or height, weight or muscle tone that are within "normal range". See 29 C.F.R. pt. 1630, app. § 1630.2(h).

The lower courts generally have treated as impairments only conditions that are considered "abnormal". For pre-ADAAA rulings, see, e.g., EEOC v. Watkins Motor Lines, Inc., 463 F.3d 436 (6th Cir. 2006) (non-physiologically caused "morbid obesity" not an impairment); Francis v. City of Meriden, 129 F.3d 281 (2d Cir.1997) (since being overweight is not an impairment, being regarded as overweight is also not); Tsetseranos v. Tech Prototype, Inc., 893 F.Supp. 109, 119 (D.N.H.1995) (pregnancy not an impairment); de la Torres v. Bolger, 781 F.2d 1134, 1138 (5th Cir.1986) (left-handedness not an impairment). But cf. EEOC v. Res. for Human Dev., Inc., 827 F.Supp.2d 688, 694–95 (E.D. La. 2011) ("severe obesity, which has been defined as body weight more than 100% over the norm, is clearly an impairment" even without a "physiological basis"); Chicago Reg'l Council of Carpenters v. Thorne Associates, Inc., 893 F.Supp.2d 952 (N.D. Ill. 2012) (assuming 5′3″ male is impaired because of height). Can "normal" be defined objectively, or must it implicitly include socially defined standards for what is desirable and or at least not stigmatized?

11. *Protection of Individuals with Disease-Associated Genes.* Genetic testing may help predict predisposition to certain diseases or personality disorders. See Larry Gostin, Genetic Discrimination: The Use of Genetically Based Diagnostic and Prognostic Tests by Employers and Insurers, 17 Am. J.L. & Med. 109, 116 (1991). Does the ADA prevent employers from not hiring or firing workers because the workers' genes predict some future impairment? Is carrying the genes itself an "impairment"? The EEOC's Interpretive Guidance states that "the term impairment * * * does not include characteristic predisposition to illness or disease." 29 C.F.R. pt. 1630, app. § 1630.2(h).

With the enactment of the Genetic Information Nondiscrimination Act of 2008 (GINA), 122 Stat. 881, 42 U.S.C. § 2000ff, federal law prohibits all employers with 15 or more employees, from discriminating on the basis of genetic information. Though it does not authorize use of the disparate-impact approach, GINA also bans employers from collecting genetic information, except for limited acceptable purposes. Under EEOC covered regulations, 29 C.F.R. Part 1635, a "request" for genetic information may include "conducting an Internet search"; "actively listening to third party conversations or searching an individual's personal effects"; and "making requests for information about an individual's current health status in a way that is likely to result in a covered entity obtaining genetic information." Id. § 1635.8(a). The regulations list six exceptions to the prohibition on the acquisition of genetic information: (1) inadvertent requests or acquisitions; (2) acquisition through voluntary wellness programs; (3) requests related to family and medical leave certifications or policies; (4) acquisition from commercially and publicly available documents; (5) acquisition to monitor the effects of toxic substances in the workplace; and (6) DNA analysis for law enforcement. 29 C.F.R. § 1635.8(b).

NOTE: DRUG AND ALCOHOL ADDICTION

Section 104(a) of the ADA provides that protected individuals "shall not include any employee or applicant who is currently engaging in the illegal use of drugs, when the covered entity acts on the basis of such use." This exclusion from ADA coverage does not extend to those who have successfully completed a supervised drug rehabilitation program, or are currently in such a program and not engaged in drug use, or are "erroneously regarded as engaged in such use." (§ 104(b)) Section 510 of the ADA also amends § 504 of the Rehabilitation Act to effect a similar exclusion of illegal drug users. The EEOC's Interpretive Guidance states that the "term 'currently engaging' is not intended to be limited to the use of drugs on the day of, or within a matter of days or weeks before, the employment action in question. Rather, the provision is intended to apply to the illegal use of drugs that has occurred recently enough to indicate that the individual is actively engaged in such conduct." 29 C.F.R. pt. 1630, app. § 1630.3(a) through (c). See also Shafer v. Preston Memorial Hosp. Corp., 107 F.3d 274, 278 (4th Cir.1997) (current use of drugs can be within prior week or month even where individual is in a rehabilitation program at time of allegedly discriminatory act).

The ADA does not exclude current alcoholics from coverage, although § 104(c)(4) expressly authorizes employers to hold alcoholics as well as drug users to the same job standards applicable to other employees. See Mararri v. WCI Steel, Inc., 130 F.3d 1180 (6th Cir.1997) (current alcoholics may be protected). The courts have not treated alcohol or drug addiction as per se disabilities. See, e.g., Burch v. Coca-Cola Co., 119 F.3d 305 (5th Cir.1997) (alcoholism is not always a disability; plaintiff must show substantial limitation).

The ADA can protect those who are not current drug users from discrimination based on a record of a prior disability which may include some forms of drug addiction. In Raytheon Co. v. Hernandez, 540 U.S. 44, 124 S.Ct. 513, 157 L.Ed.2d 357 (2003), however, the Court held that an employer did not engage in ADA-proscribed disparate treatment by refusing to rehire a past drug-user based on the company's neutral rule against hiring previously terminated workers.

C. THE DUTY OF REASONABLE ACCOMMODATION

The ADA's imposition of a duty of reasonable accommodation toward individuals with disabilities presents the statute's sharpest contrast with prior employment discrimination law. This duty appears in several key provisions of Title I of the Act. First, the core prohibition of employment discrimination expressed in § 102(a) provides that "[n]o covered entity shall discriminate against a qualified individual on the basis of disability," and § 101(8) defines "qualified individual" to mean "an individual who, *with or without reasonable accommodation*, can perform the essential functions of the employment position that such individual holds or desires." (Emphasis supplied). This definition requires employers to evaluate disabled individuals' job performance potential taking into account reasonable accommodation of their disabilities.

Second, § 102(b) lists several ways in which the proscribed discrimination against a "qualified individual with a disability" can occur, including (in subsection (b)(5)):

> (A) not making reasonable accommodation to the known physical or mental limitations of an otherwise qualified individual with a disability who is an applicant or employee, unless [the alleged discriminator] can demonstrate that the accommodation would impose an undue hardship on the operation of the business * * * ; or (B) denying employment opportunities to a job applicant or employee who is an otherwise qualified individual with a disability, if such denial is based on the need * * * to make reasonable accommodation to the physical or mental impairments of the employee or applicant;

42 U.S.C. § 12112(b)(5). These provisions together pose a number of difficult procedural and substantive issues.

US AIRWAYS, INC. V. BARNETT
Supreme Court of the United States, 2002.
535 U.S. 391, 122 S.Ct. 1516, 152 L.Ed.2d 589.

JUSTICE BREYER delivered the opinion of the Court.

I

In 1990, Robert Barnett, the plaintiff and respondent here, injured his back while working in a cargo-handling position at petitioner US Airways, Inc. He invoked seniority rights and transferred to a less physically demanding mailroom position. Under US Airways' seniority system, that position, like others, periodically became open to seniority-based employee bidding. In 1992, Barnett learned that at least two employees senior to him intended to bid for the mailroom job. He asked US Airways to accommodate his disability-imposed limitations by making an exception that would allow him to remain in the mailroom. After permitting Barnett to continue his mailroom work for five months while it considered the matter, US Airways eventually decided not to make an exception. And Barnett lost his job.

Barnett then brought this ADA suit claiming, among other things, that he was an "individual with a disability" capable of performing the essential functions of the mailroom job, that the mailroom job amounted to a "reasonable accommodation" of his disability, and that US Airways, in refusing to assign him the job, unlawfully discriminated against him. US Airways moved for summary judgment. It supported its motion with appropriate affidavits, Fed. Rule Civ. Proc. 56, contending that its "well-established" seniority system granted other employees the right to obtain the mailroom position.

The District Court found that the undisputed facts about seniority warranted summary judgment in US Airways' favor. * * *

An en banc panel of the United States Court of Appeals for the Ninth Circuit reversed. It said that the presence of a seniority system is merely "a factor in the undue hardship analysis." And it held that "[a] case-by-case fact intensive analysis is required to determine whether any particular reassignment would constitute an undue hardship to the employer." * * *

II

[W]e must consider the following statutory provisions. First, the ADA says that an employer may not "discriminate against a qualified individual with a disability." 42 U.S.C. § 12112(a). Second, the ADA says that a "qualified" individual includes "an individual with a disability who, *with* or without *reasonable accommodation*, can perform the essential functions of" the relevant "employment position." § 12111(8). Third, the ADA says that "discrimination" includes an employer's *"not making reasonable accommodations* to the known physical or mental limitations of an otherwise qualified . . . employee, *unless* [the employer] can demonstrate that the accommodation would impose an *undue hardship* on the operation of [its] business." § 12112(b)(5)(A) (emphasis added). Fourth, the ADA says that the term " 'reasonable accommodation' may include . . . reassignment to a vacant position." § 12111(9)(B).

* * *

A

US Airways' claim that a seniority system virtually always trumps a conflicting accommodation demand rests primarily upon its view of how the Act treats workplace "preferences." Insofar as a requested accommodation violates a disability-neutral workplace rule, such as a seniority rule, it grants the employee with a disability treatment that other workers could not receive. Yet the Act, US Airways says, seeks only "equal" treatment for those with disabilities See, e.g., 42 U.S.C. § 12101(a)(9). It does not, it contends, require an employer to grant preferential treatment. Cf. H. R. Rep. No. 101–485, pt. 2, p. 66 (1990); S. Rep. No. 101–116, pp. 26–27 (1989) (employer has no "obligation to prefer *applicants* with disabilities over other *applicants*"). Hence it does not require the employer to grant a request that, in violating a disability-neutral rule, would provide a preference.

While linguistically logical, this argument fails to recognize what the Act specifies, namely, that preferences will sometimes prove necessary to achieve the Act's basic equal opportunity goal. The Act requires preferences in the form of "reasonable accommodations" that are needed for those with disabilities to obtain the *same* workplace opportunities that those without disabilities automatically enjoy. By definition any special "accommodation" requires the employer to treat an employee with a disability differently, i.e., preferentially. And the fact that the difference in treatment violates an employer's disability-neutral rule cannot by itself place the accommodation beyond the Act's potential reach.

Were that not so, the "reasonable accommodation" provision could not accomplish its intended objective. Neutral office assignment rules would automatically prevent the accommodation of an employee whose disability-imposed limitations require him to work on the ground floor. Neutral "break-from-work" rules would automatically prevent the accommodation of an individual who needs additional breaks from work, perhaps to permit medical visits. Neutral furniture budget rules would automatically prevent the accommodation of an individual who needs a different kind of chair or desk. Many employers will have neutral rules governing the kinds of actions most needed to reasonably accommodate a worker with a disability. See 42 U.S.C. § 12111(9)(b) (setting forth examples such as "job restructuring," "part-time or modified work schedules," "acquisition or modification of equipment or devices," "and other similar accommodations"). Yet Congress, while providing such examples, said nothing suggesting that the presence of such neutral rules would create an automatic exemption. * * *

In sum, the nature of the "reasonable accommodation" requirement, the statutory examples, and the Act's silence about the exempting effect of neutral rules together convince us that the Act does not create any such automatic exemption. The simple fact that an accommodation would provide a "preference"—in the sense that it would permit the worker with a disability to violate a rule that others must obey—cannot, *in and of itself*, automatically show that the accommodation is not "reasonable." * * *

US Airways also points to the ADA provisions stating that a "'reasonable accommodation' may include . . . reassignment to a *vacant* position." § 12111(9)(B). And it claims that the fact that an established seniority system would assign that position to another worker automatically and always means that the position is not a "vacant" one. Nothing in the Act, however, suggests that Congress intended the word "vacant" to have a specialized meaning. And in ordinary English, a seniority system can give employees seniority rights allowing them to bid for a "vacant" position. The position in this case was held, at the time of suit, by Barnett, not by some other worker; and that position, under the US Airways seniority system, became an "open" one. * * * Moreover, US Airways has said that it "reserves the right to change any and all" portions of the seniority system at will. Consequently, we cannot agree with US Airways about the position's vacancy; nor do we agree that the Act would automatically deny Barnett's accommodation request for that reason.

B

Barnett argues that the statutory words "reasonable accommodation" mean only "effective accommodation," authorizing a court to consider the requested accommodation's ability to meet an individual's disability-related needs, and nothing more. On this view, a seniority rule violation, having nothing to do with the accommodation's effectiveness, has nothing to do with its "reasonableness." It might, at most, help to prove an "undue hardship on the operation of the business." But, he adds, that is a matter that the statute requires the employer to demonstrate, case by case.

In support of this interpretation Barnett points to Equal Employment Opportunity Commission (EEOC) regulations stating that "reasonable accommodation means. . . . modifications or adjustments . . . that *enable* a qualified individual with a disability to perform the essential functions of [a] position." 29 CFR § 1630(*o*)(ii) (2001). See also H.R. Rep. No. 101–485, pt. 2, at 66; S. Rep. No. 101–116, at 35 (discussing reasonable accommodations in terms of "effectiveness," while discussing costs in terms of "undue hardship"). Barnett adds that any other view would make the words "reasonable accommodation" and "undue hardship" virtual mirror images—creating redundancy in the statute. And he says that any such other view would create a practical burden of proof dilemma.

The practical burden of proof dilemma arises, Barnett argues, because the statute imposes the burden of demonstrating an "undue hardship" upon the employer, while the burden of proving "reasonable accommodation" remains with the plaintiff, here the employee. This allocation seems sensible in that an employer can more frequently and easily prove the presence of business hardship than an employee can prove its absence. But suppose that an employee must counter a claim of "seniority rule violation" in order to prove that an "accommodation" request is "reasonable." Would that not force the employee to prove what is in effect an absence, i.e., an absence of hardship, despite the statute's insistence that the employer "demonstrate" hardship's presence?

These arguments do not persuade us that Barnett's legal interpretation of "reasonable" is correct. For one thing, in ordinary English the word "reasonable" does not mean "effective." It is the word "accommodation," not the word "reasonable," that conveys the need for effectiveness. An *ineffective* "modification" or "adjustment" will not *accommodate* a disabled individual's limitations. Nor does an ordinary English meaning of the term "reasonable accommodation" make of it a simple, redundant mirror image of the term "undue hardship." The statute refers to an "undue hardship on the operation of the business." 42 U.S.C. § 12112 (b)(5)(A). Yet a demand for an effective accommodation could prove unreasonable because of its impact, not on business operations, but on fellow employees—say because it will lead to dismissals, relocations, or modification of employee benefits to which an employer, looking at the matter from the perspective of the business itself, may be relatively indifferent.

Neither does the statute's primary purpose require Barnett's special reading. The statute seeks to diminish or to eliminate the stereotypical thought processes, the thoughtless actions, and the hostile reactions that far too often bar those with disabilities from participating fully in the Nation's life, including the workplace. See generally § 12101(a) and (b). These objectives demand unprejudiced thought and reasonable responsive reaction on the part of employers and fellow workers alike. They will sometimes require affirmative conduct to promote entry of disabled people into the workforce. They do not, however, demand action beyond the realm of the reasonable.

Neither has Congress indicated in the statute, or elsewhere, that the word "reasonable" means no more than "effective." The EEOC regulations do say that reasonable accommodations "enable" a person with a disability to perform the essential functions of a task. But that phrasing simply emphasizes the statutory provision's basic objective. The regulations do not say that "enable" and "reasonable" mean the same thing. * * *

Finally, an ordinary language interpretation of the word "reasonable" does not create the "burden of proof" dilemma to which Barnett points. Many of the lower courts, while rejecting both US Airways' and Barnett's more absolute views, have reconciled the phrases "reasonable accommodation" and "undue hardship" in a practical way.

They have held that a plaintiff/employee (to defeat a defendant/employer's motion for summary judgment) need only show that an "accommodation" seems reasonable on its face, i.e., ordinarily or in the run of cases. See, e.g., *Reed v. LePage Bakeries, Inc.*, 244 F.3d 254, 259 (CA1 2001) (plaintiff meets burden on reasonableness by showing that, "at least on the face of things," the accommodation will be feasible for the employer) * * * .

Once the plaintiff has made this showing, the defendant/employer then must show special (typically case-specific) circumstances that demonstrate undue hardship in the particular circumstances. See *Reed*, 244 F.3d at 258–259 ("undue hardship inquiry focuses on the hardships imposed . . . in the context of the particular [employer's] operations' ") * * * .

* * * In our opinion, that practical view of the statute, applied consistently with ordinary summary judgment principles, see Fed. Rule Civ. Proc. 56, avoids Barnett's burden of proof dilemma, while reconciling the two statutory phrases ("reasonable accommodation" and "undue hardship").

III

The question in the present case focuses on the relationship between seniority systems and the plaintiff's need to show that an "accommodation" seems reasonable on its face, i.e., ordinarily or in the run of cases. We must assume that the plaintiff, an employee, is an "individual with a disability." He has requested assignment to a mailroom position as a "reasonable accommodation." We also assume that normally such a request would be reasonable within the meaning of the statute, were it not for one circumstance, namely, that the assignment would violate the rules of a seniority system. See § 12111(9) ("reasonable accommodation" may include "reassignment to a vacant position"). Does that circumstance mean that the proposed accommodation is not a "reasonable" one?

In our view, the answer to this question ordinarily is "yes." The statute does not require proof on a case-by-case basis that a seniority system should prevail. That is because it would not be reasonable in the run of cases that the assignment in question trump the rules of a seniority system. To the contrary, it will ordinarily be unreasonable for the assignment to prevail.

A

Several factors support our conclusion that a proposed accommodation will not be reasonable in the run of cases. Analogous case law supports this conclusion, for it has recognized the importance of seniority to employee-management relations. This Court has held that, in the context of a Title VII religious discrimination case, an employer need not adapt to an employee's special worship schedule as a "reasonable accommodation" where doing so would conflict with the seniority rights of other employees. *Trans World Airlines, Inc. v. Hardison,* 432 U.S. 63, 79–80, 53 L. Ed. 2d 113, 97 S.Ct. 2264 (1977). The lower courts have unanimously found that collectively bargained seniority trumps the need for reasonable accommodation in the context of the linguistically similar Rehabilitation Act. * * * And several Circuits, though differing in their reasoning, have reached a similar conclusion in the context of seniority and the ADA. * * * All these cases discuss collectively bargained seniority systems, not systems (like the present system) which are unilaterally imposed by management. But the relevant seniority system advantages, and related difficulties that result from violations of seniority rules, are not limited to collectively bargained systems.

For one thing, the typical seniority system provides important employee benefits by creating, and fulfilling, employee expectations of fair, uniform treatment. These benefits include "job security and an opportunity for steady and predictable advancement based on objective standards." [citations omitted] They include "an element of due process," limiting "unfairness in personnel decisions." Gersuny, Origins of Seniority Provisions in Collective Bargaining, 33 Lab.L.J. 518, 519 (1982). And they consequently encourage employees to invest in the employing company, accepting "less than their value to the firm early in their careers" in return for greater benefits in later years. J. Baron & D. Kreps, Strategic Human Resources: Frameworks for General Managers 288 (1999).

Most important for present purposes, to require the typical employer to show more than the existence of a seniority system might well undermine the employees' expectations of consistent, uniform treatment— expectations upon which the seniority system's benefits depend. That is because such a rule would substitute a complex case-specific "accommodation" decision made by management for the more uniform, impersonal operation of seniority rules. Such management decision making, with its inevitable discretionary elements, would involve a matter of the greatest importance to employees, namely, layoffs; it would take place outside, as well as inside, the confines of a court case; and it might well take place fairly often. Cf. ADA, 42 U.S.C. § 12101(a)(1), (estimating that some 43 million Americans suffer from physical or mental disabilities). We can find nothing in the statute that suggests Congress intended to undermine seniority systems in this way. And we consequently conclude that the employer's showing of violation of the rules of a seniority system is by itself ordinarily sufficient.

B

The plaintiff (here the employee) nonetheless remains free to show that special circumstances warrant a finding that, despite the presence of a seniority system (which the ADA may not trump in the run of cases), the requested "accommodation" is "reasonable" on the particular facts. That is because special circumstances might alter the important expectations described above. * * * The plaintiff might show, for example, that the employer, having retained the right to change the seniority system unilaterally, exercises that right fairly frequently, reducing employee expectations that the system will be followed—to the point where one more departure, needed to accommodate an individual with a disability, will not likely make a difference. The plaintiff might show that the system already contains exceptions such that, in the circumstances, one further exception is unlikely to matter. We do not mean these examples to exhaust the kinds of showings that a plaintiff might make. But we do mean to say that the plaintiff must bear the burden of showing special circumstances that make an exception from the seniority system reasonable in the particular case. And to do so, the plaintiff must explain why, in the particular case, an exception to the employer's seniority policy can constitute a "reasonable accommodation" even though in the ordinary case it cannot.

IV

In its question presented, US Airways asked us whether the ADA requires an employer to assign a disabled employee to a particular position even though another employee is entitled to that position under the employer's "established seniority system." We answer that *ordinarily* the ADA does not require that assignment. Hence, a showing that the assignment would violate the rules of a seniority system warrants summary judgment for the employer—unless there is more. The plaintiff must present evidence of that "more," namely, special circumstances surrounding the particular case that demonstrate the assignment is nonetheless reasonable.

Because the lower courts took a different view of the matter, and because neither party has had an opportunity to seek summary judgment in accordance with the principles we set forth here, we vacate the Court of Appeals' judgment and remand the case for further proceedings consistent with this opinion.

JUSTICE STEVENS, concurring. [omitted]

JUSTICE O'CONNOR, concurring.

I agree with portions of the opinion of the Court, but I find problematic the Court's test for determining whether the fact that a job reassignment violates a seniority system makes the reassignment an unreasonable accommodation under the Americans with Disabilities Act of 1990 (ADA or Act), 42 U.S.C. §§ 12101 et seq. (1994 ed. and Supp. V). Although a seniority system plays an important role in the workplace, for the reasons I explain below, I would prefer to say that the effect of a seniority system on the reasonableness of a reassignment as an accommodation for purposes of the ADA depends on whether the seniority system is legally enforceable. * * * [I]n order that the Court may adopt a rule, and because I believe the Court's rule will often lead to the same outcome as the one I would have adopted, I join the Court's opinion despite my concerns. * * *

* * * In the context of a workplace, a vacant position is a position in which no employee currently works and to which no individual has a legal entitlement. For example, in a workplace without a seniority system, when an employee ceases working for the employer, the employee's former position is vacant until a replacement is hired. Even if the replacement does not start work immediately, once the replacement enters into a contractual agreement with the employer, the position is no longer vacant because it has a "possessor." In contrast, when an employee ceases working in a workplace with a legally enforceable seniority system, the employee's former position does not become vacant if the seniority system entitles another employee to it. Instead, the employee entitled to the position under the seniority system immediately becomes the new "possessor" of that position. In a workplace with an unenforceable seniority policy, however, an employee expecting assignment to a position under the seniority policy would not have any type of contractual right to the position and so could not be said to be its "possessor." The position therefore would become vacant.

* * *

Although I am troubled by the Court's reasoning, I believe the Court's approach for evaluating seniority systems will often lead to the same outcome as the test I would have adopted. Unenforceable seniority systems are likely to involve policies in which employers "retain the right to change the system," and will often "permit exceptions". They will also often contain disclaimers that "reduce employee expectations that the system will be followed." Thus, under the Court's test, disabled employees seeking accommodations that would require exceptions to unenforceable seniority systems may be able to show circumstances that make the accommodation "reasonable in their particular case." Because I think the Court's test will often lead to the correct outcome, and because I think it important that a majority of the Court agree on a rule when interpreting statutes, I join the Court's opinion.

JUSTICE SCALIA, with whom JUSTICE THOMAS joins, dissenting.

* * * The right to be given a vacant position so long as there are no obstacles to that appointment (including another candidate who is better qualified, if "best qualified" is the workplace rule) is of considerable value. If an employee is hired to fill a position but fails miserably, he will typically be fired. Few employers will search their organization charts for vacancies to which the low-performing employee might be suited. The ADA, however, prohibits an employer from firing a person whose disability is the cause of his poor performance without first seeking to place him in a vacant job where the disability will not affect performance. Such reassignment is an accommodation to the *disability* because it removes an obstacle (the inability to perform the functions of the assigned job) arising solely from the disability. * * *

The phrase "reassignment to a vacant position" appears in a subsection describing a variety of potential "reasonable accommodations":

(A) making existing facilities used by employees readily accessible to and usable by individuals with disabilities; and

(B) job restructuring, part-time or modified work schedules, *reassignment to a vacant position*, acquisition or modification of equipment or devices, appropriate adjustment or modifications of examinations, training materials or policies, the provision of qualified readers or interpreters, and other similar accommodations for individuals with disabilities." § 12111(9) (emphasis added).

Subsection (A) clearly addresses features of the workplace that burden the disabled *because of* their disabilities. Subsection (B) is broader in scope but equally targeted at disability-related obstacles. Thus it encompasses "modified work schedules" (which may accommodate inability to work for protracted periods), "modification of equipment and devices," and "provision of qualified readers or interpreters." There is no reason why the phrase "reassignment to a vacant position" should be thought to have a uniquely different focus. It envisions elimination of the obstacle of the *current position* (which requires activity that the disabled employee cannot tolerate) when there is an alternate position freely available. If he is qualified for that position, and no one else is seeking it, or no one else who seeks it is better qualified, he *must* be given the position. But "reassignment to a vacant position" does not envision the elimination of obstacles to the employee's service in the new position that have nothing to do with his disability—for example, another employee's claim to that position under a seniority system, or another employee's superior qualifications. Cf. 29 CFR pt. 1630, App. 1630.2(*o*), p. 357 (2001) (explaining "reasonable accommodation" as "any change in the work environment or in the way things are customarily done that enables an individual with a disability to enjoy *equal employment opportunities*") * * * .

JUSTICE SOUTER, with whom JUSTICE GINSBURG joins, dissenting.

With US Airways itself insisting that its seniority system was noncontractual and modifiable at will, there is no reason to think that Barnett's accommodation would have resulted in anything more than minimal disruption to US Airways's operations, if that. Barnett has shown his requested accommodation to be "reasonable," and the burden ought to shift to US Airways if it wishes to claim that, in spite of surface appearances, violation of the seniority scheme would have worked an undue hardship. I would therefore affirm the Ninth Circuit.

NOTES AND QUESTIONS

Test Your Understanding of the Material

1.   On what basis does the *US Airways* Court conclude that a requested accommodation that "conflicts with the rules of a seniority system" is "ordinarily" not reasonable? What "special circumstances" does the Court indicate might require an accommodating departure from a seniority system?

2.   Is the Court's holding limited to situations where coworker seniority interests are implicated? Is there any basis in the ADA for special protection of seniority systems? Compare § 703(h) of Title VII, discussed pp. 245–261 supra.

Related Issues

3.   *Burden of Proof on Reasonable Accommodation.* Under *US Airways* does the plaintiff ultimately have the burden of persuasion on the reasonableness of the particular accommodation he or she is seeking? Which party has the burden of proof on undue hardship?

4.   *Must Disabled Individuals Qualified for a Vacant Position Be Given Preferences over Those Deemed More Qualified?* Are employers, at least in some circumstances, obligated to reassign disabled employees to vacant positions for which they are qualified, even though the employer would prefer assigning

other employees whom they deem more qualified? The Supreme Court first granted, and then after settlement dismissed, a writ of certiorari on this issue in Huber v. Wal-Mart Stores, Inc., 486 F.3d 480 (8th Cir.), cert. granted, 552 U.S. 1074, 128 S.Ct. 742, 169 L.Ed.2d 579 (2007) (ADA does not require employers to give disabled employees preferences in reassignments over more qualified non-disabled applicants). For a different view, see Smith v. Midland Brake, Inc., 180 F.3d 1154 (10th Cir.1999) (en banc) (unless it would impose an undue hardship, qualified individual with a disability must be reassigned a vacant position even if a "better qualified" employee is available); accord, EEOC v. United Airlines, 693 F.3d 760 (7th Cir. 2012). Is it clear why an employer must prefer an existing disabled employee for a new job with that employer if no such preference would be required for a worker seeking a job with a new employer?

5. *For Which Positions Must Reassignment Be Considered?* The ADA obligates employers to consider disabled employees' reassignment to existing vacant jobs that would not constitute a promotion. The EEOC's Interpretive Guidance would impose a duty to consider also reassignment to "wholly distinct and different" positions in "different offices and facilities." See Gile v. United Airlines, Inc., 95 F.3d 492 (7th Cir.1996). Should employers be required to consider positions outside commuting distance from the employee's home if the employee expresses a willingness to move and to pay moving expenses? The EEOC Enforcement Guidance on Reasonable Accommodation states that an employer's obligation is not necessarily limited by "department, facility, personnel system, or geographical area"; the obligation is limited only by "undue hardship." But cf. 29 C.F.R. § 1614.203(g) (Rehabilitation Act regulation requiring reassignment only in the "same commuting area").

Does the reasonable accommodation obligation include offering an individual with a disability who can no longer perform his current position a reassignment to an inferior position with a lower wage? Does such an offer have to be made or can an employer invoke a neutral policy against demotions? See Dalton v. Subaru-Isuzu Automotive, Inc., 141 F.3d 667 (7th Cir.1998) (suggesting that employers may have legitimate nondiscriminatory reasons for such policies).

6. *For How Long Must an Employer Consider Reassignment?* How long does the employer have to keep looking for another position for a newly disabled employee? Until he informs them that he is no longer interested or at least ceases cooperating with them? Or does the statutory definition of a "qualified individual with a disability" suggest a more limited duration for the obligation to consider reassignment? The Interpretive Guidance only directs employers to consider "equivalent" positions that will become vacant "within a reasonable amount of time * * * in light of the totality of circumstances", giving the example of a position that would become open in a week. 29 C.F.R. pt. 1630, app. § 1630.2(*o*). In its Enforcement Guidance on Reasonable Accommodation, the EEOC uses examples with periods between 4 weeks and six months.

NOTE: "INTERACTIVE PROCESS" AND THE ADA

Employer's Failure to Engage in "Interactive Process" as Itself a Violation of the ADA? The *U.S. Airways* majority did not address the ruling of the court of appeals below that the airline violated the ADA "by failing to engage in an interactive process" concerning Barnett's proposed accommodations. Does an employer have a statutory duty to engage in such a process? If so, what is the remedy for an employer's failure to engage in the process? Does the employee have to prove that a reasonable accommodation actually existed? See, e.g., Smith v. Midland Brake; Mengine v. Runyon, 114 F.3d 415 (3d Cir.1997) (yes). But cf. Hendricks-Robinson v. Excel Corp., 154 F.3d 685 (7th Cir.1998) (employer may have violated ADA by implementing medical layoff policy that did not provide adequate opportunity to identify reasonable accommodations). See also 29 C.F.R. § 1630.2(*o*)(3), and the accompanying Interpretive Guidance, see 29 C.F.R. pt. 1630, app. 1630.9 (Process of Determining the Appropriate Reasonable Accommodation).

Effect of Employee's Failure to Engage in the Interactive Process of Identifying Accommodations? If a plaintiff can demonstrate reasonable accommodation during a trial, is her claim nonetheless defective if she failed previously to suggest such an accommodation to the employer? It may depend on whether her failure to do so derived from the employer's nonresponsiveness or from her failure to work with the employer in exploring alternatives. In Beck v. University of Wisconsin Bd. of Regents, 75 F.3d 1130, 1135–36 (7th Cir.1996), the Seventh Circuit affirmed summary judgment for the employer because the court concluded that the plaintiff employee had failed to participate in good faith with the employer in an effort to identify a reasonable accommodation. See also Colwell v. Rite Aid Corp., 602 F.3d 495 (3rd Cir. 2010) (once nature of disability is provided, both parties have a duty to assist in search for an accommodation in good faith); Derbis v. United States Shoe Corp., 67 F.3d 294 (4th Cir.1995) (plaintiff failed to provide employer with information about the injury to her injured hand necessary to identify reasonable accommodations).

Relevance of Defendant's Knowledge of Plaintiff's Disability? Section 102(b)(5)(A) proscribes "not making reasonable accommodation to the *known* physical or mental limitation of an otherwise qualified individual with a disability" (emphasis supplied). This presumably means that an employer that has not been apprised of the existence of a disability has no accommodation responsibilities and can take adverse action against the employee for conduct or performance issues which may turn out to be caused by his disability. See 29 C.F.R. pt. 1630, app. § 1630.9 ("an employer would not be expected to accommodate disabilities of which it is unaware"). See also, e.g., Hedberg v. Indiana Bell Tel. Co., Inc., 47 F.3d 928, 931 (7th Cir.1995) (employer can discharge employee because of behavior caused by disability, where employer did not know of disability's existence); Miller v. National Casualty Co., 61 F.3d 627, 629–30 (8th Cir.1995) (accord). Are there circumstances where employers are required to ask employees or applicants if they need accommodation? See Bultemeyer v. Fort Wayne Community Sch., 100 F.3d 1281, 1285 (7th

Cir.1996) ("properly participating in the interactive process means that an employer cannot expect an employee to read its mind and know that he or she must specifically say I want a reasonable accommodation, particularly when the employee has a mental illness.").

If an employer learns of a disability and the possible need for accommodation only after the disability has caused inadequate performance or other delinquencies that would normally result in a discharge, does the employer have an obligation to attempt reasonable accommodation first? See Brady v. Wal Mart Stores, Inc., 531 F.3d 127 (2d Cir. 1008). At what point does the employer have to duty to inquire into whether the employee in question needs a reasonable accommodation? Can this inquiry be readily undertaken given the ADA proscription of employer inquiry into physical or mental disabilities? See p. 557, infra.

Employer Requests for Documentation. The ADA permits employers to request medical documentation of a disability and need for accommodation. See Grenier v. Cyanamid Plastics, 70 F.3d 667, 675 (1st Cir.1995) (permissible to request medical documentation to establish claim of disability and ability to perform job); EEOC's Enforcement Guidance on Reasonable Accommodation.

VANDE ZANDE V. STATE OF WISCONSIN DEPARTMENT OF ADMINISTRATION

United States Court of Appeals, Seventh Circuit, 1995.
44 F.3d 538.

POSNER, J.

It is plain enough what "accommodation" means. The employer must be willing to consider making changes in its ordinary work rules, facilities, terms, and conditions in order to enable a disabled individual to work. The difficult term is "reasonable." The plaintiff in our case, a paraplegic, argues in effect that the term just means apt or efficacious. An accommodation is reasonable, she believes, when it is tailored to the particular individual's disability. A ramp or lift is thus a reasonable accommodation for a person who like this plaintiff is confined to a wheelchair. Considerations of cost do not enter into the term as the plaintiff would have us construe it. Cost is, she argues, the domain of "undue hardship"—a safe harbor for an employer that can show that it would go broke or suffer other excruciating financial distress were it compelled to make a reasonable accommodation in the sense of one effective in enabling the disabled person to overcome the vocational effects of the disability".

These are questionable interpretations both of "reasonable" and of "undue hardship." To "accommodate" a disability is to make some change that will enable the disabled person to work. * * * So "reasonable" may be intended to qualify (in the sense of weaken) "accommodation," in just the same way that if one requires a "reasonable effort" of someone this means less than the maximum possible effort, or in law that the duty of "reasonable care," the cornerstone of the law of negligence, requires something less than the maximum possible care. It is understood in that law that in deciding what care is reasonable the court considers the cost of increased care. (This is explicit in Judge Learned Hand's famous formula for negligence. *United States v. Carroll Towing Co.*, 159 F.2d 169, 173 (2d Cir.1947).) Similar reasoning could be used to flesh out the meaning of the word "reasonable" in the term "reasonable accommodations." It would not follow that the costs and benefits of altering a workplace to enable a disabled person to work would always have to be quantified, or even that an accommodation would have to be deemed unreasonable if the cost exceeded the benefit however slightly. But, at the very least, the cost could not be disproportionate to the benefit. Even if an employer is so large or wealthy—or, like the principal defendant in this case, is a state, which can raise taxes in order to finance any accommodations that it must make to disabled employees—that it may not be able to plead "undue hardship," it would not be required to expend enormous sums in order to bring about a trivial improvement in the life of a disabled employee. If the nation's employers have potentially unlimited financial obligations to 43 million disabled persons, the Americans with Disabilities Act will have imposed an indirect tax potentially greater than the national debt. We do not find an intention to bring about such a radical result in either the language of the Act or its history. The preamble actually "markets" the Act as a cost saver, pointing to "billions of dollars in unnecessary expenses resulting from dependency and nonproductivity." § 12101(a)(9). The savings will be illusory if employers are required to expend many more billions in accommodation than will be saved by enabling disabled people to work.

The concept of reasonable accommodation is at the heart of this case. The plaintiff sought a number of accommodations to her paraplegia that were turned down. The principal defendant as we have said is a state, which does not argue that the plaintiff's proposals were rejected because accepting them would have imposed undue hardship on the state or because they would not have done her any good. The district judge nevertheless granted summary judgment for the defendants on the ground that the evidence obtained in discovery, construed as favorably to the plaintiff as the record permitted, showed that they had gone as far to accommodate the plaintiff's demands as reasonableness, in a sense distinct from either aptness or hardship—a sense based, rather, on considerations of cost and proportionality—required. On this analysis, the function of the "undue hardship" safe harbor, like the "failing company" defense to antitrust liability, * * * is to excuse compliance by a firm that is financially distressed, even though the cost of the accommodation to the firm might be less than the benefit to disabled employees.

This interpretation of "undue hardship" is not inevitable—in fact probably is incorrect. It is a defined term in the Americans with Disabilities Act, and the definition is "an action requiring significant difficulty or expense." 42 U.S.C. § 12111(10)(A). The financial condition of the employer is only one consideration in determining whether an accommodation otherwise reasonable would impose an undue hardship. See 42 U.S.C. §§ 12111(10)(B)(ii), (iii). The legislative history equates "undue hardship" to "unduly costly." These are terms of relation. We must ask, "undue" in relation to what? Presumably (given the statutory definition and the legislative history) in relation to the benefits of the accommodation to the disabled worker as well as to the employer's resources.

So it seems that costs enter at two points in the analysis of claims to an accommodation to a disability. The employee must show that the accommodation is reasonable in the sense both of efficacious and of proportional to costs. Even if this prima facie showing is made, the employer has an opportunity to prove that upon more careful consideration the costs are excessive in relation either to the benefits of the accommodation or to the employer's financial survival or health. In a classic negligence case, the idiosyncrasies of the particular employer are irrelevant. Having above-average costs, or being in a precarious financial situation, is not a defense to negligence. *Vaughan v. Menlove*, 3 Bing. (N.C.) 468, 132 Eng.Rep. 490 (Comm. Pl.1837). One interpretation of "undue hardship" is that it permits an employer to escape liability if he can carry the burden of proving that a disability accommodation reasonable for a normal employer would break him. *Barth v. Gelb*, 2 F.3d 1180, 1187 (D.C.Cir.1993).

Lori Vande Zande, aged 35, is paralyzed from the waist down as a result of a tumor of the spinal cord. Her paralysis makes her prone to develop pressure ulcers, treatment of which often requires that she stay at home for several weeks. * * * We hold that Vande Zande's pressure ulcers are a part of her disability, and therefore a part of what the State of Wisconsin had a duty to accommodate—reasonably.

Vande Zande worked for the housing division of the state's department of administration for three years, beginning in January 1990. The housing division supervises the state's public housing programs. Her job was that of a program assistant, and involved preparing public information materials, planning meetings, interpreting regulations, typing, mailing, filing, and copying. In short, her tasks were of a clerical, secretarial, and administrative-assistant character. In order to enable her to do this work, the defendants, as she acknowledges, "made numerous accommodations relating to the plaintiff's disability." As examples, in her words, "they paid the landlord to have bathrooms modified and to have a step ramped; they bought special adjustable furniture for the plaintiff; they ordered and paid for one-half of the cost of a cot that the plaintiff needed for daily personal care at work; they sometimes adjusted the plaintiff's schedule to perform backup telephone duties to accommodate the plaintiff's medical appointments; they made changes to the plans for a locker room in the new state office building; and they agreed to provide some of the specific accommodations the plaintiff requested in her October 5, 1992 Reasonable Accommodation Request."

But she complains that the defendants did not go far enough in two principal respects. One concerns a period of eight weeks when a bout of pressure ulcers forced her to stay home. She wanted to work full time at home and believed that she would be able to do so if the division would provide her with a desktop computer at home (though she already had a laptop). Her supervisor refused, and told her that he probably would have only 15 to 20 hours of work for her to do at home per week and that she would have to make up the difference between that and a full work week out of her sick leave or vacation leave. In the event, she was able to work all but 16.5 hours in the eight-week period. She took 16.5 hours of sick leave to make up the difference. As a result, she incurred no loss of income, but did lose sick leave that she could have carried forward indefinitely. She now works for another agency of the State of Wisconsin, but any unused sick leave in her employment by the housing division would have accompanied her to her new job. Restoration of the 16.5 hours of lost sick leave is one form of relief that she seeks in this suit.

She argues that a jury might have found that a reasonable accommodation required the housing division either to give her the desktop computer or to excuse her from having to dig into her sick leave to get paid for the hours in which, in the absence of the computer, she was unable to do her work at home. No jury, however, could in our view be permitted to stretch the concept of "reasonable accommodation" so far. Most jobs in organizations public or private involve team work under supervision rather than solitary unsupervised work, and team work under supervision generally cannot be performed at home without a substantial reduction in the quality of the employee's performance. This will no doubt change as communications technology advances, but is the situation today. Generally, therefore, an employer is not required to accommodate a disability by allowing the disabled worker to work, by himself, without supervision, at home. * * * An employer is not required to allow disabled workers to work at home, where their productivity inevitably would be greatly reduced. No doubt to this as to any generalization about so complex and varied an activity as employment there are exceptions, but it would take a very extraordinary case for the employee to be able to create a triable issue of the employer's failure to allow the employee to work at home.

And if the employer, because it is a government agency and therefore is not under intense competitive pressure to minimize its labor costs or maximize the value of its output, or for some other reason, bends over backwards to accommodate a disabled worker—goes further than the law requires—by allowing the worker to work at home, it must not be punished for its generosity by being deemed to have conceded the reasonableness of so far-reaching an accommodation. That would hurt rather than help disabled workers. Wisconsin's housing division was not required by the Americans with Disabilities Act to allow Vande Zande to work at home; even more clearly it was not required to install a computer in her home so that she could avoid using up 16.5 hours of sick leave. It is conjectural that she will ever need those 16.5 hours; the expected cost of the loss must, therefore, surely be slight. An accommodation that allows a disabled worker to work at home, at full pay, subject only to a slight loss of sick leave that may never be needed, hence never missed, is, we hold, reasonable as a matter of law.

Her second complaint has to do with the kitchenettes in the housing division's building, which are for the use of employees during lunch and coffee breaks. Both the sink and the counter in each of the kitchenettes were 36 inches high, which is too high for a person in a wheelchair. The building was under construction, and the kitchenettes not yet built, when the plaintiff complained about this feature of the design. But the defendants refused to alter the design to lower the sink and counter to 34 inches, the height convenient for a person in a wheelchair. Construction of the building had begun before the effective date of the Americans with Disabilities Act, and Vande Zande does not argue that the failure to include 34-inch sinks and counters in the design of the building violated the Act. She could not argue that; the Act is not retroactive. * * * But she argues that once she brought the problem to the attention of her supervisors, they were obliged to lower the sink and counter, at least on the floor on which her office was located but possibly on the other floors in the building as well, since she might be moved to another floor. All that the defendants were willing to do was to install a shelf 34 inches high in the kitchenette area on Vande Zande's floor. That took care of the counter problem. As for the sink, the defendants took the position that since the plumbing was already in place it would be too costly to lower the sink and that the plaintiff could use the bathroom sink, which is 34 inches high.

Apparently it would have cost only about $150 to lower the sink on Vande Zande's floor; to lower it on all the floors might have cost as much as $2,000, though possibly less. Given the proximity of the bathroom sink, Vande Zande can hardly complain that the inaccessibility of the kitchenette sink interfered with her ability to work or with her physical comfort. Her argument rather is that forcing her to use the bathroom sink for activities (such as washing out her coffee cup) for which the other employees could use the kitchenette sink stigmatized her as different and inferior; she seeks an award of compensatory damages for the resulting emotional distress. We may assume without having to decide that emotional as well as physical barriers to the integration of disabled persons into the workforce are relevant in determining the reasonableness of an accommodation. But we do not think an employer has a duty to expend even modest amounts of money to bring about an absolute identity in working conditions between disabled and nondisabled workers. The creation of such a duty would be the inevitable consequence of deeming a failure to achieve identical conditions "stigmatizing." That is merely an epithet. We conclude that access to a particular sink, when access to an equivalent sink, conveniently located, is provided, is not a legal duty of an employer. The duty of reasonable accommodation is satisfied when the employer does what is necessary to enable the disabled worker to work in reasonable comfort.

NOTES AND QUESTIONS

Test Your Understanding of the Material

1.   Note that Vande Zande, also without success, made the same argument about the meaning of "reasonable"—that it requires only efficacious accommodations—made in *US Airways*. What definition of "reasonable" does the *Vande Zande* court embrace? Is this definition consistent with the Supreme Court's later opinion in *US Airways*?

2.   What did Vande Zande argue concerning the meaning of "undue hardship"? How did the court of appeals treat that argument? What interpretation does the plain language of the statute suggest? See ADA § 101(10)(B); 42 U.S.C. § 12111.

3.   In *Vande Zande*, the court states that "it would take a very extraordinary case for the employee to be able to create a triable issue of the employer's failure to allow the employee to work at home." Is it always the case that employers need to monitor their employees at work or that employees must work in face-to-face settings? See note 5 below.

4.   Does the court in *Vande Zande* in fact apply the cost-benefit standard it purports to embrace? Consider the lowering of the sink on Vande Zande's floor. Apparently that would have cost only $150. Is the court including the benefit to Vande Zande in its analysis? Is there a benefit to the employer in not having to replace Vande Zande through this expenditure?

Related Issues

5.   *Telecommuting as a Reasonable Accommodation.* Permitting a disabled employee to work from home may be a reasonable accommodation depending on the job at issue and whether other similarly situated employees are allowed to work from home. See Langon v. Department of Health & Human Services, 959 F.2d 1053, 1055 (D.C.Cir.1992) (denying summary judgment to defendant, noting that it often allowed home work). Given the rapid development of communications technology, should courts question the durability of any general rules on home work? See EEOC v. Ford Motor Co., 752 F.3d 634, 647 (6th Cir. 2014) (finding working at home could be reasonable for resale steel buyer: "given the state of modern technology, it is no longer the case that jobs suitable for telecommuting are 'extraordinary' or 'unusual' ").

6.   *Weight That Should Be Given to the Employer's Overall Efforts at Accommodation?* The court seems to be influenced by the numerous

accommodations that Wisconsin did afford Vande Zande. Does the ADA direct an assessment of the overall efforts of an employer toward a particular employee, or should the level of accommodation to each need of a disabled employee be evaluated separately?

7. *Discrimination Between Disabled Individuals?* The court of appeals suggests that Wisconsin did more than the ADA requires by allowing Vande Zande to work many hours at home. What if Wisconsin had disallowed this home-work accommodation for another disabled worker whose duties were similar to those of Vande Zande? Would the second worker have a strong claim of discrimination under the ADA, even if her disability had a different cause and was less severe?

In Olmstead v. L.C. *ex rel.* Zimring, 527 U.S. 581 (1999), a majority of the Court held that a state could discriminate against some mentally ill individuals by failing to provide them with the community care services granted to other mentally ill persons. In a portion of her opinion joined by five Justices, Justice Ginsburg, responding to a dissent by Justice Thomas that no case of discrimination was presented, cited O'Connor v. Consolidated Coin Caterers Corp., 517 U.S. 308, 116 S.Ct. 1307, 134 L.Ed.2d 433 (1996), supra p. 440, for the proposition that discrimination can occur within a protected class. See also Jeannette Cox, Disability Stigma and Intraclass Discrimination, 62 Fla. L. Rev. 429 (2010).

8. *Providing Leave as a Reasonable Accommodation.* The EEOC's Interpretive Guidance states that other reasonable accommodations "could include permitting the use of accrued paid leave or providing additional unpaid leave for necessary treatment." 29 C.F.R. pt. 1630, app. 1630.2(*o*). Requests for leaves for an indefinite period or for over a year are not likely to be considered reasonable. See, e.g., Wood v. Green, 323 F.3d 1309 (11th Cir. 2003); Hudson v. MCI Telecommunications Corp., 87 F.3d 1167, 1169 (10th Cir.1996) (employer not required by ADA to provide indefinite leave, but a "reasonable allowance of time for medical care and treatment" may be mandated in some cases); Myers v. Hose, 50 F.3d 278, 283 (4th Cir.1995); employee must be qualified in the present "or in the immediate future"). Should reasonableness also turn on the probability that the treatment will be successful? See, e.g., Humphrey v. Memorial Hosps. Ass'n, 239 F.3d 1128, 1136 (9th Cir. 2001) (specified leave period must "plausibly enable" employee to be qualified on return). See generally Stephen F. Befort, The Most Difficult ADA Reasonable Accommodation Issues: Reassignment and Leave of Absence, 37 Wake For. L. Rev. 439 (2002).

Note that the ADA covers employees who may not be able to claim the benefits of the Family Medical Leave Act (FMLA), 29 U.S.C. § 2601 et seq., see pp. 897 infra. This may be true for a number of reasons, including working insufficient hours or employment at a worksite with fewer than 50 employees or exhaustion of twelve workweeks of unpaid leave in the past twelve months.

9. *Accommodations Beyond Those Necessary for Job Performance.* The EEOC's Regulations define "reasonable accommodation" to include

"[m]odifications or adjustments to a job application process that enable a qualified applicant with a disability to be considered for the position such qualified applicant desires", and "[m]odifications or adjustments that enable a covered entity's employee with a disability to enjoy equal benefits and privileges of employment as are enjoyed by its other similarly situated employees without disabilities." 29 C.F.R. § 1630.2(*o*)(1). Other courts of appeals, in addition to the Seventh Circuit in *Vande Zande*, have agreed that employers should consider the reasonableness of transfers that would enable an adequately performing disabled employee to get better medical treatment. See, e.g., Sanchez v. Vilsack, 695 F.3d 1174 (10th Cir. 2012) (citing other cases).

Must employers in some cases also provide disabled employees with benefits, such as convenient parking spaces for those whose walking is impaired, even where nondisabled employees are not provided comparable benefits? Should any obligation here depend on whether the disabled employee requires the accommodation in order to perform his job? Compare Lyons v. Legal Aid Society, 68 F.3d 1512, 1517 (2d Cir.1995) (convenient parking might be required because plaintiff could not work without parking close to office), with Harmer v. Virginia Elec. & Power Co., 831 F.Supp. 1300, 1307 (E.D.Va.1993) (asthmatic employee cannot demand smoking ban because he could perform essential functions even in smoke-filled room). The EEOC's Interpretive Guidance on Reasonable Accommodation states that only job-related needs must be specially addressed. The Guidance also states that "if an adjustment or modification assists the individual throughout his or her daily activities, on and off the job, it will be considered a personal item that the employer is not required to provide. Accordingly, an employer would generally not be required to provide an employee with a disability with a prosthetic limb, wheelchair, or eyeglasses." 29 C.F.R. pt. 1630, app. § 1630.9.

10. *Duty to Accommodate an Employee's Relationship or Association with an Individual with a Disability?* Section 102(b)(4) of the ADA proscribes discrimination against a qualified individual because of his or her "relationship or association" with another individual with a "known disability." Does this mean that the association or relationship must be reasonably accommodated? For instance, what if Vande Zande had requested to work at home sometimes to care for a disabled child? See, e.g., Magnus v. St. Mark United Methodist Church, 688 F.3d 331 (7th Cir. 2012); Den Hartog v. Wasatch Academy, 129 F.3d 1076, 1083–84 (10th Cir.1997) (both holding no accommodation was required); 29 C.F.R. pt. 1630, app. § 1630.8 (same). Note, however, that such employees may be entitled to unpaid leave under the FMLA, 29 U.S.C. § 2601 et seq; see discussion in Chapter 19 at pp. 897–899.

11. *Does the Reasonable Accommodation Obligation Help or Hinder the Disabled?* For studies suggesting that the imposition of costly accommodations discourage employers from hiring disabled workers, see Daron Acemoglu & Joshua D. Angrist, Consequences of Employment Protection? The Case of the Americans with Disabilities Act, 109 J. Po. Econ. 915 (2001); Thomas DeLeire, The Wage and Employment Effects of the Americans with Disabilities Act, 35 J. Hum. Res. 691 (2000). But see Susan Schwochau & Peter David Blanck, The

Economics of the Americans with Disabilities Act, Part III: Does the ADA Disable the Disabled, 21 Berk. J. Emp. & Lab. L. 271 (2000); Michael Ashley Stein, Empirical Implications of Title I, 85 Iowa L. Rev. 1671 (2000) (criticizing the methodologies of the studies).

What should be the legislative response, if any? Should Congress increase the penalties for discriminating against disabled employment applicants? Should it provide subsidies for the costs of accommodation? Should Congress permit employers to pay the disabled less to compensate for the extra costs of accommodation? Or should at least some decline in the quantity of jobs for the disabled be accepted as the cost of improving the quality of accommodated employment for those who obtain jobs? See Christine Jolls, Accommodation Mandates, 53 Stan. L. Rev. 223 (2000);. See also Sharona Hoffman, Settling the Matter: Does Title I of the ADA Work?, 59 Ala. L. Rev. 305 (2008).

DEANE v. POCONO MEDICAL CENTER

United States Court of Appeals, Third Circuit, 1998 (en banc).
142 F.3d 138.

BECKER, J.

I.

In April 1990, PMC hired Deane as a registered nurse to work primarily on the medical/surgical floor. On June 22, 1991, while lifting a resistant patient, she sustained a cartilage tear in her right wrist causing her to miss approximately one year of work. In June 1992, Deane and Barbara Manges, a nurse assigned to Deane's workers' compensation case, telephoned PMC and advised Charlene McCool, PMC's Benefits Coordinator, that Deane intended to return to work with certain restrictions. According to Deane, she informed McCool that she was unable to lift more than 15–20 pounds or perform repetitive manual tasks such as typing, but that her physician, Dr. Osterman, had released her to return to "light duty" work. Deane further explained to McCool that, if she could not be accommodated in a light duty position on the medical/surgical floor, she was willing to move to another area of the hospital, as long as she could remain in nursing. Unfortunately, this telephone call was PMC's only meaningful interaction with Deane during which it could have assessed the severity of or possible accommodation for her injuries. PMC never requested additional information from Deane or her physicians, and, according to Deane, when she subsequently attempted to contact PMC on several occasions, she was treated rudely by McCool and told not to call again.

After speaking with Deane and Manges, McCool advised Barbara Hann, PMC's Vice President of Human Resources, of Deane's request to return to work, of her attendant work restrictions, and of her stated need for accommodation. Shortly after considering the information conveyed by McCool and after comparing it to the job description of a medical/surgical nurse at PMC, Hann determined that Deane was unable to return to her previous position. Hann then asked Carol Clarke, PMC's Vice President of Nursing, and Susan Stine, PMC's Director of Nursing Resources/Patient Care Services, to review Deane's request to return to PMC and to explore possible accommodations for her. Both Clarke and Stine concluded that Deane could not be accommodated in her previous job as a nurse on the medical/surgical floor or in any other available position at the hospital. Finally, Hann asked Marie Werkheiser, PMC's Nurse Recruiter, whether there were any current or prospective job openings for registered nurses at PMC. According to Werkheiser, there were no such openings at that time.

As a result of the collective determination that Deane could not be accommodated in her previous job or in any other available position in the hospital, PMC sent Deane an "exit interview" form on August 7, 1992. On August 10, 1992, Hann notified Deane by telephone that she could not return to work because of her "handicap", and this litigation ensued. In March 1993, Deane accepted a registered nurse position at a non-acute care facility, where she remained until May 1993. Deane has been employed by a different non-acute care facility since July 1993. Neither of these positions require heavy lifting, bathing patients, or the like. * * *

* * * [Deane contends] that she was disabled under the terms of the ADA by virtue of the fact that PMC regarded her limitations as being far worse than they actually were, that PMC failed to accommodate her lifting restriction, and that she was eventually terminated on account of PMC's perception that she was disabled. In support of her perception claim, Deane relies on a "laundry list" of PMC's allegedly erroneous perceptions. According to Deane, PMC believed that she was unable to lift more than ten pounds, push or pull anything, assist patients in emergency situations, move or assist patients in the activities of daily living, perform any patient care job at PMC or any other hospital, perform CPR, use the rest of her body to assist patients, work with psychiatric patients, or use medical equipment. Deane refutes each of these perceptions—or, in her view, misperceptions—and contends that her injury was, in fact, relatively minor in nature. Deane further contends that PMC should be held responsible for these misperceptions because they were the result of PMC's "snap judgment" arrived at without making a good faith analysis, investigation, or assessment of the nature of her injury.

Finally, Deane maintains that she requires and is entitled to accommodation for her lifting restriction. In this regard, Deane contends that she could be accommodated either in her previous position as a nurse on the medical/surgical floor or through reassignment to another position that would not require heavy lifting. As to the former, Deane has suggested the following accommodations: (1) use of an assistant to help her move or lift patients; (2) implementation of a functional nursing approach, in which nurses would perform only certain types of nursing tasks; and (3) use of a

Hoyer lift to move patients. Deane also maintains that she could have been transferred to another unit within the medical center such as the pediatrics, oncology, or nursery units, which would not have required heavy lifting. In the alternative, Deane submits that she can perform the essential functions of her previous job in the medical/surgical floor without accommodation because lifting is not an essential function of nursing. * * *

II.

A.

[*Eds.* The court first concluded that Deane adduced sufficient evidence to create an issue of material fact over whether PMC regarded her as being disabled: "there are factual disputes over how impaired PMC regarded Deane as being compared with her actual level of impairment, and whether PMC's perception of Deane constituted a 'significant[ ] restriction in [Deane's] ability to perform either a class of jobs or a broad range of jobs in various classes as compared to the average person having comparable training, skills and abilities.' " 29 C.F.R. § 1630.2(j)(3)(i).]

B.

The second element of Deane's prima facie case under the ADA requires her to demonstrate that she is a "qualified individual". The ADA defines this term as an individual "who, with or without reasonable accommodation, can perform the essential functions of the employment position that such individual holds or desires." 42 U.S.C. § 12111(8). * * *

Determining whether an individual can, with or without reasonable accommodation, perform the essential functions of the position held or sought * * * is relatively straightforward. First, a court must consider whether the individual can perform the essential functions of the job without accommodation. If so, the individual is qualified (and, *a fortiori*, is not entitled to accommodation). If not, then a court must look to whether the individual can perform the essential functions of the job with a reasonable accommodation. If so, the individual is qualified. If not, the individual has failed to set out a necessary element of the prima facie case. * * *

* * *

2.

* * * [W]e must now determine whether Deane has, in fact, adduced sufficient evidence to survive summary judgment on the question whether she can perform the essential functions of the job without accommodation as to those functions. Deane claims that the heavy lifting she is restricted from doing is not an essential job function of a nurse. Deane describes nursing as a profession that focusses primarily on skill, intellect, and knowledge. While conceding that lifting constitutes part of a nurse's duties, she submits that it is only a small part.

* * *

PMC responds that lifting *is* an essential function of a nurse. In support, PMC cites its job description, which details under the heading "MAJOR TASKS, DUTIES AND RESPONSIBILITIES" that one of the "WORKING CONDITIONS" for a staff registered nurse is the "frequent lifting of patients." PMC also notes that Deane conceded that the PMC job description was "an accurate reflection of the tasks, duties and responsibilities as well as the qualifications, physical requirements and working conditions of a registered nurse at [PMC]," and that among her "critical job demands" at PMC were: (1) the placement of patients in water closets, tub chairs or gurneys, (2) the changing of position of patients, and (3) the lifting of laundry bags. These pieces of evidence, contends PMC, constitute multiple admissions by Deane that lifting is an essential function of a staff registered nurse at PMC. Finally, PMC asserts that the consequences of a nurse's inability to lift patients could create a dangerous situation in the hospital for Deane and her patients.

We decline to apply conclusive effect to either the job description or PMC's judgment as to whether heavy lifting is essential to Deane's job. The EEOC's Interpretive Guidance indicates that "the employer's judgment as to which functions are essential" and "written job descriptions prepared before advertising or interviewing applicants" are two possible types of evidence for determining the essential functions of a position, but that such evidence is not to be given greater weight simply because it is included in the non-exclusive list set out in 29 C.F.R. § 1630.2(n)(3). See 29 C.F.R. pt. 1630, app. § 1630.2(n). Thus, the job description is not, as PMC contends, incontestable evidence that unassisted patient lifting is an essential function of Deane's job. Moreover, the EEOC Regulations also provide that while "inquiry into the essential functions is not intended to second guess an employer's business judgment with regard to production standards," whether a particular function is essential "is a factual determination that must be made on a case by case basis [based upon] *all* relevant evidence." *Id.* (emphasis added). Finally, the import of the rest of PMC's evidence (e.g., her alleged admissions, etc.) is disputed by Deane. For all these reasons, we find that there is a genuine issue of material fact on the issue of whether Deane was a qualified individual under the ADA. * * *

GREENBERG, J., dissenting.

The majority believes that there is a genuine issue of material fact as to "whether PMC misperceived Deane as being disabled." But that dispute does not matter, for the critical issue is not how PMC viewed Deane because there is simply no escape from the fact that an essential element of Deane's case is that "PMC failed to accommodate her lifting restriction." After all, as the majority explains, "Deane maintains that she requires and is entitled to accommodation for her lifting restriction." * * * Thus, even if PMC regarded her as more substantially impaired than she actually was, this misperception does not matter for she was not entitled to any accommodation. * * *

The majority indicates that there is a genuine dispute of material fact regarding whether heavy lifting is an essential function of her former job. I agree that there is a genuine dispute of fact as to whether heavy lifting is an essential function of the job. But, just as the dispute of fact regarding PMC's perception of Deane does not matter, neither does the heavy lifting dispute because it is not material. Inasmuch as Deane is not actually disabled, she has no right to an accommodation whether or not the accommodation would impact on her ability to perform the essential functions of the job.

NOTES AND QUESTIONS

Test Your Understanding of the Material

1. How would the *Deane* case be decided under the ADAAA?

2. Why does the *Deane* court not give "conclusive effect" to the medical center's judgment and job description in deciding whether heavy lifting was essential to Deane's job? Note the last sentence in § 101(8) of the ADA. Consider also the non-exhaustive lists of reasons for finding a job function essential, or "fundamental" rather than "marginal," as presented in the EEOC's regulations, 29 C.F.R. § 1630.2(n)(2) and (3), and explained further in its Interpretive Guidance, 29 C.F.R. pt. 1630, app. § 1630.2(n).

Related Issues

3. *Nonessential Job Functions.* Based on the language of the statute, did the *Deane* court correctly conclude that in order to be a "qualified individual" under the ADA a plaintiff must be able to perform, with or without reasonable accommodation, only the "essential functions" of the relevant job, rather than all of its functions? Does this mean that an actually disabled individual's inability to perform non-essential functions cannot be taken into account by the employer if the employee can perform the essential functions? See, e.g., Lovejoy-Wilson v. NOCO Motor Fuel, Inc., 263 F.3d 208 (2d Cir. 2001) (employer could not refuse to promote epileptic, based on her inability to drive, to position for which driving was not an essential job function).

The essential-function analysis can be helpful in cases where plaintiffs claim that employers should accommodate their disabilities by restructuring job duties between employees. See § 101(9)(b) (expressly listing "job restructuring" as a possible reasonable accommodation); Kuntz v. City of New Haven, 2 A.D. Cases (BNA) 905 (D.Conn. 1993), affirmed without opinion, 29 F.3d 622 (2d Cir.1994) ("physically strenuous aspects" of New Haven police lieutenant's job are proportionately insignificant relative to supervisory and administrative duties).

4. *Job Attendance as an Essential Function.* The import of "essential function" analysis and of the EEOC's regulations on this issue may turn in part on the essential function claimed by the employer and the accommodation

desired by the employee. For instance, employers sued under the ADA have often claimed that the disability-caused absences of plaintiffs from work render the plaintiffs unqualified because adherence to attendance rules is an essential function of their employment. The plaintiffs in these cases claim that flexibility on attendance would be a reasonable accommodation to their disabilities.

Employees who commit serious breaches of an employer's attendance policies are not considered qualified individuals with a disability. See, e.g., Spangler v. Federal Home Loan Bank, 278 F.3d 847 (8th Cir. 2002); EEOC v. Yellow Freight Sys., 253 F.3d 943 (7th Cir. 2001); Hypes v. First Commerce Corp., 134 F.3d 721 (5th Cir.1998); Price v. S-B Power Tool, 75 F.3d 362, 365–66 (8th Cir.1996); Tyndall v. National Educ. Ctrs., Inc., 31 F.3d 209, 213–14 (4th Cir.1994); Jackson v. Veterans Admin., 22 F.3d 277, 278–79 (11th Cir.1994). Temporary medical leave, however, might constitute a reasonable accommodation in some cases. See, e.g., Cehrs v. Northeast Ohio Alzheimer's Research Center, 155 F.3d 775 (6th Cir.1998) (severe psoriasis flareup); Criado v. IBM Corp., 145 F.3d 437 (1st Cir.1998) (mental depression).

5. *Are Infrequent Tasks Nonessential?* It depends on the relative importance of the task. The EEOC's Interpretive Guidance notes that "although a firefighter may not regularly have to carry an unconscious adult out of a burning building, the consequence of failing to require the firefighter to be able to perform this function would be serious." 29 C.F.R. pt. 1630, app. § 1630.2(n).

6. *Hiring Assistants as an Accommodation.* Section 101(9)(B) of the ADA lists "the provision of qualified readers or interpreters" as a reasonable accommodation. The EEOC's Interpretive Guidance further states that a reasonable accommodation may include providing personal assistants, "such as a page turner for an employee with no hands or a travel attendant to act as a sighted guide to assist a blind employee on occasional business trips." 29 C.F.R. pt. 1630, app. § 1630.2(o). However, the Guidance also states that employers need not "reallocate essential functions" to assistants:

> For example, suppose a security guard position requires the individual who holds the job to inspect identification cards. An employer would not have to provide an individual who is legally blind with an assistant to look at the identification cards for the legally blind employee. In this situation the assistant would be performing the job for the individual with a disability rather than assisting the individual to perform the job.

Id. If an employee must turn pages in his job, why is page turning merely assisting rather than performing an essential function of a job? Is the EEOC suggesting that employers may have to provide assistants to help disabled employees perform relatively mundane parts of their jobs that do not require use of the disabled employees' special skills, but they do not have to provide assistants to do part of disabled employees' skill-demanding work? Absent a showing of undue hardship, must employers sometimes pay for as well as allow assistants?

7. *Attractiveness to Customers as an Essential Function?* Do employers violate the ADA by including job qualifications only to appeal to customer stereotypes and prejudices? Consider, for instance, the claim of a dwarf that he should be able to be employed as a guard at an exclusive, high fashion store despite the employer's desire to project a glamorous image. Or the claim of a cosmetically disfigured woman that she should be able to be employed as a receptionist at a restaurant despite the employer's demand for an especially attractive greeter. Would the woman's claim be stronger than if she applied for work as a model or an exotic dancer? Compare the *Wilson v. Southwest Airlines Co.* case at p. 358 and the accompanying notes. Compare Kuehl v. Wal-Mart Stores, Inc., 909 F.Supp. 794, 801 (D.Colo.1995) (Wal-Mart door greeter must be able to greet standing, rather than sitting, because essence of Wal-Mart's greeting policy was aggressive hospitality), with EEOC v. Wal-Mart Stores, Inc., 477 F.3d 561 (8th Cir. 2007) (EEOC presented prima facie case that applicant with cerebral palsy could be greeter with use of motorized scooter).

8. *Can an Individual Receiving Social Security or Other Disability Benefits Be a "Qualified Individual with a Disability"?* If an individual successfully applies for disability benefits from the social security system, from a state's workers' compensation system or from a private disability insurer, should that individual be estopped from claiming that she "can perform the essential functions of the employment position" that she seeks? Indeed, should an individual's mere assertion of "total and permanent disability" in an application for benefits be sufficient to preclude her from claiming that she is capable of fulfilling the functions of any job? In Cleveland v. Policy Management Systems Corp., 526 U.S. 795, 119 S.Ct. 1597, 143 L.Ed.2d 966 (1999), the Supreme Court held that the pursuit and receipt of social security benefits for total disability does not "estop" or even "erect a strong presumption against the recipient's success under the ADA."

NOTE: ESTABLISHING DISCRIMINATORY INTENT UNDER THE ADA

In few cases litigated under Title I of the ADA have plaintiffs had to establish the basic element of a disparate-treatment case—that the defendant took into account plaintiff's protected status in making a personnel decision adverse to the plaintiff. Instead, in most ADA employment discrimination cases, like *US Airways*, *Vande Zande,* and *Deane*, plaintiffs have claimed that defendant employers have failed to provide reasonable accommodations. Defendants have responded, not by claiming neutrality toward plaintiffs' physical or mental conditions and the behavior caused by such conditions, but rather by denying (i) that these conditions constitute disabilities under the ADA's definition, (ii) that the plaintiffs' requested accommodations that would be reasonable, or (iii) that plaintiffs' requested accommodations that could be granted without undue hardship.

Where more traditional disparate-treatment claims have been asserted in Rehabilitation Act cases, however, the lower courts generally have applied the *McDonnell Douglas-Burdine* burden-shifting rules. See, e.g., Crawford v.

Runyon, 37 F.3d 1338, 1341 (8th Cir.1994); Teahan v. Metro-North Commuter R.R. Co., 951 F.2d 511, 514 (2d Cir.1991); Smith v. Barton, 914 F.2d 1330, 1339–40 (9th Cir.1990); Norcross v. Sneed, 755 F.2d 113, 116–17 (8th Cir.1985). The courts in ADA cases have followed this precedent. See, e.g., Ennis v. NABER, Inc., 53 F.3d 55, 57 (4th Cir.1995).

In ADA cases, however, the lower courts do not follow Rehabilitation Act cases holding that a plaintiff must prove that his disability was the sole cause of the adverse personnel action he challenges. See, e.g., McNely v. Ocala Star-Banner Corp., 99 F.3d 1068, 1076–77 (11th Cir.1996) (but-for causation). The *McNely* court stressed legislative history suggesting that Congress intended to reject a sole causation standard when it did not repeat in the ADA the "solely by reason of her or his disability" phrase of § 504 of the Rehabilitation Act. 99 F.3d at 1076. The lower courts in ADA cases are now following the Court's decision in Gross v. FBL Financial Services, Inc., 557 U.S. 167, 129 S.Ct. 2343, 174 L.Ed.2d 119 (2009), at page 446 supra, setting but-for causation as the default rule. See, e.g. Lewis v. Humboldt Acquisition Corp., 681 F.3d 312 (6th Cir 2012) (*en banc*).

Employers might acknowledge that they have treated an employee adversely because of inappropriate or unproductive behavior associated with his disability, but deny that discrimination against that behavior should be treated as discrimination "because of" the disability. In Raytheon Co. v. Hernandez, 540 U.S. 44, 124 S.Ct. 513, 157 L.Ed.2d 357 (2003), the Supreme Court seemed to approve such a defense by noting that in *Hazen Paper Co. v. Biggins*, supra p. 470, it had rejected an argument that discrimination against something "related to" a protected status is discrimination against that status. Thus, the Court suggested, termination for "testing positive" for drugs would be termination because of violation of a rule against illegal drug use, and not because of a related drug addiction. See also, e.g., Despears v. Milwaukee County, 63 F.3d 635, 636 (7th Cir.1995) (discharging an alcoholic for having his license revoked for multiple convictions of drunk driving was not a decision based on his alcoholism because the alcoholism did not compel him to drive while drunk); EEOC v. Amego, Inc., 110 F.3d 135, 149 (1st Cir.1997) (firing employee for abuse of drug prescribed for her disabling depression not caused by disability); Palmer v. Circuit Court of Cook County, 117 F.3d 351 (7th Cir.1997) ("if an employer fires an employee because of the employee's unacceptable behavior, the fact that that behavior was precipitated by a mental illness does not present an issue" under the ADA).

Section 103 of the ADA provides an express general defense for even overt intentional discrimination against individuals with disabilities. Section 103(a) allows qualification standards, tests, or selection criteria that deny a job or benefit to an individual with a disability if they are "shown to be job-related and consistent with business necessity" and job "performance cannot be accomplished by reasonable accommodation. * * * "

These qualification standards can include a requirement "that an individual shall not pose a direct threat to the health or safety of other individuals in the workplace." Section 101(3) defines "direct threat" as a "significant risk to the health or safety of others that cannot be eliminated by reasonable accommodation." The EEOC regulations state that the "determination that an individual poses a 'direct threat' shall be based on an individualized assessment of the individual's present ability to safely perform the essential functions of the job." 29 C.F.R. § 1630.2(r). The EEOC directs consideration of four factors: "(1) The duration of the risk; (2) The nature and severity of the potential harm; (3) The likelihood that the potential harm will occur; and (4) The imminence of the potential harm." Id.

Consider how the Court in *Bragdon* viewed a parallel defense applicable to public accommodation discrimination claims under Title III of the ADA:

BRAGDON V. ABBOTT

Supreme Court of the United States, 1998.
524 U.S. 624, 118 S.Ct. 2196, 141 L.Ed.2d 540.

[*Eds.* As explained on p. 506 supra, this case was brought under the public accommodations provisions of Title III of the ADA, and involved a patient with an HIV infection who was denied dental services. The Court first held that the patient's HIV infection met the ADA's definition of disability, and then proceeded to review the Court of Appeals' affirmation of a grant of summary judgment determining as a matter of law that the infection did not pose a direct threat to the health and safety of the treating dentist.]

JUSTICE KENNEDY delivered the opinion of the Court.

III

* * * Notwithstanding the protection given respondent by the ADA's definition of disability, petitioner could have refused to treat her if her infectious condition "pose[d] a direct threat to the health or safety of others." 42 U.S.C. § 12182(b)(3). The ADA defines a direct threat to be "a significant risk to the health or safety of others that cannot be eliminated by a modification of policies, practices, or procedures or by the provision of auxiliary aids or services." Ibid. Parallel provisions appear in the employment provisions of Title I. §§ 12111(3), 12113(b).

The ADA's direct threat provision stems from the recognition in *School Bd. of Nassau Cty. v. Arline*, 480 U.S. 273, 287, 107 S.Ct. 1123, 1130–1131, 94 L.Ed.2d 307 (1987), of the importance of prohibiting discrimination against individuals with disabilities while protecting others from significant health and safety risks, resulting, for instance, from a contagious disease. In *Arline*, the Court reconciled these objectives by construing the Rehabilitation Act not to require the hiring of a person who posed "a significant risk of communicating an infectious disease to others." *Id.*, at 287, n. 16, 107 S.Ct., at 1131, n. 16. Congress amended the Rehabilitation Act and the Fair Housing Act to incorporate the language. See 29 U.S.C. § 706(8)(D) (excluding individuals who "would constitute a direct threat to the health or safety of other individuals"); 42 U.S.C. § 3604(f)(9) (same). It later relied on the same language in enacting the ADA. See 28 CFR pt. 36, App. B, p. 626 (1997) (ADA's direct threat provision codifies *Arline*). Because few, if any, activities in life are risk free, *Arline* and the ADA do not ask whether a risk exists, but whether it is significant. *Arline*, supra, at 287, and n. 16, 107 S.Ct., at 1131, and n. 16; 42 U.S.C. § 12182(b)(3).

The existence, or nonexistence, of a significant risk must be determined from the standpoint of the person who refuses the treatment or accommodation, and the risk assessment must be based on medical or other objective evidence. *Arline*, supra, at 288, 107 S.Ct., at 1131; 28 CFR § 36.208(c) (1997); id., pt. 36, App. B, p. 626. As a health care professional, petitioner had the duty to assess the risk of infection based on the objective, scientific information available to him and others in his profession. His belief that a significant risk existed, even if maintained in good faith, would not relieve him from liability. To use the words of the question presented, petitioner receives no special deference simply because he is a health care professional. * * *

Our conclusion that courts should assess the objective reasonableness of the views of health care professionals without deferring to their individual judgments does not answer the implicit assumption in the question presented, whether petitioner's actions were reasonable in light of the available medical evidence. In assessing the reasonableness of petitioner's actions, the views of public health authorities, such as the U.S. Public Health Service, CDC, and the National Institutes of Health, are of special weight and authority. *Arline*, supra, at 288, 107 S.Ct., at 1130–1131; 28 CFR pt. 36, App. B, p. 626 (1997). The views of these organizations are not conclusive, however. A health care professional who disagrees with the prevailing medical consensus may refute it by citing a credible scientific basis for deviating from the accepted norm. See W. Keeton, D. Dobbs, R. Keeton, & D. Owen, Prosser and Keeton on Law of Torts § 32, p. 187 (5th ed.1984).

We have reviewed so much of the record as necessary to illustrate the application of the rule to the facts of this case. For the most part, the Court of Appeals followed the proper standard in evaluating the petitioner's position and conducted a thorough review of the evidence. Its rejection of the District Court's reliance on the Marianos affidavits was a correct application of the principle that petitioner's actions must be evaluated in light of the available, objective evidence. The record did not show that CDC had published the conclusion set out in the affidavits at the time petitioner refused to treat respondent.

* * * Petitioner testified that he believed hospitals had safety measures, such as air filtration, ultraviolet lights, and respirators, which would reduce the risk of HIV transmission. Petitioner made no showing,

however, that any area hospital had these safeguards or even that he had hospital privileges. His expert also admitted the lack of any scientific basis for the conclusion that these measures would lower the risk of transmission. Petitioner failed to present any objective, medical evidence showing that treating respondent in a hospital would be safer or more efficient in preventing HIV transmission than treatment in a well-equipped dental office.

We are concerned, however, that the Court of Appeals might have placed mistaken reliance upon two other sources. In ruling no triable issue of fact existed on this point, the Court of Appeals relied on the 1993 CDC Dentistry Guidelines and the 1991 American Dental Association Policy on HIV. This evidence is not definitive. As noted earlier, the CDC Guidelines recommended certain universal precautions which, in CDC's view, "should reduce the risk of disease transmission in the dental environment." * * * In our view, the Guidelines do not necessarily contain implicit assumptions conclusive of the point to be decided. The Guidelines set out CDC's recommendation that the universal precautions are the best way to combat the risk of HIV transmission. They do not assess the level of risk.

Nor can we be certain, on this record, whether the 1991 American Dental Association Policy on HIV carries the weight the Court of Appeals attributed to it. The Policy does provide some evidence of the medical community's objective assessment of the risks posed by treating people infected with HIV in dental offices. * * *

We note, however, that the Association is a professional organization, which, although a respected source of information on the dental profession, is not a public health authority. It is not clear the extent to which the Policy was based on the Association's assessment of dentists' ethical and professional duties in addition to its scientific assessment of the risk to which the ADA refers. * * *

* * *

There are reasons to doubt whether petitioner advanced evidence sufficient to raise a triable issue of fact on the significance of the risk. Petitioner relied on two principal points: First, he asserted that the use of high-speed drills and surface cooling with water created a risk of airborne HIV transmission. The study on which petitioner relied was inconclusive, however, determining only that "[f]urther work is required to determine whether such a risk exists." Johnson & Robinson, Human Immunodeficiency Virus-1 (HIV-1) in the Vapors of Surgical Power Instruments, 33 J. of Medical Virology 47, 47 (1991). Petitioner's expert witness conceded, moreover, that no evidence suggested the spray could transmit HIV. His opinion on airborne risk was based on the absence of contrary evidence, not on positive data. Scientific evidence and expert testimony must have a traceable, analytical basis in objective fact before it may be considered on summary judgment. See *General Electric Co. v. Joiner*, 522 U.S. 136, 118 S.Ct. 512, 518, 519, 139 L.Ed.2d 508 (1997).

Second, petitioner argues that, as of September 1994, CDC had identified seven dental workers with possible occupational transmission of HIV. These dental workers were exposed to HIV in the course of their employment, but CDC could not determine whether HIV infection had resulted. It is now known that CDC could not ascertain whether the seven dental workers contracted the disease because they did not present themselves for HIV testing at an appropriate time after their initial exposure. It is not clear on this record, however, whether this information was available to petitioner in September 1994. If not, the seven cases might have provided some, albeit not necessarily sufficient, support for petitioner's position. Standing alone, we doubt it would meet the objective, scientific basis for finding a significant risk to the petitioner.

Our evaluation of the evidence is constrained by the fact that on these and other points we have not had briefs and arguments directed to the entire record. * * *

We conclude the proper course is to give the Court of Appeals the opportunity to determine whether our analysis of some of the studies cited by the parties would change its conclusion that petitioner presented neither objective evidence nor a triable issue of fact on the question of risk. In remanding the case, we do not foreclose the possibility that the Court of Appeals may reach the same conclusion it did earlier. A remand will permit a full exploration of the issue through the adversary process.

CHIEF JUSTICE REHNQUIST, with whom JUSTICE SCALIA and JUSTICE THOMAS join, and with whom JUSTICE O'CONNOR joins as to Part II, concurring in the judgment in part and dissenting in part.

I agree with the Court that "the existence, or nonexistence, of a significant risk must be determined from the standpoint of the person who refuses the treatment or accommodation," as of the time that the decision refusing treatment is made. I disagree with the Court, however, that "[i]n assessing the reasonableness of petitioner's actions, the views of public health authorities * * * are of special weight and authority." Those views are, of course, entitled to a presumption of validity when the actions of those authorities themselves are challenged in court, and even in disputes between private parties where Congress has committed that dispute to adjudication by a public health authority. But in litigation between private parties originating in the federal courts, I am aware of no provision of law or judicial practice that would require or permit courts to give some scientific views more credence than others simply because they have been endorsed by a politically appointed public health authority (such as the Surgeon General). In litigation of this latter sort, which is what we face here, the credentials of the scientists employed by the public health authority, and the soundness of their studies, must stand on their own. * * *

NOTES AND QUESTIONS

> *Ruling on Remand*
>
> On remand in *Bragdon* the First Circuit held that Bragdon's evidence of a direct threat in performing the dental work with proper precautions in his office rather than in a hospital was too speculative to present a genuine issue of material fact. See Abbott v. Bragdon, 163 F.3d 87 (1st Cir.1998).

Test Your Understanding of the Material

1.　Why does the Court reject a subjective, good-faith standard for the "health and safety" defense?

2.　*Bragdon* was litigated under Title III of the ADA (access to public accommodations), not Title I (employment). Is a subjective, good-faith standard available in the employment context?

3.　Note the *Bragdon* Court's statement that the "views of public health authorities * * * are of special weight and authority", though "not conclusive", in assessing the reasonableness of exclusionary decisions like that of Abbott's. Note also the Court's treatment of the 1993 Center for Disease Control (CDC) Dentistry Guidelines and the 1991 American Dental Association (ADA) Policy on HIV. Had the CDC Guidelines directly assessed risk, should the lower court have given them "special weight"?

Related Issues

4.　*Special Regulatory Authority for Food Handling*. The ADA provides express administrative authority for one category of health risk. Section 103(d) of the ADA directs the Secretary of HHS to promulgate a list of infectious and communicable diseases that may be transmitted through the handling of food. Employers may refuse to assign a job involving food handling to any individual with a listed disease for which the risk of transmission cannot be eliminated by reasonable accommodation.

5.　*Treatment of HIV Infection Risk in the Lower Courts*. A number of courts have recognized that there is no evidence of HIV being transmitted through the air, rather than through bodily fluids. See, e.g., Chalk v. United States District Ct., 840 F.2d 701, 706 (9th Cir.1988) (AIDS-infected teacher may be returned to classroom, in view of "an overwhelming evidentiary consensus of medical and scientific opinion regarding the nature and transmission of AIDS"); Harris v. Thigpen, 941 F.2d 1495, 1525 (11th Cir.1991) (must do case-by-case determination of risk of transmission of AIDS virus). Jobs involving invasive surgical procedures may present a reasonable risk of transmission. See, e.g., Mauro v. Borgess Medical Center, 137 F.3d 398 (6th Cir.1998); Bradley v. University of Texas M.D. Anderson Cancer Ctr., 3 F.3d 922, 924 (5th Cir.1993); Doe v. Washington Univ., 780 F.Supp. 628, 632–34 (E.D.Mo.1991).

6.   *"Direct Threat" to the Individual with a Disability.* Note again the ADA's definition of "direct threat" as a "significant risk to the health or safety of others." In light of this definition can an employer refuse to hire an individual because the individual's disability poses a direct threat to his or her own safety, regardless of whether the disability also threatens others? In Chevron U.S.A. Inc. v. Echazabal, 536 U.S. 73, 122 S.Ct. 2045, 153 L.Ed.2d 82 (2002), a unanimous Court sustained an EEOC regulation stating that an employer can guard against a "direct threat" to the health or safety of the "individual" as well as to others. 29 C.F.R. § 1630.2(r).

7.   *Safety as an Essential Function of the Job?* The *Bragdon* Court assumes that Bragdon had the burden of proving the direct threat as an affirmative defense. Can an employer effectively reverse the burden of proof by asserting that a plaintiff is not a qualified individual with a disability because safe operation to herself and others is an essential function of the job she seeks? See Bates v. United Parcel Service, Inc., 511 F.3d 974 (9th Cir.2007) (hearing impaired plaintiffs must show that they are capable of safely filling driving positions they seek, but employer would have to prove its hearing standard was a business necessity). See also Albertson's, Inc. v. Kirkingburg, 527 U.S. 555, 578, 119 S.Ct. 2162, 2174, 144 L.Ed.2d 518 (1999) (Thomas, J. concurring) (suggesting that plaintiffs should have burden of proving safety where it is essential to job); see generally Ann Hubbard, Understanding and Implementing the ADA's Direct Threat Defense, 95 Nw. L. Rev. 1279 (2001).

NOTE: ADA AND MEDICAL EXAMINATIONS AND INQUIRIES

Section 102(d) of the ADA may discourage some intentional discrimination against disabled workers by restricting the use of medical examinations and inquiries (other than testing for the illegal use of drugs, which § 104(d)(1) provides "shall not be considered a medical examination.") Section 102(d)(2) is designed to discourage intentional hiring discrimination by prohibiting medical exams or inquiries of "a job applicant as to whether such applicant is an individual with a disability or as to the nature or severity of such disability." Section 102(d)(3) allows an offer of employment to be conditioned on the results of a post-offer, confidential medical examination required of all entering employees. It is presumably difficult to revoke an offer after a medical examination without highlighting the results of the exam as the probable cause of the revocation.

Section 102(d)(2)(B), however, raises a challenging interpretive issue by permitting pre-employment offer "inquiries into the ability of an applicant to perform job-related functions." What kind of inquiries only probe the ability to perform job functions without also probing the existence or the nature of a disability?

The EEOC's "Enforcement Guidance" on "Preemployment Disability-Related Questions and Medical Examinations" (October, 1995) defines a prohibited medical inquiry broadly as one "likely to elicit information" about a disability. An "employer cannot ask questions that are closely related to disability." However, "if there are many possible answers to a question and only some of those answers would contain disability-related information", the question may be asked. For instance, an employer may ask whether an applicant "can perform any or all job functions." An employer also may inquire about attendance records in prior employment, but may not ask about the applicant's worker-compensation claims history because this would be likely to elicit information about the individual's disability.

Tests that measure a candidate's ability to perform a discrete task, such as a physical fitness test or a simulated task test, are not improper pre-offer tests under the ADA. Similarly, psychological tests used to measure an applicant's ability or propensity to perform a job successfully, such as personality or honesty tests, are not automatically barred, unless application of the test shows that it is designed to detect mental disability. *See, e.g.,* Karraker v. Rent-A-Center, Inc., 411 F.3d 831 (7th Cir. 2005) (barring use of test originally designed to detect mental disorders). Vision tests are not automatically barred, but may constitute a medical exam if they are likely to reveal an applicant's disability. For further elaboration, see also the EEOC's "Enforcement Guidance: Disability-Related Inquiries and Medical Examinations of Employees Under the Americans with Disabilities Act (ADA)" (July, 2000).

Section 102(d)(4)(A) also prohibits any medical examination or inquiry of current employees concerning disability status, "unless such examination or inquiry is shown to be job-related and consistent with business necessity." The EEOC's Interpretive Guidance states:

> The purpose of this provision is to prevent the administration to employees of medical tests or inquiries that do not serve a legitimate business purpose. For example, if an employee suddenly starts to use increased amounts of sick leave or starts to appear sickly, an employer could not require that employee to be tested for AIDS, HIV infection, or cancer unless the employer can demonstrate that such testing is job-related and consistent with business necessity. 29 C.F.R. pt. 1630, app. § 1630.13(b).

Would the EEOC's interpretation prevent an employer from protecting against employee abuse of sick leave by requiring employees to provide some general medical documentation before returning from substantial leave? Would it prevent an employer from requiring employees returning from substantial leave to provide medical certification that they do not pose a threat to the safety or health of other workers? See Conroy v. New York State Dept. of Correctional Services, 333 F.3d 88 (2d Cir. 2003) (to show business necessity, employer must justify policy requiring medical certification by demonstrating reason to believe covered jobs might pose threat to health or safety or that covered employees might be abusers of sick leave). On April 20, 2015, the EEOC also proposed regulations to govern disability-related inquiries or medical examinations that are part of increasingly popular employee "wellness" programs. See 80 Fed. Reg. 21,659.

Some states also have passed laws barring the use of medical tests for determining the presence of particular physical or mental conditions. See, e. g., Vt. Stat. Ann. Tit. 21, 495 (1995); Wis. State. Ann. § 103.15 (West 1996) (both restricting HIV testing). Other states have prohibited pre-employment genetic screening. See, e.g., Or.Rev.Stat. § 659A.300 (2001); Iowa Code § 729.6(2) (1995).

NOTE: ADA AND DISPARATE IMPACT

The list of alternative definitions of disability discrimination contained in § 102(b) of the ADA expressly authorizes disparate impact challenges. Section 102(b)(3) prohibits "utilizing standards, criteria, or methods of administration—(A) that have the effect of discrimination on the basis of disability. * * * " Section 102(b)(6) prohibits "using qualification standards, employment tests or other selection criteria that screen out or tend to screen out an individual with a disability or a class of individuals with disabilities unless the standard, test or other selection criteria * * * is shown to be job-related * * * and is consistent with business necessity. * * * " And § 102(b)(1), which prohibits "limiting, segregating, or classifying a job applicant or employee in a way that adversely affects the opportunities or status of such applicant or employee because of the disability of such applicant or employee", seems more clearly to rest on disparate effects than § 703(a)(2) of Title VII, on which disparate-impact theory was first based. But see 29 C.F.R. pt. 1630, app. § 1630.5 (suggesting that the EEOC views (b)(1) to cover only intentional discrimination).

Only the § (b)(6) provision includes an express job relatedness and business necessity qualification; however, the EEOC's ADA regulations also include the qualification when repeating the § (b)(3) prohibition. See 29 C.F.R. § 1630.7. Can the disparate-impact theory be applied without allowing some kind of cost-based defense? Should the qualification also be applied to the prohibition in § 102(b)(1)? These questions are further complicated by the statute's additional express inclusion in § 103(a) of the ADA of a job-relatedness and business necessity "defense" to charges framed under language that tracks only § 102(b)(6), and by the fact that this defense is framed to be advanced in tandem with a demonstration that no "reasonable accommodation" can be accomplished.

The EEOC's Interpretive Guidance states that the selection criteria that may be challenged under § (b)(6) include "all types of selection criteria, including safety requirements, vision or hearing requirements, walking requirements, lifting requirements, and employment tests." 29 C.F.R. pt. 1630, app. § 1630.10. The Guidance also asserts that although "it is not the intent of this part to second guess an employer's judgment with regard to production standards", selection criteria that "do not concern an essential function of the job would not be consistent with business necessity", and even "selection criteria that are related to an essential function of the job may not be used to exclude an individual with a disability if that individual could satisfy the criteria with the provision of a reasonable accommodation." Id.

Can disparate impact be used to challenge limitations or exclusions in employer-provided health or disability insurance plans? Most such limitations or exclusions disproportionately affect some group of disabled workers, but do not seem to be reachable by the reasonable accommodation requirements in § 102(b)(5). Are they reachable by § 102(b)(3) or even § 102(b)(1)? The EEOC has taken the position that benefit limitations that are framed neutrally toward all disabilities, are not adopted for the purpose of affecting the disabled, and have only a disparate impact on individuals with disabilities, are permissible. "Thus, for example, an employer that reduces the number of paid sick leave days that it will provide to all employees, or reduces the amount of medical insurance coverage that it will provide to all employees, is not in violation of [§ 102(b)(3)], even if the benefits reduction has an impact on employees with disabilities in need of greater sick leave and medical coverage. * * * See Alexander v. Choate, 469 U.S. 287, 105 S.Ct. 712, 83 L.Ed.2d 661 (1985)." 29 U.S.C. pt. 1630, app. § 1630.5. In *Choate* the Supreme Court assumed that § 504 of the Rehabilitation Act could be applied against some practices that have an unjustified impact on the disabled, but held that § 504 of the Rehabilitation Act did not reach a decision by the State of Tennessee to limit the number of annual days of inpatient hospital care covered by its state Medicaid program, without proof of a discriminatory motive. As explained in the following Note, ADA challenges to employer-provided health or disability insurance plans based on allegations of discriminatory intent remain possible.

NOTE: ADA AND INSURANCE

Section 102(a) of the ADA prohibits discrimination against a qualified individual with a disability in regard to "terms, conditions, and privileges of employment." Furthermore, § 102(b)(2) provides that this discrimination includes "participating in a contractual or other arrangement or relationship", including a "relationship with * * * an organization providing fringe benefits", that subjects a qualified applicant or employee to disability discrimination. In an "Interim Enforcement Guidance", the EEOC interpreted § 102 to cover employers' discrimination on the basis of disability in the provision of health insurance to their employees. See EEOC Interim Enforcement Guidance on the Application of the ADA to Disability-Based Distinctions in Employer Provided Health Insurance (Aug. 7, 2000).

The EEOC's 2000 Enforcement Guidance further states that "disability-based insurance plan distinctions are permitted only if they are within the protective ambit of section 501(c) of the ADA." Section 501(c) states that the Act's employment provisions shall not be construed to prohibit insurers or self-insured employers or health care organizations that administer bona fide benefit plans from "underwriting risks, classifying risks, or administering such risks that are based on or not inconsistent with State law", unless such decisions are "used as a subterfuge to evade the purposes" of the employment provisions. As explained in the Senate Committee Report:

> [W]hile a plan which limits certain kinds of coverage based on classification of risk would be allowed under this section, the plan

may not refuse to insure, or refuse to continue to insure, or limit the amount, extent, or kind of coverage available to an individual, or charge a different rate for the same coverage solely because of a physical or mental impairment, except where the refusal, limitation, or rate differential is based on sound actuarial principles or is related to actual or reasonably anticipated experience.

S.Rep. No. 101–116, 101st Cong., 1st Sess. at 85 (1989), reprinted in 1 Legislative History of the Americans with Disabilities Act, at 183 (1991).

The EEOC's 2000 Guidance states that limitations or exclusions in employer-provided health benefit plans are proscribed by the ADA only if they are both (1) intentionally based on disability and (2) not "within the protective ambit of section 501(c) * * * ." EEOC Interim Enforcement Guidance on the Application of the ADA to Disability-Based Distinctions in Employer Provided Health Insurance, supra. The first condition is based on the assumption, as explained in the prior Note, that the disparate "impact theory of discrimination is unavailable in this context". Id. at n.7. It also conveys the agency's view that universal, nondisease-specific restrictions on coverage, such as limits on "mental/nervous" conditions or "eye care," blanket preexisting condition clauses or caps on annual benefits for the treatment of any physical condition, do not constitute intentional discrimination on the basis of disability. The Interim Guidance states: "Such broad distinctions, which apply to the treatment of a multitude of dissimilar conditions and which constrain individuals both with and without disabilities, are not distinctions based on disability." However, "[a] term or provision is 'disability-based' if it singles out a particular disability (e.g. deafness, AIDS, schizophrenia), a discrete group of disabilities (e.g., cancers, muscular dystrophies, kidney diseases), or disability in general * * * ."

Do you understand the EEOC's distinction between broad exclusions, such as for "mental/nervous" conditions, and exclusions of a class of diseases, such as cancers? Is it not disability discrimination to deny a benefit because of a disability because some individuals also denied the benefit are not disabled? In any event, notwithstanding *Choate,* why should the ADA not condemn limitations or exclusions that have the effect of disproportionately disadvantaging the disabled, even if they also may disadvantage some who are not disabled? Compare the treatment of pregnancy-related benefits, pages 330–347 supra.

The 2010 Affordable Care Act, 124 Stat. 119, fills some of the insurance gaps that the ADA leaves unaddressed. The ACA prohibits health insurers from refusing to cover preexisting conditions and from discriminating against participants based on their health status. ACA § 1201, codified at 42 U.S.C. § 300gg. It also requires all health insurers to provide certain minimum "essential health benefits" such as mental health care, rehabilitative services, and chronic disease management. ACA § 1201, codified at 42 U.S.C. § 300gg–6; ACA § 1302, codified at 42 U.S.C. § 18022.

CHAPTER 10

RELIGIOUS DISCRIMINATION

■ ■ ■

Introduction

This chapter addresses the special issues raised by the prohibition of discrimination on account of religious belief and practices found in Title VII of the Civil Rights Act of 1964 and related state law. The concept of "reasonable accommodation," which figures centrally in disability discrimination law, first appears as a matter of federal law in the definition of religion protected under Title VII.

A. NATURE OF RELIGIOUS DISCRIMINATION

In many respects discrimination against religious minorities can be likened to discrimination against racial and ethnic minorities. Certainly, some of history's more vicious religious bigots have considered those who practice particular religions to constitute a different and inferior race. Not surprisingly, the Supreme Court has ruled that the proscription of "racial" discrimination in the 1866 Civil Rights Act, 42 U.S.C. §§ 1981, 1982, 1985(3), encompasses discrimination against Jews and certain other forms of ancestry bias. See Shaare Tefila Congregation v. Cobb, 481 U.S. 615, 107 S.Ct. 2019, 95 L.Ed.2d 594 (1987); Saint Francis College v. Al-Khazraj, 107 S.Ct. 2019 (1987). Furthermore, discrimination against religious minorities sometimes also may be closely related to bias on account of national origin.

But existing law cannot be explained completely in these terms. For example, Title VII defines discrimination on account of "religion" to include "all aspects of religious observance and practice, as well as belief," § 701, 42 U.S.C. § 2000e(j), and explicitly requires "reasonable accommodat[ion]" of an employee's or applicant's religious observance or practice. As suggested in the last chapter, a duty of reasonable accommodation reflects a qualified claim to special treatment. Similarly, the Constitution requires government in some cases to suppress legitimate interests in deference to a claim of free exercise of religion under the First Amendment. The decision to protect religious observance and practices, even at some cost to the efficiency of government programs or private employer policies, may reflect a judgment that religious choices are critical to human dignity and autonomy, and therefore should be given special protection. It may also reflect a societal commitment to religious pluralism. Without protection of religious practices, as well as beliefs, religious minorities might be driven either to assimilate or to accept confinement in isolated communities where they could find employment with coreligionists. Either choice could impoverish the larger society.

B. THE TITLE VII DUTY OF ACCOMMODATION

TRANS WORLD AIRLINES, INC. v. HARDISON
Supreme Court of the United States, 1977.
432 U.S. 63, 97 S.Ct. 2264, 53 L.Ed.2d 113.

MR. JUSTICE WHITE delivered the opinion of the Court.

Petitioner Trans World Airlines (TWA) operates a large maintenance and overhaul base in Kansas City, Mo. On June 5, 1967, respondent Larry G. Hardison was hired by TWA to work as a clerk in the Stores Department at its Kansas City base. Because of its essential role in the Kansas City operation, the Stores Department must operate 24 hours per day, 365 days per year, and whenever an employee's job in that department is not filled, an employee must be shifted from another department, or a supervisor must cover the job, even if the work in other areas may suffer.

Hardison, like other employees at the Kansas City base, was subject to a seniority system contained in a collective-bargaining agreement that TWA maintains with petitioner International Association of Machinists and Aerospace Workers (IAM). The seniority system is implemented by the union steward through a system of bidding by employees for particular shift assignments as they become available. The most senior employees have first choice for job and shift assignments, and the most junior employees are required to work when the union steward is unable to find enough people willing to work at a particular time or in a particular job to fill TWA's needs.

In the spring of 1968 Hardison began to study the religion known as the Worldwide Church of God. One of the tenets of that religion is that one must observe the Sabbath by refraining from performing any work from sunset on Friday until sunset on Saturday. The religion also proscribes work on certain specified religious holidays.

When Hardison informed Everett Kussman, the manager of the Stores Department, of his religious conviction regarding observance of the Sabbath, Kussman agreed that the union steward should seek a job swap for Hardison or a change of days off; that Hardison would have his religious holidays off whenever possible if Hardison agreed to work the traditional holidays when asked; and that Kussman would try to find Hardison another job that would be more compatible with his religious beliefs. The problem was temporarily solved when Hardison transferred to the 11 p.m.–7 a.m. shift. Working this shift permitted Hardison to observe his Sabbath.

The problem soon reappeared when Hardison bid for and received a transfer from Building 1, where he had been employed, to Building 2, where he would work the day shift. The two buildings had entirely separate seniority lists; and while in Building 1 Hardison had sufficient seniority to observe the Sabbath regularly, he was second from the bottom on the Building 2 seniority list.

In Building 2 Hardison was asked to work Saturdays when a fellow employee went on vacation. TWA agreed to permit the union to seek a change of work assignments for Hardison, but the union was not willing to violate the seniority provisions set out in the collective-bargaining contract, and Hardison had insufficient seniority to bid for a shift having Saturdays off.

A proposal that Hardison work only four days a week was rejected by the company. Hardison's job was essential and on weekends he was the only available person on his shift to perform it. To leave the position empty would have impaired supply shop functions, which were critical to airline operations; to fill Hardison's position with a supervisor or an employee from another area would simply have undermanned another operation; and to employ someone not regularly assigned to work Saturdays would have required TWA to pay premium wages.

When an accommodation was not reached, Hardison refused to report for work on Saturdays. A transfer to the twilight shift proved unavailing since that schedule still required Hardison to work past sundown on Fridays. After a hearing, Hardison was discharged on grounds of insubordination for refusing to work during his designated shift.

* * *

III

The Court of Appeals held that TWA had not made reasonable efforts to accommodate Hardison's religious needs under the 1967 EEOC guidelines in effect at the time the relevant events occurred. In its view, TWA had rejected three reasonable alternatives, any one of which would have satisfied its obligation without undue hardship. First, within the framework of the seniority system, TWA could have permitted Hardison to work a four-day week, utilizing in his place a supervisor or another worker on duty elsewhere. * * * Second—according to the Court of Appeals, also within the bounds of the collective-bargaining contract—the company could have filled Hardison's Saturday shift from other available personnel competent to do the job, of which the court said there were at least 200. * * * Third, TWA could have arranged a "swap between Hardison and another employee either for another shift or for the Sabbath days." * * *

We disagree with the Court of Appeals in all relevant respects. It is our view that TWA made reasonable efforts to accommodate and that each of the Court of Appeals' suggested alternatives would have been an undue hardship within the meaning of the statute as construed by the EEOC guidelines.

A

It might be inferred from the Court of Appeals' opinion and from the brief of the EEOC in this Court that TWA's efforts to accommodate were no more than negligible. The findings of the District Court, supported by the record, are to the contrary. In summarizing its more detailed findings, the District Court observed:

> "TWA established as a matter of fact that it did take appropriate action to accommodate as required by Title VII. It held several meetings with plaintiff at which it attempted to find a solution to plaintiff's problems. It did accommodate plaintiff's observance of his special religious holidays. It authorized the union steward to search for someone who would swap shifts, which apparently was normal procedure."

It is also true that TWA itself attempted without success to find Hardison another job. The District Court's view was that TWA had done all that could reasonably be expected within the bounds of the seniority system.

The Court of Appeals observed, however, that the possibility of a variance from the seniority system was never really posed to the union. This is contrary to the District Court's findings and to the record. The District Court found that when TWA first learned of Hardison's religious observances in April 1968, it agreed to permit the union's steward to seek a swap of shifts or days off but that "the steward reported that he was unable to work out scheduling changes and that he understood that no one was willing to swap days with plaintiff". Later, in March 1969, at a meeting held just two days before Hardison first failed to report for his Saturday shift, TWA again "offered to accommodate plaintiff's religious observance by agreeing to any trade of shifts or change of sections that plaintiff and the union could work out * * *. Any shift or change was impossible within the seniority framework and the union was not willing to violate the seniority provisions set out in the contract to make a shift or change." As the record shows, Hardison himself testified that Kussman was willing, but the union was not, to work out a shift or job trade with another employee.

* * *

B

We are also convinced, contrary to the Court of Appeals, that TWA itself cannot be faulted for having failed to work out a shift or job swap for Hardison. Both the union and TWA had agreed to the seniority system; the union was unwilling to entertain a variance over the objections of men senior to Hardison; and for TWA to have arranged unilaterally for a swap would have amounted to a breach of the collective-bargaining agreement.

Hardison and the EEOC insist that the statutory obligation to accommodate religious needs takes precedence over both the collective-bargaining contract and the seniority rights of TWA's other employees. We agree that neither a collective-bargaining contract nor a seniority system may be employed to violate the statute, but we do not believe that the duty to accommodate requires TWA to take steps inconsistent with the otherwise valid agreement.

* * *

It was essential to TWA's business to require Saturday and Sunday work from at least a few employees even though most employees preferred those days off. Allocating the burdens of weekend work was a matter for collective bargaining. In considering criteria to govern this allocation, TWA and the union had two alternatives: adopt a neutral system, such as seniority, a lottery, or rotating shifts; or allocate days off in accordance with the religious needs of its employees. TWA would have had to adopt the latter in order to assure Hardison and others like him of getting the days off necessary for strict observance of their religion, but it could have done so only at the expense of others who had strong, but perhaps nonreligious, reasons for not working on weekends. There were no volunteers to relieve Hardison on Saturdays, and to give Hardison Saturdays off, TWA would have had to deprive another employee of his shift preference at least in part because he did not adhere to a religion that observed the Saturday Sabbath.

Title VII does not contemplate such unequal treatment. The repeated, unequivocal emphasis of both the language and the legislative history of Title VII is on eliminating discrimination in employment, and such discrimination is proscribed when it is directed against majorities as well as minorities. Indeed, the foundation of Hardison's claim is that TWA and IAM engaged in religious *discrimination* in violation of § 703(a)(1) when they failed to arrange for him to have Saturdays off. It would be anomalous to conclude that by "reasonable accommodation" Congress meant that an employer must deny the shift and job preference of some employees, as well as deprive them of their contractual rights, in order to accommodate or prefer the religious needs of others, and we conclude that Title VII does not require an employer to go that far.

Our conclusion is supported by the fact that seniority systems are afforded special treatment under Title VII itself. * * * "[T]he unmistakable purpose of § 703(h) was to make clear that the routine application of a bona fide seniority system would not be unlawful under Title VII." *International Brotherhood of Teamsters v. United States*, 431 U.S. 324, 352, 97 S.Ct. 1843, 1863, 52 L.Ed.2d 396 (1977). See also *United Air Lines, Inc. v. Evans*, 431 U.S. 553, 97 S.Ct. 1885, 52 L.Ed.2d 571 (1977). * * *

There has been no suggestion of discriminatory intent in this case. * * * The Court of Appeals' conclusion that TWA was not limited by the terms of its seniority system was in substance nothing more than a ruling that operation of the seniority system was itself an unlawful employment practice even though no discriminatory purpose had been shown. That ruling is plainly inconsistent with the dictates of § 703(h), both on its face and as interpreted in the recent decisions of this Court. * * *

C

The Court of Appeals also suggested that TWA could have permitted Hardison to work a four-day week if necessary in order to avoid working on his Sabbath. Recognizing that this might have left TWA shorthanded on the one shift each week that Hardison did not work, the court still concluded that TWA would suffer no undue hardship if it were required to replace Hardison either with supervisory personnel or with qualified personnel from other departments. Alternatively, the Court of Appeals suggested that TWA could have replaced Hardison on his Saturday shift with other available employees through the payment of premium wages. Both of these alternatives would involve costs to TWA, either in the form of lost efficiency in other jobs or higher wages.

To require TWA to bear more than a *de minimis* cost in order to give Hardison Saturdays off is an undue hardship.[1] Like abandonment of the seniority system, to require TWA to bear additional costs when no such costs are incurred to give other employees the days off that they want would involve unequal treatment of employees on the basis of their religion. By suggesting that TWA should incur certain costs in order to give Hardison Saturdays off the Court of Appeals would in effect require TWA to finance an additional Saturday off and then to choose the employee who will enjoy it on the basis of his religious beliefs. While incurring extra costs to secure a replacement for Hardison might remove the necessity of compelling another employee to work involuntarily in Hardison's place, it would not change the fact that the privilege of having Saturdays off would be allocated according to religious beliefs.

As we have seen, the paramount concern of Congress in enacting Title VII was the elimination of discrimination in employment. In the absence of clear statutory language or legislative history to the contrary, we will not readily construe the statute to require an employer to discriminate against some employees in order to enable others to observe their Sabbath.

---

[1] The dissent argues that "the costs to TWA of either paying overtime or not replacing respondent would [not] have been more than *de minimis*." This ignores, however, the express finding of the District Court that "[b]oth of these solutions would have created an undue burden on the conduct of TWA's business," and it fails to take account of the likelihood that a company as large as TWA may have many employees whose religious observances, like Hardison's, prohibit them from working on Saturdays or Sundays.

MR. JUSTICE MARSHALL, with whom MR. JUSTICE BRENNAN joins, dissenting.

* * *

Once it is determined that the duty to accommodate sometimes requires that an employee be exempted from an otherwise valid work requirement, the only remaining question is whether this is such a case: Did TWA prove that it exhausted all reasonable accommodations, and that the only remaining alternatives would have caused undue hardship on TWA's business?

* * *

To begin with, the record simply does not support the Court's assertion, made without accompanying citations, that "[t]here were no volunteers to relieve Hardison on Saturdays." Everett Kussman, the manager of the department in which respondent worked, testified that he had made no effort to find volunteers, and the union stipulated that its steward had not done so either. * * * Of course, it is * * * possible that no trade—or none consistent with the seniority system—could have been arranged. But the burden under the EEOC regulation is on TWA to establish that a reasonable accommodation was not possible. 29 CFR § 1605.1(c) (1976). Because it failed either to explore the possibility of a voluntary trade or to assure that its delegate, the union steward, did so, TWA was unable to meet its burden.

Nor was a voluntary trade the only option open to TWA that the Court ignores; to the contrary, at least two other options are apparent from the record. First, TWA could have paid overtime to a voluntary replacement for respondent—assuming that someone would have been willing to work Saturdays for premium pay—and passed on the cost to respondent. In fact, one accommodation Hardison suggested would have done just that by requiring Hardison to work overtime when needed at regular pay. Under this plan, the total overtime cost to the employer—and the total number of overtime hours available for other employees—would not have reflected Hardison's Sabbath absences. Alternatively, TWA could have transferred respondent back to his previous department where he had accumulated substantial seniority, as respondent also suggested. Admittedly, both options would have violated the collective-bargaining agreement; the former because the agreement required that employees working over 40 hours per week receive premium pay, and the latter because the agreement prohibited employees from transferring departments more than once every six months. But neither accommodation would have deprived any other employee of rights under the contract or violated the seniority system in any way.

ANSONIA BOARD OF EDUC. v. PHILBROOK

Supreme Court of the United States, 1986.
479 U.S. 60, 107 S.Ct. 367, 93 L.Ed.2d 305.

CHIEF JUSTICE REHNQUIST delivered the opinion of the Court.

Petitioner Ansonia Board of Education has employed respondent Ronald Philbrook since 1962 to teach high school business and typing classes in Ansonia, Connecticut. In 1968, Philbrook was baptized into the Worldwide Church of God. The tenets of the church require members to refrain from secular employment during designated holy days, a practice that has caused respondent to miss approximately six school days each year.

* * *

Since the 1967–1968 school year, the school board's collective-bargaining agreements with the Ansonia Federation of Teachers have granted to each teacher 18 days of leave per year for illness, cumulative to 150 and later to 180 days. Accumulated leave may be used for purposes other than illness as specified in the agreement. A teacher may accordingly use five days' leave for a death in the immediate family, one day for attendance at a wedding, three days per year for attendance as an official delegate to a national veterans organization, and the like. With the exception of the agreement covering the 1967–1968 school year, each contract has specifically provided three days' annual leave for observance of mandatory religious holidays, as defined in the contract. Unlike other categories for which leave is permitted, absences for religious holidays are not charged against the teacher's annual or accumulated leave.

The school board has also agreed that teachers may use up to three days of accumulated leave each school year for "necessary personal business." Recent contracts limited permissible personal leave to those uses not otherwise specified in the contract. This limitation dictated, for example, that an employee who wanted more than three leave days to attend the convention of a national veterans organization could not use personal leave to gain extra days for that purpose. Likewise, an employee already absent three days for mandatory religious observances could not later use personal leave for "[a]ny religious activity," or "[a]ny religious observance."

* * * Until the 1976–1977 year, Philbrook observed mandatory holy days by using the three days granted in the contract and then taking unauthorized leave. His pay was reduced accordingly. In 1976, however, respondent stopped taking unauthorized leave for religious reasons, and began scheduling required hospital visits on church holy days. He also worked on several holy days. Dissatisfied with this arrangement, Philbrook repeatedly asked the school board to adopt one of two alternatives. His preferred alternative would allow use of personal business leave for religious observance, effectively giving him three additional days of paid leave for that purpose. Short of this arrangement, respondent suggested that he pay the cost of a substitute and receive full pay for additional days off for religious observances.[3] Petitioner has consistently rejected both proposals.

* * *

We find no basis in either the statute or its legislative history for requiring an employer to choose any particular reasonable accommodation. By its very terms the statute directs that any reasonable accommodation by the employer is sufficient to meet its accommodation obligation. The employer violates the statute unless it "demonstrates that [it] is unable to reasonably accommodate * * * an employee's * * * religious observance or practice without undue hardship on the conduct of the employer's business." Thus, where the employer has already reasonably accommodated the employee's religious needs, the statutory inquiry is at an end. The employer need not further show that each of the employee's alternative accommodations would result in undue hardship. As *Hardison* illustrates, the extent of undue hardship on the employer's business is at issue only where the employer claims that it is unable to offer any reasonable accommodation without such hardship. Once the Court of Appeals assumed that the school board had offered to Philbrook a reasonable alternative, it erred by requiring the board to nonetheless demonstrate the hardship of Philbrook's alternatives.

* * *

The remaining issue in the case is whether the school board's leave policy constitutes a reasonable accommodation of Philbrook's religious beliefs. Because both the District Court and the Court of Appeals applied what we hold to be an erroneous view of the law, neither explicitly considered this question. We think that there are insufficient factual findings as to the manner in which the collective bargaining agreement has been interpreted in order for us to make that judgment initially. We think that the school board policy in this case, requiring respondent to take unpaid leave for holy day observance that exceeded the amount allowed by the collective-bargaining agreement, would generally be a reasonable one. In enacting § 701(j), Congress was understandably motivated by a desire to assure the individual additional opportunity to observe religious practices, but it did not impose a duty on the employer to accommodate at all costs. *TWA v. Hardison,* 432 U.S. 63, 97 S.Ct. 2264, 53 L.Ed.2d 113 (1977). The provision of unpaid leave eliminates the conflict between employment requirements and religious practices by allowing the individual to observe fully religious holy days and requires him only to give

---

[3] The suggested accommodation would reduce the financial costs to Philbrook of unauthorized absences. In 1984, for example, a substitute cost $30 per day, and respondent's loss in pay from an unauthorized absence was over $130.

up compensation for a day that he did not in fact work. Generally speaking, "[t]he direct effect of [unpaid leave] is merely a loss of income for the period the employee is not at work; such an exclusion has no direct effect upon either employment opportunities or job status." *Nashville Gas Co. v. Satty*, 434 U.S. 136, 145, 98 S.Ct. 347, 353, 54 L.Ed.2d 356 (1977).

But unpaid leave is not a reasonable accommodation when paid leave is provided for all purposes *except* religious ones. A provision for paid leave "that is part and parcel of the employment relationship may not be doled out in a discriminatory fashion, even if the employer would be free * * * not to provide the benefit at all." *Hishon v. King & Spalding*, 467 U.S. 69, 75, 104 S.Ct. 2229, 2234, 81 L.Ed.2d 59 (1984). Such an arrangement would display a discrimination against religious practices that is the antithesis of reasonableness. Whether the policy here violates this teaching turns on factual inquiry into past and present administration of the personal business leave provisions of the collective-bargaining agreement. The school board contends that the necessary personal business category in the agreement, like other leave provisions, defines a limited purpose leave. Philbrook, on the other hand, asserts that the necessary personal leave category is not so limited, operating as an open-ended leave provision that may be used for a wide range of secular purposes in addition to those specifically provided for in the contract, but not for similar religious purposes. We do not think that the record is sufficiently clear on this point for us to make the necessary factual findings, and we therefore affirm the judgment of the Court of Appeals remanding the case to the District Court.

JUSTICE MARSHALL, concurring in part and dissenting in part.

* * * I do not find the specificity of the personal business leave, or the possibility that it may be used for activities similar to the religious activities Philbrook seeks leave to pursue, necessarily dispositive of whether the board has satisfied its affirmative duty under § 701(j), 42 U.S.C. § 2000e(j), to reasonably accommodate Philbrook's religious needs. Even if the District Court should find that the personal leave is restricted to specific secular uses having no similarity with Philbrook's religious activities, Philbrook would still encounter a conflict between his religious needs and work requirements. In my view, the question would remain whether, without imposing an undue hardship on the conduct of its educational program, the school board could further reasonably accommodate Philbrook's need for additional religious leave.

If, for example, the personal business leave were so limited that it allowed teachers paid leave for the sole purpose of meeting with their accountants to prepare their income tax returns (a purely secular activity), a proposal from Philbrook that he be allowed to prepare his tax return on his own time and use this paid leave for religious observance might be found imminently reasonable and lacking in undue hardship. The board's prior determination that the conduct of its educational program can withstand the paid absence of its teachers for up to six days each year for religious and personal reasons tends to indicate that granting Philbrook's similar request in this case for a total of six days paid religious leave and no personal leave is reasonable, would cause the board no undue hardship, and hence falls within the scope of the board's affirmative obligation under Title VII.

JUSTICE STEVENS, concurring in part and dissenting in part.

* * * The existing leave policy denies paid days to any teacher who proposes to take more paid days of personal business leave per year to fulfill his or her commitments than the contract allows. Respondent's wish to use his secular leave for religious purposes is thwarted by the same policy that denies an avid official delegate to a National Veterans' Organization use of secular leave days for that activity in excess of the days specifically allotted for it under the contract. In fact, since three days are expressly authorized for mandated religious observances—events that recur each year—whereas most other categories of paid leave cover relatively infrequent contingencies such as a death in the family or attendance at a family wedding, it is highly probable that the leave policy as a whole tends to favor, rather than to disfavor, persons who must observe religious days during the school year. For example, an atheist who attends a wedding, a funeral, and a graduation on school days receives a total of three days of paid personal leave, but a religious person who attends the same three events on paid days also receives pay for three religious days.

NOTES AND QUESTIONS

Test Your Understanding of the Material

1.   Absent the seniority system and the union's resistance to accommodating Hardison, would assigning other employees to Saturday work have been unreasonable or have imposed an undue hardship?

2.   Does the Court in *Philbrook* hold that Ansonia had a duty to reasonably accommodate Philbrook with paid leave, or simply that it had a duty not to discriminate against religious purposes in the allocation of such leave? What is the district court to determine on remand?

Related Issues

3.   *Did* Hardison *Turn on the Existence of a Collectively Bargained Seniority System?* Lower courts have held that departures from seniority systems in nonunion firms, where terms are unilaterally set but adhered to by employers, can create an undue hardship. Cf. Harrell v. Donahue, 638 F.3d 975, 981 (8th Cir. 2011) (seniority system not in collective bargaining agreement, but accommodation creates an undue hardship if it causes more than *de minimis* impact on co-workers); Balint v. Carson City, 180 F.3d 1047 (9th Cir.1999) (en banc) (accommodation is reasonable only if no disruption to

any seniority system and no more than *de minimis* cost). Note that the seniority system in *US Airways, Inc. v. Barnett*, p. 524 supra, had been unilaterally promulgated by a nonunion employer.

4. *No "More than a* De Minimis *Cost"?* If, as the Court states, requiring "TWA to bear more than a *de minimis* cost in order to give Hardison Saturdays off is an undue hardship", and if Title VII does not require subordination of the secular interests of some employees to the religious interests of others, what content is left of the reasonable-accommodation requirement? Does it require employers to incur some minimal administrative costs to accommodate religious practices? The lower courts have so held. See, e.g., Adeyeye v. Heartland Sweeteners, LLC, 721 F.3d 444, 455 (7th Cir. 2013) ("[i]n light of the evidence of high turnover, frequent use of temporary workers, and a ready supply of substitutes, a reasonable jury would not be required to find that an unpaid leave of several weeks . . . would have imposed an undue burden"); Baker v. The Home Depot, 445 F.3d 541 (2d Cir. 2006) (employer may have to allow employee to have Sundays free if no cost in doing so); EEOC v. Ilona of Hungary, Inc., 108 F.3d 1569, 1576 (7th Cir.1997) (employer must provide two employees unpaid day off for Yom Kippur); Opuku-Boateng v. California, 95 F.3d 1461, 1470 (9th Cir.1996) (employer may have to accommodate Seventh Day Adventist who could not work on Saturdays); Protos v. Volkswagen of America, Inc., 797 F.2d 129 (3d Cir.1986) (employer who had crew of relief operators to substitute for absent employees could reasonably accommodate plaintiff's religious need to have Saturdays free).

5. *Hardison and the ADA.* Is the *Hardison* Court's interpretation of "reasonable accommodation" and "undue hardship" relevant to the meaning of these terms in the American with Disabilities Act (ADA)? Based in part on the ADA's definition of "undue hardship" and legislative history, the EEOC has taken the position that the *Hardison* standard does not apply in the ADA context; "[t]o demonstrate undue hardship pursuant to the ADA * * * , an employer must show substantially more difficulty or expense than would be needed to satisfy the 'de minimis' Title VII standard of undue hardship." 29 C.F.R. § 1630.15(d).

6. *Discrimination Against the Non-Religious?* Title VII's prohibitions of discrimination are generally symmetrical, applying to discrimination in favor of, as well as against, any particular protected group. But see General Dynamics Land Systems, Inc. v. Cline, 540 U.S. 581 (2004) (ADEA does not prohibit favoring older over younger workers). Does this symmetry also apply to the prohibition against religious discrimination? Does Title VII proscribe discrimination against an employee for rejecting a favored religious faith? For rejecting religion altogether? See, e.g., Shapolia v. Los Alamos Nat'l Lab., 992 F.2d 1033, 1038 (10th Cir.1993) (plaintiff stated cause of action by claiming he was terminated for not being a Mormon like his supervisors). Does protection of the atheist from discrimination under Title VII require the accommodation of his rejection of religious practices? See, e.g., Young v. Southwestern Savings & Loan Association, 509 F.2d 140 (5th Cir.1975) (atheist cannot be required by secular employer to participate in prayer activities).

7.   *Do Employers Have to Tolerate Religious Proselytizing by Employees?*
Does Title VII require that employers tolerate the efforts of employees to press
their religious views on fellow workers and customers? Non-disruptive
assertion of religious beliefs around the workplace may have to be tolerated,
but employers do not have to allow employees' religious activity that adversely
affects working relationships or productivity. See, e.g., Peterson v. Hewlett-
Packard Co., 358 F.3d 599 (9th Cir. 2004) (employer could terminate employee
for refusing to remove prominent posting in his work cubicle of Biblical
passages condemning homosexuality in violation of employer's anti-
harassment policy); Knight v. State of Connecticut Dept. Of Public Health, 275
F.3d 156 (2d Cir.2001) (public health professionals may be barred from
evangelizing while delivering services to clients); Anderson v. U.S.F. Logistics
(IMC), Inc., 274 F.3d 470 (7th Cir.2001) (employer can prohibit employee using
"Have a Blessed Day" in communications with customers).

8.   *Religious   Harassment.*   The   basic   prohibition   of   religious
discrimination in Title VII condemns discharge or other adverse action against
an employee because of that employee's religion. Conditioning an employee's
job on the employee's willingness to suppress his religious identity indeed
would seem analogous to "quid pro quo" sexual harassment violative of Title
VII. See, e.g. Venters v. City of Delphi, 123 F.3d 956, 975–76 (7th Cir.1997).
See also Kent Greenawalt, Title VII and Religious Liberty, 33 Loy. Univ. Ch.
L.J. 1 (2001). Furthermore, an employer's acceptance of religiously bigoted
remarks by its workforce could constitute a hostile work environment.

9.   *"Affinity Groups."* In order to improve morale and productivity, a
large automobile manufacturer uses company resources to support "affinity
groups" among its employees. These groups are to be based on the status
characteristics of employees, and the company has supported disability and
gay and lesbian as well as various ethnically defined groups such as African-
Americans, Hispanics, and Chinese-Americans. Company guidelines prohibit
affinity groups being based on interests, such as theatre or golf, however, and
the guidelines also prohibit any group being based on religious affiliation or
interest. Does the company violate Title VII by refusing the request of
employees to establish a non-denominational "Christian affinity group"? See
Moranski v. General Motors Corp., 433 F.3d 537 (7th Cir. 2005) (treating all
religious positions alike did not constitute actionable discrimination).

EEOC v. ABERCROMBIE & FITCH STORES, INC.

Supreme Court of the United States, 2015.
575 U.S. ___, 135 S. Ct. 2028, 192 L.Ed.2d 35.

JUSTICE SCALIA delivered the opinion of the Court.

* * * We summarize the facts in the light most favorable to the Equal
Employment Opportunity Commission (EEOC), against whom the Tenth
Circuit granted summary judgment. Respondent Abercrombie & Fitch
Stores, Inc., operates several lines of clothing stores, each with its own
"style." Consistent with the image Abercrombie seeks to project for each

store, the company imposes a Look Policy that governs its employees' dress. The Look Policy prohibits "caps"—a term the Policy does not define—as too informal for Abercrombie's desired image.

Samantha Elauf is a practicing Muslim who, consistent with her understanding of her religion's requirements, wears a headscarf. She applied for a position in an Abercrombie store, and was interviewed by Heather Cooke, the store's assistant manager. Using Abercrombie's ordinary system for evaluating applicants, Cooke gave Elauf a rating that qualified her to be hired; Cooke was concerned, however, that Elauf's headscarf would conflict with the store's Look Policy.

Cooke sought the store manager's guidance to clarify whether the headscarf was a forbidden "cap." When this yielded no answer, Cooke turned to Randall Johnson, the district manager. Cooke informed Johnson that she believed Elauf wore her headscarf because of her faith. Johnson told Cooke that Elauf's headscarf would violate the Look Policy, as would all other headwear, religious or otherwise, and directed Cooke not to hire Elauf.

The EEOC sued Abercrombie on Elauf's behalf, claiming that its refusal to hire Elauf violated Title VII. The District Court granted the EEOC summary judgment on the issue of liability, 798 F.Supp.2d 1272 (N.D.Okla.2011), held a trial on damages, and awarded $20,000. The Tenth Circuit reversed and awarded Abercrombie summary judgment. 731 F.3d 1106 (2013). It concluded that ordinarily an employer cannot be liable under Title VII for failing to accommodate a religious practice until the applicant (or employee) provides the employer with actual knowledge of his need for an accommodation. * * *

Abercrombie's primary argument is that an applicant cannot show disparate treatment without first showing that an employer has "actual knowledge" of the applicant's need for an accommodation. We disagree. Instead, an applicant need only show that his need for an accommodation was a motivating factor in the employer's decision.

The disparate-treatment provision forbids employers to: (1) "fail . . . to hire" an applicant (2) "because of" (3) "such individual's . . . religion" (which includes his religious practice). Here, of course, Abercrombie (1) failed to hire Elauf. The parties concede that (if Elauf sincerely believes that her religion so requires) Elauf's wearing of a headscarf is (3) a "religious practice." All that remains is whether she was not hired (2) "because of" her religious practice.

The term "because of" appears frequently in antidiscrimination laws. It typically imports, at a minimum, the traditional standard of but-for causation. *University of Tex. Southwestern Medical Center v. Nassar*, 570 U.S. ___, 133 S.Ct. 2517, 186 L.Ed.2d 503 (2013). Title VII relaxes this standard, however, to prohibit even making a protected characteristic a "motivating factor" in an employment decision. 42 U.S.C. § 2000e–2(m). "Because of" in § 2000e–2(a)(1) links the forbidden consideration to each of the verbs preceding it; an individual's actual religious practice may not be a motivating factor in failing to hire, in refusing to hire, and so on.

It is significant that § 2000e–2(a)(1) does not impose a knowledge requirement. As Abercrombie acknowledges, some antidiscrimination statutes do. For example, the Americans with Disabilities Act of 1990 defines discrimination to include an employer's failure to make "reasonable accommodations to the *known* physical or mental limitations" of an applicant. § 12112(b)(5)(A) (emphasis added). Title VII contains no such limitation.

Instead, the intentional discrimination provision prohibits certain *motives*, regardless of the state of the actor's knowledge. Motive and knowledge are separate concepts. An employer who has actual knowledge of the need for an accommodation does not violate Title VII by refusing to hire an applicant if avoiding that accommodation is not his *motive*. Conversely, an employer who acts with the motive of avoiding accommodation may violate Title VII even if he has no more than an unsubstantiated suspicion that accommodation would be needed.

Thus, the rule for disparate-treatment claims based on a failure to accommodate a religious practice is straightforward: An employer may not make an applicant's religious practice, confirmed or otherwise, a factor in employment decisions. For example, suppose that an employer thinks (though he does not know for certain) that a job applicant may be an orthodox Jew who will observe the Sabbath, and thus be unable to work on Saturdays. If the applicant actually requires an accommodation of that religious practice, and the employer's desire to avoid the prospective accommodation is a motivating factor in his decision, the employer violates Title VII. * * *

Abercrombie argues * * * that a claim based on a failure to accommodate an applicant's religious practice must be raised as a disparate-impact claim, not a disparate-treatment claim. We think not. That might have been true if Congress had limited the meaning of "religion" in Title VII to religious *belief*—so that discriminating against a particular religious *practice* would not be disparate treatment though it might have disparate impact. In fact, however, Congress defined "religion," for Title VII's purposes, as "includ[ing] all aspects of religious observance and practice, as well as belief." 42 U.S.C. § 2000e(j). Thus, religious practice is one of the protected characteristics that cannot be accorded disparate treatment and must be accommodated.

Nor does the statute limit disparate-treatment claims to only those employer policies that treat religious practices less favorably than similar secular practices. Abercrombie's argument that a neutral policy cannot constitute "intentional discrimination" may make sense in other contexts.

But Title VII does not demand mere neutrality with regard to religious practices—that they be treated no worse than other practices. Rather, it gives them favored treatment, affirmatively obligating employers not "to fail or refuse to hire or discharge any individual . . . because of such individual's" "religious observance and practice." An employer is surely entitled to have, for example, a no-headwear policy as an ordinary matter. But when an applicant requires an accommodation as an "aspec[t] of religious . . . practice," it is no response that the subsequent "fail[ure] . . . to hire" was due to an otherwise-neutral policy. Title VII requires otherwise-neutral policies to give way to the need for an accommodation.

JUSTICE ALITO, concurring in the judgment. * * *

The opinion of the Court states that "§ 2000e–2(a)(1) does not impose a knowledge requirement," *ante*, at 2032, but then reserves decision on the question whether it is a condition of liability that the employer know or suspect that the practice he refuses to accommodate is a religious practice, but in my view, the answer to this question, which may arise on remand, is obvious. I would hold that an employer cannot be held liable for taking an adverse action because of an employee's religious practice unless the employer knows that the employee engages in the practice for a religious reason. If § 2000e–2(a)(1) really "does not impose a knowledge requirement," it would be irrelevant in this case whether Abercrombie had any inkling that Elauf is a Muslim or that she wore the headscarf for a religious reason. That would be very strange. * * *

[T]he statutory provisions . . . prohibit intentional discrimination, which is blameworthy conduct, but if there is no knowledge requirement, an employer could be held liable without fault. The prohibition of discrimination because of religious practices is meant to force employers to consider whether those practices can be accommodated without undue hardship. See § 2000e(j). But the "no-knowledge" interpretation would deprive employers of that opportunity. For these reasons, an employer cannot be liable for taking adverse action because of a religious practice if the employer does not know that the practice is religious.

A plaintiff need not show, however, that the employer took the adverse action because of the religious nature of the practice. Suppose, for example, that an employer rejected all applicants who refuse to work on Saturday, whether for religious or nonreligious reasons. Applicants whose refusal to work on Saturday was known by the employer to be based on religion will have been rejected because of a religious practice.

This conclusion follows from the reasonable accommodation requirement imposed by § 2000e(j). If neutral work rules (*e.g.,* every employee must work on Saturday, no employee may wear any head covering) precluded liability, there would be no need to provide that defense, which allows an employer to escape liability for refusing to make an exception to a neutral work rule if doing so would impose an undue hardship. * * *

JUSTICE THOMAS, concurring in part and dissenting in part. * * *

I would hold that Abercrombie's conduct did not constitute "intentional discrimination." Abercrombie refused to create an exception to its neutral Look Policy for Samantha Elauf's religious practice of wearing a headscarf. In doing so, it did not treat religious practices less favorably than similar secular practices, but instead remained neutral with regard to religious practices. To be sure, the *effects* of Abercrombie's neutral Look Policy, absent an accommodation, fall more harshly on those who wear headscarves as an aspect of their faith. But that is a classic case of an alleged disparate impact. It is not what we have previously understood to be a case of disparate treatment because Elauf received the *same* treatment from Abercrombie as any other applicant who appeared unable to comply with the company's Look Policy. Because I cannot classify Abercrombie's conduct as "intentional discrimination," I would affirm. * * *

NOTES AND QUESTIONS

Abercrombie's Look Policy

  In April 2015, a few months before the ruling in *EEOC v. Abercrombie*, the company abandoned its Look Policy which "banned French-tip manicures, certain hair-styling products and, among other things, mustaches." The company also rescinded its hiring criteria based on an applicant's "appearance and sense of style." Lindsay Rupp, interviewed in Bloomberg Business, April 23, 2015.

Test Your Understanding of the Material

1. Does the Court in *Abercrombie* hold that an employer can discriminate against an employee because of her religious practice without having any reason to believe that the practice is religion-based? In order to demonstrate motive, must the plaintiff at least demonstrate that the employer had some reason to "suspect" the practice is religion-based? Did Johnson, the decision-maker in *Abercrombie*, have reason to suspect that Elauf wore scarfs for religious reasons?

2. Would Elauf's case have been different had she come to her interview with nose piercings that her unusual religious beliefs dictated, but that contravened an Abercrombie policy on which the rejection of her application was based?

3. Is Justice Thomas correct that Abercrombie's Look Policy was neutral in intent toward religion-based practices and only disadvantaged Elauf as a Muslim woman because of its disparate impact? Or is Justice Alito correct that Abercrombie's application of its formally neutral rule against a religious

practice was intentionally discriminatory? See Michael C. Harper, Confusion on the Court; Distinguishing Disparate Treatment from Disparate Impact in Young v. UPS and EEOC v. Abercrombie & Fitch, Inc., 96 B.U. L. Rev. 541 (2016).

Related Issues

4.   *Accommodation of Religious Garb and Grooming.* Could Abercrombie successfully argue that making an exception to its Look Policy for Muslim women wearing head coverings would impose an undue hardship on the implementation of its marketing plan? Must an employer like Abercrombie provide some reason, other than the prejudice of customers or coworkers, why allowing a departure from a dress and grooming code for religious reasons would impose more than de minimis costs? Would every variation from an established uniform or conventional grooming be likely to impose such costs? See, e.g., Cloutier v. Costco Wholesale Corp., 390 F.3d 126 (1st Cir. 2004) (employer may require member of "Church of Body Modification" to cover facial piercing to avoid "undue hardship" of losing "control over its public image"); EEOC v. United Parcel Serv., 94 F.3d 314, 320 (7th Cir.1996) (whether UPS policy of placing employees who are not clean shaven in positions without public contact reasonably accommodates religious reasons for not shaving is a question of material fact). Cf. Goldman v. Weinberger, 475 U.S. 503, 106 S.Ct. 1310, 89 L.Ed.2d 478 (1986) (First Amendment does not restrict Air Force's application of general dress code to prohibit observant Jew's wearing of a yarmulke).

Might an employer, such as a public school, justify refusing to allow employees in public positions to assert their religious beliefs through their clothing, while allowing other employees to dress unusually for secular purposes? In United States v. Board of Educ. for Sch. Dist. of Philadelphia, 911 F.2d 882 (3d Cir.1990), the court held that the state's interest in preserving religious neutrality in the public classroom justified a "religious garb" prohibition that barred a teacher from wearing Muslim religious dress. Cf. Webb v. Philadelphia, 562 F.3d 256 (3d Cir. 2009) (city may prohibit police officer from wearing head scarf in order to maintain appearance of neutrality to public).

C. THE CONSTITUTIONAL SETTING

THORNTON V. CALDOR

Supreme Court of the United States, 1985.
472 U.S. 703, 105 S.Ct. 2914, 86 L.Ed.2d 557.

CHIEF JUSTICE BURGER delivered the opinion of the Court.

I

* * * In 1977, following the state legislature's revision of the Sunday-closing laws,[2] respondent opened its Connecticut stores for Sunday business. In order to handle the expanded store hours, respondent required its managerial employees to work every third or fourth Sunday. Thornton, a Presbyterian who observed Sunday as his Sabbath, initially complied with respondent's demand and worked a total of 31 Sundays in 1977 and 1978. In October 1978, Thornton was transferred to a management position in respondent's Torrington store; he continued to work on Sundays during the first part of 1979. In November 1979, however, Thornton informed respondent that he would no longer work on Sundays because he observed that day as his Sabbath; he invoked the protection of Conn.Gen.Stat. § 53–303e(b) (1985), which provides:

> "No person who states that a particular day of the week is observed as his Sabbath may be required by his employer to work on such day. An employee's refusal to work on his Sabbath shall not constitute grounds for his dismissal."

Thornton rejected respondent's offer either to transfer him to a management job in a Massachusetts store that was closed on Sundays, or to transfer him to a nonsupervisory position in the Torrington store at a lower salary.[4] In March 1980, respondent transferred Thornton to a clerical position in the Torrington store; Thornton resigned two days later and filed a grievance with the State Board of Mediation and Arbitration alleging that he was discharged from his manager's position in violation of Conn.Gen.Stat. § 53–303e(b) (1985).

[*Eds.* On review of the Board's decision sustaining Thornton's grievance, the Supreme Court of Connecticut reversed, holding that the statute did not have "a clear secular purpose."]

---

[2]   The state legislature revised the Sunday-closing laws in 1976 after a state court held that the existing laws were unconstitutionally vague. *State v. Anonymous*, 33 Conn.Supp. 55, 364 A.2d 244 (Com.Pl.1976). The legislature modified the laws to permit certain classes of businesses to remain open. Conn.Gen.Stat. § 53–302a (1985). At the same time, a new provision was added, § 53–303e, which prohibited employment of more than six days in any calendar week and guaranteed employees the right not to work on the Sabbath of their religious faith.

[4]   The collective-bargaining agreement in effect for nonsupervisory employees provided that they were not required to work on Sundays if it was "contrary [to the employee's] personal religious convictions."

II

Under the Religion Clauses, government must guard against activity that impinges on religious freedom, and must take pains not to compel people to act in the name of any religion. In setting the appropriate boundaries in Establishment Clause cases, the Court has frequently relied on our holding in *Lemon* [*v. Kurtzman*, 403 U.S. 602, 619 (1971)], for guidance, and we do so here. To pass constitutional muster under *Lemon* a statute must not only have a secular purpose and not foster excessive entanglement of government with religion, its primary effect must not advance or inhibit religion.

The Connecticut statute challenged here guarantees every employee, who "states that a particular day of the week is observed as his Sabbath," the right not to work on his chosen day. Conn.Gen.Stat. § 53–303e(b) (1985). The State has thus decreed that those who observe a Sabbath any day of the week as a matter of religious conviction must be relieved of the duty to work on that day, no matter what burden or inconvenience this imposes on the employer or fellow workers. The statute arms Sabbath observers with an absolute and unqualified right not to work on whatever day they designate as their Sabbath.[8]

In essence, the Connecticut statute imposes on employers and employees an absolute duty to conform their business practices to the particular religious practices of the employee by enforcing observance of the Sabbath the employee unilaterally designates. The State thus commands that Sabbath religious concerns automatically control over all secular interests at the workplace; the statute takes no account of the convenience or interests of the employer or those of other employees who do not observe a Sabbath. The employer and others must adjust their affairs to the command of the State whenever the statute is invoked by an employee.

There is no exception under the statute for special circumstances, such as the Friday Sabbath observer employed in an occupation with a Monday through Friday schedule—a school teacher, for example; the statute provides for no special consideration if a high percentage of an employer's work force asserts rights to the same Sabbath. Moreover, there is no exception when honoring the dictates of Sabbath observers would cause the employer substantial economic burdens or when the employer's compliance would require the imposition of significant burdens on other employees required to work in place of the Sabbath observers.[9] Finally, the statute

---

[8]   The State Board of Mediation and Arbitration construed the statute as providing Thornton with the absolute right not to work on his Sabbath. *Caldor, Inc. v. Thornton*, Conn.Bd.Med. & Arb.No. 7980–A–727 (Oct. 20, 1980) * * * .

[9]   Section 53–303e(b) gives Sabbath observers the valuable right to designate a particular weekly day off—typically a weekend day, widely prized as a day off. Other employees who have strong and legitimate, but non-religious, reasons for wanting a weekend day off have no rights under the statute. For example, those employees who have earned the privilege through seniority

allows for no consideration as to whether the employer has made reasonable accommodation proposals.

This unyielding weighting in favor of Sabbath observers over all other interests contravenes a fundamental principle of the Religion Clauses, so well articulated by Judge Learned Hand:

> "The First Amendment . . . gives no one the right to insist that in pursuit of their own interests others must conform their conduct to his own religious necessities." *Otten v. Baltimore & Ohio R. Co.,* 205 F. 2d 58, 61 (CA2 1953).

As such, the statute goes beyond having an incidental or remote effect of advancing religion. See, *e.g., Roemer v. Maryland Bd. of Public Works,* 426 U. S. 736, 747 (1976); *Board of Education v. Allen,* 392 U. S. 236 (1968). The statute has a primary effect that impermissibly advances a particular religious practice.

JUSTICE O'CONNOR, with whom JUSTICE MARSHALL joins, concurring.

I do not read the Court's opinion as suggesting that the religious accommodation provisions of Title VII of the Civil Rights Act of 1964 are similarly invalid. . . . Like the Connecticut Sabbath law, Title VII attempts to lift a burden on religious practice that is imposed by *private* employers, and hence it is not the sort of accommodation statute specifically contemplated by the Free Exercise Clause. See *Wallace v. Jaffree,* 472 U.S. 38, 83–84, 105 S.Ct. 2479, 2504–2505, 86 L.Ed.2d 29 (1985) (opinion concurring in judgment). The provisions of Title VII must therefore manifest a valid secular purpose and effect to be valid under the Establishment Clause. In my view, a statute outlawing employment discrimination based on race, color, religion, sex, or national origin has the valid secular purpose of assuring employment opportunity to all groups in our pluralistic society. See *Trans World Airlines, Inc. v. Hardison,* 432 U.S. 63, 90, n. 4, 97 S.Ct. 2264, 2280, n. 4, 53 L.Ed.2d 113 (1977) (Marshall, J., dissenting). Since Title VII calls for reasonable rather than absolute accommodation and extends that requirement to all religious beliefs and practices rather than protecting only the Sabbath observance, I believe an objective observer would perceive it as an anti-discrimination law rather than an endorsement of religion or a particular religious practice.

---

to have weekend days off may be forced to surrender this privilege to the Sabbath observer; years of service and payment of "dues" at the workplace simply cannot compete with the Sabbath observer's absolute right under the statute. Similarly, those employees who would like a weekend day off, because that is the only day their spouses are also not working, must take a back seat to the Sabbath observer.

NOTES AND QUESTIONS

Test Your Understanding of the Material

1.   Does the holding in *Caldor* call into question the constitutionality of the religious-accommodation provision of Title VII? Consider footnote 9 in the majority opinion.

2.   Does *Caldor* suggest that Title VII's reasonable-accommodation clause would not pass constitutional muster if it required employers to subordinate the secular interests of some employees in competitive seniority rights to the religious interests of less senior employees?

Related Issues

3.   *Free Exercise Claims for Reasonable Accommodation?* Does the First Amendment's free exercise clause require governments to accommodate religious beliefs and practices? In three cases, the Supreme Court invalidated state unemployment compensation rules that conditioned the availability of benefits upon an applicant's willingness to work under conditions forbidden by his religion. See Sherbert v. Verner, 374 U.S. 398, 83 S.Ct. 1790, 10 L.Ed.2d 965 (1963); Thomas v. Review Bd. of Indiana Employment Sec. Div., 450 U.S. 707, 101 S.Ct. 1425, 67 L.Ed.2d 624 (1981); Hobbie v. Unemployment Appeals Comm'n of Florida, 480 U.S. 136, 107 S.Ct. 1046, 94 L.Ed.2d 190 (1987). In *Sherbert* and its progeny the Court required the state to justify a substantial burden on a religious practice with some "compelling governmental interest." It might be argued that these cases limit the reach of *Caldor* by not only permitting, but also requiring at least public employers to give some degree of special treatment to religiously motivated requests for exemption from general work rules, and perhaps also requiring state regulation to account for the special needs of the religious.

However, in Employment Div., Oregon Dept. of Human Resources v. Smith, 494 U.S. 872, 110 S.Ct. 1595, 108 L.Ed.2d 876 (1990), the Court held that the *Sherbert* line of cases stand only "for the proposition that where the State has in place a system of individual exemptions, it may not refuse to extend that system to cases of 'religious hardship' without compelling reason." 494 U.S. at 884. In other situations, "generally applicable, religion-neutral laws that have the effect of burdening a particular religious practice need not be justified by a compelling governmental interest." Id. at 886 n.3.

4.   *Religious Freedom Restoration Act of 1993 (RFRA).* Essentially overturning the *Smith* decision, Congress passed the Religious Freedom Restoration Act of 1993, 107 Stat. 1488, 42 U.S.C. § 2000bb to bb–4 (1994). RFRA announced that "Government shall not substantially burden a person's exercise of religion even if the burden results from a rule of general applicability, except * * * in furtherance of a compelling governmental interest * * * [and where it uses] the least restrictive means of furthering that compelling governmental interest."

The Court applied RFRA in Burwell v. Hobby Lobby Stores, Inc., 134 S. Ct. 2751 (2014), to prevent the Department of Health and Human Services

(HHS) from requiring for-profit closed corporations controlled by owners with religion-based objections to include contraception as a preventative benefit in insurance plans offered to employees in satisfaction of their Affordable Care Act obligations. The Court held that the contraception mandate substantially burdened the exercise of religion, and the HHS could not satisfy RFRA's less-restrictive-alternative test because HHS had itself provided to religious nonprofit organizations a less restrictive accommodation that does not impose costs on employees or insurers. See also Zubik v. Burwell, 578 U.S. ___ (2016) (declining to rule on whether requiring employers to file a notice of religious objections to the ACA's contraceptive services violates the RFRA but instructing lower courts to explore ways to address the Government's interest in providing "seamless" coverage to employees of those services without directly involving the religious employers).

D. DISCRIMINATION BY RELIGIOUS INSTITUTIONS

Section 702(a) of Title VII provides that the statute "shall not apply * * * to a religious corporation, association, educational institution, or society with respect to the employment of individuals of a particular religion to perform work connected with the carrying on by such corporation, association, educational institution, or society of its activities." Prior to 1972, § 702 exempted only the religious activities of such employers, but the provision was then amended to reach all activities of religious organizations, to "take the political hands of Caesar off of the institutions of God, where they have no place to be." 118 Cong.Rec. 4503 (1972) (remarks of Sen. Ervin). In a 1987 ruling, the Supreme Court held that application of the amended exemption to the nonprofit activities of such organizations—in that case, a public gymnasium operated by the Church of Jesus Christ of the Latter Day Saints—does not contravene the establishment clause. Corporation of Presiding Bishop of Church of Jesus Christ of Latter-Day Saints v. Amos, 483 U.S. 327, 107 S.Ct. 2862, 97 L.Ed.2d 273 (1987).

Justice White's majority opinion in *Amos* finds acceptable under the establishment clause Congress's purpose in expanding the exemption: minimizing governmental "interfer[ence] with the decision-making process in religions." Justice White acknowledged that an employee's freedom of choice in religious matters could be affected by decisions of employers insulated from challenge by the expanded § 702 exemption, but stressed that this effect would derive from choices forced on employees by religious employers, rather than directly by the government. The Court distinguished *Caldor* as a case where "Connecticut had given the force of law to the employee's designation of a Sabbath day and required accommodation by the employer regardless of the burden which that constituted for the employer or other employees." 483 U.S. at 337 n.15.

Amos leaves open whether § 702's categorical exemption can be constitutionally applied to commercial, for-profit activities of religious organizations. The lower courts generally have avoided ruling on the constitutionality of applying a categorical exemption to for-profit activities by rejecting a commercial enterprise's claim to be "religious" for purposes of § 702(a). For example, in EEOC v. Townley Engineering & Mfg. Co., 859 F.2d 610 (9th Cir.1988), the court held that a mining equipment company that was founded as a Christian, "faith-oriented" business, included bible tracts in every piece of outgoing mail, and conducted devotional services in the workplace, had to permit an atheist employee to excuse himself from mandatory prayer services. The court rejected Townley's contention that it was a "religious employer" on the ground that its business was "primarily secular." Judge Noonan dissented on free exercise grounds.

Even if construed not to exempt for-profit commercial activities, does § 702(a), as applied in *Amos*, provide too great an insulation of religious-based discrimination? Does § 702(a), for instance, apply to the activities of charitable organizations dedicated to a religious mission, even if not owned or affiliated with any formal religious entity? See, e.g., Spencer v. World Vision, Inc. 633 F.3d 723 (9th Cir. 2011) (exemption applies if entity "is organized for a religious purpose, is engaged primarily in carrying out that religious purpose, holds itself out to the public as an entity for carrying out that religious purpose, and does not engage primarily or substantially in the exchange of goods or services for money beyond nominal amounts"). Does § 702(a) allow a religious organization not only to discriminate on the basis of religion in its hiring policies, but also to subject employees to religious-based harassment and retaliation? See, e.g., Kennedy v. St. Joseph's Ministries, Inc., 657 F.3d 189 (4th Cir. 2011) (Congress exempted religious organizations from all of Title VII's religious discrimination prohibitions).

Does § 702(a) also mean that any research university owned and operated under religious auspices could refuse to hire members of other religious faiths to teach secular subjects or to perform other nonsectarian duties? Might many such universities, like most commercial enterprises, be outside the protection of § 702(a) because they are not primarily "religious"? Cf. EEOC v. Kamehameha Schools/Bishop Estate, 990 F.2d 458, 460 (9th Cir.1993) (applying *Townley* to find particular private primary and secondary schools to be primarily secular rather than religious). Might the provision of significant government grants to research universities classified as "religious" for purposes of the § 702(a) exemption be challenged under the establishment clause?

Educational institutions can also assert another exemption from Title VII's prohibition of religious discrimination. Section 703(e)(2) provides: "[I]t shall not be an unlawful employment practice for a school, college, university, or other educational institution or institution of learning to hire and employ employees of a particular religion" if the discriminating employer "is, in whole or in substantial part, owned, supported, controlled, or managed by a particular religion" or religious institution, or if the curriculum "is directed toward the propagation of a particular religion." This exemption was included in Title VII as originally enacted and was not amended when the § 702(a) exemption was enlarged. Are some educational institutions, whose instruction and activities are not primarily religious, insulated by § 703(e)(2), perhaps because they receive substantial support from some religious denomination? Cf. Killinger v. Samford University, 113 F.3d 196 (11th Cir.1997) (university exempt under § 702(a) also exempt under § 703(e)(2) because it received substantial support from Baptist church). In light of *Amos* and *Caldor*, is § 703(e)(2) constitutional?

Even if an institution with a religious affiliation is not within the protective ambit of § 702(a) or § 703(e)(2), it may still attempt to invoke Title VII's bona fide occupational qualification (BFOQ) defense to religion-based discrimination. For instance, in Pime v. Loyola University of Chicago, 803 F.2d 351 (7th Cir. 1986), the court upheld the right of a university with a Jesuit tradition that was not a religious employer for § 702(a) purposes to reserve seven out of 31 positions in its philosophy department for those with Jesuit training. The court stated that "[i]t appears to be significant to the educational tradition and character of the institution that students be assured a degree of contact with teachers who have received the training and accepted the obligations which are essential to membership in the Society of Jesus." Id. at 353. Is this approach consistent with the treatment of the BFOQ defense in cases like *Johnson Controls*, supra page 347, and *Criswell*, supra page 454? Was Jesuit training "reasonably necessary" to advance the "central mission" or "essence" of the university's philosophy department?

The § 702(a) exemption does not authorize race, color, national origin or sex discrimination by religious institutions. Similarly, courts have held that the ADEA does not contain an implied exemption for religious institutions. See, e.g., DeMarco v. Holy Cross High School, 4 F.3d 166 (2d Cir.1993). Does this mean that the employment discrimination statutes can be invoked to control a religious denomination's choice of its religious leaders? If so, does this comport with the free exercise and establishment clauses?

HOSANNA-TABOR EVANGELICAL LUTHERAN CHURCH & SCHOOL v. EEOC

Supreme Court of the United States, 2012.
565 U.S. ___, 132 S.Ct. 694, 181 L.Ed.2d 650.

CHIEF JUSTICE ROBERTS delivered the opinion of the Court.

I

* * *

Petitioner Hosanna-Tabor Evangelical Lutheran Church and School is a member congregation of the Lutheran Church—Missouri Synod, the second largest Lutheran denomination in America. Hosanna-Tabor operated a small school in Redford, Michigan, offering a "Christ-centered education" to students in kindergarten through eighth grade.

The Synod classifies teachers into two categories: "called" and "lay." "Called" teachers are regarded as having been called to their vocation by God through a congregation. To be eligible to receive a call from a congregation, a teacher must satisfy certain academic requirements. One way of doing so is by completing a "colloquy" program at a Lutheran college or university. The program requires candidates to take eight courses of theological study, obtain the endorsement of their local Synod district, and pass an oral examination by a faculty committee. A teacher who meets these requirements may be called by a congregation. Once called, a teacher receives the formal title "Minister of Religion, Commissioned." A commissioned minister serves for an open-ended term; at Hosanna-Tabor, a call could be rescinded only for cause and by a supermajority vote of the congregation.

"Lay" or "contract" teachers, by contrast, are not required to be trained by the Synod or even to be Lutheran. At Hosanna-Tabor, they were appointed by the school board, without a vote of the congregation, to one-year renewable terms. Although teachers at the school generally performed the same duties regardless of whether they were lay or called, lay teachers were hired only when called teachers were unavailable.

Respondent Cheryl Perich was first employed by Hosanna-Tabor as a lay teacher in 1999. After Perich completed her colloquy later that school year, Hosanna-Tabor asked her to become a called teacher. Perich accepted the call and received a "diploma of vocation" designating her a commissioned minister.

Perich taught kindergarten during her first four years at Hosanna-Tabor and fourth grade during the 2003–2004 school year. She taught math, language arts, social studies, science, gym, art, and music. She also taught a religion class four days a week, led the students in prayer and devotional exercises each day, and attended a weekly school-wide chapel service. Perich led the chapel service herself about twice a year.

Perich became ill in June 2004 with what was eventually diagnosed as narcolepsy. Symptoms included sudden and deep sleeps from which she could not be roused. Because of her illness, Perich began the 2004–2005 school year on disability leave. * * *

On January 30, [2005,] Hosanna-Tabor held a meeting of its congregation at which school administrators stated that Perich was unlikely to be physically capable of returning to work that school year or the next. The congregation voted to offer Perich a "peaceful release" from her call, whereby the congregation would pay a portion of her health insurance premiums in exchange for her resignation as a called teacher. Perich refused to resign and produced a note from her doctor stating that she would be able to return to work on February 22. The school board urged Perich to reconsider, informing her that the school no longer had a position for her, but Perich stood by her decision not to resign.

On the morning of February 22—the first day she was medically cleared to return to work—Perich presented herself at the school. Hoeft asked her to leave but she would not do so until she obtained written documentation that she had reported to work. Later that afternoon, Hoeft called Perich at home and told her that she would likely be fired. Perich responded that she had spoken with an attorney and intended to assert her legal rights.

Following a school board meeting that evening, board chairman Scott Salo sent Perich a letter stating that Hosanna-Tabor was reviewing the process for rescinding her call in light of her "regrettable" actions. Salo subsequently followed up with a letter advising Perich that the congregation would consider whether to rescind her call at its next meeting. As grounds for termination, the letter cited Perich's "insubordination and disruptive behavior" on February 22, as well as the damage she had done to her "working relationship" with the school by "threatening to take legal action." The congregation voted to rescind Perich's call on April 10, and Hosanna-Tabor sent her a letter of termination the next day.

Perich filed a charge with the Equal Employment Opportunity Commission, alleging that her employment had been terminated in violation of the Americans with Disabilities Act, 104 Stat. 327, 42 U. S. C. § 12101 *et seq.* (1990). The ADA prohibits an employer from discriminating against a qualified individual on the basis of disability. § 12112(a). It also prohibits an employer from retaliating "against any individual because such individual has opposed any act or practice made unlawful by [the ADA] or because such individual made a charge, testified, assisted, or participated in any manner in an investigation, proceeding, or hearing under [the ADA]." § 12203(a).

II

* * *

Until today, we have not had occasion to consider whether th[e] freedom of a religious organization to select its ministers is implicated by a suit alleging discrimination in employment. The Courts of Appeals, in contrast, have had extensive experience with this issue. Since the passage of Title VII of the Civil Rights Act of 1964, 42 U. S. C. § 2000e et seq., and other employment discrimination laws, the Courts of Appeals have uniformly recognized the existence of a "ministerial exception," grounded in the First Amendment, that precludes application of such legislation to claims concerning the employment relationship between a religious institution and its ministers.

We agree that there is such a ministerial exception. The members of a religious group put their faith in the hands of their ministers. Requiring a church to accept or retain an unwanted minister, or punishing a church for failing to do so, intrudes upon more than a mere employment decision. Such action interferes with the internal governance of the church, depriving the church of control over the selection of those who will personify its beliefs. By imposing an unwanted minister, the state infringes the Free Exercise Clause, which protects a religious group's right to shape its own faith and mission through its appointments. According the state the power to determine which individuals will minister to the faithful also violates the Establishment Clause, which prohibits government involvement in such ecclesiastical decisions.

The EEOC and Perich acknowledge that employment discrimination laws would be unconstitutional as applied to religious groups in certain circumstances. They grant, for example, that it would violate the First Amendment for courts to apply such laws to compel the ordination of women by the Catholic Church or by an Orthodox Jewish seminary. According to the EEOC and Perich, religious organizations could successfully defend against employment discrimination claims in those circumstances by invoking the constitutional right to freedom of association—a right "implicit" in the First Amendment. *Roberts v. United States Jaycees*, 468 U. S. 609, 622 (1984). The EEOC and Perich thus see no need—and no basis—for a special rule for ministers grounded in the Religion Clauses themselves.

We find this position untenable. The right to freedom of association is a right enjoyed by religious and secular groups alike. It follows under the EEOC's and Perich's view that the First Amendment analysis should be the same, whether the association in question is the Lutheran Church, a labor union, or a social club. That result is hard to square with the text of the First Amendment itself, which gives special solicitude to the rights of religious organizations. We cannot accept the remarkable view that the

Religion Clauses have nothing to say about a religious organization's freedom to select its own ministers.

The EEOC and Perich also contend that our decision in *Employment Div., Dept. of Human Resources of Ore. v. Smith*, 494 U. S. 872 (1990), precludes recognition of a ministerial exception. In *Smith*, two members of the Native American Church were denied state unemployment benefits after it was determined that they had been fired from their jobs for ingesting peyote, a crime under Oregon law. We held that this did not violate the Free Exercise Clause, even though the peyote had been ingested for sacramental purposes, because the "right of free exercise does not relieve an individual of the obligation to comply with a valid and neutral law of general applicability on the ground that the law proscribes (or prescribes) conduct that his religion prescribes (or proscribes)." *Id.*, at 879 (internal quotation marks omitted).

It is true that the ADA's prohibition on retaliation, like Oregon's prohibition on peyote use, is a valid and neutral law of general applicability. But a church's selection of its ministers is unlike an individual's ingestion of peyote. *Smith* involved government regulation of only outward physical acts. The present case, in contrast, concerns government interference with an internal church decision that affects the faith and mission of the church itself. See *id.*, at 877 (distinguishing the government's regulation of "physical acts" from its "lend[ing] its power to one or the other side in controversies over religious authority or dogma"). The contention that *Smith* forecloses recognition of a ministerial exception rooted in the Religion Clauses has no merit.

III

* * * We are reluctant [ ] to adopt a rigid formula for deciding when an employee qualifies as a minister. It is enough for us to conclude, in this our first case involving the ministerial exception, that the exception covers Perich, given all the circumstances of her employment.

To begin with, Hosanna-Tabor held Perich out as a minister, with a role distinct from that of most of its members. When Hosanna-Tabor extended her a call, it issued her a "diploma of vocation" according her the title "Minister of Religion, Commissioned." She was tasked with performing that office "according to the Word of God and the confessional standards of the Evangelical Lutheran Church as drawn from the Sacred Scriptures." * * *

Perich's title as a minister reflected a significant degree of religious training followed by a formal process of commissioning. To be eligible to become a commissioned minister, Perich had to complete eight college-level courses in subjects including biblical interpretation, church doctrine, and the ministry of the Lutheran teacher. She also had to obtain the endorsement of her local Synod district by submitting a petition that contained her academic transcripts, letters of recommendation, personal statement, and written answers to various ministry-related questions. Finally, she had to pass an oral examination by a faculty committee at a Lutheran college. It took Perich six years to fulfill these requirements. And when she eventually did, she was commissioned as a minister only upon election by the congregation, which recognized God's call to her to teach. At that point, her call could be rescinded only upon a supermajority vote of the congregation—a protection designed to allow her to "preach the Word of God boldly."

Perich held herself out as a minister of the Church by accepting the formal call to religious service, according to its terms. She did so in other ways as well. For example, she claimed a special housing allowance on her taxes that was available only to employees earning their compensation " 'in the exercise of the ministry.' " * * * In a form she submitted to the Synod following her termination, Perich again indicated that she regarded herself as a minister at Hosanna-Tabor, stating: "I feel that God is leading me to serve in the teaching ministry. . . . I am anxious to be in the teaching ministry again soon."

Perich's job duties reflected a role in conveying the Church's message and carrying out its mission. Hosanna-Tabor expressly charged her with "lead[ing] others toward Christian maturity" and "teach[ing] faithfully the Word of God, the Sacred Scriptures, in its truth and purity and as set forth in all the symbolical books of the Evangelical Lutheran Church." In fulfilling these responsibilities, Perich taught her students religion four days a week, and led them in prayer three times a day. Once a week, she took her students to a school-wide chapel service, and—about twice a year—she took her turn leading it, choosing the liturgy, selecting the hymns, and delivering a short message based on verses from the Bible. During her last year of teaching, Perich also led her fourth graders in a brief devotional exercise each morning. As a source of religious instruction, Perich performed an important role in transmitting the Lutheran faith to the next generation.

In light of these considerations—the formal title given Perich by the Church, the substance reflected in that title, her own use of that title, and the important religious functions she performed for the Church—we conclude that Perich was a minister covered by the ministerial exception. * * *

[T]he Sixth Circuit placed too much emphasis on Perich's performance of secular duties. It is true that her religious duties consumed only 45 minutes of each work-day, and that the rest of her day was devoted to teaching secular subjects. * * *

* * * The issue before us, however, is not one that can be resolved by a stopwatch. The amount of time an employee spends on particular activities is relevant in assessing that employee's status, but that factor cannot be

considered in isolation, without regard to the nature of the religious functions performed and the other considerations discussed above.

* * *

Perich no longer seeks reinstatement, having abandoned that relief before this Court. But that is immaterial. Perich continues to seek frontpay in lieu of reinstatement, backpay, compensatory and punitive damages, and attorney's fees. An award of such relief would operate as a penalty on the Church for terminating an unwanted minister, and would be no less prohibited by the First Amendment than an order overturning the termination. * * * The EEOC and Perich suggest that Hosanna-Tabor's asserted religious reason for firing Perich—that she violated the Synod's commitment to internal dispute resolution—was pretextual. That suggestion misses the point of the ministerial exception. The purpose of the exception is not to safeguard a church's decision to fire a minister only when it is made for a religious reason. The exception instead ensures that the authority to select and control who will minister to the faithful—a matter "strictly ecclesiastical," *Kedroff* [*v. Saint Nicholas Cathedral*], 344 U.S. [94,], 119 [(1952)]—is the church's alone.

IV

The EEOC and Perich foresee a parade of horribles that will follow our recognition of a ministerial exception to employment discrimination suits. According to the EEOC and Perich, such an exception could protect religious organizations from liability for retaliating against employees for reporting criminal misconduct or for testifying before a grand jury or in a criminal trial. What is more, the EEOC contends, the logic of the exception would confer on religious employers "unfettered discretion" to violate employment laws by, for example, hiring children or aliens not authorized to work in the United States.

Hosanna-Tabor responds that the ministerial exception would not in any way bar criminal prosecutions for interfering with law enforcement investigations or other proceedings. Nor, according to the Church, would the exception bar government enforcement of general laws restricting eligibility for employment, because the exception applies only to suits by or on behalf of ministers themselves. Hosanna-Tabor also notes that the ministerial exception has been around in the lower courts for 40 years, see *McClure v. Salvation Army*, 460 F.2d 553, 558 (CA5 1972), and has not given rise to the dire consequences predicted by the EEOC and Perich.

The case before us is an employment discrimination suit brought on behalf of a minister, challenging her church's decision to fire her. Today we hold only that the ministerial exception bars such a suit. We express no view on whether the exception bars other types of suits, including actions by employees alleging breach of contract or tortious conduct by their religious employers. There will be time enough to address the applicability of the exception to other circumstances if and when they arise.

NOTES AND QUESTIONS

Test Your Understanding of the Material

1. After *Hosanna-Tabor*, is it sufficient that a religious employer confer in good faith a "ministerial" label on an employee? Is there a minimum substantive content for ministerial status?

2. Did the Court persuasively distinguish its earlier *Smith* decision (superseded as a matter of statutory law by RFRA) allowing Oregon to deny employment compensation to individuals who were fired for ingesting peyote for religious reasons? If the state can apply a neutral law to penalize a religious practice, why can it not apply a neutral law to penalize a religious institution's personnel decision that may have no religious basis? Does the Court's distinction of *Smith* show a preference for religions whose practices are administered through organized institutions rather than directly experienced by the faithful?

3. The EEOC argued that courts should be able to determine whether the assertion of a religious justification for a discriminatory act was pretextual and that the real reason was a proscribed discriminatory or retaliatory motivation. Would this approach provide adequate protection to religious practices, such as the Catholic Church's hiring of only male priests?

Related Issues

4. *Harassment Cases?* Does the "ministerial exception" extend to hostile work-environment harassment cases that do not involve allegations of discriminatory terminations or job assignments? Does judicial review of a religious institution's response to such harassment affect the institution's control of its "faith and mission" by penalizing it for not exercising more centralized control of its ministerial staff? But see, e.g., Bollard v. California Province of the Soc'y of Jesus, 196 F.3d 940 (9th Cir. 1999) (ministerial exception does not apply where religious organization does not attempt to justify the harassment on the basis of religious doctrine).

5. *Relevance to Tort, Criminal, and Contract Law?* The Court declines to express a "view on whether the exception bars other types of suits," and also notes that Hosanna-Tabor stated that the exception "would not in any way bar criminal prosecutions for interfering with law enforcement investigations or other proceedings." Is there any basis for distinguishing common law, tort-based protection of ministerial whistle blowers from the statutory protection from retaliation offered by employment discrimination statutes? Does *Hosanna-Tabor* suggest that a priest cannot sue his employer-church for discharging him because he reported to appropriate authorities a fellow priest's sexual harassment of parishioners or subordinate employees?

Can contract-based actions be distinguished from statutory or tort-based actions for purposes of the ministerial exception? Consider a suit by a minister alleging discharge in violation of a term in her contract that guaranteed employment for a defined period absent "cause" for discharge. Could the minister claim that her religious employer voluntarily subjected its personnel decision to external review by entering into the contract? See Kirby v. Lexington Theological Seminary, 426 S.W.3d 597, 617 (Ken. S. Ct. 2014) (ministerial exception applies to race discrimination claim, but not to claim based on voluntary contract); Minker v. Baltimore Annual Conf. of United Methodist Church, 894 F.2d 1354 (D.C. Cir. 1990) (action based on voluntary oral contract may proceed unless "ecclesiastical matters" are implicated); Ira C. Lupu & Robert W. Tuttle, Courts, Clergy and Congregations: Disputes Between Religious Leaders and Their Congregations, 7 Geo. J. L. & Pub. Pol'y 119 (2009) (suggesting the ministerial exception should apply only if the clerical performance is at issue).

PART 3

PROTECTION AGAINST RETALIATION

■ ■ ■

This Part shifts attention from employment regulations framed to prevent unfair treatment of individuals because of an immutable status, to laws intended to protect certain kinds of employee conduct. Chapter 11 reviews legislatively and judicially created rules designed to protect employees' efforts to claim some substantive, government-conferred right, including the right to be free of status discrimination. Chapter 12 considers the emerging common law and statutory protection of the decisions of employees to discharge some duty that they owe, or that they believe they owe, society. Finally, Chapter 13 considers the protection afforded by the First Amendment to public employees' choice of particular forms of expressive activity.

Society may choose to protect particular forms of employee activity based on at least three instrumental justifications. First, society may recognize that the effective enforcement of particular substantive rights may require some protection of employee efforts to assert those rights. If employers can use their power over personnel decisionmaking to penalize such efforts with impunity, the underlying substantive rights may be robbed of all practical significance. Although some employee self-help may be very disruptive and impose substantial costs, the protection of other efforts may require little more justification than the original justifications for the underlying rights.

Second, society may determine that protecting certain employee self-help efforts is an effective way not only to protect rights granted by the state, but also to promote a process for determining terms and conditions of employment that is thought to be preferable to direct government regulation. Such a determination in part underlies the National Labor Relations Act's protection of employee efforts to organize unions and to bargain collectively with their employer. Unions might insure the protection of rights more effectively than can governmental action because they have continuing and internal relationships with employers.

Third, society might wish to protect employee activity because of its contribution to goals that are not related to employee, or employer, interests. The readiest justification for such regulatory protection is simply that employees cannot be expected to bargain for third parties, or for the general society. Employer-employee bargains will not account for the external effects of certain types of employment decisionmaking. If society wants employees to engage in activity that will in some way be costly to employers, but will not directly benefit employees, it must offer employees a guarantee of protection against employer retaliation.

This last instrumental reason for choosing particular activity to protect from retaliation, however, may be the most open-ended. It may warrant protection of a broad range of activity that would impose substantial costs on employers. In this section of the book, as in the previous section, our analysis must include consideration of the costs as well as the benefits of particular forms of regulation.

Our analysis in this Part may also have to consider some issues that were not salient in the previous section. Two should be noted here. First, the common law development of some of the regulations included in this section raises the legal process issue of whether protection of socially valued employee activity is best undertaken by legislatures or by courts. Second, the First Amendment chapter highlights the important issue of whether there are strong justifications for offering different protection to public sector employees than to those in the private sector. Is regulation of the private sector likely to entail higher costs of enforcement and over-enforcement?

CHAPTER 11

RETALIATION FOR ASSERTION OF STATUTORY RIGHTS

■ ■ ■

Introduction

Virtually every federal and most state employment laws contain some form of express antiretaliation provision. See, e.g., FLSA, § 15(a)(3), 29 U.S.C. § 215(a)(3); Occupational Safety and Health Act, § 11(c), 29 U.S.C. § 660(c); the Employee Retirement Security Act of 1974 (ERISA), §§ 502(a), 510, 29 U.S.C. §§ 1132(a), 1140. These provisions, however, come in different stripes. The narrower variant provides protection only for invoking or participating in the formal processes of the statute. Thus, § 704(a) of Title VII prohibits discrimination against an employee or applicant "because he has made a charge, testified, assisted, or participated in any manner in an investigation, proceeding, or hearing under this title." This type of clause is often referred to as a "participation" clause. In addition, a broader form of antiretaliation provision privileges some forms of self-help opposition to unlawful practices. Section 704(a) also contains an "opposition" clause prohibiting discrimination against an employee or applicant "because he has opposed any practice made an unlawful employment practice by this title." Section 510 of ERISA, 29 U.S.C. § 1140, is a third type of antiretaliation provision. Section 510, in addition to protecting the assertion of statutory claims, also reaches a form of status discrimination—that which occurs for the purpose of interfering with employees obtaining contractual benefits regulated by ERISA. See, e.g., Dister v. The Continental Group, Inc., 859 F.2d 1108 (2d Cir.1988) (employee fired on the eve of entitlement to enhanced pension benefits for the retaliatory purpose of preventing the obtainment of such benefits).

A. EXPRESS ANTIRETALIATION PROVISIONS: PARTICIPATION CLAUSE

BURLINGTON NORTHERN V. WHITE

Supreme Court of the United States, 2006.
548 U.S. 53, 126 S.Ct. 2405, 165 L.Ed.2d 345.

JUSTICE BREYER delivered the opinion of the Court.

I

A

This case arises out of actions that supervisors at petitioner Burlington Northern & Santa Fe Railway Company took against respondent Sheila White, the only woman working in the Maintenance of Way department at Burlington's Tennessee Yard. In June 1997, Burlington's roadmaster, Marvin Brown, interviewed White and expressed interest in her previous experience operating forklifts. Burlington hired White as a "track laborer," a job that involves removing and replacing track components, transporting track material, cutting brush, and clearing litter and cargo spillage from the right-of-way. Soon after White arrived on the job, a co-worker who had previously operated the forklift chose to assume other responsibilities. Brown immediately assigned White to operate the forklift. While she also performed some of the other track laborer tasks, operating the forklift was White's primary responsibility.

In September 1997, White complained to Burlington officials that her immediate supervisor, Bill Joiner, had repeatedly told her that women should not be working in the Maintenance of Way department. Joiner, White said, had also made insulting and inappropriate remarks to her in front of her male colleagues. After an internal investigation, Burlington suspended Joiner for 10 days and ordered him to attend a sexual-harassment training session.

On September 26, Brown told White about Joiner's discipline. At the same time, he told White that he was removing her from forklift duty and assigning her to perform only standard track laborer tasks. Brown explained that the reassignment reflected co-worker's complaints that, in fairness, a "more senior man" should have the "less arduous and cleaner job" of forklift operator. 364 F.3d 789, 792 (CA 6 2004).

On October 10, White filed a complaint with the Equal Employment Opportunity Commission (EEOC or Commission). She claimed that the reassignment of her duties amounted to unlawful gender-based discrimination and retaliation for her having earlier complained about Joiner. In early December, White filed a second retaliation charge with the Commission, claiming that Brown had placed her under surveillance and was monitoring her daily activities. That charge was mailed to Brown on December 8.

A few days later, White and her immediate supervisor, Percy Sharkey, disagreed about which truck should transport White from one location to another. The specific facts of the disagreement are in dispute, but the upshot is that Sharkey told Brown later that afternoon that White had been insubordinate. Brown immediately suspended White without pay. White invoked internal grievance procedures. Those procedures led Burlington to conclude that White had *not* been insubordinate. Burlington reinstated White to her position and awarded her backpay for the 37 days she was suspended. White filed an additional retaliation charge with the EEOC based on the suspension.

B

After exhausting administrative remedies, White filed this Title VII action against Burlington in federal court. As relevant here, she claimed that Burlington's actions—(1) changing her job responsibilities, and (2) suspending her for 37 days without pay—amounted to unlawful retaliation in violation of Title VII. § 2000e–3(a). A jury found in White's favor on both of these claims. It awarded her $43,500 in compensatory damages, including $3,250 in medical expenses. The District Court denied Burlington's post-trial motion for judgment as a matter of law. See Fed. Rule Civ. Proc. 50(b).

Initially, a divided Sixth Circuit panel reversed the judgment and found in Burlington's favor on the retaliation claims. The full Court of Appeals vacated the panel's decision, however, and heard the matter en banc. The court then affirmed the District Court's judgment in White's favor on both retaliation claims. While all members of the en banc court voted to uphold the District Court's judgment, they differed as to the proper standard to apply. Compare 364 F.3d at 795–800, with id., at 809 (Clay, J., concurring).

II

Title VII's anti-retaliation provision forbids employer actions that "discriminate against" an employee (or job applicant) because he has "opposed" a practice that Title VII forbids or has "made a charge, testified, assisted, or participated in" a Title VII "investigation, proceeding, or hearing." § 2000e–3(a). No one doubts that the term "discriminate against" refers to distinctions or differences in treatment that injure protected individuals. * * * But different Circuits have come to different conclusions about whether the challenged action has to be employment or workplace related and about how harmful that action must be to constitute retaliation. * * *

A

Petitioner and the Solicitor General both argue that the Sixth Circuit is correct to require a link between the challenged retaliatory action and the terms, conditions, or status of employment. They note that Title VII's substantive anti-discrimination provision protects an individual only from employment-related discrimination. They add that the anti-retaliation provision should be read *in pari materia* with the anti-discrimination provision. And they conclude that the employer actions prohibited by the anti-retaliation provision should similarly be limited to conduct that "affects the employee's compensation, terms, conditions, or privileges of employment."

We cannot agree. The language of the substantive provision differs from that of the anti-retaliation provision in important ways. Section 703(a) sets forth Title VII's core anti-discrimination provision in the following terms:

> "It shall be an unlawful employment practice for an employer—
>
> "(1) *to fail or refuse to hire or to discharge* any individual, or otherwise to discriminate against any individual *with respect to his compensation, terms, conditions, or privileges of employment*, because of such individual's race, color, religion, sex, or national origin; or
>
> "(2) to limit, segregate, or classify his employees or applicants for employment in any way *which would deprive or tend to deprive any individual of employment opportunities or otherwise adversely affect his status as an employee*, because of such individual's race, color, religion, sex, or national origin." § 2000e–2(a) (emphasis added).

Section 704(a) sets forth Title VII's anti-retaliation provision in the following terms: "It shall be an unlawful employment practice for an employer *to discriminate against* any of his employees or applicants for employment . . . because he has opposed any practice made an unlawful employment practice by this subchapter, or because he has made a charge, testified, assisted, or participated in any manner in an investigation, proceeding, or hearing under this subchapter." § 2000e–3(a) (emphasis added).

The underscored words in the substantive provision—"hire," "discharge," "compensation, terms, conditions, or privileges of employment," "employment opportunities," and "status as an employee"— explicitly limit the scope of that provision to actions that affect employment or alter the conditions of the workplace. No such limiting words appear in the anti-retaliation provision. Given these linguistic differences, the question here is not whether identical or similar words should be read *in* *pari materia* to mean the same thing. * * * Rather, the question is whether Congress intended its different words to make a legal difference. We normally presume that, where words differ as they differ here, "Congress acts intentionally and purposely in the disparate inclusion or exclusion." *Russello v. United States*, 464 U.S. 16, 23, 104 S. Ct. 296, 78 L. Ed. 2d 17 (1983).

There is strong reason to believe that Congress intended the differences that its language suggests, for the two provisions differ not only in language but in purpose as well. The anti-discrimination provision seeks a workplace where individuals are not discriminated against because of their racial, ethnic, religious, or gender-based status. See *McDonnell Douglas Corp. v. Green*, 411 U.S. 792, 800–801, 93 S. Ct. 1817, 36 L. Ed. 2d 668 (1973). The anti-retaliation provision seeks to secure that primary objective by preventing an employer from interfering (through retaliation) with an employee's efforts to secure or advance enforcement of the Act's basic guarantees. The substantive provision seeks to prevent injury to individuals based on who they are, *i.e.*, their status. The anti-retaliation provision seeks to prevent harm to individuals based on what they do, *i.e.*, their conduct.

To secure the first objective, Congress did not need to prohibit anything other than employment-related discrimination. The substantive provision's basic objective of "equality of employment opportunities" and the elimination of practices that tend to bring about "stratified job environments," *id.*, at 800, 93 S. Ct. 1817, 36 L. Ed. 2d 668, would be achieved were all employment-related discrimination miraculously eliminated.

But one cannot secure the second objective by focusing only upon employer actions and harm that concern employment and the workplace. Were all such actions and harms eliminated, the anti-retaliation provision's objective would *not* be achieved. An employer can effectively retaliate against an employee by taking actions not directly related to his employment or by causing him harm *outside* the workplace. See, *e.g., Rochon v. Gonzales*, 438 F.3d at 1213 (FBI retaliation against employee "took the form of the FBI's refusal, contrary to policy, to investigate death threats a federal prisoner made against [the agent] and his wife"); *Berry v. Stevinson Chevrolet*, 74 F.3d 980, 984, 986 (CA10 1996) (finding actionable retaliation where employer filed false criminal charges against former employee who complained about discrimination). A provision limited to employment-related actions would not deter the many forms that effective retaliation can take. Hence, such a limited construction would fail to fully achieve the anti-retaliation provision's "primary purpose," namely, "maintaining unfettered access to statutory remedial mechanisms." *Robinson v. Shell Oil Co.*, 519 U.S. 337, 346, 117 S. Ct. 843, 136 L. Ed. 2d 808 (1997).

* * *

[W]e conclude that Title VII's substantive provision and its anti-retaliation provision are not coterminous. The scope of the anti-retaliation provision extends beyond workplace-related or employment-related retaliatory acts and harm. We therefore reject the standards applied in the Courts of Appeals that have treated the anti-retaliation provision as forbidding the same conduct prohibited by the anti-discrimination provision and that have limited actionable retaliation to so-called "ultimate employment decisions." * * *

B

The anti-retaliation provision protects an individual not from all retaliation, but from retaliation that produces an injury or harm. As we have explained, the Courts of Appeals have used differing language to describe the level of seriousness to which this harm must rise before it becomes actionable retaliation. * * * In our view, a plaintiff must show that a reasonable employee would have found the challenged action materially adverse, "which in this context means it well might have dissuaded a reasonable worker from making or supporting a charge of discrimination." *Rochon*, 438 F.3d at 1219 (quoting *Washington*, 420 F.3d at 662).

We speak of *material* adversity because we believe it is important to separate significant from trivial harms. Title VII, we have said, does not set forth "a general civility code for the American workplace." *Oncale v. Sundowner Offshore Services, Inc.,* 523 U.S. 75, 80, 118 S. Ct. 998, 140 L. Ed. 2d 201 (1998); see *Faragher*, 524 U.S., at 788, 118 S. Ct. 2275, 141 L. Ed. 2d 662 (judicial standards for sexual harassment must "filter out complaints attacking the ordinary tribulations of the workplace, such as the sporadic use of abusive language, gender-related jokes, and occasional teasing"). An employee's decision to report discriminatory behavior cannot immunize that employee from those petty slights or minor annoyances that often take place at work and that all employees experience. See 1 B. Lindemann & P. Grossman, Employment Discrimination Law 669 (3d ed. 1996) (noting that "courts have held that personality conflicts at work that generate antipathy" and "snubbing by supervisors and co-workers" are not actionable under § 704(a)). The anti-retaliation provision seeks to prevent employer interference with "unfettered access" to Title VII's remedial mechanisms. *Robinson*, 519 U.S., at 346, 117 S. Ct. 843, 136 L. Ed. 2d 808. It does so by prohibiting employer actions that are likely "to deter victims of discrimination from complaining to the EEOC," the courts, and their employers. *Ibid.* And normally petty slights, minor annoyances, and simple lack of good manners will not create such deterrence. See 2 EEOC 1998 Manual § 8, p. 8–13.

We refer to reactions of a *reasonable* employee because we believe that the provision's standard for judging harm must be objective. An objective standard is judicially administrable. It avoids the uncertainties and unfair discrepancies that can plague a judicial effort to determine a plaintiff's unusual subjective feelings. We have emphasized the need for objective standards in other Title VII contexts, and those same concerns animate our decision here. See, *e.g.*, [*Pa. State Police v.*] *Suders*, 542 U.S. [129,] 141, 124 S. Ct. 2342, 159 L. Ed. 2d 204 [(2004)] (constructive discharge doctrine); *Harris v. Forklift Systems, Inc.*, 510 U.S. 17, 21, 114 S. Ct. 367, 126 L. Ed. 2d 295 (1993) (hostile work environment doctrine).

We phrase the standard in general terms because the significance of any given act of retaliation will often depend upon the particular circumstances. Context matters. "The real social impact of workplace behavior often depends on a constellation of surrounding circumstances, expectations, and relationships which are not fully captured by a simple recitation of the words used or the physical acts performed." *Oncale, supra*, at 81–82, 118 S. Ct. 998, 140 L. Ed. 2d 201. A schedule change in an employee's work schedule may make little difference to many workers, but may matter enormously to a young mother with school age children. Cf., *e.g., Washington, supra*, at 662 (finding flex-time schedule critical to employee with disabled child). A supervisor's refusal to invite an employee to lunch is normally trivial, a nonactionable petty slight. But to retaliate by excluding an employee from a weekly training lunch that contributes significantly to the employee's professional advancement might well deter a reasonable employee from complaining about discrimination. See 2 EEOC 1998 Manual § 8, p. 8–14. Hence, a legal standard that speaks in general terms rather than specific prohibited acts is preferable for an "act that would be immaterial in some situations is material in others." *Washington, supra*, at 661.

* * *

III

Applying this standard to the facts of this case, we believe that there was a sufficient evidentiary basis to support the jury's verdict on White's retaliation claim. See *Reeves v. Sanderson Plumbing Products, Inc.*, 530 U.S. 133, 150–151, 120 S. Ct. 2097, 147 L. Ed. 2d 105 (2000). The jury found that two of Burlington's actions amounted to retaliation: the reassignment of White from forklift duty to standard track laborer tasks and the 37-day suspension without pay.

Burlington does not question the jury's determination that the motivation for these acts was retaliatory. But it does question the statutory significance of the harm these acts caused. The District Court instructed the jury to determine whether respondent "suffered a materially adverse change in the terms or conditions of her employment," and the Sixth Circuit upheld the jury's finding based on that same stringent interpretation of the anti-retaliation provision (the interpretation that limits § 704 to the same employment-related conduct forbidden by § 703). Our holding today makes clear that the jury was not required to find that the challenged actions were related to the terms or conditions of employment. And insofar as the jury also found that the actions were "materially adverse," its findings are adequately supported.

First, Burlington argues that a reassignment of duties cannot constitute retaliatory discrimination where, as here, both the former and present duties fall within the same job description. We do not see why that is so. Almost every job category involves some responsibilities and duties that are less desirable than others. Common sense suggests that one good way to discourage an employee such as White from bringing discrimination charges would be to insist that she spend more time performing the more arduous duties and less time performing those that are easier or more agreeable. That is presumably why the EEOC has consistently found "retaliatory work assignments" to be a classic and "widely recognized" example of "forbidden retaliation." 2 EEOC 1991 Manual § 614.7, pp. 614–31 to 614–32; see also 1972 Reference Manual § 495.2 (noting Commission decision involving an employer's ordering an employee "to do an unpleasant work assignment in retaliation" for filing racial discrimination complaint); EEOC Dec. No. 74–77, 1974 EEOC LEXIS 2, 1974 WL 3847, *4 (Jan. 18, 1974) ("Employers have been enjoined" under Title VII "from imposing unpleasant work assignments upon an employee for filing charges").

To be sure, reassignment of job duties is not automatically actionable. Whether a particular reassignment is materially adverse depends upon the circumstances of the particular case, and "should be judged from the perspective of a reasonable person in the plaintiff's position, considering all the circumstances." *Oncale*, 523 U.S., at 81, 118 S. Ct. 998, 140 L. Ed. 2d 201. But here, the jury had before it considerable evidence that the track labor duties were "by all accounts more arduous and dirtier"; that the "forklift operator position required more qualifications, which is an indication of prestige"; and that "the forklift operator position was objectively considered a better job and the male employees resented White for occupying it." 364 F.3d at 803 (internal quotation marks omitted). Based on this record, a jury could reasonably conclude that the reassignment of responsibilities would have been materially adverse to a reasonable employee.

Second, Burlington argues that the 37-day suspension without pay lacked statutory significance because Burlington ultimately reinstated White with backpay. Burlington says that "it defies reason to believe that Congress would have considered a rescinded investigatory suspension with full back pay" to be unlawful, particularly because Title VII, throughout much of its history, provided no relief in an equitable action for victims in White's position.

We do not find Burlington's last mentioned reference to the nature of Title VII's remedies convincing. After all, throughout its history, Title VII has provided for injunctions to "bar like discrimination in the future," *Albemarle Paper Co. v. Moody*, 422 U.S. 405, 418, 95 S. Ct. 2362, 45 L. Ed. 2d 280 (1975) (internal quotation marks omitted), an important form of relief. Pub. L. 88–352, § 706(g), 78 Stat. 261, as amended, 42 U.S.C. § 2000e–5(g). And we have no reason to believe that a court could not have issued an injunction where an employer suspended an employee for retaliatory purposes, even if that employer later provided backpay. In any event, Congress amended Title VII in 1991 to permit victims of intentional discrimination to recover compensatory (as White received here) and punitive damages, concluding that the additional remedies were necessary to "help make victims whole." *West v. Gibson*, 527 U.S. 212, 219, 119 S. Ct. 1906, 144 L. Ed. 2d 196 (1999) (quoting H. R. Rep. No. 102–40, pt. 1, pp. 64–65 (1991)); see 42 U.S.C. §§ 1981a(a)(1), (b). We would undermine the significance of that congressional judgment were we to conclude that employers could avoid liability in these circumstances.

Neither do we find convincing any claim of insufficient evidence. White did receive backpay. But White and her family had to live for 37 days without income. They did not know during that time whether or when White could return to work. Many reasonable employees would find a month without a paycheck to be a serious hardship. And White described to the jury the physical and emotional hardship that 37 days of having "no income, no money" in fact caused. ("That was the worst Christmas I had out of my life. No income, no money, and that made all of us feel bad. . . . I got very depressed"). Indeed, she obtained medical treatment for her emotional distress. A reasonable employee facing the choice between retaining her job (and paycheck) and filing a discrimination complaint might well choose the former. That is to say, an indefinite suspension without pay could well act as a deterrent, even if the suspended employee eventually received backpay. Cf. *Mitchell*, 361 U.S., at 292, 80 S. Ct. 332, 4 L. Ed. 2d 323 ("It needs no argument to show that fear of economic retaliation might often operate to induce aggrieved employees quietly to accept substandard conditions"). Thus, the jury's conclusion that the 37-day suspension without pay was materially adverse was a reasonable one.

JUSTICE ALITO, concurring in the judgment. [omitted]

NOTES AND QUESTIONS

Test Your Understanding of the Material

1.   What is the Court's holding in *Burlington*? Did the Court have to decide whether § 704 reaches "materially adverse" employer conduct that does not affect terms and conditions of employment?

2.   How does the Court define "material adversity"? Is it different from the EEOC definition in the agency's manual: whether a reasonable employee

would be deterred from making or supporting a charge of discrimination or complaining about discrimination? What employer conduct would not meet that standard?

Related Issues

3.   Burlington's *"Material Adversity" Standard in the Lower Courts*. For applications, see, e.g., Rivera v. Rochester Genesee Reg'l Transp. Auth., 743 F.3d 11, 26 (2d Cir. 2012) (threats of discharge and racial slurs sufficient to deter); Zelnik v. Fashion Institute of Technology, 464 F.3d 217, 227 (2d Cir. 2006) (reasonable employee would not be dissuaded by denial of emeritus status carrying no benefits); Kessler v. Westchester County Dept. of Social Services, 461 F.3d 199 (2d Cir. 2006) (jury could find that transfer to job with same salary, but less prestige and power, could deter complaint); Moore v. City of Philadelphia, 461 F.3d 331 (3d Cir. 2006) (jury could find that transfer to different precinct, mandatory psychiatric evaluation, and negative evaluation could deter).

4.   *Retaliatory Harassment*. After *Burlington*, actionable retaliation for protected activity need not involve a "tangible employment action" under *Faragher* and *Ellerth*. The Court thus rejects the view previously held by the Fifth Circuit that § 704(a) reaches only "ultimate" employment decisions—a position that effectively precluded § 704(a) protection for retaliatory workplace harassment not implicating formal employment decisions such as hiring, firing, promotion and pay. See Aryain v. Wal-Mart Stores Tex. LP, 534 F.3d 473, 484 n. 9 (5th Cir.2008) (recognizing *Burlington*'s abrogation of court's "ultimate" decision doctrine).

5.   *Reprisals Against Third Parties*. Are reprisals against spouses or others close to the employee who engaged in protected activity actionable under § 704? In Thompson v. North American Stainless, LP, 562 U.S. 170, 131 S.Ct. 863, 178 L.Ed.2d 694 (2011), the Court held that Thompson could sue under § 704 for being discharged in retaliation for his fiancee's filing of a charge of sex discrimination with the EEOC. The Court stated that it is "obvious that a reasonable worker might be dissuaded from engaging in protected activity if she knew that her fiancé would be fired." The Court declined "to identify a fixed class of relationships for which third-party reprisals are unlawful," but stated "that firing a close family member will almost always meet the *Burlington* standard, and inflicting a milder reprisal on a mere acquaintance will almost never do so." 131 S. Ct. at 688–689.

6.   *Causation*. Proving causation is critical to establishing retaliation under § 704(a), as it is to establishing discrimination under § 703. In University of Texas Southwestern Medical Center v. Nassar, 133 S.Ct. 2517 (2013), the Court held that § 704(a) retaliation claims must meet the "but-for" cause standard adopted in *Gross v. FBL Financial Services*, page 446 supra, for age discrimination claims, rather than the "motivating factor" standard set in § 703 for Title VII discrimination claims. The Court in *Nassar* explained that § 703(m), added by the 1991 amendments to Title VII, which provides that a complaining party can "demonstrate[ ] that race, color, religion, sex, or

national origin was a motivating factor," does not apply to § 704(a) actions. The Court concluded that the but-for standard set in *Gross* should be used as a default causation standard in the absence of any contrary statutory directive.

How might plaintiffs prove but-for causation? Should a short time span between the protected activity and the adverse action raise an inference of § 704(a) discrimination sufficient to require some explanation from the employer? Cf. Clark County School Dist. v. Breeden, 532 U.S. 268, 273, 274, 121 S.Ct. 1508, 149 L.Ed.2d 509 (2001) (cases relying on temporal proximity alone suggest that such proximity must be "very close"; "[a]ction taken (as here) 20 months later suggests, by itself, no causality at all").

7. *False or Baseless Accusation in EEOC Charges*. Some courts have ruled that employees are not protected by the participation clause of § 704 when they file charges that are facially invalid or not legally cognizable because they fail to allege discrimination on the basis of one of the five Title VII categories. See, e.g., Slagle v. County of Clarion, 435 F.3d 262 (3d Cir. 2006); Balazs v. Liebenthal, 32 F.3d 151, 159–60 (4th Cir. 1994). The courts, however, have not required that a facially valid charge in fact be meritorious or have even a reasonable basis. See, e.g., Wyatt v. Boston, 35 F.3d 13, 15 (1st Cir.1994); Novotny v. Great American Federal Savings & Loan Assn., 539 F.Supp. 437 (W.D.Pa.1982), on remand from 442 U.S. 366, 99 S.Ct. 2345, 60 L.Ed.2d 957 (1979). See also EEOC Guidance on Investigating, Analyzing Retaliation Claims, reprinted in (BNA) Daily Labor Report, No. 100, May 26, 1998, pp. E-3, E-6.

8. *Former Employees*. Section 704(a) proscribes any form of retaliation against "employees or applicants for employment." Does *Burlington* confirm that it also proscribes retaliation, such as through a negative letter of reference, against former employees? In Robinson v. Shell Oil Co., 519 U.S. 337, 117 S.Ct. 843, 136 L.Ed.2d 808 (1997), discussed in *Burlington*, the Supreme Court unanimously held that former employees are protected by § 704(a).

9. *Retaliation for Refusing to Release Claims*. As a condition of continued employment, can an employer require its at-will employees to sign releases of all past claims against the employer, including those under the anti-discrimination laws? Would the termination of an employee who refused to release claims constitute retaliation? Would the answer be different if the employer was converting employees to independent contractors and conditioned the conversion on the release of claims? In EEOC v. Allstate Ins. Co., 778 F.3d 444 (7th Cir. 2015), employee sales agents were terminated but offered the option of a continued relationship with Allstate as independent contractors, provided they signed a release. While the EEOC conceded that a release would be permissible had the employees been terminated, it argued that the agents were "not terminated in any normal sense" and the option to continue as contractors was insufficient consideration to support the release. The Seventh Circuit disagreed, noting the tangible benefits afforded by the continued relationship, the fact that Allstate was not legally required to offer a continued relationship, and that the "financial pressure" associated with

such offer was no more offensive than the pressure associated with an offer of severance pay. See also Employment Restatement § 5.02 (wrongful termination in violation of public policy claim available where employee "refuses to waive . . . a nonwaivable right when the employer's insistence on the waiver as a condition of employment . . . would violate well-established public policy.")

10. *Scope of Participation Clause.* Does the participation clause reach statements made by employees during an employer's internal investigation of a discrimination or harassment complaint after or prior to the filing of an EEOC charge? The question is important because the participation clause, unlike the opposition clause, does not require that the alleged activity be "an unlawful employment practice." Note that the Court in *Crawford*, the decision below, declined to rule on the applicability of the participation clause in that case.

The Title VII participation clause refers to participation in proceedings "under this title." Its protective reach presumably extends to filings with state civil rights deferral agencies, which constitute formal "participation" required by Title VII as a prelude to filing a charge with the EEOC. See Title VII, § 706 (b)–(d), 29 U.S.C. § 2000e–5(b)–(d). Some lower courts have held that participation in internal investigations following an EEOC charge are covered by the participation clause. See, e.g., Clover v. Total System Services, Inc., 176 F.3d 1346 (11th Cir.1999) (§ 704(a) extends to an employer's internal investigation when conducted in response to notice of an EEOC charge); Townsend v. Benjamin Enters., Inc., 679 F.3d 41, 48 n.6 (2d Cir. 2012) (declining to rule on whether the participation clause covers internal investigations following an EEOC charge). However, lower courts have declined to extend the protection of the participation clause to internal investigations initiated prior to an EEOC charge. See, e.g., EEOC v. Total System Services, Inc., 221 F.3d 1171 (11th Cir. 2000).

B. EXPRESS ANTIRETALIATION PROVISIONS: OPPOSITION CLAUSE AND SELF-HELP REMEDIES

CRAWFORD V. METROPOLITAN GOVERNMENT OF NASHVILLE

Supreme Court of the United States, 2009.
555 U.S. 271, 129 S.Ct. 846, 172 L.Ed.2d 650.

JUSTICE SOUTER delivered the opinion of the Court.

Title VII of the Civil Rights Act of 1964, 78 Stat. 253, as amended, 42 U.S.C. 2000e *et seq.* (2000 ed. and Supp. V), forbids retaliation by employers against employees who report workplace race or gender discrimination. The question here is whether this protection extends to an employee who speaks out about discrimination not on her own initiative, but in answering questions during an employer's internal investigation. We hold that it does.

I

In 2002, respondent Metropolitan Government of Nashville and Davidson County, Tennessee (Metro), began looking into rumors of sexual harassment by the Metro School District's employee relations director, Gene Hughes. 211 Fed. Appx. 373, 374 (CA6 2006). When Veronica Frazier, a Metro human resources officer, asked petitioner Vicky Crawford, a 30-year Metro employee, whether she had witnessed "inappropriate behavior" on the part of Hughes, *id.*, at 374–375, Crawford described several instances of sexually harassing behavior: once, Hughes had answered her greeting, " 'Hey Dr. Hughes, what's up?,' " by grabbing his crotch and saying " '[Y]ou know what's up' "; he had repeatedly " 'put his crotch up to [her] window' "; and on one occasion he had entered her office and " 'grabbed her head and pulled it to his crotch,' " *id.*, at 375, and n. 1. Two other employees also reported being sexually harassed by Hughes. *Id.*, at 375. Although Metro took no action against Hughes, it did fire Crawford and the two other accusers soon after finishing the investigation, saying in Crawford's case that it was for embezzlement. Ibid. Crawford claimed Metro was retaliating for her report of Hughes's behavior and filed a charge of a Title VII violation with the Equal Employment Opportunity Commission (EEOC), followed by this suit in the United States District Court for the Middle District of Tennessee. Ibid.

The Title VII antiretaliation provision has two clauses, making it "an unlawful employment practice for an employer to discriminate against any of his employees . . . [1] because he has opposed any practice made an unlawful employment practice by this subchapter, or [2] because he has made a charge, testified, assisted, or participated in any manner in an investigation, proceeding, or hearing under this subchapter." 42 U.S.C. 2000e–3(a). The one is known as the "opposition clause," the other as the "participation clause," and Crawford accused Metro of violating both.

The District Court granted summary judgment for Metro. It held that Crawford could not satisfy the opposition clause because she had not "instigated or initiated any complaint," but had "merely answered questions by investigators in an already-pending internal investigation, initiated by someone else." Memorandum Opinion, No. 3:03–cv–00996 (MD Tenn., Jan. 6, 2005), App. C to Pet. for Cert. 16a–17a. It concluded that her claim also failed under the participation clause, which Sixth Circuit precedent confined to protecting " 'an employee's participation in an employer's internal investigation . . . where that investigation occurs pursuant to a pending EEOC charge' " (not the case here). *Id.*, at 15a (emphasis omitted) (quoting *Abbott v. Crown Motor Co.*, 348 F.3d 537, 543 (CA6 2003)).

The Court of Appeals affirmed on the same grounds, holding that the opposition clause " 'demands active, consistent "opposing" activities to warrant . . . protection against retaliation,' " 211 Fed. Appx., at 376 (quoting *Bell v. Safety Grooving & Grinding, LP*, 107 Fed. Appx. 607, 610 (CA6 2004)), whereas Crawford did "not claim to have instigated or initiated any complaint prior to her participation in the investigation, nor did she take any further action following the investigation and prior to her firing." 211 Fed. Appx., at 376. Again like the trial judge, the Court of Appeals understood that Crawford could show no violation of the participation clause because her " 'employer's internal investigation' " was not conducted " 'pursuant to a pending EEOC charge.' " Ibid. (quoting *Abbott, supra*, at 543). * * *

II

The opposition clause makes it "unlawful . . . for an employer to discriminate against any . . . employe[e] . . . because he has opposed any practice made . . . unlawful . . . by this subchapter." 2000e–3(a). The term "oppose," being left undefined by the statute, carries its ordinary meaning, *Perrin v. United States*, 444 U.S. 37, 42, 100 S. Ct. 311, 62 L. Ed. 2d 199 (1979): "to resist or antagonize . . . ; to contend against; to confront; resist; withstand," Webster's New International Dictionary 1710 (2d ed. 1958). Although these actions entail varying expenditures of energy, "RESIST frequently implies more active striving than OPPOSE." *Ibid.*; see also Random House Dictionary of the English Language 1359 (2d ed. 1987) (defining "oppose" as "to be hostile or adverse to, as in opinion").

The statement Crawford says she gave to Frazier is thus covered by the opposition clause, as an ostensibly disapproving account of sexually obnoxious behavior toward her by a fellow employee, an answer she says antagonized her employer to the point of sacking her on a false pretense. Crawford's description of the louche goings-on would certainly qualify in the minds of reasonable jurors as "resist[ant]" or "antagoni[stic]" to Hughes's treatment, if for no other reason than the point argued by the Government and explained by an EEOC guideline: "When an employee communicates to her employer a belief that the employer has engaged in . . . a form of employment discrimination, that communication" virtually always "constitutes the employee's *opposition* to the activity." Brief for United States as Amicus Curiae 9 (citing 2 EEOC Compliance Manual §§ 8-II-B(1), (2), p. 614:0003 (Mar. 2003)); see also *Federal Express Corp. v. Holowecki*, 552 U.S. 389, 128 S. Ct. 1147, 1156, 170 L. Ed. 2d 10, 21 (2008) (explaining that EEOC compliance manuals "reflect 'a body of experience and informed judgment to which courts and litigants may properly resort for guidance' " (quoting *Bragdon v. Abbott*, 524 U.S. 624, 642, 118 S. Ct. 2196, 141 L. Ed. 2d 540 (1998))). It is true that one can imagine exceptions, like an employee's description of a supervisor's racist joke as hilarious, but these will be eccentric cases, and this is not one of them.

The Sixth Circuit thought answering questions fell short of opposition, taking the view that the clause " 'demands active, consistent 'opposing' activities to warrant . . . protection against retaliation,' " 211 Fed. Appx., at 376 (quoting *Bell*, supra, at 610), and that an employee must "instigat[e] or initiat[e]" a complaint to be covered, 211 Fed. Appx., at 376. But though these requirements obviously exemplify opposition as commonly understood, they are not limits of it.

"Oppose" goes beyond "active, consistent" behavior in ordinary discourse, where we would naturally use the word to speak of someone who has taken no action at all to advance a position beyond disclosing it. Countless people were known to "oppose" slavery before Emancipation, or are said to "oppose" capital punishment today, without writing public letters, taking to the streets, or resisting the government. And we would call it "opposition" if an employee took a stand against an employer's discriminatory practices not by "instigating" action, but by standing pat, say, by refusing to follow a supervisor's order to fire a junior worker for discriminatory reasons. Cf. *McDonnell*, supra, at 262 (finding employee covered by Title VII of the Civil Rights Act of 1964 where his employer retaliated against him for failing to prevent his subordinate from filing an EEOC charge). There is, then, no reason to doubt that a person can "oppose" by responding to someone else's question just as surely as by provoking the discussion, and nothing in the statute requires a freakish rule protecting an employee who reports discrimination on her own initiative but not one who reports the same discrimination in the same words when her boss asks a question.

Metro and its amici support the Circuit panel's insistence on "active" and "consistent" opposition by arguing that the lower the bar for retaliation claims, the less likely it is that employers will look into what may be happening outside the executive suite. As they see it, if retaliation is an easy charge when things go bad for an employee who responded to enquiries, employers will avoid the headache by refusing to raise questions about possible discrimination.

The argument is unconvincing, for we think it underestimates the incentive to enquire that follows from our decisions in *Burlington Industries, Inc. v. Ellerth*, 524 U.S. 742, 118 S. Ct. 2257, 141 L. Ed. 2d 633 (1998), and *Faragher v. Boca Raton*, 524 U.S. 775, 118 S. Ct. 2275, 141 L. Ed. 2d 662 (1998). * * * The possibility that an employer might someday want to fire someone who might charge discrimination traceable to an internal investigation does not strike us as likely to diminish the attraction of an *Ellerth-Faragher* affirmative defense.

That aside, we find it hard to see why the Sixth Circuit's rule would not itself largely undermine the *Ellerth-Faragher* scheme, along with the statute's " 'primary objective' " of "avoid[ing] harm" to employees. * * * The appeals court's rule would [ ] create a real dilemma for any knowledgeable employee in a hostile work environment if the boss took steps to assure a defense under our cases. If the employee reported discrimination in response to the enquiries, the employer might well be free to penalize her for speaking up. But if she kept quiet about the discrimination and later filed a Title VII claim, the employer might well escape liability, arguing that it "exercised reasonable care to prevent and correct [any discrimination] promptly" but "the plaintiff employee unreasonably failed to take advantage of . . . preventive or corrective opportunities provided by the employer." *Ellerth*, supra, at 765, 118 S. Ct. 2257, 141 L. Ed. 2d 633. Nothing in the statute's text or our precedent supports this catch-22.

Because Crawford's conduct is covered by the opposition clause, we do not reach her argument that the Sixth Circuit misread the participation clause as well. But that does not mean the end of this case, for Metro's motion for summary judgment raised several defenses to the retaliation charge besides the scope of the two clauses; the District Court never reached these others owing to its ruling on the elements of retaliation, and they remain open on remand.

[*Eds.* The opinion of JUSTICE ALITO, joined in by JUSTICE THOMAS, concurring in the judgment, is omitted.]

NOTES AND QUESTIONS

Test Your Understanding of the Material

1.   Why did Congress enact an opposition clause in addition to the participation clause in § 704(a) of Title VII? The legislative history on Section 704 is quite sparse. An interpretive memorandum submitted to the House of Representatives in connection with the legislation characterized the antiretaliation provisions as follows: "[it] prohibits discrimination by an employer or labor organization against persons for opposing discriminatory practices, and for bringing charges before the Commission or otherwise participating in proceedings under the title." 110 Cong. Rec. 7213 (April 8, 1964).

2.   Under *Crawford*, are all communications by an employee to an employer concerning what the employee believes to be discrimination protected by § 704(a)? Does the Court suggest any limitations?

Related Issues

3.   *Opposition on Behalf of Third Parties.* Under *Crawford* is an employee protected from retaliation for opposing discrimination against other employees? The courts had so held before *Crawford*. See, e.g., EEOC v. Navy Fed. Credit Union, 424 F.3d 397, 407 (4th Cir. 2005) (supervisor protected from retaliation for refusing to participate in scheme to discriminate against subordinate); Childress v. City of Richmond, 134 F.3d 1205 (4th Cir. 1998) (holding that white male employees opposing hostile work environment discrimination directed at black coworkers were protected from retaliation under § 704(a)). See also Thompson v. North American Stainless, LP, 562 U.S. 170, 131 S.Ct. 863 (2011) (employee fired after fiancé filed an EEOC charge had a cognizable retaliation claim even though employee did not himself engage in any protected conduct); Alex B. Long, The Troublemaker's Friend:

Retaliation against Third Parties and the Right of Association in the Workplace, 59 Fla. L. Rev. 931 (2007).

4. *Erroneous, Good Faith Opposition.* Given that protected opposition must be to a practice "made unlawful by this title," is 704(a) protection limited to opposition to practices that in fact violate Title VII? In Clark County School District v. Breeden, 532 U.S. 268, 270, 121 S.Ct. 1508, 149 L.Ed.2d 509 (2001), the Court left this question open, but held that Title VII's opposition clause at least does not protect opposition to activity that the employee could not reasonably believe violated the statute. Most courts have held that reasonable, good-faith opposition is protected even if the underlying practice is found to be lawful. See, e.g., Jordan v. Alternative Resources Corp., 447 F.3d 324 (4th Cir. 2006); Higgins v. New Balance Athletic Shoe, Inc., 194 F.3d 252 (1st Cir. 1999). See generally Matthew W. Green Jr., What's So Reasonable About Reasonableness?, 62 Kan. L. Rev. 759 (2014).

HOCHSTADT V. WORCESTER FOUNDATION

United States Court of Appeals, First Circuit, 1976.
545 F.2d 222.

CAMPBELL, J.

The Worcester Foundation for Experimental Biology is a nonprofit institution primarily committed to basic biomedical research, employing some 250 persons. The Foundation devotes $1.8 million of its annual budget to cancer research in what is known as the Cell Biology Program. The principal investigator is Dr. Mahlan Hoagland, who is also the Director of the Foundation. Dr. Hoagland has recruited other scientists to join the program since its inception, and in 1971 recruited Dr. Harvey Ozer, a virologist, to fill a specific need in the program.

Dr. Ozer informed Dr. Hoagland of the availability and interest of his wife, Dr. Joy Hochstadt, in joining the Foundation. Dr. Hochstadt is a microbiologist, whose research into cell membrane functions, described by one scientist at the hearing as "pioneering", fit into the Foundation's research program. In September, 1971, Dr. Hoagland offered both Dr. Ozer and Dr. Hochstadt positions as senior scientists. Dr. Ozer's salary was set at $24,000, while Dr. Hochstadt's salary was set at $18,000. These salaries reflected the needs of the institution. Dr. Ozer and Dr. Hochstadt accepted the employment offers on October 1, but thereafter Dr. Hochstadt sought to renegotiate her salary, claiming it was discriminatory and illegal. The Foundation reluctantly acceded to readjust the salaries of Dr. Hochstadt and Dr. Ozer so that each would receive $21,000.

After starting her employment in January, 1972, Dr. Hochstadt joined the small group of cell biologists and participated in the periodic meetings of the group held to discuss policies, recruitment, and direction of research. At these meetings, Dr. Hochstadt early began to interpose personal grievances and salary complaints, to discuss the inadequacy of the

Foundation's affirmative action program, and to criticize the Foundation's administration and its director, Dr. Hoagland, and assistant director, Dr. Welsch. These complaints interfered with the meetings, disrupted the discussions, and eventually caused discontinuation of the meetings.

In January, 1973, after they had been at the Foundation for over a year, Dr. Hochstadt and Dr. Ozer each sought from the Foundation $3,000 in lump sum back pay and a $3,000 salary increase to compensate for unanticipated moving expenses and the cost of living increase. In March, 1973, plaintiff was given a $1,500 (4.5%) increase as a result of the Foundation's annual salary review. Dr. Hoagland indicated that she would receive a larger raise the following year "when you've effectively joined the team."

In July, 1973, Dr. Hochstadt filed formal charges with the Massachusetts Commission Against Discrimination (MCAD), the EEOC, and the Department of Labor, alleging that the Foundation had discriminated against her by setting her starting salary much lower than that for male scientists starting work at the same time. One month later, she filed a class action complaint with the Department of Health, Education, and Welfare on behalf of all female employees at the Foundation. The complaint filed with HEW caused the Department to request the Foundation to implement an affirmative action plan. In June, 1974, the MCAD found reasonable cause to credit Dr. Hochstadt's complaint, but deferred further consideration of the charge pending action by the EEOC. In September, 1974, Dr. Hochstadt filed suit against the Foundation pursuant to § 2000e–5(f)(1), removing the case from the jurisdiction of the EEOC. In December, 1974, the Foundation settled with Dr. Hochstadt for $20,000.

Subsequent to her minimal increase and the filing of these charges, plaintiff sought to elicit salary information from other scientists and personnel at the Foundation, and on several occasions this conduct interfered with ongoing research and upset the other scientists and research assistants who were approached.

Plaintiff also circulated rumors that the Foundation would lose much of its federal funding because it was not complying with regulations concerning affirmative action programs. To allay the apprehension created by these rumors, on at least three occasions the Foundation had to invite an official from HEW to assure scientists at the Foundation that they were in no danger of losing federal funding.

In April, 1974, Dr. Hochstadt invited Dr. Helene Guttman, an officer of the Association of Women in Science, to conduct a covert affirmative action survey at the Foundation, ostensively [sic] while attending a scientific seminar. Dr. Guttman later wrote to Congressman Edwards indicating her findings that the Foundation was not in compliance with federal regulations and [was] critical of HEW's handling of Dr. Hochstadt's complaint of discrimination against the Foundation, and she sent copies of the letter to eight other members of Congress.

Also in 1974, Dr. Hochstadt invited a reporter from the Worcester Telegram to examine her files containing confidential salary information for employees at the Foundation. The reporter wrote several articles in the Telegram.

In mid-1974, the associate director, Dr. Welsch, complained to Dr. Hochstadt about her use of the Foundation's telephone for personal calls to her lawyer and to Dr. Guttman amounting to over $950 and her misuse of secretarial assistance and Xeroxing services.

In late 1974, two research assistants in Dr. Hochstadt's laboratory left the Foundation because of their difficulties with Dr. Hochstadt. Complaints from subordinates in other laboratories never reached the level of the complaints of Dr. Hochstadt's research assistants.

* * *

[The question in this case is] whether plaintiff's overall conduct was so generally inimical to her employer's interests, and so "excessive", as to be beyond the protection of section 704(a) even though her actions were generally associated with her complaints of illegal employer conduct. We conclude that although plaintiff's original salary complaint may have been justified, and although her later complaint over her poor rating—whether or not justified—was one which she was entitled to make in an appropriate way, still neither of these could insulate her deportment from adverse scrutiny insofar as it went beyond the pale of reasonable opposition activity.

* * *

* * * Congress certainly did not mean to grant sanctuary to employees to engage in political activity for women's liberation on company time, and an employee does not enjoy immunity from discharge for misconduct merely by claiming that at all times she was defending the rights of her sex by "opposing" discriminatory practices. An employer remains entitled to loyalty and cooperativeness from employees:

> "[M]anagement prerogatives * * * are to be left undisturbed to the greatest extent possible. Internal affairs of employers * * * must not be interfered with except to the limited extent that correction is required in discrimination practices."

Additional views on H.R. 7152, U.S.Code Cong. & Admin.News, p. 2516 (88th Cong., 2d Sess., 1964). On the other hand, section 704(a) clearly does protect an employee against discharge for filing complaints in good faith before federal and state agencies and for registering grievances through channels appropriate in the particular employment setting.

It is less clear to what extent militant self-help activity falling between these two poles, such as particular types of on-the-job opposition to alleged discrimination, vociferousness, expressions of hostility to an employer or superior and the like, are protected. In the instant case, the issue is clouded by a sophisticated employment setting which lacks a rigid structure and within which it is not always easy to assess when an employee—in this case a highly educated senior scientist—clearly oversteps the bounds.

In such instances, we think courts have in each case to balance the purpose of the Act to protect persons engaging reasonably in activities opposing sexual discrimination, against Congress' equally manifest desire not to tie the hands of employers in the objective selection and control of personnel. Allowing an employee to invoke the protection of section 704(a) for conduct aimed at achieving purely ulterior objectives, or for conduct aimed at achieving even proper objectives through the use of improper means, could have an effect directly contrary to Congress' goal, by discouraging employers from hiring persons whom the Act is designed to protect. The standard can be little more definitive than the rule of reason applied by a judge or other tribunal to given facts. The requirements of the job and the tolerable limits of conduct in a particular setting must be explored. The present case, therefore, raises the question, put simply, of whether plaintiff went "too far" in her particular employment setting.

This approach is consistent with that taken by other courts when interpreting section 704(a). In *EEOC v. Kallir, Philips, Ross, Inc.,* 401 F.Supp. 66 (S.D.N.Y.1975), a case cited by both parties, the plaintiff was discharged for discreetly obtaining from a customer of her employer a written description of her job which had been requested by the New York City Commission on Human Rights during its investigation of the employee's charge of sex discrimination. Stressing the broad language of section 704(a) protecting an employee for assisting "in any manner" with a proceeding under Title VII, the court held that plaintiff's solicitation of the letter was protected. Noting that plaintiff's action had no negative effect on the client relationship, the court observed:

> "Under some circumstances, an employee's conduct in gathering or attempting to gather evidence to support his charge may be so excessive and so deliberately calculated to inflict needless economic hardship on the employer that the employee loses the protection of section 704(a), just as other legitimate civil rights activities lose the protection of section 704(a) when they progress to deliberate and unlawful conduct against the employer."

Id. at 71–72. The Supreme Court too has made passing reference to the limits of protected conduct under section 704(a), stating that an employer may properly deny employment to a former employee who participated in an unlawful "stall-in" to protest the employer's civil rights record. "Nothing in Title VII compels an employer to absolve and rehire one who has engaged

in such deliberate, unlawful activity against it." *McDonnell Douglas Corp.
v. Green*, 411 U.S. 792, 803, 93 S.Ct. 1817, 1825, 36 L.Ed.2d 668 (1973).

* * *

Cases discussing limitations upon the right of union employees to
engage in "concerted activity" against their employer provide a helpful
point of comparison. Even if the ends sought to be achieved by the
employees are protected by the National Labor Relations Act, the means
chosen by the employees may be excessive. For example, in *NLRB v. Local
1229, IBEW, (Jefferson Standard Broadcasting Co.)*, 346 U.S. 464, 74 S.Ct.
172, 98 L.Ed. 195 (1953), the Court reinstated the Board's order upholding
an employer's discharge of nine employees for distributing during lawful
picketing handbills accusing the employer television station of not serving
the public interest.

* * *

Under the principles of the labor cases, the district court was entitled
to conclude that Dr. Hochstadt's actions went beyond the scope of protected
opposition because they damaged the basic goals and interests of the
Foundation. * * * The district court was entitled to find that Dr.
Hochstadt's constant complaints to colleagues damaged relationships
among members of the cell biology group and sometimes even interfered
with laboratory research. Even if justified, they occurred upon some
occasions when the employer was entitled to expect her full commitment
and loyalty. Section 704(a) does not afford an employee unlimited license
to complain at any and all times and places.

* * *

Keeping in mind the legitimate interests both of Dr. Hochstadt and the
Foundation, we face the ultimate question, whether the district court could
properly on this record determine that Dr. Hochstadt "went too far" in her
activities and deportment. We think it could. A permissible interpretation
of the evidence was that the Foundation had wiped the slate clean in
December, 1974, after its settlement with Dr. Hochstadt, and that the
administration was willing to accept her as a member of the team. But Dr.
Hochstadt's extreme hostility toward Dr. Welsch, Dr. Gibbons,[7] and Dr.
Hoagland in response to the April, 1975, evaluation indicated that there
would be no change in her attitude or her behavior from that encountered
since she was hired in 1972. The continuation of the general conflict forced

---

[7] Because Dr. Gibbons was the EEOC officer at the Foundation, there is some merit in the
plaintiff's argument that she was entitled to show a high degree of hostility towards the
Foundation in her conversation with Dr. Gibbons charging that her low evaluation was
discriminatory. Even assuming, however, that a higher degree of protection attaches to an
employee's contacts with her employer's EEOC officer, Dr. Hochstadt's hostile confrontation with
Dr. Welsch, the assistant director of the Foundation, must be judged against the normal standard
for protected opposition, and that confrontation, the precipitating factor of her discharge, went
beyond the scope of protected activity.

the Foundation to make a critical choice: either it would retain Dr. Hochstadt and tolerate not only her complaints against the Foundation but also the complaints against Dr. Hochstadt's behavior raised by other scientists and research personnel, or it would terminate her employment. We cannot disagree with the district court's conclusion that the Foundation was justified in choosing the latter course.

NOTES AND QUESTIONS

Test Your Understanding of the Material

1.   *Hochstadt* involves the question of how far an employee may pursue self-help opposition while remaining within the protection of § 704(a). In what precise ways did the plaintiff go beyond the pale?

Related Issues

2.   *Disruptive Conduct as Basis for Termination.* Courts of Appeals continue to cite *Hochstadt* for the proposition that excessively disruptive conduct is unprotected by Title VII. See e.g. Kempcke v. Monsanto Co., 132 F.3d 442 (8th Cir. 1998); Laughlin v. Metropolitan Washington Airports Authority, 149 F.3d 253 (1998). Some courts, however, have been reluctant to decide the issue as a matter of law, and instead permit the employer to present a "mixed motive" defense to the jury. See, e.g., Matima v. Celli, 228 F.3d 68 (2d Cir. 2000); Wolinsky v. Standard Oil of Connecticut, Inc., 712 F.Supp.2d 46 (D. Conn. 2010). The employer then must proffer evidence that it would have fired the employee for disruptive behavior regardless of the protected activity.

3.   *Public Opposition.* Under what circumstances can an employee go public with her opposition? Note that Dr. Hochstadt invited assistance not only from an officer of the Association of Women in Science, but also from a newspaper reporter. Is it realistic to expect lone employees, not represented by unions, to engage in opposition without attempting to secure assistance from the outside community? See Wrighten v. Metropolitan Hosps., supra (black nurse held press conference to charge employer with poor health care for black patients); EEOC v. Crown Zellerbach Corp., 720 F.2d 1008 (9th Cir.1983) (employees sent letter to local school board, which was a major customer of their employer, protesting manager's receipt of affirmative action award).

4.   *Oppositional Activity in Violation of Other Laws.* Can a Title VII court take into account the fact that the oppositional activity contravenes other laws? Or does the congressional policy embodied in § 704(a) require a measure of protection even in such circumstances? Note that in *McDonnell Douglas Corp. v. Green*, p. 104 supra, Green's opposition activity took the form of a "stall-in" tactic whereby he parked his car on an access road to the plant causing serious traffic problems. Green's § 704(a) claim was rejected by the district court, and he did not take a further appeal. The Supreme Court observed: "Nothing in Title VII compels an employer to absolve and rehire one who has engaged in * * * deliberate, unlawful activity against it." 411 U.S. at 803.

5. *When Can the Employer's EEO Personnel Be Said to Engage in Oppositional Activity?* The Company's EEO/HR officers often provide advice regarding whether the employer is complying with regulatory requirements. How does such an employee signal protected opposition rather than merely the giving of advice as part of the employee's job? Cf. Garcetti v. Ceballos, 547 U.S. 410 (2006); discussed p. 691 infra. See generally Deborah L. Brake, Retaliation in the EEO Office, 50 Tulsa L. Rev. 1 (2014).

6. *Opposition to Practices of Prior Employer or Other Third-Party Employer.* Does the entity charged with retaliation under § 704(a) have to be the same entity that was the object of the plaintiff's opposition? Does § 704(a), for instance, protect employees who complain about discriminatory treatment by some other employer with whom their employer has a business relationship? Compare Flowers v. Columbia College Chicago, 397 F.3d 532 (7th Cir. 2005) (Easterbrook, J.) (finding § 704(a) coverage), with Dellinger v. Science Applications Int'l Corp., 649 F.3d 226 (4th Cir. 2011) (FLSA's anti-retaliation provision does not protect employees from discrimination by prospective employers for suing prior employer).

7. *Implied Opposition Clause?* Some statutes, like the Fair Labor Standards Act (FLSA), including its Equal Pay Act amendment, 29 U.S.C. § 206(d), do not contain an express opposition clause. The anti-retaliation provision in the FLSA, 29 U.S.C. § 215(a)(3), provides that it is unlawful for any person

> to discharge or in any other manner discriminate against any employee because such employee has filed any complaint or instituted or caused to be instituted any proceedings under or related to this chapter, or has testified or is about to testify in any such proceeding * * * .

Lower courts have differed over whether this provision protects activity prior to the filing of a complaint or administrative charge. Compare, e.g., Lambert v. Genesee Hospital, 10 F.3d 46, 55 (2d Cir. 1993) (the "plain language of this provision limits the cause of action to retaliation for filing formal complaints, instituting a proceeding, or testifying, but does not encompass complaints made to a supervisor"), with Lambert v. Ackerley, 180 F.3d 997, 1004 (9th Cir.1999) (en banc) (provision protects employees who file complaints internally with employer).

In Kasten v. Saint-Gobain Performance Plastics, 563 U.S. 1, 131 S.Ct. 1325, 179 L.Ed.2d 379 (2011), the Court held that oral complaints may be protected under § 215(a)(3). The Court vacated a lower court decision that held a discharged employee did not engage in FLSA-protected activity when he made several verbal efforts to inform his employer that the location of the employers' time clocks prevented employees from being paid for time doffing and donning their gear. The Supreme Court stated a complaint, whether written or oral, "must be sufficiently clear and detailed for a reasonable employer to understand it." Although the Court left open whether a complaint to an employer rather than to the government was protected by § 215(a)(3), the decision has "impelled and guided" the Court of Appeals for the Second Circuit to reverse its precedent and join sister circuits in finding complaints to an employer protected. See Greathouse v. JHS Security Inc., 784 F.3d 105, 111 (2d Cir. 2015). Accord, e.g., Minor v. Bostwick Laboratories, Inc. 669 F.3d 428 (4th Cir. 2012).

WHIRLPOOL CORP. V. MARSHALL, SECRETARY OF LABOR

Supreme Court of the United States, 1980.
445 U.S. 1, 100 S.Ct. 883, 63 L.Ed.2d 154.

MR. JUSTICE STEWART delivered the opinion of the Court.

The Occupational Safety and Health Act of 1970 (Act) prohibits an employer from discharging or discriminating against any employee who exercises "any right afforded by" the Act.[2] The Secretary of Labor (Secretary) has promulgated a regulation providing that, among the rights that the Act so protects, is the right of an employee to choose not to perform his assigned task because of a reasonable apprehension of death or serious injury coupled with a reasonable belief that no less drastic alternative is available.[3] The question presented in the case before us is whether this regulation is consistent with the Act.

---

[2]   Section 11(c)(1) of the Act, 84 Stat. 1603, 29 U.S.C. § 660(c)(1), provides in full:

"No person shall discharge or in any manner discriminate against any employee because such employee has filed any complaint or instituted or caused to be instituted any proceeding under or related to this Act or has testified or is about to testify in any such proceeding or because of the exercise by such employee on behalf of himself or others of any right afforded by this Act."

[3]   The regulation, 29 CFR § 1977.12 (1979), provides in full:

"(a)   In addition to protecting employees who file complaints, institute proceedings, or testify in proceedings under or related to the Act, section 11(c) also protects employees from discrimination occurring because of the exercise 'of any right afforded by this Act.' Certain rights are explicitly provided in the Act; for example, there is a right to participate as a party in enforcement proceedings (sec. 10). Certain other rights exist by necessary implication. For example, employees may request information from the Occupational Safety and Health Administration; such requests would constitute the exercise of a right afforded by the Act. Likewise, employees interviewed by agents of the Secretary in the course of inspections or investigations could not subsequently be discriminated against because of their cooperation.

"(b)(1) On the other hand, review of the Act and examination of the legislative history discloses that, as a general matter, there is no right afforded by the Act which would entitle employees to walk off the job because of potential unsafe conditions at the workplace. Hazardous conditions which may be violative of the Act will ordinarily be corrected by the employer, once brought to his attention. If corrections are not accomplished, or if there is dispute about the existence of a hazard, the employee will normally have opportunity to request inspection of the workplace pursuant to section 8(f) of the Act, or to seek the assistance of other public agencies which have responsibility in the field of safety and health. Under such circumstances, therefore, an employer would not ordinarily be in violation of section 11(c) by taking action to discipline an employee for refusing to perform normal job activities because of alleged safety or health hazards.

"(2)   However, occasions might arise when an employee is confronted with a choice between not performing assigned tasks or subjecting himself to serious injury or death arising from a hazardous condition at the workplace. If the employee, with no reasonable alternative, refuses in good faith to expose himself to the dangerous condition, he would be protected against subsequent discrimination. The condition

I

The petitioner company maintains a manufacturing plant in Marion, Ohio, for the production of household appliances. Overhead conveyors transport appliance components throughout the plant. To protect employees from objects that occasionally fall from these conveyors, the petitioner has installed a horizontal wire-mesh guard screen approximately 20 feet above the plant floor. This mesh screen is welded to angle-iron frames suspended from the building's structural steel skeleton.

Maintenance employees of the petitioner spend several hours each week removing objects from the screen, replacing paper spread on the screen to catch grease drippings from the material on the conveyors, and performing occasional maintenance work on the conveyors themselves. To perform these duties, maintenance employees usually are able to stand on the iron frames, but sometimes find it necessary to step onto the steel mesh screen itself.

In 1973, the company began to install heavier wire in the screen because its safety had been drawn into question. Several employees had fallen partly through the old screen, and on one occasion an employee had fallen completely through to the plant floor below but had survived. A number of maintenance employees had reacted to these incidents by bringing the unsafe screen conditions to the attention of their foremen. The petitioner company's contemporaneous safety instructions admonished employees to step only on the angle-iron frames.

On June 28, 1974, a maintenance employee fell to his death through the guard screen in an area where the newer, stronger mesh had not yet been installed.[4] Following this incident, the petitioner effectuated some repairs and issued an order strictly forbidding maintenance employees from stepping on either the screens or the angle-iron supporting structure. An alternative but somewhat more cumbersome and less satisfactory method was developed for removing objects from the screen. This procedure required employees to stand on power-raised mobile platforms and use hooks to recover the material.

---

causing the employee's apprehension of death or injury must be of such a nature that a reasonable person, under the circumstances then confronting the employee, would conclude that there is a real danger of death or serious injury and that there is insufficient time due to the urgency of the situation, to eliminate the danger through resort to regular statutory enforcement channels. In addition, in such circumstances, the employee, where possible, must also have sought from his employer, and been unable to obtain, a correction of the dangerous condition."

[4]   As a result of this fatality, the Secretary conducted an investigation that led to the issuance of a citation charging the company with maintaining an unsafe walking and working surface in violation of 29 U.S.C. § 654(a)(1). The citation required immediate abatement of the hazard and proposed a $600 penalty. Nearly five years following the accident, the Occupational Safety and Health Review Commission affirmed the citation, but decided to permit the petitioner six months in which to correct the unsafe condition. *Whirlpool Corp.,* 1979 CCH OSHD ¶ 23,552. A petition to review that decision is pending in the United States Court of Appeals for the District of Columbia Circuit.

On July 7, 1974, two of the petitioner's maintenance employees, Virgil Deemer and Thomas Cornwell, met with the plant maintenance superintendent to voice their concern about the safety of the screen. The superintendent disagreed with their view, but permitted the two men to inspect the screen with their foreman and to point out dangerous areas needing repair. Unsatisfied with the petitioner's response to the results of this inspection, Deemer and Cornwell met on July 9 with the plant safety director. At that meeting, they requested the name, address, and telephone number of a representative of the local office of the Occupational Safety and Health Administration (OSHA). Although the safety director told the men that they "had better stop and think about what [they] were doing," he furnished the men with the information they requested. Later that same day, Deemer contacted an official of the regional OSHA office and discussed the guard screen.

The next day, Deemer and Cornwell reported for the night shift at 10:45 p.m. Their foreman, after himself walking on some of the angle-iron frames, directed the two men to perform their usual maintenance duties on a section of the old screen.[6] Claiming that the screen was unsafe, they refused to carry out this directive. The foreman then sent them to the personnel office, where they were ordered to punch out without working or being paid for the remaining six hours of the shift.[7] The two men subsequently received written reprimands, which were placed in their employment files.

A little over a month later, the Secretary filed suit in the United States District Court for the Northern District of Ohio, alleging that the petitioner's actions against Deemer and Cornwell constituted discrimination in violation of § 11(c)(1) of the Act. * * *

Following a bench trial, the District Court found that the regulation in question justified Deemer's and Cornwell's refusals to obey their foreman's order on July 10, 1974. * * * The District Court nevertheless denied relief, holding that the Secretary's regulation was inconsistent with the Act and therefore invalid.

The Court of Appeals for the Sixth Circuit reversed the District Court's judgment. * * *

II

The Act itself creates an express mechanism for protecting workers from employment conditions believed to pose an emergent threat of death or serious injury. Upon receipt of an employee inspection request stating reasonable grounds to believe that an imminent danger is present in a workplace, OSHA must conduct an inspection. 29 U.S.C. § 657(f)(1). In the

---

[6]   This order appears to have been in direct violation of the outstanding company directive that maintenance work was to be accomplished without stepping on the screen apparatus.

[7]   Both employees apparently returned to work the following day without further incident.

event this inspection reveals workplace conditions or practices that "could reasonably be expected to cause death or serious physical harm immediately or before the imminence of such danger can be eliminated through the enforcement procedures otherwise provided by" the Act,[11] 29 U.S.C. § 662(a), the OSHA inspector must inform the affected employees and the employer of the danger and notify them that he is recommending to the Secretary that injunctive relief be sought. § 662(c). At this juncture, the Secretary can petition a federal court to restrain the conditions or practices giving rise to the imminent danger. By means of a temporary restraining order or preliminary injunction, the court may then require the employer to avoid, correct, or remove the danger or to prohibit employees from working in the area. § 662(a).[12]

To ensure that this process functions effectively, the Act expressly accords to every employee several rights, the exercise of which may not subject him to discharge or discrimination. An employee is given the right to inform OSHA of an imminently dangerous workplace condition or practice and request that OSHA inspect that condition or practice. 29 U.S.C. § 657(f)(1). He is given a limited right to assist the OSHA inspector in inspecting the workplace, §§ 657(a)(2), (e), and (f)(2), and the right to aid a court in determining whether or not a risk of imminent danger in fact exists. See § 660(c)(1). Finally, an affected employee is given the right to bring an action to compel the Secretary to seek injunctive relief if he believes the Secretary has wrongfully declined to do so. § 662(d).

In the light of this detailed statutory scheme, the Secretary is obviously correct when he acknowledges in his regulation that, "as a general matter, there is no right afforded by the Act which would entitle employees to walk off the job because of potential unsafe conditions at the workplace."

* * *

As this case illustrates, however, circumstances may sometimes exist in which the employee justifiably believes that the express statutory arrangement does not sufficiently protect him from death or serious injury. Such circumstances will probably not often occur, but such a situation may arise when (1) the employee is ordered by his employer to work under conditions that the employee reasonably believes pose an imminent risk of

---

[11] These usual enforcement procedures involve the issuance of citations and imposition of penalties. When an OSHA inspection reveals a violation of 29 U.S.C. § 654 or of any standard promulgated under the Act, the Secretary may issue a citation for the alleged violation, fix a reasonable time for the dangerous condition's abatement, and propose a penalty. §§ 658(a), 659(a), 666. The employer may contest the citation and proposed penalty. § 659(a), (c). Should he do so, the effective date of the abatement order is postponed until the completion of all administrative proceedings initiated in good faith. §§ 659(b), 666(d). Such proceedings may include a hearing before an administrative law judge and review by the Occupational Safety and Health Review Commission. §§ 659(c), 661(i).

[12] Such an order may continue pending the consummation of the Act's normal enforcement proceedings. § 662(b).

death or serious bodily injury, and (2) the employee has reason to believe that there is not sufficient time or opportunity either to seek effective redress from his employer or to apprise OSHA of the danger.

Nothing in the Act suggests that those few employees who have to face this dilemma must rely exclusively on the remedies expressly set forth in the Act at the risk of their own safety. But nothing in the Act explicitly provides otherwise. Against this background of legislative silence, the Secretary has exercised his rulemaking power under 29 U.S.C. § 657(g)(2) and has determined that, when an employee in good faith finds himself in such a predicament, he may refuse to expose himself to the dangerous condition, without being subjected to "subsequent discrimination" by the employer.

The question before us is whether this interpretative regulation constitutes a permissible gloss on the Act by the Secretary, in light of the Act's language, structure, and legislative history. Our inquiry is informed by an awareness that the regulation is entitled to deference unless it can be said not to be a reasoned and supportable interpretation of the Act. *Skidmore v. Swift & Co.,* 323 U.S. 134, 139–140, 65 S.Ct. 161, 164, 89 L.Ed. 124. See *Ford Motor Credit Co. v. Milhollin,* 444 U.S. 555, 100 S.Ct. 790, 63 L.Ed.2d 22; *Mourning v. Family Publications Service, Inc.,* 411 U.S. 356, 93 S.Ct. 1652, 36 L.Ed.2d 318.

The regulation clearly conforms to the fundamental objective of the Act—to prevent occupational deaths and serious injuries.

* * *

To accomplish this basic purpose, the legislation's remedial orientation is prophylactic in nature. See *Atlas Roofing Co. v. Occupational Safety and Health Review Comm'n,* 430 U.S. 442, 444–445, 97 S.Ct. 1261, 1263–1264, 51 L.Ed.2d 464. The Act does not wait for an employee to die or become injured. It authorizes the promulgation of health and safety standards and the issuance of citations in the hope that these will act to prevent deaths or injuries from ever occurring. It would seem anomalous to construe an Act so directed and constructed as prohibiting an employee, with no other reasonable alternative, the freedom to withdraw from a workplace environment that he reasonably believes is highly dangerous.

Moreover, the Secretary's regulation can be viewed as an appropriate aid to the full effectuation of the Act's "general duty" clause. That clause provides that "[e]ach employer * * * shall furnish to each of his employees employment and a place of employment which are free from recognized hazards that are causing or are likely to cause death or serious physical harm to his employees." 29 U.S.C. § 654(a)(1). As the legislative history of this provision reflects, it was intended itself to deter the occurrence of occupational deaths and serious injuries by placing on employers a mandatory obligation independent of the specific health and safety standards to be promulgated by the Secretary. Since OSHA inspectors cannot be present around the clock in every workplace, the Secretary's regulation ensures that employees will in all circumstances enjoy the rights afforded them by the "general duty" clause.

The regulation thus on its face appears to further the overriding purpose of the Act, and rationally to complement its remedial scheme.

[*Eds.* The Court's discussion of the legislative history is omitted. For a general description of OSHA regulation, see p. 749 infra.]

NOTES AND QUESTIONS

Test Your Understanding of the Material

1.   Suppose that OSHA inspectors arrived immediately following Deemer and Cornwell's call on July 7, 1974, and declared the screen safe. Deemer and Cornwell nevertheless refuse to perform the maintenance, based on their previously articulated objections. Would Deemer and Cornwell still have a claim under the standard articulated in *Whirlpool*?

Related Issues

2.   *Limits of Self-Help Remedy.* The OSHA regulation, sustained in *Whirlpool*, does not create a general right to walk off the job whenever workers suspect a safety hazard. Rather, the workers must show that (i) they have a good faith, reasonably grounded fear of "a real danger of death or serious injury"; (ii) "there is insufficient time due to the urgency of the situation, to eliminate the danger through resort to regular statutory channels"; and (iii) "where possible," they "have sought from the employer, and been unable to obtain, a correction of the dangerous condition." 29 C.F.R. § 1977.12(b)(2), quoted in footnote 3 of the *Whirlpool* opinion.

3.   *Self-Help Under Federal Labor Law.* Federal labor law provides additional self-help protection. Workers have a statutory right to strike over safety issues, see NLRB v. Washington Aluminum Co., 370 U.S. 9, 82 S.Ct. 1099, 8 L.Ed.2d 298 (1962), and under § 502 of the LMRA, 29 U.S.C. § 143, may even strike in the face of a contractual no-strike promise if they have an objective, good-faith fear of "abnormally dangerous conditions," see Gateway Coal v. United Mine Workers, 414 U.S. 368, 385–86, 94 S.Ct. 629, 640–41, 38 L.Ed.2d 583 (1974); e.g., TNS, Inc. v. NLRB, 296 F.3d 384 (6th Cir. 2002). The collective bargaining agreement may itself privilege refusals to perform work under unsafe conditions, thus creating an exception to a general "work now/grieve later" principle, see NLRB v. City Disposal Systems, 465 U.S. 822, 104 S.Ct. 1505, 79 L.Ed.2d 839 (1984).

4.   *"Constructive Discharge" Doctrine.* Are there circumstances where § 704(a) of Title VII protects oppositional activity taking the form of a refusal to work? Can an employee subjected to insufferably discriminatory working conditions refuse to work as long as those conditions continue? Courts have developed a "constructive discharge" doctrine to allow employees to quit their employment in circumstances where reasonable persons would not continue

working without the quit being treated as a voluntary separation. See, e.g., Pennsylvania State Police v. Suders, 542 U.S. 129, 124 S.Ct. 2342, 159 L.Ed.2d 204 (2004). See Restatement of Employment Law § 5.01, Comment c (2015).

C. IMPLIED ANTIRETALIATION PROVISIONS

As noted above, most federal and state employment statutes now include some form of antiretaliation provision. As the next decision suggests, however, this is not universally the case. Furthermore, some federal and state statutes that do contain antiretaliation provisions expressly authorize only administrative or criminal enforcement; they do not expressly provide a private right of action to workers claiming to be victims of retaliation. When should courts both imply antiretaliation guarantees and also afford employees a right of action to enforce them? Does a statutory scheme that does not provide for such actions reflect a considered legislative judgment that they are inappropriate? May a court infer from the existence of substantive restrictions on employer action and the provision of some remedies a declaration of legislative policy permitting judicial implication of a private right of action?

KELSAY V. MOTOROLA, INC.
Supreme Court of Illinois, 1978.
74 Ill.2d 172, 23 Ill.Dec. 559, 384 N.E.2d 353.

RYAN, J.

Plaintiff, Marilyn Jo Kelsay, filed a complaint in the circuit court of Livingston County, seeking compensatory and punitive damages against her ex-employer, Motorola, Inc. The plaintiff alleged that her employment with defendant had been terminated as retaliation for her filing a workmen's compensation claim. The trial court directed a verdict in plaintiff's favor and the jury assessed damages in the amount of $1,000 compensatory damages and $25,000 punitive damages. The court remitted the compensatory damages to $749, which represents the wages plaintiff lost between the time she was discharged and the time she found a new job. On appeal, the Fourth District Appellate Court reversed the judgment of the trial court, holding that an employee has no cause of action against an employer for retaliatory discharge.

* * *

The Workmen's Compensation Act (Ill.Rev.Stat.1973, ch. 48, par. 138.1 *et seq.*) substitutes an entirely new system of rights, remedies, and procedure for all previously existing common law rights and liabilities between employers and employees subject to the Act for accidental injuries or death of employees arising out of and in the course of the employment. (37 Ill.L. & Prac. *Workmen's Compensation* sec. 2 (1958).) Pursuant to the statutory scheme implemented by the Act, the employee gave up his common law rights to sue his employer in tort, but recovery for injuries arising out of and in the course of his employment became automatic without regard to any fault on his part. The employer, who gave up the right to plead the numerous common law defenses, was compelled to pay, but his liability became fixed under a strict and comprehensive statutory scheme, and was not subjected to the sympathies of jurors whose compassion for fellow employees often led to high recovery. (See 81 Am.Jur.2d *Workmen's Compensation* sec. 1 *et seq.* (1976).) This trade-off between employer and employee promoted the fundamental purpose of the Act, which was to afford protection to employees by providing them with prompt and equitable compensation for their injuries.

* * *

While noting that in 1975, subsequent to plaintiff's discharge, the Workmen's Compensation Act was amended making it unlawful for an employer to interfere with or to coerce the employee in the exercise of his rights under the Act (Ill.Rev.Stat.1975, ch. 48, par. 138.4(h)), the employer argues that as of the time of plaintiff's discharge, the legislature had neither prohibited nor provided for any remedy for a discharge resulting from the filing of a workmen's compensation claim. As such, its authority to terminate the employee, whose contract was at will, was absolute.

* * *

We are not convinced that an employer's otherwise absolute power to terminate an employee at will should prevail when that power is exercised to prevent the employee from asserting his statutory rights under the Workmen's Compensation Act. As we have noted, the legislature enacted the workmen's compensation law as a comprehensive scheme to provide for efficient and expeditious remedies for injured employees. This scheme would be seriously undermined if employers were permitted to abuse their power to terminate by threatening to discharge employees for seeking compensation under the Act. We cannot ignore the fact that when faced with such a dilemma many employees, whose common law rights have been supplanted by the Act, would choose to retain their jobs, and thus, in effect, would be left without a remedy either common law or statutory. This result, which effectively relieves the employer of the responsibility expressly placed upon him by the legislature, is untenable and is contrary to the public policy as expressed in the Workmen's Compensation Act. We cannot believe that the legislature, even in the absence of an explicit proscription against retaliatory discharge, intended such a result.

* * *

The employer argues that the exclusivity provision of section 11 of the Act, which provides that the provisions of the Act "shall be the measure of the responsibility of any employer" (Ill.Rev.Stat.1973, ch. 48, par. 138.11), precludes an action for retaliatory discharge. Motorola argues that this conclusion is compelled because the section clearly shows that the legislature intended that the Act should be exclusive in providing for employees' rights and remedies. We do not agree. First, that section was meant to limit recovery by employees to the extent provided by the Act in regard to work-related injuries, and was not intended to insulate the employer from independent tort actions. Second, we cannot accept a construction of section 11 which would allow employers to put employees in a position of choosing between their jobs and seeking their remedies under the Act.

* * *

The employer argues that the absence of any provisions for civil remedies for retaliatory discharge in the 1975 amendments, which make it a criminal offense for an employer to threaten or effect such a discharge (Ill.Rev.Stat.1975, ch. 48, par. 138.4(h)), is a conscious decision by the legislature that no such civil remedy shall exist. We do not agree. As we have noted, retaliatory discharge is offensive to the public policy of this State as stated in the Workmen's Compensation Act. This policy can only be effectively implemented and enforced by allowing a civil remedy for damages, distinct from any criminal sanctions which may be imposed on employers for violating the Act after 1975. The imposition of a small fine, enuring to the benefit of the State, does nothing to alleviate the plight of those employees who are threatened with retaliation and forgo their rights, or those who lose their jobs when they proceed to file claims under the Act. It is conceivable, moreover, that some employers would risk the threat of criminal sanction in order to escape their responsibility under the Act. Further, the fact that an act is penal in nature does not bar a civil remedy, and where a statute is enacted for the benefit of a particular class of individuals a violation of its terms may result in civil as well as criminal liability, even though the former remedy is not specifically mentioned. *Heimgaertner v. Benjamin Electric Manufacturing Co.* (1955), 6 Ill.2d 152, 128 N.E.2d 691.

* * *

We now consider the award of $25,000 punitive damages. In this connection, two points merit consideration, first, whether punitive damages may generally be awarded in cases for retaliatory discharge, and second, whether the jury's award for such damages was proper in the instant case.

* * *

In the absence of the deterrent effect of punitive damages there would be little to dissuade an employer from engaging in the practice of discharging an employee for filing a workmen's compensation claim. For example in this case, the plaintiff was entitled to only $749 compensatory damages. We noted above the very real possibility that some employers would risk the threat of criminal sanction in order to escape their responsibilities under the Act. The statute makes such conduct, as is involved in this case, a petty offense (Ill.Rev.Stat.1975, ch. 48, par. 138.26), which is punishable by a fine not to exceed $500 (Ill.Rev.Stat.1975, ch. 38, par. 1005–9–1(4)). The imposition on the employer of the small additional obligation to pay a wrongfully discharged employee compensation would do little to discourage the practice of retaliatory discharge, which mocks the public policy of this State as announced in the Workmen's Compensation Act. In the absence of other effective means of deterrence, punitive damages must be permitted to prevent the discharging of employees for filing workmen's compensation claims.

* * *

However, under the facts of the present case, we are compelled to conclude that the award of $25,000 as punitive damages was improper. [T]he function of punitive damages is similar to that of a criminal penalty, *i.e.,* as a punishment to the wrongdoer and as a means to deter such a wrongdoer and others from committing like offenses in the future. (See *Mattyasovszky v. West Towns Bus Co.* (1975), 61 Ill.2d 31, 330 N.E.2d 509.) Because of their penal nature, punitive damages are not favored in the law, and the courts must take caution to see that punitive damages are not improperly or unwisely awarded. (See *Eshelman v. Rawalt* (1921), 298 Ill. 192, 197, 131 N.E. 675.) Adherence to this rule compels us to conclude that punitive damages should not be awarded where, as here, the cause of action forming the basis for their award is a novel one.

* * *

At the time of plaintiff's discharge there was no provision in the Act making it unlawful to discharge an employee for seeking relief under its provisions. Also, at that time there was no decision of this court holding that a retaliatory discharge in such cases was actionable.

[*Eds*. For a discussion of the role of Workers' Compensation Laws, see pp. 730–734 infra.]

NOTES AND QUESTIONS

Test Your Understanding of the Material

1.   Why might the Illinois legislature prior to 1975 have established a workers' compensation scheme without making it unlawful for an employer to retaliate against an employee for filing a claim under that scheme? Is the case for an implied right of action stronger or weaker after 1975, when the Illinois legislature provided for criminal remedies? For an example of judicial reluctance to recognize a supplementary civil action, see Bottijliso v. Hutchison Fruit Co., 96 N.M. 789, 635 P.2d 992 (1981).

2. Are you persuaded by the *Kelsay* court's refusal to sustain the award of punitive damages?

Related Issues

3. *Implied Antiretaliation Protections.* The Supreme Court in this century has implied anti-retaliation protections for several federal anti-discrimination rights. For instance, in Jackson v. Birmingham Bd. of Educ., 544 U.S. 167, 174, 125 S.Ct. 1497, 161 L.Ed.2d 361 (2005), the Court held that protection against retaliation for filing a complaint with the government could be implied from the prohibition of gender discrimination in Title IX of the Education Amendments of 1972, 20 U.S.C. § 1681 et seq.: "when a funding recipient retaliates against a person because he complains of sex discrimination, this constitutes intentional discrimination 'on the basis of sex,' in violation of Title IX." The Court has also held that federal-sector employees have an implied retaliation claim under Section 15 of ADEA, 29 U.S.C. § 633a, Gomez-Perez v. Potter, 553 U.S. 474, 128 S.Ct. 1931, 170 L.Ed.2d 887 (2008), and that plaintiffs have such a claim under 42 U.S.C. § 1981, CBOCS West, Inc. v. Humphries, 552 U.S. 1172, 128 S.Ct. 1183, 169 L.Ed.2d 959 (2008).

4. *Implied Federal Causes of Action.* The Court, however, seems now more hesitant to supplement express public enforcement of regulations with implied private rights of action. The Supreme Court once articulated in Cort v. Ash, 422 U.S. 66, 95 S.Ct. 2080, 45 L.Ed.2d 26 (1975), a set of criteria for deciding whether to recognize an implied right of action:

> First, is the plaintiff "one of the class for whose especial benefit the statute was enacted"—that is, does the statute create a federal right in favor of the plaintiff? Second, is there any indication of legislative intent, explicit or implicit, either to create such a remedy or to deny one? Third, is it consistent with the underlying purpose of the legislative scheme to imply such a remedy? And finally, is the cause of action one traditionally relegated to state law, so that it would be inappropriate to infer a cause of action based solely on federal law?

Id. at 78 (citations and emphasis omitted). Applying this test, the Court recognized an implied right of action under § 901(a) of Title IX of the Education Amendments of 1972, 42 U.S.C. § 681, in Cannon v. University of Chicago, 441 U.S. 677, 99 S.Ct. 1946, 60 L.Ed.2d 560 (1979). However, in post-*Cannon* decisions, the Court has stressed the second factor, insisting that Congress signal its intent to authorize private actions. See, e.g., Alexander v. Sandoval, 532 U.S. 275, 287, 121 S.Ct. 1511, 149 L.Ed.2d 517 (2001) ("[l]ike substantive federal law itself, private rights of action to enforce federal law must be created by Congress").

CHAPTER 12

"PUBLIC POLICY" CAUSE OF ACTION; PROTECTION OF "WHISTLEBLOWERS"

▪ ▪ ▪

Introduction

Chapter 11 addressed rules protecting employee activity for its contribution to a statutory scheme that is intended to secure benefits for employees. In this chapter, we consider more generally the extent to which common law decisions and statutes protect employee activity that is protected primarily because of benefits that may be generated for third parties, typically the general public.

As reflected in the Employment Restatement provision below, the majority of states recognize a cause of action for wrongful termination in violation of public policy. The primary rationale for the "public policy" cause of action is that employers should not use their contractual right to terminate the employment relationship in a manner that might frustrate the third-party interests of the public. Such frustration is likely where a retaliatory termination discourages employee activity that may serve some public interest. Just as courts declare certain contracts void as a matter of public policy, recognition of a wrongful termination in violation of public policy claim is "aimed at controlling the external effects" of private employment decisionmaking. See Jeffrey L. Harrison, "New" Terminable-at-Will Employment Contract: An Interest and Cost Incidence Analysis, 69 Iowa L.Rev. 327, 349 (1984). The public policy cause of action also owes an intellectual debt to Lawrence Blades, Employment at Will vs. Individual Freedom: On Limiting the Abusive Exercise of Employer Power, 67 Colum.L.Rev. 1404 (1967), which argued that much like the French doctrine of *abus de droit* and the American tort doctrines of malicious prosecution and abuse of process, American employment law should restrict abusive exercise of employer power for a socially unjustified purpose.

RESTATEMENT OF EMPLOYMENT LAW, §§ 5.01–5.03
American Law Institute (2015).

§ 5.01   Wrongful Discharge in Violation of Public Policy

An employer that discharges an employee because the employee engages in activity protected by a well-established public policy as described in § 5.02 is subject to liability in tort for wrongful discharge in violation of public policy, unless the statute or other law forming the basis of the applicable public policy precludes tort liability or otherwise makes judicial recognition of a tort claim inappropriate.

§ 5.02 Wrongful Discharge in Violation of Public Policy: Protected Activities

An employer is subject to liability in tort under § 5.01 for discharging an employee because the employee, acting in a reasonable manner,

(a) refuses to commit an act that the employee reasonably and in good faith believes violates a law or other well-established public policy, such as a professional or occupational code of conduct protective of the public interest;

(b) performs a public duty or obligation that the employee reasonably and in good faith believes the law imposes;

(c) file a charge or claims a benefit in good faith under an employment statute or law, whether or not the charge or claim is meritorious;

(d) refuses to waive a nonnegotiable or nonwaivable right when the employer's insistence on the waiver as a condition of employment, or the court's enforcement of the waiver, would violate well-established public policy;

(e) reports or inquires about conduct that the employee reasonably and in good faith believes violates a law or an established principle of a professional or occupational code of conduct protective of the public interest; or

(f) engages in other activity directly furthering a well-established public policy.

§ 5.03 Wrongful Discharge in Violation of Public Policy: Sources of Public Policy

Sources of public policy for the tort of wrongful discharge in violation of public policy under § 5.01 include:

(a) federal and state constitutions;

(b) federal, state, and local statutes, ordinances, and decisional law;

(c) federal, state, and local administrative regulations, decisions, and orders; and

(d) well-established principles in a professional or occupational code of conduct protective of the public interest.

NOTE: EVOLUTION OF PUBLIC POLICY CAUSE OF ACTION

The chapter starts by chronicling the evolution of the common law claim for wrongful termination in violation of public policy, starting with *Nees v. Hocks* and *Tameny v. Atlantic Richfield Co.* These two cases, along with *Kelsay v. Motorola* (the concluding case in Chapter 11) represent three stages in the judicial recognition of the public policy cause of action. *Kelsay* involves judicial implication of a private civil remedy for employees who have been retaliated against for the assertion of a statutory claim. In *Kelsay*, the public policy is defined by the statute, and the court engages in the traditional enterprise of deciding whether a private right of action is necessary to effectuate the scheme and consistent with the legislative design. *Nees* involves a somewhat more difficult problem because the public policy is not centrally located in a particular statute, but must be gleaned from a variety of state statutory and constitutional provisions. *Tameny* requires the court to determine whether in some circumstances employee refusals to perform assigned work contravenes public policy. See Samuel Estreicher & Beverly Wolff, At-Will Employment and the Problem of Unjust Dismissal, 36 Record of the Assn. of the Bar of the City of N.Y. 170 (April 1981).

The early cases in this chapter involve so-called "passive whistleblowers"—those forced to choose between their jobs and fulfilling a legal duty or complying with the law. Later cases examine the more complex case of "active whistleblowers"—those who oppose or complain about their employer's unlawful activity on their own initiative. The chapter concludes with an overview of statutory protections for whistleblowers, and how those statutes may affect the availability of common law claims.

A. PERFORMANCE OF PUBLIC OBLIGATIONS

NEES V. HOCKS

Supreme Court of Oregon, 1975.
272 Or. 210, 536 P.2d 512.

DENECKE, J.

The jury found for plaintiff; therefore, we must consider the facts as established by the evidence most favorable to plaintiff. The plaintiff performed clerical duties for defendants. She started work in 1971. In 1972 she was called for jury duty; however, as she informed defendants, she requested and was granted a 12-month postponement because of her honeymoon. On February 2, 1973, plaintiff was again subpoenaed to serve on the jury. She told defendants and they stated that a month was too long for her "to be gone." Defendants gave her a letter which stated defendants could spare plaintiff "for awhile" but not for a month and asked that she be excused. Plaintiff presented this letter to the court clerk and told the clerk that she had been called before and had to be excused, but she would like to serve on jury duty. The clerk told plaintiff she would not be excused. The plaintiff immediately came back to the office and told defendants that she would have to serve a minimum of two weeks' jury duty. She did not tell defendants she had told the court clerk she really wanted to serve.

Plaintiff started her jury duty on February 26, 1973. On March 1, 1973, she received a termination letter from defendants. The letter stated, in part: "Although we asked you to request an excusal from Jury Duty and wrote a letter confirming the [defendants'] position, it has been brought to our attention you, in fact, requested to be placed on Jury Duty." The letter went on to state the defendants also were not otherwise satisfied with plaintiff's work. Based upon other evidence, however, the jury could have found plaintiff was not terminated because of dissatisfaction with the quality of plaintiff's work.

* * *

We recognize, as defendants assert, that, generally, in the absence of a contract or legislation to the contrary, an employer can discharge an employee at any time and for any cause. Conversely, an employee can quit at any time for any cause. Such termination by the employer or employee is not a breach of contract and ordinarily does not create a tortious cause of action. The question to us is, however, are there instances in which the employer's reason or motive for discharging harms or interferes with an important interest of the community and, therefore, justifies compensation to the employee?

* * *

We conclude that there can be circumstances in which an employer discharges an employee for such a socially undesirable motive that the employer must respond in damages for any injury done. The next question is, does the evidence in this case permit a finding that such circumstances are present?

There is evidence from which the jury could have found that the defendants discharged the plaintiff because, after being subpoenaed, and contrary to the defendants' wishes, plaintiff told the clerk she would like to serve and she did serve on jury duty.[2] Therefore, the immediate question can be stated specifically—is the community's interest in having its citizens serve on jury duty so important that an employer, who interferes with that interest by discharging an employee who served on a jury, should be required to compensate his employee for any damages she suffered?

Art. VII, § 3, of the Oregon Constitution provides that jury trial shall be preserved in civil cases. Art. I, § 11, provides a defendant in a criminal case has a right of trial by jury. Art. VII, § 5, provides: "The Legislative

---

[2]   If the only evidence was that the defendants would have suffered a substantial hardship if plaintiff served this particular month [and] defendants requested only a postponement of jury service but the plaintiff nevertheless asked to serve this particular month, we probably would regard the discharge as justifiable.

Assembly shall so provide that the most competent of the permanent citizens of the county shall be chosen for jurors."

ORS 10.040 provides for certain exemptions from jury duty. ORS 10.050 provides for certain excuses from jury duty including health, age and "(c) When serving as a juror would result in extreme hardship to the person including but not limited to unusual and extraordinary financial hardship." ORS 10.055 provides for deferment of jury duty "for good cause shown" for not more than one year. ORS 10.990 provides that if a juror "without reasonable cause" neglects to attend for jury service the sheriff may impose a fine, not exceeding $20 for each day the juror does not attend.

People v. Vitucci, 49 Ill.App.2d 171, 199 N.E.2d 78 (1964), stated that an employer who discharged an employee who was absent because of jury duty was guilty of contempt of court. Massachusetts has a statute making such conduct contemptuous. 44 Mass.G.L.A., ch. 268, § 14A.

These actions by the people, the legislature and the courts clearly indicate that the jury system and jury duty are regarded as high on the scale of American institutions and citizen obligations. If an employer were permitted with impunity to discharge an employee for fulfilling her obligation of jury duty, the jury system would be adversely affected. The will of the community would be thwarted. For these reasons we hold that the defendants are liable for discharging plaintiff because she served on the jury.

NOTES AND QUESTIONS

Test Your Understanding of the Material

1.   When representing an employee with a wrongful termination in violation of public policy claim, an attorney, after collecting the facts, must identify sources of law that establish a public policy. Identify the types of legal sources that the Court in *Nees* recognizes to support the public policy at issue. Under which provision of the Employment Restatement § 5.02 would the plaintiff's claim fall?

2.   Why did the employer terminate *Nees*? Suppose the plaintiff had volunteered for jury duty. Does the reasoning of *Nees* bar an employer from advising his employee not to volunteer his or her availability for jury duty and then discharging the employee for volunteering such availability? What if the employer had a special need for the plaintiff's services during a particular period?

3.   In wrongful termination claims, courts typically expect plaintiffs to explain (a) how the cited legislation reflects a fundamental public policy interest, and (b) why common law protection of the plaintiff's conduct is important to advancing or preserving that public policy interest. Suppose that you represent the plaintiff in *Nees*. Review the language in Ore.Rev.Stat. 10.050 (quoted in the case), and explain how it reflects a fundamental public

policy interest, why Nees' actions advance or preserve that interest, and why a discharge would violate that policy.

Related Issues

4. *Statutory Developments.* The holding of *Nees* has now been codified. See Ore.Rev.Stat. 10.090. Many states have comparable provisions. See, e.g., West's Ann.Cal.Labor Code § 230(a); N.Y.Jud.Law § 532; Tex.Civ.Code Art. § 122.001–003. Some statutes also expressly protect employees who leave work to testify as witnesses in court, see, e.g., West's Ann.Cal.Labor Code § 230; N.Y.-McKinney's Penal Law § 215.11; Or.Rev.Stat. 659.270, or before a legislature, see, e.g., Nev.Rev.Stat. 50.070. Also, the Federal Jury System Improvement Act, 28 U.S.C. § 1875, prohibits penalizing employees who serve on a federal court jury. See Shea v. County of Rockland, 810 F.2d 27 (2d Cir.1987) (only lost wages, not compensatory damages, may be recovered). If the jury in *Nees* were a federal jury, what provision would the employer have violated?

5. *"Citizen Crime Fighters."* How broadly does the *Nees* rationale extend? Law enforcement authorities in some sense also rely on public cooperation in detecting and apprehending wrongdoers. Yet, under current law, while citizens may be obligated to respond honestly to grand jury inquiries, in most states they are under no affirmative duty to report suspected wrongdoing. *Palmateer v. International Harvester Co.*, p. 656 infra, examines the question of whether employees who report illegal behavior by their fellow employees or employer should be protected from employer retaliation. 85 Ill.2d 124, 52 Ill.Dec. 13, 421 N.E.2d 876 (1981). See the materials on "whistleblowers," at p. 660 infra. Does the Employment Restatement § 5.02 have any relevance here?

B. REFUSAL TO PERFORM ASSIGNMENT IN CONTRAVENTION OF PUBLIC POLICY

TAMENY v. ATLANTIC RICHFIELD CO.
Supreme Court of California, 1980.
27 Cal.3d 167, 164 Cal.Rptr. 839, 610 P.2d 1330.

TOBRINER, J.

Plaintiff Gordon Tameny instituted the present action against his former employer, Atlantic Richfield Company (Arco), alleging that Arco had discharged him after 15 years of service because he refused to participate in an illegal scheme to fix retail gasoline prices. Plaintiff sought recovery from Arco on a number of theories, contending, inter alia, that Arco's conduct in discharging him for refusing to commit a criminal act was tortious and subjected the employer to liability for compensatory and punitive damages under normal tort principles.

* * *

Because this appeal arises from a judgment entered after the sustaining of a general demurrer, we must, under established principles, assume the truth of all properly pleaded material allegations of the complaint in evaluating the validity of the trial court's action.

* * *

According to the complaint, plaintiff was hired by Arco as a relief clerk in 1960, received regular advancements, merit increases and commendatory evaluations in his initial years with the company, and, in 1966, was promoted to the position of retail sales representative, the position he held when discharged by Arco in 1975. His duties as a retail sales representative included among other matters the management of relations between Arco and the various independent service station dealers (franchisees) in his assigned territory of Bakersfield.

The complaint alleges that beginning in the early 1970s, Arco, Arco's district manager McDermott, and others engaged in a combination "for the purpose of reducing, controlling, stabilizing, fixing, and pegging the retail gasoline prices of Arco service station franchisees." According to the complaint, defendants' conduct in this regard violated express provisions of the Sherman Antitrust Act (15 U.S.C. § 1 et seq.), the Cartwright Act (Bus. & Prof.Code, § 16720 et seq.), and a specific consent decree which had been entered in a federal antitrust prosecution against Arco.

The complaint further asserts that during the early 1970s, defendants increasingly pressured plaintiff to "threaten [and] cajole * * * the so-called 'independent' service station dealers in [his] territory to cut their gasoline prices to a point at or below a designated level specified by Arco." When plaintiff refused to yield to his employer's pressure to engage in such tactics, his supervisor told him that his discharge was imminent, and soon thereafter plaintiff was fired, effective March 25, 1975. Although at the time of the discharge Arco indicated in its personnel records that plaintiff was being fired for "incompetence" and for "unsatisfactory performance," the complaint alleges that "the sole reason" for plaintiff's discharge was his refusal to commit the "grossly illegal and unlawful acts which defendants tried to force him to perform."

* * *

Under the traditional common law rule, codified in Labor Code section 2922,[6] an employment contract of indefinite duration is in general terminable at "the will" of either party. Over the past several decades, however, judicial authorities in California and throughout the United States have established the rule that under both common law and the statute an employer does not enjoy an absolute or totally unfettered right to discharge even an at-will employee. In a series of cases arising out of a

---

[6] Section 2922 provides in relevant part: "An employment, having no specified term, may be terminated at the will of either party on notice to the other. * * * "

variety of factual settings in which a discharge clearly violated an express statutory objective or undermined a firmly established principle of public policy, courts have recognized that an employer's traditional broad authority to discharge an at-will employee "may be limited by statute * * * or by considerations of public policy." (*Petermann v. International Brotherhood of Teamsters* (1959) 174 Cal.App.2d 184, 188, 344 P.2d 25, 27 (discharge for refusal to commit perjury); see, e.g., * * * *Nees v. Hocks* (1975) 272 Or. 210, 536 P.2d 512 (discharge for serving on jury); *Frampton v. Central Indiana Gas Co.* (1973) 260 Ind. 249, 297 N.E.2d 425 (discharge for filing worker's compensation claim); *Harless v. First Nat. Bank in Fairmont* (W.Va.1978) 246 S.E.2d 270 (discharge for reporting violations of consumer protection laws).)

Petermann v. International Brotherhood of Teamsters, supra, one of the seminal California decisions in this area, imposes a significant condition upon the employer's broad power of dismissal by nullifying the right to discharge because an employee refuses to perform an unlawful act. In *Petermann,* the plaintiff, who had been employed as a business agent by defendant union, brought a "wrongful discharge" action against the union alleging that he had been dismissed from his position because he had refused to follow his employer's instructions to testify falsely under oath before a legislative committee, and instead had given truthful testimony. Emphasizing that the employer's instructions amounted to a directive to commit perjury, a criminal offense, plaintiff maintained that the employer acted illegally in discharging him for refusing to follow such an order.

The *Petermann* court recognized that in the absence of contractual limitations an employer enjoys broad discretion to discharge an employee, but concluded that as a matter of "public policy and sound morality" the employer's conduct, as alleged in the complaint, could not be condoned. The court explained: "The commission of perjury is unlawful. (Pen.Code, § 118). * * * It would be obnoxious to the interests of the state and contrary to public policy and sound morality to allow an employer to discharge any employee, whether the employment be for a designated or unspecified duration, on the ground that the employee declined to commit perjury, an act specifically enjoined by statute. * * * The public policy of this state as reflected in the penal code sections referred to above would be seriously impaired if it were to be held that one could be discharged by reason of his refusal to commit perjury. To hold that one's continued employment could be made contingent upon his commission of a felonious act at the instance of his employer would be to encourage criminal conduct upon the part of both the employee and employer and serve to contaminate the honest administration of public affairs. * * * " (174 Cal.App.2d at pp. 188–189, 344 P.2d at p. 27.)

Thus, *Petermann* held that even in the absence of an explicit statutory provision prohibiting the discharge of a worker on such grounds, fundamental principles of public policy and adherence to the objectives underlying the state's penal statutes require the recognition of a rule barring an employer from discharging an employee who has simply complied with his legal duty and has refused to commit an illegal act.[8]

As the statement of facts set out above demonstrates, the present case closely parallels *Petermann* in a number of essential respects. Here, as in *Petermann*, the complaint alleges that the defendant employer instructed its employee to engage in conduct constituting a criminal offense. Plaintiff, like the employee in *Petermann*, refused to violate the law and suffered discharge as a consequence of that refusal.

Arco concedes, as it must in light of *Petermann,* that the allegations of the complaint, if true, establish that defendants acted unlawfully in discharging plaintiff for refusing to participate in criminal activity. Arco maintains, however, that plaintiff's remedy for such misconduct sounds only in contract and not in tort. Accordingly, Arco asserts that the trial court properly sustained its demurrer to plaintiff's tort causes of action, and correctly precluded plaintiff from recovering either compensatory tort damages or punitive damages.

In support of its contention that an action for wrongful discharge sounds only in contract and not in tort, Arco argues that because of the contractual nature of the employer-employee relationship, an injury which an employer inflicts upon its employee by the improper termination of such a relationship gives rise only to a breach of contract action. California decisions, however, have long recognized that a wrongful act committed in the course of a contractual relationship may afford both tort and the contractual relief, and in such circumstances the existence of the contractual relationship will not bar the injured party from pursuing redress in tort.

* * *

[W]e conclude that an employee's action for wrongful discharge is ex delicto and subjects an employer to tort liability. As the *Petermann* case indicates, an employer's obligation to refrain from discharging an employee who refuses to commit a criminal act does not depend upon any express or implied " 'promises set forth in the [employment] contract' " * * *, but rather reflects a duty imposed by law upon all employers in order to implement the fundamental public policies embodied in the state's penal

---

[8] Although the *Petermann* court did not rely upon Labor Code section 2856, that statute provides additional support for the *Petermann* ruling. Section 2856 declares that "[a]n employee shall substantially comply with all the directions of his employer concerning the service on which he is engaged, *except where such obedience is* impossible or *unlawful* * * * " (Italics added.) While this statute does not specifically refer to an employer's authority to discharge an employee, the statute does reflect direct legislative approval of the basic proposition that an employer enjoys no authority to direct an employee to engage in unlawful conduct.

statutes. As such, a wrongful discharge suit exhibits the classic elements of a tort cause of action. * * *

We hold that an employer's authority over its employee does not include the right to demand that the employee commit a criminal act to further its interests, and an employer may not coerce compliance with such unlawful directions by discharging an employee who refuses to follow such an order. An employer engaging in such conduct violates a basic duty imposed by law upon all employers, and thus an employee who has suffered damages as a result of such discharge may maintain a tort action for wrongful discharge against the employer.

CLARK, J., dissenting.

In the instant case the alleged actionable conduct is only contractual, that is, the alleged wrongful termination of an employment contract. In terminating that contract defendant did not *also* breach a duty giving rise to a cause of action in tort. (See *Petermann v. International Brotherhood of Teamsters, supra*, 174 Cal.App.2d 184, 344 P.2d 25.) As in *Petermann* there is no delictual breach in the termination itself, although it is alleged that defendants' *reason* for the termination—plaintiff's refusal to cooperate with defendants in committing acts contrary to public policy—was improper. There does not exist in the instant case * * * the least connection between defendants' actionable conduct (breach of contract) and *any* tort.

NOTES AND QUESTIONS

Test Your Understanding of the Material

1. Both *Tameny* and the *Petermann* decision on which it relies seek to relieve an employee from a pernicious Hobson's choice: either comply with the employer's directive and violate the law, or refuse to comply and suffer discharge. In both, to allow the employer to use the power of discharge to enlist employee intermediaries in unlawful conduct would be to permit the employer to do indirectly what it could not do directly. Revisit the facts in *Nees v. Hocks*. Did the plaintiff in that case face a Hobson's choice?

2. Look at the statutory language cited in footnotes 6 and 8 (Cal. Lab. Code §§ 2922 and 2856). Could the plaintiff have brought a claim solely based on the statutory language? Which provision(s) of the Employment Restatement § 5.02 could have been invoked?

3. Reexamine the facts of *Nees*, *Tameny* and *Petermann* in light of the disruption the plaintiff's actions created for the employer. Which plaintiff was most disruptive? Should disruption to the employer be a legitimate factor in weighing the plaintiff's case? The next case, *Pierce v. Ortho Pharmaceutical Inc.*, examines this question.

Related Issues

4. *Adverse Actions Short of Discharge.* Would Tameny have had a cause of action if instead of being discharged, he was reassigned to a less desirable

position or was presented with a cut in salary? What reason(s) are there for limiting the public-policy cause of action to discharges rather than including other retaliatory personnel decisions? Cf. Scott v. Pacific Gas and Electric Co., 11 Cal.4th 454, 46 Cal.Rptr.2d 427, 904 P.2d 834 (1995) (recognized implied-in-fact contract cause of action for "wrongful demotion"). The Employment Restatement does not take a position on whether the public-policy cause of action should be extended beyond discharges. See § 5.01, Comment b, at 189. Many antidiscrimination statutes do cover "material adverse action" falling short of discharge. See, e.g., Burlington Ry. v. White, 548 U.S. 53 (2006), supra p. 600 (Title VII of the Civil Rights Act of 1964, 42 U.S.C. § 2000e–3). As of this writing, only two state high courts recognize a cause of action for wrongful demotion or discipline in violation of public policy. See Trosper v. Bag 'N Save, 273 Neb. 855, 734 N.W.2d 704 (2007); Brigham v. Dillon Companies, Inc., 262 Kan. 12, 935 P.2d 1054 (1997).

5. *Refusal to Perform Assignment Erroneously Believed to be Unlawful.* Should employees be protected from discharge for refusing to perform work that they sincerely and reasonably thought was illegal, even if it turns out that there was no illegality? See Employment Restatement § 5.02(a), (b), and (e).

6. *Contract vs. Tort.* Whether a claim sounds in contract, tort (or both) is a recurring issue in the cases. Why is it important that *Tameny* permits a plaintiff to sue in either contract or tort? In Foley v. Interactive Data Corp., 47 Cal.3d 654, 254 Cal.Rptr. 211, 765 P.2d 373 (1988), reprinted in part at pp. 52–56 supra, the California high court offered the following explanation for why a *Tameny* claim affords a tort recovery:

> As *Tameny* explained, the theoretical reason for labeling the discharge wrongful in such a case is not based on the terms and conditions of the contract but rather arises out of duty implied in law on the part of the employer to conduct its affairs in compliance with public policy. * * * [T]here is no logical basis to distinguish in cases of wrongful termination for reasons violative of fundamental principles of public policy between situations in which the employee is an at-will employee and [those] in which the employee has a contract for a specified term. The tort is independent of the term of employment.

Id. at 667, 254 Cal.Rptr. at 215, 765 P.2d at 377, citing Koehrer v. Superior Court, 181 Cal.App.3d 1155, 1166, 226 Cal.Rptr. 820, 826 (1986). Most courts follow *Tameny*, *Foley* and *Cloutier* in permitting tort recovery; see Employment Restatement § 5.02. But see Johnson v. Kreiser's Inc., 433 N.W.2d 225 (S.D.1988) (contract recovery only). When is it more advantageous to sue in contract?

7. *"In Violation of Public Policy."* As Section 5.03 of the Employment Restatement suggests, many different sources of law can support a wrongful termination claim. However, the plaintiff must articulate how that law (and the plaintiff's actions) advances a public, rather than a private, interest, as listed in § 5.02. See Campbell v. Ford Industries, Inc., 274 Or. 243, 546 P.2d 141 (1976).

In *Foley v. Interactive Data Corp.*, supra, plaintiff who worked as defendant's product manager had learned that his new supervisor was under FBI investigation for embezzlement from his former employer, the Bank of America. Believing that corporate management would want to know of a high executive's alleged prior criminal conduct, he disclosed this information to his former supervisor, and was allegedly fired for that reason. The California high court held that these facts did not state a claim under California law:

> In the present case, plaintiff alleges that defendant discharged him in "sharp derogation" of a substantial public policy that imposes a legal duty on employees to report relevant business information to management. * * *

> Whether or not there is a statutory duty requiring an employee to report information relevant to his employer's interest, we do not find a substantial public policy prohibiting an employer from discharging an employee for performing that duty. * * * When the duty of an employee to disclose information to his employer serves only the private interest of the employer, the rationale underlying the *Tameny* cause of action is not implicated.

47 Cal.3d at 669–71, 254 Cal.Rptr. at 217–18, 765 P.2d at 379–80. If Foley had reported his suspicion to the police, would he have been able to sue on a public-policy cause of action under *Petermann*? Does it make sense to limit protection to situations where the individual reports directly to a government body or media without bringing the matter to the attention of corporate management first? How does the Employment Restatement § 5.02 handle this?

By contrast, in Paolella v. Browning-Ferris, Inc., 158 F.3d 183 (3d Cir.1998), the Third Circuit (applying Delaware law) held that an employee fired after making an accusation to company officers that his supervisors fraudulently inflated client bills stated a "public policy" claim under state law. Acknowledging that retaliation for the "mere questioning of the propriety of a supervisor's business practices" is not actionable under E.I. DuPont de Nemours & Co. v. Pressman, 679 A.2d 436 (Del. 1996), the appeals court emphasized that plaintiff's accusation raised legal rather than merely ethical concerns; Paolella presented evidence that the supervisor's billing practice "was illegally designed to defraud customers by leading them to believe the increase in their monthly fees was due solely to a state imposed increase in dumping costs and was therefore authorized under the terms of the service agreements." 158 F.3d at 191. Was there a third-party interest present in *Paolella* that was not present in *Foley*? N.J. Stat. § 34:19–3, subd. c. (protecting employee refusal to participate in violation of any law, rule or regulation "involving deception of, or misrepresentation to, any shareholder, investor. . . . "). See also, Notes: The Sarbanes-Oxley Act of 2002, infra p. 664; and Incentive Awards Under the Dodd-Frank Wall Street and Consumer Protection Act, infra p. 666.

C. REFUSAL TO VIOLATE
PROFESSIONAL OBLIGATIONS

PIERCE V. ORTHO PHARMACEUTICAL CORP.

Supreme Court of New Jersey, 1980.
84 N.J. 58, 417 A.2d 505.

POLLOCK, J.

Ortho specializes in the development and manufacture of therapeutic and reproductive drugs. Dr. Pierce is a medical doctor who was first employed by Ortho in 1971 as an Associate Director of Medical Research. She signed no contract except a secrecy agreement, and her employment was not for a fixed term. She was an employee at will. In 1973, she became the Director of Medical Research/Therapeutics, one of three major sections of the Medical Research Department. Her primary responsibilities were to oversee development of therapeutic drugs and to establish procedures for testing those drugs for safety, effectiveness, and marketability. Her immediate supervisor was Dr. Samuel Pasquale, Executive Medical Director.

In the spring of 1975, Dr. Pierce was the only medical doctor on a project team developing loperamide, a liquid drug for treatment of diarrhea in infants, children, and elderly persons. The proposed formulation contained saccharin. Although the concentration was consistent with the formula for loperamide marketed in Europe, the project team agreed that the formula was unsuitable for use in the United States. An alternative formulation containing less saccharin might have been developed within approximately three months.

By March 28, however, the project team, except for Dr. Pierce, decided to continue with the development of loperamide. That decision was made apparently in response to a directive from the Marketing Division of Ortho. This decision meant that Ortho would file an investigational new drug application (IND) with the Federal Food and Drug Administration (FDA), continuing laboratory studies on loperamide, and begin work on a formulation. FDA approval is required before any new drug is tested clinically on humans. 21 U.S.C. § 355; 21 C.F.R. §§ 310.3 *et seq.* Therefore, loperamide would be tested on patients only if the FDA approved the saccharin formulation.

Dr. Pierce knew that the IND would have to be filed with and approved by the FDA before clinical testing could begin. Nonetheless, she continued to oppose the work being done on loperamide at Ortho. On April 21, 1975, she sent a memorandum to the project team expressing her disagreement with its decision to proceed with the development of the drug. In her opinion, there was no justification for seeking FDA permission to use the drug in light of medical controversy over the safety of saccharin.

Dr. Pierce met with Dr. Pasquale on May 9 and informed him that she disagreed with the decision to file an IND with the FDA. She felt that by continuing to work on loperamide she would violate her interpretation of the Hippocratic oath. She concluded that the risk that saccharin might be harmful should preclude testing the formula on children or elderly persons, especially when an alternative formulation might soon be available.

Dr. Pierce recognized that she was joined in a difference of "viewpoints" or "opinion" with Dr. Pasquale and others at Ortho concerning the use of a formula containing saccharin. In her opinion, the safety of saccharin in loperamide pediatric drops was medically debatable. She acknowledged that Dr. Pasquale was entitled to his opinion to proceed with the IND. On depositions, she testified concerning the reason for her difference of opinion about the safety of using saccharin in loperamide pediatric drops:

> Q.   That was because in your medical opinion that was an unsafe thing to do. Is that so?
>
> A.   No. I didn't know. The question of saccharin was one of potential harm. It was controversial. Even though the rulings presently look even less favorable for saccharin it is still a controversial issue.

After their meeting on May 9, Dr. Pasquale informed Dr. Pierce that she would no longer be assigned to the loperamide project. On May 14, Dr. Pasquale asked Dr. Pierce to choose other projects. After Dr. Pierce returned from vacation in Finland, she met on June 16 with Dr. Pasquale to discuss other projects, but she did not choose a project at that meeting. She felt she was being demoted, even though her salary would not be decreased. Dr. Pierce summarized her impression of that meeting in her letter of resignation submitted to Dr. Pasquale the following day. In that letter, she stated:

> Upon learning in our meeting June 16, 1975, that you believe I have not 'acted as a Director', have displayed inadequacies as to my competence, responsibility, productivity, inability to relate to the Marketing Personnel, that you, and reportedly Dr. George Braun and Mr. Verne Willaman consider me to be non-promotable and that I am now or soon will be demoted, I find it impossible to continue my employment at Ortho.

The letter made no specific mention of her difference of opinion with Dr. Pasquale over continuing the work on loperamide. Nonetheless, viewing the matter most favorably to Dr. Pierce, we assume the sole reason for the termination of her employment was the dispute over the loperamide project. Dr. Pasquale accepted her resignation.

In her complaint, which was based on principles of tort and contract law, Dr. Pierce claimed damages for the termination of her employment. Her complaint alleged:

> The Defendant, its agents, servants and employees requested and demanded Plaintiff follow a course of action and behavior which was impossible for Plaintiff to follow because of the Hippocratic oath she had taken, because of the ethical standards by which she was governed as a physician, and because of the regulatory schemes, both federal and state, statutory and case law, for the protection of the public in the field of health and human well-being, which schemes Plaintiff believed she should honor.

However, she did not specify that testing would violate any state or federal statutory regulation. Similarly, she did not state that continuing the research would violate the principles of ethics of the American Medical Association. She never contended her participation in the research would expose her to a claim for malpractice.

* * *

As discussed below, our careful examination of Dr. Pierce's allegations and the record reveals no genuine issue of material fact requiring disposition at trial. Although this case raises important policy considerations, all the relevant facts are before us, and there is no reason to defer a decision. Accordingly, we reverse the Appellate Division and reinstate the summary judgment in favor of defendant.

* * *

In recognizing a cause of action to provide a remedy for employees who are wrongfully discharged, we must balance the interests of the employee, the employer, and the public. Employees have an interest in knowing they will not be discharged for exercising their legal rights. Employers have an interest in knowing they can run their businesses as they see fit as long as their conduct is consistent with public policy. The public has an interest in employment stability and in discouraging frivolous lawsuits by dissatisfied employees.

Although the contours of an exception are important to all employees at will, this case focuses on the special considerations arising out of the right to fire an employee at will who is a member of a recognized profession. * * *

Employees who are professionals owe a special duty to abide not only by federal and state law, but also by the recognized codes of ethics of their professions. That duty may oblige them to decline to perform acts required by their employers. However, an employee should not have the right to prevent his or her employer from pursuing its business because the employee perceives that a particular business decision violates the employee's personal morals, as distinguished from the recognized code of ethics of the employee's profession. *See* Comment, 28 *Vand.L.Rev.* 805, 832 (1975).

We hold that an employee has a cause of action for wrongful discharge when the discharge is contrary to a clear mandate of public policy. The sources of public policy include legislation; administrative rules, regulations or decisions; and judicial decisions. In certain instances, a professional code of ethics may contain an expression of public policy. However, not all such sources express a clear mandate of public policy. For example, a code of ethics designed to serve only the interests of a profession or an administrative regulation concerned with technical matters probably would not be sufficient. Absent legislation, the judiciary must define the cause of action in case-by-case determinations. An employer's right to discharge an employee at will carries a correlative duty not to discharge an employee who declines to perform an act that would require a violation of a clear mandate of public policy. However, unless an employee at will identifies a specific expression of public policy, he may be discharged with or without cause.

* * *

We now turn to the question whether Dr. Pierce was discharged for reasons contrary to a clear mandate of public policy. As previously stated, granting Ortho's motion for summary judgment is appropriate at this juncture only if there is no genuine issue as to any material fact.

The material facts are uncontroverted. In opposing the motion for summary judgment, Dr. Pierce did not contend that saccharin was harmful, but that it was controversial. Because of the controversy she said she could not continue her work on loperamide. Her supervisor, Dr. Pasquale, disagreed and thought that research should continue.

As stated above, before loperamide could be tested on humans, an IND had to be submitted to the FDA to obtain approval for such testing. 21 U.S.C. § 355. The IND must contain complete manufacturing specifications, details of pre-clinical studies (testing on animals) which demonstrate the safe use of the drug, and a description of proposed clinical studies. The FDA then has 30 days to withhold approval of testing. 21 C.F.R. § 312.1. Since no IND had been filed here, and even giving Dr. Pierce the benefit of all doubt regarding her allegations, it is clear that clinical testing of loperamide on humans was not imminent.

Dr. Pierce argues that by continuing to perform research on loperamide she would have been forced to violate professional medical ethics expressed in the Hippocratic oath. She cites the part of the oath that reads: "I will prescribe regimen for the good of my patients according to my ability and my judgment and never do harm to anyone." Clearly, the general language of the oath does not prohibit specifically research that does not involve tests on humans and that cannot lead to such tests without governmental approval.

We note that Dr. Pierce did not rely on or allege violation of any other standards, including the "codes of professional ethics" advanced by the dissent. Similarly, she did not allege that continuing her research would constitute an act of medical malpractice or violate any statute, including N.J.S.A. 45:9–16(h).

In this case, Dr. Pierce has never contended that saccharin would necessarily cause harm to anyone. She alleged that the current controversy made continued investigation an unnecessary risk. However when she stopped work on loperamide, there was no risk. Our point here is not that participation in unethical conduct must be imminent before an employee may refuse to work. The more relevant consideration is that Dr. Pierce does not allege that preparation and filing of the IND was unethical. Further Dr. Pierce does not suggest that Ortho would have proceeded with human testing without FDA approval. The case would be far different if Ortho had filed the IND, the FDA had disapproved it, and Ortho insisted on testing the drug on humans. The actual facts are that Dr. Pierce could not have harmed anyone by continuing to work on loperamide.

Viewing the matter most favorably to Dr. Pierce, the controversy at Ortho involved a difference in medical opinions. Dr. Pierce acknowledged that Dr. Pasquale was entitled to his opinion that the oath did not forbid work on loperamide. Nonetheless, implicit in Dr. Pierce's position is the contention that Dr. Pasquale and Ortho were obliged to accept her opinion. Dr. Pierce contends, in effect, that Ortho should have stopped research on loperamide because of her opinion about the controversial nature of the drug.

Dr. Pierce espouses a doctrine that would lead to disorder in drug research. Under her theory, a professional employee could redetermine the propriety of a research project even if the research did not involve a violation of a clear mandate of public policy. Chaos would result if a single doctor engaged in research were allowed to determine, according to his or her individual conscience, whether a project should continue. *Cf. Report of the Ad Hoc Committee on the Principles of Medical Ethics*, American Medical Association 3 (1979). An employee does not have a right to continued employment when he or she refuses to conduct research simply because it would contravene his or her personal morals. An employee at will who refuses to work for an employer in answer to a call of conscience should recognize that other employees and their employer might heed a different call. However, nothing in this opinion should be construed to restrict the right of an employee at will to refuse to work on a project that he or she believes is unethical. In sum, an employer may discharge an employee who refuses to work unless the refusal is based on a clear mandate of public policy.

PASHMAN, J., dissenting.

Three * * * points made by the majority require discussion, for they reflect the majority's failure to follow the well-established rule that the claims of a party opposing summary judgment are to be "indulgently treated" * * * . The first is the majority's characterization of the effect of plaintiff's ethical position. It appears to believe that Dr. Pierce had the power to determine whether defendant's proposed development program would continue at all. This is not the case, nor is plaintiff claiming the right to halt defendant's development efforts. Interpreted "indulgently," yet realistically, plaintiff claims only the right to her professional autonomy. She contends that she may not be discharged for expressing her view that the clinical program is unethical or for refusing to continue her participation in the project. She has done nothing else to impede continued development of defendant's proposal; moreover, it is undisputed that defendant was able to continue its program by reassigning personnel. Thus, the majority's view that granting doctors a right to be free from abusive discharges would confer on any one of them complete veto power over desirable drug development is ill-conceived.

The second point concerns the role of governmental approval of the proposed experimental program. In apparent ignorance of the past failures of official regulation to safeguard against pharmaceutical horrors, the majority implies that the necessity for administrative approval for human testing eliminates the need for active, ethical professionals within the drug industry. * * * But we do not know whether the United States Food and Drug Administration (FDA) would be aware of the safer alternative to the proposed drug when it would pass upon defendant's application for the more hazardous formula. The majority professes no such knowledge. We must therefore assume the FDA would have been left in ignorance. This highlights the need for ethically autonomous professionals within the pharmaceutical industry—a need which the majority's approach does nothing to satisfy.

The final point to which I must respond is the majority's observation that plaintiff expressed her opposition prematurely, before the FDA had approved clinical experimentation. * * * Essentially, the majority holds that a professional employee may not express a refusal to engage in illegal or clearly unethical conduct until his actual participation and the resulting harm is imminent. This principle grants little protection to the ethical autonomy of professionals that the majority proclaims. Would the majority have Dr. Pierce wait until the first infant was placed before her, ready to receive the first dose of a drug containing 44 times the concentration of saccharin permitted in 12 ounces of soda? The majority minimizes the scope of plaintiff's ethical obligation. The "clear mandate of public policy" was no less clear when she made known her opposition and refusal to participate. A professional's opposition to unethical conduct should not be considered untimely when its unethical nature is apparent. By contrast, the majority's requirement that proposed conduct be imminent would require, for example, an associate in a law firm to withhold his opposition to the preparation of perjured testimony or false evidence, see *DR 7–102(A)(4), (5) & (6)*, until he is actually ordered to begin the preparation. This narrow view of an employee's duty to obey codes of ethics does little to promote such clear mandates of public policy. It will allow unscrupulous employers to forestall discussion on proposed unethical conduct, and to evade the spirit of the majority's new principle by carefully timing such conduct to prevent meaningful dissent.

NOTES AND QUESTIONS

Test Your Understanding of the Material

1. Given the New Jersey Supreme Court's reasoning in *Pierce*, under what circumstances would Dr. Pierce have been protected by the public-policy cause of action when (i) expressing her concerns to her superiors; (ii) refusing to work further on a particular project; or (iii) reporting her objections to the FDA? Under the Employment Restatement §§ 5.02–5.03?

2. *Pierce* raises the question of whether "public policy" may be found in sources other than state constitutional, statutory, or administrative provisions. What justification is there for incorporating private professional codes of ethics into the public policy of a state? Can you think of any counter-arguments?

Related Issues

3. *Policy Trade-Offs in Drug Research.* Should Dr. Pierce have been protected from discharge if, while continuing work on the loperamide project, she informed the FDA that the company could have produced a safer alternative formula? On the one hand, government regulators are limited in their ability to assess independently the safety of a new drug or product and hence are critically dependent on the information they receive from regulated firms. Creation of a privilege of professional dissent might well aid the government's regulatory objectives. On the other hand, protection of the confidentiality of internal company deliberations and research may help encourage the development of drugs that produce substantial benefits. A drug may promote the well-being of the vast majority of its intended users while causing great harm to a small subset of users whose characteristics may not be readily identifiable at the early stages of a drug's development and use. See generally Whistleblowing in Biomedical Research (J. Swazey and S. Scher eds. 1981).

4. *Statutory Supersession.* The cause of action recognized in *Pierce* led to the enactment of New Jersey's "Conscientious Employee Protection Act," N.J. Stat. 34:19–1 to 19–8 (Stat. Supp.). The New Jersey law protects a medical-licensed professional employee's reports of, and refusal to participate in, any activity which constitutes "improper quality of patient care." Id. § 34–

19–3, subd. c. Section 34:19–8 provides for an election of remedies but also states that "[n]othing in this act shall be deemed to diminish the rights, privileges, or remedies of any other federal or State law or regulation. . . ."

5. *Professional Norms as Source of Public Policy vs. Internal Rules of the Profession?* The *Pierce* court drew a distinction between professional norms that "contain an expression of public policy" and "a code of ethics designed to serve only the interests of a profession or an administrative regulation concerned with technical matters * * * ." In Warthen v. Toms River Hospital, 199 N.J.Super. 18, 488 A.2d 229, appeal denied, 101 N.J. 255, 501 A.2d 926 (1985), a nurse claimed that ethical considerations in the Code for Nurses supported her refusal to dialyze a terminally-ill patient. The Code provided in relevant part:

> The nurse's concern for human dignity and the provision of quality nursing care is not limited by personal attitudes or beliefs. If personally opposed to the delivery of care in a particular case because of the nature of the health problem or the procedures to be used, the nurse is justified in refusing to participate. Such refusal should be made known in advance and in time for other appropriate arrangements to be made for the client's nursing care.

The state intermediate appellate court held that this passage "defines a standard of conduct beneficial only to the individual nurse and not to the public at large. The overall purpose of the language cited by plaintiff is to preserve human dignity; however, it should not be at the expense of the patient's life or contrary to the family's wishes." 199 N.J.Super. at 27, 488 A.2d at 233.

6. *Relevance of Extensive Government Regulation of Employer? Of the Profession or Occupation?* Should the claim of professional autonomy be rejected when government extensively regulates the conduct of the employer? See Suchodolski v. Michigan Consol. Gas Co., 412 Mich. 692, 316 N.W.2d 710 (1982) (rejecting public-policy cause of action based on Code of Ethics of Institute of Internal Auditors, in view of extensive state regulation of the accounting systems of public utilities and fact that plaintiff did not allege he was discharged for falsifying reports to regulatory commission).

7. *Effect on Attorney-Client Privilege?* Retaliation claims by in-house lawyers present difficult issues for courts because the underlying dispute often relates to privileged information. Courts are reluctant to allow such claims to proceed where such litigation would undermine the attorney-client privilege. See, e.g., Balla v. Gambro, 145 Ill.2d 492, 164 Ill.Dec. 892, 584 N.E.2d 104 (1991) (attorney-client privilege bars retaliatory discharge suit even though in-house counsel had operational as well as legal responsibilities and his disclosures led to FDA removal of defective dialyzers from market); GTE Products Corp. v. Stewart, 421 Mass. 22, 653 N.E.2d 161, 166 (Mass. 1995) (retaliatory discharge claim lies "if it depends on 1) explicit and unequivocal statutory or ethical norms, 2) [that] embody policies of importance to the public at large in the circumstances of the particular case, and 3) the claim can be proved without any violation of the attorney's obligation to respect client

confidences and secrets."); General Dynamics Corp. v. Superior Ct. of San Bernardino Co., 7 Cal.4th 1164, 32 Cal.Rptr.2d 1, 876 P.2d 487 (1994) (cause of action can be maintained provided there is no breaching of attorney-client privilege or "unduly endangering the values lying at the heart of the professional relationship"). See also Note: The Sarbanes-Oxley Act of 2002, p. 664 infra.

D. WHISTLEBLOWERS

GEARY V. UNITED STATES STEEL CORP.

Supreme Court of Pennsylvania, 1974.
456 Pa. 171, 319 A.2d 174.

POMEROY, J.

The complaint avers that appellant, George B. Geary, was continuously employed by appellee, United States Steel Corporation (hereinafter "company"), from 1953 until July 13, 1967, when he was dismissed from his position. Geary's duties involved the sale of tubular products to the oil and gas industry. His employment was at will. The dismissal is said to have stemmed from a disagreement concerning one of the company's new products, a tubular casing designed for use under high pressure. Geary alleges that he believed the product had not been adequately tested and constituted a serious danger to anyone who used it; that he voiced his misgivings to his superiors and was ordered to "follow directions", which he agreed to do; that he nevertheless continued to express his reservations, taking his case to a vice-president in charge of sale of the product; that as a result of his efforts the product was reevaluated and withdrawn from the market; that he at all times performed his duties to the best of his ability and always acted with the best interests of the company and the general public in mind; and that because of these events he was summarily discharged without notice. Geary asserts that the company's conduct in so acting was "wrongful, malicious and abusive", resulting in injury to his reputation in the industry, mental anguish, and direct financial harm, for which he seeks both punitive and compensatory damages.[2]

The case having been dismissed on a demurrer, all properly pleaded facts are taken as admitted for the purpose of testing the sufficiency of the complaint.[3]

* * *

---

[2] Following his discharge Geary filed a claim for unemployment benefits with the Bureau of Employment Security. The Unemployment Compensation Board of Review found that Geary was not guilty of willful misconduct in the company's employ, and allowed the claim. * * *

[3] The company in its brief denies that the new product was withdrawn from the market as a result of Geary's efforts, and has offered to prove that it has been marketed successfully without incident for several years. This factual contention is irrelevant at the preliminary objection stage.

* * * The facts alleged show only that there was a dispute over the merits of the new product; that Geary vigorously expressed his own point of view in the matter, by-passing his immediate superiors and taking his case to a company vice-president, and that he was ultimately discharged. There is nothing here from which we could infer that the company fired Geary for the specific purpose of causing him harm, or coercing him to break any law[9] or otherwise to compromise himself. According to his own averments, Geary had already won his own battle within the company. The most natural inference from the chain of events recited in the complaint is that Geary had made a nuisance of himself, and the company discharged him to preserve administrative order in its own house. * * *

Appellant's final argument is an appeal to considerations of public policy. Geary asserts in his complaint that he was acting in the best interests of the general public as well as of his employer in opposing the marketing of a product which he believed to be defective. Certainly, the potential for abuse of an employer's power of dismissal is particularly serious where an employee must exercise independent, expert judgment in matters of product safety, but Geary does not hold himself out as this sort of employee. So far as the complaint shows, he was involved only in the sale of company products. There is no suggestion that he possessed any expert qualifications, or that his duties extended to making judgments in matters of product safety. In essence, Geary argues that his conduct should be protected because his intentions were good. No doubt most employees who are dismissed from their posts can make the same claim. We doubt that establishing a right to litigate every such case as it arises would operate either in the best interest of the parties or of the public.

[E]ven an unusually gifted person may be of no use to his employer if he cannot work effectively with fellow employees. Here, for example, Geary's complaint shows that he by-passed his immediate superiors and pressed his views on higher officers, utilizing his close contacts with a company vice president.[14] The praiseworthiness of Geary's motives does not detract from the company's legitimate interest in preserving its normal operational procedures from disruption.[15] In sum, while we agree that

---

[9] Appellant suggests in his brief that continued sale of the defective product might have entailed both criminal and civil liability. This is mere speculation, particularly since the product was allegedly withdrawn from the market.

[14] " * * * [T]he claimant was critical of the program and objected to his superiors * * * . [He] was ordered to follow directions and agreed that he would do so even though he was still opposed to the program * * * . [He] took the problem to a vice president of the company with whom he was in close contact and as a result of re-evaluation the program was withdrawn * * * ." Findings of Fact of Unemployment Compensation Board, attached to and made a part of the amended complaint as Exhibit "A". In pursuing this course, Geary exceeded any duty imposed on him under the rule of the Restatement (Second) of Agency § 381: Duty to Give Information, cited in the dissenting opinion. We do not conceive that § 381 bears any relation to the case before us.

[15] We see no basis for inferring that Geary's discharge was a spiteful retaliatory gesture designed to punish him for noticing and calling attention to the asserted defect in the company's product. This is particularly true in view of the fact that the product was withdrawn from the market. It does not follow that, because Geary's motives were good, the company's motives in

employees should be encouraged to express their educated views on the quality of their employer's products, we are not persuaded that creating a new non-statutory cause of action of the sort proposed by appellant is the best way to achieve this result. On balance, whatever public policy imperatives can be discerning here seem to militate against such a course.

ROBERTS, J., dissenting.

As a salesman, Geary was required to know intimately the products he was selling. He represented United States Steel and it was expected that he would be alert to protect his employer's reputation. Likewise, it was natural that he would seek to shield himself and his employer from the consequences of a dangerous product. When he correctly recognized that the defective steel pipe had strong potential for causing injury and damage, he immediately notified his superiors. His reward for loyalty was dismissal. Of course, had Geary not informed his superiors of the defective product, he may well have been discharged for his failure to do so.

Geary's assessment of the danger of the steel pipe was correct, since after his notification, the corporation removed the steel pipe from the market. On these pleadings, it is manifestly clear that the employer realized Geary was right and that its interest lay in withdrawing from the market the dangerous product. Despite Geary's candor in seeking within the corporation family to advance the corporation's best interest, his employer fired him.

There is no doubt that strong public policies of this Commonwealth have been offended by Geary's discharge. First, the product asserted by appellant to be defective was, after appellant notified his superiors, withdrawn from the market. The manufacture and distribution of defective and potentially dangerous products does not serve either the public's or the employer's interest. Our courts have granted relief to those injured by defective merchandise. E.g., *Kassab v. Central Soya*, 432 Pa. 217, 246 A.2d 848 (1968); *Webb v. Zern*, 422 Pa. 424, 220 A.2d 853 (1966). See Restatement (Second) of Torts § 402A (1965). The majority, however, fails to perceive that the prevention of injury is a fundamental and highly desirable objective of our society.

Second, appellant as an employee was "subject to a duty to use reasonable efforts to give his [employer] information which is relevant to affairs entrusted to him, and which, as the [employee] has notice, the [employer] would desire to have and which can be communicated without violating a superior duty to a third person." Restatement (Second) of Agency § 381 (1958). Had Geary refrained from notifying his superiors of the defective product, he could have been discharged for violating this duty to come forward with information. No responsible policy is served which

---

discharging him were bad. In scrutinizing the complaint we are not required to put aside our common sense or attribute to parties a perversity which the facts alleged do not warrant.

permits an employee to be discharged solely for obeying his legal duty to communicate information to his superiors. Indeed, the policy underlying this duty to communicate is frustrated by denying Geary the opportunity to present his case to the court.

PALMATEER V. INTERNATIONAL HARVESTER CO.

Supreme Court of Illinois, 1981.
85 Ill.2d 124, 52 Ill.Dec. 13, 421 N.E.2d 876.

SIMON, J.

The plaintiff, Ray Palmateer, complains of his discharge by International Harvester Company (IH). He had worked for IH for 16 years, rising from a unionized job at an hourly rate to a managerial position on a fixed salary. Following his discharge, Palmateer filed a four-count complaint against IH, alleging in count II that he had suffered a retaliatory discharge. According to the complaint, Palmateer was fired both for supplying information to local law-enforcement authorities that an IH employee might be involved in a violation of the Criminal Code of 1961 (Ill.Rev.Stat.1979, ch. 38, par. 1–1 *et seq.*) and for agreeing to assist in the investigation and trial of the employee if requested. The circuit court of Rock Island County ruled the complaint failed to state a cause of action and dismissed it; the appellate court affirmed in a divided opinion. We granted Palmateer leave to appeal to determine the contours of the tort of retaliatory discharge approved in *Kelsay v. Motorola, Inc.* (1978), 74 Ill.2d 172, 23 Ill.Dec. 559, 384 N.E.2d 353.

* * *

By recognizing the tort of retaliatory discharge, *Kelsay* acknowledged the common law principle that parties to a contract may not incorporate in it rights and obligations which are clearly injurious to the public. * * * But the Achilles heel of the principle lies in the definition of public policy. When a discharge contravenes public policy in any way the employer has committed a legal wrong. However, the employer retains the right to fire workers at will in cases "where no clear mandate of public policy is involved" (*Leach v. Lauhoff Grain Co.,* 51 Ill.App.3d 1022, 1026, 9 Ill.Dec. 634, 366 N.E.2d 1145 (1977)). But what constitutes clearly mandated public policy?

There is no precise definition of the term. In general, it can be said that public policy concerns what is right and just and what affects the citizens of the State collectively. It is to be found in the State's constitution and statutes and, when they are silent, in its judicial decisions. (*Smith v. Board of Education* (1950), 405 Ill. 143, 147, 89 N.E.2d 893.) Although there is no precise line of demarcation dividing matters that are the subject of public policies from matters purely personal, a survey of cases in other States involving retaliatory discharges shows that a matter must strike at the heart of a citizen's social rights, duties, and responsibilities before the tort will be allowed.

* * *

It is clear that Palmateer has here alleged that he was fired in violation of an established public policy. The claim is that he was discharged for supplying information to a local law-enforcement agency that an IH employee might be violating the Criminal Code, for agreeing to gather further evidence implicating the employee, and for intending to testify at the employee's trial, if it came to that. Because of the procedural posture of the case, these allegations must be accepted as true. (*Fitzgerald v. Chicago Title & Trust Co.* (1978), 72 Ill.2d 179, 187, 20 Ill.Dec. 581, 380 N.E.2d 790.) There is no public policy more basic, nothing more implicit in the concept of ordered liberty (see *Palko v. Connecticut* (1937), 302 U.S. 319, 325, 58 S.Ct. 149, 152, 82 L.Ed. 288, 292), than the enforcement of a State's criminal code. (See *Hewitt v. Hewitt* (1979), 77 Ill.2d 49, 61–62, 31 Ill.Dec. 827, 394 N.E.2d 1204; *Jarrett v. Jarrett* (1979), 78 Ill.2d 337, 345, 36 Ill.Dec. 1, 400 N.E.2d 421.) There is no public policy more important or more fundamental than the one favoring the effective protection of the lives and property of citizens. See Ill. Const.1970, Preamble; *Marbury v. Madison* (1803), 5 U.S. (1 Cranch) 137, 163, 2 L.Ed. 60, 69.

No specific constitutional or statutory provision requires a citizen to take an active part in the ferreting out and prosecution of crime, but public policy nevertheless favors citizen crime-fighters. "Public policy favors the exposure of crime, and the cooperation of citizens possessing knowledge thereof is essential to effective implementation of that policy. Persons acting in good faith who have probable cause to believe crimes have been committed should not be deterred from reporting them by the fear of unfounded suits by those accused." (*Joiner v. Benton Community Bank* (1980), 82 Ill.2d 40, 44, 44 Ill.Dec. 260, 411 N.E.2d 229.) Although *Joiner* involved actions for malicious prosecution, the same can be said for the citizen employee who fears discharge. Public policy favors Palmateer's conduct in volunteering information to the law-enforcement agency. Once the possibility of crime was reported, Palmateer was under a statutory duty to further assist officials when requested to do so. (Ill.Rev.Stat.1979, ch. 38, par. 31–8). Public policy thus also favors Palmateer's agreement to assist in the investigation and prosecution of the suspected crime.

The foundation of the tort of retaliatory discharge lies in the protection of public policy, and there is a clear public policy favoring investigation and prosecution of criminal offenses. Palmateer has stated a cause of action for retaliatory discharge.

RYAN, J. * * * dissenting.

Kelsay relied on the fact that the legislature had clearly established the public policy that injured workers had a right to file claims for compensation with the Industrial Commission. We there held that discharging the employee for filing such a claim violated that public policy. Here the public policy supporting the cause of action cannot be found in any expression of the legislature, but only in the vague belief that public policy requires that we all become "citizen crime-fighters" (85 Ill.2d at 132, 52 Ill.Dec. at 17, 421 N.E.2d at 880).

NOTES AND QUESTIONS

Test Your Understanding of the Material

1.   Geary's *Status Within Pennsylvania*. *Geary* has been cited for the proposition that Pennsylvania recognizes a common law claim for wrongful termination in violation of public policy. See, e.g., Borse v. Piece Goods Inc., 963 F.2d 611 (1992), excerpted infra at pp. 755–758. Can you find any support for that interpretation in the *Geary* opinion? Why was Geary's claim dismissed?

2.   *Palmateer* is subject to multiple interpretations. On what grounds was Palmateer's claim upheld? What is the broadest formulation of the holding consistent with its facts? The narrowest?

Palmateer's status as precedent within Illinois is not clear. See Turner v. Memorial Medical Center, 233 Ill.2d 494, 331 Ill.Dec. 548, 911 N.E.2d 369 (2009) (public-policy cause of action is narrow exception to employment at-will rule and requires identification of "specific," apparently statutory "expression of public policy").

3.   Recall the distinction between "passive whistleblowers" forced to choose between their job and compliance with the law and "active whistleblowers" who report employer illegality but have not been instructed by the employer to further the unlawful conduct. Which category does Geary's conduct fall under? Does he fall under both? Does this distinction offer a proper line for common law decisions? Should it be followed when enacting a whistleblower-protection statute?

Related Issues

4.   *"Internal" Whistleblowing*. Whistleblowing within an organization raises conflicting policy considerations. Employers generally prefer internal whistleblowing because it allows them to avoid government scrutiny in responding to the information. Recent federal legislation containing whistleblower provisions tends to protect internal disclosures. See, e.g., Sarbanes Oxley Act, § 806; Affordable Care Act § 1558, p. 668. See also 17 C.F.R. § 205 (attorneys "appearing and practicing before" the SEC must disclose securities violations internally to chief legal officer and CEO, and, if unsuccessful, to the board or audit committee); ABA Model Rule 1.13 (requiring lawyers to internally report legal violations "likely to result in substantial injury to the organization", and only authorizing external disclosures where the highest authority in the organization refuses to address the violation or insists upon a clear violation of the law). See also note on

Incentive Awards Under the Dodd-Frank Wall Street & Consumer Protection Act, infra.

Some courts will not protect internal disclosures only. See, e.g., Wholey v. Sears Roebuck, 370 Md. 38, 803 A.2d 482 (2002) (recognizing claim in principle based on criminal statute outlawing retaliation against those reporting crimes, but protecting only reports to appropriate law enforcement authorities).

Some statutory schemes *require* exhaustion of internal remedies. Whistleblower claims can also fail where the employee fails to follow an established mechanism for complaining or disregards the chain of command. Cf. Faragher v. City of Boca Raton, 524 U.S. 775, 118 S.Ct. 2275, 141 L.Ed.2d 662 (1998) (recognizing an affirmative defense in Title VII cases where supervisors engage in sexual harassment not resulting in a termination or other "tangible employment action"—in part to encourage plaintiffs to minimize harm by utilizing effective internal complaint procedure). What position does the Employment Restatement take on an exhaustion requirement?

5. *Relevance of Expertise of Whistleblower?* Should courts make some assessment of the expertise of the employee whistleblower? Note that in *Geary*, the plaintiff made disclosures about matters that were within the subject matter of his job. Was Geary, a salesman, nevertheless not sufficiently "expert"? See Smith v. Calgon Carbon Corp., 917 F.2d 1338 (3d Cir.1990) (*Geary* extended to internal disclosure of plant operations causing environmental hazard by employee "not charged with the specific responsibility of protecting the public's interest in health and safety"); Elizabeth Tippett, The Promise of Compelled Whistleblowing: What the Corporate Governance Provisions of Sarbanes Oxley Mean for Employment Law, 11 Employee Rights & Employment Policy J. 1 (2007) (Sarbanes Oxley places whistleblower-like duties on certain employees most likely to understand and learn of financial discrepancies).

6. *Erroneous, Good-Faith Whistleblowing.* Should employees be protected for erroneous, good-faith, reporting of suspected illegality? See Employment Restatement § 5.02(a).

7. *First Amendment Protections for Public Employees.* The public employee whistleblower enjoys substantial protection under the First Amendment for disclosures on matters of public interest but not if making of such disclosures is part of the employee's job duties. See Garcetti v. Ceballos, 547 U.S. 410, 128 S.Ct. 1951, 164 L.Ed. 2d 689 (2006): Lane v. Franks, 573 U.S. ___, 134 S.Ct. 2369, 189 L.Ed 2d 312 (2014).

E. STATUTORY PROTECTIONS FOR WHISTLEBLOWERS

1. STATE LEGISLATION

Some state laws provide broad protection to whistleblowers, protecting refusals to violate state laws, as well as reasonable, good-faith disclosures of legal violations. For an example of a statute affording broad protections, the California Labor Code § 1102.5 provides:

> (b) An employer, or any person acting on behalf of the employer, shall not retaliate against an employee for disclosing information, or because the employer believes that the employee disclosed or may disclose information, to a government or law enforcement agency, to a person with authority over the employee or another employee who has the authority to investigate, discover, or correct the violation or noncompliance, or for providing information to, or testifying before, any public body conducting an investigation, hearing, or inquiry, if the employee has reasonable cause to believe that the information discloses a violation of a state or federal statute, or a violation of or noncompliance with a local, state, or federal rule or regulation, regardless of whether disclosing the information is part of the employee's job duties.

> (c) An employer, or any person acting on behalf of the employer, shall not retaliate against an employee for refusing to participate in an activity that would result in a violation of [a] state or federal statute, or a violation of or noncompliance with a local, state, or federal rule or regulation.

See also N.J.Stat.Ann. §§ 34:19–1 et seq. (similarly broad); 43 Pa.Stat. §§ 1421 et seq. (protects internal disclosures, and external disclosures if first reported internally).

Other states protect only disclosures made to government agencies. See, e.g., Fla. Stat. § 448.102 (protecting disclosures to government agencies if the employee has first disclosed the practice internally and provided the employer with a reasonable opportunity to address the wrongdoing); Mich.Comp.Laws Ann. §§ 15.361–15.369; Minn. Stat. § 181.932.

Some state statutes define protected activity more narrowly. New York's statute is especially narrow, applying only to disclosures of wrongdoing presenting "a substantial and specific danger to public health or safety". See Remba v. Federation Empl. & Guidance Serv., 76 N.Y.2d 801, 559 N.Y.S.2d 961, 559 N.E.2d 655 (1990); Vail-Ballou Press, Inc. v. Tomasky, 266 A.D.2d 662, 698 N.Y.S.2d 98 (3d Dept.1999). The New York law also contains an election-of-remedies provision foreclosing other state-law claims. See Pipas v. Syracuse Home Assn., 226 A.D.2d 1097, 641

N.Y.S.2d 768 (4th Dept.1996). Similarly, Ohio Rev. Code Ann. § 4113.52 requires a reasonable belief "that the violation either is a criminal offense that is likely to cause an imminent risk of physical harm to persons or a hazard to public health or safety or is a felony[.]" See Brooks v. Martin Marietta Utility Serv., 166 F.3d 1213 (6th Cir. 1998) (unpublished) (employee belief of a likely criminal violation, not simply a regulatory violation, required).

Most of the laws protect erroneous whistleblowing as long as the plaintiff reasonably believed illegality had occurred. Compare, e.g., 43 Pa.Stat. § 1423(a), with N.Y.Labor Law § 740(6). New York's law has been interpreted, however, to require proof of actual violations. See Bordell v. General Electric Co., 88 N.Y.2d 869, 644 N.Y.S.2d 912, 667 N.E.2d 922 (1996).

State laws protecting whistleblowing in the public sector are even more common. See, e.g. 5 Texas Gov. Code § 554.001 et seq., excerpted in Statutory Supplement.

2. FEDERAL LEGISLATION

While state legislation tends to cover a broad swath of whistleblowing, federal legislation has a piecemeal quality. Like the anti-retaliation provisions covered in Chapter 11, federal statutes protect only whistleblowing related to violations of that statute. Federal statutes containing whistleblower provisions also tend to define the protected forms of disclosure (e.g. internal and/or external to a specific government agency).

This section provides an overview of federal statutes containing whistleblower provisions, starting with the oldest statute—the 1863 False Claims Act. In recent years, whistleblowers have come into Congressional favor, with whistleblower provisions tacked onto major legislation.

a. "Qui Tam" and Whistleblower Provisions of the False Claims Act

The civil False Claims Act (FCA), 31 U.S.C. §§ 3729–31, provides a means for whistleblowers (or others) to sue employers (or their agents) who present false or fraudulent claims to the government. The suit is in the nature of a *qui tam* action on behalf of the government (which has the right to assume primary responsibility for the suit or, with court approval, seek its dismissal). In 1986, the civil penalty was increased to "not less than $5,000 and not more than $10,000 plus 3 times the amount of damages which the government sustains because of the act of that person," id. § 3729, of which the private plaintiff can recover 15–25%.

As part of the 1986 amendments to the FCA, P.L. 99–562, 100 Stat. 3153 (1986) Congress provided affirmative protection for a limited category of employee whistleblowers:

Any employee, contractor, or agent shall be entitled to all relief necessary to make that employee, contractor, or agent whole, if that employee, contractor, or agent is discharged, demoted, suspended, threatened, harassed, or in any other manner discriminated against in the terms and conditions of employment because of lawful acts done by the employee, contractor, agent or associated others in furtherance of an action under this section or other efforts to stop 1 or more violations of this subchapter. 31 U.S.C. § 3730(h).

Most often, the employee-whistleblower invokes § 3730(h) in tandem with the *qui tam* recovery provisions. Whistleblower protection under § 3730(h) may be limited, however, to actions taken "in furtherance of an action" under the FCA or "in furtherance of efforts to stop" a violation of the FCA. The FCA protects internal reports of government fraud, provided that they are based on a reasonable, good faith belief. McKenzie v. BellSouth Telecommunications, Inc., 219 F.3d 508, 516 (6th Cir.2000). To ultimately prove retaliation, the employee must show that the employer knew about the protected activity. Id.

Whether the underlying *qui tam* action can be brought will depend on (i) whether the information on which the action was brought was "publicly disclos[ed] * * * in a Federal criminal, civil, or administrative hearing * * * in a congressional, Government Accountability Office, or other Federal report, hearing, audit, or investigation, or from news media"; and (ii) if such "public disclosure" has occurred, whether the plaintiff nevertheless was "an original source of the information." 31 U.S.C. § 3730(e)(4)(A)–(B). However, § 10104(j)(2) of the 2010 federal healthcare reform legislation expands the definition of "an original source" under § 3730(e)(4)(A) of the FCA to include "individual who either (1) prior to a public disclosure under subsection (e)(4)(A), has voluntarily disclosed to the Government the information on which allegations or transactions in a claim are based, or (2) who has knowledge that is independent of and materially adds to the publicly disclosed allegations or transactions, and who has voluntarily provided the information to the Government before filing an action under this section."

In State of Vermont Agency of Natural Resources v. United States ex rel. Stevens, 529 U.S. 765, 120 S.Ct. 1858, 146 L.Ed.2d 836 (2000), the Supreme Court held that qui tam relators have article III standing to bring FCA suits because the FCA in effect makes a partial assignment of the Government's claim to the private relator.

Some states have passed statutes modeled after the FCA. See Calif.Government Code § 10548, a part of the Reporting of Improper Government Activities Act of 1986, Stats.1986, ch. 353, §§ 4–5. See Steve Seidenberg, Joining the Feds: States Passing Whistleblower Statutes, National L. J., Jan. 13, 2003, p. A24.

Example of Qui Tam Litigation

In 2004, whistleblower David Franklin received $24 million as part of a settlement over a qui tam claim against Warner-Lambert (a pharmaceutical company later acquired by Pfizer). As part of the settlement, the company pled guilty to criminal charges and agreed to pay $240 million in criminal penalties, and more than $100 million in civil damages. The qui tam suit alleged that Warner-Lambert defrauded the government by illegally promoting off-label use of the drug Neurontin. Franklin's lawsuit alleged that Warner-Lambert "suppressed study results, planted people in medical audiences to ask questions intended to put [the drug] in a good light, lavished perks on doctors, used ghostwriters . . . and used psychological profiling of doctors" to help promote the drug. Franklin was a microbiologist that worked for a subsidiary of Warner-Lambert. Warner-Lambert settled the case after a federal district court in Massachusetts denied the company's motion for summary judgment on Franklin's qui tam claim. Quoted from Jeanne Lenzer, Pfizer pleads guilty, but drug sales continue to soar, 328 British Medical Journal 7450 (2004); U.S. ex rel. Franklin v. Parke-Davis, Div. of Warner-Lambert, Case No. Civ.A. 96–11651PBS (D. Mass. 2003), 2003 WL 22048255; United States Department of Justice, Warner-Lambert to Pay $430 Million to Resolve Criminal & Civil Health Care Liability Relating to Off-Label Promotion, http://www.justice.gov/archive/opa/pr/2004/May/04_civ_322.htm.

b. Federal Health and Safety Legislation

Virtually every federal health and safety law contains an antiretaliation provision. See generally Eugene R. Fidell, Federal Protection of Private Sector Health and Safety Whistleblowers, 2 Admin.L.J. 1 (1988). Courts have shown some reluctance to interpret these provisions to cover whistleblowing in the absence of an express protection to that effect. For example, the federal courts of appeals are split over whether nuclear facility inspectors who file intracorporate quality control reports without contacting federal authorities are covered by a provision protecting participation "in any other action to carry out the purposes of" the Energy Reorganization Act, 42 U.S.C. § 5851(a)(3). Compare Brown & Root v. Donovan, 747 F.2d 1029 (5th Cir.1984) (not protected), with Kansas Gas & Electric Co. v. Brock, 780 F.2d 1505 (10th Cir.1985); Mackowiak v. University Nuclear Systems, 735 F.2d 1159 (9th Cir.1984); Consolidated Edison v. Donovan, 673 F.2d 61 (2d Cir.1982).

Rulings holding that flight officers complaining of a discharge for refusal to fly allegedly unsafe aircraft lack protection under the Federal

Aviation Act or the regulations of the Federal Aviation Administration, see Buethe v. Britt Airlines, Inc., 749 F.2d 1235 (7th Cir.1984); Pavolini v. Bard-Air Corp., 645 F.2d 144 (2d Cir.1981), would seem superseded by the 1999 "Whistleblower Protection Program" (WPP) amendment to the Airline Deregulation Act, 49 U.S.C. § 42121. The WPP requires the filing of a complaint with the Secretary of Labor, id. § 42121(b)(1), and does not appear to authorize a private right of action.

c. The Sarbanes-Oxley Act of 2002

Sarbanes-Oxley was passed in reaction to accounting scandals that resulted in the failure of Enron, a major public company, and significant regulatory problems for other corporations. Pub. L. 107–204, 116 Stat. 745 (enacted July 30, 2002), codified at 18 U.S.C. §§ 1513, 1514A. The Act contains two whistleblower provisions, sections 806 and 1107. Section 806 protects individuals who report or cooperate in the investigation of conduct alleged to violate certain federal securities and antifraud laws, and provides a private civil action. Section 1107 makes it a felony to intentionally retaliate against individuals who provide a law enforcement officer with "truthful information" concerning the actual or potential commission of "any Federal offense," id. Section 806 complaints have to be lodged initially with the U.S. Department of Labor (DOL).

1. Section 806—Civil Whistleblower Provision

a. *Scope.* Individuals employed by any public company, or its agents, are protected against retaliation "because of any act done" to provide information or assist in an investigation "regarding any conduct which the employee reasonably believes" to violate 18 U.S.C. §§ 1341 (mail fraud), 1343 (fraud by wire, radio or television), 1344 (bank fraud), 1348 (securities fraud), or "any rule or regulation of the Securities and Exchange Commission [(SEC)], or any provision of Federal law relating to fraud against shareholders. . . ." 18 U.S.C. § 1514(a)(1). In Lawson v. FMR LLC, 134 S. Ct. 1158 (2014), the Court held that § 806 protects from retaliation for whistleblowing activity not only employees of publicly-traded companies but also employees of private companies, like law firms or accountants or investment advisors, that contract with public companies. The information or assistance has to be provided to an investigation conducted by a federal agency, a member of Congress or any committee of Congress, or "a person with supervisory authority over the employee (or such other person working for the employer who has the authority to investigate, discover, or terminate misconduct). . . ." This whistleblower provision does not preempt other federal or state law retaliation claims or collectively bargained rights, 18 U.S.C. § 1514(A)(d).

The Act also contains a "participation" clause, § 1514(a)(2), protecting individuals who "file, cause to be filed, testify, participate in, or otherwise assist in a proceeding filed or about to be filed (with any knowledge of the employer) relating to an alleged violation" of the enumerated federal statutes, rules and regulations. Section 806's structure suggests that the reasonable-belief requirement applies only to § 1514(a)(1) disclosure or assistance, not participation activity under § 1514(a)(2).

b. *Procedure.* An employee seeking relief under § 806 must file a complaint with OSHA within 180 days of the alleged violation. 29 C.F.R. § 1980.103(d). OSHA shares the complaint with the SEC but handles the investigation. Parties can appeal OSHA's findings by requesting a hearing with an administrative law judge. The ALJ determination can then be appealed to the DOL's administrative review board. Id. § 29 C.F.R. 1980.106. The review board's final order is appealable to a court of appeals.

If the OSHA filing does not result in a final order within 180 days, through no fault of the employee, she or he may bring a claim directly in federal district court.

c. *Remedies.* An employee prevailing in a § 806 action is entitled to "make whole" relief, including reinstatement, back pay, and "compensation for any special damages sustained as a result of the discrimination, including litigation costs, expert witness fees, and reasonable attorney fees." 18 U.S.C. § 1514A(c). There is no express provision for compensatory or punitive damages.

The Act also authorizes a provisional reinstatement remedy. See generally Samuel Estreicher & Wendy C. Butler, Preliminary Reinstatement Under Sarbanes-Oxley, N.Y.L.J., May 9, 2006, p. 3. In Bechtel v. Competitive Techs., Inc., 369 F.Supp.2d 233 (D.Conn. 2005), vacated, 448 F.3d 469 (2d Cir. 2006), the district court enforced an ALJ order under Sarbanes-Oxley requiring preliminary reinstatement of former vice presidents of a technology company fired after complaining about corporate fraud. The Second Circuit, however, reversed, holding that the district court lacked jurisdiction because the statute did not authorize judicial enforcement of the Secretary's preliminary reinstatement orders.

2. *Section 1107—Criminal Sanctions*

Section 1107 of the Act makes it a felony to "knowingly, with the intention to retaliate, take[ ] any action harmful to any person, including interference with lawful employment or livelihood of any person, for providing to a law enforcement officer any truthful information relating to the commission or possible commission of any Federal offense." 18 U.S.C. § 1513(e). Note that the criminal provision covers disclosures of any violations of federal law, not just employee reports of securities violations or shareholder fraud.

d. Incentive Awards Under the Dodd-Frank Wall Street & Consumer Protection Act

On May 25, 2011, by a 3–2 vote, the SEC adopted final rules under Section 21F of the Securities Exchange Act of 1934, providing for whistleblower protections and an incentive award, or bounty, program. Enacted as Section 922 of the Dodd-Frank Wall Street Reform and Consumer Protection Act, 15 U.S.C. § 784–b, Section 21F requires the SEC to pay incentive awards, or bounties, "subject to certain limitations and conditions, to whistleblowers who provide the Commission with original information about violations of the federal securities laws." The provision also expands protection against employer retaliation for employees who provide information regarding possible violations to the SEC or make disclosures "required or protected" under the Sarbanes-Oxley Act of 2002 and other securities laws.

Perhaps the most controversial aspect of the rules is the agency's determination that whistleblowers are under no obligation to first report violations through the applicable company's internal compliance or legal programs in order to qualify for an award. Although the rules do not require internal disclosures, they provide some incentives for whistleblowers to report their complaints internally. Specifically, whether the whistleblower reported his complaint internally before going to the SEC will be a factor in determining the size of any incentive award. Additionally, when the whistleblower first reports internally and the company submits the information to the SEC leading to a successful enforcement action, the whistleblower will be fully credited for the award. In addition, a whistleblower who first reports to the company's internal compliance program receives the benefit of a 120-day "lookback period," meaning that information will be considered "original" for a period up to 120 days from the time the employee reported the information to the internal compliance program. Critics of Rule 21F argue that failure to require initial internal disclosures will undermine the ability of companies to promote internal compliance programs.

The criteria for whistleblower-award eligibility are: (i) an individual, alone or in conjunction with others, (ii) who voluntarily provides the SEC on or after July 21, 2010, (iii) with original information of a securities law violation, (iv) that leads to successful enforcement by the SEC of a federal court or administrative action, (v) where the SEC obtains monetary sanctions in an amount greater than $1 million. Whistleblowers meeting these criteria are eligible for an award of 10 to 30 percent of the monetary sanctions.

A submission of information to the SEC is made "voluntarily" if the information is provided "before a request, inquiry, or demand that relates to the subject matter" of the submission is directed to the whistleblower or his representative. Legally-compelled disclosures, and information covered by reporting obligations or SEC agreements are not considered voluntary. Information obtained during a company's internal investigation or gathered by the employer in response to a government inquiry is, however, considered voluntary. The SEC illustrates the distinction as follows: "An examination request directed to a broker-dealer or an investment adviser would not automatically foreclose whistleblower submissions related to the subject matter of the exam from all employees of the entity. However, if a firm employee were interviewed by examiners, the employee could not later make a 'voluntary' submission related to the subject matter of the interview."

The whistleblower seeking a bounty must provide "original information," defined as (i) "[d]erived from [the individual's] independent knowledge" or independent analysis; (ii) "[n]ot already known" to the SEC; and (iii) "[n]ot exclusively derived from" allegations in a government hearing or investigation or from the news media. Information obtained through a communication protected by the attorney-client privilege or from legal representation of a client is not considered original, unless the attorney is permitted to make the disclosure under SEC Rule 205 pursuant to the Sarbanes-Oxley Act or applicable state attorney conduct rules. Even if the information is not secret, a whistleblower may be eligible for an award based on disclosure of information derived from his or her "independent analysis," which can include information based upon the whistleblower's evaluation or analysis of publicly available sources.

Neither company compliance officers nor legal personnel are per se excluded from protection as whistleblowers or from eligibility for a bounty award. Admittedly, information received in the course of legal representation of the client, obtained by an employee whose principal duties involve compliance or internal audit functions, or received by employees or consultants retained to conduct an investigation into possible violations of law or to perform public accountant services is not considered "original information." However, the SEC has carved out areas of whistleblower eligibility for lawyers who make permitted disclosures under SEC Rule 205 and employees or consultants in the following circumstances:

(A) You have a reasonable basis to believe that the disclosure of the information to the Commission is necessary to prevent the relevant entity from engaging in conduct that is likely to cause substantial injury to the financial interest or property of the entity or investors;

(B) You have a reasonable basis to believe that the relevant entity is engaging in conduct that will impede an investigation of the misconduct; or

(C) At least 120 days have elapsed since you provided the information to the relevant entity's audit committee, chief legal officer, chief compliance officer (or their equivalents), or your supervisor, or since you received the information [under circumstances where any of the foregoing were already aware of the information].

A whistleblower's original information can lead to a successful enforcement by the SEC of a federal court or administrative action in several ways. Specifically, (i) where the information is sufficiently specific, credible, and timely to enable the Commission to open a new examination or investigation, reopen a closed investigation, or open a new line inquiry in an existing examination or investigation or (ii) where the conduct was already under investigation when the information was submitted, and the original information from the whistleblower "significantly contributed" to the success of the action. The proposed rules would have required a whistleblower to demonstrate both that the information would not have been otherwise acquired and that the information was *essential to the success of the action*. After soliciting comments and letters on the required standard for original information, the Commissioners were ultimately "persuaded by those commenters who stated that the [essential success of the action] standards . . . were too high."

e.   The Affordable Care Act of 2010

Section 1558 of the 2010 federal healthcare reform legislation, 124 Stat. 1991, codified at 29 U.S.C. § 218c (enacted March 23, 2010), amends the Fair Labor Standards Act of 1938 (see Chapter 18) to prohibit retaliation against an employee who provides or is about to provide to an employer, the federal government, or a state attorney general, information that the employee reasonably believes to be a violation of Title I of the law. Title I contains a broad range of rules governing health insurance, including a prohibition against denying coverage based upon preexisting conditions, policy and financial reporting requirements and prohibitions against discrimination based upon an individual's receipt of health insurance subsidies. Section 1558 extends protection to individuals who participate in investigations or object to or refuse to participate in any activity that the employee reasonably believes to be a violation of Title I.

The procedures, burden of proof, and remedies applicable to this new retaliation claim are set forth in the Consumer Product Safety Improvement Act of 2008, 15 U.S.C. § 2087(b). They include (1) a 180-day statute of limitations; (2) a requirement to initially file the complaint with OSHA, which will investigate the complaint and can order preliminary reinstatement; (3) the option to litigate the claim before a Department of Labor ALJ or to file an action in federal court 210 days after filing the complaint; (4) a right to a jury trial; and (5) a broad range of remedies, including reinstatement, back pay, special damages, and attorney's fees. The causation standard and burden-shifting framework is similar to Section 806 of the Sarbanes-Oxley Act.

f. Federal Employees Whistleblowers

As a result of the Civil Service Reform Act of 1978 (CSRA), 5 U.S.C. § 2301 et seq., federal employees are protected from reprisals for whistleblowing. Title I of the CSRA provides:

Employees should be protected against reprisal for the lawful disclosure of information which the employees reasonably believe evidences—

(A) a violation of any law, rule, or regulation, or

(B) mismanagement, a gross waste of funds, an abuse of authority, or a substantial danger to public health or safety.

Id. § 2301(b)(9). "[P]rohibited personnel practices" include actions taken in retaliation for whistleblowing, id. § 2302(b)(8), and those taken as a reprisal "for the exercise of any appeal right granted by any law, rule, or regulation," id. § 2302(b)(9). Challenges to adverse personnel decisions may be brought by individual employees to the Merit Systems Protections Board (MSPB) for final administrative determination. Alternatively, in the case of nontenured employees, the Special Counsel may petition the MSPB for "corrective action" against agencies or employees engaged in prohibited personnel practices. The courts have generally held that there is no private right of action; redress must be sought either through an appeal of agency-employer action to the MSPB or through a petition for corrective action with the Special Counsel. See Borrell v. United States International Communications Agency, 682 F.2d 981 (D.C.Cir.1982). This legislation is usefully described in Robert G. Vaughn, Statutory Protection of Whistleblowers in the Federal Executive Branch, 1982 U.Ill.L.Rev. 615.

NOTE: INTERACTIONS BETWEEN STATUTORY AND COMMON LAW CLAIMS

1. *Implied Federal Causes of Action.* Whether a court will recognize a federal civil action for discharge in violation of federal statutory norms will turn on whether Congress has signaled an intent to create a right of action. See, e.g., Alexander v. Sandoval, 532 U.S. 275, 287, 121 S.Ct. 1511, 149 L.Ed.2d 517(2001). The Court's earlier approach in Cort v. Ash, 422 U.S. 66, 95 S.Ct. 2080, 45 L.Ed.2d 26 (1975), envisioned a more receptive inquiry into whether private suits would promote the purpose of the legislation. For an illustration of the shift, see, e.g., Le Vick v. Skaggs Companies, Inc., 701 F.2d 777 (9th Cir.1983) (overruling earlier decision that private right of action exists under 15 U.S.C. § 1674(a) for discharge of an employee because his wages had been subjected to garnishment).

2. *State Common Law Claims Based on Federal Statutes.* To what extent may or should the public policy of a state incorporate federal concerns? Compare, e.g., Guy v. Travenol Labs., Inc., 812 F.2d 911 (4th Cir.1987) (claim of retaliatory discharge for refusing to falsify records required by federal law;

federal diversity decision holding that North Carolina has no obligation to use its tort system to supplement federal scheme); Rachford v. Evergreen Int'l Airlines, 596 F.Supp. 384 (N.D.Ill.1984) (state has general policy in favor of aviation safety, but it has no interest in enforcing FAA regulations), with Coman v. Thomas Mfg. Co., 325 N.C. 172, 381 S.E.2d 445 (1989) (discharge allegedly for refusing to violate federal safety and recordkeeping requirements); Phipps v. Clark Oil & Refining Corp., 408 N.W.2d 569 (Minn.1987) (service station employee discharged for refusing to violate federal law by pumping leaded gasoline into vehicle designed for only unleaded gasoline states claim); Thompson v. St. Regis Paper Co., 102 Wash.2d 219, 685 P.2d 1081 (1984) (accountant fired for instituting accurate accounting system in compliance with Foreign Corrupt Practices Act of 1977).

Is there a danger that state courts will misconstrue complex federal regulations? Consider Green v. Ralee Engineering Co., 19 Cal.4th 66, 78 Cal.Rptr.2d 16, 960 P.2d 1046 (1998), where the California high court held that the *Tameny* "public policy" cause of action could be based on federal safety regulations of the Federal Aviation Authority (FAA) implementing the Federal Aviation Act of 1958 (FAA), 49 U.S.C. formerly § 1301 et seq., now § 40101 et seq. Justice Chin's opinion for the majority states:

> Plaintiff performed the FAA-required inspections on the parts intended for use in Boeing aircraft to further a fundamental public policy: "to ensure that each article produced conforms to the type design and is in a condition for safe operation." (14 C.F.R. § 21.143(a).) Therefore, this regulation-based fundamental public policy may serve as the foundation for plaintiff's *Tameny* claim. * * *
>
> * * *
>
> * * * By informing defendant that he believed it was shipping defective parts for use in passenger aircraft, plaintiff gave defendant adequate notice that his concern involved potentially significant public policy matters because the FAA requires manufacturers to establish quality control procedures for the component parts they produce (14 C.F.R. § 21.143.) Thus, unlike some cases where an employer's violations of its own procedures does not implicate public policy, the internal quality control procedures at issue in this case are part of a statutory and regulatory scheme established by Congress and the FAA, designed to ensure the manufacture of safe aircraft.
>
> * * *
>
> To the extent defendant * * * claims that the FAA regulations do not even apply to its operations because it apparently never applied for certification under the FAA provisions, its argument * * * fails at the summary judgment stage of proceedings. If plaintiff's allegations are true, then defendant arguably misinterpreted the safety of the parts shipped to prime manufacturers such as Boeing, on which information these manufacturers would foreseeably rely for their own certification program. * * *

78 Cal.Rptr.2d at 24–26, 28–29, 960 P.2d at 1054–56, 1058–59.

Justice Baxter's dissent charges the majority with judicial activism, noting in part:

> [T]he majority never explains why a parts manufacturer such as defendant should have thought to focus upon a regulation pertaining to FAA certification and oversight of prime manufacturers. Indeed, the majority apparently are unable to identify any FAA regulation applicable to parts suppliers.

Id. at 34, 960 P.2d at 1064.

3. *Preclusion of Common Law Remedy by Available Administrative Remedy.* The courts may have been receptive to the public-policy cause of action in *Kelsay* and *Tameny* in part because of the absence of any retaliatory discharge remedy in the statute that gave rise to the public policy claim. Should courts recognize an additional tort remedy even where the statute provides an administrative remedy? A private cause of action? Consider the Employment Restatement § 5.01(a), which recognizes the public-policy cause of action "unless the statute or other law forming the basis of the applicable public policy precludes tort liability or otherwise makes judicial recognition of a tort claim inappropriate."

For decisions on the question of statutory preclusion, compare, e.g., Makovi v. Sherwin-Williams Co., 316 Md. 603, 561 A.2d 179 (1989) (state antidiscrimination remedy precludes wrongful termination claim based on pregnancy); Wolk v. Saks Fifth Ave., Inc., 728 F.2d 221 (3d Cir.1984) (exclusive remedy for sexual harassment is state civil rights statute), with Mendoza v. Western Medical Center Santa Ana, 222 Cal.App.4th 1334 (Cal.App.4th 2014) (citing Rojo v. Kliger, 52 Cal.3d 65, 276 Cal.Rptr. 130, 801 P.2d 373 (1990)) (statutory remedy does not bar public policy tort action for workplace sexual harassment); Collins v. Elkay Mining Co., 179 W.Va. 549, 371 S.E.2d 46, 48 (W.Va. 1988) (failure to file charge under Federal Coal Mine Safety Act or West Virginia Mine Safety Act does not bar retaliatory discharge claim by coal mine foreman for refusing to falsify company safety reports); Holien v. Sears, Roebuck and Co., 298 Or. 76, 689 P.2d 1292 (1984) (same); Phillips v. Gemini Moving Specialists, 63 Cal.App.4th 563, 74 Cal.Rptr.2d 29 (1998) (employee fired after complaining about improper wage setoff may proceed under *Tameny* theory, despite statutory remedy).

To what extent should the question of statutory preclusion turn on whether a common law action could provide more extensive remedies than the statutory claim? See, e.g., Campbell v. Husky Hogs, 292 Kan. 225, 236, 255 P.3d 1 (2011) (state wage payment statute does not bar a public policy suit challenging retaliatory discharge for filing a wage payment claim as "the wage claim redresses a different harm. The [wage payment] suit and its statutory remedy relate to Campbell's claim that Husky Hogs did not pay him all earned wages. But the retaliatory discharge claim would redress the employment termination.").

4. *Federal Preemption.* In English v. General Electric Co., 496 U.S. 72, 110 S.Ct. 2270, 110 L.Ed.2d 65 (1990), the Supreme Court unanimously held that a state-law intentional infliction of emotional distress claim by a laboratory technician who was allegedly terminated for reporting violations of nuclear-safety standards was not preempted by the antiretaliation provision of § 210 of the Energy Reorganization Act of 1974 (see Statutory Supplement). Relying on the Court's easing of federal preemption principles for state-law claims in nuclear safety disputes in Silkwood v. Kerr-McGee Corp., 464 U.S. 238, 104 S.Ct. 615, 78 L.Ed.2d 443 (1984) (allowing punitive damages for plutonium radiation injuries), Justice Blackmun's opinion notes: "Ordinarily, the mere existence of a federal regulatory or enforcement scheme, even one as detailed as § 210, does not by itself imply pre-emption of state remedies." 496 U.S. at 80. See also Schweiss v. Chrysler Motors Corp., 922 F.2d 473 (8th Cir.1990) (rejecting OSHA preemption argument in light of *English*); Sargent v. Central National Bank & Trust Co. of Enid, 809 P.2d 1298 (Okla.1991) (bank officer's claim of discharge in retaliation for refusing to destroy or alter bank records not preempted by § 24 (Fifth) of National Bank Act's authorization of bank directors to dismiss officers "at pleasure").

Federal preemption of state whistleblower protection may be an issue in some cases. See, e.g., Branche v. Airtran Airways, Inc., 342 F.3d 1248 (11th Cir. 2003) (state retaliatory discharge action held not preempted by Airline Deregulation Act, 49 U.S.C. § 41713, whose preemptive force is limited to matters relating to airline prices, routes or services; 1999 WPP amendment to the Act, 49 U.S.C. § 42121, did not expand preemptive scope of the Deregulation Act); Botz v. Omni Air Int'l, 286 F.3d 488, 496 (8th Cir. 2002) (invocation of state whistleblower law by flight attendant refusing a flight assignment for safety reasons held preempted by Deregulation Act because state law claim would interfere with "carrier's ability to provide its scheduled services"). The general issue of coordination between federal and state remedies in this area is surveyed in Trystan Phifer O'Leary, Silencing the Whistleblower: The Gap Between Federal and State Retaliatory Discharge Laws, 85 Iowa L. Rev. 663 (2000).

CHAPTER 13

FIRST AMENDMENT PROTECTION OF GOVERNMENT EMPLOYEE EXPRESSION AND ASSOCIATION

■ ■ ■

Introduction

In addition to civil service laws and collective bargaining agrements, government employees enjoy an additional source of protection in the First Amendment's guarantee of freedom of speech and assembly.

Two dominant approaches help explain the reach of the First Amendment. The first posits that the primary purpose of the First Amendment is the protection of the preconditions for public debate. As originally formulated, this justification was thought limited to those matters of government and public affairs directly relevant to an informed citizenry intelligently exercising its franchise. See, e.g., Alexander Meikeljohn, Free Speech and Its Relation to Self-Government (1948). In time, the range of topics has been expanded to include "expression about philosophical, social, artistic, economic, literary, or ethical matters," Abood v. Detroit Bd. of Educ., 431 U.S. 209, 231, 97 S.Ct. 1782, 1797, 52 L.Ed.2d 261 (1977), and indeed any matter of general interest.

Under this view, the First Amendment values unrestrained debate for an instrumental reason: it is more likely to yield an enlightened public. In Justice Holmes's famous formulation, the First Amendment assures a "marketplace of ideas" in which competing conceptions of the good are ventilated for citizens to digest, appraise and possibly act upon. Government's role in this marketplace should be one of neutrality between competing viewpoints.

A rival conception of the First Amendment holds that human expressive activity is valued not merely because it may contribute to enlightenment on political, or even more personal, questions, but also because such activity, like religious activity for many, may have intrinsic value. It may contribute to a sense of personal autonomy or to the full development of the human potential. This formulation of the purpose of the constitutional guarantee argues for even broader restrictions on personnel decisions, because it does not require that the communication make any contribution to public debate or enlightenment.

HISTORICAL NOTE

The courts did not employ the First Amendment to impose restrictions on public employers' personnel decisions until the 1950s. During the 1800s and the first half of the 1900s, the view prevailed that a citizen "may have a constitutional right to talk politics, but he has no constitutional right to be a policeman." McAuliffe v. Mayor of New Bedford, 155 Mass. 216, 220, 29 N.E. 517 (1892) (Holmes, J.). This position made the First Amendment largely irrelevant as a legal limitation on the decisions of public employers, and it corresponded to the prevailing doctrine of employment "at will" that governed the decisions of their private counterparts (see Chapter 2). The Supreme Court adhered to this view as late as 1952. See Adler v. Board of Educ., 342 U.S. 485, 72 S.Ct. 380, 96 L.Ed. 517 (1952) (upholding a New York law barring from public school employment anyone who advocated the violent overthrow of the government or belonged to an organization found to advocate or teach such an overthrow).

However, in the same year that *Adler* was decided, the Court began eroding the absolute position suggested by Holmes' formulation. In Wieman v. Updegraff, 344 U.S. 183, 73 S.Ct. 215, 97 L.Ed. 216 (1952), it struck down on due process grounds an oath requiring public employees to affirm the absence of past affiliation with the Communist Party irrespective of whether the employee had knowledge of any unlawful or subversive activity by that organization. The erosion of the Holmes dictum continued apace in the 1960s. For instance, in Shelton v. Tucker, 364 U.S. 479, 81 S.Ct. 247, 5 L.Ed.2d 231 (1960), the Court invalidated as an impairment of First Amendment-protected associational rights an Arkansas statute that required public school teachers to make annual disclosure of their organizational affiliations.

Perhaps most importantly, in a series of cases invalidating state government loyalty oaths, the Court in the sixties elaborated on the implications of *Wieman* to expand the protection of public employees. See Cramp v. Board of Pub. Instruc., 368 U.S. 278, 82 S.Ct. 275, 7 L.Ed.2d 285 (1961); Baggett v. Bullitt, 377 U.S. 360, 84 S.Ct. 1316, 12 L.Ed.2d 377 (1964); Elfbrandt v. Russell, 384 U.S. 11, 86 S.Ct. 1238, 16 L.Ed.2d 321 (1966); Keyishian v. Board of Regents, 385 U.S. 589, 87 S.Ct. 675, 17 L.Ed.2d 629 (1967). These cases found oaths to threaten First Amendment-protected activity because they were excessively vague. *Keyishian* was the culminating decision. Not only did it reject the New York law originally upheld in *Adler,* but it also expressly repudiated the "major premise" of that opinion—"that public employment, including academic employment, may be conditioned upon the surrender of constitutional rights which could not be abridged by direct government action." Id. at 605, 87 S.Ct. at 681.

The repudiation of Holmes's premise that public employment is a privilege that can be denied for any reason, forced the Court to confront more directly the extent to which the First Amendment should restrict public employers. What kinds of employee speech, or other expressive activity, should receive protection from adverse personnel decisions? What kinds of governmental justifications should be adequate to warrant the inhibition of public-employee speech?

A. FREEDOM OF SPEECH AND PUBLIC EMPLOYMENT

PICKERING V. BOARD OF EDUCATION
Supreme Court of the United States, 1968.
391 U.S. 563, 88 S.Ct. 1731, 20 L.Ed.2d 811.

JUSTICE MARSHALL delivered the opinion of the Court.

Appellant Marvin L. Pickering, a teacher in Township High School District 205, Will County, Illinois, was dismissed from his position by the appellee Board of Education for sending a letter to a local newspaper in connection with a recently proposed tax increase that was critical of the way in which the Board and the district superintendent of schools had handled past proposals to raise new revenue for the schools.

* * *

In February of 1961 the appellee Board of Education asked the voters of the school district to approve a bond issue to raise $4,875,000 to erect two new schools. The proposal was defeated. Then, in December of 1961, the Board submitted another bond proposal to the voters which called for the raising of $5,500,000 to build two new schools. This second proposal passed and the schools were built with the money raised by the bond sales. In May of 1964 a proposed increase in the tax rate to be used for educational purposes was submitted to the voters by the Board and was defeated. Finally, on September 19, 1964, a second proposal to increase the tax rate was submitted by the Board and was likewise defeated. It was in connection with this last proposal of the School Board that appellant wrote the letter to the editor that resulted in his dismissal.

* * *

The letter constituted, basically, an attack on the School Board's handling of the 1961 bond issue proposals and its subsequent allocation of financial resources between the schools' educational and athletic programs. It also charged the superintendent of schools with attempting to prevent teachers in the district from opposing or criticizing the proposed bond issue.

The Board dismissed Pickering for writing and publishing the letter. Pursuant to Illinois law, the Board was then required to hold a hearing on the dismissal. At the hearing the Board charged that numerous statements in the letter were false and that the publication of the statements unjustifiably impugned the "motives, honesty, integrity, truthfulness, responsibility and competence" of both the Board and the school administration. The Board also charged that the false statements damaged the professional reputations of its members and of the school administrators, would be disruptive of faculty discipline, and would tend to foment "controversy, conflict and dissension" among teachers, administrators, the Board of Education, and the residents of the district. * * * The Board found the statements to be false as charged. No evidence was introduced at any point in the proceedings as to the effect of the publication of the letter on the community as a whole or on the administration of the school system in particular, and no specific findings along these lines were made.

* * *

The Board contends that "the teacher by virtue of his public employment has a duty of loyalty to support his superiors in attaining the generally accepted goals of education and that, if he must speak out publicly, he should do so factually and accurately, commensurate with his education and experience." Appellant, on the other hand, argues that the test applicable to defamatory statements directed against public officials by persons having no occupational relationship with them, namely, that statements to be legally actionable must be made "with knowledge that [they were] * * * false or with reckless disregard of whether [they were] * * * false or not," *New York Times Co. v. Sullivan*, 376 U.S. 254, 280, 84 S.Ct. 710, 726, 11 L.Ed.2d 686 (1964), should also be applied to public statements made by teachers. * * *

An examination of the statements in appellant's letter objected to by the Board reveals that they, like the letter as a whole, consist essentially of criticism of the Board's allocation of school funds between educational and athletic programs, and of both the Board's and the superintendent's methods of informing, or preventing the informing of, the district's taxpayers of the real reasons why additional tax revenues were being sought for the schools. The statements are in no way directed towards any person with whom appellant would normally be in contact in the course of his daily work as a teacher. Thus no question of maintaining either discipline by immediate superiors or harmony among coworkers is presented here. Appellant's employment relationships with the Board and, to a somewhat lesser extent, with the superintendent are not the kind of close working relationships for which it can persuasively be claimed that personal loyalty and confidence are necessary to their proper functioning. Accordingly, to the extent that the Board's position here can be taken to suggest that even comments on matters of public concern that are substantially correct * * * may furnish grounds for dismissal if they are sufficiently critical in tone, we unequivocally reject it.[3]

---

[3] It is possible to conceive of some positions in public employment in which the need for confidentiality is so great that even completely correct public statements might furnish a permissible ground for dismissal. Likewise, positions in public employment in which the relationship between superior and subordinate is of such a personal and intimate nature that certain forms of public criticism of the superior by the subordinate would seriously undermine the

We next consider the statements in appellant's letter which we agree to be false. The Board's original charges included allegations that the publication of the letter damaged the professional reputations of the Board and the superintendent and would foment controversy and conflict among the Board, teachers, administrators, and the residents of the district. However, no evidence to support these allegations was introduced at the hearing. So far as the record reveals, Pickering's letter was greeted by everyone but its main target, the Board, with massive apathy and total disbelief. The Board must, therefore, have decided, perhaps by analogy with the law of libel, that the statements were *per se* harmful to the operation of the schools.

However, the only way in which the Board could conclude, absent any evidence of the actual effect of the letter, that the statements contained therein were *per se* detrimental to the interest of the schools was to equate the Board members' own interests with that of the schools. Certainly an accusation that too much money is being spent on athletics by the administrators of the school system (which is precisely the import of that portion of appellant's letter containing the statements that we have found to be false) cannot reasonably be regarded as *per se* detrimental to the district's schools. Such an accusation reflects rather a difference of opinion between Pickering and the Board as to the preferable manner of operating the school system, a difference of opinion that clearly concerns an issue of general public interest.

In addition, the fact that particular illustrations of the Board's claimed undesirable emphasis on athletic programs are false would not normally have any necessary impact on the actual operation of the schools, beyond its tendency to anger the Board. For example, Pickering's letter was written after the defeat at the polls of the second proposed tax increase. It could, therefore, have had no effect on the ability of the school district to raise necessary revenue, since there was no showing that there was any proposal to increase taxes pending when the letter was written.

More importantly, the question whether a school system requires additional funds is a matter of legitimate public concern on which the judgment of the school administration, including the School Board, cannot, in a society that leaves such questions to popular vote, be taken as conclusive. On such a question free and open debate is vital to informed decision-making by the electorate. Teachers are, as a class, the members of a community most likely to have informed and definite opinions as to how funds allotted to the operation of the schools should be spent. Accordingly, it is essential that they be able to speak out freely on such questions without fear of retaliatory dismissal.

---

effectiveness of the working relationship between them can also be imagined. We intimate no views as to how we would resolve any specific instances of such situations, but merely note that significantly different considerations would be involved in such cases.

In addition, the amounts expended on athletics which Pickering reported erroneously were matters of public record on which his position as a teacher in the district did not qualify him to speak with any greater authority than any other taxpayer. The Board could easily have rebutted appellant's errors by publishing the accurate figures itself, either via a letter to the same newspaper or otherwise. We are thus not presented with a situation in which a teacher has carelessly made false statements about matters so closely related to the day-to-day operations of the schools that any harmful impact on the public would be difficult to counter because of the teacher's presumed greater access to the real facts. Accordingly, we have no occasion to consider at this time whether under such circumstances a school board could reasonably require that a teacher make substantial efforts to verify the accuracy of his charges before publishing them.[4]

What we do have before us is a case in which a teacher has made erroneous public statements upon issues then currently the subject of public attention, which are critical of his ultimate employer but which are neither shown nor can be presumed to have in any way either impeded the teacher's proper performance of his daily duties in the classroom[5] or to have interfered with the regular operation of the schools generally. In these circumstances we conclude that the interest of the school administration in limiting teachers' opportunities to contribute to public debate is not significantly greater than its interest in limiting a similar contribution by any member of the general public.

* * *

While criminal sanctions and damage awards have a somewhat different impact on the exercise of the right to freedom of speech from dismissal from employment, it is apparent that the threat of dismissal from public employment is nonetheless a potent means of inhibiting speech. * * * [I]n a case such as the present one, in which the fact of employment is only tangentially and insubstantially involved in the subject matter of the public communication made by a teacher, we conclude that it is necessary to regard the teacher as the member of the general public he seeks to be.[6]

---

[4] There is likewise no occasion furnished by this case for consideration of the extent to which teachers can be required by narrowly drawn grievance procedures to submit complaints about the operation of the schools to their superiors for action thereon prior to bringing the complaints before the public.

[5] We also note that this case does not present a situation in which a teacher's public statements are so without foundation as to call into question his fitness to perform his duties in the classroom. In such a case, of course, the statements would merely be evidence of the teacher's general competence, or lack thereof, and not an independent basis for dismissal.

[6] Because we conclude that appellant's statements were not knowingly or recklessly false, we have no occasion to pass upon the additional question whether a statement that was knowingly or recklessly false would, if it were neither shown nor could reasonably be presumed to have had any harmful effects, still be protected by the First Amendment. See also n. 5, supra.

GIVHAN V. WESTERN LINE CONSOLIDATED SCHOOL DISTRICT

Supreme Court of the United States, 1979.
439 U.S. 410, 99 S.Ct. 693, 58 L.Ed.2d 619.

MR. JUSTICE REHNQUIST delivered the opinion of the Court.

Petitioner Bessie Givhan was dismissed from her employment as a junior high English teacher at the end of the 1970–1971 school year. * * * In an effort to show that its decision was justified, respondent School District introduced evidence of, among other things, a series of private encounters between petitioner and the school principal in which petitioner allegedly made "petty and unreasonable demands" in a manner variously described by the principal as "insulting," "hostile," "loud," and "arrogant." After a two-day bench trial, the District Court held that petitioner's termination had violated the First Amendment. Finding that petitioner had made "demands" on but two occasions and that those demands "were neither 'petty' nor 'unreasonable,' insomuch as all the complaints in question involved employment policies and practices at [the] school which [petitioner] conceived to be racially discriminatory in purpose or effect," the District Court concluded that "the primary reason for the school district's failure to renew [petitioner's] contract was her criticism of the policies and practices of the school district, especially the school to which she was assigned to teach."

* * * Although it found the District Court's findings not clearly erroneous, the Court of Appeals concluded that because petitioner had privately expressed her complaints and opinions to the principal, her expression was not protected under the First Amendment. * * * We are unable to agree that private expression of one's views is beyond constitutional protection, and therefore reverse the Court of Appeals' judgment and remand the case so that it may consider the contentions of the parties freed from this erroneous view of the First Amendment.[4]

NOTES AND QUESTIONS

Test Your Understanding of the Material

1.   Does the Court in *Pickering* engage in a multifactor balancing test? What factors were taken into account in determining that Pickering's speech

---

[4]   Although the First Amendment's protection of government employees extends to private as well as public expression, striking the *Pickering* balance in each context may involve different considerations. When a teacher speaks publicly, it is generally the *content* of his statements that must be assessed to determine whether they "in any way either impeded the teacher's proper performance of his daily duties in the classroom or * * * interfered with the regular operation of the schools generally." Private expression, however, may in some situations bring additional factors to the *Pickering* calculus. When a government employee personally confronts his immediate superior, the employing agency's institutional efficiency may be threatened not only by the content of the employee's message but also by the manner, time, and place in which it is delivered.

could not be the basis for his dismissal? How was each factor relevant? Is there some underlying principle?

2.   Consider also the factor added in footnote 4 in the *Givhan* opinion. Why does the Court suggest that time, place, and manner of the express are relevant to determining the protection of nonpublic, internal expressions of views? Are comments critical of a superior at general employee meetings more or less likely to be protected than comments in private, individual conferences with the superior?

3.   Has the Court in *Givhan* adopted the personal autonomy, noninstrumental view of the First Amendment? Or is the decision better understood as holding that although speech must contribute to public debate, the relevant "public" may be the employer and coworkers in the restricted internal "polity" of the workplace?

Related Issues

4.   *Relevance of Truth or Falsity.* Does the *Pickering* Court place sufficient weight on whether Pickering's accusations were true or false? On the one hand, given New York Times v. Sullivan, 376 U.S. 254, 84 S.Ct. 710, 11 L.Ed.2d 686 (1964), which permits libel suits to proceed against speakers uttering knowing or intentionally false statements about public officials or public figures, is there any reason why such statements when uttered by public employees about their employer should ever receive the special protection of the Constitution? Justice White argued not, in a separate opinion in *Pickering* (not included above). Cf. also Johnson v. Multnomah County, Oregon, 48 F.3d 420, 423–24 (9th Cir.1995) (holding that even "recklessly false statements are not per se unprotected", but noting split in circuits on issue.)

5.   *Can the Government Regulate Truthful Speech Without a Showing of Harm?* Does the government have to show some harm that derives from the manner of the speech, rather than its content? Harm to the "clients" of the government services being challenged, rather than on general public opinion? See generally Craig v. Rich Twp. High Sch. Dist. 227, 736 F.3d 1110, 1120 (7th Cir. 2013) (school had a sufficiently compelling interest in maintaining the integrity of its guidance program to discharge a guidance counselor who published a sexually-charged book on relationship advice); Andersen v. McCotter, 100 F.3d 723, 728 (10th Cir.1996) (government must show actual undermining of public confidence); Jefferson v. Ambroz, 90 F.3d 1291, 1297 (7th Cir.1996) (government could discharge probation officer for calling talk show and criticizing criminal justice system, in part because of effect on officer's probationers' confidence in system).

6.   *Threats to Working Relationships.* The Court stresses that Pickering's statements were not "directed towards any person with whom [he] would normally be in contact in the course of his daily work as a teacher." Cases where an employee breaches a duty of confidentiality or publicly criticizes a superior for whom he or she serves as a close personal assistant seem easily distinguishable. But should all employee criticism of immediate superiors or coworkers be unprotected? Should a public employer at least be required to

wait until the impairment of a working relationship harms its operations before disciplining an employee for making such statements? Compare Tyler v. City of Mountain Home, Arkansas, 72 F.3d 568 (8th Cir.1995) (no showing of harm required where police officer wrote an "argumentative" letter that disregarded chain of command), with Voigt v. Savell, 70 F.3d 1552, 1560 (9th Cir.1995) (employee affidavits about the disruptive effect of plaintiff's complaints on office harmony sufficient to establish harm under *Pickering* standard).

7.   *Prospective Prohibitions of Expressive Activity.* In United States v. National Treasury Employees Union, 513 U.S. 454, 115 S.Ct. 1003, 130 L.Ed.2d 964 (1995), the Court applied the *Pickering* analysis to strike down a law that prohibited federal employees from accepting any compensation, including honoraria and traveling expenses, for making speeches or writing articles having nothing to do with their official duties. The Court held that the government's burden under *Pickering* was especially "heavy" because the challenged ban applied prospectively to a broad range of speech, rather than just to that of particular individual employees, and that the "speculative benefits" of the ban were not sufficient "to justify this crudely crafted burden" on the speech of federal workers. Id. at 477.

8.   *Limited Protection for Policymaking Employees?* Does *Pickering* apply to public officials in a policymaking position? Should elected public officials be able to demand unqualified loyalty from those with significant delegated policymaking authority? See, e.g., Bardzik v. Cnty. of Orange, 635 F.3d 1138, 1151 (9th Cir. 2011) ("plaintiff's status as policymaker is dispositive" even though he accused superior of corruption); Silberstein v. City of Dayton, 440 F.3d 306 (6th Cir. 2006) (when employee is in policymaking position, there is a "presumption" that balance favors the government); Bonds v. Milwaukee County, 207 F.3d 969, 981 (7th Cir.2000) (policymaking exception does not apply to nonpolitical speech, but "policymaking status remains critical factor" in balance); McEvoy v. Spencer, 124 F.3d 92, 103 (2d Cir.1997) ("an employee's policymaking role does not provide an employer with complete insulation for adverse employment action, but does weigh, normally heavily, on the employer's side in the *Pickering* balance").

9.   *Remedies for First Amendment Violations.* In Bush v. Lucas, 462 U.S. 367, 103 S.Ct. 2404, 76 L.Ed.2d 648 (1983), the Court held that it would not create a damages remedy for nonprobationary federal employees in the civil service who are subjected to an adverse personnel action on account of protected First Amendment activity. The Court explained that the comprehensive civil service system established by Congress made it unnecessary to recognize an implied cause of action for the violation of First Amendment rights.

CONNICK V. MYERS

Supreme Court of the United States, 1983.
461 U.S. 138, 103 S.Ct. 1684, 75 L.Ed.2d 708.

JUSTICE WHITE delivered the opinion of the Court.

I

The respondent, Sheila Myers, was employed as an Assistant District Attorney in New Orleans for five and a half years. She served at the pleasure of petitioner Harry Connick, the District Attorney for Orleans Parish. During this period Myers competently performed her responsibilities of trying criminal cases.

In the early part of October 1980, Myers was informed that she would be transferred to prosecute cases in a different section of the criminal court. Myers was strongly opposed to the proposed transfer[1] and expressed her view to several of her supervisors, including Connick. Despite her objections, on October 6 Myers was notified that she was being transferred. Myers again spoke with Dennis Waldron, one of the First Assistant District Attorneys, expressing her reluctance to accept the transfer. A number of other office matters were discussed and Myers later testified that, in response to Waldron's suggestion that her concerns were not shared by others in the office, she informed him that she would do some research on the matter.

That night Myers prepared a questionnaire soliciting the views of her fellow staff members concerning office transfer policy, office morale, the need for a grievance committee, the level of confidence in supervisors, and whether employees felt pressured to work in political campaigns. Early the following morning, Myers typed and copied the questionnaire. She also met with Connick who urged her to accept the transfer. She said she would "consider" it. Connick then left the office. Myers then distributed the questionnaire to 15 Assistant District Attorneys. Shortly after noon, Dennis Waldron learned that Myers was distributing the survey. He immediately phoned Connick and informed him that Myers was creating a "mini-insurrection" within the office. Connick returned to the office and told Myers that she was being terminated because of her refusal to accept the transfer. She was also told that her distribution of the questionnaire was considered an act of insubordination.

* * *

---

[1] Myers' opposition was at least partially attributable to her concern that a conflict of interest would have been created by the transfer because of her participation in a counseling program for convicted defendants released on probation in the section of the criminal court to which she was to be assigned.

Myers filed suit under 42 U.S.C. § 1983 (1976 ed., Supp. V), contending that her employment was wrongfully terminated because she had exercised her constitutionally protected right of free speech.

* * *

II

* * * Our task, as we defined it in *Pickering*, is to seek "a balance between the interests of the [employee], as a citizen, in commenting upon matters of public concern and the interest of the State, as an employer, in promoting the efficiency of the public services it performs through its employees." 391 U.S., at 568, 88 S.Ct., at 1734. The District Court, and thus the Court of Appeals as well, misapplied our decision in *Pickering* and consequently, in our view, erred in striking the balance for respondent.

* * *

The District Court got off on the wrong foot in this case by initially finding that, "[t]aken as a whole, the issues presented in the questionnaire relate to the effective functioning of the District Attorney's Office and are matters of public importance and concern." Connick contends at the outset that no balancing of interests is required in this case because Myers' questionnaire concerned only internal office matters and that such speech is not upon a matter of "public concern," as the term was used in *Pickering*. Although we do not agree that Myers' communication in this case was wholly without First Amendment protection, there is much force to Connick's submission. The repeated emphasis in *Pickering* on the right of a public employee "as a citizen, in commenting upon matters of public concern," was not accidental. This language, reiterated in all of *Pickering*'s progeny, reflects both the historical evolvement [sic] of the rights of public employees, and the common-sense realization that government offices could not function if every employment decision became a constitutional matter.

* * *

In all of these cases, the precedents in which *Pickering* is rooted, the invalidated statutes and actions sought to suppress the rights of public employees to participate in public affairs. The issue was whether government employees could be prevented or "chilled" by the fear of discharge from joining political parties and other associations that certain public officials might find "subversive." The explanation for the Constitution's special concern with threats to the right of citizens to participate in political affairs is no mystery. The First Amendment "was fashioned to assure unfettered interchange of ideas for the bringing about of political and social changes desired by the people." *Roth v. United States*, 354 U.S. 476, 484, 77 S.Ct. 1304, 1308, 1 L.Ed.2d 1498 (1957); *New York Times Co. v. Sullivan*, 376 U.S. 254, 269, 84 S.Ct. 710, 720, 11 L.Ed.2d 686

(1964). "[S]peech concerning public affairs is more than self-expression; it is the essence of self-government." *Garrison v. Louisiana*, 379 U.S. 64, 74–75, 85 S.Ct. 209, 215–216, 13 L.Ed.2d 125 (1964). Accordingly, the Court has frequently reaffirmed that speech on public issues occupies the " 'highest rung of the hierarchy of First Amendment values,' " and is entitled to special protection.

* * *

Pickering, its antecedents, and its progeny lead us to conclude that if Myers' questionnaire cannot be fairly characterized as constituting speech on a matter of public concern, it is unnecessary for us to scrutinize the reasons for her discharge. When employee expression cannot be fairly considered as relating to any matter of political, social, or other concern to the community, government officials should enjoy wide latitude in managing their offices, without intrusive oversight by the judiciary in the name of the First Amendment.

* * *

We do not suggest, however, that Myers' speech, even if not touching upon a matter of public concern, is totally beyond the protection of the First Amendment. "[T]he First Amendment does not protect speech and assembly only to the extent it can be characterized as political. 'Great secular causes, with smaller ones, are guarded.' " *Mine Workers v. Illinois Bar Assn.*, 389 U.S. 217, 223, 88 S.Ct. 353, 356, 19 L.Ed.2d 426 (1967), quoting *Thomas v. Collins*, 323 U.S. 516, 531, 65 S.Ct. 315, 323, 89 L.Ed. 430 (1945). We in no sense suggest that speech on private matters falls into one of the narrow and well-defined classes of expression which carries so little social value, such as obscenity, that the State can prohibit and punish such expression by all persons in its jurisdiction. See *Chaplinsky v. New Hampshire*, 315 U.S. 568, 62 S.Ct. 766, 86 L.Ed. 1031 (1942); *Roth v. United States, supra; New York v. Ferber*, 458 U.S. 747, 102 S.Ct. 3348, 73 L.Ed.2d 1113 (1982). For example, an employee's false criticism of his employer on grounds not of public concern may be cause for his discharge but would be entitled to the same protection in a libel action accorded an identical statement made by a man on the street. We hold only that when a public employee speaks not as a citizen upon matters of public concern, but instead as an employee upon matters only of personal interest, absent the most unusual circumstances, a federal court is not the appropriate forum in which to review the wisdom of a personnel decision taken by a public agency allegedly in reaction to the employee's behavior. Our responsibility is to ensure that citizens are not deprived of fundamental rights by virtue of working for the government; this does not require a grant of immunity for employee grievances not afforded by the First Amendment to those who do not work for the State.

Whether an employee's speech addresses a matter of public concern must be determined by the content, form, and context of a given statement, as revealed by the whole record. In this case, with but one exception, the questions posed by Myers to her co-workers do not fall under the rubric of matters of "public concern." We view the questions pertaining to the confidence and trust that Myers' co-workers possess in various supervisors, the level of office morale, and the need for a grievance committee as mere extensions of Myers' dispute over her transfer to another section of the criminal court. Unlike the dissent, we do not believe these questions are of public import in evaluating the performance of the District Attorney as an elected official. Myers did not seek to inform the public that the District Attorney's Office was not discharging its governmental responsibilities in the investigation and prosecution of criminal cases. Nor did Myers seek to bring to light actual or potential wrongdoing or breach of public trust on the part of Connick and others. Indeed, the questionnaire, if released to the public, would convey no information at all other than the fact that a single employee is upset with the status quo. While discipline and morale in the workplace are related to an agency's efficient performance of its duties, the focus of Myers' questions is not to evaluate the performance of the office but rather to gather ammunition for another round of controversy with her superiors. These questions reflect one employee's dissatisfaction with a transfer and an attempt to turn that displeasure into a cause celebre.[8]

To presume that all matters which transpire within a government office are of public concern would mean that virtually every remark—and certainly every criticism directed at a public official—would plant the seed of a constitutional case. While as a matter of good judgment, public officials should be receptive to constructive criticism offered by their employees, the First Amendment does not require a public office to be run as a roundtable for employee complaints over internal office affairs.

One question in Myers' questionnaire, however, does touch upon a matter of public concern. Question 11 inquires if assistant district attorneys "ever feel pressured to work in political campaigns on behalf of office supported candidates." We have recently noted that official pressure upon employees to work for political candidates not of the worker's own choice constitutes a coercion of belief in violation of fundamental constitutional rights. *Branti v. Finkel*, 445 U.S. [507,] 515–516, 100 S.Ct. [1287 (1980)]; *Elrod v. Burns*, 427 U.S. 347, 96 S.Ct. 2673, 49 L.Ed.2d 547 (1976). In addition, there is a demonstrated interest in this country that government service should depend upon meritorious performance rather than political service. *CSC v. Letter Carriers*, 413 U.S. 548, 93 S.Ct. 2880, 37 L.Ed.2d 796 (1973); *Public Workers v. Mitchell*, 330 U.S. 75, 67 S.Ct.

---

[8] This is not a case like *Givhan*, where an employee speaks out as a citizen on a matter of general concern, not tied to a personal employment dispute, but arranges to do so privately. Mrs. Givhan's right to protest racial discrimination—a matter inherently of public concern—is not forfeited by her choice of a private forum. * * *

556, 91 L.Ed. 754 (1947). Given this history, we believe it apparent that the issue of whether assistant district attorneys are pressured to work in political campaigns is a matter of interest to the community upon which it is essential that public employees be able to speak out freely without fear of retaliatory dismissal.

Because one of the questions in Myers' survey touched upon a matter of public concern and contributed to her discharge, we must determine whether Connick was justified in discharging Myers.

* * *

The *Pickering* balance requires full consideration of the government's interest in the effective and efficient fulfillment of its responsibilities to the public.

* * *

We agree with the District Court that there is no demonstration here that the questionnaire impeded Myers' ability to perform her responsibilities. The District Court was also correct to recognize that "it is important to the efficient and successful operation of the District Attorney's office for Assistants to maintain close working relationships with their superiors." Connick's judgment, and apparently also that of his first assistant Dennis Waldron, who characterized Myers' actions as causing a "mini-insurrection," was that Myers' questionnaire was an act of insubordination which interfered with working relationships.[11] When close working relationships are essential to fulfilling public responsibilities, a wide degree of deference to the employer's judgment is appropriate. Furthermore, we do not see the necessity for an employer to allow events to unfold to the extent that the disruption of the office and the destruction of working relationships is manifest before taking action. We caution that a stronger showing may be necessary if the employee's speech more substantially involved matters of public concern.

* * * Questions, no less than forcefully stated opinions and facts, carry messages and it requires no unusual insight to conclude that the purpose, if not the likely result, of the questionnaire is to seek to precipitate a vote of no confidence in Connick and his supervisors. Thus, Question 10, which asked whether or not the Assistants had confidence in and relied on the word of five named supervisors, is a statement that carries the clear potential for undermining office relations.

---

[11] Waldron testified that from what he had learned of the events on October 7, Myers "was trying to stir up other people not to accept the changes [transfers] that had been made on the memorandum and that were to be implemented." In his view, the questionnaire was a "final act of defiance" and that, as a result of Myers' action, "there were going to be some severe problems about the changes." Connick testified that he reached a similar conclusion after conducting his own investigation. "After I satisfied myself that not only wasn't she accepting the transfer, but that she was affirmatively opposing it and disrupting the routine of the office by this questionnaire. I called her in * * * [and dismissed her]."

Also relevant is the manner, time, and place in which the questionnaire was distributed. * * * Here the questionnaire was prepared and distributed at the office; the manner of distribution required not only Myers to leave her work but others to do the same in order that the questionnaire be completed.[13] Although some latitude * * * is to be allowed when professional employees are involved, and Myers did not violate announced office policy, the fact that Myers, unlike Pickering, exercised her rights to speech at the office supports Connick's fears that the functioning of his office was endangered.

Finally, the context in which the dispute arose is also significant. This is not a case where an employee, out of purely academic interest, circulated a questionnaire so as to obtain useful research. Myers acknowledges that it is no coincidence that the questionnaire followed upon the heels of the transfer notice. When employee speech concerning office policy arises from an employment dispute concerning the very application of that policy to the speaker, additional weight must be given to the supervisor's view that the employee has threatened the authority of the employer to run the office. Although we accept the District Court's factual finding that Myers' reluctance to accede to the transfer order was not a sufficient cause in itself for her dismissal, and thus does not constitute a sufficient defense under *Mt. Healthy City Board of Ed. v. Doyle*, 429 U.S. 274, 97 S.Ct. 568, 50 L.Ed.2d 471 (1977), this does not render irrelevant the fact that the questionnaire emerged after a persistent dispute between Myers and Connick and his deputies over office transfer policy.

III

Myers' questionnaire touched upon matters of public concern in only a most limited sense; her survey, in our view, is most accurately characterized as an employee grievance concerning internal office policy. The limited First Amendment interest involved here does not require that Connick tolerate action which he reasonably believed would disrupt the office, undermine his authority, and destroy close working relationships. Myers' discharge therefore did not offend the First Amendment.

JUSTICE BRENNAN, with whom JUSTICE MARSHALL, JUSTICE BLACKMUN, and JUSTICE STEVENS join, dissenting.

The Court seeks to distinguish *Givhan* on the ground that speech protesting racial discrimination is "inherently of public concern." In so doing, it suggests that there are two classes of speech of public concern: statements "of public import" because of their content, form, and context, and statements that, by virtue of their subject matter, are "inherently of

---

[13] The record indicates that some, though not all, of the copies of the questionnaire were distributed during lunch. Employee speech which transpires entirely on the employee's own time, and in nonwork areas of the office, bring different factors into the *Pickering* calculus, and might lead to a different conclusion. Cf. *NLRB v. Magnavox Co.*, 415 U.S. 322, 94 S.Ct. 1099, 39 L.Ed.2d 358 (1974).

public concern." In my view, however, whether a particular statement by a public employee is addressed to a subject of public concern does not depend on where it was said or why. The First Amendment affords special protection to speech that may inform public debate about how our society is to be governed—regardless of whether it actually becomes the subject of a public controversy.

* * * I would hold that Myers' questionnaire addressed matters of public concern because it discussed subjects that could reasonably be expected to be of interest to persons seeking to develop informed opinions about the manner in which the Orleans Parish District Attorney, an elected official charged with managing a vital governmental agency, discharges his responsibilities.

* * *

The Court's adoption of a far narrower conception of what subjects are of public concern seems prompted by its fears that a broader view "would mean that virtually every remark—and certainly every criticism directed at a public official—would plant the seed of a constitutional case." Obviously, not every remark directed at a public official by a public employee is protected by the First Amendment.[3] But deciding whether a particular matter is of public concern is an inquiry that, by its very nature, is a sensitive one for judges charged with interpreting a constitutional provision intended to put "the decision as to what views shall be voiced largely into the hands of each of us." *Cohen v. California*, 403 U.S. 15, 24, 91 S.Ct. 1780, 1788, 29 L.Ed.2d 284 (1971).

NOTE: RANKIN V. MCPHERSON

Rankin v. McPherson, 483 U.S. 378, 381, 107 S.Ct. 2891, 2895, 97 L.Ed.2d 315 (1987), involved a 19 year old clerical employee of a county law enforcement agency who reacted to news of an attempted assassination of President Reagan by remarking to her co-worker and apparent boyfriend "he's cutting back Medicaid and food stamps * * * shoot, if they go for him again, I hope they get him." The remark was overheard by another of McPherson's co-workers and resulted in her discharge. The Court, in an opinion by Justice Marshall, held that the statement was on a matter of public concern protected by *Pickering*:

> Considering the statement in context, as *Connick* requires, discloses that it plainly dealt with a matter of public concern. The statement was made in the course of a conversation addressing the policies of the President's administration. It came on the heels of a news bulletin

---

[3] Perhaps the simplest example of a statement by a public employee that would not be protected by the First Amendment would be answering "No" to a request that the employee perform a lawful task within the scope of his duties. Although such a refusal is "speech," which implicates First Amendment interests, it is also insubordination, and as such it may serve as the basis for a lawful dismissal.

regarding what is certainly a matter of heightened public attention
* * * . The inappropriate or controversial character of a statement is
irrelevant to the question whether it deals with a matter of public
concern.

Id. at 386–87, 107 S.Ct. at 2897–98. Having found the *Pickering* threshold
satisfied, the Court proceeded to inquire whether the statement impaired the
effective functioning of the constable's office. The defendant acknowledged that
McPherson's conduct had not interfered with the internal operations of its
office. Nor was there any danger that the plaintiff had discredited the office by
making her statement in public. Given her level of responsibility within the
agency, the statement did not compromise the mission of the employer:
"Where, as here, an employee serves no confidential, policymaking, or public
contact role, the danger to the agency's successful function from that
employee's speech is minimal." Id. at 391–92, 107 S.Ct. at 2900. Justice Scalia,
joined by Chief Justice Rehnquist and Justices White and O'Connor, dissented.

NOTES AND QUESTIONS

Test Your Understanding of the Material

1.   Does *Connick* mean that public employee speech on matters not of
"public concern" enjoys no protection under the First Amendment from
injunctions, criminal prosecution, or other forms of state censorship? Does this
"public concern" limitation apply to government in its role as law enforcement
authority rather than as public employer?

2.   Was *Rankin* consistent with *Connick*? Would the Court have
protected McPherson's speech had she said that "I hope they get" some private
citizen who had been unkind to her family?

3.   Do you agree with the Court's conclusion that only one of Myer's
questions related to a matter of "public concern"? How are courts to determine
what is a matter of public concern?

Related Issues

4.   *Relevance of Myers's Motivation?* Was Myers's apparent motivation
for distributing the questionnaire the critical fact in *Connick?* Should the level
of First Amendment protection turn on the altruism or civic-mindedness of the
speaker? Most courts have focused on the content, as well as form and context,
of the speech, rather than on its motivation. See, e.g., Meade v. Moraine Valley
Cmty. Coll., 770 F.3d 680, 685–86 (7th Cir. 2014); (Sousa v. Roque, 578 F.3d
164 (2d Cir. 2009); Banks v. Wolfe County Bd. of Educ., 330 F.3d 888 (6th Cir.
2003); Azzaro v. County of Allegheny, 110 F.3d 968, 978 (3d Cir. 1997) (en
banc); Rode v. Dellarciprete, 845 F.2d 1195, 1201 (3d Cir.1988) (all cases
holding that an employee's personal stake in a matter of public concern does
not require *Connick* treatment).

5.   *Was* Connick *a "Mixed Motive" Case?* Should the mode of proof for
"mixed motive" § 1983 cases set out in Mt. Healthy City School Dist. Bd. of
Educ. v. Doyle, 429 U.S. 274, 97 S.Ct. 568, 50 L.Ed.2d 471 (1977), have been

used in *Connick*? Under *Mt. Healthy*, if a plaintiff proves that protected speech was a motivating factor in an adverse personnel decision, the defendant employer must prove that it would have made the same decision but for this illegitimate motive. Could Connick probably have demonstrated that he would have dismissed Myers had the questionnaire not contained question 11? Compare Desert Palace, Inc. v. Costa, 539 U.S. 90, 123 S.Ct. 2148, 156 L.Ed.2d 84 (2003), excerpted on page 126, supra (mixed motive standard in Title VII context).

6. *Misconstrued Speech*. Does the *Connick* test turn on what the public employer thought was said, or on what the trier of fact determines was actually said? In Waters v. Churchill, 511 U.S. 661, 667, 114 S.Ct. 1878, 128 L.Ed.2d 686 (1994), the Supreme Court concluded that governmental managers could discharge an employee for making statements that they "reasonably found", based on interviews with two witnesses, included comments that criticized her supervisor and discouraged transfers into her department and thus were not protected under *Connick*'s restatement of the *Pickering* balance (whether or not the comments also involved a matter of "public concern").

Justice O'Connor, writing for herself, Chief Justice Rehnquist, and Justices Souter and Ginsburg, held that an employer need only conduct an investigation that is reasonable in light of what the employee has been alleged to have said: "This need not be the care with which trials, with their rules or evidence and procedure, are conducted. It should, however, be the care that a reasonable manager would use before making an employment decision * * * of the sort involved in the particular case." Id. at 677–78. Justice Scalia, joined by Justices Kennedy and Thomas, objected to requiring any investigation, contending that the First Amendment only demands that the employer not assert a legitimate reason as a pretext in bad faith. Justice Stevens, joined by Justice Blackmun, penned a strong dissent, arguing that the First Amendment is violated "when a public employee is fired for uttering speech on a matter of public concern that is not unduly disruptive of the operation of the relevant agency," regardless of whether "the firing was based upon a reasonable mistake about what the employee said." Id. at 698.

In Heffernan v. City of Patterson, 136 S.Ct. 1412 (2016) , the Court, addressing a related question, held that an employee can sue his public employer for taking an adverse employment action against him because it mistakenly believed he had engaged in First Amendment-protected activity.

7. *Protection of Artistic or Personal Expression?* Under *Connick* can the writing of fictional works be protected from adverse personnel actions by the First Amendment? The presentation of photographs, paintings, music, or dance? Must the employee-artist first establish that his work somehow conveys a "message" of "public concern"? In City of San Diego v. Roe, 543 U.S. 77, 125 S.Ct. 521, 160 L.Ed.2d 410 (2004), the Court held that a police officer's videotapes featuring him performing sexual acts in a police uniform did not involve a matter of public concern under *Connick*.

8.   *Does* Pickering *Apply to Restrictions on Government Contractors? Do Government Contractors Have the Same Protection as Employees?* In Board of County Comm's v. Umbehr, 518 U.S. 668, 116 S.Ct. 2342, 2348–49, 135 L.Ed.2d 843 (1996), the Court held that *Pickering* balancing provides the appropriate mode of analysis for claims of government retaliation against government contractors for engaging in protected speech activities.

9.   Connick *and the Petition Clause of the First Amendment.* The First Amendment protects "the right of the people . . . to petition the Government for a redress of grievances." In Borough of Duryea v. Guarnieri, 564 U.S. 379, 131 S.Ct. 2488, 180 L.Ed.2d 408 (2011), the Court held that the "matter of public concern" limitation recognized in *Connick* also applies to claims under the petition clause. *Borough of Duryea* involved a claim of public-employer retaliation for filing both a grievance under a collective bargaining agreement and a lawsuit claiming a contract violation. The Court assumed that each constituted a "petition" under the First Amendment, but decided that neither would be protected from employment retaliation if it concerned only a private matter.

GARCETTI V. CEBALLOS

Supreme Court of the United States, 2006.
547 U.S. 410, 126 S.Ct. 1951, 164 L.Ed.2d 689.

JUSTICE KENNEDY delivered the opinion of the Court.

I

Respondent Richard Ceballos has been employed since 1989 as a deputy district attorney for the Los Angeles County District Attorney's Office. During the period relevant to this case, Ceballos was a calendar deputy in the office's Pomona branch, and in this capacity he exercised certain supervisory responsibilities over other lawyers. In February 2000, a defense attorney contacted Ceballos about a pending criminal case. The defense attorney said there were inaccuracies in an affidavit used to obtain a critical search warrant. The attorney informed Ceballos that he had filed a motion to traverse, or challenge, the warrant, but he also wanted Ceballos to review the case. According to Ceballos, it was not unusual for defense attorneys to ask calendar deputies to investigate aspects of pending cases.

After examining the affidavit and visiting the location it described, Ceballos determined the affidavit contained serious misrepresentations. The affidavit called a long driveway what Ceballos thought should have been referred to as a separate roadway. Ceballos also questioned the affidavit's statement that tire tracks led from a stripped-down truck to the premises covered by the warrant. His doubts arose from his conclusion that the roadway's composition in some places made it difficult or impossible to leave visible tire tracks.

Ceballos spoke on the telephone to the warrant affiant, a deputy sheriff from the Los Angeles County Sheriff's Department, but he did not receive a satisfactory explanation for the perceived inaccuracies. He relayed his findings to his supervisors, petitioners Carol Najera and Frank Sundstedt, and followed up by preparing a disposition memorandum. The memo explained Ceballos' concerns and recommended dismissal of the case. On March 2, 2000, Ceballos submitted the memo to Sundstedt for his review. A few days later, Ceballos presented Sundstedt with another memo, this one describing a second telephone conversation between Ceballos and the warrant affiant.

Based on Ceballos' statements, a meeting was held to discuss the affidavit. Attendees included Ceballos, Sundstedt, and Najera, as well as the warrant affiant and other employees from the sheriff's department. The meeting allegedly became heated, with one lieutenant sharply criticizing Ceballos for his handling of the case.

Despite Ceballos' concerns, Sundstedt decided to proceed with the prosecution, pending disposition of the defense motion to traverse. The trial court held a hearing on the motion. Ceballos was called by the defense and recounted his observations about the affidavit, but the trial court rejected the challenge to the warrant.

Ceballos claims that in the aftermath of these events he was subjected to a series of retaliatory employment actions. The actions included reassignment from his calendar deputy position to a trial deputy position, transfer to another courthouse, and denial of a promotion. Ceballos initiated an employment grievance, but the grievance was denied based on a finding that he had not suffered any retaliation. Unsatisfied, Ceballos sued in the United States District Court for the Central District of California, asserting, as relevant here, a claim under Rev. Stat. § 1979, 42 U.S.C. § 1983. He alleged petitioners violated the First and Fourteenth Amendments by retaliating against him based on his memo of March 2.

* * *

II

* * *

* * * Government employers, like private employers, need a significant degree of control over their employees' words and actions; without it, there would be little chance for the efficient provision of public services. Cf. *Connick* [*v. Myers*, 461 U.S. 138,] 143, 103 S. Ct. 1684, 75 L. Ed. 2d 708 ("[G]overnment offices could not function if every employment decision became a constitutional matter"). Public employees, moreover, often occupy trusted positions in society. When they speak out, they can express views that contravene governmental policies or impair the proper performance of governmental functions.

At the same time, the Court has recognized that a citizen who works for the government is nonetheless a citizen. The First Amendment limits the ability of a public employer to leverage the employment relationship to restrict, incidentally or intentionally, the liberties employees enjoy in their capacities as private citizens. See *Perry v. Sindermann*, 408 U.S. 593, 597, 92 S. Ct. 2694, 33 L. Ed. 2d 570 (1972). So long as employees are speaking as citizens about matters of public concern, they must face only those speech restrictions that are necessary for their employers to operate efficiently and effectively. See, *e.g., Connick, supra*, at 147, 103 S. Ct. 1684, 75 L. Ed. 2d 708 ("Our responsibility is to ensure that citizens are not deprived of fundamental rights by virtue of working for the government").

* * *

The Court's decisions, then, have sought both to promote the individual and societal interests that are served when employees speak as citizens on matters of public concern and to respect the needs of government employers attempting to perform their important public functions. * * * Underlying our cases has been the premise that while the *First Amendment* invests public employees with certain rights, it does not empower them to "constitutionalize the employee grievance." *Connick*, 461 U.S., at 154, 103 S. Ct. 1684, 75 L. Ed. 2d 708.

III

With these principles in mind we turn to the instant case. Respondent Ceballos believed the affidavit used to obtain a search warrant contained serious misrepresentations. He conveyed his opinion and recommendation in a memo to his supervisor. That Ceballos expressed his views inside his office, rather than publicly, is not dispositive. Employees in some cases may receive First Amendment protection for expressions made at work. See, *e.g., Givhan v. Western Line Consol. School Dist.*, 439 U.S. 410, 414, 99 S. Ct. 693, 58 L. Ed. 2d 619 (1979). Many citizens do much of their talking inside their respective workplaces, and it would not serve the goal of treating public employees like "any member of the general public," *Pickering* [*v. Board of Educ.*], 391 U.S. [563,] 573, 88 S. Ct. 1731, 20 L. Ed. 2d 811, to hold that all speech within the office is automatically exposed to restriction.

The memo concerned the subject matter of Ceballos' employment, but this, too, is nondispositive. The First Amendment protects some expressions related to the speaker's job. See, *e.g., ibid.*; *Givhan, supra*, at 414, 99 S. Ct. 693, 58 L. Ed. 2d 619. As the Court noted in *Pickering*: "Teachers are, as a class, the members of a community most likely to have informed and definite opinions as to how funds allotted to the operation of the schools should be spent. Accordingly, it is essential that they be able to speak out freely on such questions without fear of retaliatory dismissal." 391 U.S., at 572, 88 S. Ct. 1731, 20 L. Ed. 2d 811. The same is true of many other categories of public employees.

The controlling factor in Ceballos' case is that his expressions were made pursuant to his duties as a calendar deputy. That consideration—the fact that Ceballos spoke as a prosecutor fulfilling a responsibility to advise his supervisor about how best to proceed with a pending case—distinguishes Ceballos' case from those in which the First Amendment provides protection against discipline. We hold that when public employees make statements pursuant to their official duties, the employees are not speaking as citizens for First Amendment purposes, and the Constitution does not insulate their communications from employer discipline.

Ceballos wrote his disposition memo because that is part of what he, as a calendar deputy, was employed to do. It is immaterial whether he experienced some personal gratification from writing the memo; his First Amendment rights do not depend on his job satisfaction. The significant point is that the memo was written pursuant to Ceballos' official duties. Restricting speech that owes its existence to a public employee's professional responsibilities does not infringe any liberties the employee might have enjoyed as a private citizen. It simply reflects the exercise of employer control over what the employer itself has commissioned or created. Cf. *Rosenberger v. Rector and Visitors of Univ. of Va.*, 515 U.S. 819, 833, 115 S. Ct. 2510, 132 L. Ed. 2d 700 (1995) ("[W]hen the government appropriates public funds to promote a particular policy of its own it is entitled to say what it wishes"). Contrast, for example, the expressions made by the speaker in *Pickering*, whose letter to the newspaper had no official significance and bore similarities to letters submitted by numerous citizens every day.

Ceballos did not act as a citizen when he went about conducting his daily professional activities, such as supervising attorneys, investigating charges, and preparing filings. In the same way he did not speak as a citizen by writing a memo that addressed the proper disposition of a pending criminal case. When he went to work and performed the tasks he was paid to perform, Ceballos acted as a government employee. The fact that his duties sometimes required him to speak or write does not mean his supervisors were prohibited from evaluating his performance.

This result is consistent with our precedents' attention to the potential societal value of employee speech. Refusing to recognize First Amendment claims based on government employees' work product does not prevent them from participating in public debate. The employees retain the prospect of constitutional protection for their contributions to the civic discourse. This prospect of protection, however, does not invest them with a right to perform their jobs however they see fit.

Our holding likewise is supported by the emphasis of our precedents on affording government employers sufficient discretion to manage their operations. Employers have heightened interests in controlling speech made by an employee in his or her professional capacity. Official communications have official consequences, creating a need for substantive consistency and clarity. Supervisors must ensure that their employees' official communications are accurate, demonstrate sound judgment, and promote the employer's mission. Ceballos' memo is illustrative. It demanded the attention of his supervisors and led to a heated meeting with employees from the sheriff's department. If Ceballos' superiors thought his memo was inflammatory or misguided, they had the authority to take proper corrective action.

Ceballos' proposed contrary rule, adopted by the Court of Appeals, would commit state and federal courts to a new, permanent, and intrusive role, mandating judicial oversight of communications between and among government employees and their superiors in the course of official business. This displacement of managerial discretion by judicial supervision finds no support in our precedents. When an employee speaks as a citizen addressing a matter of public concern, the First Amendment requires a delicate balancing of the competing interests surrounding the speech and its consequences. When, however, the employee is simply performing his or her job duties, there is no warrant for a similar degree of scrutiny. To hold otherwise would be to demand permanent judicial intervention in the conduct of governmental operations to a degree inconsistent with sound principles of federalism and the separation of powers.

* * *

Proper application of our precedents * * * leads to the conclusion that the First Amendment does not prohibit managerial discipline based on an employee's expressions made pursuant to official responsibilities. Because Ceballos' memo falls into this category, his allegation of unconstitutional retaliation must fail.

Two final points warrant mentioning. First, as indicated above, the parties in this case do not dispute that Ceballos wrote his disposition memo pursuant to his employment duties. We thus have no occasion to articulate a comprehensive framework for defining the scope of an employee's duties in cases where there is room for serious debate. We reject, however, the suggestion that employers can restrict employees' rights by creating excessively broad job descriptions. The proper inquiry is a practical one. Formal job descriptions often bear little resemblance to the duties an employee actually is expected to perform, and the listing of a given task in an employee's written job description is neither necessary nor sufficient to demonstrate that conducting the task is within the scope of the employee's professional duties for First Amendment purposes.

Second, Justice Souter suggests today's decision may have important ramifications for academic freedom, at least as a constitutional value. There is some argument that expression related to academic scholarship or classroom instruction implicates additional constitutional interests that are not fully accounted for by this Court's customary employee-speech jurisprudence. We need not, and for that reason do not, decide whether the analysis we conduct today would apply in the same manner to a case involving speech related to scholarship or teaching.

IV

Exposing governmental inefficiency and misconduct is a matter of considerable significance. As the Court noted in *Connick*, public employers should, "as a matter of good judgment," be "receptive to constructive criticism offered by their employees." 461 U.S., at 149, 103 S. Ct. 1684, 75 L. Ed. 2d 708. The dictates of sound judgment are reinforced by the powerful network of legislative enactments—such as whistle-blower protection laws and labor codes—available to those who seek to expose wrongdoing. See, *e.g.*, 5 U.S.C. § 2302(b)(8); Cal. Govt. Code Ann. § 8547.8 (West 2005); Cal. Lab. Code Ann. § 1102.5 (West Supp. 2006). Cases involving government attorneys implicate additional safeguards in the form of, for example, rules of conduct and constitutional obligations apart from the First Amendment. See, *e.g.*, Cal. Rule Prof. Conduct 5–110 (2005) ("A member in government service shall not institute or cause to be instituted criminal charges when the member knows or should know that the charges are not supported by probable cause"); *Brady v. Maryland*, 373 U.S. 83, 83 S. Ct. 1194, 10 L. Ed. 2d 215 (1963). These imperatives, as well as obligations arising from any other applicable constitutional provisions and mandates of the criminal and civil laws, protect employees and provide checks on supervisors who would order unlawful or otherwise inappropriate actions.

We reject, however, the notion that the First Amendment shields from discipline the expressions employees make pursuant to their professional duties. Our precedents do not support the existence of a constitutional cause of action behind every statement a public employee makes in the course of doing his or her job.

JUSTICE STEVENS, dissenting.

* * * The notion that there is a categorical difference between speaking as a citizen and speaking in the course of one's employment is quite wrong. Over a quarter of a century has passed since then-Justice Rehnquist, writing for a unanimous Court, rejected "the conclusion that a public employee forfeits his protection against governmental abridgment of freedom of speech if he decides to express his views privately rather than publicly." *Givhan v. Western Line Consol. School Dist.*, 439 U.S. 410, 414, 99 S. Ct. 693, 58 L. Ed. 2d 619 (1979). We had no difficulty recognizing that the First Amendment applied when Bessie Givhan, an English teacher, raised concerns about the school's racist employment practices to the principal. See *id.*, at 413–416, 99 S. Ct. 693, 58 L. Ed. 2d 619. Our silence as to whether or not her speech was made pursuant to her job duties demonstrates that the point was immaterial. That is equally true today, for it is senseless to let constitutional protection for exactly the same words hinge on whether they fall within a job description. Moreover, it seems perverse to fashion a new rule that provides employees with an incentive to voice their concerns publicly before talking frankly to their superiors.

JUSTICE SOUTER, with whom JUSTICE STEVENS and JUSTICE GINSBURG join, dissenting.

* * * As all agree, the qualified speech protection embodied in *Pickering* balancing resolves the tension between individual and public interests in the speech, on the one hand, and the government's interest in operating efficiently without distraction or embarrassment by talkative or headline-grabbing employees. The need for a balance hardly disappears when an employee speaks on matters his job requires him to address; rather, it seems obvious that the individual and public value of such speech is no less, and may well be greater, when the employee speaks pursuant to his duties in addressing a subject he knows intimately for the very reason that it falls within his duties. * * *

Two reasons in particular make me think an adjustment using the basic *Pickering* balancing scheme is perfectly feasible here. First, the extent of the government's legitimate authority over subjects of speech required by a public job can be recognized in advance by setting in effect a minimum heft for comments with any claim to outweigh it. Thus, the risks to the government are great enough for us to hold from the outset that an employee commenting on subjects in the course of duties should not prevail on balance unless he speaks on a matter of unusual importance and satisfies high standards of responsibility in the way he does it. The examples I have already given indicate the eligible subject matter, and it is fair to say that only comment on official dishonesty, deliberately unconstitutional action, other serious wrongdoing, or threats to health and safety can weigh out in an employee's favor. If promulgation of this standard should fail to discourage meritless actions premised on 42 U.S.C. § 1983 (or *Bivens v. Six Unknown Fed. Narcotics Agents*, 403 U.S. 388, 91 S. Ct. 1999, 29 L. Ed. 2d 619 (1971)) before they get filed, the standard itself would sift them out at the summary-judgment stage.

My second reason for adapting *Pickering* to the circumstances at hand is the experience in Circuits that have recognized claims like Ceballos's here. First Amendment protection less circumscribed than what I would recognize has been available in the Ninth Circuit for over 17 years, and neither there nor in other Circuits that accept claims like this one has there been a debilitating flood of litigation. For that matter, the majority's position comes with no guarantee against factbound litigation over whether a public employee's statements were made "pursuant to . . . official duties,". In fact, the majority invites such litigation by describing the enquiry as a "practical one," apparently based on the totality of employment circumstances. Are prosecutors' discretionary statements about cases addressed to the press on the courthouse steps made "pursuant to their official duties"? Are government nuclear scientists' complaints to their supervisors about a colleague's improper handling of radioactive materials made "pursuant" to duties? * * *

JUSTICE BREYER, dissenting [omitted].

NOTES AND QUESTIONS

Test Your Understanding of the Material

1.   The Court in *Garcetti* adds a second threshold—in addition to the "matter of public concern" requirement from *Connick*—that public employees claiming First Amendment protection must cross before they can subject their employers' personnel actions to the judicial balancing of *Pickering*. How does the Court articulate this threshold?

2.   Would First Amendment protection have extended to Ceballos if he was retaliated against for a speech delivered to the Mexican-American Bar Association about misconduct in the Sheriff's Department in the criminal case on which he wrote the disposition memorandum? For testifying in the hearing to suppress evidence in the case that the affidavit he investigated contained intentional fabrications? Consider *Lane v. Franks*, described in note 4 below.

3.   Justice Kennedy, for the Court in *Garcetti*, rejects "the suggestion that employers can restrict employees' rights by creating excessively broad job descriptions." The majority states that "[f]ormal job descriptions" are not controlling, and that the "proper inquiry" is instead a "practical one" to determine whether "conducting the task is within the scope of the employee's professional duties." Would your answers to the questions in Note 2, above, be influenced by the description of Ceballos's job in formal documents? By what was taken into account in his job evaluations?

Related Issues

4.   *Job-Required or Job-Related?* In Lane v. Franks, 134 S.Ct. 2369, 2378 (2014), the Court held that "[t]ruthful testimony under oath by a public employee outside the scope of his ordinary duties is speech as a citizen for First Amendment purposes . . . even when the testimony relates to his public employment or concerns information learned during that employment." Lane, the plaintiff, had been dismissed from his position as head of a statewide program for underprivileged youth after testifying under subpoena at a trial concerning corruption he discovered during an audit of the program's expenses. Lane alleged he was fired in retaliation for his testimony. The Court did not seem to rest on the employee's speech being under oath; instead, it pronounced more generally that "the mere fact that a citizen's speech concerns information acquired by virtue of his public employment does not transform that speech into employee—rather than citizen—speech. The critical question under *Garcetti* is whether the speech at issue is itself ordinarily within the scope of an employee's duties, not whether it merely concerns those duties." Id. at 2379. In a footnote, the *Lane* Court stated that since Lane's "ordinary job

responsibilities did not include testifying in court proceedings," it "need not address in this case whether truthful sworn testimony would constitute citizen speech under *Garcetti* when given as part of a public employee's ordinary job duties." Id. at 2378 n.4.

5.   *Internal Complaints*. If Ceballos had filed a complaint with the office of Garcetti, the District Attorney, alleging that his superiors were colluding with the Sheriff's Department to obtain evidence illegally, would Ceballos have been engaged in employee speech or citizen speech protected by the First Amendment? Should it matter whether Garcetti had required his subordinates to file any such complaints with him? Cf. Matthews v. City of New York, 779 F.3d 167, 174 (2d Cir, 2015) (complaint about arrest quota system was "policy-oriented speech . . . neither part of [plaintiff's] job description nor part of the reality of his everyday work"); Hagen v. City of Eugene, 73 F.3d 1251, 1258 (9th Cir. 2013) (when police officer raises complaints up the chain of command about his job, including public safety, it ordinarily is part of performing his job); Weintraub v. Board of Education, 593 F.3d 196 (2d Cir. 2010) (speech in internal union grievance is not protected because no citizen analogue as with external complaints).

6.   *Constitutional Protection of "Whistleblowers"*? After *Garcetti* and *Lane*, to what extent does the First Amendment provide employees' protection for the public disclosure of potential wrongdoing by their public employer? Should any protection depend upon the allegations being accurate? Should protection depend on following "proper channels" before going public? Even if internal complaints are not protected under *Garcetti*? Congress has provided significant protections for federal-sector employees engaged in whistleblowing activity, and many state legislatures have provided comparable protections for state and local government employees. See the discussion of whistleblower protections at pp. 653–669 infra.

7.   *Relevance of Alternative Legal Remedies?* Is it relevant to the reach of the First Amendment that public employees who suffer retaliation for work-related expression may have alternative legal remedies like those noted at the end of *Garcetti*? Even if expression like that of Ceballos's memorandum is not protected under some whistleblower law, might it be protected by an implied contractual covenant from an employer toward its employees that it will not terminate their employment for their good faith and effective performance of their jobs? This is the position of the Employment Restatement § 2.06(c)(2) (implied duty of good faith and fair dealing not to "retaliate against the employee for performing the employee's obligations under the employment contract or law"). See generally Cynthia Estlund, Harmonizing Work and Citizenship: A Due Process Solution to a First Amendment Problem, Sup. Ct. Rev. 2006, 115 (2007) (suggesting that such an interest could be protected under the due process clause and thus require that an employer provide "some kind of hearing" to insure against its deprivation).

8.   *Academic Freedom*. Note the *Garcetti* Court's reservation of whether its analysis "would apply in the same manner to a case involving speech related to scholarship or teaching." But cf. Mayer v. Monroe County, 474 F.3d 477 (7th

Cir. 2007) (teacher did not have a right to depart from curriculum of public school to express criticism of Iraqi war). Application of *Connick*'s "public concern" limit on the protection of public employee speech also could result in the exemption of much academic expression from *Pickering* balancing. Should "academic freedom" be equally protected on all subjects, no matter how esoteric or of limited public interest? Cf. Keyishian v. Board of Regents, 385 U.S. 589, 603, 87 S.Ct. 675, 17 L.Ed.2d 629 (1967) (academic freedom is a "special concern of the First Amendment"). See generally Richard H. Hiers, New Restrictions on Academic Free Speech, 2 J.C. & U.L. 217 (1995).

B. FREEDOM OF ASSOCIATION AND PUBLIC EMPLOYMENT

McLAUGHLIN V. TILENDIS
United States Court of Appeals, Seventh Circuit, 1968.
398 F.2d 287.

CUMMINGS, J.

This action was brought under Section 1 of the Civil Rights Act of 1871 (42 U.S.C. § 1983) by John Steele and James McLaughlin who had been employed as probationary teachers by Cook County, Illinois, School District No. 149. Each sought damages of $100,000 from the Superintendent of School District No. 149 and the elected members of the Board of Education of that District.

Steele was not offered a second-year teaching contract and McLaughlin was dismissed before the end of his second year of teaching. Steele alleged that he was not rehired and McLaughlin alleged that he was dismissed because of their association with Local 1663 of the American Federation of Teachers, AFL-CIO. Neither teacher had yet achieved tenure.

* * *

It is settled that teachers have the right of free association, and unjustified interference with teachers' associational freedom violates the Due Process clause of the Fourteenth Amendment. *Shelton v. Tucker,* 364 U.S. 479, 485–487, 81 S.Ct. 247, 5 L.Ed.2d 231.

* * *

The trial judge was motivated by his conclusion that more than free speech was involved here, stating:

"The union may decide to engage in strikes, to set up machinery to bargain with the governmental employer, to provide machinery for arbitration, or may seek to establish working conditions. Overriding community interests are involved. The very ability of the governmental entity to function may be affected. The judiciary, and particularly this Court, cannot interfere with the power or discretion of the state in handling these matters."

It is possible of course that at some future time plaintiffs may engage in union-related conduct justifying their dismissal. But the Supreme Court has stated that

> "Those who join an organization but do not share its unlawful purposes and who do not participate in its unlawful activities surely pose no threat, either as citizens or as public employees." *Elfbrandt v. Russell*, 384 U.S. 11, 17, 86 S.Ct. 1238, 1241, 16 L.Ed.2d 321.

Even if this record disclosed that the union was connected with unlawful activity, the bare fact [of] membership does not justify charging members with their organization's misdeeds. A contrary rule would bite more deeply into associational freedom than is necessary to achieve legitimate state interests, thereby violating the First Amendment.

Illinois has not prohibited membership in a teachers' union, and defendants do not claim that the individual plaintiffs engaged in any illegal strikes or picketing.[3] Moreover, collective bargaining contracts between teachers' unions and school districts are not against the public policy of Illinois. *Chicago, etc., Education Association v. Board of Education of City of Chicago*, 76 Ill.App.2d 456, 222 N.E.2d 243 (1966). Illinois even permits the automatic deduction of union dues from the salaries of employees of local governmental agencies. Ill.Rev.Stats.1967, Ch. 85, Sec. 472. These very defendants have not adopted any rule, regulation or resolution forbidding union membership. Accordingly, no paramount public interest of Illinois warranted the limiting of Steele's and McLaughlin's right of association.

NOTES AND QUESTIONS

Related Issues

1. *Protecting Freedom of Association.* Although the First Amendment does not expressly mention freedom of association, the Supreme Court in *Shelton v. Tucker*, relied upon in *McLaughlin* and in the loyalty oath cases, see, e.g., Elfbrandt v. Russell, 384 U.S. 11, 86 S.Ct. 1238, 16 L.Ed.2d 321 (1966), held that the amendment's express protection of free speech, assembly and the right to petition government implicitly includes the guaranty of free association.

The right of association also includes a right to avoid political associations. Thus, the Court has held that public employees who do not occupy policymaking or confidential positions have a constitutional right not to be discharged solely because of their failure to affiliate with a particular political

---

[3] In Illinois, strikes and certain picketing by public employees are enjoinable. Board of Education of Community Unit School Dist. No. 2 v. Redding, 32 Ill.2d 567, 207 N.E.2d 427 (1965).

party. Branti v. Finkel, 445 U.S. 507, 100 S.Ct. 1287, 63 L.Ed.2d 574 (1980); Elrod v. Burns, 427 U.S. 347, 96 S.Ct. 2673, 49 L.Ed.2d 547 (1976). But cf. Wallace v. Benware, 67 F.3d 655, 662 (7th Cir.1995) (finding *Elrod*'s policymaking exception not to extend to harassment for political affiliation).

2.   *Freedom of Association After* Connick. Is *McLaughlin* still good law? Does *Connick* suggest that to be protected from adverse personnel actions, a public employee's association must relate to an issue of "public concern"? Or does *Connick* limit only the protection of expression, without limiting the protection of association? Compare Cobb v. Pozzi, 363 F.3d 89 (2d Cir. 2004) (*Connick* applies to free association claims), with Hatcher v. Board of Public Educ., 809 F.2d 1546, 1558 (11th Cir.1987) (*Connick* does not apply).

In *O'Hare Truck Service*, supra, the Court distinguished cases like *Pickering*, and *Umbehr*, discussed in Note 8 at p. 691, where specific speech activity is punished and a balancing of governmental interests is required, from cases "where the raw test of political affiliation [is] suffic[ient] to show a constitutional violation, without the necessity of an inquiry more detailed than asking whether the requirement was appropriate for the employment in question." 518 U.S. at 719.

3.   *Protecting Partisan Political Activity in the Workplace?* Does the right of association include public employee participation in partisan political campaigns? The Court has broadly sustained civil service law restrictions on such participation. See United Public Workers of America v. Mitchell, 330 U.S. 75, 67 S.Ct. 556, 91 L.Ed. 754 (1947) (provision of federal Hatch Act, 5 U.S.C. § 7324(a)), reaffirmed in a pair of post-*Pickering* decisions, see Broadrick v. Oklahoma, 413 U.S. 601, 93 S.Ct. 2908, 37 L.Ed.2d 830 (1973); United States Civil Serv. Comm'n v. National Ass'n of Letter Carriers, 413 U.S. 548, 93 S.Ct. 2880, 37 L.Ed.2d 796 (1973). Justice White's opinion for the *Letter Carriers* Court explains that Congress could act to ensure that "the rapidly expanding Government work force should not be employed to build a powerful, invincible, and perhaps corrupt political machine," and that government employees not be pressured to "vote in a certain way or perform political chores in order to curry favor with their superiors rather than to act out their own beliefs." Id. at 565–66, 93 S.Ct. at 2890–91.

Do these rulings effectively deprive public employees of the full rights of citizenship in the service of a sanitized conception of the political process? Do they permit bans on mere affiliation with political parties? Do they bar public employees from wearing partisan political buttons or displaying party propaganda in their lockers or on their bumper stickers? See Biller v. U.S. Merit Sys. Protection Bd., 863 F.2d 1079 (2d Cir.1988) (union president's statement of support of a Presidential candidate does not violate Hatch Act absent showing of concerted action with campaign); Blaylock v. U.S. Merit Sys. Protection Bd., 851 F.2d 1348 (11th Cir.1988) (same); but cf. Burrus v. Vegliante, 336 F.3d 82 (2d Cir. 2003) (upholding United States Postal Service (USPS) removal from union bulletin boards in nonpublic areas of post offices, of posters comparing positions of candidates in the 2000 presidential election).

PART 4

TORTS IN THE EMPLOYMENT RELATIONSHIP

■ ■ ■

We have previously considered the "public policy" cause of action which is treated as a tort claim in many jurisdictions. Part 4 of the book considers other torts that arise in the in the workplace. Chapter 14 addresses the torts of misrepresentation, tortious interference with contract, and defamation.

In many cases, workplace injuries are subject to exclusive remedies provided through the applicable state workers' compensation scheme. Chapter 15 examines how courts approach state workers' compensation preclusion.

Chapter 16 takes up the issue of workplace privacy—an area of law that is fairly well-developed for government employees, but is still in its nascent stages for private sector workers. The final chapter in this presents the law governing post-termination restraints: the common law duty of loyalty and restrictive covenants. Employee violations of such restraints may give rise to contract, tort, or fiduciary remedies (see Chapter 20).

CHAPTER 14

MISREPRESENTATION, WRONGFUL INTERFERENCE, AND DEFAMATION

■ ■ ■

Introduction

This chapter addresses three important torts as they arise in the employment context.

Because these torts do not deal with physical injury, they tend not to be excluded under the exclusivity provision of most workers' compensation laws. Each of these torts presents distinct issues.

A. FRAUD AND DECEIT

RESTATEMENT OF EMPLOYMENT LAW §§ 6.05–6.06
American Law Institute (2015).

§ 6.05. Employer's Fraudulent Misrepresentation Inducing the Initiation, Maintenance, or Cessation of an Employment Relationship

An employer is subject to liability for intentionally inducing a current or prospective employee, through a knowingly false representation of fact, current intent, opinion, or law

    (1) to enter into, to maintain, or leave an employment relationship with the employer, or

    (2) to refrain from entering into or maintaining an employment relationship with another employer.

§ 6.06. Employer's Negligent Provision of False Information to Employees

    (a) An employer has a duty to a current or prospective employee to exercise reasonable care not to provide false information on a topic about which the employer has special knowledge and that the employee may reasonably rely on in deciding whether to enter into or maintain an employment relationship.

    (b) An employer is subject to liability for a current or prospective employee's pecuniary loss if the employer intentionally induced the employee to enter into or to maintain an employment relationship with the employer by breaching this duty.

HUNTER V. UP-RIGHT, INC.

Supreme Court of California, 1993.
6 Cal.4th 1174, 26 Cal.Rptr.2d 8, 864 P.2d 88.

PANELLI, J.

We granted review in this case to determine whether *Foley v. Interactive Data Corp.* (1988) 47 Cal.3d 654 [, 254 Cal.Rptr. 211, 765 P.2d 373] (*Foley*) precludes recovery of tort damages for fraud and deceit predicated on a misrepresentation made to effect termination of employment. *Foley* made clear that the employment relationship is "fundamentally contractual," and that—terminations in violation of public policy aside—contract damages are the appropriate remedy for wrongful termination. * * * Analyzing the circumstances of this case in light of *Foley* and of the traditional elements of fraud, we conclude that wrongful termination of employment ordinarily does not give rise to a cause of action for fraud or deceit, even if some misrepresentation is made in the course of the employee's dismissal. Tort recovery is available only if the plaintiff can establish all of the elements of fraud with respect to a misrepresentation that is separate from the termination of the employment contract, i.e., when the plaintiff's fraud damages cannot be said to result from termination itself. The record in this case does not support such recovery. Accordingly, we reverse the judgment of the Court of Appeal.

* * * Charles Hunter began working as a welder for Up-Right, Inc. (Up-Right) in January 1973. In 1980 he was promoted to welding supervisor and worked in that capacity until his employment was terminated on September 10, 1987.

In August 1988 Hunter sued Up-Right and his former supervisor, Pat Nelson, alleging causes of action for breach of contract, breach of the implied covenant of good faith and fair dealing, and various torts. After this court filed its decision in *Foley v. Interactive Data Corp.* 47 Cal.3d 654, 254 Cal.Rptr. 211, 765 P.2d 373 (1988) (*Foley*), Hunter sought and obtained permission to amend his complaint to allege a cause of action for fraud, based on the same facts as alleged in the original complaint.

The evidence presented at trial was in conflict regarding the circumstances of Hunter's termination. Hunter testified that he enjoyed his job at Up-Right, got along well with coworkers, and received excellent performance evaluations. He testified that at the end of the workday on September 10, 1987, he was called in to meet with Nelson. According to Hunter, Nelson told him that there had been a corporate decision to eliminate his position and that if he did not resign he would be terminated.

Hunter testified he asked Nelson for the opportunity to work in a lesser position within the company, but was refused. Hunter then signed a document setting forth his resignation. The next day he picked up his final paycheck, which included $5,200 in severance pay.

Nelson testified to a different series of events. On several occasions during a period prior to September 9, 1987, Nelson testified he had admonished Hunter regarding excessive absences to attend to personal matters. On September 9, 1987, Nelson testified, Hunter told him he was thinking of resigning due to personal problems. Nelson told him to think about it overnight and come back the next day. Nelson directed his secretary, Catherine Olson, to prepare a resignation form for Hunter's signature. On September 10, Hunter returned and told Nelson he had decided to resign. Hunter then signed the resignation form. Nelson had Olson prepare a final paycheck. Nelson testified that no corporate decision had been made to eliminate Hunter's job.

John Maricich, who had been plant superintendent for Up-Right for eight years until his resignation in January 1988, testified that Up-Right had a policy of terminating employees only for good cause. He testified that Hunter was an excellent employee.

* * *

The jury found in favor of Hunter on three theories: breach of implied contract not to terminate employment without good cause, breach of implied covenant of good faith and fair dealing, and fraud. By special verdict, it awarded Hunter $38,013 on the contractual theories and $120,000 for misrepresentation. The parties agreed that the $120,000 figure represented the jury's finding as to Hunter's total damages, and thus included the $38,013 awarded as contractual damages. The trial court entered judgment in favor of Hunter in the amount of $120,000, and the Court of Appeal affirmed.

* * *

The Court of Appeal erred in inferring that an employer that misrepresents a fact in the course of wrongfully terminating an employee has committed a fraud. The court contrasted Hunter's testimony (that Nelson told him his job had been eliminated by corporate decision) with Nelson's testimony (that no such corporate decision had been made and that Hunter would not have been dismissed had he not signed a resignation). From this, the court concluded that Hunter had proved a knowing misrepresentation (the supposed corporate decision) that was intended to defraud Hunter into resigning his job, Hunter's detrimental reliance (in resigning), and his resulting damage. Thus, according to the Court of Appeal, Hunter established each of the elements of fraud: (a) misrepresentation; (b) defendant's knowledge of the statement's falsity; (c) intent to defraud (i.e., to induce action in reliance on the misrepresentation); (d) justifiable reliance; and (e) resulting damage. (5 Witkin, Summary of Cal. Law (9th ed. 1988) Torts, § 676, p. 778; Civ. Code, § 1709; *Hobart v. Hobart Estate Co.* (1945) 26 Cal.2d 412, 422 [159 P.2d 958].)

The problem with the Court of Appeal's analysis is that the result of Up-Right's misrepresentation is indistinguishable from an ordinary constructive wrongful termination. The misrepresentation transformed what would otherwise have been a resignation into a constructive termination. As the jury found that Up-Right lacked good cause to dismiss Hunter, the constructive termination was wrongful. Thus, Up-Right simply employed a falsehood to do what it otherwise could have accomplished directly. It cannot be said that Hunter relied to his detriment on the misrepresentation in suffering constructive dismissal. Thus, the fraud claim here is without substance.

Moreover, it is difficult to conceive of a wrongful termination case in which a misrepresentation made by the employer to effect termination could ever rise to the level of a separately actionable fraud. In essence, such misrepresentations are merely the means to the end desired by the employer, i.e., termination of employment. They cannot serve as a predicate for tort damages otherwise unavailable under *Foley*. If the termination itself is wrongful, either because it breaches the employment contract or because it violates some well-established public policy articulated in a statute or constitutional provision, then the employee is entitled to recover damages sounding in contract or tort, respectively. But no independent fraud claim arises from a misrepresentation aimed at termination of employment.

Recognition of a fraud cause of action in the context of wrongful termination of employment not only would contravene the logic of *Foley*, but also potentially would cause adverse consequences for industry in general. Fraud is easily pleaded, and in all likelihood it would be a rare wrongful termination complaint that omitted to do so. Much harder, however, is the defense of such claims and their resolution at the summary judgment or demurrer stage of litigation. The resultant costs and inhibition of employment decisionmaking are precisely the sort of consequences we cited in *Foley* in disapproving tort damages for breaches of the implied covenant of good faith and fair dealing.

We note, however, that a misrepresentation not aimed at effecting termination of employment, but instead designed to induce the employee to alter detrimentally his or her position in some other respect, might form a basis for a valid fraud claim even in the context of a wrongful termination. The Court of Appeals for the Ninth Circuit addressed such a situation in *Miller v. Fairchild Industries, Inc.* (9th Cir.1989) 885 F.2d 498, 509–510. In that case, the employees had filed complaints against Fairchild with the Equal Employment Opportunity Commission, which resulted in negotiation of settlement agreements by which the employees gave up their right to sue under title VII of the 1964 Civil Rights Act (42 U.S.C. § 2000e–3(a)) in return for Fairchild's promise to provide training opportunities. Soon after the settlement, however, the employees were laid off. They sued Fairchild, alleging, as one of their causes of action, that Fairchild fraudulently induced them to enter into the settlement agreements by concealing the fact that they were probable candidates for future layoff, and by making promises that Fairchild had no intention of keeping. The court concluded that Fairchild's failure to provide the promised training opportunities supported an inference that it had not intended to perform when it signed the settlement agreements. (885 F.2d at p. 509.) Thus, the trial court's entry of directed verdict on the fraud causes of action was improper. (Id. at p. 510.)

In *Miller v. Fairchild Industries, Inc.*, supra, the allegedly fraudulent settlement agreement was collateral to the employment contract itself. The *Miller* plaintiffs demonstrated that they had changed their position in reliance on Fairchild's misrepresentations by foregoing their rights to sue under title VII. *Miller* is thus readily distinguishable from the present case, where plaintiff has shown only that Up-Right engineered his resignation without good cause by telling him his position had been eliminated.

* * * Although tort damages are unavailable in this case, Hunter has established his claim to contractual damages for constructive wrongful termination, and on remand the judgment must be modified accordingly.

MOSK, J. [dissenting].

* * * [W]hile the duty to treat a party with whom one enters into contract in good faith can be seen as only a contractual duty, the obligation to refrain from committing fraud is a duty imposed by society to govern commercial and other human relationships, regardless of whether those relationships are contractual. And, unlike the tortious breach of the covenant of good faith and fair dealing, the tort of fraud has never depended on the existence of a "special relationship" between the tortfeasor and the tort victim. * * *

[I]n the promissory fraud cases, tort recovery is allowed, despite the fact that fraud and contract damages arise from the same set of facts, because the judicial system seeks to vindicate a social policy of preventing injurious, deliberate falsehoods. Although it is a fact of life that parties breach contracts because of changes in circumstance, the tort system is used to send a signal that the breach of a contract a party calculatingly never intended to fulfill is a different, and greater, wrong than an ordinary breach, and should receive greater sanction.

The circumstances in the present case are analogous to promissory fraud. Although plaintiff's damages are presumably the same for being tricked into resigning as they would be if he had been simply wrongfully discharged outright, the former behavior involves a fraud for which the law of tort provides special disincentives. The purpose of the fraud in this case, as the jury fairly inferred, was to dupe plaintiff into forfeiting his contractual and employment rights by deceiving him into resigning. The corporation sought through this artful deception to extricate itself from its contractual obligations, rather than to straightforwardly discharge him and risk potential liability for breach of contract. The law of fraud is designed to deter the use of such stratagems.

NOTES AND QUESTIONS

Test Your Understanding of the Material

1.   Identify the elements of a fraud claim. Did Hunter satisfy each element of the claim?

2.   Is *Hunter v. Up-Right* consistent with §§ 6.05 and 6.06 of the Employment Restatement?

3.   What public purpose would be served by allowing tort damages for a fraudulently induced resignation when a direct termination of employment would result only in a claim for contract damages? Justice Mosk asserts that an employee whose resignation is fraudulently induced is "in a different, and worse, position than an employee who is straightforwardly discharged." Why? Is the employer's misrepresentation a basis for tolling the applicable statute of limitations until the employee knew or should have known he was terminated without good cause?

Related Issues

4.   *The Detrimental Reliance Factor*. Andrew Lazar, who worked for a family business in New York for 20 years, was lured to California by a new employer promising a long-term job in a thriving business. The California firm, however, was having serious financial problems when the representations were made, and, moreover, was planning a merger that eventually would result in the elimination of Lazar's position. Two years after his move to California, Lazar's position was eliminated. He sued for damages for lost income, loss of contact with New York market, payments on his California home he could no longer afford, and emotional distress. The California Supreme Court held that his action could proceed, distinguishing *Hunter* on the ground that, in this case, the plaintiff detrimentally relied on the employer's misrepresentations by taking actions (moving to California and resigning his prior employment) that placed him in a worse position. Lazar v. Superior Court of Los Angeles Co., 12 Cal.4th 631, 49 Cal.Rptr.2d 377, 909 P.2d 981 (1996); accord, Stewart v. Jackson & Nash, 976 F.2d 86, 88 (2d Cir. 1992) (plaintiff's injuries, which involved damage to her career growth, "commenced well before her termination and were, in several respects, unrelated to it"; extended in Hyman v. IBM Corp., 2000 WL 1538161 (S.D.N.Y.2000); both applying New York law); Kidder v. AmSouth Bank, N.A., 639 So.2d 1361 (1994). See also the discussion of *Miller* in the *Hunter* decision.

Like California, other states have recognized a fraud claim where an employee detrimentally relied on a promise of employment. See, e.g., Meade v. Cedarapids, Inc., 164 F.3d 1218 (9th Cir. 1999) (misrepresentation to induce employee to resign from secure job to take employment with defendant); Sea-Land Service, Inc. v. O'Neal, 224 Va. 343, 297 S.E.2d 647 (1982) (action against employer for intentionally breaching promise of employment in a particular new position if she resigned from her present job with the company); O'Neal v. Stifel, Nicolaus & Co., 996 S.W.2d 700 (Mo. App. 1999) (same); cf. Bower v. AT&T Technologies, Inc., 852 F.2d 361 (8th Cir.1988) (damages for "detrimental reliance" on promise that employees would be rehired as clerical employees after their telephone repair jobs were phased out as a result of divestiture of subsidiaries).

5. *Fraudulent Inducement to Continue Employment.* Does the tort of fraudulent inducement also extend to misrepresentations that induce an at-will employee to continue employment? A number of courts have so held in cases where the employee gave up another employment opportunity in reliance on the misrepresentation. See, e.g., Cole v. Kobs & Draft Advertising, Inc., 921 F.Supp. 220 (S.D.N.Y. 1996); LaFont v. Taylor, 902 S.W.2d 375 (Mo. Ct. App. 1995); Spoljaric v. Percival Tours, Inc., 708 S.W.2d 432 (Tex. 1986). But see Mackenzie v. Miller Brewing Co., 241 Wis.2d 700, 623 N.W.2d 739 (2001) (rejecting claim as impermissible blurring of the line between contract and tort). What is the appropriate remedy in such cases?

6. *Remedy for Fraudulent Inducement?* If an employer fraudulently induces an employee to enter into an employment relationship, what should be the remedy? If an employee is fraudulently induced to leave his prior at-will employment, what is the appropriate remedy? See generally Employment Restatement Ch. 9.

7. *Negligent Misrepresentation.* The tort of negligent misrepresentation does not impose a "general duty to disclose information to employees or prospective employees, even if the employer knows the information might be material to their employment decisions[.]" Employment Restatement § 6.06, comment d. Rather, it arises only where the employer has "special knowledge" and disclosure of that information "is necessary to prevent the employer's partial or ambiguous statement of material facts from being misleading[.]" Id. See e.g. Griesi v. Atlantic Gen. Hosp. Corp., 360 Md. 1, 756 A.2d 548 (2000) (negligent misrepresentation based on offer of employment that suggested the interview process was complete, and not subject to further approvals or processes); Gayer v. Bath Iron Works Corp., 687 A.2d 617, 621 (Me. 1996) (negligent misrepresentation where company officials extended offers for apprenticeship program despite knowledge that program would not be feasible).

8. *Statutes Addressing Employer Misrepresentations.* California Labor Code § 970 prohibits employers from inducing "employees to move to, from, or within California by misrepresentation of the nature, length or physical conditions of employment." Tyco Indus. v. Superior Court (Richards), 164 Cal.App.3d 148, 155, 211 Cal.Rptr. 540, 544 (1985); see Funk v. Sperry Corp.,

842 F.2d 1129, 1133–34 (9th Cir.1988) (§ 970 claim requires proof of knowingly false representations).

9. *Tort of Negligent Breach.* A few courts have used negligence concepts to permit tort recovery for breach of the employment contract. See, e.g., Flanigan v. Prudential Federal, 221 Mont. 419, 720 P.2d 257 (1986) (negligent failure to follow employer's stated termination policies; tort recovery not barred by exclusivity of workers' compensation scheme); Chamberlain v. Bissell, Inc., 547 F.Supp. 1067 (W.D.Mich.1982). Contra, Heltborg v. Modern Machinery, 244 Mont. 24, 795 P.2d 954, 962 (1990); Demars v. General Dynamics Corp., 779 F.2d 95, 99–100 (1st Cir.1985) (Massachusetts law); Boresen v. Rohm & Haas, Inc., 526 F.Supp. 1230, 1235–36 (E.D.Pa.1981) (Pennsylvania law).

In Huegerich v. IBP Inc., 547 N.W.2d 216 (Iowa 1996), plaintiff argued that his discharge for violating IBP's policy prohibiting on-premises possession of illegal drugs or "look-alike" drugs (having the same appearance or effect of an illegal drug) should be set aside because IBP was negligent in failing to specifically advise him that possession of "look-alike" drugs violated company policy. The Iowa high court set aside a damages verdict for "negligent discharge": "To recognize a theory of negligent discharge would require the imposition of a duty of care upon an employer when discharging an employee. Such a duty would radically alter the long recognized doctrine allowing discharge for any reason or no reason at all." Id. at 220.

B. WRONGFUL INTERFERENCE WITH CONTRACTUAL RELATIONS

The wrongful-interference tort has a long lineage, beginning, interestingly, with the employment contract case of Lumley v. Gye, 2 El. & Bl. 216, 118 Eng.Rep. 749 (1853), in which a singer under contract to sing at plaintiff's theater was induced by the defendant, who owned a rival theater, to break her contract with plaintiff in order to perform for defendant. Even though no violence, fraud or defamation was alleged, such enticement of another's servants was held tortious. See also Walker v. Cronin, 107 Mass. 555 (1871) (union held liable for inducing its members to leave their jobs in the course of a strike). See generally Harvey S. Perlman, Interference with Contract and Other Economic Expectancies: A Clash of Tort and Contract Doctrine, 49 U.Chi.L.Rev. 61 (1982).

RESTATEMENT OF EMPLOYMENT LAW §§ 6.03–6.04
American Law Institute (2015).

§ 6.03. Employer's Wrongful Interference with an Employee's Employment Relationship with Another Employer

(a) An employer wrongly interferes with an employee's employment or prospective employment with another employer when the employer, by improper means or without a legitimate business interest, intentionally causes another employer (i) to terminate its employment of the employee; or (ii) not to enter into an employment relationship with the employee.

(b) An employer does not wrongly interfere with an employee's employment with another employer by making a statement about the employee that is privileged under § 6.02. [*Eds.*, see pp. 718–719 infra.]

§ 6.04. Employer Does Not Wrongfully Interfere with Its Own Employment Relationship

(a) An employer is not subject to liability for wrongful interference with the employer's own present or prospective employment relationships.

(b) An employee may be subject to liability for wrongful interference with another employee's employment relationship with the interfering employee's employer only if the employer does not authorize or ratify the interfering employee's actions and those actions are not within the scope of the employee's employment.

GRUHLKE V. SIOUX EMPIRE FED. CREDIT UNION, INC.

Supreme Court of South Dakota, 2008.
756 NW 2d 399.

KONENKAMP, J.

CU Mortgage employed Becky Gruhlke as a senior mortgage underwriter. She was hired in January 2004, with an employment contract renewable annually. CU Mortgage renewed her contract in 2004 and 2005, but did not renew it thereafter. The renewal clause stated: "This Agreement shall be renewed with the same provisions for additional one-year terms, unless either party gives written notice of termination thereof to the other party at least thirty (30) days prior to the end of any such term." As Gruhlke's complaint acknowledged, the "contract was essentially a one year employment-at-will agreement."

Gruhlke brought suit against Sioux Empire Federal Credit Union and CU Mortgage Direct alleging wrongful discharge and breach of contract. She also sued David Bednar, the chief operating officer at CU Mortgage, alleging "wrongful interference with [her] business relationship/contract." This appeal addresses only the suit against Bednar.

In her complaint, Gruhlke averred that Bednar "acted intentionally and was unjustified in his actions" and "acted out of his personal interests" when he "advocated for the termination of Gruhlke's business relationship with CU Mortgage." According to Gruhlke, Bednar asked her to submit false and misleading information to investment mortgage companies in order to secure financing for certain home loans. When she refused, Bednar "yelled at her and tried to intimidate her into complying with his requests." Gruhlke reported Bednar to her direct supervisor. In December 2006, CU Mortgage chose not to renew Gruhlke's employment contract. * * *

In general, the tort of intentional interference with contractual relations serves as a remedy for contracting parties against interference from outside intermeddlers. To prevail on a claim of tortious interference, "there must be a 'triangle'—a plaintiff, an identifiable third party who wished to deal with the plaintiff, and the defendant who interfered with" the contractual relations. *Id.* ¶ 38 (quoting *Landstrom v. Shaver*, 1997 SD 25, ¶ 75, 561 N.W.2d 1, 16). South Dakota has long recognized this tort. *See Lien v. Nw. Eng'g Co.*, 73 S.D. 84, 88, 39 N.W.2d 483, 485 (1949); *see also Tibke v. McDougall*, 479 N.W.2d 898, 908 (S.D.1992); *Groseth Int'l, Inc. v. Tenneco, Inc.*, 410 N.W.2d 159, 172 (S.D.1987).

In this case, we must decide the narrower question: whether South Dakota will recognize a cause of action against a corporate officer for tortious interference with the corporation's employment contract with another. Only then can we determine whether Gruhlke has adequately pleaded the action. * * *

In the employment context, we think a claim of tortious interference with contractual relations may be made against a corporate officer, director, supervisor, or co-worker, who acts wholly outside the scope of employment, and who acts through improper means or for an improper purpose. Such individuals should not stand immune from their independently improper acts committed entirely for personal ends. * * *

Because this tort could eclipse wrongful termination actions by the maneuver of simply pleading around at-will employment law, many courts place a heavy burden on plaintiffs. We believe the Restatement formulation adequately protects the interests involved when its conditions are strictly complied with. Thus, to state a claim against a corporate officer for intentional interference with corporate contractual relations with another, a plaintiff must allege and prove each of the following elements: (1) the existence of a valid contractual relationship, (2) intentional interference with that relationship, (3) by a third party, (4) accomplished through improper means or for an improper purpose, (5) a causal effect between the interference and damage to the relationship, and (6) damages. *See Tibke*, 479 N.W.2d at 908 (following Restatement (Second) of Torts §§ 766, 766B). * * *

Third Party—Conduct Outside Scope of Employment

A third party is an indispensable element in the tort of intentional interference with contractual relations. With interference suits against corporate officers, determination of such element precedes any further analysis. "Without the protection of the third party element of the tort, virtually every supervisory decision affecting employment status would be subject to judicial challenge through the Trojan horse of the intentional interference tort." In what circumstances, then, will a corporate officer's actions be considered the actions of a third party? In keeping with the principle of respondeat superior, when employees act within the scope of their employment, their acts are the acts of their company. State v. Hy Vee Food Stores, Inc., 533 N.W.2d 147, 149 (S.D.1995). A corporate entity cannot contractually interfere with itself. "[W]hen an employee is acting within the scope of the employee's employment, and the employer, as a result, breaches a contract with another party, that employee is not a third party for the tort of intentional interference with economic relations." McGanty [v. Staudenraus, 321 Or. 532, 901 P.2d 841, 846 (1995)].

Accordingly, when claiming tortious interference with a contractual relationship, the plaintiff must plead and prove that the officer acted outside the scope of employment. See Mueller, 2002 SD 38, ¶ 38, 643 N.W.2d at 68–69 (quoting Landstrom, 1997 SD 25, ¶ 75, 561 N.W.2d at 16). "Generally, if an act is connected either directly or indirectly with the business of the employer (designed to benefit the employer's business), that act is conducted within the scope of employment." * * * The following considerations are relevant: (1) did the officer's acts occur substantially within the time and space limits authorized by the employment; (2) were the actions motivated, at least in part, by a purpose to serve the employer; and (3) were the actions of a kind that the officer was hired to perform. See id.; see also McGanty, 901 P.2d at 846 n. 3. If the officer's actions were at least in part motivated by a purpose to serve the employer, then those actions cannot be the acts of a third party. * * *

"Improper" Means or Purpose

After it is established that an intentional interference was committed by a third party, then it must be determined whether the interference was improper. The following elements from the Restatement (Second) of Torts § 767 should be considered in assessing whether a defendant's interference with a contractual relation was improper: (a) the nature of the actor's conduct, (b) the actor's motive, (c) the interests of the other with which the actor's conduct interferes, (d) the interests sought to be advanced by the actor, (e) the societal interests in protecting the freedom of action of the actor and the contractual interests of the other, (f) the proximity or remoteness of the actor's conduct to the interference, and (g) the relations between the parties. St. Onge Livestock Co., Ltd. v. Curtis, 2002 SD 102, ¶ 16, 650 N.W.2d 537, 542 (quoting Restatement (Second) of Torts § 767 (1979)). * * *

We now turn to Gruhlke's complaint to determine whether she has sufficiently pleaded her claim against Bednar for intentional interference with her employment contract. * * *

Gruhlke did not specifically assert that Bednar acted improperly, one of the required elements of proof, but she alleged that Bednar "acted intentionally and was unjustified in his actions in advocating the termination of Gruhlke's business relationship with CU Mortgage." She also gave a detailed recitation of the facts she believed supported her assertions. She alleged that Bednar "did not want Gruhlke at CU Mortgage because she would not sign off on fraudulent and misleading mortgages that Bednar originated . . . [and] because Gruhlke would not sign off on the fraudulent mortgages, Bednar lost commissions and/or had to sign off on the fraudulent mortgages himself." * * * These assertions, as far as they go, are sufficient to form part of the elements required for the tortious interference action.

On the other hand, with respect to the third-party element, nowhere in her complaint does Gruhlke allege that Bednar acted as a third party or that he acted beyond the scope of his employment. Gruhlke contends it is sufficient that she alleged that Bednar "acted out of his personal interests when he advocated for the termination of [her] business relationship with CU Mortgage." Yet, as we have said, corporate officers cannot be considered third parties to contracts between the corporate employer and another if the actions of the officers were even partially motivated to serve employer interests. Gruhlke did not allege that Bednar acted "solely" for his personal benefit when he advocated for her dismissal. In oral argument and in the appellate briefs, counsel for Gruhlke contended that acting "solely" for personal interest was not a necessary element of proof. On the contrary, in suits against corporate officers for tortious interference with the corporation's contract with another, pleading this allegation is indispensible.

To establish that a corporate officer interfered as a third party in the company's contract with another, the plaintiff must plead and prove that the officer "acted solely 'in furtherance of [his or her] personal interests so as to preserve the logically necessary rule that a party cannot tortiously interfere with its own contract.'" *Latch v. Gratty, Inc.*, 107 S.W.3d 543, 545 (Tex.2003) (quoting *Holloway v. Skinner*, 898 S.W.2d 793, 796 (Tex. 1995)). "It is now settled law that corporate agents are not liable for tortious interference with the corporation's contracts unless they acted solely for their own benefit with no benefit to the corporation." *Reed v. Michigan Metro Girl Scout Council*, 201 Mich.App. 10, 506 N.W.2d 231, 233 (1993) (citation omitted).

Because we regard this type of action with high vigilance, we require strict adherence to the pleading requirements. * * * Although Gruhlke's complaint does set forth detailed facts, it fails to contain a recitation of the required elements for a cause of action against a corporate officer for tortious interference. Thus, it fails to state a claim upon which relief can be granted.

NOTES AND QUESTIONS

Test Your Understanding of the Material

1.   Why didn't Gruhlke satisfy the "third party" element of the tortious interference claim?

2.   How might Gruhlke amend her complaint to address the deficiencies identified by the court?

Related Issues

3.   *Third-Party Requirement.* The third-party requirement included in Section 6.04(a) of the Employment Restatement reflects the nearly unanimous judicial position. Employees sometimes assert tortious interference claims against other employees as third parties. Supervisors acting in good faith within the scope of their authority in effecting a discharge will not be held liable under this tort. See, e.g., McGanty v. Staudenraus, 321 Or. 532, 538, 901 P.2d 841 (1995) ("when an employee is acting within the scope of the employee's employment, and the employer, as a result, breaches a contract with another party, that employee is not a third party for the tort of intentional interference with economic relations").

Individual employees, including supervisors, can be held liable for interference "to further their personal goals or to injure the other party [where] contrary to the best interest of the corporation." George A. Fuller Co. v. Chicago Coll. of Osteopathic Med., 719 F.2d 1326, 1333 (7th Cir. 1983). See e.g., Haupt v. International Harvester Co., 582 F.Supp. 545 (N.D.Ill.1984) (denying summary judgment where supervisor planned employee's termination to preserve "improper favoritism" towards a vendor); Miller v. Mount Sinai Medical Ctr., 288 A.D.2d 72 (2001) (no tortious interference claim based on negative reference unless supervisor's "sole purpose" was to harm plaintiff).

4.   *Improper Means or Absence of Legitimate Business Justification.* The Employment Restatement requires proof that the defendant acted "by improper means or without a legitimate business interest." The Restatement defines improper means and legitimate business justifications as follows:

> Improper means include those defined by common or statutory law as wrongful. Intentional misrepresentation, whether or not defamatory, is an improper means. Legitimate business justifications include competition with other employers and anticipated business benefit from other employers, as when multiple employers exchange information about their employees. Legitimate business justifications, however, do not include a desire to retaliate against an employee out of spite or vindictiveness when the employer's actions serve no legitimate business purpose.

Employment Restatement § 6.03, comment b.

5.   *Privileged Conduct.* Under the Employment Restatement § 6.03, employers have an affirmative defense where their conduct falls within a recognized privilege. Truthful statements to prospective employers for a

legitimate business purpose are privileged. Id. § 6.02. Litigation or the threat of litigation is also privileged, unless made (1) without "probable cause to believe the suit will succeed" and (2) for a purpose other than to "properly adjudicate claims." See, e.g., G.S. Enterprises, Inc. v. Falmouth Marine, Inc., 410 Mass. 262, 571 N.E.2d 1363 (Mass 1991); Restatement (Second) of Torts § 767 (comment c). But see Guinn v. Applied Composites Eng. Inc., 994 N.E.2d 1256 (Ind. Ct. App. 2013) (also examining "the degree of coercion involved, the extent of harm that it threatens . . . and the general reasonableness" of former employer's threat of litigation).

C. DEFAMATION

Traditional formulations of the tort of defamation require "publication" as an essential element of the claim—meaning that the defendant made the defamatory statement to a third party. See Restatement (Second) of Torts § 577(1) (1977). The next case, *Lewis v. Equitable Life*, addresses the question of whether a defamation claim can arise from a statement made only to the employee.

RESTATEMENT OF EMPLOYMENT LAW §§ 6.01–6.02
American Law Institute (2015).

§ 6.01. Employer's Liability to Employee for Defamation

(a) Subject to the privilege stated in § 6.02 and to other applicable privileges, an employer publishing a false and defamatory statement about an employee is subject to liability for the harm the publication causes.

(b) An employer publishes a statement about an employee when the employer makes the statement:

    (1) to any third party, including prospective employers, regulatory authorities, or employment agencies;

    (2) to employees or others within the employer's organization; or

    (3) to the employee, if the employer knows or should know that the employee will have to disclose the statement to prospective employers or others, the employee asks the employer to promise not to disclose the statement to any third party, and the employer refuses to promise.

§ 6.02. Employer Qualified Privilege to Publish Statements Concerning an Employee or Former Employee

(a) Unless denied under (b), an employer has a privilege to publish statements about an employee to:

    (1) prospective employers and employment agencies;

(2) public or private regulatory or licensing authorities; and

(3) the employer's own employees and agents.

(b) An employer is denied this privilege when the employer abuses it by publishing a statement, described in subsection (a), that the employer either (i) knows is false or acts with reckless disregard of its truth or falsity, or (ii) knows or should know that neither the employer nor the recipient has a legitimate interest in the recipient receiving the statement.

LEWIS V. EQUITABLE LIFE ASSUR. SOCIETY
Supreme Court of Minnesota, 1986.
389 N.W.2d 876.

AMDAHL, C.J.

Plaintiffs, Carole Lewis, Mary Smith, Michelle Rafferty, and Suzanne Loizeaux, former employees of defendant, the Equitable Life Assurance Society of the United States (company), all hired for indefinite, at-will terms, were discharged for the stated reason of "gross insubordination." They claim that they were discharged in breach of their employment contracts, as determined by an employee handbook, and that they were defamed because the company knew that they would have to repeat the reason for their discharges to prospective employers. A Ramsey county jury awarded plaintiffs compensatory and punitive damages. The Minnesota Court of Appeals affirmed the award but remanded on the issue of contract damages for future harm. We affirm in full the award of compensatory damages but reverse the award of punitive damages.

* * *

In seeking new employment, plaintiffs were requested by prospective employers to disclose their reasons for leaving the company, and each indicated that she had been "terminated." When plaintiffs received interviews, they were asked to explain their terminations. Each stated that she had been terminated for "gross insubordination" and attempted to explain the situation. The company neither published nor stated to any prospective employer that plaintiffs had been terminated for gross insubordination. Its policy was to give only the dates of employment and the final job title of a former employee unless specifically authorized in writing to release additional information.

Only one plaintiff found employment while being completely forthright with a prospective employer about her termination by the company. A second plaintiff obtained employment after she misrepresented on the application form her reason for leaving the company. She did, however, explain the true reason in her interview. A third plaintiff obtained employment only when she left blank the question on the application form requesting her reason for leaving her last employment; the issue never arose in her interview. The fourth plaintiff has been unable to find full-time employment. All plaintiffs testified to suffering emotional and financial hardship as a result of being discharged by the company.

* * *

Defamation Claim

With regard to plaintiffs' defamation claims, the company argues that the trial court's conclusion of liability on the part of the company was erroneous because: (1) the only publications of the allegedly defamatory statement were made by plaintiffs; (2) the statement in question was true; and (3) the company was qualifiedly privileged to make the statement.

1. *Publication*

In order for a statement to be considered defamatory, it must be communicated to someone other than the plaintiff, it must be false, and it must tend to harm the plaintiff's reputation and to lower him or her in the estimation of the community. * * * Generally, there is no publication where a defendant communicates a statement directly to a plaintiff, who then communicates it to a third person. Restatement (Second) of Torts § 577, comment m (1977). Company management told plaintiffs that they had engaged in gross insubordination, for which they were being discharged. This allegedly defamatory statement was communicated to prospective employers of each plaintiff. The company, however, never communicated the statement. Plaintiffs themselves informed prospective employers that they had been terminated for gross insubordination. They did so because prospective employers inquired why they had left their previous employment. The question raised is whether a defendant can ever be held liable for defamation when the statement in question was published to a third person only by the plaintiff.

We have not previously been presented with the question of defamation by means of "self-publication." Courts that have considered the question, however, have recognized a narrow exception to the general rule that communication of a defamatory statement to a third person by the person defamed is not actionable. See, e.g., *McKinney v. County of Santa Clara*, 110 Cal.App.3d 787, 168 Cal.Rptr. 89 (1980); *Colonial Stores, Inc. v. Barrett,* 73 Ga.App. 839, 38 S.E.2d 306 (1946); *Belcher v. Little,* 315 N.W.2d 734 (Iowa 1982); *Grist v. Upjohn Co.,* 16 Mich.App. 452, 168 N.W.2d 389 (1969); *Bretz v. Mayer*, 1 Ohio Misc. 59, 203 N.E.2d 665 (1963); *First State Bank of Corpus Christi v. Ake,* 606 S.W.2d 696 (Tex.Civ.App.1980). These courts have recognized that if a defamed person was in some way compelled to communicate the defamatory statement to a third person, and if it was foreseeable to the defendant that the defamed person would be so compelled, then the defendant could be held liable for the defamation.

* * *

The company presents two arguments against recognition of the doctrine of compelled self-publication. It argues that such recognition amounts to creating tort liability for wrongful discharge which, it asserts, has been rejected by this court. In *Wild v. Rarig*, 302 Minn. [419,] 442, 234 N.W.2d [775, 790 (1975)], we held that bad-faith termination of contract is not an independent tort of the kind that will permit a tort recovery. The company, however, misreads our holding regarding tort liability for wrongful discharge. We did not hold that the harm resulting from a bad-faith termination of a contract could never give rise to a tort recovery. Indeed, we recognized such a possibility by stating that a plaintiff is limited to contract damages "except in exceptional cases where the defendant's breach of contract constitutes or is accompanied by an independent tort." Id. at 440, 234 N.W.2d at 789. If plaintiffs here can establish a cause of action for defamation, the fact that the defamation occurred in the context of employment discharge should not defeat recovery.

The company also argues that recognition of the doctrine of self-publication would discourage plaintiffs from mitigating damages. This concern does not appear to be a problem, however, if liability for self-publication of defamatory statements is imposed *only* where the plaintiff was in some significant way compelled to repeat the defamatory statement and such compulsion was, or should have been, foreseeable to the defendant. Also, the duty to mitigate can be further protected by requiring plaintiffs when they encounter a situation in which they are compelled to repeat a defamatory statement to take all reasonable steps to attempt to explain the true nature of the situation and to contradict the defamatory statement. In such circumstances, there would be no voluntary act on the part of a plaintiff that would constitute a failure to mitigate. This point is clearly illustrated by the present action. The company points to no reasonable course of conduct that plaintiffs could have taken to mitigate their damages.

The trend of modern authority persuades us that Minnesota law should recognize the doctrine of compelled self-publication. We acknowledge that recognition of this doctrine provides a significant new basis for maintaining a cause of action for defamation and, as such, it should be cautiously applied. However, when properly applied, it need not substantially broaden the scope of liability for defamation. The concept of compelled self-publication does no more than hold the originator of the defamatory statement liable for damages caused by the statement where the originator knows, or should know, of circumstances whereby the defamed person has no reasonable means of avoiding publication of the statement or avoiding the resulting damages; in other words, in cases where the defamed person was compelled to publish the statement. In such circumstances, the damages are fairly viewed as the direct result of the originator's actions.

* * *

In the present action, the record indicates that plaintiffs were compelled to repeat the allegedly defamatory statement to prospective employers and that the company knew plaintiffs would be so compelled. The St. Paul office manager admitted that it was foreseeable that plaintiffs would be asked by prospective employers to identify the reason that they were discharged. Their only choice would be to tell them "gross insubordination" or to lie. Fabrication, however, is an unacceptable alternative.

2.   Issue of Truth

Finding that there was a publication, we next turn to the issue of truth. True statements, however disparaging, are not actionable. * * * Since it is true that plaintiffs were fired for gross insubordination, the company argues, they cannot maintain an action for defamation. The company contends the relevant statement to consider when analyzing the defense of truth is the one that plaintiffs made to their prospective employers, that is, that they had been fired for gross insubordination. Plaintiffs counter that it is the truth or falsity of the underlying statement—that plaintiffs engaged in gross insubordination—that is relevant.

The company relies for its authority solely upon language of this court in *Johnson v. Dirkswager*, 315 N.W.2d 215, 218–19 (Minn.1982), where we raised the question whether truth as a defense goes to the verbal accuracy of the statement or to the underlying implication of the statement. In *Dirkswager*, however, it was unnecessary to resolve the question. Moreover, that case is distinguishable from the present case because there the underlying statements were presented merely as "allegations of misconduct." Id. at 219 n. 4. Here, the company's charges against plaintiffs went beyond accusations and were conclusory statements that plaintiffs had engaged in gross insubordination.

Requiring that truth as a defense go to the underlying implication of the statement, at least where the statement involves more than a simple allegation, appears to be the better view. *See* Restatement (Second) of Torts § 581A, comment e (1977). Moreover, the truth or falsity of a statement is inherently within the province of the jury. This court will not overturn a jury finding on the issue of falsity unless the finding is manifestly and palpably contrary to the evidence. Thus, we find no error on this point because the record amply supports the jury verdict that the charge of gross insubordination was false.

3.   Qualified Privilege

* * *

The doctrine of privileged communication rests upon public policy considerations. As other jurisdictions recognize, the existence of a privilege results from the court's determination that statements made in particular contexts or on certain occasions should be encouraged despite the risk that the statements might be defamatory. See *Calero v. Del Chemical Corp.,* 68 Wis.2d 487, 498, 228 N.W.2d 737, 744 (1975). Whether an occasion is a proper one upon which to recognize a privilege is a question of law for the court to determine. *Jacron Sales Co. v. Sindorf,* 276 Md. 580, 350 A.2d 688 (1976); *Fisher v. Myers,* 339 Mo. 1196, 100 S.W.2d 551 (1936); *Cash v. Empire Gas Corp.,* 547 S.W.2d 830, 833 (Mo.Ct.App.1976). In the context of employment recommendations, the law generally recognizes a qualified privilege between former and prospective employers as long as the statements are made in good faith and for a legitimate purpose.

* * *

* * * A qualified privilege may be lost if it is abused. The burden is on the plaintiff to show that the privilege has been abused. While the initial determination of whether a communication is privileged is a question of law for the court to decide, the question of whether the privilege was abused is a jury question. Restatement (Second) of Torts, § 619 (1977). * * *

The company * * * argues that the court's instructions incorrectly stated the standard of malice which plaintiffs must prove if the existence of a qualified privilege is demonstrated. The law recognizes essentially two definitions of malice in defamation cases: the "actual malice" definition as set forth in *New York Times Co. v. Sullivan,* 376 U.S. 254, 279–80, 84 S.Ct. 710, 726, 11 L.Ed.2d 686 (1964), and the common-law definition. See *Stuempges* [*v. Parke, Davis & Co.,* 297 N.W.2d 252, 257 (Minn.1980)]. The common-law definition is more appropriate in the employer-employee situation because it focuses on the employer's attitude toward the plaintiff. *See id.* at 258. Under the common-law definition, malice exists where the defendant " 'made the statement from ill will and improper motives, or causelessly and wantonly for the purpose of injuring the plaintiff.' " Id. at 257 (quoting *McKenzie v. William J. Burns International Detective Agency, Inc.,* 149 Minn. 311, 312, 183 N.W. 516, 517 (1921)). In its instructions, the court informed the jurors that if they found that the company was entitled to a qualified privilege, plaintiff had to prove that the statement was made "with actual malice." In defining malice for the jury, the court correctly set forth the common-law definition. We therefore find no error in the jury instructions.

Damages

1.   *Compensatory Damages*

* * * Neither expungement of the company's records nor vindication at trial eliminate all future harm to the plaintiffs' earning capacity. The fact that plaintiffs brought suit against the company may itself have future detrimental effects. A person who brings suit against a former employer is likely to be a less attractive employment candidate to prospective employers. No amount of vindication with respect to the gross insubordination charge can eliminate this impact on plaintiffs' future work lives. We conclude that there was no error in including damages for future harm in plaintiffs' awards. The trial court awards of compensatory damages are supported by the evidence, and we therefore reverse the court of appeals directive remanding the issue of compensatory damages.

2.   Punitive Damages

* * * [W]e deny the imposition of punitive damages in defamation actions involving compelled self-publication. We are concerned that the availability of punitive damages may tend to encourage publication of defamatory statements in actions where the plaintiff, rather than the defendant, does the actual publication. More importantly, in the context of an employee discharge, the availability of punitive damages in such an action may significantly deter employer communication of the reason for discharge.

NOTES AND QUESTIONS

Test Your Understanding of the Material

1.   How does the court get around the publication requirement in *Lewis*? Compare the court's definition of self-publication to the articulation in Section § 6.01(b)(3) of the Employment Restatement.

2.   How does the court in *Lewis* formulate the qualified privilege? Is it consistent with Section § 6.02 of the Restatement?

3.   What would be the optimal regulatory regime for employment references? Consider the following possible regimes: (a) strict employer liability; (b) an absolute privilege; (c) a qualified privilege; (d) mandatory disclosure by the employer. See J. Hoult Verkerke, Legal Regulation of Employment Reference Practices, 65 U. Chi.L. Rev. 115 (1998).

Related Issues

History of Self-Publication

The "self-publication" concept originated in the wartime case of Colonial Stores, Inc. v. Barrett, 73 Ga.App. 839, 38 S.E.2d 306 (1946). Under the regulations of the War Manpower Commission, employers were required to furnish discharged employees with written statements of availability, and prospective employees were required to display this certificate to prospective employers. Barrett's former employer wrote on the certificate that he had been fired for "improper conduct toward fellow employees." The writing violated the regulations' prohibition of information "prejudicial to the employee in seeking new employment." Id. at 841, 38 S.E.2d at 308.

4. *Self-Publication.* Most jurisdictions reject a broad doctrine of compulsory "self-publication." See, e.g., Cweklinsky v. Mobil Chem. Co., 267 Conn. 210, 837 A.2d 759, 761–763 (2004); White v. Blue Cross & Blue Shield of Mass., Inc., 442 Mass. 64, 809 N.E.2d 1034 (2004); Sullivan v. Baptist Memorial Hosp., 995 S.W.2d 569, 570–575 (Tenn. 1999); Gore v. Health-Tex, Inc., 567 So.2d 1307, 1308–1309 (Ala. 1990). Compare Employment Restatement § 6.01(b)(3) & Comment d.

5. *Internal Communications.* In many jurisdictions, publication may be found in internal communications between employees or officers of the same corporation. See, e.g., Dube v. Likins, 216 Ariz. 406, 417–418, 167 P.3d 93 (2007) (finding a majority of jurisdictions in favor of recognizing intrafirm publication); Torosyan v. Boehringer Ingelheim Pharm., 234 Conn. 1, 27–28, 662 A.2d 89 (1995); Employment Restatement § 6.01(b)(2) & Comment b. Restatement (Second) of Torts § 577(1), Comment (i); Rodney Smolla, Law of Defamation Sec. 15.02 (1994). But see Otteni v. Hitachi America Ltd., 678 F.2d 146 (11th Cir.1982) (no publication if communication is limited to employer's officers or members of their immediate staff).

6. *Privileges.* Privilege and malice are often central to employment-related defamation claims.

    a. *Absolute Privilege.* The "litigation privilege" affords an absolute privilege to statements made in judicial and quasi-judicial proceedings. See, e.g., Rogozinski v. Airstream by Angell, 152 N.J.Super. 133, 377 A.2d 807, 816 (1977) (statements mandated by an unemployment compensation commission are entitled only to qualified privilege because no judicial or quasi-judicial proceeding was pending at the time); Cal. Civ. Code § 47(2) (covering publication in "any (1) legislative or (2) judicial proceeding, or (3) in any other official proceeding authorized by law"). Some courts have extended an absolute privilege to statements required by collective bargaining agreements or arising out of grievance proceedings. See Hasten v. Phillips Petroleum Co., 640 F.2d 274 (10th Cir.1981); General Motors Corp. v. Mendicki, 367 F.2d 66 (10th Cir.1966). But see Overall v. University of Pennsylvania, 412 F.3d 492 (3d Cir.2005).

    b. *Qualified Privilege.* For statements made in the course of internal company investigations or in response to inquiries about the performance of former employees, only a qualified privilege is likely to be available. Such a privilege is defeated, as was the case in *Lewis,* on a showing of "malice." As the *Lewis* court states, the Supreme Court's First Amendment decision in *New York Times v. Sullivan* offered a definition of malice that differs from the common law definition adopted in *Lewis.* The *Sullivan* definition requires the publisher either to know that the defamatory statement is false or to have reckless disregard of its truth or falsity. This definition has been accepted by an increasing number of jurisdictions. See, e.g., McIntyre v. Jones,

194 P.3d 519, 530 (Colo. App. 2008); Denardo v. Bax, 147 P.3d 672, 679 (Alaska 2006); Ball v. British Petroleum Oil, 108 Ohio App.3d 129, 670 N.E.2d 289, 293, 295 (1995). Which definition of malice states a preferable standard?

6. *Retaliatory References.* Former employees may have a claim under the discrimination laws if negative references are used as a means of retaliating against them for their prior claims or oppositional activity, even if the claimed retaliation occurs after employment is terminated. See *Burlington Northern v. White*, supra at p. 600.

State and Federal Legislation Relating to Employer References

7. *Securities Industry Reporting.* In the securities industry, employers are required by the stock exchanges to complete a Form U-5 setting forth the reasons for every termination of employment of a registered representative. Information contained in the Form U-5 is available to prospective employers and investors. Responding to a certified question from the Second Circuit, the New York Court of Appeals held in Rosenberg v. MetLife, Inc., 8 N.Y.3d 359, 834 N.Y.S.2d 494, 866 N.E.2d 439 (2007), that an employer's statements on a National Association of Securities Dealers' (NASD)'s, now the Financial Industry Regulation Authority (FINRA)'s, employee termination notice (Form U-5) are protected by an absolute privilege in defamation lawsuits. The court emphasized the public function of the Form U-5 reporting system: "The Form U-5 plays a significant role in the NASD's self-regulatory process. * * * Upon receipt of the Form U-5, the NASD routinely investigates terminations for cause to determine whether the representative violated any securities rules." Id. at 367.

8. *Reporting Child Abuse.* Many jurisdictions have passed laws requiring individuals working in certain professions to report suspected child abuse, and impose civil or criminal penalties for failing to report. See Child Abuse Prevention and Treatment Act, 42 U.S, § 5106(b)(2)(B)(I) (federal funds conditional on state mandatory reporting laws). The reporting obligation attaches to the individual, rather than the employer. See Elizabeth Tippett, Child Abuse as an Employment Dispute, 17 Quinnipiac Health L. J. 16 (2014).

Nevertheless, employers can face substantial liability for failing to respond effectively to reports of potential abuse. See CNN.com, "Penn State paying $59.7 million to settle Sandusky cases" (Oct 28, 2013). See also Randi W. v. Muroc Joint Unified School Dist., 14 Cal.4th 1066, 60 Cal.Rptr.2d 263, 929 P.2d 582 (1997) (fraud and negligence claim by victim against school district that had no obligation to provide any reference but in fact provided an unqualified letter of reference for employee subject to numerous allegations of sexual impropriety).

States typically provide statutory immunity for reports to state child welfare agencies. See, e.g., N.Y. Social Svcs. Law § 419. However, accused employees sometimes bring defamation claims for statements to other employees or third parties. See, e.g., Washington v. Vogel, 2011 WL 2923862 (Tenn. Ct. App. 2011) (dismissing defamation claim based on memo advising staff to keep student away from teacher accused of hitting him with a purse); Morley v. Crawford, 2012 WL 2579676 (dismissing defamation claim on governmental immunity grounds).

9. *Missouri's "Service Letter" Statute.* Missouri requires employers on request to furnish a written statement "setting forth the nature and character of service rendered by such employee * * * and truly stating for what cause, if any, such employee was discharged or voluntarily quit such service." Inaccuracies in such a "service letter" may result in liability for compensatory but not punitive damages. Vernon's Ann.Mo.Stat. § 290.140; see Neb.Rev.Stat. § 48–211; Vernon's Texas Ann.Civ.St. art. 5196, subd. 3. For a decision under the Missouri statute, see Gibson v. Hummel, 688 S.W.2d 4 (Mo.App.1985).

10. *Access to Personnel Files.* Following the Federal Privacy Act, 5 U.S.C. § 552a, some states have also mandated employee access to personnel files and a right to correct inaccurate information in such files. See, e.g., Cal. Labor Code § 1198.5; Conn. Gen. Stat. Ann. § 21–128e (West 1997); Nev.Rev.Stat. 613.075; Wis.Stat.Ann. 103.13. See pp. 773–775 infra for discussion of the Fair Credit Reporting Act, and the Federal Privacy Act.

11. *Anti-"Blacklisting" Laws.* A few states also prohibit employers from "blacklisting" or from conspiring or acting to prevent a discharged employee from securing new employment. See, e.g., Cal. Labor Code § 1050; Nev.Rev.Stat. 613.210; Vernon's Ann.Texas Civ.St. art. 5196. Typically, such provisions privilege "truthfully stating in writing, on request of such former employee or other persons to whom such former employee has applied for employment, the reason why such employee was discharged, and why his relationship to such company ceased." Vernon's Ann. Texas Civ.St. art. 5196, subd. 1.

12. *"Qualified Immunity" Laws.* In an effort to encourage employers to avoid "no comment" letters which may hamstring reemployment of the former employee and certainly deprive new employers of material information about the prospective employee they are not likely to acquire from interviews and background checks, a number of states have enacted statutes conferring a "good faith" immunity on those who provide employment references. See, e.g., Alaska Stat. § 9.65.10 (Michie 1996); Colo. Rev. Stat. § 8–2–114 (1997); Ill. Comp. Stat. Ann. 46/10 (West Supp. 1997); Mich. Comp. Laws Ann. 423.452 (West Supp. 1998) These laws typically take the form of a presumption of an employer's good faith in providing a reference, to be rebutted on a showing of reckless, knowing or maliciously motivated disclosure of false or misleading information.

CHAPTER 15

WORKPLACE INJURIES

■ ■ ■

Employers have common law duties to provide a safe workplace and to warn of risks to employees (and other invitees). However, few civil actions are brought because an employee's exclusive remedy is in the workers' compensation system for most workplace injuries arising in the course of employment. These laws generally provide compensation on a no-fault basis, requiring only that the injury be otherwise covered and occur in the course and within the scope of employment. Awards cover medical expenses and partial wage replacement while the employee is unable to work. Wage replacement rates vary between 60% and 80% of the employee's average weekly wage, depending on the state. Damages for pain and suffering are generally unavailable. See generally Samuel Estreicher & Gillian Lester, Employment Law ch. 17 (2008).

A. DUTY TO PROVIDE A SAFE WORKPLACE

RESTATEMENT OF EMPLOYMENT LAW § 4.05
American Law Institute (2015).

§ 4.05. Employer's Duty to Provide Safe Conditions and to Warn of Risk

Except to the extent precluded by a workers' compensation statute or other law, an employer is subject to liability for harm caused to an employee by failing:

(a) to provide a reasonably safe workplace, including reasonably safe equipment; or

(b) to warn of the risk of dangerous working conditions that the employer, but not the harmed employee, knew or should have known.

NOTES AND QUESTIONS

1. *Duty to Provide Safe Working Conditions.* All states recognize a duty to provide a safe workplace. Employment Restatement § 4.05, Reporters' Notes, Comment a. As with other common law negligence claims, recovery for breach of this duty requires the plaintiff to prove both the breach and that the breach caused the harm. See Foote v. Simek, 2006 WY 96 (Wyo. 2006); Jackson

v. Murphy Farm & Ranch, Inc. 982 So.2d 1000 (Miss. 2008). The duty to provide safe working conditions also includes a duty to take reasonable precautions against the risk of criminal attacks on employees in the workplace. Employment Restatement § 4.05, Comment d. Lawsuits alleging a breach of the duty to provide a safe workplace or breach of the duty to warn of workplace hazards are uncommon because most negligence claims are precluded by a state workers' compensation scheme.

2. *Duty to Rescue.* The employer's duty to provide a safe workplace also includes a limited duty "to help employees who became vulnerable to harm in the workplace because of an injury or illness, even if the employer is not responsible for that injury or illness." Employment Restatement § 4.05, Comment e. See Nurredin v. Northeast Ohio Regional Sewer Dist., 104 Ohio App.3d 672 (Oh. 1995) (employer had a duty to protect employee from imminent harm when it delayed calling an ambulance for an employee suffering from a heart attack); Dupont v. Aavid Thermal Tech., 798 A.2d 587, 147 NH 706 (N.H. 2002) (recognizing duty to protect employee from imminent harm where employer failed to contact the police when a coworker confronted an employee with a loaded handgun).

B. PRECLUSION BY WORKERS' COMPENSATION LAWS

Workers' compensation legislation was developed in the early twentieth century. These laws replaced the employee's common law negligence action against his or her employer with a no-fault insurance scheme funded by mandatory employer contributions. The legislation reflected a compromise between employees who were blocked from receiving compensation in the common law courts because of several defenses to negligence liability (i.e., fellow-servant doctrine, assumption of risk, and contributory negligence) and employers (and their insurers) eager to avoid the risk of high or unpredictable jury awards. See generally Samuel Estreicher & Gillian Lester, Employment Law ch.7 (2008); Lawrence M. Friedman, A History of American Law, ch. 14 (1973); Richard A. Epstein, The Historical Origins and Economic Structure of Workers' Compensation Law, 16 Ga.L.Rev. 775 (1982).

In general terms, employees can file a workers' compensation claim for injuries arising in the course and within the scope of their employment. Workers' compensation is an exclusive remedy, meaning that employees cannot bring a common law cause of action for injuries covered by workers' compensation. Employees cannot avoid the exclusivity of the workers' compensation remedy by electing a tort remedy instead; covered tort claims are barred as a matter of law. Larson's Worker's Compensation Law § 100.01 (2015) (Larson's Workers Comp.).

The exclusivity of the workers' compensation remedy applies to injuries covered by the workers' compensation statute, which varies by state. If the plaintiff is a bona fide independent contractor, the contractor will not be covered by workers' compensation. See e.g. McCown v. Hones, 353 N.C. 683 (N.C. 2001). Likewise, if the employer is not covered by the workers' compensation act, or has willfully failed to purchase workers' compensation insurance, the injured employee will not be limited to a workers' compensation remedy. See e.g. Mass. Gen. Laws ch. 152 §§ 66–67 (employees of uninsured employer may bring tort claims); 77 Pa. Stat. § 501 (same); Ala. Code § 25–5–50 (domestic employees, farm laborers and casual employees excluded from coverage); Larson's Workers Comp. § 102.02. Two states now permit employers to opt out of the workers' compensation scheme. See Texas Lab. Code § 406.002; 85A Okla. Stat § 85A–202 (2014). See generally Alison D, Morantz, Rethinking the Great Compromise: What Happens When Large Companies Opt Out of Workers' Compensation? (SSRN, Oct. 15, 2015).

Where the workers' compensation regime is limited to physical injuries, some states permit employees to assert tort claims based solely on mental injuries. See e.g. Onstad v. Payless Shoesource, 301 Mont. 259, 9 P3d. 38 (Mont. 2000) (permitting tort claim for posttraumatic stress caused by sexual assault from customers). But see Bias v. Eastern Assoc. Coal Corp, 220 W. Va. 190, 640 S.E.2d 540 (W.Va. 2006) (workers' compensation statute barred tort claims arising from mental injuries, even though mental injuries are not compensable under the statute regime); Slaymaker v. Archer-Daniels-Midland Co., 540 N.W. 2d 459 (Iowa Ct. App. 1995) (intentional infliction of emotional distress claim barred when both mental and physical injuries are compensable). An employee may also have a tort remedy where the injury does not arise in the course or within the scope of employment. See e.g. Yunker v. Honeywell, infra (tort remedy available where employee murdered by co-employee at home); Potts v. Uap-Ga Ag. Chem., 270 Ga. 14, 506 S.E.2d 101 (Georgia 1998) (permitting fraud claim based on statement made outside of employment).

Many states recognize an exception to workers' compensation exclusivity for assault and battery (the "assault exception") or more broadly, for intentional torts committed by the employer or its agents. See e.g. Ariz. Rev. Stat. § 23–1022 (exception for "wilful misconduct" by the employer); Cal. Lab. Code § 3602 (assault exception); N.J. Stat § 34:15–8 (exception for "intentional wrong"). But see *Potts*, supra (claims based on intentional misconduct barred if arising in the course of employment).

BOWDEN V. YOUNG

Supreme Court of Mississippi, 2013.
120 So.3d 971.

KITCHENS, J.

This is an interlocutory appeal from the trial court's denial of the defendant Vaughn, Bowden, PA's (V & B) (f/k/a Vaughn, Bowden &

Wooten, PA) motion to dismiss for failure to state a claim upon which relief can be granted. * * *

The plaintiffs, Cherie Brott Blackmore and Diane Young, sued their former employer, the law firm of V & B[.]

Cheri Blackmore and Diane Young were legal assistants at V & B. Blackmore worked at V & B from 2006 until December 2009. Young worked at the firm from August 2009 until December 2009. In 2006, Blackmore worked in one of the firm's buildings on 23rd Avenue in Gulfport (Building A). Blackmore contends that her health deteriorated significantly during her time at that building as a result of exposure to toxic mold there. She alleges that several others at the office experienced similar symptoms, and that one employee was even fired for failing to show up for work on account of poor health. This led Blackmore to fear that any complaints or excessive absences would cost her her job. She alleges that the supervisors at the firm ignored her complaints and told the employees to stop whining.

In February 2009, the firm moved all of its employees to a new building on 25th Avenue in Gulfport (Building B). * * * V & B admit that this building suffered from moisture intrusion. Blackmore claims that, when she moved to Building B, she continued to suffer the same mold-exposure symptoms she had suffered at Building A. The building also had a gas leak which exposed workers to natural-gas fumes. Several raw-sewage backups occurred in the women's restroom, which flooded into the front of the office. The plaintiffs claim that Lowry Development and V & B were informed repeatedly about the presence of mold in Building B, but did nothing to remediate it. In June 2009, a "Mold Killer Spray" was applied to the surfaces of the office in Building B. The plaintiffs claim this also damaged the health of the V & B employees. In August 2009, Young began working at Building B. She claims that she immediately began to suffer health problems because of exposure to mold. Throughout the time the plaintiffs claim they were exposed to toxic mold at Building B, the partners who have been named defendants also worked in the same building. * * *

The plaintiffs brought claims against V & B for battery, intentional infliction of emotional distress, aiding and abetting the maintenance of a public and private nuisance, and conspiracy. * * *

This Court repeatedly has held that, "in order for a willful tort to be outside the exclusivity of the Mississippi Workers' Compensation Act [(MWCA)], the employe[r]'s action must be done 'with an actual intent to injure the employee.'" * * *] "[A] mere willful and malicious act is insufficient to give rise to the intentional tort exception to the exclusive remedy provisions of the [MWCA]. . . . Reckless or grossly negligent conduct is not enough to remove a claim from the exclusivity of the [MWCA]." * * * [Citations omitted] As recently as 2009, this Court found that "Mississippi is in concurrence with an overwhelming majority of states in requiring an 'actual intent to injure' the employee." * * *

* * * We will examine each claim to determine whether it falls outside the exclusivity provision of the MWCA.

A.   Battery

The plaintiffs allege that they were exposed intentionally to toxic mold, to a toxic Mold Killer Spray designed to get rid of the mold, and to poisonous fumes from a sewage leak. * * *

With regard to the toxic mold, the plaintiffs contend that V & B battered the plaintiffs when it failed to remediate the mold conditions, and the plaintiffs thereafter inhaled the toxic mold. However, none of the claims asserts that V & B acted with "actual intent" to batter and injure the plaintiffs. Several of the alleged acts of battery involved the use of the Mold Killer Spray, which was being used to kill the mold that was causing injury to the plaintiffs. It is not possible that the defendants were allowing the mold to exist with the intent of injuring the plaintiffs while at the same time attempting to destroy the mold. Further, the application of the Mold Killer Spray clearly was not done with any "actual intent" to injure the plaintiffs. Rather, it was applied in an attempt to remediate the mold situation. Similarly, the plaintiffs contend that they were battered by toxic gas emanating from sewage backup. This claim must fail because there is no allegation that the defendants permitted the sewage backup to exist with the actual intent to injure the plaintiffs. * * *

B.   Intentional Infliction of Emotional Distress

* * * Taking the allegations of the plaintiffs' complaint as true, they have failed to state a claim upon which relief can be granted. V & B initially denied that there was any mold in the building. Management suggested other potential causes of the plaintiffs' ailments. When it became apparent that mold was in fact present in the building, V & B attempted to remediate the situation by applying the Mold Killer Spray. Once the October Lab Report was received, V & B specifically informed the plaintiffs that it would search for new office space. While the defendants' handling of the mold problem may have been negligent, the allegations do not rise to the level of outrageous and extreme conduct that is necessary to support a claim for intentional infliction of emotional distress. Further, the plaintiffs still must be able to show that the actions of the defendants were conducted with "actual intent" to injure the plaintiffs. The fact that V & B attempted to remediate the mold issue, and ultimately decided to relocate its offices due to the mold, leads to the inevitable conclusion that the actions of V & B were not done with the actual intent to inflict emotional distress upon the plaintiffs. * * *

C. Conspiracy and Aiding and Abetting

* * *

Because the claims for battery and intentional infliction of emotional distress fail because they do not allege, and the facts of the case do not support, that V & B acted with "actual intent" to injure the plaintiffs, the claims for aiding and abetting in the commission of battery and intentional infliction of emotional distress or conspiracy to commit battery and intentional infliction of emotional distress must fail as well.

NOTES AND QUESTIONS

Test Your Understanding of the Material

1. The Mississippi workers' compensation statute in *Bowden* provided:

"Compensation shall be payable for disability or death of an employee from injury or occupational disease arising out of and in the course of employment, without regard to fault as to the cause of the injury or occupational disease. An occupational disease shall be deemed to arise out of and in the course of employment when there is evidence that there is a direct causal connection between the work performed and the occupational disease." Miss. Code § 71–3–7.

Would the plaintiffs' claims have been compensable under the Mississippi statute? According to the U.S. Centers for Disease Control and Prevention, mold is found indoors and outdoors, in thousands of varieties. Mold does not affect everyone in the same way; some people are more sensitive to mold and may have more severe reactions. See Centers for Disease Control and Prevention, "Molds in the Environment" available at http://www.cdc.gov/mold/faqs.htm. Should mold-sensitive employees be able to recover under the workers' compensation scheme? Compare Connolly v. Covanta Energy Corp, 123 A.D.3d. 1394, 1 N.Y.S.3d 404 (N.Y. App. 3d Div. 2014) (plaintiff failed to prove mold exposure caused occupational disease because he "could have been exposed to it anywhere at any time"); to Sillitti v. Liberty Travel, Inc., 83 A.D.3d 1169, 920 N.Y.S.2d 477 (N.Y. App. 3d. Div. 2011) (mold exposure compensable where it exacerbated preexisting pulmonary disease).

2. The "intent" element of an intentional tort must be inferred from the facts and circumstances. Did the employer commit an intentional wrong in *Bowden*?

3. Did the employer in *Bowden* violate the "general duty" clause, § 5(a)(1), of the Occupational Safety and Health Act of 1974 (OSHA), 29 U.S.C. § 654(a)(1), which requires employers "to "furnish to each of his employees employment and a place of employment which are free from recognized hazards that are causing or are likely to cause death or serious physical harm to his employees"? What about the Department of Labor's OSHA regulations regarding sanitation, 29 C.F.R. 1910.141? Note that "[t]here is no private right

of action under the General Duty Clause; any proceedings must be brought by the agency." Estreicher & Lester, Employment Law, at 220.

Related Issues

4. *Tort Claims Arising from Sexual and Other Workplace Harassment.* As a general matter, claims under state antidiscrimination statutes are not precluded by workers' compensation. See e.g. Horodyskyj v. Karanian, 32 P.3d 470 (Colo. 2001) (applying exclusivity principles to sexual harassment claim would undermine legislative purpose of eliminating discrimination in the workplace). Claims arising under Title VII and the ADA are also unaffected by workers' compensation exclusivity provisions.

However, the exclusivity issue is more salient when plaintiffs bring state tort actions for injuries alongside harassment claims brought under a state statute. States have reached different results on this question. Compare, e.g., Konstantopoulos v. Westvaco Corp., 690 A.2d 936 (Del.1996) (no sexual-harassment or sexual-assault exception to exclusivity provision); Hibben v. Nardone, 137 F.3d 480 (7th Cir.1998) (exclusivity provision under Wisconsin law applies to emotional-distress claims even when such claims are based on sexual harassment by coworker), with *Horodyskyj v. Karanian*, supra ("Although the Act was designed to provide exclusive remedies for employees suffering work-related injuries, it was not intended to cover injuries resulting from the usual case of workplace sexual harassment; specific federal and state anti-discrimination laws cover those cases . . . therefore, his . . . related torts are not barred by the Act.")

5. *Retaliation for Filing Workers' Compensation Claims.* As a general matter, employees discriminated against in their job conditions for filing a workers' compensation have an action in the courts as a matter of statute or common law. See Larson's Workers' Comp. § 104.07. *See also Kelsay v. Motorola*, p. 628 supra.

NOTE: PRINCIPLES OF EMPLOYER LIABILITY

If we assume that an employee's claim is not barred by the workers' compensation regime, an employee alleging a tort claim against his/her employer must prove that the employer is either directly or vicariously liable for the tortious conduct.

RESTATEMENT OF EMPLOYMENT LAW §§ 4.01–4.03
American Law Institute (2015).

§ 4.01. Scope of Employer's Liability to Employees Generally

Except to the extent precluded by a workers'-compensation statute or other law, an employer is subject to liability in tort to an employee for harm caused in the course of employment by:

(a) the tortious conduct of the employer, as set forth in § 4.02;

(b) the tortious conduct of the employer's employees and nonemployee agents, to the extent set forth in § 4.03; and

(c) the breach by the employer of its tort-based affirmative duties, including those set forth in §§ 4.04 and 4.05.

§ 4.02. Employer's Direct Liability to Employees for Its Own Conduct

Except to the extent precluded by a workers'-compensation statute or other law, an employer is subject to liability in tort to an employee for harm caused in the course of employment by the tortious conduct of the employer or controlling owner.

§ 4.03. Employer's Liability to Employees for Acts of Employees or Agents

Except to the extent precluded by a workers'-compensation statute or other law, an employer is subject to liability in tort to an employee for harm caused in the course of employment:

(a) by an employee's or nonemployee agent's conduct authorized or ratified by the employer;

(b) by an employee's tortious conduct undertaken within the scope of employment;

(c) by the tortious abuse or threatened abuse of a supervisory or managerial employee's authority, to the extent authorized by applicable law, even if the abuse or threatened abuse is not within the scope of employment, unless the employer can demonstrate that:

   (1) the employer took reasonable care to prevent and promptly correct the actual or threatened abuse of authority; and

   (2) the employee unreasonably failed either to:

      (A) take advantage of any preventive or corrective opportunity the employer provided, or

      (B) otherwise avoid the harm.

NOTES AND QUESTIONS

1. *Entity Liability for Acts of Controlling Owners.* Under § 4.02, Comment e, an employer that is a legal entity is "also subject to liability for the tortious acts of an individual who owns or, through an ownership interest, controls all or a significant part of the entity." Such individuals may also be liable in their own right.

2. *Entity Liability for "Tangible Employment Decisions" and Other Corporate Acts.* As the Supreme Court stated in Faragher v. Boca Raton, 524

U.S. 775, 118 S.Ct. 2275 (1998), excerpted supra at p. 374: "[T]here is nothing remarkable in the fact that claims against employers for discriminatory employment actions with tangible results, like hiring, firing, promotion, compensation, and work assignment, have resulted in employer liability once the discrimination was shown." The employer is liable for the "racially motivated discharge by [a] low-level supervisor, although the 'record clearly shows that [its] record in race relations . . . is exemplary.'" Id. (citation omitted). Such "tangible employment decisions" are made for the employer with delegated authority and thus are treated as acts of the employer for which the employer is subject to liability even if the decisions contravene well-established company policy. See Employment Restatement § 4.03(a).

3.   *Entity Liability for the Acts of its Employees in the Scope of Employment.* As a general matter, employers are also derivatively liability for the torts of employees committed in the scope of their employment. Some workplace torts, including negligent breaches of duties, are not likely to involve "tangible" or "corporate" decisions made with delegated corporate authority, but they may be wrongs committed by employees within the scope of their employment. Such acts are "of the kind [an employee] is employed to perform," occurring "substantially within the authorized time and space limits," and "actuated, at least in part, by a purpose to serve the master[.]" *Faragher*, 524 U.S. at 793, quoting Restatement Second of Agency § 219(1). Employees are responsible for such acts (although they may be judgment-proof) but so is the employer under principles of derivative liability. See Employment Restatement § 4.03(b).

4.   Faragher-*Type Entity Liability.* Section 4.03(c) introduces a *Faragher*-type of entity liability for torts committed by employees outside the scope of employment. *Faragher* involved sexual harassment by supervisors who abused their authority over subordinate employees. Should courts recognize *Faragher*-type liability in other circumstances? For an argument that the Court's interpretation of Title VII in *Faragher* should influence state common law, see Michael C. Harper, Fashioning a General Common Law of Employment in an Age of Statutes, 100 Cornell L. Rev. 1281, 1308 (2015).

C. INTENTIONAL TORTS

This section provides the elements of intentional tort claims that commonly arise in the employment context, followed by a series of fact patterns. For each fact pattern, assess whether (a) the plaintiff satisfied the elements of the claim; and (b) the employer is directly or vicariously liable for the tortious conduct.

1. INTENTIONAL INFLICTION OF EMOTIONAL DISTRESS

RESTATEMENT THIRD OF TORTS: LIABILITY FOR PHYSICAL AND EMOTIONAL HARM § 46

American Law Institute (2012).

§ 46.   Intentional (or Reckless) Infliction of Emotional Harm

An actor who by extreme and outrageous conduct intentionally or recklessly causes severe emotional harm to another is subject to liability for that emotional harm and, if the emotional harm causes bodily harm, also for that bodily harm.

A defendant's conduct is "outrageous" when it is so extreme that it exceeds "all possible bounds of decency, . . . atrocious, and utterly intolerable in a civilized community." Robel v. Roundup Corp., 148 Wash.2d 35 (Wash. 2002) (disputed issue of fact on whether calling plaintiff vulgar names in the workplace was outrageous); Carnemolla v. Walsh, 75 Conn.App. 319 (2003) (accusing employee of embezzling funds not outrageous). Some jurisdictions also require that the emotional distress is accompanied by physical injury. Compare Forde v. Royal's, Inc., 537 F.Supp. 1173 (S.D.Fla.1982) ("plaintiff cannot recover damages for mental anguish and suffering absent physical injury or some other type of tortious conduct"). To Sisco v. Fabrication Tech., Inc. 350 F.Supp.2d 932 (D. Wyo. 2004) (mental injury sufficient).

Applications

1.   "Debra Agis was employed by the Howard Johnson Company as a waitress in a restaurant known as the Ground Round. On or about May 23, 1975, the [restaurant manager] notified all waitresses that a meeting would be held at 3 P.M. that day. At the meeting, he informed the waitresses that 'there was some stealing going on,' but that the identity of the person or persons responsible was not known, and that, until the person or persons responsible were discovered, he would begin firing all the present waitresses in alphabetical order, starting with the letter 'A.' [The manager] then fired Debra Agis * * * Mrs. Agis became greatly upset, began to cry, sustained emotional distress, mental anguish, and loss of wages and earnings." Agis v. Howard Johnson Co., 371 Mass. 140, 355 N.E.2d 315 (1976).

2.   "Plaintiffs' second amended complaint alleges that defendants tested plaintiffs for the Human Immunodeficiency Virus (HIV) after plaintiffs applied for positions as Chicago police officers. Plaintiffs claim that their applications were rejected after plaintiffs tested positive for HIV. Plaintiffs were required to take a physical examination. John Doe received

a letter prior to the physical purporting to be a conditional offer of employment. The offer was conditioned on the completion of a background investigation and Doe passing both the physical examination and the Illinois law enforcement physical fitness test * * * USOH conducted HIV testing on both plaintiffs as part of the physical examination. Neither plaintiff gave consent to the HIV test or [was] provided counseling prior to or during the test. Plaintiffs were subsequently notified that they had tested positive for HIV * * * Defendants did not provide plaintiffs counseling regarding the results of the HIV test. Thereafter, the processing of plaintiffs' employment applications stopped, and both candidates were denied employment by the police department." Doe v. City of Chicago, 883 F.Supp. 1126 (N.D. Ill. 1994) (applying Illinois law).

3. "Several witnesses testified that [supervisor] Shields used the word 'f——' as part of his normal pattern of conversation, and that he regularly heaped abusive profanity on the employees. [Plaintiff] Linda Davis testified that Shields used this language to get a reaction. [Plaintiff] Gene Martin, another GTE employee, testified that Shields used the words 'f——' and 'motherf——er' frequently when speaking with the employees. On one occasion when [Plaintiff] Bruce asked Shields to curb his language because it was offensive, Shields positioned himself in front of her face, and screamed, 'I will do and say any damn thing I want. And I don't give a s—— who likes it.' * * * There was evidence that Shields was continuously in a rage, and that Shields would frequently assault each of the employees by physically charging at them. When doing so, Shields would bend his head down, put his arms straight down by his sides, ball his hands into fists, and walk quickly toward or 'lunge' at the employees, stopping uncomfortably close to their faces while screaming and yelling. The employees were exceedingly frightened by this behavior. * * * Bruce testified that, on one occasion, Shields began beating a banana on his desk, and when he jumped up and slammed the banana into the trash, Bruce thought he would hit her . . . Bruce also told of an occasion when Shields entered Bruce's office and went into a rage because Davis had left her purse on a chair and Bruce had placed her umbrella on a filing cabinet in the office." GTE Southwest, Inc. v. Bruce, 998 S.W.2d 605 (Tx 1999).

4. "Upon [plaintiff] Darboe's return from sick leave on August 1, [store manager] Mullins invited Darboe into his office and closed the door. Mullins told Darboe of his demotion to Sales Associate, which became effective that day. Id. [The employer] alleges that Mullins called Darboe into his office to remind him of the demotion, which he had already informed Darboe of on July 21. In contrast, Darboe claims that this was the first time that he learned of his demotion. Darboe further alleges that he told Mullins that he was the top selling salesman, to which Mullins responded: 'Now you're nothing,' or 'Now you're nobody.'" Darboe v. Staples, Inc. 243 F.Supp.2d 5 (2003).

2.   FALSE IMPRISONMENT

RESTATEMENT SECOND OF TORTS § 35
American Law Institute (1965).

§ 35.   False Imprisonment

(1)   An actor is subject to liability to another for false imprisonment if (a) he acts intending to confine the other or a third person within the boundaries fixed by the actor, and (b) his act directly or indirectly results in such a confinement of the other, and (c) the other is conscious of the confinement or is harmed by it.

———————————

Confinement need not be by physical force, it can also arise by threat of force, physical barriers or "any other form of unreasonable duress." Fermino v. Fedco, Inc., 872 P.2d 559, 7 Cal.4th 701, 30 Cal. Rptr.2d 18 (Cal. 1994). Even a brief confinement satisfies the requirements for the tort. Id.

Applications

1.   Plaintiff Fermino was employed as a salesclerk in defendant's department store, working in the jewelry department. The store's personnel manager summoned her to a windowless room, and proceeded to interrogate her concerning her alleged theft of the proceeds of a $4.95 sale to a customer. The personnel manager was joined by the store's loss prevention manager and by two security agents. One of the security agents stated that a customer and an employee, who were waiting in the next room, had witnessed the theft. He then demanded that Fermino confess. He told her that the interrogation could be handled in two ways: the 'Fedco way' or the 'system way.' The 'Fedco way' was to award points each time she denied her guilt. When 14 points were reached, she would be handled the 'system' way, i.e., handed over to the police. After each of plaintiff's repeated and vehement denials, the security agent said 'one point.' The loss prevention manager 'hurled profanities' and demanded that Fermino confess.

Fermino's repeated requests to leave the room and to call her mother were denied. She was physically compelled to remain in the room for more than one hour. At one point Fermino rose out of her chair and walked toward the door of the interrogation room in an attempt to leave; however, as soon as she made a move toward the door, one of the security guards slid in front of the door, threw up a hand and gestured her to stop.

Finally, Fermino became hysterical, and broke down in tears. At this point her interrogators departed from the room. Upon returning, they admitted no employee or customer was waiting to testify against her. They further stated they believed her, and that she could leave. Fermino v. Fedco, Inc. 7 Cal.4th 701 (Cal. 1994)

2.   William J. Krochalis worked for INA * * * [as] Director of Market Development. In 1981, INA's Corporate Audit Department conducted an audit of the operations of the Marketing Department including the expense accounts of the employees in the Market Development Department, which was then headed by Krochalis. The audit revealed several irregularities in Krochalis' expense reports, and, on February 1, 1982, Krochalis' supervisor, James E. Malling, gave Krochalis the choice of resigning or being terminated. Krochalis resigned and informed the INA employees in his department of his decision to resign on February 1, 1982. Later that day, after he left the office, Krochalis apparently changed his mind about resigning and dictated two memoranda to his secretary over the telephone. One memorandum, addressed to Malling, stated that Krochalis was not resigning, despite his statements of that morning. * * *

The next morning, February 2, 1982, Krochalis came to work. Pat Hasson, Director of Personnel, requested that Krochalis come to see him in the Personnel Office. Under Hasson's threat either to have security guards come and bring Krochalis to the Personnel Office or to have security guards remove Krochalis from the premises, Krochalis agreed to go to the Personnel Office to meet with Hasson. Hasson told him that his employment was terminated and instructed him to leave the premises. Krochalis left the building after this meeting with Hasson. Krochalis v. Ins. Co. of North Amer., 629 F.Supp. 1360 (E.D.Pa. 1985) (applying Pennsylvania law).

3.   On August 20, 1976, a workday for Mrs. Faniel, a supervisor asked her to step into a conference room. There she was introduced to Mr. Aussem, who was identified as an AT&T security supervisor from New York, responsible for investigating misuse of equipment by AT&T employees. Mr. Aussem informed Mrs. Faniel that routine testing had revealed excessive electronic resistance on her line, suggesting the presence of an unauthorized telephone installation. When asked, Mrs. Faniel told Mr. Aussem she had two phones. Later she admitted having a third, unauthorized telephone, and signed a written statement to that effect. After signing the statement, Mrs. Faniel was told a trip to her home would be necessary to recover the equipment. She did not object, because, as she testified at trial, "I just assumed that I had to go." Appellant testified that her request to call her husband first was denied by Mr. Aussem. However, appellant's supervisor, Mrs. Powell, testified that she placed a call to Mr. Faniel, at appellant's request, from the conference room, and left a message that his wife would be leaving early.

Accompanied by Mr. Aussem and Mrs. Powell, appellant was driven to her home, stopping briefly at a C&P facility in Maryland to pick up a C&P security officer. Mrs. Faniel testified that the stop came as a surprise, although Mr. Aussem testified that he advised her of the need to pick up the C&P security man who had the actual authority to recover the equipment. During the brief stop at the C&P building, Mrs. Faniel again asked to call her husband. According to appellant's version of the facts, Mrs. Powell refused permission.

The foursome proceeded to Mrs. Faniel's home where they were greeted at the door by her husband. The telephone was found unplugged and lying on the floor. After recovering the equipment, the telephone company employees left. Faniel v. Chesapeake and Potomac Telephone Co. Of Maryland, 404 A.2d 147 (1979).

3.   ASSAULT AND BATTERY

RESTATEMENT THIRD OF TORTS §§ 103, 101
American Law Institute (Discussion draft April 3, 2014).

§ 103   Assault

An actor is subject to liability to another for assault if:

(a)   the actor intends to cause the other to apprehend that a harmful or offensive contact with his or her person is imminent;

(b)   the actor's conduct causes the other to apprehend that a harmful or offensive contact with his or her person is imminent; and

(c)   the actor does not actually consent to the apprehension or to the conduct causing the apprehension.

§ 101   Battery

(1)   An actor is subject to liability to another for battery if:

(a)   the actor intends to cause a contact with the person of the other;

(b)   the actor's conduct causes such a contact;

(c)   the contact (i) is offensive or (ii) causes bodily harm to the other; and

(d)   the other does not actually consent to the contact [or to the conduct that causes the contact].

(2)   A contact is offensive if:

(a)   the contact offends a reasonable sense of personal dignity; or

(b)   the actor knows that the contact seriously offends the other's sense of personal dignity, and it is not unduly burdensome for the actor to refrain from causing the contact.

Applications

1.   Plaintiffs [Barnes and Evans] allege that they had been employees of defendant at its Chicago plant for varying periods prior to February 16, 1944. [They] further allege by affidavit that on February 16, 1944, they had been selected, at the instance of the defendant's superintendent, by certain employees to present grievances to the management of defendant corporation; and that thereafter, at about 1 p.m. on February 16, 1944, they were informed by defendant's superintendent that they were discharged and should go to the assistant foreman's office to be cleared; and that on arriving in said office, they were imprisoned therein for several hours and suffered physical injury at the hands of plant guards or auxiliary military police. Barnes v. Chrysler Corp., 65 F.Supp. 806 (N.D. Ill. 1946) (applying Illinois law)

2.   The incident occurred shortly before closing time on July 18, 1973. Plaintiff had a large J. C. Penney store sack containing a pantsuit she had brought from home and some T-shirts which she had purchased from a fellow employee. Plaintiff stopped to talk to another employee when the security officer came up to plaintiff and said, "What have we got here?" or, "What have we got in the sack?" According to plaintiff, the security officer had her feet between plaintiff's, touching plaintiff. She reached over plaintiff's shoulder, pulled out the top of the pantsuit and, in doing so, brushed against plaintiff. After removing part of the pantsuit, the security officer started to reach into the sack again. However, plaintiff pushed her hand away and removed the T-shirts, as well as the rest of the suit, and showed them to the officer. Plaintiff became extremely upset over the incident, both at the time it occurred and later. Her distress eventually caused her to secure medical treatment. Bakker v. Baza'r, Inc. 275 Or. 245, 551 P.2d 1269 (1976)

3.   In 1987, Jim Hennly, the vice president of First Federal Savings and Loan Association (First Federal) and a pipe smoker, began working in an office close to the desk of Bonnie Richardson, a receptionist/switchboard operator at First Federal. [Plaintiff] Richardson has severe reactions to pipe smoke, and while the frequency and intensity of her exposure to Hennly's pipe smoke are disputed, it is undeniable that at the time of her termination by First Federal Richardson was experiencing physical illness because of the smoke * * * First Federal did not have a policy restricting or prohibiting smoking. Hennly v. Richardson, 264 Ga. 355, 444 S.E.2d 317 (1994).

4.   McCullough was employed as a Unit Nursing Manage at Liberty Heights. Sometime in early June of 2010, McCullough began searching for

a housekeeper, and a friend recommended Judith Chase. McCullough contacted Chase, and Chase began working for McCullough at McCullough's residence.

Soon thereafter a dispute arose between McCullough and Chase over the payment of wages. The specifics of that disputed are not relevant here. The morning of June 16, 2010, Chase telephoned McCullough to say that she was coming to McCullough's office to discuss payment. McCullough objected, and protested that any such discussion should take place over the phone. At no point did McCullough tell anyone at Liberty Heights about her dispute with Chase or Chase's threat to show up there. . . . McCullough never expressed concern or requested that Liberty Heights take measures to protect her against Chase, such as denying Chase entry to the building.

At approximately 12:30 p.m. Karen Marshall, a Liberty Heights employee, was leaving the facility for a meeting when she noticed McCullough and Chase fighting in the parking lot. According to Marshall, Chase attempted to get into her car, on both the driver's and passenger's side, but McCullough repeatedly pulled her from the vehicle. When the confrontation degenerated into blows and hair pulling, Marshall went inside and informed Sandra Durham, Liberty Heights' Executive Director.

Durham went to investigate and found the two women yelling at one another. She stepped between the two, ordered McCullough to go back inside, and told Chase to leave the premises. Instead, Chase said something to the "effect of I want my money" and struck Durham in the forehead. . . . [E]ventually the police were summoned and restored order. McCullough emerged with bruises and a bite to her right index finger.

McCullough claims that Durham "in an attempt to stop the fight held Mrs. McCullough and restrained her long enough for her to be bitten on her index finger & bruises inflicted all over her body by her attacker," and that "[s]uch restraining of the Plaintiff's body by Ms. Durham was intentional, harmful & offensive." McCullough v. Liberty Heights Health & Rehabilitation Ctr. 830 F.Supp.2d 94 (D. Md. 2011) (applying Maryland law).

D. NEGLIGENT HIRING AND SUPERVISION

Employers are liable under negligence principles for failing to exercise care in selecting, supervising, and retaining employees. If an employer knows or should know that an employee or agent currently in its service has been engaging in conduct unreasonably dangerous to coworkers, the employer has a duty to end the conduct. That may require the employer to discharge the employee or agent, move them to different positions, or limit their authority to act.

This liability extends to customers and other third parties, as well as fellow employees injured by the conduct.

RESTATEMENT OF EMPLOYMENT LAW § 4.04
American Law Institute (2015).

§ 4.04 Employer's Duty to Exercise Care in Selecting, Retaining, and Supervising Employees or Agents

Except to the extent precluded by a workers' compensation statute or other law, an employer is subject to liability for the harm caused an employee by negligence in selecting, retaining, or supervising employees or agents whose tortious acts resulted in the harm.

YUNKER V. HONEYWELL, INC.
Minnesota Court of Appeals, 1993.
496 N.W.2d 419.

LANSING, J.

On motion for summary judgment, the district court held, as a matter of law, that an employer breached no ascertainable duty of care in hiring, retaining, and supervising an employee who shot and killed a coemployee off the premises. The employee had been rehired following imprisonment for the strangulation death of another coemployee. We affirm the district court's ruling as it applies to the theories of negligent hiring and supervision, but reverse the summary judgment as it applies to negligent retention and remand that part of the action to the district court. * * *

[Negligent Hiring and Supervision]

Honeywell employed Randy Landin from 1977 to 1979 and from 1984 to 1988. From 1979 to 1984 Landin was imprisoned for the strangulation death of Nancy Miller, a Honeywell coemployee. On his release from prison, Landin reapplied at Honeywell. Honeywell rehired Landin as a custodian in Honeywell's General Offices facility in South Minneapolis in August 1984. Because of workplace confrontations Landin was twice transferred, first to the Golden Valley facility in August 1986, and then to the St. Louis Park facility in August 1987.

Kathleen Nesser was assigned to Landin's maintenance crew in April 1988. Landin and Nesser became friends and spent time together away from work. When Landin expressed a romantic interest, Nesser stopped spending time with Landin. Landin began to harass and threaten Nesser both at work and at home. At the end of June, Landin's behavior prompted Nesser to seek help from her supervisor and to request a transfer out of the St. Louis Park facility.

On July 1, 1988, Nesser found a death threat scratched on her locker door. Landin did not come to work on or after July 1, and Honeywell accepted his formal resignation on July 11, 1988. On July 19, approximately six hours after her Honeywell shift ended, Landin killed

Nesser in her driveway with a close-range shotgun blast. Landin was convicted of first degree murder and sentenced to life imprisonment.

Jean Yunker, as trustee for the heirs and next-of-kin of Kathleen Nesser, brought this wrongful death action based on theories of negligent hiring, retention, and supervision of a dangerous employee. Honeywell moved for summary judgment and, for purposes of the motion, stipulated that it failed to exercise reasonable care in the hiring and supervision of Landin. The trial court concluded that Honeywell owed no legal duty to Nesser and granted summary judgment for Honeywell. * * *

Minnesota first explicitly recognized a cause of action based on negligent hiring in *Ponticas* in 1983. [*Ponticas v. K.M.S. Investments*, 331 N.W.2d 907 (Minn. 1983)]

Ponticas involved the employment of an apartment manager who sexually assaulted a tenant. The supreme court upheld a jury verdict finding the apartment operators negligent in failing to make a reasonable investigation into the resident manager's background before providing him with a passkey. The court defined negligent hiring as predicated on the negligence of an employer in placing a person with known propensities, or propensities which should have been discovered by reasonable investigation, in an employment position in which, *because of the circumstances of the employment,* it should have been foreseeable that the hired individual posed a threat of injury to others. 331 N.W.2d at 911 (emphasis added).

Honeywell argues that under *Ponticas* it is not liable for negligent hiring because, unlike providing a dangerous resident manager with a passkey, Landin's employment did not enable him to commit the act of violence against Nesser. This argument has merit, and we note that a number of jurisdictions have expressly defined the scope of an employer's duty of reasonable care in hiring as largely dependent on the type of responsibilities associated with the particular job. See *Connes,* [*v. Molalla Transp. Sys.,* 831 P.2d 1316, 1320–21 (Colo.1992)] (employer's duty in hiring is dependent on anticipated degree of contact between employee and other persons in performing employment duties); *Tallahassee Furniture Co. v. Harrison,* 583 So.2d 744, 750 (Fla.Dist.Ct.App.1991) (employer's responsibility to investigate an employee's background is defined by the type of work to be done by the employee), *pet. for rev. denied* 595 So.2d 558 (Fla.1992).

Ponticas rejected the view that employers are required to investigate a prospective employee's criminal background in every job in which the individual has regular contact with the public. *Ponticas,* 331 N.W.2d at 913. Instead, liability is determined by the totality of the circumstances surrounding the hiring and whether the employer exercised reasonable care. The court instructed that "[t]he scope of the investigation is directly related to the severity of the risk third parties are subjected to by an incompetent employee. Although only slight care might suffice in the hiring of a yardman, a worker on a production line, or other types of employment where the employee would not constitute a high risk of injury to third persons, * * * when the prospective employee is to be furnished a passkey permitting admittance to living quarters of tenants, the employer has the duty to use reasonable care to investigate his competency and reliability prior to employment (citations omitted)." Id.

Applying these principles, we conclude that Honeywell did not owe a duty to Nesser at the time of Landin's hire. Landin was employed as a maintenance worker whose job responsibilities entailed no exposure to the general public and required only limited contact with coemployees. Unlike the caretaker in *Ponticas,* Landin's duties did not involve inherent dangers to others, and unlike the tenant in *Ponticas*, Nesser was not a reasonably foreseeable victim at the time Landin was hired. * * *

Honeywell did not breach a legal duty to Nesser by hiring Landin because the specific nature of his employment did not create a foreseeable risk of harm, and public policy supports a limitation on this cause of action. The district court correctly determined that Honeywell is not liable to Nesser under a theory of negligent hiring. * * *

[Negligent Retention]

Although some jurisdictions apparently aggregate the theories of "negligent hiring" and "negligent retention" into a single doctrine, Minnesota case law refers to them separately, suggesting that they are related, but distinct theories of recovery. * * * The difference between negligent hiring and negligent retention focuses on when the employer was on notice that an employee posed a threat and failed to take steps to insure the safety of third parties. * * *

In analyzing whether Honeywell owed Nesser a duty under a theory of negligent retention, we are obligated to review the facts in a light most favorable to Yunker. [Citation omitted.] The record contains evidence of a number of episodes in Landin's postimprisonment employment at Honeywell that demonstrate a propensity for abuse and violence towards coemployees.

While at the Golden Valley facility, Landin sexually harassed female employees and challenged a male coworker to fight. After his transfer to St. Louis Park, Landin threatened to kill a coworker during an angry confrontation following a minor car accident. In another employment incident, Landin was hostile and abusive toward a female coworker after problems developed in their friendship. Landin's specific focus on Nesser was demonstrated by several workplace outbursts occurring at the end of June, and on July 1 the words "one more day and you're dead" were scratched on her locker door.

Landin's troubled work history and the escalation of abusive behavior during the summer of 1988 relate directly to the foreseeability prong of duty. The facts, in a light favorable to Yunker, show that it was foreseeable that Landin could act violently against a coemployee, and against Nesser in particular.

This foreseeability gives rise to a duty of care to Nesser that is not outweighed by policy considerations of employment opportunity. An ex-felon's "opportunity for gainful employment may spell the difference between recidivism and rehabilitation," *Haddock v. City of New York,* 553 N.E.2d 987, 992 (1990), but it cannot predominate over the need to maintain a safe workplace when specific actions point to future violence.

Our holding is narrow and limited only to the recognition of a legal duty owed to Nesser arising out of Honeywell's continued employment of Landin. It is important to emphasize that in reversing the summary judgment on negligent retention, we do not reach the remaining significant questions of whether Honeywell breached that duty by failing to terminate or discipline Landin, or whether such a breach was a proximate cause of Nesser's death. These are issues generally decided by a jury after a full presentation of facts.

[*Eds.* The Court concludes that the claim is not barred by workers compensation exclusivity because the assault did not occur "in the course of employment" and fell within the state "assault exception."]

NOTES AND QUESTIONS

Test Your Understanding of the Material

1. Compare the *Yunker* opinion to the Employment Restatement § 4.04. Is *Yunker* consistent with the Restatement?

2. What policy arguments does the court in *Yunker* provide to support its ruling on the negligent hiring claim? For more on the policy implications of criminal background checks, see Chapter 16, Note: Regulating Background Checks.

3. At what point in time should Landin's behavior have triggered more aggressive intervention by the employer? What could or should the employer have done?

Related Issues

4. *Prevalence of Workplace Violence.* Homicide represents 10% of workplace fatalities. More than 40% of fatalities are transportation-related, and 30% are from slips, falls, or being struck by an object or equipment. Bureau of Labor Statistics, US Department of Labor, available at http://www.bls.gov/iif/oshwc/cfoi/cfch0011.pdf. Only a small proportion of homicides are committed by coworkers. More commonly, workplace homicides occur in connection with a crime by a third party. In those circumstances, preventative approaches such as lighting, surveillance, signage and employee training have been effective at

reducing the risk. Centers for Disease Control, Workplace Violence Prevention Strategies and Research Needs (2004) available at http://www.cdc.gov/niosh/docs/2006–144/pdfs/2006–144.pdf.

5.   *Temporary Restraining Orders Against Employees*. Many states authorize employers to file for an order that precludes the restrained individual from entering the workplace. See, e.g., Cal. Civ. Proc. Code § 527.8; Colo Rev. Stat. 13–14–102(4)(B); Nev. Rev. Stat. § 33.200–.360. Employers can seek a restraining order on an emergency basis in the form of a temporary restraining order (TRO), and subsequently seek an injunction upon the expiration of the TRO. Workplace restraining orders have been used against former employees who present a credible threat of violence. They can also serve to protect employees from certain third parties, such as abusive domestic partners or stalkers, who may present a violent threat at the workplace.

E. OCCUPATIONAL SAFETY AND HEALTH ACT

PRACTITIONER'S PERSPECTIVE
Willis J. Goldsmith
Partner, Jones Day.

I started out in practice when it was expected that a management labor lawyer could advise and try cases concerning virtually any aspect of the employer/employee relationship. The law under the Occupational Safety and Health Act of 1970 (OSHA) quickly became one of my preferred areas.

OSHA litigation resembles tort litigation in its scientific focus, heavy reliance on expert testimony, extensive discovery and implications for the client's operations.

OSHA litigation typically starts with a call from the client saying that an OSHA Compliance Safety and Health Officer ("CSHO") from the U.S. Department of Labor has arrived at the facility and has asked to inspect. (Of course, sometimes the first time the lawyers know anything has happened is after the inspection occurs and the citation has been issued. At that point, it can be very difficult to re-create what happened during the inspection.) It is crucial for the company to do whatever can be done to control both the nature and scope of the inspection. This requires its lawyer to fully understand an employer's rights and obligations with respect to everything the CSHO does from the moment the inspector appears at the front door of the facility. The employer should immediately ask the reason for the inspection (e.g., an employee complaint, a planned inspection, or an injury or fatality) as well as the anticipated scope of the inspection. It must also consider and resolve issues during the inspection regarding document handling, witness interviews, and employee and/or union rights. How the employer handles this initial phase of the matter can often be dispositive of the ultimate outcome in litigation.

If OSHA issues a citation following the inspection, the company has an opportunity to contest it. Litigation is then underway. A visit by the company's lawyer to the cited facility, if it has not already occurred, is a must; interviews with supervisors, and others are likewise critical; understanding the scope of applicable privileges and deciding what will and will not be produced in discovery is also critical. Perhaps most importantly, it is critical to focus on the specific language of the cited items, understanding both what the cited standard (or general duty clause) requires the government to prove, as well as the precise conditions that OSHA alleges were violative of the Act. It is also extremely important to understand what the client will be required to do to abate, or fix, the cited conditions. Many OSHA citations are litigated not necessarily because of the civil penalties involved, but because of the impact the abatement may have on the employer's ability to continue to operate.

Much as in civil litigation, discovery, especially depositions, will determine whether the case will be resolved or tried. The depositions of the inspector and others within the Agency responsible for issuing the citation are especially important. Since the more complex cases often involve health issues, and since all but the most simple cases involve complicated scientific or technical issues, it is important that the lawyer representing the company either have a sound footing in the science and math that likely will come into play or co-counsel with a colleague who does. If the case proceeds to trial, it may take years until resolution. An unfortunate example in this regard is one high-profile OSHA matter I tried which lingered in litigation for close to 20 years.

The Occupational Safety and Health Act of 1970 (OSHA), 29 U.S.C. § 651 et seq., requires every employer engaged in interstate commerce to adhere to minimum safety and health standards. OSHA imposes a general duty on a covered employer to "furnish to each of his employees employment and a place of employment which are free from recognized hazards that are causing or are likely to cause death or serious physical harm to his employees." 29 U.S.C. § 654. The statute authorizes the Department of Labor to set specific health and safety standards, grouped by industry. The standards, for instance, specify the types of protective equipment required, the level of ventilation, and the physical layout of the workplace. 29 C.F.R. 1910 et seq. See generally Estreicher & Lester, Employment Law ch.12.

OSHA Citation Against Sea World

In 2010, OSHA issued a citation to Sea World after a killer whale drowned an animal trainer. The animal was previously involved in the death of another trainer in 1991. OSHA fined Sea World $70,000 for violating the general duties clause by allowing trainers to swim with the animal despite "his dangerous past behavior." See www.osha.gov/dep/citations/seaworld-citation-notification-of-penalty.pdf.

OSHA is enforced exclusively by the federal government; there is no private right of action. The Occupational Safety and Health Administration, located in the Department of Labor, is responsible for issuing regulations, conducting inspections and issuing citations. The adjudication of violations of the statute is committed to the Occupational Safety and Health Review Commission (OSHRC), an independent agency that acts as the adjudicatory body. Legislation like OSHA—which is more common on the state level and in other countries—may have a number of justifications, some of which concern weaknesses in the operations of labor markets. OSHA's standards for labeling hazardous materials, for example, attempt to address disparate access to information between employers and workers. Employers are better situated to know of hidden or long-term hazards and have little incentive to explain these hazards to their employees. See Mary Loring Lyndon, Information Economics and Chemical Toxicity: Designing Laws to Produce and Use Data, 87 Mich.L.Rev. 1795 (1989).

OSHA's minimum safety and health standards cannot be waived by employees irrespective of information availability. This suggests that the Act also rests on the assumption that even fully informed workers may not be able fully to appreciate long-term, probabilistic risk. See generally Cass R. Sunstein, Legal Interference with Private Preferences, 53 U.Chi.L.Rev. 1129 (1986). In addition, unregulated bargaining may not fully account for the external or public costs of declining worker health and safety. See Susan Rose-Ackerman, Progressive Law and Economics—And the New Administrative Law, 98 Yale L.J. 341, 356 (1988). Like the FLSA and child labor laws, OSHA may also express a collective social judgment that people should not be subjected to work unless certain minimum standards are met.

CHAPTER 16

WORKPLACE PRIVACY

■ ■ ■

Introduction

This chapter explores the growing protection of employee privacy interests in U.S. law. Unlike most of our European trading partners, the United States has no general privacy legislation or even a strong underlying common law framework. Most legislation, federal or state, deals with specific areas of concern. In 2015, the Restatement of Employment Law formulated a framework for decisional law treating employee privacy.

A. PHYSICAL INTRUSIONS

RESTATEMENT OF EMPLOYMENT LAW
§§ 7.01–7.03, 7.06–7.07
American Law Institute (2015).

§ 7.01. Employee Right of Privacy

Employees have a right not to be subjected to wrongful employer intrusions upon their protected privacy interests. Protected employee privacy interests are listed in § 7.02, and further defined in §§ 7.03–7.05. Employer intrusions into those interests are defined in §§ 7.03–7.05. The term "wrongful employer intrusion" is defined in § 7.06.

§ 7.02. Protected Employee Privacy Interests

Protected employee privacy interests include:

(a) the privacy of the employee's person (including aspects of his physical person, bodily functions, and personal possessions) as well as the privacy of the physical and electronic locations, including work locations provided by the employer, as to which the employee has a reasonable expectation of privacy (as provided in § 7.03);

(b) the privacy of the employee's information of a personal nature (as provided in § 7.04); and

(c) the privacy of the employee's information of a personal nature disclosed in confidence to the employer (as provided in § 7.05).

§ 7.03. Protected Employee Privacy Interests in the Employee's Physical Person and in Physical and Electronic Locations

(a) An employee has a protected privacy interest against employer intrusion into:

   (1) the employee's physical person, bodily functions, and personal possessions; and

   (2) physical and electronic locations, including employer-provided locations, as to which the employee has a reasonable expectation of privacy.

(b) An employee has a reasonable expectation in the privacy of a physical or electronic work location provided by the employer if:

   (1) the employer has provided express notice that the location or aspects of the location are private for employees; or

   (2) the employer has acted in a manner that treats the location or aspects of the location as private for employees, the type of location is customarily treated as private for employees, and the employee has made reasonable efforts to keep the location private.

(c) An employer intrudes upon an employee's protected privacy interest under this Section by such means as an examination, search, or surveillance into the locations discussed in subsection (a).

§ 7.06. Wrongful Employer Intrusions

(a) An employer is subject to liability for a wrongful intrusion upon an employee's protected privacy interest (see §§ 7.03–7.05) if the intrusion would be highly offensive to a reasonable person under the circumstances.

(b) An intrusion is highly offensive under subsection (a) if the nature, manner, and scope of the intrusion are clearly unreasonable when judged against the employer's legitimate business interests or the public's interests in intruding.

§ 7.07. Discharge in Retaliation for Refusing Privacy Invasions

An employer who discharges an employee for refusing to consent to a wrongful employer intrusion upon a protected employee privacy interest under this Chapter is subject to liability for wrongful discharge in violation of well-established public policy under Chapter 5. [*Eds.* Chapter 5 of the Employment Restatement is covered at p. 633 supra.]

BORSE V. PIECE GOODS SHOP, INC.

United States Court of Appeals for the Third Circuit, 1992.
963 F.2d 611.

BECKER, J.

Plaintiff Sarah Borse brought suit against her former employer, Piece Goods Shop, Inc. ("the Shop"), in the district court for the Eastern District of Pennsylvania. She claimed that, by dismissing her when she refused to submit to urinalysis screening and personal property searches (conducted by her employer at the workplace pursuant to its drug and alcohol policy), the Shop violated a public policy that precludes employers from engaging in activities that violate their employees' rights to privacy and to freedom from unreasonable searches. [T]he district court dismissed her complaint for failure to state a claim on which relief could be granted. * * *

Because of the procedural posture of this case, we begin with a summary of the allegations of the complaint. Borse was employed as a sales clerk by the Piece Goods Shop for almost fifteen years. In January 1990, the Shop adopted a drug and alcohol policy which required its employees to sign a form giving their consent to urinalysis screening for drug use and to searches of their personal property located on the Shop's premises.

Borse refused to sign the consent form. On more than one occasion, she asserted that the drug and alcohol policy violated her right to privacy and her right to be free from unreasonable searches and seizures as guaranteed by the United States Constitution. The Shop continued to insist that she sign the form and threatened to discharge her unless she did. On February 9, 1990, the Shop terminated Borse's employment.

The complaint alleges that Borse was discharged in retaliation for her refusal to sign the consent form and for protesting the Shop's drug and alcohol policy. It asserts that her discharge violated a public policy, embodied in the First and Fourth Amendments to the United States Constitution, which precludes employers from engaging in activities that violate their employees' rights to privacy and to freedom from unreasonable searches of their persons and property. Plaintiff seeks compensatory damages for emotional distress, injury to reputation, loss of earnings, and diminished earning capacity. She also alleges that the discharge was willful and malicious and, accordingly, seeks punitive damages.

* * *

Because the Pennsylvania Supreme Court has not addressed the question [of] whether discharging an at-will employee who refuses to consent to urinalysis and to searches of his or her personal property located on the employer's premises violates public policy, we must predict how that court would resolve the issue should it be called upon to do so. * * *

In order to evaluate Borse's claim, we must attempt to "discern whether any public policy is threatened" by her discharge. As evidence of a public policy that precludes employers from discharging employees who refuse to consent to the practices at issue, Borse primarily relies upon the First and Fourth Amendments to the United States Constitution and the right to privacy included in the Pennsylvania Constitution. As will be seen, we reject her reliance on these constitutional provisions, concluding instead that, to the extent that her discharge implicates public policy, the source of that policy lies in Pennsylvania common law. * * *

Although we have rejected Borse's reliance upon constitutional provisions as evidence of a public policy [*Eds.* in a portion of the opinion not reprinted here] allegedly violated by the Piece Goods Shop's drug and alcohol program, our review of Pennsylvania law reveals other evidence of a public policy that may, under certain circumstances, give rise to a wrongful discharge action related to urinalysis or to personal property searches. Specifically, we refer to the Pennsylvania common law regarding tortious invasion of privacy. Pennsylvania recognizes a cause of action for tortious "intrusion upon seclusion." *Marks v. Bell Telephone Co.*, 460 Pa. 73, 331 A.2d 424, 430 (1975). The Restatement defines the tort as follows:

> One who intentionally intrudes, physically or otherwise, upon the solitude or seclusion of another or his private affairs or concerns, is subject to liability to the other for invasion of his privacy, if the intrusion would be highly offensive to a reasonable person.

Restatement (Second) of Torts § 652B.

Unlike the other forms of tortious invasion of privacy, an action based on intrusion upon seclusion does not require publication as an element of the tort. *Harris by Harris v. Easton Publishing Co.*, 335 Pa. Super. 141, 483 A.2d 1377, 1383 (1984). The tort may occur by (1) physical intrusion into a place where the plaintiff has secluded himself or herself; (2) use of the defendant's senses to oversee or overhear the plaintiff's private affairs; or (3) some other form of investigation or examination into plaintiff's private concerns. 483 A.2d at 1383. Liability attaches only when the intrusion is substantial and would be highly offensive to "the ordinary reasonable person." *Id.* at 1383–84.

We can envision at least two ways in which an employer's urinalysis program might intrude upon an employee's seclusion. First, the particular manner in which the program is conducted might constitute an intrusion upon seclusion as defined by Pennsylvania law. The process of collecting the urine sample to be tested clearly implicates "expectations of privacy that society has long recognized as reasonable," *Skinner v. Railway Labor Executives Association*, 489 U.S. 602, 109 S. Ct. 1402, 1413, 103 L. Ed. 2d 639 (1989). In addition, many urinalysis programs monitor the collection of the urine specimen to ensure that the employee does not adulterate it or substitute a sample from another person. See, for example, 109 S. Ct. at

1413 (noting that in some cases, visual or aural observation of urination is required). * * *

Second, urinalysis "can reveal a host of private medical facts about an employee, including whether she is epileptic, pregnant, or diabetic." *Skinner*, 109 S. Ct. at 1413. A reasonable person might well conclude that submitting urine samples to tests designed to ascertain these types of information constitutes a substantial and highly offensive intrusion upon seclusion.

The same principles apply to an employer's search of an employee's personal property. If the search is not conducted in a discreet manner or if it is done in such a way as to reveal personal matters unrelated to the workplace, the search might well constitute a tortious invasion of the employee's privacy. See, for example, *K-Mart Corp. Store No. 7441 v. Trotti*, 677 S.W.2d 632 (Tex. App. 1984) (search of employee's locker). See also *Bodewig v. K-Mart, Inc.*, 54 Or. App. 480, 635 P.2d 657 (1981) (subjecting cashier accused of stealing to strip search). * * *

Only a handful of other jurisdictions have considered urinalysis programs implemented by private employers. The majority of these decisions balance the employee's privacy interest against the employer's interests in order to determine whether to uphold the programs. See, for example, *Luedtke v. Nabors Alaska Drilling, Inc.*, 768 P.2d 1123 (Alaska 1989). In *Luedtke*, two employees challenged their employer's urinalysis program, alleging violation of their state constitutional right of privacy, common-law invasion of privacy, wrongful discharge, and breach of the covenant of good faith and fair dealing. (Under Alaska law, the public policy exception to the employment-at-will doctrine is "largely encompassed within the implied covenant of good faith and fair dealing." 768 P.2d at 1130 * * *. After determining that the relevant provision of the Alaska constitution did not apply to private action, the Alaska Supreme Court concluded that a public policy protecting an employee's right to withhold private information from his employer exists in Alaska and that violation of that policy "may rise to the level of a breach of the implied covenant of good faith and fair dealing," 768 P.2d at 1130.

* * *

Although most ... jurisdictions have applied a balancing test to urinalysis programs conducted by private employers, not all have done so. In *Jennings v. Minco Technology Labs, Inc.*, 765 S.W.2d 497 (Tex. App. 1989), for example, the Texas Court of Appeals upheld an employer's random urinalysis program without balancing the employee's interests against the employer's. The court upheld the program for two reasons. First, the court reasoned that although the Texas Supreme Court had on one occasion recognized an exception to the employment-at-will doctrine based on public policy, see *Sabine Pilot, Inc. v. Hauck*, 687 S.W.2d 733 (Tex.

1985), the "lower courts are not free to create additional exceptions," 765 S.W.2d at 501, particularly in the absence of a statute explicitly recognizing the public policy allegedly violated by the discharge, *id*. at 501 & 501 n3. Second, the court reasoned that the employer's urinalysis program would not violate plaintiff's privacy because her urine would be tested only if she consented. *Id*. at 502. Jennings argued that her consent would be ineffective because if she did not consent, she would lose her job, which she could not afford to do. The court rejected her argument, however, because "there cannot be one law of contracts for the rich and another for the poor." *Id*. * * *

In view of the foregoing analysis, we predict that the Pennsylvania Supreme Court would apply a balancing test to determine whether the Shop's drug and alcohol program (consisting of urinalysis and personal property searches) invaded Borse's privacy. Indeed, determining whether an alleged invasion of privacy is substantial and highly offensive to the reasonable person necessitates the use of a balancing test. The test we believe that Pennsylvania would adopt balances the employee's privacy interest against the employer's interest in maintaining a drug-free workplace in order to determine whether a reasonable person would find the employer's program highly offensive.

We recognize that other jurisdictions have considered individualized suspicion and concern for safety as factors to be considered in striking the balance, see, for example, *Twigg* [v. *Hercules Corp*., 185 W.Va. 155, 406 406 S.E.2d [52,] 55 [(1990)] (allowing urinalysis based on individualized suspicion or when employee's job implicates safety concerns). We do not doubt that, in an appropriate case, Pennsylvania would include these factors in the balance, but we do not believe that the Pennsylvania Supreme Court would require private employers to limit urinalysis programs or personal property searches to employees suspected of drug use or to those performing safety-sensitive jobs.

NOTES AND QUESTIONS

Test Your Understanding of the Material

1.   How is an employee's privacy invaded by a urinalysis when the urine specimen is given behind a closed stall with no one else present? Is it because the urine sample may reveal private medical information? What if the sample is analyzed not by the employer directly but by a laboratory and the employer is informed only of the presence of an illegal drug? The Supreme Court dealt with this question in the public-employment context in Skinner v. Railway Labor Executive Assn., 469 U.S. 602, 109 S.Ct. 1402, 103 L.E.2d 639 (1989).

2.   In what sense is there an invasion of privacy where the employee refuses to give his or her consent and is discharged for that reason? See Employment Restatement § 7.07.

3.   What legitimate interests does an employer have in requiring a drug test as a condition of employment? Courts have been receptive to the argument that employees in safety-sensitive positions may be subjected to drug tests because impairment of the employee may imperil the safety of the employees, coworkers, or the public. See e.g. Webster v. Motorola, Inc., 637 N.E.2d 203, 418 Mass. 425 (1994) (driver's privacy interest outweighed by employer's interest in ensuring that its vehicle was not operated by a person under the influence of illegal drugs); Folmsbee v. Tech Tool Grinding & Supply, Inc., 417 Mass. 388, 630 N.E.2d 586 (1994) (rejecting public policy challenge to drug testing where workplace safety depended upon "extreme alertness and precision").

What interest did the store in *Borse* have for its drug-testing program? Is an interest in a drug-free workplace simpliciter sufficient?

4.   Do employees have a stronger privacy interest than job applicants in resisting a drug test as a condition of continued employment? Put differently, do employers have a stronger interest in using such tests because they have not had an opportunity to evaluate job applicants over a significant period of time? See Loder v. City of Glendale, 14 Cal.4th 846, 897, 59 Cal.Rptr.2d 696, 728–29, 927 P.2d 1206, 1234 (1997).

5.   What is the effect of employee consent to a drug test if it is obtained on threat of dismissal? See Employment Restatement § 7.06, Comment h.

6.   Does the balancing test articulated in *Borse* provide sufficient guidance to employers or employees? Does § 7.06 of the Employment Restatement offer a better approach?

Related Issues

7.   *"Public Policy" Cause of Action for Invasion of Privacy. Borse* involved a public policy cause of action where the source of the public policy was tort decisional law protecting a privacy right. A few other states have also recognized a public-policy claim in the workplace privacy area. See, e.g., Baughman v. Wal-Mart Stores, Inc., 215 W.Va. 45, 592 S.E.2d 824 (2003) (state public policy permits pre-employment testing of applicants but not incumbent employees absent safety concerns or "good faith objective suspicion" of drug use); Hennessey v. Coastal Eagle Point Oil Co., 129 N.J. 81, 609 A.2d 11 (1992) (recognizing "public policy" cause of action in the drug-testing context; however, firing oil refinery employee in safety-sensitive position for failing urine test deemed permissible); Luedtke v. Nabors Alaska Drilling Inc., 768 P.2d 1123, 1133 (Alaska 1989) (recognizing that "there exists a public policy protecting spheres of employee conduct into which employers may not intrude", but upholding monitoring of oil rig employees for off-duty drug use).

8.   *General Privacy Protections.* Only a handful of states provide general privacy protection whether by statute, see Mass. G.L. c. 214, § 1B, or state constitutional provision. See White v. Davis, 13 Cal.3d 757, 120 Cal.Rptr. 94, 533 P.2d 222 (1975); Hill v. National Collegiate Athletic Assn., 7 Cal.4th 1, 26 Cal.Rptr. 2d 834, 865 P.2d 633 (1994) (en banc) (recognizing a constitutional privacy interest for student athletes but finding that the NCAA's interest in

maintaining fair competition outweighed those interests). Most states reaching the issue have not interpreted their state constitutions to reach private-sector activity. See, e.g., Cisco v. United Parcel Services, 328 Pa.Super. 300, 476 A.2d 1340 (1984) (employer need not rehire former employee acquitted of suspected theft; state constitution does not extend to private-sector employees).

9.   *State Drug Testing Laws.* A number of state laws regulate workplace drug testing programs. See, e.g., Conn. Gen. Stat. Ann., § 31–51t et seq. (permitting random testing of applicants only, where authorized by federal law or in positions that are "high-risk" or "safety-sensitive"; otherwise, "reasonable suspicion" required); Vt. Stat. Ann., tit. 21 §§ 511–20 (random testing permitted only of applicants and where required by federal law; otherwise, only probable-cause testing is permitted and only where employer has an employee assistance program (EAP) and will not terminate employee unless employee tests positive after completion of EAP). Drug testing can also give rise to liability under the Americans with Disabilities Act (ADA) and cognate state law where a failed drug tests compels the employee to disclose an underlying medical condition for which the employee is receiving treatment with prescription drugs. See e.g. Warshaw v. Concentra Health Svcs., 719 F.Supp.2d 484 (E.D. Pa. 2010) (employee removed from project after failing drug test for ADHD medication).

10.   *Supreme Court Law on Drug Testing.* Skinner v. Railway Labor Executives' Association 489 U.S. 602, 109 S.Ct. 1402, 103 L.Ed.2d 639 (1989), addressed the constitutionality of a Federal Railroad Administration (FRA) regulation requiring blood and urine tests of railroad employees involved in certain train accidents. The FRA also has adopted regulations that authorized railroads to administer breath and urine tests to employees who violate certain safety rules.

> Unlike the blood-testing procedure at issue in *Schmerber* [v. *California,* 384 U.S. 757 (1966),] the procedures prescribed by the FRA regulations for collecting and testing urine samples do not entail a surgical intrusion into the body. It is not disputed, however, that chemical analysis of urine, like that of blood, can reveal a host of private medical facts about an employee, including whether she is epileptic, pregnant, or diabetic. Nor can it be disputed that the process of collecting the sample to be tested, which may in some cases involve visual or aural monitoring of the act of urination, itself implicates privacy interests. * * *
>
> By and large, intrusions on privacy under the FRA regulations are limited. To the extent transportation and like restrictions are necessary to procure the requisite blood, breath, and urine samples for testing, this interference alone is minimal given the employment context in which it takes place. Ordinarily, an employee consents to significant restrictions in his freedom of movement where necessary for his employment, and few are free to come and go as they please during working hours. See, *e.g., INS v. Delgado,* 466 U.S., at 218, 104 S.Ct., at 1763. Any additional interference with a railroad employee's

freedom of movement that occurs in the time it takes to procure a blood, breath, or urine sample for testing cannot, by itself, be said to infringe significant privacy interests. * * *

The breath tests authorized by Subpart D of the regulations are even less intrusive than the blood tests prescribed by Subpart C. Unlike blood tests, breath tests do not require piercing the skin and may be conducted safely outside a hospital environment and with a minimum of inconvenience or embarrassment. Further, breath tests reveal the level of alcohol in the employee's bloodstream and nothing more. * * *

A more difficult question is presented by urine tests. Like breath tests, urine tests are not invasive of the body and, under the regulations, may not be used as an occasion for inquiring into private facts unrelated to alcohol or drug use. We recognize, however, that the procedures for collecting the necessary samples, which require employees to perform an excretory function traditionally shielded by great privacy, raise concerns not implicated by blood or breath tests. While we would not characterize these additional privacy concerns as minimal in most contexts, we note that the regulations endeavor to reduce the intrusiveness of the collection process. The regulations do not require that samples be furnished under the direct observation of a monitor, despite the desirability of such a procedure to ensure the integrity of the sample. See 50 Fed.Reg. 31555 (1985). See also Field Manual B-15; *id.,* at D-1. The sample is also collected in a medical environment, by personnel unrelated to the railroad employer, and is thus not unlike similar procedures encountered often in the context of a regular physical examination.

More importantly, the expectations of privacy of covered employees are diminished by reason of their participation in an industry that is regulated pervasively to ensure safety, a goal dependent, in substantial part, on the health and fitness of covered employees.

* * *

By contrast, the government interest in testing without a showing of individualized suspicion is compelling. Employees subject to the tests discharge duties fraught with such risks of injury to others that even a momentary lapse of attention can have disastrous consequences. * * * An impaired employee, the Agency found, will seldom display any outward "signs detectable by the lay person or, in many cases, even the physician." 50 Fed.Reg. 31526 (1985). * * *

While no procedure can identify all impaired employees with ease and perfect accuracy, the FRA regulations supply an effective means of deterring employees engaged in safety-sensitive tasks from using controlled substances or alcohol in the first place. 50 Fed.Reg. 31541 (1985). * * * By ensuring that employees in safety-sensitive positions know they will be tested upon the occurrence of a triggering event, the timing of which no employee can predict with certainty, the regulations significantly increase the deterrent effect of the administrative penalties associated with the prohibited conduct, * * * concomitantly increasing the likelihood that employees will forgo using drugs or alcohol while subject to being called for duty.

NOTE: INVESTIGATIONS

Privacy issues commonly arise in the context of investigations into employee misconduct. Private employers face two sources of liability in conducting investigations—the common law tort of invasion of privacy, discussed supra, and statutory liability under federal and state law, which prohibit certain types of employer investigations.

Invasion of Privacy Tort

As reflected in in Sections 7.01–7.03 of the Employment Restatement, employees can bring common law privacy claims for wrongful intrusions into "work locations provided by the employer, as to which the employee has a reasonable expectation of privacy[.]" How do Courts determine whether an employee has a "reasonable expectation of privacy" in a particular location? Consider the following excerpt from the Supreme Court's Fourth Amendment ruling in O'Connor v. Ortega, 480 U.S. 709, 107 S.Ct. 1492, 94 L.Ed.2d 714 (1987):

> Dr. Magno Ortega, a physician and psychiatrist, held the position of Chief of Professional Education at Napa State Hospital (Hospital) for 17 years, until his dismissal from that position in 1981. As Chief of Professional Education, Dr. Ortega had primary responsibility for training young physicians in psychiatric residency programs.
>
> In July 1981, Hospital officials, including Dr. Dennis O'Connor, the Executive Director of the Hospital, became concerned about possible improprieties in Dr. Ortega's management of the residency program. In particular, the Hospital officials were concerned with Dr. Ortega's acquisition of an Apple II computer for use in the residency program. The officials thought that Dr. Ortega may have misled Dr. O'Connor into believing that the computer had been donated, when in fact the computer had been financed by the possibly coerced contributions of residents. Additionally, the Hospital officials were concerned with charges that Dr. Ortega had sexually harassed two female Hospital employees, and had taken inappropriate disciplinary action against a resident.
>
> On July 30, 1981, Dr. O'Connor requested that Dr. Ortega take paid administrative leave during an investigation of these charges. * * *
>
> Dr. O'Connor selected several Hospital personnel to conduct the investigation, including an accountant, a physician, and a Hospital security officer. Richard Friday, the Hospital Administrator, led this "investigative team." At some point during the investigation, Mr. Friday made the decision to enter Dr. Ortega's office. The specific

reason for the entry into Dr. Ortega's office is unclear from the record. The petitioners claim that the search was conducted to secure state property. Initially, petitioners contended that such a search was pursuant to a Hospital policy of conducting a routine inventory of state property in the office of a terminated employee. At the time of the search, however, the Hospital had not yet terminated Dr. Ortega's employment; Dr. Ortega was still on administrative leave. Apparently, there was no policy of inventorying the offices of those on administrative leave. Before the search had been initiated, however, the petitioners had become aware that Dr. Ortega had taken the computer to his home. Dr. Ortega contends that the purpose of the search was to secure evidence for use against him in administrative disciplinary proceedings. The resulting search of Dr. Ortega's office was quite thorough. The investigators entered the office a number of times and seized several items from Dr. Ortega's desk and file cabinets, including a Valentine's card, a photograph, and a book of poetry all sent to Dr. Ortega by a former resident physician. These items were later used in a proceeding before a hearing officer of the California State Personnel Board to impeach the credibility of the former resident, who testified on Dr. Ortega's behalf. The investigators also seized billing documentation of one of Dr. Ortega's private patients under the California Medicaid program. The investigators did not otherwise separate Dr. Ortega's property from state property because, as one investigator testified, "[t]rying to sort State from non-State, it was too much to do, so I gave it up and boxed it up." Thus, no formal inventory of the property in the office was ever made. Instead, all the papers in Dr. Ortega's office were merely placed in boxes, and put in storage for Dr. Ortega to retrieve. * * *

Given the societal expectations of privacy in one's place of work * * * , we reject the contention made by the Solicitor General and petitioners that public employees can never have a reasonable expectation of privacy in their place of work. Individuals do not lose Fourth Amendment rights merely because they work for the government instead of a private employer. The operational realities of the workplace, however, may make *some* employees' expectations of privacy unreasonable when an intrusion is by a supervisor rather than a law enforcement official. Public employees' expectations of privacy in their offices, desks, and file cabinets, like similar expectations of employees in the private sector, may be reduced by virtue of actual office practices and procedures, or by legitimate regulation. Indeed, in *Mancusi* itself, the Court suggested that the union employee did not have a reasonable expectation of privacy against his union supervisors. 392 U.S., at 369, 88 S.Ct., at 2124. The employee's expectation of privacy must be assessed in the context of the employment relation. An office is seldom a private enclave free from entry by supervisors, other employees and business and personal invitees. Instead, in many cases offices are continually entered by fellow employees and other visitors during the workday for conferences, consultations, and other work-related visits. Simply put, it is the nature of government offices that others—such as fellow employees, supervisors, consensual visitors, and the general public—may have frequent access to an individual's office. * * * Given the great variety of work environments in the public sector, the question of whether an employee has a reasonable expectation of privacy must be addressed on a case-by-case basis.

The Court of Appeals concluded that Dr. Ortega had a reasonable expectation of privacy in his office, and five Members of this Court agree with that determination. * * * Because the record does not reveal the extent to which Hospital officials may have had work-related reasons to enter Dr. Ortega's office, we think the Court of Appeals should have remanded the matter to the District Court for its further determination. But regardless of any legitimate right of access the Hospital staff may have had to the office as such, we recognize that the undisputed evidence suggests that Dr. Ortega had a reasonable expectation of privacy in his desk and file cabinets. The undisputed evidence discloses that Dr. Ortega did not share his desk or file cabinets with any other employees. Dr. Ortega had occupied the office for 17 years and he kept materials in his office, which included personal correspondence, medical files, and correspondence from private patients unconnected to the Hospital, personal financial records, teaching aids and notes, and personal gifts and mementos. The files on physicians in residency training were kept outside Dr. Ortega's office. Indeed, the only items found by the investigators were apparently personal items because, with the exception of the items seized for use in the administrative hearings, all the papers and effects found in the office were simply placed in boxes and made available to Dr. Ortega.

O'Connor was decided under the Fourth Amendment which bars the government from engaging in unreasonable search and seizure. Nevertheless, the Court's reasoning regarding an employee's reasonable expectation of privacy is relevant for a common law tort claim. In which portions of the workplace did Ortega have a reasonable expectation of privacy? Is the Court's reasoning consistent with Section 7.03(b)(2) of the Employment Restatement?

State and Federal Statutes Relating to Investigations

Surveillance. Several states prohibit employers from hiring detectives to spy on employees for any purpose, or at least for the purpose of interfering with the exercise of labor rights. See e.g., West's Ann. Cal. Pub. Utility Code § 8251 (public agency may not terminate or discipline an employee based on "upon a report by such special agent, detective, or spotter", involving a "question of integrity, honesty, or a breach of rules of the employer" without notice and a hearing); Kan. Stat. Ann. § 44–808(6) (unlawful to "employ any person to spy upon employees or their representatives respecting their exercise of any right created or approved by this act", many of which relate to union organizing);

Nev. Rev. Stat., vol. 32, Detectives & Spotters Law § 613.160 (prohibits employers from hiring a "special agent, detective or person commonly known as a spotter for the purpose of investigating, obtaining and reporting to the employer . . . information concerning his or her employees"); N.Y. Labor Law § 704(1) (unlawful "[t]o spy upon or keep under surveillance, whether directly or through agents or any other person, any activities of employees or their representatives in the exercise" of labor rights).

Lie Detectors. Under the Employee Polygraph Protection Act, 29 U.S.C. §§ 2001–09 (see Statutory Supplement), private and government employers are generally restricted in their use of a "lie detector," defined to include "a polygraph, deceptograph, voice stress analyzer, psychological stress evaluator, or any other similar device (whether mechanical or electrical) that is used . . . for the purpose of rendering a diagnostic opinion regarding the honesty or dishonesty of an individual. . . . " Id. § 2001. Unless the employer provides security services or lawfully handles controlled substances, lie detectors are permitted only for testing of incumbent employees in connection with "an ongoing investigation involving economic loss or injury to the employer's business." The employee must have had access to the property in question and the employer must have a reasonable suspicion of the employee's involvement. The employer must also provide a statement of the basis for its suspicion, and comply with other limitations in the questioning, subsequent documentation, and discipline on the basis of the results. Some state laws further restrict the use of polygraphs. See, e.g., D.C. Code § 36–802 (prohibiting all use of lie detector tests).

Medical Examinations. The ADA, 29 U.S.C. § 12112(d), restricts an employer's ability to conduct a pre-employment medical examination. See p. 557 supra. Some state laws limit certain personal inquiries on employment applications and the like. See, e.g., Md. Ann. Code, art. 100, § 95A (questions pertaining to any physical, psychological or psychiatric illness or treatment not bearing "a direct, material, and timely relationship" to applicant's fitness); Cort v. Bristol-Meyers Co., 431 N.E.2d 908 (Mass. 1982) (no invasion of privacy where employees refused to answer certain questions on a questionnaire; no public policy claim available where those questions did not represent an "unreasonable, substantial or serious interference with his privacy"). See also Genetic Information Nondiscrimination Act of 2007, 42 U.S.C. § 2000ff–5; Employment Restatement § 7.04 ("[a]n employee has a protected privacy interest in information relating to the employee that is of a personal nature and that the employee has made reasonable efforts to keep private. . . . An employer intrudes upon this protected privacy interest by requiring that the employee provide [such] information").

B. INTRUSIONS INTO ELECTRONIC "LOCATIONS"

NOTE: REGULATING INTERCEPTION OF COMMUNICATIONS

Consistent with decisional and statutory developments, the Employment Restatement §§ 7.02–7.03 addresses employer intrusions into electronic locations in which employees have a reasonable expectation of privacy. An employer that violates that right may be liable for a common law tortious invasion of privacy claim.

Wiretap Act

Before the advent of digital technology, conversations on landlines were monitored through the physical placement of an electrical phone-line tap, which intercepted communications over the phone wires. The federal wiretapping statute, Title III of the Omnibus Crime Control and Safe Streets Act of 1968, 18 U.S.C. § 2510 et seq., prohibits "interceptions" of telephone calls and other communications without the consent of at least one party. See id. § 2511(2)(d). Some states like Maryland require the consent of both parties to a communication. See Md. Ann. Code, Cts. & Jud. Proc., § 10–401 to 410 (regulating willful interception of any wire, oral or electronic communication absent consent of all of the parties); Cal. Penal Code § 632 (monitoring of cellular communication requires consent of all parties). Some states also have anti-hacking statutes. See e.g. Cal. Penal Code § 502.

The courts are generally disinclined to find implied consent. See Watkins v. L.M. Berry & Co., 704 F.2d 577 (11th Cir.1983) (employer's announced policy of intercepting sales calls did not establish consent to monitoring of personal calls beyond determining the nature of the call). Title III of the Omnibus Crime Control Act, 18 U.S.C. § 2510(5)(a)(i), contains an exception for interceptions resulting from use of equipment "in the ordinary course of business." The *Watkins* court held that this exception applies only to intercepted business calls and to other calls only to determine whether the call was personal or not; "a personal call may be intercepted in the ordinary course of business to determine its nature but never its contents." 704 F.2d at 583.

Electronic Communications Privacy Act

In 1986, Congress enacted the Electronic Communications Privacy Act (ECPA), 18 U.S.C. §§ 2510–20, which largely amended Title III of the Omnibus Crime Control Act, to address electronic communications. An ECPA violation requires an "interception" of the communication, i.e., obtaining the contents of the communication during transmission—thus limiting the statute's applicability to email systems where interception usually occurs after the message has been sent and stored. See, e.g., Konop v. Hawaiian Airlines, Inc., 302 F.3d 868 (9th Cir.2002) (employer's unauthorized access of an employee website not an "interception"); United S. v. Ropp, 347 F.Supp.2d 831 (S.D. Ohio 2013) (keystroke monitoring software did not intercept electronic communications).

The ECPA contains an exception for service providers. 18 U.S.C. § 2701(c). Employers have successfully used this exception for accessing information stored on their own networks. Bohach v. City of Reno, 932 F.Supp. 1232, 1236 (D.Nev.1996) (no ECPA violation where employer accessed pager messages stored on its network because the ECPA "allows service providers to do as they wish when it comes to accessing communications in electronic storage."). The statute also contains an exception for authorized users. See Konop v. Hawaiian

Airlines, Inc., 302 F.3d 868 (2002) (reversing summary judgment for employer that logged onto employee's private website using credentials obtained from other employees); Ehling v. Monmouth-Ocean Hospital Svcs. Corp, 961 F.Supp.2d 659 (D.N.J. 2013) (no ECPA violation where employer passively received screenshots of employee's private Facebook wall from co-worker "friend" authorized to access the posts).

Stored Communications Act

Unauthorized access to electronic communications while they are in electronic storage is addressed in the Stored Communications Act (SCA), which was enacted as Title II of the ECPA, 18 U.S.C. § 2701 et seq. SCA violations tend to arise in the context of unauthorized access of an employee's personal email from a third party server. See, e.g., Doe v. County of San Francisco, Case No. C10–04700 (N.D.Cal. 2012) 2012 WL 2132398 (upholding jury verdict against employer for opening and "sifting through" employee's personal webmail inbox); Mintz v. Bartelstein and Assoc. Inc., 906 F.Supp.2d 1017 (C.D.Cal. 2012) (privacy invasion when employer obtained temporary passwords to plaintiff's Gmail account and read his email for "at least twenty minutes").

The statutory exception for an employer's own network allows employers to recover any personal email stored locally on the employer's computers. Computer forensics experts can often recover snippets of personal email stored in computer temp files, as well as internet browsing history. In Sunbelt Rentals v. Victor 43 F.Supp.3d 1026 (N.D. Cal. 2014), a former employee inadvertently synced a new iPad and iPhone with an old device in the possession of the prior employer. The prior employer, a competitor, thereby received all of the employee's current text messages. The court ruled the employer did not violate the SCA in reading the text messages because it took no actions to download the messages from a third party server.

Employees generally are treated as having a lesser expectation of privacy in company-owned equipment than in their own computers or other possessions. See Restatement § 7.03, comment g; Sunbelt Rentals, supra (dismissing privacy claim, noting the employer owned the device in question). Courts have even allowed employers to search personal computers when (a) they were used for work-related purposes and (b) the employer had previously warned of a possible search. TBG. Ins. Svcs. Corp. v. Superior Ct. 117 Cal.Rptr.2d 155 (Cal. App. 2002) (ordering employee to produce personal computer for search where employee consented to monitoring of that computer in an employer policy); Sitton v. Print Direction, Inc. 312 Ga.App. 365 (Ga. App. 2011) (reviewing and printing personal email open on personal laptop at work not "offensive or objectionable to a reasonable person" given suspicion of misconduct and warning in Employee Handbook).

C. INFORMATIONAL PRIVACY

RESTATEMENT OF EMPLOYMENT LAW §§ 7.04–7.05
American Law Institute (2015).

§ 7.04. Protected Employee Privacy Interest in Information of a Personal Nature

(a) An employee has a protected privacy interest in information relating to the employee that is of a personal nature and that the employee has made reasonable efforts to keep private.

(b) An employer intrudes upon this protected privacy interest by requiring that the employee provide information described in this subsection (a) or by obtaining the information through deceit.

(c) An employer does not intrude upon the protected privacy interest stated in subsection (a) by requiring the employee to provide (i) personal information the employer is required by law to obtain from employees or (ii) personal information that is relevant to the employer's business needs and is customarily required by employers in the course of employment.

§ 7.05. Protected Employee Privacy Interest Against Employer Disclosure of Employee Personal Information

(a) An employee has a protected privacy interest in personal information related to the employee that is provided in confidence to the employer in the course of the employment relationship.

(b) An employer intrudes upon the privacy interest stated in subsection (a) by providing or allowing third parties access to such employee information without the employee's consent. For purposes of this Section, third parties include an employer's employees or agents who have no legitimate business reason to access the information.

(c) An employer does not intrude upon the privacy interest stated in subsection (a) if the employer is compelled by law to provide or allow a third party access to the employee information described in the subsection.

CITY OF ONTARIO V. QUON

Supreme Court of the United States, 2010.
560 U.S. 746, 130 S.Ct. 2619, 177 L.Ed.2d 216.

KENNEDY, J. delivered the opinion of the Court.

I

A

The City of Ontario (City) is a political subdivision of the State of California. The case arose out of incidents in 2001 and 2002 when respondent Jeff Quon was employed by the Ontario Police Department (OPD). He was a police sergeant and member of OPD's Special Weapons and Tactics (SWAT) Team. The City, OPD, and OPD's Chief, Lloyd Scharf, are petitioners here. As will be discussed, two respondents share the last name Quon. In this opinion "Quon" refers to Jeff Quon, for the relevant events mostly revolve around him.

In October 2001, the City acquired 20 alphanumeric pagers capable of sending and receiving text messages. Arch Wireless Operating Company provided wireless service for the pagers. Under the City's service contract with Arch Wireless, each pager was allotted a limited number of characters sent or received each month. Usage in excess of that amount would result in an additional fee. The City issued pagers to Quon and other SWAT Team members in order to help the SWAT Team mobilize and respond to emergency situations.

Before acquiring the pagers, the City announced a "Computer Usage, Internet and E-Mail Policy" (Computer Policy) that applied to all employees. Among other provisions, it specified that the City "reserves the right to monitor and log all network activity including e-mail and Internet use, with or without notice. Users should have no expectation of privacy or confidentiality when using these resources." In March 2000, Quon signed a statement acknowledging that he had read and understood the Computer Policy.

The Computer Policy did not apply, on its face, to text messaging. Text messages share similarities with e-mails, but the two differ in an important way. In this case, for instance, an e-mail sent on a City computer was transmitted through the City's own data servers, but a text message sent on one of the City's pagers was transmitted using wireless radio frequencies from an individual pager to a receiving station owned by Arch Wireless. It was routed through Arch Wireless' computer network, where it remained until the recipient's pager or cellular telephone was ready to receive the message, at which point Arch Wireless transmitted the message from the transmitting station nearest to the recipient. After delivery, Arch Wireless retained a copy on its computer servers. The message did not pass through computers owned by the City.

Although the Computer Policy did not cover text messages by its explicit terms, the City made clear to employees, including Quon, that the City would treat text messages the same way as it treated e-mails. At an April 18, 2002, staff meeting at which Quon was present, Lieutenant Steven Duke, the OPD officer responsible for the City's contract with Arch Wireless, told officers that messages sent on the pagers "are considered e-mail messages. This means that [text] messages would fall under the City's policy as public information and [would be] eligible for auditing." Duke's comments were put in writing in a memorandum sent on April 29, 2002, by Chief Scharf to Quon and other City personnel.

Within the first or second billing cycle after the pagers were distributed, Quon exceeded his monthly text message character allotment. Duke told Quon about the overage, and reminded him that messages sent on the pagers were "considered e-mail and could be audited." Duke said, however, that "it was not his intent to audit [an] employee's text messages to see if the overage [was] due to work related transmissions." Duke suggested that Quon could reimburse the City for the overage fee rather than have Duke audit the messages. Quon wrote a check to the City for the overage. Duke offered the same arrangement to other employees who incurred overage fees.

Over the next few months, Quon exceeded his character limit three or four times. Each time he reimbursed the City. Quon and another officer again incurred overage fees for their pager usage in August 2002. At a meeting in October, Duke told Scharf that he had become " 'tired of being a bill collector.' " Scharf decided to determine whether the existing character limit was too low—that is, whether officers such as Quon were having to pay fees for sending work-related messages—or if the overages were for personal messages. Scharf told Duke to request transcripts of text messages sent in August and September by Quon and the other employee who had exceeded the character allowance.

At Duke's request, an administrative assistant employed by OPD contacted Arch Wireless. After verifying that the City was the subscriber on the accounts, Arch Wireless provided the desired transcripts. Duke reviewed the transcripts and discovered that many of the messages sent and received on Quon's pager were not work related, and some were sexually explicit. Duke reported his findings to Scharf, who, along with Quon's immediate supervisor, reviewed the transcripts himself. After his review, Scharf referred the matter to OPD's internal affairs division for an investigation into whether Quon was violating OPD rules by pursuing personal matters while on duty.

The officer in charge of the internal affairs review was Sergeant Patrick McMahon. Before conducting a review, McMahon used Quon's work schedule to redact the transcripts in order to eliminate any messages Quon sent while off duty. He then reviewed the content of the messages

Quon sent during work hours. McMahon's report noted that Quon sent or received 456 messages during work hours in the month of August 2002, of which no more than 57 were work related; he sent as many as 80 messages during a single day at work; and on an average workday, Quon sent or received 28 messages, of which only 3 were related to police business. The report concluded that Quon had violated OPD rules. Quon was allegedly disciplined.

B

Raising claims under Rev. Stat. § 1979, 42 U.S.C. § 1983; 18 U.S.C. § 2701 et seq., popularly known as the Stored Communications Act (SCA); and California law, Quon filed suit against petitioners in the United States District Court for the Central District of California. Arch Wireless and an individual not relevant here were also named as defendants. * * * Among the allegations in the complaint was that petitioners violated respondents' Fourth Amendment rights and the SCA by obtaining and reviewing the transcript of Jeff Quon's pager messages and that Arch Wireless had violated the SCA by turning over the transcript to the City. * * *

II

* * *

The [Court in *O'Connor v. Ortega*, 480 U.S. 709 (1987),] did disagree on the proper analytical framework for Fourth Amendment claims against government employers. A four-Justice plurality concluded that the correct analysis has two steps. First, because "some government offices may be so open to fellow employees or the public that no expectation of privacy is reasonable," a court must consider "[t]he operational realities of the workplace" in order to determine whether an employee's Fourth Amendment rights are implicated. On this view, "the question whether an employee has a reasonable expectation of privacy must be addressed on a case-by-case basis." Next, where an employee has a legitimate privacy expectation, an employer's intrusion on that expectation "for noninvestigatory, work-related purposes, as well as for investigations of work-related misconduct, should be judged by the standard of reasonableness under all the circumstances." * * *

III

A

Before turning to the reasonableness of the search, it is instructive to note the parties' disagreement over whether Quon had a reasonable expectation of privacy. The record does establish that OPD, at the outset, made it clear that pager messages were not considered private. The City's Computer Policy stated that "[u]sers should have no expectation of privacy or confidentiality when using" City computers. Chief Scharf's memo and Duke's statements made clear that this official policy extended to text messaging. The disagreement, at least as respondents see the case, is over whether Duke's later statements overrode the official policy. Respondents contend that because Duke told Quon that an audit would be unnecessary if Quon paid for the overage, Quon reasonably could expect that the contents of his messages would remain private.

At this point, were we to assume that inquiry into "operational realities" were called for, it would be necessary to ask whether Duke's statements could be taken as announcing a change in OPD policy, and if so, whether he had, in fact or appearance, the authority to make such a change and to guarantee the privacy of text messaging. It would also be necessary to consider whether a review of messages sent on police pagers, particularly those sent while officers are on duty, might be justified for other reasons, including performance evaluations, litigation concerning the lawfulness of police actions, and perhaps compliance with state open records laws. See Brief for Petitioners 35–40 (citing Cal. Public Records Act, Cal. Govt. Code Ann. 6250 et seq. (West 2008)). These matters would all bear on the legitimacy of an employee's privacy expectation.

The Court must proceed with care when considering the whole concept of privacy expectations in communications made on electronic equipment owned by a government employer. The judiciary risks error by elaborating too fully on the Fourth Amendment implications of emerging technology before its role in society has become clear. [I]n *Katz v. United States,* 389 U.S. 347, 353, 88 S. Ct. 507, 19 L. Ed. 2d 576 (1967)[,] the Court relied on its own knowledge and experience to conclude that there is a reasonable expectation of privacy in a telephone booth. It is not so clear that courts at present are on so sure a ground. Prudence counsels caution before the facts in the instant case are used to establish far-reaching premises that define the existence, and extent, of privacy expectations enjoyed by employees when using employer-provided communication devices.

Rapid changes in the dynamics of communication and information transmission are evident not just in the technology itself but in what society accepts as proper behavior. * * *

Even if the Court were certain that the *O'Connor* plurality's approach were the right one, the Court would have difficulty predicting how employees' privacy expectations will be shaped by those changes or the degree to which society will be prepared to recognize those expectations as reasonable. Cell phone and text message communications are so pervasive that some persons may consider them to be essential means or necessary instruments for self-expression, even self-identification. That might strengthen the case for an expectation of privacy. On the other hand, the ubiquity of those devices has made them generally affordable, so one could counter that employees who need cell phones or similar devices for personal matters can purchase and pay for their own. And employer policies concerning communications will of course shape the reasonable expectations of their employees, especially to the extent that such policies are clearly communicated.

A broad holding concerning employees' privacy expectations vis-a-vis employer-provided technological equipment might have implications for future cases that cannot be predicted. It is preferable to dispose of this case on narrower grounds. For present purposes we assume several propositions arguendo: First, Quon had a reasonable expectation of privacy in the text messages sent on the pager provided to him by the City; second, petitioners' review of the transcript constituted a search within the meaning of the Fourth Amendment; and third, the principles applicable to a government employer's search of an employee's physical office apply with at least the same force when the employer intrudes on the employee's privacy in the electronic sphere. * * *

NOTES AND QUESTIONS

Test Your Understanding of the Material

1. Recall that the City had a policy through which it "reserve[d] the right to monitor and log all network activity including e-mail and Internet use, with or without notice." It also warned users that they "should have no expectation of privacy or confidentiality when using these resources." What did the City do to undermine that policy? If this policy had been consistently maintained, would the police officers still have had a valid invasion of privacy claim under the Fourth Amendment?

2. Review Employment Restatement Section § 7.01–7.03. Had *Quon* been a private sector employee, would he have had a cognizable common law claim for invasion of privacy?

NOTE: REGULATING BACKGROUND CHECKS

Fair Crediting Report Act of 1970

Under the Fair Credit Reporting Act of 1970 (FCRA), 15 U.S.C. §§ 1681*l*–1681t, employers must obtain consent from the employee or applicant before "the collection of any information" for the purpose of requesting a "consumer report" or an "investigative consumer report." Before taking adverse action based on a consumer report, the employer also must provide the employee with a copy of the report and written explanation of the employee's rights under the FCRA. Id. § 1681b(b)(1)–(3).

Consumer reports have traditionally consisted of credit reports and criminal background checks. Investigative consumer reports have traditionally consisted of reference checks. However, the statutory definitions could encompass a broader array of employer inquiries:

- A "consumer report" is defined as "any written, oral, or other communication of any information by a consumer reporting agency bearing on a consumer's credit worthiness, credit standing, credit capacity, character, general reputation, personal characteristics, or mode of living." 15 U.S.C. § 1681a(d)

- "Investigative consumer reports" refers to "a consumer report or portion thereof in which information on a consumer's character, general reputation, personal characteristics, or mode of living is obtained through personal interviews with neighbors, friends, or associates of the consumer reported on or with others with whom he is acquainted." 15 U.S.C. § 1681a(e)

- "Credit reporting agencies" refers to entities that regularly "assembl[e] or evaluat[e] consumer credit information or other information on consumers for the purpose of furnishing consumer reports to third parties" 15 U.S.C. § 1681a(f)

15 U.S.C. § 1681a(d)–(f). After the Federal Trade Commission took the position that third parties hired by employers to investigate harassment claims qualify as "credit reporting agencies," Congress amended FCRA to exclude employer investigations of misconduct. Fair and Accurate Credit Transactions Act of 2003, Pub. L. 108–159, 15 U.S.C. § 1681a(y).

State Laws

A number of states have enacted "ban the box" laws prohibiting employers from inquiring about an applicant's criminal history on the initial screening of employment applications. See Hawai'i Rev. Stat. § 378–2.5; Ill. St. Ch. 820 § 75//15; Mass. G.L.A. 151B § 4 9 1/2. These statutes permit employers to inquire about a criminal history later in the hiring process. Some laws restrict only public employers, and some require that adverse actions be job-related. Cal. Lab. Code § 432.9; Del Cod. Ann. Tit. 19, § 711(g)(2); Minn. Stat. Ann. § 364.03. Some states also prohibit employers from using credit checks unless the employee works in certain enumerated positions. Cal. Lab. Code § 1024.5; Col. Rev. Stat. Ann. § 8–2–126; 820 Ill. Comp. Stat. Ann. 70/10.

NOTE: RECORDS PRIVACY LAWS

Medical Records Privacy

The Health Insurance Portability and Accountability Act of 1996 (HIPAA), 15 U.S.C. §§ 1681*l*–1681t, restricts the disclosure of individually identifiable information by health plans and health care providers. 45 C.F.R. § 160.103. In general, these regulations require that (1) all "protected health information" (identifiable health information provided by health care providers and insurers relating to the physical or mental health of individuals or payments for provision of health care) be held confidential, unless a specific exemption applies to the information; (2) all entities subject to the regulations treat such information as confidential; and (3) patients are given certain protections against the misuse or disclosure of their health record. See generally Kathryn L. Bakich, Countdown to HIPAA Compliance: Understanding EDI, Privacy, and Security, 15 Benefits L.J. 45 (Summer 2002).

Employers and employment records are generally excluded from HIPAA unless the employer acts as a health care provider or health care insurer for its employees. HIPAA prohibits health care providers from releasing patient information directly to employers without an employee's written authorization or a subpoena. 45 C.F.R. § 164.512; 45 C.F.R. § 164.508. The regulations also contain an exception for employer-requested medical evaluations of work-related injuries. 45 C.F.R. § 164.512(b)(1)(v). Some state laws provide additional protections for health-related information. See Pettus v. Cole, 49 Cal.App.4th 402, 57 Cal.Rptr.2d 46 (1996) (employer requested psychiatric evaluation in connection with disability leave; psychiatrist violated California Medical Information Act by disclosing report to employer without employee's consent).

Government Records Privacy

Another important federal measure is the Privacy Act of 1974, 5 U.S.C. § 552(a), which grants certain rights and remedies to individuals who are the subject of records maintained by federal agencies, see, e.g., NASA v. Nelson, 562 U.S. 134 (2011); Dickson v. Office of Personnel Management, 828 F.2d 32 (D.C.Cir.1987) (agency's maintenance of record in violation of statutory fairness standard exposes agency to liability for damages); Brune v. Internal Revenue Service, 861 F.2d 1284 (D.C.Cir.1988) (agency not required by Privacy Act to interview employees under investigation for possible misconduct before questioning third parties about the incident).

Access to Personnel Records

Some state laws provide a right for private sector employees to have access to their personnel files and the right to correct inaccurate information in such files. See, e.g., Mich.Comp.Laws Ann. §§ 423.501–.512.

Data Breach Security Laws

Some state laws require employers to notify employees if a network security breach has resulted in the disclosure of personal data, such as social security numbers. See, e.g., Ca. Civ. Code § 1798.80 et seq.; N.Y. Gen. Bus. Law. § 899–aa.

D. PERSONAL AUTONOMY

NOVOSEL V. NATIONWIDE INSURANCE CO.

United States Court of Appeals, Third Circuit, 1983.
721 F.2d 894.

ADAMS, J.

Novosel was an employee of Nationwide from December 1966 until November 18, 1981. He had steadily advanced through the company's ranks in a career unmarred by reprimands or disciplinary action. At the time his employment was terminated, he was a district claims manager and one of three candidates for the position of division claims manager.

In late October 1981, a memorandum was circulated through Nationwide's offices soliciting the participation of all employees in an effort to lobby the Pennsylvania House of Representatives. Specifically, employees were instructed to clip, copy, and obtain signatures on coupons bearing the insignia of the Pennsylvania Committee for No-Fault Reform. This Committee was actively supporting the passage of House Bill 1285, the "No-Fault Reform Act," then before the state legislature.

The allegations of the complaint charge that the sole reason for Novosel's discharge was his refusal to participate in the lobbying effort and his privately stated opposition to the company's political stand. Novosel contends that the discharge for refusing to lobby the state legislature on the employer's behalf constituted the tort of wrongful discharge on the grounds it was willful, arbitrary, malicious and in bad faith, and that it was contrary to public policy.

* * *

Novosel's tort allegations raise two separate issues: first, whether a wrongful discharge claim is cognizable under Pennsylvania law; second, if such a claim can go forward under state law, by what standard is a court to determine whether the facts set forth in the complaint present a sufficient basis for a successful tort action.

* * *

Applying the logic of *Geary* [*v. United States Steel Corp.*, 456 Pa. 171, 319 A.2d 174 (1974),] we find that Pennsylvania law permits a cause of action for wrongful discharge where the employment termination abridges a significant and recognized public policy.

* * *

An extensive case law has developed concerning the protection of constitutional rights, particularly First Amendment rights, of government employees.

* * *

In striking down the use of patronage appointments for federal government employees, the [Supreme Court has] noted that one of its goals was to insure that "employees themselves are to be sufficiently free from improper influences." *CSC v. Letter Carriers*, 413 U.S. 548, 564, 93 S.Ct. 2880, 2890, 37 L.Ed.2d 796 (1973). It was not, however, simply the abuse of state authority over public employees that fueled the Court's concern over patronage political appointments; no less central is the fear that the political process would be irremediably distorted. If employers such as federal, state or municipal governments are allowed coercive control of the scope and direction of employee political activities, it is argued, their influence will be geometrically enhanced at the expense of both the individual rights of the employees and the ability of the lone political actor to be effectively heard.

We further note that the Pennsylvania Supreme Court has similarly voiced its concern over the threat posed by discharges to the constitutionally protected rights of employees. In *Sacks v. Commonwealth of Pennsylvania, Department of Public Welfare*, 502 Pa. 201, 465 A.2d 981 (Pa.Sup.Ct.1983), the court ordered a state employee reinstated following a discharge for public comments critical of his agency employer.

* * *

Although Novosel is not a government employee, the public employee cases do not confine themselves to the narrow question of state action. Rather, these cases suggest that an important public policy is in fact implicated wherever the power to hire and fire is utilized to dictate the terms of employee political activities. In dealing with public employees, the cause of action arises directly from the Constitution rather than from common law developments. The protection of important political freedoms, however, goes well beyond the question whether the threat comes from state or private bodies. The inquiry before us is whether the concern for the rights of political expression and association which animated the public employee cases is sufficient to state a public policy under Pennsylvania law. While there are no Pennsylvania cases squarely on this point, we believe that the clear direction of the opinions promulgated by the state's courts suggests that this question be answered in the affirmative. * * * The Pennsylvania Supreme Court's rulings in *Geary* and *Sacks* are thus interpreted to extend to a non-constitutional claim where a corporation conditions employment upon political subordination. * * *

RESTATEMENT OF EMPLOYMENT LAW § 7.08
American Law Institute (2015).

§ 7.08   Intrusions upon Employee Personal Autonomy

(a) Employees have protected interests in personal autonomy outside of the employment relationship. Such interests include:

(1) engaging in lawful conduct that occurs outside of the locations, hours, and responsibilities of employment and does not refer to or otherwise involve the employer or its business;

(2) adhering to political, moral, ethical, religious, or other personal beliefs or expressing such beliefs outside of the locations, hours, and responsibilities of employment in a manner that does not refer to or otherwise involve the employer or its business; or

(3) belonging to or participating in lawful associations when that membership or participation does not refer to or otherwise involve the employer or its business.

(b) Unless the employer and employee agree otherwise, an employer is subject to liability for intruding upon an employee's personal autonomy interests if the employer discharges the employee because the employee exercises a personal autonomy interest under § 7.08(a).

(c) The employer is not liable under § 7.08(b) if it can prove that it had a reasonable and good faith belief that the employee's exercise of an autonomy interest interfered with the employer's legitimate business interests, including its orderly operations and reputation in the marketplace.

NOTES AND QUESTIONS

Test Your Understanding of the Material

1. In *Novosel*, the Court uses First Amendment principles applicable to government employers as a source of public policy to support a common law claim against a private employer. Can you think of any reasons why public employers might be distinct from private employers as it relates to political speech? Did Nationwide have a legitimate interest in enlisting its employees to support its position on the no-fault legislation? Would Novosel have had a claim under § 7.08 of the Employment Restatement?

2. Consider how the holding of *Novosel* might be applied to advocacy organizations such as the ACLU and the National Right to Work League. Would *Novosel* undermine the *raison d'etre* of such organizations? Even where a corporation is principally concerned with the sale of goods or services, rather than advocacy of a cause, it has a First Amendment right to be a partisan on matters of concern to it (or at least to assert the public's First Amendment right to receive such partisan views). See First National Bank of Boston v. Bellotti, 435 U.S. 765, 98 S.Ct. 1407, 55 L.Ed.2d 707 (1978).

Related Issues

3. Novosel's *Questionable Viability*. The Third Circuit, sitting in diversity, may have gone beyond the position of the Pennsylvania courts in holding that the state's public policy incorporated federal constitutional norms. See Burkholder v. Hutchison, 403 Pa.Super. 498 (Pa. Super 1991) (declining to follow *Novosel*). Most courts have rejected a direct application of public-sector speech protections to the private sector. See, e.g., Dixon v. Coburg Dairy, Inc., 330 F.3d 250, 262 (4th Cir. 2003) (applying S.C. law) reversed on other grounds, 369 F.3d 811 (4th Cir. 2004) (en banc); Grinzi v. San Diego Hospice Corp., 120 Cal.App.4th 72, 14 Cal.Rptr.3d 893, 900 (2004); Edmondson v. Shearer Lumber Products, 139 Idaho 172, 75 P.3d 733, 738–739 (2003); Shovelin v. Central New Mexico Elec. Co-op., Inc., 115 N.M. 293, 850 P.2d 996, 1010 (1993); Tiernan v. Charleston Area Medical Center, Inc., 203 W.Va. 135,

506 S.E.2d 578, 588–591 (1998); Barr v. Kelso-Burnett Co., 106 Ill.2d 520, 478 N.E.2d 1354, 1356 (1985).

4. *Statutes Protecting Lawful Off-Duty Conduct.* A few states broadly protect employees for engaging in lawful off-duty conduct. See, e.g., Cal. Lab. Code § 98.6; New York Labor Law § 201–d; Miss. Code. Ann. § 79–1–9; Colo. Rev. Stat. § 24–34–402.5. See also Coates v. Dish Network, LLC, 303 P.3d 147 (Colo. Ct. App. Div. A 2013) (medical use of marijuana not protected by lawful off-duty conduct statute because such use remains prohibited under federal law).

5. *Statutes Protecting Political Activity.* Several states have passed statutes expressly barring employers from using the threat of discharge or loss of job rights as a means of coercing or influencing employees "to adopt or follow or refrain from adopting or following any particular course or line of political action or political activity." Cal. Labor Code § 1102. See Conn.Pub. Act 83–578 (barring discharge on grounds violative of the First Amendment); La. Rev.Stat. §§ 23:961–962; Nev.Rev.Stat. §§ 614.040.

6. *Use of "Public Policy" Cause of Action in the Absence of a "Political Activity" Law.* Can an attorney in a law firm be discharged for representing an unpopular client with which the attorney finds common political cause? Is the state-law "public policy" cause of action available in jurisdictions lacking express statutory protection for employee political activity? See Greenwood v. Taft, Stettinius & Hollister, 105 Ohio App.3d 295, 663 N.E.2d 1030 (Ohio App. 1995), lv. denied, 75 Ohio St.3d 1204, 662 N.E.2d 22 (1996) (denying attorney's claim that he was fired for representing gay-rights organization because alleged public policy against discrimination in employment for participation in the political process not of requisite "uniform statewide application").

7. *Statutory Extension of Constitutional Protections.* A Connecticut statute applies federal and state free-speech guarantees to the private sector, "provided such activity does not substantially or materially interfere with the employee's bona fide job performance or the working relationship between the employee and the employer * * * ." Conn. Gen. Stat. § 31–51q. See Cotto v. United Technologies Corp., 251 Conn. 1, 738 A.2d 623 (1999) (statute provides remedy for private-sector employees, but court rejects employee's challenge to requirement that American flags be placed at employee workstations because of absence of allegations that employee was directed to manifest his patriotism in a particular way or to affix the flag to his personal property).

8. *Off-Duty Smoking and Other Health-Related Conduct.* Some state laws protect smokers from adverse employment action for off-duty tobacco use. See, e.g., Conn. Gen. Stat. Ann. § 31–40s; W.Va. Code § 21–3–19. For an anti-discrimination analysis, see Jessica Roberts, Healthism and the Law of Employment Discrimination, 99 Iowa L. Rev. 571 (2014).

Absent statutory protections, employees who have suffered an adverse employment action for health-related conduct may not have no redress. See Rodrigues v. EG Systems, Inc. (D. Mass. 2009) (no protected privacy interest in employee's nicotine use); City of North Miami v. Kurtz, 653 So.2d 1025 (Fla.

1995) (smoker refused to sign pre-employment statement that he had not smoked in previous two years; rejecting state constitutional challenge). Courts have also permitted employers to refuse employment on the basis of body mass index, unless the employee qualifies as disabled under the ADA. Michigan also protects employees from discrimination on the basis of "weight." Mich. Comp. L. Ann. § 37.2102.

9. *Labor Law Protection for Internet Posts.* The National Labor Relations Act, 29 U.S.C. § 157 (NLRA) protects employees for engaging in "concerted activity"—two or more employees working together to improve wages or working conditions. The National Labor Relations Board, the agency administering the NLRA, has ruled that Facebook discussions among coworkers about staffing levels and job performance qualifies as concerted activity. NLRB Office of the General Counsel, Memo OM 11–74 (August 18, 2011).

10. *Anti-Fraternization Policies.* Some employers prohibit dating among co-workers. Do anti-fraternization polices violate state laws barring discrimination on account of "marital status," on the theory that married couples are more favorably treated under these policies? Do these laws protect only those who are married or do they also protect discrimination against the non-married? For a decision sustaining a challenge to an anti-fraternization policy alleging discrimination against the non-married, see Ross v. Stouffer Hotel Co., 72 Haw. 350, 816 P.2d 302 (1991). For Title VII challenges, see Sarsha v. Sears, Roebuck & Co., 3 F.3d 1035 (7th Cir.1993) (rejecting Title VII sex-discrimination challenge to no-dating policy applied to supervisory employees); Yuhas v. Libbey-Owens-Ford Co., 562 F.2d 496 (7th Cir.1977) (finding employer's "no spouse" policy had disparate impact on women under Title VII, but was job related as rule to minimize perception of favoritism among coworkers). See generally Timothy D. Chandler, Rafael Gely, Jack Howard & Robin Cheramie, Spouses Need Not Apply: The Legality of Antinepotism and Non-Spouse Rules, 39 San Diego L. Rev. 31 (2002)

NOTE: PRIVATE-SECTOR EMPLOYEES WORKING UNDER A COLLECTIVE BARGAINING AGREEMENT

Union-represented private sector employees generally enjoy more protection of their privacy, as well as of their job security, than do their nonunionized counterparts. Unions can help protect employee privacy both by the negotiation of express contractual provisions and by encouraging arbitrators to find implied protections when construing labor agreements. The National Labor Relations Board (NLRB) has ruled that employers subject to the National Labor Relations Act of 1935 (NLRA), 29 U.S.C. §§ 151–169, have a duty to bargain with exclusive bargaining representatives before implementing a drug testing program for existing employees, see Johnson-Bateman Co., 295 N.L.R.B. No. 26 (1989), but need not bargain over the testing of applicants who are not yet part of the bargaining unit, see Minneapolis Star Tribune, 295 N.L.R.B. No. 63 (1989). The Supreme Court, however, has held that an employer subject to the Railway Labor Act could implement a drug testing program without bargaining when it had an "arguable" claim that it was authorized to initiate the program by the union's acceptance of its past practices during periodic examinations. This claim was to be resolved by the Act's grievance and arbitration process as a "minor dispute." See Consolidated Rail Corp. v. Railway Labor Executives' Ass'n, 491 U.S. 299, 109 S.Ct. 2477, 105 L.Ed.2d 250 (1989); see also Teamsters v. Southwest Airlines, Inc., 875 F.2d 1129 (5th Cir.1989) (arguable justification for drug program in management rights clause).

Even where unions have not negotiated explicit privacy-protective provisions, they have often been successful in persuading arbitrators to find in the labor agreement implied privacy guarantees. Such arbitrators have used as bases for such awards the same sources that have been invoked for construing the meaning of "just cause": past firm or industry practice, negotiating history, or perhaps general social standards of fairness that the parties can be assumed to have accepted. There is a division among arbitrators over the extent to which the "just cause" standard incorporates constitutional norms limiting unreasonable searches and discipline for off-premises conduct. The majority of arbitrators reject per se application of constitutional doctrine, but some nonetheless refer to the doctrine as a guide for gauging past practice or accepted principles defining the "common law of the shop." See generally Proceedings of the 23rd Annual Meeting of the National Academy of Arbitrators, Surveillance and the Labor Arbitration Process: Arbitration and the Expanding Role of Neutrals (G. Somers & B. Dennis, eds. 1970).

Arbitration cases treating employee drug testing are illustrative. Although these cases evidence a division of authority, they also indicate that even in the absence of any specific restrictions on employer authority, many arbitrators have questioned both the institution of drug tests and discipline resulting from such tests. Arbitrators have sometimes demanded individualized suspicion of impairment or on-the-premises drug use; they have sometimes imposed a higher standard of proof for discipline based on positive test results; and they have sometimes required, under progressive discipline principles, an opportunity for rehabilitation before discharge. See generally Denenberg & Denenberg, Drug Testing from the Arbitrator's Perspective, 11 Nova L.Rev. 377 (1987); Levin & Denenberg, How Arbitrators View Drug Abuse, 31 Arb.J. 97 (1976); Wynns, Arbitration Standards in Drug Discharge Cases, 34 Arb.J. 19 (1976). For arbitrator scrutiny of employer surveillance practices, see Edward Hertenstein, Electronic Monitoring in the Workplace: How Arbitrators Have Ruled, Dispute Resol. J. (Fall 1997), p. 36ff.

In framing its disclosure requirements, the NLRB is obligated to balance employee privacy interests. See Detroit Edison Co. v. NLRB, 440 U.S. 301, 99 S.Ct. 1123, 59 L.Ed.2d 333 (1979). In NLRB v. United States Postal Service, 660 F.3d 65 (1st Cir. 2011), the agency found that USPS violated the NLRA by refusing to turn over to the union the personal aptitude scores of 22 employees unless the union first obtained their consent. The First Circuit denied enforcement, finding that the employees had a sufficient confidentiality interest in their test scores to require the agency to balance that interest against the union's interest in obtaining the information.

NOTE: CONSTITUTIONAL PRIVACY PROTECTIONS FOR PUBLIC-SECTOR EMPLOYEES

1. *Fourth Amendment.* Public sector employees are protected from unreasonable searches by their government employers under the Fourth Amendment. Where an employee can establish a reasonable expectation of privacy in the area searched, courts will then assess whether the search was reasonable in inception and scope:

> * * * In sum, we conclude that the "special needs, beyond the normal need for law enforcement make the * * * probable-cause requirement impracticable," * * * , for legitimate work-related, noninvestigatory intrusions as well as investigations of work-related misconduct. A standard of reasonableness will neither unduly burden the efforts of government employers to ensure the efficient and proper operation of the workplace, nor authorize arbitrary intrusions upon the privacy of public employees. We hold, therefore, that public employer intrusions on the constitutionally protected privacy interests of government employees for noninvestigatory, work-related purposes, as well as for investigations of work-related misconduct, should be judged by the standard of reasonableness under all the circumstances. Under this reasonableness standard, both the inception and the scope of the intrusion must be reasonable.

> Ordinarily, a search of an employee's office by a supervisor will be "justified at its inception" when there are reasonable grounds for suspecting that the search will turn up evidence that the employee is guilty of work-related misconduct, or that the search is necessary for a noninvestigatory work-related purpose such as to retrieve a needed file.

O'Connor v. Ortega, 480 U.S. 709 (1987).

2. *Fifth Amendment Privilege Against Self-Incrimination.* Because blood or urine samples do not violate the Fifth Amendment in the criminal context, they are likely permissible under the Fifth Amendment in the employment context. See Schmerber v. California, 384 U.S. 757, 86 S.Ct. 1826, 16 L.Ed.2d 908 (1966). (Such tests are however, subject to Fourth Amendment scrutiny. See Skinner v. Railway Labor Executives' Ass'n, 489 U.S. 602 (1989)). The self-incrimination clause may nevertheless restrict more traditional employer investigations absent disallowance of use of any compelled employee statements in subsequent prosecution. See Gardner v. Broderick, 392 U.S. 273, 88 S.Ct. 1913, 20 L.Ed.2d 1082 (1968) (reinstating police officer terminated for refusing to sign immunity waiver in grand jury proceeding). See also NASA v. Nelson, 562 U.S. 134 (2011) (questions in background investigation about illegal drug use permissible where applicant informed would not be used in subsequent criminal proceedings).

3. *Due Process Right to Informational Privacy*. In National Aeronautics and Space Administration v. Nelson, 562 U.S. 134, 131 S.Ct. 746, 178 L.Ed.2d 667 (2011), the Court addressed the issue of government background checks in light of a constitutional privacy "interest in avoiding disclosure of personal matters" recognized in Whalen v. Roe, 429 U.S. 589, 599–600, 97 S.Ct. 869, 51 L.Ed.2d 64 (1977); and Nixon v. Administrator of General Services, 433 U.S. 425, 457, 97 S.Ct. 2777, 53 L.Ed.2d 867 (1977). In *Nelson*, federal contract employees at a Government laboratory, claimed unsuccessfully that two parts of a standard employment background investigation violated their rights under *Whalen* and *Nixon*. The Court, per Justice Alito, writing for himself and five other Justices, assumed *arguendo* that the Constitution protects a privacy right of the sort mentioned in *Whalen* and *Nixon*. However, "the challenged portions of the Government's background check do not violate this right in the present case. The Government's interests as employer and proprietor in managing its internal operations, combined with the protections against public dissemination provided by the Privacy Act of 1974, 5 U.S.C. § 552a, satisfy any 'interest in avoiding disclosure' that may 'arguably ha[ve] its roots in the Constitution.' *Whalen*, supra, at 599, 605, 97 S.Ct. 869, 51 L.Ed.2d 64."

4. *Due Process Right to Associational Privacy*. Public sector employees have challenged anti-fraternization policies on the basis of associational privacy. While courts recognize an associational privacy interest, they have applied rational basis scrutiny to such policies. Shawgo v. Spradlin, 701 F.2d 470 (5th Cir.1983) (police anti-fraternization policy survived rational basis scrutiny in associational privacy claim); also Montgomery v. Carr, 101 F.3d 1117 (6th Cir. 1996) (upholding school district's anti-fraternization policy under rational basis scrutiny). Compare City of Sherman v. Henry, 39 Tex. Sup. J. 920, 928 S.W.2d 464 (1996) (rejecting constitutional privacy claim where police officer's promotion was denied for affair with coworker's spouse, noting "adultery is not a fundamental right").

5. *First Amendment*. Questions unjustifiably probing into beliefs or associations are vulnerable to First Amendment challenges. See, e.g., Shelton v. Tucker, 364 U.S. 479, 81 S.Ct. 247, 5 L.Ed.2d 231 (1960); NAACP v. Alabama ex rel. Patterson, 357 U.S. 449, 78 S.Ct. 1163, 2 L.Ed.2d 1488 (1958). First Amendment rights of government employees are the subject of Chapter 13.

CHAPTER 17

EMPLOYEE DUTIES

■ ■ ■

Introduction

The chapter explores the extent to which employees both during and after their employment are under a common law obligation not to divulge confidential information obtained from their employer; and whether agreements may restrict the freedom of departing employees to compete in the same business and/or to use information these employees acquired in their prior positions. The issues treated here have taken on greater saliency in recent decades as "knowledge" workers have become a growing segment of the U.S. workforce and employees change jobs with greater frequency.

A. COMMON LAW DUTY OF LOYALTY

RESTATEMENT OF EMPLOYMENT LAW § 8.01
American Law Institute (2015).

§ 8.01. Employee Duty of Loyalty

(a) Employees in a position of trust and confidence with their employer owe a fiduciary duty of loyalty to the employer in matters related to their employment. Other employees who come into possession of the employer's trade secrets owe a limited fiduciary duty of loyalty with regard to those trade secrets. In addition, employees may, depending on the nature of the employment position, owe an implied contractual duty of loyalty to the employer in matters related to their employment.

(b) Employees breach their duty of loyalty to the employer by

    (1) disclosing or using the employer's trade secrets (as defined in § 8.02) for any purpose adverse to the employer's interest, including after termination of the employment relationship (§ 8.03);

    (2) competing with the employer while employed by the employer (§ 8.04); or

    (3) misappropriating the employer's property, whether tangible or intangible, or otherwise engaging in self-

dealing through the use of the employee's position with the employer.

(c) The employee's duty of loyalty must be interpreted in a manner consistent with the employee's rights and responsibilities as set forth in Chapter 5 and under employment and other law, as well as with any right or privilege provided by law to cooperate with regulatory authorities.

NOTES AND QUESTIONS

1.   Where does the "duty of loyalty" come from? Is it an implied term of every employment contract? Are employers under a reciprocal duty to their employees?

2.   Why are only employees in a position of trust and confidence subject to fiduciary duties? What are examples of such positions? Under § 8.01(a), when are employees not working in a position subject to a duty of loyalty? See generally Deborah A. DeMott, Relationships of Trust and Confidence in the Workplace, 100 Cornell L. Rev. 1255 (2015).

3.   Does the Employment Restatement suggest there are only three categories of conduct that implicate the employee's duty of loyalty?

4.   What conduct is being shielded by § 8.01(c)?

1.   TRADE SECRETS

RESTATEMENT OF EMPLOYMENT LAW §§ 8.02–8.03
American Law Institute (2015).

§ 8.02.   Definition of Employer's Trade Secret

An employer's information is a trade secret under this Chapter if

(a) it derives independent economic value from being kept secret,

(b) the employer has taken reasonable measures to keep it secret, and

(c) the information is not

   (1) generally known to the public or in the employer's industry;

   (2) readily obtainable by others through proper means; or

   (3) acquired by employees through their general experience, knowledge, training, or skills during the ordinary course of their employment.

§ 8.03. Disclosure or Use by Employee or Former Employee of Employer's Trade Secrets

(a) An employee or former employee breaches the duty of loyalty to the employer if, without the employer's consent, the employee discloses to a third party or uses for the employee's own benefit or a third party's benefit the employer's trade secrets, as that term is defined in § 8.02.

(b) The duty stated in subsection (a) is not breached if the employee acts under a legal duty, legal protection, or other legal permission in making the disclosure or use.

(c) The employee's obligation not to disclose or use the employer's trade secrets lasts as long as the information remains a trade secret under § 8.02, and continues beyond termination of the employment relationship regardless of the reason for termination.

AMP INC. v. FLEISCHHACKER
U.S. Court of Appeals for the Seventh Circuit, 1987.
823 F.2d 1199.

CUMMINGS, J.

Plaintiff appeals the district court's entry of final judgment in favor of the defendants after a bench trial. We affirm.

The plaintiff, AMP Incorporated, brought this action against a former employee, James Fleischhacker, and one of its competitors, Molex, alleging unfair competition and misappropriation of trade secrets. AMP is the world's leading producer of electrical and electronic connection devices. It is by far the largest company in the connector industry, with over 21,000 employees and 1983 reported sales of over one-and-one-half billion dollars and net income of about $163 million. AMP's Components & Assemblies Division, headquartered in Winston-Salem, North Carolina, is one of its major divisions, generating in excess of $100 million in gross sales per year.

Molex is a principal competitor of AMP's Components & Assemblies Division and has its principal place of business in Lisle, Illinois. Molex's annual sales are in excess of $250 million, with foreign sales accounting for over half of that total. A significant portion of Molex's total sales is attributable to products that compete directly with products manufactured by AMP's Components & Assemblies Division.

The present controversy involves the 1984 hiring by Molex of defendant James Fleischhacker, formerly the Division Manager of AMP's Components & Assemblies Division, to fill the position of Director of Marketing for Molex's Commercial Products Division. Mr. Fleischhacker, who holds a Bachelor of Science degree from the University of Minnesota and a Master's degree from the Massachusetts Institute of Technology, joined AMP in 1973. He rapidly advanced through the corporation and in 1982 was named Manager of the Components & Assemblies Division, the position he held until he resigned in 1984. As Division Manager, Mr. Fleischhacker supervised approximately 1200 people who were responsible for the manufacture and sale of 10,000 different component parts. His duties as Division Manager included reviewing and approving business programs, interfacing with group management, implementing strategic policies and plans, and developing personnel. * * *

In 1982 Molex decided to create a new position, Director of Marketing, in its Commercial Products Division. An executive search firm directed Molex to Mr. Fleischhacker, whom Molex found to be a desirable and highly qualified candidate for the position as a result of his background, education, skill, and ability, including demonstrated product management capabilities, and especially because of his knowledge of the connector industry. Molex made a written offer of employment to Mr. Fleischhacker at the end of 1983, which he accepted in February 1984.

AMP has alleged that Molex's hiring of Mr. Fleischhacker is part of a larger pattern of conduct by Molex involving the misappropriation and threatened misappropriation of AMP's trade secrets and other confidential information, and the solicitation and hiring of AMP personnel. Given the nature of the competition between Molex and AMP, the nature of the respective positions held by Mr. Fleischhacker at AMP and Molex, and an alleged propensity on the part of Molex to misappropriate AMP's internal information without regard to its proprietary nature, AMP maintains that it is inevitable that Mr. Fleischhacker and other AMP personnel hired by Molex will use and disclose AMP trade secrets and confidential information for the benefit and unjust enrichment of Molex. * * *

[T]he initial question to be resolved is whether Mr. Fleischhacker was bound by a valid and enforceable restrictive covenant or was merely restricted by common law principles. The record indicates that he was not bound by a restrictive covenant not to compete. He did, however, sign a confidentiality agreement when he first became employed at AMP whereby he agreed inter alia:

> (3) To keep confidential during and subsequent to the period of said employment, except for those whom his authorized activities for the Company require should be informed, all information relating to the Company's business, its research or engineering activities, its manufacturing processes or trade secrets, its sources of supply or lists of customers and its plans or contemplated actions.

* * * The language of this confidentiality agreement purports to prohibit Mr. Fleischhacker from disclosing to any non-AMP personnel any information relating to AMP and its operations forever. The Illinois courts

have held unenforceable nearly identical provisions in confidentiality agreements because (1) they contain no limitation on the duration of the nondisclosure provision, instead restricting disclosure "during and subsequent to the period of said employment," and (2) they contain no geographical limitation or other kind of limit on the parties to whom the employee is prohibited from disclosing information. See *Cincinnati Tool Steel Co. v. Breed*, 136 Ill. App. 3d [267,] 275–276, 482 N.E.2d [170,] 175 [(2d Dist. 1985)]; *Disher v. Fulgoni*, 124 Ill. App. 3d 257, 262, 464 N.E.2d 639, 643, 79 Ill. Dec. 735 (1st Dist. 1984). Confidentiality agreements without such limitations constitute, in the view of the Illinois courts, unreasonable restraints on trade which unduly restrict the free flow of information necessary for business competition. * * *

Because Mr. Fleischhacker is not subject to any enforceable contractual restrictions, AMP was first required to establish the existence of genuine trade secrets in order for injunctive relief to be warranted. The Illinois Supreme Court has defined a trade secret as "a plan or process, tool, mechanism, compound, or informational data utilized by a person in his business operations and known only to him and such limited other persons to whom it may be necessary to confide it." *ILG Industries, Inc. v. Scott*, 49 Ill. 2d 88, 92, 273 N.E.2d 393, 395 (1971). It is generally recognized in Illinois that at the termination of employment, an employee may not take with him confidential, particularized plans or processes developed by his employer and disclosed to him while the employer-employee relationship existed, which are unknown to others in the industry and which give the employer an advantage over his competitors. On the other hand, an employee is free to take with him general skills and knowledge acquired during his tenure with his former employer. * * *

The district court initially found that AMP had failed to establish any protectable trade secrets with respect to the products manufactured by its Components & Assemblies Division. The court found that the electronic components produced were low technology commodity products which could be easily reproduced, and that much of the AMP product information possessed by Mr. Fleischhacker was already known to virtually all of AMP's competitors and easily available from widely circulated public sources. AMP does not contest this finding on appeal, asserting that it never contended that its connectors themselves constituted trade secrets. * * * Rather AMP contends that it has protectible trade secrets in a host of confidential information to which Mr. Fleischhacker had access during the course of his employment at AMP. This information, it alleges, includes: business and strategic planning information for the Components & Assemblies Division; new product development information; manufacturing information, including equipment, processes, cost and capacity information; financial information, including product-line profit-margin, sales, and budget information; and marketing and customer information.

AMP has consistently failed throughout this litigation to identify any particularized trade secrets actually at risk. Prior to trial, AMP submitted six single-spaced, typewritten pages listing by general item and category hundreds of pieces of AMP internal information. Other courts have warned plaintiffs of the risks they run by failing to identify specific trade secrets and instead producing long lists of general areas of information which contain unidentified trade secrets. See, e.g., *Litton Systems, Inc. v. Sundstrand Corp.*, 750 F.2d 952, 954, 956–957, 224 U.S.P.Q. (BNA) 252 (1984). * * *

Our examination of Illinois law reveals that the district court erred as a matter of law when it held that the general confidential information identified by AMP constituted protectible business secrets. As explained above, where the parties have entered into a restrictive covenant not to compete, the scope of protection afforded a former employer is quite broad and may extend to the type of generalized confidential business information to which AMP points. * * * Absent such a covenant, however, the plaintiff must demonstrate the existence of a genuine trade secret to obtain injunctive relief. As Judge Shadur noted in *Fleming Sales Co. v. Bailey*, 611 F. Supp. 507, 511 (N.D.Ill.1985), the "right to impose contractual restraints does not render the same knowledge 'trade secrets' in the absence of such restraints."

In marked contrast to those cases involving the enforceability of a restrictive covenant, the Illinois courts have not extended protection under the common law of trade secrets to the kind of generalized confidential business information on which AMP relies. In *Cincinnati Tool Steel Co. v. Breed*, 136 Ill. App. 3d 267, 482 N.E.2d 170, 90 Ill. Dec. 463, the plaintiff alleged that a former office manager/sales manager had misappropriated confidential pricing information, including cost, special discounts and supply information. The court refused to find that the plaintiff had a protectible interest in this information warranting injunctive relief. The defendant former manager had not taken any documents or other material with her when she left the plaintiff's employ, and the court concluded that the fact that the defendant might be able to recollect pricing information that could potentially be used to the plaintiff's detriment while later working for one of plaintiff's competitors was simply too conjectural to establish a prima facie showing of a protectible interest. Similarly, in *Smith Oil Corp. v. Viking Chemical Co.*, 127 Ill. App. 3d 423, 468 N.E.2d 797, 82 Ill. Dec. 250, the plaintiff alleged that former employees had misappropriated customer lists, customer orders, pricing information, cost information, sample formulas, product formulas, customer correspondence and other special customer information when they left to work for a competitor. Other than the exact formulas for the plaintiff's products, the court held that the information which the plaintiff wanted protected fell into the category of "general skills and knowledge" which an employee is free to take with him when his employment is terminated. * * *

These cases are controlling here. The district court credited the testimony of Mr. Fleischhacker that after he tendered his resignation he hurriedly packed his personal papers and belongings under the surveillance of an AMP employee and did not deliberately take with him anything of a confidential nature. AMP has offered no proof to the contrary. See *Smith Oil Corp.*, 127 Ill. App. 3d at 431, 468 N.E.2d at 802–803 (injunctive relief requires that plaintiff produce evidence that former employee actually took or possessed trade secret information)[.] * * * The record is similarly devoid of any evidence that Mr. Fleischhacker ever systematically recorded, copied, compiled, or even purposefully memorized any of AMP's confidential business information while he was still employed at AMP for use in his new position at Molex. * * *

This is not a case where the plaintiff can point to any tangible work product, such as blueprints, designs, plans, processes, or other technical specifications, at risk of misappropriation. * * * Nor is this a case, like many cited by AMP, involving a former employee who held a technical or engineering position and was responsible for distinct areas of technology and research. Mr. Fleischhacker was a high-level managerial executive who had broad supervisory responsibility for 1200 employees and over 10,000 different products at AMP. AMP now requests that we restrain him from in any way making use of or relying on his independent recollections of generalized business and technical information to which he had access while employed at AMP. Illinois law simply does not authorize such relief.

* * *

* * * [T]he practical effect of any grant of injunctive relief in favor of AMP would be to prohibit Mr. Fleischhacker from working in the connector industry. In its brief AMP disingenuously claims that the injunctive relief requested would not deny Mr. Fleischhacker his choice of employer, i.e., Molex, but would only remove him from the conflicting position he now holds. Molex, however, obviously hired Mr. Fleischhacker as a result of his expertise, skill, and experience as a Director of Marketing in the connector industry. It is unlikely that Mr. Fleischhacker would be of much use to Molex in a position wholly unrelated to the duties he performed at AMP. The same would undoubtedly be true of any other company in the connector industry.

Our holding by no means leaves an employer helpless against a former employee using the skills and knowledge he acquired during the course of employment to obtain an undue competitive advantage. An employer is always free to protect its interests through a reasonable, restrictive covenant not to compete.

NOTES AND QUESTIONS

Test Your Understanding of the Material

1.   *AMP* was decided before Illinois's adoption of the Uniform Trade Secrets Act (UTSA) in 1988. Forty-eight states have enacted the UTSA in one form or another since its promulgation in 1979; two states have not (Massachusetts and New York). Massachusetts has its own trade secrets law that is not based on the UTSA. See Mass. Ann. Laws ch. 93, §§ 42–42A. New York has developed decisional law based in part on § 757 of the Restatement (First) of Torts. See 2 Melvin F. Jager, Trade Secrets Law (1985).

2.   Did Fleischhacker breach a duty of loyalty to AMP, as formulated in Employment Restatement § 8.01?

3.   Consider the difficulty that AMP had in establishing the existence of any trade secrets (albeit under a common law definition). The Employment Restatement, quoted above, adopts the definition of "trade secret" articulated in the UTSA. (See Statutory Supplement.) Would AMP have had an easier time under the Employment Restatement?

4.   What role should the absence of an enforceable no-compete covenant, see pp. 806–817, play in the analysis? Given the nature of the information AMP was concerned about, is a reasonable restriction on competition a more direct approach than protecting that information as a trade secret?

5.   Some commentators have suggested that trade-secret protection should not extend to "research methods, marketing strategies, advertising campaigns, business plans, payroll and profit data, and pricing schemes" because such protection interferes with employee mobility. Orly Lobel, Talent Wants to Be Free: Why We Should Learn to Love Leaks, Raids and Free Riding 105–106 (2013). What legitimate interests would be undermined by this proposed regime? Are the limits on protection in § 8.02 of the Employment Restatement sufficient to protect legitimate employee interests? Which additional limits would you suggest? What steps would employers take to protect sharing or other dissemination of the items information listed by Professor Lobel if trade secret information were withheld?

Related Issues

6.   *Defend Trade Secrets Act of 2016.* The Defend Trade Secrets Act of 2016, Pub. L. 114–153 (May 11, 2016) creates a private civil cause of action for trade secret misappropriation related to a product or service in interstate or foreign commerce. It draws its definition of "trade secret" from the Economic Espionage Act, codified at 18 U.S.C. § 1839. Equitable relief and damages are available. The statute of limitation is set at three years from the date of discovery of the misappropriation. A trade secret owner may apply for and a court may grant a seizure order to prevent dissemination of the trade secret if the court makes specific findings, including that an immediate and irreparable injury will occur if seizure is not ordered. Any party harmed by the order may move to dissolve or modify the order and may also seek relief against the applicant of the seizure order for wrongful or excessive seizure. The statute

also provides that an employee is immune from liability under the Act for confidential disclosure of trade secrets to a government official or to an attorney for the purpose of investigating a suspected violation or for such disclosure in a complaint or other litigation-related filing made under seal.

7.   *Preclusion of Common Law Claims by the Uniform Trade Secrets Act.* The model UTSA, by its terms, does not preempt contract claims. UTSA § 7(b), excerpted in statutory supplement ("This Act does not affect contractual remedies, whether or not based upon misappropriation of a trade secret.") Thus, the UTSA would not disturb the aspect of the employee's duty of loyalty that bars use or disclosure of employer confidential information. Employment Restatement § 8.01(b)(1). However, most state versions of the UTSA contain some preemption of tort claims. See UTSA § 7(a) ("this [Act] displaces conflicting tort, restitutionary, and other law of this State providing civil remedies for misappropriation of a trade secret"). See Charles Tait Graves & Elizabeth Tippett, UTSA Preemption and the Public Domain: How Courts Have Overlooked Patent Preemption of State Law Claims Alleging Employee Wrongdoing, 65 Rutgers L. Rev. 1 (2012).

In the next case, an employer seeks an injunction against a former executive employee who has gone to work for its principal competitor on the grounds that the new employment will lead to "inevitable disclosure" of the prior employer's confidential information.

RESTATEMENT OF EMPLOYMENT LAW § 8.05
American Law Institute (2015).

§ 8.05.   Competition by Former Employee with Former Employer

A former employee may compete with, or work for a competitor of, the former employer, including by soliciting customers or recruiting employees, unless

(a)   the former employee is bound by an agreement not to compete (or not to solicit or recruit) enforceable under §§ 8.06 or 8.07; or

(b)   in doing so the former employee discloses, uses, or by words or conduct threatens to disclose or use, specifically identifiable trade secrets of the former employer in violation of § 8.03.

PEPSICO, INC. V. REDMOND

U.S. Court of Appeals for the Seventh Circuit, 1995.
54 F.3d 1262.

FLAUM, J.

* * * William Redmond, Jr. worked for PepsiCo in its PepsiCola North America division ("PCNA") from 1984 to 1994. Redmond became the General Manager of the Northern California Business Unit in June, 1993, and was promoted one year later to General Manager of the business unit covering all of California, a unit having annual revenues of more than 500 million dollars and representing twenty percent of PCNA's profit for all of the United States.

Redmond's relatively high-level position at PCNA gave him access to inside information and trade secrets. Redmond, like other PepsiCo management employees, had signed a confidentiality agreement with PepsiCo. That agreement stated in relevant part that he

> would not disclose at any time, to anyone other than officers or employees of [PepsiCo], or make use of, confidential information relating to the business of [PepsiCo] * * * obtained while in the employ of [PepsiCo], which shall not be generally known or available to the public or recognized as standard practices.

Donald Uzzi, who had left PepsiCo in the beginning of 1994 to become the head of Quaker's Gatorade division, began courting Redmond for Quaker in May, 1994. Redmond met in Chicago with Quaker officers in August, 1994, and on October 20, 1994, Quaker, through Uzzi, offered Redmond the position of Vice President—On Premise Sales for Gatorade. Redmond did not then accept the offer but continued to negotiate for more money. Throughout this time, Redmond kept his dealings with Quaker secret from his employers at PCNA.

On November 8, 1994, Uzzi extended Redmond a written offer for the position of Vice President—Field Operations for Gatorade and Redmond accepted. Later that same day, Redmond called William Bensyl, the Senior Vice President of Human Resources for PCNA, and told him that he had an offer from Quaker to become the Chief Operating Officer of the combined Gatorade and Snapple company but had not yet accepted it. Redmond also asked whether he should, in light of the offer, carry out his plans to make calls upon certain PCNA customers. Bensyl told Redmond to make the visits.

Redmond also misstated his situation to a number of his PCNA colleagues, including Craig Weatherup, PCNA's President and Chief Executive Officer, and Brenda Barnes, PCNA's Chief Operating Officer and Redmond's immediate superior. As with Bensyl, Redmond told them that he had been offered the position of Chief Operating Officer at Gatorade and that he was leaning "60/40" in favor of accepting the new position.

On November 10, 1994, Redmond met with Barnes and told her that he had decided to accept the Quaker offer and was resigning from PCNA. Barnes immediately took Redmond to Bensyl, who told Redmond that PepsiCo was considering legal action against him.

True to its word, PepsiCo filed this diversity suit on November 16, 1994, seeking a temporary restraining order to enjoin Redmond from assuming his duties at Quaker and to prevent him from disclosing trade secrets or confidential information to his new employer. * * *

From November 23, 1994, to December 1, 1994, the district court conducted a preliminary injunction hearing on the same matter. At the hearing, PepsiCo offered evidence of a number of trade secrets and confidential information it desired protected and to which Redmond was privy. First, it identified PCNA's "Strategic Plan," an annually revised document that contains PCNA's plans to compete, its financial goals, and its strategies for manufacturing, production, marketing, packaging, and distribution for the coming three years. Strategic Plans are developed by Weatherup and his staff with input from PCNA's general managers, including Redmond, and are considered highly confidential. The Strategic Plan derives much of its value from the fact that it is secret and competitors cannot anticipate PCNA's next moves. PCNA managers received the most recent Strategic Plan at a meeting in July, 1994, a meeting Redmond attended. PCNA also presented information at the meeting regarding its plans for Lipton ready-to-drink teas and for All Sport for 1995 and beyond, including new flavors and package sizes.

Second, PepsiCo pointed to PCNA's Annual Operating Plan ("AOP") as a trade secret. The AOP is a national plan for a given year and guides PCNA's financial goals, marketing plans, promotional event calendars, growth expectations, and operational changes in that year. The AOP, which is implemented by PCNA unit General Managers, including Redmond, contains specific information regarding all PCNA initiatives for the forthcoming year. The AOP bears a label that reads "Private and Confidential—Do Not Reproduce" and is considered highly confidential by PCNA managers.

In particular, the AOP contains important and sensitive information about "pricing architecture"—how PCNA prices its products in the marketplace. Pricing architecture covers both a national pricing approach and specific price points for given areas. Pricing architecture also encompasses PCNA's objectives for All Sport and its new age drinks with reference to trade channels, package sizes and other characteristics of both the products and the customers at which the products are aimed. Additionally, PCNA's pricing architecture outlines PCNA's customer development agreements. These agreements between PCNA and retailers provide for the retailer's participation in certain merchandising activities for PCNA products. As with other information contained in the AOP, pricing architecture is highly confidential and would be extremely valuable to a competitor. Knowing PCNA's pricing architecture would allow a competitor to anticipate PCNA's pricing moves and underbid PCNA strategically whenever and wherever the competitor so desired. PepsiCo introduced evidence that Redmond had detailed knowledge of PCNA's pricing architecture and that he was aware of and had been involved in preparing PCNA's customer development agreements with PCNA's California and California-based national customers. Indeed, PepsiCo showed that Redmond, as the General Manager for California, would have been responsible for implementing the pricing architecture guidelines for his business unit.

PepsiCo also showed that Redmond had intimate knowledge of PCNA "attack plans" for specific markets. Pursuant to these plans, PCNA dedicates extra funds to supporting its brands against other brands in selected markets. To use a hypothetical example, PCNA might budget an additional $500,000 to spend in Chicago at a particular time to help All Sport close its market gap with Gatorade. Testimony and documents demonstrated Redmond's awareness of these plans and his participation in drafting some of them.

Finally, PepsiCo offered evidence of PCNA trade secrets regarding innovations in its selling and delivery systems. Under this plan, PCNA is testing a new delivery system that could give PCNA an advantage over its competitors in negotiations with retailers over shelf space and merchandising. Redmond has knowledge of this secret because PCNA, which has invested over a million dollars in developing the system during the past two years, is testing the pilot program in California.

Having shown Redmond's intimate knowledge of PCNA's plans for 1995, PepsiCo argued that Redmond would inevitably disclose that information to Quaker in his new position, at which he would have substantial input as to Gatorade and Snapple pricing, costs, margins, distribution systems, products, packaging and marketing, and could give Quaker an unfair advantage in its upcoming skirmishes with PepsiCo. Redmond and Quaker countered that Redmond's primary initial duties at Quaker as Vice President—Field Operations would be to integrate Gatorade and Snapple distribution and then to manage that distribution as well as the promotion, marketing and sales of these products. Redmond asserted that the integration would be conducted according to a pre-existing plan and that his special knowledge of PCNA strategies would be irrelevant. This irrelevance would derive not only from the fact that Redmond would be implementing pre-existing plans but also from the fact that PCNA and Quaker distribute their products in entirely different ways: PCNA's distribution system is vertically integrated (i.e., PCNA owns the system) and delivers its product directly to retailers, while Quaker ships its product to wholesalers and customer warehouses and relies on independent distributors. The defendants also pointed out that Redmond had signed a confidentiality agreement with Quaker preventing him from disclosing "any confidential information belonging to others," as well as the Quaker Code of Ethics, which prohibits employees from engaging in "illegal or improper acts to acquire a competitor's trade secrets." Redmond additionally promised at the hearing that should he be faced with a situation at Quaker that might involve the use or disclosure of PCNA information, he would seek advice from Quaker's in-house counsel and would refrain from making the decision. * * *

On December 15, 1994, the district court issued an order enjoining Redmond from assuming his position at Quaker through May, 1995, and permanently from using or disclosing any PCNA trade secrets or confidential information. The court entered its findings of fact and conclusions of law on January 26, 1995, nunc pro tunc December 15, 1994. The court, which completely adopted PepsiCo's position, found that Redmond's new job posed a clear threat of misappropriation of trade secrets and confidential information that could be enjoined under Illinois statutory and common law. The court also emphasized Redmond's lack of forthrightness both in his activities before accepting his job with Quaker and in his testimony as factors leading the court to believe the threat of misappropriation was real. This appeal followed.

Both parties agree that the primary issue on appeal is whether the district court correctly concluded that PepsiCo had a reasonable likelihood of success on its various claims for trade secret misappropriation and breach of a confidentiality agreement. * * *

The Illinois Trade Secrets Act ("ITSA"), which governs the trade secret issues in this case, provides that a court may enjoin the "actual or threatened misappropriation" of a trade secret. 765 ILCS 1065/3(a) * * * . A party seeking an injunction must therefore prove both the existence of a trade secret and the misappropriation. The defendants' appeal focuses solely on misappropriation; although the defendants only reluctantly refer to PepsiCo's marketing and distribution plans as trade secrets, they do not seriously contest that this information falls under the ITSA.

The question of threatened or inevitable misappropriation in this case lies at the heart of a basic tension in trade secret law. Trade secret law serves to protect "standards of commercial morality" and "encourage[ ] invention and innovation" while maintaining "the public interest in having free and open competition in the manufacture and sale of unpatented goods." 2 [Melvin F.] Jager, [Trade Secrets Law] § IL.03, at IL-12 [Clark Boardman rev. ed. 1994)]. Yet that same law should not prevent workers from pursuing their livelihoods when they leave their current positions. * * *

This tension is particularly exacerbated when a plaintiff sues to prevent not the actual misappropriation of trade secrets but the mere threat that it will occur. While the ITSA plainly permits a court to enjoin the threat of misappropriation of trade secrets, there is little law in Illinois or in this circuit establishing what constitutes threatened or inevitable misappropriation. * * *

In *AMP* [*Inc. v. Fleischhacker*, 823 F.2d 1199 (7th Cir.1987), see p. 787 supra] we affirmed the denial of a preliminary injunction on the grounds that the plaintiff AMP had failed to show either the existence of any trade secrets or the likelihood that defendant Fleischhacker, a former AMP employee, would compromise those secrets or any other confidential business information. * * *

It should be noted that *AMP*, which we decided in 1987, predates the ITSA, which took effect in 1988. The ITSA abolishes any common law remedies or authority contrary to its own terms. 765 ILCS 1065/8. The ITSA does not, however, represent a major deviation from the Illinois common law of unfair trade practices. * * * The ITSA mostly codifies rather than modifies the common law doctrine that preceded it. Thus, we believe that *AMP* continues to reflect the proper standard under Illinois's current statutory scheme.[7]

The ITSA * * * and *AMP* lead to the same conclusion: a plaintiff may prove a claim of trade secret misappropriation by demonstrating that defendant's new employment will inevitably lead him to rely on the plaintiff's trade secrets. * * * Questions remain, however, as to what constitutes inevitable misappropriation and whether PepsiCo's submissions * * * meet that standard. We hold that they do.

PepsiCo presented substantial evidence at the preliminary injunction hearing that Redmond possessed extensive and intimate knowledge about PCNA's strategic goals for 1995 in sports drinks and new age drinks. The district court concluded on the basis of that presentation that unless Redmond possessed an uncanny ability to compartmentalize information, he would necessarily be making decisions about Gatorade and Snapple by relying on his knowledge of PCNA trade secrets. It is not the "general skills and knowledge acquired during his tenure with" PepsiCo that PepsiCo seeks to keep from falling into Quaker's hands, but rather "the particularized plans or processes developed by [PCNA] and disclosed to him while the employer-employee relationship existed, which are unknown to others in the industry and which give the employer an advantage over his competitors." *AMP*, 823 F.2d at 1202. The [plaintiff in] *AMP* * * * could do nothing more than assert that skilled employees were taking their skills elsewhere; PepsiCo has done much more.

---

[7] The ITSA has overruled *AMP's* implications regarding the durability of an agreement to protect trade secrets. *AMP* followed a line of Illinois cases questioning the validity of agreements to keep trade secrets confidential where those agreements did not have durational or geographical limits. *AMP,* 823 F.2d at 1202. The ITSA, in reversing those cases, provides that "a contractual or other duty to maintain secrecy or limit use of a trade secret shall not be deemed to be void or unenforceable solely for lack of durational or geographical limitation on the duty." 765 ILCS 1065/8(b)(1). * * *

Admittedly, PepsiCo has not brought a traditional trade secret case, in which a former employee has knowledge of a special manufacturing process or customer list and can give a competitor an unfair advantage by transferring the technology or customers to that competitor. * * * PepsiCo has not contended that Quaker has stolen the All Sport formula or its list of distributors. Rather PepsiCo has asserted that Redmond cannot help but rely on PCNA trade secrets as he help plots Gatorade and Snapple's new course, and that these secrets will enable Quaker to achieve a substantial advantage by knowing exactly how PCNA will price, distribute, and market its sports drinks and new age drinks and being able to respond strategically. * * *

Quaker and Redmond assert that they have not and do not intend to use whatever confidential information Redmond has by virtue of his former employment. They point out that Redmond has already signed an agreement with Quaker not to disclose any trade secrets or confidential information gleaned from his earlier employment. They also note with regard to distribution systems that even if Quaker wanted to steal information about PCNA's distribution plans, they would be completely useless in attempting to integrate the Gatorade and Snapple beverage lines.

The defendants' arguments fall somewhat short of the mark. Again, the danger of misappropriation in the present case is not that Quaker threatens to use PCNA's secrets to create distribution systems or coopt PCNA's advertising and marketing ideas. Rather, PepsiCo believes that Quaker, unfairly armed with knowledge of PCNA's plans, will be able to anticipate its distribution, packaging, pricing, and marketing moves. Redmond and Quaker even concede that Redmond might be faced with a decision that could be influenced by certain confidential information that he obtained while at PepsiCo. In other words, PepsiCo finds itself in the position of a coach, one of whose players has left, playbook in hand, to join the opposing team before the big game. Quaker and Redmond's protestations that their distribution systems and plans are entirely different from PCNA's are thus not really responsive.

The district court also concluded from the evidence that Uzzi's actions in hiring Redmond and Redmond's actions in pursuing and accepting his new job demonstrated a lack of candor on their part and proof of their willingness to misuse PCNA trade secrets, findings Quaker and Redmond vigorously challenge. * * *

The facts of the case do not ineluctably dictate the district court's conclusion. Redmond's ambiguous behavior toward his PepsiCo superiors might have been nothing more than an attempt to gain leverage in employment negotiations. The discrepancy between Redmond's and Uzzi's comprehension of what Redmond's job would entail may well have been a simple misunderstanding. * * * The court also pointed out that Quaker, through Uzzi, seemed to express an unnatural interest in hiring PCNA employees: all three of the people interviewed for the position Redmond ultimately accepted worked at PCNA. Uzzi may well have focused on recruiting PCNA employees because he knew they were good and not because of their confidential knowledge. Nonetheless, the district court, after listening to the witnesses, determined otherwise. That conclusion was not an abuse of discretion. * * *

Thus, when we couple the demonstrated inevitability that Redmond would rely on PCNA trade secrets in his new job at Quaker with the district court's reluctance to believe that Redmond would refrain from disclosing these secrets in his new position (or that Quaker would ensure Redmond did not disclose them), we conclude that the district court correctly decided that PepsiCo demonstrated a likelihood of success on its statutory claim of trade secret misappropriation.

* * *

For the same reasons we concluded that the district court did not abuse its discretion in granting the preliminary injunction on the issue of trade secret misappropriation, we also agree with its decision on the likelihood of Redmond's breach of his confidentiality agreement should he begin working at Quaker. Because Redmond's position at Quaker would initially cause him to disclose trade secrets, it would necessarily force him to breach his agreement not to disclose confidential information acquired while employed in PCNA. Cf. *George S. May Int'l*, 628 N.E.2d at 653 ("An employer's trade secrets are considered a protectable interest for a restrictive covenant under Illinois law.").

Quaker and Redmond do not assert that the confidentiality agreement is invalid; such agreements are enforceable when supported by adequate consideration.

NOTES AND QUESTIONS

Pepsi's Motivation for the Lawsuit?

Professor Alan Hyde's later interview with Pepsi's outside counsel suggests that the protection of trade secrets was not the primary motivation for the lawsuit. Pepsi wanted to "send a message to Quaker" and "to their own employees. . . . They wanted to get Quaker to stop [targeting their employees] and to signal strongly to those employees that they could not expect to depart to a rival without litigation." Alan Hyde, The Story of PepsiCo., Inc. v. Redmond: How the Doctrine of Inevitable Disclosure of the Trade Secrets of Marketing Sports Beverages Was Brewed, in Employment Law Stories ch. 5 (Samuel Estreicher & Gillian Lester eds. 2007).

Test Your Understanding of the Material

1.   Was a protectable trade secret at risk in *Redmond*? In *AMP v. Fleischhacker*, the court faulted AMP for its "fail[ure] to list any particular pieces or type of information that warranted protection." Did PepsiCo in *Redmond* do a better job in that regard? If so, how? Consider also the reference to "specifically identifiable trade secrets" in § 8.05(b) of the Restatement of Employment Law.

2.   Review the excerpt from the Uniform Trade Secrets Act in the Statutory Supplement. Under UTSA § 1(2), was Redmond or Quaker guilty of actual or threatened "misappropriation" of PepsiCo's trade secrets? Were the conditions set out in Employment Restatement§ 8.05(b) met?

3.   What inference can be drawn from Redmond's misstatement of his future intentions at important corporate meetings? Consider Bimbo Bakeries USA Inc. v. Botticella, 613 F.3d 102, 118 (3d Cir.2010) (applying Pennsylvania law), where the court sustained a preliminary injunction on an "inevitable disclosure" rationale in part because of "evidence of Botticella's suspicious conduct during his final weeks at Bimbo":

> In the period between when Botticella accepted the Hostess offer on October 15, 2009, and when he ceased working for Bimbo on January 13, 2010, he continued to have all the access to Bimbo's confidential and proprietary information befitting a trusted senior executive. For instance, Botticella attended a meeting with Bimbo's present and other Bimbo officers in December 2009 at which the participants discussed confidential information regarding the company's strategic plan for California.

If you were representing an employee in Redmond's or Bimbo's situation who was planning to leave to work for a competitor, what advice would you give to avoid any misstatements of future intention or other conduct that may encourage a grant to grant an injunction?

4.   What effect should be given to PepsiCo's failure to procure an enforceable no-compete agreement from Redmond?

Related Issues

5.   *"Inevitable Disclosure"*. The theory of inevitable disclosure appeared in a New York decision as early as 1919 in Eastman Kodak Co. v. Powers Film Products, Inc., 189 A.D. 556, 179 N.Y.S. 325, 330 (4th Dept. 1919). However, the doctrine is in decline. Recent decisions invoking the doctrine as an independent basis for injunctive relief are rare. See Employment Restatement § 8.05, Comment b.

For a decision questioning the "inevitable disclosure" doctrine, see EarthWeb, Inc. v. Schlack, 71 F.Supp.2d 299 (S.D.N.Y.1999), vacated and remanded (to clarify basis for denying plaintiff's motion for preliminary injunctive relief), 205 F.3d 1322 (2d Cir.2000) (unpubl.). Schlack was responsible for overseeing the editorial content of the EarthWeb website, which licensed content from third parties. After less than a year with EarthWeb,

Schlack left to join ITworld.com, which generated its own editorial content. Schlack's agreement with EarthWeb included a broad confidentiality provision, and a narrow non-compete provision under which ITworld.com was not considered a competitor. The court refused to enjoin Schlack from working for ITworld.

6. *Enforceability of Confidentiality Provisions.* Contrary to the *AMP* ruling, the majority of states do not require a temporal limitation on confidentiality provisions. See M. Scott McDonald & Jacqueline C. Johnson, Unfair Competition and Intellectual Property Protection in Employment Law at 191 (2014). Does the Employment Restatement § 8.03(c) recognize such a limitation? The Illinois statute adopting the UTSA included a provision specifying that confidentiality agreements "shall not be deemed to be void or unenforceable solely for lack of durational or geographic limitation on the duty." 765 Ill. Comp. Stat. Ann. 1065/8. (The Uniform Act iself does not contain that particular provision.)

Likewise, many courts do not scrutinize the geographic scope of a confidentiality provision because a limited scope "would defeat the entire purpose of restricting disclosure, since confidentiality knows no temporal or geographic boundaries." Revere Transducers, Inc. v. Deere & Co., 595 N.W.2d 751 (Iowa 1999), quoting 2 Rudolf Callman, The Law of Unfair Competition, Trademarks & Monopolies § 14.04 (Supp. 1998).

From a practical standpoint, all confidential information has a temporal limitation—the point at which the information becomes commonly known within an industry or public knowledge.

PRACTITIONER'S PERSPECTIVE
Marina Tsatalis
Partner, Wilson Sonsini Goodrich & Rosati.

LOHR, J.

Employee mobility is the ER in the hospital of employment law. A client will call with an emergency: a key employee just resigned and is joining a competitor despite the employee's contract with the employer prohibiting such competition. Making the matter more urgent, the employee is steeped in the employer's trade secrets, and may even have downloaded pivotal company confidential information prior to resigning.

A call of this nature requires immediate action. The first step is making sure the employer has battened down the hatches with regard to its trade secrets. Has the employee been locked out of the company's server? Has the employee's email account been disabled? Has the employee's office been checked to make sure company materials are accounted for? Have the employee's company-issued electronic devices been collected? Another important step is guiding the employer through an exit interview with the departing employee, including preparing talking points and sometimes even attending the interview in person, to make sure we obtain all relevant information about the employee's activities and plans.

At the same time, our team will prepare the documents to file in court to obtain a temporary restraining order (TRO) to stop the employee from beginning his or her employment with the competing employer, and to force the return of our client's property. Time is of the essence. A TRO is emergency relief, and unless we get in to court quickly, we will undermine the emergent nature of our request. Equally important, however, is making sure we have collected the evidence required to convince the court that our client is likely to succeed on the merits—that the employee has an enforceable covenant not to compete, that the employee's anticipated activities with the new employer will violate its terms, and that the ensuing harm will be irreparable. This requires reviewing documents and interviewing witnesses who can help me to understand what the employee did for the prior employer and the significance and meaning of the non-public business information to which he or she had access, which often entails quickly coming up to speed on technology and business concepts so that I can convince the court that the new employer is indeed competitive and that my client's valuable trade secrets will be jeopardized if the employee is permitted to work there.

From the moment the call comes from the client, to the point of standing in the courtroom advocating for a TRO, our team is absorbed in an intense whirlwind of activity. The issues are all-encompassing for our clients as well, whose very businesses are sometimes riding on the successful prosecution of our claims and our ability to protect their trade secrets. These are some of the reasons why my practice is focused on this exciting area of employment law.

---

2. COMPETITION WITH A CURRENT OR FORMER EMPLOYER

Even without an express agreement, employees are under a common law duty not to compete against their employer. In the interest of facilitating the ability to pursue new employment, employees may engage in preparatory steps towards seeking new employment such as inquiring with prospective employers, and once they decide to leave, they may give notice of such departure to coworkers and clients of the employer. See, e.g., Maryland Metals, Inc. v. Metzner, 282 Md. 31, 382 A.2d 564, 568–69 (1978) ("A departing employee may not solicit his employer's customers but he may advise the customers of his intention to leave and set up a competing business."). This common law duty does not apply to former employees.

RESTATEMENT OF EMPLOYMENT LAW § 8.04
American Law Institute (2015).

§ 8.04. Competition by Employee with Current Employer

(a) Except as otherwise provided in subsections (b) and (c), an employee breaches the duty of loyalty to the employer if, without the employer's express or implied consent, the employee, while employed by the employer, works for a competitor or otherwise competes with the employer.

(b) Competition with the employer under subsection (a) includes solicitation of the employer's customers to divert their business to a competitor and recruitment of other employees to work for a competitor, but does not include reasonable preparation by an employee or group of employees to compete with the employer.

(c) Absent an agreement with their first employer to the contrary, employees, other than employees in a position of trust and confidence with their first employer under § 8.01(a), may work for a competitor of the first employer as long as the work is not done during time committed to the first employer, does not involve the use or disclosure of the first employer's trade secrets, and does not injure the employer to any greater extent than would any other individual working for the competitor.

JET COURIER SERVICE, INC. V. MULEI
Supreme Court of Colorado, 1989.
771 P.2d 486.

Jet [Courier Service, Inc. ("Jet")] is an air courier company engaged principally in supplying a specialized transportation service to customer banks. Jet provides air and incidental ground courier service to carry canceled checks between banks to facilitate rapid processing of those checks through the banking system. * * * [*Eds.* Jet was based in Ohio, and hired Anthony Mulei to open and manage its Denver office.]

In the course of seeking other employment opportunities and while still employed by Jet, Mulei began to investigate setting up another air courier company that would compete with Jet in the air courier business. In January 1983, Mulei spoke with John Towner, a Kansas air charter operator who was in the business of supplying certain air transportation services, about going into business together. In February 1983, Mulei met with Towner and two Jet employees to discuss setting up this new business and obtaining customers. [*Eds.* Mulei and Towner named the new business American Check Transport, Inc. ("ACT").]

On February 27, 1983, Mulei, while still employed by Jet and on Jet business in Phoenix, talked to two of Jet's customer banks to inform them he would be leaving Jet in mid-March and to tell them he "would try to give them the same service." He engaged in similar discussions with two bank customers of Jet in Dallas while still employed by Jet. Early in March 1983, Mulei met with representatives of three of Jet's Denver customers, First Interstate Bank of Denver, Central Bank of Denver, and United Bank of Denver, and discussed the new air courier company that Mulei and Towner were forming. Mulei told the United Bank of Denver float manager that "if they wished to give us [ACT] the business," then ACT would be able to serve them without any break in the service, and that ACT would be able to take over their business and fully satisfy their air courier service needs. Mulei further told United Bank of Denver that "by minimizing expenses, I would be in a position, sometime later, to reduce cost." Mulei had similar conversations with representatives of First Interstate Bank of Denver.

Prior to the termination of Mulei's employment by Jet on March 10, 1983, Mulei met with nine pilots who were flying for Jet to discuss his formation of ACT. Before his termination, Mulei also met with Jet's Denver office staff and with its ground couriers to discuss potential future employment with ACT. Mulei offered Jet's office staff better working conditions, including health and dental insurance and part ownership of ACT, if they were to join ACT. Mulei did not inform [Jet management] of any of these activities with respect to Jet customers, contractors or employees.

ACT was incorporated on February 28, 1983. Mulei was elected president at the first shareholders meeting. [Jet] fired Mulei on March 10, 1983, when [the CEO] first learned of Mulei's organization of a competing enterprise. On that same day Mulei caused ACT to become operational and compete with Jet. Five Denver banks that had been Jet customers became ACT customers at that time. Additionally, when Mulei was fired, three of the four other employees in Jet's Denver office also left Jet and joined ACT. All of Jet's ground carriers in Denver immediately left Jet and joined ACT. All nine of Jet's pilots in Denver either quit or were fired. Jet was able to maintain its Denver operations only through a rapid and massive transfer of resources, including chartered aircraft and ground couriers, from Jet's other offices. * * *

The court of appeals affirmed the trial court's holding that Mulei's pre-termination meetings with customers did not violate a duty of loyalty since ACT did not become operational and commence competing with Jet until after Mulei left Jet's employ. * * * This reasoning fails to accord adequate scope to the [employee's] duty of loyalty. . . . * * * While still employed by Jet, Mulei was subject to a duty of loyalty to act solely for the benefit of Jet in all matters connected with his employment. * * * [T]he key inquiry is whether Mulei's meetings amounted to solicitation, which would be a breach of his duty of loyalty. Generally under his privilege to make preparations to compete after the termination of his employment, an employee may advise current customers that he will be leaving his current employment. * * * However, any pre-termination solicitation of those customers for a new competing business violates an employee's duty of loyalty.

NOTES AND QUESTIONS

Test Your Understanding of the Material

1. *"Preparing to Compete"*. How does one draw the line between competition, which breaches the employee's duty of loyalty, and taking reasonable preparatory steps to compete, which does not? Can employees jointly agree to leave the employer's business and form a competitive firm? Can they do so without giving reasonable notice and an opportunity to adjust quickly? Again, the *Jet Courier Service* court states:

> It is normally permissible for employees of a firm, or for some of its partners, to agree among themselves, while still employed, that they will engage in a competition with the firm. * * * However, a court may find that it is a breach of duty for a number of the key officers or employees to agree to leave their employment simultaneously and without giving the employer an opportunity to hire and train replacements.

771 P.2d at 497. See Employment Restatement § 8.04, Comment c. Does this elevate form over substance? If employees have agreed to leave to join a competitor, why can't they do so at the same time? Is there an obligation to give notice to the prior employer? At what point is the harm to the employer from the employees' departure sufficient to enable the prior employer to establish a breach of the duty of loyalty and/or obtain an injunction against the departure? See id. § 9.08.

2. *Permissible "Moonlighting"?* Does the common law duty of loyalty bar nonsupervisory employees from working for competitors on their own time? What if the harm to the first employer is no different than the harm from any other individual working for the competitor? See Employment Restatement Section 8.04, Comment b.

3. *"Corporate Opportunities"*. Does the employee's common law duty of loyalty include an obligation not to use for the employee's own benefit corporate opportunities that the employee becomes aware of only because of his employment relationship? See id., Comment e.

B. RESTRICTIVE COVENANTS

All of the cases we have covered thus far involve an employer's ability to restrain a former employee's activities in the absence of a non-competition covenant. In some states, most notably California, covenants not to compete are unenforceable. See Cal. Bus. & Prof. Code § 16600 (non-competes unenforceable, except in connection with the sale of a business). See also Colo. C.R.S. 8–2–113 (non-competes only enforceable to recover education and training costs for certain employees). In others, state statutes define the contours of permissible non-competes. See Oregon Rev. State § 653.295; Fla. St. § 542.335. Most states enforce covenants not to compete as a matter of decisional law, along the lines of the Restatement provisions below.

RESTATEMENT OF EMPLOYMENT LAW §§ 8.06–8.08
American Law Institute (2015).

§ 8.06. Enforcement of Restrictive Covenant in Employment Agreement

Except as otherwise provided by other law or applicable professional rules, a covenant in an agreement between an employer and a former employee restricting the former employee's working activities is enforceable only if it is reasonably tailored in scope, geography, and time to further a protectable interest of the employer, as defined in§ 8.07, unless:

(a) the employer discharges the employee on a basis that makes enforcement of the covenant inequitable;

(b) the employer acted in bad faith in requiring or invoking the covenant;

(c) the employer materially breached the underlying employment agreement; or

(d) in the geographic region covered by the restriction a great public need for the special skills and services of the former employee outweighs any legitimate interest of the employer in enforcing the covenant.

§ 8.07. Protectable Interests for Restrictive Covenants

(a) A restrictive covenant is enforceable only if the employer can demonstrate that the covenant furthers a legitimate interest of the employer.

(b) An employer has a legitimate interest in protecting, by means of a reasonably tailored restrictive covenant with its employee, the employer's:

(1) trade secrets, as defined in § 8.02, and other protectable confidential information that does not meet the definition of trade secret,

(2) customer relationships,

    (3)   investment in the employee's reputation in the market, or

    (4)   purchase of a business owned by the employee.

§ 8.08.   Modification of Unreasonable Restrictive Covenant

A court may delete or modify provisions in an overbroad restrictive covenant in an employment agreement and then enforce the covenant as modified unless the agreement does not allow for modification or the employer lacked a reasonable and good-faith basis for believing the covenant was enforceable. Lack of a reasonable and good-faith basis for believing a covenant was enforceable may be manifested by its gross overbreadth alone, or by overbreadth coupled with other evidence that the employer sought to do more than protect its legitimate interests.

BDO SEIDMAN V. HIRSHBERG

Court of Appeals of New York, 1999.
93 N.Y.2d 382, 690 N.Y.S.2d 854, 712 N.E.2d 1220.

LEVINE, J.

BDO Seidman (BDO), a general partnership of certified public accountants, appeals from the affirmance of an order of the Supreme Court granting summary judgment dismissing its complaint against defendant, who was formerly employed as an accountant with the firm. The central issue before us is whether the "reimbursement clause" in an agreement between the parties, requiring defendant to compensate BDO for serving any client of the firm's Buffalo office within 18 months after the termination of his employment, is an invalid and unenforceable restrictive covenant. The courts below so held. * * *

BDO is a national accounting firm having 40 offices throughout the United States, including four in New York State. Defendant began employment in BDO's Buffalo office in 1984, when the accounting firm he had been working for was merged into BDO, its partners becoming BDO partners. In 1989, defendant was promoted to the position of manager, apparently a step immediately below attaining partner status. As a condition of receiving the promotion, defendant was required to sign a "Manager's Agreement," the provisions of which are at issue. In Paragraph "SIXTH" defendant expressly acknowledged that a fiduciary relationship existed between him and the firm by reason of his having received various disclosures which would give him an advantage in attracting BDO clients. Based upon that stated premise, defendant agreed that if, within 18 months following the termination of his employment, he served any former client of BDO's Buffalo office, he would compensate BDO "for the loss and damages suffered" in an amount equal to one and one half times the fees BDO had charged that client over the last fiscal year of the client's patronage. Defendant was to pay such amount in five annual installments.

Defendant resigned from BDO in October 1993. This action was commenced in January 1995. During pretrial discovery, BDO submitted a list of 100 former clients of its Buffalo office, allegedly lost to defendant, who were billed a total of $138,000 in the year defendant left the firm's practice.

Defendant denied serving some of the clients, averred that a substantial number of them were personal clients he had brought to the firm through his own outside contacts, and also claimed that with respect to some clients, he had not been the primary BDO representative servicing the account. * * *

Concededly, the Manager's Agreement defendant signed does not prevent him from competing for new clients, nor does it expressly bar him from serving BDO clients. Instead, it requires him to pay "for the loss and damages" sustained by BDO in losing any of its clients to defendant within 18 months after his departure, an amount equivalent to one and one half times the last annual billing for any such client who became the client of defendant.

Nonetheless, it is not seriously disputed that the agreement, in its purpose and effect, is a form of ancillary employee anti-competitive agreement that is not per se unlawful but will be carefully scrutinized by the courts. * * *

The modern, prevailing common law standard of reasonableness for employee agreements not to compete applies a three-pronged test. A restraint is reasonable only if it: (1) is no greater than is required for the protection of the legitimate interest of the employer, (2) does not impose undue hardship on the employee, and (3) is not injurious to the public (see, e.g., *Technical Aid Corp. v. Allen*, 134 N.H. 1, 8, 591 A.2d 262, 265–266 * * *; Restatement [Second] of Contracts § 188). A violation of any prong renders the covenant invalid.

New York has adopted this prevailing standard of reasonableness in determining the validity of employee agreements not to compete. "In this context a restrictive covenant will only be subject to specific enforcement to the extent that it is reasonable in time and area, necessary to protect the employer's legitimate interests, not harmful to the general public and not unreasonably burdensome to the employee" (*Reed, Roberts Assocs. v. Strauman*, 40 N.Y.2d 303, 307, 386 N.Y.S.2d 677, 353 N.E.2d 590).

In general, we have strictly applied the rule to limit enforcement of broad restraints on competition. Thus, in *Reed, Roberts Assocs.* (supra), we limited the cognizable employer interests under the first prong of the common law rule to the protection against misappropriation of the employer's trade secrets or of confidential customer lists, or protection from competition by a former employee whose services are unique or extraordinary (40 N.Y.2d at 308).

With agreements not to compete between professionals, however, we have given greater weight to the interests of the employer in restricting competition within a confined geographical area. * * * [However, t]his Court's rationale for giving wider latitude to covenants between members of a learned profession[1] because their services are unique or extraordinary does not realistically apply to the actual context of the anti-competitive agreement here. In the instant case, BDO is a national accounting firm seeking to enforce the agreement within a market consisting of the entirety of a major metropolitan area. Moreover, defendant's unchallenged averments indicate that his status in the firm was not based upon the uniqueness or extraordinary nature of the accounting services he generally performed on behalf of the firm, but in major part on his ability to attract a corporate clientele. Nor was there any proof that defendant possessed any unique or extraordinary ability as an accountant that would give him a competitive advantage over BDO. Moreover, the contexts of the agreements not to compete in *Karpinski* and *Gelder Medical Group* were entirely different. In each case, the former associate would have been in direct competition with the promisee-practitioner for referrals from a narrow group of primary health providers in a rural, geographical market for their medical or dental practice specialty.

Thus, our learned profession precedents do not obviate the need for independent scrutiny of the anti-competitive provisions of the Manager's Agreement under the tripartite common law standard. Close analysis of Paragraph SIXTH of the agreement under the first prong of the common law rule, to identify the legitimate interest of BDO and determine whether the covenant is no more restrictive than is necessary to protect that interest, leads us to conclude that the covenant as written is overbroad in some respects. BDO claims that the legitimate interest it is entitled to protect is its entire client base, which it asserts a modern, large accounting firm expends considerable time and money building and maintaining. However, the only justification for imposing an employee agreement not to compete is to forestall unfair competition (see, *Columbia Ribbon & Carbon Mfg. Co. v. A-1-A Corp.*, 42 N.Y.2d at 499). It seems self-evident that a former employee may be capable of fairly competing for an employer's clients by refraining from use of unfair means to compete. If the employee abstains from unfair means in competing for those clients, the employer's interest in preserving its client base against the competition of the former employee is no more legitimate and worthy of contractual protection than when it vies with unrelated competitors for those clients.

---

[1] Law firm partnership agreements represent an exception to the liberality with which we have previously treated restraints on competition in the learned professions. Our decisions invalidating anti-competitive clauses in such agreements were not based on application of the common law rule, but upon enforcement of the public policy reflected in DR 2–108(A) of the Code of Professional Responsibility (see, 22 NYCRR 1200.13). There is no counterpart to DR 2–108(A) in the rules regulating the ethical conduct of accountants. * * *

* * * Protection of customer relationships the employee acquired in the course of employment may indeed be a legitimate interest. [Where employees work closely with clients or customers over a long period of time,] the employee has been enabled to share in the goodwill of a client or customer which the employer's overall efforts and expenditures created. The employer has a legitimate interest in preventing former employees from exploiting or appropriating the goodwill of a client or customer, which had been created and maintained at the employer's expense, to the employer's competitive detriment.

It follows from the foregoing that BDO's legitimate interest here is protection against defendant's competitive use of client relationships which BDO enabled him to acquire through his performance of accounting services for the firm's clientele during the course of his employment. Extending the anti-competitive covenant to BDO's clients with whom a relationship with defendant did not develop through assignments to perform direct, substantive accounting services would, therefore, violate the first prong of the common law rule: it would constitute a restraint "greater than is needed to protect" these legitimate interests (Restatement [Second] of Contracts § 188[1][a]). * * *

To the extent, then, that paragraph SIXTH of the Manager's Agreement requires defendant to compensate BDO for lost patronage of clients with whom he never acquired a relationship through the direct provision of substantive accounting services during his employment, the covenant is invalid and unenforceable. By a parity of reasoning, it would be unreasonable to extend the covenant to personal clients of defendant who came to the firm solely to avail themselves of his services and only as a result of his own independent recruitment efforts, which BDO neither subsidized nor otherwise financially supported as part of a program of client development. Because the goodwill of those clients was not acquired through the expenditure of BDO's resources, the firm has no legitimate interest in preventing defendant from competing for their patronage. Indeed, enforcement of the restrictive covenant as to defendant's personal clients would permit BDO to appropriate goodwill created and maintained through defendant's efforts, essentially turning on its head the principal justification to uphold any employee agreement not to compete based on protection of customer or client relationships.

Except for the overbreadth in the foregoing two respects, the restrictions in paragraph SIXTH do not violate the tripartite common law test for reasonableness. The restraint on serving BDO clients is limited to 18 months, and to clients of BDO's Buffalo office. The time constraint appears to represent a reasonably brief interlude to enable the firm to replace the client relationship and goodwill defendant was permitted to acquire with some of its clients. Defendant is free to compete immediately for new business in any market and, if the overbroad provisions of the covenant are struck, to retain his personal clients and those clients of BDO's that he had not served to any significant extent while employed at the firm. He has averred that BDO's list of lost accounts contains a number of clients in both categories. Thus, there is scant evidence suggesting that the covenant, if cured of overbreadth, would work an undue hardship on defendant.

Moreover, given the likely broad array of accounting services available in the greater Buffalo area, and the limited remaining class of BDO clientele affected by the covenant, it cannot be said that the restraint, as narrowed, would seriously impinge on the availability of accounting services in the Buffalo area from which the public may draw, or cause any significant dislocation in the market or create a monopoly in accounting services in that locale. These factors militate against a conclusion that a reformed paragraph SIXTH would violate the third prong of the common law test, injury to the public interest. * * *

[Severance or Partial Enforcement]

We conclude that the Appellate Division erred in holding that the entire covenant must be invalidated, and in declining partially to enforce the covenant to the extent necessary to protect BDO's legitimate interest. * * *

Here, the undisputed facts and circumstances militate in favor of partial enforcement. The covenant was not imposed as a condition of defendant's initial employment, or even his continued employment, but in connection with promotion to a position of responsibility and trust just one step below admittance to the partnership. There is no evidence of coercion or that the Manager's Agreement was part of some general plan to forestall competition. Moreover, no proof was submitted that BDO imposed the covenant in bad faith, knowing full well that it was overbroad. Indeed, as already discussed, the existence of our "learned profession" precedents, and decisions in other States upholding the full terms of this type of agreement, support the contrary conclusion. Therefore, partial enforcement of Paragraph SIXTH is warranted.

The Appellate Division's fear that partial enforcement will require rewriting the parties' agreement is unfounded. No additional substantive terms are required. The time and geographical limitations on the covenant remain intact. The only change is to narrow the class of BDO clients to which the covenant applies. * * *

[Damages]

Since defendant does not dispute that at least some BDO clients to which the restrictive covenant validly applies were served by him during the contractual duration of the restraint, plaintiff is entitled to partial summary judgment on the issue of liability. Remittal is required in order to establish plaintiff's damages, including resolution of any contested issue as to which of BDO's former clients served by defendant the restrictive covenant validly covers.

As to those clients, the measure of plaintiff's damages will depend in the first instance on the validity of the clause in paragraph SIXTH of the Manager's Agreement requiring defendant to compensate BDO "for the loss and damages suffered" in an amount equal to one and one half times the fees charged each lost client over the last full year the client was served by the firm. This provision essentially represents a liquidated damages clause, as BDO conceded at nisi prius.

Liquidated damages provisions, under our precedents, are valid if the "damages flowing from a breach are difficult to ascertain [and under] a provision fixing damages in advance * * * the amount is a reasonable measure of the anticipated probable harm" (*City of Rye v. Public Serv. Mut. Ins. Co.*, 34 N.Y.2d 470, 473, 358 N.Y.S.2d 391, 315 N.E.2d 458). On the other hand, if "the amount fixed is plainly or grossly disproportionate to the probable loss, the provision calls for a penalty and will not be enforced" (*Truck Rent-A-Center, Inc. v. Puritan Farms 2nd, Inc.*, 41 N.Y.2d 420, 425, 393 N.Y.S.2d 365, 361 N.E.2d 1015).

The damages here are sufficiently difficult to ascertain to satisfy the first requirement of a valid liquidated damages provision. Because of the inability to project with any degree of certainty how long a given client would have remained with BDO if defendant had not made himself available as an alternative source of accounting services, BDO's actual lost profits from defendant's breach would be impossible to determine with any precision.

In our view, however, the averment regarding the basis of the liquidated damages formula by no means conclusively demonstrates the absence of gross disproportionality. * * * We note that other courts have remitted on the issue of the validity of these types of liquidated damages provisions in accountant employee anti-competitive agreements when they found the record insufficiently developed to establish that the amount fixed in the agreement was not so excessive to actual damages as to constitute a penalty * * * . The sparse proof on this issue here persuades us that we, similarly, should remit for further development of the record on the liquidated damages formula.

NOTES AND QUESTIONS

Test Your Understanding of the Material

1.   What aspect(s) of Seidman's non-compete clause was overbroad? What does the court mean when it uses the term "goodwill"?

2.   How might a court's willingness to modify an agreement alter the way a covenant is drafted? Consider Section 8.08 of the Employment Restatement's conditions on judicial modification of overbroad covenants. Do

they sufficiently curb incentives employers may have to insist on overbroad covenants?

3. Consider a number of possible justifications for restricting an employer's ability to impose post-termination no-compete covenants:

    a.   "Employers should not be able to insulate themselves from competition by precluding highly-skilled employees from working for their competitors."

    b.   "Employees should not be able to bind themselves in a way that hampers their ability to exit the firm and thereby tempt their employers to impose unreasonable terms during the employment relationship."

    c.   "Employees should not be able to bind themselves in a way that hampers their ability to exit the firm because employees will not be able properly to value the opportunity costs of such restraints, particularly at the stage when they are hired."

Which of these justifications for regulation do you find persuasive? Do these justifications provide support for a per se rule barring no-compete covenants, or for something more akin to New York's or the Employment Restatement's approach? Do these justifications retain any force where the previous employer continues the employee's salary during the no-compete period (what in the United Kingdom is called a "gardening leave")? Cf. Maltby v. Harlow Meyer Savage, Inc., 166 Misc.2d 481, 633 N.Y.S.2d 926 (N.Y.Sup.1995).

Related Issues

4. *Inquiry into Reasonable Scope of Constraint.* Even where a protectable interest is found, courts will still inquire whether the geographical and durational limits on the no-compete clause are reasonable within the applicable business context. For a holding that a one-year limitation can be unreasonable in the IT industry, see EarthWeb, Inc. v. Schlack, 71 F.Supp.2d 299 (S.D.N.Y.1999): "When measured against the IT industry in the internet environment, a one-year hiatus from the workforce is several generations, if not an eternity." 71 F.Supp.2d at 316.

5. *Consideration.* Presumably, consideration is not a problem when new employees are required to sign no-compete agreements as a condition of obtaining employment. Is separate consideration required to support no-compete agreements signed by incumbent employees? Some courts hold that continued at-will employment beyond the date of signing of the agreement provides sufficient consideration. See, e.g., Copeco, Inc. v. Caley, 91 Ohio App.3d 474, 632 N.E.2d 1299 (1992). Other courts require that employment continue for a "substantial" or "reasonable" time before a no-compete promise will be enforced—a kind of ex post theory of consideration. See, e.g., Zellner v. Conrad, 183 A.D.2d 250, 589 N.Y.S.2d 903 (2d Dept. 1992). Still others require separate consideration for incumbent employees, such as promise of continued employment, a raise, or a promotion. See Softchoice, Inc. v. Schmidt, 763

N.W.2d 660 (Minn. Ct. App. 2009) (applying Missouri law); Access Organics, Inc. v. Hernandez, 2008 MT 4, 175 P.3d 899 (Mont. 2008). Compare Employment Restatement § 8.06, Illus. 12 & Reporters' Notes.

6. *Involuntary Termination.* Under § 8.06(a)–(c) of the Employment Restatement, courts will not enforce even otherwise reasonable covenants where the employer materially breaches the underlying employment agreement or the circumstances indicate that enforcement would be inequitable. When the employer decides that the employee is no longer a valuable asset to the company, it can be difficult for the employer to later explain why it has a legitimate business interest in restraining the employee from working for others. See Insulation Corp. Of America v. Brobston, 667 A.3d 729 (Pa. Super. Ct. 1995).

7. *Wrongful Discharge for Refusing to Sign a No-Compete Agreement.* Can an incumbent employee lawfully be fired for refusing to sign a no-compete agreement in a jurisdiction that enforces "reasonable" agreements? Under § 5.02(d) of the Employment Restatement, the employer does not violate public policy when it requires employees, as a condition of employment, to sign an agreement that is judicially enforceable, even if the agreement involves a waiver of modifiable rights. Courts differ where the employee is discharged for refusing to sign an agreement that would be unenforceable. Compare, e.g., Tatge v. Chambers & Owen, Inc., 219 Wis.2d 99, 579 N. 2d 217, 224 (Wis.1998) (employees are protected from compliance with an unreasonable covenant "by rendering that covenant void and unenforceable. * * * The public policy is not to create a cause of action, but to void the covenant"), with D'sa v. Playhut, Inc., 85 Cal.App.4th 927, 102 Cal.Rptr.2d 495 (2000) (in view of state's prohibition of no-compete covenants, discharge for failure to sign a confidentiality agreement containing such a covenant states "public policy" cause of action, despite severability provisions).

8. *Choice of Law Issues.* AGI, a California corporation, and Hunter, a Maryland firm, are competitors providing computer consulting services for businesses that use human resources software. Pike, a Maryland resident, worked for Hunter for 16 months in Baltimore. Her employment agreement contained a one-year no-compete clause and a Maryland choice of law clause, both of which are lawful under Maryland law. AGI recruits Pike to work in California during the one-year period. Does California's statute prohibiting no-compete agreements apply? See The Application Group, Inc. v. The Hunter Group, 61 Cal.App.4th 881, 892, 72 Cal.Rptr.2d 73, 86 (1998) (holding it does):

> We are * * * convinced that California has a materially greater interest than does Maryland in the application of its law to the parties' dispute, and that California's interests would be more seriously impaired if its policy were subordinated to the policy of Maryland. Accordingly, the trial court did not err when it declined to enforce the contractual conflict of law provision in Hunter's employment agreements. To have done so would have been to allow an out-of-state employer/competitor to limit employment and business opportunities in California.

9. *"No-Solicitation" Agreements.* Should the law treat differently agreements that allow the employee to enter into a competitive business but do not allow raiding of employees or customers of the previous employer? The California courts, for example, have held that restrictions on client solicitations are enforceable despite the statutory ban on no-compete covenants. See Loral Corp. v. Moyes, 174 Cal.App.3d 268, 219 Cal.Rptr. 836 (1985). In Chernoff Diamond & Co. v. Fitzmaurice, 234 A.D.2d 200, 203, 651 N.Y.S.2d 504, 505-506 (1996), a two-year bar on solicitation of an insurance agency's clients was upheld but on an analysis that presumably also would have been used in evaluating a no-compete agreement:

> * * * [N]either the duration of the restriction, i.e., two years, nor its scope is unduly burdensome. The covenant does not prohibit defendant from pursuing his profession * * * or limit him geographically. Indeed, the only restriction imposed upon him is that he is not permitted to deal with [his previous employer's] clients. There is no reason to suppose that this limitation will prevent defendant * * * from operating a successful insurance agency.

> Although, within the context of this case, the restriction imposed is relatively limited in scope, we are mindful that even such a restriction on defendant's right to pursue his livelihood should not be enforced if it is not necessary to protect the employer's "legitimate interests". * * * In this regard, the issue is not only whether plaintiff's client list was confidential (which it apparently was, but only in part) but also whether defendant obtained, while in plaintiff's employ, invaluable and otherwise unobtainable information concerning the business practices and resulting insurance needs of these clients due to his position as their trusted professional advisor.

NOTE: FORFEITURE-FOR-COMPETITION CLAUSES

Some agreements may provide that employees who violate an otherwise reasonable restrictive covenant forfeit bonuses or other benefits. To the extent the forfeited benefits are vested pension benefits, such clauses may violate ERISA, see Clark v. Lauren Young Tire Ctr. Profit Sharing Trust, 816 F.2d 480 (9th Cir.1987); cf. *Nationwide v. Darden*, supra p. 11. To the extent the benefits are earned compensation, such clauses may violate state wage-payment laws, see supra p. 860.

One important question is whether such forfeiture-for-compensation provisions should receive the same level of judicial scrutiny as a non-compete clause. Like *Seidman*, some courts treat contracts providing for a penalty or forfeiture as indistinguishable from a no-compete clause. See e.g. Edwards v. Arthur Andersen, 44 Cal.4th 937 (2008); Food Fair Stores, Inc. v. Greeley, 264 Md. 105 (1972); Medtronic, Inc. v. Hedemark, Case No. A08–0987, 2009 WL 511760 (Minn. Ct. App. 2009). Others may engage in more lenient scrutiny, on the reasoning that a forfeiture clause restrains an employee's ability to earn a livelihood in a more limited way than does a blanket prohibition on competition. See Fraser v. Nationwide Mutual Ins. Co., 334 F.Supp.2d 755

(2004) (applying Pennsylvania law). New Jersey scrutinizes forfeiture clauses as a form of liquidated damages clause. Borteck v. Riker, Danzig, Scherer, Hypand and Perretti LLP, 179 N.J. 246 (2004). See also Burzee v. Park Ave Ins. Agency, Inc., 946 So. 2d 1200 (Fla. 5th D.C.A. 2007).

New York takes an unusual approach to forfeiture clauses in compensation and benefit-related agreements, known as the "employee choice" doctrine. If the employee quits voluntarily, New York courts will generally enforce the forfeiture clause without regard to its reasonableness. See Post v. Merrill Lynch, Pierce, Fenner & Smith, 48 N.Y.2d 84, 421 N.Y.S.2d 847, 397 N.E.2d 358 (1979). However, if the employee was terminated without cause, the clause is evaluated for the presence of a protectable interest and reasonableness of scope and duration. See e.g., Wrigg v. Junkermier, Clark, Campanella, 362 Mont. 496, 505, 265 P.3d 646 (2011) ("an employer normally lacks a legitimate business interest in a covenant when it chooses to terminate the employment relationship.")

C. EMPLOYEE INVENTIONS

RESTATEMENT OF EMPLOYMENT LAW § 8.09
American Law Institute (2015).

§ 8.09. Rights of Employees to Inventions

(a) Unless otherwise agreed between the employer and the employee (§ 8.11), when an employee has not been hired or assigned to do inventive work, the employee has the right to patent an invention the employee creates, even if the invention is created during working hours or with the use of the employer's resources.

(b) Unless otherwise agreed between the employer and the employee (§ 8.11), an employee hired or assigned to do inventive work has presumptively assigned to the employer any patents on inventions relating to the work for which the employee was hired (compare § 8.11).

NOTES AND QUESTIONS

1. *Different Default Rules in Copyright Law vs. Patent Law.* Under U.S. copyright law, the employer is considered to be the author of a "work made for hire" when it is prepared by an employee in the scope of his employment. The default rule under U.S. patent law, however, is different: absent agreement, the invention belongs to the inventing party, whether the inventor be an employee or an independent contractor, unless the employee was hired to invent. "Unless the employee is hired to perform inventive work, the law assumes the employee is the rightful owner of any inventions the employee creates. An employee hired to perform inventive work, by contrast, is typically bound by an agreement to assign the patent rights to any resulting invention

to the employer." Employment Restatement § 8.09. Comment a. See Bruce H. Little & Craig W. Trepanier, Untangling the Intellectual Property Rights of Employers, Employees, Inventors, and Independent Contractors, 22 Employee Rels. 49, 56 (No. 4, Spring 1997); see also Samuel Estreicher & Kristina Yost, University IP: The University as Coordinator of the Team Production Process, 91 Indiana L. J. 4 (2016).

2. *Statutory Restrictions on Assignment of Inventions.* Employers often require their employees to assign their inventions to the firm. Some states restrict such assignments. For example, Cal. Labor Code § 2870 (1999) provides in relevant part:

> ### § 2870   Application of provision that employee shall assign or offer to assign rights to invention to employer
>
> (a)   Any provision in an employment agreement which provides that an employee shall assign, or offer to assign, any of his or her rights to an invention to his or her employer shall not apply to an invention that the employee developed entirely on his or her own time without using the employer's equipment, supplies, facilities, or trade secret information except for those inventions that either:
>
>> (1)   Relate at the time of conception or reduction to practice of the invention to the employer's business, or actual or demonstrably anticipated research or development of the employer; or
>>
>> (2)   Result from any work performed by the employee for the employer.

3. *"Holdover" Agreements.* Some employers also require employees to sign so-called "holdover" agreements, which purport to reach inventions conceived after termination of employment "if conceived as a result of and attributable to work done during such employment and [which] relate[ ] to a method, substance, machine, article of manufacture or improvements therein within the scope of business" of the employer. Ingersoll-Rand Co. v. Ciavatta, 110 N.J. 609, 615, 641, 542 A.2d 879 (1988). Recognizing the value of a company-sponsored culture of "creative brainstorming" and the legitimacy in some circumstances of providing protection to employers even in the absence of trade secrets or other confidential information, the *Ingersoll-Rand* court declined to adopt a rule of per se invalidity but barred enforcement of the putative assignment in that case as a matter of state common law:

> The roofs and walls of underground mines]. * * * Ingersoll-Rand did not assign Ciavatta to a "think tank" division in which he would likely have encountered on a daily basis the ideas of fellow Ingersoll-Rand personnel regarding how the split set stabilizer could be improved or how a more desirable alternative stabilizer might be designed.
>
> More importantly, the information needed to invent the split set stabilizer is not that unique type of information that we would deem protectable even under our expanded definition of a protectable

interest. All of the specifications and capabilities of the Ingersoll-Rand split set stabilizer were widely publicized throughout industry and trade publications.

110 N.J. at 609. See Catherine L. Fisk, The Story of *Ingersoll-Rand v. Ciavatta:* Employee Inventors in Corporate Research & Development: Reconciling Innovation with Entrepreneurship, Ch. 6 in Employment Law Stories (Samuel Estreicher & Gillian Lester eds. 2007).

PART 5

REGULATION OF COMPENSATION AND BENEFITS

■ ■ ■

Until this point the book has treated two principal approaches of the American legal regime toward the regulation of employer decisions; first, the prohibition of decisions having particular "bad" reasons or unjustified "bad" effects; and second, the enforcement of contractual commitments, both express and implied. In general, U.S. employment law allows the parties to the relationship to write their own contracts, unlike the tradition in at least continental Europe of a significant government role in the process.

In this part, we look at two areas where the federal government has established minimum substantive standards that set a floor for private bargaining. Chapter 18 explores the federal requirement that employers pay specified minimum wages and overtime premiums to certain employees for work in excess of 40 hours in a workweek. Chapter 19 covers federal statutes regulating employee benefits and leaves.

CHAPTER 18

COMPENSATION

■ ■ ■

Introduction

Compensation is, of course, a fundamental term of the employment contract. It is a subject determined by the agreement of the parties. This chapter focuses on statutory .systems that set the legal framework for bargaining over wages and salary.

A. WAGE AND HOUR LAWS

The principal federal law regulating compensation and work hours is the Fair Labor Standards Act of 1938 (FLSA). The purpose of the FLSA, in President Franklin D. Roosevelt's words, was to give "all our able-bodied working men and women a fair day's pay for a fair day's work. * * * A self-supporting and self-respecting democracy can plead no justification for the existence of child labor, no economic reason for chiseling workers' wages or stretching workers' hours." Franklin D. Roosevelt, Message to Congress on Establishing Minimum Wages and Maximum Hours, May 24, 1937, quoted in Jonathan Grossman, Fair Labor Standards Act of 1938: Maximum Struggle for a Minimum Wage, 101 Monthly Lab. Rev. 22 (1978).

The FLSA contains three core substantive obligations: (1) payment of a prescribed minimum wage (§ 206(a)); (2) payment of an overtime premium (1 1/2 times the employee's basic rate of pay) for work in excess of 40 hours in any workweek (§ 207(a)); and (3) prohibition of employment of children under the age of 12, with special exceptions for certain types of agricultural work and child actors (§ 212). Other provisions impose on employers (4) recordkeeping (§ 211) and (5) non-retaliation (§ 215(a)(3)) duties.

The Act is enforced by the Wage and Hour Division of the Department of Labor (DOL). DOL has authority to subpoena records and bring lawsuits for injunctive relief and for back-pay relief on behalf of present or former employees. Employees also may sue on their own, without any requirement to file a complaint with DOL, and can do so both individually and on behalf of others "similarly situated" (who consent to be represented in this manner).

PRACTITIONER'S PERSPECTIVE

Molly Biklen

Supervising Attorney, U.S. Department of Labor, Office of the Solicitor.

As a trial attorney in the New York Regional Office of the U.S. Department of Labor (DOL), I represent the Secretary of Labor in all trial level enforcement activity for Region II, which covers New York, New Jersey, Puerto Rico, and the U.S. Virgin Islands. Our office handles the major statutes enforced by the Department, including the Fair Labor Standards Act, the Occupational Safety and Health Act, the Employee Retirement and Income Security Act, the Mine Safety and Health Act, Davis Bacon and Related Acts, Executive Order 11246 (employment discrimination), and many others.

At the regional office, we are trial attorneys and our practice is focused on preparing cases for trial: advising on investigations; analyzing cases; deposing witnesses; writing briefs and motions; and trying cases in U.S. district courts and before administrative law judges. My practice is mainly in the wage and hour area and focuses on protecting workers' rights to fair wages, but I also take cases in other areas as well. On any given day, I might be advising DOL investigators on their investigation of a particularly complex worker misclassification scheme, speaking with an expert about a valuation in an ERISA matter to protect workers' retirement savings, drafting discovery requests in a case involving farmworkers in Puerto Rico, conducting settlement negotiations, or interviewing construction workers in New York City to prepare for a trial in a prevailing wage case. Usually, I do some combination of all of those things.

However, if I receive a call from investigators about an employer retaliating or threatening to retaliate against employees who cooperate with the Department of Labor, I will drop everything to focus on filing a motion for a temporary restraining order and a preliminary injunction to stop the harassment. In a recent matter, we learned that the employer had removed the time clock in the warehouse we were investigating and told employees to lie to DOL investigators about its existence and the number of hours they worked each week. We moved quickly to speak with the workers and gather evidence. We soon filed a complaint and prepared papers asking the court to issue emergency relief. Just a few weeks later, we obtained an order from the district court requiring, among other things, that the employees receive written and oral notice that they had the right to speak truthfully to the DOL about their working conditions without threat of firing or immigration consequences. Although these cases are a lot of work in a very short time, they are quite fulfilling. You can go from the initial investigation stage to conducting a full evidentiary hearing before a district judge in just a few weeks.

I find my practice rewarding because every day I am working to protect vulnerable workers and improve the working conditions for America's workforce. It also provides me with constant challenges and new things to learn as employment practices evolve and change.

---

1. MINIMUM WAGE LAWS

The FLSA acts as a wage floor, upon which state or local governments can build. As of January 2016, the federal minimum wage is $7.25. (The Department of Labor's website provides the current minimum wage.) A majority of states have enacted minimum wages exceeding the federal minimum. Some states have passed laws providing for a gradual increase in the minimum wage over time or that indexes their minimum wage to the rate of inflation. In recent years, a national "fight for 15" movement has prompted California and New York to adopt $15 per hour minimum wage laws.

Generally the minimum wage, if applicable, must be paid in cash or negotiable instruments. However, under § 3(m) the "wage" paid can include "the reasonable cost, as determined by the Secretary of Labor, to the employer of furnishing such employee with board, lodging or other facilities, if such board, lodging or other facilities are customarily furnished by such employer to his employees * * * ." 29 U.S.C. § 203(m). An employer may not, however, set off against the required minimum wages the value of goods, including gas and supplies from the company store, furnished to employees. See, e.g., Brennan v. Heard, 491 F.2d 1 (5th Cir.1974).

Economic Research Supporting Minimum Wage Hikes

Proposed increases to the minimum wage are often opposed on the ground that higher wages will cause employers to respond by reducing work hours or by declining to hire new workers. To test this argument, economists David Card and Alan Krueger devised an ingenious study of the labor effects of minimum wage increases. Before a planned 1992 increase in the New Jersey minimum wage from $4.25 to $5.05 per hour, they called fast food restaurants in both New Jersey and Pennsylvania, where the minimum wage remained flat. They called the restaurants again after the New Jersey increase. They observed a 10% rise in the starting wage in the New Jersey restaurants, and a small increase in the number and percentage of full-time employees. The average number of hours the restaurants were open was unaffected by the wage increase. See David Card and Alan Krueger, Minimum Wages and Employment: A Case Study of the Fast-Food Industry in New Jersey and Pennsylvania, 84 Amer. Econ. Rev.774 (1994); and their Myth and Measurement: The New Economics of the Minimum Wage (1997).

The Card-Krueger study markedly influenced policy debates over the 1996–97 increase in the federal minimum wage.

In a subsequent law review article, Professor Daniel Shaviro[*] observed that the "widely shared view, based on empirical research concerning teenagers that was assumed to apply more generally, was that a 10 percent increase in the minimum wage would likely reduce the hours worked by low wage workers by 1 to 3 percent, while a 25 percent hike would reduce such hours by 3.5 to 5.5 percent." Where increases in the minimum wage reduce available hours, "the resulting disemployment might be borne disproportionately by those who were both least skilled and least affiliated in the workplace. . . . *Second*, suppose that low-wage jobs are an important stepping stone to better work opportunities in the future. If the reduction in hours worked means fewer jobs, not just fewer hours per job, then a minimum wage increase might reduce the present value of expected lifetime income for low-wage workers, even if upon enactment it increased their current-year income."

Consider also the contrary perspective of Jared Bernstein, Vice-President Biden's former chief economist and policy advisor (from 2009–11)[**]:

---

[*]   Daniel Shaviro, The Minimum Wage, the Earned Income Tax Credit, and Optimal Subsidy Policy, 64 U. Chi. L. Rev. 405 (1997).

[**]   The Minimum Wage: Reviewing Recent Evidence of Its Impact on Poverty, Hearing Before the U.S. House of Representatives Committee on Education and the Workforce (1999) (statement of Jared Bernstein, Economist, Economic Policy Institute, Washington, D.C.

"[O]pponents of increases in the minimum continue to raise the same objection: the increase will lead to job loss. * * * The state of economists' understanding of the issue was recently summarized by Nobel laureate Robert Solow, who noted that 'the main thing about this research is that the evidence of job loss is weak. And the fact that the evidence is weak suggests that the impact on jobs is small.' "

NOTES AND QUESTIONS

1. Subsequent research generally supports the Card-Krueger results for certain levels of minimum-wage rise. See Hristos Doucouliagos and T.D. Stanley, Publication Selection Bias in Minimum-Wage Research? A Meta-Regression Analysis, 47 British J. Of Ind. Rel. 406 (2009) (meta-analysis finding no effect on employment from minimum wage increase); Arindrajit Dube, T. William Lester & Michael Reich, Minimum Wage Effects Across State Borders: Estimates Using Contiguous Counties, 92 Rev. of Econ. & Stat. 945 (2010) (comparing adjacent counties in different states and finding no effect on employment rates); but see David Neumark, J.M. Ian Salas & William Wascher, More on Recent Evidence on the Effects of Minimum Wages in the United States, NBER Working Paper 20619 (Oct. 2014) (questioning Dube et al. methodology).

2. *Policy Goals of Minimum Wage Increases.* What are the social benefits of a minimum-wage increase? Consider the following arguments:

a. *Wealth Redistribution.* Professor Gottesman argues that minimum wage laws offer a politically feasible, if less than optimal, means of effecting progressive wealth redistribution to the less well-off, because political majorities will support "making work pay" where they will not vote for outright wealth transfers. Michael H. Gottesman, Whither Goest Labor Law: Law and Economics in the Workplace, 100 Yale L.J. 2767, 2790–93 (1991). In his view, the redistributive (and any displacement) effects of a minimum wage increase are multiplied because pay structures in collective bargaining agreements (and even among nonunion employers that pay wages comparable to the union sector) are often keyed to a multiple of the statutory minimum wage.

b. *Strengthening Workplace Affiliation.* A related argument for "making work pay" is that higher wages will improve incentives for marginal workers to leave welfare rolls and enter (and remain) in the workforce. Nobel laureate economist Edmund Phelps is prominently associated with this view. See Edmund S. Phelps, Rewarding Work: How to Restore Participation and Self-Support to Free Enterprise (1997). Phelps's policy recommendation, however, is not to legislate increases in the minimum wage but, rather, to offer firms a subsidy for each low income worker they hire.

3. *Accounting for Conditions of the Local Economy?* One problem with a nationally uniform minimum wage is that it fails to reflect the diversity of local conditions; the FLSA permits "upward" variability—as states can enact higher minimum wages—but not "downward" variability below the FLSA "floor". Would it be preferable, instead of the FLSA model, to adopt (i) the one-time British approach of allowing regional and local wage councils (comprised of workers' and employers' representatives with an odd number of independent members) to set wage minima (see David Metcalf, The Low Pay Commission and the National Minimum Wage, 109 Econ. J. F46 (No. 453, Feb. 1999)); or (ii) the former German approach of dispensing with statutory wage minima in favor of collectively bargained standards that could be applied industry-wide once a certain percentage of the industry worked under collective agreement?

The FLSA's "Hot Cargo" Provision

The Department of Labor (DOL) in the Obama administration has sought to improve wage-hour compliance by invoking § 15(a) of the FLSA. This "hot cargo" provision authorizes the government to seize good manufactured in violation of the FLSA. By threatening to enforce the "hot cargo" provision, the DOL, it is claimed, was able to negotiate more robust compliance agreements with manufacturers, providing for better screening and oversight of contractor practices. See David Weil, Improving Workplace Conditions through Strategic Enforcement: A Report to the Wage and Hour Division at 29–30 (May 2010), available at http://www.dol.gov/whd/resources/strategicEnforcement.pdf.

---

4. *"Prevailing Wage" Laws.* Entities that contract with the federal government on public projects are subject to federal "prevailing wage" statutes. See Davis-Bacon Act, 40 U.S.C. §§ 276a et seq. (requires prevailing wages and benefits for laborers and mechanics engaged in the construction, alteration or repair of a public work project pursuant to a federal contract in excess of $2000); Walsh-Healy Government Contracts Act, 41 U.S.C. § 35 et seq. (covers companies engaged in providing manufacturing services or supplies pursuant to federal contracts in excess of $10,000); Service Contract Labor Standards Act, 41 U.S.C. §§ 351 et seq. (covers all contracts for services to the federal government in excess of $2500); Contract Work Hours and Safety Standards Act, 40 U.S.C. § 327 et seq. (overtime obligations for federal construction contractors).

Unlike the federal minimum wage law, the "prevailing wage" is not a single federal rate, but a rate calculated at the state and county level that takes into account the type of service provided. (The applicable prevailing wage rates are available at www.wdol.gov.) The federal agency seeking bids from contractors is responsible for providing applicable prevailing wage rates in document soliciting bids. Many states impose similar or more demanding obligations on their contractors. See e.g., Cal. Labor Code § 1815.

2. DEFINING COMPENSABLE WORKING TIME

The FLSA does not set a limit on the numbers of hours a day or week an individual can work, other than to require payment of the overtime premium for work in excess of 40 hours a week. California imposes an overtime premium for work beyond 8 hours a day and for the first 8 hours worked on the seventh consecutive day of work in a workweek; double pay for hours above this threshold. Cal. Labor Code § 510 (a). New York has a "spread of hours" (i.e., the interval between the beginning and end of an employee's workday, including time off for meals) law requiring an additional hour of pay for workdays that exceed 10 hours. See 12 NYCRR §§ 142–2.4(a) & 142–2.18.

For employers to record, calculate and pay wages, they must first determine what does and does not qualify as working time. As you may recall from Chapter 1, the FLSA broadly defines "[e]mploy" to include "suffer or permit to work" (29 U.S.C. § 203(g)).

In 1947, Congress amended the FLSA through the Portal-to-Portal Act, 61 Stat. 86, 29 U.S.C. § 254 et seq., in reaction to a series of Supreme Court decisions which held that the FLSA required compensation for time spent by employees traveling from "portal to portal" (the cases involved walking from iron ore portals to underground working areas and walking from time clocks located near the plant entrance to the areas where they began productive labor.) 29 U.S.C. § 254 seq. In these rulings, the Court also defined "workweek" for FLSA purposes to include all time the employee was required to be on the employer's premises. See Tennessee Coal, Iron & R. Co. v. Muscoda Local No. 123, 321 U.S. 590, 64 S.Ct. 698, 88 L.Ed. 949 (1944); Armour & Co. v. Wantock, 323 U.S. 126, 65 S.Ct. 165, 89 L.Ed. 118 (1944); Anderson v. Mt. Clemens Pottery Co., 328 U.S. 680, 66 S.Ct. 1187, 90 L.Ed. 1515 (1946).

Under the Portal-to-Portal Act amendments, the following activities are generally non-compensable: (1) "walking, riding, or traveling to or from the actual place of performance of the principal activity activities which [the] employee is employed to perform"; and (2) "activities which are preliminary or postliminary to said principal activity or activities, which occur either prior to the time on any particular workday at which such employee commences, or subsequent to the time on any particular workday at which he ceases, such principal activity or activities." 29 U.S.C. § 254(a).

In Steiner v. Mitchell, 350 U.S. 247, 76 S.Ct. 330, 100 L.Ed. 267 (1956), the question was whether workers in a battery plant must be paid as a part of their "principal" activities for the time incident to changing clothes at the beginning of the shift and showering at the end, where they must make extensive use of dangerously materials, to change clothes and are required to shower in state-law mandated facilities. The Court held that these activities were compensable; "activities performed either before or after the regular work shift, on or off the production line, are compensable . . . [T]hose activities are an integral and indispensable part of the principal activities for which covered workmen are employed and are not specifically excluded by [29 U.S.C. § 254 (a)(1)]." 350 U.S. at 256. See also IBP, Inc. v. Alvarez, 546 U.S. 21, 126 S.Ct. 514, 163 L.Ed.2d 288 (2005) (walking from changing area to place of production and waiting to take off required equipment held compensable but not walking to the changing area and waiting to put on required equipment). See also Integrity Staffing Sol. Inc. v. Busk, 574 U.S. ___, 135 S.Ct. 513, 190 L. Ed.2d 410 (2014) (time Amazon warehouse staffers waited to go through security held not compensable).

Once work has begun, courts apply the concept of a "continuous workday." The Court held in *Alvarez* that "any activity that is 'integral and indispensable' to a 'principal activity' is itself a 'principal activity' under [§ 254(a)]. Moreover, during a continuous workday, any walking time that occurs after the beginning of the employee's first principal activity and before the end of the employee's last principal activity is excluded from the scope of that provision, and as a result is covered by the FLSA." 546 U.S. at 37.

The next case, *Bright v. Houston Northwest Medical Center Survivor, Inc.* examines the related question of whether time spent "on call" qualifies as working time.

BRIGHT V. HOUSTON NORTHWEST MEDICAL CENTER SURVIVOR, INC.

U.S. Court of Appeals for the Fifth Circuit (en banc), 1991.
934 F.2d 671.

GARWOOD, J.

This is a former employee's suit for overtime compensation under section 7(a)(1) of the Fair Labor Standards Act (FLSA), 29 U.S.C. § 207(a)(1). The question presented is whether "on-call" time the employee spent at home, or at other locations of his choosing substantially removed from his employer's place of business, is to be included for purposes of section 7 as working time in instances where the employee was not actually "called." The district court granted the motion for summary judgment of the employer, defendant-appellee Houston Northwest Medical Center Survivor, Inc. (Northwest), ruling that this on-call time was not working time and dismissing the suit of the employee. * * * We * * * affirm the district court's summary judgment for the employer.

Bright went to work for Northwest at its hospital in Houston in April 1981 as a biomedical equipment repair technician, and remained in that employment until late January 1983 when, for reasons wholly unrelated to any matters at issue here, he was in effect fired. Throughout his employment at Northwest, Bright worked a standard forty-hour week at the hospital, from 8:00 a.m. to 4:30 p.m., with half an hour off for lunch, Monday through Friday, and he was paid an hourly wage. Overtime in this standard work week was compensated at time and a half rates, and it was understood that overtime work required advance approval by the department head, Jim Chatterton. When Bright started at the hospital, his immediate supervisor was Howard Culp, the senior biomedical equipment repair technician. Culp had the same work schedule as Bright. However, throughout his off-duty hours, Culp was required to wear an electronic paging device or "beeper" and to be "on call" to come to the hospital to make emergency repairs on biomedical equipment. Culp, as Bright knew, was not compensated for this "on-call" time (although Culp apparently was compensated when he was called). In February 1982 Culp resigned, and Bright succeeded him as the senior biomedical equipment repair technician and likewise succeeded Culp in wearing the beeper and being on call throughout all his off-duty time. Bright remained in that role throughout the balance of his employment at Northwest. The only period of time at issue in this lawsuit is that when Bright had the beeper, namely from February 1982 to the end of his employment in January 1983.

Bright was not compensated for his on-call time, and knew this was the arrangement with him as it had been with Culp. During the "on-call" time, if Bright were called, and came to the hospital, he was compensated by four hours [of] compensatory time at his then regular hourly rate (which apparently was some $9 or $10 per hour) for each such call. This compensation was effected by Bright simply working that many less hours the following workday or days: for example, if Bright were called on a Monday evening, he might work in his regular workshift only from 8:00 a.m. until noon on the following Tuesday, but would be paid for the entire eight hours on that day. There is no evidence that these calls on average (or, indeed, in any given instance) took as much as two hours and forty minutes (two-thirds of four hours) of Bright's time. This case does not involve any claim respecting entitlement to compensation (overtime or otherwise) for time that Bright actually spent pursuant to a call from Northwest received while he was on call.

It is undisputed that during the on-call time at issue Bright was not required to, and did not, remain at or about the hospital or any premises of or designated by his employer. He was free to go wherever and do whatever he wanted, subject only to the following three restrictions: (1) he must not be intoxicated or impaired to the degree that he could not work on medical equipment if called to the hospital, although total abstinence was not required (as it was during the daily workshift); (2) he must always be reachable by the beeper; and (3) he must be able to arrive at the hospital within, in Bright's words, "approximately twenty minutes" from the time he was reached on the beeper. Bright's answer to interrogatories reflect that in February 1982, when he commenced wearing the beeper and being on call, he was living about three miles, on average a fifteen-minute drive, from the hospital, but that in about July 1982 he moved his residence to a location some seventeen miles, on average a thirty-minute drive, from the hospital, and continued living there throughout all the remaining some five or six months of his Northwest employment. * * * Bright admitted while on call he not only stayed at home and watched television and the like, but also engaged in other activities away from home, including his "normal shopping" (including supermarket and mall shopping) and "occasionally" going out to restaurants to eat. * * * Bright also testified on deposition that he was "called" on "average" two times during the working week (Monday through Friday) and "ordinarily two to three times" on the weekend. * * *

At issue here is whether the time Bright spent on call, but uncalled on, is working time under section 7, which provides in relevant part as follows:

"Except as otherwise provided in this section, no employer shall employ any of his employees * * * for a workweek longer than forty hours unless such employee receives compensation for his employment in excess of the hours above specified at a rate not less than one and one-half times the regular rate at which he is employed." 29 U.S.C. § 207(a)(1).

* * *

Here, the undisputed facts show that the on-call time is not working time. In such a setting, we have not hesitated to so hold as a matter of law. * * *

Armour [*& Co. v. Wantock*, 323 U.S. 126, 65 S. Ct. 165, 89 L.Ed. 118 (1944)], and *Skidmore* [*v. Swift & Co.*, 323 U.S. 134, 65 S.Ct. 161, 89 L.Ed. 124 (1944)] clearly stand for the proposition that, in a proper setting, on-call time may be working time for purposes of section 7. But those decisions also plainly imply that that is not true of employer-required on-call time in all settings. In *Skidmore* the Court noted, with at least some degree of implied approval, the administrative interpretations that

"in some occupations * * * periods of inactivity are not properly counted as working time even though the employee is subject to call. Examples are an operator of a small telephone exchange where the switchboard is in her home and she ordinarily gets several hours of uninterrupted sleep each night; or a pumper of a stripper well or watchman of a lumber camp during the off season, who may be on duty twenty-four hours a day but ordinarily 'has a normal night's sleep, has ample time in which to eat his meals, and has a certain amount of time for relaxation and entirely private pursuits.' Exclusion of all such hours the Administrator thinks may be justified." Id. 65 S. Ct. at 163–64.

* * *

Bright's case is wholly different from *Armour* and *Skidmore* and similar cases in that Bright did not have to remain on or about his employer's place of business, or some location designated by his employer, but was free to be at his home or at any place or places he chose, without advising his employer, subject only to the restrictions that he be reachable by beeper, not be intoxicated, and be able to arrive at the hospital in "approximately" twenty minutes. During the period in issue he actually moved his home—as Northwest knew and approved—to a location seventeen miles and twenty-five or thirty minutes away from the hospital, as compared to the three miles (and some fifteen minutes) away that it had been when he started carrying his beeper. Bright was not only able to carry on his normal personal activities at his own home, but could also do normal shopping, eating at restaurants, and the like, as he chose. * * *

[W]e have described "the critical issue" in cases of this kind as being "whether the employee can use the [on-call] time effectively for his or her own purposes." *Halferty* [*v. Pulse Drug Co., Inc.*], 864 F.2d [1185,] 1189 [(5th Cir.1989)]. This does not imply that the employee must have substantially the same flexibility or freedom as he would if not on call, else all or almost all on-call time would be working time, a proposition that the settled case law and the administrative guidelines clearly reject. Only in the very rarest of situations, if ever, would there be any point in an employee being on call if he could not be reached by his employer so as to shortly thereafter—generally at least a significant time before the next regular workshift could take care of the matter—be able to perform a needed service, usually at some particular location.

Within such accepted confines, Bright was clearly able to use his on-call time effectively for his own personal purposes. * * *

The panel majority * * * placed crucial reliance on the fact that Bright throughout the nearly one year in issue never had any relief from his on-call status during his nonworking hours. * * * [T]he panel majority inferentially conceded that for any given day or week of on-call time, Bright was as free to use the time for his own purposes. * * * But the panel majority claims that a different result should apply here because Bright's arrangement lasted nearly a year.

We are aware of no authority that supports this theory, and we decline to adopt it. * * *

Further, the FLSA is structured on a workweek basis. Section 7, at issue here, requires time and a half pay "for a workweek longer than forty hours." What Bright was or was not free to do in the last week in September is wholly irrelevant to whether he worked any overtime in the first week of that month. As we said in *Halferty*, the issue "is whether the employee can use the time effectively for his or her own purposes," and that must be decided, under the statutory framework, on the basis of each workweek at the most.

JERRE S. WILLIAMS, J., with whom JOHNSON, J., joins, dissenting.

Admittedly, there are jobs which because of location are in isolated areas. That is in the nature of the jobs. But the isolation is not the result of an employer's direction requiring employee on-call availability during off-duty hours. The employer has nothing to do with the restricted recreational and living accommodations in an isolated job. That is not an on-call situation at all. In contrast, here it is the employer who is enforcing a unique restriction upon a particular employee as part of the particular on-call work assignment. This is of the essence of the thrust of potential work time under the Fair Labor Standards Act.

NOTES AND QUESTIONS

Test Your Understanding of the Material

1. Suppose that a firefighter's job duties require him to be on call for 24 hours at a time. While on call, the firefighter must report to the firehouse within 20 minutes of being paged. The firefighter receives an average of 3 to 5 calls per on-call period. Applying the standard articulated in *Bright v. Houston*, is the firefighter's on-call time compensable? See Renfro v. City of Emporia, Kansas, 948 F.2d 1529 (10th Cir.1991); 29 C.F.R. §§ 553.221, 785.17.

2. In 2009, a class of T-Mobile employees brought an FLSA claim for unpaid wages, alleging:

> Throughout the relevant period, Plaintiffs were provided with a Company Blackberry [smartphone] or other smart device and were required to review and respond to T-Mobile-related emails and text messages at all hours of the day, whether or not they were punched into T-Mobile's computer-based timecard system. Plaintiffs were also required to take and place telephone calls to other T-Mobile personnel and customers relating to store staffing, sales, and/or discounting of handsets, customer satisfaction concerns and other T-Mobile business. Plaintiffs were also required to participate on frequent conference calls, typically at least one time per week[.]

See Agui v. T-Mobile USA, Case No. 1:09–cv–02955–RJD–RML (E.D.N.Y. filed July 7, 2009). The case settled in 2010 for an undisclosed amount. Was the time the T-Mobile employees spent after hours answering calls and responding to emails compensable? Was the time waiting for such calls or emails compensable?

3. An employer cannot avoid its obligations under the FLSA by adopting a policy prohibiting employees from working overtime when its work assignments effectively require overtime work. See Lyle v. Food Lion, Inc., 954 F.2d 984 (4th Cir.1992) (employer must pay for unauthorized overtime work). Suppose you represent an employer that has adopted a no-overtime policy, where an employee consistently works in excess of 40 hours per week. What advice would you give to that employer on how to (a) handle the employee that

worked overtime, and (b) prevent the problem from recurring? Does the FLSA prohibit discharging the employee?

Related Issues

4. *"Sleep Time"*. The Labor Department's regulations permit agreements between an employer and an employee on 24-hour duty to exclude not more than 8 hours for "a bona fide regularly scheduled sleeping period," provided (i) adequate facilities are provided, (ii) the employee can usually enjoy an uninterrupted night's sleep, (iii) sleep time interruptions are compensated, and (iv) the entire sleep period is compensated if the employee cannot receive at least 5 hours' sleep during the scheduled period. 29 C.F.R. § 785.22. For employees residing at their employer's premises on a permanent basis or "for extended periods of time," the regulations take into account a reasonable agreement between the parties. Id. 785.23.

5. *Live-In Domestic Workers*. When an employee, such as a nanny or housekeeper, lives and works in a private residence, demarcations between working and non-working time can be unclear. As with other employees, the definition of working time depends upon the agreement between the parties. However, for free time to qualify as non-working, it must be of "sufficient duration to enable the employee to make effective use of time," and the employee must have "complete freedom from all duties [and] may either leave the premises or stay on the premises for purely personal pursuits." 29 C.F.R. § 552.102. See also id. § 530.1(d) (regulating "homework"—the industrial production of goods from one's home).

6. *Impact of Small Discrepancies*. Seemingly small discrepancies in timekeeping can result in large damage awards when applied to many employees over a long period of time. In Penaloza v. PPG Indus. Inc., Case No. BC471369, 2013 WL 2917624 (Cal Super. Ct. May 20, 2013), an employer's practice of rounding employee timecards at the start and end of a shift underpaid employees nearly 80,000 hours in the aggregate, producing unpaid wage liability of $1.3 million. Cf. See's Candy Shops, Inc. v. Superior Court, 210 Cal.App.4th 889 (2012) (rounding permissible where it produces no aggregate loss to employees).

7. *Sending Workers Home Early Without Pay for the Full Day*. The FLSA does not penalize employers for not providing advance notice of a change in scheduled work hours or sending workers home early. However, some state or local laws provide for "reporting time" pay, requiring employers to pay for a certain number of hours when they send an employee home early. See e.g. 12 N.Y.C.R.R. § 142–2.3, 8 Cal. Code Regs. § 11040. See generally Charlotte Alexander, Anna Haley-Lock & Nantiya Ruan, Stabilizing Low-Wage Work, 50 Harv. C.R.-C.L. L. Rev. 1 (2015).

PRACTITIONER'S PERSPECTIVE

Jahan Sagafi
Partner, Outten & Golden.

As an employment rights advocate litigating wage and hour and discrimination class actions, I help workers achieve fair treatment in the workplace.

Wage and hour litigation plays an important role in my effort to enforce these laws and help achieve a more just society. One common problem is misclassification of white collar workers, such as assistant managers at retail stores, technical support workers, bank employees, etc. Misclassification of an employee as exempt from the FLSA and state law requirements enables the employer to require the employee to work more than 40 hours in a week without paying for those hours at the overtime premium under these laws. Likewise, hourly workers are often required to work "off the clock," before their shift, after their shift, or during their breaks, to keep up with productivity requirements. Lesser known violations include requiring workers to pay for their own equipment or uniforms, or stripping employees of vacation pay they have earned.

In wage and hour cases, plaintiffs' attorneys must carefully select cases through interviews of the potential class representative and other class members to assess (1) individual liability, (2) whether a class of similarly situated individuals exists, such that the same evidence will be relevant to multiple people's claims, and (3) whether there are sufficient damages to justify the huge investment by our law firm of out-of-pocket costs (hundreds of thousands or even millions of dollars) and time (often millions of dollars' worth of lawyer and paralegal time). We spend significant time speaking with class members to learn about their job duties, the employer's policies and practices, and hours worked.

In discovery, we need to penetrate the defendant's reluctance to share information about the merits, through extensive conversations with opposing counsel, carefully crafted discovery requests, targeted Rule 30(b)(6) depositions, and (where needed) motions to compel. Procedural maneuvering in class actions is often critical—the interplay between the merits and Rule 23 (or the FLSA's analogous procedure) can be quite intricate and challenging, implicating issues of arbitration, discovery, class certification, class member communications, settlement, fees, and more. We also often work with statisticians to calculate damages (or perhaps calculate them ourselves, so quantitative skills are important too). Due to their huge size and the risks involved for both sides, class actions rarely go to trial. Cases typically settle in 2–4 years.

Representing employees in employment class actions is profoundly rewarding, both because of the satisfaction of working on behalf of people of modest means who have been taken advantage of by powerful corporations, and because of the difficult intellectual challenges inherent in complex litigation. It is hard to imagine a more fun and meaningful way to pursue social justice in a private law firm.

---

3. REGULAR RATE AND OVERTIME-PREMIUM PAY

The FLSA requires employers to pay a premium rate of 1.5 times their regular rate for each hour worked in excess of 40 hours in a week. To calculate the overtime premium, an employer must first calculate the "regular rate" of an employee's pay. See 29 U.S.C. § 207(e) (the "regular rate" includes "all remuneration for employment paid to, or on behalf of, the employee.")

In general, the overtime calculation—both the "regular rate" and hours worked—is based on each workweek. This calculation is straightforward for employees that are compensated on an hourly basis. Calculating an employee's overtime-premium pay becomes more complicated when employees are paid additional amounts (such as a piece rate pay or commissions).

Some forms of compensation are included in the regular rate and others are not. Non-discretionary bonuses, commissions, and piece rate pay are included in the "regular rate." Bonuses awarded at the employer's sole discretion, gifts, employee benefits, and stock options are not included in the regular rate. See 29 U.S.C. § 207(e); 29 USC § 203(t) (tips count towards minimum wage but are generally not included in the regular rate). To calculate the regular rate for non-hourly forms of compensation, the employer must add up the total weekly compensation, and then divide it by the number of hours worked. That provides a regular rate from which the overtime premium can be calculated. Suppose that a hotel cleaning employee gets paid $3 per room (a form of piece rate compensation). If the employee cleans 150 rooms over the course of 50 hours in a week, the employee's regular rate is $9.00 per hour ($3 × 150/50). The employee is owed an overtime rate of $13.50, and the employer should pay the employee $495 (40 × $9 + 10 × 13.50) for that week's work.

In the case of a non-discretionary bonus, calculating the regular rate associated with the bonus can be difficult where the bonus is earned over many weeks or months. In such cases, the regulations permit the employer to defer payment of the fractional increase in overtime premium until such time as the bonus is "ascertainable." 29 C.F.R. § 778.209. Once ascertainable, "it must be apportioned back over the workweeks of the period during which it may be said to have been earned. The employee must then receive an additional amount of compensation for each workweek that he worked overtime during the period equal to one-half of the hourly rate of pay allocable to the bonus for that week multiplied by the number of statutory overtime hours worked during the week." Id.

NOTES AND QUESTIONS

Test Your Understanding of the Material

1. Following the example above, suppose that a less productive hotel cleaning employee is paid $3 per room, but only cleans 100 rooms in 50 hours. How much must the employee be paid to comply with the FLSA's minimum wage and overtime rules? See McLaughlin v. Dial America Mktg., Inc., 716 F.Supp. 812 (D.N.J.1989).

2. An investment bank provides its traders an annual "discretionary performance bonus" keyed to the profitability of the firm generally and the profits generated by the trading department. In existence for five years, the bank has awarded such a bonus, amounting to 25% of average compensation, in four of the years. Is the bonus part of "regular pay"? See 29 C.F.R. § 778.211(b).

3. *Justifications for Overtime Regulation.* Consider the following justifications for regulating overtime work. What assumptions does each make about the way employers and employees make decisions?

   a. *Work-Sharing.* A principal justification offered for requiring payment of an overtime premium is that employment levels should increase when it becomes more expensive for employers to use incumbent workers for work beyond the normal workweek. But see John T. Addison & Barry T. Hirsch, The Economic Effects of Employment Regulation: What Are the Limits?, 141–42 in Government Regulation of the Employment Relationship 145 (Bruce E. Kaufman ed., 1997).

   b. *Expanding Leisure Time.* A related justification for the overtime premium is that by creating a financial disincentive for work beyond the regular workweek, the FLSA expands the leisure time (with associated health benefits) available to workers. Note that the FLSA, unlike some of the European laws, does not prohibit employers from compelling employees to work overtime as long as the overtime premium is paid. See generally Todd D. Rakoff, A Time for Every Purpose: Law and the Balance of Life 65–66 (2002); Shirley Lung, Overwork and Overtime, 34 Ind.L.Rev. 51 (2005).

   c. *"Making Work Pay".* Like the minimum wage requirement, the overtime premium requirement benefits incumbent workers who would not receive such a premium in the absence of a legal mandate.

Related Issues

4. *"Comp" Time.* The FLSA does not permit employers in lieu of overtime pay to provide "compensatory time," i.e, paid time off equivalent to the hours of overtime work. 29 U.S.C. § 207(*o*)(1) (compensatory time only permissible for state and local government employees).

5. *The "Fluctuating Work Week" Method.* After Walling v. Belo Corp., 316 U.S. 624 (1992), the DOL has permitted use of a "fluctuating work week" method of calculating pay and overtime for employees with irregular schedules. See 29 C.F.R. § 778.114 ("An employee employed on a salary basis may have hours of work which fluctuate from week to week and the salary may be paid him pursuant to an understanding with his employer that he will receive such fixed amount as straight time pay for whatever hours he is called upon to work in a workweek, whether few or many.") See also Overnight Motor Transp. Co., Inc. v. Missel, 316 U.S. 572, 62 S. Ct. 1216, 86 L. Ed. 1682 (1942). The method may also be used in calculating damages in overtime misclassification cases. See Urnikis-Negro v. American Family Property Services, 616 F.3d 665 (7th Cir. 2010).

B. EXEMPTIONS FROM MINIMUM WAGE AND OVERTIME COVERAGE

The FLSA contains exemptions from minimum wage and/or overtime obligations for several categories of employees. Table 1, below, summarizes several of these exclusions, too numerous to list in complete form. The broadest and most complex of these are the so-called "white collar" exemptions, which we will examine in detail.

The employer bears the burden of establishing that an employee's position satisfies the requirements for an exemption. Mitchell v. Kentucky Finance Co., 359 U.S. 290 (1959). The damages associated with misclassifying a position as exempt can be substantial, especially where the classification affects many employees and the employees are highly compensated. Employers do not in general track the hours worked by salaried employees; the employer will often lack documentation of hours worked when salaried employees have been found to be misclassified as overtime-exempt. As the Court held in Anderson v. Mt. Clemens Pottery Co., 328 U.S. 680, 66 S.Ct. 1187, 90 L.Ed. 1515 (1946), an employer's violation of its recordkeeping obligations under 29 U.S.C. § 211(c), does not provide a defense to liability and indeed can give rise to a reasonable inference for the employee not properly paid. "[E]ven where the lack of accurate records grows out of a *bona fide* mistake as to whether certain activities or nonactivities constitute work, the employer, having received the benefits of such work, cannot object to the payment for the work on the most accurate basis possible under the circumstances. . . . Unless the employer can provide accurate estimates, it is the duty of the trier of facts to draw whatever reasonable inferences can be drawn from the employees' evidence as to the amount of time spent in these activities in excess of the productive working time." 328 U.S. at 688, 694, superseded on other grounds by Integrity Staffing Solutions, Inc. v. Busk, 657 U.S. ___ (2014).

Table 1. Exemptions from the FLSA's Minimum Wage and Overtime Provisions

Exempt from Minimum Wage and Overtime
• "White collar" exemptions for executive, administrative, professional, and computer employees, as well as outside salespersons § 213(a)(1)
• Highly-compensated workers paid a total annual compensation of $100,000 or more 29 C.F.R. § 541.601
• Certain agricultural employees § 213(a)(6)
• Newspaper deliverers § 213(d)
• Casual babysitters § 213(a)(15)
• Domestic workers providing companionship to the aged or infirm § 213(a)(15)
• Seasonal amusement park, camp or recreational employees 29 U.S.C. § 213(a)(3)
• Workers paid an "opportunity wage" § 206(g)
• Learners, apprentices and disabled workers approved by Secretary of Labor § 213(a)(7) & 214
Exempt from Overtime but Not Minimum Wage
• Commissioned retail sales employees paid at least 1.5x the minimum wage § 207(i)
• Live-in domestic service workers § 213(b)(21)
• Tipped workers § 203(t)

For most of the white collar exemptions, the employer must establish that (1) the employee is paid on a "salary basis" (the so-called "salary basis" test), and (2) the employee's work predominantly involves exempt duties (the so-called "duties" test).

1. "SALARY BASIS" TEST

AUER V. ROBBINS

Supreme Court of the United States, 1997.
519 U.S. 452, 117 S.Ct. 905, 137 L.Ed.2d 79.

JUSTICE SCALIA delivered the opinion of the Court.

I

Petitioners are sergeants and a lieutenant employed by the St. Louis Police Department. They brought suit in 1988 against respondents, members of the St. Louis Board of Police Commissioners, seeking payment of overtime pay that they claimed was owed under § 7(a)(1) of the FLSA, 29 U.S.C. § 207(a)(1). Respondents argued that petitioners were not entitled to such pay because they came within the exemption provided by § 213(a)(1) for "bona fide executive, administrative, or professional" employees.

Under regulations promulgated by the Secretary, one requirement for exempt status under § 213(a)(1) is that the employee earn a specified minimum amount on a "salary basis." 29 CFR §§ 541.1(f), 541.2(e), 541.3(e) (1996). According to the regulations, "an employee will be considered to be paid 'on a salary basis' * * * if under his employment agreement he regularly receives each pay period on a weekly, or less frequent basis, a predetermined amount constituting all or part of his compensation, which amount is not subject to reduction because of variations in the quality or quantity of the work performed." § 541.118(a). Petitioners contended that the salary-basis test was not met in their case because, under the terms of the St. Louis Metropolitan Police Department Manual, their compensation could be reduced for a variety of disciplinary infractions related to the "quality or quantity" of work performed. Petitioners also claimed that they did not meet the other requirement for exempt status under § 213(a)(1): that their duties be of an executive, administrative, or professional nature. See §§ 541.1(a)–(e), 541.2(a)–(d), 541.3(a)–(d).

The District Court found that petitioners were paid on a salary basis and that most, though not all, also satisfied the duties criterion. The Court of Appeals affirmed in part and reversed in part, holding that both the salary-basis test and the duties test were satisfied as to all petitioners. * * *

II

The FLSA grants the Secretary broad authority to "define and delimit" the scope of the exemption for executive, administrative, and professional employees. § 213(a)(1). Under the Secretary's chosen approach, exempt status requires that the employee be paid on a salary basis, which in turn requires that his compensation not be subject to reduction because of variations in the "quality or quantity of the work performed," 29 CFR § 541.118(a) (1996). Because the regulation goes on to carve out an exception from this rule for "penalties imposed * * * for infractions of safety rules of major significance," § 541.118(a)(5), it is clear that the rule embraces reductions in pay for disciplinary violations. The Secretary is of the view that employees whose pay is adjusted for disciplinary reasons do not deserve exempt status because as a general matter true "executive, administrative, or professional" employees are not "disciplined" by piecemeal deductions from their pay, but are terminated, demoted, or given restricted assignments.

The FLSA did not apply to state and local employees when the salary-basis test was adopted in 1940. See 29 U.S.C. § 203(d) (1940 ed.); 5 Fed. Reg. 4077 (1940) (salary-basis test). In 1974 Congress extended FLSA coverage to virtually all public-sector employees, Pub. L. 93–259, § 6, 88 Stat. 58–62, and in 1985 we held that this exercise of power was consistent with the Tenth Amendment, *Garcia v. San Antonio Metropolitan Transit Authority,* 469 U.S. 528, 83 L.Ed. 2d 1016, 105 S.Ct. 1005 (1985) * * * . (Respondents * * * contend * * * that the "no disciplinary deductions" element of the salary-basis test is invalid for public-sector employees because as applied to them it reflects an unreasonable interpretation of the statutory exemption. That is so, they say, because the ability to adjust public-sector employees' pay—even executive, administrative or professional employees' pay—as a means of enforcing compliance with work rules is a necessary component of effective government. In the public-sector context, they contend, fewer disciplinary alternatives to deductions in pay are available [because of civil-service requirements].

Because Congress has not "directly spoken to the precise question at issue," we must sustain the Secretary's approach so long as it is "based on a permissible construction of the statute." *Chevron U.S.A. Inc.* v. *Natural Resources Defense Council, Inc.,* 467 U.S. 837, 842–843, 81 L.Ed.2d 694, 104 S.Ct. 2778 (1984). While respondents' objections would perhaps support a different application of the salary-basis test for public employees, we cannot conclude that they compel it. The Secretary's view that public employers are not so differently situated with regard to disciplining their employees as to require wholesale revision of his time-tested rule simply cannot be said to be unreasonable. * * *

Respondents appeal to the "quasi military" nature of law enforcement agencies such as the St. Louis Police Department. The ability to use the full range of disciplinary tools against even relatively senior law enforcement personnel is essential, they say, to maintaining control and discipline in organizations in which human lives are on the line daily. It is far from clear, however, that only a pay deduction, and not some other form of discipline—for example, placing the offending officer on restricted duties—will have the necessary effect. Because the FLSA entrusts matters of judgment such as this to the Secretary, not the federal courts, we cannot say that the disciplinary-deduction rule is invalid as applied to law enforcement personnel. * * *

III

A primary issue in the litigation unleashed by application of the salary-basis test to public-sector employees has been whether, under that test, an employee's pay is "subject to" disciplinary or other deductions whenever there exists a theoretical possibility of such deductions, or rather only when there is something more to suggest that the employee is actually vulnerable to having his pay reduced. Petitioners in effect argue for something close to the former view; they contend that because the police manual nominally subjects all department employees to a range of disciplinary sanctions that includes disciplinary deductions in pay, and because a single sergeant was actually subjected to a disciplinary deduction, they are "subject to" such deductions and hence non-exempt under the FLSA. * * *

The Secretary of Labor, in an amicus brief filed at the request of the Court, interprets the salary-basis test to deny exempt status when employees are covered by a policy that permits disciplinary or other deductions in pay "as a practical matter." That standard is met, the Secretary says, if there is either an actual practice of making such deductions or an employment policy that creates a "significant likelihood" of such deductions. The Secretary's approach rejects a wooden requirement of actual deductions, but in their absence it requires a clear and particularized policy—one which "effectively communicates" that deductions will be made in specified circumstances. This avoids the imposition of massive and unanticipated overtime liability * * * (including the possibility of a doubling of economics losses as liquidated damages * * *) in situations in which a vague or broadly worded policy is nominally applicable to a whole range of personnel but is not "significantly likely" to be invoked against salaried employees. * * *

The Secretary's approach is usefully illustrated by reference to this case. The policy on which petitioners rely is contained in a section of the police manual that lists a total of 58 possible rule violations and specifies the range of penalties associated with each. All department employees are nominally covered by the manual, and some of the specified penalties involve disciplinary deductions in pay. Under the Secretary's view, that is not enough to render petitioners' pay "subject to" disciplinary deductions within the meaning of the salary-basis test. This is so because the manual does not "effectively communicate" that pay deductions are an anticipated form of punishment for employees in petitioners' category, since it is perfectly possible to give full effect to every aspect of the manual without drawing any inference of that sort. If the statement of available penalties applied solely to petitioners, matters would be different; but since it applies both to petitioners and to employees who are unquestionably not paid on a salary basis, the expressed availability of disciplinary deductions may have reference only to the latter. No clear inference can be drawn as to the likelihood of a sanction's being applied to employees such as petitioners. Nor, under the Secretary's approach, is such a likelihood established by the one-time deduction in a sergeant's pay, under unusual circumstances. * * *

IV

One small issue remains unresolved: the effect upon the exempt status of Sergeant Guzy, the officer who violated the residency requirement, of the one-time reduction in his pay. The Secretary's regulations provide that if deductions which are inconsistent with the salary-basis test—such as the deduction from Guzy's pay—are made in circumstances indicating that "there was no intention to pay the employee on a salary basis," the exemption from the FLSA is "[not] applicable to him during the entire period when such deductions were being made." 29 CFR § 541.118(a)(6) (1996). Conversely, "where a deduction not permitted by [the salary-basis test] is inadvertent, or is made for reasons other than lack of work, the exemption will not be considered to have been lost if the employer reimburses the employee for such deductions and promises to comply in the future." *Ibid.*

Petitioners contend that the initial condition in the latter provision (which enables the employer to take corrective action) is not satisfied here because the deduction from Guzy's pay was not inadvertent. That it was not inadvertent is true enough, but the plain language of the regulation sets out "inadvertence" and "made for reasons other than lack of work" as alternative grounds permitting corrective action. Petitioners also contend that the corrective provision is unavailable to respondents because Guzy has yet to be reimbursed for the residency-based deduction; in petitioners' view, reimbursement must be made immediately upon the discovery that an improper deduction was made. The language of the regulation, however, does not address the timing of reimbursement, and the Secretary's amicus brief informs us that he does not interpret it to require immediate payment. Respondents are entitled to preserve Guzy's exempt status by complying with the corrective provision in § 541.118(a)(6).

NOTES AND QUESTIONS

Test Your Understanding of the Material

    1.   What do you think is the policy justification for the salary-basis test and its exceptions?

    2.   Is the standard adopted by the Court sufficient to deter employers from making regular deductions from an exempt employee's salary and still retain the employee's FLSA-exempt status? Note that the DOL regulations do not permit employers to avail themselves of the "window of correction" defense where there has been a pattern of improper deductions. See 29 C.F.R. § 541.603(a) ("An actual current practice of making improper deductions demonstrates that the employer did not intend to pay employees on a salary basis."); Hoffmann v. Sbarro, Inc., 982 F.Supp. 249, 256 (S.D.N.Y.1997) (deferring to DOL appellate counsel's statement of agency policy that this defense is not "available in cases of multiple or recurring improper deductions or a longstanding policy permitting such deductions"). But see Moore v. Hannon Food Serv., Inc., 317 F.3d 489 (5th Cir.2003) (exempt status of fast-food restaurant managers retained despite employer's deduction of cash register shortfalls from their paychecks for four months because employer repaid improper deductions and dropped the practice).

Related Issues

    3.   *Exceptions to the "Salary Basis" Test.* The regulations recognize several exceptions to the salary-basis rule:

a. deductions for absences from work "for one or more full days for personal reasons, other than sickness or disability" (29 C.F.R. § 541.602(b)(1));

b. deductions for absences "of a day or more occasioned by sickness or disability" in accordance with a bona-fide plan or policy (§ 541.602(b)(2));

c. "[p]enalties imposed in good faith for infractions of safety rules of major significance," i.e., "those relating to the prevention of serious danger in the workplace or to other employees" (§ 541.602(b)(4));

d. employees "need not be paid for any workweek in which they perform no work" (§ 541.602(a));

e. full workweek or multiple-period suspensions for violations of non-safety-related work rule, see Hackett v. Lane County, 91 F.3d 1289 (9th Cir.1996);

f. charging partial-day absences against accrued leave time, provided no salary deductions occur if accrued leave is exhausted, see Aaron v. City of Wichita, 54 F.3d 652 (10th Cir.1995); and

g. partial-day deductions for intermittent or reduced-schedule leaves pursuant to the Family and Medical Leave Act (29 U.S.C. § 825.206(a)).

4. *Prospective Salary Reductions.* In In re Wal-Mart Stores, 395 F.3d 1177, 1184 (10th Cir.2005), the court held that prospective salary reductions do not violate the salary-basis test: "[A]n employer may prospectively reduce salary to accommodate the employer's business needs unless it is done with such frequency that the salary is the functional equivalent of an hourly wage. . . . [W]e would read the regulation as prohibiting only reductions in pay made in response to certain events in a period for which the pay had been set, not salary reductions to take effect in future pay periods."

PRACTITIONER'S PERSPECTIVE

Samuel S. Shaulson
Partner, Morgan, Lewis & Bockius LLP.

One of the things I like most about being an employment lawyer is the variety of the practice. I might be litigating a single-plaintiff sexual harassment case in federal court on one day, negotiating an executive employment contract on another day, and appearing before the Equal Employment Opportunity Commission on yet another day. But the complexity of our laws and legal system forces even employment practitioners to specialize in one or more sub-specialties. One of my specialties is representing employers in wage and hour class and collective actions. This, for example, could involve defending claims brought on behalf of a class of hundreds or even tens of thousands of employees that they were misclassified as exempt from overtime. Or it could involve claims that employee class members were required to work "off the clock" without being paid for all hours worked, were subject to improper wage deductions, or were not provided required meal and rest breaks. Not all claims are meritorious, not all class claims are justified by the facts or the law.

While some of my practice involves appellate work, I love the strategy involved in litigating cases at the trial court level, particularly complex class actions. After appropriate factual investigation, I need to develop a strategy that will meet my client's objectives (what I call "a victory for the client"). In any given class case, I need to decide, for example, how to get useful admissions from the class representatives in their depositions, whether our client should first fight class certification or the merits, or whether we can moot the class claims by offering full relief at the onset of the case. In addition, I may need to determine how we can reduce the overall settlement value of the case by incremental litigation victories, such as narrowing the scope of discovery, obtaining the dismissal of certain claims, or limiting the scope of the class. Ultimately, I need to figure out how we can marshal the facts and the law to secure a victory for the client.

I have found that litigating, especially class cases, can be likened to an intellectual sport. Within the rules of the game (the law and the procedural and ethical rules), it is my job to create and implement a strategy that maximizes the chances that my client will win. And like most athletes and coaches, my job involves constant feedback. I learn whether potential clients have decided to retain my firm and me rather than competing law firms, whether courts have ruled in my clients' favor, and whether I have been successful in resolving a case to my client's satisfaction. Competing every day, helping clients achieve their objectives, and affecting change in the law has made my career intellectually stimulating and incredibly rewarding.

---

2. THE "DUTIES" TEST

DAVIS V. J.P. MORGAN CHASE & CO.

U.S. Court of Appeals for the Second Circuit, 2009.
587 F.3d 529.

LYNCH, J.

This appeal requires us to decide whether underwriters tasked with approving loans, in accordance with detailed guidelines provided by their employer, are administrative employees exempt from the overtime requirements of the Fair Labor Standards Act. Andrew Whalen was employed by J.P. Morgan Chase ("Chase") for four years as an underwriter. As an underwriter, Whalen evaluated whether to issue loans to individual loan applicants by referring to a detailed set of guidelines, known as the Credit Guide, provided to him by Chase. The Credit Guide specified how underwriters should determine loan applicant characteristics such as qualifying income and credit history, and instructed underwriters to compare such data with criteria, also set out in the Credit Guide, prescribing what qualified a loan applicant for a particular loan product. Chase also provided supplemental guidelines and product guidelines with information specific to individual loan products. An underwriter was expected to evaluate each loan application under the Credit Guide and approve the loan if it met the Guide's standards. If a loan did not meet the Guide's standards, certain underwriters had some ability to make exceptions or variances to implement appropriate compensating factors. Whalen and Chase provide different accounts of how often underwriters made such exceptions.

* * *

At the time of Whalen's employment by Chase, Chase treated underwriters as exempt from the FLSA's overtime requirements. Whalen sought a declaratory judgment that Chase violated the FLSA by treating him as exempt and failing to pay him overtime compensation. Both Whalen and Chase filed motions for summary judgment. The district court denied Whalen's motions and granted Chase's motion, dismissing Whalen's complaint. This appeal followed.

* * *

The statute specifying that employees who work in "bona fide executive, administrative, or professional capacit[ies]" are exempt from the FLSA overtime pay requirements does not define "administrative." 29 U.S.C. § 213(a)(1). Federal regulations specify, however, that a worker is employed in a bona fide administrative capacity if she performs work "directly related to management policies or general business operations" and "customarily and regularly exercises discretion and independent judgment." 29 C.F.R. § 541.2(a).[2] Regulations further explain that work directly related to management policies or general business operations consists of "those types of activities relating to the administrative operations of a business as distinguished from 'production' or, in a retail or service establishment, 'sales' work." 29 C.F.R. § 541.205(a).[3] Employment may thus be classified as belonging in the administrative category, which

---

[2] The Department of Labor issued new regulations defining the administrative exemption in 2004. Unless otherwise specified, reference to the regulations is to the pre-2004 regulations.

[3] Although there are other requirements to fall within the exemption, such as customarily and regularly exercising discretion, because we conclude that Whalen's work was not "administrative," we need not decide whether Whalen's employment as an underwriter met those requirements.

falls squarely within the administrative exception, or as production/sales work, which does not.

Precedent in this circuit is light but provides the framework of our analysis to identify Whalen's job as either administrative or production. In *Reich v. State of New York*, 3 F.3d 581 (2d Cir.1993), overruled by implication on other grounds by *Seminole Tribe v. Florida*, 517 U.S. 44, 116 S. Ct. 1114, 134 L. Ed. 2d 252 (1996), we held that members of the state police assigned to the Bureau of Criminal Investigation (BCI), known as BCI Investigators, were not exempt as administrative employees. BCI Investigators are responsible for supervising investigations performed by state troopers and conducting their own investigations of felonies and major misdemeanors. Applying the administrative versus production analysis, we then reasoned that because "the primary function of the Investigators . . . is to conduct—or 'produce'—its criminal investigations," the BCI Investigators fell "squarely on the 'production' side of the line" and were not exempt from the FLSA's overtime requirements.

* * *

The line between administrative and production jobs is not a clear one, particularly given that the item being produced—such as "criminal investigations"—is often an intangible service rather than a material good. Notably, the border between administrative and production work does not track the level of responsibility, importance, or skill needed to perform a particular job.[4] * * * The Department of Labor has attempted to clarify the classification of jobs within the financial industry through regulations and opinion letters. In 2004, the Department of Labor promulgated new regulations discussing, among other things, employees in the financial services industry. Although these regulations were instituted after Whalen's employment with Chase ended, the Department of Labor noted that the new regulations were "[c]onsistent with existing case law." 69 Fed. Reg. 22,122, 22,145 (Apr. 23, 2004). The regulation states:

> Employees in the financial services industry generally meet the duties requirements for the administrative exemption if their duties include work such as collecting and analyzing information regarding the customer's income, assets, investments or debts; determining which financial products best meet the customer's needs and financial circumstances; advising the customer regarding the advantages and disadvantages of different financial products; and marketing, servicing or promoting the employer's financial products. However, an employee whose primary duty is

---

[4]   Such considerations may be relevant to other, independent, requirements for exemption from the FLSA overtime provisions. The responsibility exercised by an employee, for example, would affect whether that employee "customarily and regularly exercise[d] discretion and independent judgment." 29 C.F.R. § 541.2. Such a determination, however, is entirely separate from whether an employee's function may be classified as administrative or production-related.

selling financial products does not qualify for the administrative exemption.

29 C.F.R. § 541.203(b).

The Department of Labor explained that the new regulation was sparked by growing litigation in the area and contrasted two threads of case law. On the one hand, some courts found that "employees who represent the employer with the public, negotiate on behalf of the company, and engage in sales promotion" were exempt from overtime requirements. 69 Fed. Reg. 22,122, 22,145 (Apr. 23, 2004), citing *Hogan v. Allstate Ins. Co.*, 361 F.3d 621, 2004 WL 362378 (11th Cir.2004); *Reich v. John Alden Life Ins. Co.*, 126 F.3d 1 (1st Cir.1997); *Wilshin v. Allstate Ins. Co.*, 212 F. Supp. 2d 1360 (M.D.Ga.2002). On the other hand, the Department cited a Minnesota district court, which found that "employees who had a 'primary duty to sell [the company's] lending products on a day-to-day basis' directly to consumers" were not exempt. 69 Fed. Reg. 22,122, 22,145 (Apr. 23, 2004), quoting *Casas v. Conseco Fin. Corp.*, No. Civ. 00–1512(JRT/SRN), 2002 WL 507059, at *9 (D.Minn.2002). The regulation thus helped to clarify the distinction between employees performing substantial and independent financial work and employees who merely sold financial products. * * *

We * * * turn to the job of underwriter at Chase to assess whether Whalen performed day-to-day sales activities or more substantial advisory duties. As an underwriter, Whalen's primary duty was to sell loan products under the detailed directions of the Credit Guide. There is no indication that underwriters were expected to advise customers as to what loan products best met their needs and abilities. Underwriters were given a loan application and followed procedures specified in the Credit Guide in order to produce a yes or no decision. Their work is not related either to setting "management policies" nor to "general business operations" such as human relations or advertising, 29 C.F.R. § 541.2, but rather concerns the "production" of loans—the fundamental service provided by the bank.

Chase itself provided several indications that they understood underwriters to be engaged in production work. Chase employees referred to the work performed by underwriters as "production work." Within Chase, departments were at least informally categorized as "operations" or "production," with underwriters encompassed by the production label. Underwriters were evaluated not by whether loans they approved were paid back, but by measuring each underwriter's productivity in terms of "average of total actions per day" and by assessing whether the underwriters' decisions met the Chase credit guide standards.

Underwriters were occasionally paid incentives to increase production, based on factors such as the number of decisions underwriters made. While being able to quantify a worker's productivity in literal numbers of items produced is not a requirement of being engaged in production work, it illustrates the concerns that motivated the FLSA. The overtime requirements of the FLSA were meant to apply financial pressure to "spread employment to avoid the extra wage" and to assure workers "additional pay to compensate them for the burden of a workweek beyond the hours fixed in the act." *Overnight Motor Transp. Co., Inc. v. Missel*, 316 U.S. 572, 577–78, 62 S. Ct. 1216, 86 L. Ed. 1682 (1942) * * * . While in the abstract any work can be spread, there is a relatively direct correlation between hours worked and materials produced in the case of a production worker that does not exist as to administrative employees. Paying production incentives to underwriters shows that Chase believed that the work of underwriters could be quantified in a way that the work of administrative employees generally cannot.

We conclude that the job of underwriter as it was performed at Chase falls under the category of production rather than of administrative work. Underwriters at Chase performed work that was primarily functional rather than conceptual. They were not at the heart of the company's business operations. They had no involvement in determining the future strategy or direction of the business, nor did they perform any other function that in any way related to the business's overall efficiency or mode of operation. It is undisputed that the underwriters played no role in the establishment of Chase's credit policy. Rather, they were trained only to apply the credit policy as they found it, as it was articulated to them through the detailed Credit Guide.

Furthermore, we have drawn an important distinction between employees directly producing the good or service that is the primary output of a business and employees performing general administrative work applicable to the running of any business. In *Reich*, for example, BCI Investigators "produced" law enforcement investigations. By contrast, administrative functions such as management of employees through a human resources department or supervising a business's internal financial activities through the accounting department are functions that must be performed no matter what the business produces. For this reason, the fact that Whalen assessed creditworthiness is not enough to determine whether his job was administrative. The context of a job function matters: a clothing store accountant deciding whether to issue a credit card to a consumer performs a support function auxiliary to the department store's primary function of clothes. An underwriter for Chase, by contrast, is directly engaged in creating the "goods"—loans and other financial services—produced and sold by Chase.

* * *

Accordingly, we hold that Whalen did not perform work directly related to management policies or general business operations. Because an administrative employee must both perform work directly related to management policies or general business operations and customarily and regularly exercise discretion and independent judgment, we thus hold that

Whalen was not employed in a bona fide administrative capacity. We need not address whether Whalen customarily and regularly exercised discretion and independent judgment.

NOTES AND QUESTIONS

Test Your Understanding of the Material

1. What is the source of the production-administrative dichotomy? Is it in the statute? The DOL regulations? What are the policy reasons behind the dichotomy? Can there be administrative jobs that also involve responsibility for production?

2. Is a night manager in a fast-food restaurant involved in production work as well as supervision? Can you be an effective night-shift supervisor without also engaging in some production work? Might any exemptions other than the administrative exemption apply?

3. A law firm's unit of production usually is the billable hour. Under which side of the production/administration dichotomy do associate attorneys fall? Do attorneys fall under any other FLSA exemption? 29 C.F.R. §§ 541.300–304.

4. Would it make more sense as a policy matter to abolish the duties test and make any exemption rest exclusively on the employee's compensation (which could be set at an appropriate multiple of the minimum wage)? Such a change would reduce administrative costs and promote compliance by simplifying this area of the law. Should traditional hourly workers who work considerable amounts of regularly scheduled overtime be included in such an exemption? Note also the provision for highly-compensated employees in 29 C.F.R. § 541.601.

Related Issues

5. *Marketing Representatives.* Insurance companies increasingly rely on contractors to sell insurance directly to customers. These marketing representatives are not directly involved in product design, generation, or sales of insurance. Assuming they satisfy the salary-basis requirement and are otherwise employees, do these representatives fall within the administrative exemption? See Reich v. John Alden Life Ins. Co., 126 F.3d 1 (1st Cir.1997).

6. *Pharmaceutical Representatives.* Sales representatives for pharmaceutical companies spend most of their time traveling to doctors' offices and attempting to persuade them to prescribe their company's products. Because patients fill prescriptions for a drug, the doctor does not purchase the drug or place an order with the sales representatives.

The FLSA defines sale as "sale, exchange, contract to sell, consignment for sale, shipment for sale, or other disposition." 29 U.S.C. § 203(k). The DOL regulations refer to the FLSA's definition, but further define "sales" to mean "the transfer of title to tangible property, and in certain cases, of tangible and valuable evidences of intangible property." 29 C.F.R. § 541.501. The regulations also provide that "promotion work" is "often performed by persons who make sales" and is considered exempt when made incidental to an employee's own sales, but not to sales by others. 29 C.F.R. § 541.503.

In Christopher v. SmithKline Beecham Corp., 567 U.S. ___, 132 S.Ct. 2156, 183 L. Ed.2d 153 (2012), the Supreme Court decided that pharmaceutical sales representatives were overtime-exempt under the outside-sales exemption. The Court explained that "[t]he specific list of transactions that precedes the phrase "other disposition" [in the statute] represents an attempt to accommodate industry-by-industry variations in methods of selling commodities. Consequently, we think that the catchall phrase "other disposition" is most reasonably interpreted as including those arrangements that are tantamount, in a particular industry, to a paradigmatic sale of a commodity. . . . Obtaining a nonbinding commitment from a physician to prescribe one of respondent's drugs is the most that [the sales representatives] were able to do [by law] to ensure the eventual disposition of the products that respondent sells." 567 U.S. at ___.

7.   *Service Advisors.* In Encino Motorcars, LLC v. Navarro, No. 15-415, the Court will decide whether "service advisors" at a car dealership whose primary job responsibilities involve identifying service needs and selling service solutions to the dealership's customers are exempt from overtime requirements for "any salesman, partsman, or mechanic primarily engaged in selling or servicing automobiles." 29 U.S.C. § 213(b)(10)(A).

C. COMPENSATION DISPUTES ARISING FROM STATE CONTRACT AND WAGE-PAYMENT LAWS

In addition to federal and state wage-hour laws, compensation disputes may also involve breach of contracts claims and actions under state wage-payment laws.

1. IMPLIED COVENANT OF GOOD FAITH AND FAIR DEALING

The implied covenant of good faith and fair dealing can be viewed as an example of contract law supplying the implied background rules which inform the expectations of the parties when they enter into a particular contract. Absent such implied terms, the parties would have to negotiate prolix documents setting forth all of the obligations underlying their proposed relationship. You may recall Wood v. Lucy, Lady Duff-Gordon, 222 N.Y. 88, 118 N.E. 214 (1917) from your first-year contracts class. In that case, a well-known creator of fashions gave the exclusive right to market her designs for a period of at least a year to Wood in return for half of the proceeds he obtained from such marketing, but the agreement said nothing about Wood's duty to market the designs. Lady Duff Gordon's attempt to justify a breach of the agreement because of lack of consideration was rejected by the New York Court of Appeals. Judge

Cardozo explained that in view of the "exclusive privilege" granted to Wood, the court would not "suppose that one party was to be placed at the mercy of the other," and held that consideration was supplied by Wood's implied promise to use "reasonable efforts to * * * market her designs * * * ." Id. at 90–91, 118 N.E. at 214.

RESTATEMENT OF EMPLOYMENT LAW § 3.05
American Law Institute (2015).

§ 3.05 Implied Duty of Good Faith and Fair Dealing

(a) Each party to an employment relationship, including at-will employment, owes a nonwaivable duty of good faith and fair dealing to the other party, which includes a party's obligation not to hinder the other party's performance under, or to deprive the other party of the benefit of, their contractual relationship (§ 2.07). The duty applies whether the relationship is terminable at will (as set forth in subsection (b)) or only for cause.

(b) The implied duty of good faith and fair dealing applies to at-will employment relationships in a manner consistent with the essential nature of such an at-will relationship.

(c) The employer's duty of good faith and fair dealing includes the duty not to terminate or seek to terminate the employment relationship or effect other adverse employment action for the purpose of

(1) preventing the vesting or accrual of an employee right or benefit, or

(2) retaliating against the employee for refusing to consent to a change in earned compensation or benefits.

FORTUNE V. NATIONAL CASH REGISTER CO.
Supreme Judicial Court of Massachusetts, 1977.
373 Mass. 96, 364 N.E.2d 1251.

ABRAMS, J.

Orville E. Fortune (Fortune), a former salesman of The National Cash Register Company (NCR), brought a suit to recover certain commissions allegedly due as a result of a sale of cash registers to First National Stores Inc. (First National) in 1968. Counts 1 and 2 of Fortune's amended declaration claimed bonus payments under the parties' written contract of employment. The third count sought recovery in quantum meruit for the reasonable value of Fortune's services relating to the same sales transaction. Judgment on a jury verdict for Fortune was reversed by the Appeals Court, and this court granted leave to obtain further appellate review. We affirm the judgment of the Superior Court. We hold, for the reasons stated herein, there was no error in submitting the issue of "bad faith" termination of an employment at will contract to the jury.

The issues before the court are raised by NCR's motion for directed verdicts. Accordingly, we summarize the evidence most favorable to the plaintiff. * * *

Fortune was employed by NCR under a written "salesman's contract" which was terminable at will, without cause, by either party on written notice. The contract provided that Fortune would receive a weekly salary in a fixed amount plus a bonus for sales made within the "territory" (i.e., customer accounts or stores) assigned to him for "coverage or supervision," whether the sale was made by him or someone else.[2] The amount of the bonus was determined on the basis of "bonus credits," which were computed as a percentage of the price of products sold. Fortune would be paid a percentage of the applicable bonus credit as follows: (1) 75% if the territory was assigned to him at the date of the order, (2) 25% if the territory was assigned to him at the date of delivery and installation, or (3) 100% if the territory was assigned to him at both times. The contract further provided that the "bonus interest" would terminate if shipment of the order was not made within eighteen months from the date of the order unless (1) the territory was assigned to him for coverage at the date of delivery and installation, or (2) special engineering was required to fulfil the contract. In addition, NCR reserved the right to sell products in the salesman's territory without paying a bonus. However, this right could be exercised only on written notice.

In 1968, Fortune's territory included First National. This account had been part of his territory for the preceding six years; he had been successful in obtaining several orders from First National, including a million dollar order in 1963. Sometime in late 1967, or early 1968, NCR introduced a new model cash register, Class 5. Fortune corresponded with First National in an effort to sell the machine. He also helped to arrange for a demonstration of the Class 5 to executives of First National on October 4, 1968. NCR had a team of men also working on this sale.

On November 27, 1968, NCR's manager of chain and department stores, and the Boston branch manager, both part of NCR's team, wrote to First National regarding the Class 5. The letter covered a number of subjects, including price protection, trade-ins, and trade-in protection against obsolescence. While NCR normally offered price protection for only an eighteen-month term, apparently the size of the proposed order from First National caused NCR to extend its price protection terms for either a two-year or four-year period. On November 29, 1968, First National signed

---

[2]   Apparently, NCR's use of a "guaranteed territory" was designed to motivate "the salesman to develop good will for the company and also avoided a damaging rivalry among salesmen." D. Boorstin, The Americans: The Democratic Experience at 202 (1973).

an order for 2,008 Class 5 machines to be delivered over a four-year period at a purchase price of approximately $5,000,000. Although Fortune did not participate in the negotiation of the terms of the order,[3] his name appeared on the order form in the space entitled "salesman credited." The amount of the bonus credit as shown on the order was $92,079.99.

On January 6, 1969, the first working day of the new year, Fortune found an envelope on his desk at work. It contained a termination notice addressed to his home dated December 2, 1968. Shortly after receiving the notice, Fortune spoke to the Boston branch manager with whom he was friendly. The manager told him, "You are through," but, after considering some of the details necessary for the smooth operation of the First National order, told him to "stay on," and to "[k]eep on doing what you are doing right now." Fortune remained with the company in a position entitled "sales support." In this capacity, he coordinated and expedited delivery of the machines to First National under the November 29 order as well as servicing other accounts.

Commencing in May or June, Fortune began to receive some bonus commissions on the First National order. Having received only 75% of the applicable bonus due on the machines which had been delivered and installed, Fortune spoke with his manager about receiving the full amount of the commission. Fortune was told "to forget about it." Sixty-one years old at that time, and with a son in college, Fortune concluded that it "was a good idea to forget it for the time being."

NCR did pay a systems and installations person the remaining 25% of the bonus commissions due from the First National order although contrary to its usual policy of paying *only* salesmen a bonus. NCR, by its letter of November 27, 1968, had promised the services of a systems and installations person; the letter had claimed that the services of this person, Bernie Martin (Martin), would have a forecasted cost to NCR of over $45,000. As promised, NCR did transfer Martin to the First National account shortly after the order was placed.

Approximately eighteen months after receiving the termination notice, Fortune, who had worked for NCR for almost twenty-five years, was asked to retire. When he refused, he was fired in June of 1970. Fortune did not receive any bonus payments on machines which were delivered to First National after this date.

At the close of the plaintiff's case, the defendant moved for a directed verdict, arguing that there was no evidence of any breach of contract, and adding that the existence of a contract barred recovery under the quantum meruit count. Ruling that Fortune could recover if the termination and firing were in bad faith, the trial judge, without specifying on which count,

---

[3] Fortune was not authorized to offer the price protection terms which appeared in the November 27 letter, as special covenant A, par. 3 of his contract prohibited him from varying the prices of items.

submitted this issue to the jury. NCR then rested and, by agreement of counsel, the case was sent to the jury for special verdicts on two questions:

"1. Did the Defendant act in bad faith * * * when it decided to terminate the Plaintiff's contract as a salesman by letter dated December 2, 1968, delivered on January 6, 1969?

"2. Did the Defendant act in bad faith * * * when the Defendant let the Plaintiff go on June 5, 1970?"

The jury answered both questions affirmatively, and judgment entered in the sum of $45,649.62.[6]

* * *

The contract at issue is a classic terminable at will employment contract. It is clear that the contract itself reserved to the parties an explicit power to terminate the contract without cause on written notice. It is also clear that under the express terms of the contract Fortune has received all the bonus commissions to which he is entitled. Thus, NCR claims that it did not breach the contract, and that it has no further liability to Fortune.[7] According to a literal reading of the contract, NCR is correct.

However, Fortune argues that, in spite of the literal wording of the contract, he is entitled to a jury determination on NCR's motives in terminating his services under the contract and in finally discharging him. We agree. We hold that NCR's written contract contains an implied covenant of good faith and fair dealing, and a termination not made in good faith constitutes a breach of the contract.

We do not question the general principles that an employer is entitled to be motivated by and to serve its own legitimate business interests; that an employer must have wide latitude in deciding whom it will employ in the face of the uncertainties of the business world; and that an employer needs flexibility in the face of changing circumstances. We recognize the employer's need for a large amount of control over its work force. However, we believe that where, as here, commissions are to be paid for work performed by the employee, the employer's decision to terminate its at will employee should be made in good faith. NCR's right to make decisions in

---

[6] The amount apparently represented 25% of the commission due during the eighteen months the machines were delivered to First National, and which was paid to Martin, and 100% of the commissions on the machines delivered after Fortune was fired.

[7] Damages were, by stipulation of the parties, set equal to the unpaid bonus amounts. Thus we need not consider whether other measures of damages might be justified in cases of bad faith termination. Nor do we now decide whether a tort action, with possible punitive damages, might lie in such circumstances. See, e.g., Blades, Employment at Will vs. Individual Freedom: On Limiting the Abusive Exercise of Employer Power, 67 Colum.L.Rev. 1404, 1421–1427 (1967).

Although the order called for purchase of 2,008 Class 5 machines for a total sale of $5,040,080, at trial the parties stipulated that "1,503 machines were actually delivered and installed" under the First National order. The stipulated damages in the instant case were based on the number of registers actually delivered and installed.

its own interest is not, in our view, unduly hampered by a requirement of adherence to this standard.

On occasion some courts have avoided the rigidity of the "at will" rule by fashioning a remedy in tort. We believe, however, that in this case there is remedy on the express contract. In so holding we are merely recognizing the general requirement in this Commonwealth that parties to contracts and commercial transactions must act in good faith toward one another. Good faith and fair dealing between parties are pervasive requirements in our law; it can be said fairly, that parties to contracts or commercial transactions are bound by this standard. See G.L. c. 106, § 1–203 (good faith in contracts under Uniform Commercial Code); G.L. c. 93B, § 4(3)(c) (good faith in motor vehicle franchise termination).

* * *

In the instant case, we need not * * * speculate as to whether the good faith requirement is implicit in every contract for employment at will. It is clear, however, that, on the facts before us, a finding is warranted that a breach of the contract occurred. Where the principal seeks to deprive the agent of all compensation by terminating the contractual relationship when the agent is on the brink of successfully completing the sale, the principal has acted in bad faith and the ensuing transaction between the principal and the buyer is to be regarded as having been accomplished by the agent. Restatement (Second) of Agency § 454, and Comment a (1958). The same result obtains where the principal attempts to deprive the agent of any portion of a commission due the agent. Courts have often applied this rule to prevent overreaching by employers and the forfeiture by employees of benefits almost earned by the rendering of substantial services. See, e.g., *RLM Assocs. v. Carter Mfg. Corp.,* 356 Mass. 718, 248 N.E.2d 646 (1969); *Lemmon v. Cedar Point, Inc.,* 406 F.2d 94, 97 (6th Cir.1969); *Coleman v. Graybar Elec. Co.,* 195 F.2d 374 (5th Cir.1952); *Zimmer v. Wells Management Corp.,* 348 F.Supp. 540 (S.D.N.Y.1972); *Sinnett v. Hie Food Prods., Inc.,* 185 Neb. 221, 174 N.W.2d 720 (1970). In our view, the Appeals Court erroneously focused only on literal compliance with payment provisions of the contract and failed to consider the issue of bad faith termination. Restatement (Second) of Agency § 454, and Comment a (1958).

NCR argues that there was no evidence of bad faith in this case; therefore, the trial judge was required to direct a verdict in any event. We think that the evidence and the reasonable inferences to be drawn therefrom support a jury verdict that the termination of Fortune's twenty-five years of employment as a salesman with NCR the next business day after NCR obtained a $5,000,000 order from First National was motivated by a desire to pay Fortune as little of the bonus credit as it could. The fact that Fortune was willing to work under these circumstances does not constitute a waiver or estoppel; it only shows that NCR had him "at their mercy." *Commonwealth v. DeCotis,* 366 Mass. 234, 243, 316 N.E.2d 748 (1974).

NCR also contends that Fortune cannot complain of his firing in June, 1970, as his employment contract clearly indicated that bonus credits would be paid only for an eighteen-month period following the date of the order. As we have said, the jury could have found that Fortune was stripped of his "salesman" designation in order to disqualify him for the remaining 25% of the commissions due on cash registers delivered prior to the date of his first termination. Similarly, the jury could have found that Fortune was fired (or not assigned to the First National account) so that NCR could avoid paying him *any* commissions on cash registers delivered after June, 1970.

Conversely, the jury could have found that Fortune was assigned by NCR to the First National account; that all he did in this case was arrange for a demonstration of the product; that he neither participated in obtaining the order nor did he assist NCR in closing the order; and that nevertheless NCR credited him with the sale. This, however, did not obligate the trial judge to direct a verdict.

NOTES AND QUESTIONS

Test Your Understanding of the Material

1. Did National Cash Register breach the express terms of the "salesman contract"?

2. Does the implied covenant of good faith and fair dealing represent an exception to the employment-at-will rule? Consider Employment Restatement § 2.07, Comment b: "As in all contracts, the implied duty of good faith and fair dealing serves as a supplementary aid in implementing the parties' reasonable expectations and should not be read as a means of overriding the basic terms of, or otherwise undermining the essential nature of their contractual relationship. Jurisdictions that recognize the implied duty also recognize that the duty applies in at-will employment in a manner consistent with the essential nature of such an at-will relationship—namely, except to the extent provided by law or public policy, either party may terminate the relationship, with or without cause."

3. Was National Cash Register acting unfairly by terminating Fortune? Richard Epstein argues:

> The contractual provisions concerning commissions represent a rough effort to match payment with performance where the labor of more than one individual was necessary to close the sale. The case is not simply one where a strategically timed firing allowed the company to deprive a dismissed employee of the benefits due him upon completion of performance. Indeed, the firm kept none of the commission at all, so that when the case went to the jury, the only issue was whether the company should be called upon to pay the

same commission twice. * * * In its enthusiastic meddling in private contracts, the court nowhere suggested an alternative commission structure that would have better served the joint interests of the parties at the time of contract formation.

Epstein, In Defense of the Contract at Will, 51 U.Chi.L.Rev. 947, 981–82 (1984). Do you agree?

Related Issues

4.   *Recovery of Lost Commissions Only?* Is Fortune seeking recovery only for commissions withheld or was he also seeking recovery for lost future compensation due to his alleged bad-faith termination?

As interpreted by the Massachusetts courts, *Fortune* seems confined to situations involving forfeiture of compensation for past services on the eve of entitlement. See Gram v. Liberty Mutual Ins. Co., 384 Mass. 659, 666–67, 429 N.E.2d 21, 25–26 (1981). Moreover, the *Fortune* ruling has been construed to provide a basis only for securing the compensation withheld rather than for overturning the termination itself. See Wakefield v. Northern Telecom, Inc., 769 F.2d 109 (2d Cir.1985) (applying either New York or New Jersey law). Judge Winter observed in *Wakefield*:

> Wakefield may not * * * recover for his termination *per se*. However, the contract for payment of commissions creates rights distinct from the employment relation, and * * * obligations derived from the covenant of good faith implicit in the commission contract may survive the termination of the employment relationship.
>
> * * *
>
> A covenant of good faith should not be implied as a modification of an employer's right to terminate an at-will employee because even a whimsical termination does not deprive the employee of benefits expected in return for the employee's performance. This is so because performance and the distribution of benefits occur simultaneously, and neither party is left high and dry by the termination. Where, however, a covenant of good faith is necessary to enable one party to receive the benefits promised for performance, it is implied by the law as necessary to effectuate the intent of the parties.

Id. at 112. For rulings similar to *Fortune* and *Wakefield,* see Metcalf v. Intermountain Gas Co., 116 Idaho 622, 627, 778 P.2d 744, 749 (1989); Wagenseller v. Scottsdale Memorial Hospital, 147 Ariz. 370, 710 P.2d 1025, 1040 (1985) (en banc); Nolan v. Control Data Corp., 243 N.J.Super. 420, 579 A.2d 1252 (App.Div.1990).

The good-faith covenant plays a significant role in deferred compensation cases. See generally Samuel J. Samaro, The Case for Fiduciary Duty as a Restraint on Employer Opportunism Under Sales Commission Agreements, 8 U. Pa. L. Rev. J. of Lab. & Emp. L. 441 (2006). See Employment Restatement § 3.05.

5. *The Good-Faith Covenant in New York.* The New York courts have insisted that an implied good-faith covenant cannot be read so as to override an at-will employment contract: "[I]t would be incongruous to say that an inference may be drawn that the employer impliedly agreed to a provision which would be destructive of his right of termination." Murphy v. American Home Products Corp., 58 N.Y.2d 293, 304–05, 461 N.Y.S.2d 232, 237, 448 N.E.2d 86, 91 (1983).

In Wieder v. Skala, 80 N.Y.2d 628, 593 N.Y.S.2d 752, 609 N.E.2d 105 (1992), New York opened the door a crack, in a case involving a law firm's discharge of an associate allegedly for reporting the professional misconduct of another associate to disciplinary authorities as required by the legal profession's Code of Professional Responsibility. The high court held that the plaintiff stated a claim for breach of contract based on an "implied-in-law obligation" inherent in his relationship with his employer. *Wieder*'s potential reach was narrowed in Horn v. New York Times Co., 100 N.Y.2d 85, 790 N.E.2d 753, 760 N.Y.S.2d 378 (2003).

6. *Securities Industry Arbitration.* Arbitration disputes before the Financial Industry Regulatory Authority often involve implied-covenant and industry-practice claims. For a plaintiff lawyer'sperspective in this context, see Ethan A. Brecher, Compensation Claims in Securities Industry Arbitration, ch. 13 in Compensation, Work Hours and Benefits; Proc. N.Y.U. 57th Ann. Conf. on Labor (Jeffrey M. Hirsch & Samuel Estreicher eds. 2009).

2. STATUTORY WAGE CLAIMS ARISING FROM CONTRACT

TRUELOVE V. NORTHEAST CAPITAL & ADVISORY, INC.
Court of Appeals of New York, 2000.
95 N.Y.2d 220, 738 N.E.2d 770, 715 N.Y.S.2d 366.

LEVINE, J.

Plaintiff William B. Truelove, Jr. brought this action against his former employer, defendant Northeast Capital & Advisory, Inc., under article 6 of the Labor Law to recover the unpaid balance of a bonus he was awarded in December 1997, payable in quarterly installments through the following year. His complaint alleges that his bonus constituted "wages" within the meaning of Labor Law § 190(1) and that, following his resignation after the first bonus payment, defendant violated Labor Law § 193 by enforcing an express condition in the bonus plan predicating payment of each quarterly installment on continued employment. We agree with Supreme Court and the Appellate Division that plaintiff's bonus does not fall within the definition of wages protected by Labor Law article 6.

Defendant, a small investment banking firm, hired plaintiff in June 1996 as a financial analyst in a non-revenue generating position. Plaintiff elected a compensation plan under which he was to receive an annual salary of $40,000 and be eligible to participate in a bonus/profit sharing pool. Plaintiff's offer of employment stated that a "bonus, if paid, would reflect a combination of the individual's performance and Northeast Capital's performance."

The terms of the bonus plan were further clarified in two memoranda by defendant's Chief Executive Officer. The memoranda explained that a bonus/profit sharing pool would be established only if the firm generated a certain stated minimum of revenues and that the pool, once established, would be calculated pursuant to a graduated percentage schedule of firm revenues. The memoranda further stipulated that bonus/profit sharing distributions would be allocated in the CEO's sole discretion and would be paid in quarterly installments, with each payment contingent upon the recipient's continued employment at the firm. Employees were required to have an "acceptable" performance rating to participate in the bonus/profit sharing pool.

At the end of 1997, defendant established a bonus/profit sharing pool of $240,000 based upon firm revenues of approximately $1.6 million for that year. Defendant's CEO allocated $160,000 of that pool to plaintiff. Defendant paid plaintiff an initial bonus installment of $40,000, but refused to make any further payments after plaintiff's resignation.

Plaintiff brought this suit under Labor Law article 6, alleging that his bonus fell within the definition of wages set forth in Labor Law § 190(1). Plaintiff claimed that defendant's failure to pay him the three remaining bonus installment payments for 1997 violated Labor Law § 193, which provides that "no employer shall make any deduction from the wages of an employee, except" under certain limited circumstances not relevant here. Supreme Court granted summary judgment to defendant on the ground that plaintiff's bonus did not constitute wages within the meaning of Labor Law article 6. The Appellate Division affirmed. * * *

Article 6 of the Labor Law sets forth a comprehensive set of statutory provisions enacted to strengthen and clarify the rights of employees to the payment of wages. * * * An employer who violates the requirements of Labor Law article 6 is subject to civil liability and criminal penalties (see, Labor Law §§ 198 and 198–a). The dispositive issue in this case is whether plaintiff's bonus constitutes "wages" within the meaning of the Labor Law.

Although New York has provided statutory protection for workers' wages for more than a century * * *, the Legislature first defined the term "wages" in the 1966 enactment of Labor Law article 6 (L 1996, ch. 548). Labor Law § 190(1) defines "wages" as "the earnings of an employee for labor or services rendered, regardless of whether the amount of earnings is determined on a time, piece, commission or other basis". Courts have construed this statutory definition as excluding certain forms of "incentive compensation" that are more in the nature of a profit-sharing arrangement and are both contingent and dependent, at least in part, on the financial success of the business enterprise (see, *International Paper Co. v. Suwyn*, 978 F.Supp. 506, 514; *Tischmann v. ITT/Sheraton Corp.*, 882 F.Supp. 1358, 1370; see also, *Magness v. Human Resource Servs., Inc.*, 161 A.D.2d 418, 419, 555 N.Y.S.2d 347). We arrive at the same conclusion with respect to plaintiff's bonus compensation arrangement.

The terms of defendant's bonus compensation plan did not predicate bonus payments upon plaintiff's own personal productivity nor give plaintiff a contractual right to bonus payments based upon his productivity. To the contrary, the declaration of a bonus pool was dependent solely upon his employer's overall financial success. In addition, plaintiff's share in the bonus pool was entirely discretionary and subject to the non-reviewable determination of his employer. These factors, we believe, take plaintiff's bonus payments out of the statutory definition of wages.

Unlike in other areas where the Legislature chose to define broadly the term "wages" to include every form of compensation paid to an employee, including bonuses (see Unemployment Insurance Law §§ 517, 518), the Legislature elected not to define that term in Labor Law § 190(1) so expansively as to cover all forms of employee remuneration. We therefore agree with those courts that have concluded that the more restrictive statutory definition of "wages," as "earnings for labor or services rendered," excludes incentive compensation "based on factors falling outside the scope of the employee's actual work" * * *. In our view, the wording of the statute, in expressly linking earnings to an employee's labor or services personally rendered, contemplates a more direct relationship between an employee's own performance and the compensation to which that employee is entitled. Discretionary additional remuneration, as a share in a reward to all employees for the success of the employer's entrepreneurship, falls outside the protection of the statute.

* * *

Finally, we reject plaintiff's argument that he had a vested right to the bonus payments once defendant declared that a bonus would be paid and calculated the amount of that bonus. In *Hall v. United Parcel Serv.* (76 N.Y.2d 27, 36, 556 N.Y.S.2d 21, 555 N.E.2d 273), we held that an "employee's entitlement to a bonus is governed by the terms of the employer's bonus plan." Here, the bonus plan explicitly predicated the continuation of bonus payments upon the recipient's continued employment status. Because plaintiff resigned shortly after he received his first quarterly payment, he was not entitled to receive the remaining three payments.

NOTES AND QUESTIONS

Test Your Understanding of the Material

1. Under current FLSA regulations, would Truelove likely have qualified as exempt from minimum wage and overtime? Which provision?

2. Assume that Truelove would have been eligible for overtime. Should the bonus have been included in his "regular rate"?

3. Would the bonus payment in *Fortune v. National Cash Register* have qualified as a "wage" under the standard articulated in *Truelove*?

Related Issues

4. *"Earned" Wages.* Wage claims involving commissions often turn on whether the commission was "earned" under terms of the applicable contract or plan. These disputes become even more complex when the applicable provision does not define "earned", as illustrated in the case of *Pachter v. Bernard Hodes Group, Inc.*, 10 N.Y.3d 609 (2008), on certified questions from 505 F.3d 129 (2d Cir.2007):

> Pachter's commission earnings were calculated using a formula. When a client of Hodes agreed to a media buy, Hodes would advance payment to the media company and the client would subsequently reimburse Hodes and pay a fee for Pachter's services. When the client was billed, Pachter received a percentage of the amount billed minus particular charges that are central to the dispute in this case—client receipts were reduced by certain business costs, such as finance charges for late payments, losses attributable to errors in placing advertisements, uncollectible debts and Pachter's travel and entertainment expenses. In addition, she chose to work with an assistant, and half of the assistant's salary was deducted from Pachter's percentage of billings. Each month, Pachter received a commission statement that listed her total billings and the percentage of those billings that represented her gross commission. The expenses attributed to her activities and any advances she had drawn from her commission account were then deducted to reach the net amount of income she had earned for that period. Pachter concedes that she was aware of the charges Hodes subtracted from her gross commissions and acquiesced in the compensation scheme for over a decade. * * * .

> The lack of a specific written contract on when commissions were earned is not determinative because the record in the case—the evidence of the parties' extensive course of dealings for more than 11 years and the written monthly compensation statements issued by Hodes and accepted by Pachter—provided ample support for the conclusion that there was an implied contract under which the final computation of the commissions earned by Pachter depended on first making adjustments for nonpayments by customers and the cost of Pachter's assistant, as well as miscellaneous work-related expenses

* * * . Notably, Pachter understood the adjustments and acquiesced in them—the District Court found that Pachter consented to the compensation plan and that Hodes complied with it in all respects, thereby establishing that the parties mutually agreed to depart from the common-law rule, i.e., commissions are earned when the broker procures a customer "ready and willing to enter into a contract upon [the salesmen's] employer's terms," Feinberg Bros. Agency, Inc. v. Berted Realty Co., Inc., 70 N.Y.2d 828, 830, 517 N.E.2d 1325, 523 N.Y.S.2d 439 (1987).

We therefore conclude that neither section 193 nor any other provision of article 6 of the Labor Law prevented the parties in this case from structuring the compensation formula so that Pachter's commission would be deemed earned only after specific deductions were taken from her percentage of gross billings. Consequently, we answer the second certified question by stating that, in the absence of a governing written instrument, when a commission is "earned" and becomes a "wage" for purposes of Labor Law article 6 is regulated by the parties' express or implied agreement; or, if no agreement exists, by the default common-law rule that ties the earning of a commission to the employee's production of a ready, willing and able purchaser of the services.

10 N.Y.3d at 618.

5. *Vacation and Sick Pay.* Employers typically structure their vacation policies to allow employees to accrue a certain number of days or hours of vacation pay over a period of months or years of service. Sick pay, by contrast, is often structured as an allotment of usable days over the course of a year to be used for specific purposes.

Some states characterize vacation pay as a wage, non-forfeitable once earned. Characterizing vacation pay as a wage limits an employer's ability to erase an employee's vacation balance from year to year, and requires an employer to pay out unused vacation upon termination. See Cal. Lab. § 227.3; Thompson v. Cheyenne Mountain Sch. Dist. No. 12, 844 P.2d 1235 (Colo. App. Ct. 1992) (unused vacation must be paid upon termination absent express agreement providing for forfeiture).

Sick pay tends to be excluded from the definition of "wage" although states vary. See e.g. 7 D.C.M.R. § 3204.3 (D.C. sick leave statute does not require payout upon termination); Schwartz v. Gary Comm. Sch. Corp, 762 N.E.2d 192 (Ind. Ct. App. 2002) (sick pay is a wage where no restrictions are placed on its use); Souto v. Sovereign Realty Assoc., 23 Mass. L. Rptr. 386 (Ma. Super. 2007) (no right to sick pay upon termination absent express agreement).

6. *Are Stock Options "Wages"?* In Schachter v. Citigroup, Inc., 47 Cal.4th 610, 101 Cal. Rptr. 3d 2 (2009), the plaintiff signed a restricted stock agreement upon hire, which provided for a compensation reduction in exchange for discounted restricted stock, vesting over two years. The terms also provided that the employee would forfeit the stock if the employee they

terminated employment voluntarily prior to vesting. When Schachter resigned prior to the vesting date, he brought a wage claim alleging that the stock represented a wage and could not be forfeited under California's wage-payment statutes.

The Court agreed that stock qualified as a wage but treated Schachter's stock as equivalent to incentive compensation. Like commissions and bonuses, California law permits employers to place conditions precedent upon "earning" incentive compensation. Because Schachter had not yet "earned" the stock under the restricted stock agreement, Citigroup did not violate wage laws by refusing to provide the stock.

7. *Penalties for Delay in Paying Final Wages.* Several states impose penalties on employers that fail to deliver a final paycheck within a specified period following termination or resignation (known as "waiting time" penalties). See e.g. Cal. Lab. Code § 203 (willful failure to pay final paycheck "immediately" upon termination or within 72 hours of a resignation, liable for 1 days' wages for each day of delay, up to 30 days); Md. Lab & Emp Art. § 3–505 (liquidated damages of up to 3 times unpaid wage where employers fails to pay undisputed wages by next regular payday); Minn. Stat. § 181.14 (penalty of up to 14 days wages for delay in payment).

8. *Improper Deductions from Wages.* Many state wage-payment laws restrict an employer from making deductions from an employee's paycheck, regardless of whether the employee is exempt. See e.g. N.Y. Labor Law § 193 ("no employer shall make any deduction from the wages of an employee, except" under certain specified circumstances); N.J. Stat. § 34:11–4.4 ("no employer may withhold or divert any portions of an employee's wages" unless "required or empowered to do so by" state or federal law, or the contributions are used for certain permissible purposes).

Several state labor agencies have interpreted their wage-payment laws to prohibit deductions based on cash shortages or inventory shortfalls or damage. See e.g. Cal. Dep. of Ind. Rel., Deductions, available at www.dir.ca.gov/dlse/faq_deductions.html; But see Colo. Rev. Stat. § 8–4–105(e) (permits deductions for an employee's failure to pay for or return property).

9. *"Wages" vs. "Company Funds"?* Consider In the Matter of Hudacs v. Frito-Lay, Inc., 90 N.Y.2d 342, 344–45, 660 N.Y.S.2d 700, 683 N.E.2d 322 (1997):

> Respondent Frito-Lay, Inc. manufactures and distributes snack foods. As part of its distribution process, it employs route salespeople who pick up the snack food from the company's wholesale distribution warehouses, deliver them to retailers and collect payments from those stores on behalf of the company. * * *

> When a salesperson picks up the product each morning from the Frito-Lay warehouse, the amount taken and the cost is verified by both the salesperson and a warehouse employee. The salesperson then delivers the product to various retail markets, and collects payment from the retailer for the product delivered. * * * The

company requires cash receipts to be converted into either checks or money orders, which are then mailed directly to Frito-Lay along with checks from retailers and charge tickets. The company reimburses employees for the costs of money orders; however, the checks forwarded by employees come directly from their personal checking accounts.

Every 20 business days, the company issues an accounting report to each employee. * * * The reports show any discrepancies between the amount of product taken by a salesperson, and the amount of money remitted to Frito-Lay. The salespeople are required to reimburse the company for any deficit shown on the report. * * * Frito-Lay provides the employees an opportunity to demonstrate that the deficit is the result of such things as damaged or stale product, bounced checks, or third-party theft of either product or cash. Frito-Lay does not attempt to recoup those types of losses from its employees. Moreover, wages are paid regardless of any outstanding account deficiencies existing at the time of payment, although the company does impose other sanctions [including discipline] for the failure to make up account deficits.

Has Frito-Lay violated New York Labor Law § 193? Is the case distinguishable from that of more typical service workers such as supermarket cashiers or waiters whom the New York Legislature presumably intended to protect from payback schemes?

CHAPTER 19

BENEFITS

■ ■ ■

Introduction

Employee benefits in addition to wages or salary are often an important part of compensation. The tax system generally favors employer provision of certain benefits by not treating their receipt as taxable income for employees. The value of such benefits is leveraged by this preferential tax treatment. In addition, in some situations, employers because of economies of scale may be able to provide benefits to employees that are better or cheaper than the employees could obtain on the open market. See Samuel Estreicher & Gillian Lester, Employment Law 228–30 (2008).

A. HEALTH AND WELFARE BENEFITS

M&G POLYMERS USA, LLC v. TACKETT

Supreme Court of the United States, 2015.
574 U.S. ___, 135 S.Ct. 926, 190 L.Ed.2d 809.

JUSTICE THOMAS delivered the opinion of the Court.

This case arises out of a disagreement between a group of retired employees and their former employer about the meaning of certain expired collective-bargaining agreements. The retirees (and their former union) claim that these agreements created a right to lifetime contribution-free health care benefits for retirees, their surviving spouses, and their dependents. The employer, for its part, claims that those provisions terminated when the agreements expired. * * *

I

Respondents Hobert Freel Tackett, Woodrow K. Pyles, and Harlan B. Conley worked at (and retired from) the Point Pleasant Polyester Plant in Apple Grove, West Virginia (hereinafter referred to as the Plant). * * * They represent a class of retired employees from the Plant, along with their surviving spouses and other dependents. Petitioner M&G Polymers USA, LLC, is the current owner of the Plant.

When M&G purchased the Plant in 2000, it entered a master collective-bargaining agreement and a Pension, Insurance, and Service Award Agreement (P&I agreement) with the Union, generally similar to agreements the Union had negotiated with M & G's predecessor. The P&I agreement provided for retiree health care benefits as follows:

> "Employees who retire on or after January 1, 1996 and who are eligible for and receiving a monthly pension under the 1993 Pension Plan . . . whose full years of attained age and full years of attained continuous service . . . at the time of retirement equals 95 or more points will receive a full Company contribution towards the cost of [health care] benefits described in this Exhibit B-1. . . . Employees who have less than 95 points at the time of retirement will receive a reduced Company contribution. The Company contribution will be reduced by 2% for every point less than 95. Employees will be required to pay the balance of the health care contribution, as estimated by the Company annually in advance, for the [health care] benefits described in this Exhibit B-1. Failure to pay the required medical contribution will result in cancellation of coverage." * * *

Exhibit B-1, which described the health care benefits at issue, opened with the following durational clause: "Effective January 1, 1998, and for the duration of this Agreement thereafter, the Employer will provide the following program of hospital benefits, hospital-medical benefits, surgical benefits and prescription drug benefits for eligible employees and their dependents. . . ." * * * The P&I agreement provided for renegotiation of its terms in three years.

In December 2006, M&G announced that it would begin requiring retirees to contribute to the cost of their health care benefits. Respondent retirees, on behalf of themselves and others similarly situated, sued M&G and related entities, alleging that the decision to require these contributions breached both the collective-bargaining agreement and the P&I agreement, * * * and § 502(a)(1)(B) of the Employee Retirement Income Security Act of 1974 (ERISA), 88 Stat. 891. Specifically, the retirees alleged that M&G had promised to provide lifetime contribution-free health care benefits for them, their surviving spouses, and their dependents. They pointed to the language in the 2000 P&I agreement providing that employees with a certain level of seniority "will receive a full Company contribution towards the cost of [health care] benefits described in. . . ." * * * The retirees alleged that, with this promise, M&G had created a vested right to such benefits that continued beyond the expiration of the 2000 P&I agreement.

The District Court dismissed the complaint for failure to state a claim. * * * The Court of Appeals reversed based on the reasoning of its earlier decision in [*International Union, United Automobile Workers v. Yard-Man*, 716 F.2d 1476 (6th Cir. 1983), which] involved a similar claim that an employer had breached a collective-bargaining agreement when it terminated retiree benefits. 716 F.2d, at 1478. * * *

The Court of Appeals [concluded] * * * that, "in the absence of extrinsic evidence to the contrary, the agreements indicated an intent to vest lifetime contribution-free benefits." * * *

II

This case is about the interpretation of collective-bargaining agreements that define rights to welfare benefits plans. * * * When collective-bargaining [or other] agreements create pension or welfare benefits plans, those plans are subject to rules established in ERISA. ERISA defines pension plans as plans, funds, or programs that "provid[e] retirement income to employees" or that "resul[t] in a deferral of income." § 1002(2)(A). It defines welfare benefits plans as plans, funds, or programs established or maintained to provide participants with additional benefits, such as life insurance and disability coverage. § 1002(1).

ERISA treats these two types of plans differently. Although ERISA imposes elaborate minimum funding and vesting standards for pension plans, §§ 1053, 1082, 1083, 1084, it explicitly exempts welfare benefits plans from those rules, §§ 1051(1), 1081(a)(1). Welfare benefits plans must be "established and maintained pursuant to a written instrument," § 1102(a)(1), but "[e]mployers or other plan sponsors are generally free under ERISA, for any reason at any time, to adopt, modify, or terminate welfare plans," *Curtiss-Wright Corp. v. Schoonejongen,* 514 U.S. 73, 78, 115 S.Ct. 1223, 131 L.Ed.2d 94 (1995). As we have previously recognized, "[E]mployers have large leeway to design disability and other welfare plans as they see fit." *Black & Decker Disability Plan v. Nord,* 538 U.S. 822, 833, 123 S.Ct. 1965, 155 L.Ed.2d 1034 (2003). And, we have observed, the rule that contractual "provisions ordinarily should be enforced as written is especially appropriate when enforcing an ERISA [welfare benefits] plan." * * *

We interpret collective-bargaining agreements, including those establishing ERISA plans, according to ordinary principles of contract law, at least when those principles are not inconsistent with federal labor policy. See *Textile Workers v. Lincoln Mills of Ala.,* 353 U.S. 448, 456–457, 77 S.Ct. 912, 1 L.Ed.2d 972 (1957). "In this endeavor, as with any other contract, the parties' intentions control." *Stolt-Nielsen S.A. v. AnimalFeeds Int'l Corp.,* 559 U.S. 662, 682, 130 S.Ct. 1758, 176 L.Ed.2d 605 (2010). * * *

III

The Court of Appeals has long insisted that its *Yard-Man* inferences are drawn from ordinary contract law. In *Yard-Man* itself, the court purported to apply "traditional rules for contractual interpretation." 716 F.2d, at 1479. The court first concluded that the provision governing retiree insurance benefits—which stated only that the employer "will provide" such benefits—was ambiguous as to the duration of those benefits. *Id.,* at 1480. To resolve that ambiguity, it looked to other provisions of the agreement. The agreement included provisions for terminating active employees' insurance benefits in the case of layoffs and for terminating benefits for a retiree's spouse and dependents in case of the retiree's death before the expiration of the collective-bargaining agreement, but no provision specifically addressed the duration of retiree health care benefits. *Id.,* at 1481–1482. From the existence of these termination provisions and the absence of a termination provision specifically addressing retiree benefits, the court inferred an intent to vest those retiree benefits for life.

The court then purported to apply the rule that contracts should be interpreted to avoid illusory promises. It noted that the retiree insurance provisions "contain[ed] a promise that the company will pay an early retiree's insurance upon such retiree reaching age 65 but that the retiree must bear the cost of company insurance until that time." *Id.,* at 1481. Employees could retire at age 55, but the agreement containing this promise applied only for a 3-year term. *Ibid.* Thus, retirees between the ages of 55 and 62 would not turn 65 and become eligible for the company contribution before the 3-year agreement expired. In light of this fact, the court reasoned that the promise would be "completely illusory for many early retirees under age 62" if the retiree benefits terminated when the contract expired. *Ibid.* * * *

Although the contract included a general durational clause—meaning that the contract itself would expire at a set time—the court concluded that these contextual clues "outweigh[ed] any contrary implications derived from a routine duration clause." *Id.,* at 1483.

* * *

We disagree with the Court of Appeals' assessment that the inferences applied in *Yard-Man* and its progeny represent ordinary principles of contract law.

As an initial matter, *Yard-Man* violates ordinary contract principles by placing a thumb on the scale in favor of vested retiree benefits in all collective-bargaining agreements. That rule has no basis in ordinary principles of contract law. And it distorts the attempt "to ascertain the intention of *the parties*." 11 Williston [on Contracts] § 30:2, at 18 * * * ; see also *Stolt-Nielsen,* 559 U.S., at 682, 130 S.Ct. 1758. *Yard-Man*'s assessment of likely behavior in collective bargaining is too speculative and too far removed from the context of any particular contract to be useful in discerning the parties' intention.

And the Court of Appeals derived its assessment of likely behavior not from record evidence, but instead from its own suppositions about the intentions of employees, unions, and employers negotiating retiree benefits. See *Yard-Man,* 716 F.2d, at 1482. For example, it asserted, without any foundation, that, "when . . . parties contract for benefits which accrue upon achievement of retiree status, there is an inference that the parties likely intended those benefits to continue as long as the beneficiary remains a retiree." *Ibid.*; see also *ibid.* ("[I]t is unlikely that [retiree] benefits ... would be left to the contingencies of future negotiations"). Although a court may look to known customs or usages in a particular industry to determine the meaning of a contract, the parties must prove those customs or usages using affirmative evidentiary support in a given case. 12 Williston § 34:3; accord, *Robinson v. United States,* 13 Wall. 363, 366, 20 L.Ed. 653 (1872); *Oelricks v. Ford,* 23 How. 49, 61–62, 16 L.Ed. 534 (1860). *Yard-Man* relied on no record evidence indicating that employers and unions in that industry customarily vest retiree benefits. * * *

Yard-Man also relied on the premise that retiree benefits are a form of deferred compensation, but that characterization is contrary to Congress' determination otherwise. In ERISA, Congress specifically defined plans that "resul[t] in a deferral of income by employees" as pension plans, § 1002(2)(A)(ii), and plans that offer medical benefits as welfare plans, § 1002(1)(A). Thus, retiree health care benefits are not a form of deferred compensation.

Further compounding this error, the Court of Appeals has refused to apply general durational clauses to provisions governing retiree benefits. Having inferred that parties would not leave retiree benefits to the contingencies of future negotiations, and that retiree benefits generally last as long as the recipient remains a retiree, the court in *Yard-Man* explicitly concluded that these inferences "outweigh[ed] any contrary implications derived from a routine duration clause terminating the agreement generally." 716 F.2d, at 1482–1483. * * *

Perhaps tugged by these inferences, the Court of Appeals misapplied other traditional principles of contract law, including the illusory promises doctrine. That doctrine instructs courts to avoid constructions of contracts that would render promises illusory because such promises cannot serve as consideration for a contract. See 3 Williston § 7:7 (4th ed. 2008). But the Court of Appeals construed provisions that admittedly benefited some class of retirees as "illusory" merely because they did not equally benefit *all* retirees. See *Yard-Man, supra,* at 1480–1481. That interpretation is a contradiction in terms—a promise that is "partly" illusory is by definition not illusory. * * *

The Court of Appeals also failed even to consider the traditional principle that courts should not construe ambiguous writings to create lifetime promises. See 3 A. Corbin, Corbin on Contracts § 553, p. 216 (1960) (explaining that contracts that are silent as to their duration will ordinarily be treated not as "operative in perpetuity" but as "operative for a reasonable time" (internal quotation marks omitted)). * * * Because vesting of welfare plan benefits is not required by law, an employer's commitment to vest such benefits is not to be inferred lightly; the intent to vest must be found in the plan documents and must be stated in clear and express language" (internal quotation marks omitted)). The different treatment of these two types of employment contracts only underscores *Yard-Man*'s deviation from ordinary principles of contract law.

* * * We vacate the judgment of the Court of Appeals and remand the case for that court to apply ordinary principles of contract law in the first instance.

NOTES AND QUESTIONS

Test Your Understanding of the Material

1. In what respects was the Court of Appeal's *Yard-Man* approach consistent with common law contract principles? What happens on remand? As a lawyer for the plaintiffs, how would you frame the issue for the trier of fact? Is the Supreme Court's analysis in *M&G Polymers* limited to collective bargaining agreements or to ERISA benefit plans generally or does it also apply to individual employment agreements? Consider the treatment of indefinite-term employment agreements in the Employment Restatement §§ 2.03(a)(2)–2.04.

Related Issues

2. *Welfare-Benefit Plans*. ERISA defines an employee welfare benefit plan as "any plan * * * which * * * is hereafter established or maintained * * * for the purpose of providing for its participants or their beneficiaries * * * medical, surgical, or hospital care or benefits, or benefits in the event of sickness, accident, disability, death or unemployment, or vacation benefits, apprenticeship or other training programs, or day care centers, scholarship funds, or prepaid legal services * * * ." 29 U.S.C. § 1002(1). ERISA's fiduciary, disclosure, and recordkeeping requirement apply to welfare plan benefits, but unlike pension-plan benefits, the statute does not require that the benefits become vested or that they employer-sponsor fund the benefits in any particular manner. They do not require advance funding by the employer-sponsor. ERISA generally preempts state regulation of employees, whether pension-plan or welfare-plan benefits. *M&G Polymers* illustrates how courts have developed an ERISA "common law" as a gap-filler. See, e.g., Noorily v. Thomas & Betts Corp., 188 F.3d 153 (3d Cir.1999) (employer initially announced that employees choosing not to relocate would receive severance payments from unfunded benefit plan, but changed policy when it became clear that most of its product managers and engineers would not be relocating; plaintiffs, after this policy change, declined to transfer and sued unsuccessfully to recover once-promised severance pay).

3. *Continuation of Healthcare Benefits*. Before the advent of the Affordable Care Act (ACA), P.L. 111–148, 42 U.S.C. § 1800, many health insurance plans would deny, or charge more for, coverage of "pre-existing conditions." This created serious problems for employees who lost their jobs and or had to change jobs. To mitigate this problem, Congress in the Consolidated Omnibus Budget Reconciliation Act (COBRA), 29 U.S.C. § 1161 et seq., requires employee health care benefit plans to permit former employees to continue coverage for 18 months (in some situations, 36 months), provided

the employee pays the cost. COBRA requires employers to send a notice to terminated employees advising them of their eligibility for continued coverage. Under the ACA, healthcare plans can no longer refuse to cover pre-existing conditions. See 29 C.F.R. § 2590.715–2704; 29 U.S.C. §§ 1181–2.

4. *ERISA Enforcement Provisions.* The Department of Labor is charged with the responsibility of interpreting and enforcing the labor provisions of ERISA. However, the statute authorizes private rights of action. Participants or beneficiaries may bring a civil action in federal court for any violation of the statute, including breach of fiduciary duties. 29 U.S.C. § 1132(a)(3). In addition, individuals challenging a retaliatory discharge have a remedy under § 510 of ERISA, 29 U.S.C. § 1140.

FMC CORPORATION V. HOLLIDAY

Supreme Court of the United States, 1990.
498 U.S. 52, 111 S.Ct. 403, 112 L.Ed.2d 356.

JUSTICE O'CONNOR delivered the opinion of the Court.

This case calls upon the Court to decide whether the Employee Retirement Income Security Act of 1974 (ERISA) as amended pre-empts a Pennsylvania law precluding employee welfare benefit plans from exercising subrogation rights on a claimant's tort recovery.

* * *

Petitioner, FMC Corporation (FMC), operates the FMC Salaried Health Care Plan (Plan), an employee welfare benefit plan within the meaning of ERISA that provides health benefits to FMC employees and their dependents. The Plan is self-funded; it does not purchase an insurance policy from any insurance company in order to satisfy its obligations to its participants. Among its provisions is a subrogation clause under which a Plan member agrees to reimburse the Plan for benefits paid if the member recovers on a claim in a liability action against a third party.

* * *

* * * Three provisions of ERISA speak expressly to the question of pre-emption:

> "Except as provided in subsection (b) of this section [the saving clause], the provisions of this subchapter and subchapter III of this chapter shall supersede any and all State laws insofar as they may now or hereafter relate to any employee benefit plan." § 514(a), as set forth in 29 U.S.C. § 1144(a) (pre-emption clause).

> "Except as provided in subparagraph (B) [the deemer clause], nothing in this subchapter shall be construed to exempt or relieve any person from any law of any State which regulates insurance, banking, or securities." § 514(b)(2)(A), as set forth in 29 U.S.C. § 1144(b)(2)(A) (saving clause).

"Neither an employee benefit plan * * * nor any trust established under such a plan, shall be deemed to be an insurance company or other insurer, bank, trust company, or investment company or to be engaged in the business of insurance or banking for purposes of any law of any State purporting to regulate insurance companies, insurance contracts, banks, trust companies, or investment companies." § 514(b)(2)(B), as set forth in 29 U.S.C. § 1144(b)(2)(B) (deemer clause).

We indicated in *Metropolitan Life Ins. Co. v. Massachusetts,* 471 U.S. 724, 105 S.Ct. 2380, 85 L.Ed.2d 728 (1985), that these provisions "are not a model of legislative drafting." Id., at 739, 105 S.Ct., at 2389. Their operation is nevertheless discernible. The pre-emption clause is conspicuous for its breadth. It establishes as an area of exclusive federal concern the subject of every state law that "relates to" an employee benefit plan governed by ERISA. The saving clause returns to the States the power to enforce those state laws that "regulate insurance," except as provided in the deemer clause. Under the deemer clause, an employee benefit plan governed by ERISA shall not be "deemed" an insurance company, an insurer, or engaged in the business of insurance for purposes of state laws "purporting to regulate" insurance companies or insurance contracts.

* * *

Pennsylvania's antisubrogation law "relates to" an employee benefit plan. We made clear in *Shaw v. Delta Air Lines* [463 U.S. 85, 103 S.Ct. 2890, 77 L.Ed.2d 490 (1983)], that a law relates to an employee welfare plan if it has "a connection with or reference to such a plan." Id., at 96–97, 103 S.Ct., at 2899–2900 (footnote omitted). We based our reading in part on the plain language of the statute. Congress used the words " 'relate to' in § 514(a) [the pre-emption clause] in their broad sense." Id., at 98, 103 S.Ct., at 2900. It did not mean to pre-empt only state laws specifically designed to affect employee benefit plans. That interpretation would have made it unnecessary for Congress to enact ERISA § 514(b)(4), which exempts from pre-emption "generally" applicable criminal laws of a State. We also emphasized that to interpret the pre-emption clause to apply only to state laws dealing with the subject matters covered by ERISA, such as reporting, disclosure, and fiduciary duties, would be incompatible with the provision's legislative history because the House and Senate versions of the bill that became ERISA contained limited pre-emption clauses, applicable only to state laws relating to specific subjects covered by ERISA. These were rejected in favor of the present language in the Act, "indicating that the section's pre-emptive scope was as broad as its language." [*Shaw v. Delta Air Lines,* 463 U.S.] at 98, 103 S.Ct., at 2901.

Pennsylvania's antisubrogation law has a "reference" to benefit plans governed by ERISA. The statute states that "in actions arising out of the maintenance or use of a motor vehicle, there shall be no right of subrogation or reimbursement from a claimant's tort recovery with respect to * * * benefits * * * paid or payable under section 1719." 75 Pa. Cons.Stat. § 1720 (1987). Section 1719 refers to "any program, group contract or other arrangement for payment of benefits." These terms "include, but [are] not limited to, benefits payable by a hospital plan corporation or a professional health service corporation." § 1719.

The Pennsylvania statute also has a "connection" to ERISA benefit plans. In the past, we have not hesitated to apply ERISA's pre-emption clause to state laws that risk subjecting plan administrators to conflicting state regulations. See, e.g., *Shaw v. Delta Air Lines,* supra, at 95–100, 103 S.Ct., at 2898–2902 (state laws making unlawful plan provisions that discriminate on the basis of pregnancy and requiring plans to provide specific benefits "relate to" benefit plans); *Alessi v. Raybestos-Manhattan, Inc.,* 451 U.S. 504, 523–526, 101 S.Ct. 1895, 1906–1908, 68 L.Ed.2d 402 (1981) (state law prohibiting plans from reducing benefits by amount of workers' compensation awards "relates to" employee benefit plan). To require plan providers to design their programs in an environment of differing State regulations would complicate the administration of nationwide plans, producing inefficiencies that employers might offset with decreased benefits. See *Fort Halifax Packing Co. v. Coyne,* 482 U.S. 1, 10, 107 S.Ct. 2211, 2216, 96 L.Ed.2d 1 (1987). Thus, where a "patchwork scheme of regulation would introduce considerable inefficiencies in benefit program operation," we have applied the pre-emption clause to ensure that benefit plans will be governed by only a single set of regulations. Id., at 11, 107 S.Ct., at 2217.

There is no dispute that the Pennsylvania law falls within ERISA's insurance saving clause. * * * Section 1720 directly controls the terms of insurance contracts by invalidating any subrogation provisions that they contain. See *Metropolitan Life,* 471 U.S., at 740–741, 105 S.Ct., at 2389–2390. It does not merely have an impact on the insurance industry; it is aimed at it. See *Pilot Life Ins. Co. v. Dedeaux,* 481 U.S. 41, 50, 107 S.Ct. 1549, 1554, 95 L.Ed.2d 39 (1987). This returns the matter of subrogation to state law. Unless the statute is excluded from the reach of the saving clause by virtue of the deemer clause, therefore, it is not pre-empted.

We read the deemer clause to exempt self-funded ERISA plans from state laws that "regulate insurance" within the meaning of the saving clause. By forbidding States to deem employee benefit plans "to be an insurance company or other insurer * * * or to be engaged in the business of insurance," the deemer clause relieves plans from state laws "purporting to regulate insurance." As a result, self-funded ERISA plans are exempt from state regulation insofar as that regulation "relates to" the plans. State laws directed toward the plans are pre-empted because they relate to an employee benefit plan but are not "saved" because they do not regulate insurance. State laws that directly regulate insurance are "saved" but do not reach self-funded employee benefit plans because the plans may not be deemed to be insurance companies, other insurers, or engaged in the business of insurance for purposes of such state laws. On the other hand, employee benefit plans that are insured are subject to indirect state insurance regulation. An insurance company that insures a plan remains an insurer for purposes of state laws "purporting to regulate insurance" after application of the deemer clause. The insurance company is therefore not relieved from state insurance regulation. The ERISA plan is consequently bound by state insurance regulations insofar as they apply to the plan's insurer.

* * *

Congress intended by ERISA to "establish pension plan regulation as exclusively a federal concern." *Alessi v. Raybestos-Manhattan, Inc.,* 451 U.S., at 523, 101 S.Ct., at 1906 (footnote omitted). Our interpretation of the deemer clause makes clear that if a plan is insured, a State may regulate it indirectly through regulation of its insurer and its insurer's insurance contracts; if the plan is uninsured, the State may not regulate it. As a result, employers will not face " 'conflicting or inconsistent State and local regulation of employee benefit plans.' " *Shaw v. Delta Air Lines, Inc.,* 463 U.S., at 99, 103 S.Ct., at 2901 (quoting remarks of Sen. Williams). A construction of the deemer clause that exempts employee benefit plans from only those state regulations that encroach upon core ERISA concerns or that apply to insurance as a business would be fraught with administrative difficulties, necessitating definition of core ERISA concerns and of what constitutes business activity. It would therefore undermine Congress' desire to avoid "endless litigation over the validity of State action," see 120 Cong.Rec. 29942 (1974) (remarks of Sen. Javits), and instead lead to employee benefit plans' expenditure of funds in such litigation.

NOTES AND QUESTIONS

Test Your Understanding of the Material

1. ERISA preemption principles apply to both employee pension plans as well as employee welfare plans. Although ERISA requires advance funding, vesting requirements, and disclosure and fiduciary stanrards in the case of pension plans, its regulation of welfare plans is limited to disclosure and fiduciary requirements. Can you determine from FMC Corporation why Congress chose to preempt state regulation of welfare benefit plans as well?

2. Why do employers self-insure? Under *Holliday*, are self-insured plans exempt from all state insurance laws, even though plans using insurance companies for underwriting their risks are subject to state insurance laws? Consider also Paul Secunda, Samuel Estreicher & Rosalind Connor, Global Issues in Employee Benefits Law 131(2008) (self-insured plans can purchase "stop-loss" insurance policies which provide that "the insurer will step in and

pay claims once such claims exceed a specified dollar amount"—without jeopardizing ERISA preemption).

Related Issues

3.   *Other Express Exemptions from § 514 Preemption.* State laws "regulating insurance, banking, or securities" are not the only state laws that "relate to" ERISA regulated plans that are nonetheless exempted from ERISA preemption. Section 514 contains other limited exemptions, including "any generally applicable criminal law of a state", 29 U.S.C. § 1144(b)(4). Furthermore, § 514(d) provides that the preemption provision shall not "be construed to alter, amend, modify, invalidate, impair, or supersede any law of the United States * * * ." The latter provision was interpreted in Shaw v. Delta Air Lines, Inc., 463 U.S. 85, 103 S.Ct. 2890, 77 L.Ed.2d 490 (1983), to exempt from preemption state antidiscrimination laws that assist the Title VII enforcement scheme by prohibiting practices that are unlawful under Title VII, but not to exempt state anti-discrimination laws relating to ERISA benefit plans that prohibit practices that are lawful under Title VII.

The *Shaw* Court also interpreted another important limitation on the scope of ERISA preemption. Section 514(a) is not applicable to state laws that relate to benefit plans that are exempt from ERISA regulation, including plans that are "maintained solely for the purpose of complying with applicable workmen's compensation laws or unemployment compensation or disability insurance laws." 29 U.S.C. § 1003(b)(3). The *Shaw* Court held that only "separately administered * * * plans maintained solely to comply" with the kinds of state laws covered by § 1003(b)(3) are exempt from ERISA coverage, but that states may require employers to maintain separate plans to make possible the enforcement of their disability insurance (or presumably workers' compensation or unemployment compensation) laws.

4.   *§ 502 Preemption of State Tort and Contract Claims.* Section 514(a) is not the only provision of ERISA that bears on preemption. In Pilot Life Insurance Co. v. Dedeaux, 481 U.S. 41, 107 S.Ct. 1549, 95 L.Ed.2d 39 (1987), the Supreme Court held preempted tort and breach of contract claims for an employer's failure to pay benefits under an ERISA-regulated disability benefits plan. Although the Court relied on § 514, it also stressed that under § 502 of ERISA a plan participant or beneficiary may sue to recover or clarify rights to benefits. It then concluded that Congress intended § 502 to be "the exclusive vehicle for * * * asserting improper processing of a claim for benefits * * * ." 481 U.S. at 52.

In Ingersoll-Rand Co. v. McClendon, 498 U.S. 133, 111 S.Ct. 478, 112 L.Ed.2d 474 (1990), the Court held preempted by ERISA a state common law claim that an employee was unlawfully discharged to prevent his attainment of pension benefits. All members of the Court agreed that *Dedeaux* stands for the proposition that § 502 of ERISA provides the exclusive remedy for rights guaranteed under the substantive provisions of ERISA, including § 510— which makes it unlawful to discriminate against a benefit plan participant "for the purpose of interfering with the attainment of any right to which such participant may become entitled under the plan". The preemptive force of § 502 is not limited to state actions seeking recovery of benefits; it extends to state actions providing remedies not afforded by § 510.

In 1999, however, in UNUM Life Insurance Co. of America v. Ward, 526 U.S. 358, 119 S.Ct. 1380, 143 L.Ed.2d 462 (1999), the Court held that *Dedeaux* does not bar a participant from invoking in a § 502 action to recover benefits from an ERISA plan a state common law rule that prevents an insurer from asserting a defense of untimely notice unless it can prove prejudice. The *Ward* Court held that this state law is not preempted under § 514 because it is saved as a law that regulates insurance. The Court therefore concluded that the state law can be asserted in an action brought under § 502, as the latter provision preempts only independent common law actions.

B. PENSION BENEFITS

There are two basic types of ERISA pension plans: "defined contribution" plans that provide for an individual account for each participant and for benefits based solely upon the amount contributed to that account plus any income or other gain (earned by the contributions); and "defined benefit" plans which promise to pay a specific or definitely determinable benefit. In defined-benefit, the employer-sponsor assumes the market risk that contributions it makes to the plan will not yield promised pension benifits. In defined-contribution plan, the employee-participants has to invest the employer's contributions as best he or she can and assumes the attendant market risk. See generally Samuel Estreicher & Laurence Gold, The Shift from Defined Benefit to Defined Contribution Pension Plans, 11 Lewis & Clark L. Rev. 101 (2007).

ERISA regulations of pension plans fall into three basic categories: (i) minimum standards designed to promote nonforfeitable pension rights, such as vesting (initially, after 10 years of service, now reduced to 5 years' "cliff" vesting or 3–7 years' phased vesting as a result of 1986 tax reform legislation), benefit accrual, and minimum age and service conditions; (ii) plan funding requirements to ensure that defined-benefit pension plans will have adequate assets to meet promised benefits; and (iii) fiduciary standards and reporting and disclosure obligations.

WILLIAMS V. WRIGHT
U.S. Court of Appeals for the Eleventh Circuit, 1991.
927 F.2d 1540.

ANDERSON, J.

This appeal raises issues involving the Employee Retirement Income Security Act of 1974 ("ERISA"), 29 U.S.C. §§ 1001–1461, and state contract law. Appellant James T. Williams ("Williams") brought an action under § 502 of ERISA, 29 U.S.C. § 1132, against appellees Fred P. Wright ("Wright") and Wright Pest Control Co. ("WPCC"), alleging violations of

ERISA. Williams also included a state law claim for breach of a retirement contract. The district court eventually granted summary judgment in favor of appellees on all counts. * * *

James T. Williams began working for WPCC in 1947. In October of 1981, Williams and Fred P. Wright, Jr., president of WPCC, discussed the possibility and terms of Williams' retirement. Although these talks were inconclusive, on October 23, 1981, Wright presented to Williams the letter set out in the [Appendix below] (the "1981 letter").

Williams received benefits in accordance with this letter until September, 1984. On September 7, 1984, "Wright informed [Williams] that for business reasons it would be necessary 'to slow the gravy train down from a race to a crawl.' " Subsequently, WPCC reduced the country club, telephone, and automobile expenses, but continued the monthly payments of $500.00 and the insurance benefits.

On September 1, 1985, Wright informed Williams that WPCC's dissolution and imminent asset sale to Terminex Service, Inc. necessitated termination of Williams' retirement benefits. Accordingly, after the asset sale and dissolution occurred, in December, 1985, WPCC terminated Williams' benefits. Wright did transfer title to the company car that Williams had been using to Williams and forgive $1,906.63 in personal debt owed to WPCC by Williams. This lawsuit followed. * * *

The ERISA Claim * * *

ERISA recognizes two types of plans, "employee welfare benefit plans"[4] and "employee pension benefit plans."[5] In order for appellant to invoke ERISA's substantive provisions covering either type, appellant must prevail on the threshold question of whether the benefits

---

[4]   29 U.S.C. § 1002(1) provides:

The terms "employee welfare benefit plan" and "welfare plan" mean any plan, fund, or program which was heretofore or is hereafter established or maintained by an employer or by an employee organization, or by both, to the extent that such plan, fund, or program was established or is maintained for the purpose of providing for its participants or their beneficiaries, through the purchase of insurance or otherwise, (A) medical, surgical, or hospital care or benefits, or benefits in the event of sickness, accident, disability, death or unemployment, or vacation benefits, apprenticeship or other training programs, or day care centers, scholarship funds, or prepaid legal services, or (B) any benefit described in section 186(c) of this title (other than pensions on retirement or death, and insurance to provide such pensions).

[5]   29 U.S.C. Sec. 1002(2)(A) provides:

Except as provided in subparagraph (B), the terms "employee pension benefit plan" and "pension plan" mean any plan, fund, or program which was heretofore or is hereafter established or maintained by an employer or by an employee organization, or by both, to the extent that by its express terms or as a result of surrounding circumstances such plan, fund, or program—

    (i)   provides retirement income to employees, or

    (ii)   results in a deferral of income by employees for periods extending to the termination of covered employment or beyond, regardless of the method of calculating the contributions made to the plan, the method of calculating the benefits under the plan or the method of distributing benefits from the plan.

arrangement set out in the 1981 letter is a "plan, fund, or program" covered by ERISA. *Donovan v. Dillingham*, 688 F.2d 1367 (11th Cir.1982) (en banc); 29 U.S.C. §§ 1002(1) and (2)(A). Although the definition of these terms has proved to be elusive at best, *Donovan* at 1372, this court has prescribed general guidelines for resolving the threshold question: "[A] 'plan, fund, or program' under ERISA is established if from the surrounding circumstances a reasonable person can ascertain the intended benefits,[7] a class of beneficiaries, the source of financing, and procedures for receiving benefits." Id. at 1373. * * *

The district court applied the *Donovan* analysis and concluded that the retirement arrangement at issue was not covered by ERISA. The district court was troubled by the fact that the only ascertainable source of financing for Williams' benefits was the general assets of the corporation rather than any separate fund or trust, that the class of beneficiaries was limited to Williams and his wife, and that, in the court's view, there were no procedures for receiving benefits. The district court also viewed the arrangement as, at best, "an individual employment contract which included post-retirement compensation" rather than an ERISA "plan, fund, or program." * * * [W]e conclude that the district court erred in holding that the letter from Wright to Williams did not establish a plan covered by ERISA.

1. The Donovan Analysis

a. Source of Financing

Although noting that the source of financing for the benefits at issue was the general assets of WPCC, the district court found no ascertainable source of financing under *Donovan*. Although, with some exceptions, it is true that the assets of employee benefit plans are required to be held in trust, see 29 U.S.C. § 1103, it is equally true that an employer's failure to meet an ERISA requirement does not exempt the plan from ERISA coverage. *Scott v. Gulf Oil Corp.*, 754 F.2d 1499, 1503 (9th Cir.1985). "An employer * * * should not be able to evade the requirements of the statute merely by paying * * * benefits out of general assets." *Fort Halifax Packing Co., Inc. v. Coyne*, 482 U.S. 1, 18, 107 S.Ct. 2211, 2221, 96 L.Ed.2d 1 (1987). Therefore, we conclude that the payment of benefits out of an employer's general assets does not affect the threshold question of ERISA coverage. See also U.S. Dept. of Labor Opinion Letters 78–18 (Sept. 20, 1978) and 79–75 (Oct. 29, 1979) (finding ERISA coverage where benefit payments were made from general assets of employer and other requirements satisfied).

---

[7] With regard to this first prong of *Donovan*, we can easily ascertain the benefits intended by Wright's October 23, 1981 letter. The promise of monthly payments of $500.00 and group health and life insurance coverage is certainly not ambiguous.

b. *Procedures for Receiving Benefits*

Relying in part on *Fort Halifax*, supra, the district court held that the instant case lacked the administrative program or procedures characteristic of ERISA plans. However, *Fort Halifax* does not support the conclusion that the retirement arrangement at issue is not covered by ERISA for this reason. Although the procedures for receiving benefits provided by the 1981 letter are simple, they are sufficiently ascertainable under the *Donovan* analysis.

In *Fort Halifax*, after the employer closed its poultry packaging and processing plant, the state of Maine sued to enforce a state statute requiring the employer to provide a one-time severance payment to certain employees. The employer argued, inter alia, that the state statute was preempted by ERISA and therefore unenforceable. The Supreme Court held that ERISA was inapplicable because a one-time payment did not require the sort of ongoing administrative scheme characteristic of an ERISA plan. The Court reasoned that a purpose of ERISA preemption, "to afford employers the advantages of a uniform set of administrative procedures governed by a single set of regulations," *Fort Halifax* at 11, 107 S. Ct. at 2217, was not compromised where "the employer assumes no responsibility to pay benefits on a regular basis." Id. at 12, 107 S.Ct. at 2218. The Court concluded that "the theoretical possibility of a one-time obligation in the future simply creates no need for an ongoing administrative program for processing claims and paying benefits." Id.

The situation in *Fort Halifax* is easily distinguishable from the instant case which does involve a continuing obligation necessitating ongoing, though simple, procedures. The letter of October 23, 1981 expressly provides that the company "will issue you a check * * * each month * * * until your death or when you have no use for [the benefits]." In addition the letter provides that in the event that the arrangement does not "fill all needs as anticipated," revisions will be considered after April 1, 1982. Therefore, we conclude that the 1981 letter provides for sufficiently ascertainable procedures or receiving benefits under *Donovan*.

c. *The Class of Beneficiaries*

The requirement of an ascertainable class of beneficiaries is perhaps more troublesome. However, we do not interpret *Donovan*'s use of the word "class" as an absolute requirement of more than one beneficiary or that a plan tailored to the needs of a single employee can not be within ERISA. Rather, Donovan referred only to the fact that most pension plans falling within ERISA involve identical treatment of a group of employees.

Furthermore, we find nothing in the ERISA legislation pointing to the exclusion of plans covering only a single employee. In fact, ERISA's predecessor statute, the Welfare and Pension Plans Disclosure Act, Pub.L. No. 85–836, § 4(b)(4), 72 Stat. 998–999 (1958), expressly excluded plans covering less than 25 employees. Congress was aware of this limitation in the prior legislation but apparently decided not to include it in ERISA. See S.Rep. No. 127, 93d Cong., 1st Sess., at 6 (1973).

It is also significant that Department of Labor regulations refer to a plan covering one or more employees as within ERISA. See, e.g., 29 C.F.R. § 2510.3–3(b) (1988) ("[A] Keogh plan under which *one or more* common law employees, in addition to the self-employed individuals, are participants covered under the plan, will be covered under Title I [of ERISA].") (emphasis added). See also 29 C.F.R. § 2510.3–2(d) (under some circumstances, individual retirement accounts or annuities are covered by ERISA).

* * *

2. The Employment Contract Cases

Aside from the *Donovan* analysis, further support for our conclusion that the 1981 letter establishes an ERISA plan or program is found in the cases that appellee cites for the opposite conclusion. For example, in *Jervis v. Elerding*, 504 F. Supp. 606 (C.D.Cal.1980), an owner of apartment buildings, Elerding, entered into an employment contract with his apartment manager, Jervis, agreeing to provide Jervis with an apartment upon her retirement or termination after at least ten years in his employ. After Jervis terminated her employment, Elerding refused to provide the apartment as agreed. The court held that "a contract between an employer and an individual employee providing for post-retirement or post-termination in-kind compensation is not a 'plan, fund, or program' within the definitional framework of ERISA." Id. at 608. The court based this holding on its observation that the agreement to provide the apartment "was part of the present compensation arrangement, inserted as consideration for plaintiff's continued services to defendant, *rather than as part of a 'plan' providing for retirement income or deferral of income.*" Id. at 609 (emphasis added). Also, the court noted that the employer's promise of a rent-free apartment was not conditioned on the employee's retirement and that "the parties merely memorialized their employee-employer relationship; they did not enter into an agreement for a *separate and specific retirement plan.*" Id. (emphasis added).

Similarly, other cases cited by appellee and relied on by the district court generally involve the promise of post-retirement payments offered only incidentally to a present individual employment agreement. * * *

The distinction between payments after retirement or termination pursuant to a current employment contract and a plan to specifically provide for an employee's retirement was perhaps made most clearly in *Murphy v. Inexco Oil Co.*, 611 F.2d 570 (5th Cir.1980). In *Murphy*, Murphy, the president of Inexco, was one of a number of employees given a bonus in the form of royalties from the company's drilling projects. Murphy eventually sued the company, alleging various violations of ERISA. The court did not address the substantive ERISA violations because it concluded that the bonus program was not a pension plan covered by ERISA. * * *

* * * The court's rationale for excluding the bonus program from ERISA was expressed in the following language: "[The bonus program] was evidently designed to provide *current* rather than *retirement* income to Inexco's employees." *Murphy*, 611 F.2d at 575–76 (emphasis added). The court interpreted "the words 'provides retirement income' [in 29 U.S.C. § 1002(2)(A)(i) as referring] only to plans *designed for the purpose of paying retirement income* whether as a result of their express terms or surrounding circumstances." Id. at 575 (emphasis added). The *Murphy* analysis would not include within ERISA payments that incidentally might be made after retirement but were not designed for retirement purposes. Id. at 574–75. * * *

The facts of this case reveal that the letter presented to Williams by Wright on October 23, 1981 contemplated Williams immediate retirement. We initially note that the letter itself expressly changed Williams' status at WPCC as of October 26, 1981, just three days after the date of the letter. Furthermore, although the letter states that "in exchange for these payments and benefits, you will be expected to function for the company in the manner of consultant and advisor on pest control matters * * * ," the record shows that Williams performed only minimal, if any, consulting services after October 26, 1981 * * * In fact, Wright stated that he typed and presented the letter to Williams specifically for the purpose of procuring Williams' retirement, or, as Wright put it, Williams' termination. * * * In addition, in a letter dated April 3, 1987, Wright stated that "the money paid by Wright Pest Control to James Williams was retirement pay and not salary." * * * Finally, in defense of appellant's contract claims, appellees stated in the joint proposed pretrial order that the letter was "a gratuitous promise to pay retirement income * * * ."

Therefore, it is clear that the 1981 letter's arrangement primarily constituted payment of retirement income and was not an employment contract outside the scope of ERISA. * * *

Although ERISA does not mandate the establishment of employee benefit plans, a primary purpose of the legislation is to protect employees once a plan is established and certain other requirements are met. In light of this purpose, we conclude that the district court erred in ruling that the 1981 letter did not establish a "plan" or "program" within ERISA. * * *

[*Eds*. The *Wright* court's discussion of ERISA preemption is omitted.]

Appendix

The letter reads [in relevant part] as follows:

* * *

Dear Jim:

This letter is to formalize our earlier conversations regarding your compensation as General Manager of Wright Pest Control as of January 1, 1982 and your duties thereafter.

After consultation with attorneys and accountants, I have arrived at the following plan, which will provide for an uninterrupted continuation of cash as you gradually alter your work schedule to a retirement status.

Your current net pay is $1200.00 per month, plus or minus $50.00. I understand that you have applied for social security benefits beginning January 1, 1982, and that these benefits will net you approximately $700.00 per month.

As of January 1, 1982, you are permitted to earn up to $6000.00 per year without any effect on your social security benefits. The company will issue you a check in the amount of $500.00 each month, on the first of each month. This amount will completely take care of your allowed earned income under social security regulations.

The total of your social security benefits, plus this monthly amount[,] should equal the $1200.00 target amount, plus or minus $50.00. In addition, we will also:

Pay all dues and fees at the Augusta Country Club, including meal tickets when appropriate receipts are executed.

Furnish you with a vehicle, equal or better than that which has been furnished you in the past. All expenses are to be paid, including gasoline. A radio will also be furnished for communication with the company. The vehicle is to be returned to the company should you ever become unable to drive.

Pay all premiums for yourself and Mrs. Williams on the company's group medical insurance plan, and the maximum available term life insurance available through the plan for your age group.

These benefits will continue until your death or when you have no use for them. It is understood that your country club membership will be made available to me personally when you no longer have use for it.

In exchange for these payments and benefits, you will be expected to function for the company in the manner of consultant and advisor on pest control matters, and various activities of a social nature related to sales activity or general public relations. You will not have any operational authority or duties except in a life or death situation, such as when observing an unsafe act by a company employee.

Your office and desk will be maintained as per your wishes, until an acute need for space in the office should dictate otherwise. Your desk will be kept locked, but for security reasons we ask that all company documents of a confidential or sensitive nature be destroyed. This will include any past profit and loss statements, personnel records, etc. In a like manner we can not be responsible for any personal items of a confidential or sensitive nature.

As this program is as we agreed, but in fact may not fill all needs as anticipated, future revisions are to be expected, but no changes will be considered until a sufficient amount of time has passed. April 1, 1982 will be the earliest date that revisions will be considered. * * *

Sincerely,

Fred P. Wright, Jr., President

NOTES AND QUESTIONS

Related Issues

1. *Plaintiffs Claiming ERISA Preemption?* It is unusual for a plaintiff, as in *Wright*, to argue that his benefits are governed by an ERISA plan, because a typical consequence of finding a plan to be covered by ERISA is preemption of all state-law claims. The opinion does not reveal why Wright's lawyer made the ERISA argument; perhaps the lawyer was seeking the benefit of ERISA-authorized attorney's fees. As *Wright* illustrates, the absence of a separate trust fund or violations of the disclosure and reporting requirements of ERISA do not negate the preemptive force of ERISA.

2. *Eligible "Participants."* As is true of virtually all employment regulations, and as we have seen in connection with the *Darden* decision, p. 11 supra, ERISA's protections extend only to "employees". Federal law does not require an employer to provide all undisputed common-law employees with pension or welfare benefits, but the language used in plan documents and ERISA regulations may make it difficult for employers to limit plans to particular employees while excluding others who are similarly situated. See Vizcaino v. Microsoft Corporation 120 F.3d 1006 (9th Cir.1997).

3. *Stock Option Plans.* A considerable portion of compensation for U.S. managers, and increasingly for nonmanagerial personnel as well, takes the form of stock options. See David Lebow, Louise Sheiner, Larry Slifman & Martha Starr-McCluer, Recent Trends in Compensation Practices (July 15, 1999); Employment Restatement § 2.02, Comment d. A stock option gives the holder the right (but not the obligation) to purchase a specified number of shares of company stock at a price that is fixed at the date of the grant of the option. Stock option plans are not currently regulated by ERISA or comprehensively regulated by the federal securities laws. See In re Cendant Corporation Securities Litigation, 76 F.Supp. 2d 539 (D.N.J.1999). The *Cendant* court dismissed any transactional fraud claim under § 10(b) of the Securities Exchange Act of 1934, 15 U.S.C. § 78j(b), because no "purchase or sale" of a security occurs where plaintiff acquired her options, at no direct cost

to herself, "when she was already employed by Cendant under a plan that offered the options not to her as an individual, but as a member of an employee group"; compulsory, noncontributory stock options plans do not require an employee "to make an affirmative investment decision * * * ." As for the ERISA claim, the court noted that optionholders merely have an expectancy interest, "a contractual right to purchase an equitable interest in a corporation at some later date." Whatever discretionary authority the company's Compensation Committee had over the stock option plan, the court held, did not implicate ERISA because stock option plans do not fit within the statute's definitional framework. See generally Matthew T. Bodie, Aligning Incentives with Equity: Employee Stock Options and Rule 10b–5, 88 Iowa L. Rev. 539 (2003); Susan J. Stabile, Another Look at 401(k) Plan Investments in Employer Securities, 35 John Marshall L. Rev. 539 (2002); and her earlier article, Motivating Executives: Does Performance-Based Compensation Positively Affect Managerial Performance?, 2 U.Pa. J. Lab. & Employ. L. 227 (1999).

4. *Payroll Deductions for IRA Accounts.* Department of Labor regulations state that payroll deduction plans for individual retirement accounts are not ERISA plans, provided "(i) No contributions are made by the employer or employee association; (ii) Participation is completely voluntary for employees or members; (iii) The sole involvement of the employer or employee organization is . . . to collect contributions through payroll deductions or dues checkoffs and to remit them to the sponsor; and (iv) The employer or employee organization receives no consideration in the form of cash or otherwise, other than reasonable compensation for services actually rendered in connection with payroll deductions or dues checkoffs." 29 C.F.R. § 2510.3–2; Cline v. Indus. Maintenance Eng. & Contracting, 200 F.3d 1223 (9th Cir. 2000) (applying regulations).

5. *ERISA's Non-Interference Provision.* Section 510 prohibits an employer from discharging an employee "for the purpose of interfering with the attainment of any right to which [an employee] may become entitled" under an employee pension or welfare benefit plan. Although the principal purpose of § 510 was to ensure the integrity of the vesting rules by preventing discharges strategically timed to prevent vesting from occurring, the courts have held that even employees who are fully qualified for benefits may state a § 510 claim. Such an action may also lie for discharges allegedly motivated by a desire to stop paying welfare benefits which are not vested under ERISA. See Inter-Modal Rail Employees Assn. v. Atchison, Topeka and Santa Fe Railway Co., 520 U.S. 510 (1997).

Recall that in Hazen Paper Co. v. Biggins, 507 U.S. 604, 113 S.Ct. 1701, 123 L.Ed.2d 338 (1993), p. 470, supra, the Supreme Court held that terminating an employee to prevent vesting of a pension benefit did not state a claim of intentional age discrimination in violation of ADEA. Reliance on a factor such as length of service that merely correlated with age—here, length of service—could not be equated with reliance on age. The *Hazen* Court suggested, however, that the plaintiff in that case may have stated a claim under § 510 of ERISA. The Court also intimated that where eligibility for pension benefits is based on a combination of age and length of service, a similarly motivated discharge might also violate ADEA.

Practitioner's Perspective

Mark E. Brossman
Partner, Schulte Roth & Zabel LLP.

There is an ongoing national debate about how best to provide retirement security and health insurance to our nation's workers. Regardless of the ultimate result, the field of employee benefits continues to be highly regulated and the statutory framework governing pension and health plans continue to constantly change and evolve.

My practice group advises employers on complying with the Employee Retirement Income Security Act ("ERISA") with respect to their employee benefit plans. In the pension area, due to increasing liabilities and unfunded plans, employers are moving away from defined-benefit pension plans to defined-contribution plans. Instead of promising a defined benefit payable at retirement, where the employer bears the risk of delivering the promised pension benefit at retirement, employers are now making or matching defined contributions to a plan, and the individual employees' actual retirement benefit is the amount contributed plus or minus investment gains or losses.

We advise both single-employer benefit plans and trustees of multiemployer benefit plans. We often serve as general counsel to the plan, which can have assets in the multi-millions or even billions of dollars. We advise the fiduciaries of the plan on their responsibilities and compliance with the complex legal framework governing the design and operation of such plans. We also represent clients in government investigations and oversight (Internal Revenue Service, U.S. Department of Labor, Pension Benefit Guaranty Corporation, etc.).

We play an important role advising our corporate and institutional clients on benefits issues in mergers and acquisitions, as well as issues arising out of the investment of employee benefit plan assets. We represent clients in novel issues of employee benefits law involving plan mergers, terminations, spin-offs, fiduciary duties, prohibited transactions, and withdrawal liability. We also engage in collective bargaining negotiations involving health and pension benefits for unionized workers.

We also represent companies and executives with respect to the negotiation and drafting of executive employee agreements, separation agreements, and deferred compensation arrangements, including stock options and all forms of non-qualified compensation.

With respect to welfare benefits, the Affordable Care Act has revolutionized how health benefits are delivered in the U.S. We advise employers, funds, and insurers on the law, and carefully follow new developments and regulations.

We are engaged in litigation of employee benefit issues ranging from fiduciary issues, collection of contributions and withdrawal liability, and retiree health benefits. Most of this litigation is in federal courts throughout the nation.

Due to the varied nature of our practice, I interact with actuaries, accountants, trustees, investment consultants, investment advisors, and other plan professionals, and negotiate with government personnel on a variety of issues. It is complex, intellectually challenging, ever-changing, and has a profound impact on the lives of real people.

C. TERMINATION NOTICE AND SEVERANCE PAY

FORT HALIFAX PACKING CO., INC. v. COYNE

Supreme Court of the United States, 1987.
482 U.S. 1, 107 S.Ct. 2211, 96 L.Ed.2d 1.

JUSTICE BRENNAN delivered the opinion of the Court.

In this case we must decide whether a Maine statute requiring employers to provide a one-time severance payment to employees in the event of a plant closing, Me.Rev.Stat.Ann., Tit. 26, § 625–B (Supp.1986–1987),[1] is pre-empted by either the Employee Retirement Income Security Act of 1974, 88 Stat. 832, as amended, 29 U.S.C. §§ 1001–1381 (ERISA), or the National Labor Relations Act, 49 Stat. 452, as amended, 29 U.S.C. §§ 157–158 (NLRA).

---

[1] The statute provides in pertinent part:

"2. Severance pay. Any employer who relocates or terminates a covered establishment shall be liable to his employees for severance pay at the rate of one week's pay for each year of employment by the employee in that establishment. The severance pay to eligible employees shall be in addition to any final wage payment to the employee and shall be paid within one regular pay period after the employee's last full day of work, notwithstanding any other provisions of law.

"3. Mitigation of severance pay liability. There shall be no liability for severance pay to an eligible employee if:

"A. Relocation or termination of a covered establishment is necessitated by a physical calamity;

"B. The employee is covered by an express contract providing for severance pay;

"C. That employee accepts employment at the new location; or

"D. That employee has been employed by the employer for less than 3 years."

§ 625–B(1)(A) defines "covered establishment" as a facility that employs 100 or more persons, while § 625–B(1)(F) defines "relocation" as the removal of all or substantially all operations at least 100 miles away from their original location.

* * *

II

Appellant's basic argument is that any state law pertaining to a type of employee benefit listed in ERISA necessarily regulates an employee benefit plan, and therefore must be pre-empted. Because severance benefits are included in ERISA, see 29 U.S.C. § 1002(1)(B), appellant argues that ERISA pre-empts the Maine statute.[5] In effect, appellant argues that ERISA forecloses virtually all state legislation regarding employee benefits. This contention fails, however, in light of the plain language of ERISA's pre-emption provision, the underlying purpose of that provision, and the overall objectives of ERISA itself.

A

The first answer to appellant's argument is found in the express language of the statute. ERISA's pre-emption provision does not refer to state laws relating to "employee benefits," but to state laws relating to "employee benefit *plans*":

> "[T]he provisions of this subchapter * * * shall supersede any and all State laws insofar as they may now or hereafter relate to any *employee benefit plan* described in § 1003(a) of this title and not exempt under § 1003(b) of this title." 29 U.S.C. § 1144(a) (emphasis added).

We have held that the words "relate to" should be construed expansively: "[a] law 'relates to' an employee benefit plan, in the normal sense of the phrase, if it has a connection with or reference to such a plan." *Shaw v. Delta Air Lines, Inc.,* 463 U.S. 85, 96–97, 103 S.Ct. 2890, 2900, 77 L.Ed.2d 490 (1983). Nothing in our case law, however, supports appellant's position that the word "plan" should in effect be read out of the statute.

* * *

B

The second answer to appellant's argument is that pre-emption of the Maine statute would not further the purpose of ERISA pre-emption. * * *

Statements by ERISA's sponsors in the House and Senate clearly disclose the problem that the pre-emption provision was intended to address. In the House, Representative Dent stated that "with the pre-emption of the field [of employee benefit plans], we round out the protection

---

[5]   Section 1002(1)(B) defines an employee welfare benefit plan as a plan that pays, *inter alia,* benefits described in 29 U.S.C. § 186(c). The latter section includes, *inter alia,* money paid by an employer to a trust fund to pay for severance benefits. Section 1002(1)(B) has been construed to include severance benefits paid out of general assets, as well as out of a trust fund. See *Holland v. Burlington Industries, Inc.,* 772 F.2d 1140 (C.A.4 1985), summarily aff'd, 477 U.S. 901, 106 S.Ct. 3267, 91 L.Ed.2d 559 (1986); *Gilbert v. Burlington Industries, Inc.,* 765 F.2d 320 (C.A.2 1985), summarily aff'd, 477 U.S. 901, 106 S.Ct. 3267, 91 L.Ed.2d 558 (1986); *Scott v. Gulf Oil Corp.,* 754 F.2d 1499 (C.A.9 1985); 29 CFR § 2510.3–1(a)(3) (1986).

afforded participants by eliminating the threat of conflicting and inconsistent State and local regulation." 120 Cong.Rec. 29197 (1974). Similarly, Senator Williams declared, "It should be stressed that with the narrow exceptions specified in the bill, the substantive and enforcement provisions of the conference substitute are intended to preempt the field for Federal regulations, thus eliminating the threat of conflicting or inconsistent State and local regulation of employee benefit plans." Id., at 29933.

* * *

It is thus clear that ERISA's pre-emption provision was prompted by recognition that employers establishing and maintaining employee benefit plans are faced with the task of coordinating complex administrative activities. A patchwork scheme of regulation would introduce considerable inefficiencies in benefit program operation, which might lead those employers with existing plans to reduce benefits, and those without such plans to refrain from adopting them. Pre-emption ensures that the administrative practices of a benefit plan will be governed by only a single set of regulations.

* * *

The Maine statute neither establishes, nor requires an employer to maintain, an employee benefit *plan.* The requirement of a one-time lump-sum payment triggered by a single event requires no administrative scheme whatsoever to meet the employer's obligation. The employer assumes no responsibility to pay benefits on a regular basis, and thus faces no periodic demands on its assets that create a need for financial coordination and control. Rather, the employer's obligation is predicated on the occurrence of a single contingency that may never materialize. The employer may well *never* have to pay the severance benefits. To the extent that the obligation to do so arises, satisfaction of that duty involves only making a single set of payments to employees at the time the plant closes. To do little more than write a check hardly constitutes the operation of a benefit plan. Once this single event is over, the employer has no further responsibility. The theoretical possibility of a one-time obligation in the future simply creates no need for an ongoing administrative program for processing claims and paying benefits.

* * *

C

* * * [T]he Maine statute not only fails to implicate the concerns of ERISA's pre-emption provision, it fails to implicate the regulatory concerns of ERISA itself. The Congressional declaration of policy, codified at 29 U.S.C. § 1001, states that ERISA was enacted because Congress found it desirable that "disclosure be made and safeguards be provided with respect to the establishment, operation, and administration of [employee benefit] plans." § 1001(a). Representative Dent, the House sponsor of the legislation, represented that ERISA's fiduciary standards "will prevent abuses of the special responsibilities borne by those dealing with plans." 120 Cong.Rec. 29197 (1974). Senator Williams, the Senate sponsor, stated that these standards would safeguard employees from "such abuses as self-dealing, imprudent investing, and misappropriation of plan funds." Id., at 29932. The focus of the statute thus is on the administrative integrity of benefit plans—which presumes that some type of administrative activity is taking place. * * *

The foregoing makes clear both why ERISA is concerned with regulating benefit "plans," and why the Maine statute does not establish one. Only "plans" involve administrative activity potentially subject to employer abuse. The obligation imposed by Maine generates no such activity. There is no occasion to determine whether a "plan" is "operated" in the interest of its beneficiaries, because nothing is "operated." No financial transactions take place that would be listed in an annual report, and no further information regarding the terms of the severance pay obligation is needed because the statute itself makes these terms clear. It would make no sense for pre-emption to clear the way for exclusive federal regulation, for there would be nothing to regulate. Under such circumstances, pre-emption would in no way serve the overall purpose of ERISA.

* * *

JUSTICE WHITE, with whom THE CHIEF JUSTICE, JUSTICE O'CONNOR, and JUSTICE SCALIA join, dissenting.

* * * By making pre-emption turn on the existence of an "administrative scheme," the Court creates a loophole in ERISA's pre-emption statute, 29 U.S.C. § 1144, which will undermine Congress' decision to make employee-benefit plans a matter of exclusive federal regulation. The Court's rule requiring an established "administrative scheme" as a prerequisite for ERISA pre-emption will allow States to effectively dictate a wide array of employee benefits that must be provided by employers by simply characterizing them as non-"administrative."

NOTES AND QUESTIONS

Test Your Understanding of the Material

Is *Halifax* limited to a one-time plant closing? Does ERISA preempt state laws requiring companies to provide severance pay of one day per month of service for all employees who have worked for the company for at least five years?

ALLEN v. SYBASE, INC.

U.S. Court of Appeals for the Tenth Circuit, 2006.
468 F.3d 642.

SEYMOUR, J.

Plaintiffs, twenty-six former employees of Financial Fusion, Inc. (FFI), filed suit against FFI and its parent company, Sybase, Inc., (Sybase) (defendants), for violations under the Worker Adjustment and Retraining Notification Act (WARN). 29 U.S.C. § 2101 *et seq.* The parties filed cross motions for summary judgment, and the district court ruled for plaintiffs. The court subsequently entered final judgment ordering defendant companies to pay damages, interest and attorneys fees to plaintiffs in accordance with WARN. Defendants appeal. We affirm in part, reverse in part, and remand for further proceedings.

* * * WARN directs that an employer can be liable for up to sixty days' back pay and benefits to certain employees who lose their jobs as part of a plant closing or mass layoff without receiving sixty days' advanced notice. See 29 U.S.C. § 2104(a)(1). An employer may be excused from the sixty-day notice requirement where a mass layoff was the result of an unforseen business circumstance. Id. at § 2102(b)(2)(A). Nevertheless, an employer "shall give as much notice as is practicable and at that time shall give a brief statement of the basis for reducing the notification period." Id. at § 2102(b)(3). WARN also directs that a number of smaller employment losses over a ninety-day period may be aggregated to constitute a mass layoff, thereby imposing on an employer the obligation to provide either statutory notice or sixty days' back pay in lieu of notice to relevant employees. Id. at § 2102(d). In these situations, however, the employer may disprove the existence of a mass layoff if it shows that the individual sets of employment losses were for separate and distinct causes. Id.; 20 C.F.R. § 639.5(a)(1)(ii).

* * * Plaintiffs were employed by FFI, a software company specializing in retail banking and capital markets software, * * * [which] is a wholly owned subsidiary of Sybase. Sybase acquired FFI in March 2000. During the 2000 fiscal year, FFI reported an operating loss of approximately $20.3 million. * * *

In an effort to meet Sybase's financial targets, FFI engaged in a series of small layoffs during the first two quarters of 2001. The company dismissed four employees during the first quarter and five in the second quarter. But FFI's operating costs still exceeded its revenues: during the first quarter of 2001, FFI operated at a loss of $11 million; during the second quarter, the loss was $5.6 million.

In early August 2001, the middle of the third quarter, FFI cancelled production for a product scheduled to be released during the first quarter of 2002. It then moved all the project engineers who were assigned to the

2002 product, including a majority of plaintiffs, to work on a different product with a release date of September 24. During this same time frame, FFI planned a layoff in comparable size to the job terminations earlier in the year. On September 7, 2001, the company terminated four employees at the Orem location, all of whom eventually became plaintiffs in the instant case. FFI did not provide the employees with advance notice of the terminations, nor sixty days' pay in lieu of such notice pursuant to WARN.

* * *

On September 24, 2001, FFI met its release date for the new product. Four days later, on or about September 28, 2001, and two weeks after the September 11, 2001 airplane bombings of the World Trade Center and the Pentagon (9/11 bombings), FFI dismissed forty-one employees, many of whom had worked to ensure that FFI's new product was released on time. As with the employees dismissed on September 7, none were provided advance written notice of the terminations nor, in the alternative, sixty days' pay and benefits under WARN. * * * Twenty-four of these fired employees became the remaining plaintiffs in this case. FFI's third quarter losses were slightly improved, equaling $4.9 million, but nonetheless contributed to a total of $21.5 million in losses thus far in 2001.

In October, Sybase's Chief Financial Officer initiated "a plan to restructure and consolidate on a company-wide basis Sybase's Information Technology ('IT') operations." * * * . In accordance with this plan, "Sybase directed FFI to eliminate 6 IT positions at its Orem, Utah site. The elimination of these 6 positions was the result of Sybase's corporate consolidation and was unrelated to FFI's financial condition." * * * In conjunction with the six dismissals ordered by Sybase, FFI decided to terminate an additional five employees from its Orem office "in an effort to cut fourth quarter expenses." * * * The dismissals occurred on October 31, 2001.

FFI's human resources director, Neil Morris, was aware of WARN's notice and payment requirements and recognized that with the October 31 dismissals, the company had fired more than fifty employees over a ninety-day period at the Orem site. Therefore, FFI provided the eleven employees fired on October 31 with sixty days' pay and benefits "in satisfaction of any obligations [the company might] owe under state or Federal law." Id. at 196. In January 2002, Sybase proudly reported that FFI "bettered its [fourth quarter] forecast revenues and expenses to produce the company's first profitable quarter." Id. at 79.

Plaintiffs filed this action on February 7, 2003, claiming they were fired without notice in a mass layoff and defendants were therefore obligated to provide them with sixty days' back pay and benefits. * * *

Plaintiffs filed a motion for summary judgment on May 2, 2003, contending they lost their jobs in a mass layoff without notice in violation of WARN. [Defendants also filed a summary judgment motion.] * * * The district court subsequently granted summary judgment in favor of plaintiffs[.]

     * * * Defendants raise a number of issues on appeal in challenging the district court's ruling. * * * [T]hey assert there was no mass layoff under WARN because the three sets of employee terminations were for separate and distinct causes. Defendants also argue they should have been excused from any WARN obligations because the forty-one layoffs in September were precipitated by the unforeseeable financial impact of the 9/11 bombings. * * *

     We begin by examining whether defendants can be held liable to plaintiffs for a mass layoff under WARN. In this regard, defendants concede the number of employees fired over a ninety-day period exceeded fifty. They argue that even so, the different layoffs were for separate and distinct causes and did not constitute a mass layoff.

WARN Liability Generally

     * * * Unfortunately, WARN is less than clear with respect to mass layoffs occurring in an aggregation setting. As we highlight below, the statute and regulations generally speak in terms of planned, proposed, and foreseeable mass layoffs and employer liability that arises from failure to provide notice in those settings. Although WARN creates employer liability for aggregated mass layoffs under [29 U.S.C.] § 2102(d), it does not explicitly state how and when employer duties arise in an aggregated setting. * * *

     We begin with the portion of the statute that specifically outlines the terms of an employer's liability. Section 2104(a) of WARN states * * *

A "mass layoff" is

> a reduction in force which—(A) is not the result of a plant closing; and (B) results in an employment loss at the single site of employment during any 30-day period for—(i)(I) at least 33 percent of the employees (excluding any part-time employees); and (II) at least 50 employees (excluding any part-time employees); or (ii) at least 500 employees (excluding any part-time employees) . . .

Id. at § 2101(a)(3).

     In further fleshing out the pertinent terms in § 2104(a)(1), the relevant portion of § 2102 of WARN dictates that "[a]n employer shall not order a . . . mass layoff until the end of a 60-day period after the employer serves written notice of such an order—(1) to each . . . affected employee. . . ." Id. at § 2102(a). * * *

     Generally, therefore, when an employer foresees it could lay off enough employees to constitute a mass layoff under WARN, the employer must provide its employees with sixty days' advance notice. When the employer fails to do so, it must pay the terminated employees up to sixty days' back pay and benefits in lieu of notice. But as this case illustrates, business layoffs are not always so tidy or contained. Section 2102(d) of the statute acknowledges that sometimes the requisite number of employment losses sufficient to constitute a mass layoff might not occur during a single thirty-day period. Rather, they might occur in smaller increments, which in the aggregate and over a ninety-day period will constitute a mass layoff. WARN specifically directs that

> in determining whether a . . . mass layoff has occurred or will occur, *employment losses for 2 or more groups at a single site* of employment, each of which is less than the minimum number of employees specified in section [2101(a)(3)] of this title but *which in the aggregate exceed that minimum number,* and which occur *within any 90-day period shall be considered* to be a plant closing or *mass layoff unless the employer demonstrates that the employment losses are the result of separate and distinct actions and causes and are not an attempt by the employer to evade the requirements of this chapter.*

Id. at § 2102(d) (emphasis added).

The statute thus "imposes an affirmative burden on the employer to prove that the court should disaggregate employment losses that occurred during the 90-day period." [citation omitted]. If the employer does not satisfy this burden, the aggregate number of employees who have lost their jobs, "*shall be considered* to be a . . . mass layoff. . . ." 29 U.S.C. § 2102(d) (emphasis added).

Between September 7 and October 31—a fifty-eight-day period—defendants dismissed fifty-six employees. * * *

"Separate and Distinct" Causes

A mass layoff will not be deemed to have occurred if the employer can show the employment losses were the "result of separate and distinct actions and causes and are not an attempt by the employer to evade the requirements of" WARN. Id. at § 2102(d). We agree with the district court that defendants have not sufficiently raised an issue of fact on this point to survive summary judgment.

Defendants' argument regarding the separate and distinct causes for the three sets of layoffs represents a moving target. In their motion for summary judgment they argued that

> *six of the employees* terminated by FFI on October 31, 2001, were laid off due to the "separate and distinct cause" of Sybase's IT reorganization plan. . . . FFI's termination of these six IT

employees was unrelated to the financial difficulties that precipitated the other layoffs at Orem within the 90-day period.

* * * They appeared to contend that the six Sybase IT October layoffs were separate and distinct from the September employment losses, and therefore no mass layoff occurred. On appeal, however, defendants shift their argument somewhat. In their opening brief they contend each of the layoffs in this case arose from distinct causes. They assert the four September 7 job terminations were caused by FFI's financial difficulties, while the forty-one employment losses on September 28 were the result of "the significant financial fallout from the events of 9/11." * * * Finally, they maintain the October 31 layoff of eleven employees was due to Sybase's reorganization of its IT department. * * *

We are underwhelmed by defendants' inconsistent arguments and limit our review to the position they presented to the district court. [citation omitted]. As to defendants' initial argument, it is immaterial that the separate and distinct cause for six of the employment losses on October 31 was Sybase's reorganization of its company-wide IT department. Even excluding those six employees from the mass layoff calculation, FFI made the independent decision to fire another five employees "in an effort to cut fourth quarter expenses." * * * When one adds together the four employees from the September 7 job terminations, the forty-one employees from the September 28 terminations, and the five employees from the October 31 terminations, the total employment losses equals fifty. * * * In the absence of evidence showing the employment losses were for separate and distinct causes and not all the result of FFI's precarious financial situation, the job terminations were properly aggregated to constitute a mass layoff under § 2102(d) of WARN.

NOTES AND QUESTIONS

Test Your Understanding of the Material

1. What is the purpose of requiring notice of a plant closing or mass layoff, if the law does not require bargaining over the closing or layoff and the employees are not likely to have any leverage to wrest concessions from the employer? If the employees have a collective bargaining representative under the National Labor Relations Act, 29 U.S.C. §§ 151–169, the employer will have a duty to bargain in good faith with the employees' representative over the effects of the plant closing. See First National Maintenance Corp. v. NLRB, 452 U.S. 666 (1981); Fibreboard Paper Products Corp. v. NLRB, 379 U.S. 203 (1964) ; Samuel Estreicher & Matthew T. Bodie, Labor Law: Concepts and Insights Ch. 7 (2016). Unions also may sue on behalf of represented employees to enforce WARN obligations. UFCW Local 751 v. Brown Group, Inc., 517 U.S. 544, 116 S.Ct. 1529, 134 L.Ed.2d 758 (1996).

2.   WARN does not preclude states from enacting supplementary protections. How far could states go in requiring severance payments in the event of a plant closing or mass layoff?

Related Issues

3.   *Release Agreements.* Layoffs are a common juncture at which companies seek advice from employment lawyers, who are often called upon to prepare separation and release agreements. These agreements typically provide severance in exchange for a release of all claims. Releasing age claims for employees covered by the ADEA can be somewhat complex because the release must comply with OWBPA to be effective. See supra page 495.

D. PAID AND UNPAID LEAVE LAWS

1. FAMILY AND MEDICAL LEAVE ACT

The federal Family and Medical Leave Act (FMLA), 29 U.S.C. § 2601 et seq., requires covered employers to grant eligible employees a total of twelve (12) workweeks of unpaid or paid leave during any twelve month period for one or more of the following reasons: (a) to care for a child born within the last year; (b) to care for a child who has been adopted or placed in foster care with the employee during the past year; (c) to care for a spouse, child, or parent with a serious health condition; (d) because of a serious health condition that renders the employee unable to perform the functions of his or her position; or (e) qualifying exigencies relating to military service. 29 U.S.C. § 2612(a). A total of 26 weeks of leave is available for military caregivers. 29 U.S.C. § 2612(a)(3).

The FMLA covers only entities employing 50 or more employees for each working day during each of 20 or more calendar weeks in the current or preceding calendar year. Even when an employer is covered by the FMLA, an individual employee may not be eligible for leave. To be eligible, an employee (1) must have worked for the employer for at least twelve months and (2) for at least 1,250 hours during the previous year and (3) at a worksite where their employer employs at least 50 employees within a 75-mile radius.

The FMLA requires employers to reinstate any employee who takes such a leave to the position of employment held by the employee when the leave commenced, or to an equivalent position with equivalent pay, benefits, and other terms and conditions of employment. Id. at § 2614(a). (Reinstatement of employees in the top 10% of the payroll may be denied, however, after giving notice of an opportunity to return, where "necessary to prevent substantial and grievous economic injury to the operations of the business." Id. at § 2614(b).) Furthermore, employers must continue to provide health insurance coverage during FMLA leave, id. at § 2614(c), and may not deny employees who return from taking an FMLA leave any employment benefit, such as accumulated seniority, accrued prior to the date on which the leave commenced, id. at § 2614(a)(2). An employer may not "interfere with, restrain, or deny the exercise of or the attempt to exercise" any of these employee rights. Id. at § 2615(a).

The Supreme Court has upheld the application of the FMLA to state governments as an exercise of Congressional power under § 5 of the Fourteenth Amendment to "enact so-called prophylactic legislation that proscribes facially constitutional conduct, in order to prevent and deter unconstitutional conduct." Nevada Dept. of Human Resources v. Hibbs, 538 U.S. 721, 727, 123 S.Ct. 1972, 1977, 155 L.Ed.2d 953 (2003). Chief Justice Rehnquist reasoned for the Court:

> By creating an across-the-board, routine employment benefit for all eligible employees, Congress sought to ensure that family-care leave would no longer be stigmatized as an inordinate drain on the workplace caused by female employees, and that employers could not evade leave obligations simply by hiring men. By setting a minimum standard of family leave for all eligible employees, irrespective of gender, the FMLA attacks the formerly state-sanctioned stereotype that only women are responsible for family caregiving, thereby reducing employers' incentives to engage in discrimination by basing hiring and promotion decisions on stereotypes.

Id. at 737. But see Coleman v. Court of Appeals of Maryland, 132 S.Ct. 1327,182 L.Ed.2d 296 (2012) (11th Amendment bars suits against the states for money damages under FMLA's self-care provision).

The FMLA requires employees requesting leave to give their employer 30 days' notice if the need for leave is foreseeable, based on "expected birth or placement" or "planned medical treatment", or at least such notice "as is practicable." 29 U.S.C. § 2612(e). In addition, an employer may request that employees provide the "certification" of a health care provider as a condition of requesting leave based on the serious health condition of a family member or of their own. Notice requirements also are imposed on employers. Id. at § 2613. Employers must give employees notice of their FMLA rights "in conspicuous places on the premises of the employer". Id. at § 2619. Moreover, the Department of Labor, pursuant to regulations promulgated under its authority to implement the FMLA, requires employers to give notice of employee FMLA rights in employee handbooks or other such written material, and also to give employees notice of their rights and responsibilities under the FMLA when they request leave. The regulations specifically require employers to designate leave as FMLA leave and to notify affected employees of this designation and any responsibility to provide medical certification.

In Ragsdale v. Wolverine World Wide, Inc., 535 U.S. 81, 122 S.Ct. 1155, 152 L.Ed.2d 167 (2002), the Court held that the Department's regulation requiring an employer to designate leave as FMLA leave was invalid in so far as it mandated the tolling of the running of the twelve week period until the employee was advised of the designation. The *Ragsdale* Court found that the regulation was inconsistent with the FMLA because the statute requires employees to prove that an employer's actions or lapses caused "real impairment of their rights and resulting prejudice." Id. at 90. Since *Ragsdale,* courts have found that an employer's failure to give notice of rights or responsibilities could cause such prejudice in some cases, however. See, e.g., Lubke v. City of Arlington, 455 F.3d 489 (5th Cir.2006) (employer's failure to notify employee of responsibility of providing medical certification was prejudicial because employee could have avoided discharge by providing doctors' reports earlier); Conoshenti v. Public Service Electric & Gas Co., 364 F.3d 135 (3d Cir.2004) (employer's failure to advise employee of his rights to only twelve weeks of FMLA leave may have prejudiced employee who might have postponed surgery to return to work).

The degree to which the FMLA has contributed to achieving greater gender equality at the workplace is not clear. It seems not to have resulted in a significantly greater sharing of family responsibilities. FMLA leave has been most often taken by employees because of their own medical condition. About 75% of leave-eligible men with young children take some form of leave to care for a newborn or newly adopted child, although leave-eligible women with young children take leave at higher rates when maternity-disability leave is included. Department of Labor Wage and Hour Division, 2000 Survey Report, available at http://www.dol.gov/whd/fmla/chapter4.htm#4.6. The availability of FMLA leave might help some women keep jobs and stay on a career path, however. See Jean Kimmel & Catalina Amuedo-Dorantes, The Effects of Family Leave on Wages, Employment and the Family Wage Gap: Distributorial Implications, 15 Wash. U. J. L. & Pol'y 115 (2004).

The FMLA does not require employers to continue paying workers while they are on leave. However, the FMLA permits the employer to require employees to use any paid leave accrued pursuant to the employer's own leave policies while they are on FMLA leave, provided the employer includes such requirement in its written leave policies. 29 C.F.R. § 825.207.

2. STATE PAID FAMILY-MEDICAL LEAVE LAWS

In 2002, California became the first state to require employers to provide paid family leave. Cal. Unemp. Ins. Code § 984(a)(2)(B). The California law establishes a disability insurance program to provide up to six weeks of replacement benefits for employees who are caring for a seriously ill child, spouse, parent, or domestic partner, or bonding with a new child. As of 2015, eligible employees are to be paid 55% of their salary up to a maximum of $1,104 per week. The benefit is financed through payroll deductions. Subsequently, Washington also established an insurance program to fund a paid family leave benefit, see Wash. Rev. Code § 49.86, and New Jersey provides for unemployment insurance after the birth or adoption of a child, see N.J. Rev. Stat. §§ 43.21–4 and 43:21–7.

Comparative Note

Western European nations and Canada also require more generous benefits to employees out on family leave. Most require some degree of wage replacement as well as more extended periods during which leave is allowed. See Linda White, The United States in Comparative Perspective: Maternity and Parental Leave and Childcare Benefits in Liberal Welfare States, 21 Yale J. of L. and Feminism 185 (2009); Richard N. Block, Work-Family Legislation in the United States, Canada, and Western Europe: A Quantitative Comparison, 34 Pepp. L. Rev. 333 (2007); Annie Pelletier, The Family Medical Leave Act of 1993—Why Does Parental Leave in the United States Fall So Far Behind Europe?, 42 Gonz. L. Rev. 547 (2007); Dorothea Alewell and Kerstin Pull, An International Comparison and Assessment of Maternity Legislation, 22 Comp. Lab.L. & Po. J. 297 (2001).

Employers can adopt voluntary policies to facilitate the exit and reentry of primary parents, such as parenting leaves and day care benefits. Are there any reasons why employers should not permit flexible periods of consideration for key promotional decisions such as selection to partnership or a tenured faculty position? See generally Kathy Abrams, Gender Discrimination and the Transformation of Workplace Norms, 42 Vand.L.Rev. 1184, 1233–46 (1989); Nancy Dowd, Work and Family: The Gender Paradox and the Limitations of Discrimination Analysis in Restructuring the Workplace, 24 Harv.Civ.Rts.-Civ.Libs.L.Rev. 79 (1989).

PART 6

REMEDIAL ISSUES IN
EMPLOYMENT LAW

■ ■ ■

The remedies a claimant may obtain in litigation is an important determinant of whether to bring a lawsuit, and will also shape the possibility of a settlement short of trial. Chapter 20 explores the remedies available in common law cases. Chapter 21 looks to procedural issues that principally arise in cases governed by statutes but that cut across many substantive areas.

CHAPTER 20

REMEDIES

■ ■ ■

Introduction

Obtainable remedies usually are the principal motivation for a lawsuit. An understanding of available remedies also helps shape settlement negotiations. The discussion in this chapter of remedies in employment related actions is organized in terms of claims against employers and claims against employees and is further broken down between contract, tort, and statutory causes of action.

A. CLAIMS AGAINST EMPLOYERS

1. CONTRACT CLAIMS

RESTATEMENT OF EMPLOYMENT LAW § 9.01

American Law Institute (2015).

§ 9.01. Damages—Employer Termination in Breach of an Agreement for a Definite or Indefinite Term of Employment or of a Binding Employer Promise of Employment

    (a) An employer who lacks cause for terminating the employment of an employee with an unexpired agreement for a definite term (§§ 2.03–2.04) is subject to liability to the discharged employee for

        (1) all compensation that the employee would have received under the remaining term of the agreement, less mitigation of losses (such as the compensation earned and that reasonably could have been earned from comparable alternative employment during the remaining term);

        (2) reasonably foreseeable consequential damages; and

        (3) the expenses of reasonable effort (whether or not successful) to mitigate losses.

    (b) An employer who lacks cause for terminating the employment of an employee with an agreement for an indefinite term requiring cause for termination (§§ 2.03–2.04) is subject to liability to the discharged employee for:

    (1)   all compensation that the employee would have received under that agreement, less mitigation of losses (such as the compensation earned and that reasonably could have been earned from comparable alternative employment);

    (2)   reasonably foreseeable consequential damages; and

    (3)   the expenses of reasonable effort (whether or not successful) to mitigate losses.

(c)   The employer and employee may specify in the agreement a reasonable amount to be paid by the employer for termination with or without cause in lieu of the measure of damages stated in (a) and (b).

(d)   An employer who breaches a promise that limits the employer's right to terminate employment and that induces reasonable and detrimental reliance by the employee (§ 2.02, Comment c) is subject to liability to the discharged employee for:

    (1)   damages (including reasonably foreseeable consequential damages) caused by the employee's reasonable reliance on that promise;

    (2)   less mitigation of losses (such as the compensation earned and that reasonably could have been earned from comparable alternative employment during the period covered by the promise); and

    (3)   the expenses of reasonable effort (whether or not successful) to mitigate losses.

SHIRLEY MACLAINE PARKER V. TWENTIETH CENTURY-FOX FILM CORP.

Supreme Court of California, 1970.
3 Cal.3d 176, 89 Cal.Rptr. 737, 474 P.2d 689.

BURKE, J.

Defendant Twentieth Century-Fox Film Corporation appeals from a summary judgment granting to plaintiff the recovery of agreed compensation under a written contract for her services as an actress in a motion picture. * * *

Plaintiff is well known as an actress, and in the contract between plaintiff and defendant is sometimes referred to as the "Artist." Under the contract, dated August 6, 1965, plaintiff was to play the female lead in defendant's contemplated production of a motion picture entitled "Bloomer Girl." The contract provided that defendant would pay plaintiff a minimum "guaranteed compensation" of $53,571.42 per week for 14 weeks commencing May 23, 1966, for a total of $750,000. [*Eds.* In inflation adjusted figures, the contract would be worth $4.5 million today.] Prior to May 1966 defendant decided not to produce the picture and by a letter dated April 4, 1966, it notified plaintiff of that decision and that it would not "comply with our obligations to you under" the written contract.

By the same letter and with the professed purpose "to avoid any damage to you," defendant instead offered to employ plaintiff as the leading actress in another film tentatively entitled "Big Country, Big Man" (hereinafter, "Big Country"). The compensation offered was identical, as were 31 of the 34 numbered provisions or articles of the original contract. Unlike "Bloomer Girl," however, which was to have been a musical production, "Big Country" was a dramatic "western type" movie. "Bloomer Girl" was to have been filmed in California; "Big Country" was to be produced in Australia. Also, certain terms in the proffered contract varied from those of the original.[2] Plaintiff was given one week within which to accept; she did not and the offer lapsed. Plaintiff then commenced this action seeking recovery of the agreed guaranteed compensation.

The complaint sets forth two causes of action. The first is for money due under the contract; the second, based upon the same allegations as the first, is for damages resulting from defendant's breach of contract. Defendant in its answer admits the existence and validity of the contract, that plaintiff complied with all the conditions, covenants and promises and stood ready to complete the performance, and that defendant breached and "anticipatorily repudiated" the contract. It denies, however, that any money is due to plaintiff either under the contract or as a result of its breach, and pleads as an affirmative defense to both causes of action plaintiff's allegedly deliberate failure to mitigate damages, asserting that

---

[2]   Article 29 of the original contract specified that plaintiff approved the director already chosen for "Bloomer Girl" and that in case he failed to act as director plaintiff was to have approval rights of any substitute director. Article 31 provided that plaintiff was to have the right of approval of the "Bloomer Girl" dance director, and Article 32 gave her the right of approval of the screenplay.

Defendant's letter of April 4 to plaintiff, which contained both defendant's notice of breach of the "Bloomer Girl" contract and offer of the lead in "Big Country," eliminated or impaired each of those rights. It read in part as follows: "The terms and conditions of our offer of employment are identical to those set forth in the 'BLOOMER GIRL' Agreement, Articles 1 through 34 and Exhibit A to the Agreement, except as follows:

"1. Article 31 of said Agreement will not be included in any contract of employment regarding 'BIG COUNTRY, BIG MAN' as it is not a musical and it thus will not need a dance director.

"2. In the 'BLOOMER GIRL' agreement, in Articles 29 and 32, you were given certain director and screenplay approvals and you had preapproved certain matters. Since there simply is insufficient time to negotiate with you regarding your choice of director and regarding the screenplay and since you already expressed an interest in performing the role in 'BIG COUNTRY, BIG MAN,' we must exclude from our offer of employment in 'BIG COUNTRY, BIG MAN' any approval rights as are contained in said Articles 29 and 32; however, we shall consult with you respecting the director to be selected to direct the photoplay and will further consult with you with respect to the screenplay and any revisions or changes therein, provided, however, that if we fail to agree . . . the decision of . . . [defendant] with respect to the selection of a director and to revisions and changes in the said screenplay shall be binding upon the parties to said agreement."

she unreasonably refused to accept its offer of the leading role in "Big Country."

Plaintiff moved for summary judgment under Code of Civil Procedure section 437c, the motion was granted, and summary judgment for $750,000 plus interest was entered in plaintiff's favor. This appeal by defendant followed. * * *

As stated, defendant's sole defense to this action which resulted from its deliberate breach of contract is that in rejecting defendant's substitute offer of employment plaintiff unreasonably refused to mitigate damages.

The general rule is that the measure of recovery by a wrongfully discharged employee is the amount of salary agreed upon for the period of service, less the amount which the employer affirmatively proves the employee has earned or with reasonable effort might have earned from other employment. * * * However, before projected earnings from other employment opportunities not sought or accepted by the discharged employee can be applied in mitigation, the employer must show that the other employment was comparable, or substantially similar, to that of which the employee has been deprived; the employee's rejection of or failure to seek other available employment of a different or inferior kind may not be resorted to in order to mitigate damages. [Citations omitted]

In the present case defendant has raised no issue of *reasonableness of efforts* by plaintiffs to obtain other employment; the sole issue is whether plaintiff's refusal of defendant's substitute offer of "Big Country" may be used in mitigation. Nor, if the "Big Country" offer was of employment different or inferior when compared with the original "Bloomer Girl" employment, is there an issue as to whether or not plaintiff acted reasonably in refusing the substitute offer. Despite defendant's arguments to the contrary, no case cited or which our research has discovered holds or suggests that reasonableness is an element of a wrongfully discharged employee's option to reject, or fail to seek, different or inferior employment lest the possible earnings therefrom be charged against him in mitigation of damages.[5]

Applying the foregoing rules to the record in the present case, with all intendments in favor of the party opposing the summary judgment motion-here, defendant-it is clear that the trial court correctly ruled that plaintiff's failure to accept defendant's tendered substitute employment could not be applied in mitigation of damages because the offer of the "Big Country" lead was of employment both different and inferior, and that no factual dispute was presented on that issue. The mere circumstance that "Bloomer Girl" was to be a musical review calling upon plaintiff's talents as a dancer as well as an actress, and was to be produced in the City of Los Angeles,

---

[5] Instead, in each case the reasonableness referred to was that of the *efforts* of the employee to obtain other employment that was not different or inferior; his right to reject the latter was declared as an unqualified rule of law. * * *

whereas "Big Country" was a straight dramatic role in a "Western Type" story taking place in an opal mine in Australia, demonstrates the difference in kind between the two employments; the female lead as a dramatic actress in a western style motion picture can by no stretch of imagination be considered the equivalent of or substantially similar to the lead in a song-and-dance production.

Additionally, the substitute "Big Country" offer proposed to eliminate or impair the director and screenplay approvals accorded to plaintiff under the original "Bloomer Girl" contract (see fn. 2, *ante*), and thus constituted an offer of inferior employment. No expertise or judicial notice is required in order to hold that the deprivation or infringement of an employee's rights held under an original employment contract converts the available "other employment" relied upon by the employer to mitigate damages, into inferior employment which the employee need not seek or accept. * * *

NOTES AND QUESTIONS

Test Your Understanding of the Material

1.   Is *Parker* a special case for high-end actors for whom each film project is viewed as a unique opportunity? Assume Jim Jones is a movie set cameraman who was initially offered work on "Bloomer Girl," which did not materialize and was then offered work at the same pay and benefits for "Big Country, Big Man," which he turns down? Would this be viewed by the California court as a failure to mitigate damages? See Employment Restatement § 9.01.

2.   Applying the Employment Restatement provision above, outline plaintiff's measure of damages. Note that the relevant California Civil Jury Instructions provide: "[Name of plaintiff] also must prove the amount of [his/her/its] damages according to the following instructions. [He/She/It] does not have to prove the exact amount of damages. You must not speculate or guess in awarding damages." CACI No. 350, Judicial Council of California Civil Jury Instruction (June 2015 Supp.).

3.   What position does the Employment Restatement take on recovery of future economic losses? Consider § 9.05, Comment e:

> Although some courts continue to be skeptical of claims of future economic harm, courts in a considerably larger number of jurisdictions, perhaps influenced by the availability of "front pay" in lieu of reinstatement for statutory employment-law violations (see § 9.04, Comment *c*), show increasing receptivity to allowing well-grounded claims of reasonably certain future economic loss to be submitted to the trier of fact. This Section adopts the view of the latter jurisdictions, that ordinarily the trier of fact should be allowed to consider whether claims of future economic loss are well-founded by assessing the injured party's probable compensation over his likely work expectancy minus earnings the employee would, or could

(through reasonable effort), obtain had he not been injured. These courts do not require expert vocational testimony in all cases but do insist on a reasonable factual basis for awarding damages for future economic loss.

Related Issues

4. *Specific Performance of Employment Contracts?* Could Ms. Parker have obtained an order requiring the defendant to place her in "Bloomer Girl"? As a general matter, courts will not grant specific performance of personal services contracts. Note in Ms. Parker's case such an order may be particularly infeasible because the court would be ordering the production of a film that the defendant had taken off the boards. In most employment terminations, reinstatement is not as infeasible but is still difficult when a replacement has been hired or there are continuing tensions between the plaintiff and the former employer. See Employment Restatement § 9.04.

5. *Consequential Damages.* Should Ms. Parker be able to recover consequential damages for harm to her reputation as a result of losing the "Bloomer Girl" opportunity? See. Id. § 9.01, Comment h.

2. TORT CLAIMS

RESTATEMENT OF EMPLOYMENT LAW § 9.05
American Law Institute (2015).

§ 9.05. Damages—Employer Breach of Tort-Based Duty

(a) An employer who breaches a tort-based duty to an employee is subject to liability in damages to the affected employee for foreseeable harms caused by the wrong.

(b) To the extent not precluded by workers'-compensation law or other applicable law, available items of damages that may be sought under (a) include past and reasonably certain future economic loss, noneconomic loss, the expenses of reasonable efforts to mitigate damages, and reasonably foreseeable consequential damages. An employee may also recover punitive damages if the employer was sufficiently culpable, or nominal damages if no actual damages are proven.

(c) Unless otherwise provided by law, an employer who breaches a tort-based duty is not subject to liability for the attorney's fees incurred by the employee in maintaining the employee's claim.

FOLEY V. INTERACTIVE DATA CORP.

Supreme Court of California, En Banc 1988.
47 Cal.3d 654, 254 Cal.Rptr. 211, 765 P.2d 373.

[*Eds.* For previous excerpt from this decision, see p. 52 supra.]

We turn now to plaintiff's cause of action for tortious breach of the implied covenant of good faith and fair dealing. Relying on *Cleary* [*v. American Airlines, Inc.*,] (1980), 111 Cal.App.3d 443, 168 Cal.Rptr. 722, and subsequent Court of Appeal cases, plaintiff asserts we should recognize tort remedies for such a breach in the context of employment termination.

The distinction between tort and contract is well grounded in common law, and divergent objectives underlie the remedies created in the two areas. Whereas contract actions are created to enforce the intentions of the parties to the agreement, tort law is primarily designed to vindicate "social policy." (Prosser, Law of Torts (4th ed. 1971) p. 613.) The covenant of good faith and fair dealing was developed in the contract arena and is aimed at making effective the agreement's promises. Plaintiff asks that we find that the breach of the implied covenant in employment contracts also gives rise to an action seeking an award of tort damages.

* * *

"Every contract imposes upon each party a duty of good faith and fair dealing in its performance and its enforcement." (Rest.2d Contracts, § 205.) This duty has been recognized in the majority of American jurisdictions, the Restatement, and the Uniform Commercial Code. (Burton, *Breach of Contract and the Common Law Duty to Perform in Good Faith* (1980) 94 Harv.L.Rev. 369.) Because the covenant is a contract term, however, compensation for its breach has almost always been limited to contract rather than tort remedies. * * *

An exception to this general rule has developed in the context of insurance contracts where, for a variety of policy reasons, courts have held that breach of the implied covenant will provide the basis for an action in tort. California has a well-developed judicial history addressing this exception. In *Comunale v. Traders & General Ins. Co.* (1958) 50 Cal.2d 654, 658, 328 P.2d 198, we stated, "There is an implied covenant of good faith and fair dealing in every contract that neither party will do anything which will injure the right of the other to receive the benefits of the agreement." (See also *Egan v. Mutual of Omaha Ins. Co., supra,* 24 Cal.3d 809, 818, 169 Cal.Rptr. 691, 620 P.2d 141.) Thereafter, in *Crisci v. Security Ins. Co.* (1967) 66 Cal.2d 425, 58 Cal.Rptr. 13, 426 P.2d 173, for the first time we permitted an insured to recover in tort for emotional damages caused by the insurer's breach of the implied covenant. We explained in *Gruenberg v. Aetna Ins. Co.* (1973) 9 Cal.3d 566, 108 Cal.Rptr. 480, 510 P.2d 1032, * * *. Accordingly, when the insurer unreasonably and in bad faith withholds payment of the claim of its insured, it is subject to liability in tort." (Id., at p. 575, 108 Cal.Rptr. 480, 510 P.2d 1032.)

* * *

* * * An allegation of breach of the implied covenant of good faith and fair dealing is an allegation of breach of an "ex contractu" obligation, namely one arising out of the contract itself. The covenant of good faith is read into contracts in order to protect the express covenants or promises of the contract, not to protect some general public policy interest not directly tied to the contract's purposes. The insurance cases thus were a major departure from traditional principles of contract law. We must, therefore, consider with great care claims that extension of the exceptional approach taken in those cases is automatically appropriate if certain hallmarks and similarities can be adduced in another contract setting. With this emphasis on the historical purposes of the covenant of good faith and fair dealing in mind, we turn to consider the bases upon which extension of the insurance model to the employment sphere has been urged.

The "special relationship" test gleaned from the insurance context has been suggested as a model for determining the appropriateness of permitting tort remedies for breach of the implied covenant of the employment context. One commentary has observed, "[j]ust as the law of contracts fails to provide adequate principles for construing the terms of an insurance policy, the substantial body of law uniquely applicable to insurance contracts is practically irrelevant to commercially oriented contracts * * * . These [unique] features characteristic of the insurance contract make it particularly susceptible to public policy considerations." (Louderback & Jurika, *Standards for Limiting the Tort of Bad Faith Breach of Contract* (1982) 16 U.S.F.L.Rev. 187, 200–201, fns. omitted.) These commentators assert that tort remedies for breach of the covenant should not be extended across the board in the commercial context, but that, nonetheless, public policy considerations suggest extending the tort remedy if certain salient factors are present. (Id., at pp. 216–218.) "The tort of bad faith should be applied to commercial contracts only if four of the features characteristic of insurance bad faith actions are present. The features are: (1) one of the parties to the contract enjoys a superior bargaining position to the extent that it is able to dictate the terms of the contract; (2) the purpose of the weaker party in entering into the contract is not primarily to profit but rather to secure an essential service or product, financial security or peace of mind; (3) the relationship of the parties is such that the weaker party places its trust and confidence in the larger entity; and (4) there is conduct on the part of the defendant indicating an intent to frustrate the weaker party's enjoyment of the contract rights." (Id., at p. 227.) The discussion of these elements includes an assumption that a tort remedy should be recognized in employment relationships within the stated limitations.

* * *

[W]e are not convinced that a "special relationship" analogous to that between insurer and insured should be deemed to exist in the usual employment relationship which would warrant recognition of a tort action for breach of the implied covenant. Even if we were to assume that the special relationship model is an appropriate one to follow in determining whether to expand tort recovery, a breach in the employment context does not place the employee in the same economic dilemma that an insured faces when an insurer in bad faith refuses to pay a claim or to accept a settlement offer within policy limits. When an insurer takes such actions, the insured cannot turn to the marketplace to find another insurance company willing to pay for the loss already incurred. The wrongfully terminated employee, on the other hand, can (and must, in order to mitigate damages [see *Parker v. Twentieth Century-Fox Film Corp.* (1970) 3 Cal.3d 176, 181–182, 89 Cal.Rptr. 737, 474 P.2d 689] make reasonable efforts to seek alternative employment. * * * Moreover, the role of the employer differs from that of the "quasi-public" insurance company with whom individuals contract specifically in order to obtain protection from potential specified economic harm. The employer does not similarly "sell" protection to its employees; it is not providing a public service. Nor do we find convincing the idea that the employee is necessarily seeking a different kind of financial security than those entering a typical commercial contract. If a small dealer contracts for goods from a large supplier, and those goods are vital to the small dealer's business, a breach by the supplier may have financial significance for individuals employed by the dealer or to the dealer himself. Permitting only contract damages in such a situation has ramifications no different from a similar limitation in the direct employer-employee relationship.

Finally, there is a fundamental difference between insurance and employment relationships. In the insurance relationship, the insurer's and insured's interest are financially at odds. If the insurer pays a claim, it diminishes its fiscal resources. The insured of course has paid for protection and expects to have its losses recompensed. When a claim is paid, money shifts from insurer to insured, or, if appropriate, to a third party claimant.

Putting aside already specifically barred improper motives for termination which may be based on both economic and noneconomic considerations, as a general rule it is to the employer's economic benefit to retain good employees. The interests of employer and employee are most frequently in alignment. If there is a job to be done, the employer must still pay someone to do it. This is not to say that there may never be a "bad motive" for discharge not otherwise covered by law. Nevertheless, in terms of abstract employment relationships as contrasted with abstract insurance relationships, there is less inherent relevant tension between the interests of employers and employees than exists between that of insurers and insureds. Thus the need to place disincentives on an employer's conduct in addition to those already imposed by law simply does not rise to the same level as that created by the conflicting interests at stake in the insurance context. Nor is this to say that the Legislature would have no basis for affording employees additional protections. It is, however, to say that the need to extend the special relationship model in the form of judicially created relief of the kind sought here is less compelling.

* * * [I]n traditional contract law, the *motive* of the breaching party generally has no bearing on the scope of damages that the injured party may recover for the breach of the implied covenant; the remedies are limited to contract damages. Thus, recitation of the parameters of the implied covenant alone is unsatisfactory. If the covenant is implied in every contract, but its breach does not in every contract give rise to tort damages, attempts to define when tort damages are appropriate simply by interjecting a requirement of "bad faith" do nothing to limit the potential reach of tort remedies or to differentiate between those cases properly and traditionally compensable by contract damages and those in which tort damages should flow. Virtually any firing (indeed any breach of a contract term in any context) could provide the basis for a pleading alleging the discharge was in bad faith under the cited standards.

NOTES AND QUESTIONS

Test Your Understanding of the Material

1. Does the *Foley* court persuasively distinguish the insurance law principle of "bad-faith breach," which states a tort in California and other states? Only Nevada has applied the insurance precedent to certain employment cases. In K Mart Corp. v. Ponsock, 103 Nev. 39, 732 P.2d 1364 (1987), the court held that an employee discharged after nearly 10 years of service for the purpose of preventing the vesting of retirement benefits could recover in tort. Apparently, Nevada limits the bad-faith discharge theory recognized in *K Mart* to contexts where employers breach without justification a "contractual obligation of continued employment". Sands Regent v. Valgardson, 105 Nev. 436, 777 P.2d 898, 899 (1989). Should tort damages be available in a case like *Fortune*, p. 853 supra?

2. What are differences, if any, between recovery in tort and recovery under contract? As the Restatement provisions indicate, in both cases mitigation of damages is required, see Employment Restatement § 9.05, Comment c, and recovery for non-speculative future losses is possible. Punitive damages would not be available in a contract case. Would damages for emotional distress be available as an element of damages for a contract case? Would they be available in a tort case outside the parameters of the intentional infliction of emotional distress tort? See Employment Restatement, § 9.01, Comment j.

Related Issues

3. *Punitive Damages*. The commission of an otherwise actionable tort by an agent of the employer does not necessarily translate into employer liability for punitive damages. Calif. Civil Code Sec. 3294, subd. (a), for example, allows a plaintiff to seek punitive damages "for the breach of an obligation not arising from contract" when the plaintiff can show by "clear and convincing evidence" that a defendant "has been guilty of oppression, fraud or malice." However, subd. (b), added in 1980, states that an employer cannot be held liable for punitive damages unless

> the employer has advance knowledge of the unfitness of the employee and employed him with a conscious disregard of the rights or safety of others or authorized or ratified the wrongful conduct for which the damages are awarded or was personally guilty of oppression, fraud or malice.

The statute also includes an additional requirement for corporate employers who will not be liable for punitive damages unless "the advance knowledge and conscious disregard, authorization, ratification or act of oppression, fraud, or malice [is] on the part of an officer, director, or managing agent of the corporation." See also White v. Ultramar, 21 Cal.4th 563, 88 Cal.Rptr.2d 19, 981 P.2d 944 (1999) ("'managing agent' [includes] only those corporate employees who exercise substantial independent authority and judgment in their corporate decisionmaking so that their decisions ultimately determine corporate policy.") 21 Cal.App.4th at 566, 577, 981 P.2d at 947, 954. The New York rule can be found in Loughry v. Lincoln First Bank, 67 N.Y.2d 369, 494 N.E.2d 70, 502 N.Y.S.2d 965 (1986).

The Efficacy of Reputational Sanctions

Will reputational harms be sufficient to curb any tendency by employers to contravene implied understandings with employees?

> In most employment settings, reliable information about the firm's record of promise-keeping is not readily obtainable. Current employees are likely to be the best source of such information but, under real world conditions, they are not likely to transmit this information to job applicants. Moreover, they are unlikely to transmit clear informational signals by exiting employment, because it is difficult to evaluate why employees are leaving and, given the lock-in effect of the internal labor market contract, it is difficult to evaluate why they stay.

Samuel Estreicher, Employer Reputation at Work, 27 Hofstra Lab. & Emp. L. J. 1 (2009). Have you ever looked up information about an employer's reputation online, including "Best Employer" websites, before taking a job? What sort of information was there on its employment policies? Was it useful in assessing the likelihood of fair treatment on the job?

3. STATUTORY CLAIMS

NOTES AND QUESTIONS

1. *Reinstatement with Back Pay.* At least in statutory employment cases, courts award reinstatement of the wronged employee to the position the employee would have had but for the employer's wrongdoing, coupled with back pay for lost compensation during the period before reinstatement, is the usual remedy. An unconditional offer to reinstate a terminated employee generally cuts off back pay and front pay damages as of the date of the offer. Ford Motor Co. v. EEOC, 458 U.S. 219 (1982) ([T]he legal rules fashioned to implement Title VII should be designed . . . to encourage Title VII defendants promptly to make curative, unconditional job offers to Title VII claimants, thereby bringing defendants into 'voluntary compliance.' . . . The victims of job discrimination want jobs, not lawsuits.")

Courts award back pay "as a matter of course" to further the employment statute's "make whole purpose." Albemarle Paper Co. v. Moody, 422 U.S. 405 (1975):

> [G]iven a finding of unlawful discrimination, backpay should be denied only for reasons which, if applied generally, would not frustrate the central statutory purposes of eradicating discrimination throughout the economy and making persons whole for injuries suffered through past discrimination[.] * * * The District Court's stated grounds for denying backpay * * * was that Albermarle's breach of Title VII had not been in 'bad faith.' This is not a sufficient reason for denying backpay.

Prior to the 1991 amendments, Title VII courts were limited to awarding reinstatement and back pay—both types of equitable relief. In assessing the appropriateness of reinstatement in the Title VII context, courts consider the plaintiff's situation, including subsequent employment, career goals, and ability to return to work. They also consider such factors as whether the employer remains in business, the availability of a comparable position, and the displacement of other employees. They consider the parties' feelings towards reinstatement, including hostility or animosity between the parties, hostility in the workplace, and the parties' agreement as to the viability of reinstatement. Ogden v. Wax Work, Inc., 29 F.Supp.2d 1003 (N.D. Iowa 1998). After acquired evidence of terminable misconduct precludes both reinstatement and front pay. See *McKennon v. Nashville,* supra at p. 135.

2. *Front Pay in Lieu of Reinstatement.* In Title VII cases, courts do not consider awarding front pay until they are "assured that reinstatement is an infeasible or otherwise inappropriate remedy." Williams v. Valentec Kisco, Inc., 964 F.2d 723 (8th Cir.1992). Often the employer is reluctant to reinstate a formerly discharged employee. The employee also may be reluctant to return to the same place of employment. Courts in Title VII and other statutory contexts have developed an equitable award of front pay in lieu of reinstatement. Where an employee has been working for an indefinite term,

the court must determine the effect of the termination on the employee's future wages. Front pay is also a helpful remedy in ADEA cases where an older plaintiff faces a low likelihood of reemployment.

Employees injured by statutory violations generally have a duty to mitigate losses. This requires searching for alternate employment. Where an employee has obtained alternate but inferior employment, the court must estimate (often with the help of experts) the difference in earnings between the substitute employment and the original job. Goss v. Exxon Office Sys. Co., 747 F.2d 885 (3d. Cir.1984) (awarding front pay for the estimated period it would take plaintiff to reach a compensation level equivalent to what she would have received absent discrimination); Koyen v. Consolidated Edison Co. Of New York, Inc., 560 F.Supp. 1161 (S.D.N.Y.1983).

The courts generally have treated front pay under Title VII as a form of equitable relief over which district courts have wide discretion. Hukkanen v. Int'l Union of Operating Engineers, 3 F.3d 281 (8th Cir.1993). See, e.g., Padilla v. Metro-North Commuter R.R., 92 F.3d 117, 126 (2d Cir.1996) (sustaining award to plaintiff in his 40s, "in the amount of the difference between his salary as a train dispatcher and the salary paid to the superintendent of train operations until he reaches the age of 67"); Kelley v. Airborne Freight Corp., 140 F.3d 335, 355–56 (1st Cir.1998) (sustaining $1 million award because plaintiff was six years away from becoming fully vested in pension plan).

In Pollard v. E.I. du Pont de Nemours & Co., 532 U.S. 843, 121 S.Ct. 1946, 150 L.Ed.2d 62 (2001), the Court held that front pay is an instance of equitable relief authorized by § 706(g), and is not an element of compensatory damages under § 1981a and hence not subject to the damages "caps" in § 1981a(b)(3) of the 1991 Civil Rights Act.

3. *After-Acquired Evidence of Employee Misconduct.* Recall from Chapter 3 that evidence of terminable misconduct uncovered in a subsequent lawsuit serves to limit an employee's damages in a Title VII or ADEA case. Courts have invoked the doctrine to limit recovery in other contexts as well. See Silver v. CPC-Sherwood Manor, Inc., 2006 OK 97, 151 P.3d 127 (Okl.2006) (public-policy claim). See Riddle v. Wal-Mart Stores, Inc., 27 Kan.App.2d 79 (Kan. App.2000) (public-policy claim); Gassman v. Evangelical Lutheran Good Samaritan Soc., Inc., 933 2d. 743 (Kan.1997) (implied-contract claim).

4. *Pre- and Post-Judgment Interest.* The lower courts have held that an award of prejudgment interest, although routinely made, is discretionary. See, e.g., Hunter v. Allis-Chalmers Corp., 797 F.2d 1417 (7th Cir.1986)—a position endorsed (in dicta) in Loeffler v. Frank, 486 U.S. 549, 108 S.Ct. 1965, 100 L.Ed.2d 549 (1988), and codified at 42 U.S.C. § 2000e–16(d) ("the same interest to compensate for delay in payment shall be available as in cases involving nonpublic parties").

Some decisions hold that in ADEA cases prejudgment interest on back pay awards is not available because the cost of delay is already accounted for in the provision of liquidated damages. See Shea v. Galaxie Lumber & Construction Co., Ltd., 152 F.3d 729, 733–34 (7th Cir.1998); McCann v. Texas City Refining,

Inc., 984 F.2d 667 (5th Cir.1993); Linn v. Andover Newton Theological School, Inc., 874 F.2d 1 (1st Cir.1989); but see Starceski v. Westinghouse Electric Corp., 54 F.3d 1089, 1099–1100 (3d Cir.1995) (liquidated damages are "punitive" under Trans World Airlines, Inc. v. Thurston, 469 U.S. 111, 105 S.Ct. 613, 83 L.Ed.2d 523 (1985), and do not foreclose prejudgment interest).

5. *Non-Economic Damages.* For statutory claims, the availability of non-economic damages—such as pain and suffering, humiliation, or out-of-pocket expenses—is governed by the statute. Title VII permits plaintiffs to recover non-economic damages subject to a cap based on the employer's size. 42 U.S.C. § 1981(b)(3).

Courts generally decline to award non-economic damages under the ADEA, principally because of the availability of liquidated damages, which amounts to a doubling of economic loss. See, e.g., Flamand v. American International Group, 876 F.Supp. 356 (D.P.R.1994). The Seventh Circuit takes the view that a 1977 amendment to the FLSA authorizes compensatory damage awards in FLSA and EPA retaliation cases. See Shea v. Galaxie Lumber & Constr. Co., 152 F.3d 729 (7th Cir.1998); Avitia v. Metropolitan Club of Chicago, Inc., 49 F.3d 1219, 1226 n. 2 (7th Cir.1995); see also Moore v. Freeman, 355 F.3d 558 (6th Cir. 2004).

6. *Recovery of Attorney's Fees.* Absent a statutory provision awarding attorney's fees, each party must pay their own attorneys' fees (known as the "American Rule"). Alyeska Pipeline Co. v. Wilderness Soc'y, 421 U.S. 240 (1975). As a result, plaintiffs pursuing state law contract and tort claims ordinarily cannot recover attorney's fees even if they prevail. However, most employment statutes allow prevailing plaintiffs to recover such fees. See e.g. 29 U.S.C. § 216(b) (FLSA); 29 U.S.C. § 626(b) (ADEA); 29 U.S.C. § 2617(a)(3) (FMLA); 18 U.S.C. 1514(a)(c)(2)(C) (Sarbanes-Oxley Act).

Recall from Chapter 3 that plaintiffs in Title VII cases are eligible for a fee award even under a "mixed motive" analysis, where the employer can show that it would have made the same decision in any event. § 706(g)(2)(B)(i). As a general matter, prevailing defendants cannot recover attorney's fees unless the lawsuit was "groundless or without foundation" "frivolous" or "vexatiously brought." Christiansburg Garment Co. v. EEOC, 434 US 412 (1978).

Courts calculate attorneys' fees using the "lodestar" method. Under this method, the "initial estimate of a reasonable attorney's fee is properly calculated by multiplying the number of hours reasonably expended on the litigation times a reasonable hourly rate." Blum v. Stenson, 465 U.S. 886, 888, 104 S.Ct. 1541, 1543 (1984). The reasonableness of an hourly rate and of the hours expended may turn on a range of factors, including "the novelty and difficulty of the questions"; "the skill requisite to perform the legal service properly"; "the preclusion of employment * * * due to acceptance of the case"; "the customary fee"; "time limitations imposed by the client or the case"; "the amount involved and the results obtained"; "the experience, reputation, and ability of the attorneys"; "the 'undesirability' of the case"; "the nature and length of the professional relationship with the client"; and "awards in similar cases". Johnson v. Georgia Highway Express, Inc., 488 F.2d 714 (5th Cir.1974).

7. *Penalties.* Employment statutes sometimes use penalties and liquidated damages to deter employer violations and encourage private enforcement. Penalties are especially prevalent in the wage and hour context. The FLSA provides for liquidated damages equal to the amount of unpaid wages, doubling the plaintiff's potential recovery. 29 U.S.C. § 216. Although punitive damages are not available in ADEA actions, the statute authorizes an award of liquidated damages (doubling the unpaid wages due) for "willful" violations. The Supreme Court in Trans World Airlines v. Thurston, 469 U.S. 111, 126, 105 S.Ct. 613, 624, 83 L.Ed.2d 523 (1985), held that such an award serves a punitive purpose and is available only where the employer "knew or showed reckless disregard . . . whether its conduct was prohibited by the ADEA."

Several states provide for penalties where the employer fails to deliver a terminated employee's final paycheck within the statutory period. See p. 865 supra, Chapter 18 (state "waiting time" penalties).

Some statutes provide for penalties to be assessed by government agencies, where penalties ultimately become a function of available government resources to investigate and enforce violations. For example, many states empower state workers' compensation and unemployment insurance agencies to assess fines for misclassifying independent contractors. See e.g. Ind. Code § 22–3–1–3(15); In re: Body Electric Corp of Amer., 89 A.D. 3d 1331 (N.Y.App.Div.2011) (upholding penalty and unpaid contributions assessed by state unemployment insurance agency).

To mitigate the resource limitations of government agencies, the California Private Attorneys General Act provides a private right of action to enforce any penalty-bearing provision of the labor code. Cal. Lab. § 2698 et seq. The statute also imposes default penalties for all other labor code violations except posting and filing requirements, also recoverable through a private right of action.

A number of employment-related statutes have criminal penalties, although employees are rarely prosecuted. See e.g. 29 U.S.C. § 216 (willful violation of certain provisions of FLSA); 18 U.S.C. 1030 (Computer Fraud and Abuse Act); 43 Penn. Stat. § 933.1 et seq. (criminalizing independent contractor misclassification in the construction industry); Cal. Labor Code §§ 510, 1109 (misdemeanor to violate minimum wage order and overtime provisions); 18 U.S.C. § 1513(e) (up to 10 years imprisonment for retaliation against any person for providing truthful information to law enforcement officer regarding a possible federal offense).

8. *Punitive Damages.* Where available, punitive damages can "be awarded for conduct that is outrageous, because of the defendant's evil motive or his reckless indifference to the rights of others." Restatement (Second) of Torts § 908(2).

KOLSTAD V. AMERICAN DENTAL ASSOCIATION

Supreme Court of the United States, 1999.
527 U.S. 526, 119 S.Ct. 2118, 144 L.Ed.2d 494.

JUSTICE O'CONNOR delivered the opinion of the Court. * * *

I

A

In September 1992, Jack O'Donnell announced that he would be retiring as the Director of Legislation and Legislative Policy and Director of the Council on Government Affairs and Federal Dental Services for respondent, American Dental Association (respondent or Association). Petitioner, Carole Kolstad, was employed with O'Donnell in respondent's Washington, D.C., office, where she was serving as respondent's Director of Federal Agency Relations. When she learned of O'Donnell's retirement, she expressed an interest in filling his position. Also interested in replacing O'Donnell was Tom Spangler, another employee in respondent's Washington office. At this time, Spangler was serving as the Association's Legislative Counsel, a position that involved him in respondent's legislative lobbying efforts. Both petitioner and Spangler had worked directly with O'Donnell, and both had received "distinguished" performance ratings by the acting head of the Washington office, Leonard Wheat.

Both petitioner and Spangler formally applied for O'Donnell's position, and Wheat requested that Dr. William Allen, then serving as respondent's Executive Director in the Association's Chicago office, make the ultimate promotion decision. After interviewing both petitioner and Spangler, Wheat recommended that Allen select Spangler for O'Donnell's post. Allen notified petitioner in December 1992 that he had, in fact, selected Spangler to serve as O'Donnell's replacement. Petitioner's challenge to this employment decision forms the basis of the instant action.

B

The District Court denied petitioner's request for a jury instruction on punitive damages. The jury concluded that respondent had discriminated against petitioner on the basis of sex and awarded her backpay totaling $52,718. Although the District Court subsequently denied respondent's motion for judgment as a matter of law on the issue of liability, the court made clear that it had not been persuaded that respondent had selected Spangler over petitioner on the basis of sex, and the court denied petitioner's requests for reinstatement and for attorney's fees.

Petitioner appealed from the District Court's decisions denying her requested jury instruction on punitive damages and her request for reinstatement and attorney's fees. [After the D.C. Circuit agreed to hear the case en banc] the court affirmed the decision of the District Court. The en banc majority concluded that, "before the question of punitive damages can go to the jury, the evidence of the defendant's culpability must exceed what is needed to show intentional discrimination." Based on the 1991 Act's structure and legislative history, the court determined, specifically, that a defendant must be shown to have engaged in some "egregious" misconduct before the jury is permitted to consider a request for punitive damages. Although the court declined to set out the "egregiousness" requirement in any detail, it concluded that petitioner failed to make the requisite showing in the instant case. * * *

II

A

Prior to 1991, only equitable relief, primarily backpay, was available to prevailing Title VII plaintiffs; the statute provided no authority for an award of punitive or compensatory damages. See *Landgraf v. USI Film Products*, 511 U.S. 244, 252–253, 128 L. Ed. 2d 229, 114 S. Ct. 1483 (1994). With the passage of the 1991 Act, Congress provided for additional remedies, including punitive damages, for certain classes of Title VII and ADA violations.

The 1991 Act limits compensatory and punitive damages awards, however, to cases of "intentional discrimination"—that is, cases that do not rely on the "disparate impact" theory of discrimination. 42 U.S.C. § 1981a(a)(1). Section 1981a(b)(1) further qualifies the availability of punitive awards:

> "A complaining party may recover punitive damages under this section against a respondent (other than a government, government agency or political subdivision) if the complaining party demonstrates that the respondent engaged in a discriminatory practice or discriminatory practices *with malice or with reckless indifference to the federally protected rights of an aggrieved individual.*" (Emphasis added.)

The very structure of § 1981a suggests a congressional intent to authorize punitive awards in only a subset of cases involving intentional discrimination. Section 1981a(a)(1) limits compensatory and punitive awards to instances of intentional discrimination, while § 1981a(b)(1) requires plaintiffs to make an additional "demonstration" of their eligibility for punitive damages. Congress plainly sought to impose two standards of liability—one for establishing a right to compensatory damages and another, higher standard that a plaintiff must satisfy to qualify for a punitive award.

The Court of Appeals sought to give life to this two-tiered structure by limiting punitive awards to cases involving intentional discrimination of an "egregious" nature. We credit the en banc majority's effort to effectuate congressional intent, but, in the end, we reject its conclusion that eligibility for punitive damages can only be described in terms of an employer's "egregious" misconduct. The terms "malice" and "reckless" ultimately focus on the actor's state of mind. See, e.g., Black's Law Dictionary 956–957, 1270 (6th ed. 1990); see also W. Keeton, D. Dobbs, R. Keeton, & D. Owen, Prosser and Keeton, Law of Torts 212–214 (5th ed. 1984) (defining "willful," "wanton," and "reckless"). While egregious misconduct is evidence of the requisite mental state, * * * § 1981a does not limit plaintiffs to this form of evidence, and the section does not require a showing of egregious or outrageous discrimination independent of the employer's state of mind. * * * The employer must act with "malice or with reckless indifference *to [the plaintiff's] federally protected rights.*" § 1981a(b)(1) (emphasis added). The terms "malice" or "reckless indifference" pertain to the employer's knowledge that it may be acting in violation of federal law, not its awareness that it is engaging in discrimination.

* * *

There will be circumstances where intentional discrimination does not give rise to punitive damages liability under this standard. In some instances, the employer may simply be unaware of the relevant federal prohibition. There will be cases, moreover, in which the employer discriminates with the distinct belief that its discrimination is lawful. The underlying theory of discrimination may be novel or otherwise poorly recognized, or an employer may reasonably believe that its discrimination satisfies a bona fide occupational qualification defense or other statutory exception to liability. See, e.g., 42 U.S.C. § 2000e–2(e)(1) (setting out Title VII defense "where religion, sex, or national origin is a bona fide occupational qualification"); see also § 12113 (setting out defenses under ADA). In *Hazen Paper Co. v. Biggins*, 507 U.S. 604, 616, 123 L. Ed. 2d 338, 113 S. Ct. 1701 (1993), we thus observed that, in light of statutory defenses and other exceptions permitting age-based decisionmaking, an employer may knowingly rely on age to make employment decisions without recklessly violating the Age Discrimination in Employment Act of 1967 (ADEA). Accordingly, we determined that limiting liquidated damages under the ADEA to cases where the employer "knew or showed reckless disregard for the matter of whether its conduct was prohibited by the statute," without an additional showing of outrageous conduct, was sufficient to give effect to the ADEA's two-tiered liability scheme. 507 U.S. at 616, 617.

* * *

Egregious misconduct is often associated with the award of punitive damages, but the reprehensible character of the conduct is not generally considered apart from the requisite state of mind. * * * [U]nder § 1981a(b)(1), pointing to evidence of an employer's egregious behavior would provide one means of satisfying the plaintiff's burden to "demonstrate" that the employer acted with the requisite "malice or * * * reckless indifference." See 42 U.S.C. § 1981a(b)(1); see, e.g., 3 BNA EEOC

Compliance Manual N:6085–N6084 (1992) (Enforcement Guidance: Compensatory and Punitive Damages Available Under § 102 of the Civil Rights Act of 1991) (listing "the degree of egregiousness and nature of the respondent's conduct" among evidence tending to show malice or reckless disregard). Again, however, respondent has not shown that the terms "reckless indifference" and "malice," in the punitive damages context, have taken on a consistent definition including an independent, "egregiousness" requirement * * * .

B

The inquiry does not end with a showing of the requisite "malice or * * * reckless indifference" on the part of certain individuals, however. * * * The plaintiff must impute liability for punitive damages to respondent. The en banc dissent recognized that agency principles place limits on vicarious liability for punitive damages. Likewise, the Solicitor General as amicus acknowledged during argument that common law limitations on a principal's liability in punitive awards for the acts of its agents apply in the Title VII context. * * * While we decline to engage in any definitive application of the agency standards to the facts of this case, * * * it is important that we address the proper legal standards for imputing liability to an employer in the punitive damages context. * * *

* * *

The common law has long recognized that agency principles limit vicarious liability for punitive awards. * * *

We have observed that, "in express terms, Congress has directed federal courts to interpret Title VII based on agency principles." *Burlington Industries, Inc. v. Ellerth*, 524 U.S. 742, 754, 141 L. Ed. 2d 633, 118 S. Ct. 2257 (1998); see also *Meritor Savings Bank, FSB v. Vinson*, 477 U.S. 57, 72, 91 L. Ed. 2d 49, 106 S. Ct. 2399 (1986) * * * .

* * * [O]ur interpretation of Title VII is informed by "the general common law of agency, rather than * * * the law of any particular State." *Burlington Industries, Inc.*, supra, at 754 (internal quotation marks omitted). The common law as codified in the Restatement (Second) of Agency (1957), provides a useful starting point for defining this general common law. * * * The Restatement of Agency places strict limits on the extent to which an agent's misconduct may be imputed to the principal for purposes of awarding punitive damages:

"Punitive damages can properly be awarded against a master or other principal because of an act by an agent if, but only if:

"(a) the principal authorized the doing and the manner of the act, or

"(b) the agent was unfit and the principal was reckless in employing him, or "(c) the agent was employed in a managerial capacity and was acting in the scope of employment, or

"(d) the principal or a managerial agent of the principal ratified or approved the act." Restatement (Second) of Agency, supra, § 217 C.

See also Restatement (Second) of Torts § 909 (same).

The Restatement, for example, provides that the principal may be liable for punitive damages if it authorizes or ratifies the agent's tortious act, or if it acts recklessly in employing the malfeasing agent. The Restatement also contemplates liability for punitive awards where an employee serving in a "managerial capacity" committed the wrong while "acting in the scope of employment." Restatement (Second) of Agency, supra, § 217 C; see also Restatement (Second) of Torts, supra, § 909 (same). "Unfortunately, no good definition of what constitutes a 'managerial capacity' has been found," 2 J. Ghiardi [& J. Kircher, Punitive Damages: Law and Practice], § 24.05, at 14 [(1998)], and determining whether an employee meets this description requires a fact-intensive inquiry. * * * Suffice it to say here that the examples provided in the Restatement of Torts suggest that an employee must be "important," but perhaps need not be the employer's "top management, officers, or directors," to be acting "in a managerial capacity." Ibid.; see also 2 Ghiardi, supra, § 24.05, at 14; Restatement (Second) of Torts, § 909, at 468, Comment b and Illus. 3.

Additional questions arise from the meaning of the "scope of employment" requirement. The Restatement of Agency provides that even intentional torts are within the scope of an agent's employment if the conduct is "the kind [the employee] is employed to perform," "occurs substantially within the authorized time and space limits," and "is actuated, at least in part, by a purpose to serve the" employer. Restatement (Second) of Agency, supra, § 228(1), at 504. According to the Restatement, so long as these rules are satisfied, an employee may be said to act within the scope of employment even if the employee engages in acts "specifically forbidden" by the employer and uses "forbidden means of accomplishing results." Id. § 230, at 511, Comment b; see also *Burlington Industries, Inc.*, supra, at 756. * * * On this view, even an employer who makes every effort to comply with Title VII would be held liable for the discriminatory acts of agents acting in a "managerial capacity."

Holding employers liable for punitive damages when they engage in good faith efforts to comply with Title VII, however, is in some tension with the very principles underlying common law limitations on vicarious liability for punitive damages—that it is "improper ordinarily to award punitive damages against one who himself is personally innocent and therefore liable only vicariously." Restatement (Second) of Torts, supra, § 909, at 468, Comment b. Where an employer has undertaken such good faith efforts at Title VII compliance, it "demonstrates that it never acted in reckless disregard of federally protected rights." * * * ; see also *Harris*, 132 F.3d at 983, 984 (observing that, "in some cases, the existence of a written policy instituted in good faith has operated as a total bar to employer liability for punitive damages" and concluding that "the institution of a written sexual harassment policy goes a long way towards dispelling any claim about the employer's 'reckless' or 'malicious' state of mind").

Applying the Restatement of Agency's "scope of employment" rule in the Title VII punitive damages context, moreover, would reduce the incentive for employers to implement antidiscrimination programs. In fact, such a rule would likely exacerbate concerns among employers that § 1981a's "malice" and "reckless indifference" standard penalizes those employers who educate themselves and their employees on Title VII's prohibitions. * * * Dissuading employers from implementing programs or policies to prevent discrimination in the workplace is directly contrary to the purposes underlying Title VII. The statute's "primary objective" is "a prophylactic one," *Albemarle Paper Co. v. Moody*, 422 U.S. 405, 417, 45 L. Ed. 2d 280, 95 S. Ct. 2362 (1975); it aims, chiefly, "not to provide redress but to avoid harm," *Faragher*, 524 U.S. at 806. With regard to sexual harassment, "for example, Title VII is designed to encourage the creation of antiharassment policies and effective grievance mechanisms." *Burlington Industries, Inc.*, 524 U.S. at 764. The purposes underlying Title VII are similarly advanced where employers are encouraged to adopt antidiscrimination policies and to educate their personnel on Title VII's prohibitions.

In light of the perverse incentives that the Restatement's "scope of employment" rules create, we are compelled to modify these principles to avoid undermining the objectives underlying Title VII. * * * Recognizing Title VII as an effort to promote prevention as well as remediation, and observing the very principles underlying the Restatements' strict limits on vicarious liability for punitive damages, we agree that, in the punitive damages context, an employer may not be vicariously liable for the discriminatory employment decisions of managerial agents where these decisions are contrary to the employer's "good-faith efforts to comply with Title VII." * * *

We have concluded that an employer's conduct need not be independently "egregious" to satisfy § 1981a's requirements for a punitive damages award, although evidence of egregious misconduct may be used to meet the plaintiff's burden of proof. We leave for remand the question whether petitioner can identify facts sufficient to support an inference that the requisite mental state can be imputed to respondent. The parties have not yet had an opportunity to marshal the record evidence in support of their views on the application of agency principles in the instant case, and the en banc majority had no reason to resolve the issue because it concluded that petitioner had failed to demonstrate the requisite "egregious" misconduct. Although trial testimony established that Allen made the ultimate decision to promote Spangler while serving as petitioner's interim executive director, respondent's highest position, * * * it remains to be seen whether petitioner can make a sufficient showing that Allen acted with malice or reckless indifference to petitioner's Title VII rights. Even if it could be established that Wheat effectively selected O'Donnell's replacement, moreover, several questions would remain, e.g., whether Wheat was serving in a "managerial capacity" and whether he behaved with malice or reckless indifference to petitioner's rights. It may also be necessary to determine whether the Association had been making good faith efforts to enforce an antidiscrimination policy. We leave these issues for resolution on remand.

CHIEF JUSTICE REHNQUIST, with whom JUSTICE THOMAS joins, concurring in part and dissenting in part.

* * * I would hold that Congress' two-tiered scheme of Title VII monetary liability implies that there is an egregiousness requirement that reserves punitive damages only for the worst cases of intentional discrimination. Since the Court has determined otherwise, however, I join that portion of Part II-B of the Court's opinion holding that principles of agency law place a significant limitation, and in many foreseeable cases a complete bar, on employer liability for punitive damages.

NOTES AND QUESTIONS

Test Your Understanding of the Material

1. To what extent does the Court adopt the principles in the Restatement Second of Agency that it cites?

2. On balance, is *Kolstad* a plaintiff victory (because the Court rejects an "egregiousness" standard, hence limiting occasions for court review of punitive awards by juries) or a defense victory (because agency principles may insulate the employer from liability)?

3. Make a list of evidence that Kolstad or the American Dental Association might present to support or defend Kolstad's claim for punitive damages on remand.

Related Issues

4. *"Managerial Capacity"*. Does the reference to "managerial capacity" in *Kolstad* refer to all supervisors or only a more limited class of senior managers? Lower courts are more likely to deem low-level supervisors "managerial" where the company has failed to take preventative measures. See Lowery v. Circuit City Stores, 206 F.3d 431, 446 (4th Cir.2000) (punitive damages may be appropriate despite formal anti-discrimination policy where evidence of "top" executives' bias and policy "to keep African-Americans in low level positions"); Tisdale v. Federal Express Corp., 415 F.3d 516 (6th Cir.2005) ("non-senior management employees can serve in a managerial capacity" for

purposes of punitive damages in absence of "good-faith" company efforts); EEOC v. Wal-Mart Stores, 187 F.3d 1241 (10th Cir.1999) (punitive damages for ADA violation appropriate under *Kolstad* where discriminating store managers acted within scope of employment and company failed to disseminate or provide training on its antidiscrimination policy).

5. *Punitive Damages for Discriminatory Harassment.* As suggested by *Faragher* and *Oncale,* harassment is generally considered outside the scope of employment when it does not result in a "tangible" employment decision such as a refusal to hire or promote or a termination. Plaintiffs in such cases must rely on other principles of agency law to obtain punitive damages. See Kimbrough v. Loma Linda Development, 183 F.3d 782 (8th Cir.1999) (finding ratification in manager's approval of harassment); Swinton v. Potomac Corp., 270 F.3d 794, 811 (9th Cir.2001) (supervisor's knowledge of harassment and failure to respond establishes lack of "good faith"); Deters v. Equifax Credit Information Services, Inc., 202 F.3d 1262 (10th Cir.2000) (no good faith defense available because of failure by "final decision-making authority" in plaintiff's office to respond to complaints). For a criticism of decisions like *Deters* and *Swinton* holding that a rogue manager or supervisor's failure to implement an anti-harassment policy is sufficient to establish a lack of corporate good faith, see Michael C. Harper, Eliminating the Need for Caps on Title VII Damage Awards: The Shield of *Kolstad v. American Dental Association*, 14 N.Y.U. J. of Leg. & Pub. Pol. 477, 496–596 (2011).

6. *Proportionality of Punitive Awards.* The Supreme Court has held that a punitive damages award may be an unconstitutional deprivation of property without due process, depending in substantial part on its proportionate relationship to the compensable harm caused by the wrongdoer. See State Farm Mut. Auto Ins. co. v. Campbell, 538 U.S. 408, 123 S.Ct. 1513, 155 L.Ed.2d 585 (2002); BMW of North America v. Gore, 517 U.S. 559, 116 S.Ct. 1589, 134 L.Ed.2d 809 (1996). Does this mean that a Title VII court cannot approve the award of punitive damages in a case where the jury declines to award compensatory damages? For cases holding that a punitive award is permissible in these circumstances, see, e.g., Abner v. Kansas City Southern Railroad Co., 513 F.3d 154 (5th Cir.2008) ("combination of the statutory cap and high threshold of culpability for any award confines the amount of the award to a level tolerable by due process"); Cush-Crawford v. Adchem Corp., 271 F.3d 352 (2d Cir. 2001); Timm v. Progressive Steel Treating, Inc., 137 F.3d 1008 (7th Cir.1998); but see Kerr-Selgas v. American Airlines, Inc., 69 F.3d 1205, 1214 (1st Cir.1995) (Title VII award of compensatory or nominal damages is required; discounting damages allocated to claims under Puerto Rico law).

7. *Punitive Damages Under State Law.* Some state civil rights law permit recovery of punitive damages, see, e.g., Rush v. Scott Specialty Gases, Inc., 914 F.Supp. 104 (E.D.Pa.1996) (43 Pa. Cons. Stat. Ann. §§ 951–63); Arthur Young & Co. v. Sutherland, 631 A.2d 354 (D.C.App.1993) (D.C. Human Rights Law), while others do not, see, e.g., Thoreson v. Penthouse Int'l, 179 A.D.2d 29, 583 N.Y.S.2d 213 (1992) (N.Y. Human Rights Law).

B. CLAIMS AGAINST EMPLOYEES

RESTATEMENT OF EMPLOYMENT LAW, §§ 9.07–9.09
American Law Institute (2015).

§ 9.07. Damages—Employee Breach of Agreement

(a) An employee who breaches any obligation that the employment agreement clearly states is a basis for damages liability is subject to liability for that breach of contract. The employer may recover damages for foreseeable economic loss that the employer could not have reasonably avoided, including any reasonably foreseeable consequential damages and the expenses of reasonable efforts to mitigate damages.

(b) Economic loss under subsection (a) does not include lost profits caused by the employee's breach unless the agreement expressly provides for such recovery or the employee knew or should have known that the employee would be held responsible for lost profits caused by the employee's breach. (For employees who have breached a tort-based or fiduciary duty to the employer, see § 9.09(b).)

§ 9.08. Injunctive Relief—Employee Breach of Agreement

(a) An employer may not obtain specific performance of the employee's promise to work.

(b) An employer may obtain injunctive relief to enforce any other obligation expressly stated in the employment agreement if the employer satisfies the traditional requirements for obtaining equitable relief.

§ 9.09. Damages and Restitution—Employee Breach of Tort-Based Duty or Fiduciary Duty

(a) An employee who breaches a tort-based duty or any fiduciary duty the employee owes the employer (Chapter 8) is subject to liability for foreseeable harm to the employer caused by the breach, including the expenses of reasonable efforts to mitigate damages, less damages that the employer could reasonably have avoided.

(b) Available items of damages that may be obtained under (a) include past and reasonably certain future economic loss and noneconomic loss, punitive damages, reasonably foreseeable lost profits, and reasonably foreseeable consequential damages.

(c) Except to the extent the employer would obtain double recovery for the same loss, and subject to applicable state wage-payment legislation and other law, an employer may deny any compensation owed, and recover any compensation paid, to an employee who breaches the employee's fiduciary duty of loyalty owed the employer (§ 8.01), where

(1) the employee's compensation cannot be apportioned between the employee's disloyal services and the employee's loyal services, and

(2) the nature of the employee's disloyalty is such that there is no practicable method for making a reasonable calculation of the harm caused the employer by the employee's disloyal services.

If the employee's compensation can be reasonably apportioned between the employee's loyal and disloyal services, then the employer may deny any compensation owed, and recover any compensation paid, for the disloyal services.

(d) If an employee personally profits from a breach of fiduciary duty, the employer can recover those profits from the employee.

(e) Unless otherwise provided by law, an employee who breaches a tort-based duty or a fiduciary duty owed to the employer (Chapter 8) is not subject to liability for the attorney's fees incurred by the employer in maintaining the employer's claim.

PURE POWER BOOT CAMP, INC. V. WARRIOR FITNESS BOOT CAMP, LLC

United States District Court, S.D. New York, 2011.
813 F.Supp.2d 489.

KATZ, J.

Plaintiffs Pure Power Boot Camp, Inc., Pure Power Boot Camp Franchising Corporation, Pure Power Camp Jericho Inc., and Lauren Brenner (collectively "Plaintiffs" or "Pure Power"), brought this action against Defendants Warrior Fitness Boot Camp, LLC, Alexander Kenneth Fell, Ruben Dario Belliard, Jennifer J. Lee, and Nancy Baynard (collectively "Defendants" or "Warrior Fitness"), accusing Defendants of stealing their business model, customers, and confidential and commercially sensitive documents, breaching contractual and employee fiduciary duties, and infringing Plaintiffs' trade-dress. * * *

Pure Power Boot Camp is modeled, in part, after United States Marine Corps training facilities. It is designed in military camouflage colors and decor and, unlike traditional gyms, does not have a membership fee;

instead, clients sign renewable contracts for "tours of duty," meaning that "recruits"—as Pure Power clients are called—sign up for a program to attend a certain number of sessions per week for a set number of weeks. If a recruit does not show up for a scheduled class, Pure Power personnel contacts them directly. * * *

Pure Power was a unique concept and unlike most other exercise facilities. It was an immediate success, garnering attention from a variety of media outlets, including MSNBC and Inside Edition. Brenner personally appeared on a variety of television shows, including NBC's The Today Show, the Donny Deutsch Show, and the Anderson Cooper Show on CNN. Brenner's intent when she created Pure Power was not to have one location, but to develop a business plan that could be rolled out as a national franchise. In 2006, she took steps to franchise the Pure Power concept. * * *

In preparation for Pure Power's franchising roll-out, Brenner had the drill instructors sign an Employment Agreement as a condition of continued employment. With the exception of Fell, every drill instructor, Belliard included, admits to having signed an Employment Agreement. * * *

[Breach of Contract]

The Employment Agreement contains a number of contractual provisions, including: * * * a non-disclosure provision[.] * * *

[*Eds*. The court found that Defendant Belliard breached the non-disclosure provision for stealing and disclosing the company's "business plan, start-up manual, and operations manual" and customer list.]

Plaintiffs argue that they are entitled to recover, as compensatory damages for Belliard's breach of the non-disclosure provision, the lost profit Pure Power incurred as a consequence of the breach, from May 2008 to December 2010. Plaintiffs propose two alternative calculations. First, attributing all of Warrior Fitness's revenue as properly belonging to Pure Power and applying Pure Power's purported 58% profit margin, Plaintiffs claim $1,368,247.00 in lost profits from May 2008 to December 2010. Second, considering only the 147 allegedly solicited Pure Power clients, and assuming that Pure Power clients, on average, generate $2,655.00 per year in revenue, Plaintiffs calculate total lost profits from May 2008 through December 2010, in an amount of $354,177.00.

Under New York law, the measure of damages for a violation of a restrictive covenant is the loss sustained by reason of the breach, including "the net profits of which the plaintiff was deprived" by the defendant's acts. *See Weinrauch v. Kashkin*, 64 A.D.2d 897, 898, 407 N.Y.S.2d 885 (2d Dep't 1978); *see also Cargill v. Sears Petroleum & Transp. Corp.*, 388 F.Supp.2d 37, 70 (N.D.N.Y.2005) (stating that the proper measure of damages for breach of a non-disclosure agreement is the net profits of which plaintiff was deprived as a consequence of the breach). Lost profits may be recovered only if: (1) lost profits were "fairly within the contemplation of the parties to the contract at the time it was made;" (2) lost profits were caused by the defendant's breach; and (3) damages are "capable of proof with reasonable certainty." *Kenford Co. v. Cnty. of Erie*, 67 N.Y.2d 257, 261, 502 N.Y.S.2d 131, 132, 493 N.E.2d 234 (1986); * * * "[D]amages may not be merely speculative, possible or imaginary, but must be reasonably certain and directly traceable to the breach, not remote or the result of other intervening causes." *Kenford*, 67 N.Y.2d at 261, 502 N.Y.S.2d at 132, 493 N.E.2d 234; *see also Toltec Fabrics, Inc. v. August Inc.*, 29 F.3d 778, 784 (2d Cir.1994) (finding evidence of lost profits insufficient where there was no reasonable certainty of future sales and plaintiff failed to demonstrate "proof of a consistent pattern of frequent ordering by a specific customer"); *Trademark Research Corp. v. Maxwell Online, Inc.*, 995 F.2d 326, 332–33 (2d Cir.1993) (finding no reasonable certainty of lost profits despite evidence of expert calculation of lost profits based on performance of comparable companies, market studies, business and promotional plans, subsequent sales, and earnings).

Plaintiffs fail to satisfy all three necessary elements to recover lost profits for Belliard's breach of contract. First, the Employment Agreement does not make any reference to lost profits, and Plaintiffs failed to introduce any evidence into the record suggesting that the parties contemplated such damages. *See, e.g., Spherenomics Global Contact Ctrs. v. vCustomer Corp.*, 427 F.Supp.2d 236, 252 (E.D.N.Y.2006) (finding that parties did not contemplate lost profits liability when the non-compete was silent as to such damages).

Second, regardless of the alternative measures of lost profits offered by Plaintiffs, Plaintiffs failed to establish that lost profits were caused by Belliard's breach of the non-disclosure provision. The preponderance of the evidence does not support the conclusion that, but for Belliard's stealing and disclosing Pure Power's business documents and the customer list, Warrior Fitness would not have opened. Indeed, Belliard and Fell already knew how to operate a gym. They were familiar with Brenner's teaching methods and techniques. They learned how to do the training. They knew Pure Power's pricing structure. And, Lee, their partner, had a business degree and business experience. There is no sound basis to conclude that information contained in the stolen business documents, or the client list itself, was necessary to open Warrior Fitness. Accordingly, it is not appropriate to consider all of Warrior Fitness's revenues as Pure Power's lost profits.

Likewise, as discussed, Plaintiffs failed to prove that the disclosure or use of the client list was the reason why the 147 former Pure Power clients signed up for classes at Warrior Fitness. Moreover, there is no support for Plaintiffs' contention that, had Belliard not breached the non-disclosure provision of the Employment Agreement, every one of these 147 Warrior Fitness clients would have enrolled in Pure Power.

Third, and finally, Plaintiffs failed to establish lost profit damages with reasonable certainty. Plaintiffs' lost profit calculation attributing all of Warrior Fitness's revenue to Pure Power is overreaching, inherently speculative, and cannot be tied to the breach of the non-disclosure provision. Moreover, although the relevant information was available to Plaintiffs throughout the course of this litigation, Plaintiffs ignored the actual data in the case and chose, instead, to rely on the discredited "mass asset" theory of their damages expert—which was precluded by this Court. * * *

Accordingly, for all these reasons, Plaintiffs failed to establish all of the required elements of their breach of contract claim against Defendants Belliard and Fell.

Breach of the Duty of Loyalty

Plaintiffs contend that Defendants Belliard and Fell breached the common law duty of loyalty owed to Pure Power as employees of Pure Power. * * *

Here, the preponderance of the evidence establishes numerous breaches by Defendants Belliard and Fell of their duty of loyalty to Pure Power. Defendant Belliard stole Pure Power documents, including Pure Power's business plan, start-up manual, and operations manual. Belliard also stole personnel files from Brenner's private office, and destroyed his and other employees' signed Employment Agreements. After Belliard destroyed the original Employment Agreements, he sent an email to Fell, boasting that the "cat is in the bag," to which Fell responded "hallelujah." Belliard shared the other stolen materials with Fell, who did not return them to Pure Power, but, instead, destroyed them. Belliard also provided a copy of Pure Power's business plan, operations manual, and start-up manual to Lee, who referred to these documents in drafting business documents for Warrior Fitness. Belliard and Fell were also aware that, on their behalf, Lee was soliciting current Pure Power clients to join Warrior Fitness, while she was still a member of Pure Power.

Both Belliard and Fell collected and maintained Pure Power client contact information, while on Pure Power's payroll and at the Pure Power facility, in anticipation of opening Warrior Fitness. In addition, Belliard, without permission, downloaded a copy of Pure Power's customer list onto a thumb-drive and disclosed the confidential contact information contained therein to, at a minimum, Baynard, with the intention that this information be used to solicit Pure Power customers to join Warrior Fitness. * * *

Plaintiffs seek as compensatory damages for Belliard and Fell's breach of their duty of loyalty to Pure Power a disgorgement of all revenues earned by Warrior Fitness from 2008 through 2010, in the amount of $2,390,082.00.

Under New York law, an employer alleging a breach of the common law duty of loyalty against an employee may choose whether to seek damages (1) through an accounting of the disloyal employee's gain (profit disgorgement) or (2) as a calculation of what the employer would have made had the employee not breached his or her duty of loyalty to the employer. *See Gomez v. Bicknell*, 302 A.D.2d 107, 114, 756 N.Y.S.2d 209, 214–15 (2d Dep't 2002); *accord Phansalkar*, 344 F.3d at 211 n. 23. If the plaintiff chooses profit disgorgement (i.e., restitution), then the plaintiff must also establish that the breach of duty by the defendant was a "substantial factor" contributing to the defendant's profits. *See Am. Fed. Grp., Ltd. v. Rothenberg*, 136 F.3d 897, 907 n. 7 (2d Cir.1998) * * * . * * *

New York courts generally find disgorgement of profits or restitution is appropriate only in "a straightforward case in which an employee makes a profit or receives a benefit in connection with transactions conducted by him on behalf of his employer." *Phansalkar [v. Andersen Weinroth & Co., L.P.*, 344 F.3d 184, 200 (2d Cir.2003).] * * *

As an initial matter, because Defendants Belliard and Fell opened Warrior Fitness *after* their employment by Pure Power had been terminated, the gross profit generated by Warrior Fitness from 2008 to 2010, which Plaintiffs now seek to have fully disgorged, was not earned by Defendants Belliard and Fell in connection with transactions conducted by them on behalf of Pure Power. Plaintiffs mistakenly conflate Defendants breaches of loyalty with the profit they earned by opening a competing business; however, opening the business was not a breach of the duty of loyalty. While Plaintiffs are of the view that Defendants would not have been able to open their business but for their breaches, the Court disagrees. As discussed in several other sections, the documents Defendants stole were not a substantial factor that enabled them to open Warrior Fitness. It was the knowledge Belliard and Fell gained as trainers at Pure Power that was key.

In addition, Plaintiffs have failed to establish that they had a "tangible expectancy" in many of the Pure Power clients allegedly solicited by Defendants. Pure Power had no tangible expectancy in clients who merely chose not to renew their subscriptions at Pure Power. * * * Moreover, only approximately 20 of the allegedly solicited clients who joined Warrior Fitness were, in fact, enrolled in Pure Power as of 2008. But, even with respect to these 20 or so clients, in whose contracts Pure Power may have had a tangible expectancy for some subsequent period of time, Plaintiffs failed to establish that Defendants' breach of their duty of loyalty was a "substantial factor" in contributing to the clients' decisions to leave Pure Power and to enroll in Warrior Fitness. In any event, Plaintiffs failed to establish damages with respect to these 20 or so clients, and any reasonable estimate would surely not approach the $2,390,082.00 Plaintiffs presently seek in profit disgorgement.

Accordingly, Plaintiffs have [ ] failed to establish that they are entitled to disgorgement of Warrior Fitness's gross profit, or that a corporate opportunity of Pure Power's has been usurped, on the basis of Defendant Belliard's and Fell's breach of their duty of loyalty.

New York's Faithless Servant Doctrine

As an additional measure of compensatory damages for Defendants' breach of their duty of loyalty to Pure Power, Plaintiffs contend that, pursuant to New York's faithless servant doctrine, they are entitled to the compensation Belliard and Fell earned while working as fitness instructors at Pure Power.

Unlike a traditional breach of fiduciary duty claim, which requires a showing of actual damages, to prove a violation of New York's faithless servant doctrine, an employer is not obligated to show that it "suffered . . . provable damage as a result of the breach of fidelity by the agent." *Feiger v. Iral Jewelry, Ltd.,* 41 N.Y.2d 928, 929, 394 N.Y.S.2d 626, 363 N.E.2d 350 (1977); *see also Webb v. Robert Lewis Rosen Assoc., Ltd.,* No. 03 Civ. 4275(HB), 2003 WL 23018792, at *6 (S.D.N.Y. Dec. 23, 2003) ("[While] proving a breach of fiduciary duty claim requires a showing of damages . . . the faithless servant doctrine [ ] provides an additional mechanism for relief, notwithstanding that [the employer] suffered no damage."). * * *

In determining whether an employee's conduct warrants forfeiture under the faithless servant doctrine, New York courts continue to apply two alternative standards. *See Phansalkar,* 344 F.3d at 200–02. The first standard requires that "misconduct and unfaithfulness . . . substantially violate [ ] the contract of service." *Id.* at 201 (quoting *Turner v. Konwenhoven,* 100 N.Y. 115, 2 N.E. 637, 639 (1885)). The second standard requires only that an agent "act [ ] adversely to his employer in any part of [a] transaction, or omit [ ] to disclose any interest which would naturally influence his conduct in dealing with the subject of [his] employment." *Id.* (quoting *Murray v. Beard,* 102 N.Y. 505, 7 N.E. 553, 554 (1886)).

Here, the Court concludes that forfeiture is appropriate under either standard. In particular, forfeiture is warranted under the *Murray* standard because Defendants Belliard and Fell acted "adversely to [their] employer." As discussed, among other such adverse actions taken by Belliard and Fell, Belliard destroyed Pure Power files and stole confidential business documents, and shared them with Fell, as well as Baynard and Lee. Belliard and Fell, in league with Baynard and Lee, caused negative rumors about Pure Power, and Brenner specifically. Defendants took affirmative steps to hamstring Pure Power and at no point disclosed their plans to open a competing business, using many of Pure Power's ideas and concepts, a mere fifteen blocks away from Pure Power. Likewise, applying *Turner,* forfeiture is warranted on the grounds that Belliard and Fell committed a "substantial violation" of the terms of their employment. Although the Second Circuit has not provided express criteria for determining whether a given violation of an employee's duty of loyalty is substantial, "[l]ower New York courts . . . have found disloyalty not to be 'substantial' only where the disloyalty consisted of a single act, or where the employer knew of and tolerated the behavior." *Phansalkar*, 344 F.3d at 201–02. Here, in addition to the Court's findings regarding Belliard's and Fell's disloyal conduct, Belliard and Fell cannot avoid forfeiture by contending that their disloyalty consisted of a "single act," or that Brenner was aware of, or in any way approved of, Defendants' ongoing disloyal conduct. * * *

The forfeiture of Belliard's and Fell's compensation, however, is limited to the "time period of disloyalty." *Design Strategy, Inc. v. Davis*, 469 F.3d 284, 301 (2d Cir.2006); [citations omitted].

The Court finds that the time period of disloyalty for both Belliard and Fell began in August 2007. On or about this time, Belliard stole Pure Power's confidential business plan and shared it with Fell, as well as Lee, who relied upon the business plan to draft Warrior Fitness's business plan. Belliard and Fell's disloyal scheme to use or destroy stolen confidential Pure Power information in furtherance of their opening a competing gym continued throughout the duration of their employment at Pure Power. As discussed, Belliard stole Employment Agreements, Pure Power's customer list, and other confidential documents, all in furtherance of his and Fell's plan to open a competing gym. Brenner fired Fell on March 16, 2008. Belliard quit Pure Power on April 1, 2008.

Accordingly, the Court concludes that Belliard must forfeit $55,196.70 in total compensation ($20,280.00 (2008 salary) + $34,916.70 (42% of 2007 salary)). Likewise, Fell must forfeit $40,177.00 in total compensation ($14,200.00 (2008 salary) + $25, 977. 00 (42% of 2007 salary)). (*See* Pls.' Exs. 162–63.) * * *

NOTES AND QUESTIONS

Test Your Understanding of the Material

1. Is the District Court's ruling in *Pure Power* as to the breach of the non-disclosure provision consistent with § 9.07 of the Employment Restatement?

2. The defendants in this case were subject to a non-compete covenant, which the court declared overbroad and unenforceable. Could the *Pure Power* court have enjoined the defendants from further disclosure or misuse of its confidential information? Could the court have enjoined the defendants from working for Warrior Fitness on the basis of their misuse of its confidential information? Consider § 9.08 of the Employment Restatement.

3. Section 9.09(a) of the Employment Restatement provides that "an employee who breaches a tort-based duty . . . is subject to liability for foreseeable harm to the employer caused by the breach[.]" Did the Court award damages for the harm caused by the breach of the duty of loyalty? Why or why not?

4. Section 9.09(c) of the Employment Restatement provides that the forfeiture of employee wages for breaches of the duty of loyalty should be "apportioned between the employee's disloyal services and the employee's loyal services" where practicable, otherwise the "employer may deny any compensation owed, and recover any compensation paid, for the disloyal services." Did the Court attempt an apportionment of the defendants' wages in applying the faithless servant doctrine? Applying § 9.09 of the Employment Restatement in its entirety, would the court have decided differently on the forfeiture issue?

Related Issues

5. *New York's "Faithless Service" Doctrine.* If an employee performs disloyal acts, should he or she forfeit all compensation during the period of disloyalty, even if the company receives value from his or her services? In Astra USA Inc. v. Bildman, 455 Mass. 116, 130, 914 N.E.2d 36 (2009), the Court held that "law of New York requires the disloyal employee to forfeit his compensation even if he otherwise performed valuable services for the principal" during the period of disloyalty. See also Phansalkar v. Andersen Weinroth & Co., LP, 344 F.3d 184, 205–207 (2d Cir. 2003) (applying New York law, declining to limit forfeiture to undisclosed board payments and instead ordering forfeiture of all compensation during period of disloyalty). Would the court in *Astra* have reached the same result under the Employment Restatement Section 9.09(c)?

6. *State Wage-Payment Laws and Forfeiture.* Not all states permit employers to withhold or recover compensation associated with a period of disloyalty. See Employment Restatement § 9.09 (forfeiture principles "subject to state wage-payment legislation and other law"). Many states have strict wage and hour rules that forbid unauthorized deductions from employee paychecks, or that impose penalties where the employer fails to timely pay an employee's final paycheck. See notes 7 & 8 on pp. 865–865.

7. *Damages Against Employees for Premature Quits.* When an employee has a contractual duty to work for an employer for a definite period, the employee can be held liable for quitting prematurely. However, damages are generally limited to the employer's costs in connection with replacing the employee. See e.g. Handicapped Children's Education Board of Sheboygan County v. Lukaszewiski, 112 Wis. 2d 197 (1983) (ordering employee to pay difference in salary between breaching employee and replacement); GME v. Carter, 120 Idaho 517, 817 P.2d 183 (1991) (employer suffered no damages where employee terminated contract prematurely but employer replaced him with someone at a lower salary). Where the contract specifies an amount of damages, courts will scrutinize them as liquidated damages provisions. Allied

Informatics, Inc. v. Yeruva, 251 Ga.App. 404, 554 S.E.2d 550 (Ga. Ct. App. 2001) (refusing to enforce $5,000 liquidated damages clause associated with resignation prior to the end of the employment term); Arrowhead School Dist. No. 75 v. Kylap, 2003 MT 294, 318 Mont. 103, 79 P.3d 250, 267 (2003) (enforcing liquidated damages of 20% of teacher's salary when teacher quit 2 weeks prior to the start of the school year).

8.   *Lost Profits.* As Section 9.07(b) of the Employment Restatement suggests, courts generally decline to award lost profits to a former employer when an employee breaches a contract by resigning prematurely. See e.g. Med+Plus Neck & Back Pain Center, S.C. v. Noffsinger, 311 Ill.App.3d 853, 726 N.E.2d 687 (2d Dist. 2000). However, courts have awarded lost profits where an employee breaches a non-compete agreement. See e.g. B & Y Metal Printing, Inc. v. Ball, 279 N.W.2d 813, 816 (Minn. 1979); Arabesque Studios, Inc. v. Academy of Fine Arts, Intern. Inc., 529 S.W.2d 564 (Tx. App. 1975). To recover lost profits, the plaintiff must prove that "(a) profits were lost, (b) the loss was directly caused by the breach of the covenant not to compete, and (c) the amount of such causally related loss is capable of calculation with reasonable certainty rather than benevolent speculation." B & Y Metal Printing, 279 N.W.2d at 816.

CHAPTER 21

PROCEDURAL ISSUES

∎ ∎ ∎

Introduction

In this closing chapter, we look at procedural issues that cross many different theories of recovery—much as they would in litigation. These issues should be borne in mind by the policymaker and students of the system.

A. THE ROLE OF THE ADMINISTRATIVE AGENCY

Crafting a regulatory scheme requires making difficult policy choices in the resolution of procedural, as well as substantive, issues. Perhaps the most important procedural decision is the choice of enforcement vehicle: whether to rely exclusively on the private suit or on a specialized administrative agency, or to utilize some mixture of both.

The private-suit model of enforcement offers several distinct advantages. First, because private suits draw from the general resources of the court system, regulatory norms can be promulgated without special allocation of scarce government agency budgetary resources for enforcement. Second, at least where legal assistance is available, claimants enjoy direct access to the remedial scheme. Third, where courts are receptive to the substantive claims, they may be quite vigorous enforcement agents; where jury trials are afforded, there also may be a distinctly pro-claimant tilt.

Each of these advantages, however, has its corresponding disadvantages. First, congestion in the courts may lead to multiple-year delay in the redress of wrongs. Second, even where attorney's fees are recoverable by successful claimants, the availability of legal counsel may be problematic. Third, courts may not be very good at coherent development of the subsidiary policy decisions that have to be made under any statutory scheme. Judicial agreement on particular issues also may be long in coming. Moreover, private suits usually turn not on legal issues of general importance but on fact-specific disputes. Judges who have too steady a diet of such cases may develop undesirable predispositions toward them. This in turn may lead to distortions in the actual development of the statutory scheme. Also, even judges free of such predispositions do not generally have any expertise with most regulatory statutes; their answers to novel, difficult questions may resolve a particular dispute, but often without a full appreciation of competing considerations or of the effect of their ruling on the statute as a whole.

These difficulties can generally be avoided by administrative enforcement—if the administrative agency is given sufficient resources, develops a good esprit de corps, is relatively free from political influences, and commands respect in the courts by the quality of its work. This ideal is, however, not always achieved. Reliance on agencies can result in under enforcement of the statute, either because of budgetary cutbacks, poor internal management, or the hostility of new administrations to the goals of the statutory scheme. It can also result in over enforcement, when political criteria rather than fidelity to the statutory design explain staffing and enforcement decisions.

1. EXCLUSIVE RELIANCE ON PRIVATE SUITS

Examples of exclusive reliance on private suits include state-law private tort and contract actions and suits under 42 U.S.C. § 1981 and 1983. For the private tort/contract claimant or § 1981 plaintiff, there are no administrative exhaustion requirements; access to the courts requires only the securing of counsel. The action is often one for damages, and there is a right to a jury trial for disputed issues of fact. Broad-based, systemic litigation is possible with the advent of the modern class action. Judicial opinions elaborate regulatory norms in the course of litigation of private wrongs.

Typically, use of the private-suit model entails reliance on the civil courts. This need not be so. The European countries which have enacted "unjust dismissal" legislation have also provided for special labor courts to adjudicate privately-initiated and privately-prosecuted claims. See Samuel Estreicher & Jeffrey M. Hirsch, Comparative Wrongful Dismissal Law: Reassessing American Exceptionalism, 92 N.C. L. Rev. 342 (2014). In our country, unemployment compensation and workers' compensation claims are initiated by private claimants but processed in an administrative adjudication. Many state civil rights laws provide a choice between private suit in the courts and an administrative adjudication before a civil rights agency.

The National Labor Relations Act of 1935, 29 U.S.C. § 151 et seq., presents a good example of exclusive reliance on an administrative agency. A worker seeking union representation or complaining of an unfair labor practice must secure the assistance of the NLRB. Representation proceedings take place solely on the administrative level; a decision of the director of a regional office of the NLRB on matters of representation, unit determination or voter eligibility may be reviewed by the five-member Board in Washington, D.C., but there is no direct recourse to the courts. See Michael C. Harper, The Case for Limiting Judicial Review of Labor Board Certification Decisions, 55 Geo.Wash.L.Rev. 262 (1987). Unfair labor practice proceedings occur only upon the issuance of a complaint by the General Counsel; with the exception of secondary boycott violations, there is no private right of action to secure relief from an alleged unfair labor practice. Once a complaint issues, an adjudicatory proceeding occurs before an administrative law judge. At this proceeding, an agent of the NLRB represents the Government; private charging parties may only intervene to supplement the Board's presentation. The decision of the administrative law judge may be reviewed by the Board in Washington, D.C. Persons aggrieved by the Board's order may also secure judicial review in the U.S. Courts of Appeals. That review is, however, of an appellate nature; the statute and administrative law principles require deference to agency findings of fact and discretionary policy decisions.

The nondiscrimination and affirmative action obligations of federal government contractors, particularly in connection with Executive Order 11246 and § 503 of the Rehabilitation Act, are also enforced through the agency model. Here, exclusive enforcement responsibility is lodged with the Office of Federal Contract Compliance Programs (OFCCP) of the Department of Labor. There is no private right of action, see, e.g., Cohen v. Illinois Institute of Technology, 524 F.2d 818 (7th Cir.1975) (Executive Order 11246); Simpson v. Reynolds Metals Co., 629 F.2d 1226 (7th Cir.1980) (§ 503), although some courts have permitted private parties to sue, in the nature of mandamus, to compel OFCCP enforcement of nondiscretionary duties, see, e.g., Legal Aid Soc'y of Alameda County v. Brennan, 608 F.2d 1319 (9th Cir.1979), and as third-party beneficiaries of affirmative action agreements, see, e.g., Jones v. Local 520, International Union of Operating Engineers, 603 F.2d 664 (7th Cir.1979).

2. HYBRID SYSTEMS

In contrast, Title VII, ADEA, ADA (§ 107 of the latter incorporates Title VII procedures) are "hybrid regulatory systems," borrowing features from both the private suit and administrative enforcement models. Claimants ultimately have a private right of action in state or federal courts, and the courts have been the principal formulators of the substantive policy choices left open by the statutes.

Unlike the pure private-suit model, however, Title VII, ADEA and ADA also give administrative processes a prominent role. Claimants must first file charges with the EEOC. (Charges under ADEA were processed by the Department of Labor until July 1, 1979, when the EEOC was given compliance responsibility under Reorganization Plan No. 1 of 1978, 43 Fed.Reg. 19,807.) The purpose of such filings is to take advantage of the agency's investigative capacity and to permit an opportunity for informal conciliation. Prior to the 1972 amendments to Title VII, the EEOC did not have authority to file suit, although the Justice Department could institute "pattern and practice" litigation under § 707 of Title VII. Now, the EEOC can file suits on behalf of individuals under § 706 and systemic actions under § 707. It enjoys comparable authority under ADEA and ADA; the Justice Department retains authority for "pattern and practice" suits against state and local government employers. Issues arising under both private- and EEOC-initiated litigation are discussed below in this chapter.

Yet another approach is suggested by statutes like the FLSA, which authorize a private cause of action without any requirement of resort to administrative remedies, but provide that a government enforcement suit in the courts, once it has been filed, displaces the opportunity to bring a private suit. The ADEA and the Equal Pay Act incorporate (to some extent) the FLSA's enforcement provisions. In Lorillard v. Pons, 434 U.S. 575, 98 S.Ct. 866, 55 L.Ed.2d 40 (1978), the Supreme Court held that Congress's decision to utilize FLSA procedures required that a private action for unpaid wages under ADEA be treated the same as a jury-tried action for unpaid wages under § 16(b) of FLSA. Congress in 1978 amended § 7(c) of ADEA, 29 U.S.C. § 626(c)(2), to expressly provide for a right to a jury trial in private suits "regardless of whether equitable relief is sought by any party in such action." A private EPA action for unpaid wages is similarly likened to a FLSA § 16(b) action. Although EEOC actions under FLSA § 17 are viewed as bench-tried actions to redress a public offense even where unpaid wages are sought in addition to equitable relief, see *Lorillard,* 434 U.S. at 580 n. 7, 98 S.Ct. at 870 n. 7, it remains unresolved whether EEOC-maintained ADEA or EPA actions on behalf of individuals under FLSA § 16(c) are triable before a jury.

3. AVAILABILITY OF JURY TRIALS

Even where private suits are available, policymakers also have to decide whether judges or juries will be the trier of fact. Jury trials are common in actions seeking damages under the various contract and tort theories explored earlier in this book. Under the 1991 Civil Rights Act, jury trials are available for claims for compensatory or punitive damages resulting from intentional discrimination in violation of Title VII, ADA and the Rehabilitation Act of 1973. Generally, the lower courts have held that a jury trial is available for actions seeking compensatory damages under § 1981.

Jury trials are not available for Title VII disparate-impact claims or failure of reasonable-accommodation claims under the ADA or § 501 of the Rehabilitation Act (where a good faith effort to accommodate has been made). However, claimants may append jury-triable claims under Title VII, ADA, ADEA, EPA, § 1981 or state laws, in order to obtain a jury trial over issues of fact common to the non-jury Title VII (or ADA) claim. See also Lytle v. Household Mfg., Inc., 494 U.S. 545, 110 S.Ct. 1331, 108 L.Ed.2d 504 (1990) (plaintiffs securing a reversal on appeal of an erroneous dismissal of their § 1981 claim have a right to a jury trial on that claim free of any issue preclusive effect inhering in the adjudication of their Title VII claim before an appeal could be taken).

B. ADMINISTRATIVE FILING REQUIREMENTS

Administrative exhaustion or filing requirements refer to a common statutory requirement that a claimant-plaintiff invoke or, more often, complete any administrative remedies and related procedures before filing a civil claim in court. A plaintiff's failure to exhaust administrative procedures within the regulatory filing period can result in dismissal of the plaintiff's lawsuit or, in some cases, a stay of the civil action.

State contract and tort actions can be brought directly without exhausting administrative procedures. State antidiscrimination laws tend to follow the approach of the FLSA in providing an administrative investigation and possible enforcement proceeding as an optional alternative to a private suit. See, e.g., N.Y. Human Rts. L., N.Y. Executive L., § 297. Federal government employees face a somewhat similar choice. See Title VII, 42 U.S.C. § 2000e–16; ADEA, 29 U.S.C. § 633a(b)–(c).

By contrast, for employees of private employers and state and local government, the administrative filing requirements of Title VII, ADEA and ADA are prerequisites to bringing a lawsuit. Common issues relating to administrative-filing requirements are discussed below.

1. *De Facto 300-Day Filing Period?*

Title VII, ADEA and ADA provide a 180-day period for filing a charge with the EEOC. However, as a practical matter most claimants have 300 days from the occurrence of the unlawful employment decision to make such a filing. In EEOC v. Commercial Office Products Co., 486 U.S. 107, 108 S.Ct. 1666, 100 L.Ed.2d 96 (1988), the Supreme Court effectively extended the filing period to 300 days for claimants living in states with civil rights agencies approved as § 706 deferral agencies. The Court there approved "worksharing" agreements between the EEOC and the state agency whereby charges "filed" with the state agency can be "terminated" for § 706(c) purposes without sacrificing the state agency's authority later to reactivate those charges under state law. In Love v. Pullman Co., 404 U.S. 522, 92 S.Ct. 616, 30 L.Ed.2d 679 (1972), the Court upheld the EEOC's deferral procedure, under which the EEOC itself refers a charge to an appropriate state deferral agency, and then begins its own processing of the charge 60 days later or on termination of the state agency proceeding, whichever occurs first. By treating the EEOC filing as being in a state of "suspended animation" until the expiration of the deferral period, the Court enabled Title VII claimants, who are often unrepresented by counsel, to avoid having to make an independent filing with the state agency.

2. *Statutory Prerequisites to Suit*

a. *Conciliation.* Before the EEOC can bring suit under Title VII it must investigate the discrimination charge and find "reasonable cause" to believe the charge has merit. The agency must then initially "endeavor to eliminate [the] alleged unlawful employment practice by informal methods of conference, conciliation and persuasion." 42 U.S.C. 2000e–5(b). To ensure candor during these discussions, the statute provides: "Nothing said or done during . . . such informal endeavors" may be publicized by the agency or "used as evidence in a subsequent proceeding without the written consent of the persons concerned." Id. Rebuffing lower-court decisions that allowed extensive discovery of the conciliation process to determine its adequacy, the Supreme Court in Mach Mining, LLC v. EEOC,135 S.Ct. 1645, 191 L.Ed.2d 607 (2015), unanimously ruled that although the EEOC's conciliation activities are reviewable, the scope of judicial review is quite narrow. The employer must be given notice that "properly describes both what the employer has done and which employees . . . have suffered as a result." The agency must then "try to engage the employer in some form of discussion (whether written or oral), so as to the give the employer an opportunity to remedy the allegedly discriminatory practice." 135 S.Ct. at 1655–56. If the court finds that the EEOC has not provided the requisite information or attempted to engage in informal conciliation discussions, "the appropriate remedy is to order the EEOC to undertake the mandated efforts to obtain voluntary compliance." Id. at 1656.

b. *EEOC "Cause" Determination.* The EEOC plays no screening function. Whereas it must under § 706(b) find "reasonable cause" before it can bring a lawsuit, such a finding is not required for the issuance of a right-to-sue letter authorizing a private suit. See McDonnell Douglas Corp. v. Green, 411 U.S. 792, 798–99, 93 S.Ct. 1817, 1822–23, 36 L.Ed.2d 668 (1973).

c. *Scope of Charge vs. Scope of Suit.* The scope of a Title VII-ADA-ADEA lawsuit is only loosely determined by the scope of the charge filed with the EEOC. Although additional parties cannot be named in the suit unless they were the subject of conciliation, the scope of the charge itself is not determinative. An influential liberal standard can be found in Sanchez v. Standard Brands, Inc., 431 F.2d 455, 466 (5th Cir.1970):

> [T]he allegations in a judicial complaint filed pursuant to Title VII "may encompass any kind of discrimination like or related to allegations contained in a charge and growing out of such allegation during the pendency of the case before the Commission". . . . In other words, the "scope" of the judicial complaint is limited to the "scope" of the EEOC investigation which can reasonably be expected to grow out of the charge of discrimination.

In *Sanchez,* the suit added a new basis of discrimination (national origin) and a new incident (discharge) not recited in the charge. Should claimants be able to add entirely new theories of discrimination not recited in their charge? Although many Title VII claimants proceed *pro se,* some are represented by counsel even when filing a charge. Should this liberal approach be available to the counseled claimant? To cases initiated by a Commissioner's charge?

In Edelman v. Lynchburg College, 535 U.S. 106, 122 S.Ct. 1145, 152 L.Ed.2d 188 (2002), the Court upheld an EEOC interpretation that deemed the requirement in § 706(b) that a charge of discrimination be "under oath or affirmation" to be satisfied by a later oath that had been omitted from what otherwise would have been a timely filing under § 706(e)(1).

3. *Tolling of the 180/300 Day Charge-Filing Period*

The Court in *McDonnell Douglas v. Green,* supra, used the term "jurisdictional prerequisite" in referring to the 180/300 day filing requirements in § 706(c). However, in Zipes v. Trans World Airlines, Inc., 455 U.S. 385, 393, 102 S.Ct. 1127, 1132, 71 L.Ed.2d 234 (1982), the Court stated that the requirement of filing a timely charge "is subject to waiver, estoppel and equitable tolling." The issue in that case was whether a defendant waived its right to object to an untimely filing by failing to plead untimeliness.

Although the Court generally has given little guidance as to the kinds of situations in which tolling should be recognized, it has established at least two rules. First, recourse to the grievance procedure of a collective bargaining agreement will not toll the 180/300 day filing period. Electrical Workers (IUE) Local 790 v. Robbins & Myers, Inc., 429 U.S. 229, 97 S.Ct. 441, 50 L.Ed.2d 427 (1976). Is this decision consistent with the solicitude for lay claimants expressed in *Commercial Office Products* and the Congressional emphasis on informal conciliation? Is it explainable as a means of preserving the independence of the Title VII cause of action?

Second, the filing of a class action will toll the filing period for members of the class, so that if the class is not certified, particular class members "may choose to file their own suits or to intervene as plaintiffs in the pending action." Crown, Cork & Seal Co. v. Parker, 462 U.S. 345, 354, 103 S.Ct. 2392, 2398, 76 L.Ed.2d 628 (1983) (addressing requirement to file suit within 90 days of receipt of EEOC "right to sue" letter). See also Tolliver v. Xerox Corp., 918 F.2d 1052 (2d Cir.1990) (approving "single filing" ruling for ADEA representative action, thus permitting separate ADEA suits after decertification of representative action without requiring filing of separate, individually timely administrative charges). At what point does the tolling effect of a class action filing cease: (i) the entry of an order denying class certification or (ii) completion of an appeal from the order denying certification? See Armstrong v. Martin Marietta Corp., 138 F.3d 1374 (11th Cir.1998) (en banc) (adopting the former position).

Does the notion that Title VII filing periods are subject to "waiver, estoppel and equitable tolling" provide some allowance for erroneous filings with other federal agencies? See, e.g., Bethel v. Jefferson, 589 F.2d 631 (D.C.Cir.1978) (filing with OFCCP); but see Stafford v. Muscogee County Bd. of Educ., 688 F.2d 1383 (11th Cir.1982).

4. *90-Day Period for Filing Court Action*

Part of the Court's rationale in *Zipes* was that the administrative filing requirement was not contained in § 706(f)(1), the provision authorizing the private civil action. Section 706(f)(1) does, however, require suit by a person aggrieved within 90 days of receipt of the Commission's "right to sue" letter—a requirement that the Court in *McDonnell Douglas* also termed a "jurisdictional prerequisite." Does the placement of the 90-day period in § 706(f)(1) suggest that this requirement is truly "jurisdictional" and hence not subject to "waiver, estoppel and equitable tolling"? Cf. Irwin v. Department of Veterans Affairs, 498 U.S. 89, 111 S.Ct. 453, 112 L.Ed.2d 435 (1990).

5. *Statutory Cap on Backpay Liability*

The timing of the filing of a charge will also determine the scope of liability. Under § 706(g) "[b]ack pay liability shall not accrue from a date more than two years prior to the filing of a charge with the Commission." There is no similar provision under the ADEA or the Rehabilitation Act.

C. STATUTES OF LIMITATIONS

1. RANGE OF LIMITATIONS PERIODS

Congress has not provided a traditional statute of limitations for claims under Title VII, ADA or ADEA. A suit must be brought within 90 days of the EEOC's issuance of a right-to-sue letter, but otherwise there is no requirement that a suit be brought within a certain period of time from the occurrence of the violation. In the context of EEOC suits, the Supreme Court held in Occidental Life Insurance Co. v. EEOC, 432 U.S. 355, 97 S.Ct. 2447, 53 L.Ed.2d 402 (1977), that while the agency is free of any federal or state statute of limitations, it is subject to the unreasonable-delay and prejudice restraints of the doctrine of laches. Compare, e.g., EEOC v. Alioto Fish Co., 623 F.2d 86 (9th Cir. 1980) (finding prejudice in 62-month delay where key witnesses for the employer had retired or were deceased), with EEOC v. Great Atlantic & Pacific Tea Co., 735 F.2d 69 (3d Cir.1984) (nine-year delay held excusable).

Under § 706(f)(1), a Title VII claimant may request a right-to-sue letter from the EEOC 180 days after filing a charge. Should a claimant who awaits the completion of a multi-year EEOC investigation and conciliation, before making such a request, ever be barred from suit by laches? See, e.g.,

Cleveland Newspaper Guild, Local 1 v. Plain Dealer Publishing Co., 839 F.2d 1147 (6th Cir.1988) (en banc).

Congress has provided a statute of limitations for FLSA claims: a two-year period for filing suit, extended for an additional year for "willful" violations by § 6 of the 1947 Portal-to-Portal Act, 29 U.S.C. § 255(a). See McLaughlin v. Richland Shoe Co., 486 U.S. 128, 108 S.Ct. 1677, 100 L.Ed.2d 115 (1988). In addition, some state wage-and-hour laws like New York's provide a limitations period as long as six years, see N.Y. Labor L. § 663.

Initially, Congress utilized the FLSA limitations system for ADEA claims. Because of EEOC backlogs during the 1980s, ADEA claimants awaiting the outcome of the administrative process risked having their civil actions time-barred by the limitations period. The 1991 Civil Rights Act (§ 115) discarded the FLSA-based limitations period, and ADEA claimants, like Title VII (and ADA) claimants, face only the 180/300 day filing requirements and the same 90-day period (from receipt of the EEOC's right-to-sue letter) within which to file suit. However, unlike Title VII (and ADA) claimants, individuals with ADEA claims are not expressly subject to the same 2-year limit on pre-charge backpay liability.

In 1990 Congress enacted a default four-year statute of limitations for actions arising under federal statutes enacted after December 1, 1990. See 28 U.S.C. § 1658(a). This statute posed a special issue for § 1981, which like § 1983, does not contain a statute of limitations, but whose scope was expanded by amendments included in the Civil Rights Act of 1991. In Goodman v. Lukens Steel Co., 482 U.S. 656, 107 S.Ct. 2617, 96 L.Ed.2d 572 (1987), before the passage of § 1658, the Court had held that the courts should apply "the most appropriate or analogous state statute of limitations" to claims based on alleged violations of § 1981. In Jones v. R.R. Donnelley & Sons Co., 541 U.S. 369, 124 S.Ct. 1836, 158 L.Ed.2d 645 (2004), however, the Court held that § 1658's four-year statute of limitations governs any § 1981 cause of action, such as those against racial harassment, made possible by the 1991 amendments' expansion of § 1981's scope.

For other federal statutes affecting the employment area, the Court has heeded the general directive of 42 U.S.C. § 1988, which requires resort to "not inconsistent" state laws to fill in gaps in the federal scheme. The Court in Wilson v. Garcia, 471 U.S. 261, 105 S.Ct. 1938, 85 L.Ed.2d 254 (1985), held that the appropriate state statute of limitations for § 1983 claims was the statute for personal injury actions. In states having statutes of limitations for enumerated intentional torts and a residual statute for all other personal injury actions, the residual or general personal injury statute applies. See Owens v. Okure, 488 U.S. 235, 109 S.Ct. 573, 102 L.Ed.2d 594 (1989). The residual statute at issue in *Owens* provided for a three-year period. The Court left open whether a residual statute providing a shorter period would be "inconsistent with federal interests." 109 S.Ct. at 582 n. 13.

2.   TIMING OF VIOLATION

Perhaps the most important question in applying a statute of limitations or administrative-filing requirement is determining when a violation has commenced. The timing of a violation triggers the start of the period for filing a charge with an administrative agency; it may also start or be relevant to the period for filing a lawsuit.

NATIONAL R.R. PASSENGER CORP. V. MORGAN
Supreme Court of the United States, 2002.
536 U.S. 101, 122 S.Ct. 2061, 153 L.Ed.2d 106.

JUSTICE THOMAS delivered the opinion of the Court. * * *

I

On February 27, 1995, Abner J. Morgan, Jr., a black male, filed a charge of discrimination and retaliation against Amtrak with the EEOC and cross-filed with the California Department of Fair Employment and Housing. Morgan alleged that during the time period that he worked for Amtrak he was "consistently harassed and disciplined more harshly than other employees on account of his race." The EEOC issued a "Notice of Right to Sue" on July 3, 1996, and Morgan filed this lawsuit on October 2, 1996. While some of the allegedly discriminatory acts about which Morgan complained occurred within 300 days of the time that he filed his charge with the EEOC, many took place prior to that time period. Amtrak filed a motion, arguing, among other things, that it was entitled to summary judgment on all incidents that occurred more than 300 days before the filing of Morgan's EEOC charge. The District Court granted summary judgment in part to Amtrak, holding that the company could not be liable for conduct occurring before May 3, 1994, because that conduct fell outside of the 300-day filing period. * * *

Morgan appealed. The United States Court of Appeals for the Ninth Circuit reversed, relying on its previous articulation of the continuing violation doctrine, which "allows courts to consider conduct that would ordinarily be time barred 'as long as the untimely incidents represent an ongoing unlawful employment practice.' " * * *

II

* * *

[*Eds*. The Court discusses its prior decisions in Delaware State College v. Ricks, 449 U.S. 250, 101 S.Ct. 498, 66 L.Ed.2d 431 (1980), and United Air Lines, Inc. v. Evans, 431 U.S. 553, 97 S.Ct. 1885, 52 L.Ed.2d 571 (1977).] We derive several principles from these cases. [D]iscrete discriminatory acts are not actionable if time barred, even when they are related to acts alleged in timely filed charges. Each discrete discriminatory act starts a new clock for filing charges alleging that act. The charge, therefore, must be filed within the 180- or 300-day time period after the discrete discriminatory act occurred. The existence of past acts and the employee's prior knowledge of their occurrence, however, does not bar employees from filing charges about related discrete acts so long as the acts are independently discriminatory and charges addressing those acts are themselves timely filed. Nor does the statute bar an employee from using the prior acts as background evidence in support of a timely claim.

* * *

Discrete acts such as termination, failure to promote, denial of transfer, or refusal to hire are easy to identify. Each incident of discrimination and each retaliatory adverse employment decision constitutes a separate actionable "unlawful employment practice." Morgan can only file a charge to cover discrete acts that "occurred" within the appropriate time period.[7] While Morgan alleged that he suffered from numerous discriminatory and retaliatory acts from the date that he was hired through March 3, 1995, the date that he was fired, only incidents that took place within the timely filing period are actionable. Because Morgan first filed his charge with an appropriate state agency, only those acts that occurred 300 days before February 27, 1995, the day that Morgan filed his charge, are actionable. During that time period, Morgan contends that he was wrongfully suspended and charged with a violation of Amtrak's "Rule L" for insubordination while failing to complete work assigned to him, denied training, and falsely accused of threatening a manager. All prior discrete discriminatory acts are untimely filed and no longer actionable.[9]

B

Hostile environment claims are different in kind from discrete acts. Their very nature involves repeated conduct. See 1 B. Lindemann & P. Grossman, Employment Discrimination Law 348–349 (3d ed. 1996) (hereinafter Lindemann) ("The repeated nature of the harassment or its intensity constitutes evidence that management knew or should have known of its existence"). The "unlawful employment practice" therefore cannot be said to occur on any particular day. It occurs over a series of days or perhaps years and, in direct contrast to discrete acts, a single act of harassment may not be actionable on its own. See *Harris v. Forklift Systems, Inc.*, 510 U.S. 17, 21, 126 L.Ed.2d 295, 114 S.Ct. 367 (1993) ("As

---

[7] * * * There may be circumstances where it will be difficult to determine when the time period should begin to run. One issue that may arise in such circumstances is whether the time begins to run when the injury occurs as opposed to when the injury reasonably should have been discovered. But this case presents no occasion to resolve that issue.

[9] We have no occasion here to consider the timely filing question with respect to "pattern-or-practice" claims brought by private litigants as none are at issue here.

we pointed out in *Meritor* [*Savings Bank, FSB v. Vinson*, 477 U.S. 57, 67, 91 L.Ed. 2d 49, 106 S.Ct. 2399 (1986)], 'mere utterance of an . . . epithet which engenders offensive feelings in a[n] employee,' ibid. (internal quotation marks omitted) does not sufficiently affect the conditions of employment to implicate Title VII"). Such claims are based on the cumulative effect of individual acts.

In determining whether an actionable hostile work environment claim exists, we look to "all the circumstances," including "the frequency of the discriminatory conduct; its severity; whether it is physically threatening or humiliating, or a mere offensive utterance; and whether it unreasonably interferes with an employee's work performance." *Id.*, at 23. To assess whether a court may, for the purposes of determining liability, review all such conduct, including those acts that occur outside the filing period, we again look to the statute. It provides that a charge must be filed within 180 or 300 days "after the alleged unlawful employment practice occurred." A hostile work environment claim is comprised of a series of separate acts that collectively constitute one "unlawful employment practice." 42 U.S.C. § 2000e–5(e)(1). The timely filing provision only requires that a Title VII plaintiff file a charge within a certain number of days after the unlawful practice happened. It does not matter, for purposes of the statute, that some of the component acts of the hostile work environment fall outside the statutory time period. Provided that an act contributing to the claim occurs within the filing period, the entire time period of the hostile environment may be considered by a court for the purposes of determining liability.

That act need not, however, be the last act. As long as the employer has engaged in enough activity to make out an actionable hostile environment claim, an unlawful employment practice has "occurred," even if it is still occurring. Subsequent events, however, may still be part of the one hostile work environment claim and a charge may be filed at a later date and still encompass the whole.

It is precisely because the entire hostile work environment encompasses a single unlawful employment practice that we do not hold, as have some of the Circuits, that the plaintiff may not base a suit on individual acts that occurred outside the statute of limitations unless it would have been unreasonable to expect the plaintiff to sue before the statute ran on such conduct. The statute does not separate individual acts that are part of the hostile environment claim from the whole for the purposes of timely filing and liability. And the statute does not contain a requirement that the employee file a charge prior to 180 or 300 days "after" the single unlawful practice "occurred." Given, therefore, that the incidents comprising a hostile work environment are part of one unlawful employment practice, the employer may be liable for all acts that are part of this single claim. In order for the charge to be timely, the employee need only file a charge within 180 or 300 days of any act that is part of the hostile work environment.

The following scenarios illustrate our point: (1) Acts on days 1–400 create a hostile work environment. The employee files the charge on day 401. Can the employee recover for that part of the hostile work environment that occurred in the first 100 days? (2) Acts contribute to a hostile environment on days 1–100 and on day 401, but there are no acts between days 101–400. Can the act occurring on day 401 pull the other acts in for the purposes of liability? In truth, all other things being equal, there is little difference between the two scenarios as a hostile environment constitutes one "unlawful employment practice" and it does not matter whether nothing occurred within the intervening 301 days so long as each act is part of the whole. Nor, if sufficient activity occurred by day 100 to make out a claim, does it matter that the employee knows on that day that an actionable claim happened; on day 401 all incidents are still part of the same claim. On the other hand, if an act on day 401 had no relation to the acts between days 1–100, or for some other reason, such as certain intervening action by the employer, was no longer part of the same hostile environment claim, then the employee can not recover for the previous acts, at least not by reference to the day 401 act.

* * *

With respect to Morgan's hostile environment claim, the Court of Appeals concluded that "the pre- and post-limitations period incidents involved the same type of employment actions, occurred relatively frequently, and were perpetrated by the same managers." To support his claims of a hostile environment, Morgan presented evidence from a number of other employees that managers made racial jokes, performed racially derogatory acts, made negative comments regarding the capacity of blacks to be supervisors, and used various racial epithets. Although many of the acts upon which his claim depends occurred outside the 300 day filing period, we cannot say that they are not part of the same actionable hostile environment claim. On this point, we affirm.

C

Our holding does not leave employers defenseless against employees who bring hostile work environment claims that extend over long periods of time. Employers have recourse when a plaintiff unreasonably delays filing a charge. * * *

* * *

In addition to other equitable defenses, . . . an employer may raise a laches defense, which bars a plaintiff from maintaining a suit if he unreasonably delays in filing a suit and as a result harms the defendant. This defense " 'requires proof of (1) lack of diligence by the party against whom the defense is asserted, and (2) prejudice to the party asserting the defense.'" *Kansas v. Colorado*, 514 U.S. 673, 687, 131 L.Ed.2d 759, 115 S.Ct. 1733 (1995) * * * .

[*Eds*. The partial dissent of JUSTICE O'CONNOR, joined in different parts by CHIEF JUSTICE REHNQUIST and JUSTICES SCALIA, KENNEDY and BREYER, is omitted.]

NOTES AND QUESTIONS

Test Your Understanding of the Material

1. Consider the Court's examples of "discrete acts." Are they the same as the "tangible" employment decisions for which an employer can be directly liable under *Faragher* and *Ellerth*, p. 374 supra?

2. In determining timeliness, why does the Court treat acts that create a hostile work environment differently than "discrete acts," like a continuing "failure to promote, denial of transfer, or refusal to hire," that may be part of the same continuing course of discrimination?

3. Consider the Court's second hypothetical: "Acts contribute to a hostile environment on days 1–100 and on day 401, but there are no acts between days 101–400." Whether the employee can recover for acts between days 1–100 depends on whether the acts on day 401 are related to the earlier acts. Devise a hypothetical in which the acts would be related, and one where they would not.

4. When might prior non-discrete discriminatory acts not be part of the same hostile environment? Note the Court's suggestion that "certain intervening action" by the employer may indicate that prior conduct is "no longer part of the same hostile environment claim." Note also the court's reference to the doctrine of laches.

Related Issues

5. *Start of Filing Period for Constructive Discharge?* Assume that Morgan had resigned from his position with Amtrak claiming that he should recover back pay from the time of his resignation because he faced a discriminatory hostile work environment so severe and pervasive that a reasonable person would have felt compelled to resign. This is the Title VII standard for "constructive discharge" endorsed by the Court in 2004 in *Pennsylvania State Police v. Suders*, supra p. 388. Would the filing period for this claim commence at the time of the last hostile discriminatory act or at the time of his resignation? See Green v. Brennan, No. 14-613, 578 U.S. ___ (decided May 23, 2016) (filing period for constructive discharge claims commences upon resignation).

LEDBETTER V. GOODYEAR TIRE & RUBBER CO.

Supreme Court of the United States, 2007.
550 U.S. 618, 127 S.Ct. 2162, 167 L.Ed.2d 982.

JUSTICE ALITO delivered the opinion of the Court.

This case calls upon us to apply established precedent in a slightly different context. We have previously held that the time for filing a charge of employment discrimination with the Equal Employment Opportunity Commission (EEOC) begins when the discriminatory act occurs. We have explained that this rule applies to any "discrete act" of discrimination, including discrimination in "termination, failure to promote, denial of transfer, [and] refusal to hire." *National Railroad Passenger Corporation v. Morgan*, 536 U.S. 101, 114, 122 S. Ct. 2061, 153 L. Ed. 2d 106 (2002). Because a pay-setting decision is a "discrete act," it follows that the period for filing an EEOC charge begins when the act occurs. Petitioner, having abandoned her claim under the Equal Pay Act, asks us to deviate from our prior decisions in order to permit her to assert her claim under Title VII. Petitioner also contends that discrimination in pay is different from other types of employment discrimination and thus should be governed by a different rule. But because a pay-setting decision is a discrete act that occurs at a particular point in time, these arguments must be rejected. We therefore affirm the judgment of the Court of Appeals.

I

Petitioner Lilly Ledbetter (Ledbetter) worked for respondent (Goodyear) at its Gadsden, Alabama, plant from 1979 until 1998. During much of this time, salaried employees at the plant were given or denied raises based on their supervisors' evaluation of their performance. In March 1998, Ledbetter submitted a questionnaire to the EEOC alleging certain acts of sex discrimination, and in July of that year she filed a formal EEOC charge. After taking early retirement in November 1998, Ledbetter commenced this action, in which she asserted, among other claims, a Title VII pay discrimination claim and a claim under the Equal Pay Act of 1963 (EPA), 29 U.S.C. § 206(d).

The District Court granted summary judgment in favor of Goodyear on several of Ledbetter's claims, including her Equal Pay Act claim, but allowed others, including her Title VII pay discrimination claim, to proceed to trial. In support of this latter claim, Ledbetter introduced evidence that during the course of her employment several supervisors had given her poor evaluations because of her sex, that as a result of these evaluations her pay was not increased as much as it would have been if she had been evaluated fairly, and that these past pay decisions continued to affect the amount of her pay throughout her employment. Toward the end of her time with Goodyear, she was being paid significantly less than any of her male colleagues. Goodyear maintained that the evaluations had been nondiscriminatory, but the jury found for Ledbetter and awarded her backpay and damages.

On appeal, Goodyear contended that Ledbetter's pay discrimination claim was time barred with respect to all pay decisions made prior to September 26, 1997—that is, 180 days before the filing of her EEOC questionnaire. And Goodyear argued that no discriminatory act relating to Ledbetter's pay occurred after that date.

The Court of Appeals for the Eleventh Circuit reversed, holding that a Title VII pay discrimination claim cannot be based on any pay decision that occurred prior to the last pay decision that affected the employee's pay during the EEOC charging period. 421 F.3d 1169, 1182–1183 (2005). The Court of Appeals then concluded that there was insufficient evidence to prove that Goodyear had acted with discriminatory intent in making the only two pay decisions that occurred within that time span, namely, a decision made in 1997 to deny Ledbetter a raise and a similar decision made in 1998. *Id.*, at 1186–1187.

* * *

II

* * *

In addressing the issue whether an EEOC charge was filed on time, we have stressed the need to identify with care the specific employment practice that is at issue. *Morgan*, 536 U.S., at 110–111, 122 S. Ct. 2061, 153 L. Ed. 2d 106. Ledbetter points to two different employment practices as possible candidates. Primarily, she urges us to focus on the paychecks that were issued to her during the EEOC charging period (the 180-day period preceding the filing of her EEOC questionnaire), each of which, she contends, was a separate act of discrimination. Alternatively, Ledbetter directs us to the 1998 decision denying her a raise, and she argues that this decision was "unlawful because it carried forward intentionally discriminatory disparities from prior years." Both of these arguments fail because they would require us in effect to jettison the defining element of the legal claim on which her Title VII recovery was based.

Ledbetter asserted disparate treatment, the central element of which is discriminatory intent. * * * However, Ledbetter does not assert that the relevant Goodyear decisionmakers acted with actual discriminatory intent either when they issued her checks during the EEOC charging period or when they denied her a raise in 1998. Rather, she argues that the paychecks were unlawful because they would have been larger if she had been evaluated in a nondiscriminatory manner prior to the EEOC charging period. Similarly, she maintains that the 1998 decision was unlawful because it "carried forward" the effects of prior, uncharged discrimination decisions. In essence, she suggests that it is sufficient that discriminatory acts that occurred prior to the charging period had continuing effects during that period. * * * This argument is squarely foreclosed by our precedents.

In *United Air Lines, Inc. v. Evans*, 431 U.S. 553, 97 S. Ct. 1885, 52 L. Ed. 2d 571 (1977), we rejected an argument that is basically the same as Ledbetter's. Evans was forced to resign because the airline refused to employ married flight attendants, but she did not file an EEOC charge regarding her termination. Some years later, the airline rehired her but treated her as a new employee for seniority purposes. *Id.*, at 554–555, 97 S. Ct. 1885, 52 L. Ed. 2d 571. Evans then sued, arguing that, while any suit based on the original discrimination was time barred, the airline's refusal to give her credit for her prior service gave "present effect to [its] past illegal act and thereby perpetuated the consequences of forbidden discrimination." *Id.*, at 557, 97 S. Ct. 1885, 52 L. Ed. 2d 571.

We agreed with Evans that the airline's "seniority system [did] indeed have a continuing impact on her pay and fringe benefits," id., at 558, 97 S. Ct. 1885, 52 L. Ed. 2d 571, but we noted that "the critical question [was] whether any present *violation* existed." *Ibid.* (emphasis in original). We concluded that the continuing effects of the precharging period discrimination did not make out a present violation. As Justice Stevens wrote for the Court:

> "United was entitled to treat [Evans' termination] as lawful after respondent failed to file a charge of discrimination within the 90 days then allowed by § 706(d). A discriminatory act which is not made the basis for a timely charge . . . is merely an unfortunate event in history which has no present legal consequences." *Ibid.*

It would be difficult to speak to the point more directly.

Equally instructive is *Delaware State College v. Ricks*, 449 U.S. 250, 101 S. Ct. 498, 66 L. Ed. 2d 431 (1980), which concerned a college librarian, Ricks, who alleged that he had been discharged because of race. In March 1974, Ricks was denied tenure, but he was given a final, nonrenewable one-year contract that expired on June 30, 1975. *Id.*, at 252–253, 101 S. Ct. 498, 66 L. Ed. 2d 431. Ricks delayed filing a charge with the EEOC until April 1975, *id.*, at 254, 101 S. Ct. 498, 66 L. Ed. 2d 431, but he argued that the EEOC charging period ran from the date of his actual termination rather than from the date when tenure was denied. In rejecting this argument, we recognized that "one of the *effects* of the denial of tenure," namely, his ultimate termination, "did not occur until later." *Id.*, at 258, 101 S. Ct. 498, 66 L. Ed. 2d 431 (emphasis in original). But because Ricks failed to identify any specific discriminatory act "that continued until, or occurred at the time of, the actual termination of his employment," *id.*, at 257, 101 S. Ct. 498, 66 L. Ed. 2d 431, we held that the EEOC charging period ran from "the time the tenure decision was made and communicated to Ricks," *id.*, at 258, 101 S. Ct. 498, 66 L. Ed. 2d 431.

This same approach dictated the outcome in *Lorance v. AT&T Technologies, Inc.*, 490 U.S. 900, 109 S. Ct. 2261, 104 L. Ed. 2d 961 (1989), which grew out of a change in the way in which seniority was calculated under a collective-bargaining agreement. Before 1979, all employees at the plant in question accrued seniority based simply on years of employment at the plant. In 1979, a new agreement made seniority for workers in the more highly paid (and traditionally male) position of "tester" depend on time spent in that position alone and not in other positions in the plant. Several years later, when female testers were laid off due to low seniority as calculated under the new provision, they filed an EEOC charge alleging that the 1979 scheme had been adopted with discriminatory intent, namely, to protect incumbent male testers when women with substantial plant seniority began to move into the traditionally male tester positions. *Id.*, at 902–903, 109 S. Ct. 2261, 104 L. Ed. 2d 961.

We held that the plaintiffs' EEOC charge was not timely because it was not filed within the specified period after the adoption in 1979 of the new seniority rule. We noted that the plaintiffs had not alleged that the new seniority rule treated men and women differently or that the rule had been applied in a discriminatory manner. Rather, their complaint was that the rule was adopted originally with discriminatory intent. *Id.*, at 905, 109 S. Ct. 2261, 104 L. Ed. 2d 961. And as in *Evans* and *Ricks,* we held that the EEOC charging period ran from the time when the discrete act of alleged intentional discrimination occurred, not from the date when the effects of this practice were felt. 490 U.S., at 907–908, 109 S. Ct. 2261, 104 L. Ed. 2d 961. We stated:

> "Because the claimed invalidity of the facially nondiscriminatory and neutrally applied tester seniority system is wholly dependent on the alleged illegality of signing the underlying agreement, it is the date of that signing which governs the limitations period." *Id.*, at 911, 109 S. Ct. 2261, 104 L. Ed. 2d 961.[2]

Our most recent decision in this area confirms this understanding. In *Morgan*, we explained that the statutory term "employment practice" generally refers to "a discrete act or single 'occurrence' " that takes place at a particular point in time. 536 U.S., at 110–111, 122 S. Ct. 2061, 153 L. Ed. 2d 106. We pointed to "termination, failure to promote, denial of transfer, [and] refusal to hire" as examples of such "discrete" acts, and we held that a Title VII plaintiff "can only file a charge to cover discrete acts that

---

[2] After *Lorance*, Congress amended Title VII to cover the specific situation involved in that case. See 42 U.S.C. § 2000e–5(e)(2) (allowing for Title VII liability arising from an intentionally discriminatory seniority system both at the time of its adoption and at the time of its application). * * * For present purposes, what is most important about the amendment in question is that it applied only to the adoption of a discriminatory seniority system, not to other types of employment discrimination. *Evans* and *Ricks*, upon which *Lorance* relied, 490 U.S., at 906–908, 109 S. Ct. 2261, 104 L. Ed. 2d 961, and which employed identical reasoning, were left in place, and these decisions are more than sufficient to support our holding today.

'occurred' within the appropriate time period." *Id.*, at 114, 122 S. Ct. 2061, 153 L. Ed. 2d 106.

* * *

A disparate-treatment claim comprises two elements: an employment practice, and discriminatory intent. Nothing in Title VII supports treating the intent element of Ledbetter's claim any differently from the employment practice element.[3] If anything, concerns regarding stale claims weigh more heavily with respect to proof of the intent associated with employment practices than with the practices themselves. For example, in a case such as this in which the plaintiff's claim concerns the denial of raises, the employer's challenged acts (the decisions not to increase the employee's pay at the times in question) will almost always be documented and will typically not even be in dispute. By contrast, the employer's intent is almost always disputed, and evidence relating to intent may fade quickly with time. * * * [4]

III

A

In advancing her two theories Ledbetter * * * argues that our decision in *Bazemore v. Friday*, 478 U.S. 385, 106 S. Ct. 3000, 92 L. Ed. 2d 315 (1986) (per curiam), requires different treatment of her claim because it relates to pay. Ledbetter focuses specifically on our statement that "each week's paycheck that delivers less to a black than to a similarly situated white is a wrong actionable under Title VII." *Id.*, at 395, 106 S. Ct. 3000, 92 L. Ed. 2d 315. She argues that in *Bazemore* we adopted a "paycheck accrual rule" under which each paycheck, even if not accompanied by discriminatory intent, triggers a new EEOC charging period during which the complainant may properly challenge any prior discriminatory conduct that impacted the amount of that paycheck, no matter how long ago the discrimination occurred. On this reading, *Bazemore* dispensed with the need to prove actual discriminatory intent in pay cases and, without giving

---

[3] Of course, there may be instances where the elements forming a cause of action span more than 180 days. Say, for instance, an employer forms an illegal discriminatory intent towards an employee but does not act on it until 181 days later. The charging period would not begin to run until the employment practice was executed on day 181 because until that point the employee had no cause of action. The act and intent had not yet been joined. Here, by contrast, Ledbetter's cause of action was fully formed and present at the time that the discriminatory employment actions were taken against her, at which point she could have, and should have, sued.

[4] [T]his case illustrates the problems created by tardy lawsuits. Ledbetter's claims of sex discrimination turned principally on the misconduct of a single Goodyear supervisor, who, Ledbetter testified, retaliated against her when she rejected his sexual advances during the early 1980's, and did so again in the mid-1990's when he falsified deficiency reports about her work. His misconduct, Ledbetter argues, was "a principal basis for [her] performance evaluation in 1997." Brief for Petitioner 6; see also id., at 5–6, 8, 11 (stressing the same supervisor's misconduct). Yet, by the time of trial, this supervisor had died and therefore could not testify. A timely charge might have permitted his evidence to be weighed contemporaneously.

any hint that it was doing so, repudiated the very different approach taken previously in *Evans* and *Ricks*. Ledbetter's interpretation is unsound.

Bazemore concerned a disparate-treatment pay claim brought against the North Carolina Agricultural Extension Service (Service). 478 U.S., at 389–390, 106 S. Ct. 3000, 92 L. Ed. 2d 315. Service employees were originally segregated into "a white branch" and "a Negro branch," with the latter receiving less pay, but in 1965 the two branches were merged. *Id.*, at 390–391, 106 S. Ct. 3000, 92 L. Ed. 2d 315. After Title VII was extended to public employees in 1972, black employees brought suit claiming that pay disparities attributable to the old dual pay scale persisted. *Id.*, at 391, 106 S. Ct. 3000, 92 L. Ed. 2d 315. The Court of Appeals rejected this claim, which it interpreted to be that the "discriminatory difference in salaries should have been affirmatively eliminated." *Id.*, at 395.

This Court reversed in a per curiam opinion, 478 U.S., at 386–388, 106 S. Ct. 3000, 92 L. Ed. 2d 315, but all of the Members of the Court joined Justice Brennan's separate opinion, see *id.*, at 388, 106 S. Ct. 3000, 92 L. Ed. 2d 315 (opinion concurring in part). Justice Brennan wrote:

"The error of the Court of Appeals with respect to salary disparities created prior to 1972 and perpetuated thereafter is too obvious to warrant extended discussion: that the Extension Service discriminated with respect to salaries prior to the time it was covered by Title VII does not excuse perpetuating that discrimination *after* the Extension Service became covered by Title VII. To hold otherwise would have the effect of exempting from liability those employers who were historically the greatest offenders of the rights of blacks. A pattern or practice that would have constituted a violation of Title VII, but for the fact that the statute had not yet become effective, became a violation upon Title VII's effective date, and to the extent an employer continued to engage in that act or practice, it is liable under that statute. While recovery may not be permitted for pre-1972 acts of discrimination, to the extent that this discrimination was perpetuated after 1972, liability may be imposed." *Id.*, at 395, 106 S. Ct. 3000, 92 L. Ed. 2d 315 (emphasis in original).

Far from adopting the approach that Ledbetter advances here, this passage made a point that was "too obvious to warrant extended discussion," ibid.; namely, that when an employer adopts a facially discriminatory pay structure that puts some employees on a lower scale because of race, the employer engages in intentional discrimination whenever it issues a check to one of these disfavored employees. An employer that adopts and intentionally retains such a pay structure can surely be regarded as intending to discriminate on the basis of race as long as the structure is used.

* * *

Bazemore stands for the proposition that an employer violates Title VII and triggers a new EEOC charging period whenever the employer issues paychecks using a discriminatory pay structure. But a new Title VII violation does not occur and a new charging period is not triggered when an employer issues paychecks pursuant to a system that is "facially nondiscriminatory and neutrally applied." *Lorance*, 490 U.S., at 911, 109 S. Ct. 2261, 104 L. Ed. 2d 961. The fact that precharging period discrimination adversely affects the calculation of a neutral factor (like seniority) that is used in determining future pay does not mean that each new paycheck constitutes a new violation and restarts the EEOC charging period.

Because Ledbetter has not adduced evidence that Goodyear initially adopted its performance-based pay system in order to discriminate on the basis of sex or that it later applied this system to her within the charging period with any discriminatory animus, *Bazemore* is of no help to her. Rather, all Ledbetter has alleged is that Goodyear's agents discriminated against her individually in the past and that this discrimination reduced the amount of later paychecks. Because Ledbetter did not file timely EEOC charges relating to her employer's discriminatory pay decisions in the past, she cannot maintain a suit based on that past discrimination at this time.

B

The dissent also argues that pay claims are different. Its principal argument is that a pay discrimination claim is like a hostile work environment claim because both types of claims are "based on the cumulative effect of individual acts," but this analogy overlooks the critical conceptual distinction between these two types of claims. And although the dissent relies heavily on *Morgan*, the dissent's argument is fundamentally inconsistent with *Morgan*'s reasoning.

Morgan distinguished between "discrete" acts of discrimination and a hostile work environment. A discrete act of discrimination is an act that in itself "constitutes a separate actionable 'unlawful employment practice'" and that is temporally distinct. *Morgan*, 536 U.S., at 114, 117, 122 S. Ct. 2061, 153 L. Ed. 2d 106. As examples we identified "termination, failure to promote, denial of transfer, or refusal to hire." *Id.*, at 114, 122 S. Ct. 2061, 153 L. Ed. 2d 106. A hostile work environment, on the other hand, typically comprises a succession of harassing acts, each of which "may not be actionable on its own." In addition, a hostile work environment claim "cannot be said to occur on any particular day." *Id.*, at 115–116, 122 S. Ct. 2061, 153 L. Ed. 2d 106. In other words, the actionable wrong is the environment, not the individual acts that, taken together, create the environment.

* * *

[I]f a single discriminatory pay decision made 20 years ago continued to affect an employee's pay today, the dissent would presumably hold that the employee could file a timely EEOC charge today. And the dissent would presumably allow this even if the employee had full knowledge of all the circumstances relating to the 20-year-old decision at the time it was made. The dissent, it appears, proposes that we adopt a special rule for pay cases based on the particular characteristics of one case that is certainly not representative of all pay cases and may not even be typical. We refuse to take that approach.

IV

In addition to the arguments previously discussed, Ledbetter relies largely on analogies to other statutory regimes and on extrastatutory policy arguments to support her "paycheck accrual rule."

A

Ledbetter places significant weight on the EPA, which was enacted contemporaneously with Title VII and prohibits paying unequal wages for equal work because of sex. 29 U.S.C. § 206(d). Stating that "the lower courts routinely hear [EPA] claims challenging pay disparities that first arose outside the limitations period," Ledbetter suggests that we should hold that Title VII is violated each time an employee receives a paycheck that reflects past discrimination.

The simple answer to this argument is that the EPA and Title VII are not the same. In particular, the EPA does not require the filing of a charge with the EEOC or proof of intentional discrimination. See § 206(d)(1) (asking only whether the alleged inequality resulted from "any other factor other than sex"). Ledbetter originally asserted an EPA claim, but that claim was dismissed by the District Court and is not before us. If Ledbetter had pursued her EPA claim, she would not face the Title VII obstacles that she now confronts. * * *

Ledbetter, finally, makes a variety of policy arguments in favor of giving the alleged victims of pay discrimination more time before they are required to file a charge with the EEOC. Among other things, she claims that pay discrimination is harder to detect than other forms of employment discrimination.[10] * * *

Ledbetter's policy arguments for giving special treatment to pay claims find no support in the statute and are inconsistent with our precedents. We apply the statute as written, and this means that any unlawful employment practice, including those involving compensation, must be presented to the EEOC within the period prescribed by statute.

---

[10] We have previously declined to address whether Title VII suits are amenable to a discovery rule. *National Railroad Passenger Corporation v. Morgan,* 536 U.S. 101, 114, n. 7, 122 S.Ct. 2061, 153 L.Ed.2d 106 (2002). Because Ledbetter does not argue that such a rule would change the outcome in her case, we have no occasion to address this issue.

JUSTICE GINSBURG, with whom JUSTICES STEVENS, SOUTER and BREYER join, dissenting.

The Court's insistence on immediate contest overlooks common characteristics of pay discrimination. Pay disparities often occur, as they did in Ledbetter's case, in small increments; cause to suspect that discrimination is at work develops only over time. Comparative pay information, moreover, is often hidden from the employee's view. Employers may keep under wraps the pay differentials maintained among supervisors, no less the reasons for those differentials. Small initial discrepancies may not be seen as meet for a federal case, particularly when the employee, trying to succeed in a nontraditional environment, is averse to making waves. * * *

* * *

Ledbetter's petition presents a question important to the sound application of Title VII: What activity qualifies as an unlawful employment practice in cases of discrimination with respect to compensation. One answer identifies the pay-setting decision, and that decision alone, as the unlawful practice. Under this view, each particular salary-setting decision is discrete from prior and subsequent decisions, and must be challenged within 180 days on pain of forfeiture. Another response counts both the pay-setting decision and the actual payment of a discriminatory wage as unlawful practices. Under this approach, each payment of a wage or salary infected by sex-based discrimination constitutes an unlawful employment practice; prior decisions, outside the 180-day charge-filing period, are not themselves actionable, but they are relevant in determining the lawfulness of conduct within the period. The Court adopts the first view, but the second is more faithful to precedent, more in tune with the realities of the workplace, and more respectful of Title VII's remedial purpose.

* * *

Pay disparities, of the kind Ledbetter experienced, have a closer kinship to hostile work environment claims than to charges of a single episode of discrimination. Ledbetter's claim, resembling Morgan's, rested not on one particular paycheck, but on "the cumulative effect of individual acts." Initially in line with the salaries of men performing substantially the same work, Ledbetter's salary fell 15 to 40 percent behind her male counterparts only after successive evaluations and percentage-based pay adjustments. Over time, she alleged and proved, the repetition of pay decisions undervaluing her work gave rise to the current discrimination of which she complained. Though component acts fell outside the charge-filing period, with each new paycheck, Goodyear contributed incrementally to the accumulating harm. See *Morgan*, 536 U.S., at 117, 122 S. Ct. 2061, 153 L. Ed. 2d 106; *Bazemore*, 478 U.S., at 395–396, 106 S. Ct. 3000, 92 L.

Ed. 2d 315; cf. *Hanover Shoe, Inc. v. United Shoe Machinery Corp.*, 392 U.S. 481, 502, n. 15, 88 S. Ct. 2224, 20 L. Ed. 2d 1231 (1968).

The problem of concealed pay discrimination is particularly acute where the disparity arises not because the female employee is flatly denied a raise but because male counterparts are given larger raises. Having received a pay increase, the female employee is unlikely to discern at once that she has experienced an adverse employment decision. She may have little reason even to suspect discrimination until a pattern develops incrementally and she ultimately becomes aware of the disparity. Even if an employee suspects that the reason for a comparatively low raise is not performance but sex (or another protected ground), the amount involved may seem too small, or the employer's intent too ambiguous, to make the issue immediately actionable—or winnable.

NOTES AND QUESTIONS

Test Your Understanding of the Material

1. Review the majority and dissenting opinions in *Ledbetter*. Are discriminatory pay decisions fully completed when implemented or do they continue on with each paycheck into the filing period?

2. How does the *Ledbetter* Court distinguish its earlier decision in *Bazemore v. Friday*? Is the distinction persuasive? Should employers be expected to counter plaintiffs' allegations of covert discriminatory events that may stem from discrete events distant in time?

Related Issues

3. *"Discovery" Rule?* Would a "discovery" rule (a point left open in footnote 10 of the Court's opinion) be preferable to the rule adopted by the majority? Under a "discovery" rule, the plaintiff's claim would accrue when the plaintiff learns or should have known of the discriminatory pay practice. The Court earlier reserved decision on whether a "discovery" rule was appropriate in Mohasco Corp. v. Silver, 447 U.S. 807, 818 n. 22, 100 S.Ct. 2486, 2493 n. 22, 65 L.Ed.2d 532 (1980). In Reeb v. Economic Opportunity Atlanta, Inc., 516 F.2d 924 (5th Cir.1975), the plaintiff had been terminated on grounds of "limitations of funds" but subsequently learned that her previous position had been filled by a presumably less qualified male employee; the court held that the filing period began with the subsequent discovery. Does *Reeb* provide support for a general "discovery" rule or is it an instance of equitable tolling because of defendant's concealment of the true facts? See Kale v. Combined Insurance Co. of America, 861 F.2d 746 (1st Cir.1988) (recognizing tolling because of "equitable estoppel" due to employer misrepresentations).

4. *Lilly Ledbetter Fair Pay Act of 2009 (LLA).* On January 29, 2009, President Obama signed legislation intended to overturn *Ledbetter*. The legislation, Pub. L. 111–2, 123 Stat. 5, amends § 706(e) of Title VII (with conforming amendments to ADEA, ADA, and the Rehabilitation Act), codified now as 42 U.S.C. § 2000e–5(e)(3)(A), to provide:

> An unlawful employment practice occurs, with respect to discrimination in compensation in violation of this title, when a discriminatory compensation decision or other practice is adopted, when an individual becomes subject to a discriminatory compensation decision or other practice, or when an individual is affected by application of a discriminatory compensation decision or other practice, including each time wages, benefits, or other compensation is paid, resulting in whole or in part from such a decision or other practice.

The Act was made retroactive to the date of the *Ledbetter* decision, May 28, 2007, and applies to all cases pending on that date. How would a case like that of Lilly Ledbetter's now be decided? Might an employer still be able to assert the equitable doctrine of *laches* in an appropriate case?

5. *Discharge and Promotion Decisions After the Lilly Ledbetter Act.* To what extent does the amendment affect the beginning of the filing period in a discharge case like that of *Ricks*, discussed in the *Ledbetter* decision? What about a case where an employee claims discrimination in the denial of a promotion that would have been accompanied by a pay raise? See Noel v. Boeing Co., 622 F.3d 266 (3d Cir. 2010); Schuler v. Pricewaterhouse Coopers, LLP, 595 F.3d 370 (D.C. Cir. 2010) (both holding failure-to-promote claim does not fall within purview of Ledbetter Act because they are not "discriminatory compensation decision[s] . . . or practice[s].")). In Almond v. Unified School District #501, 665 F.3d 1174 (10th Cir. 2011), the court of appeals held that the LLA does not apply to claims involving transfer to lower-paying jobs absent allegations of "unequal pay for equal work".

6. *Intentionally Discriminatory Seniority Systems.* The LLA was not the first time Congress reversed a decision of the Court that refused to start a new filing period with each application of a prior discriminatory decision. Note the *Ledbetter* Court's discussion of *Lorance v. AT&T Technologies*. In § 112 of the Civil Rights Act of 1991, Congress overturned the holding in *Lorance*, by amending § 706(e) of Title VII to provide that, for challenges "to a seniority system that has been adopted for an intentionally discriminatory purpose in violation of this title (whether or not that discriminatory purpose is apparent on the face of the seniority provision), when the seniority system is adopted, when an individual becomes subject to the seniority system, or when a person aggrieved is injured by the application of the seniority system or provision of the system."

7. *Adoption vs. Application of Practice with Disparate Impact.* In Lewis v. City of Chicago, 560 U.S. 205, 130 S.Ct. 2191, 176 L.Ed.2d 967 (2010), the Supreme Court addressed the question of whether the filing period for a disparate-impact claim starts upon the adoption of a practice or whether it also starts upon the later application of that practice. In 1995, the Chicago Fire Department adopted a selection practice whereby applicants scoring about 89 on a written test would be eligible to be selected for a position, whereas those scoring between 65 and 88 were kept on a wait list. The plaintiffs filed a disparate impact claim challenging the city's selection practices. The challenge

to the 1995 adoption was untimely but subsequent application of the selection procedure could be challenged. The Court concluded that both the adoption and application of the practice gave rise to a cause of action:

> It may be true that the City's January 1996 decision to adopt the cutoff score (and to create a list of the applicants above it) gave rise to a freestanding disparate-impact claim. But it does not follow that no new violation occurred—and no new claims could arise—when the City implemented that decision down the road. If petitioners could prove that the City "use[d]" the "practice" that "causes a disparate impact," they could prevail.

> [Our] cases establish only that a Title VII plaintiff must show a "present violation" within the limitations period. *Evans, supra,* at 558, 97 S. Ct. 1885, 52 L. Ed. 2d 571 (emphasis deleted). What that requires depends on the claim asserted. For disparate-treatment claims—and others for which discriminatory intent is required—that means the plaintiff must demonstrate deliberate discrimination within the limitations period. See *Ledbetter, supra,* at 624–629, 127 S. Ct. 2162, 167 L. Ed. 2d 982; *Lorance, supra,* at 904–905, 109 S. Ct. 2261, 104 L. Ed. 2d 961 * * * . But for claims that do not require discriminatory intent, no such demonstration is needed. 560 U.S. at 215.

D. CLASS ACTIONS

GENERAL TELEPHONE COMPANY OF THE SOUTHWEST V. FALCON

Supreme Court of the United States, 1982.
457 U.S. 147, 102 S.Ct. 2364, 72 L.Ed.2d 740.

JUSTICE STEVENS delivered the opinion of the Court.

The question presented is whether respondent Falcon, who complained that petitioner did not promote him because he is a Mexican-American, was properly permitted to maintain a class action on behalf of Mexican-American applicants for employment whom petitioner did not hire.

I

In 1969 petitioner initiated a special recruitment and training program for minorities. Through that program, respondent Falcon was hired in July 1969 as a groundman, and within a year he was twice promoted, first to lineman and then to lineman-in-charge. He subsequently refused a promotion to installer-repairman. In October 1972 he applied for the job of field inspector; his application was denied even though the promotion was granted several white employees with less seniority.

Falcon thereupon filed a charge with the Equal Employment Opportunity Commission stating his belief that he had been passed over for promotion because of his national origin and that petitioner's promotion policy operated against Mexican-Americans as a class. In due course he received a right-to-sue letter from the Commission and, in April 1975, he commenced this action under Title VII of the Civil Rights Act of 1964, 78 Stat. 253, as amended, 42 U.S.C. § 2000e *et seq.* (1976 ed. and Supp. IV), in the United States District Court for the Northern District of Texas. His complaint alleged that petitioner maintained "a policy, practice, custom, or usage of: (a) discriminating against [Mexican-Americans] because of national origin and with respect to compensation, terms, conditions, and privileges of employment, and (b) * * * subjecting [Mexican-Americans] to continuous employment discrimination." Respondent claimed that as a result of this policy whites with less qualification and experience and lower evaluation scores than respondent had been promoted more rapidly. The complaint contained no factual allegations concerning petitioner's hiring practices.

Respondent brought the action "on his own behalf and on behalf of other persons similarly situated, pursuant to Rule 23(b)(2) of the Federal Rules of Civil Procedure." The class identified in the complaint was "composed of Mexican-American persons who are employed, or who might be employed, by GENERAL TELEPHONE COMPANY at its place of business located in Irving, Texas, who have been and who continue to be or might be adversely affected by the practices complained of herein."

After responding to petitioner's written interrogatories, respondent filed a memorandum in favor of certification of "the employees who have been employed, are employed, or may in the future be employed and all those Mexican-Americans who have applied or would have applied for employment had the Defendant not practiced racial discrimination in its employment practices." His position was supported by the ruling of the United States Court of Appeals for the Fifth Circuit in *Johnson v. Georgia Highway Express, Inc.,* 417 F.2d 1122 (1969), that any victim of racial discrimination in employment may maintain an "across the board" attack on all unequal employment practices alleged to have been committed by the employer pursuant to a policy of racial discrimination. Without conducting an evidentiary hearing, the District Court certified a class including Mexican-American employees and Mexican-American applicants for employment who had not been hired.

Following trial of the liability issues, the District Court entered separate findings of fact and conclusions of law with respect first to respondent and then to the class. The District Court found that petitioner had not discriminated against respondent in hiring, but that it did discriminate against him in its promotion practices. The court reached converse conclusions about the class, finding no discrimination in promotion practices, but concluding that petitioner had discriminated against Mexican-Americans at its Irving facility in its hiring practices.

* * *

Both parties appealed. The Court of Appeals rejected respondent's contention that the class should have encompassed all of petitioner's operations in Texas, New Mexico, Oklahoma, and Arkansas. On the other hand, the court also rejected petitioner's argument that the class had been defined too broadly. For, under the Fifth Circuit's across-the-board rule, it is permissible for "an employee complaining of one employment practice to represent another complaining of another practice, if the plaintiff and the members of the class suffer from essentially the same injury. In this case, all of the claims are based on discrimination because of national origin."

* * *

II

* * *

We have repeatedly held that "a class representative must be part of the class and 'possess the same interest and suffer the same injury' as the class members." *East Texas Motor Freight System, Inc. v. Rodriguez,* 431 U.S. 395, 403, 97 S.Ct. 1891, 1896, 52 L.Ed.2d 453 (quoting *Schlesinger v. Reservists Committee to Stop the War,* 418 U.S. 208, 216, 94 S.Ct. 2925, 2929–2930, 41 L.Ed.2d 706.)

* * *

We cannot disagree with the proposition underlying the across-the-board rule—that racial discrimination is by definition class discrimination. But the allegation that such discrimination has occurred neither determines whether a class action may be maintained in accordance with Rule 23 nor defines the class that may be certified. Conceptually, there is a wide gap between (a) an individual's claim that he has been denied a promotion on discriminatory grounds, and his otherwise unsupported allegation that the company has a policy of discrimination, and (b) the existence of a class of persons who have suffered the same injury as that individual, such that the individual's claim and the class claims will share common questions of law or fact and that the individual's claim will be typical of the class claims. For respondent to bridge that gap, he must prove much more than the validity of his own claim. Even though evidence that he was passed over for promotion when several less deserving whites were advanced may support the conclusion that respondent was denied the promotion because of his national origin, such evidence would not necessarily justify the additional inferences (1) that this discriminatory treatment is typical of petitioner's promotion practices, (2) that petitioner's promotion practices are motivated by a policy of ethnic discrimination that pervades petitioner's Irving division, or (3) that this policy of ethnic discrimination is reflected in petitioner's other employment practices, such as hiring, in the same way it is manifested in the promotion practices. These additional inferences demonstrate the tenuous character of any presumption that the class claims are "fairly encompassed" within respondent's claim.

* * * Without any specific presentation identifying the questions of law or fact that were common to the claims of respondent and of the members of the class he sought to represent, it was error for the District Court to presume that respondent's claim was typical of other claims against petitioner by Mexican-American employees and applicants. If one allegation of specific discriminatory treatment were sufficient to support an across-the-board attack, every Title VII case would be a potential companywide class action. We find nothing in the statute to indicate that Congress intended to authorize such a wholesale expansion of class-action litigation.

The trial of this class action followed a predictable course. Instead of raising common questions of law or fact, respondent's evidentiary approaches to the individual and class claims were entirely different. He attempted to sustain his individual claim by proving intentional discrimination. He tried to prove the class claims through statistical evidence of disparate impact. Ironically, the District Court rejected the class claim of promotion discrimination, which conceptually might have borne a closer typicality and commonality relationship with respondent's individual claim, but sustained the class claim of hiring discrimination. As the District Court's bifurcated findings on liability demonstrate, the individual and class claims might as well have been tried separately. It is clear that the maintenance of respondent's action as a class action did not advance "the efficiency and economy of litigation which is a principal purpose of the procedure." *American Pipe & Construction Co. v. Utah,* 414 U.S. 538, 553, 94 S.Ct. 756, 766, 38 L.Ed.2d 713.

NOTES AND QUESTIONS

Test Your Understanding of the Material

1.   In light of *Falcon* what must Title VII plaintiffs establish in order to satisfy the typicality and commonality requirements of Rule 23?

2.   Why did the *Falcon* Court reject the Fifth Circuit's "across the board" approach to Title VII certifications? Was the Court concerned about potential conflicts of interest between incumbent employees and disappointed applicants, or between past employees and current employees?

Related Issues

3.   *Advantages of Class Actions.* Class actions have been lauded as important to antidiscrimination and wage-and-hour litigation because they enable individual claimants and advocacy organizations to mount systemic,

high-impact challenges to employer decisionmaking. Class actions enable large numbers of victims of discrimination to obtain relief from the outcome of a single disparate impact or systemic disparate treatment suit. The filing of such actions offers other advantages to claimants. The Court held in Albemarle Paper Co. v. Moody, 422 U.S. 405 (1975), that a class action may be brought on behalf of individuals who have not themselves filed charges with the EEOC; and in Crown, Cork and Seal Co. v. Parker, 462 U.S. 345 (1983), it held that the filing of such an action tolls Title VII filing periods for members of the class with viable claims at the time of filing who might wish to initiate or join in an individual suit if the class is not certified. Moreover, once a class action has been certified, it acquires a life of its own, surviving the death or resolution of the individual claims of the representative parties. See Sosna v. Iowa, 419 U.S. 393, 95 S.Ct. 553, 42 L.Ed.2d 532 (1975). A denial of class certification may be reviewed on appeal despite the fact that the representative party's claim has become moot. See Parole Comm'n v. Geraghty, 445 U.S. 388, 100 S.Ct. 1202, 63 L.Ed.2d 479 (1980); Deposit Guaranty National Bank v. Roper, 445 U.S. 326, 100 S.Ct. 1166, 63 L.Ed.2d 427 (1980).

4. *"Across the Board" Certifications After* Falcon? Does *Falcon* rule out all "across the board" actions which allege discriminatory treatment of both applicants and incumbent employees? What about challenges to discriminatory systems? Consider footnote 15 of the decision in *Falcon* (not reprinted in the excerpt):

> If petitioner used a biased testing procedure to evaluate both applicants for employment and incumbent employees, a class action on behalf of every applicant or employee who might have been prejudiced by the test clearly would satisfy the commonality and typicality requirements of Rule 23(a). Significant proof that an employer operated under a general policy of discrimination conceivably could justify a class of both applicants and employees if the discrimination manifested itself in hiring and promotion practices in the same general fashion, such as through entirely subjective decisionmaking processes.

5. *Notice and "Opt-Out" Rights in Discrimination Class Actions.* Class actions of the Rule 23 variety purport to have binding effect on the members of the class; if the class loses, individual suits by class members generally cannot be brought. This raises concerns because many class actions are brought under Rule 23(b)(2) of the F.R.Civ.P., which, unlike Rule 23(b)(3), does not by its terms require that notice and an opportunity to opt out be furnished to class members. The Court mitigated somewhat the harshness of this rule in Cooper v. Federal Reserve Bank, 467 U.S. 867, 104 S.Ct. 2794, 81 L.Ed.2d 718 (1984), by confining the binding effect of a Title VII class action to the issues actually litigated therein, and holding that a court's rejection of a systemic disparate treatment case does not necessarily foreclose individual discrimination claims. The dilemma nevertheless remains to the extent the class action purports to resolve individual claims or will have that effect as a practical matter. Some courts have required notice to class members before foreclosure of their

individual claims may occur. See, e.g., Johnson v. General Motors Corp., 598 F.2d 432 (5th Cir.1979).

6. *Class Action Settlements.* How should settlements of Rule 23(b)(2) class actions be treated? Rule 23(e) requires notice to class members and the holding of a "fairness" hearing by the district court before approval of a settlement. At the hearing, class members opposed to the settlement may seek to intervene or simply voice their objections. The Fifth and Eleventh Circuits have held that while there is no absolute opt-out right, the trial court must be assured of the continuing homogeneity of interests between class representatives and passive class members at the settlement stage. See Cox v. American Cast Iron Pipe Co., 784 F.2d 1546 (11th Cir.1986); Holmes v. Continental Can Co., 706 F.2d 1144 (11th Cir.1983); Penson v. Terminal Transport Co., 634 F.2d 989 (5th Cir.1981). For data on employment class action settlements, see Samuel Estreicher & Kristina Yost, Measuring the Value of Employment Class Action Settlements: A Preliminary Assessment, 6 J. of Empirical Legal Studies 768 (Dec. 2009).

7. *"Opt-In" Collective Actions Under FLSA, EPA and ADEA.* Representative actions differ under ADEA and EPA. These statutes utilize the enforcement procedures of the FLSA, rather than Rule 23, and thus permit only "opt-in" collective actions; individuals can be bound only if they have opted in to the lawsuit. See 29 U.S.C. § 216(b). In Hoffman-La Roche, Inc. v. Sperling, 493 U.S. 165, 110 S.Ct. 482, 107 L.Ed.2d 480 (1989), the Court held that district courts may facilitate notice of ADEA representative actions to potential plaintiffs by allowing discovery of names and addresses of similarly situated employees, provided the appearance of judicial endorsement of the merits of the action is avoided.

FLSA-model collective actions may be brought only on behalf of employees who are "similarly situated" to the named plaintiffs. See 29 U.S.C. § 216(b). Some courts take the view that the "similarly situated" standard is "considerably less stringent than the requirement of Fed.R.Civ.P. 23(b)(3) that common questions 'predominate.'" In re Food Lion, Inc., 151 F.3d 1029 (4th Cir. 1998) (unpublished); Hoffmann v. Sbarro, Inc., 982 F.Supp. 249, 261 (S.D.N.Y.1997) ("plaintiffs can meet this burden by making a modest factual showing sufficient to demonstrate that they and potential plaintiffs together were victims of a common policy or plan").

A court has two opportunities to decide whether to permit the collective action to proceed. First, upon the plaintiffs' request to send a notice to the prospective class, it may "conditionally certify" a class using the fairly lenient approach to the "similarly situated" standard stated above. After discovery has been completed, the court may use a more demanding version of the "similarly situated" standard. See, e.g., Thiessen v. General Electric Capital Corp., 996 F.Supp. 1071, 1080 n. 13 (D.Kan.1998); Vaszlavik v. Storage Tech. Corp., 175 F.R.D. 672, 678–79 (D.Colo.1997).

WAL-MART STORES, INC. v. DUKES

Supreme Court of the United States, 2011.
564 U.S. 338, 131 S.Ct. 2541, 180 L.Ed.2d 374.

JUSTICE SCALIA delivered the opinion of the Court.

We are presented with one of the most expansive class actions ever. The District Court and the Court of Appeals approved the certification of a class comprising about one and a half million plaintiffs, current and former female employees of petitioner Wal-Mart who allege that the discretion exercised by their local supervisors over pay and promotion matters violates Title VII by discriminating against women. In addition to injunctive and declaratory relief, the plaintiffs seek an award of backpay. We consider whether the certification of the plaintiff class was consistent with Federal Rules of Civil Procedure 23(a) and (b)(2).

I

A

Petitioner Wal-Mart is the Nation's largest private employer. It operates four types of retail stores throughout the country: Discount Stores, Supercenters, Neighborhood Markets, and Sam's Clubs. Those stores are divided into seven nationwide divisions, which in turn comprise 41 regions of 80 to 85 stores apiece. Each store has between 40 and 53 separate departments and 80 to 500 staff positions. In all, Wal-Mart operates approximately 3,400 stores and employs more than one million people.

Pay and promotion decisions at Wal-Mart are generally committed to local managers' broad discretion, which is exercised "in a largely subjective manner." 222 F.R.D. 137, 145 (ND Cal. 2004). Local store managers may increase the wages of hourly employees (within limits) with only limited corporate oversight. As for salaried employees, such as store managers and their deputies, higher corporate authorities have discretion to set their pay within preestablished ranges.

Promotions work in a similar fashion. Wal-Mart permits store managers to apply their own subjective criteria when selecting candidates as "support managers," which is the first step on the path to management. Admission to Wal-Mart's management training program, however, does require that a candidate meet certain objective criteria, including an above-average performance rating, at least one year's tenure in the applicant's current position, and a willingness to relocate. But except for those requirements, regional and district managers have discretion to use their own judgment when selecting candidates for management training. Promotion to higher office—e.g., assistant manager, co-manager, or store manager—is similarly at the discretion of the employee's superiors after prescribed objective factors are satisfied.

B

The named plaintiffs in this lawsuit, representing the 1.5 million members of the certified class, are three current or former Wal-Mart employees who allege that the company discriminated against them on the basis of their sex by denying them equal pay or promotions, in violation of Title VII of the Civil Rights Act of 1964, 78 Stat. 253, as amended, 42 U.S.C. § 2000e–1 *et seq.*

Betty Dukes began working at a Pittsburgh, California, Wal-Mart in 1994. She started as a cashier, but later sought and received a promotion to customer service manager. After a series of disciplinary violations, however, Dukes was demoted back to cashier and then to greeter. Dukes concedes she violated company policy, but contends that the disciplinary actions were in fact retaliation for invoking internal complaint procedures and that male employees have not been disciplined for similar infractions. Dukes also claims two male greeters in the Pittsburgh store are paid more than she is.

Christine Kwapnoski has worked at Sam's Club stores in Missouri and California for most of her adult life. She has held a number of positions, including a supervisory position. She claims that a male manager yelled at her frequently and screamed at female employees, but not at men. The manager in question "told her to 'doll up,' to wear some makeup, and to dress a little better."

The final named plaintiff, Edith Arana, worked at a Wal-Mart store in Duarte, California, from 1995 to 2001. In 2000, she approached the store manager on more than one occasion about management training, but was brushed off. Arana concluded she was being denied opportunity for advancement because of her sex. She initiated internal complaint procedures, whereupon she was told to apply directly to the district manager if she thought her store manager was being unfair. Arana, however, decided against that and never applied for management training again. In 2001, she was fired for failure to comply with Wal-Mart's timekeeping policy.

These plaintiffs, respondents here, do not allege that Wal-Mart has any express corporate policy against the advancement of women. Rather, they claim that their local managers' discretion over pay and promotions is exercised disproportionately in favor of men, leading to an unlawful disparate impact on female employees, see 42 U.S.C. § 2000e–2(k). And, respondents say, because Wal-Mart is aware of this effect, its refusal to cabin its managers' authority amounts to disparate treatment, see § 2000e–2(a). Their complaint seeks injunctive and declaratory relief, punitive damages, and backpay. It does not ask for compensatory damages.

Importantly for our purposes, respondents claim that the discrimination to which they have been subjected is common to *all* Wal-

Mart's female employees. The basic theory of their case is that a strong and uniform "corporate culture" permits bias against women to infect, perhaps subconsciously, the discretionary decisionmaking of each one of Wal-Mart's thousands of managers—thereby making every woman at the company the victim of one common discriminatory practice. Respondents therefore wish to litigate the Title VII claims of all female employees at Wal-Mart's stores in a nationwide class action.

C

[R]espondents moved the District Court to certify a plaintiff class consisting of " '[a]ll women employed at any Wal-Mart domestic retail store at any time since December 26, 1998, who have been or may be subjected to Wal-Mart's challenged pay and management track promotions policies and practices.' " 222 F.R.D., at 141–142, As evidence that there were indeed "questions of law or fact common to" all the women of Wal-Mart, as Rule 23(a)(2) requires, respondents relied chiefly on three forms of proof: statistical evidence about pay and promotion disparities between men and women at the company, anecdotal reports of discrimination from about 120 of Wal-Mart's female employees, and the testimony of a sociologist, Dr. William Bielby, who conducted a "social framework analysis" of Wal-Mart's "culture" and personnel practices, and concluded that the company was "vulnerable" to gender discrimination. 603 F.3d 571, 601 (CA9 2010) (en banc).

Wal-Mart unsuccessfully moved to strike much of this evidence. It also offered its own countervailing statistical and other proof in an effort to defeat Rule 23(a)'s requirements of commonality, typicality, and adequate representation. Wal-Mart further contended that respondents' monetary claims for backpay could not be certified under Rule 23(b)(2), first because that Rule refers only to injunctive and declaratory relief, and second because the backpay claims could not be manageably tried as a class without depriving Wal-Mart of its right to present certain statutory defenses. With one limitation not relevant here, the District Court granted respondents' motion and certified their proposed class.

D

A divided en banc Court of Appeals substantially affirmed the District Court's certification order. 603 F.3d 571. The majority concluded that respondents' evidence of commonality was sufficient to "raise the common question whether Wal-Mart's female employees nationwide were subjected to a single set of corporate policies (not merely a number of independent discriminatory acts) that may have worked to unlawfully discriminate against them in violation of Title VII." *Id.*, at 612 (emphasis deleted). It also agreed with the District Court that the named plaintiffs' claims were sufficiently typical of the class as a whole to satisfy Rule 23(a)(3), and that they could serve as adequate class representatives, see Rule 23(a)(4). *Id.*, at 614–615. With respect to the Rule 23(b)(2) question, the Ninth Circuit held that respondents' backpay claims could be certified as part of a (b)(2) class because they did not "predominat[e]" over the requests for declaratory and injunctive relief, meaning they were not "superior in strength, influence, or authority" to the nonmonetary claims. *Id.*, at 616 (internal quotation marks omitted).[4]

Finally, the Court of Appeals determined that the action could be manageably tried as a class action because the District Court could adopt the approach the Ninth Circuit approved in *Hilao v. Estate of Marcos*, 103 F.3d 767, 782–787 (1996). There compensatory damages for some 9,541 class members were calculated by selecting 137 claims at random, referring those claims to a special master for valuation, and then extrapolating the validity and value of the untested claims from the sample set. See 603 F.3d at 625–626. The Court of Appeals "s[aw] no reason why a similar procedure to that used in *Hilao* could not be employed in this case." *Id.*, at 627. It would allow Wal-Mart "to present individual defenses in the randomly selected 'sample cases,' thus revealing the approximate percentage of class members whose unequal pay or nonpromotion was due to something other than gender discrimination." *Ibid.* at 628, n. 56 (emphasis deleted). * * *

II

* * * Rule 23(a) ensures that the named plaintiffs are appropriate representatives of the class whose claims they wish to litigate. The Rule's four requirements—numerosity, commonality, typicality, and adequate representation—"effectively 'limit the class claims to those fairly encompassed by the named plaintiff's claims.' " *General Telephone Co. of Southwest v. Falcon*, 457 U.S. 147, 156, 102 S. Ct. 2364, 72 L. Ed. 2d 740 (1982) (quoting *General Telephone Co. of Northwest v. EEOC*, 446 U.S. 318, 330, 100 S. Ct. 1698, 64 L. Ed. 2d 319 (1980)).

A

The crux of this case is commonality—the rule requiring a plaintiff to show that "there are questions of law or fact common to the class." Rule 23(a)(2). That language is easy to misread, since "[a]ny competently crafted class complaint literally raises common 'questions.' " Nagareda, Class Certification in the Age of Aggregate Proof, 84 N.Y.U. L. Rev. 97, 131–132 (2009). * * * Quite obviously, the mere claim by employees of the same company that they have suffered a Title VII injury, or even a disparate-impact Title VII injury, gives no cause to believe that all their claims can productively be litigated at once. Their claims must depend upon a common

---

4   To enable that result, the Court of Appeals trimmed the (b)(2) class in two ways: First, it remanded that part of the certification order which included respondents' punitive-damages claim in the (b)(2) class, so that the District Court might consider whether that might cause the monetary relief to predominate. 603 F.3d at 621. Second, it accepted in part Wal-Mart's argument that since class members whom it no longer employed had no standing to seek injunctive or declaratory relief, as to them monetary claims must predominate. It excluded from the certified class "those putative class members who were no longer Wal-Mart employees *at the time Plaintiffs' complaint was filed*," *id.*, at 623 (emphasis added).

contention—for example, the assertion of discriminatory bias on the part of the same supervisor. That common contention, moreover, must be of such a nature that it is capable of classwide resolution—which means that determination of its truth or falsity will resolve an issue that is central to the validity of each one of the claims in one stroke.

> "What matters to class certification . . . is not the raising of common 'questions'—even in droves—but, rather the capacity of a classwide proceeding to generate common *answers* apt to drive the resolution of the litigation. Dissimilarities within the proposed class are what have the potential to impede the generation of common answers." Nagareda, *supra*, at 132.

Rule 23 does not set forth a mere pleading standard. A party seeking class certification must affirmatively demonstrate his compliance with the Rule—that is, he must be prepared to prove that there are *in fact* sufficiently numerous parties, common questions of law or fact, etc. We recognized in *Falcon* that "sometimes it may be necessary for the court to probe behind the pleadings before coming to rest on the certification question," 457 U.S., at 160, 102 S. Ct. 2364, 72 L. Ed. 2d 740, and that certification is proper only if "the trial court is satisfied, after a rigorous analysis, that the prerequisites of Rule 23(a) have been satisfied," *id.*, at 161, 102 S. Ct. 2364, 72 L. Ed. 2d 740; see *id.*, at 160, 102 S. Ct. 2364, 72 L. Ed. 2d 740 ("[A]ctual, not presumed, conformance with Rule 23(a) remains . . . indispensable"). Frequently that "rigorous analysis" will entail some overlap with the merits of the plaintiff's underlying claim. That cannot be helped. " '[T]he class determination generally involves considerations that are enmeshed in the factual and legal issues comprising the plaintiff's cause of action.' " *Falcon*, *supra*, at 160, 102 S. Ct. 2364, 72 L. Ed. 2d 740 (quoting *Coopers & Lybrand v. Livesay*, 437 U.S. 463, 469, 98 S. Ct. 2454, 57 L. Ed. 2d 351 (1978); some internal quotation marks omitted).[6] Nor is there anything unusual about that consequence: The necessity of touching aspects of the merits in order to resolve preliminary matters, *e.g.*, jurisdiction and venue, is a familiar feature of litigation. See *Szabo v. Bridgeport Machines, Inc.*, 249 F.3d 672, 676–677 (CA7 2001) (Easterbrook, J.).

In this case, proof of commonality necessarily overlaps with respondents' merits contention that Wal-Mart engages in a *pattern or*

---

[6] A statement in one of our prior cases, *Eisen v. Carlisle & Jacquelin*, 417 U.S. 156, 177, 94 S. Ct. 2140, 40 L. Ed. 2d 732 (1974), is sometimes mistakenly cited to the contrary: "We find nothing in either the language or history of Rule 23 that gives a court any authority to conduct a preliminary inquiry into the merits of a suit in order to determine whether it may be maintained as a class action." But in that case, the judge had conducted a preliminary inquiry into the merits of a suit, not in order to determine the propriety of certification under Rules 23(a) and (b) (he had already done that, see *id.*, at 165, 94 S. Ct. 2140, 40 L. Ed. 2d 732), but in order to shift the cost of notice required by Rule 23(c)(2) from the plaintiff to the defendants. To the extent the quoted statement goes beyond the permissibility of a merits inquiry for any other pretrial purpose, it is the purest dictum and is contradicted by our other cases. * * *

practice of discrimination. That is so because, in resolving an individual's Title VII claim, the crux of the inquiry is "the reason for a particular employment decision," *Cooper v. Federal Reserve Bank of Richmond*, 467 U.S. 867, 876, 104 S. Ct. 2794, 81 L. Ed. 2d 718 (1984). Here respondents wish to sue about literally millions of employment decisions at once. Without some glue holding the alleged *reasons* for all those decisions together, it will be impossible to say that examination of all the class members' claims for relief will produce a common answer to the crucial question *why was I disfavored*.

B

This Court's opinion in *Falcon* describes how the commonality issue must be approached. There an employee who claimed that he was deliberately denied a promotion on account of race obtained certification of a class comprising all employees wrongfully denied promotions and all applicants wrongfully denied jobs. 457 U.S., at 152, 102 S. Ct. 2364, 72 L. Ed. 2d 740. We rejected that composite class for lack of commonality and typicality, explaining:

> "Conceptually, there is a wide gap between (a) an individual's claim that he has been denied a promotion [or higher pay] on discriminatory grounds, and his otherwise unsupported allegation that the company has a policy of discrimination, and (b) the existence of a class of persons who have suffered the same injury as that individual, such that the individual's claim and the class claim will share common questions of law or fact and that the individual's claim will be typical of the class claims." *Id.*, at 157–158, 102 S. Ct. 2364, 72 L. Ed. 2d 740.

Falcon suggested two ways in which that conceptual gap might be bridged. First, if the employer "used a biased testing procedure to evaluate both applicants for employment and incumbent employees, a class action on behalf of every applicant or employee who might have been prejudiced by the test clearly would satisfy the commonality and typicality requirements of Rule 23(a)." *Id.*, at 159, n. 15, 102 S. Ct. 2364, 72 L. Ed. 2d 740. Second, "[s]ignificant proof that an employer operated under a general policy of discrimination conceivably could justify a class of both applicants and employees if the discrimination manifested itself in hiring and promotion practices in the same general fashion, such as through entirely subjective decisionmaking processes." *Ibid.* We think that statement precisely describes respondents' burden in this case. The first manner of bridging the gap obviously has no application here; Wal-Mart has no testing procedure or other company-wide evaluation method that can be charged with bias. The whole point of permitting discretionary decisionmaking is to avoid evaluating employees under a common standard.

The second manner of bridging the gap requires "significant proof" that Wal-Mart "operated under a general policy of discrimination." That is entirely absent here. Wal-Mart's announced policy forbids sex discrimination, and as the District Court recognized the company imposes penalties for denials of equal employment opportunity, 222 F.R.D., at 154. The only evidence of a "general policy of discrimination" respondents produced was the testimony of Dr. William Bielby, their sociological expert. Relying on "social framework" analysis, Bielby testified that Wal-Mart has a "strong corporate culture," that makes it " 'vulnerable' " to "gender bias." Id., at 152. He could not, however, "determine with any specificity how regularly stereotypes play a meaningful role in employment decisions at Wal-Mart. At his deposition . . . Dr. Bielby conceded that he could not calculate whether 0.5 percent or 95 percent of the employment decisions at Wal-Mart might be determined by stereotyped thinking." 222 F.R.D. 189, 192 (ND Cal. 2004). The parties dispute whether Bielby's testimony even met the standards for the admission of expert testimony under Federal Rule of Evidence 702 and our *Daubert* case, see *Daubert v. Merrell Dow Pharmaceuticals, Inc.*, 509 U.S. 579, 113 S. Ct. 2786, 125 L. Ed. 2d 469 (1993). The District Court concluded that Daubert did not apply to expert testimony at the certification stage of class-action proceedings. 222 F.R.D., at 191. We doubt that is so, but even if properly considered, Bielby's testimony does nothing to advance respondents' case. "[W]hether 0.5 percent or 95 percent of the employment decisions at Wal-Mart might be determined by stereotyped thinking" is the essential question on which respondents' theory of commonality depends. If Bielby admittedly has no answer to that question, we can safely disregard what he has to say. It is worlds away from "significant proof" that Wal-Mart "operated under a general policy of discrimination."

C

The only corporate policy that the plaintiffs' evidence convincingly establishes is Wal-Mart's "policy" of *allowing discretion* by local supervisors over employment matters. On its face, of course, that is just the opposite of a uniform employment practice that would provide the commonality needed for a class action; it is a policy *against having* uniform employment practices. It is also a very common and presumptively reasonable way of doing business—one that we have said "should itself raise no inference of discriminatory conduct," *Watson v. Fort Worth Bank & Trust*, 487 U.S. 977, 990, 108 S. Ct. 2777, 101 L. Ed. 2d 827 (1988).

To be sure, we have recognized that, "in appropriate cases," giving discretion to lower-level supervisors can be the basis of Title VII liability under a disparate-impact theory—since "an employer's undisciplined system of subjective decisionmaking [can have] precisely the same effects as a system pervaded by impermissible intentional discrimination." *Id.*, at 990–991, 108 S. Ct. 2777, 101 L. Ed. 2d 827. But the recognition that this type of Title VII claim "can" exist does not lead to the conclusion that every employee in a company using a system of discretion has such a claim in common. To the contrary, left to their own devices most managers in any corporation—and surely most managers in a corporation that forbids sex discrimination—would select sex-neutral, performance-based criteria for hiring and promotion that produce no actionable disparity at all. Others may choose to reward various attributes that produce disparate impact—such as scores on general aptitude tests or educational achievements, see *Griggs v. Duke Power Co.*, 401 U.S. 424, 431–432, 91 S. Ct. 849, 28 L. Ed. 2d 158 (1971). And still other managers may be guilty of intentional discrimination that produces a sex-based disparity. In such a company, demonstrating the invalidity of one manager's use of discretion will do nothing to demonstrate the invalidity of another's. A party seeking to certify a nationwide class will be unable to show that all the employees' Title VII claims will in fact depend on the answers to common questions.

Respondents have not identified a common mode of exercising discretion that pervades the entire company—aside from their reliance on Dr. Bielby's social frameworks analysis that we have rejected. In a company of Wal-Mart's size and geographical scope, it is quite unbelievable that all managers would exercise their discretion in a common way without some common direction. Respondents attempt to make that showing by means of statistical and anecdotal evidence, but their evidence falls well short.

The statistical evidence consists primarily of regression analyses performed by Dr. Richard Drogin, a statistician, and Dr. Marc Bendick, a labor economist. Drogin conducted his analysis region-by-region, comparing the number of women promoted into management positions with the percentage of women in the available pool of hourly workers. After considering regional and national data, Drogin concluded that "there are statistically significant disparities between men and women at Wal-Mart . . . [and] these disparities . . . can be explained only by gender discrimination." 603 F.3d at 604 (internal quotation marks omitted). Bendick compared work-force data from Wal-Mart and competitive retailers and concluded that Wal-Mart "promotes a lower percentage of women than its competitors." *Ibid.*

Even if they are taken at face value, these studies are insufficient to establish that respondents' theory can be proved on a classwide basis. In *Falcon*, we held that one named plaintiff's experience of discrimination was insufficient to infer that "discriminatory treatment is typical of [the employer's employment] practices." 457 U.S., at 158, 102 S. Ct. 2364, 72 L. Ed. 2d 740. A similar failure of inference arises here. As Judge Ikuta observed in her dissent, "[i]nformation about disparities at the regional and national level does not establish the existence of disparities at individual stores, let alone raise the inference that a company-wide policy of discrimination is implemented by discretionary decisions at the store and district level." 603 F.3d at 637. A regional pay disparity, for example, may be attributable to only a small set of Wal-Mart stores, and cannot by itself establish the uniform, store-by-store disparity upon which the plaintiffs' theory of commonality depends.

There is another, more fundamental, respect in which respondents' statistical proof fails. Even if it established (as it does not) a pay or promotion pattern that differs from the nationwide figures or the regional figures in *all* of Wal-Mart's 3,400 stores, that would still not demonstrate that commonality of issue exists. Some managers will claim that the availability of women, or qualified women, or interested women, in their stores' area does not mirror the national or regional statistics. And almost all of them will claim to have been applying some sex-neutral, performance-based criteria—whose nature and effects will differ from store to store. In the landmark case of ours which held that giving discretion to lower-level supervisors can be the basis of Title VII liability under a disparate-impact theory, the plurality opinion *conditioned* that holding on the corollary that merely proving that the discretionary system has produced a racial or sexual disparity *is not enough*. "[T]he plaintiff must begin by identifying the specific employment practice that is challenged." *Watson*, 487 U.S., at 994, 108 S. Ct. 2777, 101 L. Ed. 2d 827; accord, *Wards Cove Packing Co. v. Atonio*, 490 U.S. 642, 656, 109 S. Ct. 2115, 104 L. Ed. 2d 733 (1989) (approving that statement), superseded by statute on other grounds, 42 U.S.C. § 2000e–2(k). That is all the more necessary when a class of plaintiffs is sought to be certified. Other than the bare existence of delegated discretion, respondents have identified no "specific employment practice"—much less one that ties all their 1.5 million claims together. Merely showing that Wal-Mart's policy of discretion has produced an overall sex-based disparity does not suffice.

* * *

In sum, we agree with Chief Judge Kozinski that the members of the class:

> "held a multitude of different jobs, at different levels of Wal-Mart's hierarchy, for variable lengths of time, in 3,400 stores, sprinkled across 50 states, with a kaleidoscope of supervisors (male and female), subject to a variety of regional policies that all differed. . . . Some thrived while others did poorly. They have little in common but their sex and this lawsuit." 603 F.3d at 652 (dissenting opinion).

III

We also conclude that respondents' claims for backpay were improperly certified under Federal Rule of Civil Procedure 23(b)(2). Our opinion in *Ticor Title Ins. Co. v. Brown*, 511 U.S. 117, 121, 114 S. Ct. 1359,

128 L. Ed. 2d 33 (1994) *(per curiam)* expressed serious doubt about whether claims for monetary relief may be certified under that provision. We now hold that they may not, at least where (as here) the monetary relief is not incidental to the injunctive or declaratory relief.

Rule 23(b)(2) allows class treatment when "the party opposing the class has acted or refused to act on grounds that apply generally to the class, so that final injunctive relief or corresponding declaratory relief is appropriate respecting the class as a whole." One possible reading of this provision is that it applies *only* to requests for such injunctive or declaratory relief and does not authorize the class certification of monetary claims at all. We need not reach that broader question in this case, because we think that, at a minimum, claims for *individualized* relief (like the backpay at issue here) do not satisfy the Rule. The key to the (b)(2) class is "the indivisible nature of the injunctive or declaratory remedy warranted—the notion that the conduct is such that it can be enjoined or declared unlawful only as to all of the class members or as to none of them." Nagareda, 84 N. Y. U. L. Rev., at 132. In other words, Rule 23(b)(2) applies only when a single injunction or declaratory judgment would provide relief to each member of the class. It does not authorize class certification when each individual class member would be entitled to a *different* injunction or declaratory judgment against the defendant. Similarly, it does not authorize class certification when each class member would be entitled to an individualized award of monetary damages.

* * *

[W]e think it clear that individualized monetary claims belong in Rule 23(b)(3). The procedural protections attending the (b)(3) class—predominance, superiority, mandatory notice, and the right to opt out—are missing from (b)(2) not because the Rule considers them unnecessary, but because it considers them unnecessary *to a (b)(2) class*. When a class seeks an indivisible injunction benefitting all its members at once, there is no reason to undertake a case-specific inquiry into whether class issues predominate or whether class action is a superior method of adjudicating the dispute. Predominance and superiority are self-evident. But with respect to each class member's individualized claim for money, that is not so—which is precisely why (b)(3) requires the judge to make findings about predominance and superiority before allowing the class. Similarly, (b)(2) does not require that class members be given notice and opt-out rights, presumably because it is thought (rightly or wrongly) that notice has no purpose when the class is mandatory, and that depriving people of their right to sue in this manner complies with the Due Process Clause. In the context of a class action predominantly for money damages we have held that absence of notice and opt-out violates due process. See *Phillips Petroleum Co. v. Shutts*, 472 U.S. 797, 812, 105 S. Ct. 2965, 86 L. Ed. 2d 628 (1985). While we have never held that to be so where the monetary claims do not predominate, the serious possibility that it may be so provides an additional reason not to read Rule 23(b)(2) to include the monetary claims here.

Contrary to the Ninth Circuit's view, Wal-Mart is entitled to individualized determinations of each employee's eligibility for backpay. Title VII includes a detailed remedial scheme. If a plaintiff prevails in showing that an employer has discriminated against him in violation of the statute, the court "may enjoin the respondent from engaging in such unlawful employment practice, and order such affirmative action as may be appropriate, [including] reinstatement or hiring of employees, with or without backpay . . . or any other equitable relief as the court deems appropriate." § 2000e–5(g)(1). But if the employer can show that it took an adverse employment action against an employee for any reason other than discrimination, the court cannot order the "hiring, reinstatement, or promotion of an individual as an employee, or the payment to him of any backpay." § 2000e–5(g)(2)(A).

We have established a procedure for trying pattern-or-practice cases that gives effect to these statutory requirements. When the plaintiff seeks individual relief such as reinstatement or backpay after establishing a pattern or practice of discrimination, "a district court must usually conduct additional proceedings . . . to determine the scope of individual relief." *Teamsters*, 431 U.S., at 361, 97 S. Ct. 1843, 52 L. Ed. 2d 396. At this phase, the burden of proof will shift to the company, but it will have the right to raise any individual affirmative defenses it may have, and to "demonstrate that the individual applicant was denied an employment opportunity for lawful reasons." *Id.*, at 362, 97 S. Ct. 1843, 52 L. Ed. 2d 396.

The Court of Appeals believed that it was possible to replace such proceedings with Trial by Formula. A sample set of the class members would be selected, as to whom liability for sex discrimination and the backpay owing as a result would be determined in depositions supervised by a master. The percentage of claims determined to be valid would then be applied to the entire remaining class, and the number of (presumptively) valid claims thus derived would be multiplied by the average backpay award in the sample set to arrive at the entire class recovery—without further individualized proceedings. 603 F.3d at 625–627. We disapprove that novel project. Because the Rules Enabling Act forbids interpreting Rule 23 to "abridge, enlarge or modify any substantive right," 28 U.S.C. § 2072(b); . . . a class cannot be certified on the premise that Wal-Mart will not be entitled to litigate its statutory defenses to individual claims. And because the necessity of that litigation will prevent backpay from being "incidental" to the classwide injunction, respondents' class could not be certified even assuming, *arguendo*, that "incidental" monetary relief can be awarded to a 23(b)(2) class.

* * *

JUSTICE GINSBURG, with whom JUSTICE BREYER, JUSTICE SOTOMAYOR, and JUSTICE KAGAN join, concurring in part and dissenting in part.

* * *

Whether the class the plaintiffs describe meets the specific requirements of Rule 23(b)(3) is not before the Court, and I would reserve that matter for consideration and decision on remand. The Court, however, disqualifies the class at the starting gate, holding that the plaintiffs cannot cross the "commonality" line set by Rule 23(a)(2). In so ruling, the Court imports into the Rule 23(a) determination concerns properly addressed in a Rule 23(b)(3) assessment.

NOTES AND QUESTIONS

Test Your Understanding of the Material

1. What was deficient in plaintiffs' proof regarding whether Wal-Mart "operated under a general policy of discrimination"? To what extent should a trial court evaluate the merits of the claim in deciding class certification?

2. What was the nature of the plaintiffs' expert testimony, what role did it play in the plaintiffs' "commonality" showing, and what was the Court's criticism of the testimony?

3. What is the significance of the Court's unanimous holding that claims for individual backpay relief had to be brought, if it all, as a Federal Rule 23(b)(3) rather than (b)(2) class actions? Will this significantly hamper plaintiff class actions? If so, why? Could actions be brought under (b)(2) for injunctive relief only?

4. If you represented the plaintiffs, how would you replead or restructure the case to satisfy the Court's strictures on the "commonality" requirement of Rule 23(a)?

Related Issues

5. *Continued Viability of Cases Challenging Subjective Employment Practices? Dukes v. Wal-Mart* is technically a Rule 23 case. However, the commonality standard articulated in *Wal-Mart* may present particular difficulty for plaintiffs challenging subjective employment practices; the effect of subjective practices can vary widely across worksites and individual managers. See Elizabeth Tippett, Robbing a Barren Vault: The Implications of Dukes v. Wal-Mart for Cases Challenging Subjective Employment Practices, 29 Hofstra Lab. & Emp. L.J. 433 (2012).

Nevertheless, plaintiffs have been successful in meeting *Wal-Mart's* commonality standard in certain disparage impact challenges. See Brown v. Nucor, 785 F.3d 895 (4th Cir. 2015) (vacating decertification of disparate impact claim based on single employment site); McReynolds v. Merrill Lynch, Pierce, Fenner & Smith, Inc., 672 F.3d 482 (7th Cir. 2012) (reversing denial of class certification for issues-only disparate impact challenge to team-based compensation practices, which may have the effect of excluding minority brokers); Ellis v. Costco Wholesale Corp. 285 F.R.D. 492 (N.D.Cal. 2012) (applying *Wal-Mart* on remand from 657 F.3d 970 (9th Cir. 2011) (granting certification in challenge to subjective promotion practices where plaintiff identified a "pervasive company culture that, along with common policies and practices, guide" promotion decisions, and showed classwide effects across all regions). See generally Michael C. Harper, Class-Based Adjudication of Title VII Claims in the Age of the Roberts Court, 95 B.U. L. Rev. 1099, 1111–1113 (2015).

6. *Managing a Large (b)(3) Class.* Note that the "predominance" and "superiority" requirements for certification of a (b)(3) class are to include consideration of "the likely difficulties in managing a class action." This "manageability" consideration may be particularly important in putative class actions where the individualized legal relief sought would require a jury to determine a variant level of damages for each class member. Consider the *Wal-Mart* Court's rejection, as a "Trial by Formula", of the use of a "sample set of the class members" to determine the aggregate level of damages. Does this rejection pose a high barrier to the certification of many large (b)(3) employment discrimination classes seeking variant individualized legal damages before a jury? Some courts have addressed manageability concerns by invoking Rule 23(c)(4), which permits a court to issue certification for "a class action with respect to particular issues." For instance, in *McReynolds v. Merrill Lynch*, supra, the Seventh Circuit ruled that certification should have been granted on the issue of whether the company's team-based compensation practices violated Title VII. See also *Harper*, supra, at 1115–1122.

In Tyson Foods, Inc. v. Bouaphakeo, 136 S. Ct. 2036 (2016), a case involving claims for unpaid overtime, the Court limited the implications of its "Trial by Formula" language in *Wal-Mart*. The Court in *Tyson Foods* held that representative or statistical evidence—such as the average time needed for compensable donning and doffing in that case—that could be used to establish liability in an individual action also can be used to establish liability for all class members in a collective or class action.

7. *Collective Claims Unaffected by* Wal-Mart. *Wal-Mart* does not directly affect group claims that are not based on Rule 23 of the FRCP. Following the FLSA enforcement model, claims brought under the FLSA, EPA and ADEA are brought as collective actions, rather than class actions. See supra note 7 at p. 967. Moreover, state-law discrimination class action claims brought in state court are not directly controlled by the Court's interpretation of Rule 23.

NOTE ON EEOC LITIGATION

The 1972 amendments to Title VII transformed the EEOC from a predominantly investigative and conciliation body to an agency with substantial independent litigation authority. Responsibility for "pattern or practice" litigation under § 707, see, e.g., International Broth. of Teamsters v. United States, 431 U.S. 324, 97 S.Ct. 1843, 1865, 52 L.Ed.2d 396 (1977), was transferred from the Justice Department to the Commission. In addition, the

EEOC was expressly given the authority to sue on behalf of charging parties under § 706(f)(1). EEOC § 706 actions can be brought on behalf of both individuals and groups.

The Supreme Court has held that an EEOC action seeking classwide relief is in the nature of a public action not governed by Rule 23 of the Federal Rules of Civil Procedure, and hence findings rejecting liability will not have binding effects on individual employees. See General Telephone Co. v. EEOC, 446 U.S. 318, 100 S.Ct. 1698, 64 L.Ed.2d 319 (1980). The Court also has ruled that the EEOC may seek both prospective and victim-specific relief on behalf of individual employees who have entered into otherwise valid arbitration agreements that would require arbitration of their individual claims were they to bring suit on their own. See EEOC v. Waffle House, Inc., 534 U.S. 279, 122 S.Ct. 754, 151 L.Ed.2d 755 (2002). Moreover, the lower courts have held that settlements with individual charging parties do not moot the EEOC's right of action to seek injunctive relief. See, e.g., EEOC v. United Parcel Service, 860 F.2d 372 (10th Cir.1988); EEOC v. Goodyear Aerospace Corp., 813 F.2d 1539 (9th Cir.1987).

Under § 706(b), members of the Commission may file charges that form the basis of an EEOC suit under § 706(f)(1) or § 707. In EEOC v. Shell Oil Co., 466 U.S. 54, 104 S.Ct. 1621, 80 L.Ed.2d 41 (1984), the Court sustained an EEOC subpoena issued in connection with a Commissioner's "pattern or practice" charge that did not identify victims of discrimination or the precise manner in which they were injured. The Court did require that—

> Insofar as he is able, the Commissioner should identify the groups of persons that he has reason to believe have been discriminated against, the categories of employment positions from which they have been excluded, the methods by which the discrimination may have been effected, and the periods of time in which he suspects the discriminations to have been practiced.

Id. at 73, 104 S.Ct. at 1633.

Under § 706(f)(1), an EEOC suit against a respondent named in a charge cuts off the charging party's right to bring an action, but the charging party has a statutory right to intervene. Similarly, an EEOC suit on behalf of a charging party under § 7(c)(1) of ADEA "terminates" the charging party's right of action. See also EEOC v. United States Steel Corp., 921 F.2d 489 (3d Cir.1990) (discussion of doctrine of "representative claim preclusion"). Can the EEOC file an independent ADEA action on behalf of an individual who has already brought suit? See EEOC v. Wackenhut Corp., 939 F.2d 241 (5th Cir.1991).

EEOC subpoena authority can also help private charging parties obtain far-reaching discovery of firm practices. See EEOC v. Morgan Stanley & Co., Inc., 1999 WL 756206, Civ. Action M 18–304 (DLC) (S.D.N.Y.1999).

E. PRIVATE GRIEVANCE ARBITRATION AND FEDERAL STATUTORY CLAIMS

GILMER V. INTERSTATE/JOHNSON LANE CORP.

Supreme Court of the United States, 1991.
500 U.S. 20, 111 S.Ct. 1647, 114 L.Ed.2d 26.

JUSTICE WHITE delivered the opinion of the Court.

Respondent Interstate/Johnson Lane Corporation (Interstate) hired petitioner Robert Gilmer as a Manager of Financial Services in May 1981. As required by his employment, Gilmer registered as a securities representative with several stock exchanges, including the New York Stock Exchange (NYSE). His registration application, entitled "Uniform Application for Securities Industry Registration or Transfer," provided, among other things, that Gilmer "agreed to arbitrate any dispute, claim or controversy" arising between him and Interstate "that is required to be arbitrated under the rules, constitutions or by-laws of the organizations with which I register." Of relevance to this case, NYSE Rule 347 provides for arbitration of "any controversy between a registered representative and any member or member organization arising out of the employment or termination of employment of such registered representative."

* * *

Interstate terminated Gilmer's employment in 1987, at which time Gilmer was 62 years of age. After first filing an age discrimination charge with the Equal Employment Opportunity Commission (EEOC), Gilmer subsequently brought suit in the United States District Court for the Western District of North Carolina, alleging that Interstate had discharged him because of his age, in violation of the ADEA. In response to Gilmer's complaint, Interstate filed in the District Court a motion to compel arbitration of the ADEA claim. In its motion, Interstate relied upon the arbitration agreement in Gilmer's registration application, as well as the Federal Arbitration Act (FAA), 9 U.S.C. § 1 *et seq.* The District Court denied Interstate's motion, based on this Court's decision in *Alexander v. Gardner-Denver Co.,* 415 U.S. 36, 94 S.Ct. 1011, 39 L.Ed.2d 147 (1974), and because it concluded that "Congress intended to protect ADEA claimants from the waiver of a judicial forum." The United States Court of Appeals for the Fourth Circuit reversed.

* * *

The FAA was originally enacted in 1925, 43 Stat. 883, and then reenacted and codified in 1947 as Title 9 of the United States Code. Its purpose was to reverse the longstanding judicial hostility to arbitration agreements that had existed at English common law and had been adopted by American courts, and to place arbitration agreements upon the same footing as other contracts. *Dean Witter Reynolds, Inc. v. Byrd,* 470 U.S. 213, 219–220, and n. 6, 105 S.Ct. 1238, 1241–1242, and n. 6, 84 L.Ed.2d 158 (1985); *Scherk v. Alberto-Culver Co.,* 417 U.S. 506, 510, n. 4, 94 S.Ct. 2449, 2453, n. 4, 41 L.Ed.2d 270 (1974). Its primary substantive provision states that "[a] written provision in any maritime transaction or a contract evidencing a transaction involving commerce to settle by arbitration a controversy thereafter arising out of such contract or transaction * * * shall be valid, irrevocable, and enforceable, save upon such grounds as exist at law or in equity for the revocation of any contract." 9 U.S.C. § 2. The FAA also provides for stays of proceedings in federal district courts when an issue in the proceeding is referable to arbitration, § 3, and for orders compelling arbitration when one party has failed, neglected, or refused to comply with an arbitration agreement, § 4. These provisions manifest a "liberal federal policy favoring arbitration agreements." *Moses H. Cone Memorial Hospital v. Mercury Construction Corp.,* 460 U.S. 1, 24, 103 S.Ct. 927, 941, 74 L.Ed.2d 765 (1983).[2]

It is by now clear that statutory claims may be the subject of an arbitration agreement, enforceable pursuant to the FAA. Indeed, in recent years we have held enforceable arbitration agreements relating to claims arising under the Sherman Act, 15 U.S.C. §§ 1–7; §§ 10(b) of the Securities Exchange Act of 1934, 15 U.S.C. § 78j(b); the civil provisions of the Racketeer Influenced and Corrupt Organizations Act (RICO), 18 U.S.C. § 1961 *et seq.;* and § 12(2) of the Securities Act of 1933, 15 U.S.C. § 77l(2). See *Mitsubishi Motors Corp. v. Soler Chrysler-Plymouth, Inc.,* 473 U.S. 614, 105 S.Ct. 3346, 87 L.Ed.2d 444 (1985); *Shearson/American Express Inc. v. McMahon,* 482 U.S. 220, 107 S.Ct. 2332, 96 L.Ed.2d 185 (1987); *Rodriguez de Quijas v. Shearson/American Express, Inc.,* 490 U.S. 477, 109 S.Ct. 1917, 104 L.Ed.2d 526 (1989). In these cases we recognized that "by agreeing to arbitrate a statutory claim, a party does not forgo the substantive rights afforded by the statute; it only submits to their resolution in an arbitral, rather than a judicial, forum." *Mitsubishi, supra,* at 628, 105 S.Ct., at 3354.

Although all statutory claims may not be appropriate for arbitration, "having made the bargain to arbitrate, the party should be held to it unless Congress itself has evinced an intention to preclude a waiver of judicial

---

[2] Section 1 of the FAA provides that "nothing herein contained shall apply to contracts of employment of seamen, railroad employees, or any other class of workers engaged in foreign or interstate commerce." 9 U.S.C. Sec. 1. Several *amici curiae* in support of Gilmer argue that that section excludes from the coverage of the FAA all "contracts of employment." Gilmer, however, did not raise the issue in the courts below, it was not addressed there, and it was not among the questions presented in the petition for certiorari. In any event, it would be inappropriate to address the scope of the Sec. 1 exclusion because the arbitration clause being enforced here is not contained in a contract of employment. The FAA requires that the arbitration clause being enforced be in writing. See 9 U.S.C. Secs. 2, 3. The record before us does not show, and the parties do not contend, that Gilmer's employment agreement with Interstate contained a written arbitration clause. Rather, the arbitration clause at issue is in Gilmer's securities registration application, which is a contract with the securities exchanges, not with Interstate. * * * Consequently, we leave for another day the issue raised by *amici curiae.*

remedies for the statutory rights at issue." *Ibid.* In this regard, we note that the burden is on Gilmer to show that Congress intended to preclude a waiver of a judicial forum for ADEA claims. See *McMahon,* 482 U.S., at 227, 107 S.Ct., at 2337–2338. If such an intention exists, it will be discoverable in the text of the ADEA, its legislative history, or an "inherent conflict" between arbitration and the ADEA's underlying purposes. See *ibid.* Throughout such an inquiry, it should be kept in mind that "questions of arbitrability must be addressed with a healthy regard for the federal policy favoring arbitration." *Moses H. Cone,* 460 U.S., at 24, 103 S.Ct., at 941.

* * *

As Gilmer contends, the ADEA is designed not only to address individual grievances, but also to further important social policies. See, e.g., *EEOC v. Wyoming,* 460 U.S. 226, 231, 103 S.Ct. 1054, 1057–1058, 75 L.Ed.2d 18 (1983). We do not perceive any inherent inconsistency between those policies, however, and enforcing agreements to arbitrate age discrimination claims. It is true that arbitration focuses on specific disputes between the parties involved. The same can be said, however, of judicial resolution of claims. Both of these dispute resolution mechanisms nevertheless also can further broader social purposes. The Sherman Act, the Securities Exchange Act of 1934, RICO, and the Securities Act of 1933 all are designed to advance important public policies, but, as noted above, claims under those statutes are appropriate for arbitration. "So long as the prospective litigant effectively may vindicate [his or her] statutory cause of action in the arbitral forum, the statute will continue to serve both its remedial and deterrent function." *Mitsubishi, supra,* at 637, 105 S.Ct., at 3359.

We also are unpersuaded by the argument that arbitration will undermine the role of the EEOC in enforcing the ADEA. An individual ADEA claimant subject to an arbitration agreement will still be free to file a charge with the EEOC, even though the claimant is not able to institute a private judicial action. Indeed, Gilmer filed a charge with the EEOC in this case. In any event, the EEOC's role in combating age discrimination is not dependent on the filing of a charge; the agency may receive information concerning alleged violations of the ADEA "from any source," and it has independent authority to investigate age discrimination. See 29 CFR §§ 1626.4, 1626.13 (1990). Moreover, nothing in the ADEA indicates that Congress intended that the EEOC be involved in all employment disputes. Such disputes can be settled, for example, without any EEOC involvement. See, e.g., *Coventry v. United States Steel Corp.,* 856 F.2d 514, 522 (C.A.3 1988); *Moore v. McGraw Edison Co.,* 804 F.2d 1026, 1033 (C.A.8 1986);

Runyan v. National Cash Register Corp., 787 F.2d 1039, 1045 (CA6), cert. denied, 479 U.S. 850, 107 S.Ct. 178, 93 L.Ed.2d 114 (1986).[3] * * *

Gilmer also argues that compulsory arbitration is improper because it deprives claimants of the judicial forum provided for by the ADEA. Congress, however, did not explicitly preclude arbitration or other nonjudicial resolution of claims, even in its recent amendments to the ADEA. * * * Moreover, Gilmer's argument ignores the ADEA's flexible approach to resolution of claims. The EEOC, for example, is directed to pursue "informal methods of conciliation, conference, and persuasion," 29 U.S.C. § 626(b), which suggests that out-of-court dispute resolution, such as arbitration, is consistent with the statutory scheme established by Congress. In addition, arbitration is consistent with Congress' grant of concurrent jurisdiction over ADEA claims to state and federal courts, see 29 U.S.C. § 626(c)(1) (allowing suits to be brought "in any court of competent jurisdiction"), because arbitration agreements, "like the provision for concurrent jurisdiction, serve to advance the objective of allowing [claimants] a broader right to select the forum for resolving disputes, whether it be judicial or otherwise." *Rodriguez de Quijas,* 490 U.S., at 483, 109 S.Ct., at 1921.

* * *

In arguing that arbitration is inconsistent with the ADEA, Gilmer also raises a host of challenges to the adequacy of arbitration procedures. * * *

Gilmer first speculates that arbitration panels will be biased. However, "we decline to indulge the presumption that the parties and arbitral body conducting a proceeding will be unable or unwilling to retain competent, conscientious and impartial arbitrators." *Mitsubishi, supra,* at 634. In any event, we note that the NYSE arbitration rules, which are applicable to the dispute in this case, provide protections against biased panels. The rules require, for example, that the parties be informed of the employment histories of the arbitrators, and that they be allowed to make further inquiries into the arbitrators' backgrounds. In addition, each party is allowed one peremptory challenge and unlimited challenges for cause. Moreover, the arbitrators are required to disclose "any circumstances which might preclude [them] from rendering an objective and impartial determination." The FAA also protects against bias, by providing that courts may overturn arbitration decisions "where there was evident partiality or corruption in the arbitrators." 9 U.S.C. § 10(b). There has been no showing in this case that those provisions are inadequate to guard against potential bias.

---

[3]   In the recently enacted Older Workers Benefit Protection Act, Pub.L. 101–433, 104 Stat. 978, Congress amended the ADEA to provide that "an individual may not waive any right or claim under this Act unless the waiver is knowing and voluntary." See Sec. 201. Congress also specified certain conditions that must be met in order for a waiver to be knowing and voluntary. *Ibid.*

Gilmer also complains that the discovery allowed in arbitration is more limited than in the federal courts, which he contends will make it difficult to prove discrimination. It is unlikely, however, that age discrimination claims require more extensive discovery than other claims that we have found to be arbitrable, such as RICO and antitrust claims. Moreover, there has been no showing in this case that the NYSE discovery provisions, which allow for document production, information requests, depositions, and subpoenas, will prove insufficient to allow ADEA claimants such as Gilmer a fair opportunity to present their claims. Although those procedures might not be as extensive as in the federal courts, by agreeing to arbitrate, a party "trades the procedures and opportunity for review of the courtroom for the simplicity, informality, and expedition of arbitration." *Mitsubishi, supra,* at 628, 105 S.Ct., at 3354. Indeed, an important counterweight to the reduced discovery in NYSE arbitration is that arbitrators are not bound by the rules of evidence.

A further alleged deficiency of arbitration is that arbitrators often will not issue written opinions, resulting, Gilmer contends, in a lack of public knowledge of employers' discriminatory policies, an inability to obtain effective appellate review, and a stifling of the development of the law. The NYSE rules, however, do require that all arbitration awards be in writing, and that the awards contain the names of the parties, a summary of the issues in controversy, and a description of the award issued. In addition, the award decisions are made available to the public. Furthermore, judicial decisions addressing ADEA claims will continue to be issued because it is unlikely that all or even most ADEA claimants will be subject to arbitration agreements. Finally, Gilmer's concerns apply equally to settlements of ADEA claims, which, as noted above, are clearly allowed.[4]

It is also argued that arbitration procedures cannot adequately further the purposes of the ADEA because they do not provide for broad equitable relief and class actions. As the court below noted, however, arbitrators do have the power to fashion equitable relief. Indeed, the NYSE rules applicable here do not restrict the types of relief an arbitrator may award, but merely refer to "damages and/or other relief." The NYSE rules also provide for collective proceedings. * * * Finally, it should be remembered that arbitration agreements will not preclude the EEOC from bringing actions seeking class-wide and equitable relief.

* * *

An additional reason advanced by Gilmer for refusing to enforce arbitration agreements relating to ADEA claims is his contention that

---

[4]   Gilmer also contends that judicial review of arbitration decisions is too limited. We have stated, however, that "although judicial scrutiny of arbitration awards necessarily is limited, such review is sufficient to ensure that arbitrators comply with the requirements of the statute" at issue. *Shearson American Express Inc. v. McMahon,* 482 U.S. 220, 232, 107 S.Ct. 2332, 2340, 96 L.Ed.2d 185 (1987).

there often will be unequal bargaining power between employers and employees. Mere inequality in bargaining power, however, is not a sufficient reason to hold that arbitration agreements are never enforceable in the employment context. Relationships between securities dealers and investors, for example, may involve unequal bargaining power, but we nevertheless held in *Rodriguez de Quijas* and *McMahon* that agreements to arbitrate in that context are enforceable. See 490 U.S., at 484, 109 S.Ct., at 1921–1922; 482 U.S., at 230, 107 S.Ct., at 2339–2340. As discussed above, the FAA's purpose was to place arbitration agreements on the same footing as other contracts. Thus, arbitration agreements are enforceable "save upon such grounds as exist at law or in equity for the revocation of any contract." 9 U.S.C. § 2. "Of course, courts should remain attuned to well-supported claims that the agreement to arbitrate resulted from the sort of fraud or overwhelming economic power that would provide grounds 'for the revocation of any contract.' " *Mitsubishi*, 473 U.S., at 627, 105 S.Ct., at 3354. There is no indication in this case, however, that Gilmer, an experienced businessman, was coerced or defrauded into agreeing to the arbitration clause in his registration application. As with the claimed procedural inadequacies discussed above, this claim of unequal bargaining power is best left for resolution in specific cases.

* * *

In addition to the arguments discussed above, Gilmer vigorously asserts that our decision in *Alexander v. Gardner-Denver Co.,* 415 U.S. 36, 94 S.Ct. 1011, 39 L.Ed.2d 147 (1974), and its progeny—*Barrentine v. Arkansas-Best Freight System, Inc.,* 450 U.S. 728, 101 S.Ct. 1437, 67 L.Ed.2d 641 (1981), and *McDonald v. City of West Branch,* 466 U.S. 284, 104 S.Ct. 1799, 80 L.Ed.2d 302 (1984)—preclude arbitration of employment discrimination claims. Gilmer's reliance on these cases, however, is misplaced.

* * *

There are several important distinctions between the *Gardner-Denver* line of cases and the case before us. First, those cases did not involve the issue of the enforceability of an agreement to arbitrate statutory claims. Rather, they involved the quite different issue whether arbitration of contract-based claims precluded subsequent judicial resolution of statutory claims. Since the employees there had not agreed to arbitrate their statutory claims, and the labor arbitrators were not authorized to resolve such claims, the arbitration in those cases understandably was held not to preclude subsequent statutory actions. Second, because the arbitration in those cases occurred in the context of a collective-bargaining agreement, the claimants there were represented by their unions in the arbitration proceedings. An important concern therefore was the tension between collective representation and individual statutory rights, a concern not applicable to the present case. Finally, those cases were not decided under the FAA, which, as discussed above, reflects a "liberal federal policy favoring arbitration agreements." *Mitsubishi,* 473 U.S., at 625, 105 S.Ct., at 3353. Therefore, those cases provide no basis for refusing to enforce Gilmer's agreement to arbitrate his ADEA claim.

JUSTICE STEVENS, with whom JUSTICE MARSHALL joins, dissenting.

Section 1 of the Federal Arbitration Act (FAA) states:

> "[N]othing herein contained shall apply to contracts of employment of seamen, railroad employees, or any other class of workers engaged in foreign or interstate commerce." 9 U.S.C. § 1.

The Court today, in holding that the FAA compels enforcement of arbitration clauses even when claims of age discrimination are at issue, skirts the antecedent question of whether the coverage of the Act even extends to arbitration clauses contained in employment contracts, regardless of the subject matter of the claim at issue.

* * *

There is little dispute that the primary concern animating the FAA was the perceived need by the business community to overturn the common-law rule that denied specific enforcement of agreements to arbitrate in contracts between business entities. The Act was drafted by a committee of the American Bar Association (ABA), acting upon instructions from the ABA to consider and report upon "the further extension of the principle of commercial arbitration." Report of the Forty-third Annual Meeting of the ABA, 45 A.B.A.Rep. 75 (1920). At the Senate Judiciary Subcommittee hearings on the proposed bill, the chairman of the ABA committee responsible for drafting the bill assured the Senators that the bill "is not intended [to] be an act referring to labor disputes, at all. It is purely an act to give the merchants the right or the privilege of sitting down and agreeing with each other as to what their damages are, if they want to do it. Now that is all there is in this." Hearing on S. 4213 and S. 4214 before a Subcommittee of the Senate Committee on the Judiciary, 67th Cong., 4th Sess., 9 (1923). At the same hearing, Senator Walsh stated:

> "The trouble about the matter is that a great many of these contracts that are entered into are really not [voluntary] things at all. Take an insurance policy; there is a blank in it. You can take that or you can leave it. The agent has no power at all to decide it. Either you can make that contract or you can not make any contract. It is the same with a good many contracts of employment. A man says, 'These are our terms. All right, take it or leave it.' Well, there is nothing for the man to do except to sign it; and then he surrenders his right to have his case tried by the court, and has to have it tried before a tribunal in which he has no confidence at all." *Ibid.*

Given that the FAA specifically was intended to exclude arbitration agreements between employees and employers, I see no reason to limit this exclusion from coverage to arbitration clauses contained in agreements entitled "Contract of Employment." In this case, the parties conceded at oral argument that Gilmer had no "contract of employment" as such with respondent. Gilmer was, however, required as a condition of his employment to become a registered representative of several stock exchanges, including the New York Stock Exchange (NYSE).

* * *

Not only would I find that the FAA does not apply to employment-related disputes between employers and employees in general, but also I would hold that compulsory arbitration conflicts with the congressional purpose animating the ADEA, in particular. As this Court previously has noted, authorizing the courts to issue broad injunctive relief is the cornerstone to eliminating discrimination in society. *Albemarle Paper Co. v. Moody,* 422 U.S. 405, 415, 95 S.Ct. 2362, 2370, 45 L.Ed.2d 280 (1975). The ADEA, like Title VII, authorizes courts to award broad, class-based injunctive relief to achieve the purposes of the Act. 29 U.S.C. § 626(b). Because commercial arbitration is typically limited to a specific dispute between the particular parties and because the available remedies in arbitral forums generally do not provide for class-wide injunctive relief, see Shell, ERISA and Other Federal Employment Statutes: When is Commercial Arbitration an "Adequate Substitute" for the Courts?, 68 Texas L.Rev. 509, 568 (1990), I would conclude that an essential purpose of the ADEA is frustrated by compulsory arbitration of employment discrimination claims. * * * The Court's holding today clearly eviscerates the important role played by an independent judiciary in eradicating employment discrimination.

When the FAA was passed in 1925, I doubt that any legislator who voted for it expected it to apply to statutory claims, to form contracts between parties of unequal bargaining power, or to the arbitration of disputes arising out of the employment relationship. In recent years, however, the Court "has effectively rewritten the statute", and abandoned its earlier view that statutory claims were not appropriate subjects for arbitration.

NOTES AND QUESTIONS

Gilmer's Case After the Supreme Court Decision

Gilmer ultimately pursued his case in arbitration and was awarded $250,000 by the arbitrator. His lawyer reported that he "did not work again because he was 'devastated' by his termination from Interstate." See Samuel Estreicher, The Story of Gilmer v. Interstate/Johnson Lane Corp.: The Emergence of Employment Arbitration, in Employment Law Stories, ch. 7 (Samuel Estreicher & Gillian Lester eds. 2007).

Test Your Understanding of the Material

1. What are the grounds for the Court's statement that "the burden is on Gilmer to show that Congress intended to preclude a waiver of a judicial forum for ADEA claims"? The lower courts have agreed that arbitration agreements are enforceable with respect to Title VII, see, e.g., EEOC v. Luce, Forward, Hamilton & Scripps, 345 F.3d 742 (9th Cir. 2003), and FLSA claims, see, e.g., Sutherland v. Ernst & Young LLP, 726 F.3d 290 (2d Cir. 2013).

Related Issues

2. *Jury Trial Waivers.* After the 1991 Title VII amendments, employees seeking damages have a right to a jury trial in actions brought in court. A jury trial is inconsistent with arbitration. The effect of enforcing an arbitration agreement on a damages claim thus is to foreclose a jury trial. On the effect of arbitration agreements, see Note on Class Action Waivers and Arbitration, infra p. 995.

3. *"Save upon Such Grounds as Exist at Law or in Equity for the Revocation of Any Contract."* The FAA provides that arbitration agreements shall be enforceable "save upon such grounds as exist at law or in equity for the revocation of any contract." 9 U.S.C. § 2. This provision authorizes review of such agreements under generally applicable contract law, but does not permit courts to craft special rules for arbitration agreements. See AT&T Mobility LLC v. Concepcion, 563 U.S. 333 (2011). Preston v. Ferrer, 552 U.S. 346, 128 S.Ct. 978, 169 L.Ed.2d 917 (2008); Doctor's Associates, Inc. v. Casarotto, 517 U.S. 681, 687, 116 S.Ct. 1652, 134 L.Ed.2d 902 (1996).

4. *Exception for "Contracts of Employment if Seamen, Railroad Employees, or Any Other Class of Workers Engaged in . . . Commerce"?* What does the FAA § 1 exception for "contracts of employment" mean? In *Gilmer,* the Court found that the arbitration agreement was a condition of registration with the NYSE, not an employment contract. However, in Circuit City Stores, Inc. v. Adams, 532 U.S. 105, 121 S.Ct. 1302, 149 L.Ed.2d 234 (2001), the Court adopted a transportation-worker-only interpretation of the FAA § 1 exclusion, exempting only contracts of employment of seamen, railroad employees and any other class of workers similarly directly engaged in foreign or interstate commerce. For pre-*Circuit City* commentary, compare, e.g., Samuel Estreicher, Predispute Agreements to Arbitrate Statutory Employment Claims, 72 N.Y.U.

L.Rev. 1344, 1369–71 (1997), with Matthew Finkin, "Workers' Contracts" Under the United States Arbitration Act: An Essay in Historical Clarification, 17 Berkeley J.Emp. & Lab.L. 282, 298 (1996).

5. *Applicability to EEOC.* Is the EEOC bound by an arbitration agreement between the employee and the employer? See EEOC v. Waffle House, Inc., 534 U.S. 279, 122 S.Ct. 754, 151 L.Ed.2d 755 (2002) (EEOC is a third party to the agreement and represents the public interest, not simply the individual employee).

6. *Preemption of State Law Barring Arbitration of State Statutory Claims.* Can a state adopt a policy more restrictive of statutory claim arbitration than federal courts under the FAA? Can a state law bar the enforcement of predispute arbitration agreements for claims made under its own law? Such state law restriction of arbitration is preempted by the FAA under controlling Supreme Court precedent. See, e.g., Southland Corp. v. Keating, 465 U.S. 1, 104 S.Ct. 852, 79 L.Ed.2d 1 (1984) (holding preempted a California law requiring claims brought under it to have judicial consideration); Perry v. Thomas, 482 U.S. 483, 107 S.Ct. 2520, 96 L.Ed.2d 426 (1987) (holding preempted private employees' wage payment claims despite the state's declared policy that such actions "may be pursued without regard to private arbitration agreements"); Allied-Bruce Terminix Cos. v. Dobson, 513 U.S. 265, 115 S.Ct. 834, 130 L.Ed.2d 753 (1995) (confirming the *Southland* Court's holding that "state courts cannot apply state statutes that invalidate arbitration agreements") See generally Christopher R. Drahozal, Federal Arbitration Act Preemption, 79 Ind. L.J. 393 (2002).

7. *"Knowing Waiver" of Right of Access to Judicial Forum.* The Court in *Gilmer* holds that a "take-it-or-leave-it" employment agreement like that which Gilmer signed is sufficiently *voluntary* to be an effective waiver. Might a court still find an employee's agreement to an arbitration system to be defective because it does not reflect a "knowing waiver"? In a series of cases the Ninth Circuit has held that "[a]ny bargain to waive the right to a judicial forum for civil rights claims * * * in exchange for employment or continued employment must at the least be express: The choice must be explicitly presented to the employee and the employee must explicitly agree to waive the specific right in question." Nelson v. Cyprus Bagdad Copper Corp., 119 F.3d 756, 762 (9th Cir.1997).

Is the Ninth Circuit position here consistent with *Gilmer*? With the FAA requirement that courts may apply only generally applicable principles for contract revocation in declining to enforce arbitration agreements? Most courts do not require arbitration agreements to spell out the particular statutory claims that are encompassed by the arbitration promise as long as employees are made aware that judicial remedies are being waived and that agreement encompasses employment disputes. In Campbell v. General Dynamics Government Systems Corp., 407 F.3d 546 (1st Cir. 2005), the court refused to compel arbitration of an ADA claim because the arbitration program had been distributed to employees by email without sufficiently alerting them to the fact that they were asked to agree to a waiver of judicial remedies. Links were provided to the full text of the arbitration program but the cover email was held not to contain sufficiently clear notice, nor were employees asked to acknowledge receipt or take some other affirmative step that might have provided a basis for establishing notice. Id. at 555.

8.   *Delegating to the Arbitrator Power to Decide Arbitrability?* In Rent-A-Center, West, Inc. v. Jackson, 561 U.S. 63, 130 S.Ct. 2772, 177 L.Ed.2d 403 (2010), the Court held that a challenge to the validity of an arbitration agreement that contains a clause delegating to the arbitrator the exclusive authority to resolve threshold issues of validity, including unconscionability under state law, is to be decided by the arbitrator, not the court, unless the challenge is specifically directed to the validity of the delegation provision itself.

9.   *Judicial Scrutiny of Fairness of Arbitration Procedure.* Does a court have authority to refuse to compel arbitration if dissatisfied with the essential fairness of the arbitration's procedures? Without clear articulation of the source of their authority, lower courts since *Gilmer* have been prepared to judge the adequacy of arbitration systems before compelling arbitration. Arbitration agreements that provide for lesser remedies than would be available in court for statutory violations would seem to contravene the Supreme Court's insistence that arbitration involves the waiver of a judicial forum, not the waiver of any substantive right. See, e.g. Paladino v. Avnet Computer Technologies, Inc., 134 F.3d 1054 (11th Cir.1998) (arbitration clause that does not authorize full statutory remedies is not enforceable); Graham Oil Co. v. ARCO Prods. Co., 43 F.3d 1244, 1248–49 (9th Cir.1994) (arbitration agreement that denied statutory remedies and shortened statutory statute of limitations periods is unenforceable). Might a failure to provide for neutral selection of the arbitrator also be treated as a waiver of a substantive right? See, e.g., Hooters of America v. Phillips, 173 F.3d 933, 938–40 (4th Cir.1999) (Hooters promulgated egregiously unfair arbitration rules, including selection procedures ensuring company control of membership of arbitration panel).

> *The Due Process Protocol for Employment Arbitration*
>
> A "Due Process Protocol for Arbitration of Statutory Disputes" has been developed and endorsed by the Labor & Employment Law Section of the American Bar Association as well as by major arbitration associations. See Disp. Resol. J. Oct.–Dec. 1995, at 37. The protocol posits seven minimum standards: (1) a jointly selected arbitrator who knows the applicable law; (2) simple but adequate discovery; (3) some cost-sharing between the parties to ensure arbitrator neutrality and to deter frivolous claims, though the employer should pay a higher percentage; (4) employee selection of own representative; (5) availability of all remedies provided by law; (6) opinion and award with reasoning from arbitrator; and (7) judicial review of legal issues. See generally Samuel Estreicher & Zev Eigen, The Forum for Adjudication of Employment Disputes, ch. 14 in Research Handbook on the Economics of Labor and Employment Law (Cynthia L. Estlund & Michael L. Wachter eds. 2012).

10. *Cost-Sharing Provisions.* As Due Process Protocol standard (3) indicates, "cost-sharing" can be viewed as a means of ensuring arbitrator neutrality, but the costs of arbitration—both the fees of the arbitration organization and the fees charged by the arbitrator—can erect a prohibitive barrier for claimants of average income. See, e.g., Cole v. Burns Int'l Sec. Serv., 105 F.3d 1465, 1483–85 (D.C.Cir.1997) (an agreement that obligated the employee to pay all or part of the arbitrators' fees would undermine substantive rights by creating costly barrier to assertion of claims). Can courts refuse to enforce arbitration agreements that impose costs on claimants higher than the nominal filing fees assessed in commencing a suit in the courts? In Green Tree Financial Corp. v. Randolph, 531 U.S. 79, 90–92, 121 S.Ct. 513, 148 L.Ed.2d 373 (2000), involving a consumer dispute under the Truth in Lending Act, 15 U.S.C. § 1601 *et seq.*, the Court held that a mere "risk" that a plaintiff "will be saddled with prohibitive costs" is insufficient to invalidate an arbitration agreement. However, a party may prove that arbitrator fees would be prohibitive in his/her individual case. As of 2015, the American Arbitration Association ("AAA") charges employees a $200 filing fee for disputes "arising out of employer-promulgated plans" (as opposed to "individually negotiated employment agreements"), and requires the employer to pay the arbitrator's fees. AAA, Employment Arbitration Rules (May 15, 2013), available at www.adr.org. Employees that individually negotiate their employment agreements, in contrast, must pay a filing fee ranging from $775 to $10,200, depending on the amount of their claim, and arbitrator fees "are subject to allocation by the arbitrator in an award." Id.

11. *Effect of Arbitration on Employee Outcomes.* For the affirmative case for arbitration if properly designed, see, e.g., Zev J. Eigen & David Sherwyn, A Model of Dispute Resolution Fairness, in Beyond Elite Law: Access to Civil

Justice in American (Samuel Estreicher & Joy Radice eds. 2016). David Sherwyn, Samuel Estreicher & Michael Heise, Assessing the Case for Employment Arbitration: A New Path for Empirical Research, 57 Stan. L. Rev. 1557 (2005); Saturns for Rickshaws: The Stakes in the Debate over Mandatory Employment Arbitration, 16 Ohio St. J. on Disp. Resol. 559 (2001). For the negative case, see, e.g., Judith Resnik, Diffusing Disputes: The Public in the Private of Arbitration, the Private in the Courts, and the Erasure of Rights, 124 Yale L.J. 2804 (2015); Alexander J.S. Colvin, An Empirical Assessment of Employment Arbitration: Case Outcomes and Processes, 8 J. Empirical Legal Studies 1 (2011).

PRACTITIONER'S PERSPECTIVE

Ethan Brecher
Law Office of Ethan A. Brecher, LLC.

Conventional wisdom teaches that employers prefer arbitration to court with former employees. Arbitration, however, holds many benefits for employees, too, and employees can use the arbitration process to their benefit.

Arbitrations trend to be shorter, involve less discovery and are far less expensive than court actions. An employee thus has a more direct road to a hearing and timely resolution of his case than in court. Typically the most useful discovery comes from emails and other electronic sources, and arbitrators are inclined to permit sufficiently robust electronic discovery so as to place it on par with what can be obtained in court.

Arbitrators are generally not inclined to allow or grant dispositive motions (especially because of the lack of viable appellate options from arbitration awards), and an employee can reasonably expect his claim to go to trial, where he will be able to examine key witnesses with the most pertinent documents.

Further, arbitrators are generally not strictly bound by the law, and thus an employee with a compelling equitable claim has a better chance of a favorable outcome than in court. See Silverman v. Benmor Coats, Inc., 61 NY2d 299, 308 (1984). Strong legal claims generally also prevail in arbitration, as they would in court.

The fact that an employee can succeed on equity also enhances the possibility of a favorable settlement, because employers might be unwilling to risk an adverse award with an employee with a weak legal but strong equitable claim.

Arbitrators are also human and want to appear fair, so employers cannot count on arbitrators doing their bidding simply because they are better resourced. Nevertheless, employees should approach the arbitrator selection process with care and eliminate through due diligence those who have an obvious pro-employer track record. In doing so, employees can maximize the chance that the arbitrator is a well-respected neutral who will fairly and impartially preside over their case.

Moreover, if an employee prevails in arbitration, an employer has little chance of reversing that result on appeal. By contrast, it's almost a certainty that if an employee loses a jury trial he will have little chance of reviving his claim on appeal. Thus, the lack of a plenary appeal process in arbitration should not be too concerning, because an employee will have his "day in court" and his claims heard by an impartial neutral.

Arbitration has undeservedly earned a bad name among plaintiff's employment lawyers. Employees, though, should not view arbitration as a death knell to their claims, but rather as an opportunity to secure favorable outcome for their legally or equitably meritorious cases.

NOTE: CLASS ACTION WAIVERS AND ARBITRATION

1. *When an Agreement is "Silent" on the Issue of Class Arbitrability.* The Supreme Court first ruled that a state court lacks authority to compel classwide arbitration of claims where the underlying arbitration agreement is silent on the question; a plurality of Justices determined that the availability of classwide arbitration is an issue for the arbitrator to decide. See Green Tree Financial Corp. v. Bazzle, 539 U.S. 444, 123 S.Ct. 2402, 156 L.Ed.2d 414 (2003). In Stolt-Nielsen S.A. v. AnimalFeeds Int'l Corp., 559 U.S. 662, 130 S.Ct. 1758, 176 L.Ed.2d 605 (2010), the Court held 5–3 that an arbitration agreement that the parties agree is "silent" on class arbitration may not proceed on a class basis. The arbitration panel below exceeded its authority in violation of the FAA when it found that the agreement permitted class arbitration. Justice Alito, writing for the Court, stated that the panel had acted according to its own sense of public policy, rather than within the scope of authority provided by the agreement. Because the parties acknowledged that the agreement was "silent" and there had been "no agreement" on class arbitration, there was no need to ascertain the parties' intent on the subject. Instead, the panel's proper task was to determine whether, in the face of that silence, class arbitration was permitted by an underlying default rule of law. The Court then considered the appropriate default rule under the FAA. Arbitration, the Court explained, has always been considered a matter of consent. Class arbitration "changes the nature of arbitration to such a degree" that consent to class arbitration cannot be presumed. Commonly touted benefits of arbitration such as speed, cost savings, efficiency, and privacy may be lost in a class setting, and new concerns added related to the greater potential for a multiplicity of claims, absent parties, and high stakes. Thus, the Court ruled that "a party may not be compelled under the FAA to submit to class arbitration unless there is a contractual basis for concluding that the party agreed to do so." Because the parties here conceded that there was no

such agreement, there could be no mandated class arbitration. The Court remanded the case, but ruled that rehearing by the arbitration panel on the class issue was not warranted given the parties stipulation on "silence."

2. *Class Action Waivers and State-Law Unconscionability Review.* After the Supreme Court's 2003 decision in *Bazzle* suggested that arbitrators could interpret silence in an arbitration agreement to authorize class proceedings, some companies responded by inserting provisions in their arbitration agreements waiving class actions or the consolidation of claims. Attorneys seeking to preserve the availability of claim consolidation in the face of such provisions have used several kinds of arguments.

First, the waiver provisions have been challenged under state-law unconscionability doctrine. This doctrine arguably is relevant under section 2 of the FAA, which allows invalidation or non-enforcement of arbitration agreements on "grounds as exist at law or in equity for the revocation of any contract." Thus, the California Supreme Court in Discover Bank v. Superior Court, 36 Cal.4th 148, 30 Cal.Rptr.3d 76, 113 P.3d 1100 (2005), declared class action waivers in arbitration agreement unconscionable when applied to consumer claims involving contracts of adhesion and small amounts of money.

In AT&T Mobility LLC v. Vincent Concepcion, 563 U.S. 333, 131 S.Ct. 1740, 179 L.Ed.2d 742 (2011), however, the Supreme Court held that the FAA precludes application of California's *Discover Bank* unconscionability doctrine. It reasoned that the doctrine created barriers to the effectuation of arbitration agreements by conditioning enforcement of the arbitration agreement on the company's consenting to a classwide arbitral proceeding.

Vincent and Liza Concepcion had entered into an agreement with AT&T Mobility LLC, a wireless subsidiary of AT&T, ("AT&T") in February 2002 for the sale and servicing of "free" wireless telephones. The Concepcions were not charged for the retail value of the phones, but were responsible for $30.22 in sales tax, a cost that was not disclosed in AT&T's advertisement. The Concepcions filed a complaint in the United States District Court for the Southern District of California in March 2006 alleging violations of California consumer protection laws based on AT&T's non-disclosure of the state sales tax.

The Concepcions' wireless service agreement incorporated a one-page statement of "Terms and Conditions," which contained an agreement to arbitrate any disputes under the agreement and barred consolidation or class arbitration. The agreement also allowed unilateral amendments of the contract by AT&T at any time. AT&T exercised this right following initiation of the Concepcions' lawsuit by adding a "premium payment clause" to the agreement, which provided for a minimum payment of $7,500 to a California customer if an arbitral award was greater than AT&T's last written settlement offer prior to selection of an arbitrator. In March 2008, AT&T moved to compel individual arbitration. Relying on *Discover Bank,* the District Court denied AT&T's motion and concluded that the class action ban in the parties' arbitration agreement was both procedurally and substantively unconscionable under California law. The Ninth Circuit affirmed. 584 F.3d 849 (9th Cir. 2009).

The U.S. Supreme Court, in a 5–4 decision, reversed. In the majority opinion, authored by Justice Scalia, the Court noted that arbitration is a matter of contract and a predominant purpose of the FAA is to "ensur[e] that private arbitration agreements are enforced according to their terms." Justice Scalia's opinion explained

> [A]lthough [FAA] § 2's saving clause preserves generally applicable contract defenses, nothing in it suggests an intent to preserve state-law rules that stand as an obstacle to the accomplishment of the FAA's objectives . . . [and] the overarching purpose of the FAA . . . is to ensure the enforcement of arbitration agreements according to their terms. . . .

With respect to California's *Discover Bank* rule, the majority concluded, "although the rule does not *require* classwide arbitration," it interfered with the FAA's objective of enforcing arbitration agreements according to their terms because the *Discover Bank* rule "allows any party to a consumer contract to demand it *ex post*."

The Court reasoned that the *Discover Bank* rule conflicted with the congressional purpose in enacting the FAA in three principal ways. First, class arbitration "sacrifices the principal advantage of arbitration—its informality—and makes the process slower, more costly, and more likely to generate procedural morass than final judgment." Class certification in the arbitration context adds additional obstacles that must be resolved before arbitration can begin. Next, class arbitration requires a level of procedural formality that, could not possibly have been envisioned by Congress when it passed the FAA in 1925. Particularly, the majority noted, "it is at the very least odd to think that an arbitrator would be entrusted with ensuring that third parties' due process rights are satisfied." Third, informal arbitration procedures pose a risk to defendants where, in the absence of the multilayered review available in court proceedings, errors are more likely to go uncorrected and in the class context their impact may increase exponentially. According to the majority, defendants are often willing to accept the costs of errors in arbitration given the size and possible damages of individual disputes. Conversely, "when damages allegedly owed to tens of thousands of potential claimants are aggregated and decided at once, the risk of error will often become unacceptable" to businesses. In addition, the majority rejected the argument that the California rule is a generally applicable defense to contract formation and therefore not preempted by the FAA. According to the majority, even a state contract law of general applicability will be preempted where it "stand[s] as an obstacle to the accomplishment of the FAA's objectives."

Justice Breyer, with whom Justices Ginsberg, Sotomayor and Kagan joined, filed a dissenting opinion. The dissent argued that the *Discover Bank* rule is consistent with both the FAA's language and the "purpose behind" the Act, and that *Discover Bank* cannot be viewed as an attack on arbitration as the state law imposes comparable limitations on arbitration and court litigation. Further, under the express terms of the FAA Section 2, the dissent argued that "California is free to define unconscionability as it sees fit, and its common law is of no federal concern so long as the State does not adopt a special rule that disfavors arbitration."

3. *Class Action Waivers as Waivers of Substantive Rights.* Although the *Concepcion* decision concluded that California's unconscionability doctrine violated the FAA, the Court seemed to leave the door ajar for the argument that in cases involving small sums not likely to attract a competent lawyer in individual arbitrations, some further accommodation might be required. The Concepcions had maintained that their claim "was most unlikely to go unresolved," but the Court noted that in its agreement AT&T promised it would pay claimants "a minimum of $7,500 and twice their attorney's fees if they obtain an arbitration award greater than AT&T's last settlement offer."

In American Express Co. v. Italian Colors Restaurant, U.S., 133 S.Ct. 2304 (2013), however, the Court seemingly closed the door on this argument. In this case, Italian Colors and other merchants brought a class action in court against American Express, alleging that its credit card acceptance agreement violated antitrust law. The Court held that the merchants could not bring the action because the agreement included a commitment to arbitrate claims without use of class arbitration. The merchants contended that enforcing the class waiver would prevent the "effective vindication" of their rights because none of the merchants individually would have an adequate incentive to pay for the expert analysis necessary to prove the claim. The Court rejected the broadly framed "effective vindication" formulation of the Second Circuit in this case; it instead asserted that the doctrine applies only where there is an obstruction of access to a forum to vindicate the rights. The Court did note, however, that the arbitration agreements did not prevent plaintiffs from pooling their resources in mounting the costs of an expert witness in an individual arbitration. See 133 S.Ct. at ___ n.4. Furthermore, although the Court does not discuss the point, expert testimony in one arbitration presumably would be admissible evidence in another arbitration involving common facts. Cf. Parklane Hosiery Co. v. Shore, 439 U.S. 322 (1979) (nonmutual issue preclusion as federal common law rule).

4. *Validity of Class Action Waivers Under the Federal Law Forming the Basis of the Plaintiff's Claim.* Class action waivers in arbitration agreements still could be ineffective in cases brought to enforce a federal statutory right that includes a guarantee of access to consolidated litigation in court. In CompuCredit Corp. v. Greenwood, 565 U.S. ___, 132 S.Ct. 665, 181 L.Ed.2d 586 (2012), consumers filed a class action against a credit corporation and a bank, claiming that petitioners violated the Credit Repair Organizations Act (CROA), 15 U.S.C. § 1679 et seq. The district court denied petitioners' motion to compel arbitration on the ground that the CROA itself expressly contemplated, in the notice the statute required these organizations to provide consumers, a right to bring class actions to redress CROA violations. The Ninth Circuit affirmed. The Supreme Court reversed, finding no basis in the CROA

to overcome *Gilmer's* presumption of arbitrability. Writing for himself and five other Justices, Justice Scalia reasoned:

> Respondents suggest that the CROA's civil-liability provision, § 1679g * * * demonstrates that the Act provides consumers with a "right" to bring an action in court. They cite the provision's repeated use of the terms "action," "class action," and "court"—terms that they say call to mind a judicial proceeding. These references cannot do the heavy lifting that respondents assign them. It is utterly commonplace for statutes that create civil causes of action to describe the details of those causes of action, including the relief available, in the context of a court suit. If the mere formulation of the cause of action in this standard fashion were sufficient to establish the "contrary congressional command" overriding the FAA, valid arbitration agreements covering federal causes of action would be rare indeed. But that is not the law. * * * [I]f a cause-of-action provision mentioning judicial enforcement does not create a right to initial judicial enforcement, the waiver of initial judicial enforcement is not the waiver of a "right of the consumer," § 1679f(a).

Given *CompuCredit,* do plaintiffs challenging a class action waiver have a viable argument that they cannot be forced to arbitrate their Title VII systemic disparate treatment claims because such claims contemplate a classwide vehicle given the burden-shifting framework of *Teamsters,* supra p. 148? See *Parisi v. Goldman, Sachs & Co.,* 710 F.3d 483 (2d Cir. 2013) (class action arbitration provision did not prevent plaintiff from vindicating her Title VII statutory rights because employees can challenge discriminatory policies in an individual arbitration and there is no substantive Title VII right to bring a systemic disparate-treatment claim on a class basis).

INDEX

References are to Pages